Contemporary Social Problems

Contributors

John A. Clausen   *University of California, Berkeley*
Albert K. Cohen   *University of Connecticut*
James S. Coleman   *The Johns Hopkins University*
Donald R. Cressey   *University of California, Santa Barbara*
Kingsley Davis   *University of California, Berkeley*
Amitai Etzioni   *Columbia University*
Jack P. Gibbs   *Washington State University*
William J. Goode   *Columbia University*
David Matza   *University of California, Berkeley*
David Riesman   *Harvard University*
Arnold M. Rose   *University of Minnesota*
James F. Short, Jr.   *Washington State University*
Robert Straus   *University of Kentucky*
Robert S. Weiss   *Brandeis University*

Contemporary Social Problems

second edition

EDITED BY

Robert K. Merton
Columbia University

AND

Robert A. Nisbet
University of California, Riverside

HARCOURT, BRACE & WORLD, INC.

New York / Chicago / Burlingame

© 1961, 1966 BY HARCOURT, BRACE & WORLD, INC.

LIBRARY OF CONGRESS CATALOG CARD NUMBER: 66-15611

PRINTED IN THE UNITED STATES OF AMERICA

Preface

THREE CENTRAL IDEAS GOVERN THE SCOPE AND CHARACTER OF THIS BOOK. First, that with the growth of sociological knowledge, the "field" of social problems has increasingly become an array of associated sociological specialties; second, that a comprehensive theory of social problems does not yet exist, although it may be in the making; and third, that the student can best be led to an understanding of social problems by having him focus on the problems of a complex, industrial society, seen in the broader context provided by comparison with other types of societies. A few words about each of these governing ideas will introduce the reader to the plan and rationale of the book.

In sociology, as in other learned disciplines, specialization increases as more and more knowledge accumulates through the combined efforts of more and more scholars and scientists. The sociologist of a generation or two ago could acquire a thoroughgoing knowledge of just about everything that was then known about social problems, for as compared with today, relatively few sociologists were investigating these problems. With the increased pace of research, however, it has become a formidable task to keep up with the work being done on even a few of these problems and almost impossible to keep thoroughly abreast of the work going forward on all of them. The sociology of population and the sociology of mental health, for example, are developing at such a pace that the sociologist who would remain abreast of either of these subjects recognizes that he cannot be equally informed about specialized inquiries in the fields, say, of race and ethnic relations or of family disorganization.

As sociologists generally realize, this development has led to the course on social problems becoming a set of associated sociological specialties: specialties dealing with forms of deviant behavior expressed, for example, in crime and juvenile delinquency, mental illness and drug addiction, suicide and prostitution; and specialties dealing with forms of social disorganization such as those found in relations between racial and ethnic collectivities, in various patterns of population change, in the place of work, in the home, and in the local community. One way of acquainting the student with detailed knowledge of each of these subjects is to have a curriculum of specialized courses, each devoted to a single subject. This is what many departments of sociology actually do. But most undergraduates do not go on to these advanced courses. Besides, there is added value in introducing the student, whether he continues his sociological studies or not, to an overview of social problems in a single course, for this helps him see the many interconnections between these problems and the ways in which general sociological ideas bring some understanding of seemingly disparate problems.

One way, then, of providing a comprehensive and authoritative overview of these associated special subjects is to have the essentials of each subject distilled by specialists. This affords the student an introduction to each subject under the guidance of a sociologist who knows that subject in depth since he is concentrating his research efforts on it. The specialist can inform the student of what is currently known in a particular field and, no less important, give him a sense of ongoing sociological inquiry by authoritatively but not pessimistically indicating the limits of current knowledge in that field. This is one of the assumptions underlying this book.

From the outset, all of us collaborating on the book foresaw the difficulty that might arise from having each specialist deal with a separate social problem: the student might receive a suitable introduction to each subject *seriatim* but be left, in the end, with a disjointed assortment of sociological information. This point brings us to our second governing idea. Sociologists today generally recognize that there is no single comprehensive and tight-knit "sociological theory of social problems," in the sense of a logically articulated set of precisely formulated propositions from which many empirical uniformities are rigorously derived. Instead, the condition is one often found when a discipline is still in its early phases of development: the presence of a good many confirmed hypotheses of fairly limited scope. In the area of social problems, however, a theoretical *orientation* of much broader scope has also been emerging, which has been found useful in directing the observations of sociologists at work in the different specialties encompassed by the subject. This theoretical orientation, rather than a still unformed comprehensive theory, unifies the chapters of the book.

The reader will identify this general orientation for himself in the following pages, but it may nevertheless be useful to summarize its principal components here.

1. The same social structure and culture that in the main make for conforming and organized behavior also generate tendencies toward distinctive kinds of deviant behavior and potentials of social disorganization. In this sense, the problems current in a society register the social costs of a particular organization of social life.

2. From this premise, it can be seen that the sociological orientation rejects as demonstrably inadequate the commonly held doctrine that "evil is the cause of evil" in society. Instead, it alerts us to search out the ways in which socially prized arrangements and values in society can produce socially condemned results.

3. It follows also that, to a substantial extent, social problems are the unwilled, largely indirect, and often unanticipated consequences of institutionalized patterns of social behavior.

4. From what precedes, it follows further that in order to study and understand disorganization in particular departments of social life, it is necessary to study and understand the social framework of their organization. The two—disorganization and organization, seemingly at odds in the commonsense view—are theoretically inseparable.

5. From these related premises, it can be concluded that each social and cultural structure will have its distinctive kinds and degrees of social problems.

6. Another major premise in this sociological orientation takes note that social structures are variously differentiated into social statuses, roles, and strata, having their distinctive as well as their shared values and interests. This premise directs us to recognize the differing pressures upon people differently located in the structure to engage in certain forms of deviant behavior and to be diversely subject to the consequences of social disorganization. People in different social positions are variously exposed to the hazards of aberrant behavior and are variously vulnerable to these hazards.

7. The preceding two premises—#5 and #6—lead us to anticipate that people occupying different positions in the social structure will ordinarily differ in their appraisal of the same social situations as problems requiring social action. Only in the exceptional and limiting case do people in all groups, social strata, organizations, communities, and regions in a complex society agree that particular conditions are social problems requiring solution.

8. Since, as was noted in premise #7, people variously located in the social structure differ in their appraisal of a particular situation

as a social problem, we should be prepared to find (and in fact we do find) that the "solutions" proposed for coping with these problems also differ; these too are limited and partly shaped by the social structure. As a result, the changes represented by the proposed solutions will accord with the interests and values of some and run counter to the interests and values of others. It is, therefore, often difficult to develop and put into effect public policies designed to solve social problems.

9. Owing to the systemic interdependence among the parts of a social structure, efforts to do away with one social problem will often introduce other (either more or less damaging) problems. Sociologists have long noted this tendency; so far as we can now say, the image of a problem-less society, in which all is as all men would wish it to be, must be regarded as fantasy. But it does not follow that public policy cannot result in the progressive curbing of particular social problems and be the better prepared to cope with the new ones coming along.

It is not the function of a textbook to set out new theoretical systems with which the authors are currently experimenting. The orientation that pervades the chapters of this book is not peculiar to it; it has emerged from the collective results of inquiry by sociologists over a span of generations. It is held in common by the various "schools of sociology," differing somewhat in other respects but not, we believe, in the main substance of the premises we have just sketched out.

The third idea governing the plan of the book has to do with its scope and with the particular problems selected for examination. As will become apparent to the reader, the book focuses on contemporary social problems in the United States, considered as an instance of complex industrial society. However, even though the greater part of the factual evidence has been drawn from American society, the book is by no means confined to it. The chapter on the world's population crisis, of course, presents comparative materials drawn from various types of society, but so do many of the others—always with an eye to clarifying the spectrum of American social problems by comparison with problems found elsewhere.

The particular subjects selected are for the most part those kinds of deviant behavior and social disorganization which have long been at the center of sociological research on social problems. Once again, this decision was largely dictated to us by our plan for a textbook rather than a specialized monograph.

This collaborative effort, then, is designed to introduce the student to the sociology of social problems by giving him an overview of forms of deviant behavior and social disorganization and by showing him how sociologists identify, acquire, and interpret the evidence to arrive at what is now known about the subject.

* * *

This second edition retains the basic structure and governing ideas of the first, but its content has been substantially changed to take account of new developments in the field and the experience with the book reported to us by teachers and students. The changes are of three kinds: (1) Statistical and quantitative materials in all chapters have been brought up to the latest possible date. These changes are reflected in the text as well as in tables and graphs. (2) Most of the chapters have been considerably rewritten to embody recent developments in sociological research and analysis and to improve their organization and exposition. (3) Three new chapters have been introduced—on alcohol, poverty, and war and disarmament—to deal with vital problems of contemporary society not included in the first edition. These additions have been at a price: to avoid lengthening an already long book, it was necessary to drop the chapters on problems of military life, of disaster and catastrophe, and of transportation in the metropolis, which proved to be more appropriate for graduate students than for undergraduates. Advanced students will want to consult those chapters in the first edition to learn how the sociological orientation helps to clarify problems once assumed to be the exclusive province of other specialists.

We are greatly indebted to the many college and university teachers whose detailed suggestions and comments have been invaluable to us in planning this second edition.

ROBERT K. MERTON
Columbia University

ROBERT A. NISBET
University of California

Contents

PART TWO: SOCIAL DISORGANIZATION

INTRODUCTION

The Study of Social Problems

by Robert A. Nisbet

THERE ARE MANY APPROACHES TO THE UNDERSTANDING OF A SOCIETY: through its dominant personalities, its major institutions, its modes of technology, its idea systems, or art forms. Each way is, as the philosopher Whitehead has told us, "a sort of searchlight, elucidating some of the facts, and retreating the remainder into an omitted background."

In this book we approach society through the perspective formed by some major social problems. We do this partly because of the significance, often imperative, of the problems themselves and partly because through observation and analysis of these problems we are afforded insight into the distinctive nature of our society: its social structures, codes, and norms; its processes of organization as well as disorganization; its patterns of conformity as well as deviation. It is one of the major arguments of this book, amply reinforced by each of the chapters that follow, that there is a close and even predictable relation between the recurrent social problems of a culture and the identifying values and institutions of that culture.

Fourteen major problems are dealt with: mental disorders, juvenile delinquency, crime, drug addiction, alcohol, suicide, prostitution and sexual deviation, population, ethnic relations, family disorganization, work and automation, poverty, community conflict, and war and disarmament. That each is important, though in varying degree, is obvious. That all are widely recognized as social problems is equally obvious. We do not suggest that these are the only significant problems in twentieth-century America or even that, in all instances, they are among the most vital. It might well be contended that political apathy, debasement of popular taste, mediocrity of leadership, or impoverishment of culture and education are problems of greater importance to the present and future of the nation than some of those selected for treatment here. No doubt, it is unlikely that any nation or community ever declined as the consequence of prostitution, narcotics addiction, or high suicide rates, whereas there is little question that whole nations have lost the capacity for maintaining their full social organization as the result of weak or perverse leadership, failure of nerve, or endemic apathy.

All of this is true as far as it goes. But two points must be noted that are relevant to the choice of the problems in this book. First, there would be little agreement, even among scholars, as to what constitutes inadequate leadership, intellectual mediocrity, or debasement of culture. From a scientist's point of view there is too little precision in these conceptions to make them suitable for objective treatment. They fall within more speculative types of discourse.

Second, this is a textbook in sociology. Sociology is a special science, distinguished by its own problems, methodology, concepts, and insights. It does not purport to deal with all problems of popular concern. The problems that have been selected for treatment here are manifestly significant, and they have the added character of being problems on which a substantial body of research has been done by sociologists, using methods and reaching conclusions based on systematic investigation. In sum, while this book is an introduction to the study of social problems, it is also an introduction to the sociological study of human behavior.

The Cultural Base of Social Problems

In the popular view, largely as the result of our religious and moral heritage, there is a common tendency to think of social problems as the consequences of "antisocial" behavior, as the embodiment of patently evil elements. For many centuries, Western ethics rested upon the view that, as only good can come from good, so the causes of evil must be located in the residually evil. If there is crime, it is because there are evil persons, evil groups, evil values.

Yet, as every chapter of this book makes clear, the crucial contexts of social problems are, in many cases, accepted by society as unobjectionable, even good. Thus the social *problem* of alcohol in American culture is largely inseparable from the social *function* that alcohol holds in literally scores of cherished contexts of association, ranging from the family cocktail before dinner through religious ceremonies to the indispensable diplomatic reception. Similarly, there is a close relation between certain social problems and urbanism. Apart from city life, whose cultural values attract people in large numbers, many of the ills would not exist. The same is true of the difficulties presented by population growth. Obviously, there is nothing intrinsically evil in having large families; an entire morality rests upon the Biblical injunction to be fruitful and multiply. For thousands of years high birth rates were necessary and functional for the preservation of society. But today, in many areas, as the result of sharply lowered death rates, the growth of population has become one of society's most formidable problems.

In crime, suicide, and family disorganization, we often discover processes of behavior that, if not necessarily beneficent, are at least normal to human endeavor in our society. This is not said in moral exoneration. Stealing is wrong, and it can constitute a serious problem to any community that prizes its own maintenance and integrity. Sociologists interested in the causal conditions of types of crime, however, cannot overlook their effective contexts: the incentives, goals, status drives, and role needs that characterize the society. We may deplore our rates of suicide and of divorce—as measured in lives taken, in broken homes, and in personalities set adrift—but we cannot isolate these rates from a culture that sets high value upon individualism, secularism, and contractual ties.

Too often the popular view of social problems likens them to cancers: for most citizens, the image of society and its problems is that of an essentially healthy organism invaded by alien substances. The legislator, or the policeman, is thought of as a kind of physician, bound to remove the cyst, destroy the virus, but without altering the character of the organism itself.

Such an analogy seriously distorts social reality. We shall discover in the chapters of this book that social problems, even the worst of them, often have a functional relationship to the institutions and values by which we live. We cannot divorce racial and ethnic discrimination from the complex of customs that have sometimes given discrimination a wide variety of functions in our economic, political, domestic, and recreational life. We cannot separate many of the discontents of work from our own development of more cultivated standards of existence, of leisure values that we properly cherish. Even prostitution exists only as a dark reflection of the value we place on the monogamous family and the sanctity of marriage.

This is not to argue that social problems are so closely or so organically related to all parts of their social framework that the only possibility of their solution is a total change of society. This view, to be sure, has been taken by many a moral prophet and philosopher of history. We see it in revolutionary Marxism and in other doctrines which contend that social evils and corruptions are so inextricably embedded in the central character of society that until this character has been purified or cauterized, as it were, by the fire of revolt, specific evils of crime and discrimination will no more be banished than would a malaria epidemic through case-by-case treatment. The intoxicating and ever alluring essence of the total, or chiliastic, approach is plain enough. In his historical study, *The Pursuit of the Millennium*,[1] Norman Cohn has shown how, from the late Middle Ages on, European society has been recurrently seized by messianic movements, ranging from those that drew eschatological inspiration from the Book of Daniel or the Sybilline Oracles five centuries ago to those of the twentieth century that have drawn it from the Communist Manifesto or Mein Kampf. The messianic or revolutionary view is inevitably attractive to those obsessed by the monolithic vision of a sick or degenerate society, but it has no more place in scientific sociology than does any other form of apocalyptic vision.

Modern sociology—as exemplified in the chapters of this book—maintains simply that social behavior, whether moral or immoral, legal or illegal, can be understood only in light of the values that give it meaning and the institutions that provide the channels for achievement of these values. What we observe repeatedly in deviant behavior is the pursuit of the values sought by the rest of society, but through channels or by means that are condemned. As Robert Merton has observed, ". . . when a system of cultural values extols, virtually above all else, certain common success goals for the population at large while the social structure rigorously restricts or completely closes access to approved modes of reaching these goals for a considerable part of the population, deviant behavior ensues on a large scale." [2]

The Historical Variability of Social Problems

A. J. Toynbee [3] has emphasized that the history of civilization may be seen as a succession of challenges—physical, technological, intellectual, and moral—to the intellect and conscience of man, each demanding unwonted mobilization of thought and energy. When successful solutions are found, a society moves on to new and higher

---

[1] Norman Cohn, *The Pursuit of the Millennium*, 2nd ed. (New York: Harper, 1961), especially the Conclusion.

[2] Robert K. Merton, *Social Theory and Social Structure*, rev. ed. (New York: Free Press, 1957), p. 146.

[3] *A Study of History* (New York: Oxford University Press, 1933), Vol. 1, *passim*.

levels; when solutions are not found, stagnation and decline are the frequent consequences. Proper assessment of the priority of the challenges which confront a society is, of course, the main responsibility of leadership. When leadership misjudges the order of priority—placing, for example, conquest of outer space ahead of urban development, education, or civil rights—it inevitably influences the future of democratic society.

Social problems are distinguished from other problems by their close relation with institutional and normative contexts. They are social in the sense that they pertain to human relationships and to the value contexts in which human relationships exist. They are problems in the sense that they represent interruptions in the socially expected or morally desired scheme of things. They are violations of the good and right, as a society defines these moral attributes; dislocations of the social patterns and relationships that a society approves or takes for granted. Family disorganization, ethnic discrimination, poverty, and explosive population growth are considered social problems because their primary contexts are recognized as institutional, formed by human beings in interaction, and because the conditions they reflect are regarded as destructive of prized institutions and values: family solidarity, democratic equality, material and cultural well being, and so on.

Just as there is a reciprocal relation between individual thought, properly called, and the recognition of cognitive problems, so is there a reciprocal relation between moral consciousness in a society and the perceived existence of social problems. We may cite here Émile Durkheim's famous thesis of the "functional necessity of crime" in which he argued that a certain amount of crime is necessary to the stability of a moral order because without occasional violations there would be no occasions on which society could reaffirm the essential tenets of its moral code. Durkheim's thesis doubtless says more than most of us would care to conclude, but we may extract from it the important and paradoxical truth that while moral consciousness indeed underlies perception of social problems, it is only the recognition of, and response to, social problems that creates or reinforces the moral consciousness of any age. When a society pronounces narcotics addiction, poverty, or mental illness a social problem, it is saying something about, and *doing something for,* its level of moral regard. The gin-ridden slums of eighteenth-century London that William Hogarth sketched did not seem a social problem to the average Englishman of that day, any more than did the generally appalling lives of the indigent, the delinquent, and the mentally ill. This is not to say that the eighteenth century was without moral consciousness but only that such conditions, wretched though they seem to us in retrospect, had not yet seriously entered the province of moral consciousness, except in the minds of a very few.

While it would be presumptuous to claim for ourselves a higher level of morality than that of two centuries ago in England, we are certainly justified in saying that for more and more of us today these conditions have disturbing impact. Making all allowance for lethargy and for the hypocrisy and the parochially selective character of much of our response to poverty, narcotics addiction, alcoholism, juvenile delinquency, and prostitution, these have become active moral, and therefore social, problems for us in a way they were not in the earlier age.

To be sure, we do not have to go back to the eighteenth century for negative examples of this point. After all, for how long can discrimination in civil rights be said to have existed in the domain of active moral consciousness and considered as one of America's social problems? There are curious fluctuations of moral regard for some problems: poverty, for instance. Once it was a staple of every textbook on the social ills of America. Then for two or three decades it largely disappeared, only to return to active attention in the 1960's, surrounded (as the chapter on poverty makes arrestingly evident) by a plethora of issues—moral, semantic and political—that complicate even its study.

Another fluctuation of moral attitude has been occurring with respect to fertility. Traditionally fertility has been a positive value—sanctified by religious dogma and attested to by folk rituals. Today, however, we are in the presence of what can only be called a confrontation between the traditional religious ethic on fertility and a new ethic, that of control of fertility, born of scientific understanding. Here are two conflicting activations of moral consciousness: one in the ranks of those for whom defense of the ancient ethic of fertility is urgent—for whom birth *control* is the social problem; the other in the ranks of those for whom the unrestrained increase of population ranks as perhaps the greatest single problem faced by mankind.

The Modern Recognition of Social Problems

In our study of social problems, we must consider not only their intrinsic cognitive, moral, and social elements, but the historical currents through which social problems have gained the status of popular recognition in modern Western society.[4] Two historical currents are of greatest significance: secular rationalism and humanitarianism.

The essence of *secular rationalism* in modern Europe has been its conceptual conversion of problems and conditions from the ancient theological contexts of good and evil to the rationalist contexts of analytical understanding and of control. Control is the essential element. If we did not think there was something that could be *done* about social problems, if we regarded them—as some of those in this book were once universally regarded—as ineffaceable elements of the human condition, we probably would not have included them in our contemporary lexicon of social problems. We would not define them, nor indeed even see them, as social problems. It is no accident that serious awareness of social problems in western Europe first entered the European mind during the Enlightenment, an age when reason, extolled by earlier philosophers such as Bacon and Descartes on behalf of the control or "reform" of *nature,* was now extolled on behalf of the control or reform of *society.* This was the age when, for the first time in many centuries—since, perhaps, the age of Socrates—men were inspired by the possibilities of putting reason in service to man's earthly estate and happiness. And, given this new vision of reason and its potentialities, it was not strange that social conditions that had heretofore been regarded by even the most humane minds as, at best, distressing and regrettable aspects of man's sojourn on earth began to be noticed as "problems."

After the Enlightenment, the condition of the working class, poverty, crime, family disorganization, and similar conditions would be regarded by an ever widening public as matters about which something should and could be done. All too often, then as now, what was proposed as a cure could be worse then the ill—as in some of Jeremy Bentham's well-meant, scrupulously rational, but nevertheless merciless projects for the care of the indigent, delinquent, and mentally disturbed. His celebrated Panopticon (an ingenious mode of concentric architecture in which a centrally placed overseer could keep the delinquent or indigent inmates under constant and relentless eye, at little cost) was, as Disraeli later observed, the unlovable issue of a marriage between reason and inhumanity.[5]

It does not matter. Even if, as more than one student of the utilitar-

---

[4] See the Epilogue (pp. 780-99) for an analysis of the sociological criteria for the recognition of social problems.

[5] For an account of Bentham's Panopticon principle see Gertrude Himmelfarb's "The Haunted House of Jeremy Bentham" in *Ideas in History: Essays in Honor of Louis Gottschalk* (Durham, N. C.: Duke University Press, 1965).

ians has been led to conclude, it was the illogicality rather than the moral degradation or inhumanity of social conditions that spurred Bentham and his followers, the central point is that through their unrelenting effort one of the two essential conditions of the modern recognition of social problems was fulfilled: that is, the intellectual conversion of the "timeless and inevitable" into concrete problems that not only should, but *could* be met by human reason.

The second historical condition, also an emergent of the early nineteenth century, is *humanitarianism*. We may define humanitarianism as the gradual widening and institutionalization of compassion. Compassion is an individual sentiment, but its sway is largely established by socially prescribed channels and boundaries. There is, it is worth emphasizing, a history and a sociology of compassion just as there is a history and sociology of jealousy, affection, and other emotions that, though assuredly individual, nevertheless manifest themselves in ways largely prescribed by social norms. Compassion is a timeless and universal human sentiment, but its objects and intensity vary from age to age. In the same way that certain social conditions became, at the beginning of the nineteenth century, objects of rationalist regard, conceived as intellectual problems, they became also objects of moral regard, conceived as moral problems. Sudden reflections of this growing compassion are reflected in the literature of the age, notably in the English social novel, where such problems were just brought to the attention of society.

Histories of modern European humanitarianism sometimes interpret this widening of compassion as the consequence of a humanization of the upper classes. While there may be something in this, the major reason lies, as Alexis de Tocqueville saw so vividly, in the tendency toward equalization of social ranks that followed the American and French revolutions. One of the by-products of the age of democratic revolution was a widening of the social area within which human compassion tended to operate. Tocqueville's illustrations of his thesis are vivid, and since the sociological elements remain as relevant today as then, they are worth repeating. He cites the following passage from a letter written in 1675 by a gentlewoman, Madame de Sévigné, to a friend about the brutal civil repression that followed an abortive tax revolt by the hard-pressed peasants of her area of Brittany:

> You talk very pleasantly about our miseries, but we are no longer so jaded with capital punishments; only one a week now, just to keep up appearances. It is true that hanging now seems to me quite a cooling entertainment. I have got a wholly new idea of justice since I have

been in this region. Your galley slaves seem to me a society of good people who have retired from the world in order to lead a quiet life.[6]

These lines were written, as Tocqueville notes, not by a selfish and cruel, much less a sadistic, person, but by a woman passionately attached to her children, always ready to sympathize in the sorrows of her friends, and notably indulgent to servants and retainers. "But," writes Tocqueville, "Madame de Sévigné *had no clear notion of suffering in anyone who was not a person of quality*" (italics added). It was not a want of compassion that produced the cruel jocularity and insensitivity of Madame de Sévigné's words; it was the existence of a *social limit* of compassion that, try as she might have, she could not have gone beyond.

Why, Tocqueville asks, would such a letter from a person widely regarded as cultivated and humane be inconceivable in Tocqueville's own day? Not, he concludes, because of any intrinsic elevation of upper-class character, but instead because of a fundamental change in the relation of the ranks of society to one another, a change produced by the tides of political and civil democracy that were beginning to engulf social parochialisms and insensitivities that neither Christianity nor Renaissance humanism had had any marked effect upon. The widening of political democracy has had, Tocqueville suggests, the effect of widening the effective social field of recognition of suffering.

> When all the ranks of a community are nearly equal, as all men then think and feel in nearly the same manner, each of them may judge in a moment the sensations of all the others; he casts a rapid glance upon himself, and that is enough. There is no wretchedness into which he cannot readily enter, and a secret instinct reveals to him its extent. It signifies that not strangers or foes are the sufferers; imagination puts him in their place; something like a personal feeling is mingled with his pity and makes himself suffer while the body of his fellow creature is in torture.

Tocqueville offers a positive and a negative demonstration of his thesis, each highly germane to a chapter in this book. In the first, drawn from penology, Tocqueville adduces "the model system of criminal justice" that existed in the early nineteenth century in the United States (and was indeed the prime reason for Tocqueville's visit to this country, as it was of the visits of some other Europeans). "In no country is criminal justice administered with more mildness

---

[6] Alexis de Tocqueville, *Democracy in America* (New York: Knopf, 1945). This passage and those which follow are contained in Volume II, Book III, Chapter 1.

than in the United States. . . . North America is, I think, the only country upon earth in which the life of not one citizen has been taken for a political offense in the course of the last fifty years." And the reason for this, Tocqueville thought, was that Americans, by and large, could see those charged with criminal offenses as of like social class and, therefore, perceivable within the social limits of their compassion.

He draws the second, and negative, demonstration of his equalitarian thesis from the treatment of Negro slaves. Tocqueville, like other visitors to the South at that time, was appalled by the "frightful misery" and the "cruel punishments" inflicted on the Negroes by Southern whites who were, in many instances, like Madame de Sévigné, notably kind and generous in their own circles. The Negro was, however, even farther outside the pale of social compassion than was the French peasant in the seventeenth century. He and his sufferings were, so to speak, invisible.

"Thus," Tocqueville concludes, "the same man who is full of humanity toward his fellow creatures when they are at the same time his equals becomes insensible of their afflictions as soon as that equality decreases. His mildness should therefore be attributed to the equality of conditions rather than to civilization and education."

Two further conclusions might be added, neither of which Tocqueville lived long enough to draw, but both of which add cognate illumination to his thesis. In penology, the mid-nineteenth-century beginnings of the deterioration of the "model system of criminal justice" that had so impressed Tocqueville coincided almost exactly with the changing composition of the American prison population. As the number of impoverished, lower-class Irish, Italians, and, then, eastern Europeans in the prison population increased—a consequence of the sudden increase of these nationalities in the larger population—the capacity of the middle-class American to conceive their plight compassionately declined notably. The results are written in a system of justice and prison administration that, by the late nineteenth century, brought few if any admiring European visitors.

The other illustration is the twentieth-century history of the Negro in America. What has manifestly been required to alter the position of the Negro in American society is exactly what was required in early nineteenth-century Europe to alter the position of the peasant: an extension of, first, political and civil equality and then, gradually, equality in economic and social areas. And if it be true that the French Revolution was required for the elevation of the status of the European peasant, it is equally true that the contemporary "civil rights revolution" is required in the case of the Negro.

The Comparative Study of Social Problems

It is one of the merits of the chapters in this book that they place American social problems against the background of other peoples—historic and contemporary, non-Western and Western. No society, however simple and stable, is altogether free of social dislocations and deviations, but the comparative study of human behavior makes it clear that both types and intensities of social problems differ widely from culture to culture, from age to age. In part this is the consequence, as we have just noted, of contrasting states of moral consciousness. It is also the result of contrasting standards of living and patterns of social authority, function, and membership.

Nonliterate and folk societies, largely organized in terms of kinship and other close personal ties, tend to have few, if any, of the social problems we consider in this book. For these societies other problems, chiefly those of adjustment to the physical environment—the need for food, shelter, physical security—loom much larger. When the basic problems of physical survival dominate a society's attention, there is less likelihood of those breakdowns in social relationships and deviations from social codes that are the stuff of social problems in present-day America. The raw challenge of physical environment has something of the same integrating effect upon social organization that catastrophe and disaster can have. In time of war, disaster, and physical calamity, as has often been noted, crimes, suicides, divorces, and community conflicts tend to diminish in number. Within a military organization itself there is a sudden reduction of tensions and delinquencies when war comes. The very mobilization of human energies elicited by a harsh physical environment or threat of a catastrophe has a tonic effect upon human relationships, resulting in a stronger moral consensus and a more integrated social system.

In America today we live in what is often called an affluent society. It is a society characterized by imposing command of physical resources, high standards of private consumption, effective maintenance of public order and security, freedom from most of the uncertainties of life that plagued our ancestors, and relatively high livels of humanitarianism. There are also, of course, squalid slums, both urban and rural; occasional epidemics of disease; sudden eruptions of violence or bigotry, even in the most civilized of communities; people for whom the struggle for food and shelter yet remains obsessing and precarious. Thus, we are not free of social problems, and some of them seem to grow almost in direct proportion to our affluence. That there may indeed be a fundamental conflict between material welfare and social or moral consensus is a thought that has crossed the minds of philosophers from Hesiod to Schweitzer. Such philosophers have argued that in the process of developing wealth and power a society must draw upon personal qualities—avarice, ambition, egoism, and others—which are the very antithesis of the qualities upon which social harmony and moral consensus rest.

Whether so fundamental a conflict in civilization exists is not, however, one of the questions dealt with by this book. However fascinating it may be as a problem in social ethics, it is not a question easily amenable to the concepts and methods of social science. It remains in the realm of moral philosophy, always interesting, always provocative, but basically unanswerable in the terms with which the sociologist seeks to clarify the social environment.

What we do know as social scientists emphasizes that there is no paradox in a civilization of high order containing certain social problems in greater number and intensity than are to be found in the kind of simple society that some philosophers have thought to be nearer man's essential nature. There is no paradox in relatively high rates of crimes against property in an advanced society that sets a high premium upon worldly goods and quick access to them. There is no paradox in the presence of racial and ethnic tensions in a society that, on the one hand, fosters equality through its constitution and laws but, on the other, maintains, through processes of use and wont, enclaves of discrimination and differential privilege.

Nor is there any paradox involved in the other problems that flourish, as this book makes plain, amid the opulence and aspirations of present-day America. Poverty, population tensions, social discontents in work, community conflicts, and divorce all have, in the form in which we know them, a close relation to the social patterns and values that we prize as elements of an advanced and free society. This does not mean that the problems are therefore ineradicable. Slavery and epidemic disease, once thought to be inextinguishable features of the human scene, have today largely disappeared. We therefore have every right to believe that our other problems are similarly subject to solution, given increasing knowledge and the moral will to use it.

Approaches to Social Problems

It will be clarifying to our understanding of the distinctiveness of the sociological approach to social problems if we examine briefly four other possible approaches: religion, law, journalism, and art. Let us begin with one of the oldest and most deeply seated: religion.

RELIGION. For thousands of years religious and legal codes have been the major perspectives through which social problems have been defined and acted upon. And, as we shall have repeated occasion to note, one of the major difficulties experienced by the contemporary social scientist in his own approach to social problems is the ancient and insistent tendency of the human mind to foreclose consideration of matters like juvenile delinquency and alcoholism by simply pronouncing them illegal or evil.

Whatever else religion is, it is an alembic of social experience. It distills and also composes the data of experience. It is not what religion says *about* social problems that is crucial; it is the way religion perceives, identifies, and relates these problems that gives it powerful sway. Religion identifies the transcendental essence in the mundane. The realm of the sacred, Durkheim emphasized, was the most powerful realm in the early development of human consciousness. From it and from the differentiation made between it and the profane, the merely utilitarian, arose many of our moral and even metaphysical perspectives. It is hardly strange, therefore, that social problems should still, for most persons, be subjects in the sovereign realm of the sacred—the realm, that is, of good and evil, of right and wrong.

From a theological point of view, many of the problems treated in this book are, first and last, violations of a divinely sanctioned moral order. As such they are often considered to be manifestations of evil, of original sin. The theologian will concede readily that such acts as murder, adultery, and theft are susceptible in part to nonreligious explanations, to influences of environment, and, if he is engaged in pastoral work, he will not hesitate to avail himself of the help of legal and social agencies. But, as a theologian, he will probably choose to see the final explanation of these acts in religious terms, as violations of God's commandments, as sin. And, like the explanation, the ultimate solution is put by the theologian in religious terms: expiation through prayer and penance.

LAW. There is both a logical and historical relationship between the religious and the legal approaches to social problems. In law, as in religious morality, such acts as murder and theft are conceived, fundamentally, as violations of a normative order—in this instance, the duly constituted and sanctioned law of the society concerned. From a strictly juridical point of view, the only reality that a social problem has is its legal reality as a crime, tort, or other breach of the legal order. A murder is not something for either study or redemptive prayer; it is the signal for mobilization of the whole retributive apparatus of the state, a mobilization that does not end until judicial determination of guilt is concluded. To be sure, the modern legal process increasingly avails itself of the resources of medicine, psychiatry, and the social sciences. A case that begins as a hard and fast legal matter—with apprehension, prosecution, and punishment the sole ends in view—may, in some of the more enlightened halls of justice today, end therapeutically rather than retributively. The borrowed objective is cure rather than punishment. And that social prevention of crime, rather than repression alone, has become more widely accepted in many communities is a mark both of rising recognition of the practical contributions of the social sciences and of more humane objectives of law-enforcement agencies. Nevertheless, with all allowance for its liaisons with therapeutic and scientific disciplines, the sovereign end of the legal process remains that of enforcement and, where necessary, punishment for violations. There remains for most persons a strongly religious element in law and its relation to crime. The guilty person, we are prone to say, must pay his debt to society—that is, do penance—through various expiatory means, ranging from fines through imprisonment to execution.

JOURNALISM. A very different approach to social problems is the journalistic approach. Ever since the eighteenth century, newspapers and magazines have been notable organs of exposure of and protest against exploitation, corruption, and degradation in society. Not infrequently has honest and accurate exposure been the real basis of charges of sensationalism and yellow journalism in this country and elsewhere in the world. In the United States, early in this century, it was the writings of the so-called Muckrakers—a group of courageous and perceptive journalists that included Lincoln Steffens, Ida Tarbell, and Upton Sinclair, working for such publishers as E. H. Scripps and Frank Munsey—that, perhaps above any other single force, first shocked the American public into awareness of social problems, particularly those of the burgeoning cities, and helped force public agencies into action. Today, the newspaper and the magazine remain valuable instruments for awakening popular response to narcotics, poverty, slums, prostitution, delinquency, and other ills that all too easily take refuge behind public lethargy or official incompetence. Modern thought as well as modern life would be the poorer but for the arts of cartoonists, the denunciations of editors, and the often brilliant exposures by newspaper reporters.

In journalism, the primary intent, however, is that of shocking or shaming the public into awareness of violations of the legal or moral order. Exposure is the overriding aim; all else—whether understanding, prevention, cure, or punishment—is secondary. The method is consequently impressionistic and rarely dispassionate.

ART. A fourth approach to social problems, that of the artist, is to be seen in all spheres of art, painting, drama, poetry, but nowhere so compellingly as in the social novel. Some of the most celebrated literary works of the past century have been conceived by their authors in hatred of poverty, injustice, and inequality. In the nineteenth century, the mordant depictions of lower-class misery under the impact of the new industrialism contained in the works of Mrs. Gaskell, Charles Kingsley, Charles Dickens, and Émile Zola were, for many millions of readers, the indispensable means of perceiving what actually lay around them. So too, in a later period, did the works of Henrik Ibsen, H. G. Wells, Samuel Butler, George Bernard Shaw, and John Galsworthy bring to attention the cankering social and moral problems that had lain long concealed behind the thick folds of Victorian respectability. In Europe, the social novel and play attained, in the late nineteenth and early twentieth centuries, much of the appeal to popular taste that the picaresque or romantic novel had held earlier. It was therefore an effective vehicle of the development of humanitarianism.

In America, the social novel has been a conspicuous part of the literary tradition throughout the present century. The novels of David Graham Phillips, Upton Sinclair, Theodore Dreiser, John Steinbeck, James Farrell, Charles Jackson, Nelson Algren, Ralph Ellison, and many others have laid bare, often hauntingly, sometimes with genius, the essential human elements of social problems dealt with in this book. Merely to list such titles as *Susan Lenox, The Jungle, An American Tragedy, The Grapes of Wrath, Studs Lonigan, The Lost Weekend, The Man With the Golden Arm,* and *Invisible Man* is to be reminded of novels that, quite apart from their varying worth as imaginative literature, have had enormous impact in their illumination of prostitution, poverty, crime, job and family dislocation, juvenile delinquency, alcoholism, narcotics, ethnic segregation, and other social problems. At their best these works have conveyed to their readers a sense of poignant immediacy, of vicarious experience, that is always the test and essence of art.

What all four of these approaches to social problems—religious, legal, journalistic, and artistic—have in common is their moral commitment. By their very nature they are caught up in, and are inseparable from ethical codes or ethical intent: in the case of religion or law, the governing end is that of inducing conformity to the moral or legal order, and in the case of the journalist or novelist, the end is that of arousing moral sympathy, passion, resentment, or hatred.

Sociology and Social Problems

Very different from the four approaches just discussed is the sociological approach to social problems. Here the objective is not dramatization, exposure, condemnation, or repression. The primary objective of the sociologist is to uncover the causes of the problems, to seek their determining contexts and their relation to other areas of social behavior. The sociologist is interested in understanding pathological social actions in exactly the same way that he is interested in understanding the normal and the good. In his strict role of scientist, as seeker of knowledge, he cannot be interested in exhortation or repressive sanctions except insofar as these responses are themselves involved in the nature of the social problems he is concerned with. What the scientist, as scientist, seeks is knowledge of the conditions involved, how the problems have come to be as we find them, and what the crucial factors are in their incidence. It is not action that the scientist seeks but hypothesis—clear, verifiable, and valid statements of causation.

Nothing could be more false than the occasional charge that sociologists are indifferent to moral standards; that for them one form of behavior is as good or bad as the next; that relativism is the moral code by which men should live. It would be as false as suggesting that the medical scientist is indifferent to the agonies of cancer because, instead of relying simply upon prayer or anesthetics, he insists upon the long-run study of this disease, upon approaching it in the same way that he would approach benign or normal aspects of organic functioning.

The social scientist is interested in making the protection of society his first responsibility, in seeing society reach higher levels of moral decency, and, when necessary, in promoting such legal actions as are necessary in the short run for protection or decency. But, as a scientist, it is his professional responsibility to deal with such matters as crime, suicide, narcotics, and ethnic tensions exactly in the manner in which he deals with other forms of human behavior.

Concern with social problems—including those treated in this book—has been an integral part of the main tradition of sociology. Emphasis on this point is valuable at the present time when, as Robert Merton suggests in the epilogue, an ambivalence exists toward the sociology of social problems and toward applied social science in general. Let it be emphasized, therefore, that modern systematic sociology was born in the practical interests of its titans quite as much as in their theoretical interests. Two classic works, each immensely influential on the subsequent course of sociological theory, admirably illustrate this: *Suicide* by Émile Durkheim and *The Polish Peasant* by William I. Thomas and Florian Znaniecki, the first published in France in 1896, the second in the United States in 1918-1920. Durkheim took as his point of departure the social problem posed by the rising rate of suicide in European society; Thomas and Znaniecki began with the high reported incidence of delinquency and crime among the Polish population of Chicago. That we tend today to think of each of these momentous studies as falling in the main tradition of sociology, rather than in the literature of social problems, is tribute, of course, to the overriding scientific intent of their authors. The essential point, however, for our purposes is that each work, in the process of illuminating the nature of a widely recognized social problem (and also, be it emphasized, of seeking a practical answer to the problem), was led to theoretical analyses of the social order, of personality, social interaction, and social norms that were to have quite as much effect upon the subsequent study of social organization as of disorganization, of theory as well as practice. It is perhaps the crowning merit of each work that it lifted its problem from the simple and sterile perspectives in which it had previously lain—perspectives of "pathology," "evil," and the like—and related it significantly to some of the main currents and contexts of modern Western society: individualism, secularism, urbanism, and industrialism.

All of this is not to suggest that social problems—of the kind represented in this book—are the constitutive problems of sociology as a science. Such a suggestion would be wide of reality. For sociology, like any other analytical science, is built around a different type of problem: that which emerges from theoretical reflection and dispassionate observations. Even if we lived in a social order miraculously exempt from all the problems dealt with in this book, man—blessed (or cursed) by what William James called the "divine itch of curiosity" —would still be interested in his own nature and society, and, therefore, in problems of social structure, social interaction, social change, and the others that give distinctive identity to sociology as a basic science. The itch of curiosity has generally had more to do with the history of science than has the spur of moral conscience.

So much is incontestable. But having said this, two conclusions remain vital: first, in the actual history of modern sociology, it was the attention, as much moral as theoretical or analytical, that such pioneers as Le Play, Durkheim, Weber, Thomas, and Cooley paid to social problems like family disorganization, suicide, and delinquency that provided much of the base on which the relevance to society of sociology's *theoretical* problems and conclusions was first established. The major figures in the history of sociology have never been constrained by methodological or theoretical fastidiousness from dealing directly with social problems. After all, as John Dewey tirelessly emphasized, it is method, not subject, that identifies a science.

The second conclusion, no more than an extension of the first, is that even today, when sociology has built up an imposing body of empirical fact, method, and verified conclusion that separates it as clearly from social work and reform as modern physiology is separated from medicine and public health, sociologists continue to find in their studies of crime, narcotics, alcohol, delinquency, and other social problems, insights into the nature of human behavior with implications that reach far beyond the empirical area from which they are drawn. It is hardly possible to read the chapters of this book and not realize frequently, and sometimes poignantly, the applicability of their main concepts to nondeviant behavior.

Historical Background of Contemporary Social Problems

In a society as complex as ours, no single or simple background of its problems can be offered. History is plural, and so are the contexts of the various types of deviation and disorganization presented in this book. All we can do by way of introduction is identify some of the larger and more general processes of change in modern society: processes which, in ways too numerous and too varied to identify here, have entered into the specific causes of contemporary social problems.

These general processes involve, of course, the larger contexts of human association: kinship systems, communities, and moral codes; social functions and patterns of authority; the allegiances and cross-allegiances of individuals to institutions; and the relationship of norms to human action. Seen from a sociological point of view, the whole history of civilization is one of repeated changes in these systems, functions, and structures. But human history also contains innumerable examples of social fixity, of institutional persistence; many of our most pressing problems have taken their form as the result of unresolved tensions between the new and the old, existing side by side in a culture.

We often refer to urbanism and technology as major forces involved in the social dislocations of Western society. While there is truth in this, we must understand clearly what is meant. It is not the city as such, any more than it is technology, that directly causes such phenomena as crime, delinquency, and ethnic tensions. There are far more examples of stable and constructive behavior in urban and industrial settings than there are of the reverse. Inherently, there is no more reason for technology to be associated with social disorganization and moral alienation than there is for agricultural life. Today indeed, as many studies have shown, some of the most marked manifestations of disorganization and deviation are to be found in rural environments.

Even though the physical facts of technology and the city are not themselves necessarily involved in the background of our social problems, certain historically related social processes are definitely visible. Careful reading of the chapters that follow will make clear that implicit in the oft-cited references to urbanism and technology are more fundamental and relevant references to processes that are social and normative—processes that share in the substance of the problems themselves.

Four such processes are particularly significant: *conflict of institutions, social mobility, individuation,* and *anomie.* Although these processes are rarely, if ever, found in isolated, discrete form in human history, we shall deal with them individually here for purposes of clarification.

CONFLICT OF INSTITUTIONS. Every institution—family, community, trade union, church—is a pattern of ends, functions, and authorities, commanding varying degrees of allegiance from its members. Each institution is potentially capable of extending itself in virtually complete fashion over the lives of its individual members, dominating all aspects of their existence. For example, there are societies in which the family itself—the extended family—is sovereign and all-encompassing. Economic, religious, and political functions are all performed within the kinship group; there is no competing type of authority; the individual's allegiance to family is undivided. In the same way, there are other societies, and other historical ages, in which the church possesses this comprehensive and total role; in contemporary totalitarian societies, the political state is a monolith of authority and function.

But what we see more commonly in a society is a plurality of institutions, each with its own authority and functions, each limited, so to speak, by the presence of others, and all forming together the larger pattern of authority, function, and allegiance by which a society comes to be known. Such pluralism is also to be seen historically, and most especially in Western history. We can see a succession of dominant social influences and, in our own day, a kind of composite of them all.

In the early Middle Ages, kinship and local community held the greatest influence in the lives of individuals; the church, as we know, acceded to eminence before the period was over. Still later it was the national state, and then, in vast sections, industry.

This pluralism cannot be overlooked in our study of the background of modern social problems, for it is frequently at the bottom of those conflicts and dislocations which form the substance of deviant behavior. We may, as historians, choose to see such pluralism and conflict of institutions over the long span, but it is deeply involved in recent and present history, as well: in the migration of peoples and cultures from the old world to the new; in the passage of American society from rural to urban; in the changed position of the generations to one another; and in the rise of such new institutions as the labor union, mass communication media, political parties, and the suburban complex. Where there is plurality there is competition and even conflict of ends, influences, and functions.

Such competition and conflict in the institutional scene are often reflected within the minds and personalities of the people concerned. We see this reflection throughout Western history, sometimes in epic and convulsive degree. Social change is at bottom the reaction of people to intrusions into, or alterations of, their environment. Social change appears when the results of such intrusion or alteration are incorporated, however confusedly, in the personalities of individuals, and come thus to exert influence upon their purposes. The conflict between established habits and new values, between old allegiances and new authorities, can sometimes be drastic and difficult. Each institution is a web of functions, allegiances, and meanings in the lives of individuals. The change in one institution—the loss or addition of functions and meanings that are vital—must frequently react upon the structure of some other institution and thus awaken conflicting responses in the minds of individuals.

Nowhere has such conflict been more vivid, and frequently agonizing, than in the transplanting of peoples from Europe or Africa or Asia to the United States. Much of American social history is made up of this transplanting. And with it there has been a frequent conflict of institutional loyalties, of old memberships and new. Out of such conflicts have come some of the great intellectual and moral achievements of American civilization, but out of them have also come some of our bitterest problems.

SOCIAL MOBILITY. Closely related to conflict among institutions and cultures is the mobility of persons and groups that has been so revolutionary a feature of the modern West, especially since the eighteenth century. It has been a horizontal mobility, carrying tens of millions of persons across oceans, plains, and mountains; but, more significantly, it has also been a vertical mobility, involving countless shifts of personal and family status. Relationships of social classes have been profoundly affected; the legal, economic, and social positions of ethnic and racial groups have been altered; patterns of influence, prestige, and power in society have been transformed or sharply modified.

In this process, many influences have been at work: mercantilism, spurring the quest for new lands and wealth; industrialism, with its frequently isolating and fragmenting effects upon established communities and statuses; political centralization, leading to a sharp reduction in influence of local and regional authorities; religious individualism, with its atomizing effects upon older ecclesiastical structures and codes; and, finally, the advent of modern democracy, with its relentless and radical stress upon social equality. All these forces have been connected with the powerful processes of social mobility.

With this mobility there has inevitably been a release from social and cultural isolation. It is difficult for us in the contemporary world to realize the extent to which isolation has characterized most of the groups and communities in the history of the world. Often this has been geographical isolation, with whole societies insulated from physical contact with other peoples. But even where there has been physical propinquity, there has been a striking tendency for religions, ethnic groups, guilds, communities, and families to maintain privacy from one another, so far as possible, and to guard their respective cultures and values. Often this isolation has been imposed upon groups, as in the case of racial or religious minorities where assimilation with the majority was forbidden by law or custom.

The last century has seen dramatic changes in this pattern. With the advent of legal equalitarianism, industrialization, and a general rise in humanitarianism, social fixity has been succeeded, for thousands of groups, by a high degree of mobility. With the blurring of traditional social class lines and the removal of the more flagrant legal and economic privileges of certain classes, there has been marked change in the whole status structure of modern society. With a culture in which the ethic of success is compelling, it is only to be expected that status-striving will become obsessive for large numbers of persons. The struggle to succeed, to belong, to influence, lies behind remarkable achievements in all areas of our society. But it also lies behind some of the tragedies: lives broken by the struggle; individuals driven to means that are not tolerated by society, even though the ends which dictate the means are tolerated; children, as well as adults, who seek status security where they can find it, even when it lies in illegal or unmoral contexts. There is wreckage as well as achievement written in the story of social mobility.

INDIVIDUATION. One of the fundamental differences between modern and traditional society is the degree of legal and moral autonomy possessed by individuals. Our society is less likely to be based upon the corporate communities of interest that were so distinct in earlier kinship, neighborhood, parish, and guild. Many sociologists have called attention to the contrast, among them Maine, Tönnies, Durkheim, and Simmel. These men have seen forces in modern history leading to a movement away from the centrality of the social group, with its attributes of ascribed status and close membership, to the primacy of the legally autonomous individual and impersonal relations of contract. Tönnies emphasized the historical weakening of the ties of *Gemeinschaft*—the communal ties of family, village, and guild—and the maximization, in modern times, of the more impersonal, atomistic, and mechanical relationships of *Gesellschaft*. Simmel dealt extensively with the mechanizing and frequently isolating influence of the market economy with its depersonalizing influence upon traditional moral and social patterns. Because of the easy convertibility of all qualitative values and status relationships into fluid relationships of contract, based upon money, he saw a fragmenting effect upon the established contexts of status and morality. And Durkheim wrote: "What is characteristic of our development, is that it has successively destroyed all the established social contexts; one after another they have been banished either by the slow erosion of time or by violent revolution, and in such fashion that nothing has been developed to replace them."

It would be easy to exaggerate this process of individuation and depersonalization. There can be no such thing in either society or nature as a complete vacuum. The decline of the extended family, the corporate parish, the guild, traditional class, and the various other forms of traditional society has never been complete; new associations have arisen in many parts of society to replace them. The labor union, the school, the business enterprise all reflect modern forms of organization that can often be as rigorous in their influences as the older groups.

But it is equally true that there are many areas in which the newer forms of association have not proved to be as encompassing; associational ties are plainly weaker than they once were, and in these areas a good deal of behavior can be interpreted in terms of a drive toward functional significance, close membership, and clear and meaningful status. We see this in behavior that is in no sense deviant or patho-logical—an aspect of what Riesman has called the Lonely Crowd—but we see it also in juvenile delinquency, alcoholism, and community disorganization.

ANOMIE. One of the most striking features of modern Western history has been the set of changes affecting the character of moral values and the relationships between these values and dominant insti-tutions. All human behavior is normative. It is directed to ends and draws its meaning and importance in terms of these ends. When moral values are widely accepted in a society, they form the basis on which the society achieves consensus and integration. Such values are also essential to the integrity and successful functioning of individual per-sonality. When values become confused, when they conflict with one another, or when they lose their immediacy to human beings, both individual behavior and the social order are affected.

Much of the history of modern Western society is the history of the dislocation or changed emphasis of traditional values. Many of the values that are characteristically Western developed from the matrix of Judeo-Christianity and were given their institutional setting during centuries in which the economic order was largely agrarian and in which the typical units of society were small and homogeneous. The rise of capitalism, religious individualism, and democracy has inevita-bly affected the character of traditional values. It has done so by alter-ing, often transforming, the social contexts of the traditional values, and by spawning new values more directly related to the nature of the modern order. Such doctrines as critical rationalism and utilitarian-ism have taken their toll from the traditional values of the past. It is difficult for a set of values to maintain clear moral ascendancy when the presumed sanctity or divinity of its roots is challenged by the secular ideas of rationalism and science.

Modern history has frequently been an arena for conflicts between such values, on the one hand, as patriarchalism, religious corporatism, and fixed social status, and, on the other hand, individualism of faith and morals, self-interest in economic and political affairs, and a belief in the right of all individuals to those things for which their individual talents and virtues qualify them. Such conflicts of values can be seen in many parts of the world today. We see it in India where ancient values of family and caste are being challenged on a widening front by the values of individualism, democracy, and the scientific-techno-logical order. We also see this conflict in our own society: it often occurs when families come from the traditional culture of eastern Europe, Latin America, or the Middle East and settle in the more impersonal and secular atmosphere of an American city. Anomie, with its implicit tensions of moral conflict, alienation, and meaninglessness, is a notable and persisting aspect of contemporary social problems, even as it is an aspect of the whole history of man.

Conclusion

Much of what we value in American society—personal freedom, liberal democracy, economic and social opportunity—would be inconceivable apart from the processes of conflict, mobility, individuation, and anomie that we have briefly described above. Historians have pointed out that great periods of human thought and achievement are also periods of some degree of social and political dislocation, or of conflict of values. With the breaking of custom, the liberation from processes of use and wont, men's minds can be challenged in ways that have bold and creative results. What else indeed is the history of the Western mind and conscience?

But conflict of institutions and values, mobility of individuals and groups, can also have negative consequences to a civilization. Such processes can lead, and often do lead, not to creative achievement but to alienated and pathological behavior: the kinds of behavior that are regarded as social problems. These kinds of behavior, as well as the creative and good, form an essential part of the study of man, and they are the subject matter of this book.

PART ONE
DEVIANT BEHAVIOR

1

Mental Disorders

by John A. Clausen

Everyone suffers from physical ailments at one time or another. Most of us spend several days in a hospital at least once or twice in our lifetime. It is probably safe to say that most of us suffer from emotional upsets at one time or another, though most of us would balk at referring to these as "mental illness." Many of us may be surprised, nevertheless, to learn that approximately 600,000 adults are confined in the mental hospitals of the United States on any given day and that according to current estimates one person in 12 will spend some time in a mental hospital before he dies. It is probably not erroneous to say that almost all of us will at some time witness severe mental illness in a relative or close friend. Further, while mental diseases do not usually kill, they tend to be persistent, often resulting in long periods of incapacity.

We do not usually think of illness as a form of deviant behavior, although we commonly recognize the disruptive effect that illness of a key person can have in any organization. We also commonly recognize that illness is often related to life patterns and to unusual stresses upon the body. But for the diagnosis and treatment of most organic diseases, we have clearly relevant medical resources which are available to most of the population in the United States. Therefore, we generally do not regard physical illness as a major social problem but as a medical problem with important economic and social consequences. This is scarcely true, however, of mental illness.

It appears that the mentally ill have always been regarded primarily as deviants. In Biblical days, the mentally disordered were described as being possessed by demons or devils. In Colonial America, they were often regarded as witches, persecuted, and even executed; at best they were designated as "lunatics" or "madmen" and confined in jails or locked in well-barred rooms. In recent decades, however, there has been a significant social movement committed to the view that mental disorders are truly illnesses, no more to be stigmatized than any other illness. This view has had adherents at least since the rise of medicine in ancient Greece, but has only recently received even token acceptance by a significant segment of the general public.

Now that mental disorders are officially recognized as a health problem, is there any reason to regard them as a social problem beyond the fact that many persons are incapacitated and that public facilities must be provided for the patients? The question is best answered by considering a brief case description (from the author's files).

Lorraine B. was 40 years old when she was first admitted to a mental hospital. Married for seven years to Fred B., a meagerly educated but hard working and steady laborer, she was the mother of a five-year-old daughter and a three-year-old son. She had been married previously and had had two children who died in infancy. Her mother had been hospitalized with the diagnosis "schizophrenia" in 1943, staying in the hospital about six months.

Mrs. B. was committed to the hospital on certification by two physicians that she was insane. Questioned by the admitting psychiatrist as to why she was sent to the hospital, she blamed her husband. She said he was frequently drunk, sexually demanding, and running around with other women. Further, her family didn't want her to read the Bible and preach. On questioning, she acknowledged that she had seen God in the clouds and had been hearing noises which she was unable to identify. The provisional diagnosis was *schizophrenia, paranoid type.*

The B.'s lived in a small basement apartment in a metropolitan suburb. The apartment was somewhat sparsely and simply furnished. The rental was high for Mr. B.'s income, but they enjoyed the pleasant suburban neighborhood with its lawns and trees. They did not have a telephone; a television set was the one "luxury item" in their home. Mr. B. did not have a car but had the regular use of a small pick-up truck owned by his employer.

As part of a study of the impact of mental illness on the family, Mr. B. was interviewed at home soon after his wife's admission to the hospital. What had happened prior to her admission? When had he first felt that something might be wrong? Fred B. was not a highly verbal person. His education went only to the fifth grade in rural North Carolina. His answers were brief, direct, concrete—and, the interviewer felt, sincere. His wife had become violently distrustful of him, especially in the past 18 months, but the first indication had come nearly five years ago. He recalled: "It was when Sue [the daughter] was about three months old. My wife was jealous if I played with the baby. She resented it."

From this time, Mr. B. thought of his wife as having "a nasty streak in her that made her act jealous." She was frequently accusatory and he was frequently angry with her, especially when she falsely accused him of running around with other women. Still, she was a good mother to the children and when she flew off the handle, he would go out for a walk to avoid further conflict.

Had there been any other signs? "Yes, her drawing pictures." Mr. B. pointed to a crayon portrait of Christ thumb-tacked to the wall. It was striking in coloring and expression. He mused, "It just beats me. She never had no training at drawing but that's a good picture. Don't you think so? She would read the Bible and then just sit there and stare and then she'd draw. It was like she didn't know there was anyone in the room with her. Even if the kids came in and spoke to her, she just didn't notice."

When had he first thought that the problem might be serious? [We did not use the term mental illness, since we wanted his words.] It was the night, about three months before she went to the hospital, when she said someone had "done something" to the alarm clock to change its shape. Her husband had tried to reason with her, but it wasn't any more possible to get her to listen than it had been when he tried to convince her he wasn't running with other women. "Then," he said, "I thought she wasn't right in the head."

She began to restrict the children's play. When a neighbor came to see how Mrs. B. was, she ordered her former friend out of the house, waving a butcher knife. Lorraine B. moved out of her husband's bed, but frequently kept him awake much of the night while she prowled the house to "protect her papers and books."

A neighbor spoke to Mr. B., suggesting that his wife needed to see a doctor. Fred went to see the family doctor and asked him to drop by the apartment to see Mrs. B. The doctor did so. He prescribed some "nerve pills," which she threw away. Mrs. B. then "ran away" to a friend's home in another state, staying for several weeks; the friend finally called Mr. B. and asked him to take his wife home.

During the final week before hospitalization, Lorraine smashed the radio because it was making sounds even when it was turned off. When the children were invited to a friend's birthday party and went without their mother's consent, she went after them, denounced the neighbor who had invited them and screamed obscenities which aroused the whole neighborhood. Then she became mute and completely withdrawn.

Mr. B. went back to the doctor, who said he had known she was "off" when he saw her a month previously, though he hadn't told her husband then. The doctor filled out commitment papers and said Mr. B. would have to go to the county seat to arrange for taking Mrs. B. to the hospital. Mr. B. asked a police lieutenant for information about procedures. He was told to swear out a warrant so the police could transport Mrs. B. to the hospital. He did so. The police then dispatched a car to pick up Mrs. B. and take her to the county jail, overnight. The next day she was transported to the mental hospital, confused and enraged. She felt that she had been betrayed by her husband and rejected by everyone else.

The research interviewer asked Mr. B., "Looking back over this period, what would you say caused the greatest difficulty in trying to deal with your wife's problem?" His reply: "Not being able to get her to understand."

While their mother was in the hospital, the children were taken to North Carolina to stay with their paternal grandparents, on the small farm where their father had grown up.

Mrs. B. was hospitalized for approximately three months. At first she did not wish to see her husband when he came to the hospital to visit; she was alternately seclusive and hostile toward others. She was started on a course of treatment using a strong tranquillizing drug and was transferred to a "chronic" ward. In the view of the examining physician, Mrs. B. had obviously been ill for a considerable time and was unlikely to respond to therapy. Quite soon thereafter, however, she was put in the care of a physician to whom she almost immediately responded positively. It was impossible to say why, but she became cooperative and in a few days was helping other patients and participating in cleaning and kitchen work. She reported no more delusions. After she had maintained apparently normal behavior for several weeks she was permitted to go home for a week-end. Her husband was wary but glad that she could visit. After a few more weeks she went home to stay. Her husband said she had not been "so easy to live with" since before Sue was born. The one thing she was still bitter about was that she had been arrested and thrown in jail overnight before going into the hospital. Mrs. B. was eager to have the children home with her; the family was reconstituted with the children's return a week after hers.

Mrs. B.'s period of hospitalization was less than the average for patients with a diagnosis of schizophrenia, but obviously longer than would be required for most physical ailments. Her symptoms were perhaps somewhat more violently manifest than those of most patients, but were not by any means atypical. The difficulty that her husband had in assessing what was wrong and what could be done about the problem attests to the lack of clearly apparent patterns for dealing with mental illness. The indignity of a night in jail affords further testimony to a persisting difference between mental illnesses and other illnesses. For patient and family, then, and for the community as a whole, mental illness is a puzzling, disruptive phenomenon, a problem whose social aspects are not adequately encompassed within the medical context. (See Chapter 10, page 540.)

The Nature and Varieties of Mental Disorders

Mental disorders vary in kind and in degree, just as physical illnesses do. Some mental illnesses result from organic lesions (e.g., that caused by syphilis of the central nervous system); others appear to have their roots in psychological experiences and to be quite different in quality from most somatic diseases. Indeed, there is some question as to whether certain mental disorders can really be considered illnesses. The psychiatrist Thomas Szasz has written of the "myth of mental illness," [1] maintaining that all mental disorders are simply defective strategies for handling difficult life situations.

Few psychiatrists are disposed to agree with Szasz that even severe mental disorders are not to be considered illness. It is clear, however, that the general public does not tend to react to the mentally ill as it does to the physically ill, nor does the disordered person tend to see himself as ill, even though he may be desperately miserable. Ironically, the more serious the mental illness, the less likely is the patient to recognize that he is ill. Perhaps it is this aspect of mental illness—the patient's inability to realize that he is sick and needs help —along with the fact that mental illness disrupts interpersonal relationships, that has set off mental patients, not as ill persons, but as insane, "crazy," alienated.

As with other forms of illness, only the most severely impaired or acutely distressed mentally ill persons are in hospitals. Despite this fact, roughly half of the hospital beds in the United States are occupied by mental patients. Some of these patients have been hospitalized continuously not merely for years, but for decades. Contrary to popular belief, however, most persons who become patients in our mental hospitals do not stay there. Most are returned home within a matter of months, depending, of course, on the nature of the particular disorder, the home environment of the patient, and the administrative and therapeutic policies and practices of the hospital. We shall want to return to a consideration of the nature of mental disorder from a sociological perspective after we have examined both the psychiatric perspective and popular beliefs about mental illness. To begin, let us briefly consider the kinds of disorders or diseases recognized by psychiatry and the bases for their classification.

It must be acknowledged at the outset that modern psychiatry has not been conspicuously successful in the classification of mental illness. Whereas an internationally accepted nomenclature has been achieved for the classification of most other types of disease, national and even local customs and considerations have prevented agreement on all but the most gross categories of mental illness. In the United States the nomenclature—that is, the set of names or classes by which the various disorders are known—was changed shortly after World War II but remains variant from the nomenclature proposed by the

---

[1] Thomas S. Szasz, *The Myth of Mental Illness* (New York: Harper, 1961).

World Health Organization (WHO) and adopted, at least in part, by most of the other countries with advanced medical services.[2] This state of affairs exists largely because our knowledge of the etiology of major segments of mental disease is incomplete and because symptom patterns are diverse and overlapping. With symptoms still our primary basis for classification, we are at the same stage of knowledge about mental disease that medicine occupied a century ago with reference to the "fevers." Typhoid, malaria, and a number of other diseases, readily distinguishable now, were all lumped together.

Indeed, the picture for mental disorders is even more confused than was that for "fevers." The symptoms of mental disorder are ideational and behavioral. Therefore they reflect cultural emphases as well as disease processes. Many symptoms cannot be adequately interpreted without a knowledge of the norms of the subculture to which the individual belongs. For example, certain severe mental disorders are characterized by persisting delusions, such as believing oneself bewitched. In a culture in which most people believe in witches, however, such a belief cannot be considered delusional. It may be lacking in a scientific basis, but the same can be said of all beliefs in a supernatural realm. The culture not only provides the norms for assessing any given pattern of belief or behavior, but also provides the coloring or emphasis to the manifest symptomatology and the characteristic modes for dealing with such behavioral manifestations. Therefore it becomes extremely difficult to equate symptoms from one culture to another or even from one time to another.

Ideally, a classification scheme should be based upon theoretical or etiological considerations. When causes of diseases are not known, there are likely to be a number of competing etiological hypotheses, and often these become elevated to the rank of valid theories even when there is little evidence for their validity.

A substantial part of the difference in nomenclature between usage in the United States and that advanced by the WHO stems from the different preconceptions of etiology. Some conditions regarded by most American psychiatrists as "reactions" to life experience are regarded by their European counterparts as "endogenous"—i.e., constitutionally determined. Problems of nomenclature greatly increase the difficulty of comparing research results from one country to another, but they need not further detain us here. Forewarned of the

---

[2] Problems and systems of nomenclature are discussed in *Diagnostic and Statistical Manual: Mental Disorders* (Washington, D. C.: American Psychiatric Association, 1952). See also Joseph Zubin, ed., *Field Studies in the Mental Disorders* (New York: Grune and Stratton, 1961).

complexity of the problem, we can consider the major categories of mental illness recognized by psychiatry, even though specific diagnoses may vary to a degree by country and by psychiatric school.

As a starting point, we may note the traditional breakdown of mental disorders into three major classes: the psychoses, which entail a gross derangement of mental processes and inability to evaluate external reality correctly; the neuroses, which entail impairment of functioning, often of a segment of behavior, but no sharp break with reality; and the psychosomatic disorders, which entail very real organic symptoms and malfunctions caused at least in part by psychological processes.

The term *insane*—which has legal meaning but no technical status in psychiatry—is most often applicable to persons suffering from the acute or chronic phases of psychosis, though a recurrent legal problem is posed by the fact that the boundary between sane and insane is not the same as that between psychotic and nonpsychotic. Of the several classes of psychosis, we shall be most concerned with the functional psychoses or psychotic states, especially schizophrenia, and with the mental disorders of old age. These, along with the psychoses stemming from alcoholism and from syphilis of the brain, are the diagnoses given to the bulk of patients in our mental hospitals.

Our knowledge of the prevalence of the various forms of mental illness is limited to the cases that come into treatment. Intensive studies to ascertain the true prevalence of mental illnesses have clearly demonstrated that only a small proportion of neurotic and psychosomatic ailments are diagnosed and treated. It may be assumed, however, that in Western society the majority of persons who show continuing symptoms of psychosis are at some time or other hospitalized or otherwise confined or brought into treatment.

Some idea of the relative frequency of hospitalization [3] for various categories of mental disorder is given by Figure 1, which shows the rate of initial hospitalization by diagnostic category per 100,000 population of a given age group. It will at once be apparent that very few persons are hospitalized for mental illness prior to age 15 and that the major categories of disorder tend to peak at different age

---

[3] Data on the number, diagnosis, age, and sex of hospitalized patients are published each year in *Patients in Mental Institutions,* prepared by the Biometrics Branch of the National Institute of Mental Health and issued by the Dept. of Health, Education, and Welfare. This is the basic source of the data to be presented on the number and characteristics of patients in various diagnostic categories.

FIGURE 1

First Admission Rates for Selected Diagnoses by Age: State and County Mental Hospitals, United States, 1963

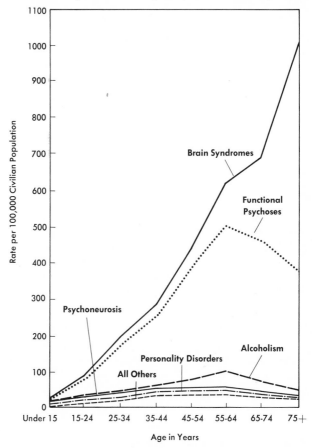

levels. But first admissions to the hospital do not tell the whole story. Persons hospitalized with a diagnosis of psychoneurosis or personality disorder are likely to have a relatively short stay in the hospital while others—notably those with a diagnosis of functional psychosis or chronic brain syndrome—may stay for much longer periods. As a result, the latter categories tend to accumulate in the hospital. Therefore the resident population at any given time is largely composed of persons with a functional psychosis or a brain syndrome (Figure 2).

FIGURE 2

Resident Patient Rates for Selected Diagnoses by Age:
State and County Mental Hospitals, United States, 1963

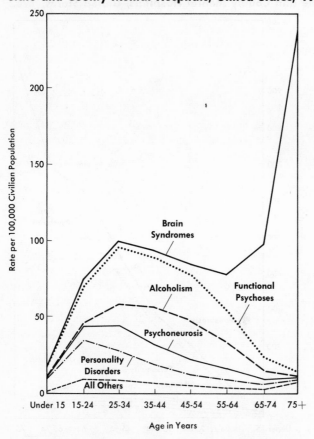

Age in Years

Schizophrenia and Other Functional Psychoses

The "functional" psychoses are so labeled because they are without clearly defined organic cause or identifiable structural change in the brain and are assumed to be psychological in origin, at least to some degree. Schizophrenia was first called *dementia praecox* (psychosis of adolescence) because of the frequency with which it occurs among young adults. The symptomatic manifestations that are labeled schizophrenia may, however, occur at any age level from childhood to senescence. Although popularly referred to as "split personality," it is doubtful that this term will connote the basic symptoms of schizophrenia to most persons. The "split" refers to the separation of emotion from cognition or intellectual functioning. But what impresses most of us is the combination of psychological withdrawal from others with a wide variety of distortions or derangements of thought processes—delusions, bizarre associations, flights of ideas, etc.

The major subtypes of schizophrenia—paranoid, hebephrenic, catatonic—are diagnosed on the basis of dominant symptomatology and course of the illness, but these diagnoses are woefully unreliable over time. Many psychiatrists now believe that schizophrenia is not a single disease, but a family of disorders. Be that as it may, the majority of hospitalized mental patients who enter a mental hospital before the age of 40 receive this diagnosis in the United States. Many return home within a matter of months, to live useful and happy lives. Others show a degree of symptomatology which may impair their relationships in day-to-day life in the community; they may return to the mental hospital for months or years at a time over several decades. Still others fail ever to leave the hospital, becoming chronic or deteriorated to such a degree that they tend to be relegated to the "back wards." Although only a minority of schizophrenic patients fail to leave the hospital, this residue accumulates and may in time comprise 50 percent or more of the hospital population because of the relatively young age at the onset of the illness and the nearly normal life expectancy of schizophrenics.

Included with schizophrenia among the functional psychotic disorders are *manic-depressive reactions* and *involutional melancholia,* both of which tend to occur in middle life. In theory, the manic-depressive patient shows alternations of extreme excitement and euphoria with periods of extreme depression and despair. In fact, however, the manic phase is relatively rare. Manic-depressive psychosis tends to be episodic. Patients given this diagnosis are more likely to recover completely than are those diagnosed schizophrenic, but recurrences of the illness are quite usual.

The diagnosis of involutional psychosis tends to be given by psychiatrists if the patient is near the phase of physical change of life. The symptoms are very difficult to distinguish from those of the depressed type of manic-depressive patient. Whether there is a valid distinction between these affective states or whether they represent a psychiatric "folkway" cannot be definitely answered at the present time.

There is room for doubt as to whether the remaining category within the class *psychotic states*—paranoia—actually exists as a distinct entity. Paranoid symptoms—delusions of grandeur, delusions of persecution, and the like—are found in paranoid schizophrenia, in manic-depressive and involutional states, in the mental disorders of old age, and indeed, in persons who are excessively suspicious of others, but who are not grossly ill. In "true paranoia" the delusional system is tremendously elaborated, but in other areas of thought and emotion the person is relatively normal. The diagnosis—now called "paranoid states"—is rarely given in most mental hospitals (.05 percent of first admissions to United States mental hospitals bore this diagnostic label in 1963), and increasingly is regarded as an extreme form of symptomatic variant of other disorders, most often schizophrenia.

Mental Disorders of Old Age

As the bulk of the population has shifted from farms and small rural communities to the cities, and as life expectancy has been increased by medical science and public health programs, the mental disorders of old age—primarily *senile dementia* and *psychosis with cerebral arteriosclerosis*—have become both more prevalent and more difficult to cope with. Rural life offered both meaningful activities and living space for grandparents; urban life tends to diminish both. It is normal (that is, usual) for older persons to become somewhat forgetful, for traits like garrulousness or suspiciousness to become somewhat accentuated, and for inhibitions and concern for the amenities to be diminished, especially as one approaches 80. In a small house or an apartment in the city, these characteristics of old age may be especially hard to live with. When the older person ceases to be responsible even for his own bodily functions, caring for him in the home may constitute an unbearable burden for the other members of the household. In the past 50 years, hospitalization of patients suffering the mental disorders of old age has increased tremendously. Senile and arteriosclerotic patients now constitute nearly 25 percent of all first admissions to mental hospitals for long-term care.

The mental disorders of old age must not, however, be thought of as representing a steady or inevitable decline in the organism. While it is true that many older patients go to the mental hospital to die there, a substantial number may be able to function with fair adequacy in a somewhat sheltered environment where they feel they have a secure place and some degree of usefulness.

Grouped with the mental disorders of old age in the category now labeled "chronic brain syndrome" are the psychoses stemming from syphilis of the brain—*dementia paralytica* or *paresis*—those resulting from chronic alcoholism, and those resulting from long-continued trauma to the brain such as is received not infrequently by professional boxers. It is of interest to note that few new cases of paresis have occurred since the advent of antibiotic treatment for syphilis, yet the proportion of cases now found in our mental hospitals is greater than in the past. The explanation is simply the greater life expectancy of patients already hospitalized. Thus our present paretic patients are a heritage from the days before effective treatment for syphilis. In another few decades, however, this form of mental disease should be relatively infrequent.

The Psychoneuroses

The terms "neurosis" and "neurotic" have achieved a wide currency in contemporary life. They call various images to mind: the complaining, never satisfied housewife; the sensitive, tortured artist who cannot accept man's inhumanity to man; the businessman obsessed with the quest for wealth and power and unable to enjoy anything else to the full. Sometimes the terms are used with a note of approbation, sometimes as derogatory epithets. Sometimes it is even suggested that we are all a bit neurotic. If this statement is intended to indicate that at times we all behave in ways that deviate from objectively sensible or fruitful behavior, it can hardly be challenged.

Just where the line between normality and psychoneurosis should be drawn, for purposes of classifying people, is a matter of opinion, because psychoneurotic reactions are disturbances in the functioning of personalities, and not diseases as usually understood. The chief characteristic of these disorders is *anxiety* which may be directly felt and expressed or which may be unconsciously and automatically controlled by the utilization of various psychological defense mechanisms. When the intensity of anxiety is so great as to produce symptoms which markedly impair the individual's ability to carry out normal activities with his fellow men, it is appropriate to label the resulting state a neurosis.

The form that the neurosis takes—that is, the kinds of symptoms that will be manifest—will depend on the way that the person has learned (whether consciously or not) to handle his anxiety. In the form called simply *anxiety reaction,* the anxiety is diffuse and uncontrolled. In *conversion reactions,* the anxiety is "converted" into organic dysfunctions—paralysis, tics, etc. In *phobic reactions,* the anxiety is expressed symbolically as fear of some specific idea, object, or situation. In *obsessive-compulsive reactions,* the anxiety is associated with the persistence of unwanted ideas and of repetitive impulses to perform acts which may be considered morbid or unreasonable by the patient. In *depressive reactions,* which are often associated with a feeling of guilt for past failures or deeds, the anxiety may be allayed and hence partially relieved by the symptoms of depression and self-depreciation.

The prevalence of psychoneurosis obviously depends upon where one draws the dividing line between normal and pathological. Selective Service rejections in World War II because of psychoneurotic tendencies amounted to more than half a million men; in addition, over 300,000—or roughly 7 percent of the population screened—were discharged from the services for psychoneurosis.[4] In a recent study of a rural county, the Leightons found that over half the population had at some time or other exhibited psychoneurotic symptoms to a significant degree.[5] The Leightons suggest that many people have a number of the symptoms of psychoneurosis most of the time, but that the degree of impairment caused by such symptoms is variable, depending upon life experiences and pressures. In any event, most psychoneurosis goes undiagnosed and untreated, accounting for a large measure of unhappiness and ineffectiveness but not for the sharp social disruptions found with psychosis.

Psychosomatic or Psychophysiological Disorders

Closely akin to the psychoneuroses are those responses to emotional stress which take the form of physiological malfunction. In mild cases they may be nothing more than a headache, an occasional attack of diarrhea, or a transitory skin rash during or after periods of tension. More severe cases, such as *ulcerative colitis, hypertension,* or *anorexia nervosa* (severe loss of appetite and vomiting) sometimes produce structural changes which may threaten life.

These disorders are readily defined as belonging in the medical context, and need not further concern us as to their dynamics or treatment. There is, however, much evidence to suggest that these disorders are related to the kinds of demands placed upon persons in various social roles. Indeed, treatment programs often combine medication with prescribed changes in the life regime (or with psychotherapy) to relieve the stresses which produced the disorder.

The psychophysiological disorders appear to be the most prevalent manifestation of emotional disorder. The Leightons found that 77 percent of their study population reported reactions of this type, and it is quite likely that everyone at some time experiences such reactions

---

[4] R. H. Felix and Morton Kramer, "Extent of the Problem of Mental Disorders," *Annals of the American Academy of Political and Social Science,* Vol. 286 (March, 1953), p. 8. See also Norman Q. Brill and Gilbert Beebe, *A Follow-up Study of War Neuroses* (Washington, D. C.: Veterans' Administration, 1955), p. 28.

[5] Dorothea C. Leighton *et al., The Character of Danger* (New York: Basic Books, 1964).

without necessarily being aware of the cause. Whether these should be regarded primarily as one of the prices we pay for our form of civilization, or whether they are rather the price that man pays for his highly developed nervous system, we cannot at present say.

Mental Deficiency

The phenomena representing mental deficiency differ significantly from those of mental illness, but like the latter term, mental deficiency encompasses a number of conditions brought about in distinctly different ways. The central circumstance is, of course, a defect of intelligence such that the person is not capable of performing normal mental tasks appropriate to his age and environment. The most extreme forms of mental deficiency—idiocy and imbecility—represent gross organic defects which not only impair the development of intelligence but markedly reduce life expectancy. The great majority of individuals so afflicted are institutionalized early in life and remain institutionalized, except for those in the upper ranges of the category called imbeciles. As of the mid-1960's, nearly 200,000 persons are confined in public institutions for mental defectives in the United States. Their maintenance entails a direct cost of over $400,000,000 per year.[6]

This chapter does not attempt to assess mental deficiency as a social problem, but merely calls attention to it. Until quite recently, mental deficiency was a topic which aroused little interest in the general public or even among physicians and psychologists. For a long time the stigma of mental deficiency led families to conceal the existence of a mentally defective or retarded child. In recent decades, however, a number of prominent persons who are parents or relatives of severely retarded children have spoken out on the need for more adequate care for such children and for research into the causes of mental deficiency. Parent organizations and professional organizations focused on dealing with mental retardation have been formed, and, especially with the impetus given by the interest of President Kennedy, there has been a great increase in support and expansion of research in this field.[7]

---

[6] These data are from Provisional Patient Movement and Administrative Data, Public Institutions for the Mentally Retarded, United States, 1964. National Clearing House for Mental Health Information (Bethesda, Maryland).

[7] See, for example, the report of the President's Advisory Panel on Mental Retardation. See also Richard Masland, Seymour Sarason, and Thomas Gladwin, *Mental Subnormality* (New York: Basic Books, 1958); and Herbert G. Birch, ed., *Brain Damage in Children: The Biological and Social Aspects* (New York: Williams and Wilkins, 1964).

While most severe mental deficiency has its origins in brain injury or organic defect, a substantial part of mental subnormality represents simply the lower end of the range of intellectual potentiality coupled with cultural and intellectual deprivation. Children from the poorest, most culturally deprived segments of the population fail to develop in the preschool years the language skills necessary for incorporation into the regular school system. This is a problem which is being tackled on a large scale for the first time under the Poverty Program of President Johnson. While efforts to provide intellectual stimulus to the deprived will probably make relatively little difference in the number of individuals who have to be institutionalized because of mental deficiency, they may decrease substantially the much larger number of individuals who are ineffective in modern society because of mental retardation deriving from cultural deprivation.

Professional Resources

Given the prevalence of mental illness and its crippling effects, how does our society mobilize its capabilities for dealing with the problem? The primary resource for diagnosing and treating the mentally ill in modern society is, of course, the psychiatric profession, together with the systems of services for which it is responsible. The plural, *systems*, is used advisedly, for there is, in the United States at least, no over-all coordination or integration of these services. The basic responsibility for caring for mental patients who are most severely ill has been taken by the states, since few families can bear the cost of private medical treatment for mental illness. But the level of budgetary support for state mental health programs has until recently been abysmally low, with the result that little more than custodial care has been provided to most patients. The most highly trained psychiatrists are seldom attracted to state hospital positions; other activities are more rewarding. Psychiatrists and other mental health specialists are in short supply, but the problem is not merely one of training additional personnel. Underlying the poor support of public mental health programs are widespread fear of mental illness and distrust of governmental involvement in medical care, both on the part of large sectors of the general public and on the part of professional groups. A substantial portion of the social problem of mental illness lies in these attitudes, which prevent the most effective use of our resources to deal with the phenomena of mental illness. To understand the complexity of the institutional and personnel programs which are entailed, let us look first at the hospitals and other services organized to provide care and treatment to the mentally ill, and then at the mental health professions and the roles that they carry out within these services.

The Mental Hospitals of the United States in 1965

There were, in the United States in 1965, roughly 300 public and 250 private hospitals for the prolonged care of mental patients, and at any given time there were roughly 575,000 patients resident in them.[8] The great majority—about 85 percent—of the patients are in state mental hospitals. Next in importance, and accounting for nearly 10 percent of all long-term patients, are the veterans' hospitals; then come county and municipal hospitals and, finally, private hospitals. Although private mental hospitals accommodate only a little over 2 percent of mental patients, their influence on psychiatric theory and practice is great, for they provide valuable facilities for training and for research. In general, because the cost of maintaining a patient in a private mental hospital is beyond the means of any but the wealthiest families, patients stay in such hospitals a relatively short time. If they are not improved, they are likely to be sent to public mental hospitals or to be maintained in the community with private psychiatric care.

In addition to hospitals for prolonged care of mental patients, general hospitals are increasingly providing psychiatric wards for short-term patients. Although the number of patients accommodated at any given time is not large, over the course of a year over 200,000 psychiatric patients are admitted and discharged from general hospitals at present.[9] Many of these patients would have gone to a state hospital a decade or so ago; a third of them are diagnosed as having functional psychoses and another fourth as suffering from psychoneuroses. Because of hospital policies and costs, mental patients seldom stay more than a few weeks in a general hospital. For many patients this period is long enough to permit them to regain equilibrium so that they can again function in the community. Moreover, by virtue of remaining in the community and not being stigmatized by hospitalization in an "insane asylum" these patients are likely to be better able to fit back into the community. On the other hand, for a significant (but unknown) proportion of these patients, a short stay in a private hospital or in the psychiatric ward of a general hospital is merely a precursor to admission to a public, prolonged-care hospital.

---

[8] Data supplied by Biometrics Branch, National Institute of Mental Health.

[9] See Part III: "Private Mental Hospitals and General Hospitals with Psychiatric Facilities," *Patients in Mental Institutions*, 1963.

The mental hospital is charged with both medical and legal responsibility for many of its patients. Most patients in our public mental hospitals are not there voluntarily (although the number of voluntary admissions has been increasing greatly in recent years); they are committed under legal provisions and procedures that vary from state to state.[10] In many states, commitment may be arranged by the filing of a certificate signed by two physicians who have examined the prospective patient and who can attest to his being of unsound mind or "insane." In other states, temporary hospitalization may be arranged by similar, relatively simple means, but indefinite commitment requires a formal hearing before a duly constituted mental hygiene commission or other official body. In Texas, it was until very recently necessary to provide for a jury trial in order to accomplish the long-term hospitalization of unwilling persons. The various procedures are designed to protect persons who are not mentally ill from being "railroaded" into the mental hospital. While it is doubtful that commitment of well persons has ever accounted for any substantial proportion of patients, there is an ever present danger that the nonconformist or the person with extreme idiosyncrasies will be committed unjustly. Commitment procedures, then, are designed to provide for that "due process of law" without which no person can be deprived of his liberty.

Once in the mental hospital, the patient becomes primarily a medical responsibility. He is usually assigned to an admission or receiving ward where he can be given close attention and, depending on available staff, such medical, psychiatric, and psychological examinations as will aid in diagnosis and the planning of treatment.

Our mental hospitals are, for the most part, understaffed and inadequately supported. Yet they must somehow cope with the anxiety-provoking propensities of the patients, provide what treatment can be managed, maintain livable quarters and physical facilities, schedule food preparation and serving, afford a program of activities for the patients, and at the same time decide when any given patient is ready to be released to the community. If they do less than a perfect job, we might well consider in what other realm of human activity we ask for such exacting performance with so little in the way of resources and support.

Because at one time the emphasis in mental hospital construction was upon building a few extremely large institutions where a great

---

[10] See Ruth Roemer, "Mental Health Legislation Affecting Patient Care," *American Journal of Public Health*, Vol. 52 (1962), pp. 592-99.

many patients could be confined at low per-person cost, usually in somewhat remote sites, the older hospitals tend to be unnecessarily prison-like in appearance. In other respects, too, mental hospitals are quite different from the usual hospital to which we take our physical ailments. First of all, most patients do not need to be in bed except for normal sleep requirements. Then, because of the hospital's legal responsibility and the nature of the symptomatic behavior of many patients at one time or another (but only a small minority at any given time), much attention is given to matters of security. More and more hospitals are managing to open—that is, to unlock—many of their wards or buildings, but in most public mental hospitals in the United States locked wards are considered a virtual necessity. Where greater freedom is accorded the patients, greater staff vigilance and availability to patients is required to prevent "elopements" or interpersonal complications of one sort or another. In most hospitals, then, such freedom as "ground privileges" or visits in the community are accorded only to those patients who are judged to be well enough to take personal responsibility.

As a social organization designed to help mentally ill or emotionally disturbed persons to achieve mental health and take up normal social roles in the community, the traditional mental hospital has many defects. Limited staff and resources, coupled with large size and isolation from the community, make many mental hospitals little more than repositories for custodial care of involuntary inmates. From the standpoint of the patient, herded as a member of a collectivity with little attention to his personal needs or desires, such hospitals are little different from prisons and concentration camps. Goffman has characterized such organizations as "total institutions" and has noted the ways in which staff and inmates interact and work out adjustments in such establishments.[11] Although supervision of the wards and decisions relating to patient care and release from the hospital are the responsibilities of the medical personnel, the limited number of psychiatrists and other physicians available in most public hospitals precludes any substantial amount of contact between doctor and pa-

_____

[11] See Erving Goffman, *Asylums* (New York: Doubleday, 1961). Other influential studies of mental hospitals include the following: Ivan Belknap, *Human Problems of a State Mental Hospital* (New York: McGraw-Hill, 1956); William Caudill, *The Mental Hospital as a Small Society* (Cambridge, Mass.: Harvard University Press, 1958); H. Warren Dunham and S. K. Weinberg, *The Culture of a State Mental Hospital* (Detroit: Wayne State University Press, 1960); and Alfred Stanton and Morris Schwartz, *The Mental Hospital* (New York: Basic Books, 1954).

tient. The doctors and even the graduate nurses must spend most of their time in maintaining records and handling problems of patient disposition. As a consequence, in many hospitals it is the attendants who control the operations of the wards, largely by their control of access of patients to physicians and of physicians to information about patients. Patients are to be fitted to the system, not the system to the needs of patients. The distressed and often disoriented patient is usually deprived of his personal possessions, deprived of the privileges that self-respecting adults take for granted, and, in short, treated in such a way as to deprive him of all the trappings of self-respect.

Large, poorly supported public mental hospitals are likely to retain the objectionable characteristics of "total institutions," but there is now at least an awareness of the problem and an increasing disposition to seek other ways of dealing with mental illness. Recent research on the effects of the hospital social structure on the rehabilitative potential of patients, together with increasing support in many states for smaller, more adequately staffed hospitals, suggests that there is a decided trend away from custodial and toward therapeutic patient care. To this topic we shall return later in the chapter.

Outpatient Services

By "outpatient services" we refer to those agencies and facilities that provide therapy or counseling to persons whose mental illness or emotional distress is not so acute or severe as to require their hospitalization. Available outpatient services include a wide variety of community clinics, counseling services, private psychiatrists, psychiatric consultants to social agencies, and clinics or therapy groups maintained by mental hospitals for former patients. The expansion of mental health services within the community has been the most significant single development in efforts to deal with mental illness in recent decades. Prior to World War II there were fewer than 200 mental health clinics in the United States. By 1963 there were nearly 1800 outpatient clinics which provided diagnostic or treatment services to an estimated 450,000 persons.[12]

The psychiatric clinic is most often a team operation in which the psychiatrist serves as director and chief therapist. The psychiatric social worker conducts intake interviews and often carries family members in psychotherapy or counseling under the guidance of the psychiatrist. The clinical psychologist brings skills in the systematic assess-

---

[12] Biometrics Branch, National Institute of Mental Health.

ment of personality and intelligence and may be called on to supply research competence in those clinics that undertake research.

The primary therapeutic technique of outpatient services for the mentally ill is psychotherapy. The essence of psychotherapy is that the distressed person is helped to examine and hopefully to understand his ways of acting, thinking, and feeling. Clinic services are utilized largely by middle-class families having a degree of familiarity with psychiatric thinking. By and large, persons with a working-class background seem less disposed to verbalize their feelings or to examine them introspectively.[13] This fact, coupled with the very great discrepancy between the things taken for granted by the middle-class psychotherapist and the working-class patient, would seem to be the major reason why working-class persons tend to find the procedures of psychotherapy unacceptable or unrewarding.

Despite the tremendous increase in available clinic services, the average mental health clinic has a long list of persons waiting for diagnosis or treatment. An emotionally upset individual who goes to a clinic seeking immediate help for an acute problem seldom receives immediate attention. He is likely to be asked to fill out an application for service and then to be placed on the waiting list. He may be seen for a general assessment of his problem in a matter of weeks, but at many clinics services other than assessment may be delayed for six months, a year, or even longer.

One of the major problems in the provision of help for the acutely distressed person is, then, that clinics are overloaded. In other fields of medicine, there is a tendency to stretch available facilities by giving less time per person, using a variety of aides, or devising new modes of coping with shortages. But psychotherapy, like college lecture courses, has almost always been organized into 50-minute hours. Only recently have serious efforts been made to develop emergency services for mentally disturbed persons in the United States, though a number of European cities have had such services for decades. Some general hospitals now maintain emergency services for the mentally ill just as they maintain them for persons injured in accidents or those with acute problems of physical illness. A few communities are even experimenting with first-aid services for the mentally ill, having workers ready to go out into the community to assess acute

---

[13] Jerome Myers and Leslie Schaffer, "Social Stratification and Psychiatric Practice: A Study of an Outpatient Clinic," *American Sociological Review*, Vol. 19 (June, 1954), pp. 307-10.

problems of emotional disturbance in the social settings in which they become manifest.[14]

As mental health services have become more closely linked with the field of public health, a variety of new forms of treatment services and aids for those who suffer from chronic forms of mental illness have been developed. In a few communities, "day-hospitals" are being tried out for acutely distressed patients who can play some role in family life but need the emotional support of the hospital staff on a regular basis. At other places there are "night-hospitals" for patients who are able to hold a job during the day but who require a measure of support when they are not at work. In general, the aim of recently developed programs has been to keep the patient in the community and functioning in at least some of his normal roles to the maximum extent possible.

From the above description of institutional resources, one might think that professional resources are primarily to be found in mental hospitals, clinics, and other public or privately organized facilities for the mentally ill. More than half of the trained psychiatrists in the United States are, however, engaged full or part time in the private practice of psychiatry, where the great majority of their practice is with persons who are relatively well-to-do and are not suffering from severe mental illness.

Mental Health Personnel

In general, facilities and services for the mentally ill are directed by psychiatrists. Like other medical specialists, the fully qualified psychiatrist must meet stringent requirements as to training, experience, and knowledge before he is certified. To qualify for examination and certification by the American Board of Psychiatry and Neurology, a medical school graduate must serve his year of internship and three years of residency training in an approved institution (including both course work and supervised experience in treating a variety of patients) and secure an additional two years of relevant experience. An even longer period of training and experience is required for psychiatrists who wish to be fully qualified as psychoanalysts. Formal psychoanalytic training is, in general, open only to physicians who have had at least a year of full-time psychiatric training and usually entails another three or more years. In addition to

---

[14] A general discussion of recent developments in outpatient care as well as in other aspects of patient care is given in Morris and Charlotte Schwartz, *Social Patterns of Mental Patient Care* (New York: Columbia University Press, 1964).

course work, the student must complete a personal psychoanalysis and must carry out a supervised psychoanalysis of one or more patients. Despite the relatively small number of psychoanalysts in the United States—about 1000—psychoanalytic thinking has been a major influence in American psychiatry.

Although the development of psychiatry in the United States originated in the mental hospitals, less than a fifth of American psychiatrists are now full-time staff members of a mental hospital.[15] Psychiatry moved out of the mental hospital in response to a number of influences in the early decades of the twentieth century: the influence of psychoanalytic theory and practice, leading to greater interest in the neuroses and in the private practice of intensive psychotherapy; the markedly greater financial rewards of private practice in an affluent society; the demands for a military psychiatry that could cope with emotional disturbances brought about by the stress of combat; the development of concern with preventive psychiatry through early treatment and through child guidance work. As a consequence of these developments, it is estimated that less than a third of American psychiatrists are now engaged primarily in providing services for the severely mentally ill.[16] For Board-certified psychiatrists the proportion is almost certainly lower.

Statistics on the number and qualifications of various categories of mental health personnel are somewhat haphazard because the use of a given title is not necessarily confined to persons who are fully qualified. For example, while there are roughly 7000 Board-certified psychiatrists in the United States, a survey by the American Psychiatric Association indicated more than 17,000 physicians designated as psychiatrists.[17] In order to qualify for associate membership in the A.P.A., a physician must have had a minimum of one year's experience in a mental hospital. Physicians with such experience and many others who have not completed a psychiatric residency may call themselves psychiatrists and treat mental patients.

Reference has already been made to the clinic team which combines the skills of psychiatrist, psychiatric social worker, and clinical psychologist. The tremendous increase in the number of outpatient facilities in recent years was possible only because of the vast expansion of training facilities for these categories of professional per-

---

[15] Estimate based on administrative data from *Patients in Mental Hospitals.*

[16] This estimate was arrived at by pooling available data from a variety of sources.

[17] Manpower Studies Unit, National Institute of Mental Health.

sonnel.[18] Psychiatric social workers and clinical psychologists also provide therapy or counseling and psychological assessment through a variety of other community organizations (family service, child welfare and other health and welfare agencies, and the schools). Within the mental hospital, psychiatric nurses constitute the largest single group of professionally trained workers. And in recent decades another category of nurse is being trained in increasing numbers—the public health nurse with mental health training. Such nurses, working largely on the staffs of local health departments, are in especially strategic positions to bring mental health services to large segments of the population.

The number of professional workers in various mental health activities has increased markedly in recent decades, yet almost all categories of professional staff are in demand. Within the field of mental patient care, however, professionals constitute only a small fraction of total personnel. In 1964, the latest year for which data on mental hospital personnel are available at this writing, there were more than 200,000 full-time employees in prolonged-care public mental hospitals alone. Relatively few of them, however, were professionally trained. Of full-time employees, less than 2 percent were psychiatrists, and less than 10 percent were professionals of any sort—physicians, psychologists, social workers, or graduate nurses. The great bulk of hospital personnel is comprised of nursing aides or "attendants"—who provide the basic care of patients—and maintenance personnel. Less than half of these nursing aides have completed even a high school education. A recent study of nursing aides revealed that only 8 percent had any relevant training prior to employment in the mental hospital where they were working.[19] The median annual income of such aides—$3,440 in 1963—was well below the median for all workers. Yet studies of the operation of public mental hospitals have revealed that the attendants frequently control the patient's access to professional personnel and set the norms for patient care.[20] Only as hospital systems come to reward the nursing assistant or attendant with an adequate salary and provide thorough training and firm but supportive supervision will the transition from custodial to therapeutic care, earlier referred to, become a reality.

---

[18] Descriptions of the qualifications of each of these categories of personnel and of trends in their training are given in George W. Albee, *Mental Health Manpower Trends* (New York: Basic Books, 1959).

[19] See *The Psychiatric Aide in State Mental Hospitals*, Public Health Service Publication No. 1286 (Washington, D.C.: U.S. Government Printing Office, 1965).

[20] See, for example, Belknap, *Human Problems of a State Mental Hospital.*

The Public Image of Mental Illness

We have seen that a considerable medical-legal machinery has been set up in Western society for dealing with mental illness, and we have noted briefly the major types of such illness recognized by the professions concerned. At the outset of this chapter, however, we noted that mental illnesses are not as readily recognized and defined by patient and family as are most physical ailments. The reasons for this, and the consequences, are important to analyze.

What do most people understand by the term "mental illness"? How do they think mental illness should be dealt with? We have evidence to help answer these questions from several sources, including public opinion surveys, community studies, studies of mental patients and their families, and observations of public reaction to mental health programs and problems.

Ignorance and Misinformation

Public opinion studies to assess attitudes toward mental illness and psychiatric services make it abundantly clear that a majority of the American public uses the term "mental illness" to refer only to the most severely disturbed persons. The National Opinion Research Center, for example, interviewed a sample of 3500 respondents on the topic, presenting them with a series of brief descriptions of persons with such disabilities as paranoid delusions leading to assaultive behavior, simple schizophrenia, obsessive-compulsive neurosis, a severe phobia, and alcoholism. Dr. Shirley Star, the study director, reports that only in the instance of the paranoid symptomatology did most respondents regard the person described as mentally ill.[21] In the other cases they "explained away" the symptoms as reflections of problems everyone has to some degree, or as transitory responses to life circumstances, needing only mild (almost mechanical) suggestion or encouragement to be overcome. Whereas programs to raise the level of public understanding of mental illness have emphasized that health and illness are a continuum, and that we all have some of the propensities that are manifest in mental illness, the popular view seems to be that any deviance which can be "explained" is not mental illness. For many persons, then, mental illness is expressed in that kind of behavior which requires that one be sent to a mental hospital. The public opinion studies of the early 1950's also suggest a high level of

---

[21] Shirley A. Star, "The Public's Ideas About Mental Illness," paper presented to the Annual Meeting of the National Association for Mental Health, November 5, 1955.

superficial familiarity and favorable response to psychiatric services but a very low level of sophistication with regard to psychiatric practice or the conditions under which a psychiatrist might fruitfully be consulted.

It is likely that there has been some increase in public sophistication after more than a decade of bombardment by the mass media with information about mental illness and psychiatry. On the other hand, as one recent study has pointed out, mass media content designed to convey correct information about mental illness is far outweighed by presentations in which the mentally ill and psychiatry are pictured in stereotyped, distorted ways.[22] The bizarre symptoms of the mentally ill are overemphasized. The occurrence of mental disorder is naïvely attributed to environmental pressures. The homespun philosopher of the "soap opera," with his trite homilies, becomes the therapist *par excellence*. In a way, then, the mass media are lagging behind public attitudes toward mental illness rather than helping to create informed attitudes.

Even members of the larger medical profession show an unfortunate lack of information about mental illness and its treatment, especially physicians trained prior to World War II. A study conducted by the Gallup Poll for the State of New Jersey revealed that 27 percent of physicians under 50 years of age and 38 percent of those 50 and over said they read little or nothing about psychiatry and mental illness.[23] Less than a fifth of the physicians interviewed knew of the existence of new state facilities (established two to five years before the survey) for the diagnosis and treatment of several categories of mentally disturbed children. Not surprisingly, the less well-informed they were about mental illness and psychiatry, the more confident they were of their own competence to treat neurotic patients. Yet studies of the general public reveal that the family physician is the first professional to whom most people would turn for help with an emotional problem, either their own or that of a family member.

The lack of knowledge about mental illness and facilities for its treatment extends throughout the structure of many of our communities. When a person requires emergency care for physical illness, in any but the most sparsely settled areas, he can be taken to help or help brought to him. The doctor's office, the emergency room of the hospital, or the plant dispensary are clearly perceived resources. When a

---

[22] Jum C. Nunnally, *Popular Conceptions of Mental Health* (New York: Holt, 1961).

[23] Robert Myers, "Influence of Age on Physicians' Views Concerning Mental Health Matters," *Public Opinion Quarterly*, Vol. 19 (Fall, 1955), pp. 252-58.

person needs emergency care for mental illness, there seldom exists a clear picture of the services available. Further, the mental illness may not itself be perceived, greatly complicating the problem of getting proper care.

In a study of the impact of mental illness on the family, it was found that the patient's problem was seldom initially recognized as mental illness.[24] Instead, as in the case described at the beginning of this chapter, the problem tends to be seen as physical illness or fatigue, as meanness or character weakness, or as "natural" response to crisis or other stress. Since the patient can seldom be reasoned with, conflict and hurt feelings take precedence over rational assessment of the nature of the problem. Yet, as would be expected, efforts to deal with the problem depend on that assessment.

> If the husband's symptomatic behavior was complicated by physical illness, the wife frequently turned or urged her husband to turn to the family doctor or another physician for treatment, or at least for diagnosis. If, on the other hand, it was seen as evidence of meanness or weak character, the wife often attempted over long periods to argue with her husband, to moralize, recriminate. Self-help tended to be stressed, though a few wives urged their husbands to talk with a clergyman. Several wives turned the husband over to his parents, suggesting that they try to do something about him. In part, this action seems to have been linked with an attitude of blaming the parents for the husband's behavior, but in some instances it appears also that the wife felt the husband's parents might be able to convince him of his need to get help. Where there was much aggression by the husband, a few wives invoked the police for protection; others temporarily escaped to the homes of friends or relatives. Typically, then, there were both professionals and non-professional associates of the family who entered into the process of trying to deal with the husband's mental illness.[25]

The commitment procedure itself, requiring certification and often the use of uniformed policemen to take the patient to the hospital, left many families shocked and bewildered at what had happened. Perhaps most difficult to reconcile with the ideals that gave rise to community psychiatric services was the fact that even in a metropolitan center such services were not, by and large, available to those patients who did recognize their desperate need for emergency help. Instead, they were put off for one reason or another. In a number of

---

[24] John A. Clausen and Marian R. Yarrow, eds., "The Impact of Mental Illness on the Family," *Journal of Social Issues,* Vol. 11, No. 4 (1955), p. 18.

[25] *Ibid.,* p. 28. Similar findings are reported from England by Enid Mills, *Living with Mental Illness* (London: Routledge and Kegan Paul, 1962).

instances, relatives seeking help and reassurance were told that nothing could be done unless the patient "got in trouble with the law," in which case he could be sent to a mental hospital. (See Chapter 10, page 540.)

The Stigma of Mental Disorder

Mental disorder is in many ways a threat to the social order. The mentally ill often violate the most sacred social norms. They offend the sensibilities. They turn against those closest to them. And they do all these things without clearly apparent reasons. The very fact that severe mental illness is seldom seen as such but is often seen as weakness or meanness suggests that a strong stigma attaches to the idea of mental disorder or derangement. This stigma has been a major factor influencing patterns of mental patient care until very recently. It constitutes a major problem for the severely disturbed individual who is an incipient mental patient and for the ex-patient. Being labeled mentally ill, insane, or crazy is itself a potential invitation to further deviance. This is a problem to which we shall return.

The dominant pattern of dealing with mental illness in contemporary America has been characterized by Elaine and John Cumming as one of "isolation and denial." [26] That is, we tend to wall off the mentally ill, both figuratively and literally, from the rest of the community and then, to all intent, we deny that they exist. The Cummings were led to this formulation as a result of their study of a community educational program aimed at changing attitudes toward mental illness. To their surprise, there was little change in attitude following intensive efforts to interest community members in the mental health aspects of everyday life. Instead, there was a good deal of anxiety and manifest hostility toward the mental health personnel who developed the program. Mental illness, like the hydrogen bomb, may be for many people too threatening a subject to confront realistically; for them it is apparently conceived of as beyond direct intervention.

There is little question that the way in which mental hospitals were located, and the size of the hospitals built in the latter half of the nineteenth century, largely reflected the view that mental illness was best walled off from view and thought. There are many other reflections of the tendency to isolation and denial. Even when mental hospitals are centrally located, there are few visitors other than patients' family members. Fund-raising drives by voluntary organizations seek-

---

[26] Elaine Cumming and John Cumming, *Closed Ranks: An Experiment in Mental Health Education* (Cambridge, Mass.: Harvard University Press, 1957) Chapter 7.

ing to provide more adequate local services to deal with mental illness are meagerly rewarded compared with drives to raise funds for associations concerned with physical ailments. The very terminology of public information programs symbolizes the nature of the problem. The widespread use of the terms "mental health" and "mental hygiene" as euphemistic ways of avoiding mention of mental illness is akin to the earlier use of the term "social hygiene" in order to avoid mention of venereal disease. Both instances reflect a recognition of stigma and contain an implicit hypothesis that nice people will be less offended or threatened by avoiding direct mention of the real concern.

Toward New Concepts of Mental Illness and Patient Care—A Historical Review

The inevitable consequence of a pattern of isolation and denial of mental illness in the general culture has been neglect and often mistreatment of the mentally ill. As early as the second century, and intermittently thereafter, voices were raised in behalf of the mentally ill, but over the centuries these voices carried only short distances and were heard but briefly.[27] When effective reforms finally came—partial reforms to be sure—they were symbolized by a few names which became rallying points: Pinel in France, striking off the chains of the patients at the Bicêtre and Salpêtrière in the 1790's; Dorothea Lynde Dix, mobilizing first the elite of New England and then that of much of the rest of the nation over four full decades from 1841 to 1881, to provide mental hospitals and decent care in place of jailing, assignment to almshouses, or neglect for the mentally ill; Clifford W. Beers, dramatizing by his autobiography, *A Mind That Found Itself*, the personal horror of hospitalization in even the best of the asylums existing around 1900, and crying for an end to cruelty and degradation of the mentally ill. Yet, if dramatic individual actions gave impetus to reform movements, it was the current of the times which permitted them to be sustained: a new concept of man's potentialities flourishing with the triumph of the Republic in France; the beginning of government responsibility (at the *state* level) for the mentally ill in mid-nineteenth-century America; and the rise of preventive medicine and public health in the first decade of the twentieth century. Albert Deutsch summarized the climate of reform in the latter period:

---

[27] This section is based primarily on Albert Deutsch, *The Mentally Ill in America* (New York: Columbia University Press, 1949).

There was a growing conviction that radical measures were required in dealing with the major social ills: poverty, delinquency, and disease. The cyclic interaction of these evils was discerned with increasing clarity. . . . To break this cycle, it was now manifest, emphasis must be placed not on therapeutics, not on patching up, but on the drastic application of preventive measures. Prevention became the keynote in social work and in public health as the new century opened.[28]

It was in this atmosphere that Clifford Beers found listeners, readers, and supporters.

The Mental Hygiene Movement

Clifford Beers's psychosis came a few years after his graduation from Yale. He must have been a difficult patient, combining paranoid symptomatology with a fierce demand for his rights and decent treatment. As a consequence, he called down upon himself the most punitive responses in the attendant staffs at the private and public hospitals in which he spent three years. He was beaten, choked, spat upon, reviled, and often imprisoned for days on end in straitjacket and padded cell. His determination, even obsession, to do something to change the lot of the mentally ill came well before his return to the community. Impressed with the success of *Uncle Tom's Cabin* more than a generation before in arousing America to the fight against slavery, he resolved to make his own life story not merely an indictment of the mental hospital, but an instrument for social change. He was convinced that mental disease was not only curable, but also preventable. In his book he outlined a plan for establishment of a national society which would undertake mental hospital reforms, public education about mental illness, research into the causes, nature, and treatment of mental disease, and the creation of services directed toward the prevention of these diseases. He was able to enlist the support of some of the leading psychiatrists of the period, and in 1909 the National Committee for Mental Hygiene was founded. Since then, it has played a major role in seeking more adequate public support for mental health services. Ironically, however, some of the very forces set in motion by the emphasis on prevention have helped to turn attention and psychiatric skill away from the mental hospital, as we have already noted.

However that may be, World War I gave impetus to the movement by calling attention to the high rate of disability from nervous and mental disorders among soldiers. Especially dramatic were the severe psychoneurotic reactions which were at the time labeled "shell shock"

[28] *Ibid.*, p. 301.

and which had been reported from other armies well before our entrance into the war. Psychiatry was incorporated into the American Army, and the language of psychiatry received greater currency.

At about the same time, the emergence of social casework as an occupational specialty, requiring graduate training in theory and technique, brought into being a new profession which quickly became devoted to the ideals of mental hygiene. Delinquency and a wide variety of behavior problems and family difficulties were seen as reflecting individual maladjustment and therefore as requiring individual casework for their solution. The development of child guidance clinics in the 1920's was a direct reflection of this orientation, supported by great enthusiasm based on the belief that a means of preventing both delinquency and mental illness was near at hand. The ensuing decades, however, have shown that neither delinquency nor mental illness is so easily dealt with.

Social movements have their origins in the disorganization or disruption of societal functioning or in manifest conflict between values and prevailing practices. Thus, the mental hygiene movement had its roots in the conflict between the value placed upon human dignity and worth in the Judeo-Christian ethic and the manifest maltreatment of mental patients (once mental disorder could be regarded as illness and not as the manifestation of sin). Those most drawn to the mental hygiene movement were persons of high ethical commitment. Many were less concerned with the treatment of the mentally ill than they were with the possibility of increasing human happiness and improving mental health generally. Moreover, they were unequivocally middle class in the goals they equated with mental health.[29] Normal or healthy behavior was equated with "adjustment" and adjustment with striving for occupational and social success in an individualistic, competitive society. Almost no recognition was given to the grossly unequal chances of achieving success for individuals in other positions within the social structure—inequalities of access to physical and emotional security in childhood, to education, to health facilities in time of need. In a way, then, the movement came to represent a strong force in behalf of conformity with middle-class aspirations and ethics.

The great depression of the 1930's served to counterbalance this bias to a considerable degree. It became no longer possible to maintain the comfortable view that men out of work were basically lazy or "psychopathic." Not individual maladjustment, but a basic societal

---

[29] The consequences of the middle-class orientation of the leaders of the mental hygiene movement have been analyzed by Kingsley Davis, "Mental Hygiene and the Class Structure," *Psychiatry*, Vol. 1 (February, 1938), pp. 55-65.

maladjustment had to be recognized. As a consequence, there seems to have been a decline in emphasis on psychiatric services and facilities during the 1930's, but at the same time a beginning of systematic inquiry into the social correlates of mental illness. Within the realm of psychiatric theory, perhaps the most influential development in the United States derived from the view, expressed by Harry Stack Sullivan and his followers, that mental illness is basically a disturbance in interpersonal relationships.[30] Its roots, he believed, lay in the realm of the social. Social and psychological were not, then, to be opposed; they were to be viewed as interacting.

With World War II, and its demand for dependable manpower, emphasis shifted to the assessment of individual capacities and vulnerabilities—capacities for specialized training, for functioning in the highly regimented social systems of the military services; vulnerabilities to breakdown under the routines of garrison life or under the stress of combat and isolation. The psychiatric disabilities of World War II took a different form than those of World War I. Their relationship to anxiety and fatigue was more clearly manifest, for they were seldom masked by the kinds of physical symptoms that led to the term "shell shock" in World War I.

Psychiatry played a more substantial role in World War II than it had in the previous conflict. It was given major responsibility for "screening" out those selectees who were likely to break down psychologically and major responsibility for returning to combat effectiveness or recommending for other dispositions those who had become ineffective by virtue of psychological impairment. But, almost certainly, the chief impact of the war on the development of psychiatry and on services for the mentally ill was an indirect one: World War II called attention as nothing else had to the magnitude of the problem of psychoneurosis and the enormous loss of productivity to which it led. Not long after the end of the war, the problem of mental illness was posed to Congress as a major public health problem, on a par with any in the realm of physical illness. In 1946, after extensive hearings, Congress passed the National Mental Health Act establishing the National Institute of Mental Health within the United States Public Health Service.[31]

---

[30] Harry Stack Sullivan, *Conceptions of Modern Psychiatry* (Washington, D. C.: William Alanson White Psychiatric Foundation, 1947).

[31] For a description of the background and implications of this act see James V. Lowry, "Public Mental Health Agencies, State and National," *Annals of the American Academy of Political and Social Science*, Vol. 286 (March, 1953), p. 103.

The establishment of the national mental health program within the context of public health, with its traditional emphasis on prevention and control of disease, served as a powerful impetus to consideration of the mass aspects of mental disorder. Federal expenditures for mental health served, moreover, to markedly stimulate state expenditures as well. Federal funds have gone primarily into research, training, and grants to states for partial support of community services. State funds have gone more largely into improvement and staffing of the mental hospitals.

In 1955, Congress passed the Mental Health Study Act, providing funds for a Joint Commission on Mental Health and Illness to analyze and evaluate the needs and resources of the mentally ill in the United States and to make recommendations for new program developments. A number of excellent monographs were produced for or by the Joint Commission, reviewing the current status of the field of mental health as of the late 1950's.[32] The final report of the Commission, entitled *Action for Mental Health*,[33] strongly emphasized the need for more adequate facilities for immediate care of acutely disturbed persons and provided impetus for substantial federal contributions to the establishment of community mental health centers.

Social Correlates of Mental Disorder

It is apparent that mental disorders constitute a major social problem in modern society, whether or not social factors are implicated in their etiology. Detailed discussion of the etiologies of the major mental disorders is beyond the scope of this chapter, but we shall briefly examine the complexity of the question of causation and then turn to a consideration of evidence relating to the distribution and correlates of mental illness in society.

Only a few mental disorders are directly and unequivocally the product of organic disease, nutritional deficiency, or heredity. Others —largely the neuroses but also some acute psychotic episodes—seem to result from certain types of life experience or extreme stress. For the disorders that afflict the majority of persons in our mental hospitals and other treatment services, however, knowledge of causation

---

[32] Of particular interest are Marie Jahoda, *Current Concepts of Positive Mental Health* and Rashi Fein, *Economics of Mental Illness* (New York: Basic Books, 1958); Gerald Gurin, Joseph Veroff, and Sheila Feld, *Americans View Their Mental Health* and Reginald Robinson, David DeMarche, and Mildred Wagle, *Community Resources in Mental Health* (New York: Basic Books, 1960).

[33] Published in 1961 by Basic Books, New York.

is at best partial. Some may be diseases in the usual sense, the psychological symptoms representing reactions to biochemical defect or other physiological malfunctions, but as yet no one has been able to demonstrate the underlying defects. Quite possibly, certain mental disorders will be found to result from the interaction of constitutional factors (biologically given tendencies or vulnerabilities) and life experiences as influenced by sociopsychological development and sociocultural patterns.

To the extent that mental disorders are not manifestations of organic disease as such, they may be regarded primarily as disorders of cognitive processes, as distortions of the personality, or as faulty strategies in interpersonal relationships. The personality is itself, at any given time, the resultant of a complex interaction between constitutional potentialities and proclivities and the sociocultural environment as mediated through the family and other agents of socialization and influence. The human organism is not only reactive to its environment but acts upon it and, beyond early childhood, to a considerable degree selects its local environment. This enormously complicates the task of establishing causal links between aspects of personality and aspects of the social and cultural order. Even the etiology of bacterial diseases turns out to be much more complex than had been assumed at the time that germ theory was evolved by Koch and Lister.[34] When one is dealing with reaction tendencies of highly differentiated personality systems, the complexities are such that the concept of cause may be inappropriate. Almost no one doubts that mental disorders are explicable in naturalistic terms; the question is whether they are explicable in terms of a relatively small number of influences whose effects can be specified with some precision.

The study of the distribution and course of disease in large populations is known as *epidemiology*.[35] Although originally developed as a methodology for studying the spread of epidemics, the epidemiological approach can be used to study the distribution of any form of disease or disability. The epidemiologist seeks to establish the characteristics which differentiate persons who are ill from those who are not. The first step in seeking to establish that any given characteristic or life circumstance is related to mental illness is to ascertain whether persons with this characteristic or subject to this circumstance have a

---

[34] See René Dubos, *The Mirage of Health* (New York: Harper, 1959), for a discussion of the complexities of disease causation.

[35] An excellent, relatively nontechnical treatment of this topic is contained in Donald D. Reid, *Epidemiological Methods in the Study of Mental Disorders* (Geneva, Switzerland: World Health Organization, 1960).

58   JOHN A. CLAUSEN

higher rate of illness. The most frequently used approximation or index of severe mental illness is hospitalization, but we now have a good deal of evidence that many factors other than degree of illness influence whether or not one is hospitalized. More people are hospitalized in communities near mental hospitals than in more remote communities, for example. Moreover, some families may attempt to take care of a markedly disturbed person in the home, while others will send him to a mental hospital. It is quite probable, then, that differences in rates of hospitalization among various population groups primarily reflect different attitudes and values toward mental illness and mental hospitals rather than different amounts of mental illness.

Similar considerations apply to data on other types of treatment as indices of the amount of mental illness in any population group; private psychiatric care is probably a better reflection of income level than it is of need for treatment. Except for a very small proportion of mental disorders, moreover, there is no technique, simple or complex, by which the presence of mental illness can be detected. All attempts to establish the frequency of mental illness rest, in the last analysis, upon an assessment of behavior by a qualified psychiatrist.

Periodic psychiatric examination of all members of the population might seem to be the most satisfactory basis for assessing mental health status, but it is not likely to be feasible for a long time to come. The cost and difficulty of recruiting and training a psychiatric staff that could examine sufficiently large samples of the population to yield stable rates of serious mental illness would be tremendous, requiring vastly more than the funds currently available for research. Further, there are attitudinal barriers to such an approach. Relatively few psychiatrists feel comfortable about examining persons who have not sought help and to whom services are not to be offered even if, in the psychiatrist's opinion, they are needed. Public attitudes toward seeking or accepting a proffered psychiatric examination pose an even more serious difficulty. Most people regard mental quirks in themselves or members of their family as something to be concealed, not exposed. Consequently, those persons who are most likely to be designated as "cases" are often the most reluctant to undergo psychiatric examination. Small-scale efforts to examine specified samples suggest that the refusal rate sometimes runs as high as 40 percent. In attempts to locate cases of severe mental illness—a phenomenon that occurs in a very small proportion of persons in a year—even a 10 percent refusal rate would make systematic estimation of the total amount of mental illness virtually impossible.

There is another side of this problem which further complicates classification through psychiatric examination or screening. Every community has some members who are regarded by their fellow citizens as "queer," "mean," "shy," "offensive," and the like. Many of these persons would be diagnosed by a psychiatrist as neurotic and some as psychotic, even though other community members may not regard them as mentally ill. Moreover, persons whose social backgrounds are grossly divergent from that of the psychiatrist (e.g., lower-class persons) tend to be seen by him as sicker than those whose attitudes and behaviors are closer to his own outlook. Unless and until there are valid tests for the diagnosis of schizophrenia and other mental illnesses, studies of so-called true prevalence must deal with biases in clinical classification due to subcultural perspectives, just as studies of treated prevalence must deal with biases of community and professional response. With these considerations in mind, let us examine what has been learned from research—most of it of quite recent origin—on the distribution of mental illness in time and space.

Mental Illness and Modern Urban Society

One frequently hears that the hectic pace of modern life has resulted in a great increase in mental disorders. Until quite recently, the population of our mental hospitals was increasing more rapidly than the rate of growth of the total population, which might seem to support the notion that more people are mentally ill at present than were in the past. Certainly more people now receive psychiatric care or enter mental hospitals than did previously. Present experience suggests the likelihood that about one person in 12 in urban America will be hospitalized for mental illness some time during his life.[36] The proportion is, of course, higher for persons who live much beyond age 70. Although this expectancy of hospitalization is higher than in the past, it does not appear that the likelihood of becoming mentally ill prior to or during the prime of life has increased. For example, statistics relating to the number of mentally ill persons confined in jails, almshouses, and other institutions in Massachusetts between 1840 and 1850 suggest that, for all but the aged, rates of severe mental illness (psychotic states) were at least as high then as they are at present.[37]

Massachusetts was a highly urbanized state even in 1840. It is likely that many of the disorganizing effects of urbanization and industrialization had already taken place. The existence of value conflicts, the

---

[36] This estimate derives from Herbert Goldhamer and Andrew Marshall, *Psychosis and Civilization* (New York: Free Press, 1953).
[37] *Ibid.*

segmentalization of relationships, and the lack of stable occupational expectations—all concomitants of social change and of urbanization— might be expected to contribute stresses leading to an increase in mental breakdown. One might ask, then, whether a comparable amount of mental illness would be expected in a population with high consensus as to values, a relatively homogeneous set of occupational and familial expectations, and close integration of the individual into the network of community relations. The Hutterite communities of Montana and the Dakotas, settled in the latter half of the nineteenth century by Anabaptist immigrants from central Europe, approximate this ideal type of homogeneous and highly integrated community. These rural villages have managed to maintain a surprising degree of resistance against the encroachments of the competitive, hedonistic emphasis in American life. Yet a careful check of Hutterite communities to locate mentally ill persons by a research team which included a psychiatrist, a psychologist, and a sociologist disclosed that the occurrence of episodes of severe mental illness among the Hutterites was roughly comparable to the occurrence of hospitalization for mental illness in New York State.[38] Among the Hutterites, however, patients were cared for at home rather than in mental hospitals. Moreover, both the duration and patterning of the symptoms manifested by members of the Hutterite communities differed somewhat from those of patients from the larger American society.

Many anthropologists, travelers, and workers in nonliterate cultures have made observations about the frequency or infrequency of mental disorder. Unfortunately, no one person's experience is likely to be an adequate basis for an estimate of the frequency of mental disorder unless systematic observations have been recorded for defined populations. Few of those who have made pronouncements in this area have been adequately trained in either psychiatry or statistics; almost none in both. A critical review of this literature suggested that the one conclusion warranted was that "the mental disorders known to Western psychiatry do occur among primitive peoples throughout the world." [39] (See Chapter 6, page 290.)

Social Status and Mental Health

The social status of one's family influences to a considerable degree the relative ease or discomfort of one's physical existence, the values

---

[38] Joseph W. Eaton and Robert J. Weil, *Culture and Mental Disorders* (New York: Free Press, 1955).

[39] Paul K. Benedict and Irving Jacks, "Mental Illness in Primitive Societies," *Psychiatry*, Vol. 17 (November, 1954), p. 389.

that one learns early in life, the opportunities that become available, and the attitudes that are expressed toward one by other persons. Social status does influence personality development. Since, however, one can move up or down the status hierarchy, the status of one's family is not in any sense determinative of personality. To what extent do mental disorders vary by social status? In seeking to answer this question, investigators have used a number of indices of social status as well as a variety of indices of mental disorder.

One of the most influential studies of the distribution of mental disorder was Faris and Dunham's *Mental Disorders in Urban Areas*.[40] These researchers plotted the residential distribution of all patients from the city of Chicago admitted to public and private mental hospitals and computed rates of hospital admission for the various diagnostic categories of illness by area. The study conclusively demonstrated that hospitalized mental illness was not randomly distributed through the city. Highest rates were found near the center of the city in areas of high population mobility and heterogeneity and low socioeconomic status. Conversely, the lowest rates were in the stable residential areas of higher socioeconomic status.

In part, this over-all distribution was influenced by the concentration of organic psychoses due to syphilis and alcohol in those "skid row" or "flophouse" areas where the homeless and workless males of any metropolis tend to collect. But Faris and Dunham found that the rate distribution of schizophrenia also tended to be much higher in these same areas of high population mobility and heterogeneity and low socioeconomic status than in stable residential areas. It did not seem likely that schizophrenics had simply drifted to these areas.

Nearly two decades after the study by Faris and Dunham, Hollingshead and Redlich [41] set out to establish whether there were significant differences in the prevalence and incidence of mental illness among the social classes in New Haven. Data were secured not only from hospitals and clinics but from private psychiatrists as well. For hospitalized mental illness, Hollingshead and Redlich found the same general pattern that Faris and Dunham had found, with highest rates in the lower social strata and substantially lower rates in the upper strata. The New Haven study contributed further evidence that schizophrenia, insofar as it results in psychiatric treatment, tends to be more prevalent in the lower social strata. On the other hand,

---

[40] Robert E. L. Faris and H. Warren Dunham, *Mental Disorders in Urban Areas* (Chicago: University of Chicago Press, 1939).

[41] A. B. Hollingshead and F. Redlich, *Social Class and Mental Illness* (New York: Wiley & Sons, 1958).

most of the differential between classes resulted from the much greater duration of hospitalization for lower-class patients. Once they came into treatment or care, they were more likely to remain there, but the frequency with which they initially became ill was only slightly greater than that of higher status patients.

The New Haven study for the first time presented evidence on the distribution of persons receiving outpatient treatment, either in clinics or from private psychiatrists. Here the picture tended to be almost the reverse of that shown for hospitalized patients—the highest rates were in the upper social strata. Hollingshead and Redlich were able to demonstrate conclusively that the way in which persons came into treatment, the kind of treatment received, and the duration of treatment all varied greatly by social class. Their study was exceedingly valuable in giving an understanding of the way in which treatment services operate; by the same token it clearly demonstrated that data on treated cases of mental illness could not be used as a basis for estimating the true prevalence of illness within the population.

The most conclusive study to date of the actual distribution of symptoms in an urban population is the Midtown Manhattan study. Its psychiatric classifications were based upon interviews of a cross section of nearly 1700 persons in a section of New York City. The interview was designed to get at such matters as the respondent's having had a "nervous breakdown" or having sought psychotherapy; the presence of somatic disorders which frequently have a psychogenic basis; acknowledgment of nervousness, restlessness, and other psychophysiologic manifestations of emotional disturbance; indications of memory difficulties; acknowledgment of difficulties in interpersonal relations; and indications of emotional disturbance given by the respondent's behavior in the interview situation.[42] Information from each of these areas of the interview was abstracted and given to a team of psychiatrists who rated the respondent as to the degree of psychiatric symptomatology, if any, and the apparent amount of impairment of functioning as a result of such symptomatology. The data provided by such a survey are generally not adequate for affixing a diagnostic label even in instances of considerable symptomatology. On the other hand, as we shall see, such studies help with the interpretation of findings relating to hospitalized or treated mental illness.

Perhaps the most startling finding of the Midtown study was the

---

[42] For a full description of the methodology see Leo Srole *et al.*, *Mental Health in the Metropolis* (New York: McGraw-Hill, 1962), Chapter 3.

very high proportion of the population rated "impaired" by psychiatric symptoms—23.4 percent.[43] Indeed, less than a fifth of the population was rated as showing no signs at all of psychiatric symptoms. There was a very substantial relationship between ratings of mental health and social status in the Midtown study: whereas 30 percent of the respondents in the highest stratum of socioeconomic status were rated "well," less than 5 percent in the lowest stratum were rated "well." In the highest stratum only 12.5 percent were rated "impaired," and of these none were "incapacitated," while in the lowest stratum 47.3 percent were rated "impaired" and 9.3 percent were rated "incapacitated." Another striking finding concerned the socioeconomic differential in rates of psychiatric treatment reported by persons who were classified "impaired." At the upper-status levels, fully a fifth of the persons rated impaired were currently receiving outpatient therapy and more than half of them had at one time or another been psychiatric patients (mostly outpatients).[44] At the lower-status levels, on the other hand, only 1 percent of the persons rated "impaired" were currently receiving outpatient treatment. Another 20 percent had previously been patients, but, unlike upper-status ex-patients, the bulk of these had been hospitalized.

Receiving a rating of "impaired" as a result of one's responses to an intensive interview is not, of course, the same thing as being diagnosed mentally ill. The surveys used in epidemiological studies of mental illness have focused upon symptoms and have tended to ignore strengths. Moreover, many of the symptoms may be primarily reflections of physical illness or of objective problems of living. Nevertheless, an examination of the interview responses of persons classified "impaired" leaves one with little doubt that most of them have emotional problems quite comparable to those of many persons who seek psychiatric help. Indeed, the finding that more than half of the upper-status impaired group had sought such help indicates something of the potential demand for psychiatric service if everyone with emotional problems were to seek it.

Very similar in approach to the Midtown Manhattan study but much more intensive in its collection of data on psychiatric status is the Stirling County study of the Leightons.[45] For nearly 15 years a team

---

[43] The impaired group is made up of three categories: marked symptom formation (13.2 percent); severe symptom formation (7.5 percent); incapacitated (2.7 percent). *Ibid.*, p. 138.

[44] *Ibid.*, p. 246.

[45] This research has been published in three volumes, of which the first, Alexander H. Leighton *et al.*, *My Name is Legion* (New York: Basic Books,

of psychiatrists and social scientists has worked in a rural county of maritime Canada, using a wide variety of approaches but basing primary classifications of psychiatric status on a survey interview somewhat similar to that of the Midtown study. In general, the Leightons found that the prevalence of symptoms increased as social status declined, though perhaps not to the same degree as in the Midtown study. The Stirling County study showed a much higher prevalence of psychoneurotic symptoms on the part of women than on the part of men. Among men, psychoneurotic symptoms were substantially more frequent in the lowest occupational group, made up of wage workers in agriculture, fishing, and forestry. Thus, if one relies on the presence of symptoms rather than on the seeking of treatment as a basis of classification, it would appear that neurosis is more prevalent in the lower class than in the middle and upper classes. It has been suggested by some that working-class life is more stressful than that of the middle class. The notion of stress is itself worthy of some consideration.[46]

Social Stress and Mental Illness

The concept of stress is a convenient means of designating the notion that external pressures or loads can lead to internal deformations or strains. There are many problems, however, in applying the concept of stress to the human personality. Certain types of experiences are probably "stressful" to everyone—experiences such as the loss of a loved one. Aside from situations in which continuing physical strain and extreme personal danger are involved, however, it appears that the psychological stressfulness of any situation depends largely upon the meaning that it derives from the individual's life history. To the extent that any given situation or event is a threat to a person's image of himself or to the values that he has incorporated in his personality, it is likely to be experienced as stressful. On the other hand, discomfort or even extremely unpleasant emotions do not necessarily impair or threaten the psychological functioning of the individual. For example, it might be assumed that under the wartime stress of bombing civilian populations would show a very high incidence of mental breakdown. Such was not, however, the case. In a thorough review of wartime experience, Donald Reid concludes

1959), and the last, Dorothea C. Leighton *et al.*, *The Character of Danger* (New York: Basic Books, 1963), are of primary importance.

[46] A particularly interesting analysis is afforded in the second volume reporting the findings of the Midtown Manhattan study. See Thomas S. Langer and Stanley T. Michael, *Life Stress and Mental Health* (New York: Free Press, 1963).

that "there was no evidence that the privations and anxieties of the War, either in the United Kingdom or in enemy-occupied countries like Denmark, had produced any major increase in serious psychosis."[47] Reid goes on to note that on the basis of data from the records of general medical practice in London, there was some evidence of a slight increase in the frequency of patients reporting sick with neurotic complaints often a week or ten days after heavy bombing. Most of these complainants had suffered from such illnesses in the past. Data on combatants themselves do, of course, indicate that the combination of extreme fatigue, terror, and guilt can lead to a high incidence of breakdown in any group. In general, however, we can say that instances of personal failure which lead to feelings of inadequacy and call for a reevaluation of who and what one is appear to be far more traumatic than is exposure to noxious stimuli as such.

There are many indications that the most significant social influences upon the likelihood of one's developing a mental illness are those which influence the early life experiences of the individual, leading him to have low self-esteem or deviant orientations. While the personality is by no means totally formed during the early years in the family, those years are of great significance. Maternal deprivation, parental rejection of the child, conflicts between parents for the allegiance of the child, overly protective maternal care—these and many other aspects of family relationship can render the child insecure or vulnerable in the sense that certain types of life situations subsequently encountered will produce a great deal of anxiety.[48] Some of the most interesting research on family relations and psychopathology has been carried out with the families of schizophrenic patients. We shall concentrate on research in this area as an illustration of the intricacy of the problem.

Social Relations and Schizophrenia

Each scientific discipline that has been involved in research on schizophrenia has tended to hypothesize that the causes of this most perplexing of mental disorders lie within that discipline's conceptual

---

[47] Donald D. Reid, "Precipitating Proximal Factors in the Occurrence of Mental Disorders: Epidemiological Evidence," *Causes of Mental Disorders: A Review of Epidemiological Knowledge, 1959* (New York: Milbank Memorial Fund, 1961).

[48] See, for example, Leon Yarrow, "Separation from Parents During Early Childhood," in Martin L. Hoffman and Lois W. Hoffman, eds., *Review of Child Development Research* (New York: Russell Sage Foundation, 1964). See also John H. Cumming, "The Family and Mental Disorder: An Incomplete Essay," *Causes of Mental Disorders: A Review of Epidemiological Knowledge, 1959.*

realm. Sociologists have proposed social isolation and the effects of status deprivation; geneticists have presented strong evidence of hereditary influence, if not complete determinism; [49] psychoanalysts have advanced theories of failure of ego differentiation largely as a result of deficient mothering; and biochemists, neuropathologists, and other scientists studying the nervous system have from time to time reported findings which differentiated study groups of schizophrenic patients from samples of the normal population.

Faris and Dunham, in seeking to explain the distribution of schizophrenia in the subcommunities of the city of Chicago, formulated the hypothesis that schizophrenics were persons who for one reason or another tended to be isolated from close social contacts with their peers. At the time of initial hospitalization, relatively few schizophrenics appear to have close personal ties. There have been a number of attempts to establish whether social isolation is in any sense causative of schizophrenia, whether it is primarily a reflection of the early stages of the disorder, or whether it is a consequence of the family patterns and early personality development of the schizophrenic. One research, which inquired into the childhood and adolescent social activities of schizophrenics and a matched control group of normal persons, suggested that only about a third of the schizophrenics were isolates from their peers early in adolescence.[50] Moreover, these individuals appeared to have been withdrawn personalities rather than casualties of isolating experiences in childhood.

Psychiatrists treating schizophrenic patients in psychotherapy or working with the families of these patients have been impressed with the frequency of certain characteristics of the parents and of relationships between parents and patient which might well be regarded as pathogenic (that is, giving rise to the illness).[51] The mothers of schizophrenics have been characterized as cold, perfectionistic, anxious, overcontrolling, and unable to give spontaneous love and acceptance to the child. They often seem unwilling to accord the child any privacy,

---

[49] The most influential American work in this area has been that of Franz Kallmann, *Genetics of Schizophrenia* (Locust Valley, N. Y.: Augustin, 1938). A recent evaluation of the status of the genetic hypothesis is contained in David Rosenthal, ed., *The Genain Quadruplets: A Case Study and Theoretical Analysis of Heredity and Environment in Schizophrenia* (New York: Basic Books, 1963).

[50] M. L. Kohn and J. A. Clausen, "Social Isolation and Schizophrenia," *American Sociological Review*, Vol. 20 (June, 1955), pp. 265-73.

[51] This literature has been reviewed by John P. Spiegel and N. W. Bell, "The Family of the Psychiatric Patient," in Sylvano Arieti, ed., *American Handbook of Psychiatry* (New York: Basic Books, 1959). Also by J. A. Clausen and M. L. Kohn, "Social Relations and Schizophrenia," in Don Jackson, ed., *Etiology of Schizophrenia* (New York: Basic Books, 1960).

attempting to intrude even into its thoughts. The fathers of schizophrenics have been described as representing three types: the first passive and immature; the second domineering and sadistic; and the third aloof and narcissistic. The family network appears to be characterized by great stress and conflict, though often this is covered over by a desire to conceal the existence of differences. The net effect of most of the patterns noted is that they would make it difficult for a child to achieve an identity of his own, to be able to confront life situations with self-reliance and confidence.

A major limitation on the inferences that can be drawn from such research, however, derives from the fact that the families can only be identified and studied after the schizophrenia has become manifest. The families, then, are confronting one of the most devastating stresses that can be imagined. In order to live with a schizophrenic child, parents may well develop behavioral patterns different from those that had characterized the family before. Here again, evidence suggestive of the importance of psychosocial development in the genesis of schizophrenia is inconclusive because of the difficulties of research. Nevertheless, recent research on social class differences in family relationships and on the dynamics of personality development increases the plausibility of the hypothesis that in the United States and Great Britain, at least, schizophrenia is more likely to occur in lower-status families than in those higher in the social structure. Lower-status families are more often characterized by the pattern of maternal dominance together with a weak or even absent father figure that so often is found in the families of schizophrenics. For the male child especially, it appears that the environment of the lower-class family less often affords adequate opportunity for the achievement of self-confidence and success in terms valued by the community at large. Indeed, it has been hypothesized by at least one influential psychiatrist that mental breakdown in this environment is one alternative solution to the developmental problems that confront children from the most underprivileged and pathological homes.[52] Another alternative is delinquency. Most of these children will not, of course, be either severely mentally ill or severely delinquent, but it does appear that personality development of children drawn from the lowest socioeconomic fifth of the population is fraught with many more hazards than is the development of more favored children.

Certainly the most tenable hypothesis as to the etiology of schizo-

---

[52] James S. Plant, *Personality and the Cultural Pattern* (New York: Commonwealth Fund, 1937).

phrenia at this time is that various combinations of hereditary vulnerability and environmental stress (either in early childhood or in later life) may lead to overt manifestation of the disorder. It seems likely that hereditary vulnerability does not rest on a single gene, but on combinations of genes, and that the incidence of these combinations is much more widespread than is the incidence of schizophrenia. In families where the infant does not receive affection and emotional nurturance and where the child does not have security in his relationships with those who are most significant to his care, vulnerable personalities may be generated. If such vulnerability is coupled with even a small degree of genetic vulnerability, schizophrenia may result. On the other hand, given a favorable family environment, another child with the same genetic potential may never manifest any of the symptoms or signs of schizophrenia. Again, a child with a strong genetic predisposition may well develop schizophrenia even under very favorable circumstances. This formulation is conjectural, but is in keeping with the evidence available from various sources in 1965. (See Chapter 10, pages 543-45.)

Social Roles and the Mental Disorders of Old Age

The current nomenclature of the American Psychiatric Association places the senile and arteriosclerotic mental disorders under the general heading *chronic brain syndrome*. Indeed, what used to be called "senile psychosis" is now called "chronic brain syndrome with senile brain disease and with psychotic reaction." This terminology is unfortunate, for the brain disease (apart from arteriosclerosis) is detectable only in behavior, and the behavior of the older patient is often strongly responsive to the social environment. Recent research has revealed that some persons perform well on psychological tests and function very well in social relationships even when they show considerable arteriosclerotic brain damage, while other patients show the symptoms of senility while manifesting little evidence of brain damage.[53] An increasing literature on social adjustment in old age also attests to the importance of continued involvement in meaningful activities and relationships. The impairment of physical and mental capacities in old age poses a problem for the older person in terms of changed activities, relationships, and self-conception. Whether or not extreme symptomatology (either neurotic or psychotic) results may depend then not so

---

[53] David Rothchild, "Senile Psychoses and Psychoses with Arteriosclerosis," in Oscar J. Kaplan, ed., *Mental Disorders in Later Life*, 2nd ed. (Stanford, Calif.: Stanford University Press, 1956).

much on the physiological changes that have occurred as on the ways that physical aging is handled, both by the older person and by those in his environment.

There is no question but that our contemporary urban society fails to provide meaningful and satisfying roles for a large number of the aged. A much higher proportion of persons survive beyond 70 than was the case even a generation ago, but the structure of occupational opportunities for older persons has not expanded. Indeed, industrial operations place a high premium on youth. Retirement programs and social security afford a greater measure of economic security than was hitherto available, but the transition to retirement often seems to entail a feeling of loss of purpose. The yielding of the occupational role is not compensated for by other prestige-giving or satisfying functions. Moreover, as a consequence of the trend away from three-generation households to the nuclear family of husband, wife, and children, associated both with high population mobility and with the small dwelling units of the modern city, the aged are increasingly isolated from kin. Some grandparents may still enjoy the possibility of serving as built-in "baby sitters," but perhaps more often the modern grandparent must be content with an occasional visit to or from children and grandchildren. (See Chapter 10, page 501.)

A recent study of the circumstances attending the hospitalization of more than 500 persons over 60 years of age in San Francisco suggests that the mental disorders of old age as such seldom lead immediately to hospitalization.[54] Most of these older people had gradually developed a wide variety of symptoms—mental, behavioral, and physical—well before they were hospitalized. Most frequently they were characterized as "confused," "mind wanders," or "disoriented." Their families and other close relatives frequently tried a number of alternative ways of trying to deal with the annoyances and disruptions caused by the senile person. In a third of the cases, this went on for five or more years before hospitalization. In the last analysis, it was the disruptiveness and potential self-destructiveness of most of these older persons which led to hospitalization. Thus, the mental disorders of old age are quite different from those of the middle years. Even though many of the same symptoms may be manifest—suspiciousness, disorientation, even hallucinations—these symptoms are not maintained with the same intensity, nor do they evoke the same intensity of reaction from others.

---

[54] See Marjorie Fiske Lowenthal, *Lives in Distress: The Paths of the Elderly to the Psychiatric Ward* (New York: Basic Books, 1964).

The Etiology of Neuroses

There is a much greater agreement as to the crucial role of psychosocial factors in the etiology of neuroses than in that of the functional psychoses or the psychoses of old age. In the United States, at least, the psychoanalytic theory of the neuroses, or some variant of it, is held by most psychiatrists. Without attempting to present this theory in detailed or technical terms, we may say that it rests upon the concept of unconscious motivation and upon the needs, vulnerabilities, and conflicts that are unconsciously internalized as a result of life experience, especially in early childhood. The biological organism, with its drives for physical gratifications and its needs for nurturance, is entirely dependent upon others for security in the satisfaction of those needs. But for a variety of reasons, such security may not be achieved. Biological needs are channeled and "disciplined"; infant strivings are often frustrated. Kubie has characterized the human child as "one helpless Lilliputian among hordes of brutal rival Lilliputians in a Brobdingnagian world of giants who are always giving too much protection or too little." [55] In attempting to ward off anxiety stemming from inevitable frustrations and frightening experiences, the child evolves various modes of psychological defense. These "defense mechanisms," which everyone uses to some extent, may permit the channeling of anxiety into relatively harmless or at times quite useful practices. Unfortunately, they may also lead to stereotyped ways of meeting situations, often quite inappropriate to the requirements of the situation. And being unaware of the reason for his stereotyped behavior, the potential neurotic is unable to modify it. When defenses patently lead to inappropriate responses or when for some reason they break down, full-blown neurosis, in one form or another, results.

Classical psychoanalytic theory placed the roots of neurosis in early life experience by postulating an inevitable conflict between man's biological nature and the demands placed on that nature by civilization. Neo-Freudians, such as Erich Fromm, Karen Horney, and Harry Stack Sullivan, however, have pointed out that Freud mistook the characteristics of middle-class Germany in the late nineteenth century for the immutable characteristics of "civilization." As a consequence, he was unaware of the enormous role played by culture in patterning interaction within the family and in setting life goals. He seems also

---

[55] Lawrence S. Kubie, "Social Forces and the Neurotic Process," in Alexander H. Leighton, John A. Clausen, and Robert N. Wilson, eds., *Explorations in Social Psychiatry* (New York: Basic Books, 1957), p. 90.

to have underestimated the importance of later childhood and subsequent experiences in generating neurotic conflicts.

In *The Neurotic Personality of Our Time*, Horney points out that our modern era is characterized by a highly individualistic, competitive striving for achievement and social status.[56] As a consequence, interpersonal relationships are suffused by hostile tension and insecurity. It is the fear of failure and the fear of one's own aggressive tendencies toward others which, according to Horney, account for the neurotic anxiety that is so prevalent today. Where Freud emphasized the frustration of libidinal (essentially sexual) needs by civilization, Horney emphasizes that Western culture itself contains conflicts that are internalized by its bearers: the conflict between competitive striving and brotherly love; the conflict between materialistic aspirations and the possibility of their fulfillment; and the conflict between the ideal of individual freedom and the reality of regimentation. This last conflict is the theme of a cogent analysis by Erich Fromm which extends consideration far beyond the realm of neurosis into that of the political dilemma of modern man.[57]

Whether or not specific cultural themes and specific aspects of social organization today have produced a demonstrable increase in neurotic breakdown, there seems but little question that the sociocultural heritage is implicated in neurotic conflicts and in psychophysiological disorders. We cannot, however, assume that the elimination of specific cultural themes (if this were possible) would automatically reduce pathology, any more than we can predict the psychological stress value of a specific situation without knowing the whole context in which it is embedded.

Mental Illness as a Social Role

The labels "crazy," "insane," or "mentally ill" all connote in our culture a kind of thinking and behaving that is uncontrolled, senseless, and frightening. Except for rare institutionalized occasions, all societies place a high value on the individual's ability to control his behavior, if not his thoughts. In mental illness, the individual loses such control. This not only poses a problem for others; it poses a persisting problem for the individual himself.

Once one is labeled a "madman," others expect him to behave in nonrational ways. Whatever the reason for his original loss of control

---

[56] Karen Horney, *The Neurotic Personality of Our Time* (New York: Norton, 1937).

[57] Erich Fromm, *Escape from Freedom* (New York: Rinehart, 1941).

or manifestation of other symptoms, being considered mentally ill by others puts one on precarious ground. Indeed, the sociologist Thomas Scheff has suggested that many persons may unconsciously take on the stereotyped role of the insane once someone has suggested that they are mentally ill.[58] Scheff observes that a great many people deviate from social norms without necessarily receiving any particular label thereby. If, however, this "residual deviance" is challenged and labeled mental illness by others, the disturbed individual may tend to let himself go and behave according to the stereotyped notion of mental illness.

It is unlikely that any substantial number of persons become mentally ill by virtue of being so labeled, but it does appear that calling a person mentally ill frequently intensifies his symptoms. Epidemiological studies support Scheff's observation that there is a very high frequency of "residual deviance" or symptomatic behavior in the population. If the general public were to use psychiatrists' ratings as the basis for classifying their colleagues and relatives, it might be very difficult to maintain the stability of our society.

The social and personal consequences of being considered mentally ill are thus very different from the consequences of physical illness. This poses a very real dilemma for those who deal with emotionally upset or confused persons. The early provision of meaningful help will frequently minimize the person's distress and prevent more severe disorder. On the other hand, actions which brand the person as mentally ill may carry the connotation that he is no longer expected to behave responsibly. Much careful study of this problem is needed in order to assess its effects on the cause and course of mental disorders and its implications for attempts to provide help to disturbed persons.

Some Recent Trends

We have seen that although the incidence of severe mental illness does not appear to have changed markedly over the past century, the development of mental hospital facilities and other services for the mentally ill has led to substantial changes in the treatment of mental patients, even in the past two or three decades. Most striking,

---

[58] Thomas Scheff, "The Role of the Mentally Ill and the Dynamics of Mental Disorder: A Research Framework," *Sociometry*, Vol. 26 (1963), pp. 436-53. See also Scheff's paper, "The Societal Reaction to Deviance: Ascriptive Elements in the Psychiatric Screening of Mental Patients in a Midwestern State," *Social Problems*, Vol. 11 (1964), pp. 401-13.

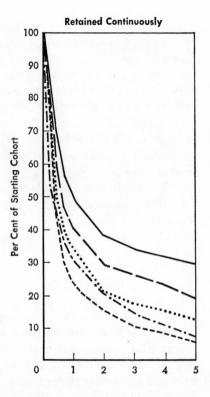

FIGURE 3

Percent of First Admissions Retained in Hospital, Released Alive, and Dead Within Specified Periods Following Admission to Warren State Hospital, Warren, Pennsylvania: 1936 to 1945

DIAGNOSTIC GROUP:

——— Schizophrenia — — – (1,271)
– – – – Manic-depressive
        Psychoses — — — — — (408)
•••••••• Involutional Psychoses – (190)
— — Syphilitic Psychoses — – (378)
—•— Mental Diseases ôf
        Senium — — — — — (1,031)

Source: Morton Kramer et al., A Historical Study of the Disposition of First Admissions to a State Mental Hospital, Dept. of Health, Education, and Welfare, Public Health Monograph No. 32 (Washington, D. C., 1955).

perhaps, has been the increase in the proportion of ill persons who come to treatment facilities, both mental hospitals and outpatient clinics. But equally important has been the decline in length of hospitalization for many categories of patients.

Trends in Mental Hospital Admissions and Discharges

While the number of first admissions to long-term mental hospitals has continued to rise each year, the resident population of those hospitals has declined slightly each year since 1955—the first such decline in the history of our mental hospital system. This decline has been achieved by virtue of the fact that newly admitted patients are, on the average, not staying as long as before; the number of these patients who become chronic hospital residents is less than the number of deaths and discharges among patients already resident in long-term mental hospitals.

Does this recent reversal of the long-time trend represent a decrease in the prevalence of mental illness? The question must be considered,

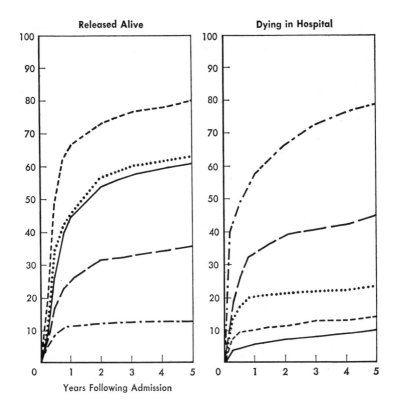

Released Alive / **Dying in Hospital**

Years Following Admission

even though we are already aware of the difficulty of arriving at a satisfactory answer. It appears that with certain types of treatment now available, patients can be released from the hospital somewhat earlier than would have been considered feasible a decade ago. Quite possibly, however, a change in administrative policies regarding discharge has been as important as changed treatment practices. There has been an increasing conviction among psychiatrists in the past decade that the effect of long hospitalization upon many acutely psychotic patients is to produce chronic, deteriorated patients who will then spend the rest of their lives in the hospital.

The probability of release from the mental hospital is highest in the first year, considerably diminished in the second year, and very low beyond that. In part, these probabilities reflect the severity of illness of various categories of patients, the least ill getting out earliest. But there is reason to believe that the social characteristics of the patients influence both their treatment and the duration of hospitalization, and that a part of the residual of chronic patients must be at-

FIGURE 4

Percent of First Admissions Retained in Hospital, Released Alive, and Dead Within Specified Periods Following Admission to Warren State Hospital, Warren, Pennsylvania: 1916 to 1950

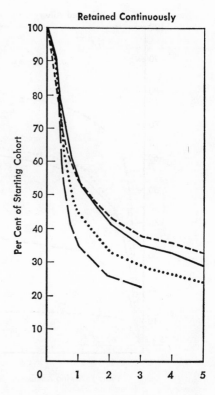

Retained Continuously

Per Cent of Starting Cohort

COHORT OF:

——— 1916-25 (1,004)
– – – 1926-35 (1,203)
•••••• 1936-45 (2,016)
— — 1946-50 (1,114)

Source: Kramer et al., A Historical Study of First Admissions.

tributed to the retention of patients who might earlier have been released to the community, even though they were not wholly recovered.

Accurate knowledge of length of stay of hospitalized patients is relatively recent. For a long time, average length of stay for various categories of patients was computed by counting all patients resident in a hospital as of a given date and calculating the average time since admission. In the course of a year, however, most of the patients discharged would have been relatively recent admissions, so the average length of stay of those remaining would greatly overstate the figure for all patients admitted to the hospital. The only appropriate measure, then, is to take a group of consecutive admissions (called a cohort) and to follow them through to discover how many have been released or have died and how many are still resident in the hospital at any given time after admission.

A careful "cohort study" conducted from the records of the Warren

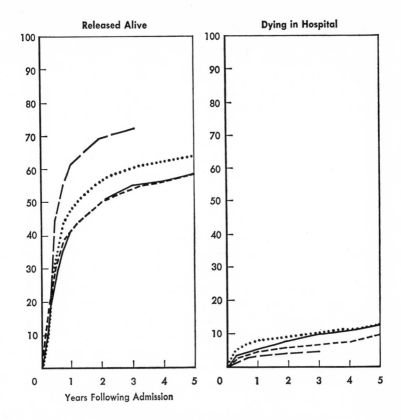

Released Alive

Dying in Hospital

Years Following Admission

State Hospital in Pennsylvania reveals rather striking changes in the experience (retention, release, or death in hospital) of patients admitted over the past several decades, as well as differences in the experience of patients of different diagnostic categories admitted in more recent years (Figure 3). It will be noted that at this hospital, among patients admitted from 1936-1945, over 65 percent of the manic-depressive patients, 45 percent of schizophrenic and involutional patients, and 11 percent of those with mental diseases of old age were released from the hospital within a year. Beyond the first year, however, release rates drop off markedly, and beyond the second year the curves flatten out. The percentage of the original group who are released in the fifth year is very small: less than 2 percent of manic depressives, involutionals, and schizophrenics and less than 0.2 percent of those suffering from psychoses of old age.

The comparison of cohorts admitted in successive decades is also enlightening. Figure 4, which confines consideration to patients admitted with a diagnosis of functional psychosis (schizophrenic, manic-depressive, or involutional), indicates little change for the decades centered on 1920 and 1930, but substantial improvement in release rates for the more recent period. In part, this reflects the introduction of shock therapy for depressed patients, cutting down deaths of these patients in the hospital, and the general increase in therapeutic measures and services available. The interpretation of such trends must, however, take into account administrative policies, community facilities for outpatient care, and a variety of other factors.

Recent studies suggest that the experience of the Warren State Hospital was typical of many public hospitals. Moreover, the upward trend in the proportion of patients released alive within the first year after admission to the mental hospital has continued during the past decade. Thus, a study of the Rochester State Hospital in Monroe County, New York, reveals that as of 1960-1962, 80 percent of the patients with diagnoses of functional psychoses were returned to the community within a year of initial hospitalization, and 90 percent were returned within two years.[59]

Other studies indicate that social status, as indicated by education or occupation, tends to be directly related to release from the hospital, so that upper-status persons generally stay in the hospital a shorter time (as was noted in connection with Hollingshead and Redlich's New Haven study). A study of schizophrenic patients in Ohio public hospitals, for example, found that 77 percent of the male patients with a college degree were released within two years as against 59 percent of those with only a grade-school education.[60] Even more striking differences were found at St. Elizabeth's hospital in Washington, D. C., by Erwin Linn.[61] In 1953-1954, prior to the use of tranquilizers by this hospital, Linn found that only 28 percent of the psychotic patients with grade-school education were released within a year as against 46 percent of those with higher educational attainment. Two years later, after tranquilizers were widely used in the hospital, the release figures for the two groups were 62 percent and 73 percent respectively. In general, tranquilizers not only stepped up release rates but also tended to be equalizers of differences between status groups.

---

[59] Elmer A. Gardner, Anita Bahn, and Harold C. Miles, "Patient Experience in Psychiatric Units of General and State Mental Hospitals," *Public Health Reports,* Vol. 79 (September, 1964), pp. 755-66.

[60] See Benn Z. Locke, "Outcome of First Hospitalization of Patients with Schizophrenia," *Public Health Reports,* Vol. 77 (September, 1962), pp. 801-05.

[61] Erwin L. Linn, "Patients' Socioeconomic Characteristics and Release from a Mental Hospital," *American Journal of Sociology,* Vol. 65 (1959), pp. 280-86.

The tranquilizing drugs have unquestionably been the most exciting therapeutic innovation of the century for chronic and acute psychotic patients. They are also widely used for the outpatient treatment of anxiety states. These drugs do not appear to cure mental illness, but to diminish the severity of certain types of symptoms (agitation, aggressive tendencies).[62] They thereby render the patient more comfortable, more socially acceptable, and possibly also more accessible to social relationships and psychotherapy. By virtue of these effects, the use of tranquilizers has greatly reduced the stresses upon staff members charged with the care of chronic patients and has permitted a more relaxed and therapeutic environment, including a much more hopeful attitude on the part of the hospital personnel. Although the downward trend in resident populations in prolonged-care public mental hospitals cannot be wholly attributed to the effects of the tranquilizers and other recently synthesized drugs, they have certainly played a significant role. Much current research is devoted to investigating the mode of drug action, not only to permit the production of even more effective pharmacological agents, but also to illuminate the physiological dynamics of mental illness.

The earlier return of patients to the community also reflects a growing awareness of the dangers associated with prolonged hospitalization. The enduring loss of normal social roles, coupled with adaptation to the hospital, tends to make the chronic patient unfit for any other mode of life. Part of the increased rate of return of patients is probably attributable also to the very real improvements in the staffing and patterns of patient care in our mental hospitals. Many are still far from adequate, but fewer can now be characterized as "snake pits." One of the major consequences of research on the mental hospital has been greater attention to its social climate.

Even in the time of Pinel there was some recognition that a brief stay in a protected, warm, accepting environment could restore many patients to more-or-less normal functioning. This was the essence of "moral treatment" and it is the essence of modern milieu therapy, but during the period of emphasis on the large public hospital this concept of patient care dropped out of sight. There are many different conceptions of the ideal nature of a therapeutic milieu,[63] but one indispensable aspect is that the patient must be treated as a person worthy of the respect of others if he is to achieve any self-respect. The

---

[62] Jonathan O. Cole and Ralph W. Gerard, *Pharmacotherapy: Problems in Evaluation* (Washington, D. C.: National Academy of Sciences, 1959).

[63] For an excellent general discussion, see Schwartz and Schwartz, *Social Approaches to Mental Patient Care,* Chapter 11.

rigid, hierarchical structure of the large mental hospital would seem to preclude its being a therapeutic milieu. Only when all categories of staff who have dealings with patients are involved in the objective of providing a therapeutic atmosphere and when patients have a considerable voice in the conduct of hospital affairs does the desired pattern of relationships begin to emerge. Especially influential have been efforts to develop "therapeutic communities," both in the United States and in Britain.[64] The first efforts along these lines came in seeking to assist long-time prisoners of war to make the difficult transition back to civilian life. Special "transitional communities" were established, in which the members were given an opportunity to redevelop and practice social skills and to acquire again the ability to make decisions for themselves.

Even an ideal therapeutic community is not, however, a viable pattern of adult life.[65] Institutional processes are inevitably different from family life. Further transitional stages seem called for, and there is currently much experimentation with "halfway houses" and other patterns which permit gradual reintegration of the patient who is not able to take on full adult responsibilities.

Recent research suggests that there are wide differences in the range of tolerance which former patients tend to receive in various living arrangements after hospitalization.[66] Patients who return to live with husband or wife are, in general, expected to perform adequately their normal roles as adults—spouse, parent, worker, neighbor, and the like. Much less is expected of those who return to the household of their parents, even if they are adults. As a consequence, former patients living in these two settings show substantial differences in degree of impairment and in the likelihood of being returned to the hospital if they become somewhat upset.

Some patients return from the mental hospital or emerge from outpatient treatment without any appreciable psychological impairment. They are effective, happy persons. Others show more or less marked impairment or unhappiness. Some had been, and again become, well integrated into a network of intimate relationships. Others had been and continue to be somewhat marginal in their social relation-

---

[64] See especially Maxwell Jones, *The Therapeutic Community* (New York: Basic Books, 1953).

[65] In *Community as Doctor: New Perspectives on a Therapeutic Community* (London: Tavistock Publications, 1960), Robert N. Rapoport analyzes the objectives, procedures, and problems of one of the best-known therapeutic communities.

[66] See, for example, Howard E. Freeman and Ozzie C. Simmons, *The Mental Patient Comes Home* (New York: Wiley & Sons, 1963).

ships. Here again, the difference between mental disorders and physical illnesses is great. The former mental patient not only has to cope with whatever degree of impairment his mental illness may have entailed, but he must also cope with the altered expectations of others. The recognition of this fact puts added stress on the desirability of attempting to prevent mental illness.

Can Mental Illness Be Prevented? [67]

Certain types of mental illness can definitely be prevented and, indeed, are now being prevented. Reference has been made to the effective treatment of general paresis by the use of drug therapy. Since paresis results only as a very late stage in the course of syphilis, the cure of syphilis in earlier stages prevents the development of the psychotic state. Psychoses associated with pellagra—once a common cause of admission to mental hospitals in the South where dietary deficiencies were widespread—are now very rare. The provision of nicotinic acid in the diet was all that was required.

When we consider the functional psychoses and the mental disorders of old age, it is more difficult to apply our knowledge of etiology to preventive programs. For one thing, our knowledge of etiology is still very meager and would afford at best only partial control. For another, it would entail public education and social change in areas remarkably resistant to change, such as patterns of family life and even of mate selection. What public health workers call "secondary prevention" may for some time be more feasible. This entails the early recognition of illness and maladjustment and the provision of ameliorative services or environmental change to limit the severity and duration of disease. School counseling services and community clinics have been organized to serve this function, but the present pattern of clinic services cannot meet the demand for help; new, more flexible programs need to be developed.

Insofar as further research supports or disproves the hypothesis that high incidence of the functional psychoses and the neuroses is linked with the social deprivation and the conflict of values confronting families and individuals at the lowest socioeconomic levels, the implications for preventive programs will be similar to those that are oriented toward limiting the incidence of some of the other social problems that are discussed in this book. If, on the other hand, organic

---

[67] Perhaps the most influential presentation of the psychiatric approach to preventive and community psychiatry is Gerald Caplan, *Principles of Preventive Psychiatry* (New York: Basic Books, 1964).

factors should be linked with severe mental illnesses in such a way that gross symptomatology can be prevented by drugs or other modes of biological control, preventive programs will be primarily a medical problem and responsibility. Even in this instance, however, it is likely that major issues of social policy will have to be dealt with. For the present, it appears that more adequate knowledge, through rigorous research which explores all possible leads, is our primary hope for preventing mental illness in the future.

Personal Disorganization and Social Disorganization

This chapter has been concerned with diagnosable mental disorder as a social problem. It has indicated some of the evidence pointing to the involvement of social factors in the complex etiology of a number of mental illnesses, but it has been more concerned with the problems of societal response and social organization for dealing with such illnesses than with the thesis that they are primarily reflections of social change and social disorganization. It will conclude by taking a more general perspective toward the relationship between social disorganization and personality development.

Personality may be conceived of as the organized totality of those aspects of behavior and tendencies to behavior which give meaning to an individual in society—his characteristic ways of acting, thinking, dealing with emergencies, relating to persons of the same or different age, sex, or social status, his view of himself, and his way of communicating that view to others. Our knowledge of the relationships of personality development to such variables as social class status, family structure, and particular parental child-rearing practices is far from complete but does very clearly demonstrate that social and cultural patterns have a manifest influence.

Gross inconsistencies in the values and behaviors to which the child is exposed, or pervasive derogation or neglect of the child are reflected in vulnerabilities which may subsequently lead to personality disorders. These vulnerabilities and disorders may come to the attention of mental health specialists, or they may be expressed in various forms of deviance and rebellious behavior. Whether or not one wants to call such problems mental illness will depend largely on philosophical grounds or on professional orientations. Much deviant behavior can legitimately be labeled as the manifestation of neurotic tendencies, but the other chapters in this section make clear that such labeling may well obscure underlying social causes. At the same time, personality dynamics cannot be ignored in trying to understand the relationship between social disorganization and forms of deviant behavior.

Very little attention has been given in this chapter to the effects of mental illness and personal disorganization upon the functioning of the larger society. Our knowledge of this area tends to be of the anecdotal sort. That is, we can all cite instances of the disruptive influence of disturbed persons upon collective enterprises. The rabble-rousing demagogue whose appeal is addressed to the insecure and the frustrated is a case in point. Such persons have, for example, greatly increased the difficulties attendant upon the securing of civil rights for Negroes in the southern states. In the realm of international relations, the threat to world peace which would be posed by mental illness in any one of a dozen political leaders is frightening to consider.

Many of us will have direct experience with mental illness. Persons on whom we depend will at one time or another seem unpredictable, angry, out of sorts. Usually these will be transitory deviations, but occasionally they will violate all our expectations and defy all our efforts to repair relationships. At such times we become most acutely aware of the nature of the personal and social problems posed by mental illness.

To the extent that a person's ties with others are already tenuous when overt symptomatology occurs, mental illness is likely to go unrecognized and hence untreated until it has taken a high toll from the sick person and from his environment. To the extent that he is integrated into the social fabric—family, community, work group— there is hope for early, and not merely punitive, response to the disturbed deviant, and the consequences of the illness, difficult as they may be for those nearest to the patient, can often be limited.

2

Juvenile Delinquency

by Albert K. Cohen and James F. Short, Jr.

Until the end of the nineteenth century, young offenders in this country were either subject to the criminal law or beyond the reach of the law. Our laws governing the treatment of young offenders were based on the ancient common law of England, which took age into account only in this respect: Children under seven were "irrebuttably presumed" to be incapable of having the "criminal intent" that is a necessary ingredient of a criminal act. Children from seven to fourteen were generally presumed to be capable of criminal intent, but this presumption could be rebutted by evidence of their immaturity. If not capable of criminal intent, a child was incapable of crime. His misconduct might be a matter for his parents or kinsmen, master or priest, but it was not a matter for the courts. If, on the other hand, he were capable of criminal intent, he might be subject to the same law, the same courts, the same procedures, and the same penalties as an adult.

The Juvenile Court

In 1899 the first juvenile court was established in Cook County, Illinois, and within a generation practically every state had enacted statutes establishing juvenile courts or their equivalent. These statutes specified certain categories of young offenders and for these they provided special procedures and special dispositions. These laws created a new kind of machinery, outside the criminal law, for handling offenders, and therefore a new category of persons: young people subject to handling by this machinery. The "delinquent child"—the legal term for a child subject to the jurisdiction of the juvenile court—was, in a sense, invented in 1899.

The manifest function of the juvenile court—that is, the acknowledged and intended function—is usually phrased in the statutes in some such words as these: to secure for each child within its jurisdiction such care, custody, and treatment as should have been provided by the child's natural parents. It is not to punish but to "help children in trouble," to do what is in the best interest of the child and the state, to "rehabilitate."

The distinctive characteristics of the juvenile court are intended to secure this rehabilitative aim. The terminology of the criminal court —e.g., indictment, trial, conviction, sentence—is largely discarded in favor of a new terminology untainted by connotations of criminality. For example, the child comes to the attention of the court by a "petition in his behalf"; he has a "hearing"; he is "adjudicated to the status of a delinquent child"; and he is "committed" to a "school." The statutes generally do not prescribe a particular disposition for a particular offense, but the judge of the juvenile court may use whichever one of a variety of dispositions provided by law seems to him best calculated to secure the interests of the child and of the state. The child remains subject to the jurisdiction of the court or of the agency to which he has been committed until he is 21, or some other age specified by the statute, unless he is discharged before then because, in the judgment of the authorities, he is no longer in need of their guidance, ministrations, and benevolent discipline.

The rehabilitative philosophy of the statutes implies a flexible procedure and a wide discretion in the hands of the court, in order that dispositions may be made that are tailored to the peculiar needs of each individual child. Therefore, the statutes define delinquency in very broad terms. The category "delinquent child" includes children, within specified age brackets, who have committed acts that would be crimes if they were committed by adults. It also includes those committing vaguely defined acts that would not be crimes and for which adults would not be legally accountable, such as: "is guilty of immoral or indecent conduct," "knowingly associates with vicious or immoral persons," "is growing up in idleness and crime," "is habitually truant from school," "is incorrigible," "habitually uses vile, indecent, or obscene language," etc. The proceedings are usually more relaxed and informal than in the criminal courts, they are closed to the public, there is less emphasis on formal rules of evidence, and names of children are withheld from the press.

There is no doubt that most people want the courts to rehabilitate offenders. But they also want the courts to administer justice under "due process of law," that is, to deprive no person of life, liberty, or property except for an offense clearly defined in the law and only if the commission of that offense has been clearly established according to certain rules of procedure and evidence. Many, perhaps most, people, especially if they themselves are the victims, also are interested in seeing the wrongdoers punished. Finally, people want the court to deal with the child in a way that will most effectively deter other children from doing as he did, to "make an object lesson of him."

In short, the community seeks to achieve through the court not only the rehabilitation of offenders but a number of different objectives. In this respect the courts are like families, universities, social clubs, churches, and, indeed, most social systems. They are instrumentalities that people try to use for a variety of ends. It is seldom possible, however, fully to realize all these ends at the same time and with the same social machinery. The pursuit of one end is likely to obstruct the realization of another, or the machinery designed to facilitate the realization of one end may be used to realize other and incompatible ends.

So it is with the juvenile court. In particular, those same features of the law and of the courts that seem necessary or at least useful to the rehabilitative function of the court may be used to frustrate the value of due process and to promote the ends of punishment and vengeance. Specifically, the discretion in the definition of "delinquent child" and in the choice of dispositions that seems necessary in order to realize the rehabilitative end may be used by the court for quite different purposes. Armed with this discretion, a judge can deprive a child of years of freedom for the commission of an act for which an adult could not even be prosecuted. It is difficult to ensure that the judge will be governed in his dispositions solely by rehabilitative considerations and not by the social position of the child's family, the social status or political power of the victim, or by his own private moral predilections. Furthermore, when delinquency is defined, as it is in the statutes, so broadly and loosely that almost any child *could* be held to be delinquent, the judge must perforce decide for himself what "delinquent child" shall mean in *his* court. Due process, however, implies that the liberties of the citizen are not to be abridged except for reasons clearly stated in the law. Therefore, the relaxed and informal procedures of the court, the lack of emphasis on adherence to strict legal rules of evidence, the privacy of the proceedings, have all been assailed by those who cherish the tradition of due process on the grounds that these conditions may confer on an incompetent or prejudiced judge great power without corresponding responsibility or assurance that the power will be exercised to the ends for which it was conferred.

The point is not that judges *will* act in a capricious, arbitrary, or punitive spirit; it is probable that, by and large, they do not act in such a spirit. We are not arguing that flexibility and discretion are undesirable. The fact remains, however, that there are real dilemmas built into the structure of the courts, and the central dilemma—the basis for most of the controversy surrounding the court—is how to provide the flexibility and discretion necessary for rehabilitative ends and, at the same time, to guarantee due process and the subordination of punishment to rehabilitation.

But even if the courts single-mindedly pursued the goal of rehabilitation, they would still be lacking a clear criterion for decisions. The field of delinquency, unlike the field of medicine, does not have a large body of verified, detailed, and precise knowledge about etiology and treatment. It is, therefore, difficult to know in any particular case what disposition is to be preferred above another *on treatment grounds*. Under these conditions, the judge, since he must decide on *some* grounds, cannot help but be influenced in a large proportion of cases by considerations other than treatment effectiveness.[1]

Delinquency as a Social Role

The word "delinquent," as it is used legally, "defines" and "places" a person so that one may know how to deal with him in the courts. The word is also used by parents, teachers, neighbors, peers, etc., for labeling people and organizing one's behavior toward them. But the category "delinquent" as a social "role" of everyday life is not identical with "delinquent" as a legal category. That is, the criteria by which the man in the street defines somebody as delinquent and the images, feelings, and dispositions that the word arouses are not identical with the criteria and consequences in the world of the courts. The social role of delinquent entails consequences over and above those provided by law. If a boy is defined as delinquent in the world of everyday life, his whole social world may be transformed—the ways in which other people see him, how they feel toward him, their willingness to asso-

---

[1] Among more extensive treatments of the development of the juvenile court are the following: Herbert H. Lou, *Juvenile Courts in the United States* (Chapel Hill: University of North Carolina Press, 1927). Frederick J. Ludwig, *Youth and the Law* (Brooklyn: Foundation Press, 1955). Paul W. Tappan, *Juvenile Delinquency* (New York: McGraw-Hill, 1959). Also his *Comparative Survey of Juvenile Delinquency: Part 1, North America* (New York: United Nations, 1952). Herbert A. Bloch and Frank T. Flynn, *Delinquency: The Juvenile Offender in America Today* (New York: Random House, 1956). David Matza, *Delinquency and Drift* (New York: Wiley & Sons, 1964), Chapter 4.

ciate with him, the activities and opportunities that are open to him. In consequence of these changes, the way in which the boy sees, labels, and evaluates himself, his estimate of his chances and prospects in the world of nondelinquent and conventional people, his notion of whether trying to avoid delinquency is worth the trouble, may be profoundly affected. It is quite possible, indeed, that being invested with the social role may so narrow a person's opportunities for the rewards and gratifications of nondelinquent society that it may strengthen his tendency to behavior that is delinquent in the legal sense.[2]

Although being a "delinquent child" and having the social role of delinquent are not the same thing, if one has been legally declared a "delinquent child" and the fact is known, he is likely to be invested with the social role. Indeed, if he has merely been processed by the courts without having been found delinquent, this may suffice to endow him with the social role. This by-product of legal processing may have more far-reaching consequences in the life of the child than what happens to him in court. For this reason, it is not possible to appraise the law and the judicial institutions without considering the extra-judicial social role of delinquency and its meaning for the child.

Defining Delinquency for Etiological Purposes

We shall be concerned in this chapter with the causes of delinquent behavior, whether or not that behavior has actually resulted in legal action. We want to explain the behavior of children, not the behavior of officials. For our present purposes, then, we shall define delinquent behavior as those actions of young people that are specified by law as grounds for an adjudication of delinquency. It will be recalled, however, that the statutes define delinquency so broadly that almost any child could, under the statutes, be declared a "delinquent child." Where, then, are the "nondelinquents"?

The problem arises only if we assume that there are really only two kinds of children, "delinquents" and "nondelinquents," and that every child is either the one or the other. It does not arise if we recognize that children, even if most of them could be labeled delinquent under the law, vary almost infinitely in their actual delinquent behavior. Children differ with respect to kinds, frequency, regularity, and versatility of their delinquent behavior. If our concern is with delinquent behavior, our task is not to sort out all children into two categories

---

[2] Frank Tannenbaum, *Crime and the Community* (New York: Ginn, 1938).

but rather to study the different varieties and patterns of delinquent behavior and to try to explain them. The perfectly nondelinquent child becomes only one—and possibly an imaginary one—of a variety of possibilities to be recognized and accounted for.[3]

The Data of Delinquency

Accurate and representative data about delinquency are essential to the development of theory and to delinquency control, for the data at hand suggest theories, provide the means for testing them, and are the indicators of the effectiveness of our attempts at control. The principal sources of data about delinquency are the following:

1. Clinical reports. These data usually take the form of intensive case studies and are invaluable for the suggestion of hypotheses. They are obtained mostly through interviews in the course of clinical practice or by researchers operating in a clinical setting.

2. Records of law-enforcement, judicial, and correctional agencies, usually in the form of statistical summaries.

3. Studies of self-reported behavior. These are attempts to obtain, from reports of the subjects themselves, detailed data about the distribution and correlates of delinquency. An example would be anonymous questionnaires about delinquency administered to total populations of high schools.

4. Participant and field observation, utilizing methods developed by anthropologists and sociologists, in which the researcher makes observations on the basis of direct contact with the groups or communities under investigation.

Statistical data on juvenile delinquency in the United States are published by the United States Children's Bureau [4] and in the Uniform Crime Reports of the Federal Bureau of Investigation.[5] The Children's Bureau data concern "alleged delinquents known to the juvenile courts"; the FBI data concern children arrested, or what might be termed "alleged delinquents known to the police."

---

[3] F. Ivan Nye and James F. Short, Jr., "Scaling Delinquent Behavior," *American Sociological Review*, Vol. 22 (June, 1957), pp. 326-31. Lester E. Hewitt and Richard L. Jenkins, *Fundamental Patterns of Maladjustment: The Dynamics of Their Origin* (Springfield: State of Illinois, 1947). John Findley Scott, "Two Dimensions of Delinquent Behavior," *American Sociological Review*, Vol. 24, No. 2 (April, 1959), pp. 240-43.

[4] Department of Health, Education, and Welfare, *Juvenile Court Statistics*, Children's Bureau Statistical Series (Washington, D. C., published annually).

[5] Federal Bureau of Investigation, *Crime in the United States*, Uniform Crime Reports (Washington, D. C., published annually).

Limitations of Official Statistics

Official statistics on juvenile delinquency are, in general, subject to the same kinds of limitations as those discussed in the chapter on crime, but the following specific limitations are especially worth noting.

1. All official statistics are the records of the activities of officials—policemen, judges, probation officers, etc.—and, in this sense, the bookkeeping records of "business transacted" in official agencies. Therefore, they are directly descriptive of the behavior of officials rather than that of children.

2. Different kinds of delinquent children and of delinquent acts have different probabilities of becoming officially known and different probabilities of reaching any given stage in the correctional process. Therefore, it is hazardous to draw inferences, from the data compiled by official agencies, about the distribution of delinquents and delinquencies in the population.

3. These statistics provide very meager information about characteristics of the offenders and the offenses which they describe, information that is important for purposes of theory-testing and delinquency control.

4. The juvenile court philosophy stresses a rehabilitative approach which prescribes that each child be dealt with in a manner calculated to serve his best interests. The appropriate disposition depends on the resources and personnel available in the court and the community and will therefore vary from one jurisdiction to another. In short, to the degree that the courts conform to the juvenile court philosophy, disposition data from one jurisdiction will not be comparable to those from another.

On the basis of *seriousness* ratings of a variety of crimes, Sellin and Wolfgang have derived an index of delinquency from *police* data.[6] They attempt to overcome the limitations of official statistics by choosing as their source of information *police descriptions of delinquency events,* and by limiting index offenses to those whose discovery and reporting involve little official activity. The resulting index is therefore limited to serious crimes that do not involve consensus of offender and victim (e.g., statutory rape). Minor delinquencies such as truancy and drinking, which bulk large in the early history of many "delinquent careers," are thus eliminated. The index is useful as a gross

---

[6] Thorsten Sellin and Marvin Wolfgang, *The Measurement of Delinquency* (New York: Wiley & Sons, 1964). In addition to detailing the derivation of the index, this book presents a comprehensive and systematic history of attempts to measure juvenile delinquency.

measure of the volume and seriousness of delinquency in a community and of the effectiveness of control programs in reducing over-all delinquency. It is of limited value, however, for delinquency studies that are concerned with variations in kinds and patterns of delinquent behavior, whether among communities or individuals.

Because of these and other limitations of official data sources, there is increasing interest among students of delinquency in the further development and application of methods of self-reported behavior and participant and field observation.

Trends

It is impossible to state unequivocally how much delinquency there is in the United States or whether it has been increasing or decreasing over the past several decades. On the basis of both Children's Bureau and FBI data, one would be tempted to conclude that delinquency in this country rose to an all-time high level in the 1960's. Both agencies report startling rises since the immediate post-World War II period. Roughly 2 percent of all children aged 10 through 17 were involved in court cases each year after 1954, in contrast to approximately 1 percent in the pre-World War II period.

We must, however, be skeptical of these findings because of the limitations of official data. Furthermore, "The delinquency rates of today (the late fifties) may be 'very high' only when we compare them to the 'very low' rates of the late thirties." [7] The latter statement is provocative but difficult to test. Two studies may be cited. (1) Teeters and Matza present data from Cuyahoga County (Cleveland), Ohio, for the years 1918-1957. From these data they infer that "the rates in Cleveland and the rest of the county were twice as high in the period during and after World War I than the rates experienced during the early and late fifties." (2) McKay has compiled data from the oldest Juvenile Court in the land since its inception. His calculation of rates of male juvenile delinquents for Cook County, Illinois, indicates that the highest rates of the entire series, 1900-1959, were reached in the *early years* of the court. The peak year was 1906. Another high level was reached during the World War I years of 1914-1918. The lowest level occurred in the late 1930's and very early 40's. After 1951, the rate climbed to a level that was slightly *below* the level for the first decade of the century.[8]

---

[7] Negley K. Teeters and David Matza, "The Extent of Delinquency in the United States," *The Journal of Negro Education*, Vol. 28 (Summer, 1959), pp. 210-11.

[8] From unpublished data, by kind permission of Henry D. McKay.

TABLE 1

Number of Persons Under 18 Years of Age Arrested for Major Crimes in Cities of the United States and Percentage of Those Arrested in Two Age Groups, 1964

Offense Charged	Number of Persons Arrested Under 18	Percentage Under 18	Percentage Over 18
Larceny; theft	193,670	54.0	46.0
All other offenses (except traffic)	149,836	29.3	70.7
Burglary; breaking or entering	96,087	51.4	48.6
Disorderly conduct	75,300	15.8	84.2
Runaways	70,517	100.0	—
Curfew and loitering-law violations	64,784	100.0	—
Auto theft	62,734	64.4	35.6
Vandalism	59,413	77.3	22.7
Liquor laws	40,044	26.0	74.0
Other assaults	26,722	14.0	86.0
Drunkenness	21,918	1.5	98.5
Suspicion	19,659	19.3	80.7
Sex offenses (except forcible rape and prostitution)	13,720	23.6	76.4
Aggravated assault	11,791	14.8	85.2
Robbery	10,790	27.6	72.4
Weapons: carrying, possessing, etc.	9,662	20.4	79.6
Vagrancy	9,052	6.8	93.2
Stolen property: buying, receiving, possessing	6,293	34.7	65.3
Arson	3,315	63.5	36.5
Narcotic drug laws	3,305	8.7	91.3
Forgery and counterfeiting	3,111	10.2	89.8
Gambling	2,270	2.2	97.8
Forcible rape	1,776	18.8	81.2
Driving under the influence	1,774	.8	99.2
Fraud	1,323	2.9	97.1
Offenses against family and children	805	1.4	99.6
Murder and nonnegligent manslaughter	546	8.5	91.5
Prostitution and commercialized vice	537	1.9	99.1
Embezzlement	193	2.2	97.8
Manslaughter by negligence	185	6.9	93.1

Source: Federal Bureau of Investigation, *Crime in the United States,* Uniform Crime Reports, 1964 (Washington, D. C., 1965), p. 111.

Major crimes as reported by the FBI have followed the pattern of court cases described by the Children's Bureau. Each year since 1952, when the FBI inaugurated the present system of reporting arrests, the number of persons under 18 years of age arrested has increased more rapidly than have arrests of older persons. It will be noted from Table 1 that, both in numbers arrested and in the percentage of all persons arrested, young people come to the attention of the police primarily for property crimes, for specifically juvenile offenses such as runaway and curfew violation, and for vandalism. With the exception of embezzlement and fraud, forgery and counterfeiting, which require greater finesse and higher social position, a large percentage of all property offenses committed annually in this country is accounted for by juveniles. The proportion of auto theft accounted for by juveniles is especially striking. For several years this proportion has been approximately two-thirds of all such offenses. It must be remembered, however, that much juvenile auto theft, in contrast to that of adults, consists of "joy-riding," which attracts the attention of police and therefore is more likely to lead to detection and apprehension.

It is possible that juvenile delinquency has been growing more violent and destructive over the past few decades, but there is no definitive evidence on this matter, and property offenses continue to bulk large among all juvenile crimes.

Age and Delinquency [9]

Most children who are brought before the court are in the *older* age categories, but apparently this figure has been dropping. In 1963, the largest *number* of persons arrested for all crimes, as reported to the FBI, were 16 years of age, with persons 17 years of age being second, and 15- and 18-year-olds following with almost equal numbers.

Sex and Delinquency

In recent years, the ratio of boys to girls appearing before juvenile courts has dropped to about 5 to 1, and this is consistent with data from other sources. This represents a considerable decrease from the 50-to-60 to 1 ratio which obtained in this country around the turn of the century.

Sex ratios are not the same for all types of delinquency. Boys tend overwhelmingly to be arrested for offenses involving stealing and mischief of one sort or another, while girls are typically brought before the court for sex offenses and for "running away," "incorrigibility" and "delinquent tendencies," which are often euphemisms for problems of sex behavior. The *sources* of case referral also differ for boys and girls. While the police and other law-enforcement agencies refer the major-

---

[9] These observations follow Walter C. Reckless, *The Crime Problem*, 2nd ed. (New York: Appleton, 1955). See especially Reckless' treatment of "categoric risks." Specific data on these matters are found in FBI and Children's Bureau reports and in special studies devoted to these topics.

ity of all delinquency cases to the court, a far higher percentage of girls' cases are referred by parents, other relatives, schools, social agencies, and other sources.

Race and Ethnicity

Racial and ethnic groups have been shown by many studies to have widely varying delinquency rates. The Negro delinquency rate, for example, is exceptionally high.[10] Estimates of the number of delinquents among Negroes range from about twice to about five times as high as would be expected on the basis of the proportion of Negroes in the total population. Puerto Ricans, Mexicans, and American Indians likewise have been found to have especially high delinquency rates. Orientals have usually been found to comprise a lower proportion of all delinquents than their proportion in the total population.

Differences such as these may be misleading, however, for numerous studies have found greater variation within these groups than between them. Intergroup comparisons are suspect also because the data upon which these observations are made are *official* data, subject to all the qualifications of official data discussed earlier, and especially subject to certain of these qualifications. Axelrad, for example, has found that Negro children were committed at younger ages, for less serious crimes, and with fewer prior court appearances and institutional commitments than were white children.[11]

Ethnic variations present a striking picture of change over time, reflecting very closely the flow of immigration to this country. As recently as 1930, for example, shortly after the sharp restrictions imposed on immigration in the mid-1920's, about one-half of the children coming to the attention of the courts were of foreign-born parentage. Today about three-fourths of such children are native-born, of native-born parentage.[12]

The findings on race and ethnicity in relation to delinquency must

---

[10] See *The Journal of Negro Education*, Vol. 28 (Summer, 1959). The issue is devoted to "Juvenile Delinquency Among Negroes in the United States."

[11] Sidney Axelrad, "Negro and White Male Institutionalized Delinquents," *American Journal of Sociology*, Vol. 57 (May, 1952), pp. 569-74. See also Don C. Gibbons and Manzer J. Griswold, "Sex Differences Among Juvenile Court Referrals," *Sociology and Social Research*, Vol. 42 (November-December, 1957), pp. 106-10.

[12] Recently Chilton has shown that the foreign-born no longer contribute significantly to delinquency arrests, but that race continues to be an important factor. See Roland J. Chilton, "Delinquency Area Research in Baltimore, Detroit, and Indianapolis," *American Sociological Review*, Vol. 29 (February, 1964), pp. 71-83.

not be interpreted as a simple function of societal and administrative bias against Negroes and other ethnic populations, though this probably operates in many cases. The juvenile court philosophy is consistent with earlier intervention of the state in the case of groups living under such conditions as poverty and family and community disorganization. Where family and community resources are questionable, this philosophy prescribes earlier action on the part of official agents and action with respect to less serious offenses which, when committed by more favored groups in society, might be handled by the family and/or community.

Social Class and Delinquency

A variety of studies indicate that lower-class individuals run greater risks of becoming officially defined as delinquent, but studies of self-reported delinquency reveal much overlapping in delinquent behavior between those who are officially delinquent and officially nondelinquent.

Studies in small cities and towns across the land fail to demonstrate differences in delinquency involvement among children in different social classes,[13] while greater involvement by lower-class youngsters is reported by studies conducted in large cities.[14]

Social class occupies such an important position in etiological theories of delinquency that systematic, objective, and relevant data on the matter are of the greatest importance. From large cities, *observational* data from lower-class areas with high rates of *official* delinquency suggest that the incidence of hidden delinquency in these areas is also extremely high. Here there appear to be both quantitative and qualitative differences in delinquency involvement among children with different social class backgrounds, with lower-class children being more seriously involved than are children in more favorable social and economic positions.[15]

---

[13] F. Ivan Nye, James F. Short, Jr., and V. J. Olson, "Socioeconomic Status and Delinquent Behavior," *American Journal of Sociology,* Vol. 63 (January, 1958), pp. 381-89. Studies currently being conducted by Himelhoch in Vermont, Empey and Erickson in Utah, and Polk in Oregon report similar findings.

[14] See James F. Short, Jr., and Fred L. Strodtbeck, *Group Process and Gang Delinquency* (Chicago: University of Chicago Press, 1965), especially Chapter 7.

[15] Walter B. Miller, Hildred S. Geertz, and Henry S. G. Cutter, "Aggression in a Boys' Street-Corner Group," *Psychiatry,* Vol. 24 (1961), pp. 283-98; James F. Short, Jr., Kenneth I. Howard, and Ray A. Tennyson, "Behavior Dimensions of Gang Delinquency," *American Sociological Review,* Vol. 28 (June, 1963), pp. 411-28; and Andrew Greeley and James Casey, "An Upper Middle Class Deviant Gang," *American Catholic Sociological Review,* Vol. 24 (Spring, 1963), pp. 33-41.

Rural-Urban Differences in Delinquency

There appears to be a direct relationship between urbanization and juvenile delinquency. Highest rates occur in urban areas, with lowest rates in rural areas, and "semiurban" areas in between.

The chief caution in interpreting these findings has to do with differences in facilities for handling cases in urban and in rural areas. It seems likely that in rural areas less serious offenses tend to be handled outside the court by parents, ministers, teachers, and others, whereas in urban areas, where facilities are more fully developed and legal controls more relied upon, similar offenses are more likely to find their way into the courts. On the other hand, when cases do reach the courts, rural areas handle a higher proportion of them officially, rather than informally and without making them part of the official record, and send a higher proportion on to institutions, than do urban areas.

Ecological Differences in Delinquency

Probably the best established patterns of variation in official delinquency are of an ecological nature. The classic works of Shaw, McKay, and their collaborators, and more recent studies reveal wide variations in the spatial concentration of delinquency, variations which occur regardless of the population groups occupying areas with different rates of delinquency.[16] Though the details of ecological patterns vary in different cities, the general nature of these patterns is remarkably consistent. Rates of juvenile delinquency and recidivism are highest in the inner-city areas characterized by physical deterioration and the concentration of other social problems such as poverty, suicide, adult crime, and mental illness. As one moves away from these "delinquency areas," rates go down fairly regularly. When studied over time these ecological distributions change little despite changes in the racial and ethnic composition of the areas studied.

The most serious criticism of the "delinquency area" concept concerns the fact that even in such areas delinquency rates are considerably below 100 percent. A delinquency rate of 25 percent (a very high rate) of all age-eligible boys in an area does not mean, however, that only 25 percent of these boys engaged in delinquent behavior. The incidence of hidden delinquency is very large. Additionally, recent studies indicate that the percentage of youngsters who come before

---

[16] Clifford Shaw *et al., Delinquency Areas* (Chicago: University of Chicago Press, 1929); Clifford Shaw and Henry McKay, *Juvenile Delinquency and Urban Areas* (Chicago: University of Chicago Press, 1942); and Bernard Lander, *Towards an Understanding of Juvenile Delinquency* (New York: Columbia University Press, 1954).

the court at some time during their period of "eligibility" is several times the *annual* rate. By carefully studying incidence figures for each age group, Ball and his associates estimate that 20.7 percent of the boys and 5.2 percent of the girls in the Lexington, Kentucky, area will appear officially in court before age 18, as compared with an annual rate for boys in 1960 of 2.3 percent, and for girls of 0.5 percent.[17] This includes neither all arrests nor *unofficial* court appearances. Monahan reports similar figures for Philadelphia, where Savitz also has reported that 59 percent of the boys in a high delinquency area had acquired delinquency records by age 18.[18] In the highest rate areas, therefore, it seems probable that a sizeable majority of boys will be officially tabbed as delinquent at some time during their period of eligibility.

Delinquency Causation: Levels of Theory

The literature on delinquency theory consists largely of arguments between partisans of "psychological" and of "sociological" theories. Underlying these arguments is the assumption that these two kinds of theory are different and incompatible ways of explaining the same thing. Much of the controversy, however, turns out to be pointless if we recognize that there are different sorts of questions that one can ask about delinquency causation and if we think of sociological theories and psychological theories as concerned with answering different questions.

1. Any act—delinquent or otherwise—depends on "something about the actor," that is, something about his values, his goals, his interests, his temperament, or, speaking inclusively, his personality, and it depends also on "something about the situation" in which he finds himself. Change either actor or situation and you get a different act. One kind of question we can ask is this: how do circumstances on the actor or personality side and on the situational side interact to determine delinquent behavior? What do you have to take into account in personality and in the situation, and what are the rules for predicting the outcomes of various combinations of personality components? For example, recent sociopsychological studies have stressed the role of

---

[17] John C. Ball, Alan Ross, and Alice Simpson, "Incidence and Estimated Prevalence of Recorded Delinquency in a Metropolitan Area," *American Sociological Review*, Vol. 29 (February, 1964), pp. 90-93.

[18] Thomas P. Monahan, "On the Incidence of Delinquency," *Social Forces*, 39 (October, 1960), pp. 66-72; and Leonard Savitz, "Delinquency and Migration," in Marvin E. Wolfgang, Leonard Savitz, and Norman Johnston, eds., *The Sociology of Crime and Delinquency* (New York: Wiley & Sons, 1962), p. 205.

group processes, involving the interaction of personality variables and the setting of group activity in the production and inhibition of delinquent behavior.[19]

2. Remembering that delinquent acts always depend on appropriate combinations of actor *and situation,* we know also that, under given conditions, people with certain kinds of personalities are more likely to commit delinquent acts than other people. We may now ask: what kinds of experiences produce what kinds of personalities and, in particular, the kinds of personalities that will produce delinquent acts under a given range of conditions? It is possible to have similar theories of motivation along with quite different theories about the origin or history of the components of motivation on the personality side. These questions are addressed by theories about learning or personality development.

3. Both of the foregoing types of theories fall within the domain of psychology or social psychology. Still another type of question, however, concerns the distribution of delinquent acts in social systems. Each type of delinquent act is distributed in a characteristic way among the various age, race, ethnic, regional, ecological, social class, and other sectors or categories of the social system. We may ask, then, this question: What is it about social systems—about their cultures and institutions and how their parts are related to one another—that explains variations in rates from one part of a system to another, from one system to another, from one time to another? This question is the concern of sociological theory.

Theories of delinquent behavior sometimes deal with one of these levels of inquiry, while ignoring the other levels or making assumptions about them which are only rarely made explicit. Several recent studies attempt to integrate these levels, both in theory and in empirical inquiry, and, in the process, to add greatly to knowledge in this area.[20]

---

[19] See Short and Strodtbeck, *Group Process and Gang Delinquency;* Lewis Yablonsky, *The Violent Gang* (New York: Macmillan, 1962); and Harold W. Pfautz, "Near-Group Theory and Collective Behavior: A Critical Reformulation," *Social Problems,* 9 (Fall, 1961), p. 173.

[20] See, for example, Alex Inkeles, "Personality and Social Structure," in Robert K. Merton, Leonard Broom, and Leonard S. Cottrell, Jr., eds., *Sociology Today* (New York: Basic Books, 1959), Chapter 11; Albert K. Cohen, "The Sociology of the Deviant Act: Anomie Theory and Beyond," *American Sociological Review* (February, 1965), pp. 5-14; Robert K. Merton, "Anomie, Anomia, and Social Interaction: Contexts of Deviant Behavior," in Marshall B. Clinard, ed., *Anomie and Deviant Behavior* (New York: Free Press, 1964), pp. 213-42. Specifically with reference to juvenile delinquency, see Short and Strodtbeck, *Group Process and Gang Delinquency.*

Psychobiological Theories [21]

We speak here of theories according to which the independent variables in the determination of delinquency are some observable or hypothetical aspect of the biological structure of the person. In the more extreme versions of such theories, variations in the situation are largely ignored, both as variables in the learning process and in motivational processes. Delinquent behavior becomes a direct manifestation of some underlying condition in the glands, the nervous system, or, more vaguely, "the constitution." These bodily characteristics are, in turn, ascribed to a defective heredity and the causation of delinquency becomes reduced to the formula: heredity determines delinquency.

The prototype of such theories is Cesare Lombroso's theory of the born criminal. Lombroso's conception of the born criminal was sharply criticized in his own day and even Lombroso, in his later work, greatly qualified himself,[22] but the general idea of a "criminal type," recognizable by his bestial or otherwise unlovely stigmata, has always attracted some scholars. Most recently, the American anthropologist, E. A. Hooton, claimed, on the basis of his comparison of criminals and noncriminals, that criminals showed various traits of biological inferiority and degeneration and that criminality was the behavioral manifestation of such biological inadequacy.[23] (See Chapter 3, pages 161-63.)

Somewhat reminiscent of Lombroso's born criminal, without the biological stigmata, is the still popular conception of the "constitutional psychopathic personality," an individual devoid of moral sense and the tender affections, ruled only by his impulses and intelligence, but never by regard for moral values or the welfare of others. This individual is presumed to be delinquent because of some underlying defect of his brain or nervous system, either inherited or acquired through organic injury or disease.[24]

Until the 1930's it was widely believed that the principal cause of delinquency lay in mental deficiency. (See Chapter 3, page 164.) Here the delinquency is not perceived as a direct expression of an

---

[21] For an excellent survey of this class of theories, see William McCord, "The Biological Basis of Juvenile Delinquency," in Joseph S. Roucek, ed., *Juvenile Delinquency* (New York: Philosophical Library, 1958), pp. 59-78.

[22] See the introduction to Gina Lombroso-Ferrero, *Criminal Man According to the Classifications of Cesare Lombroso* (New York: Putnam, 1911), pp. xiv-xv.

[23] E. A. Hooton, *Crime and the Man* (Cambridge, Mass.: Harvard University Press, 1939). See also R. K. Merton and M. F. Ashley-Montagu, "Crime and the Anthropologist," *American Anthropologist*, Vol. 42 (1940), pp. 384-468.

[24] For a critique of this concept, see Bloch and Flynn, *Delinquency*, pp. 144 ff.

organically rooted instinct but rather of mental deficiency, which is alleged to impair the capacity to acquire morality and self-control. Mental deficiency is, in turn, presumed to be inherited from tainted stock.[25]

These and most other theories that explain delinquency as a direct or indirect result of biological constitution have been largely discredited, for there is little evidence to support them. The research on which they are based has typically used poor or inadequate controls; the measuring instruments have been inadequate or unskillfully applied; and the biological connection with delinquency has been so vague and undefined as to be unfit for scientific investigation.

William H. Sheldon has developed a system for describing the varieties of human physique.[26] To one such variety, the mesomorph, characterized by a sturdy and muscular athletic frame, he ascribes an unusual propensity to delinquency. He does not assert, however, that there is something inherently and specifically delinquent about the mesomorph. The mesomorphic physique is asserted rather to be associated with a distinctive type of temperament, somatotonia, characterized by such traits as assertiveness of posture and movement, love of physical adventure, abounding and restless energy, need for and enjoyment of exercise. This temperament is not of itself necessarily predictive of delinquency. Mesomorphy and its attendant somatotonia, however, produce aggressive, energetic, daring types of people; it is the stuff of which generals, athletes, and politicians, as well as delinquents, often are made. All are callings that are congenial to the somatotonic temperament.

Sheldon's research has been the subject of devastating criticism,[27] but his ideas have been given a new lease of life by the more recent work of Sheldon Glueck and Eleanor Glueck.[28] Although their work has also been subject to criticism it is, of all the research in the field of the relationship between physique and delinquency, methodologically the most scrupulous and respectable. Their samples of delinquents and nondelinquents have been more carefully drawn, their statistical analysis more cautious, and their conclusions more limited and guarded. It seems probable that the mesomorphic physique is

---

[25] See Harry M. Shulman, "Intelligence and Delinquency," *Journal of Criminal Law and Criminology*, Vol. 41 (1951), pp. 763-81.

[26] William H. Sheldon, *Varieties of Delinquent Youth* (New York: Harper, 1949).

[27] Albert K. Cohen, Alfred R. Lindesmith, and Karl Schuessler, eds., *The Sutherland Papers* (Bloomington: Indiana University Press, 1956), pp. 279-90.

[28] Sheldon and Eleanor Glueck, *Physique and Delinquency* (New York: Harper, 1956).

disproportionately common in officially delinquent populations, although it is far from being the hallmark by which delinquents may be identified. (Even in the Glueck research, 40 percent of their delinquents *were not* predominantly mesomorphic, and 30 percent of their nondelinquents *were.*) Whether this is so because the temperament of the mesomorph, rooted in an inherited biological constitution, has an inherent propensity for danger, violence, and predatory behavior, whether it is because the strenuous and active life of the lower-class, street-dwelling delinquent tends to harden the body into a mesomorphic contour, or whether it is because the boy with the strength and energy of the mesomorph finds it easier than his scrawnier or more corpulent peers to gain status through the kinds of accomplishments that are rewarded in the delinquent gang, is uncertain.

In sum, there seems to be no evidence or logic for believing that heredity equips some people with a ready-made repertoire of delinquent actions. It does not, however, seem improbable that variations in human temperament, like variations in intelligence, may be related to variations in biological equipment. Nor does it seem inherently improbable that such variations in temperament may, in complex and subtle ways, constitute significant variables in human motivation and learning, and therefore in delinquent behavior. It would therefore seem premature to condemn as futile all further inquiry in this direction. We should not, however, expect to find any consistent relationship between specific biological traits and delinquent actions. Variations in biological structure are likely to have indirect and contingent significance for the understanding of delinquency—perhaps the same order of significance they might have for one's becoming a doctor, artist, teacher, carpenter, or drugstore clerk.

Psychoanalytical Instinct Theories [29]

Psychoanalytical theory is not a single coherent theory but a variety of theories developed by numerous writers from the original work of Sigmund Freud.

One kind of psychoanalytical theory starts from the conception of the personality as constituted of the Id, the Ego, and the Superego. The Id is the abode of impulse life, the wants and wishes that press for gratification. It includes aggressive and destructive impulses.

---

[29] See citations to theories of this class and discussion in Albert K. Cohen, *Delinquent Boys* (New York: Free Press, 1955), pp. 14-15, 181-82. See also David Abrahamsen, *Who are The Guilty?* (New York: Grove, 1952), pp. 36, 37-38, 60, 65.

Delinquent and criminal behavior represent the eruption of these impulses from the cellars and caverns of the personality.

The Ego is the "reality principle," the capacity to take thought, to take into account the environment, including the probable reactions of others, and to control and delay the free expression of the impulses proceeding from the Id in order to maximize gratification in the long run. It is one restraining force that helps to keep the Id subdued and harmless.

The Superego is the other restraining force. It is roughly equivalent to the conscience, the moral standards with which the individual identifies, and it functions as a monitor and censor over the antisocial tendencies of the Id.

Delinquent behavior results when the restraining forces are too weak to curb the pressures from the Id. In this theory of delinquent motivation, delinquency and nondelinquency are the outcomes of the battles fought within the personality by these three protagonists. Situational factors play a minor part in motivation and in the development of the delinquent impulse. In most psychoanalytical writings the Id is treated as a bundle of instincts, a species characteristic that does not differentiate one person from another. We are all, in this view, born criminals—or, at least, contain within ourselves a born criminal. The Ego and Superego, on the other hand, are the result of learning. According to this view, therefore, all young children are criminals. We do not learn to become criminals; rather, some of us learn to control our criminality and some do not.

This theory is vulnerable to all the criticisms that have been directed at attempts to account for human behavior as expressions of biologically derived instincts. The most general of these criticisms is that such explanations are circular. They say, in effect: we behave thus-and-so because of an instinct, and we know there is such an instinct because we behave thus-and-so.

Psychodynamic Problem-solving Theories [30]

There is another class of theories derived mostly from the work of psychoanalytical writers. These theories are found intertwined in their writings with theories of the instinctivist variety; because of this, they

---

[30] For a classic statement of the psychodynamic point of view, see William Healy and Augusta F. Bronner, *New Light on Delinquency and Its Treatment* (New Haven: Yale University Press, 1936). See also, D. H. Stott, *Delinquency and Human Nature* (Dumferline, Fife: The Carnegie United Kingdom Trust, 1950). For a critique of psychodynamic and instinctivist views see Michael Hakeem, "A Critique of the Psychiatric Approach," in Joseph Roucek, ed., *Juvenile Delinquency*, pp. 79-112.

are often identified with the latter, but they are in important respects different.

According to these theories, the delinquent act is not the expression of a fully formed delinquent impulse that finds its way out through a chink in the armor of the Ego and Superego. It is, rather, a form of behavior that is *contrived* by the personality as a way of dealing with some problem of adjustment. The problem takes the form of a conflict among various ingredients of the personality: wishes, strivings, fears, loyalties, the conscience, etc. One of the ingredients of the conflict is usually an internalized moral standard; one or more of the other ingredients are usually wishes or impulses that are unacceptable to the self because they conflict with the moral standards (Superego) of the person. Because they are unacceptable, the individual is reluctant to acknowledge them to himself and fails to recognize them for what they are (i.e., he is "unconscious" of them). It is not possible to give full satisfaction to all of the contending parties. The delinquent act is a partial solution because it gives partial, although disguised, satisfaction to both of them, because it gives expression to one and keeps the other under control and out of sight, or because in some way it makes it easier to live with the conflict even though it does not completely resolve it. The delinquent act, therefore, does not mean what it seems to mean. Its true meaning is obscure and is accessible to analysis only by special techniques.

In these theories, too, situational factors generally are not given a great deal of attention, because the problem is commonly thought of as something built into the personality that the person carries with him. Some situations may, however, provide a convenient occasion for the expression of a delinquent tendency that the personality has already formed and that is ready for release.

We speak of these as a "class" of theories because theories that have these characteristics in common may also differ among themselves, principally in two respects. First, they may differ with respect to the components of the problem or conflict to which the delinquent act is supposed to be a solution. Thus, different investigators are prone to discover different conflicts in the psyche of the delinquent: feminine tendencies or unconscious homosexual wishes in conflict with a masculine Ego-ideal; or unconscious hostility toward a parent or sibling, which the child cannot express because of fear or guilt; or incestuous wishes in conflict with the Superego; or innumerable other conflicts. Each of these yields a different explanation of the delinquent act.

Second, they may differ also with respect to the "psychodynamic mechanism" that is supposed to be operating; that is, the process through which the delinquent act performs its problem-solving function. Thus, two investigators might agree on the content of the problem—e.g., that the child has unconscious feelings of hatred toward his father and feels guilty about this. One, however, may interpret a destructive act against a stranger as an attack on a father-symbol, an attack which permits a partial satisfaction to the hostile wish, but which can be more easily reconciled with the Superego because its "real" meaning is disguised to the attacker himself. Another person may construe the same act as "delinquency out of a sense of guilt," that is, as the commission of a delinquent act *with an unconscious intention of being apprehended and punished,* thereby satisfying an unconscious need for punishment in order to assuage the feelings of guilt arising out of the hatred for the father. A delinquent act may be construed as an effort to provoke somebody to a show of rejection and hostility, in order to justify one's own hostility, about which one feels guilty. It may be construed as an attempt to "compensate" for a real or imagined inferiority or sense of weakness, which one is unwilling to accept in one's self. There are numerous such mechanisms differently favored by different investigators, and they form an integral part of each explanation.

As a preface to criticism of such theories, it should be remarked that people who do not formally subscribe to these theories and who may even be among their most virulent critics often make use of these modes of reasoning in their professional work and in their everyday interpretations of other people's behavior.

Among the more common defects to be found in explanations in psychodynamic terms are these:

1. It is common for investigators, trying to account for delinquent behavior, to dig around in the person's psyche till they find some sordid and ugly problem and to proclaim, "This is the reason for the delinquency." Assuming that delinquent behavior is, indeed, problem-solving, every individual has, nonetheless, numerous problems, and it is the explainer's task, often neglected, to demonstrate convincingly, or at least to argue plausibly, that *this* problem has something to do with *this* delinquency.

2. Assuming for the moment that it has been plausibly shown that the delinquency, through some mechanism, serves to solve or mitigate some problem, there remains the task of explaining why this individual found a *delinquent* solution to this problem, rather than some non-delinquent solution. To every problem there is more than one possible adjustment. If two people deal differently with the same problem,

one in a delinquent and another in a nondelinquent manner, then one has not fully explained the delinquent behavior until he has explained the choice of a *delinquent* solution.

3. It is possible that the problem of adjustment, which is alleged to *cause* the delinquent behavior, may be a *consequence* of the delinquent behavior. Delinquency, whatever its causes, often creates serious tensions with one's parents, brings rejection from one's peers, results in incarceration, and in various ways contributes to a troubled mind. It is not easy to decide whether the evidences of a troubled mind point to causes or consequences of delinquent behavior.

4. Psychodynamic theories lean heavily on assumptions about unconscious mental processes, wishes, meanings, and gratifications. It is clear, at the very least, that the imputation of unconscious states or activity is extraordinarily difficult to prove or disprove. For many people the temptation is irresistible to impute to other people's minds whatever unconscious content seems to make plausible their delinquency, with no evidence of that unconscious content except the fact of the delinquency itself, and therefore with no possibility of disproof.

Closely related to the problem-solving class of theories is the conception of delinquency as a *symptom* of a pathological state of mind. In this view, the delinquent is a sick person, and the delinquency, like a rash or a fever, is indicative of an underlying malady. The "choice of symptom," if it is explained at all, is usually explained in terms of the same psychodynamic mechanisms as in the problem-solving theories. However, not all who interpret delinquency as problem-solving behavior would accept the proposition that the delinquent is a sick person.

It should be emphasized that we have been discussing a type of theory of motivation. We have not mentioned theories about the origins of the components of the conflicts that give rise to delinquency, or theories that explain, in terms of their past histories, the dispositions of different persons to make use of different mechanisms in solving their problems. Students of delinquency who share a problem-solving conception of motivation may have quite different views about origins. Some derive certain of the components of the conflict—especially the sexual and the aggressive—from that reservoir of biologically given instincts, the Id. However, we also find a variety of theories that trace the origins of the Superego, emotional needs, and even the specific content and direction of the sexual and affectionate interests that figure in the problems of adjustment, to specific processes of social interaction, especially with parents and siblings in the very early years. These theories, too, are found most elaborately developed in the works of writers of the psychoanalytical school.

Sociological Perspectives on Motivation and Learning

Sociological students of juvenile delinquency have been more interested in learning than in motivation, and have not given much attention to working out explicit and systematic theories of delinquent motivation. We shall not, therefore, attempt to present in this section an integrated theory of delinquent motivation, but shall state a number of propositions that represent the emergent sociological perspectives on motivation in general.[31]

1. *Behavior Is Oriented to the Maintenance and Enhancement of the Self*

The expression "the self" stands for an interrelated set of beliefs and attitudes of the actor. It has three major components. The first may be referred to as the self-image. It is what the actor believes to be true about himself, the way he describes himself to himself. It is how he answers the questions: Who am I? What do I look like? How do I behave? Why do I act as I do? The second component is variously referred to as the self-demands, self-standards, self-expectations, or self-ideal. It is what the actor wants to be, and to which he compares the self-image. It includes the conscience or Superego, the moral standards by which he evaluates his self-image. The third component is self-judgment and is the result of the relationship between self-image and self-demands. Depending on the consistency or discrepancy between these two, self-judgment is one of pride or guilt, self-acceptance or self-rejection, self-satisfaction or self-hatred.

The general formula for motivation would be this: in any given situation, the actor tends to select, from the possibilities open to him, that mode of action that is most likely to reduce the discrepancy between his self-image and his self-demands, and thereby to maintain or enhance a satisfactory self-judgment.

2. *The Self Is Largely Defined in Role Terms*

People classify themselves and one another in terms of labels embedded in the language of their milieu. These labels evoke socially

---

[31] These propositions are in various degrees explicit in the following works: Tannenbaum, *Crime and the Community;* Clifford Shaw and Henry D. McKay, "Social Factors in Juvenile Delinquency," *Report on the Causes of Crime,* National Commission on Law Observance and Enforcement, Vol. 2, 1931; Cohen, *Delinquent Boys.*

standardized expectations that we may fittingly call role demands. Role demands define the full-fledged and adequate incumbent of the respective role and provide the standards in terms of which we judge him. What we have called the self-demands consists largely of a set of roles with which the individual identifies or to which he aspires, and the corresponding socially defined role demands. Therefore, how a boy reacts to his self-image, what he wants to preserve in himself, and what he wants to change in himself, depends on how he labels himself in role terms ("tough guy," "Christian," "friend," "member of the Golden Dragons," "kid," "man," "good sport," "junior scientist," and so forth) and on the expectations that attach to these roles in his cultural setting.

George Grosser's analysis of the differences between the characteristic stealing behavior of boys and girls is illustrative of motivational analysis in these terms.[32] Grosser observed that the stealing of boys typically seemed to be directed to no practical end, that they seemed to steal all sorts of things for "fun," as it were, or for "kicks." Girls seemed to steal in a more "rational" way; to take things that they could use—typically, clothing, jewelry, and cosmetics. Grosser distinguished between "role-expressive" behavior, which *fulfills* role demands, and "role-supportive" behavior, which makes possible or *facilitates* behavior corresponding directly to role demands.

Stealing as such, like "badness" in general, has connotations of masculinity in our society. The boy who steals and "tears things up" may be a "bad boy" but he is "all boy." Perhaps he does not *have* to steal in order to vindicate his claim to masculinity, but it is *consistent with* the claim to masculinity; for the young male, it is *one way* of proving to himself something of great importance: that he is authentically and indubitably masculine.

Stealing, destructiveness, and generally defiant, mischievous behavior do not, on the other hand, have the same role-expressive significance for the female role. This sort of behavior is likely to damage rather than to enhance a girl's self-conception *as a girl*. A girl is likely to be judged, and to judge herself, rather on the basis of her attractiveness to the other sex, her "looks," her "charm," her "sex appeal," the size of her male following. Fulfillment of demands of her role requires, or at least is facilitated by, the right kind of clothing, cosmetics, ornaments, and accessories. One way of getting these things is by stealing them. To steal *these things,* then, is "supportive of" the

---

[32] George Grosser, "Juvenile Delinquency and Contemporary American Sex Roles," unpublished Ph.D. dissertation, Harvard University, 1952.

female role, although stealing *as such* is not a way of validating a claim to femininity.

These concepts lend themselves to very broad application. It is apparent that fighting and having sexual experiences are strongly expressive of the male role and therefore help to solve the problem of validating one's masculinity. At the same time, behavior expressive of and compatible with the role of a "boy" or a "kid" may be inconsistent with the demands of a more "grown-up" role. Therefore, the same person who, at one age, broke windows and stole hubcaps might, a few years later, abandon such behavior because it is defined as "kid stuff." On the other hand, the almost universal participation of narcotic drug-users in our society in stealing or some other kind of "acquisitive" delinquent behavior is not fully understood in role-expressive terms. To play the role of a drug-using "cat" one must have the drug, and to buy the drug costs more money than most young people or even adults can procure by legitimate means. Illegitimate ways of getting money are necessary, therefore, to *support* the drug-user's role. (See Chapter 4, pages 217-19.)

3. *Meaning and Validity Depend on One's Normative Reference Groups*

When we choose a course of action, we do not act altogether on the basis of values, demands, and definitions that have already been internalized, once and for all, as a result of our past experience. Situations arise in which internalized standards provide no unambiguous guide to action. Our sense of the rightness, the reasonableness, the appropriateness, and even the sanity of what we do depends partly on our received notions from past experiences and partly on the current notions among those whose judgments we value. Each of us, however, is in contact with not one but a variety of groups with different cultural perspectives. Those groups whose perspectives are authoritative for us and provide standards by which we test the meaning and the rightness of our own behavior are called our *normative reference groups*. This means that, in the analysis of motivation, whether of delinquent or of nondelinquent behavior, it is necessary to take into account, on the situational side, the values and beliefs current in the normative reference groups of the particular individual in question.

Thus, whether we are even capable of thinking in terms of certain roles, like "cool cat" and "square"; whether we attach certain expectations to those roles and even to more general roles like "boy"; and whether a given role and its corresponding demands are to be desired or eschewed, all depend on the reference groups to whose perspectives we are sensitive. Reference groups are particularly important when we are morally ambiguous; for example, when we are disposed to act in a delinquent manner and, at the same time, have moral doubts about acting in this way. Unless we can "rationalize" this behavior, find some verbal formula for justifying it—e.g., "They're always picking on us; we're just defending ourselves"—we may not be able to proceed with the act, or at least to proceed with a clear conscience. Justifications and rationalizations are convincing largely to the extent to which they are shared by others whose opinions we value. Psychoanalytically oriented psychologists have long emphasized the importance of such processes of rationalization. A major contribution from sociologically trained people is emphasis on the dependence of these rationalizations on their acceptance by our reference groups.

4. Behavior Is Oriented to the Maintenance and Enhancement of Favorable Judgments from Our Status Reference Groups

The counterpart of self-acceptance and self-respect is acceptance and respect from others—that is, *status*. Again, however, we do not value status from various sources equally. We care greatly what some people think of us, and very little what some others think of us. Those groups from whom we value status we may call our *status reference groups*. Normative and status reference groups are to be distinguished because they are not necessarily identical. Even when the two sorts of groups are concretely identical, however, the normative and status-conferring functions are to be distinguished. A boy may look to his parents or to his friends or to his teachers for admiration and approval; he may look to the same people for clear guides to what is right and wrong, for standards that will define for him the meaning and appropriateness of his behavior. It is with the former function that we are, at the moment, concerned.

Our status reference groups and the standards by which they judge us also become important variables on the situational side of motivation. Different status reference groups may lay down different conditions, as it were, for the granting of status. The standards of parents or of the school, for example, may be in conflict with those of one's peers—or, happily, they may be in harmony. It then becomes important to know the relative weight or importance, for the particular individual, of status with this or that group.

Sociologists tend to emphasize the normative and status-giving functions of reference groups *in the current milieu*. They have built up a rich literature demonstrating that delinquency is normally an activity carried on in groups; that stealing, fighting, vandalism, drug use, and other forms of delinquent behavior are associated with various roles within these groups; and that, insofar as these groups function for a child as normative reference groups, they help him to clear this behavior with his conscience. In general, all the sociological perspectives that we have discussed tend to emphasize the similarity of the underlying motivational processes in delinquent and nondelinquent behavior and to account for differences in behavior in terms of differences in self-conceptions, in the cultures of normative and status reference groups, and in the ongoing processes of adjustment in each of these.

On the level of learning theory as well, the distinctively sociological contribution has been to emphasize those processes that operate *generally* in the formation of personality. The learning theories of sociologists may be characterized as cultural-transmission theories; they share the idea that the values and beliefs that favor delinquent and criminal behavior are originally part of our cultural milieus and that they are taken over in the same way that antidelinquent and anticriminal values and beliefs are taken over. The most systematic statement of a cultural-transmission view is Edwin H. Sutherland's theory of differential association, which is discussed in the chapter on crime.[33]

The Sociology of Delinquency

An adequate system of theory on the sociological level should make sense of the variations in delinquency, with respect to both kind and amount, in different areas within our cities, from one city to another, between rural and urban areas, between different societies, between males and females, in different age groups, among different racial and ethnic categories, and from time to time. There are stimulating and challenging theories, but none broad enough to comprehend all the differences in question. Here too we are confronted forcibly with the interdependence of theory and data. Because the facts about the distribution of delinquency are so poorly known, we are lacking in data for testing and settling theoretical arguments. There is scarcely an issue in the sociology of delinquency that can be regarded as settled. It will be possible in our limited space only to suggest some of the leading ideas on the subject.

Current sociological theories generally start from the assumption

---

[33] Cohen, Lindesmith, and Schuessler, eds., *The Sutherland Papers*. See also Donald R. Cressey, *Delinquency, Crime, and Differential Association* (The Hague, Netherlands: Martinus Nijhoff, 1964); and *Social Problems*, Vol. 8 (Summer, 1960), entire issue.

that most delinquent behavior is culturally patterned: that it is group activity, that it represents conformity to a set of culturally defined role expectations, and that these cultural definitions are in the nature of traditions that exhibit a high degree of stability and persistence in certain areas of our cities. These high rate areas are associated with poverty, disease, overcrowding and slum conditions, the presence of disadvantaged minorities and recently arrived immigrant groups, and proximity to centers of commercial and industrial activity. The problem then becomes one of explaining what it is about such areas that accounts for the concentration there of delinquent cultures—or *subcultures,* as they are commonly called, to signify the fact that they are specialized and differentiated versions and developments of a larger American culture.

The fact that the high delinquency areas are usually economically "underprivileged" provides a beguiling clue but a precarious foundation on which to build a theory: first, because the correlation between delinquency and indices of economic status of areas is far from perfect; second, because of the presence of "ethnic islands," e.g., areas peopled by groups of Chinese extraction, surrounded by slum conditions, and characterized by severe crowding and inferior housing, but having delinquency rates that are among the lowest to be found anywhere in our society; third, because there is no unequivocal evidence that delinquency rates, notwithstanding that they are correlated with economic status *of areas,* are correspondingly correlated with *changes in economic conditions over time.*

The *culture conflict* [34] and *social disorganization* theories [35] emphasize other characteristics of these communities that are associated with low economic status but do not make the low economic status itself the crucial variable. The culture conflict theories point to the variety of groups in these areas and especially the conflict between the cultures of the parental generation—often of European peasant or Southern rural background—and the culture of the schools and other agencies and representatives of the dominant groups in American society. The older generation could live out their lives in the old-world cultural islands that comprised the areas of first settlement. Their children, however, could not; for them, the process of adjustment to the world beyond the family was full of hazards.

The social disorganization theories emphasize the difficulty of *en-*

---

[34] Thorsten Sellin, *Culture Conflict and Crime* (New York: Social Science Research Council, 1938).

[35] Shaw and McKay, *Juvenile Delinquency and Urban Areas.* See also Shaw *et al., Delinquency Areas.*

forcing any standards of conduct in these areas. Because of the heterogeneity of the population, the recency of their arrival and consequent lack of identification with the larger community, the inability to make their wishes felt among politicians and law-enforcement officials, and the high rate of mobility within their local communities with its consequent anonymity of individuals, the residents of these communities are incapable of concerted and effective action to keep track of their own children, to discipline them effectively, and to compel public officials to provide to the community the services and the efficient law enforcement that other communities enjoy.

It is probable that all these considerations are relevant and must be taken into account by a comprehensive theory of the sociology of delinquency. Without pausing to note every criticism that may be raised, however, it is important to point out one important limitation of both these types of theory. Both essentially are *control* theories, in the sense that they explain delinquency in terms of the absence of effective controls. The implied model of motivation assumes that the impulse to delinquency is an inherent characteristic of young people and does not itself need to be explained; it is something that erupts when the lid—i.e., internalized cultural restraints or external authority—is off. They do not set forth the processes of group interaction which "build up" to delinquent episodes and which determine, to a large extent, the meaning and "pay-off" of delinquent behavior to members.

The *anomie* theory of Robert K. Merton emphasizes not so much the *absolute* economic deprivation of residents of high rate areas as their deprivation *relative to their aspirations*.[36] According to this theory, a common American culture tends to indoctrinate all groups in our society with relatively high status aspirations, and the possession of material goods and a high style of living are the sovereign symbols of status and success in American society. But different racial, ethnic, and class groupings, although more or less "equal" in their aspirations, are radically unequal in their ability to realize those aspirations by legitimate means. In those areas where the discrepancy between the "culture goals" and the "institutionalized means" is greatest, a condition of *anomie* prevails, a condition of breakdown of the regulative norms, and people have recourse to whatever means will "work." In these areas we find the highest rates of crime and delinquency. This is in contrast to other societies where different classes of people are indoctrinated with different levels of aspiration in keeping with their

---

[36] Robert K. Merton, "Social Structure and Anomie," *Social Theory and Social Structure,* rev. ed. (New York: Free Press, 1957), pp. 131-60.

respective means. In such societies one may find great deprivation without anomie or high rates of deviant behavior.

An attractive feature of this theory is its *generality;* it purports to account not only for delinquency in American society but for differences in delinquency rates among societies. In the form in which we have set it forth here, however, it fails to come to grips with certain of the features of delinquency in American society. Juvenile delinquency consists largely of violence, destruction of property, illicit sexual behavior, and the theft of goods of no value to the thief. In short, much and perhaps most delinquency appears to be "nonutilitarian" and "malicious." It is not readily intelligible as merely an alternative, albeit illegitimate, means to the acquisition of scarce worldly goods.[37]

Cohen's [38] theory of the delinquent subculture also directs attention to the discrepancy between culture goals and institutionalized means, the problems of adjustment which this entails, and the utility of delinquency as a mode of adjustment to these problems. The nature of the problems of adjustment, however, is conceived differently.

According to this theory, the delinquent subculture is a response to status problems associated primarily with the male working-class role—*male* because "being somebody" is for males, more than for females, dependent upon personal achievement; *working class* because persons in this stratum face problems not encountered by those above them. There is, apparently, no single set of criteria by which young people are evaluated in our society, and one must, therefore, be guarded in his generalizations. However, in the United States, where the value of upward mobility pervades all segments of the population, an important set of criteria is that which emphasizes those personal qualities and achievements that facilitate upward mobility and which is applied by those segments of the population that control the gateways to "getting ahead," such as teachers, business and professional people, ministers, and civic leaders. Cohen calls this set of criteria the *middle-class* criteria of status, not because they are peculiarly middle class but because they are subscribed to by middle-class people more consistently and with less ambivalence than by other classes.

These criteria include the following: ambition; a pattern of deferred

---

[37] However, see also Merton's restatement and elaboration of his position in *ibid.,* pp. 178-79.
[38] Cohen, *Delinquent Boys.* Several critiques of Cohen's position have appeared. See Gresham M. Sykes and David Matza, "Techniques of Neutralization: A Theory of Delinquency," *American Sociological Review,* Vol. 22 (1957), pp. 664-70; John I. Kitsuse and David C. Dietrich, "Delinquent Boys: A Critique," *American Sociological Review,* Vol. 24, No. 2 (April, 1959), pp. 208-15.

gratification, that is, a capacity for sustained effort, involving the subordination of immediate satisfactions in the interest of achieving long-run goals; a sense of personal responsibility for one's failures and achievements; the possession of skills of potential academic, economic, and occupational value; the rational cultivation of manners, courtesy, and personableness, which involves patience, self-discipline, and the control of emotional expression, physical aggression, and violence.

Socialization in working-class homes is less likely to produce young people with the ability to do well in terms of these criteria than is middle-class socialization. Many working-class children thus appear rough, uncouth, ill-bred, undisciplined, and lacking in ambition, ability, and drive. In school they are ill-equipped, lacking the background and the habits that would help them to master academic subjects and to perform acceptably in other ways. Furthermore, the "democratic" ethos of American society itself works against them. This ethos allows and even encourages working-class children to "better themselves" and to compete for status with middle-class children, and holds that they are entitled to the same rewards if deserving. By the same token, however, it subjects children of differing backgrounds to evaluation by the same set of standards, the "middle-class measuring rod." Thus, working-class children are systematically disadvantaged in the competitive pursuit of status and are likely to find themselves repeatedly "at the bottom of the heap" with their self-respect damaged.

This is true, however, only so long as the working-class child accepts the validity of the middle-class definitions and expectations of the child role or, in different words, if he elects to play the game and seek the prizes under the rules as defined by the dominant, middle-class culture. It is not true if the child can successfully repudiate the validity of those rules and can convince himself that the game is unworthy of his participation. To do this, however, he still needs support from others and alternative sources of status. As it happens, he is not unique. There are many "in the same boat" and for the same reasons. These individuals, says Cohen, tend to draw together and, through their sympathetic interaction, develop social systems of their own and their own rules of the game and criteria of status. The new status system, according to the theory, is fully intelligible only as a reaction to the conventional status system. Virtue comes to consist in flouting and defying middle-class morality. Orderliness, amenability to adult supervision and guidance, respect for property, polite speech and manners, the preference of diplomacy to violence—these are contemptuously spurned by the new, jointly supported way of life, the

ALBERT K. COHEN AND JAMES F. SHORT, JR.

delinquent subculture. It is to be noted that this conception of delin-quency as behavior in accordance with a subculture tailored to certain socially structured problems of adjustment of working-class boys makes sense only as a group response.

Recent theoretical and research effort has sought to comprehend the *variety* of patterns taken by gang delinquency of the sort to which Cohen directed attention. Cohen and Short [39] have suggested a classification of delinquent subcultures, which includes: a subculture with a more rational, utilitarian, "semiprofessional" style; a conflict-oriented or "bopping" subculture; a drug-users' subculture; and a "parent" subculture, which is the common or garden variety of de-linquent subculture, more versatile and less specialized than the others, and from which the other subcultures develop. These are all primarily male, working-class subcultures. They have also distin-guished a female "parent" subculture and drug-users' subculture, and a middle-class delinquent subculture. For each of these they have suggested processes of American society that generate problems of adjustment that are shared by individuals similarly located in the social structure, and to which the respective subcultures provide modes of adjustment.

The most comprehensive attempt to account for varieties of delin-quent subcultures is found in the work of Richard Cloward and Lloyd Ohlin.[40] It is not enough, they say, to point out that people have problems of status frustration. How people will deal with such prob-lems depends on the alternatives available in their social settings. The alternatives available depend on the structure of opportunities for learning and playing various delinquent roles. Areas characterized by organized and professional crime, where criminal adults are finan-cially successful and powerful and participate also in conventional institutions such as churches, credit unions, lodges, and political or-ganizations, produce one kind of delinquent opportunity structure. In these areas adult criminals are available as role models; the criminal organizations offer a variety of not unattractive jobs. Young people know of these jobs and come to aspire to them early; they know also that the criminal role, as defined by the adult criminal reference groups, places value on criminal skills, loyalty, dependability, shrewd-

[39] Albert K. Cohen and James F. Short, Jr., "Research in Delinquent Subcul-tures," *Journal of Social Issues,* Vol. 14, No. 3 (1958), pp. 20-37.

[40] Richard A. Cloward, "Illegitimate Means, Anomie, and Deviant Behavior," *American Sociological Review,* Vol. 24 (April, 1959), pp. 164-77. Richard A. Cloward and Lloyd E. Ohlin, *Delinquency and Opportunity* (New York: Free Press, 1960).

ness, and other traits, but has little use for wildness, bloodshed, irresponsibility, and, in general, the kind of behavior that imperils the success of a coolly planned businesslike enterprise. In such areas, young people who are disadvantaged in terms of legitimate opportunities are responsive to the demands and expectations of the adult criminals. Delinquent behavior is a kind of rehearsal and playing at forms of adult crime, and takes on a relatively restrained and disciplined quality. There is another kind of area in which neither conventional nor criminal elements are well organized, and in which crime itself is individual, petty, and sporadic, rather than organized, and yields little income or prestige. In these areas opportunities do not exist either to identify with criminal role models or to learn appropriate skills. Here there are no effective controls arising from any part of the adult population. There are no positive attractions toward the more disciplined, professionally oriented kinds of delinquency. In these areas, therefore, youngsters seek status by participating in the more untrammeled and violent forms of gang activity.

Lastly, there are those individuals who, by reason of internalized moral inhibitions, the lack of necessary skills, or the objective unavailability of either criminal or violence opportunity structures, can make use of neither of these patterns. Such individuals, "double failures," so to speak, tend to form their own "retreatist" subcultures, centering around the use of drugs, alcohol, or some other "kick."

In contrast to the foregoing theories is the recent work of Miller,[41] an anthropologist with extensive experience with street gangs. Miller also sees delinquent behavior as conformity to a culture pattern. However, according to Miller, what the law calls delinquent behavior and crime represents conformity not to a specialized youth subculture but to the expectations and values of the more general lower-class subculture. This culture attaches value to such personal qualities and experiences as "trouble," "toughness," "smartness," "excitement," "fate" or "luck," and "autonomy." There are different ways of realizing these values—none of them is intrinsically and necessarily delinquent—but their pursuit is highly conducive to delinquent behavior. The important respect in which Miller's theory differs from the others mentioned is that he sees the values to which delinquent behavior is oriented as deriving directly from socialization into lower-class culture; they are in the culture of the parents; they do not in any way represent a reaction against the cultural patterns and status criteria of the middle-class world.

[41] Walter B. Miller, "Lower-Class Culture as a Generating Milieu of Gang Delinquency," *Journal of Social Issues,* Vol. 14, No. 3 (1958), pp. 5-19.

Recent empirical work by Short and Strodtbeck, and their associates in Chicago, bears on these formulations and suggests modifications which incorporate sociological perspectives on motivation and learning, such as those discussed earlier. These investigators find little evidence that members of delinquent gangs (responding individually to questionnaires) reject middle-class values or those who administer the "middle-class measuring rod." [42] However, extended field observation of these boys *in the gang context* suggests that the gang actively discourages expressions of conventional values. Furthermore, values which are given active support within the context of gang interaction, such as toughness and sexual prowess, are not conducive to conventional types of achievement. Support is found for some hypothesized social structural correlates of gang delinquency and for the notion that behavior patterns of gangs vary considerably. Thus, for example, a measure of "position discontent"—the discrepancy between boys' occupational *aspirations* and their occupational *expectations*—is closely related to official delinquency rates of study groups: Negro and white lower-class gang and nongang boys, and middle-class boys of both races. Similarly, perceptions of legitimate and illegitimate opportunities by these boys confirm the Cloward and Ohlin theory. [43] Other measures are not consistent with the theories, however, and behavioral variation *within gangs* is not systematically related to the perceived opportunity scores of individual boys.

Short and Strodtbeck draw upon their own work and the work of others to explain variations in the behavior of the boys studied. The gangs studied were much less cohesive than nostalgic models of "that old gang of mine" have led us to expect, and gang boys lacked many of the personal and social skills which are associated both with satisfying interpersonal relations and with "success" in conventional institutions. [44] The "unstable poor" lack resources necessary to impart

---

[42] See Robert A. Gordon, James F. Short, Jr., Desmond S. Cartwright, and Fred L. Strodtbeck, "Values and Gang Delinquency: A Study of Street Corner Groups," *American Journal of Sociology,* Vol. 69 (September, 1963), pp. 109-28; James F. Short, Jr., Ramon Rivera, and Harvey Marshall, "Adult-Adolescent Relations and Gang Delinquency," *Pacific Sociological Review,* Vol. 7 (Fall, 1964), pp. 59-65; see also Martin Gold, *Status Forces in Delinquent Boys* (Ann Arbor: Institute for Social Research, 1963).

[43] See James F. Short, Jr., "Gang Delinquency and Anomie," a chapter in Marshall B. Clinard, ed., *Anomie and Deviant Behavior* (New York: Free Press, 1964); James F. Short, Jr., Ramon Rivera, and Ray A. Tennyson, "Perceived Opportunities, Gang Membership, and Delinquency," *American Sociological Review,* Vol. 30 (February, 1964), pp. 56-67.

[44] Robert A. Gordon, "Social Level, Social Disability, and Gang Interaction," an unpublished paper; and Short and Strodtbeck, *Group Process and Gang Delinquency,* Chapter 10.

these skills.[45] Feelings of "helplessness" in the face of life problems, a distrust of one's fellow man, and the intermingling of "respectable" and "shady" elements in many lower-class communities provide the background for gang interaction.[46] Although the solidarity of the gang is not very impressive, it does provide emotional and material support and other satisfactions of group life to boys who are not well equipped for "making it alone" or for participating successfully in more conventional and demanding contexts.

There is much variation among lower-class communities, of course, and gang life reflects these variations. The degree of "integration" between conventional and criminal ("respectable" and "shady") elements varies greatly from community to community, and these variations are reflected in the types of behavior in which gangs engage.[47] Regardless of such variation, however, the Chicago study finds evidence that role relationships and status considerations within gangs influence greatly the behavior of the boys and of their female counterparts. For example, threats to the status of a boy, or a group of boys, often precipitate delinquency episodes, as when a gang with a reputation for toughness and fighting skill is challenged by a rival group, or when a leader feels his status in the group is threatened. By contrast, a drug-using group was observed to withdraw from impending conflict and to "get high" instead, as though to dramatize their lack of concern for matters external to the group.[48]

Thus, to personality and social structural levels of causation are added community influences and processes of interaction in face-to-face groups. Hopefully, the questions of theory raised by this analysis will be the basis for further empirical inquiry and theoretical development. In the last few years there has been a surge of interest in the sociology of juvenile delinquency, but our theories are still tentative, and on some of the issues we have scarcely done more than ask

[45] S. M. Miller, "The American Lower Class: A Typological Approach," *Social Research* (Spring, 1964), republished in the Syracuse University Youth Development Reprint Series, pp. 1-22; see also Fred L. Strodtbeck, "Progress Report, the Reading Readiness Nursery: Short-Term Social Intervention Technique," University of Chicago: Social Psychology Laboratory, August, 1964 (multilith).

[46] Albert K. Cohen and Harold M. Hodges, Jr., "Characteristics of the Lower-Blue-Collar Class," *Social Problems* (Spring, 1963), pp. 303-34; and St. Clair Drake and Horace R. Cayton, *Black Metropolis: A Study of Negro Life in a Northern City* (New York: Harper, 1962), Vol. II.

[47] Solomon Kobrin, Joseph Puntil, and Emil Peluso, "Criteria of Status Among Street Gangs," paper read at the annual meetings of the American Sociological Association, 1963; Cloward and Ohlin, *Delinquency and Opportunity;* and Short and Strodtbeck, *Group Process and Gang Delinquency*, especially Chapters 5 and 9.

[48] Short and Strodtbeck, *ibid.*, Chapters 8 and 9.

the questions. The need and the opportunity for creative theoretical thinking and research are great.

There does exist, to be sure, a considerable literature that seeks to relate various aspects of the social and cultural order to delinquent behavior by comparing the backgrounds and experiences of official delinquents and of those not officially defined as delinquent.[49] These studies have yielded much data on such topics as family conditions, educational and religious experiences, and exposure to mass media within the groups studied. We do not detail these studies here because of space limitations. Certain observations, however, apply to most of them.

1. The findings are often inconclusive and inconsistent as, for instance, in the numerous studies on the relationship between delinquency and broken homes.

2. They usually define delinquency in very general terms such as residence in a particular institution or commitment for a particular type of legal offense, rather than in terms more specifically and concretely descriptive of the behavior in question.[50]

3. They deal largely with correlations, that is, the observed tendency for delinquency (as defined) to be associated with certain other events and circumstances. They do not, as a rule, deal with these correlations within the context of a general theory of delinquency which would be necessary to *explain the correlations.* The theories we have presented at some length, on the other hand, suggest ways in which the findings of these studies can be explained.

Delinquency Control: Sociology of the Correctional System [51]

The official correctional system may be visualized as a flow chart, constructed by tracing out on a route map countless and varied individual delinquent careers. The route map is a network of roles and agencies which are charged with various responsibilities with respect to law enforcement, justice, and treatment. There are various ways in which a boy or girl may enter this system and many paths which may be followed once it has been entered. The paths intersect

---

[49] For a review of these studies, see Ruth S. Cavan, *Juvenile Delinquency* (Philadelphia: Lippincott, 1962).

[50] For an exception to this, see the reported behavior studies cited earlier, and F. Ivan Nye, *Family Relationships and Juvenile Delinquency* (New York: Wiley & Sons, 1958).

[51] For more extensive treatment of the components of the delinquency control process, see Bloch and Flynn, *Delinquency,* Parts Three and Four, and other references below.

and at each intersection decisions must be made as to the next turn to be taken by the child. The ways of entry into the system and the paths which are followed differ from place to place, from time to time, and for persons occupying different roles and positions in the social order.

Our flow chart is not simply a mechanical model through which children are, like baggage, transported unchanged, but, rather, a socialization system which transforms those who pass through it. Whether or not the effect is that which is *intended* by the society which sponsors and supports this system is a question of considerable importance and one to which presently we shall return. It is necessary first of all to understand some of the elements which go into correctional decisions, and which therefore influence the process of selective movement into, through, and out of the system, as well as what happens to people at any given point in the system. (See Chapter 3, page 144.)

Elements of Correctional Decisions: Definition

Before he can act, a correctional agent must decide: what sort of child is this? He must, that is, *define* the situation. Upon this definition may depend the child's subsequent movement within the system and the content of his correctional experiences. Definition involves more than categorizing the child as "delinquent" or "nondelinquent." He may be additionally defined as "a spoiled brat," "a bum," "a bad apple," "disturbed," "rejected," "insecure," "neglected," "a ringleader," "a good kid in bad company," or in a variety of other ways. These definitions involve interpretation and diagnosis, and therefore notions about etiology, although people are often unaware of their own etiological assumptions. They reflect also the training, beliefs, prejudices, values, and interests of those who participate in the defining, and a variety of pressures from the social settings in which these people function.

Definitions are made at each point in the official correctional system: by the policeman before he makes his referral (or chooses not to do so), the probation officer, the judge, the superintendent, the psychologist, and the janitor in the institution for juvenile delinquents. They are also made, however, before, during, and after the child's sojourn in the official correctional system by "nonofficial correctional agents": parents, peers, school principals, social workers, complaining witnesses, and character witnesses. They too must define the situation before they make their "dispositions."

Elements of Correctional Decisions: Disposition

There are, in general, two types of dispositions: (a) *handling* of the case by the correctional agent himself; and (b) *referral* of the case to some other agent or agency. The policeman on the beat, for example, may decide to *handle* an altercation between two boys by "chewing them out," or he may *refer* the boys to their parents or to his own superiors, or he may do both. His superiors may in turn decide to make a "station adjustment" of the case, or they may decide to make a referral to the juvenile court, and so on. Piliavin and Briar, reporting on a study of police encounters with juveniles, found that the police officers' dispositions did not depend in any simple way on the nature of the offense alone. There was at play a process of defining the youngsters as "serious delinquents," "good boys," etc., and this definition in turn was largely based on such factors as the boys' prior offense records, race, grooming, and demeanor.[52]

Once such a decision is made, the resulting disposition in effect becomes part of the definition of the juvenile, e.g., free after a "last chance" warning, probationer, "reform school" inmate, parolee, etc. And, more important, the disposition becomes a part of the image which *others* form of the boy—others involved in the correctional process, officially and unofficially, and others not so involved in a direct sense, such as the "public" and his friends and associates.

Legal requirements and limitations provide a comparatively stable framework within which these decisions are made. They may require that a particular class of cases be tried in a criminal court rather than the juvenile court, or they may specify who shall decide which court is to receive certain types of cases. They may restrict a judge's action to either informal handling, referral to a youth commission or authority, or formal probation. Within the limits set by this framework, however, and particularly in the early stages of our flow chart, the question of who becomes involved in the legal machinery of the courts depends largely on community concern and community power structure. If, for example, the community, or some influential segment of it, has become incensed over a wave of auto thefts or gang fights, great pressure will be brought on the police and courts to "do something about" these problems, and what is done under such circumstances will be different from what is done when community pressure is not so great.

---

[52] Irving Piliavin and Scott Briar, "Police Encounters with Juveniles," *American Journal of Sociology*, Vol. 70 (September, 1964), pp. 206-14.

Nonofficial Correctional Agents

Anybody outside the formal, official correctional system who "sizes up" another person thought to have committed a delinquent act, who defines the situation, and who then does something about it (sends him to the principal's office, calls the police, advises parents to take the boy to a child guidance clinic) is making a correctional decision. Rights and obligations to make various kinds of correctional decisions may be assigned by the culture to many roles: parents, teachers, older siblings, neighbors, etc. In some societies there is no official correctional system at all; *all* correctional decisions are incidents of *other roles*. The extent to which correctional decisions are incidents of (a) such relatively unspecialized roles as those just mentioned; (b) relatively specialized but nonofficial correctional agencies (private social work agencies, Boy Scouts, Y.M.C.A., and other "youth-serving" agencies); and (c) official correctional agencies, varies with social systems.

The official correctional system, then, is an *abstraction* from the total correctional system, which includes also a "nonofficial" correctional environment that operates before, during, and after a child's contact with police, courts, and institutions. Who gets fed into the official system, in what numbers, and at what points depends on the social organization of the nonofficial correctional system. Also, when the official correctional system is "through with" a person, he is fed back into the nonofficial system, but tagged, labeled, and resocialized, for further definition and disposition. And, although the official system no longer has "responsibility," the tags it has put on him and the experiences it has given him are among the important determinants of what will happen to him "on the outside." As Tannenbaum so vividly puts it: [53]

> The first dramatization of the "evil" which separates the child out of his group for specialized treatment plays a greater role in making the criminal than perhaps any other experience. It cannot be too often emphasized that for the child the whole situation has become different. He now lives in a different world. He has been tagged. A new and hitherto non-existent environment has been precipitated out for him.

These ideas stand very much in need of empirical investigation, for the precise relationship between different definitions, dispositions, and correctional outcomes is not well understood.

A correctional career, then, is a succession of encounters with cor-

---

[53] Tannenbaum, *Crime and the Community*, p. 18.

rectional officials and nonofficial correctional agents, in which one is defined, handled, and/or transferred from one agency to another. Each official agency, i.e., each correctional institution, police department, juvenile court, etc., is a social system in its own right, with its own internal structure and public identity and reputation. Each has a characteristic *input* of numbers and kinds of children and a characteristic *output* of the same children altered by their experiences in the system. Each system has ostensible, official purposes defined by the law and by the "public," but the kinds of things that happen to juveniles as they move through the system are never a simple function of the official purposes of the agencies that comprise the system. Some of the characteristics of the system and the relationships between the system and its environment, which are most important in determining what happens to those who are its principal objects, are the following.

Recruitment of Correctional Personnel

The behavior of correctional agents depends upon their knowledge and experience, their skills, career aspirations, values, and outside involvements. These characteristics of correctional personnel, however, are not just matters of chance. They depend on how the correctional system is organized for recruiting personnel into the system, into the "correctional personnel flow chart," so to speak. Here, again, a host of considerations enters in, including: the requirements set up for various positions; the extent to which these are adhered to; the pool of human resources from which to draw; the rewards attached to the various positions in the form of pay, status, and possibilities of political advancement; and the attractiveness of competing occupational opportunities. In all these respects, there is great variation from one agency to another, whether we are speaking of policemen, probation officers, judges, or the various kinds of institutional personnel from vocational instructors to superintendents. However, there has been little research on the consequences of such variability for the functioning of correctional agencies and the behavior of their agents.

Agency Staff Culture and Socialization

Just as delinquency is often a subcultural phenomenon, so also are the subsystems within the correctional flow chart we have been discussing. That is, these systems develop their own traditional, customary, and routine ways of meeting situations, of defining and disposing of problems. The correctional agent, like the child himself, is also "processed" by the systems in which he participates. In various ways, some deliberate and contrived, some unconscious and unintended, he is modified or "socialized" by the agency culture.

These cultures may differ in important ways, even among agencies of the same general class, e.g., correctional institutions.[54] These include differences with respect to conceptions of the agency's function, its responsibility to its publics, the nature of its clients or inmates, the effectiveness and the propriety of various ways of accomplishing its job, the specific responsibilities that go with particular positions in the system, and the criteria for judging adequacy of performance and for assignment of status within the system. Notwithstanding these differences, however, agencies of the same class tend also to develop certain broad similarities of culture that differentiate them from agencies of other classes.[55] These differences often produce conflicts between police and probation officers, judges and social work agencies, etc.

Inmate Structure and Culture

One of the most important determinants of what happens to a child in such agencies as jails, detention homes, and institutions is the inmate population itself. The structure of the inmate "community" and its culture exert powerful influences on both inmates and institutional staff and on the extent to which program goals are capable of realization. In fact, the view is held by many students of correction that it is unreasonable to expect a net "therapeutic" effect on the inmate population from institutions that throw together large numbers of individuals who have in common only that they all have an experience of delinquency, and that they are segregated from their homes and communities and subordinated to a group of strange adults.

The nature of the inmate structure and culture depends partly on the kinds of children who are fed into the institution by the selective processes of the flow chart. Public institutions rarely enjoy control over their input. They take what is sent to them from courts or other agencies set up for this purpose, for example, youth authorities. Youth authorities are agencies to which courts make commitments, and which in turn are charged with the responsibility of deciding upon

---

[54] Mayer Zald, "The Correctional Institution for Juvenile Offenders: An Analysis of Organizational 'Character,'" *Social Problems,* Vol. 8 (Summer, 1960), pp. 57-67.

[55] For an expression of attitudes commonly associated with the police subculture, see *The Police Chief,* Vol. 25 (June, 1958). See also Jerome Skolnick, *Justice Without Trial, a Sociological Study of Law Enforcement* (forthcoming).

the most appropriate disposition for each child.[56] If, in states that have youth authorities, an array of differentiated institutions and other courses of action is available, different sorts of children can be assigned to different institutions, each with distinct and relatively homogeneous populations, and this, in turn, makes possible differentiated programs appropriate to the respective populations. In most states, however, there is no such over-all agency nor is there a variety of institutions. Instead, all boys and girls who receive institutional commitments must go into the one or two institutions available.

Goals

Each subsystem is called upon by the public to do a number of different things. The police, for example, are charged with preventing crime and delinquency and apprehending offenders, keeping the peace, the security of property, traffic control, responding to accident calls and all sorts of emergencies, intervening in family fights, and sometimes with social work and recreational functions. The courts, likewise, have other business than disposing of delinquency charges, and institutions have many other tasks than rehabilitation—notably the tasks of custody, plant maintenance, and feeding and clothing of inmates.

Furthermore, the operation of any kind of agency requires the performance of all sorts of tasks that have to do with maintaining the viability of the agency and the morale of its personnel: getting money and other resources from the legislature; providing for fringe benefits, security, opportunities for advancement, and the convenience and comfort of personnel; and maintaining an establishment that is physically attractive and impressive to outsiders.

There are always more goals than can be met, and the manifest or official goals often recede before the others. Housekeeping and public relations activities may enjoy such high priority and consume so much of the agency's energies that they, in fact, dictate the main content of the agency's program. They may also dictate the agency's "foreign relations," that is, its relationships to other agencies, especially if they are seen as possible competitors for funds, prestige, and public support. Miller has pointed out some of the consequences of concern with such "system-maintenance" goals:

> This paper suggests that operating philosophies which are *functional* for the purpose of maintaining institutional viability may be *non-*

---

[56] John R. Ellington and Paul W. Tappan, "The Youth Authority Plan," in Paul W. Tappan, ed., *Contemporary Correction* (New York: McGraw-Hill, 1951), Chapter 9.

functional for the purpose of reducing juvenile crime, and that a consequence of differences in institutional philosophies is that a significant proportion of energy potentially directable to delinquency reduction is instead expended in conflict between institutions and/or attempts to effect inter-institutional cooperation.[57]

No feature of staff culture is more important than staff conceptions of the relative importance of different agency goals, for differences in technology and staff organization are largely the result of attempts to implement different goals. The resultant differences in staff behavior in turn create different environments for clients or inmates. Street, reporting on a comparative study of juvenile correctional institutions, has shown how such differences in environments lead to the formation of different inmate cultures and social organizations. These may vary from "solidary opposition" to staff on the part of inmates to trust and cooperation with staff. Street found that differences in inmate systems in these and other respects were strongly related to differences in emphasis within the staff culture on "custody" versus "treatment" goals.[58]

Delinquency Control Techniques

The traditional distinction between treatment and prevention does not seem useful, for the objective of almost all approaches to delinquency control, whether they are directed at children who are only slightly, moderately, or seriously delinquent, is to prevent the further commission of delinquent acts.

The Target: Groups or Individuals

Efforts at delinquency control may focus on the behavior of selected individuals or on the jointly supported and collective activities of groups or gangs. Most traditional procedures, like those of child guidance clinics or social casework or probation officers, illustrate the former. More recent programs, like detached work with gangs, illustrate the latter. Most of the distinctions discussed below are relevant to either type of approach.

Changing the Motivational Field: The Person Versus the Situation

In the discussion of motivation, we noted that behavior varies with the situation and with the beliefs, values, and attitudes of the person.

---

[57] Walter B. Miller, "Inter-Institutional Conflict as a Major Impediment to Delinquency Prevention," *Human Organization*, Vol. 17, No. 3 (1958), pp. 20-23.

[58] David Street, "The Inmate Group in Custodial and Treatment Settings," *American Sociological Review*, Vol. 30 (February, 1965), pp. 40-55.

Efforts to change behavior may focus on effecting change in either of these components of the motivational fields, whether of selected individuals or of organized groups. Thus, psychiatrists and group workers may try, through their respective techniques, to change the self-conceptions, aspirations, and reference group orientations of their "patients" or "clients"; a community might, on the other hand, provide additional recreational facilities on the assumption that the same, essentially unchanged personalities will abandon delinquent behavior in the face of the new opportunities provided by the changed situation. Following the terminology of R. K. Merton, we will find it useful to speak of the relevant aspects of the situation as the "structure of opportunities." [59]

Ways of Altering the Child's Experiences: Direct Interaction and Environmental Manipulation

Personalities are formed and changed only through experience, through interaction with those around us. Insofar as their object is to modify values and beliefs, i.e., to change personalities, agencies with correctional objectives must intervene somehow in the experience-world of the individuals and groups concerned, i.e., somehow change the quality of their experiences. These agencies generally go about this in one or the other (or both) of two ways. They may intervene *directly* by themselves becoming part of the experience-world of the child—that is, by interacting directly with him: by preaching to him, by counseling, by yelling at him, by spanking him, by psychoanalyzing him, by playing with him. Or they may seek to alter the experience-world of the child by changing *other* aspects of the child's milieu, such as the attitudes and expectations of other individuals, so that the quality of *their* interaction with the child and therefore its consequences for the child's personality is changed. Thus, a psychiatrist or a teacher might, through conferences with parents, try to change their behavior toward the child and thereby the home as a socialization setting. A further subdivision under this heading distinguishes three ways of manipulating the environment. One is by working directly with the people who are already part of the child's existing, everyday milieu, as in the preceding example. A second is by replacing some of the child's associates by others, or in some way altering his pattern of association. This may be done through suggesting directly to the child activities which will bring him into contact with others with whom it is presumed association will be beneficial, or by

---

[59] Merton, "Social Structure and Anomie."

influencing others to accept him. Thus, a policeman may suggest to a boy that he join a boys' club or a school psychologist may suggest to a teacher that she encourage a boy to get into the drama club. A group worker might similarly try to bring a street club into an agency setting and thereby into interaction with less delinquent boys. A third way is, more or less through external constraint, to transfer the boy to a new setting believed to be beneficial, often one contrived and created for correctional purposes. Commitments to institutions and semivoluntary sojourns in foster homes, treatment camps, and special schools would be examples, as would assignments and transfers from one cottage or vocational class to another within a training school.

Different approaches to delinquency control can be distinguished on the basis of their different emphases with respect to targets, focus on one aspect or another of the motivational field, and ways in which they try to intervene in the experience-world of the child insofar as they are concerned with changing his personality. They differ also in their specific techniques for accomplishing these things. All these respects in which agency programs differ are determined, in large part, by the etiological theories with which they operate, but they differ also in part because of the various kinds of pressures operating, from without and from within, upon the correctional subsystems, as discussed in the immediately preceding section of this chapter.

In the following discussion we shall only hint at the actual variety of approaches representing various combinations of these emphases.

INTERVIEW THERAPY.[60] This procedure is best exemplified by the traditional psychiatric approach. The target is an individual; the focus is primarily on changing the person; the technique is through direct interaction of a single correctional agent with the child, usually in an office or clinic setting; the subject is perceived as a "patient," the delinquent behavior as a pathological "disturbance," the correctional agent as a "therapist," and his interaction with the child as "therapy." The therapist interacts with the child once or twice a week for perhaps an hour at a time. The nature of the interaction depends upon the way in which the therapist defines the child—that is, his diagnosis of the disturbance—and on the particular therapeutic techniques which he favors, and these vary according to the school of psychiatric thought in which he has been trained. Through talking with the child, the therapist tries to change the child's perceptions of himself and of

[60] Ralph A. Brancale and Kenneth L. M. Pray, "Psychiatric, Psychological, and Casework Services," in Tappan, ed., *Contemporary Correction*, Chapter 13. See Sheldon Glueck, ed., *The Problem of Delinquency* (Boston: Houghton Mifflin, 1959), Chapter 27.

others, to alter his values, to "work through" his problems of adjustment, and in various ways to change his perspectives so that he will handle his customary life situations differently.

There are severe limitations inherent in this type of approach, even if we assume the validity of diagnosis and the competence and skill of the therapist. It would not be remarkable if the therapist, who is not part of the child's workaday milieu and who talks to the child in a segregated and insulated setting at intervals of several days, could not counteract the influences that operate continuously and pervasively at home, in school, and on the street. Actually, the therapist has the imposing task of trying to sever the child's bonds to trusted friends, without being able to provide fully equivalent substitutes, and to define for him new roles that may have little support in his natural groupings. Research studies give little evidence that interview therapy significantly affects delinquent behavior.

There are numerous modifications of interview therapy and related techniques. Therapists may also attempt to modify the child's experiences through manipulating the environment. Some, for example, feel that it is necessary to "treat the whole family," although this is confessedly difficult with the traditional interview techniques and the usual resources of psychiatrists. Social workers often combine interview therapy in an office setting and interaction with the child in the home and elsewhere, and at the same time work with parents, teachers, and other persons in the child's everyday world. They are more likely than are psychiatrists to visit the child and his family in the home setting, and are therefore more likely to derive their information about the child from observing him and interacting with him in more "natural" life situations.[61]

The procedures of probation and parole personnel vary so widely, owing to differences in training, philosophy, legal requirements, relationships to the court and other agencies, case load, and other circumstances, that they defy generalization.[62] Some workers are trained in psychiatric social casework, clinical psychology, or sociology; others are good-hearted and well-intentioned adults without any sort

---

[61] Edwin Powers and Helen Witmer, *An Experiment in the Prevention of Delinquency: The Cambridge-Somerville Youth Study* (New York: Columbia University Press, 1951). See also New York City Youth Board, *How They Were Reached,* Monograph No. 2 (New York, November, 1954). Ruth S. Tefferteller, "Delinquency Prevention Through Revitalizing Parent-Child Relations," *Annals of the American Academy of Political and Social Science,* Vol. 322 (March, 1959), pp. 69-78.

[62] See Negley K. Teeters and John O. Reinemann, *The Challenge of Delinquency* (Englewood Cliffs, N. J.: Prentice-Hall, 1950), pp. 413-28. Sheldon Glueck, ed., *The Problem of Delinquency,* pp. 607-50.

of training, and still others are, at best, deserving Democrats or Republicans. Those who are professionally trained and professionally identified with correctional work may make diligent use of a variety of approaches, insofar as their heavy case loads permit. Efforts to change the person through direct interaction of one sort or another are likely to be central to their repertoire of techniques. However, they may also try to alter the child's attitudes and values by manipulating his milieu: by trying to create supportive and accepting attitudes in others, by trying to redirect the child's associations, and, in the event of final discouragement or pressure from the community, by recommending commitment or recommitment to some closed institution. A very important aspect of their repertoire, in addition, is changing the opportunity structure—specifically, for older children, by finding jobs and other opportunities to express and support law-abiding roles.

Generally speaking, research to date does not convincingly demonstrate the effectiveness of any of these modifications of interview therapy and their combinations with other approaches. However, research in this area is fraught with difficulties, not the least of which is the fact that practices going by a given label vary widely. Therefore, it would be premature to draw radically pessimistic conclusions from this research.

TREATMENT IN CLOSED INSTITUTIONAL SETTINGS. We have here in mind social systems, both within and without the official correctional system, in which numbers of children live for extended periods of time and which have been created and designed for specifically correctional purposes. This category includes, at the one extreme, state training schools to which children are committed by the courts and with inmate populations running into the several hundreds and, at the other extreme, treatment homes for emotionally disturbed children—not all of whom are necessarily delinquent—that may have as few as a dozen resident children. They all represent efforts to transform the experience-world through transfer to a specially contrived environment.

Within these residential communities we can find all kinds of social structures, staff and inmate (for want of a better word, although "inmate" ordinarily connotes individuals legally committed to official agencies) cultures, and correctional philosophies and techniques.

Training schools typically have quite heterogeneous populations; individuals are assigned to cottages or other residential units and to academic and vocational programs by the classification staff, the primary defining and referring agents within the institution. Few of the staff are likely to have any specialized training for this sort of work although there may be a small "professional staff" including one or more psychologists, social workers or sociologists, and possibly a psychiatrist. Activities of children are fairly regimented and supervised, although much less so than in adult penal institutions, and there is considerable anxiety about the possibility of runaways, and therefore concern about custody. It is hoped that discipline, interaction with benign adults, and training in useful arts may effect desired changes in the personality of the child. Definitive evaluation of the effectiveness of this type of program is not possible because we have no way of knowing what the outcomes of the same or comparable groups of children would have been without passing through this experience. What can be said definitively is that research studies have generally found that upward of 50 percent of children who are alumni of state training schools become recidivists in the sense of having further court appearances either as children or as adults.[63]

The structure and programs of closed institutions may diverge greatly from the pattern described. A variety of experiments in progress combine in different ways the following departures from the traditional pattern. The schools are smaller. Their populations are more homogeneous. Housekeeping functions are more subordinated to correctional objectives. There is greater freedom of movement and self-selected activity permitted to inmates and less concern with custody. Relationships with staff are likely to be more informal. Interview therapy with individuals or therapeutically oriented interaction with groups of inmates, or both, conducted by professionally trained personnel, play a central and organizing rather than an incidental role in the institution program and are an important part of each child's experience. Each child interacts rather intensively with each of a small number of adults in a variety of settings, rather than superficially with a large number of adults and with each in a specialized setting. Research indicates, to this point, that these programs result in significantly lower rates of recidivism than the traditional programs.[64]

---

[63] Clifford R. Shaw and Associates, "Subsequent Criminal Careers of Juvenile Delinquents, School Truants, and Special School Pupils," an unpublished study, Chicago: Institute of Juvenile Research, 1949 (mimeographed).

[64] Ashley Weeks, *Youthful Offenders at Highfields* (Ann Arbor: University of Michigan Press, 1958). Lloyd W. McCorkle, Albert Elias, and F. Lovell Bixby, *The Highfields Story: An Experimental Treatment Project for Youthful Offenders* (New York: Holt, 1958). See also descriptions of "milieu therapy," e.g., Fritz Redl and David Wineman, *Children Who Hate—The Disorganization and Breakdown of Behavior Controls* (New York: Free Press, 1951). Bruno Bettelheim, *Love Is Not Enough—The Treatment of Emotionally Disturbed Children* (New York: Free Press, 1950).

We intend no radical division between the "traditional" training school and the newer, "progressive" programs. No two closed institutions are identical, and many of the older institutions, originally cast in the "traditional" mold, have incorporated in various ways and degrees features of the "progressive" institutions. It should, finally, be added that *all* institutions have fairly high rates of recidivism, and it is still not definitely known how much more effective *any* of them is than the available alternatives, including the alternative of "doing nothing."

AREA PROJECTS. Area projects, which have their longest history and highest development in the city of Chicago, are based on certain sociological assumptions: that delinquency can neither be understood nor effectively combated unless it is seen as a product of the culture and social organization of the community; that significant reductions in delinquency require extensive changes in the fabric of social relationships in the community; that these changes must involve a strengthening of relationships between young people and conventional adults and institutions in such a way that the latter become more effective as role models and reference groups and provide more attractive and realistic opportunities for achieving satisfactory self-conceptions through law-abiding behavior. In short, these projects require transformation of the total milieu as a socialization setting and as an opportunity structure. Fundamental also to this approach is the assumption that important changes cannot be imposed by outsiders, no matter how sophisticated, well-trained and benevolent, but require the active initiative and participation of the residents of the community. The technique, therefore, is to provide to indigenous leaders of the community—working-class people identified with the community and respected by their friends, neighbors, and kinsmen—guidance and assistance in forming organizations and obtaining funds and resources for a variety of projects. The leadership and membership of the organizations, however, are local; the expert assistance from outside is merely consultative, and policies are adopted and carried out by residents themselves. The projects themselves vary from community to community and include sponsorship of recreational programs, campaigns for community improvement—e.g., school improvement, sanitation, traffic safety, and law enforcement—and activities directed to delinquent children, both on an individual and a group basis.[65]

---

[65] See Anthony Sorrentino, "The Chicago Area Project After Twenty-Five Years," *Federal Probation*, Vol. 23 (June, 1959), pp. 40-45.

It is the impression of those who have dedicated themselves to the promotion and guidance of these projects that they have reduced delinquency in high rate areas, but they concede that it is difficult to prove this because of difficulties in measurement.[66] They rest their defense of the area projects primarily on the grounds that their methods are consistent with contemporary sociological theory about the nature of delinquency and its sources in the social structure. This position seems reasonable to the authors of this chapter, but the fact remains that the effectiveness of these programs has yet to be demonstrated. Furthermore, the area project approach is not the only approach that is consistent with contemporary sociological theory, and there are probably severe limitations on the extent to which a local community, even with the help of knowledgeable outsiders, can mobilize its own resources and transform the pattern of its own social life to bring about drastic reductions in delinquency rates.

DETACHED WORK WITH GROUPS.[67] Efforts to work with delinquent children have been repeatedly frustrated by difficulties in establishing and maintaining contact with them, especially if these children are well-integrated members of delinquent groups that provide for their members a fairly well-rounded design for living. They are not likely to go knocking at the psychiatrist's or social worker's door for help, and, for a variety of reasons, they resist being drawn into the programs of settlement houses, teen-age canteens, boys' clubs, and other "intramural" programs supervised by adults. One of the reasons for this difficulty is the social class distance between the children and the adult correctional agents. The barriers of class and culture lead the children to resent the real or supposed condescension of the adults, to be suspicious of their intentions, and to resist their efforts to make them over in accordance with middle-class ideals and notions of respectability. For these reasons they have been called "hard to reach."

Detached work programs assign workers, detached from their agency base and intramural programs, to go out on the street and to make contact and establish relationships with street-corner groups in their natural habitat. These workers attempt, in a variety of ways depending on the individual worker and the philosophy of the sponsoring agency, to change the pattern of group life. In every instance, success depends on winning the trust and respect of the boys and on

---

[66] See Solomon Kobrin, "The Chicago Area Project—A 25-Year Assessment," *Annals of the American Academy of Political and Social Science,* Vol. 322 (March, 1959), pp. 19-29.

[67] Paul L. Crawford, Daniel L. Malamud, and James R. Dumpson, *Working with Teen-age Gangs* (New York: Welfare Council of New York City, 1950).

respecting, in turn, the boys' own culturally patterned values and ways without, however, approving or condoning their delinquent behavior. As a counselor and friend who does not moralize or preach, who is an older person with valued knowledge and skills, and who shows up "on the corner" six or seven days a week and spends long hours with the boys in their everyday activities, the worker seeks to influence their conduct. He may try to accomplish this by influencing their values and beliefs through direct interaction and by increasing the range of nondelinquent opportunities open to them by helping them acquire various skills of value in social, athletic, or occupational activities. In addition, some workers attempt to change the nature of the boys' milieu by acting as a liaison with police, schools, social agencies, neighbors, and employers, with a view to creating thereby new avenues of communication with the adult world and new opportunities for gaining status by playing conventional roles.

It should be noted that, although detached work has only recently been attempted on an ambitious scale and thus come into the public eye, it has long been one of the techniques employed in the Chicago area projects, although usually with indigenous workers rather than workers detached from a social agency.

The logic of detached work is also consistent with current knowledge and theory about delinquent behavior, and preliminary research indications are that detached work may effect significant reductions in delinquent behavior. However, most of these programs have not been in existence long enough to permit definitive study and evaluation.[68]

Conclusion

We are now entering a period of vigorous, imaginative, and varied experimentation in the field of delinquency control. This is due partly to the magnitude of the delinquency problem in our great urban concentrations; in part to the increased public attention to poverty and related problems, among which is delinquency; but mostly to the greatly increased financial support available from government and

---

[68] See H. W. Mattick and N. S. Caplan, "Stake Animals, Loud Talking, and Leadership in Do-Nothing and Do-Something Situations," in Malcolm S. Klein and Barbara G. Myerhoff, eds., *Juvenile Gangs in Context: Theory, Research, and Action* (Los Angeles: University of Southern California, Youth Studies Center, 1963); and Roger E. Rice and Stuart Adams, "The Correctional Cost of Serviced and Unserviced Juvenile Gangs: An Evaluation of a Detached-Worker Program" (Los Angeles County Probation Department Research Report No. 23, June, 1965).

private foundations. Much of this support goes to "demonstration projects" in communities all across the country. Such projects are deliberately experimental, involving new techniques, modifications of traditional techniques, and organizations mixing the traditional and the new. They are designed to test the value of fresh approaches to the delinquency problem; therefore, some provision for evaluation of the effectiveness of the program is usually built into the project itself. These demonstration projects include relatively small-scale operations, like the Provo Experiment in Provo, Utah, which is designed to explore the possibilities of "guided group interaction," a form of treatment akin to group therapy, with probationers in the open community.[69] They include also massive, broad-scale assaults on delinquency, such as New York City's Mobilization for Youth[70] —a many-sided, community-wide, multimillion dollar attempt to reduce delinquency by opening up the opportunity structure; the New York program includes such programs as a Youth Job Center; an Urban Youth Service Corps; a Homework Helper Program; Reading Clinics; an Organizing the Unaffiliated Program, designed to increase the participation of poor people in community decision-making; a Legal Services Unit, designed to lessen inequalities in the availability of legal services; and Visiting Homemakers.

It seems fair to say that, at the present moment, we do not have techniques for controlling delinquency that are demonstrably effective. Evaluation of delinquency control programs is extremely difficult and complex.[71] The identification of personality or behavioral changes in individuals and groups is itself very difficult; hence the equivocal and uncertain results of evaluative research. However, in view of the enormous ferment and unprecedented activity in this field, we have every reason to expect that our understanding of delinquency control will grow rapidly in the next few years. It is to be hoped, however, that the task of evaluation will not be neglected and much of the value of this experience thereby lost.

---

[69] LaMar T. Empey and Jerome Rabow, "The Provo Experiment in Delinquency Rehabilitation," *American Sociological Review,* Vol. 26 (October, 1961), pp. 679-95.

[70] President's Committee on Juvenile Delinquency and Youth Crime, *Counter-Attack on Delinquency: The Program of the Federal Government to Stimulate Communities to Develop Rational Answers to a Growing Crisis,* Washington, D. C., 1964 (mimeographed), pp. 24-34.

[71] Helen L. Witmer and Edith Tufts, *The Effectiveness of Delinquency Control Programs* (Washington, D. C.: Department of Health, Education and Welfare, 1954). See also "Prevention of Juvenile Delinquency," *Annals of the American Academy of Political and Social Science,* Vol. 322 (March, 1959).

3

Crime

by Donald R. Cressey

ALL SOCIETIES HAVE RULES THAT SPECIFY APPROPRIATE AND INAPPRO-
priate ways of behaving. These rules, often called "norms" or "conduct
norms," are sets of directions for behavior, and members of a society
are expected to follow them. When a child is born, he immediately
comes under the influence of the broad social organization, called
"society," in which he lives, and he also comes under the influence
of smaller social organizations such as his family. For example, what
he is fed, when he is fed, and how he is fed all are determined by
norms existing in advance of his arrival. And as he grows older and
begins to walk and talk he is increasingly expected to conform to
norms himself. He must follow certain time schedules, pay attention
to his elders, and learn many other customs.

Ordinarily, appropriate behavior is rewarded, and inappropriate behavior has some form of punishment as its consequence. We often
reward children simply for indicating that they have learned a rule,
even if they do not follow it. For example, in a large American city
a three-year-old boy may be praised for learning the meaning of hand
signals used in driving a car, although he will not actually be following
traffic rules for some time to come. Adults, on the other hand, are
rewarded and punished according to their performance, rather than
according to their knowledge of a rule. The process of giving rewards
to adults—in the form of prestige, love, economic goods, and power,
for example—is ordinarily more subtle and less dramatic than is allocation of punishments. An adult is expected to conform to the rules
of his society, and as long as he does so the other members of the
society appear to be rather neutral in their reactions toward him.
Many rewards for compliance with norms are not readily visible.
Should an adult violate an important rule, however, some kind of
negative action is taken, often in a dramatic manner. Similarly, com-

pliance with a positive rule for behavior, such as the rule in our society that a father should support his children, is not dramatically rewarded, but failure to comply may result in a collective condemnation.

Conduct Norms and the Criminal Law

The norms of a society are not all of equal importance. The most important ones have been called *mores*, and they constitute the basic rules that are widely believed to be essential to holding a society together. When the mores are violated, members of the society respond with great moral indignation; punishment is likely to be quite severe. Immoral acts, such as cannibalism, rape, and murder, are violations of mores. Less important norms are called *folkways,* and punishments for violation of them are likely to be quite mild and inconsistent. Rules about table manners, styles of dress, and etiquette are folkways. In modern societies, many mores and folkways have been codified and made into laws, so that the laws themselves are norms. Some laws are rules of fair play in personal transactions—indicating, for example, that one man must pay the amount of damage done if his negligence causes another person some financial or personal loss. This body of norms is called *tort law,* and it is ordinarily associated with folkways rather than mores. On the other hand, the *criminal law* is a body of rules stipulating that anyone violating certain folkways and mores will be considered a criminal and will be *officially* punished. Some criminals laws, such as those regulating traffic, weights and measures, and drunkenness, are codifications of folkways; those prohibiting murder and stealing are codifications of mores. Not all mores have been so codified, and many folkways receive no attention in the criminal law.

Criminal laws differ from mores and folkways because they have been established by the political authority of a society and are enforced by that authority. This political authority, "the state," may or may not be the same as the "society." Thus, some societies have not separated their bodies of conduct norms into "official" and "unofficial" rules. In nonliterate societies, organized on a kinship basis, rules prohibiting the killing of humans are not necessarily separated in a special code distinguishable from the body of rules indicating, for example, how one should behave at a wedding. The "state" is not immediately distinguishable from the "family," or the "society," and, thus, a body of official rules to be enforced by the state is not possible. In more complex societies, on the other hand, consensus about discouraging certain kinds of behavior has been embodied in an official set of rules, the criminal law. This set of rules is to be enforced by representatives of the state, as distinguished from other kinds of institutional functionaries. Here, an act can be a violation of rules for family living, for religious conduct, for economic conduct, or for educational conduct and still not stimulate an official reaction from the society. If one violates the rules for good etiquette at a wedding, one may lose favor with the participants and spectators, and such loss may have painful consequences for him; but such violation is not a crime and is of no concern to the political authorities. Yet if a participant or spectator at a wedding gets into a fight, behaves obscenely, or walks off with the wedding presents, he commits a crime. His conduct is in violation of rules which go beyond the immediate wedding situation and are of concern to the state as a whole. Hence, in such cases, policemen, jailers, prosecuting attorneys, judges, wardens, and other representatives of the state go into action against him.

In an earlier period, criminal laws were enacted when almost all the members of a society believed strongly that a particular kind of conduct was so repulsive that formal machinery for dealing with it should be set up. Thus, taboos against murder and theft were considered so important that they became institutionalized; a definite penalty for each offense was stipulated in advance, certain officials (police) were designed to apprehend offenders, other officials (judges, prosecutors) were designated to try offenders and assign penalties to the guilty, and still other officials (jailers, wardens, executioners) were asked to carry out the sentences.

Most criminal laws established in more recent times, however, do not have such a broad base in the society, for these are the laws that institutionalize folkways.[1] The same kinds of officials are given authority to enforce the laws once they are established, but the process of establishing them is different. Rather than a codification of a widespread consensus that certain conduct is morally wrong, these laws are likely to be codifications of the consensus of only a rather small segment of the society. Laws against operating a saloon on Sunday, discriminating against Negroes in employment practices, practicing certain professions without having membership in the professional association, selling merchandise above or below certain prices, building a home without a certain kind of equipment, and a host of similar laws are examples of criminal laws promulgated by special interest groups rather than by society as a whole.

---

[1] See Richard C. Fuller, "Morals and the Criminal Law," *Journal of Criminal Law and Criminology,* Vol. 32 (March-April, 1942), pp. 624-30.

Even in reference to the most ancient of criminal laws, the process of declaring an act to be crime involves a number of persons who are behaving in a certain way, a number of persons who are opposed to this kind of behavior, a struggle for legislative or judicial dominance between the two groups, and victory in this struggle by the persons opposing the behavior. For example, killing other persons became a crime because some persons persisted in the conduct, despite mores to the contrary. Other members of society, through their political institution, centralized and formalized the mechanisms for social control of the conduct, and taboo against killing became the "law of the land."

Thus, a conflict between norms is reflected in the criminal law. In complex societies such as ours, one group has one set of folkways, while another group has another set. Even the same group may hold conflicting norms. Norms of one group may not be important to another, or a group may believe that uniformity in behavior among persons is desirable while at the same time holding that individualism, inventiveness, and freedom are also desirable. It is in this kind of society that crime becomes a social problem, for a considerable proportion of the population persists in behavior which has been officially prohibited and threatened with punishment. In our society, with its emphasis on the rights and dignity of individuals, there even is a tradition which permits one to "take the law into his own hands" in some situations, even if his act is distinctly in violation of the law and normally has severe punishment as its consequence.

Criminal Law and the Definition of Crime

The rules that a state has enacted in its corporate capacity and that representatives of the state are ready to attempt to enforce are embodied in the criminal law. Behavior that is reprehensible from the standpoint of a family or other social group is not necessarily a violation of these official rules, and for that reason it is not crime. There must be violation of the criminal law. A family might be quite distraught because the father prefers spending Thanksgiving in a bar to spending the day at home, and it might take numerous courses of action to change the man's conduct. But the father has committed no crime, because the society has not officially prohibited such conduct. Students may gossip about, ridicule, and ostracize a fellow student who cheats on examinations, but the rules with which they are concerned are not the official rules of the broader society and violation of them is not, therefore, crime. Even immoral conduct is not necessarily behavior that a society has agreed to prohibit officially. A good swimmer who refuses to go to the aid of a drowning boy behaves immorally, and his action is likely to be condemned by all who hear of it; but he has not necessarily violated a criminal law. It is not correct to equate "crime" and "antisocial conduct." Behavior can be antisocial without being a violation of criminal law.

The criminal law is defined conventionally as a body of specific rules about human conduct which have been promulgated by political authority, which apply uniformly to all members of the classes to which the rules refer, and which are enforced by punishment administered by the state.[2] Hence, the criminal law is distinguishable from other bodies of rules by *politicality, specificity, uniformity, and penal sanction.* "Politicality" refers to the principle, already discussed, that only violation of official rules, those made by the state, are crimes. "Specificity" is included in order to indicate that each prohibited act is precisely defined; criminal law contains no general provision that any act that injures someone is a punishable offense. "Uniformity" is included to indicate that behavior that is crime when enacted by one person is also crime when enacted by other persons, no matter what their differences in social status.

"Penal sanction" refers to the notion that any violator will be punished or at least threatened with punishment by the state. Punishment for crime is to be imposed dispassionately by representatives of the state, and it is to be imposed in the interests of the state, rather than in the interests of any specific person such as the victim. In contrast, a violation of the tort law is viewed as an invasion of the interests of an individual. A person who attacks another and breaks his nose in a fist fight has committed both an act against the victim and an act against the state. A civil court may order him to pay $1,000 to the victim, as reimbursement for the damage to the victim's personal interests. But a criminal court may also order him to pay a $1,000 fine to the state, as punishment for violating the rules against disturbing the peace, which the state has set up to protect its corporate interests. Only the $1,000 paid to the state is punishment, and its imposition is independent of the wishes of the victim.

The individual rules within the whole body of criminal law have distinguishable characteristics in common. The characteristics of these individual rules are consistent with the characteristics of the criminal law viewed as a body of rules, and they are the criteria used to

---

[2] See Edwin H. Sutherland and Donald R. Cressey, *Principles of Criminology,* 6th ed. (Philadelphia: Lippincott, 1960), pp. 4-9.

determine whether in fact a particular act is or is not a crime. For example, penal sanction is a general characteristic of the criminal law, and liability to official punishment is a characteristic of all acts or omissions properly called crimes. If it is discovered that the act of a person being tried is in fact an act for which punishment has not been specified in advance, the act is not crime and the person goes free.

The nature of criminal law and of crimes indicates that "crime" is a technical term to be used only in special circumstances. In our everyday language we often use the term incorrectly, saying, for example, "It is a crime to make students take early morning classes," or "The way that boy snubs that girl is a crime." In the study of crime, however, we must use the term correctly—to refer only to behavior which is in violation of the criminal law. If this is not done, comparative studies will be impossible; one person will make a generalization about "crime" as he defines it, and another person will generalize about "crime" as he defines it, but neither will know what the other is talking about.[3] (See Chapter 2, page 88.)

Measuring Crime Rates

Numerous criminologists and correctional workers have reported their belief that the statistics on crime and criminals are among the most unsatisfactory of all social statistics. Six principal criticisms of the general statistics on crime have been made.[4] First, statistical data on the true crime rate cannot be compiled, for the simple reason that it is impossible to determine the amount of crime in any given locality at any particular time. Many crimes are not discovered. Others are discovered but not reported. Still others are reported but not recorded in any official way, so they do not appear in sets of crime statistics. Consequently, any record of crimes is at best an "index" of the total number of crimes committed.

Second, such "indexes" do not maintain a constant ratio with the true crime rate, whatever it may be. In crime statistics the variations in any set of figures cannot be considered a real index; the "index" items cannot be a sample of the whole because the whole cannot be specified.

Third, variation in the conditions affecting published records of

---

[3] See Donald R. Cressey, "Criminological Research and the Definition of Crimes," *American Journal of Sociology*, Vol. 56 (May, 1951), pp. 546-51.

[4] Donald R. Cressey, "The State of Criminal Statistics," *National Probation and Parole Association Journal*, Vol. 3 (July, 1957), pp. 230-41.

TABLE 1

Estimated Number of Major Crimes, and Crime Rates in the United States, 1960-1962 and 1963

Offense	Estimated Number of Offenses			Crimes per 100,000 Inhabitants	
	1960-1962 Average	1963	% Change	1963 Rate	% Change Over 3-Year Average
Murder	8,660	8,500	−2	4.5	−4
Forcible rape	16,100	16,400	+2	8.7	−1
Robbery	93,210	100,160	+7	53.1	+4
Aggravated assault	134,500	147,800	+10	78.4	+7
Burglary	854,600	975,900	+14	517.6	+11
Larceny $50 and over	505,000	611,400	+21	324.3	+17
Auto theft	334,400	399,000	+19	211.6	+16
Total	1,946,500	2,259,100	+16	1,198.3	+12

Source: Federal Bureau of Investigation, *Uniform Crime Reports for the United States, 1963* (Washington, D. C., 1964), pp. 2-3.

crime makes it foolhardy to compare crime rates in different juris-dictions, and it is hazardous even to compare the rates of the same jurisdiction (such as a city, county, state, or nation) in two different years.

Fourth, crime statistics are compiled primarily for administrative purposes, and for that reason they cannot be relied upon in scientific research. A scholar who develops a theory that accounts for variations in crime rates, whatever they may be, does so at great risk, for the extent of statistical error in any observed variation is unknown.

Fifth, statistics on the variations in the recorded rates for some crimes, such as white-collar crimes, are not routinely compiled. Many crimes committed by persons of upper socioeconomic status in the course of their business are handled by quasi-judicial bodies, such as the Federal Trade Commission, in order to avoid stigmatizing busi-nessmen as criminals, in much the way that children's cases are heard in juvenile courts rather than the criminal courts used for adults, for the same reason.

Sixth, the statistics on juvenile delinquency are subject to all of these criticisms and, in addition, are inadequate because in America delin-quency is not precisely defined. (See Chapter 2, page 90.)

"Crimes known to the police" is the set of statistics most generally accepted as the most adequate set of crime figures available. Each year the Federal Bureau of Investigation publishes a summary statement of the serious crimes known to the police departments who report to it. Table 1 summarizes these data for 1960-1962 and 1963. However, as indicated in the first three points above, this set of statistics is affected by conditions which cannot readily be taken into account in statistical reporting, conditions such as police practices, politics, laws, and public opinion. Consequently, even "crimes known to the police" may be an inadequate index of true rates. Yet the decision to use this rate is probably the best way out of a bad situation for, as Sellin, the nation's foremost expert on crime statistics, has repeatedly pointed out, "The value of criminal statistics as a basis for measurement in geographic areas decreases as the procedure takes us farther away from the offense itself." [5] Thus, crimes known to the police probably constitute a better index of the true crime rate than the arrest rate; the arrest rate, in turn, is probably more efficient than the conviction rate; and the conviction rate probably is more effective than the imprisonment rate. The "funneling effect" of law-enforcement procedures is shown in Figure 1.

Two important studies have shown that a large number of crimes are "hidden," in the sense that they do not appear in any set of crime statistics. In the first study, 1020 men and 678 women were asked to check off which of some 49 listed offenses they had ever committed. [6] An effort was made to distribute the questionnaire to a balanced religious and racial cross section of the population, but systematic sampling procedures were not used. Most of the respondents were New Yorkers, and the group of subjects contained an excess of persons from upper socioeconomic levels. Ninety-one percent of the respondents admitted that they had committed at least one offense, excluding juvenile delinquencies, for which they could have been jailed or imprisoned. Men committed an average of 18 offenses, and women had an average of 11. Twenty-six percent of the men said they had committed automobile theft, 17 percent that they had committed burglary, 13 percent grand larceny, and 11 percent robbery. Among the women, 8 percent admitted at least one automobile theft, 11 percent a burglary, 11 percent a grand larceny, and 1 percent a robbery. Sixty-four percent of the men and 27 percent of the women said they had committed at least one felony, a class of serious offenses usually punishable by at least one year in the state prison.

[5] Thorsten Sellin, "The Significance of Records of Crime," *Law Quarterly Review,* Vol. 67 (October, 1951), pp. 496-504.

[6] J. S. Wallerstein and C. J. Wyle, "Our Law-abiding Lawbreakers," *Probation,* Vol. 25 (March-April, 1947), pp. 107-12.

FIGURE 1 Procedure in Felony Cases

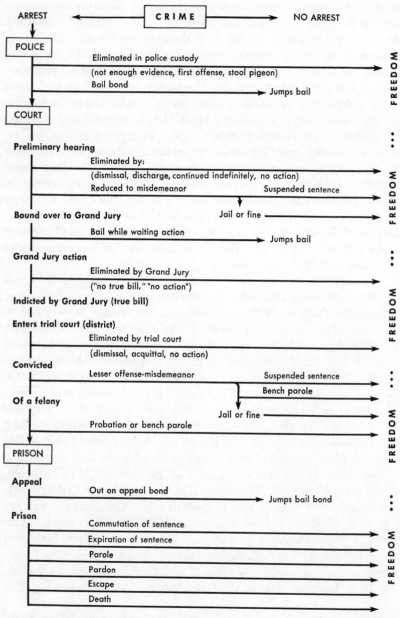

Source: Redrawn from Walter A. Lunden, "How to Beat the Rap," *American Journal of Correction,* Vol. 19, No. 10-13 (May-June, 1957), p. 13.

DONALD R. CRESSEY

In the second study, "white-collar crimes" were investigated.[7] These are crimes committed by persons of respectability and high social status in the course of their occupations. It was found that prosecution for this kind of crime often can be avoided because of the political or financial importance of the individuals involved, because of the difficulty of securing evidence, or because of the apparent triviality of the crimes. Also, the actions are punishable under criminal laws, but their perpetrators are often tried in the hearings of administrative commissions and in the civil courts, rather than being subjected to the regular criminal court procedures. In a comment on the frequency of such crimes—in the form of misrepresentation of financial statements, bribery, embezzlement, tax fraud, misrepresentation in advertising, etc.— Sutherland said:

> The manufacturers of practically every class of articles used by human beings have been involved in legal difficulties . . . with more or less frequency during the last thirty years, including the manufacturers of the surgical instruments with which an infant may be assisted into the world, the bottle and nipple from which he may secure his food, the milk in his bottle, the blanket in which he is wrapped, the flag which his father displays in celebration of the event, and so on throughout life until he is finally laid away in a casket which was manufactured and sold under conditions which violated the law.[8]

More specifically, Sutherland's study of the white-collar crimes of the 70 largest mining, manufacturing, and mercantile corporations in the United States indicated that in a period of 40 years every corporation had violated at least one of the laws outlawing restraint of trade, misrepresentation in advertising, infringement of patents, trademarks, and copyrights, violations of wartime regulations, and some miscellaneous activities. The corporations had a total of 307 adverse decisions on charges of restraint of trade, 222 adverse decisions on charges of infringements, 158 adverse decisions under the National Labor Relations Law, 97 adverse decisions under the laws regulating advertising, and 196 adverse decisions on charges of violating other laws. Generally, the official records indicated that the corporations violated the laws regulating trade with great frequency, but that such crimes do not appear in the official sets of statistics used as "indexes" of the true crime rate in the United States.

---

[7] Edwin H. Sutherland, *White-Collar Crime* (New York: Dryden, 1949).

[8] Edwin H. Sutherland, "Crime and Business," *Annals of the American Academy of Political and Social Science,* Vol. 217 (September, 1941), pp. 111-18.

Variations in Crime Rates

Despite all their limitations, statistics on crime give information important to our understanding of crime and to hypotheses and theories about it. (See Chapter 2, pages 89-97.) Similarities and differences in crime rates for certain categories of persons are so consistent that a gross relationship between the category and crime can reasonably be concluded to exist. In these cases, it is practical to assume that if the part of an observed relationship which is due merely to the methods of collecting statistics were eliminated, a real relationship would still remain. After specifying this assumption, we can go ahead and use the statistics. Even if they are gross, relationships which consistently appear and which cannot be readily "explained away" by citing the inadequacy of crime statistics must be taken into account in any theory of crime and criminality. There are at least six types of such consistent relationships that are of great theoretical significance to students of crime and criminality.

Variation by Age

Many varieties of statistics, in many jurisdictions, in many different years, collected by many types of agencies, uniformly report such a high incidence of crime among young persons, as compared with older persons, that it may reasonably be assumed that there is a statistically significant difference between the rate of crime among young adults and the rate among other age groups. Statistics are likely to exaggerate the crime rate of young adults: old people may have prestige enough to avoid fingerprinting and arrest, and young children might not be arrested as readily as either young adults or old adults, leaving young adults to bear the responsibility for more than their share of all the crimes committed. But there does seem to be a difference, even if it is not as great as the statistics indicate when they are taken at face value. In this sense, there are two general relationships between age and criminality.

A. For all crimes, taken collectively, the age of maximum criminality is in the adolescent period. American statistics on crimes known to the police show the maximum age of general criminality to be between the ages of 18 and 24, but these data probably are more subject to the bias indicated above than are the English statistics, which show that males between the ages of 12 and 13 have the highest crime rates of all male age groups, and that females aged 16 and 17 have higher crime rates than any other female age group.

B. The age of maximum criminality is not the same under all conditions. The extent to which the crime rate among young persons exceeds the crime rate among other age groups varies by offense, sex, place, and time:

1. The age of maximum criminality varies with the type of crime. Automobile theft and burglary, for example, are concentrated in the age group 15-19, while murder, embezzlement, and gambling offenses are committed by persons who are much older.

2. The age of maximum criminality varies by sex. Generally speaking, females commit crimes at later ages than do males. In 1963, for example, 54 percent of the males arrested for larceny were under 18 years of age, but only 40 percent of the females arrested for the same offense were under 18. Yet sex offenses, narcotic drug offenses, crimes against family and children, driving while intoxicated, and homicide and forgery appear earlier in the lives of women than in the lives of men. In 1963, 6 percent of the females and 1 percent of the males arrested for crimes against family and children were under age 18.[9]

3. The age of first delinquency varies from place to place. In areas of high rates of delinquency, the children who become delinquent do so at an earlier age than do the children living in areas with low rates of delinquency.[10]

4. The type of crime most frequently committed by persons of various ages varies from place to place. In some areas of Chicago, delinquent boys between 12 and 13 years old commit burglaries, while in other areas delinquent boys of those ages commit petty larcenies or engage in gang violence. In rural areas, offenders of any specified age are likely to be convicted of crimes different from those committed by offenders of the same age who live in urban areas.

5. For all crimes, and for each specific crime, the rate decreases steadily from the age of maximum criminality to the end of life. Thus, burglary and automobile theft decrease rather regularly after ages 15-19, as does the crime rate generally; homicide decreases rather regularly after ages 20-29, where it is concentrated. Consistently, the number of first offenders per 1000 persons of any given age decreases regularly after ages 15-19. Some crimes decrease more dramatically with increasing age than do others; for example, the evidence is fairly

---

[9] Federal Bureau of Investigation, *Uniform Crime Reports for the United States, 1963* (Washington, D. C., 1964), pp. 115-17.

[10] See Ernest Manheim, *Youth in Trouble* (Kansas City, Mo.: Department of Welfare, 1945), pp. 66-67.

conclusive that larceny decreases in old age more than do sex offenses.[11]

6. The crime rates among different age groups vary from time to time. The crime rate among old people seems to have declined since the time of World War I, while the crime rate among young adults seems to have been increasing.

7. Both the probability that a crime will be repeated and the length of time between first and second offenses vary with the age at which the first offense is committed. Generally speaking, the younger a person is when he commits his first offense, the higher the probability that he will commit a second offense and the shorter the interval between first offense and second offense.[12]

In sum, the available statistics on crime tell us that young persons have higher crime rates than older persons but that there are variations in the ratio of young persons to old persons in the criminal population. Thus, crime rates vary with age, but in any age group the rates vary with specific social conditions.

Variations by Sex

Sex status is of greater statistical significance in differentiating criminals from noncriminals than any other trait. If an investigator were asked to use a single trait to predict which persons in a town of 10,000 population would become criminals, he would make the fewest mistakes if he simply chose sex status and predicted criminality for the males and noncriminality for the females. He would be wrong in many cases, for most of the males would not become criminals, and a few of the females would become criminals. But he would be wrong in more cases if he used any other single trait, such as age, race, family background, or a personality characteristic. As is the case with age, there are two general relationships to be observed between crime and sex status.

A. The crime rate for men is greatly in excess of the rate for women —in all nations, all communities within a nation, all age groups, all periods of history for which organized statistics are available, and for all types of crime except those peculiar to women, such as in-

---

[11] David O. Moberg, "Old Age and Crime," *Journal of Criminal Law and Criminology*, Vol. 43 (March-April, 1953), pp. 764-76. Vernon Fox, "Intelligence, Race, and Age as Selective Factors in Crime," *Journal of Criminal Law and Criminology*, Vol. 37 (July-August, 1946), pp. 141-52.

[12] Thorsten Sellin, "Recidivism and Maturation," *National Probation and Parole Association Journal*, Vol. 4 (July, 1958), pp. 241-50. Hermann Mannheim and Leslie T. Wilkins, *Prediction Methods in Relation to Borstal Training* (London: H.M.S.O., 1955), p. 64.

fanticide and abortion. In the United States, at present, the rate of arrest of males is about ten times the rate of arrest for females; about 15 times as many males as females are committed to correctional institutions of all kinds; and about 20 times as many males as females are committed to the state and federal prisons and reformatories housing serious offenders. Even if the statistics are grossly biased against males, they can reasonably be interpreted to mean that *some* excess of crime among males is present.[13]

B. The extent to which the crime rate among males exceeds the crime rate among females is not the same under all conditions. There are variations in the sex ratio in crime, just as there are variations in the age ratio in crime:

1. The extent to which the rate for males exceeds the rate for females varies from one nation to another. In Algeria, Tunis, Japan, and Ceylon, male criminals and delinquents are seen to be 3000 or 4000 times as numerous as female criminals.[14] In Australia, Western Europe, the United States, and other nations in which females have great freedom and are viewed as almost equal in social standing to men, the rate for females is closest to the rate for males, although males remain greatly overrepresented in the criminal population.

2. The extent to which the rate for males exceeds the rate for females varies with the social positions of the sexes in different groups within a nation. An analysis of statistics in prewar Poland indicated sex ratios that ranged from 176 to 1163 in 42 groups in categories according to age, province of residence, rural-urban residence, religion, and civil status.[15] (The sex ratio always is expressed as the number of males per 100 females. A ratio over 100, therefore, means that males exceed females, while a ratio less than 100 means that females exceed males.) In the United States, the sex ratio is less extreme among Negroes than it is among whites, and it is probable that Negro males and females more closely resemble each other in social standing than do white males and females. In 1964 the sex ratio among 3000 Negroes placed on probation by the United States District Courts was 576, but the ratio among 9000 whites was 867, and the ratio among 267 American Indians was 927.[16]

[13] *Cf.* Otto Pollak, *The Criminality of Women* (Philadelphia: University of Pennsylvania Press, 1950), pp. 44-56, 154.

[14] E. Hacker, *Kriminalstatistische und Kriminalaetiologische Berichte* (Miskolc, Hungary: Ludwig, 1941).

[15] L. Radzinowicz, "Variability in the Sex Ratio of Criminality," *Sociological Review*, Vol. 29 (January, 1937), pp. 76-102.

[16] Administrative Office of the U.S. Courts, *Persons Under Supervision of the Federal Probation System; Fiscal Year 1964* (Washington, D. C., 1965), p. 17.

3. The extent to which the rate for males exceeds the rate for females varies with the size of community residence. In American cities the crime rate of females is closer to the crime rate of males than is the case in rural areas and small towns. In rural areas reporting arrests to the Federal Bureau of Investigation in 1963, the sex ratio for all crimes was 1209; for cities with over 2500 population it was 755, and for suburban areas it was 834. In the same year, the sex ratio among persons arrested for larceny was 1490 in rural areas, 396 in cities, and 441 in suburban areas. For the crime of burglary, the sex ratios were more nearly the same in the three types of community— 2960 in rural areas, 2880 in cities, and 3570 in suburban areas.[17]

4. The extent to which the crime rate among males exceeds the crime rate among females varies with age. In the United States, the sex ratio among persons committed to penal institutions tends to increase with increasing age. At ages 15-17 the sex ratio is about 1300, while at 60-64 it is about 2500. Similar variations have been found in Sweden and eight other European nations.[18]

5. The extent to which the crime rate among males exceeds the crime rate among females varies with area of residence within a city. Generally, the higher the crime rate of an area the lower the sex ratio in crime. However, it has been shown that some areas with high delinquency rates also have unusually high sex ratios among their delinquents.[19]

6. The extent to which the crime rate among males exceeds the crime rate among females varies with time. There is some evidence that the sex ratio is decreasing. Females were 5 per cent of the persons under age 18 whose arrests were reported to the FBI in 1938, 10 percent in 1947, 12.7 in 1957, and 15.3 in 1963. In time of war, when women take over some of the jobs usually performed by men, and when women in other ways tend to become more nearly equal to men in social standing, the sex ratio in crime declines.

7. Among young criminals, the extent to which the crime rate for males exceeds the crime rate for females varies with the degree of integration in the family. Among delinquents from broken homes the

---

[17] Federal Bureau of Investigation, *Uniform Crime Reports for the United States, 1963*, pp. 115, 126. See also Jackson Toby, "The Differential Impact of Family Disorganization," *American Sociological Review*, Vol. 22 (October, 1957), pp. 505-12.

[18] See Gunnar Dahlberg, "A New Method of Crime Statistics Applied to the Population of Sweden," *Journal of Criminal Law and Criminology*, Vol. 39 (September-October, 1948), pp. 327-41.

[19] Manheim, *Youth in Trouble*, pp. 64-65.

sex ratio is lower than it is among delinquents from unbroken, "integrated" homes.[20] Further, there is some evidence from specialized studies that the sex ratio in delinquency is lower in families in which male children outnumber the females than in families in which the number of each sex is more nearly equal.[21]

To summarize, the available statistics indicate that males have much higher crime rates than females but that the ratio of male criminals to female criminals varies with specific social situations.

Variations by Race

A number of studies have shown that, in the United States, Negroes are more likely to be arrested, indicted, and convicted than are whites who commit the same offenses.[22] Similarly, it has been shown that Negroes have less chance than whites to receive probation, a suspended sentence, parole, commutation of a death sentence, or a pardon.[23] Thus, almost an "index" of the crime rate is likely to exaggerate the rate for Negroes, as compared with the rate among whites. However, it is also true that many crimes committed by Negroes against other Negroes receive no official attention from the police or criminal courts, and this practice of overlooking some crimes offsets to some unknown degree the bias in other arresting, reporting, and recording practices. At least three localized studies have shown that the racial membership of the victim is of great importance in determining the official reactions to crimes committed by Negroes.[24] Like the situation with age and sex, there are two general relationships between crime and race, though here our observations are confined to the United States.

A. The official statistics indicate that the crime rate of Negroes

---

[20] Toby, "The Differential Impact of Family Disorganization."

[21] R. F. Sletto, "Sibling Position and Juvenile Delinquency," *American Journal of Sociology,* Vol. 39 (March, 1934), pp. 657-69.

[22] See, for example, Edwin M. Lemert and Judy Rosberg, "The Administration of Justice to Minority Groups in Los Angeles County," *University of California Publications in Culture and Society,* Vol. 2, No. 1 (1948), pp. 1-28.

[23] Thorsten Sellin, "Race Prejudice in the Administration of Justice," *American Journal of Sociology,* Vol. 41 (September, 1935), pp. 212-17. Also Sidney Axelrad, "Negro and White Institutionalized Delinquents," *American Journal of Sociology,* Vol. 57 (May, 1952), pp. 569-74.

[24] Guy B. Johnson, "The Negro and Crime," *Annals of the American Academy of Political and Social Science,* Vol. 217 (September, 1941), pp. 93-104. James D. Turner, "Differential Punishment in a Bi-racial Community," unpublished M.A. dissertation, Indiana University, 1948. James D. Turner, "Dynamics of Criminal Law Administration in a Bi-racial Community of the Deep South," unpublished Ph.D. dissertation, Indiana University, 1956.

exceeds the rate of whites. The number of arrests of Negroes per 100,000 Negroes is about three times the number of arrests of whites per 100,000 whites. The rate of commitment of Negroes to state and federal prisons is about six times the white rate.

B. The extent to which the crime rate of Negroes exceeds the crime rate of whites varies with social conditions. In some conditions the rate for Negroes is not as far in excess of the rate for whites as it is in other conditions, and in still other conditions the rate for Negroes is lower than the rate for whites:

1. The extent to which the rate for Negroes exceeds the rate for whites varies with regions of the United States. The excess is highest in the western states and lowest in the southern states, with northern states occupying an intermediate position.[25] In Philadelphia in 1954, Negroes made up 20 percent of the population but accounted for 50 percent of the arrests;[26] in Michigan at about the same time, Negroes were 7 percent of the population and about 40 percent of the prison population.[27] The differences in rates are not distributed in the same way for all offenses; for homicide, for example, the difference is greatest in the South and least in New England.

2. The extent to which the crime rate of Negroes exceeds the crime rate of whites varies with sex status. In 1964, 205 white women were placed on federal probation for each 100 Negro women placed on probation, but 313 white men were committed for each 100 Negro men.

3. The extent to which the crime rate of Negroes exceeds the crime rate of whites varies with offense. When based on imprisonment rates, the excess is greatest for assault and homicide and lowest for rape. One study indicated that in Virginia the rates for forgery and for drunken driving actually are lower among Negroes than among whites, but this does not take into account the fact that literacy and automobile ownership are probably less frequent among Negroes.[28] Another study indicated that large cities with a high percentage of Negroes in their populations had higher arrest rates for murder than

---

[25] The high ratio in the West may be due in part to the fact that Negroes in that area tend to be unduly concentrated in the young-adult group and in cities, both of which have high crime rates.

[26] William M. Kephart, "The Negro Offender," *American Journal of Sociology*, Vol. 60 (July, 1954), pp. 46-50.

[27] Vernon Fox and Joan Volakakis, "The Negro Offender in a Northern Industrial Area," *Journal of Criminal Law and Criminology*, Vol. 46 (January-February, 1956), pp. 641-47.

[28] Workers' Writers Program, *The Negro in Virginia* (New York: Hastings House, 1940), p. 341.

did large cities with only small percentages of Negroes.[29] It also is known that the excess of crime among Negroes is higher for second offenses than it is for first offenses.

4. The extent to which the crime rate of Negroes exceeds that of whites varies with the area of residence within a city. Studies of Houston and Baltimore show that the Negro delinquency rate is lowest in those areas having the greatest proportion of Negroes in their populations and highest in those areas with relatively low proportions of Negroes to whites.[30] In northern cities, on the other hand, the Negro crime and delinquency rates are higher in segregated than in nonsegregated areas.

5. The extent to which the crime rate of Negroes exceeds the crime rate of whites varies with time. There is no precise evidence on this point, but it seems probable that the amount of excess has been increasing. An earlier study indicated that in three decades the Negro juvenile delinquency rate in Chicago increased seven times, while the Negro population increased only three times.[31] The comparable rate and population increases for whites is not available.

In short, such statistics as are available indicate that Negroes have higher crime rates than whites but that the ratio of crime rates among Negroes to crime rates among whites varies with specific social situations.

Variations by Nativity

During the years when immigration was at its height, it was generally believed that there was an undue amount of crime among the foreign-born. While assimilation of vast numbers of immigrants is no longer a serious social problem in the United States, analysis of the data on crime among immigrants remains a sociological problem of great theoretical significance. The following two observations about nativity and crime can be made.

A. Such statistics as are available indicate that the crime rate among the foreign-born in the United States is less than that of native whites with the same age, sex, and rural-urban distribution. When computed on the basis of population numbers alone, the crime rate of immigrants

---

[29] James E. McKeown, "Poverty, Race, and Crime," *Journal of Criminal Law and Criminology,* Vol. 39 (November-December, 1948), pp. 480-83.

[30] *The Houston Delinquent in His Community Setting* (Houston: Bureau of Research, Council of Social Agencies, 1945), pp. 22-25. Bernard Lander, *Towards an Understanding of Juvenile Delinquency* (New York: Columbia University Press, 1954), p. 82.

[31] Earl R. Moses, "Community Factors in Negro Delinquency," *Journal of Negro Education,* Vol. 5 (April, 1936), pp. 220-27.

is about half that of whites.[32] Similarly, in Australia the crime rate of native Australians is about twice the rate for the immigrants arriving since World War II.[33] When correction is made for the age and sex distributions of the two groups, the crime rates become more nearly equal but still show less crime among immigrants than among native whites.

B. The extent to which the crime rate of native whites exceeds the rate among immigrants is not the same under all social conditions.

1. The extent to which the crime rate among native whites exceeds the crime rate of the foreign-born varies with offense. Certain types of crime are characteristic of one immigrant group, while another type of crime is characteristic of a different immigrant group. Usually, these same types of crime are also characteristic of the home countries. Italy has a high rate of homicide, and Italian immigrants in the United States also have a high homicide rate, as compared to either other immigrant groups or natives. Drunkenness is rare in Italy but frequent in Ireland; Italian immigrant groups have low arrest rates for drunkenness, but Irish immigrants have rather high rates for that offense.

2. The extent to which the crime rate of native whites exceeds the rate among foreign-born persons varies from one immigrant group to another. In 1955, Eastern European immigrants in Australia had crime rates about three times as high as Southern European immigrants and almost twice as high as Northern European immigrants.[34] Similarly, in the United States in the years when immigration was at its height, persons of Irish nativity had crime rates three to five times as high as German immigrants. The crime rate among Japanese immigrants is exceptionally low.[35]

3. The extent to which the crime rate of native whites exceeds the rate among the foreign-born varies from one native white group to another. The native white sons of immigrants tend to have crime rates higher than those of their fathers but lower than other native whites. In 1933, the rate of commitment of immigrants to state and federal prisons was lower than the commitment rate for the sons of immigrants

---

[32] See Arthur Lewis Wood, "Minority Group Criminality and Cultural Integration," *Journal of Criminal Law and Criminology*, Vol. 37 (March-April, 1947), pp. 498-510.

[33] Commonwealth Immigration Advisory Council, *Third Report of the Committee Established to Investigate Conduct of Migrants* (Canberra: Commonwealth Government Printer, 1957), p. 4.

[34] *Ibid.*, p. 18.

[35] Norman S. Hayner, "Delinquency Areas in the Puget Sound Area," *American Journal of Sociology*, Vol. 39 (November, 1933), pp. 314-28.

in all but one of the 28 states for which data were available.[36] Also, sons of immigrants tend to commit crimes characteristic of the receiving country, while, as indicated, the immigrants themselves commit crimes characteristic of the home country.

4. The amount of the excess of crime among the native-born varies with age. Among immigrants who arrive in the United States when they are in early childhood, the crime rate is higher than among immigrants arriving in middle age.[37] Young immigrants take on the relatively high crime rate of native whites to a greater extent than do middle-aged immigrants.

5. The extent to which the crime rate of native whites exceeds that of immigrants varies with the length of time the immigrants have been in the host country. Both immigrants and their sons tend to take on the crime rate of the specific part of the country in which they locate. A study of crime rates in France in the nineteenth century indicated that migrants moving from one province to another changed their crime rates in the direction of the rate of the host province, whether the rate in the host province was higher or lower than the rate in the province from which they migrated.[38] In the first five years of residence in an area of high delinquency in Los Angeles, 5 percent of the children in an immigrant group appeared before the juvenile court; after five more years, 46 percent appeared; and after another ten years 83 percent of the children came before the court.[39] The delinquency rate increased with length of stay in the area, presumably because the immigrant group was assimilating that part of American culture which it experienced, including the delinquency rates. It is safe to assume, on the basis of the study of France, that if the immigrant group had had a high crime rate and had settled in an area of low delinquency rates, their rate would have decreased with increased length of stay.

Variations by Size of Community

Statistics from many countries, and in many periods of time, indicate that urban areas have higher crime rates than rural areas. Again, two general types of relationship between crime and size of community can be observed.

A. Official statistics indicate that the number of serious crimes per

---

[36] Donald R. Taft, "Nationality and Crime," *American Sociological Review,* Vol. 1 (October, 1936), pp. 724-36.

[37] C. C. Van Vechten, "The Criminality of the Foreign-Born," *Journal of Criminal Law and Criminology,* Vol. 32 (July-August, 1941), pp. 139-47.

[38] Henri Joly, *La France Criminelle* (Paris: Cerf, 1889), pp. 45-46.

[39] Pauline V. Young, "Urbanization as a Factor in Juvenile Delinquency," *Publications of the American Sociological Society,* Vol. 24 (1930), pp. 162-66.

100,000 population increases with the size of the community. In 1963, the rate of robberies known to the police increased from 10.7 in rural areas to 11.1 in towns of less than 10,000 population, to 159.5 in cities of over 250,000, and to 205.8 in cities with over a million inhabitants. Offenses committed by rural criminals might not be reported or recorded as readily as offenses committed in urban areas, but the urban rate generally so far exceeds the rural rate that it is reasonable to conclude that there is in fact a great excess of crime in urban places. Moreover, a large proportion of urban crime also is overlooked, and it is not at all certain that this proportion is any less than the proportion of rural crime that is overlooked.

B. The extent to which the crime rate in urban areas exceeds the crime rate in rural areas is not the same under all conditions. In some rural areas the crime rate, especially for some types of offenses, is higher than the rate in urban areas.

1. The amount of the excess of crime in urban areas varies by offense. In American cities of over 250,000, murder and rape rates are about five times as high as the rates in towns less than 10,000; burglary and larceny rates are about twice as high; automobile theft about four times as high, and robbery about fourteen times as high.

2. The amount of the excess of crime in urban areas varies by area. In an earlier period, frontier towns, river towns, and resort towns were noted for high crime rates, despite the fact that they were not large in size. In contemporary American states containing rural mining and logging towns, the amount of excess is less than in states where rural communities are engaged in agriculture.[40] A study of the Chicago area by Sutherland indicated that burglaries and robberies of banks did not decrease steadily with distance from the city, as was the case for burglary and robbery of chain stores and drug stores; banks in the suburbs had higher rates of robbery and burglary than banks in the center of the city.[41] Similarly, Lottier found that in the Detroit area murder, assault, rape, and robbery were more concentrated in the city than were burglary, automobile theft, and larceny.[42]

3. The amount of excess of crime in urban areas varies in time. There is evidence that as improved communication and transportation

---

[40] Helen L. Yoke, "Crime in West Virginia," *Sociology and Social Research,* Vol. 16 (January, 1932), pp. 267-73. M. G. Caldwell, "The Extent of Juvenile Delinquency in Wisconsin," *Journal of Criminal Law and Criminology,* Vol. 32 (July-August, 1941), pp. 145-57. Paul Wiers, "Juvenile Delinquency in Rural Michigan," *Journal of Criminal Law and Criminology,* Vol. 30 (July-August, 1939), pp. 211-22.

[41] Sutherland and Cressey, *Principles of Criminology,* pp. 155-56.

[42] *Ibid.*

have reduced the differences between urban and rural districts, the differences in the crime rates of the two areas have decreased. In the United States, the rural rate has since about 1945 been increasing more rapidly than the urban rate. Similar trends have been noted for European countries.

Variations by Social Class

The reliability of the official statistics on the socioeconomic class backgrounds of criminals has been questioned even more severely than have statistics on variables like age, race, and area of residence. Many persons maintain that the law enforcement processes tend to select working-class persons, just as they tend to select Negroes. Thus it is believed that if a member of the working class and a member of the upper class are equally guilty of some offense, the person on the lower level is more likely to be arrested, convicted, and committed to an institution. Further, some white-collar crimes are not included in sets of official crime statistics. Reckless is confident that if statistical procedures could be corrected, the distribution of crime by social classes in the United States would show a bimodal curve, with high peaks for members of the upper class and the lower class and a low valley for members of the middle class.[43] However, the statistics on ordinary crime so consistently show an overrepresentation of lower-class persons that it is reasonable to assume that there is a real difference between the behavior of the members of this class and the members of other social classes, so far as criminality is concerned. If this assumption is made, the following two general observations are warranted.

A. In the United States, official statistics indicate that the largest proportion of criminal populations come from the working class, and there is also some evidence that the crime rate of working-class persons exceeds the crime rate of other persons. In institutionalized populations, about two-thirds to three-fourths of the men, and about nine-tenths of the women, are members of the working class. A Wisconsin study found that 12 percent of the population of the state was unskilled but that 33 percent of the parents of the state's institutionalized delinquent boys and 53 percent of the parents of its institutionalized delinquent girls were unskilled.[44] In a famous study of social classes in a New England community, it was found that the two

---

[43] Walter C. Reckless, *The Crime Problem,* 2nd ed. (New York: Appleton, 1955), pp. 28-30.

[44] M. G. Caldwell, "The Economic Status of the Families of Delinquent Boys in Wisconsin," *American Journal of Sociology,* Vol. 37 (September, 1931), pp. 231-39.

lower classes constituted 57 percent of the city's population but accounted for 90 percent of the arrests made during a seven-year period.[45] Many other studies have shown similar overrepresentations of working-class people in criminal populations. One study found that prison inmates rank themselves lower than they rank their fathers on socioeconomic status,[46] perhaps indicating that the prisoners were unable to maintain the family level of status, let alone improve it through upward mobility. Studies of the areas of criminals' residence also indicate high crime rates in areas occupied by persons of low socioeconomic status.

B. The extent of overrepresentation of working-class persons in the criminal population is not the same under all conditions. In some situations, working-class people have crime rates lower than those of other classes:

1. The ratio of working-class persons to other persons in the criminal population varies by social group. In the Japanese colony in Seattle prior to World War II, delinquency and crime rates were very low, despite the fact that the residents were of the working class and were in as great poverty as residents of the area surrounding the colony, who had high rates.[47] Members of the working class who live in rural areas, similarly, have relatively low crime rates. Females living in areas where most residents are of low socioeconomic status have low crime rates. Also, members of some groups in extreme poverty have literally starved to death rather than violate laws. Finally, it is obvious that most working-class persons do not become criminals and that, therefore, something other than working-class membership is involved. Even in areas of great poverty and high crime rates, large proportions of the residents do not become criminals.

2. The ratio of working-class persons to other persons varies by offense. Most studies showing high ratios of working-class persons have concentrated on crimes against property, such as larceny and burglary. There is some evidence, however, that the ratio is somewhat lower for sex offenses, and in fact the crime rates of the working class may be lower than those of other classes for some sex offenses.[48] Similarly, a study conducted in Detroit indicated that working-class

[45] William Lloyd Warner and Paul S. Lunt, *The Social Life of a Modern Community* (New Haven: Yale University Press, 1941), pp. 373-77.

[46] Harold Bradley and Jack D. Williams, *Intensive Treatment Program: Second Annual Report* (Sacramento, Calif.: Department of Corrections, 1958), p. 16.

[47] Hayner, "Delinquency Areas in the Puget Sound Area."

[48] A. C. Kinsey, W. B. Pomeroy, and C. E. Martin, *Sexual Behavior in the Human Male* (Philadelphia: Saunders, 1948), pp. 327-93.

persons are not as overrepresented in the population of automobile thieves as they are in other delinquent and criminal populations.[49] And, of course, working-class persons have lower crime rates than other persons for offenses such as embezzlement, misrepresentation in advertising, violation of antitrust laws, and issuing worthless stocks. The person's position in the occupational structure determines the opportunities for some kinds of crime and also determines whether or not a person will possess the skills necessary to perpetrating some types of offenses.[50]

Conclusion

Although the above are only some of the social conditions with which crime rates vary, the list is sufficiently long to enable us to draw the important conclusion that crime is social behavior that is closely associated with other kinds of social behavior. One set of facts indicates that the crime rate is higher for young adults than for persons in later life, higher for men than for women, higher for Negroes than for whites, higher for native-born than for foreign-born, higher in cities than in rural areas, and higher for the working class than for other social classes. Such differences may be described as ratios—the age ratio in crime, the sex ratio in crime, etc. A second set of facts points up the fact that these ratios are not constant. They vary in definite ways.

These ratios, and variations in ratios, make up some of the facts that a general explanation of crime must fit. They may be called definitive facts, for they define or limit the explanations of crime that can be considered valid. For example, an explanation that attributes crime to poverty helps make good sense out of the overrepresentation of Negroes and working-class persons in the general criminal population, but the theory falls flat when it is recalled that women, who are equal in poverty with men, have very low crime rates; when it is recalled that immigrants, who are probably at least as poor as their sons, sometimes have crime rates lower than their sons; when it is recalled that even poor Negroes and working-class persons do not have high crime rates if they live in rural areas, and so on. Similarly, an explanation of crime in terms of a trait of aggression or other per-

---

[49] William W. Wattenberg and James Balistrieri, "Automobile Theft: A 'Favored-Group' Delinquency," *American Journal of Sociology*, Vol. 57 (May, 1952), pp. 575-79.

[50] See Donald R. Cressey, "Application and Verification of the Differential Association Theory," *Journal of Criminal Law and Criminology*, Vol. 43 (May-June, 1952), pp. 72-80.

sonality characteristic must show that the characteristic is much more frequent among men than among women, among Negro women than white women, among young persons as compared to old persons, etc.; and it also must show that the trait occurs infrequently among immigrant groups, Negroes who live in segregated areas, middle-class persons, etc.

None of the general explanations of crime makes good sense out of *all* the ratios and variations in ratios. Some of them explain one set of facts, and others explain another set of facts, but none of them explains all the facts. However, some of the general theories make better sense out of more of the facts than do others. These are the sociological theories that have as their general point the observation that crime and criminality are products of social experience and social interaction. Some of these theories will be reviewed later, after the various approaches to the study of crime have been identified.

The Study of Crime Causation

Criminology, considered as the systematic study of the causes of crime, developed late in the United States. (See Chapter 2, pages 97-105.) Until the twentieth century, little systematic research was conducted, and few carefully written books on the subject were by Americans. In the nineteenth century, such work as was done was conducted almost completely outside academic circles by theologians, physicians and psychiatrists, and reformers. Most of these writers were not concerned with developing generalizations about criminal behavior and about the relationships between crime rates and other social conditions. Particularly, prior to the last quarter of the nineteenth century, most men who advanced theories about crime causation did so in an attempt to find a panacea for criminality. Few efforts were made to verify the many theological or moralistic assertions by actually investigating relevant situations; writers usually selected a general "cause" of all criminality and then sought to convince their readers that elimination of that cause would eradicate crime both by reforming criminals and by preventing future criminality. There was little or no attempt to "make sense," in a logical generalization, of the known facts about variations in crime rates, principally because few facts of the kind listed above were known.

It was not until the end of the nineteenth century that an interest in scientific theory of crime and criminality developed in America, although such an interest had appeared earlier in Europe. Sociology was making its way into the curricula of universities and colleges at this time, and a survey conducted in 1901 indicated that criminology and penology were among the first courses offered under the general title of "Sociology." [51] From that time to the present the main academic stronghold of criminology has been in departments of sociology. The sociological study of crime and criminality will be discussed after we have reviewed some of its early and contemporary competitors, the biological, psychiatric, and psychometric approaches.

The Biological Approach

An Italian physician of the nineteenth century, Cesare Lombroso, and his followers greatly stimulated the development of criminology both in the United States and abroad. Lombroso's theory held, essentially, that criminals are by birth a distinct biological type and can be recognized by characteristics such as a long lower jaw, flattened nose, sparse beard, and low sensitivity to pain. Further, these anatomical characteristics were said to identify a person who is a reversion to an earlier type of human, an atavism. At first the work of Lombroso and his disciples was directed against the "classical school" of criminal law and criminology, which assumed that men choose between the pleasures anticipated from a particular criminal act and the pains anticipated from the same act. The criminal was assumed to have a free will which enabled him to make his choice with reference to his balance of pleasures and pains. In contrast, the Lombrosian position was a deterministic one, holding that criminality is determined by something that the actor cannot control. Later Lombrosians directed their work against the ideas of Gabriel Tarde, a French social psychologist who attempted to refute the prevailing biological notions by developing a theory emphasizing the idea that people behave according to the customs of their society; if a man steals or murders, he is just imitating someone else. The controversy here was on the question of biological determinism versus social determinism, rather than on the question of determinism versus free will.

The English Convict, a study reported by Charles Goring, an English physician, is generally accepted in the United States as the work which finally demolished the Lombrosian notion that there is a distinct criminal type,[52] but in Italy and South America emphasis on the idea that criminals are a distinct morphological type has contin-

---

[51] Frank L. Tolman, "Study of Sociology in Institutions of Learning in the United States," *American Journal of Sociology,* Vol. 7 (May, 1902), pp. 797-838; Vol. 8 (July, 1902), pp. 85-121; Vol. 8 (September, 1902), pp. 251-72; Vol. 8 (January, 1903), pp. 531-58.

[52] Charles Goring, *The English Convict* (London: H.M.S.O., 1913).

ued. Further, research which is essentially Lombrosian in character continues in the United States.[53] Goring's conclusion, which he based on detailed comparison of over 3000 prisoners and noncriminals, was that whatever difference in physical traits exists is due to a process of selection not unlike that operating in the choice of many occupations. The work on anatomical characteristics and body-types did not purport to explain the many variations in crime rates; to do so, it would have been necessary to show differences in the frequency of anatomical characteristics in rural and urban dwellers, immigrants and native whites, working-class and middle-class persons, and other groups.

Similarly, biologically oriented persons have attempted, in various ways, to show that criminality is inherited. One school of thought was based upon the idea contained in Richard Dugdale's book, *The Jukes*, published in 1877.[54] This book traced the Jukes family through several generations beginning with an illegitimate union, and it showed an enormous concentration of feeblemindedness, delinquency, degeneracy, and crime in the family. Another school of thought more recently took its clue from a study claiming that one-egg twins more frequently resemble each other in criminality than do two-egg twins.[55] Since twins coming from a single egg have identical hereditary makeup, while twins coming from different eggs are no more similar than other brothers or sisters, the study was said to show that criminality can be inherited. Nevertheless, sociologists and biologists alike have refused to accept this study, and similar studies, as conclusive proof.[56] The wide variations in crime rates cannot be accounted for by the inherited characteristics of the persons involved.

It should be recalled that crime, by definition, contains three elements. First, a value which is appreciated by a group or a part of a group is involved. Second, another part of this group is isolated or in conflict with the first group, so that they do not appreciate the

---

[53] See Earnest A. Hooton, *Crime and the Man* (Cambridge, Mass.: Harvard University Press, 1939). William H. Sheldon, *Varieties of Delinquent Youth: An Introduction to Constitutional Psychiatry* (New York: Harper, 1949). Sheldon and Eleanor T. Glueck, *Physique and Delinquency* (New York: Harper, 1956).

[54] Richard Dugdale, *The Jukes: A Study in Crime, Pauperism, and Heredity* (New York: Putnam, 1877).

[55] Johannes Lange, *Verbrechen Als Schicksal* (Leipzig: Thieme, 1929); trans. by Charlotte Haldane with the title *Crime and Destiny* (New York: Boni, 1930).

[56] H. H. Newman, *Multiple Human Births* (New York: Doubleday, 1940), p. 160. M. F. Ashley-Montagu, "The Biologist Looks at Crime," *Annals of the American Academy of Political and Social Science*, Vol. 217 (September, 1941), pp. 46-57. Ernest R. Mowrer, "Some Factors in the Affectional Adjustment of Twins," *American Sociological Review*, Vol. 16 (August, 1954), pp. 468-71.

value or regard it less highly and, thus, tend to endanger it. Third, the first section of the group resorts to coercion, applied in a disinterested manner in the name of the entire group to those who disregard the value. Since rule violations come to be called crimes by this process, what is "crime" and what is not crime is quite arbitrary. One cannot inherit a biological predisposition to behave in a manner that is criminalistic only because it has arbitrarily been so labeled by a social group.

The Psychiatric Approach

With the development of psychiatry in the last four decades there has been an increasing tendency to apply psychiatric and psychoanalytical techniques and theories to the crime problem. This, in fact, has been the source of the most important nonacademic influence upon criminological theory. The publication of William Healy's *The Individual Delinquent* in 1915 may be taken as the event which signalized the liberation of psychiatry from Lombrosian preconceptions, opening the way for research and theorizing about crime in a manner which has profoundly influenced criminological thought.[57] Bernard Glueck provided another impetus when he published the results of his investigations of 608 inmates of Sing Sing Prison in New York.[58] He stated at about that time that "it is now universally recognized that the pauper, the prostitute, and the criminal classes are primarily the product of mental defect and degeneracy and as such must come within the purview of mental medicine." [59]

In the areas of crime causation, the contributions of psychiatry have been made in two principal ways. First, in an effort to test or prove assumptions such as those of Glueck's quoted in the preceding paragraph, studies have been designed to determine the prevalence of mental defects or disorders among criminals. This has led psychiatrists and psychiatrically oriented research workers from crude tabular presentations of percentages without the use of control groups to the refinements of current statistical techniques of sampling, correlation, and controls. The second principal contribution of psychiatry has come through the emphasis, description, and attempted explanation of the psychic aspects of criminal behavior and the insistence that these aspects must be taken into account. Psychoanalytic theory has provided

---

[57] William Healy, *The Individual Delinquent* (Boston: Little, Brown, 1915).

[58] Bernard Glueck, "Concerning Prisoners," *Mental Hygiene*, Vol. 2 (1918), pp. 85-151.

[59] Bernard Glueck, *Studies in Forensic Psychiatry* (Boston: Little, Brown, 1916), p. 68.

a system of concepts and explanatory principles which, after undergoing criticism and modification, has been influential upon psychiatrists and sociologists alike, as well as upon the public.

The early preoccupation of psychiatrists was with the assumption that criminals constitute an inferior type, characterized by feeblemindedness, mental disease, alcoholism, drug addiction, psychopathy, epilepsy, neuroticism, and the like. Unfortunately, in the effort to demonstrate the truth of this contention by statistical means, control groups were at first rarely used, and many key concepts were vaguely defined. This was true of such concepts as that of "constitutional psychopath," "inadequate personality," and many of the neuroses and psychoses. This looseness of definition made it especially easy to fall into error in the use of these terms. One of the most notable of these errors has been to assume that psychopathy is a cause of crime and in trying to prove that contention to assume that criminality alone is adequate evidence of psychopathy.[60]

In addition to the diagnosis of serious mental defects and disorders, there has been a trend toward the inclusion of all kinds of personality traits within the scope of psychiatry, on the assumption that a normal, well-balanced personality possesses adequate mental and emotional equipment and that the absence of such equipment may lead to various forms of deviant behavior, including crime. Through this type of reasoning, minor emotional disturbances are held to cause crime.

Psychiatrists at present are, to some extent, abandoning their efforts to demonstrate the prevalence of deviations from the normal among delinquents and criminals in favor of trying to describe the processes involved in the development of the criminal mentality. Psychoanalysts, by use of the intensive study of cases which characterizes their technique, have furnished particularly detailed case histories, which they have interpreted in accordance with the doctrines and concepts of their approach, emphasizing the effects of repressed conflicts, early traumatic experiences, especially those connected with sex, and other motivational aspects of behavior emphasized by the various branches of the psychoanalytical school of thought. In their intensive probing of psychic life, psychiatrists and psychoanalysts have contributed material that sociologists of the past seldom dealt with and that they are now increasingly taking into account.

In recent years there has been a growing disposition among psychiatrists and sociologists to make allowances for each other's findings

---

[60] See Michael Hakeem, "A Critique of the Psychiatric Approach to Crime and Correction," *Law and Contemporary Problems*, Vol. 23 (Autumn, 1958), pp. 650-82.

and to attempt some sort of synthesis or compromise. Some psychiatrists have sought to resolve the conflict created by the contradictory claims of sociologists and psychiatrists by contending that some classes of criminals fall into the domain of the psychiatrists and others, usually those who are relatively normal, into the field of sociology. Other psychiatrists contend that modern psychiatry is concerned not only with deviant behavior but with normal behavior as well, and they consequently see no reason for restricting their attention to the neurotic or mentally diseased criminal.

The Psychometric Approach

The interest of psychologists in the crime problem has been expressed largely through the use of tests and measurement devices. Ideally, the aim has been to measure psychological factors deemed significant in criminal behavior and, by comparisons with control groups taken from the noncriminal population, to show that the differences between the criminal and noncriminal groups are statistically significant. The assumption underlying this approach usually is that if a trait appears more frequently among a group of criminals than it does in a comparable group of noncriminals it may be regarded as a "cause" of criminality. Sometimes, however, the investigator does not make this assumption but is content merely to state the differences he finds.

Immediately before and after World War I, when intelligence testing began to come into vogue, the newly devised tests were applied to delinquents and criminals, and feeblemindedness began to be regarded as an important cause of crime by an increasing number of scholars. Henry H. Goddard was one of the most enthusiastic early advocates of the doctrine that feeblemindedness is the principal cause of crime. In 1912 he estimated that at least 25 percent of adult criminals were feebleminded and hence unable to do right; [61] by 1914, when he published his book on feeblemindedness, he estimated that the percentage was at least 50; [62] and by 1920 he believed that "nearly all" criminals and delinquents are of low-grade mentality.[63]

In 1933, L. D. Zeleny, after having examined about 200 studies of

---

[61] Henry H. Goddard, "The Responsibility of Children in the Juvenile Court," *Journal of the American Institute of Criminal Law and Criminology,* Vol. 3 (September, 1912), pp. 365-75.

[62] Henry H. Goddard, *Feeblemindedness, Its Causes and Consequences* (New York: Macmillan, 1914).

[63] Henry H. Goddard, *Human Efficiency and Levels of Intelligence* (Princeton, N. J.: Princeton University Press, 1920), pp. 73-74.

criminal intelligence, noted that marked disagreements existed among the authors, some claiming that the criminal population has a larger proportion of feebleminded persons than the noncriminal population, a second group maintaining that criminal and noncriminal populations contain like portions of feebleminded persons, and a third group contending that the proportion of feebleminded persons is smaller in the criminal population than it is in the noncriminal population. Zeleny himself concluded that there was a slight excess of feeblemindedness in the criminal population.[64] At about the same time, E. H. Sutherland analyzed about 350 reports on mental tests of criminals and noted that the proportion of delinquents diagnosed as feebleminded declined steadily from the early 1910-1914 period to 1928-1929, when he made his analysis.[65] He concluded that the delinquent population closely resembles the general population in intelligence scores and that feebleminded persons in the community at large do not show excessive rates of delinquency. These conclusions are consistent with Carl Murchison's statistical analysis in 1926[66] and with Tulchin's analysis in 1939.[67] They represent an almost complete retraction of the early conclusion that mentally defective persons are overrepresented in groups having high crime rates.

The theory and assumptions which first led to attempts to differentiate criminals from noncriminals on the basis of intelligence test scores are now most in evidence in attempts to differentiate the two groups on the basis of some other kind of test score. In trying out the notion that delinquents and criminals constitute a psychological type, psychologists and others have used dozens of tests, rating scales, and other measuring devices to study differences in emotion, temperament, character, and a host of psychological traits such as mechanical aptitude, aggressiveness, speed of decision, emotional instability, caution, self-assurance, excitability, motor inhibition, and many others. Generally speaking, the work in this area has been fragmentary in character, in the sense that a study is made without reference to a systematically developed theory of crime.

In 1950, Schuessler and Cressey summarized the results of all studies in which delinquents' and criminals' scores on objective tests of person-

---

[64] L. D. Zeleny, "Feeblemindedness and Criminal Conduct," *American Journal of Sociology*, Vol. 38 (January, 1933), pp. 564-76.

[65] Edwin H. Sutherland, "Mental Deficiency and Crime," in Kimball Young, ed., *Social Attitudes* (New York: Holt, 1931), Chapter 15, pp. 357-75.

[66] Carl Murchison, *Criminal Intelligence* (Worcester, Mass.: Clark University Press, 1926).

[67] Samuel H. Tulchin, *Intelligence and Crime* (Chicago: University of Chicago Press, 1939).

ality were compared with the scores of control groups or with the norms established for the tests.[68] A wide range of personality traits were purportedly measured by the tests, including emotional immaturity, emotional instability, and emotional disturbance. One conclusion from analysis of the 113 studies of this kind was that not a single trait had been shown to be more characteristic of criminals than of noncriminals. Their general observation was that "the doubtful validity of many of the obtained differences, as well as the lack of consistency in the combined results, makes it impossible to conclude from these data that criminality and personality elements are associated." Recent studies using the Minnesota Multiphasic Personality Inventory have shown differences between delinquents and nondelinquents in some instances but not in others.[69] A critical appraisal of criminological research and theory pointed out that establishing statistically significant differences between criminals and noncriminals, even when the statistical techniques are adequate and the sample groups are truly representative, does not in itself lead to conclusions about crime causation.[70] Variations in personality traits have not been shown to follow the variations in crime rates we described earlier.

The Sociological Approach

Perhaps it was a historical accident that the new field of criminal sociology, so widely publicized by Lombroso and his followers,[71] was at the peak of its popularity at the time sociology departments were first organized in American universities and colleges. Thus, the earliest American writing by persons who would now be identified as sociologists leaned strongly toward Lombrosian theory, though the thesis was not necessarily accepted completely.[72] Investigators in many Eu-

---

[68] Karl F. Schuessler and Donald R. Cressey, "Personality Characteristics of Criminals," *American Journal of Sociology,* Vol. 55 (March, 1950), pp. 476-84.

[69] S. R. Hathaway and Elio D. Monachesi, *Analyzing and Predicting Delinquency with the MMPI* (Minneapolis: University of Minnesota Press, 1953). Arthur P. Volkman, "A Matched-Group Personality Comparison of Delinquent and Nondelinquent Juveniles," *Social Problems,* Vol. 6 (Winter, 1959), pp. 238-45.

[70] J. Michael and M. J. Adler, *Crime, Law, and Social Science* (New York: Harcourt, Brace & World, 1933), Chapter 5.

[71] E. Ferri, *Criminal Sociology,* trans. by J. I. Kelly and John Lisle (Boston: Little, Brown, 1917). Charles R. Henderson, "General Sociology and Criminal Sociology," *Charities Review,* Vol. 5 (April, 1896), pp. 298-301. Francis A. Keller, "Criminal Sociology: The American vs. the Latin School," *Arena* (March, 1900), pp. 301-07.

[72] See, for example, Charles R. Henderson, *An Introduction to the Study of Dependent, Defective, and Delinquent Classes* (Boston: Heath, 1893). Arthur MacDonald, *Criminology* (New York: Funk and Wagnalls, 1893), and *Abnormal Man* (Washington: U.S. Bureau of Education, 1893). August Drahms, *The Criminal,*

ropean nations were making sound scientific studies of crime and criminality both before the time of Lombroso and contemporaneously with him. These studies were sociological in nature, and the great popularity of the biological thesis delayed for about 50 years the other scientific work in progress at the time.[73]

After the publication of Goring's famous study, American sociologist-criminologists turned away from the biological notions introduced by Lombroso and cultivated a strong environmentalist position. Since that time they have emphasized the relationships between social and cultural conditions and crime. As early as 1914 a sociologist wrote, "The longer the study of crime has continued in this country, the greater has grown the number of causes of crime which can be described as social. This is the aspect in the development of American criminology which has given to that study in this country the title of 'The American School.'"[74] This trend has continued down to the present.

However, of the various approaches to the study of crime by academic disciplines, the sociological is the most varied and diverse. Virtually all techniques of studying crime and all theoretical systems that are applied to it are found among sociologists. Thus, statistically trained sociologists sometimes use psychometric methods, social psychologists use the case history technique of psychiatry, and other sociologists use the prolonged interviews and the conceptual framework of psychoanalysis. In the past, as we have indicated, some sociologists even espoused biological doctrines. But ordinarily the sociologically oriented investigator emphasizes that external social and cultural conditions and processes are basic in crime causation and

---

His Personnel and Environment (New York: Macmillan, 1900). Francis A. Keller, *Experimental Sociology* (New York: Macmillan, 1901). Carrol D. Wright, *Outline of Practical Sociology* (New York: Longmans, Green, 1899). Maurice F. Parmalee, *The Principles of Anthropology and Sociology in Their Relations to Criminal Procedure* (New York: Macmillan, 1908). Phillip A. Parsons, *Responsibility for Crime* (Columbia University Studies in History, Economics, and Public Law, Vol. 24, no. 3, 1909).

[73] See Alfred Lindesmith and Yale Levin, "The Lombrosian Myth in Criminology," *American Journal of Sociology,* Vol. 42 (March, 1937), pp. 653-71. Yale Levin and Alfred Lindesmith, "English Ecology and Criminology of the Past Century," *Journal of Criminal Law and Criminology,* Vol. 27 (March-April, 1937), pp. 801-16. N. S. Timasheff, "Review of *Principles of Criminology,* by Edwin H. Sutherland and Donald R. Cressey," *American Catholic Sociological Review* (June, 1955), pp. 143-44.

[74] John L. Gillin, "Social Factors Affecting the Volume of Crime," *Physical Basis of Crime: A Symposium* (Easton, Pa.: American Academy of Medicine, 1914), pp. 53-67.

seeks to formulate his theories in these terms, even though he may at times borrow techniques and ideas from other disciplines.[75]

The central theme running through criminological studies conducted by sociologists is that crime and criminality are products of the same social conditions and processes that produce other kinds of social behavior. Analyses of these conditions and processes have taken two general forms. First, there have been attempts to show relationships between variations in crime rates and variations in social organization. Thus, the crime rates of societies, subsocieties, and groups have been shown to be connected with processes and conditions such as mobility, competition, and culture conflict; political, religious, and economic ideologies; population density and composition; and the distribution of wealth, income, and employment. This kind of analysis declined in popularity after about 1940, principally because investigators became aware of the great hazards in making generalizations about crime as measured by conventional crime statistics, but it is on the rise again at present. Second, sociologists have attempted to define and identify the processes by which persons become criminals. These analyses are social-psychological in nature, and the concepts used are related to those utilized in more general theories of social learning. Various investigators have stressed processes such as imitation, role-playing, differential association, compensation, identification, self-conception, and frustration-aggression. All these are processes by which persons learn various kinds of social behavior, and it is maintained that persons learn criminal behavior in the same way that they learn other kinds of social behavior, such as an occupational role, the role of a boy or girl, or the role of a teen-ager. The content of the learning, not the process of learning, is viewed as the important condition which determines whether a person becomes a criminal. Through a learning process a boy learns how to behave toward his family and friends; through the same learning process he learns how to behave toward unlocked automobiles which are available for theft.

The Multiple-Factor Approach

William Healy's emphasis upon multiple causation in the cases of individual delinquents,[76] combined with the then prevalent endeav-

---

[75] See Frank E. Hartung, "A Critique of the Sociological Approach to Crime and Correction," *Law and Contemporary Problems,* Vol. 23 (Autumn, 1958), pp. 703-34.

[76] Healy, *The Individual Delinquent,* pp. 16, 33-125, 130-38.

ors to discount the biological and physical conditions which were said to produce crime and criminals, played an important part in the development of the "multiple-factor" approach to crime. The revolt against the practice of stressing one cause for all crime led to the production of extensive lists of "causes" of crime, each one of which was at first said to produce a portion of all criminals. This idea that crime is a result of multifarious influences has persisted to the present, but the specific factors said to be important in crime have shifted from time to time, progressively becoming more social in nature. Also, there has been a shift toward concentration on multifarious factors in the crimes of individual offenders, rather than on multifarious factors producing high crime rates.

When the multiple-factor approach is used in the study of individual cases, it is maintained that one crime is caused by one set of "factors," and that another crime is caused by a different set of factors. Advocates of the approach pay little or no attention to developing a system of theory which would try to make sense of the relationships that might be found. Rather, one criminal is said to have become a criminal because of the influence of three or four factors, another criminal is said to be criminalistic because of other factors, and no elaboration is viewed as necessary. Some advocates of the approach hold that each factor is of equal importance, but the majority argue that the presence of one or two "important" factors or seven or eight "minor" factors will produce criminality.

When the multiple-factor approach is used in the study of variations in crime rates, the investigator simply lists conditions that are associated with crime to a high or low degree. The higher the degree of association, the more importance is ascribed to the particular condition. There is little attempt to make sense out of the statistical findings by showing that they are consistent or inconsistent with a theoretical scheme. Reckless has advocated the use of this method under the name "actuarial approach." [77] The concern is with statistical association; there is no imputation of "causal power" to any factor or set of factors. As early as 1895, criminologists were warned not to impute causal power to statistical correlations, on the dual grounds that the connection between the alleged cause and the alleged effect might merely be an accidental one and that "the coincidence of two statistical facts does not in itself determine which of the two is primary and which is secondary, nor whether both may not have in common origin a third

---

[77] Walter C. Reckless, *The Etiology of Delinquent and Criminal Behavior* (New York: Social Science Research Council, 1943), p. 74.

which, perhaps, is not included in the scope of the investigation." [78]

Advocates of the multiple-factor approach often take pride in their broadmindedness, arguing that explanations by psychiatrists, sociologists, psychologists, or members of any other academic discipline are narrow and particularistic.[79] However, in one of the best critiques of the multiple-factor approach, Albert Cohen has made three principal points.[80]

1. Persons using the multiple-factor approach confuse explanation by means of a *single theory* or set of theories with explanation by means of a *single factor*. No one explains crime by means of a single factor, but this does not mean that crime cannot be explained by means of a single theory. A single theory is a logical statement showing how variations in one thing are linked up with variations in other things. Thus, theory is concerned with many variables, but the variables are not considered as causal agents. We make statements of fact in terms of values (high, low, etc.) of variables: "The crime rate is high among persons with low incomes, among young adults, and among males." But such statements of fact, whether concerned with the relationship of the values of one variable to crime (income) or with the relationship of the values of a number of variables (income, age, sex) are not explanations of crime. A criminological theory makes sense of the facts about crime, and the best theory is the one that makes the best sense out of the most facts.

2. The "evil-causes-evil fallacy" usually characterizes the multiple-factor approach, though it is not peculiar to it. The fallacy is that results we do not like (crime) must have antecedents we do not like (alcoholism, psychopathic personality, biological inferiority, lack of love by parents, overprotection by parents, etc.). When this fallacy is present, "explanations" of crime or almost any other social problem are likely to be statements attributing causal power to a list of ugly and sordid conditions which any "decent citizen" deplores. It is very difficult to reason that crime (an evil) does not necessarily result from something also considered evil, but instead might result from something which most persons hold to be good. A "good thing" like democracy, freedom, or individualism can have unanticipated "evil" conse-

---

[78] Fredrick H. Wines, *Punishment and Reformation* (New York: Crowell, 1895), p. 267.

[79] Sheldon Glueck, "Theory and Fact in Criminology," *British Journal of Delinquency*, Vol. 7 (October, 1956), pp. 92-109.

[80] Albert K. Cohen, "Juvenile Delinquency and the Social Structure," unpublished Ph.D. dissertation, Harvard University, 1951, pp. 5-13; see also his *Delinquent Boys: The Culture of the Gang* (New York: Free Press, 1955).

quences like crime. Perhaps in criminology there is a tendency to seek the "causes" of crime in evil antecedents because this practice will enable us to denounce crime without hurting anyone's feelings and because it will enable us to attempt to eliminate crime without changing any conditions we hold dear.

3. "Factors" are confused with "causes," and each factor is assumed to contain within itself a fixed amount of crime-producing power. The fact that a person has a low income is said to have some crime-producing power; the fact that he is a young adult pushes him further in the direction of crime; and the fact that he is a male is the last straw. Sometimes the basis for imputing causal power to a factor in an individual case is high statistical association between the factor and crime rates—if in a city the areas of poor housing are also the areas of high crime rates, a person who lives in a substandard house is considered on the road to crime. Statisticians point out the fallacy of such reasoning, and it is not part of the "actuarial approach." [81] Sometimes the imputing of causal power to a factor is based only on subjective judgments of the person doing the imputing, and it cannot be determined at all by outsiders. Some people have said, for instance, that poor eyesight, or red hair, or inability to play a musical instrument is a "factor in" delinquency or crime, but no one can determine why such conditions are viewed as "pushers." Nothing in the condition of poor eyesight jumps up and pushes a person in one direction or another; if the condition is important at all, it must be related to some meaning which poor eyesight has to the person and to the effects of this meaning on some process which leads to crime. Specification of this process is a theory of criminality. (See Chapter 2, page 119.)

Some Sociological Theories of Criminal Behavior

In the years since 1915, the quantity of criminological research conducted in the United States has increased enormously, but adequate knowledge about crime causation has not increased proportionately. As indicated, much of the research has been of a descriptive, statistical nature, usually seeking neither to take into consideration much of the existing information in the same area of study nor to establish explanations of the statistical relationships revealed. But some sociologists have shown dissatisfaction with the multiple-factor approach and have attempted to integrate and to systematize the knowledge obtained from detailed and specialized studies, in an endeavor to provide a

---

[81] William S. Robinson, "Ecological Correlations and the Behavior of Individuals," *American Sociological Review,* Vol. 15 (June, 1950), pp. 351-57.

framework for a general explanation of criminal behavior. The most noteworthy of these attempts have been those made by Edwin H. Sutherland, Thorsten Sellin, Donald R. Taft, and Robert K. Merton.

Sutherland has hypothesized that persons acquire patterns of criminal behavior in the same way that they acquire patterns of lawful behavior.[82] That is, "criminal behavior is learned in interaction with persons in a pattern of communication," and the specific direction of motives, drives, rationalizations, and attitudes—whether in the direction of anticriminality or criminality—is learned from persons who define the legal codes as rules to be observed and from persons whose attitudes are favorable to violation of the legal codes. "A person becomes delinquent because of an excess of definitions favorable to violation of law over definitions unfavorable to violations of law." In American society, the two kinds of definitions of what is to be done in reference to legal codes exist side by side, and the same person might present different definitions at different times and in different situations. Sutherland has called this process "differential association," because the content of what is learned in the process of association with criminal behavior patterns differs from the content of what is learned in the process of association with anticriminal behavior patterns. "When persons become criminal, they do so because of contacts with criminal behavior patterns and also because of isolation from anticriminal patterns."

It should be noted that the theory involves much more than the old notion that delinquency and crime are caused by "bad companions." "Differential association" refers to a *ratio* of associations with both criminal behavior patterns and anticriminal behavior patterns. Moreover, the association need not be with criminal *persons;* an individual can present criminal behavior patterns even if he is not himself a criminal; and even confirmed criminals present anticriminal behavior patterns to their children and friends. Of course, many of the behavior patterns with which a person comes in contact during the course of everyday living have nothing to do with criminality one way or the other. A child who is being taught to read or to brush his teeth is being presented with behavior patterns, but these are neither favorable nor unfavorable to law violation. But a person who is taught that "honesty is the best policy" and also that "it is all right to steal a loaf of bread when you are starving" is being presented with both an anticriminal behavior pattern and a criminal behavior pattern, even if the presentations are made by his noncriminal mother.

---

[82] Sutherland and Cressey, *Principles of Criminology,* pp. 74-81.

Sutherland further hypothesizes that "the principal part of the learning of criminal behavior occurs in intimate personal groups." While the impersonal agencies of communication such as newspapers, books, moving pictures, radio, and television exert some influence through the patterns they present, they are important principally in that they render the individual either receptive or nonreceptive to the patterns of criminal behavior and of anticriminal behavior that are presented in personal association.

When it is applied to a nation, a city, or a group, the theory of differential association becomes a theory of differential social organization. A high crime rate in a city, for example, is the end product of a situation in which relatively large numbers of persons have been presented with an excess of criminal behavior patterns, as compared with anticriminal behavior patterns. From this it can be reasoned, as Sutherland has done, that a group with a high crime rate is organized for crime at the same time that it is organized against crime. Whether the crime rate is high or low depends upon the degree to which the organized system for presenting anticriminal behavior patterns is counteracted by the organized system for presenting criminal behavior patterns. In some groups, many persons are presented with an excess of criminal behavior patterns even if the group also is organized against crime.

In some nonliterate and peasant societies, the influences surrounding a person are relatively steady, uniform, harmonious, and consistent. "Society" and "family" are almost synonymous, so that the individual's career and ambitions are ascribed to him in much the way that an American family ascribes age and sex status. But in contemporary America, no such consistency and uniformity is present. Standards of conduct in one group often are extremely different from those in another group. Since crime persists despite the fact that the law-abiding culture is the dominant and more extensive one, it may be viewed as a consequence of social disorganization or unorganization. However, the social conditions in which the influences on a person are relatively inharmonious and inconsistent are themselves a kind of social organization,[83] and there are wide variations in the degree of normative conflict—the situation in which both anticriminal and criminal behavior patterns are presented. Since the rates of criminality vary with the degree of normative conflict, they can be attributed to differential social organization.

This theory of differential association and differential social organi-

---

[83] See Sutherland, *White-Collar Crime*, pp. 253-56.

zation makes understandable most of the variations in crime rates previously described. The high rates among Negroes, among working-class persons, and among young males, for example, are attributed to criminalistic traditions existing in those groups, in opposition to anticriminalistic traditions. Not all Negroes, working-class persons, etc., become criminals because some are presented with an excess of anticriminal behavior patterns, but the *chances* of being presented with an excess of criminal behavior patterns are better if one is a Negro, a member of the working class, a young male, an urban dweller, and a native American than they are if one is white, middle-class, old, a rural resident, or an immigrant. In Sutherland's words:

> Persons become criminals principally because they have been relatively isolated from the culture of law-abiding groups, by reason of their residence, employment, codes, native capacities or something else, or else have been in relatively frequent contact with a rival criminal culture. Consequently, they are lacking in the experiences, feelings, ideas, and attitudes out of which to construct a life organization that the law-abiding public will regard as desirable.[84]

This theory has frequently been criticized on the ground that it does not explain why persons have the associations they have. Sutherland replied that determining why persons have the associations they have is a desirable problem for research, but the fact that the theory of differential association does not pretend to do so cannot be considered a weakness in the theory:

> It is not necessary, at this level of explanation, to explain why a person has the associations he has; this certainly involves a complex of things. In an area where the delinquency rate is high a boy who is sociable, gregarious, active, and athletic is very likely to come in contact with the other boys in the neighborhood, learn delinquent behavior from them, and become a gangster; in the same neighborhood the psychopathic boy who is isolated, introverted, and inert may remain at home, not become acquainted with the other boys in the neighborhood, and not become delinquent. In another situation, the sociable, athletic, aggressive boy may become a member of a scout troop and not become involved in delinquent behavior. The person's associations are determined in the general context of social organization.[85]

A second major effort to formulate a general theory of criminality has been made by Thorsten Sellin. His theory, like Sutherland's, stresses the importance of conflicts between conduct norms or, more

---

[84] Sutherland and Cressey, *Principles of Criminology*, p. 323.
[85] *Ibid.*, p. 79.

generally, culture conflict.[86] He proposes that sociologists should not confine their attention to crime and criminals but should, instead, study the conflicts of conduct norms that exist when divergent rules of conduct govern the specific life situation in which a person may find himself. These rules "prohibit and conversely enjoin specific types of persons, as defined by their status in (or with reference to) the normative group, from acting in a certain specified way in certain circumstances." Conduct norms arise as a group reaction to conduct not in the interests of the social group, acquiring validity when they are incorporated into the personalities of the group members. Hence, the differentiation of the personality structure or the growth process of the violator as opposed to that of the conformist should be an important function of research on crime causation.

Both criminality and noncriminality of individual persons are attributable to the kinds of conduct norms which have been learned. But learning of divergent conduct norms presupposes the existence of a society in which the conduct norms of one group are in conflict with the conduct norms of another. Thus, the condition of "culture conflict" underlies a condition of high crime rates, for it is only when there is culture conflict that persons can learn conduct norms which permit the reaction to some situations to be one of criminality:

> Every person is identified with a number of social groups, each meeting some biologically-conditioned or socially-created need. Each of these groups is normative in the sense that within it there grow up norms of conduct applicable to situations created by that group's specific activities. As a member of a given group, a person is not only supposed to conform to the rules which it shares with other groups, but also to those which are peculiarly its own. A person who as a member of a family group—in turn the transmitting agency for the norms which governed the groups from which the parents came—possesses all its norms pertaining to conduct in routine life situations, may also as a member of a play group, a work group, a political group, a religious group, etc., acquire norms which regulate specialized life situations and which sustain, weaken, or even contradict the norms earlier incorporated in his personality. The more complex a culture becomes, the more likely it is that the number of normative groups which affect a person will be large, and the greater is the chance that the norms of these groups will fail to agree, no matter how much they may overlap as a result of common acceptance of certain norms. A conflict of norms is said to exist when more or less divergent rules of conduct govern the specific life situation in which a person may find himself. The conduct norm of one group of which he is a part may

---

[86] Thorsten Sellin, *Culture Conflict and Crime* (New York: Social Science Research Council, 1938), pp. 20-40.

permit one response to this situation, the norm of another group may permit perhaps the very opposite response.[87]

This culture conflict theory explains variations in the crime rates of various groups in terms very similar to those used by Sutherland. High or low crime rates depend upon the ratio of essentially pro-criminal and essentially anticriminal conduct norms in the situation.

The theoretical system developed by Donald R. Taft also has assumed a distinct deterministic position, and it contains a strong cultural emphasis.[88] Where the theories of Sutherland and Sellin stress the importance of transmission of criminal and delinquent behavior patterns from one person to another, Taft's theory extends beyond the individual and his personal groups to the broader culture of a people. Thus, he is concerned more with the problem of explaining why one nation has a high crime rate compared to another nation, than with the problem of which persons in the nation are criminals. Criminality is a product of culture. American culture is characterized by relatively high crime rates, and it also is characterized by conditions and processes which are "criminogenic" in their influence. Among these are the culture's dynamic, complex, and materialistic qualities, the tradition of the frontier, the breakdown of primary group relationships, political corruption and inefficiency, and others. Taft summarizes his theory as follows:

> Given a culture dynamic, complex, materialistic, admiring the successful in a competitive struggle but permitting many to fall short of success, relative failures will collect in its slums and there develop patterns of behavior hostile to the interests of the general community, but in harmony with the community's basic ideals. Assume such a society nominally approving democracy, but nevertheless in practice rating its members not because of their individual virtues but because of their accidental membership in not-all-inclusive social groups such as races, classes, nationalities or cliques. Destroy in such a culture primary group controls which prevent serious departure from approved traditional patterns. Develop in such a culture, through processes of social change, a confusion of tongues in definitions of morality, hypocritical rationalizations as to contrasts between the criminal and the noncriminal, the dangerous and the nondangerous. Permit white-collar criminals to receive but mild punishment and no loss of status. Permit also gigantic social swindles and injuries to the body politic to go unpunished while no more serious injuries, classed and treated as crime, result in severe punishment. Provide that often

---

[87] *Ibid.*, p. 130.

[88] Donald R. Taft, *Criminology*, 3rd ed. (New York: Macmillan, 1956), pp. 336-49.

the power of the fix or the fear of political loss to those in power shall permit escape from punishment. Assume in this culture a holdover of frontier traditions involving approval of the use of force, and mob action by "respectable" groups against those who oppose their interests or arouse their hostile prejudices. Grant the prevalence in that society of Puritanical traditions preventing the legal or "moral" expression of basic sex and other drives—traditions to which lip service continues to be given long after large minorities, at least, cease to follow them in their behavior. Create thus a gulf between precept and practice. Give prestige and important pattern-setting roles in that society to groups with rather unsocially oriented values which not infrequently are exploitative.

Assume, in spite of this, a great faith in law as being effective to regulate behavior so that the scope of the law is extended to forbid satisfactions that are in wide demand. Observe in such a culture, not only a competitive spirit and exploitation tending to restrict what one's fellows shall "earn," but tendencies to strive through gambling and other nonsocial practices to obtain something for nothing. Involve in this situation important social institutions of family and church so that the sincerity and moral significance of their influence is brought into question. Make education there subservient to preparation for participation in competitive nonsocial activities, rather than furthering the socialization of children. Develop there newspapers, commercialized entertainments, radio, television, and other agencies of communication and enjoyment through which the values of a competitive society may be propagated and the interests of minorities promoted. In such a culture there will be considerable conflict, often in the form of crime. The effort to make the punished feel unusual shame over their behavior, rather than mere regret that they were caught, will be ineffective. Under such conditions, indeed, the very process of punishment will appear to the punished as further evidence of discriminating exploitation. It will tend to embitter rather than reform them.

Such a culture will undoubtedly have a different behavior significance for the slum dwellers than for those who live on the boulevard, for the child from the broken home than for the child in the whole home. It may also impinge somewhat differently upon the emotionally unstable and upon the emotionally stable, upon the dull than upon the intelligent. But these differences will merely determine *the form* or degree of their exploitative behavior. "No-collar" crime, white-collar crime, and noncriminal exploitation will all tend to reflect criminogenic elements in the general culture. By and large, it is our contention, such a culture must expect considerable crime which can be attributed basically to its own inherent qualities. In this sense we get the criminals we deserve.[89]

---

[89] From Donald R. Taft, *Criminology* (New York: Macmillan, 1956), pp. 341-42. Reprinted by permission of the publisher.

According to this theory, variations in crime rates among different groups are attributable to the differential impact of the criminogenic culture on those groups. Thus, it explains that the excess of male over female crime is due to the relative protection of women from the stresses of active, competitive, economic life, to different moral codes, and to different social roles.[90] More generally, relative economic welfare, relative isolation from competition, families that give security and affection, etc., will isolate individuals from the criminogenic culture and will, thus, keep crime rates low in some groups.[91]

Robert K. Merton has developed a theory which, like Taft's, is concerned more with explaining differing rates of crime in various strata and groups within a society than with the problem of explaining which persons in a stratum or group will become criminals. The theory is part of a more general theory of deviant behavior, which need not be discussed here.[92] Of relevance is the idea that high crime rates are a reflection of the situation in which a society places great emphasis upon the goal of individual "success"—for example, the attainment of wealth and property—while effectively blocking, for some part of the population, the paths to achievement of that goal. In this situation, the generally approved "rules of the game" may be known to those who evade them, but the emotional supports which accompany conformity to the law are offset by the stress placed on achieving success. In Merton's words:

> . . . when a system of cultural values extols, virtually above all else, certain *common* success-goals for the population at large while the social structure rigorously restricts or completely closes access to approved modes of reaching these goals *for a considerable part of the population,* deviant behavior ensues on a large scale.[93]

Thus, it is maintained that in America there is a conflict between the values stressing success and the values which make achievement of success an impossibility for some, and that this conflict results in high crime rates. The theory contains three basic propositions.[94] (1)

---

[90] *Ibid.,* p. 115.

[91] *Ibid.,* pp. 338-40, 754-55.

[92] Robert K. Merton, "Social Structure and Anomie," *American Sociological Review,* Vol. 3 (October, 1938), pp. 677-82. This article has been revised and enlarged, and it now appears in Robert K. Merton, *Social Theory and Social Structure,* rev. ed. (New York: Free Press, 1957), pp. 161-94.

[93] *Ibid.,* p. 180.

[94] See Donald R. Cressey, "Criminal and Delinquent Behavior," in Leonard Broom and Philip Selznick, *Sociology: A Text with Adapted Readings,* 2nd ed. (Evanston, Ill.: Row, Peterson, 1958), Chapter 15, pp. 609-10.

Values emphasizing achievement of wealth are characteristic of American culture, and the goal of "success" is held by persons of all social classes. (2) Values in reference to the legal means for achieving this goal are such that "success" is effectively denied to many members of the lower classes. (3) This conflict leads to frequent efforts among the lower classes to achieve success by illegal means.

In America, it is emphasized, the desire for symbols of luxury, ease, and success has spread to all classes, and the doctrine of equality means that each man is to compete against all comers for these symbols, even if his social and economic status puts him at considerable disadvantage when the competition is carried out within the law. One result is a criminal subculture in which emphasis is placed on achievement of success by any means whatever, and another is a similar subculture in which the values are turned upside down, so that emphasis is placed on destruction of property rather than on acquisition of it.[95] Neither result may appear in a society in which the notion that "anyone can be successful" is not shared by considerable proportions of the population. When peasants and members of the working class have learned to live according to the economic standards of their fathers and grandfathers, and when members of an elite, rich, or "noble" class have learned to live, and are expected to live, according to the economic standards of *their* ancestors, then one of the requisite conditions for high crime rates among the peasants and working class is missing. These groups do not have the same aspirations for "success" that American groups do, and their crime rate is correspondingly low.

This theory best explains the overrepresentation of working-class persons in the criminal population of the United States, but it also makes good sense of the overrepresentation of young males, Negroes, native Americans, and urban dwellers. Each group can be viewed as sharing the goal of success but, at the same time, experiencing more frustrations in achieving that goal than does the group with which it is compared. The theory does not purport to explain why only some of the members of the deprived population commit crimes; it is concerned with the origins of the criminal subculture and with gross variations in crime rates. Even in a society disproportionately stressing the goal of success for all persons, most persons who are denied the legal means for achieving the goal do not use illegal means for achieving it. As Merton indicates in his broader theory, some persons react by "retreating"—denying the value of success. McKay has stressed the notion that in a multi-group type of social organization, alternative

---

[95] Cohen, *Delinquent Boys.*

and inconsistent standards of conduct are possessed by various groups, so that an individual who is a member of one group learns to use legal means for achieving the success goal, or learns to deny the importance of success, while an individual who is a member of another group learns to accept the importance of success and to achieve it by illegal means. Such groups exist even among the lower social classes and other populations whose path to success is generally blocked. Stated in another way, in deprived populations there are alternative educational processes in operation, varying with groups, so that a person may be educated in either conventional or criminal means of achieving success.[96] Cloward has shown that even illegal means are not available to everyone; some persons may be "double failures," in the sense that neither legal nor illegal means for achieving success are available to them.[97]

The above theories, like most of the theoretical work in criminology, are directed at explanation of crime in general. But crime in general consists of a great variety of criminal acts, ranging from traffic violations to embezzlement, robbery, and murder. Except for the fact that all such acts are violations of law, they may have very little in common. The techniques are different, the victims are different, the resulting harms are different, the reactions of the public are different, and the motives and characteristics of the criminals are different. Consequently, a theory which explains all of them must necessarily be quite general in nature. Such general theory is desirable because it organizes, integrates, and makes sense of the factual data on crime and criminals. But it also is desirable to break crime down into homogeneous units and develop theories to explain each unit.[98] In this sense, explanation of crime is like explanation of disease. A theory purporting to explain all disease must be quite general, but it is quite useful in understanding the origin and transmission of illness. Nevertheless, even general theories of disease, like the "germ theory," do not apply to all diseases, and theories about specific diseases have been

---

[96] Henry D. McKay, "The Neighborhood and Child Conduct," *Annals of the American Academy of Political and Social Science,* Vol. 261 (January, 1949), pp. 32-42. See also South Side Community Committee, *Bright Shadows in Bronzetown* (Chicago: The Committee, 1949), pp. 26-28. See also Richard A. Cloward and Lloyd E. Ohlin, *Delinquency and Opportunity* (New York: Free Press, 1960).

[97] Richard A. Cloward, "Illegitimate Means, Anomie, and Deviant Behavior," *American Sociological Review,* Vol. 24 (April, 1959), pp. 164-76.

[98] See Don C. Gibbons and Donald L. Garrity, "Some Suggestions for the Development of Etiological and Treatment Theory in Criminology," *Social Forces,* Vol. 38 (October, 1959), pp. 51-58.

developed to supplement them. Similarly, in studying crime it is desirable to supplement general theories with theories about specific units within the broad area of crime and about specific units within the legal definitions of types of crime such as embezzlement, robbery, and murder. Important theories of this kind have recently been developed to explain forgery, vandalism, the criminal violation of financial trust, professional theft, and white-collar crime.[99] General theories about criminal behavior as a whole should guide the research and theory directed at explaining particular kinds of criminal behavior, and studies of particular kinds of criminal behavior should lead to either strengthening or modifying the general theories. If no one general theory can explain all criminal behavior, then it is desirable to define precisely the areas to which it does apply, so that several congruous theories will, when taken together, explain all crime.

The Rehabilitation of Criminals [100]

General policies for dealing with lawbreakers may be considered as "societal reactions to criminality," for they are the corporate responses of the society to violation of its legal norms. (See Chapter 2, page 126.) Such reactions of societies to lawbreaking have varied tremendously from time to time. At one time the reaction was essentially punitive, at another time nonpunitive; at one time punishments were frequent and severe, at another time infrequent and mild; at one time punishment was predominantly corporal, at another time it was a certain kind of imprisonment or a fine. The societal reactions may be classified on a scale ranging from "purely punitive" to "purely nonpunitive." Although this kind of scale does not summarize all the variations, some societal reactions to crime, and hence some policies for rehabilitating criminals, have been directed primarily by punitive

---

[99] Edwin M. Lemert, "An Isolation and Closure Theory of Naïve Check Forgery," *Journal of Criminal Law and Criminology,* Vol. 44 (September-October, 1953), pp. 296-307. Marshall B. Clinard and Andrew L. Wade, "Toward the Delineation of Vandalism as a Subtype in Juvenile Delinquency," *Journal of Criminal Law and Criminology,* Vol. 48 (January, 1958), pp. 493-99. Cohen, *Delinquent Boys.* Donald R. Cressey, *Other People's Money* (New York: Free Press, 1953). Edwin H. Sutherland, *The Professional Thief* (Chicago: University of Chicago Press, 1937). Vilhelm Aubert, "White-Collar Crime and Social Structure," *American Journal of Sociology,* Vol. 58 (November, 1952), pp. 263-71.

[100] Parts of this section are adapted from Donald R. Cressey, "Hypotheses in the Sociology of Punishment," *Sociology and Social Research,* Vol. 39 (July-August, 1955), pp. 394-400; and "The Nature and Effectiveness of Correctional Techniques," *Law and Contemporary Problems,* Vol. 23 (Autumn, 1958), pp. 754-71.

considerations, others by nonpunitive treatment considerations, and a final category by a mixture of punitive and treatment considerations. We shall look first at some of the hypotheses which have been developed to explain general variations in the punitive reaction to lawbreaking, and then we shall examine the nature and effectiveness of the rehabilitation techniques used to implement the official reactions to crime in contemporary American society.

The Sociology of Punishment

The general problem in the sociology of punishment is not unlike the general problem in the study of criminality itself. The problem can be summarized by the question: why does the punitive reaction to crime vary from time to time and from place to place? An efficient answer to this question would correlate variations in the punitive reaction to lawbreaking with variations in social organization and would then account for the correlations in terms of a theoretical generalization. Here, we will only report on the theories and will not consider in detail the statistical studies which have shown the degree to which variations in the societal reaction to crime are correlated with various aspects of social organization. The attempts to give a complete answer to the question we have posed have utilized cultural, psychoanalytic, and sociological concepts.

One theory, stated by Sutherland, accounts for the many variations in the presence of the punitive reaction to lawbreaking in terms of "cultural consistency." [101] The general point is that societal reactions to crime show a tendency to be consistent with other ways of behaving in a society. For example, two centuries ago physical suffering was regarded as the natural lot of mankind, and the means of preventing pain and suffering were not well developed; it was at this time that attempts to rehabilitate criminals took the form of torture, mutilation, and degradation. Similarly, when societies were without the price system in their economic systems they also were without it in dealing with criminals; as the price system developed, monetary implications were incorporated into the societal reaction to crime, so that prisoners were viewed as "paying the price," or "owing a debt to society." Also, penalties tend to be more severe for acts that endanger the values that are highly regarded in a society, and when these values change, the societal reaction to violation changes.

A second theory, advanced by psychoanalysts, correlates variations in societal reactions to crime with variations in alternative systems for

---

[101] Sutherland and Cressey, *Principles of Criminology*, pp. 298-301.

satisfying aggressive and libidinal instincts. This may be termed a "scapegoat" theory, for the general point is that mankind possesses certain instincts which, though they are opposed to societal norms, must nevertheless be expressed, and that the criminal often serves as a scapegoat for their expression. Whether societal reactions will be punitive or nonpunitive depends upon the availability of alternative channels through which the libidinal and aggressive urges can be expressed. Thus, it has been held that in societies where the social prohibitions against sexual behavior are few and lax, the reaction to crime is nonpunitive, while in societies where sex and sexuality are declaimed against, the reaction to criminality is punitive.[102] Similarly, it has been argued that enemies in war are alternatives to criminals as scapegoats for expression of aggressive instincts,[103] and this would imply that in warring societies the reactions to crime would be nonpunitive, while in peaceful societies they would be punitive.

Third, a few social scientists, largely European, have attempted to relate variations in societal reactions to crime to variations in certain aspects of social structures. One such theory holds that the societal reaction to crime is much affected, if not determined, by the general economic conditions of a society. Rusch, for example, advanced the thesis that when the labor market is glutted and labor therefore cheap, the societal reaction is punitive, but, when the labor supply is scarce and labor therefore at a premium, the reaction is nonpunitive or only partially punitive.[104] Another theory relates variations in the societal reactions to crime to the presence of the lower middle class. The general notion is that the punitive reaction to crime is present when there is a "petite bourgeoisie" or "lower middle class," and that this reaction does not prevail in societies where that social class is of little significance.[105] Still another social structure theory attributes general variations in the punitive reaction to changes in the division of labor in society. The basic notion here is that when a society has mechanical solidarity, a solidarity based not upon division of labor but upon similarity of behavior and attitudes, the reaction to legal wrongs is punitive, but in societies whose solidarity is organic, a solidarity based

---

[102] Charles Berg, "The Psychology of Punishment," *British Journal of Medical Psychology,* Vol. 20 (October, 1945), pp. 295-313.

[103] Paul Riewald, *Society and Its Criminals* (New York: International Universities Press, 1950), p. 235. See also F. Alexander and H. Staub, *The Criminal, the Judge, and the Public,* rev. ed. (New York: Free Press, 1956), pp. 213-23.

[104] George Rusch and Otto Kirchheimer, *Punishment and Social Structure* (New York: Columbia University Press, 1939).

[105] Svend Ranulf, *Moral Indignation and Middle-Class Psychology: A Sociological Study* (Copenhagen: Levin and Munksgaard, 1938), p. 198.

upon specialization or division of labor, the reaction is restitutive or nonpunitive.[106] A final theory of this kind is stated in terms of the homogeneity and heterogeneity of societies and may be termed a theory of "social disorganization." Here, the basic notion is that in homogeneous societies the reaction to crime is nonpunitive, but in heterogeneous societies the reaction is punitive. Various indexes of homogeneity and heterogeneity have been used. Sorokin, for example, refers to "ethico-juridical heterogeneity and antagonism" of social groups and argues that when this heterogeneity is present, the reaction to criminality is punitive.[107] Znaniecki considers the variations in the presence of "insiders" and "outsiders" in societies and makes the point that when a society is homogeneous, the reaction to the crimes of outsiders is punitive; but in heterogeneous societies the distinction between insiders and outsiders is not easily made, so the reaction to crime is sometimes punitive, sometimes nonpunitive, and sometimes a mixture of the two.[108]

The Effectiveness of Rehabilitation Techniques

Closely allied to the problem of accounting for variations in the punitive reaction to crime is that of explaining variations in the use of specific methods of implementing both the punitive and nonpunitive reactions. Although it has not always been so, at present these specific methods are called "rehabilitation techniques." Two principal conceptions of rehabilitation techniques are found. One considers the techniques to be those general systems and programs used for handling criminals and assumed to be reformative. Probation, parole, and imprisonment are examples of such programs. They were introduced into American judicial procedures at least in part because it was assumed that doing so would help rehabilitate a larger number of criminals. The second conception of rehabilitation techniques places more emphasis upon the specific methods used in attempts to change individual criminals into noncriminals. Thus, within a probation or parole agency, workers may help prisoners find jobs and counsel them on psychological problems of adjustment. Similarly, prison inmates may be enrolled in schools, given vocational counseling and training, or engaged in individual or group psychotherapeutic interviews. Each of these ma-

---

[106] Émile Durkheim, *The Division of Labor in Society*, trans. by George Simpson (New York: Free Press, 1947).

[107] Pitirim A. Sorokin, *Social and Cultural Dynamics* (New York: American Book, 1937), Vol. 2, p. 595.

[108] F. Znaniecki, *Social Actions* (New York: Farrar and Rinehart, 1936), p. 376.

neuvers is designed to help criminals become noncriminals, and, thus, each is viewed as rehabilitative. An analogy with clinical medicine is made, so that utilizing such techniques is called "treatment" or "therapy."

GENERAL PROGRAMS. The principal societal reaction to criminality in the United States has always been punitive. Punishment for criminals is pain or suffering intentionally inflicted by the state because of some value the pain or suffering is assumed to have. We have assumed that one value stemming from infliction of pain on offenders is reformation or, in the newer terminology, "rehabilitation" or "correction" of those offenders. Other values, such as deterrence (punishment of criminals will frighten noncriminals so that they will not commit crimes), also are assumed. But it is the idea that punishment reforms that makes the infliction of pain a rehabilitation technique in the broadest sense of the term. As indicated, the general programs used for implementing the punitive reaction to crime also have been viewed as rehabilitative devices. Physical torture, social degradation, restriction of wealth, and restriction of freedom are among the programs used for inflicting pain on criminals. At present, the most popular technique of this sort for dealing with serious offenders is restriction of liberty (imprisonment).

As a general program for dealing with criminals, the prison performs an integrating function for society. This function is assumed to have two principal aspects. First, the prison is expected to restore society to the state of equilibrium and harmony it was in before the crime was committed. "Undesirables," "deviants," "nonconformists," and "outlaws" (all synonyms for criminals) are segregated behind walls so that they cannot disrupt society's peace and harmony at least during a specified period. Second, the prison is expected to contribute to social integration by reducing the frequency of occurrence of future crimes. It is assumed that this aspect of the prison's integrative function is performed in two ways. (1) Crime rates are kept low both by the deterrent effects of imprisonment and by the effect that imprisoning men has on reinforcing the anticriminal values of the society doing the imprisoning.[109] (2) Imprisonment reduces crime rates by changing criminals into noncriminals. It is this last goal of prisons that gives imprisonment, as a general program, the character of a rehabilitation technique.

It must be emphasized that support for continuing the punitive reaction to crime or for specifically implementing this reaction by

---

[109] Durkheim, *The Division of Labor,* pp. 70-110.

imprisonment is always based on some value which punishment generally or the specific kind of punishment inflicted by the fact of imprisonment is *assumed* to have. We do not *know* that imprisoning men deters others, reinforces anticriminal values, corrects criminals, or in some other way promotes social solidarity. However, neither do we *know* that inflicting pain by imprisonment or some other means is an *inefficient* system for maintaining, or restoring, social integration.

SPECIFIC METHODS. Statements about the effectiveness of specific procedures for rehabilitating criminals are subject to reservations identical to those that must be placed on statements about broader systems and programs. Currently, many correctional workers assume that any real rehabilitation technique is nonpunitive in nature.[110] Saying that a technique is "rehabilitative" or "therapeutic" is, then, a shorthand way of saying that those who use the technique do not make the traditional assumption that inflicting pain on criminals will rehabilitate them. For example, psychotherapy, vocational education, and counseling are considered rehabilitative principally because they are nonpunitive. But we cannot be sure that any nonpunitive rehabilitation technique of this kind is either more or less efficient than were older punitive devices such as "teaching discipline," "breaking the will," and "instilling fear of the law."

TWO PRINCIPLES FOR REHABILITATING CRIMINALS. If the work of rehabilitating criminals were scientific, we would be reasonably sure that men commit crime in certain circumstances and not in others, and then would set out to modify these circumstances. Use of each rehabilitative technique over a period of time would be an experiment designed to test a theory of crime causation. However, the various techniques currently in use were not derived from precise statements of criminological theory and cannot, therefore, be considered tests of such theory. Yet some of the rehabilitative techniques being used by probation, prison, and parole workers are fairly consistent with standard theories of personality, crime causation, and rehabilitation. Among these workers, there are two general and popular, but contradictory, principles for the rehabilitation of criminals. These two principles—the "group-relations principle" and the "clinical principle"—are, in effect, theories of rehabilitation. Some rehabilitation techniques are somewhat consistent with one or the other of them, some with both, and some with neither. The two principles are the logical outgrowths of two alternative kinds of theory about crime causation. These the-

---

110 See Donald R. Cressey, "Professional Correctional Work and Professional Work in Correction," *National Probation and Parole Association Journal,* Vol. 5 (January, 1959), pp. 1-15.

ories of crime causation, in turn, are applications explaining a specific kind of behavior (criminality) of two even more general theories treating the connection between personality and social relationships. We shall briefly identify the two theories of personality and the two criminological theories and then shall proceed to the two principles of reformation.

Stanton and Schwartz have summarized the observation, made by many sociologists, that social scientists at one pole think of the "organization" of social interaction and of "personality" as two facets of the same thing.[111] The person is viewed as a product of the kinds of social relationships and values in which he participates; he obtains his satisfactions and, in fact, his essence, from participation in the rituals, rules, schedules, customs, and regulations of various kinds which surround him. Moreover, the person (personality) is not separable from the social relationships in which he lives. He behaves according to the rules (which are sometimes contradictory) of the large organization, called "society," in which he participates; he cannot behave any other way.

On the other hand, social scientists at the opposite pole think of the individual as essentially autonomous, and they consider his interaction with rules and regulations of society and other organizations as *submission* rather than participation. "Personality" is an outgrowth of the effect that the "restrictions" necessary to organization have on an individual's expression of his own pristine needs. These social scientists emphasize "individual self-determination" and make a distinction between the "real" or "natural" part of the person and the "spurious," "artificial," or "consensual" part. The former is viewed as primary, free, and spontaneous; the latter (obtained from the social relationships making up society) is formal, secondary, and restrictive.

Certainly the two theories of the relationship between personality and culture are more complex than this simple statement implies, and few social scientists maintain one or the other of them exclusively and with no qualifications. But these two ideas have made their way into correctional work and have become the basis of correctional techniques.

Consistent with the first general theory is criminological theory that maintains, in essence, that criminality is behavior which the person in question has appropriated from the social relationships in which he has been participating. Crime, like other behaviors, attitudes, beliefs,

---

[111] Alfred H. Stanton and Morris S. Schwartz, *The Mental Hospital* (New York: Basic Books, 1954), pp. 37-38.

and values which a person exhibits, is the *property of groups,* not of individuals.[112] Criminality is not just the product of an individual's contacts with certain kinds of groups; it is, in a very real sense, behavior which is "owned" by groups rather than by individuals.

Consistent with the second general theory of personality is criminological theory maintaining, essentially, that criminality is a personal trait or characteristic of the person exhibiting the behavior. An extreme position is, as we have seen, that criminality is a biological phenomenon. Much more popular is the theoretical position that criminality is a psychological defect or disorder, or a "symptom" of either. Here, criminality is considered the *property of the individual* criminal exhibiting it. The principal point is that a "healthy" or "adjusted" personality is one that does not own criminality because it has been permitted to express itself freely in numerous alternative ways.

The *group-relations principle* for rehabilitating criminals is based on the first kind of theory about the relationship between personality and culture and on the first kind of criminological theory. It holds that attempts to change the criminal behavior of a person must be directed at modification of the groups owning the behavior. If the behavior of a man is an intrinsic part of the groups to which he belongs, then attempts to change that behavior will succeed only if the groups are somehow modified. Many rehabilitation practices and programs arising in the last century have been indirectly, at least, consistent with this principle. Among the more general programs which are consistent with it are probation and parole, where the offender's prison sentence is suspended (probation) or shortened (parole) so that he can be integrated into sets of social relationships in which criminality as a way of life is truly taboo. Similarly, even imprisonment may be viewed as a system for attempting to force criminals to become members of organizations which do not own criminality, but, instead, own anticriminal behavior.

Within probation and parole systems, a precise scientific technique which is consistent with the group-relations principle has yet to be invented. Rather than descriptions of techniques, we find statements that the individual is to be rehabilitated by "gaining his confidence

---

[112] See Dorwin Cartwright, "Achieving Change in People: Some Applications of Group Dynamics Theory," *Human Relations,* Vol. 4 (1951), pp. 381-92; Donald R. Cressey, "Changing Criminals: The Application of the Theory of Differential Association," *American Journal of Sociology,* Vol. 61 (September, 1955), pp. 116-20; and Rita Volkman and Donald R. Cressey, "Differential Association and the Rehabilitation of Drug Addicts," *American Journal of Sociology,* Vol. 69 (September, 1963), pp. 129-42.

and friendship," "stimulating his self-respect," "manipulating his environment," "providing a supportive atmosphere," or "changing his group relations." The same difficulty arises in connection with techniques used within prisons. Academic and vocational education are consistent with the group-relations principle to the extent that they are directed toward changing the offender's postinstitutional group relationships. Conceivably, this is successful in some cases. A popular but apparently fallacious assumption is that taking an educational course, such as eighth-grade arithmetic, should make bad citizens (prisoners) good ones, because passing through such courses is a characteristic of good citizens. But perhaps such courses are rehabilitative only to the degree that they change inmates' postrelease associations.

Individual and group psychotherapy are rapidly becoming popular rehabilitative devices, both in prisons and in probation and parole agencies. In individual psychotherapy, the psychological needs of individual criminals are of primary consideration, and the usual assumption is that correction of any psychological disorder or problem the criminal may have will change his criminality. Alternatively, adherents of the group-relations principle assume that individual psychotherapy is effective in changing criminality to the extent that it serves as a stimulant or inducement to changes in social relationships. The criminal's psychological problems may be relieved, but this has little or no effect on his reformation unless his relationships with groups owning the criminality he has been exhibiting are modified. Group therapy as a rehabilitative technique is not necessarily consistent with the group-relations principle. Rather, a popular assumption is that group therapy, like individual therapy, rehabilitates criminals by correcting their individual psychological disorders.[113] Criminals participate in group discussions, guided by a therapist, so as to satisfy their individual needs or to rid themselves of undesirable psychological problems. But the group-relations principle implies that for rehabilitating criminals there must be more than this—there must be opportunities for integration into groups that own an abundance of anticriminal values and behavior patterns. Thus, interaction in a clinical group might be effective as a rehabilitation technique to the extent that it gives the criminal participant experience in the role of a law-abiding person and to the extent that these experiences carry over to affect the kind of group relations the participant experiences when he becomes an ex-convict.

The *clinical principle* for rehabilitating criminals is consistent with

---

[113] Donald R. Cressey, "Contradictory Theories in Correctional Group Therapy Programs," *Federal Probation*, Vol. 18 (June, 1954), pp. 20-24.

the second type of theory about personality and the second kind of criminological theory. If criminality is an individual disorder, then, like a biological disease, it should be corrected on a clinical basis. Consistent with the most extreme position is the notion that the criminal's anatomy or physiology is to be modified through lobotomy, castration, modification of glandular functioning, or something else of like kind. Much more popular is the theory that individual disorders producing criminality are psychological and are, therefore, to be corrected through psychological attention. But in either case, the implication is that criminality should be corrected or treated clinically. In a sense, criminality is viewed as analogous to an infectious disease like syphilis —while group relationships of various kinds are necessary to the disorder, the disorder can be eradicated in a clinic, without reference to the conditions under which it was acquired. Because criminality is an expression of individual psychological disorders, it is to be corrected by elimination of the disorders. But because the disorders, in turn, spring from the restrictions society has placed on "free" individuals, correction of them must be in the form of modifying the impact of the restrictions on the individual. Although this might have reformation of society as one of its implications, individual criminals are to be corrected by giving them relief from the restrictions—in the form of "ventilation," "catharsis," "acting out," and other devices for removing "tensions," "aggression," "unconscious tendencies and wishes," and other individual disorders. Many of the rehabilitation techniques and programs arising in recent times have been indirectly consistent with this principle, as well as with the group-relations principle.

Probation and parole, as general programs, permit criminals more freedom than is possible if they are imprisoned, and, therefore, these systems reduce the intensity of the war between the individual and his society. Since criminality is an outgrowth of "undue" restriction of the individual by society, it is not logical to restrict the criminal further in attempts to correct him. Probation and parole are, then, rehabilitative, even if they are only less restrictive than imprisonment. Similarly, in recent years, adherents of the clinical principle have emphasized the importance of making the prison itself less restrictive than formerly, presumably on the assumption that a "relaxed discipline" or "therapeutic climate" will enable inmates better to "act out" and in other ways adjust to the restrictions of society.

As is the case with the group-relations principle, scientific techniques for implementing the clinical principle within probation and parole systems have not been invented. We learn that offenders are to "gain insight," "relieve emotional tensions," "sublimate," and so on; but we do not know precisely how this is to be done. Similarly, we must know how, or whether, these processes change criminals into noncriminals. Even if we had a precise technique for ridding criminals of emotional tensions, for example, this technique might have little to do with changing their criminality.

Most of the rehabilitative techniques used in prisons are consistent with the clinical principle only in very indirect ways. Perhaps academic and vocational education courses are effective rehabilitative techniques only to the extent that they permit the individual criminal to express himself, sublimate antisocial tendencies, or escape from the restrictions on uneducated persons. It is not sufficient merely to implant knowledge or vocational skills; the education in a few cases might be effective because it alleviates, partially, the criminal's personal psychological problems.

Individual and group therapy are consistent with the clinical principle, and they have been introduced into rehabilitative work by advocates of the second type of personality theory and criminological theory. Individual psychotherapy, as a system for rehabilitating criminals, is perhaps the best example of a current rehabilitative technique based on the clinical principle. Both group therapy and individual therapy enable the participants to "get beneath the surface," "adjust to reality," identify their individual traits in terms such as "resentment of authority," "feelings of guilt," "frustration," and "Oedipus complex," and to dissipate the tensions and anxieties arising from such traits.

CONCLUSION. The foregoing discussion leads to the conclusion that most of the techniques used in rehabilitating criminals are only very indirectly related to standard theories of crime causation. To a degree, this is a consequence of the kinds of theories we have. However, there also is a problem of putting the theories into practice. Many techniques consistent with the group-relations principle and the theory on which it is based could not be implemented in a society where prison and parole workers, like other men, work only an eight-hour day and a forty-hour week. And many of the "diagnoses" which are consistent with the clinical principle and its theory call for techniques and programs which no parole agency or prison could possibly afford.

4

Drug Addiction

by John A. Clausen

DRUG ADDICTION ENTAILS BOTH A PSYCHOLOGICAL AND A PHYSIOLOGI-
cal reaction to a chemical substance consumed or used to produce
pleasurable effects or to avoid pain and discomfort. The use of narcotic drugs is enmeshed in social ritual. But in the United States the
nonmedical use of narcotics is hardly a matter of conventional sociability; it is a crime, and one of the most stigmatized of crimes at that.
The mere possession of any of the opiates—opium, morphine, heroin,
dilaudid, and so on—or of marihuana, cocaine, or several other drugs,
except as these are handled within strictly regulated medical-pharma-
ceutical channels, is a violation of federal and state laws.

Drug addiction is not a widespread or pervasive problem in Western society, as are delinquency, crime, and mental illness. Even in
the United States, which has more addicts than all of Europe, there
are probably fewer than 60,000 persons addicted to drugs other than
alcohol (as against an estimated 5,000,000 alcoholics). Yet the nature
of addiction and of attitudes which have been engendered toward it
in the United States since the beginning of the twentieth century
have led to recurrent public concern, to laws imposing ever more
severe penalties on addicts as well as drug peddlers, and to a generally
ineffective, even self-defeating approach to the problem. For more
than a generation, public opinion toward drug addiction in the
United States was to a considerable degree molded by a division of
the Treasury Department—the Bureau of Narcotics—which is charged
with enforcing federal narcotics laws. Its approach was for three
decades consistently authoritarian and punitive, branding the addict
a fiend and opposing with scorn and denunciation all those who called
for a different approach to the problem. Only recently has the punitive approach been strongly challenged; the laws it spawned are still
on the statute books. Drug addiction constitutes a social problem of

changing character and response and one toward which public attitudes and perhaps public policies may be expected to undergo additional change in the next few years.

The traffic in illegal drugs has been estimated to gross tens of millions of dollars per year. Narcotics smuggling and distribution are big business for criminal syndicates. Yet at the beginning of the twentieth century the link between narcotics and crime was a rather casual affair. In fact, the possession and use of opiates was not a crime nor even strongly stigmatized unless one frequented "opium dens." Indeed, in most civilized countries at the present time, narcotics addiction is not an important social problem and is not primarily a matter for criminal prosecution; it is a medical problem to be dealt with through the doctor-patient relationship.

What is the nature of narcotics addiction that it has come to be so greatly feared? How has the problem become so many-faceted in the United States? What kind of persons become drug addicts and how does their addiction come about? What are the consequences of addiction? How are we attempting to control or prevent drug addiction in the United States? What alternative approaches exist? These are some of the questions we shall try to answer about addiction as such, the primary focus of this chapter.

But a somewhat broader perspective is called for, because drug addiction is just one aspect of several much broader social problems. One of these problems involves the widespread use in the United States of drugs that affect psychic functioning—sleeping pills, tranquilizers, energizers, hallucinogens, and other "psychoactive" drugs. Some of these drugs are used under medical supervision and are widely prescribed, despite a lack of knowledge of their long-term effects on behavior, character, and interpersonal relations. They may constitute a serious potential danger and thus represent a latent social problem. This is a problem to which pharmacologists, physicians, and social scientists are beginning to address themselves [1] but it will not be dealt with here. Other drugs, addicting and nonaddicting, are used outside of medical channels for the enjoyment of their psychic effects. Increasingly, persons arrested for drug offenses are found to be using a variety of so-called dangerous drugs (the name for all drugs whose use is subject to a physician's prescription), such as

---

[1] See, for example, S. M. Farber and R. H. L. Wilson, eds., *Control of the Mind* (New York: McGraw-Hill, 1961); Paul Talalay, ed., *Drugs in Our Society* (Baltimore, Md.: The Johns Hopkins Press, 1964); and the forthcoming report, *Drugs and Society*, prepared by Bernard Barber for the Russell Sage Foundation.

amphetamines ("benzedrine") or hallucinogens, on an occasional or "spree" basis. Such drug use or abuse does not constitute addiction. As yet we have little knowledge of the extent and character of occasional use of "dangerous drugs" beyond impressions from arrest data, reports in the public press, and the pronouncements of advocates of free drug use or their opponents. We shall deal primarily with addiction because it poses certain problems that are unique, but we shall seek a wider view from time to time in order not to lose our perspective.

The Nature of Drug Addiction

Experts have defined drug addiction in a variety of ways. Perhaps the most influential definition is that given by a committee of the World Health Organization:

> a state of periodic or chronic intoxication detrimental to the individual and to society, produced by the repeated consumption of a drug (natural or synthetic). Its characteristics include: (1) an overpowering desire or need (compulsion) to continue taking the drug and to obtain it by any means; (2) a tendency to increase the dose; (3) a psychic (psychological) and, sometimes, a physical dependence on the effects of the drug.[2]

There are a number of drugs that possess attributes leading to all three of the characteristics named in the WHO definition, but by far the most important of these are alcohol (see Chapter 5) and the opiates (along with synthetic substitutes for the latter). The opiates epitomize addicting power based on initial euphoria and subsequent physical dependence. This dependence is closely linked with *tolerance,* the ability of the body to adapt to progressive increases in the amount of the drug that can safely be taken. Indeed, such increases are required if the drug is to have an effect. In time, with continued substantial drug dosage, the body comes to require the drug for normal functioning; without the drug, an acute illness known as the *abstinence syndrome* results. Opiate addiction is, then, in every respect the kind of phenomenon referred to in the definition of the WHO.

Unfortunately, however, the term "addiction" tends to be loosely used to cover a variety of types of illegal drug use regardless of whether or not physiological dependence or proven compulsion to use

---

[2] United Nations Expert Committee on Drugs Liable to Produce Addiction, Reports 6-7, World Health Organization Technical Report Series No. 21 (New York: United Nations, 1950).

drugs are entailed. Thus lawmakers and narcotics-control personnel have frequently referred to marihuana use as addiction, though it clearly does not qualify according to the WHO definition. Many pharmacologists and other students of drug use prefer to use the term *habituation* to refer to regular use of drugs that do not entail physiological dependence. Even here, however, there are logical difficulties, for in instances where physiological dependence is lacking, it is primarily the habits and attitudes of the user, not those of the drug, that are problematic. As Isadore Chein has observed in examining the cultural and psychological contexts of drug use, some persons develop compulsive cravings for a number of substances that are not proscribed (the "coffee addict," for example), and others use proscribed drugs on an occasional basis that in no sense qualifies as either addiction or habituation.[3]

In order to understand the nature of physiological dependence on a drug, let us consider the opiate abstinence syndrome. An addict who is deprived of the drug he has been taking will experience a train of symptoms and signs that conforms to a general pattern, varying somewhat in intensity and course depending upon the particular drug and the length and strength of the addiction. For example, if morphine is suddenly and completely withdrawn, a feeling of tension sets in some 8 to 14 hours after the last shot, succeeded by restless sleep.

> About the sixteenth to the eighteenth hour of withdrawal and after the patient has awakened, slight lacrimation, rhinorrhea, perspiration, and yawning appear. Restlessness and nervousness ensue and become progressively worse as the hours go by. Twenty-four hours after the last dose of the drug is administered most patients are acutely miserable, complain of chilly sensations and of cramps in the muscles of the back and extremities. Lacrimation, rhinorrhea, perspiration, and yawning become more marked. Recurring waves of goose-flesh and dilation of the pupils appear. . . . Patients become increasingly restless and continually move from one part of the bed to the other. They twitch their arms, legs, and feet almost constantly. This twitching of the legs has given rise to the term "kicking the habit." Patients usually cover themselves with blankets even in the hottest weather, curl into a ball and present an appearance of abject misery. They may become so uncomfortable that they leave their beds and lie on a hard concrete floor in an attempt to obtain some ease from the muscular cramping and aching. They are nauseated, gag, retch, vomit, have diarrhea and may lose from five to fifteen pounds in twenty-four

---

[3] See Isadore Chein *et al.*, "Some Matters of Perspective," *The Road to H: Narcotics, Delinquency, and Public Policy* (New York: Basic Books, 1964), Chapters 13 and 14.

hours. All of these symptoms increase in intensity until the thirty-sixth to forty-eighth hour after the last dose of morphine is given. The peak intensity of abstinence symptoms from morphine is maintained from the forty-eighth to the seventy-second hour of abstinence, after which it begins to decline. Five to seven days after the last dose of morphine is given, practically all acute symptoms have disappeared and the only complaints remaining are nervousness, insomnia, and weakness. These gradually decline over a course of three to four months, but minor physiologic aberrations may persist for as long as six months.[4]

At any time during the acute abstinence period, a single dose of morphine will produce a prompt and pronounced reduction of the intensity of all the disturbances mentioned. This relief lasts 6 to 12 hours, after which time the intensity of the abstinence syndrome returns to the level it would have reached at that time if untreated. The abstinence syndrome with heroin is similar, except that withdrawal symptoms appear and reach peak intensity earlier and subside more rapidly.

Used in excessive amounts, alcohol and the barbiturates—such as seconal and nembutal—produce the physiological dependence that results in an abstinence syndrome when the drug is withdrawn. Use of cocaine, amphetamine, and marihuana, on the other hand, does not lead to tolerance nor does withdrawal of the drug produce an appreciable abstinence reaction. Drug effects are, of course, quite different. The opiates are primarily "depressants," leading to a slowing down of bodily processes. Their depressant actions include relief of pain, muscular relaxation, drowsiness or lethargy, and (before extreme tolerance has been developed) euphoria, a sense of well-being and contentment. Cocaine and amphetamine are stimulants. They "speed up" and activate the user. In place of drowsiness and lethargy, they produce feelings of elation, excitement, and relief of fatigue, but as the effect of the drug wears off, there is pronounced restlessness and depression. These drugs are seldom used alone or taken continuously. Cocaine may be paired with heroin to produce the "speedball," combining the shock power of the cocaine with the afterglow of the opiate. Benzedrine may likewise be combined with barbiturates to give similar but milder effects.

Marihuana or Indian hemp (*Cannabis Indica*) has, like the opiates, a history of varied use. In literary circles of the past century and in the Orient, from which it was first imported, it achieved fame as

---

[4] Harris Isbell, "Meeting a Growing Menace—Drug Addiction," *The Merck Report* (July, 1951).

hashish. In the United States it has been used most widely in "reefers," cigarettes made from the dried leaves of the plant. Marihuana's effects are somewhat akin to those of alcohol, and like alcohol "it does different things to different persons." Most typically, it generates feelings of well-being and relaxation; tensions are reduced. Perhaps the most striking effect, however, is that one's perception of time is markedly affected. In the early phases of use, acuity of hearing and sensitivity to rhythm appear to be enhanced, though in later phases there is marked distortion. It is this quality of marihuana, and perhaps a mythology relating to this, that seems to account for its popularity with jazz musicians, many of whom feel that performance is enhanced by the drug.

Cultural Orientations Toward Drug Use

The chemical characteristics of drugs largely determine their effects upon the organism, but cultural norms dictate the circumstances under which various drugs are used and the consequences of such use for the individual. It may be assumed that in all societies men generally want to avoid or minimize pain, fatigue, or anxiety and to achieve a level of euphoria some of the time; in most societies, there is approval of at least occasional use of stimulants, narcotics, or other chemical substances to help achieve these objectives. Alcohol is probably the most widely used of such substances, but tobacco and coffee also qualify as drugs which are important adjuncts to daily life in much of the civilized world. Most Americans are aware of the fact that alcohol was outlawed for more than a decade in the United States; they are perhaps not aware that tobacco and coffee were both outlawed in a number of countries just a few centuries ago. Indeed, the smoking of tobacco was at one time or another a crime punishable by death in Russia, Persia, Turkey, and parts of Germany.[5] Tobacco use was regarded by those who made the laws as a certain road to moral depravity, much as some contemporary legislators and custodians of morality have regarded marihuana. The parallel is perhaps worth considering briefly. Both drugs—tobacco and marihuana—are made from the leaves and tender stems of a plant; both may be smoked or used in other forms; both lead to habituation, but neither entails marked physical dependence. Tobacco may actually come

---

[5] Louis Lewin, *Phantastica: Narcotic and Stimulating Drugs, Their Use and Abuse,* trans. from 2nd German edition by P. H. A. Wirth (New York: Dutton, 1964).

closer to being truly addicting than does marihuana.[6] Marihuana has a somewhat stronger psychological effect, though that effect seems to depend very much on the attitudes and beliefs of the user. For example, marihuana (or, more accurately, *cannabis* in one form or another) is used as an adjunct to sociability in some countries, as an ingredient in religious contemplation in others, and as a means of relieving fatigue in still others. In this respect, as in the general intensity of effect, marihuana is not unlike alcohol and many other drugs; when the drug is used in moderation, the social framework and the personality of the user are as important as the drug itself in producing the psychological effect.

Tobacco use is at present unregulated by law in the United States, despite overwhelming evidence that in cigarette form it leads to a marked shortening of life expectancy.[7] As reported in Chapter 5, alcohol use is strictly regulated in only a few localities in the United States, despite the fact that millions of Americans are impaired in their functioning by virtue of excessive use of alcohol. Marihuana use is regulated by federal and state laws which call for very severe penalties if even a small quantity of the drug is found in a person's possession, despite the fact that marihuana appears to entail less danger to life than tobacco and no more than does alcohol. This is intended neither as an argument for legislation against cigarettes and alcohol nor as an assertion that there should be no control whatsoever over marihuana use. It is rather to make quite clear that cultural values and popular beliefs, as well as the objective characteristics of drugs, influence both drug use and legislation relating to drugs.

As already noted, the problems posed by addiction to the opiates are clearly different from those posed by tobacco and marihuana, and hence most of our attention will be devoted to true narcotics addiction. As we shall see, however, legislation outlawing particular drugs that are widely consumed tends to bring those drugs within a context of crime and deviance whether or not the drugs are in themselves significantly harmful. Hence the evaluation of our efforts to deal with the problem of drug addiction requires a broad perspective and a questioning both of prevailing stereotypes and of practices that are taken for granted by many persons.

---

[6] The strength of habituation to cigarettes is evidenced in William Haenszel, Michael B. Shimkin, and Herman P. Mitler, "Tobacco Smoking Patterns in the United States," *Public Health Monographs, No. 45* (Washington, D. C.: U.S. Government Printing Office, 1956).

[7] See, for example, *Smoking and Health: Report of the Advisory Committee to the Surgeon General of the Public Health Service* (Washington, D. C.: U.S. Government Printing Office, 1964).

Early History of Narcotics Use
and Narcotics Legislation in the United States [8]

The opium poppy has been the source of sleep-inducing drugs and soothing beverages since antiquity. Eventually it was learned that the ingredients responsible for the soporific properties were contained in the juice which exudes from the ripe poppy head when it is lanced. This juice, collected and dried, is opium. The opium itself contains two major components (alkaloids) which are distinct though related in drug action: morphine and codeine. They were first identified early in the nineteenth century.

Opium and its derivatives were inexpensive drugs and were used for a wide variety of human ills with almost no limitation until the early twentieth century. Indeed, the bold use of opium appears to have been the basis for the reputations of a number of famous physicians of earlier times. Not confined to use by physicians, however, opium and its derivatives were included in almost every patent medicine for the relief of painful conditions, in "soothing syrups" for babies, and in a variety of confections. Not all users received a sufficiently large or regular dosage to become addicted to these drugs, but many did. As one writer has commented:

> Addicted persons have enjoyed the appellation "dope fiend" for only some forty years, while the pusher of pre-World-War I society was usually the local pharmacist, grocer, confectioner or general store keeper. In fact, until the turn of the twentieth century, the use of opium and its derivatives was generally less offensive to Anglo-American public morals than the smoking of cigarettes.[9]

Some physicians had begun to warn against the dangers of the opiates as early as the 1830's, but by and large during the nineteenth century the problem of dependency was simply dealt with by continued consumption of the drug. The discomforts of abstinence were then just another set of aches and pains that could be alleviated by this panacea for all ills.

As an increasing number of physicians became aware of the dangers of habitual use of opium and its derivatives, there was a search

---

[8] The history of narcotics use and addiction is treated in some detail by Charles E. Terry and Mildred Pellens, *The Opium Problem* (New York: Committee on Drug Addiction, 1928), Chapter 2, and more briefly by Glenn Sonnedecker "Emergence and Concept of the Problem of Addiction," in Robert B. Livingston, ed., *Narcotic Drug Addiction Problems* (Washington, D. C.: U.S. Government Printing Office, 1963).

[9] Rufus King, "Narcotic Drug Laws and Enforcement Policies," *Law and Contemporary Problems*, Vol. 22 (Winter, 1957), p. 113.

for ways of using the drugs so as to avoid an "opium appetite." The introduction of the hypodermic needle was thought to afford such a means. It was only after the habitual hypodermic use of morphine to relieve pain by Civil War veterans that the dangers of addiction through this channel were recognized. So widespread was morphine use among ex-soldiers that it was known for a time as "army disease."

No sooner had awareness of this danger been achieved than a new one appeared. A new opiate, heroin, was produced in Germany in 1898. It was widely heralded as being free from addiction-producing properties, possessing all of the virtues but none of the dangers of morphine. It took several years' use of heroin to disprove these erroneous beliefs. Terry and Pellens observe that the widespread use of heroin as a substitute for morphine and as a more stimulating narcotic took place "first in the underworld, . . . long before the average physician had become aware of the dangers of the drug." [10] Heroin was especially convenient for underworld use, in that it was both highly potent and easy to adulterate with sugar of milk (lactose). While these characteristics were useful even before heroin could no longer be purchased freely, they became especially important after federal control of narcotics had been established.

Use of opium primarily for the sake of psychological effects achieved a vogue in some circles as a consequence of De Quincey's famous *Confessions of an English Opium-Eater,* which had appeared in 1821. Later in the century, the Chinese pattern of opium smoking was introduced to "sporting circles" in San Francisco. It spread especially among gamblers, prostitutes, and other frequenters of the demimonde. Although local ordinances were passed forbidding the practice, imports of smoking opium increased sharply and exceeded 100,000 pounds per year for every year from 1890 to 1909, when legal importation was terminated. Interestingly enough, prior to the passage of federal legislation in 1909, the only measure employed for the control of this importation of opium for nonmedicinal use was the imposition of import duties. When these became heavy, legal importation diminished and smuggling increased.

The Harrison Act

The first significant federal legislation to deal with the problems posed by narcotics addiction was an outgrowth of concern about opium smoking in Far Eastern territories. Theodore Roosevelt established

---

[10] Terry and Pellens, *The Opium Problem,* p. 84.

a commission which met in Shanghai in 1908 to discuss the abuse of drugs and recommend possible solutions. This in turn led to the first international drug conference. The Hague Opium Convention of 1912 constituted an agreement among nations to control the traffic in opium and other addicting drugs. As an expression of our adherence to that Convention, Congress in 1914 passed the Harrison Act to control the domestic sale, use, and transfer of opium and coca products. The Act provided at the same time for an excise tax and for registration of, and maintenance of exact records by, persons handling drugs, and prohibited possession of the drugs, except for "legitimate medical purposes," on the part of persons not registered under the provisions of the Act.

The primary purpose of the Act, then, appeared to be to bring the drug traffic into observable and controllable channels. The lack of adequate control and the earlier indiscriminate use of opiates by physicians had resulted in a large number of addicted persons. Estimates vary, but almost certainly there were more than 100,000 addicts in the United States in 1914, many of whom were highly respected members of society. Prior to passage of the Harrison Act, these persons could apply to any member of the medical profession for treatment, including gradual drug withdrawal, or they could purchase drugs at moderate prices direct from any supplier. At a stroke, the Harrison Act cut off the latter source of supply and left the question of medical dosage for addicts to legal interpretation. That is, the direct dispensing of drugs by a physician was permitted only "for legitimate medical purposes," but it was not clear whether a physician could provide drugs to prevent the abstinence syndrome in persons previously addicted. World War I intervened before this issue was resolved. It would appear that many addicts did receive drugs through physicians, but that the short supply of opiates during the war led to some diminution of the number of addicted persons.

Since the Harrison Act was a revenue act, enforcement of its provisions was vested in a special police unit, the Narcotics Division of the Treasury Department. In 1919, after Treasury Department officials had charged that the drug menace had greatly increased, the government brought action against a number of physicians who had prescribed opiates for addicted persons. Several of these physicians had written prescriptions for addicts on a wholesale scale, without regard for medical responsibility. They were convicted, and, on appeal, the convictions were sustained by the Supreme Court. Unfortunately, these convictions were interpreted as denying to physicians the right to prescribe narcotics to relieve suffering due to addiction. Justices

Holmes, Brandeis, and McReynolds vigorously dissented from this interpretation. Overnight, the government's action, put into effect by the Treasury Department, created a new dimension of the problem of drug addiction. The former Chairman of the Committee on Narcotics and Alcohol of the American Bar Association presents one view of the consequences:

> Armed with what came to be known as the Behrman indictment, the Narcotics Division launched a reign of terror. Doctors were bullied and threatened, and those who were adamant went to prison. Any prescribing for an addict, unless he had some other ailment that called for narcotization, was likely to mean trouble with the Treasury agents. The addict-patient vanished; the addict-criminal emerged in his place. Instead of policing a small domain of petty stamp-tax chisellers, the Narcotics Division expanded its activities until it was swelling our prison population with thousands of felony convictions each year. Many of those who were caught had been respected members of their communities until the T-men packed them off.
>
> Simultaneously with its campaign to cut the addict off from the recourse to medical help, the Narcotics Division launched an attack on him along another line as well. He was portrayed as a moral degenerate, a criminal type, and the public was told that he could only be dealt with by being isolated from all normal contacts with society; if left at large, one of his main preoccupations was allegedly contriving ways to induce others to share his misery by becoming addicted themselves. In short, he should be caught and locked up.[11]

The consequence of the interpretation and implementation of the Harrison Act was, then, to discourage the medical profession from dealing with a legitimate medical problem, to define the addict as a criminal rather than as an afflicted person, and, by branding them "dope fiends," degenerates, enemies of society, greatly to increase the difficulty of rehabilitating addicts and assimilating them into normal society. In 1925 the Supreme Court unequivocally rejected the interpretation that physicians were prohibited by the Harrison Act from treating addicts by prescribing drugs. In a unanimous decision, the Court disclaimed that the previous rulings could be

> . . . accepted as authority for holding that a physician who acts bona fide and according to fair medical standards, may never give an addict moderate amounts of drugs for self-administration in order to relieve conditions incident to addiction. Enforcement of the tax demands no such drastic rule, and if the Act had such scope it would certainly encounter grave constitutional difficulties.[12]

---

[11] King, "Narcotic Drug Laws," pp. 122-23.
[12] *Ibid.*, p. 123, quoted from the Supreme Court ruling in *Linder* v. *United States*, 268 U.S. 5 (1925).

Unfortunately, by the time this ruling was handed down, the medical profession had withdrawn from attempting to treat addicts; the field was left to the illicit drug peddler.

There were occasional waves of public concern about drug addiction between the early 1920's and World War II, even though the available evidence suggests that there was a gradual decrease in the number of addicts during this period. World War II brought about a further decline, as the channels of illegal drug distribution were disrupted by the war. It is not clear whether any substantial number of addicts were thereby freed from the drug habit or whether they became merely quiescent for a time. It does appear, however, that relatively fewer new addicts were being created during the decade before World War II and during the war itself. Within five years of the end of World War II, however, there was unmistakable evidence of a substantial increase in narcotics use. Increasing proportions of young delinquents and criminals either had on their persons the characteristic bent spoon and hypodermic needle that are the addict's standard equipment for preparing and injecting heroin or manifested the abstinence syndrome when jailed. Increasing numbers of parents appealed to police, to hospitals, and to social agencies for help in dealing with older adolescents and young adults who had become addicted to heroin. There were reports that heroin was being peddled to high school and even junior high school students and that addiction was rife in many parts of major cities. These reports were grossly exaggerated. There can be no question, however, that within relatively limited areas a major epidemic of drug use was in process.

Public concern with drug addiction has remained at a high level into the 1960's. But in recent years there has been an increasing recognition on the part of the medical and legal professions that they have a responsibility for helping to achieve a more effective program to deal with this problem. In 1962, President Kennedy convened a White House Conference on Narcotic and Drug Abuse to examine all facets of the problem.

Number and Characteristics of the Addict Population

Estimates of the extent of drug addiction are at best crude. In general, an addict becomes known only as he is arrested or seeks treatment. Even in the case of persons arrested for possession of narcotics, however, one often cannot be certain that the offender is an addict. There are a number of signs by which the drug user can be identified—

hypodermic punctures, for example—but definite evidence of addiction can be established only by the use of chemical tests or by appearance of the abstinence syndrome after drug withdrawal. Therefore, statistics of arrests for drug offenses cannot properly be interpreted as statistics on addicts, even though a majority of those arrested are drug users.

The Bureau of Narcotics, which is the policing agency for federal narcotics laws, has maintained a register of "active addicts" since 1952. Each year the Bureau has indicated the number of newly reported addicts—that is, those not previously listed in its register. By 1962 the cumulative total reached 78,209, yet the Bureau's list of "active addicts" numbered only 47,489.[13] The reason for this discrepancy is said to be that names of addicts are removed from the active list if they have not reappeared within five years. Unfortunately, there is no way that one can ascertain whether a person so dropped has died, been imprisoned, given up drugs, or simply not been rearrested. Moreover, when the Bureau's estimates are compared with those of the states that now maintain their own record systems, there are glaring discrepancies. In 1962, for example, the state of California listed 13,620 known narcotic addicts and users within the state while the Bureau of Narcotics showed only 7412 allocated to California.[14]

The divergency among estimates of the number of addicts in the United States led the Ad Hoc Panel on Drug Abuse, convened for the 1962 White House Conference, to conclude it is not possible to secure an adequate estimate. From the various fragments of data available, one can, however, hazard the estimate that the number of persons actively addicted to opiates is not less than 50,000 and not more than 100,000. This estimate does not include persons who use marihuana or various other nonaddicting drugs without also using opiates.

Of addicts known to the Bureau of Narcotics, more than two-fifths are attributed to New York State (overwhelmingly in New York City), another fourth are divided between Illinois and California (primarily in the Chicago and Los Angeles areas), and the remainder are largely concentrated in Washington, Detroit, St. Louis, Dallas, and a few other metropolitan areas.

---

[13] Estimates of the addict population are given in the annual reports of the Bureau of Narcotics, *Traffic in Opium and other Dangerous Drugs*. A cogent criticism of the inadequacy of these estimates is given in Alfred R. Lindesmith, *The Addict and the Law* (Bloomington, Ind.: Indiana University Press, 1965), Chapter 4.

[14] *Drug Arrests and Dispositions in California, 1962* (State of California, Bureau of Criminal Statistics, 1963).

No other Western nation has as many as 5000 addicts and most have only a few hundred.[15] Great Britain, France, and the Scandinavian countries all report addict populations of less than 1000. In western Europe only Germany has a sizable group of addicts—somewhat over 4000—but the nature of narcotics addiction in Germany is vastly different from that in the United States.[16] For example, more than 95 percent of German addicts are over 30 years of age. The largest single occupational group represented consists of housewives, followed by medical personnel. The drugs used are largely synthetic counterparts of the opiates; heroin is almost nonexistent. There appears to be only a slight relationship with either crime or economic deprivation. In some respects, the characteristics of the German addict population resemble those of American addicts 50 years ago. But there have been marked changes in the characteristics of narcotics users in the United States since World War II. Nearly three-fourths of the "active addicts" recorded by the Bureau of Narcotics are Negro, Puerto Rican, or Mexican-American in extraction. Thus, the problem of narcotics use in the United States is now closely entwined with minority-group status.

For nearly two decades after their establishment in the 1930's, the Public Health Service hospitals for the treatment of addicts were the only public facilities for this purpose. Statistics were compiled on the characteristics of the first thousand admissions to the Lexington, Kentucky, hospital.[17] A comparison of these early statistics with more recent compilations for the hospital (which draws patients from the whole country) reveals a striking change in the characteristics of this segment of the addict population.

Less than 10 percent of the addicts received at the Lexington Hospital during its first year were Negroes; in recent years nearly two-fifths have been Negroes. Less than 10 percent of the addicts received two decades ago were under 25 years of age; in recent years a third have been under 25, and in the early 1950's the proportion was even higher.

The same trends in changing characteristics are revealed by studies conducted in New York City and Chicago during the mid-1950's, as

---

[15] Information relating to many aspects of narcotics production and abuse is published annually by the Commission on Narcotic Drugs of the United Nations Economic and Social Council. See its *Summary of the Annual Reports of Governments Relating to Opium and Other Dangerous Drugs.*

[16] *Ibid.,* 1962, p. 27.

[17] Michael J. Pescor, "A Statistical Analysis of the Clinical Records of Hospitalized Drug Addicts," *Public Health Reports,* Supplement to No. 143 (Washington, D. C.: U.S. Government Printing Office, 1943).

compared with the results of earlier studies. In Chicago, for example, Dai analyzed the characteristics of 2439 addicts who were arrested on narcotics charges or treated for addiction during the period 1928-1934.[18] Eight percent were under 25 years of age. Seventy-seven percent were white (overwhelmingly native-born), 17 percent were Negro, and 6 percent were members of other racial groups, largely Chinese. At that time, these other racial groups comprised less than 1 percent of the Chicago population, Negroes comprised 7 percent, and whites 92 percent. In a study made two decades later, the staff of the Chicago Area Project found that nearly one-half of the approximately 5000 drug users officially known to the Police Narcotics Bureau and other agencies were under 25 years of age and that Negro narcotics users now constituted a substantial majority of those users known to official sources in Chicago.[19]

Prior to passage of the Harrison Act, it is believed that female addicts outnumbered males, largely through their habitual use of patent medicines containing opium derivatives. By the late 1920's and early 1930's, however, Dai found that nearly three-fourths of the Chicago addicts were males. Subsequent studies reveal that among the younger addicts the proportion of males is even higher. The Chicago Area Project study revealed that 83 percent of all cases known to the Police Narcotics Bureau, and a substantially higher percentage of younger cases, were males. Chein, studying the distribution of all adolescent adults known to police, hospitals, and social agencies in New York, found that roughly 85 percent were males.

Pescor's study of early admissions to the hospital at Lexington revealed an educational distribution not markedly different from that of the total population at the time, except for the unduly high proportion of graduates of professional schools. The latter finding reflects the relatively high rate of addiction among physicians, nurses, pharmacists, and dentists, all of whom have ready access to narcotics. The greatest concentration occupationally was in the domestic and personal service category, especially among waiters, porters, and the like.[20] All major occupational groups were well represented, however. Dai's Chicago study revealed a generally similar occupational distribution of addicts: disproportionately high numbers in the personal service trades and in entertainment but, nevertheless, a broad representation

---

[18] Bingham Dai, *Opium Addiction in Chicago* (Shanghai: Commercial Press, 1937).

[19] Illinois Institute for Juvenile Research, *Drug Addiction Among Young Persons in Chicago*, Chicago Area Project, 1953 (mimeographed).

[20] Pescor, "A Statistical Analysis," p. 27.

of major occupational categories.[21] Dai's sample did not include physicians and druggists, because of restrictions on the use of records relating to offenses of this group. Tabulations of recent admissions to the Public Health Service hospitals indicate little change in the occupational categories which are overrepresented in the addict population. As a consequence of the younger age of the addicts recently admitted, however, and the fact that they represent a markedly deprived segment of the population, more of them are reported as having no occupation. It must be noted that the occupational designation of many addicts does not represent a continuing or current mode of earning a living since they engage in illegal pursuits. Nevertheless, in examining the process whereby narcotics use is learned, we shall note that certain occupational groups are much more strategically placed for such learning than are others.

Perhaps the most revealing picture of the distribution of narcotics use in metropolitan populations is afforded by mapping the residences of drug users and computing the rates of known users per thousand of population. Dai carried out such an analysis in the earlier study referred to above. Nine of Chicago's 120 subcommunities, as then delineated, contained roughly 5 percent of the total population but fully half of the known narcotics users.[22] The areas with high rates of drug addicts were areas of lowest socioeconomic status and of greatest urban blight. They were characterized by low proportions of persons living in family groups, high population mobility, high rates of juvenile delinquency and adult criminality, and, indeed, high rates of a wide variety of social problems. Family groups living in such areas tended to be migrants of relatively recent years, sifted into the least desirable areas of residence, largely because they had fewer advantages in the competitive process.

The more recent researches of the staff of the Chicago Area Project reveal that the residential distribution of the great bulk of present drug users is very similar to that found by Dai two decades ago. (See Chapter 2, page 132.) In the intervening period, however, there has been a considerable change in the population of many of the areas of highest drug use. The expanding Negro population has replaced earlier foreign-born migrants who had settled in some of these deteriorated areas of the city. The personal characteristics of residents of many of these areas have, thus, changed, but the problematic social characteristics of the areas are essentially the same.

---

[21] Dai, *Opium Addiction in Chicago,* p. 53.
[22] *Ibid.,* p. 78.

A similar residential concentration of drug users was found by Chein and his associates in studies of the distribution of narcotics use among adolescents in New York City. Eighty-three percent of the adolescent users were found to live in just 15 percent of the city's census tracts.[23] These tracts constituted the poorest, most crowded, and most physically dilapidated areas of the city. Further, within these tracts, drug use was highest where income and education were lowest and where there was the greatest breakdown of normal family living arrangements. They were, in large part—but by no means exclusively—areas of residence of the Negro and Puerto Rican population of the city. On the other hand, many other areas of Negro and Puerto Rican residence that were less deprived and less socially disorganized had low rates of drug use.

In no subcommunities of New York or Chicago does it appear that a majority of the population or of any specific age group is addicted to the use of narcotics. There are areas in both cities, however, where as many as 10 percent of the young adult males have been apprehended or treated for narcotics possession or addiction. We must look, then, to the conditions of life within these areas for clues to the factors which make narcotics addiction so much more prevalent there than in the larger society.

Induction to Drug Use

Studies of drug addiction conducted over the past three decades, including the recent studies of younger addicts, suggest that addiction is not primarily to be attributed to the drug peddler or to a seeking after drugs on the part of persons intent upon trying narcotics. The most usual pattern of induction is through intimate association with one or more addicts—perhaps most often without prior knowledge of the fact of their addiction. Dai's interviews with addicts in Chicago revealed, however, that such association most often took place after the addict-to-be had already cut loose from conventional groups to which he had belonged.[24] Some of Dai's subjects were introduced to drugs at "pleasure parties," to which they were taken by more experienced friends or dates. Others were introduced to drugs by prostitutes or in homosexual relationships, through pool-hall and dance-hall associations, through association with co-workers in hotels and restaurants, or, in a few instances, by the purposive urging of peddlers.

---

[23] Chein *et al.*, *The Road to H*, p. 39.
[24] Dai, *Opium Addiction in Chicago*, p. 173.

Most of these addicts had not started life in the areas where drug use is most prevalent. They had come to such areas for a variety of reasons—in search of inexpensive living quarters, in the course of employment (as bellhops, porters, entertainers), or in search of freedom from the restraints of the moral order of the larger society. Thus, many were deviants from conventional morality well before they had tried drugs.

Few of Dai's subjects, or of other groups of addicts studied before World War II but after passage of the Harrison Act, seem to have been exposed to the opportunity to experiment with narcotics in adolescence. Among the more recently studied addicts, however, the opportunity to smoke marihuana or to try heroin frequently occurs by age 15 or 16. Even among eighth-grade students in schools located in areas of high drug use in New York City, Chein found that 45 percent claimed personal acquaintance with a heroin user.[25] Among delinquents who did *not* become heroin users, two-thirds were offered an opportunity to try heroin before they were 18; among boys who did become users, 68 percent had their first chance to try heroin by age 16.[26] In such areas, then, easy access to the use of drugs is a characteristic of the environment. Environments so drastically different from those which most of us have known demand closer scrutiny. If they present a high proportion of teen-agers with the opportunity to experiment with narcotics, it is likely that they have already presented younger children with interests and attitudes deviant from those of the larger society. Before examining the nature of the specific associations and situations in which narcotics are first tried, let us look more closely at the characteristics of these urban areas and their populations.

Social Characteristics of Areas of High Drug Use

We have already noted that in both New York and Chicago—cities that account for a very high proportion of the known drug addicts in the United States in recent years—the areas of residence of drug users are the poorest, most deteriorated areas of the city. The areas of highest rates of drug use tend to be inhabited by the most disadvantaged minority groups and by the least successful or most deviant members of other population groups. These are the areas with the highest rates

---

[25] Chein *et al., The Road to H,* p. 84.
[26] *Ibid.,* p. 153.

of adult crime, the highest rates of prostitution and illegitimacy, the highest prevalence of infant mortality and of tuberculosis, the highest proportion of broken families and of nonfamily living arrangements. They have high population density and high population turnover. As has already been suggested, residents of these areas tend to live there either because they have no alternative, by virtue of their poor competitive position in the community, or because they desire the anonymity and freedom from conventional restraints which would be found in other, more stable residential areas. The great diversity of origins of the migrant populations, the high population turnover, the pressing concern with immediate problems of subsistence, and the power of the organized underworld all conspire against the likelihood of concerted action by those residents of such areas who desire a more stable and moral order.

Within such areas, several families may share a single flat, often with no central heating and with no separate bathroom. Children may sleep two or three to a bed or they may share a bed with an adult. A high proportion of the families lack a stable male head. Marriages, whether formal or of the common-law variety, tend to be taken up readily and broken easily by simple desertion; a succession of male figures may pass through the household, contributing temporarily to its support but taking relatively little responsibility for the children of previous unions. Under these circumstances, many mothers work, leaving the child to the care of other female relatives. This pattern has been especially typical of the lower-status Negro family in the United States; it was fostered by the conditions of slavery and later by economic deprivations attendant upon the Negro male's lack of opportunity to develop competitive occupational skills. Instability of the family and related divergencies are by no means confined to the Negro population, however; the moral norms of the dominant middle class in Western society are in a number of respects rather sharply redefined within the more deprived segments of the population. This redefinition extends to the pastimes of children, as has already been noted in the chapter on delinquency. The subculture of "street-corner society" and the various forms of peer group activity within this society are most likely to be oriented toward nonconventional goals in the areas characterized by highest rates of drug addiction.

> The central feature of this society and its body of practices, or "culture," is the support it gives to behavior which is generally inconsistent with the norms of conventional society, and often openly hostile to many of its expectations. This orientation on the part of the street

boys is expressed in a variety of ways, but is most clearly and dramatically manifested in delinquency, and in the search for and exploitation of "kicks." [27]

The norms and values of street-corner society tend, then, to be inconsistent with or in conflict with those of the larger society. Yet they *are* norms and values which constrain or dictate certain types of behaviors. They are norms and values which have utility in binding the peer group together and enhancing feelings of adequacy and of power in the face of dismal living conditions and family relationships which are often lacking in nurturance and emotional support.

In a group seeking "kicks," prestige comes from willingness to experiment and let oneself go, whether in delinquent acts, in the use of intoxicants or stimulants, or in other forms of behavior which are intrinsically exhilarating, involve an element of risk, or defy convention and conformity.[28] In the language of the "cats"—originally derived from the argot of the older drug addict and from that of the jazz musician—adherence to conventional norms is for the "squares." It would appear, however, that the culture of the "cats" and the pursuit of "kicks" are much more widespread than is the use of narcotics. Even in the areas of highest drug use, as we have seen, it appears that only a minority of the boys experiment with heroin or other opiates, though most of them have incorporated some of the norms and values of street-corner society. Most have also incorporated many of the norms of conventional society.

Patterns of association are at any given time markedly influenced by the boy's relative commitment to conventional norms or to those of various deviant subcultures. It seems reasonable to surmise that those who take the course of relatively conventional behavior have opportunities to gratify their needs for social response without commitment to the delinquent activities of street-corner society. There is evidence that they are more likely to come from families that provide and enforce relatively consistent standards of behavior; they are less free from the application of social controls. At present, however, we know less about the nondelinquent, non-drug-using youth from such areas than we know about those boys who become delinquent or addicted to drugs.

---

[27] Illinois Institute for Juvenile Research, *Drug Addiction Among Young Persons in Chicago*, p. 10.

[28] See Harold Finestone, "Cats, Kicks, and Color," *Social Problems*, Vol. 5 (July, 1957), pp. 3-13.

The Process of Becoming a Drug User

We have suggested that the city areas in which drug use is most prevalent afford access to a variety of patterns of deviant behavior and peer group norms which, to some degree, encourage the adolescent to exploit opportunities for "kicks." There is a good deal of evidence that the use of heroin and other opiates tends to follow the manifestation by the adolescent or young adult of a number of other behaviors which are in conflict with the norms of the larger society. For example, the great bulk of recent addicts to opiates in urban slum areas have smoked marihuana prior to using heroin.

Marihuana was introduced into this country by migrants from Mexico and the Southwest. Prior to 1937, it was not subject to the federal controls imposed by the Harrison Act. Its use at that time among Mexican-Americans and Negroes in urban slums appears to have been more widespread than opiate use; it was easy to supply and relatively inexpensive, since the plant from which it is obtained grows wild in the Southwest and can be cultivated in most parts of the United States. The Marihuana Tax Act of 1937 extended federal controls over the production, transfer, and use of marihuana. Subsequently, distribution traffic in marihuana seems to have merged at least in part with the distribution channels for heroin.

Whatever the reason, there was a pronounced change in the relationship of marihuana use to heroin use between the late 1930's and the late 1940's. In 1938, Mayor La Guardia of New York appointed a committee to investigate the extent and consequences of marihuana use among adolescents. The committee's report, released in 1944, indicated that marihuana use was widespread in certain areas of Harlem where it was distributed through an estimated 500 "tea-pads" (places where people gather to smoke marihuana) and perhaps another 500 peddlers. Marihuana cigarettes—"reefers"—could be purchased for from 15 to 25 cents, so that they were within the purchasing power of all segments of the population.[29] Reviewing the evidence on effects of marihuana use, the committee concluded that the campaigns against marihuana as a major cause of crime and psychological degradation grossly exaggerated the dangers of the drug. Further, the committee found no evidence at that time that the use of marihuana tended to lead to the use of opiates or other addicting drugs.

---

[29] Mayor's Committee on Marihuana, *Marihuana Problem in the City of New York* (Lancaster, Pa.: Jaques Cattell, 1944), pp. 9-25.

By 1949, however, when the postwar wave of drug addiction first became a matter of great concern in a few of the largest cities, marihuana use was very frequently the harbinger of heroin use. Among the group of young heroin users studied by Chein in New York City, 86 percent had smoked marihuana prior to using heroin.[30] A few of these boys smoked their first "reefer" as early as age 10 or 11; the most frequent age at which marihuana use began was 15—on the average, about two years before their initial experience with heroin.

The process of becoming a marihuana user has been described by Becker in terms that are equally applicable to heroin use.[31] As he notes, even for the boy who has participated in occasional delinquency, a number of controls prevent his readily taking over the pattern of smoking reefers. Even in a subculture which places high value on the pursuit of "kicks," there are powerful deterrents. In general, the boy knows that marihuana or heroin use is not only illegal but is punished by severe penalties. He knows that this form of behavior can lead to social ostracism by persons who are important to him. Finally, it is likely that he has to some degree accepted traditional views which define drug use as a sign of moral degradation—and as leading to loss of will power and enslavement. As Becker notes, becoming a regular marihuana user entails learning the means of disengaging oneself from these controls as well as learning the proper techniques and definitions which insure positive pleasure from the experience.

Initially, experience of the drug comes most often from its having been made available by a friend or in a group in which he participates, some member of which has access to a source of supply. Use tends at first to be primarily a function of availability; the occasional user can become a regular user only by finding a more stable source of supply than the few users whom he knows well. He must have a "connection." But this means being identified as a drug user and introduced *to* the proper parties *by* the proper parties.

In general, the neophyte will be concerned with keeping the fact of his marihuana use a secret and will try to confine use to times and places where friends or relatives will not be likely to see him. As he participates more with other users, however, he tends either to give up most of his conventional ties and to identify completely with users or to learn to control the expression of his "highs" so that nonusers will not be aware of them.

---

[30] Chein *et al.*, *The Road to H*, p. 149.

[31] Howard S. Becker, "Marihuana Use and Social Control," *Social Problems,* Vol. 3 (July, 1955), pp. 35-44.

As he moves from occasional to regular use, from a chance source of supply to a "connection," from occasional association with other users to almost complete involvement with them, the marihuana user learns also to rationalize and redefine the meaning of use of the drug. He finds that the stereotyped description of marihuana as the source of all evils simply does not correspond to his experience. He can now take a more "emancipated" view. He can point to the harmful consequences of alcohol and argue that a comparatively mild vice like marihuana smoking cannot be seriously wrong. He can long maintain the belief that he is not really dependent upon the drug, since he can stop for periods of a week or two without the distress that withdrawal from an opiate would entail.

Thus, in the process of becoming a marihuana user, one set of norms and controls is discarded in favor of another. Many of those who try marihuana, however, do not make the full transition to a deviant subculture; the conventional controls, internal and external, never wholly cease to operate and finally win out.

Induction to heroin use likewise involves learning to define as acceptable, and indeed as the ultimate in "kicks," a practice which is generally condemned and feared. Chein found that roughly a third of the boys who became drug users in adolescence were offered their first "shot" or "snort" by a youthful friend when just the two were together. Another third experienced their first opportunity in a group setting and in response to a group atmosphere favorable to experimentation:

> I was at a party—everybody was having a good time—I wanted to be one of the crowd—I thought that if it didn't hurt them it wouldn't hurt me—that started the ball rolling. . . . They were sniffing at that time. . . . Two or three pulled out a few caps, said, "Here, if you want to try." I accepted.[32]

About 10 percent of the boys were introduced to heroin by members of their families or unrelated adults. Only 10 percent actively sought an opportunity to experience heroin, according to the statements of the boys themselves. In most instances, heroin was easy for the boys to obtain and was initially offered without cost. Few boys became addicted primarily because a peddler or "pusher" induced an innocent youth to try heroin, but it would appear that sometimes friends or associates pushed heroin with a peddler's motivations.

There are undoubtedly many variants to the modes of induction to

---

[32] Chein *et al., The Road to H,* p. 151.

drug use that have been described here. Perhaps the most markedly different from that of the young, deprived, minority-group member is the process whereby a physician, a nurse, or another professional with legitimate access to narcotics comes to draw upon and then to rely upon opiates or other drugs. Pescor's statistical analysis of the records of the first thousand addicts treated at the Lexington Hospital revealed that nearly 10 percent were professionals and semiprofessionals, largely physicians, pharmacists, and dentists. It is likely that this underrepresents the true proportion of addicts with such backgrounds since it is much easier for such persons to sustain their addictions without resorting to other criminal activities. While we have little systematic data on these persons, it appears that their initial use of narcotics was most often for the relief of pain or fatigue and that they found the drug effects so salutory that they established dependence.

Regardless of the circumstances under which initial narcotics use takes place, a new dimension is added by the first experience of withdrawal. Lindesmith notes that "awareness of addiction and the admission that one is 'hooked' date from the moment that withdrawal distress bars the way to voluntary abstinence." There comes a time when the recently initiated drug user is either without the drug or seeks to demonstrate to himself that he can stop when he wishes. If he has become physiologically dependent, he experiences withdrawal distress. Since this distress can be quickly alleviated by the drug, there is now a tremendously important additional motivation for using the drug. It becomes a symbol of security. At the same time, there comes the realization that one is "hooked."

> As soon as the user realizes that he must begin to plan for his future supply, he is ripe for assimilation into the drug addicts' culture. It is now vital to know others of his kind from whom he must obtain his supply. He thus learns the various devices and customs by means of which his problems are solved.[33]

The culture of the drug user has its symbols of status, its mythology, and, to a considerable extent, its own language. By these means, social solidarity among addicts counters their being outcasts from the larger society. The addict acquires skills at the necessary transactions to secure drug supplies, often including the skills of some type of professional criminal activity to provide a source of funds for purchasing supplies. Periodically, he may try to break away from addiction and to try for a "cure," but as we shall see, this is a formidable undertaking.

---

[33] Alfred R. Lindesmith, *Opiate Addiction* (Evanston, Ill.: Principia Press, 1947), p. 85.

Criminality and Drug Addiction

The Harrison Act, as interpreted, made it a crime to possess narcotics for the purpose of maintaining an addiction. Before its passage, as we have seen, many persons became addicted through medical use of narcotics or through the use of patent medicines and confections containing opium derivatives. It would be a mistake, however, to conclude that narcotics use was, prior to the Harrison Act, as prevalent in conventional society as it was in the underworld. The pursuit of pleasure in its nonconventional forms has always been easier for those who have already broken with conventional society than for those firmly incorporated in the social fabric. It would be strange, indeed, if any substance possessing the potentials of the opiates were to be overlooked by members of the demimonde seeking thrills and the release of tensions. The incidence of addiction seems to have been especially high among prostitutes and their pimps; it was relatively low among the more prestigeful ranks of the underworld such as safecrackers and burglars.

Since the Harrison Act, there has been a widely held belief that narcotics breed crime, especially crimes of violence. Many persons believe that the effect of heroin is to release inhibitions and to make the addict a ruthless criminal. The evidence shows that crime and narcotics use do exist side by side but that neither opiates nor marihuana generally leads to crimes of violence. The addict, unless he is wealthy or has professional access to channels of legitimate drug distribution, must rely upon crime to secure money for the purchase of illicit drugs. But his crime tends to entail various types of theft, not crimes of violence. Table 1 compares the offenses committed by known narcotics users in Chicago in 1951 with offenses committed by the population at large in the same year. Arrests for nonviolent property crimes were much more frequent among the addicts. On the other hand, violent offenses against the person—sex offenses such as rape and various forms of assault—were relatively much less frequent among the addicts than among other offenders: 2.9 percent as against 30.7 percent. Most arrests of narcotics-users are, of course, for drug-connected offenses. Comparative data such as those presented in Table 1 become available only as the result of special studies. While these data are not current, there is no reason to assume that a more recent study would show any significant change.

A similar conclusion can be drawn from studies in changes of the behavior of adolescent gangs in which a substantial number of members came to use narcotics. Following their drug use, there was a

TABLE 1

The Percentage Distribution of Arrests
for the Most Serious Types of Offenses in the Narcotics Bureau
and the Chicago Police Department, 1951

	Narcotics Bureau	Chicago Police Department
Larceny; Theft (except auto theft)	58.8	31.0
Robbery	16.2	7.3
Burglary; Breaking and entering	9.9	9.4
Stolen property: buying, receiving, possessing	5.1	3.2
Forgery and Counterfeiting; Embezzlement and Fraud	4.2	4.9
Sex offenses; Rape	1.6	11.0
Auto theft	1.5	9.1
Weapons: carrying, possessing, etc.	1.4	4.4
Aggravated assault; Other assault	1.3	19.7
Total	100.0	100.0

Source: Reproduced from Harold Finestone, "Narcotics and Criminality," *Law and Contemporary Problems*, Vol. 22 (Winter, 1957), p. 71.

decrease in such activities as gang fights and assaults as well as a decrease in participation in active sports.

The addict who is without drugs will, of course, go to any necessary lengths to obtain drugs to ward off the abstinence syndrome. Thus, the importance of narcotics as a cause of crime is not the direct effect of the drug but the meaning which it comes to possess for the addicted person. He must have a source of supply. The addicted pharmacist or physician generally commits no crime beyond his illegitimate use of drugs to which he has access; the young minority-group addict in an urban slum tends to commit many crimes to maintain his addiction. Finestone describes the young addicts who were interviewed in 1952, most of whom were in the early stages of their addiction:

> They were "snatch-and-grab" junkies, supporting their habits through petty thievery, breaking into cars, shoplifting, and a variety of "scheming," such as "laying a story" on "a sucker" in the hope of gaining sympathy and some cash. Some enterprising ones actually had girls out "hustling" for them through "boosting" [shoplifting] and "turning tricks" [prostitution]. Despite the ragged state of their clothing and the harried nature of their existence, they regarded themselves as the members of an elite, the true "down cats" on the best "kick" of them all, "Horse" [heroin]. Many of them were still living at home, although they had long since exhausted the last reserves of patience of their families and "fenced" much of their movable property. Few,

if any, of them had finished high school, and, on the average, they had little or no employment experience. Their attitudes towards work and the daily routine that steady employment presupposed were entirely negative. Their number-one hazard was the "man" [the police]. Once they became "known junkies"—that is, known to the police—they were frequently picked up and sometimes sentenced—mostly for misdemeanors and, consequently, for short sentences. . . . The police became a symbol of the "revolving door through whose entrance and exit the same persons form a constant procession."

The question arises as to the relationship of the young narcotics addict to the rest of the criminal world. The impression gained from interviewing them was that these addicts were petty thieves and petty "operators" who, status-wise, were at the bottom of the criminal population or underworld. It is difficult to see how they could be otherwise. The typical young junky spent so much of his time in a harried quest for narcotics, dodging the police, and in lockups, that he was hardly in a position to plan major crimes.[34]

It is obvious that availability of drugs and knowledge of the techniques of drug use are necessary conditions for such use. We have seen that certain urban areas afford a high degree of access both to the drugs and to the requisite knowledge. In these areas some groups have relatively favorable attitudes toward experimentation with drugs and relatively tenuous commitments to the moral norms of the larger society. Membership in such groups depends partly on residence and on chance factors of association based on social background. To what extent does it also depend upon the characteristics of individual personalities, whether pathological or simply "different"? To what extent can narcotics addicts be distinguished by their personality characteristics from nonaddicts drawn from the same general milieu?

Personality Characteristics and Drug Use

Psychiatrists who have specialized in the treatment of older addicts are in substantial agreement that addicts are not "normal" personalities. Nevertheless, less than 10 percent of the first thousand addicts hospitalized at the Lexington Public Health Service Hospital were diagnosed as psychoneurotic or psychotic.[35] Fifty-five percent of these addicts were classed as having a "psychopathic diathesis"—that is, a predisposition toward the psychopathic personality. To this group, according to the report, belong "carefree individuals on the lookout for new excitements, sensations, and pleasures." This characterization

---

[34] Harold Finestone, "Narcotics and Criminality," *Law and Contemporary Problems,* Vol. 22 (Winter, 1957), pp. 76-77.

[35] Pescor, "A Statistical Analysis," p. 17.

would well suit many of the young minority-group members—the "cats"—growing up in street-corner society.

Social scientists are more inclined to view the addict as the product of a particular type of environment and the occupant of a particular social role. That is, the patterns of behavior and attitude which characterize addict society are held to be learned by a high proportion of persons who grow up in the milieu of that society. These patterns are learned from older "role models" just as skills in sports are learned from older role models by boys growing up in middle-class suburbs.

But there is no necessary conflict between the view of the addict as a deviant personality and the view of the addict as a social type. Undoubtedly the addiction of some persons is to be understood primarily as the expression of severe psychopathology. The addiction of others has come about through being subjected to environmental pressures too strong to resist—for example, children whose parents or other relatives made drugs available to them. But personality is not independent of environmental influences and, by and large, the influences that permit heroin to be available to a teen-ager and that permit a high proportion of adolescents to become members of street-corner society also create psychological needs and vulnerabilities which enhance the value of narcotics to the person.

Studies in the United States and in England have described a number of sources of personality distortion or vulnerability that frequently characterize child rearing in urban slum areas. These include absence of a stable father figure in the family, exposure to the overtly exploitative use of sex, repeated frustrations of affectional needs, rebuffs related to minority-group status, and a host of more subtle influences. The consequences are seen in frequent manifestations of personal insecurity, problems of sexual identification on the part of males, rebellious attitudes toward authority, and various defensive maneuvers and tendencies to escape through gambling, intoxicants, and other "kicks." For example, Spinley, a psychologist who studied adolescents (not drug users) in a London slum, found that many manifested:

> . . . a basic insecurity; a serious sexual disturbance which is associated with feminine identifications; an inability to form close affectional ties; an absence of strong and efficient super-ego; an inability to postpone satisfaction and an absence of conflict over pleasures; a highly sensitive ego and marked narcissistic trends; a ready aggressiveness; a tendency to "leave the field" when circumstances are experienced as unpleasant; a rebellious attitude toward authority.[36]

---

[36] B. M. Spinley, *The Deprived and the Privileged: Personality Development in English Society* (New York: Humanities Press, 1953), p. 79.

Many of these same phrases have been used to describe the young addicts, except that they tend to be unaggressive rather than aggressive. Indeed, the pattern of drug use has been characterized as the *retreatist* form of delinquent adjustment.

If personality deviation is so widespread in the milieu of the urban slum, should we not say that drug addiction and personality deviation are simply two aspects of the same problem? To some extent this seems justified, but we must remember that only a minority of young people in these areas become seriously delinquent and far fewer become drug addicts. Psychopathology is both more frequent and more severe among young drug users than among nonusers growing up in the same environment. Moreover, the series of studies undertaken by Chein and his associates provide convincing evidence that the personality attributes of the young drug users are not merely a reflection of their deviance and the social role of the drug user but derive from family experiences which have been found generally to contribute to the development of psychopathology. As compared with nonusers from the same neighborhoods, drug users far more often came from homes characterized by absence of a father figure for a significant part of early childhood, by disturbed relationships between parents, lack of warmth, and vague and inconsistent parental standards. The absence of a positive relationship between the boy and an adult male role model was especially striking:

> In almost all the addict families (97 percent), there was a disturbed relationship between the parents, as evidenced by separation, divorce, open hostility, or lack of warmth and mutual interest. In these conditions, the mother usually became the most important parent figure in the life of the youngster. But, whatever the vicissitudes of the relationship between the boy and his mother, one theme was almost invariably the same—the absence of a warm relationship with a father figure with whom the boy could identify.[37]

We may say, then, that among the younger group of addicts whose early life was spent in the milieu of drug use, internal psychodynamics and social attitudes both play a part in leading the adolescent or young adult to experimentation with drugs and incorporation in the culture of narcotics use.

We have less adequate information on the older user prior to his addiction. We know that once he has taken on the social role of the addict and has been subjected to the experiences and social definitions attaching to addiction, his attitudes, values, and motivations will differ

---

[37] Chein *et al.*, *The Road to H*, pp. 273-74.

markedly from those of the nonaddict. A number of psychiatrists have suggested that while experimentation with drugs may not require any great degree of personality deviance, the adult who persists to the point of getting "hooked" tends to have certain "needs" other than the simple desire for euphoria, which narcotics meet more fully than does anything else.

The Psychological Functions of Narcotics Use

The attractiveness of morphine and heroin to a person seems to be related to the extent to which he is able to gratify primary bodily needs and to avoid anxiety by normally available means. Wikler points out that ". . . many normal individuals experience euphoria after administration of morphine, but they feel no great need to repeat the experience since they are able to achieve euphoria by gratification of their needs through socially acceptable channels—work, marriage, and social relationships." [38] Where "primary needs"—the needs for relief of pain, hunger, and sexual urges—are not so gratified, opiates seem to excel other drugs, including alcohol, by virtue of the specificity with which the opiates do gratify (relieve) these urges or tensions.

For certain types of personality, it appears that personal functioning approaches the normal only when the individual is taking opiates. This seems to be true of a number of the younger addicts who, as a consequence of family experiences, have been unable to achieve any sort of self-confidence in their relationships with others. It has also been noted that some physicians have taken opiates at relatively controlled dosage for years, feeling that they functioned effectively in their work only after they had begun the practice. By and large, of course, persons who have tried this have come to grief because they develop tolerance of the drug, but, up to a point, opiates can permit effective functioning without impairing either technical skills or internalized controls on behavior.

"Once an Addict—"

Most often, in contemporary America, the addict is an unhappy, insecure individual. Few addicts except medical personnel and those engaged in entertainment have significant occupational skills, and even fewer maintain any sort of regular employment once addicted. Since possession of proscribed drugs is legally defined as more reprehensible and calls for longer prison sentences than most forms of theft, there

---

[38] Abraham Wikler, *Opiate Addiction: Psychological and Neurophysiological Aspects* (Springfield, Ill.: Thomas, 1952), p. 54.

is little incentive for the addict to work. Even in Britain, where addiction and drug possession are not defined as crimes, most addicts have poor work records.[39]

The preoccupation of the addict with drug effects and drug supplies, his chaotic way of life, his devaluation by self and others, and his criminal activities to produce money for drugs make him a prime target for arrest and abuse. In many communities, known addicts and former addicts are likely to be arrested "routinely"—i.e., without any evidence that they have committed a crime.[40] If they have drugs in their possession, they can be charged with a crime that may result in a long prison term, or they can be pressured to serve as informers against other addicts and drug peddlers. Many arrests of addicts are on the fringe of legality, but the addict is in no position to claim his constitutional rights. One's assessment of the propriety of police methods is likely to depend largely on whether one views the situation from the perspective of the enforcement officer trying to get a very difficult kind of evidence or from that of an addict victimized because his addiction requires that he have at least a small supply of drugs in his possession.

Beyond the early stages of addiction there is little euphoria and much misery. It is not surprising, then, that most addicts come to the point where they want to get out from under the "monkey on their backs." This does not necessarily, or even usually, mean that they contemplate a complete change in attitudes and activities. But being hooked entails too many problems unless one has a safe source of supply and can keep his addiction secret.

Efforts to deal with the problems of drug use and addiction in the United States have been concentrated primarily on attempts to eliminate the illegal drug traffic by overseeing the medical distribution of narcotics and by making the penalties for illegal sale of such drugs so severe as to deter potential offenders. Severe penalties have not had this effect. Drug traffic continues to flourish. Moreover, the nature of addiction almost insures that addicts will supply one another in accordance with their abilities to obtain "connections." It is difficult, then, to distinguish the addict-pusher from the large distributor unless very large quantities of narcotics are entailed. The punitive approach, which calls for locking up the addict-pusher, ignores the fact that after several decades the United States has made almost no

---

[39] Edwin M. Schur, *Narcotic Addiction in Britain and America* (Bloomington, Ind.: Indiana University Press, 1962), pp. 131-35.

[40] See Lindesmith, *The Addict and the Law,* for a discussion of the ways in which addicts are handled by the police—especially Chapters 2 and 3.

progress toward solving its narcotics problem by this approach. Some measure of rehabilitation of these addicts is crucial to a successful narcotics program. As we shall see, the one-sided approach that has characterized control efforts has made much more difficult the rehabilitation of American addicts. Let us first briefly examine efforts to control the traffic and then the status of efforts to rehabilitate addicts and other drug users.

Drug Traffic and Its Control [41]

The addicting drugs, in their natural forms, are not produced in the United States, although some synthetic equivalents of opiates are produced here. As we have noted earlier, concerted action to control the international traffic in opium and other narcotics began with the Shanghai Commission in 1908 and subsequently bore fruit in the Hague Opium Convention in 1912. When the League of Nations was formed after World War I, its Covenant entrusted the League with the general supervision of the execution of agreements with regard to the traffic in opium and other dangerous drugs. The League drew up and put into effect a number of additional international agreements.

Following World War II, the United Nations took over the functions and programs which had been carried out by the League of Nations. To prevent the abuse of narcotic drugs while assuring their availability for medical and scientific purposes, the international narcotic instruments not only prescribe rules in the international field but also define the measures of control which are to be maintained within each country. The latter provide for the licensing and supervision of the manufacture and distribution of narcotics and for the recording of all transfers and dispensing of the drugs. They limit the stocks of raw materials which may be maintained by manufacturers and provide bases for the limitation of production to meet legitimate needs. These measures must, of course, be implemented by appropriate legislation by the individual countries which are signatory to the agreement.

Narcotics Control in the United States

Within the United States, elimination of illegal drug traffic is the task of the Bureau of Narcotics and the Bureau of Customs through

---

[41] A very thorough discussion of this topic is contained in Bertil Renborg, "International Control of Narcotics," *Law and Contemporary Problems*, Vol. 22 (Winter, 1957), pp. 86-112.

their agents and officers in the field. Most major seizures of narcotics are made at ports of entry or other points along the border of the United States. But "undercover" federal narcotics agents operate both abroad and throughout the United States to learn the channels of illegal drug distribution and to make purchases which will give a basis for prosecution.

In order to discourage the traffic in narcotics, Congress has on several occasions increased the penalties provided for under the Harrison Act. In recent years, there has been a sharp cleavage between the views of law-enforcement officers and those of the professional associations of physicians and lawyers. Both the American Psychiatric Association and the House of Delegates of the American Bar Association argued against the punitive orientation of recent legislation on the ground that the proposed laws were based on a misconception of the nature of drug addiction and would make even more difficult the rehabilitation of addicts.[42] On the other hand, law-enforcement officers testified that severe penalties would reduce the incidence of addiction. The legislators were primarily influenced by the testimony of the law-enforcement officers. The Narcotic Drug Control Act of 1956 provides for a sentence of not less than 2 nor more than 10 years on a first offense of illegal *possession* of narcotics or marihuana, 5 to 20 years on a second, and 10 to 40 years on a third or subsequent offense. In this category, parole or probation is possible on the first offense, but not subsequently. For illegal *sale* or for conspiring to sell narcotics or marihuana illegally, penalty for a first offense is not less than 5 nor more than 20 years and for subsequent offenses 10 to 40 years. Parole and probation are not allowed beyond the first offense. Sale of, or conspiracy to sell, heroin to a person under 18 is punishable by imprisonment from 10 years to life, or, if the jury so directs, by death.

In recent years the bulk of narcotics arrests and prosecutions have been made by local enforcement agencies operating under state laws.[43] All but a few of the states have adopted, usually with modifications, the Uniform Narcotic Drug Act, which was prepared by the National Conference of Commissioners on Uniform State Laws in

---

[42] American Medical Association, Council on Mental Health, "Report on Narcotic Addiction," *Journal of the American Medical Association*, Vol. 165, No. 13 (Nov. 30, 1957), pp. 1707-13, No. 14 (Dec. 7, 1957), pp. 1834-41, No. 15 (Dec. 14, 1957), pp. 1968-74.

[43] Lindesmith, in *The Addict and the Law*, summarizes data from several sources which suggest that at least 95 percent of all narcotics prosecutions in 1962 were nonfederal (pp. 106-07).

1932.[44] This Act was formulated to meet the need for uniform legislation in areas of narcotics activity not readily covered under the Harrison Act. All the states prohibit possession of narcotic drugs except under closely specified controls. There are some variations in the scope of state laws, but by far the greatest variation is in the penalties provided by the several legislatures. Nevertheless, a review of recent laws shows the almost unanimous trend toward increasing the severity of the penalties in all the states.[45]

One consequence of the increasing severity of penalties for narcotics offenses is that drug offenders have come to make up a considerable portion of all federal and state prisoners. Despite a declining number of federal prosecutions, the number and proportion of drug offenders in federal prisons have increased steadily, from roughly 2000 in 1950 (constituting less than ten percent of all prisoners) to over 4400 in 1962 (roughly a fifth of all federal prisoners).[46] The average length of sentences served by these prisoners increased from 20 months in 1950 to 84 in 1962. In recent years, less than half the prisoners committed to federal prisons for drug offenses have been eligible for parole. About half of these prisoners are addicts. Another 40 percent have been characterized by James V. Bennett, Director of the United States Bureau of Prisons, as "marihuana users and smalltime sellers whose basic motivation is a quick and easy dollar or . . . some temporary boost for [their] inadequacy or frustration."[47] Mr. Bennett has elsewhere noted that:

> No prison program is equipped to properly treat the addict. . . . Prisons, both State and Federal, in the years immediately ahead will be faced with problems of narcotics offenders, addict and nonaddict, who are weighed down by the hopelessness and the bitter futility of sentences which seemingly stretch into infinity.[48]

Another consequence of inflexible, severe sentences for drug possession is that they frequently seem so senseless to judges and juries that the rate of convictions drops markedly. In Michigan, for example,

---

[44] See William B. Eldridge, *Narcotics and the Law* (New York: American Bar Foundation, 1962) for the content of this Act (pp. 133-47) and for an evaluation of present state and federal laws relating to narcotics (especially Chapter 4).

[45] *Ibid.*, p. 65.

[46] Federal Bureau of Prisons, *Federal Prisons* (Annual Reports of the work of the Federal Bureau of Prisons, 1950-1962).

[47] White House Conference on Narcotic and Drug Abuse, *Proceedings* (Washington, D. C.: U.S. Government Printing Office, 1963), p. 255.

[48] James V. Bennett, quoted in "Report of the State of New York Joint Legislative Committee on Narcotic Study," State of New York Legislative Document No. 7 (1959), p. 102.

where the penalty for the first offense of selling is a minimum of 20 years, without possibility of suspension or probation, only 3 percent of the persons charged as narcotics peddlers have been convicted on this charge. A study by the American Bar Foundation reported that juries were unwilling to convict persons of sale of narcotics when the penalty was set so high.[49]

The White House Conference

The 1962 White House Conference on Narcotic and Drug Abuse highlighted the differences in perspective between enforcement personnel desirous of making it easy to arrest, convict, and incarcerate drug users and professionals whose aim is to rehabilitate as many addicts as possible.[50] Following the Conference and a review of all the testimony there presented, the President's Advisory Commission on Narcotic and Drug Abuse presented a series of recommendations.[51] These were less forthright in dealing with the crucial issues of the narcotics problem than might have been anticipated, undoubtedly because the Commission's aim was to achieve a viable set of proposals in the face of sharply conflicting points of view. Nevertheless, the Commission called for a number of changes in federal laws, policies, and procedures. It recommended a reallocation of responsibilities now lodged in the Treasury Department and called for the development of needed data collection and evaluation services within the federal government. It also recommended that "the penalty provisions of the federal narcotics and marihuana laws which now prescribe mandatory minimum sentences and prohibit probation or parole be amended to fit the gravity of the particular offense so as to provide a greater incentive for rehabilitation." [52] It recognized the inappropriateness of lumping marihuana with narcotics in existing legislation, noting that "the marihuana reefer is less harmful than any opiate" and that "sentencing of the petty marihuana offender should be left entirely to the discretion of the federal courts." [53] It called for closer regulation of the distribution of other drugs subject to abuse, such as the amphetamines and barbiturates.

The death of President Kennedy, a few weeks after transmittal of the Commission's report, undoubtedly took away much of the poten-

---

[49] Eldridge, *Narcotics and the Law,* pp. 88-89.
[50] See White House Conference on Narcotic and Drug Abuse, *Proceedings* (Washington, D. C.: U.S. Government Printing Office, 1963).
[51] President's Advisory Commission on Narcotic and Drug Abuse, *Final Report* (Washington, D. C.: U.S. Government Printing Office, 1963).
[52] *Ibid.,* p. 41.
[53] *Ibid.,* p. 42.

tial influence of the report. As of late 1965, the major legislative resultant of the Commission's recommendations has been the "Drug Use Control Amendments of 1965" extending controls over depressant and stimulant drugs.

Perhaps the single topic of greatest interest at the White House Conference was the development of "civil commitment" programs.[54] Civil commitment is a legal mechanism utilized in place of criminal commitment to insure control over addicts and other drug users. The two major civil commitment laws thus far enacted—in New York and California—differ in a number of respects but in essence provide for suspension of criminal proceedings against defendants "addicted or in imminent danger of becoming addicted" and for commitment to a rehabilitation program, provided they are regarded as good risks for rehabilitation. These programs are also available to addicts who voluntarily commit themselves and to users under 21 years of age whose next of kin apply for such commitment. In general, drug users with previous felony records or those involved in crimes of violence are excluded. The total period of commitment may not exceed three years in New York and seven in California. In each instance a part of this period—at least six months in California—is spent in a rehabilitation center, followed by close supervision after return to the community.

Civil commitment programs are not a panacea. There is a danger that civil commitment may represent little more than a change of name for imprisonment and that the rights of the individual to due process of the law may actually be infringed. Although "civil" commitment technically avoids the label of "criminal," the individual in fact may be as strongly stigmatized as if imprisoned for a criminal charge, especially if he is committed to facilities that also house convicted felons, as is the case in California. On the other hand, the development of specialized programs for drug users and the provision of close supervision in the community do offer some promise that more effective rehabilitation methods will be developed. In any case, the New York and California programs have produced some valuable information about the addict after his return to the community.

The Rehabilitation of Drug Addicts

The first step toward rehabilitation of the addict is, of course, to end his physiological dependence on the drug, a step usually referred to

---

[54] See White House Conference, *Proceedings,* pp. 173-221.

as detoxification. Detoxification may come about simply as a consequence of jailing, with sudden termination of drug use, in which case the full intensity of the abstinence syndrome will be experienced, or the process may be carried out gradually in a hospital, with considerable diminution of suffering. Despite the physical misery entailed in "kicking the habit cold turkey"—i.e., without medical aid—many addicts are willing to go through enforced abstinence in this way without intending to renounce opiates permanently. They know that when they are no longer physiologically dependent on heroin or other opiates, a much smaller dose will again produce greater pleasure. Detoxification, then, is a necessary stage toward giving up drugs, but its significance for rehabilitation is minimal.

Until the last decade or so, very few public or private hospitals were either willing or equipped to accept addicts for detoxification or long-term treatment. During the 1930's two large Public Health Service hospitals—at Fort Worth, Texas, and Lexington, Kentucky—were established for the treatment of narcotics addicts. Prison-like in appearance and only slightly less so in atmosphere, these hospitals are required by law to give priority to addicted prisoners and probationers who have been convicted of violations of federal narcotics laws. Such patients must remain in the hospital for the duration of their sentences unless transferred to other institutions. Thus they retain the status of prisoners, though they are afforded therapy. In addition to prisoner-patients, addicts who wish to try for a "cure" may be admitted to the Public Health Service hospitals to the extent that facilities will permit. Such patients may, however, request their release at any time.

The management of withdrawal is now accomplished quite simply through the use of the synthetic, methadone, which substitutes for opiates to prevent the abstinence syndrome. Once the substitution has been made, the methadone can be gradually withdrawn. It, too, produces an abstinence syndrome, but of markedly reduced intensity. The process of withdrawal may require from two weeks to a month, depending upon the degree of dependence and the physical condition of the addict.

Beyond detoxification, rehabilitation programs are in general psychiatrically oriented. Psychotherapy in one form or another—frequently group therapy—is usually provided, but vocational and educational training are also stressed. In general, the addict is not a good subject for individual psychotherapy. His cultural background and vastly different orientation from that of the well-educated therapist tend to militate against a close, trusting relationship. Beyond this, the addict's characteristic pattern of dealing with tension-producing situations by "leaving the field" leads to broken appointments and prematurely terminated treatment unless he is compelled to stay, but compulsion tends to defeat the objectives of psychotherapy. To some extent, group therapy and "therapeutic community" programs (see Chapter 1) avoid these difficulties.

The President's Commission noted that "no accepted satisfactory course of treatment has yet been established" but stressed the need for providing rehabilitation services in or near the drug user's own community and for providing extensive aftercare following detoxification.[55] Former addicts released from hospitals and jails into the community with little or no supervision have tended to revert to drug use in a relatively short time. A follow-up study of young drug users released from the Riverside Hospital in New York in the late 1950's found that of 247 only eight did not return to drug use after discharge.[56] None of these eight had been truly addicted prior to admission to the hospital. Of addicts returned to New York City from the Public Health Service Hospital at Lexington, Kentucky, during the period July, 1952, to December, 1955, only 9 percent were voluntarily abstinent six months later and less than 3 percent remained abstinent for a full five years.[57]

It appears that regular supervision and guidance after an addict's return to the community may help him to abstain from drugs. Addicts closely supervised on parole after discharge from compulsory treatment programs in both New York and California have tended to remain abstinent for considerably longer periods than those discharged without supervision. Roughly a third of a group of young New York drug users abstained for a period of three years.[58] The experience of groups followed up in California has varied somewhat, depending on the area of the state and characteristics of addicts involved, but for some samples as many as a third of the parolees have remained free of drug use for more than a year in the community.[59]

In general, follow-up studies have found that older users are more

---

[55] President's Advisory Commission, *Final Report*, pp. 53-56.

[56] Cited by Dr. Ray E. Trussell at the White House Conference. See *Proceedings*, pp. 69-70.

[57] Henrietta J. Duvall *et al.*, "Follow-up Study of Narcotic Drug Addicts Five Years After Hospitalization," *Public Health Reports*, Vol. 78 (1963), pp. 185-94.

[58] Meyer H. Diskind and George Klonsky, *Recent Developments in the Treatment of Paroled Offenders Addicted to Narcotic Drugs* (Albany, N. Y.: Division of Parole, 1964).

[59] Department of Corrections, "Narcotic Treatment Control Program" (Sacramento, Calif.: Research Report No. 19, May 1963).

likely to remain abstinent than younger. Indeed, there are a number of indications that after age 40 the rate of relapse may be appreciably lower than for younger users, though available data do not indicate what happens to the older users. Many simply disappear from view.

Follow-up studies have also found that an appreciable proportion of users die from drug overdoses. This is largely a consequence of variability in the strength of available heroin. The addict can never be sure what he is getting until he has tried it. It is probable that overdoses are more common among young and inexperienced users since they are likely not to understand the nature of drug tolerance and tend to be reckless in their use of heroin.

The Social Context of Treatment Failures

Whether the addict is treated in the community by outpatient therapy, or in a drug-free hospital, his natural environment is not drug-free, and the social ties of major consequence to him before his hospitalization or his undertaking treatment have been with other drug users. (See Chapter 3, page 188.) He has come to speak the language of the addict, a colorful argot that, although it has contributed many words to the popular idiom, remains mostly incomprehensible to the uninitiated. The addict's in-group may, to a degree, provide the same kind of social and psychological support that a family group provides for other persons. Within this group he can be himself, he can find acquiescence and enthusiasm for his views about drugs and drug effects. The addict's very sense of identity rests upon his commitment to the values and practices of the drug-using subculture. But, as already noted, he cannot fail to recognize the cost of addiction to him—not merely in the constant struggle to get drugs, the misery of enforced abstinence, the dismal pattern of life once euphoria is gone, but also in rejection by family and conventional society, poor health as a consequence of personal neglect, and disgust with self. The cycle of abstinence and relapse which tends to characterize addicts has been studied by Marsh Ray, who notes the shifting identifications of the addict and his ambivalence as to where he belongs.[60] The addict cannot readily become a full participant in the conventional culture from which he has, over a period of time, become alienated, yet he is aware of how much he would like to participate.

Many of the stereotypes that the drug user has built up, his tech-

---

[60] Marsh Ray, "The Cycle of Abstinence and Relapse among Heroin Addicts," *Social Problems*, Vol. 9 (1961), pp. 132-40.

niques of neutralizing conventional values are called into question if he attempts to affiliate with nonusers. Both the abstainer and those members of the non-drug-using community who know of his former addiction are likely to be on their guards. The widespread belief that addiction is incurable tends to become a self-fulfilling prophecy. Family and friends are constantly watching for signs of relapse, suggesting that no identity but the addict identity can last. Under these circumstances a return to affiliation with drug users and a confirmation of an identity which will be accepted by peers is likely to occur. Even if he makes a strong effort to stay off drugs, the addict who has participated fully in the subculture of addiction is likely to have closer continuing ties with some members of the addict community than with any persons in conventional society.

Synanon

One of the most novel and promising approaches to rehabilitation—Synanon—derives its strength from the character of the addicts' attitudes and social ties.[61] Synanon originated as a banding together of a number of alcoholics and drug addicts who were searching for recognition and response from others as well as some understanding of their own situations. The original group, in Santa Monica, California, set up a joint household not too dissimilar in certain respects from fraternity living, except that both sexes were included. Subsequently, a number of other Synanon units have been established, each representing a residential unit run by the addicts themselves. The principles upon which these groups are operated are quite different from those which govern rehabilitation programs run by public or private agencies. Synanon units tend to be paternalistic, to entail indoctrination and, at times, severe browbeating of members. They do not invoke the moral and religious imperatives that guide Alcoholics Anonymous. But the commitment made in joining the Synanon group, the setting of boundaries and the establishment of meaningful relationships, and the leaderless group therapy sessions all seem to contribute to stabilization of the addicts desire to stay "clean"—i.e., off drugs. No really adequate study has yet been made of Synanon; the panegyrics that are available are not careful assessments. Synanon appears to offer a viable pattern of life for some addicts for a time, but it is not clear

---

[61] Descriptions of Synanon are given in Daniel Casriel, *So Fair a House: The Story of Synanon* (Englewood Cliffs, N. J.: Prentice-Hall, 1963); Rita Volkman and Donald R. Cressey, "Differential Association and the Rehabilitation of Drug Addicts," *American Journal of Sociology*, Vol. 69 (September, 1963), pp. 129-42; and Lewis Yablonsky, *The Tunnel Back: Synanon* (New York: Macmillan, 1965).

whether most of its members will be able to make the full transition to more conventional family living. Even if they do not, however, the apparent initial success of Synanon suggests that the individual's personal commitment, coupled with group support, holds a promise that court commitments are unlikely to equal.

Treatment of Addicts in Great Britain

Great Britain has, as previously noted, only a few hundred narcotics addicts. It appears that the British have never had a major problem of drug addiction, even though prior to 1920 narcotics could be purchased from chemists (pharmacists) without a prescription. The Dangerous Drugs Act of 1920 was the British equivalent of the Harrison Act. It placed responsibility for the treatment of addicts in the hands of the medical profession. As in the case of the Harrison Act, a question arose as to the interpretation of the phrase in the law which permitted a doctor to possess, supply, or prescribe drugs "so far as necessary for the practice of his profession." The Home Office, which has general control over drug law enforcement, interpreted this to mean that doctors were not to prescribe drugs "solely for the gratification of addiction." On the other hand, rather than categorically defining the situation in legal terms, the government requested a medical committee to advise it on doubtful points and accepted the committee's report as its guide in defining the relationship of the physician to the addict. The committee recommended that:

> . . . morphine or heroin may be properly administered to addicts in the following circumstances, namely, (a) where patients are under treatment by the gradual withdrawal method with a view to cure, (b) where it has been demonstrated, after a prolonged attempt at cure, that the use of the drug cannot be safely discontinued entirely, on account of the severity of the withdrawal symptoms produced, (c) where it has been similarly demonstrated that the patient, while capable of leading a useful and relatively normal life when a certain minimum dose is regularly administered, becomes incapable of this when the drug is entirely discontinued.[62]

Thus, the addict who has become so dependent upon drugs as to be unable to get along without them may be given maintenance doses by a physician. The cost of legal opiates is modest. The addict need not, therefore, resort to crime in order to secure drugs. Equally important, the demand for illicit drugs is minimized and the traffic in such drugs is much less profitable than in the United States.

---

[62] Home Office, "The Duties of Doctors and Dentists under the Dangerous Drugs Acts," D.D. 101 (February, 1956), Appendix A, p. 10.

Until recently, the difference between the British approach and that of the United States has been either ignored or denied by American narcotics-control personnel. On the one hand, they have argued that the British have the same system as we do; on the other, they have argued that the approach may work in England but will not work here.[63] Clearly, the medical profession was not intimidated by narcotics-control personnel in Great Britain. Doctors can prescribe drugs for addicts if in their opinion such prescription is warranted, and they need not fear being hounded by narcotics agents. Addicts are not automatically criminals; drug possession is a crime only if the drugs have been obtained unlawfully. No attempt has been made to brand the addict as a "dope fiend." He is seen as a sick person needing medical help.

Drug addiction in Britain is much more an individual phenomenon than in the United States. It is not substantially linked with organized crime or with deprivation. The British system works as well as it does because the definitions of the situation, made in the interpreting legislation for the control of narcotics, have been generally accepted by all participants—enforcement personnel, medicine, the general public, even the addicts. Stereotypes that were promulgated by the Bureau of Narcotics and by frightened reformers in the United States are not consonant with the view of the addict as a sick person. The consequences are seen in the nature of the problem of drug use at the present time. It is not a phenomenon which can be dealt with in terms of the individual alone. It would be a mistake to ignore this fact and to assume that the British approach would solve our narcotics problem. But it would be equally a mistake to dismiss the British system as having no implications for the United States.

Conclusion

In perspective, the problem of drug addiction is not a major social problem. Compared with mental illness, juvenile delinquency, and other problems treated in this book, it occurs infrequently and in more delimited population groups. For these groups, it is a grave problem, but it is not clearly differentiated from a number of other difficulties and deviations. It is, indeed, primarily a symptom of a deeper pathol-

---

[63] See the discussion by Lindesmith in *The Addict and the Law*, Chapter 6. Lindesmith has for two decades attempted to make Americans aware of the British approach and as a consequence has frequently drawn attacks from the former Commissioner of Narcotics. The British approach and its implications receive the fullest treatment in Schur, *Narcotic Addiction in Britain and America*.

ogy that derives from our failure to integrate into the social fabric the more deprived migrants to our metropolitan centers, especially those disadvantaged by minority-group status. Subjected to all the stimuli which beckon Americans to participate in the joys of an affluent society, yet lacking the legitimate, socially approved means to achieve the gratifications and material rewards promised by this society, some of these persons turn to deviant and illegal means. (See the Epilogue, pages 805-17.)

The solution to the problem of drug addiction may then be approached either from the standpoint of dealing with the symptoms or from that of dealing with the underlying pathology. The elimination of drugs from the environment would relieve the symptoms of addiction. It would not transform present addicts and potential addicts into conventional, effective citizens, but it would remove from their repertoire one mode of retreat for persons whose lack of integration into satisfying relationships and opportunity-structures leads them to the pursuit of "kicks" as the chief end in life. To go beyond this limited objective (which is itself far from attainment) will require coping with the broader issue of social disorganization.

5

Alcohol

by Robert Straus

EFFORTS TO UNDERSTAND THE PHENOMENA ASSOCIATED WITH ALCOHOL
have frequently been limited by a tendency to cast the consideration
within a unilateral conceptual model, to think exclusively within the
frame of reference of morality or medicine or the law, instead of recognizing that drinking behavior has broad social implications affecting in some way almost every aspect of social life. Alcohol problems
also transcend the lines of traditional disciplines devoted to the study
of human behavior.

The nature and severity of alcohol problems found in a particular
society or at a particular time depend on the customs of drinking
which prevail in that society. However, the relationship between
drinking customs and drinking problems can be understood only if
consideration is given to the nature of alcohol, its action in the human
body, and its impact on human behavior.

The Action of Alcohol on Man

An understanding of the relationship between drinking customs and
drinking problems requires a holistic [1] conceptual model that considers the functional relationship, continuing interaction, and fundamental interdependence among the basic components of drinking behavior. These components include the nature of alcohol and its pharmacological properties; the nature of alcoholic beverages, including
the variations in the concentrations of alcohol and of other substances
found in common types of beverage; the historical role of climate and

---

[1] Named for a philosophical theory first so designated by Jan C. Smuts which
holds that organic systems have properties pertaining to the whole rather than
to its components and that the dynamics of the whole cannot be explained as
the result of its independent elements.

other geographical factors in influencing the drinking customs of various societies; the biological nature of man and his physiological and biochemical reactions to alcohol; the psychological nature of man and his psychological reactions to alcohol; the nature of beliefs about alcohol and sanctions for drinking; the customs of drinking, expressed in terms of time, context, rationale, quantity, and frequency; the impact of drinking customs on the psychological and biological experiences of drinking; and the relationship between drinking customs and the family, religious, economic, political, medical, and recreational systems of a society.

The Nature of Alcohol: Physiological Effects [2]

Beverage alcohol [3] in its pure form is a colorless, volatile, inflammable liquid. It has almost no odor, but it does possess a powerful burning taste that virtually prohibits human consumption of alcohol in full strength. Alcohol can be derived from a wide variety of fruits and grains by several processes. The oldest two processes are fermentation and brewing, which were known to many prehistoric peoples. The manufacturing of alcoholic beverages by distillation, however, is a relatively recent process.[4]

Natural fermentation involves exposing fruit juices to the air in a warm place. The process is dependent on yeast from the dust of the air which settles on the liquid and acts on the sugar in the juices. Fermentation can produce an alcohol content ranging from about 9 to 14 percent depending on the amount of sugar in the fruit. Some wines are "reinforced" or "fortified" to an alcohol content of 20 percent by the addition of distilled spirits. Brewing involves fermentation of a cereal-based broth to which malt is added to convert starch to sugar on which the yeast can act. Brewed beers and ales usually have an

---

[2] See Leon Greenberg, "Alcohol in the Body," in R. G. McCarthy, ed., *Drinking and Intoxication* (New York: Free Press, 1959), pp. 7-13; and Leonard Goldberg, "The Metabolism of Alcohol," in S. P. Lucia, ed., *Alcohol and Civilization* (New York: McGraw-Hill, 1963), pp. 23-42.

[3] Beverage alcohol, technically ethyl alcohol, is only one of numerous forms of alcohol. Unlike other alcohols, ethyl alcohol can be rapidly oxidized in the human body. A variety of nonpotable alcohols are used in industrial processes and in such common substances as automobile antifreeze, cleaning fluids, fuels, liniments, and numerous other readily available items. The ingestion of these poisonous alcohols can, and frequently does, lead to blindness, permanent nerve disorder, or death. The occasional use of nonbeverage alcohols for human consumption, either by accident or in desperation by alcoholics, poses an additional social problem of alcohol, one which is not considered in this chapter.

[4] Although the date of the first introduction of distilled spirits cannot be established, there does not appear to have been significant use in Europe until the twelfth or thirteenth century.

alcohol content of from 3 to 6 percent. Stronger beverages are manufactured through the distillation of fermented wines or brews, a process which recovers liquids with an alcohol content of 35 to 50 percent. Fermented and brewed beverages retain some of the minerals and vitamins of the fruit or cereals from which they are made, but these properties are all lost in the process of distillation.[5]

Since alcohol has a high caloric value, individuals who drink large amounts in the form of distilled spirits often meet their energy needs through alcohol and are, therefore, not hungry for foods which contain minerals, proteins, vitamins, and other essential nutrients. For this reason, a variety of serious nutritional diseases, including beriberi and pellagra, have been commonly associated with chronic and heavy consumption of alcohol. However, the prevalence of nutritional disease as a concomitant of alcoholism has decreased dramatically since the 1930's when the practice of food enrichment became widespread. With vitamins and other essential nutrients added to breads, cereals, and countless other common foods, "even the little an alcoholic might eat supplied some thiamine, some niacin, some iron, some riboflavin." [6]

In full strength, alcohol is an irritant to body tissues; however, it is seldom taken in this form because of the burning sensation it produces in the mouth and throat. Drinkers who habitually consume strong alcoholic beverages without dilution, however, may develop chronic gastritis or may damage the throat or esophagus. Unlike almost all other substances, alcohol does not require digestion. It is quickly absorbed into the blood, in part directly from the stomach and in part from the small intestine. Because it is so rapidly absorbed, the concentration of alcohol in the blood is quickly reduced to a level which is relatively nonirritating to body tissues.

The major impact of alcohol on human behavior is derived from its pharmacological properties as an anesthetic and a depressant, with an action quite similar to that of ether or chloroform. The intoxicating effect of alcohol depends on its concentration in the blood when it reaches the brain.

Roughly speaking, a man of moderate weight (155-165 pounds) who consumes an ounce of whisky or a bottle of beer might achieve an alcohol concentration in the blood of no more than 0.02 percent. However, were he to consume five or six ounces of whisky rather quickly he would achieve a concentration of about 0.1 percent.

[5] Greenberg, "Alcohol in the Body," pp. 7-8.
[6] Mark Keller, "Norman Jolliffe, 1901-1961," *Quarterly Journal of Studies on Alcohol,* Vol. 22 (December, 1961), pp. 531-34.

The effect on behavior from a concentration of 0.02 percent would be negligible for most people. But a concentration of 0.1 percent produces definite depression of sensory and motor functions (slight staggering, fumbling, and the tongue tripping over even familiar words). Despite a reduction in digital dexterity, auditory and visual discrimination, tactile perception, and the speed of motor responses, many drinkers at this level have the illusion that their reactions, perception, and discrimination are better than normal. A concentration of 0.2 percent of alcohol will incapacitate most drinkers both physically and emotionally. At 0.3 percent the drinker will be stuporous; a concentration above 0.4 percent leads to coma. A concentration of 0.6 or 0.7 percent would affect the ability to breathe and cause death.[7]

Whereas the level of the intoxicating effect depends on the level of concentration of alcohol in the blood reaching the brain, the level of concentration of alcohol in turn depends on the amount of pure or absolute alcohol ingested, the kind of alcoholic beverage, the body weight and body chemistry of the drinker, the content of the drinker's stomach, the time of day, and the speed with which a given amount of alcohol is consumed.

Once it enters the human body and is absorbed by the blood, alcohol is subject to a process of oxidation by which it is eventually reduced to carbon dioxide and water. This process occurs at a fairly constant rate for each individual, with the amount of alcohol that can be used up in a given period of time varying according to body weight. A man of moderate weight will generally dispose of about three-quarters of an ounce of whisky an hour. Since the degree of intoxication that a drinker will experience depends on the concentration of alcohol at any one time, significant intoxication will be experienced only when conditions of drinking are such that the rate of absorption is sufficiently greater than the rate of oxidation. A pint of whisky consumed gradually over a 24 hour period might produce no marked effect, while the same amount consumed in the space of an hour would lead to extreme intoxication.

It has already been noted that alcoholic beverages vary in the amount of absolute alcohol which they contain, from about 3 percent for some beers to 50 percent for many distilled spirits. The ingestion of two ounces of absolute alcohol would require drinking 40 ounces of 5 percent beer but only four ounces of 50 percent whisky. The length of time required to consume alcohol in the form of whisky as compared with beer would account for the fact that the whisky drinker

---

[7] Greenberg, "Alcohol in the Body," pp. 11-12.

achieves a greater concentration of alcohol than the beer drinker, for by the time the latter finishes his large volume of beverage, some of the alcohol in the first part of his drink has already been oxidized. Furthermore, beer contains some food substances which tend to slow absorption.

Generally speaking, other factors being equal, people who customarily consume alcohol in the form of beer or wine do not experience the same levels of effect from alcohol as those who customarily consume distilled types of beverage with higher alcohol content. Similarly, persons whose drinking is deliberately spaced over time do not experience the same effect as others who may consume the same amount or form of alcoholic beverage in a short period of time.

Because alcohol is absorbed directly from the stomach and small intestine, the rate of absorption depends on the stomach content at the time of drinking. Alcohol ingested on an empty stomach is very rapidly absorbed into the blood and sent quickly on its way to the central nervous system where maximum effect may be experienced before oxidation takes place. The same amount of alcohol ingested with food, or on a full stomach, will be absorbed much more slowly. Foods rich in protein, such as cheese, meat, and eggs, are especially effective in slowing the absorption of alcohol. When alcohol is ingested after a large protein-rich meal, oxidation is able to keep pace with absorption. Thus the drinker may feel only a minimal effect.

Another important physiological variable is the weight of the drinker. Since the volume of body fluid is roughly proportional to body weight, a person weighing 100 pounds who ingests an ounce of absolute alcohol within a minute's time will experience roughly twice the concentration of alcohol in the blood and a much greater intoxicating effect from alcohol than a person who weighs 200 pounds.

Certain characteristics of different types of alcoholic beverages may also have an important bearing on the effects upon individual drinkers. For example, carbon dioxide in a beverage appears to hasten absorption, thus enhancing the attraction of soda water and other carbonated mixers for those who want to feel maximum effect. Milk used in eggnog or butter used in hot buttered rum have the opposite effect.

Although almost all that we now know about the intoxicating properties of alcoholic beverages relates to ethyl alcohol, there are recent suggestions that other substances which are present in very minute amounts in all alcoholic beverages may help explain the apparent differences in the toxic reaction of different persons to similar amounts of alcohol consumed under similar conditions. These substances are called "congeners." They exist in several hundred varieties and are natural products of the fermentation process and of the processes whereby whiskies are aged for taste, color, and bouquet.[8] The congeners found in different types of beverage vary widely in number and level of concentration; there are few in vodka and gin and relatively many in bourbon, rum, and cognac brandy.[9] Congeners are mentioned here because a further understanding of both the transitory and potentially cumulative toxicity of certain congeners may modify current concepts regarding the toxic impact of alcoholic beverages on man.

The Impact of Drinking Customs

In a wide variety of ways, the impact of alcohol on man is also related to the society's customs regarding drinking. In historical perspective, the types of alcoholic beverages used by different societies have been determined in large part by such geographic factors as soil, climate, and terrain. Just as the wine drinking customs and wine technology of southern Europe are clearly associated with an area where geographic conditions have nurtured the growth of succulent grapes, so the varied alcoholic beverages used by peoples throughout the world reflect the prevailing natural products and technology of particular regions. Only in the recent past have technological advances in agriculture, transportation, and manufacturing removed those barriers which sharply distinguish the drinking customs of different societies. These changes have permitted the emergence of more heterogeneous drinking practices, particularly in the United States and other technologically advanced areas.

The customary contexts in which drinking takes place and the customary beliefs about the function of drinking influence the frequency and intensity of an alcohol-induced effect. People who look upon alcohol as a form of food and who customarily drink only with meals rarely achieve a high level of alcohol concentration. As mentioned above, food acts as a buffer to alcohol absorption and provides competing caloric intake. Furthermore, drinking with meals rarely involves the rapid ingestion of large amounts of alcohol required to achieve a significant effect.

It is quite otherwise when most drinking occurs on an empty stomach, such as at a late afternoon cocktail party. Drinkers generally experience quite rapid absorption and more readily achieve concentrations of alcohol sufficient to produce noticeable effects. The buffering

---

[8] Herbert McKennis, Jr., and Harvey B. Hagg, "On the Congeners of Whiskey," *Journal of the American Geriatrics Society,* Vol. 7 (1959), pp. 845-58.

[9] Berton Roueché, *The Neutral Spirit* (Boston: Little, Brown, 1960).

effect of food is missing; also, people tend to drink more rapidly when they are not eating, and more rapidly when standing up than when seated. Moreover, beverages served at cocktail parties most likely provide alcohol in high concentration, thus permitting the drinker to ingest relatively large amounts of alcohol without a large volume of dilutants.

People who consume alcohol primarily because they believe in its medicinal efficacy are apt to space their drinking regularly over time, or, as they would other medicines, use alcohol only when a specific need arises. For example, a study of the drinking practices of Italians in the United States revealed the fairly prevalent belief that alcohol in the form of wine increases the supply of blood. Some adherents to this notion faithfully increased their alcohol consumption at times of menstruation or accidents in order to replenish their blood supply. Others, with the same basic belief and under similar circumstances, were careful to abstain from alcohol lest they induce a dangerously excessive loss of blood.[10]

The Psychological Effects of Alcohol

To this point we have considered the mechanisms whereby alcohol is ingested and disposed of by the human body and the relationship between drinking customs and the physiological effects of alcohol. The primary significance of alcohol in man appears to lie in its effect on human behavior after it reaches the central nervous system, where its action is essentially that of an anesthetic and a depressant.

We will now consider the impact of alcohol on psychological behavior—on the ways in which a person may think, feel, and act when under the influence of alcohol.

The psychological effects of alcohol have been classified into two distinct but related categories.[11] First are effects on *overt* behavior, such as "sensation, perception, reaction time, the performance of motor tasks and skills and processes of learning, remembering, thinking, reasoning, and solving problems."[12] Second are the effects on *emotional* behavior, such as fear, anxiety, tension, hostility, or such feelings as being "on edge" or having a sense of well-being.

---

[10] P. H. Williams and R. Straus, "Drinking Patterns of Italians in New Haven; Utilization of the Personal Diary as a Research Technique," *Quarterly Journal of Studies on Alcohol*, Vol. 11 (March, June, September, December, 1950), pp. 50-91, 250-308, 452-83, 586-629.

[11] Edith S. Lisansky, "Psychological Effects of Alcohol," in McCarthy, ed., *Drinking and Intoxication*, pp. 18-25.

[12] *Ibid.*, p. 18.

Numerous studies have suggested clearly that alcohol, even in small amounts, does have a deleterious impact on task performance, but that the relationship depends on such variables as the complexity of the task and the familiarity of the task to the performer. E. M. Jellinek has noted that while the effect of even "small amounts of alcohol on skilled performances increases as the tasks become more complex. . . . the effect on a complex but familiar task may be less than on a simpler but unfamiliar one, and . . . the effect may be less on persons accustomed than on persons not accustomed to drinking." [13] Some experienced drinkers do appear to learn how to compensate psychologically for the sensations produced by alcohol. They learn how to present the outward manifestations of sobriety and how to carry on some kinds of familiar activities despite the handicap of alcohol's effect.

Studies of alcohol and human behavior are further complicated by the fact that alcohol may have a beneficial impact on emotional behaviors which appears to counteract its impact on task performance. The ability of many individuals to perform effectively is often seriously limited by their emotional reactions. To those who have experienced at some time the feeling that they did not perform well on a given task or examination because they were worried or wrought up, alcohol, which serves as a kind of sedative and also acts to depress inhibitory mechanisms, may provide enough relief from anxiety and tension to permit more effective performance.

In situations where "effective performance" does not demand a special skill, such as social gatherings, alcohol can produce the desired emotional feeling of well-being and relaxation. However, where some degree of efficiency is required, the relaxing qualities of alcohol may be dangerously misleading for, as Jellinek stresses, "the properties of alcohol that are conducive to sedation or relaxation are by no means conducive to task efficiency." [14]

This paradox leaves unresolved the question of how helpful or damaging the use of alcohol may be for particular individuals faced with particular tasks.[15] As a general rule drinking does not enhance task performance; however, for some individuals, especially very tense, experienced drinkers performing familiar tasks, the relaxing qualities

[13] E. M. Jellinek, *How Alcohol Affects Psychological Behavior,* Lay Supplement No. 11 (New Haven: Quarterly Journal of Studies on Alcohol, 1944), p. 12.
[14] *Ibid.*
[15] For a critical review of relevant literature since 1940, see John A. Carpenter, "The Effects of Alcohol on Some Psychological Processes," *Quarterly Journal of Studies on Alcohol,* Vol. 23 (June, 1962), pp. 274-314.

of alcohol may override its deleterious effects in terms of over-all performance.

The inexperienced drinker, however, is apt to overreact to the sensations of alcohol. He may be merely fulfilling what he perceives to be the socially expected behavior in response to drinking. Such a reaction is commonly seen in groups of young people who can behave as if hilariously intoxicated under the influence of very small amounts of alcohol (and sometimes without alcohol at all). Some drinking novices are so unaccustomed to even the mild sensations of a little alcohol that it may actually impede their task performance beyond the normal expectation for their level of blood alcohol concentration. This phenomenon contributes to a special concern over drinking and driving in young people who are neither experienced drinkers nor experienced drivers.

There is, of course, a fundamental relationship between man's physiological and psychological responses to alcohol. For example, psychological conditions can either promote or retard stomach motility, thereby increasing or decreasing the rate of alcohol absorption and directly influencing the level of effect resulting from a given amount of alcohol. The intensity of psychological effect is directly related to physiological effect. Also, some individuals appear to be psychologically more sensitive to alcohol when they are fatigued.

American Drinking Customs in Historical Perspective [16]

Drinking customs and attitudes of the American population reflect a configuration of practices, beliefs, and attitudes which have come from many parts of the world and reflect many cultures. Over the years,

[16] This section draws primarily from the following sources: H. W. Haggard and E. M. Jellinek, *Alcohol Explored* (New York: Doubleday, 1945), pp. 3-85; Raymond G. McCarthy and E. M. Douglass, *Alcohol and Social Responsibility* (New York: Crowell, 1949), p. 34; and R. Straus and S. D. Bacon, "Drinking Customs and Attitudes in American Society," *Drinking in College* (New Haven: Yale University Press, 1953), Chapter 2, pp. 20-35.

This chapter is concerned primarily with the problems of alcohol as they are manifested in the United States. A growing body of literature about the drinking customs and alcohol problems of other cultures depicts many similarities with conditions in this country but also many striking differences in the interaction of drinking customs, social structure, alcohol problems, and the mechanisms for coping with these problems. For further consideration of alcohol problems in cross-cultural perspective, readers are referred to: McCarthy, ed., *Drinking and Intoxication;* David J. Pittman and Charles R. Snyder, eds., *Society, Culture, and Drinking Patterns* (New York: Wiley & Sons, 1962); Salvatore P. Lucia, ed., *Alcohol and Civilization* (New York: McGraw-Hill, 1963); and the files of the *Quarterly Journal of Studies on Alcohol,* Vols. 1-26 (1940-1965).

there have been significant changes. Nevertheless, many of the ideas about drinking and social responses to the problems of alcohol which prevailed in the eighteenth and nineteenth centuries have resisted change. As a result, there have been striking anachronisms and much confusion in the coping mechanisms of our governmental, religious, and educational systems which have complicated society's response to drinking and have even contributed to the total constellation of problems.

The colonists who came to America from England brought with them well-established habits and attitudes about the use of alcohol. Alcoholic beverages had important religious, medical, and dietary significance; they were well integrated into family life and community recreational practices and quickly became a prominent component of commerce and of the colonial economy. At first, distilled spirits, which had not been generally available in Europe until around 1500, were secondary to beer and wine. However, due to limitations of transportation, the distilling industry was particularly well suited to the colonial economy and soon gained a prominent place. Manufactured distilled spirits were relatively less bulky to transport and less subject to spoilage on long journeys than either grains from which they were derived or beers and wines. Much lower transportation costs in relation to alcohol content and price also favored distilled spirits and seriously handicapped the brewing and wine-producing industries. By the end of the eighteenth century about 90 percent of the alcohol consumed in this country was in the form of distilled spirits. By 1807 it is recorded that Boston had one distillery for every 40 inhabitants—but only two breweries.

Prior to 1700, the use of beer and wine appears to have been primarily a family-centered and family-controlled activity. Religious sanctions were directed against drunkenness and its concomitants. The significance of distilled spirits grew coincidentally with the immigration of numbers of unattached males, whose drinking was unrelated to family sanctions and may have served to compensate for the absence of the gratifications, responsibilities, and stability of family living. The frequent use of alcohol to produce intoxication became particularly characteristic of life on the ever expanding frontier and among the less stable segments of communities during the several decades following the Revolutionary War.

Perhaps in reaction against the excesses of drinking on the frontier and in its urban counterpart, the practice of family drinking appears to have diminished by the early nineteenth century, when frequent heavy consumption of distilled spirits, much of it by unattached men, became the dominant drinking practice. Such practices, which were often accompanied by wild destructive behavior, became a major social concern. Intoxication was seen as a threat to the personal well-being and property of peaceful citizens, and the loss of productive manpower through drunkenness was seen as a threat to the national economy and vitality.

Social concern about drinking began to be expressed in the latter half of the eighteenth century through the temperance movement, which, for a century and a half, has exerted a major influence on American beliefs about alcohol and attitudes toward it. At the outset, the temperance movement was directed against excessive drinking. It was concerned specifically with distilled spirits, not with moderate drinking or the use of beers and wines. It condemned drunkenness on moral, medical, economic, and nationalistic grounds and advocated governmental controls on the liquor trade. By the end of the eighteenth century, the temperance movement gained force and influence, and the first Congress was asked to impose prohibitive tariffs on the import of distilled spirits.

The movement for temperance became identified with almost every facet of social life by the 1830's. In addition to numerous religious organizations that had quite early advocated moderation, there were now temperance societies in the national Congress and in state legislatures, among farmers and businessmen, and in schools and colleges; there were even temperance hotels that boasted that they did not offer spirits for sale. It is estimated that by the mid-1830's, when the nation's population was about 13,000,000, at least a million members were active in the movement.

The temperance movement in the United States reached a peak in 1836.[17] Up to this time, its leaders had been men who were also leaders in their respective professions; women had not been recognized for associate membership until 1833. Until 1836, the temperance movement had been relatively consistent and was clearly focused on the major problems of alcohol as they were defined by society-at-large. Its persuasion was directed at the drinking behavior of peripheral segments of society and its moderation doctrine appears to have been consistent with the prevailing attitudes and drinking behavior of the majority.

Between 1836 and 1840, however, several changes occurred in the movement's concepts and goals, as well as in the place of the temperance movement in the social structure. First, there was a shift of

---

[17] McCarthy and Douglass, *Alcohol and Social Responsibility*, p. 20.

emphasis from drunkenness to drinking, from moderation to abstinence, and from distilled spirits to all alcoholic beverages. Religious beliefs which held that alcoholic beverages were the creation of God and clearly approved in both the Old and New Testaments were radically altered to stress Biblical references implying disapproval of all alcohol consumption. Biblical statements approving wine were reinterpreted as referring to unfermented juices. Temperance philosophy also began to shift from a reliance on moral persuasion against drunkenness to proposals for legal enforcement of total abstinence. Finally, soon after women were admitted to membership, the leadership of the temperance movement quietly shifted from professional and business men to women, and the movement became clearly associated with programs for women's rights, especially suffrage and higher education. As the movement became more radical and more militant and as its leadership became increasingly dominated by persons who displayed a lack of emotional stability, it tended to lose the support of the more stable and respected community elements.

In the 1850's, more than a third of the states legislated prohibition of the manufacture, distribution, and sale of alcoholic beverages, but within a few years these laws had all been repealed or significantly modified. A second wave of prohibition in the 1880's involving eight states was also short-lived. A third wave, involving 25 states by 1917, brought about the national Prohibition Amendment in 1919 which was not repealed until 1933. Even today, legal prohibition prevails in one state (Mississippi) and in hundreds of counties under local option legislation. But legal prohibition, whether national, state, or by local option, has not always shifted drinking behavior in directions desired by the more militant advocates of temperance. It is ironical that successful efforts to legislate prohibition have frequently owed their success to the support of the bootlegging interests, and that drinking practices under prohibition have been particularly characterized by the use of high-alcohol-content beverages under conditions that have increased the prevalence of drunkenness.

Ironically, too, the shift in focus of the temperance movement to encompass all drinking and all forms of alcoholic beverage came at the very time when changes in the composition of the American population were effecting a marked alteration in drinking practices in the direction initially advocated by the adherents of temperance.

At the beginning of the nineteenth century, when the use of distilled spirits dominated American drinking, 90 percent of the white population was of British heritage. After about 1820, waves of immigrants from other nations significantly altered the ethnic composition of this country. In the next century, more than 20 million people migrated from southern, central, and eastern Europe, where the predominant alcoholic beverages were either beers or wines. By about 1840, the change in the ethnic composition of the population began to be reflected in patterns of alcohol consumption. In the 100 years from 1850 to 1950, alcohol consumed in the form of distilled spirits fell from roughly 90 percent to 40 percent of the total alcohol consumed, and per capita (those 15 and over) consumption dropped from 4.17 to 1.72 gallons. During the same period, alcohol consumed in the form of beer rose from 6 to 49 percent of the total, while that in the form of wine rose from 4 to 11 percent; per capita consumption for beer rose from 2.70 to 23.21 gallons and for wine from 0.46 to 1.27 gallons.[18] During this same period the over-all per capita consumption of absolute alcohol in various beverage forms remained virtually consistent, 2.07 gallons in 1850 and 2.04 gallons in 1950.

Changes in the types of alcoholic beverages consumed naturally reflect changes in drinking customs. Jellinek has noted that "a large consumption of distilled spirits and a small consumption of beer is generally an indication that the users are relatively few in number but individually heavy consumers. A large consumption of beer, on the other hand, is indicative of wide use and relatively small individual consumption." [19] Data on consumption from 1750 to 1850 suggest that there were relatively few moderate drinkers and that most people were either heavy drinkers or abstainers. Current estimates suggest that about 70 percent of the adult population use alcohol, but since the total per capita consumption has remained constant, it follows that per capita consumption for users has declined markedly. The shift from distilled spirits to beer has further implications in terms of effects on behavior. Whereas a person drinking whisky could easily consume a pint of alcohol in the course of a day by drinking a quart of whisky, a beer drinker would have to drink ten quarts to take in the same amount of alcohol. From our knowledge of the absorption, metabolism, and impact of alcohol in the human body, it is quite obvious that the effects of beer drinking upon intoxication are quite different from drinking which involves primarily whisky.

Although there has been some moderation in the temperance position during the past 20 years, partly in response to an expanding scientific understanding of the impact of alcohol on man, the basic

---

[18] Compiled by Mark Keller and V. Efron for Straus and Bacon, *Drinking in College*, p. 22.

[19] E. M. Jellinek, "Recent Trends in Alcoholism and in Alcohol Consumption," *Quarterly Journal of Studies on Alcohol*, Vol. 8 (June, 1947), p. 9.

temperance position remains one of unalterable opposition to drinking, based on concepts that emerged when drinking was for the most part heavy drinking leading to intoxication on the part of a marginal but conspicuous minority of the population. Although this position may seem unrealistic in a society in which at least 70 percent of the adult population use alcoholic beverages (for the most part, in moderation), it has had a profound impact on almost every form of social response to the problems involved in the use of alcohol and has helped to perpetuate the confusion and ineffectiveness of efforts by religious, educational, governmental, and medical institutions to deal with these problems.

The impact of the temperance movement in the public schools has been particularly significant. Largely as a result of temperance group pressure, every state has legislated a requirement that education about alcohol be included in the school curriculum. Until quite recently, there were few reliable educational materials and few teachers who were informed about alcohol, so that much which passed for education served to perpetuate misconceptions and stereotypes. The former deficiency no longer exists, although school systems and teachers may have difficulty sorting reliable text materials from those which reflect the biases of special interests.

The alcoholic beverage industries have invested large amounts of money and effort in opposition to the temperance or "dry" position. The "wet" position is expressed in advertising and sales promotion. Behind the scenes, a much more subtle battle has been waging for more than a century. Both the wet and dry interests maintain an extensive lobbying machinery and continuing contact with federal and state legislators and with the power structure of local communities. In recent years, both forces have tried to don the cloak of scientific respectability by offering grants in support of research and quoting extensively, though selectively, from research findings.

Contemporary American Drinking Customs

We have yet to examine the prevalence of drinking in contemporary American society. Although it may seem to be a simple matter, measurements in this field are as difficult to come by as those in fields of mental illness, crime, delinquency, poverty, and the other social problems reviewed in this book. The problem of measurement is complicated by fairly wide variations in the interpretation of just what constitutes being a drinker or an abstainer.

How frequently in a month, a year, or a lifetime, or how much does one have to drink in order to be considered or to consider himself a "drinker?" Some people who take beverage alcohol daily think of themselves as abstainers because they believe that they are drinking for reasons of health. Others who have used alcohol only on infrequent social occasions during their lifetime may classify themselves as users. Neither the general public nor the various investigators who have tried to measure the prevalence of drinking have so far agreed on criteria.

Two recent studies show that between 63 and 71 percent of the adult population (age 21 and above) in the United States drink some form of alcoholic beverages.[20] Although this figure represents about 70 to 80 million American adults, it grossly underestimates the prevalence of drinking since it omits drinkers under 21 years of age. Several studies of teen-age alcohol use in various parts of the United States between 1953 and 1963 find that most high school graduates have had some exposure to drinking.[21]

It was reported in 1953 that about 90 percent of the students 16 years and older in Nassau County, New York, drink on some occasions.[22] A study of 2000 Michigan high school students found, however, that although 92 percent had tasted alcohol at some time, only 23 percent drank in any continuing pattern.[23] Another study conducted in Kansas suggested that about half of the high school youths in that state are using alcohol with the prevalence of use increasing gradually as they progress through school.[24]

---

[20] Harold A. Mulford reports a figure of 71 percent, based on modified random sampling conducted by the Natural Opinion Research Center in 1963. See "Drinking and Deviant Drinking in the U.S.A., 1963," *Quarterly Journal of Studies on Alcohol*, Vol. 25 (December, 1964), pp. 634-50. Mulford's figure compares with 63 percent reported in 1964 by the American Institute of Public Opinion (Princeton, N. J.: Press Release 5, February, 1964). Both studies used the same basic question on prevalence, "Do you ever have occasion to use alcoholic beverages such as liquor, wine, or beer, or are you a total abstainer?" In 1946, a survey based on a sample comparable to Mulford's reported a drinking prevalence rate of 65 percent for American adults. J. W. Riley, Jr. and C. F. Marden, "The Social Pattern of Alcoholic Drinking," *Quarterly Journal of Studies on Alcohol*, Vol. 8 (September, 1947), pp. 265-73. Also in 1946, the American Institute of Public Opinion reported that 67 percent of American adults used alcohol.

[21] E. A. Shepherd and Mary R. Barber, *Teen-Age Alcohol Use* (Hartford, Conn.: Connecticut Department of Mental Health, Alcoholism Division, 1965).

[22] Hofstra College Research Bureau, *Use of the Alcoholic Beverages Among High School Students* (New York: Sheppard Foundation, 1953).

[23] G. L. Maddox and B. C. McCall, *Drinking Among Teen-Agers* (New Brunswick, N. J.: Rutgers Center of Alcohol Studies, 1964).

[24] University of Kansas, Department of Sociology and Anthropology, *Attitudes of High School Students Toward Alcoholic Beverages* (New York: Sheppard Foundation, 1956).

Straus and Bacon reported in 1953 on the drinking practices of 16,300 students in 27 American colleges throughout the country.[25] They found that 74 percent of their total sample reported some use of alcoholic beverages beyond experimental, joking, or ceremonial use in childhood or purely isolated experiences.

These various studies of the prevalence of drinking in high school and college age groups provide a basis for estimating that from 8 to 10 million young people in the age range 16 to 20 drink alcoholic beverages beyond the extent of isolated incidents. Added to the estimates for the "adult" population, this suggests that from 80 to 90 million Americans above the age of 15 can be considered as users of alcoholic beverages.

Some Social Correlates of Drinking

Actually, data on the prevalence of drinking in a total population may be quite misleading. The studies of Mulford and of Riley and Marden both reported greater use by men than by women (Mulford: men 79 percent, women 63 percent; Riley and Marden: men 75 percent, women 56 percent) and both studies found that the prevalence of drinkers tended to be greater for persons with more education, for those living in large urban centers, and for those of the Jewish and Catholic faiths. Both studies found a decreasing prevalence of drinkers with advancing age past age 35.

Mulford found that the prevalence of drinking varied regionally from 88 percent in the mid-Atlantic states to 33 percent in the East South Central region; by religion from 90 percent for Jews and 89 percent for Catholics to 48 percent for Baptists and 53 percent for small Protestant denominations; by annual income from 87 percent for those over $10,000 to 54 percent for those under $3,000. There were variations also according to occupational and marital status, years of education, and size of community. Straus and Bacon found similar variations among college students. In their study, there were twice as many abstainers among the women (39 percent) as among the men (20 percent); more users in private than public colleges; more users among students from higher income families and among Jewish and Catholic students; more users among Jews and Catholics who were *frequent* participants in religious activity, but more users among Protestants and especially Mormons who were *infrequent* church-goers; and many more users if both parents were users than if both parents abstained.

---

[25] Straus and Bacon, *Drinking in College.*

Even more striking relationships between drinking customs and the sociocultural characteristics of students are found in such matters as the types of beverages used, the quantity and frequency of drinking, usual drinking companions, the occasions or settings in which drinking normally takes place, and the stated reasons for drinking. Consistently, drinking patterns reflect the practices and sanctions of their significant reference groups—parents, close friends, and persons with similar regional, income, religious, ethnic, and educational identifications. These data, together with Mulford's findings for the adult population, firmly document the significance of reference group behavior as a primary determinant of individuals' participation or nonparticipation in the customs of drinking as well as the specific nature of the drinking patterns which may be followed. It is also clear that certain kinds of social groups attract or repel members in part because of their reputation for heavy or moderate drinking or abstaining.[26]

Alcohol and Youth

A major social problem associated with alcoholic beverages today revolves around the question of drinking by young people. The press has given special prominence to this question—in part reflecting social concern, in part creating concern and misconceptions as well. There appears to be general readiness to assume that almost any untoward behavior involving young people is due to their drinking. Such assumptions are even made in the face of clear evidence to the contrary. For example, a news item about vandalism which occurred during a college outing noted in its headline and lead paragraph that the incident was undoubtedly the result of drinking by students, while buried in the rest of the article was a police report which exonerated the students altogether. The prevailing tendency to equate disturbed behavior in young people with drinking involves both an oversimplifi-

---

[26] This review of the customs of drinking in American society has not dealt with racial differences or similarities in drinking practices simply because the question has scarcely been studied. G. L. Maddox and E. Borinski recently reported ("Drinking Behavior of Negro Collegians," *Quarterly Journal of Studies on Alcohol,* Vol. 25 [December, 1964], pp. 651-68) that in reviewing the literature they found only 17 items in the *Classified Abstract Archives of the Alcohol Literature* and only six additional occasional references. They concluded primarily that drinking is at least as prevalent among Negroes as among other Americans and that drinking among Negroes is associated with a higher incidence of personal and social complications. The lack of any significant data on the drinking practices of the largest ethnic minority in the United States leaves a glaring gap in the sociological study of alcohol problems.

cation of multiple factors and an exaggeration of the role of alcohol per se.

Adult attitudes toward teen-age drinking often confuse drinking with alcohol pathology, although there is no evidence to show that particular patterns of teen-age drinking are especially linked with alcoholism. Like many other social problems, the question of teen-age drinking elicits a wide variety of ineffectual social responses. Some people exaggerate the problem; others deny that it even exists. Parents tend to blame or impose responsibility upon schools or law-enforcement agencies. Equally, schools tend to blame parents or the police, while law-enforcement personnel in turn blame schools and parents, and churches frequently blame all three.

Available data on drinking by adolescents indicate that the vast majority of high school students who drink at all do not drink very often, nor do they consume very much at a time. However, in the college age group of 18 to 21, the prevalence of drinking equals, and the quantity and frequency may exceed, that of the general population. For teen-agers, intoxication is a special problem, perhaps because they have a limited capacity for alcohol, or perhaps because their initial psychological reaction to alcohol might be hypersensitive and complicated by their lack of experience in coping with the effects of alcohol. Therefore, when adolescents do become intoxicated they are likely to get involved in other difficulties and be conspicuous. As noted earlier, some adolescents may give the illusion of intoxication when they have consumed only a single drink. Such behavior undoubtedly contributes to a stereotype of the excesses of teen-age drinking.

Most adolescent drinking reflects the practices and sanctions of family, friends, and other reference groups.[27] However, for some young people, drinking involves breaking with family or religious convictions. The mere act of drinking, or the effects of drinking, or the behavior of drinking companions may evoke feelings of personal conflict or guilt. Or drinking may be associated with sexual behavior which evokes similar kinds of conflict. The reaction of students to the anxiety associated with drinking is complicated by the fact that pharmacological properties of alcohol can provide temporary relief for the drinker from the very anxiety that his concern about drinking has created. This is a "solace" denied to the young person who may be

---

[27] G. L. Maddox, "High School Drinking Behavior: Incidental Information from Two National Surveys," *Quarterly Journal of Studies on Alcohol,* Vol. 25 (June, 1964), pp. 339-47.

equally anxious because he has decided not to drink despite pressures from his peers. The dilemma of those who abstain in the face of pressures to drink should not be omitted from an inventory of alcohol problems.

The confusion prevailing in American society with respect to drinking by young people is compounded by a gross inconsistency between custom and law. Forty-eight states prohibit the use of distilled spirits by anyone under the age of 21. Only New York and Louisiana set the legal age at 18. All but five states prohibit the use of wine, and all but 14 prohibit the use of beer, before age 21, with six of the latter making the exception only for beer containing no more than 3.2 percent alcohol.[28] Kentucky permits voting at age 18, but not drinking.

From the standpoint of the law, drinking is clearly defined as an adult behavior. A few exceptions that involve primarily parental or medical responsibility merely emphasize the gap between law and custom. Eighteen states make exceptions for drinking in the presence of or with consent of a parent although most of these permit drinking only at home, and some make an exception only for beer. Six states exempt drinking for medicinal purposes. There is one exception for sacramental drinking. Two states waive the age limit if the drinker is married and one state exempts members of the armed services. There is only a token recognition that certain social roles, such as in marriage or the military service, may alter one's legal status with respect to adulthood.

As we have seen, the realities of drinking by high school and college youth reveal widespread disregard of legal sanctions. In fact, Straus and Bacon found that the quantity and frequency of drinking among college users appears to increase by age up to about 21, after which there is a slight decline. There is a hint here that, once drinking becomes legally permissible, it may become somewhat less important.

The college drinking survey also found a distinct correlation between formal college prohibitions on drinking and the excesses displayed by student drinkers. Although colleges with formal prohibitions had relatively fewer drinkers than those with no restrictions or only token prohibition, the students at "restricted schools" who broke the formal code by drinking generally drank more frequently, more heavily, and were more often involved in drinking-related problems than the drinking students at more "liberal" colleges. As one student noted,

---

[28] Raymond G. McCarthy, ed., *Alcohol Education for Classroom and Community* (New York: McGraw-Hill, 1964), p. 26.

"When you go to the trouble of driving fifty miles to get a drink, you don't have just two drinks." [29]

The tendency to use alcohol as a way of flaying the restrictions of authority is not restricted to adolescents. It is reminiscent of adult drinking practices under prohibition. Yet, in the 1960's, this pattern may provide a key to the special significance of drinking for young people.

Adolescence in contemporary American society has become recognized as a particularly important period of socialization. It is a period of transition from dependence on a parental family to independence in marriage, employment, and community status. In our culture, it is a period during which social and psychological maturity frequently lags behind physical maturity. The restrictions of adolescence are such that many young people develop doubts about their own manliness or womanliness. Drinking behavior for some young men provides a symbolic proof of manliness. For others, alcohol helps remove inhibitions to the actual demonstration of sexual prowess or attraction.

Adolescents in American society are faced with many discontinuities and inconsistencies. They are expected to assume certain "adult" roles and responsibilities, while many "adult" rights and privileges are withheld. Much adolescent behavior which is culturally sanctioned does little to prepare the adolescent for the roles required of an adult. For example, dating customs often bear little relevance to expected roles in marriage.

Rapid social change has imposed a barrier between roles and values of parents and those of their adolescent children. Parents can provide less meaningful role models and less security.[30]

In the face of conflict, insecurity, and confusion, adolescents have developed a distinctive subculture. They seek a self-identity. They tend to press for symbolic adult status and to reject symbols of repressive authority. Drinking behavior provides an apt symbol of the achievement of adult status since it is defined legally as an adult privilege. At the same time, restrictions against teen-age drinking provide the symbolic "red flag" for rejection of authority. Thus, many efforts to control or moderate the drinking of young people, although charged with good intent, simply serve to enhance the attractiveness and status of drinking. Drinking that is an expression of personal con-

---

[29] Straus and Bacon, *Drinking in College,* p. 69.

[30] The dilemma of adolescents in contemporary society is discussed in James S. Coleman, *The Adolescent Society* (New York: Free Press, 1961), pp. 1-57 and Paul Goodman, *Growing up Absurd* (New York: Random House, 1960).

flict or social rebellion is more apt to involve conditions conducive to intoxication: large amounts of alcohol, distilled spirits rather than beer, quick consumption, no food, and, often, the major purpose of becoming high, tight, or drunk.

A recent study of the relationship between teen-age drinking and the law has documented the long recognized anachronism of most existing age limits on drinking in terms of the realities of adolescent drinking.[31] This problem has prompted numerous recommendations for uniform state laws that would lower the legal age for purchasing and consuming alcoholic beverages to 18 since existing laws certainly do not deter teen-age drinking. A special problem in this respect is found in the states bordering New York, whose young people drive into New York to take advantage of the lower legal age for purchasing alcohol. This practice, which welds driving and drinking into a single pattern, has dramatized the need for uniformity.

Statutes regarding alcohol education, most of which call for an emphasis on the evils of alcohol and employ a psychology of fear, are equally outdated. Modern educational approaches focus on instruction about the physiological and psychological effects of alcohol in an effort to promote more responsible drinking practices on the part of those who drink and to provide peer group understanding and acceptance for those who abstain.[32]

Drinking and Driving

For many years, there has been an increasing social concern about the role played by alcohol in traffic accidents. The Attorney General of New Jersey reported in 1965 that tests performed on three-fourths of the drivers killed in his state during 1961-1964 revealed that 56 percent tested positive for alcohol and half of these had a blood alcohol content ranging from 0.15 percent to more than 0.25 percent. At the 0.15 percent level, the presumption of intoxication is legally invoked. Of the drivers killed in single-vehicle accidents, two-thirds had been drinking.[33] In many different contexts, alcohol is now identified as the leading cause of driver-caused traffic accidents and an increasing body of data from blood-alcohol measurements on drivers has been assembled to back up these claims.

The problems of drinking and driving are by no means new. They

---

[31] M. W. Sterne, D. J. Pittman, and T. Coe, "Teen-agers, Drinking, and the Law," *Crime and Delinquency*, Vol. 11 (January, 1965), pp. 78-85.

[32] See McCarthy, ed., *Alcohol Education for Classroom and Community*.

[33] *The New York Times*, April 3, 1965, p. 83.

have involved Roman chariots, clipper ships, and "mule-skinners," but they became more pronounced in the early nineteenth century with the introduction of various mechanical modes of transportation.[34] Railroad companies and unions have long had strict rules against drinking while on duty. By 1924, the automobile had developed sufficient lethal potential for the Connecticut Motor Vehicle Commission to conclude categorically that "any person who . . . drinks and then operates a motor vehicle must be considered drunk . . . no person who has been drinking ought to be allowed to operate a car." [35]

A large body of research has been concerned with the impact of various levels of alcohol in the body on psychosensory and psychomotor behavior. Numerous chemical tests have been developed for quantifying alcohol levels in blood reaching the brain by analyzing breath or samples of urine or capillary blood. In the 1930's, several "packaged laboratories" were developed for use by police departments in order to obtain quick measurements of the blood alcohol concentration of drivers from samples of blood or breath which could be obtained at the scene of an accident.[36] In 1938, a committee of the National Safety Council recommended a uniform code for designating legal evidence of intoxication. It was suggested that a blood alcohol concentration of 0.05 percent or less be recognized as evidence that alcohol influence was not sufficient to impair driving ability; levels between 0.05 and 0.15 percent were designated as relevant but not conclusive evidence of intoxication; and levels of 0.15 percent or more, as evidence of intoxication sufficient to impair driving ability. The code was formulated in an effort to provide a precise basis for nationwide standardization of statutes regarding drinking and driving and also to provide law-enforcement agencies with a basis for obtaining indisputable evidence that would stand up in court.

There has been anything but uniformity in the application of the National Safety Council's uniform code. States have varied widely both in their statutes and interpretations of the law regarding the obtaining and use of evidence from breath or blood samples, particularly if evidence is provided involuntarily. There have also been some doubts raised about the limits of alcohol concentration permitted by the code, suggesting that they may be much too liberal. There is

---

[34] R. F. Borkenstein, H. J. Trubitt, and R. J. Lease, "Problems of Enforcement and Prosecution," in B. H. Fox and J. H. Fox, eds., *Alcohol and Traffic Safety*, Public Health Service Publication No. 1043 (Washington, D.C.: U.S. Government Printing Office, 1963), pp. 137-88.

[35] *Ibid.*, p. 138.

[36] *Ibid.*, p. 191.

strong evidence to suggest that even very low levels of alcohol, well below 0.05 percent, may impair the driving of some individuals, especially of poor drivers or of young people who are both inexperienced drinkers and inexperienced drivers. Even mild sensations produced by alcohol, if they come at a time when the novice drinker-driver is called upon to respond to a unique traffic situation, might "cause" an accident. For poor-risk drinkers and poor-risk drivers, the code's implication of a "safe level" can provide a very dangerous justification of driving after drinking.

It has also been demonstrated that there are wide variations in the curve of blood-alcohol concentration so that some drivers who might test within "safe" limits shortly after an accident could have experienced a peak within the dangerous limits of alcohol concentration at the time of the accident. Such relatively precipitous but brief peaks of alcohol effect may be particularly common in persons who are driving from a late afternoon cocktail party where they have been drinking moderately but hastily and on an empty stomach.

In an effort to identify clearly "safe" and clearly "dangerous" alcohol levels for driving, the National Safety Council's code has left ambiguous the very broad range of concentrations between 0.05 and 0.15 percent. There is considerable evidence that a level of 0.15 is much too high for safety and that even a level of 0.1 percent involves risk for a majority of drivers. Yet, as we have seen, there is also some reason to believe that small amounts of alcohol may actually improve the task performance of some people, especially if they have been incapacitated by tension and anxiety.

In spite of fairly clear evidence that alcohol impairs driving ability, the issue is clouded by many variables which, as we have noted, affect the impact of a given amount of alcohol on a particular driver. These include the related factors of age, sex, and body weight; the relative degrees of experience in drinking and of learned ability to compensate for some of the effects of alcohol; [37] the nature of an individual's "normal" psychosensory and psychomotor responses; fatigue; individual body chemistry; and those aspects of the drinking custom that influence the curve of alcohol effect, such as beverage type, context of drinking, time of day, speed of drinking, and presence or absence of food.

The relevant considerations are numerous and complex, and it is clear that no uniformly safe rule for driving and drinking can be defined. Quite apart from the problem of defining criteria for establishing

---

[37] Carpenter, "The Effects of Alcohol on Some Psychological Processes."

legal intoxication, the interests of public safety clearly support a broad social movement to discourage drinking prior to driving. Yet efforts to modify drinking-and-driving customs in the United States have thus far met with abysmal failure, despite daily dramatic evidence of the impact of drinking and driving on innocent victims. Public resistance seems rooted in the strong mores which have protected the "right to drink" against legal prohibitions and in the equally strong mores which have developed around the "right to drive." Supported perhaps by an illusion of individual omnipotence or invulnerability, public sentiment in the United States has generally resisted efforts to protect the public safety which involve increasingly stringent control on the right to drive. There has been resistance to reexamining drivers, to inspecting vehicles, and to penalties on chronic traffic law violators, as well as to efforts for the control of driving while intoxicated. At this time, prevailing mores in America appear to place a higher value on the right to drink and drive than on protection from the drinking driver.[38]

Alcoholism

Most people, when they speak of the problems of alcohol, are thinking primarily of alcoholism. The term alcoholism is an elusive one that defies clear-cut, generally acceptable definition. As more and more is understood about the causes and forms of pathological drinking, it is apparent that the term alcoholism encompasses a range of pathological behavioral syndromes associated with alcohol use. If it were not semantically awkward, it would be more appropriate to speak of alcoholisms [39] rather than alcoholism, for it has become recognized that the term alcoholism has been used to describe a number of quite distinct disorders whose major common characteristic is the pathological seeking for and reaction to the effects of alcohol on the nervous system.

For purposes of clarification, the typology of alcoholism, especially as it is seen in the United States, will be considered in terms of ad-

---

[38] For further reference, see the collection of papers in Fox and Fox, eds., *Alcohol and Traffic Safety.*

[39] This thesis is detailed by E. M. Jellinek, *The Disease Concept of Alcoholism* (New Haven: Hillhouse Press, 1960). Jellinek describes five primary types of alcoholism which he designates *alpha, beta, gamma, delta,* and *epsilon.* The typology discussed here reflects the influence of Jellinek and of Mark Keller and John R. Seeley's disciplined considerations in *The Alcohol Language* (Toronto: University of Toronto Press, 1958) along with a thesis developed by the author in collaboration with Raymond G. McCarthy.

dictive and nonaddictive pathological drinking.[40] Alcoholism or pathological drinking can be defined operationally as the use of alcoholic beverages to the extent that it repeatedly "exceeds customary dietary use or ordinary compliance with the social drinking of the community, and interferes with the drinker's health, interpersonal relations, or economic functioning." [41] Associated with this condition is a state of stress, discontent, or inner tension, the origin of which may be physiological, psychological, or social, or a blending of all three. Alcohol is resorted to for the relief of these discomforts.

For some alcoholics, the recourse to alcohol is accompanied by certain characteristics of an addiction. The addictive drinker has lost control over his drinking. Once he starts, he seems impelled to continue drinking until he has reached peak intensity of intoxication. Yet an essential criterion of addiction is insatiability—a persistent seeking for the unattainable. If alcohol is withdrawn before a drinking spree has run its course, there are severe withdrawal reactions expressed in various physical forms, such as rapid heart beat, profuse sweating, severe nausea, and uncontrollable trembling. In some addictive drinkers, loss of control over drinking becomes generalized, and they are unable to abstain for even a day without suffering withdrawal symptoms.

Alcohol addiction may be defined as a condition in which the drinking of alcoholic beverages becomes persistent, repetitive, uncontrollable, and progressively destructive of the psychological and social functioning of the individual. It runs its episodic course with complete indifference to the logic or reality of the normal life situation or basic social responsibilities. For most addictive drinkers, the condition develops only after years of exposure to relatively high levels of alcohol concentration. It may be surmised that, at some point, there develops a kind of conditioned response to alcohol so that once a given concentration is reached it releases an impulsive drive to attain a peak intensity of effect.

Addictive drinking, as characterized here, represents the most commonly recognized form of alcoholism in the United States. Obviously, all addictive drinkers can be classified as alcoholics. But not every alcoholic is an alcohol addict. There are several categories of

---

[40] R. Straus and R. G. McCarthy, "Nonaddictive Pathological Drinking Patterns of Homeless Men," *Quarterly Journal of Studies on Alcohol,* Vol. 12 (December, 1951), pp. 601-11.

[41] From a definition of alcoholism in Keller and Seeley, *The Alcohol Language,* p. 19.

alcoholics whose drinking repeatedly interferes with health or personal relations, or reduces efficiency and dependability, but who never experience the criteria of alcohol addiction such as insatiability, loss of control over drinking, or withdrawal symptoms.

The nonaddictive alcoholic seems to be primarily concerned with achieving a limited level of alcohol-induced oblivion from reality and often with maintaining a state of alcohol-induced euphoria for a convenient period of time. The addictive alcoholic strives for a *peak* intensity of effect from alcohol; the nonaddictive alcoholic, on the other hand, seeks a *plateau* at much lower levels of alcohol concentration. The nonaddictive alcoholic not only can control his drinking, but often he (or she) will plan it quite carefully in order to attain the most desirable combination of effect and duration within the limits of resources for drinking and available time. He is also able to adapt his drinking practices, apparently without severe difficulty, to variations in his living conditions.

Nonaddictive alcoholism is particularly common among men who frequent skid row areas, jails, and other public institutions. Although there are also many alcohol addicts in this population, a substantial portion of homeless men present a routine of living dominated by the use of alcohol to attain relief from discomfort or escape from reality as often as possible and maintaining it as long as convenient. They may demonstrate considerable foresight in allocating their major funds for alcoholic beverages and in planning their drinking. For many, their drinking seems to be associated with unmet dependency needs. When deprived of alcohol under conditions where their particular dependency needs are fulfilled, such as in a jail or hospital, they manifest no particular urgency to drink.[42]

Other nonaddictive drinkers may plan their drinking to dull the experience of unpleasant situations. These include men who function quite successfully at work but seek an alcohol-induced escape from their marital responsibilities on evenings and weekends. Increasingly, nonaddictive alcoholism occurs among women who have failed, in their routine roles of housewife and mother, to find fulfillment for their self-expectations. Such alcoholics may never experience real in-

---

[42] See R. Straus, "Alcohol and the Homeless Man," *Quarterly Journal of Studies on Alcohol,* Vol. 7 (December, 1946), pp. 360-404; Straus and McCarthy, "Nonaddictive Pathological Drinking Patterns of Homeless Men," pp. 601-11; Joan K. Jackson and R. Connor, "The Skid Road Alcoholic," *Quarterly Journal of Studies on Alcohol,* Vol. 14 (September, 1953), pp. 468-86; E. Rubington, "The Chronic Drunkenness Offender," *Annals of the American Academy of Political and Social Science,* Vol. 315 (January, 1958), pp. 65-72.

toxication, but their daylong sipping will be sufficient to render them chronically ineffective and inefficient.

As might be expected, there are significant differences in the types of alcoholic beverage used by addictive and nonaddictive alcoholics. Addictive drinkers usually seek distilled beverages with the highest alcohol content available, for their goal is intensity of effect. Nonaddictive drinkers, however, particularly if their funds are limited, will usually drink beer or wine, which is much more suited to their goal of maintaining a limited effect from alcohol for some planned duration of time. Sherry, for example, is a common beverage for the housewife sipper.

Depending on the relation of drinking to his life pattern and on physiological variables that are not fully understood, the alcoholic may or may not develop such physical complications of alcohol as cirrhosis of the liver, polyneuropathy, gastritis, or a nutritional disease. Such complications may develop in either addictive or nonaddictive drinkers.

Theories of Etiology

The understanding of alcoholism has until quite recently been clouded by a persistent groping for unilateral theories of etiology. Much research and many efforts to explain alcoholism have been restricted by the blinders of single academic disciplines. Various theories have been based on a consideration of such important factors as liver metabolism, the function of the central nervous system, hormonal imbalances, vitamin and nutritional deficiencies, personality deviations, and the forces of culture and of social pathology.

There appears today sufficient evidence to suggest that alcoholism in its various forms is a manifestation of one or more of a number of underlying stress-producing conditions. The recognition or identification of primary etiological factors is complicated by the fact that the pathological use of alcohol in connection with what might be called primary forms of stress invariably results in the generation of additional stress-producing conditions which ultimately become an integral part of the over-all syndrome. Harold Kalant has emphasized the problem of sorting out specific processes from the viewpoint of a biological scientist:

> With the expansion of knowledge on functional interrelations, it has become clear that the metabolism of the liver affects the function of the central nervous system, that psychological and peripheral sensory stimuli acting on the central nervous system affect the release of various hormonal factors, that the resulting hormonal imbalances affect the metabolic behavior of the liver and of all other tissues, including

the brain and so on and on. Because of this, it has become very difficult indeed to pick out those effects of alcohol which are primary, and those which are secondary and nonspecific consequences of the disturbance resulting from alcohol.[43]

The social scientist faces the same kind of dilemma in his effort to understand alcoholism. Most forms of alcoholism are found in association with some form or forms of social pathology. Marital discord, job instability, social alienation, economic strain, and chronic ill health can contribute to and be supported by an alcoholic drinking pattern, and each of these problems tends to interact with the others in a complex clustering of social, psychological, and biological pathology.

As yet there are no completely satisfactory theories regarding the causes of various types of pathological drinking. Although no specific physiological or biochemical factors have yet been satisfactorily identified as causing alcoholism, the existence of some biological deficiencies or sensitivities as possible contributing factors cannot be ruled out.

A number of psychological traits have commonly been identified in individuals who drink excessively, and much has been written about the "alcoholic personality." [44] Alcoholics have been characterized as suffering from extreme feelings of inadequacy and chronic anxiety and as being excessively dependent on emotional support from others. Yet similar traits can be found in users of narcotics, individuals with various kinds of psychosomatic disease, persons addicted to food, as well as in many men and women who appear to function quite effectively within normal ranges of physical health and socially acceptable behavior. Knowledge about the psychological effects of alcohol in alleviating anxiety and providing a sense of well-being helps explain why alcohol is attractive to and functional for persons with deep feelings of emotional insecurity, but psychological theory cannot tell us, for example, why, of the people with a so-called alcoholic personality, only some become alcoholics, while others do not.

Sociologists have approached the study of alcoholism in part by considering the customs of drinking. Not only is alcoholism restricted to persons who happen to participate in the particular social custom, but striking differences in the prevalence and typology of pathological drinking have been identified with variations both in the overt customs

---

[43] Harold Kalant, "Some Recent Physiological and Biochemical Investigations on Alcohol and Alcoholism," *Quarterly Journal of Studies on Alcohol,* Vol. 23 (March, 1962), p. 53.

[44] For a summary, see John D. Armstrong, "The Search for the Alcoholic Personality," *Annals of the American Academy of Political and Social Science,* Vol. 315 (January, 1958), pp. 40-47.

of drinking and in the beliefs, attitudes, and values about alcohol which mold reference group sanctions on drinking.

A conceptual approach to the study of cultural differences in rates of alcoholism was provided by R. F. Bales in 1946, based in part on his own observations of the striking differences between drinking customs and rates of alcoholism among Irish and Orthodox Jews in the United States.[45]

Studies of the *prevalence* of drinking in the United States consistently place those who identify themselves as Jewish along with Italians at the top of a religious-ethnic scale. In both groups a majority of the adults use alcohol and report having done so since childhood. In contrast, persons of Irish background are somewhat less likely to drink as adults and much less likely to have experienced drinking in childhood.[46] When rates of drinking are compared with rates of alcohol pathology for these cultural groups an inverse relationship is found. Studies of *alcohol pathology* consistently place the rates of alcoholism among the Irish in the United States at the top of the ethnic scale, many times greater than rates for either Italians or Jews, both of which are strikingly low. It is also noteworthy that rates of alcoholism among women in most societies are much lower than those for men, a difference which is generally much greater than the sex differences in prevalence of drinking. The negative correlation between prevalence of drinking and alcoholism might be easily explained if it could be demonstrated that societies with high prevalence rates were all characterized by moderate patterns of consumption. However, numerous studies of drinking have shown that there are cultures, both primitive and advanced, that combine high prevalence with high rates of consumption.

Bales [47] has suggested three general ways in which culture and social organization may influence rates of alcoholism. First are factors which operate to create inner tension, such as culturally induced anxiety, guilt, conflict, suppressed hostility, and sexual tensions. Second are culturally supported attitudes toward drinking and intoxication which determine whether drinking is an acceptable means of relieving inner tension or whether the thought of drinking for this purpose is in itself sufficiently anxiety-provoking to preclude its use.

---

[45] Robert Freed Bales, "Cultural Differences in Rates of Alcoholism," *Quarterly Journal of Studies on Alcohol,* Vol. 6 (March, 1946), pp. 400-99.

[46] Straus and Bacon, *Drinking in College,* found that students who reported drinking in childhood included 81 percent of those who identified themselves as Jewish and 86 percent of the Italians, compared with 45 percent of the Irish.

[47] Bales, "Cultural Differences in Rates of Alcoholism," p. 482.

Third are the alternate provisions for resolving tension provided by the culture.

Bales then describes how the nineteenth-century culture in Ireland, from which the Irish migrated to the United States, supported the development of intensive inner frustration, hostility, and unrelieved sexual tension in the large numbers of males who were retained in the social status of "boy" throughout their adulthood.[48] As a form of social control for the potentially explosive force created by enforced dependency, especially mother-son dependency, and sexual deprivation, the culture supported the frequent excessive use of alcohol by single males, thus providing a relatively "safe" outlet for tension and hostility through a kind of institutionalized intoxication. After migrating to the United States, the Irish found themselves at the bottom of the socioeconomic scale. They found many factors that perpetuated the anxieties of the old country, as well as a new culture and, especially, new expectations regarding the independence of the adult male, which served merely to provoke additional anxiety. Because they brought with them practices and attitudes which supported using alcohol to the point of intoxication as a means of dealing with tension, there was a ready-made combination of cultural factors that has served to create a greater exposure to the prodromal aspects of pathological drinking for the Irish male than for most other Americans.

C. R. Snyder [49] has tested Bales's concepts in an extensive study of the use of alcohol by Jews in the United States. Particularly among the more orthodox Jews, Snyder found that drinking was an integral part of the socialization process, repeatedly experienced as a part of religious ritualism and thoroughly compatible with moral symbolism. Even though alcohol use was extensive, sobriety was maintained as a norm; the experience of intoxication was limited to culturally sanctioned, symbolically meaningful situations, and alcoholism was virtually nonexistent. As he studied Jews according to a decreasing scale of orthodoxy, Snyder found that the disruption of the traditional rites with which drinking had been integrated, the dissociation of drinking experiences from the normal socialization process, and the introduction of drinking in social contexts where its use for the purpose of achieving an individual effect from alcohol was stressed, were all associated with an increase in the rates of alcohol pathology.

Several studies of the drinking practices of Italians, both in Italy

---

[48] See the classic study, Conrad M. Arensberg, *The Irish Countryman* (New York: Macmillan, 1937).

[49] Charles R. Snyder, *Alcohol and the Jews* (New York: Free Press, 1958).

and in the United States,[50] have identified alcohol as an integral part of the dietary beliefs and practices. Drinking and eating are inseparable activities. Drinking usually involves wine (with low alcohol content), and excessive drinking usually occurs in the context of excessive eating. Even when large amounts of alcohol are consumed, they are taken slowly and interspaced with food which impedes the rate of absorption. Intoxication, when it does occur, is in the context of social conviviality and is considered in the same light as indigestion or other concomitants of gluttony. Alcoholism is rare. As in the case of the Jews, studies of Italian drinking reveal marked changes in drinking patterns according to generation and degree of acculturation in the United States. As alienation from the original Italian culture takes place, drinking occurs apart from the context of meals, involves beverages other than wine or beer, and occurs in settings where Italian group sanctions do not prevail. Under such conditions, drinking for the sake of drinking becomes more common, intoxication more frequent, and alcoholism begins to appear.

From all this it should not be conjectured that Italians or Jews have less inner tension or fewer problems of adjustment; on the contrary, both groups appear to have their expected share of various forms of mental illness, with Jews perhaps exceeding most other religious groups.[51] Both groups seem to include more than their share of individuals who eat to the point of gross obesity in an apparent effort to deal with stress.[52]

The studies cited here and many others which have considered the relationship between cultural norms and pathological drinking add convincing support to the inclusion of cultural factors in a holistic theory of the causes of alcoholism. We have seen that alcoholism becomes a response to stress primarily in those cultures where drinking customs create exposure to frequent intoxication, where intoxication is a means of fulfilling individual rather than group functions, and where there are no culturally approved alternative modes of dealing with stress.

Most theories of alcoholism emphasize the role of stress as a pre-

---

[50] See especially Giorgio Lolli *et al., Alcohol in Italian Culture* (New York: Free Press, 1958).

[51] See, for example, A. B. Hollingshead and F. C. Redlich, *Social Class and Mental Illness* (New York: Wiley & Sons, 1958), pp. 204-05; also Bales, "Cultural Differences in Rates of Alcoholism," p. 490.

[52] Snyder, *Alcohol and the Jews,* pp. 9-10; Giorgio Lolli *et al.,* "The Use of Wine and other Alcoholic Beverages by a Group of Italians and Americans of Italian Extraction," *Quarterly Journal of Studies on Alcohol,* Vol. 13 (March, 1952), pp. 27-48.

condition of alcoholism. Stress is seen as originating in a physiological condition, in personality characteristics, in adaptation to the social setting, or in combinations of these sources.

Although temperance writings for a century equated drinking and alcoholism, the role of drinking itself has generally been dismissed as a cause of alcoholism. It is pointed out that perhaps 19 out of 20 people who drink do not become alcoholics, and that the behavior of the alcoholic in using alcohol is very different from that of the average person who drinks.[53]

Certainly the maintenance of a clear distinction between drinking and alcoholism is particularly important in light of the confusion that has prevailed with respect to the phenomena generally associated with alcohol. However, since drinking itself can generate enough stress for some people, the act of drinking may contribute to a self-perpetuating syndrome, conceivably in persons for whom drinking violates such strong social norms that they come to rely on the effects of alcohol as a means of alleviating their feelings of guilt. A number of clinicians have identified deep-seated guilt about alcoholism as a serious barrier to effective therapy; Jews and Italians whose alcoholism represented alienation from their cultural background were found to be particularly recalcitrant patients. In the study of college drinking practices and attitudes it was found that Mormon students and those from fundamentalist colleges who violated their religion and cultural norms by drinking had become intoxicated, experienced social complications, and displayed some prodomal signs of pathological drinking more frequently than other student drinkers.

Magnitude of the Problem

It has been very difficult to count the number of alcoholics, not only because there is no universally accepted definition of alcoholism, but also because the condition is still shrouded in stigma and therefore frequently denied or hidden.[54] The estimate of five million alcoholics in the United States in 1965 is a reasonably conservative one. This would mean about one alcoholic for every 18 persons who customarily drink alcoholic beverages. Men outnumber women alcoholics by about five and a half to one.

---

[53] See Selden D. Bacon, "Alcoholics Do Not Drink," *Annals of the American Academy of Political and Social Science,* Vol. 315 (January, 1958), pp. 55-64.

[54] Most estimates rely on a formula devised by E. M. Jellinek that is based on projections made from reported deaths due to cirrhosis of the liver attributable to alcoholism. See World Health Organization, Expert Committee on Mental Health, *Report on the First Session of the Alcoholism Subcommittee* (WHO Technical Report Series, No. 42, 1951, Annex 2).

The magnitude of alcoholism involves much more than a count of individuals who are alcoholics. Much of the behavior associated with alcoholism is social behavior. A primary consequence of alcoholism is the inability of the alcoholic to function effectively in a variety of social roles and to carry out social responsibilities. There are perhaps ten million wives, husbands, children, or parents in the United States who live in the same household with alcoholics and are directly affected by their behavior. Most alcoholics hold jobs, and the magnitude of alcoholism should also be measured in terms of lost manpower, accidents, industrial waste, and inefficiency. Alcoholics drive cars and usually involve others when accidents occur. Alcoholics also have higher rates of most kinds of sickness than other people and place a heavy demand on already taxed medical facilities and personnel. Social consequences also include the considerable investment of public funds which communities spend on their police, courts, jails, hospitals, and other institutional responses to the problems of chronic intoxication.

Social Responses to Alcoholism

The last 25 years have witnessed a significant change in social perceptions of the problems of alcoholism and in responses to them. During this period there has emerged a substantial public health movement concerned with education about and treatment for alcoholism. There has also been a major development in research activity involving many scientific disciplines. Since 1940, the *Quarterly Journal of Studies on Alcohol* has provided a means for disseminating information and stimulating investigation.

Up to about 1940, there was little reliable scientific data on alcoholism and almost a total lack of public understanding. As we have noted, most public references to alcoholism were cast in terms of temperance philosophy which equated drinking, drunkenness, and alcoholism with immorality, lack of will power, and personal degradation. In society-at-large, alcoholism tended to be among the unmentionable stigmas. A prevailing stereotype equated alcoholism with the intemperance of the derelict whose condition was readily visible. Public provision for alcoholics was found only in jails, asylums, public infirmaries, or shelters. It was assumed that most alcoholics were men, alienated from their families, unemployed or unemployable, highly unstable, and socially irresponsible.[55] Chronic inebriates who belonged

---

[55] These characteristics did describe the more conspicuous categories of alcoholics. See, for example, S. D. Bacon, *Inebriety, Social Integration, and Mar-*

to families, who held jobs, who were relatively stable members of the community, or who happened to be women, were not usually labeled as alcoholics. They did not fit the stereotype, and their condition was generally hidden or denied by relatives and close friends.

A radical departure in social provisions for alcoholism took place in 1944 with the establishment of the first public outpatient clinics to provide treatment for alcoholics through a combination of medical, psychological, and social work therapies. These pilot clinics and others which soon followed were originally intended to help relieve the community of the high cost of maintaining alcoholics in jails and mental hospitals. Although community alcoholism clinics quickly caught on, their clients were not the typical arrested or homeless inebriates who lacked both the motivation and the stability in the community necessary for continuing contact with a clinic. Instead, the patients who quickly appeared wherever clinics were established turned out to be men, and gradually some women, whose social stability was relatively intact. Numerous studies of the social characteristics of patients seen in community treatment programs for alcoholics since the mid-1940's find that over half of the patients are married and living with their families; most live in established households and have residential stability; perhaps two-thirds are actively employed; many have been steadily employed for a number of years; and the majority work in positions involving some skill and responsibility.

By providing both hope and help, community treatment programs have gradually drawn the formerly hidden alcoholic out of the proverbial closet and have made possible a better understanding of the alcoholic's social assets and liabilities.

Ironically, the community clinic has had little impact on the chronic homeless inebriate. Although it is now estimated that he represents a relatively smaller segment of the over-all problem than was formerly believed, he has proved less accessible than most alcoholics to modern rehabilitation efforts, and he still monopolizes a large share of society's investment in its police, courts, and jails.

Along with the development of research and public programs for rehabilitation and education, another movement of considerable sociological significance has been the organization known as Alcoholics Anonymous.[56] The essential therapeutic element of Alcoholics Anony-

---

riage (New Haven: Quarterly Journal of Studies on Alcohol, 1945); and D. J. Pittman and C. W. Gordon, Revolving Door (New York: Free Press, 1958).

[56] Several sociologists have studied the phenomena of Alcoholics Anonymous. See R. F. Bales, "The Therapeutic Role of Alcoholics Anonymous as Seen by a Sociologist," Quarterly Journal of Studies on Alcohol, Vol. 5 (September, 1944),

mous appears to be the provision of a meaningful reference group concerned with maintaining sobriety.

The social impact of Alcoholics Anonymous lies perhaps not so much in the members that it has helped achieve sobriety as in its contribution to the reduction of the stigma of alcoholism and to a better public understanding of and sympathy for the alcoholic. The movement has demonstrated more dramatically than formal treatment programs that alcoholics are drawn from all walks of life and that they can be reclaimed as useful, productive, and respectable members of the community. Members of Alcoholics Anonymous have constituted a powerful lobbying force working for the development of more effective social responses to the problems of alcoholism.

Beginning in the 1940's, also, most states have established tax-supported programs for education about and treatment of alcoholism, and many communities now have voluntary or public health agencies devoted to these problems. During the last several years, the federal government has become significantly involved, and several millions of dollars have been appropriated in support of research on alcoholism and related problems.

Most social responses to alcoholism have been characterized by a "special problem" emphasis. There have been special agencies, special clinics, specially designated research funds and hospital beds, and specialized therapists and administrators. This pattern of organization has typified social efforts to deal with health and welfare problems in the United States. Proponents of the "special problem" approach point out that unless there is a specific focus on a problem and an effort to "sell" the problem to the general public, to legislators, and to the professions, it is invariably lost among traditional responses. In the case of alcoholism, the prevalence of gross misconceptions and stigma has long served as a barrier to understanding and provided a rationale for the rejection of social responsibility. Until very recently, most hospitals refused to admit patients for treatment of alcoholism, and most practicing physicians have been reluctant to accept alcoholics as patients, perhaps because they feel that they have nothing to offer, that alcoholics are unrewarding patients, that they might lose other patients, or that alcoholism is not medically respectable. As in the case of many other health problems, victims themselves and their families

pp. 267-78; O. W. Ritchie, "A Sociohistorical Survey of Alcoholics Anonymous," *Quarterly Journal of Studies on Alcohol*, Vol. 9 (June, 1948), pp. 119-56; and Milton A. Maxwell, "Alcoholics Anonymous: An Interpretation," in Pittman and Snyder, eds., *Society, Culture, and Drinking Patterns*, pp. 577-85.

have provided much of the drive behind efforts to develop effective social mechanisms for coping with alcoholism. Their work has helped to focus special emphasis on the problems of alcoholism since the 1940's and has contributed to the establishment of numerous special treatment centers throughout the country, most of them publicly supported.

However, even the best of these special resources can provide help for only a small segment of the alcoholic population. If large numbers of alcoholics are to be helped, it is essential that the general health resources of the community, including practicing physicians, become a part of this effort. Overemphasis on the need for a specialized approach can impair the attainment of this goal, particularly if alcoholic patients are referred to special resources by more comprehensive resources better equipped to deal with the medical, psychiatric, and social ramifications of prolonged excessive drinking.

Of particular concern are the special therapeutic approaches that focus on drinking to the exclusion of all other aspects of the alcoholism problem. For example, there are many alcoholics who achieve sobriety without resolving those physiological, psychological, or social factors that have contributed to their perpetual state of tension. It is not known how many of these so-called recovered alcoholics may find the stress of living without alcohol so great that they can no longer sustain family or job stability, or who may seek to resolve their stress in other excesses, such as food, sex, drugs, or hyperactivity, or who may, after alcohol is withdrawn, suffer from other serious functional diseases. As yet, there has been almost no research concerned with the complex interaction of social, psychological, and physiological processes encountered by the alcoholic, both in attaining and sustaining a reasonably comfortable adjustment to life without alcohol.

The Problems of Alcohol and Major Social Systems

The various forms of alcoholism, and the other problems associated with drinking customs, are reflected in and affected by the behavior and functions of every major social system. Bare mention of these may be enough to indicate the complex interdependence.

The national economy reflects the great size of the alcoholic beverage industry as an employer, and as a user of natural products and of such major services as transportation, advertising, and retail sales. For example, expenditures by the alcoholic beverage industries for national advertising in newspapers, magazines, and on television in

1963 amounted to almost 200 million dollars, or 6 percent of the total advertising revenue of these media.[57] Personal consumption expenditures for packaged alcoholic beverages in the United States in 1962 amounted to 10.7 billion dollars or 3 percent of all personal expenditures.[58]

The alcohol beverage industry is a significant source of tax revenue for local, state, and federal government. Federal taxes on alcoholic beverages in 1963 came to more than 3.4 billion dollars while the states collected an additional 22 million. Together these sources accounted for more than 3 percent of all federal and state tax revenue.[59]

Government in turn is actively involved in the regulation and control of alcohol beverage manufacturing, distribution, and sales. A large portion of local government expenditures for police, courts, and jails is attributable to intoxication and related problems. State governments have been concerned with legislating the legal age for drinking, alcohol education in the schools, driver safety, and have recently developed state programs to cope with problems resulting from alcoholism.

Employers in many fields of endeavor are coming to recognize the costs of alcohol problems in terms of absenteeism, accidents and injuries, job turnover, wasted time, and spoiled goods. Unfortunately, the few studies in this area fail to provide concrete cost estimates.[60] Many major industrial concerns have been reexamining their policies with respect to employees who have a drinking problem. A remarkable case of social change is provided by the instances in which business firms have established programs of alcoholism education, detection, and treatment.

Increasingly, alcohol use is identified with other leisure activities. Taverns in various parts of the country have long included shuffleboard, pinball machines, and similar diversions. More recently, bars are becoming commonplace in recreational centers ranging from bowling alleys, ball parks, and drive-in movies to legitimate theaters and concert halls. Such drinking tends to occur apart from the usually moderating influences of family sanctions and often under circumstances that require driving afterwards.

---

[57] *Statistical Abstract of the United States, 1964* (Washington, D.C.: U.S. Government Printing Office, 1964), pp. 845-46.

[58] *Ibid.*, p. 325.

[59] *Ibid.*, pp. 395, 430.

[60] Harrison M. Trice, "The Job Behavior of Problem Drinkers," in Pittman and Snyder, eds., *Society, Culture, and Drinking Patterns.*

The Family

It is within the family that the questions of drinking and the problems of alcohol are most intimately experienced. Most people are first exposed to the values, beliefs, and customs of drinking or abstaining within the context of their family. Several studies have found that the family is the most frequent setting and family members the most frequent companions at the time of earliest exposure to alcohol, and that about half of those who drink report some experiment or taste by the age of 10. The importance of the family in the transmission of drinking customs is further demonstrated by high correlations between young people and their parents in regard to the types of beverages used, frequency of drinking, and amounts consumed. The significance of the family to adolescent drinking is also seen in those whose use of alcohol does not conform to family norms, and who appear to be using alcohol as a symbol of rejecting the authority of parents and others. It is within the family that most individuals acquire traits of security or inadequacy that may influence the psychological meaning of alcohol for them and their future motivations for drinking.

The role of the family in drinking customs is recognized by 18 states which, it will be remembered, make exceptions for family drinking in their laws prohibiting alcohol use before age 21. The much-publicized incident in Darien, Connecticut, in 1964, of a fatal automobile accident involving a 17-year-old driver who had been drinking at a friend's home is testing the legal liability of parents for serving alcohol to minors in their homes and has been used symbolically to focus national attention on the problems of teen-age drinking.[61]

The family's role in the generation of a "personality" prone to alcoholism has been the subject of much debate. The life histories of alcoholics usually present clear evidence of family stress or of unresolved conflicts over ambivalent feelings toward parents as contributing factors, especially in families that generated conflict or guilt about the use of alcohol or that provided role models for the use of alcohol as a way of acting out conflict or resolving stress. Although there is no evidence to support genetic inheritance of alcoholism, the fact that children of alcoholic parents are more prone themselves to alcoholism suggests the significance of the family environment as an etiological factor.

In turn, alcoholism is clearly one of the most significant factors con-

---

[61] *The New York Times,* June 24, 1964, and almost daily for some weeks thereafter.

tributing to family stress and instability. Alcoholics are more frequently divorced or separated than nonalcoholics, and the wives, husbands, and children of alcoholics present relatively high rates of physical, emotional, and psychosomatic illness. Alcoholics usually are overdemanding of emotional support from others, while providing little or no such support for them in turn. Also, because of their preoccupation with alcohol, or because of personality traits associated with alcoholism, or merely because of the impotency resulting from the sedating impact of alcohol, alcoholics are often unsatisfying sexual partners.

Additional stress for families of alcoholics stems from the economic burdens often associated with the relatively high cost of alcohol or the loss of income due to alcohol pathology.

Some studies which have revealed certain personality traits to be fairly characteristic of the wives of alcoholics have led to the suggestion that there is a kind of mutual selection process in marriages involving known alcoholics or alcoholism-prone individuals, or that the experience of marriage to an alcoholic leads to the development of a unique pattern of social and psychological adjustment.[62] However, the possibility that alcoholism, despite its considerable stress-producing potential, may provide compensations as well is supported by the fact that a large segment of the alcoholic population does maintain family stability [63] and by the observation that some marriages collapse only after the alcoholic has ceased drinking.

The significance of the family as an important stabilizing factor must not be overlooked. Statistics reveal that persons who have never married or whose marriages have been disrupted do not live as long and have higher rates of morbidity than those who live in a family context. Studies of homeless men suggest that, while alcoholism and its underlying causes undoubtedly contribute to homelessness, the stress associated with alienation or isolation from a family clearly supports patterns of pathological drinking.[64]

Education

Alcohol problems have involved American educational systems in two distinct, though related, questions: teaching about alcohol and

---

[62] Joan K. Jackson, "The Adjustment of the Family to the Crisis of Alcoholism," *Quarterly Journal of Studies on Alcohol,* Vol. 15 (December, 1954), pp. 562-86.

[63] Margaret B. Bailey, "Alcoholism and Marriage," *Quarterly Journal of Studies on Alcohol,* Vol. 22 (March, 1961), pp. 81-94; M. B. Bailey, P. Haberman, and H. Alksne, "Outcomes of Alcoholic Marriage," *Quarterly Journal of Studies on Alcohol,* Vol. 23 (December, 1962), pp. 610-23.

[64] Straus, "Alcohol and the Homeless Man," pp. 360-404.

drinking by students. Since most state laws requiring education about alcohol in the elementary and secondary schools were introduced and supported by temperance interests, it is not surprising that the information presented and materials used have long reflected a temperance point of view. In 1943, Anne Roe surveyed 177 textbooks and related materials on alcohol education in use in American school systems. She reported that, although the materials on the effects of alcohol were presented in a scientific frame of reference, they were consistently slanted in order to indoctrinate students with a viewpoint unrelated to scientific findings.[65] Although education on alcohol has undergone many important changes during the last 20 years, it was characterized until well after World War II by erroneous biological facts and reflected the drinking customs and alcohol problems of the early nineteenth century more than those of the mid-twentieth century. It relied heavily on a psychology of fear as an instrument of indoctrination and social control. The nature of alcohol education has been drastically modified in the past 20 years. While many teachers still reflect their own childhood indoctrination, the majority of textbooks and teaching materials are oriented to providing students with a factual basis for making intelligent personal decisions.[66] Changes in the context and content of education about alcohol have occurred as part of the broader social enlightenment which has included increased scientific research, the creation of voluntary and tax-supported programs, the treatment of alcoholism, a change in the position of less militant temperance groups, and a modification of social values regarding the open discussion of alcohol problems.

On the other hand, the policies of school officials concerning drinking by students have been slower to change. Legal restrictions on drinking by minors dictate most official policy. More liberal administrators, who recognize that restrictions may invite and even encourage violations, are often caught between their obligation to uphold the law and the dictates of their judgment. As a result, many schools operate with two codes—formal rules of prohibition and informal policies which recognize the forces of custom and even try to encourage the moderate social uses of alcohol as a favorable alternative to im-

---

[65] Anne Roe, *A Survey of Alcohol Education in Elementary and High Schools in the United States* (New Haven: Quarterly Journal of Studies on Alcohol, 1943).

[66] See especially George L. Maddox, "The Work of Two Decades; The Bibliography of Raymond G. McCarthy, 1901-1964," *Bulletin of the Association for the Advancement of Instruction about Alcohol and Narcotics*, Vol. 10 (December, 1964), pp. 1-6.

moderate uses. As noted earlier, efforts to enforce restrictive school policies are generally associated with a higher prevalence of drinking problems than policies which are more in keeping with the reality of contemporary drinking customs.

Religion

It has been seen that the different religions present a broad range of conflicting positions regarding the propriety of drinking. Most major religions have at some time in their history attached symbolic importance to the ritual use of alcohol, but for many, the questions of morality associated with intoxication have become paramount, and drinking itself has become defined as a moral transgression. In historical perspective, the antialcohol position of many Christian denominations stems from about 1840 and is traceable to the close identification of churches with the temperance movement.

Religions that have retained the symbolic meaning of alcohol as a well-integrated aspect of their theology, such as Orthodox Judaism, have often been able to limit intoxication among their adherents or to confine it within the context of socially controlled ritualistic expression. But, it must be remembered that for Orthodox Jews, their religion controls almost every aspect of living. As the rigid discipline of religious orthodoxy has decreased among Jews, and as the number of activities responsive to religious laws has declined, the introduction of a more secular way of life has brought with it secular drinking patterns, a secular context for intoxication, and secular problems of alcohol.[67]

Protestant denominations are quite divided on their position toward drinking. Mormons and many of the smaller fundamentalist denominations appear to take the strongest antialcohol position, with both the Methodists and Baptists not far behind. Churches which frown upon drinking clearly have a lower prevalence of drinkers among their membership. However, as noted earlier, data from Mulford's 1963 study and the college drinking survey of 1953 [68] show that drinkers from religious groups with the lowest prevalence of drinking tend to drink more frequently, in larger amounts, and with more frequent complications than drinkers with other religious identities. An exception is the Roman Catholic Church which includes the distinct and

---

[67] See Snyder, *Alcohol and the Jews.*

[68] Mulford, "Drinking and Deviant Drinking in the USA, 1963." Straus and Bacon, *Drinking in College.*

contrasting drinking patterns of the Irish with high rates and the Italians with low rates of alcohol pathology. Because the Catholic Church recognizes drinking as a highly personal matter, ethnic and other secular norms and sanctions are more important than religious norms in determining the drinking patterns of Catholics.[69]

Since the beginnings of the temperance movement, many churches have played a leading role in temperance education. In recent years, alcohol education programs of the more liberal churches have reflected a marked change in their approach to the questions of drinking and the problems of alcohol. Increasingly, when these issues are discussed from the pulpit or in a religious publication, they are presented in the context of a scientific rather than a moral model. In keeping with the more general development of pastoral counseling as a church function, many ministers now offer counseling for alcoholics and their families.

The Medical Model

The health professions, although long involved in treating alcoholics suffering from cirrhosis of the liver, nutritional deficiency, and other specific diseases or injuries, have long resisted treating the problems of alcoholism per se. In recent years, medical, psychiatric, public health, and hospital resources have been under increasing pressure to assume greater responsibility. There has been a calculated effort to create a public health or medical model, in place of a moralistic model, for conceptualizing the problems of alcoholism and for mobilizing social responses. This movement has involved voluntary citizens' committees on alcoholism, public agencies, recovered alcoholics, and some educational and research organizations. In order to encourage alcoholics to seek treatment, and in order to create a more sympathetic public image of alcoholism and develop support for research and treatment resources, alcoholism has been defined as a "disease" and the alcoholic as a "sick person."

While the substitution of a medical model for a moralistic model appears to have been somewhat effective in modifying public attitudes and may even have contributed to some modifications in medical attitudes and practices, it perpetuates the oversimplification of a complex problem.[70] The problems of alcohol, including alcoholism,

---

[69] John C. Ford, S.J., *Man Takes a Drink* (New York: Kenedy and Sons, 1955), pp. 15-19, 112-13.

[70] See John R. Seeley, "Alcoholism Is a Disease: Implications for Social Policy," in Pittman and Snyder, eds., *Society, Culture, and Drinking Patterns*, pp. 586-93.

certainly have medical ramifications, but they continue to be moral problems as well, and they continue to involve government, religion, law, education, business, recreation, and the family.

The Current and Future Status of Alcohol Problems

It has been suggested several times in this chapter that the period since 1940 has seen a marked change in the understanding of alcohol problems and in social responses to these problems. This change has affected the attitudes and responses of the general public, of various professional groups, and of alcoholics themselves.

The stigma of alcoholism has been moderated. The alcoholic is less apt to be held morally responsible for his problem. Instead, he is depicted as the victim of a disease. He is now more likely to admit that he has a problem and to seek help.

Several different kinds of alcoholism have been identified and concepts of multiple causation have emerged, although there is as yet no generally acceptable theory of etiology. Numerous treatment resources have been developed and a variety of drugs have been found to help the alcoholic maintain sobriety, although they do not cure his alcoholism. Special clinics, special hospitals, and specially designated beds in general hospitals have become available to alcoholics in increasing numbers; even a few physicians are specializing in the treatment of alcoholism. Alcoholics Anonymous has had a significant, if unmeasurable, impact. Yet even these growing resources can serve only a small portion of the alcoholic population because they must operate within the severe limits of available knowledge. Generally, those approaches to treatment which combine medical, psychological, and social intervention have had the greatest degree of success.

A growing concept of public responsibility for the problems of alcoholism has been reflected in the increasing support provided for treatment services at the local and state levels of government and for research by the federal government. After much resistance, major employers and insurance companies are also beginning to give some attention to these problems. But, as yet, there are no sure cures and no known ways of preventing alcoholism. Nor does there appear to be any measurable reduction in the incidence or prevalence of alcoholism in the United States.

Since 1940, much progress has been made in differentiating alcoholism from some of the other problems of alcohol. Dangerously misleading educational materials used in the schools are being replaced with those designed to afford young people a basis for making intelligent decisions about drinking. The problem of drinking by young people is less often identified with the fear that they will become alcoholics. However, while most young people continue to be exposed to confusing and conflicting pressures from family, church, community, and peer groups, the use of alcohol as a way of resolving adolescent stress as well as drinking outside of the generally moderating context of the home may both be increasing.

Despite the reality of adolescent drinking, legal restrictions against drinking before the age of 21 continue and serve to enhance the symbolic status of drinking for the teen-ager. Both alcohol and the automobile have important significance in the striving for adult status, and, when combined, they comprise a potentially lethal force.

Since 1940, there is a better understanding of the impact of alcohol on driving performance. An effort is under way to redefine the public perception of this problem from that of "drunken driving" to the combination of "drinking and driving." Thus far, efforts at public education have been relatively ineffective in modifying drinking and driving behavior in this country, where the mores which uphold both the right to drink and the right to drive have prevailed against the enforcement of most laws designed to impose social control.

Conflicts between mores and laws continue to characterize many aspects of drinking behavior. The phrase "vote dry and drink wet" is an apt description, not merely of behavior associated with prohibition laws, but also of the predominant response to most other legal restrictions associated with drinking customs: the legal age laws, drinking-and-driving codes, laws regulating the hours of sale and other aspects of distribution, and laws covering manufacturing and taxation. Many people will strongly support alcohol control laws in principle but will violate them freely and, unless a violation has involved personal and direct damage to themselves, will condone their violation by others.

Experience in the United States, and elsewhere in the world, has clearly indicated that efforts to cope with problems of alcohol by legislating change will prove ineffective unless laws can be made which reflect the forces of normative behavior. Yet, in the United States, the heterogeneous nature of the population makes the task of delineating a single normative pattern of drinking behavior impossible. Drinking customs and attitudes and drinking problems in American society reflect the practices, beliefs, and values of many national, regional, ethnic, and social backgrounds. The absence of homogeneity in drinking norms itself contributes to an additional problem of alcohol—the problem of conceptualization, which has been a recurring though as yet unidentified theme of this chapter.

The Problem of Conceptualizing Alcohol Problems

The many and diverse problems of alcohol affect all segments of the population, although in very different ways, and they involve all major social institutions. They include both deviant behavior, such as alcoholism and intoxication, and social disorganization, such as the consequences of prohibition and the conflicts between mores and laws.

References to alcohol problems have tended to confuse drinking with alcoholism. References to alcoholism have tended to overlook the many different forms of pathological drinking. Much of the study of alcohol problems has been restricted by the unilateral lines of traditional academic disciplines.

More than any other factor, the existence of many conflicting conceptual models, each of limited dimensions, has restricted the understanding of alcohol problems and the development of effective social responses. Only a holistic conceptualization, which includes consideration of biological, psychological, social, cultural, environmental, and temporal factors, will facilitate an examination of the continuing interaction and fundamental interdependence of the action of alcohol on the human organism and the customs of drinking as common denominators to all of the problems of alcohol and man.

6

Suicide

by Jack P. Gibbs

Lᴵᴋᴇ ᴀɴʏ ᴏᴛʜᴇʀ ꜰᴏʀᴍ ᴏꜰ ᴅᴇᴀᴛʜ, ꜱᴜɪᴄɪᴅᴇ ᴄᴀʀʀɪᴇꜱ ᴡɪᴛʜ ɪᴛ ᴛʜᴇ ɪᴅᴇᴀ of tragedy. Unlike other forms, however, it is considered in most societies to be not only tragic but avoidable, and this avoidability stamps it as a social problem.

Cases of voluntary death are experienced by the victim's associates as a personal loss, but they also represent a societal loss. Beyond personal and ethical valuations, a person's worth can be assessed in terms of his contribution to society—as a producer, as a parent, as a soldier, and so on. Suicide is thus a social problem independent of personal grief because it represents a measurable loss to society.

This loss is greater than one might suspect. Consider, for example, the number of suicides in each of five countries in one year (Table 1).

Suicide is generally believed to be of little quantitative importance in comparison to other causes of death. The fact is, however, that it constitutes a major cause of death, at least in some societies. This is seen from the following ranking of suicide among causes of death in four countries (Table 2).

TABLE 1
Number of Suicides in Selected Countries

Country	Year	Number of Suicides
United States	1962	20,207
Japan	1962	16,439
West Germany	1961	10,116
France	1962	7,112
United Kingdom	1962	6,123

Source: Demographic Yearbook, 1963 (New York: United Nations, 1964), Table 25.

TABLE 2

Rank of Suicide as a Cause of Death, Selected Countries

Country and Year	Rank of Suicide as One of 50 Major Causes of Death	Suicides as a Percent of All Deaths
Finland, 1962	9	2.3
Hungary, 1962	10	2.3
Austria, 1962	10	1.8
United States, 1962	15	1.2

Source: Demographic Yearbook, 1963, Table 25.

If we judge contributions to society in terms of status, then married persons of between 15 and 64 years of age warrant a high position. If only the nonproductive members of a society (e.g., the extremely aged) took their lives, the collective loss would be negligible; but this is not the case. In the United States, for example, of the 50,047 suicides during 1949-1951, 50.3 percent were married persons between 15 and 64 years of age.[1] Thus, suicide represents a substantial social loss, both quantitatively and qualitatively.

Suicide and Social Disorganization

Although social disorganization is subject to various definitions, the failure of groups or individuals to conform to social norms often is viewed as indicative of disorganization, on the grounds that such behavior is not in accord with the expectations of others. On the other hand, nonconformity may be construed as evidence of a conflict in values, which in itself constitutes social disorganization.[2] However social disorganization be defined, it is generally thought to be linked to deviant behavior, and in this context suicide is a social problem beyond collective and personal loss.

In all Christian and Moslem nations, and in Israel, self-destruction violates normative expectations. It is, in fact, treated as a crime in some countries. But the moral evaluation now accorded the act is by no means as severe as it once was. In European history we find numerous instances of violent opposition to voluntary death—the victim's

---

[1] Vital Statistics—Special Reports, Selected Studies, U.S. National Office of Vital Statistics, Vol. 39 (May 8, 1956), p. 370.

[2] See Ralph H. Turner, "Value Conflict in Social Disorganization," Sociology and Social Research, Vol. 38 (May-June, 1954), pp. 301-08.

body was subject to abuse, religious services were denied, and his property confiscated.[3]

Where suicide is opposed by the mores, by the law, or by both, its occurrence is evidence of weak social norms. This is true for deviant acts generally, but it is all the more accentuated by the very nature of voluntary death—the individual not only defies collective authority but renounces his membership in the collectivity as well. (This was perhaps sensed by the citizens of Greek city-states when they demanded that the prospective victim petition for the right to take his life.) The seriousness to society of this renunciation is pointed up by its military illustration when treason and desertion in time of war are considered the gravest of crimes.

That suicide may reflect weak social norms is indicated by studies which have found it to be most prevalent in areas of a city that abound with other deviations, such as mental illness, drug addiction, and prostitution.[4] This association suggests that where some people readily renounce their membership in society, others are not prone to respect the norms which govern the living. (See Chapter 4, pages 210-12.)

In addition to the distinctly sociological correlates of suicide, the act is believed to be associated with emotional disorders and mental illness.[5] From the psychological point of view, frequent suicides may be taken as evidence of marked psychopathology in the population, and sociological studies in urban areas have produced findings that support the idea.[6] As we shall see, however, the relationship between suicide and its alleged psychological and sociological correlates is subject to debate; nevertheless, there are reasons for regarding suicide as a form of deviant behavior reflecting conditions that constitute serious social problems.[7]

---

[3] Émile Durkheim, *Suicide: A Study in Sociology,* trans. by John A. Spaulding and George Simpson (New York: Free Press, 1951), pp. 326-38.

[4] See Ruth S. Cavan, *Suicide* (Chicago: University of Chicago Press, 1928), pp. 81-105; Calvin F. Schmid, "Suicides in Seattle, 1914-1925: An Ecological and Behavioristic Study," *University of Washington Publications in the Social Sciences,* Vol. 5 (October, 1928), pp. 4-23; Calvin F. Schmid, *A Social Saga of Two Cities; An Ecological and Statistical Study of Social Trends in Minneapolis and St. Paul* (Minneapolis: Minneapolis Council of Social Agencies, Bureau of Social Research, 1937), pp. 370-80; Ernest R. Mowrer, *Disorganization: Personal and Social* (Philadelphia: Lippincott, 1942); Peter Sainsbury, *Suicide in London: An Ecological Study* (New York: Basic Books, 1956).

[5] See Karl A. Menninger, *Man Against Himself* (New York: Harcourt, Brace & World, 1938) and Simpson's observations in Durkheim, *Suicide,* pp. 20-25.

[6] See Sainsbury, *Suicide in London,* pp. 84-87.

[7] For related observations, see Erich Fromm, *The Sane Society* (New York: Rinehart, 1955), pp. 3-11.

The Prevention of Suicide

Most social problems are believed subject to remedial action. In this context suicide is unique, in that it is difficult to imagine any course of action which would substantially reduce its incidence. There have been arguments for more severe prison sentences for drug addicts, curfew laws for juveniles, and so on; but, whatever their merits as preventives of other deviant acts, such repressive devices are clearly not applicable to suicide. Punishment holds little fear for the would-be victim. Confiscation of property and punishment of relatives might act to deter self-destruction, but the public would almost certainly reject such measures. The long and short of the matter is that suicide is not subject to conventional means of control; consequently, it is all the more a social problem.

Suicide as a Sociological Problem

Few *specific* forms of deviant behavior have claimed the attention of as many scholars in a variety of fields as has suicide. Dahlgren estimates that as of 1945 there were approximately 4000 published works on the subject.[8] Sociologists have been among those drawn to the subject, and this poses a question: why should a discipline concerned with the study of society be interested in an individual and ostensibly asocial act? The question deserves an answer, if only to show that an inclination for the morbid is not an occupational prerequisite for sociologists.

The study of social norms and violations of them is fundamental to sociology; it follows, then, that the study of suicide is a legitimate part of the field. But this indicates only why the act is studied at all; it does not explain the great amount of attention devoted to the phenomenon, particularly in comparison to other deviant acts. Few sociological studies have been done on the subject of pimping; yet not only is pimping proscribed, but, unlike suicide, it also involves social relations, the touchstone of sociological subject matter. So, the answer to the question remains incomplete.

For a more adequate explanation, we turn to Émile Durkheim, who established the basic rationale for the sociological analysis of suicide. This rationale takes the form of a working postulate: the volume of suicide reflects something basic in the characteristics of

---

[8] Karl Gustav Dahlgren, *On Suicide and Attempted Suicide* (Lund, Sweden: Hakan Ohlssons Boktryskeri, 1945), p. 1.

social entities independent of the individual victims. We can best understand this postulate by analyzing everyday experience.

It is obvious that some statuses and social groups are quite different from others, and these differences are reflected both in norms and in actual behavior. True, we may be unable to specify the exact nature of such differences. But this does not alter the fact of social contrasts between men and women, the old and the young, the married and the single, Negroes and whites in the South, bankers and laborers, Catholics and Unitarians, and so on. Differences among whole societies cannot readily be experienced at first hand, but it does not require a social scientist to appreciate a variety of contrasts between, for example, Denmark and Ceylon.

The importance of these contrasts lies in the consistency with which social entities otherwise deemed dissimilar also have vastly different suicide rates.[9] Thus, we find a sharp difference between rates for men and women, the old and the young, the married and the single, Negroes and whites in the South, and between Denmark and Ceylon. Such differences were known to exist before Durkheim's research, but it was he who first showed that the suicide rate reflects something basic in the social characteristics of a population.

Note, however, that Durkheim's argument may apply to practically all forms of deviant behavior. Moreover, as suggested earlier, certain proscribed acts are ostensibly far more social than is suicide. Why, then, has suicide been selected for extensive study? Primarily because sociology, like other disciplines, has a particular axe to grind: to demonstrate the social influences upon all manner of human behavior. And what better way is there to add to the efficacy of the argument for social causation than to show that it extends even to such a personal and desperate act as suicide?

Durkheim's approach has greatly influenced later studies of suicide by setting the central problem—the explanation of differences in suicide rates. Why, for example, was Sweden's 1961 suicide rate more than twice that of Norway; and why did Finland's rate increase from 6.1 in 1901 to 22.1 in 1962?[10]

[9] A suicide rate is usually computed by the formula: $r = (S/P)100,000$, where S is the number of suicides occurring in a given year, or the average number per year, and P is the mean number of people in the population over the year or years. Thus r represents the annual number or mean annual number of suicides per 100,000 population during a year or period of years.

[10] World Health Organization, *Epidemiological and Vital Statistics Report*, Vol. 9, Table 2 and p. 251; and *Demographic Yearbook, 1963* (New York: United Nations, 1964), Table 25.

Concern with suicide rates has created still another problem for sociological research, the question of the reliability of official suicide statistics. Following Durkheim, suicide may be defined formally as "death resulting directly or indirectly from a positive or negative act of the victim himself, which he knows will produce this result." [11] But this may not be applied by persons who compile official mortality statistics. The author finds that officials (e.g., coroners) who make such decisions are not governed by a formal definition of this kind. Thus the use of official suicide statistics in research rests on the assumptions that the commonly held conception of the act: (1) corresponds to the research definition, (2) does not vary from one population to the next, and (3) is applied consistently to all cases of death.

Many observers rightly question these assumptions and thereby cast doubts on the use of official statistics. Zilboorg, for instance, argues that:

> . . . statistical data on suicide as they are compiled today deserve little if any credence; it has been repeatedly pointed out by scientific students of the problem that suicide cannot be subject to statistical evaluation. . . .[12]

But Zilboorg's evaluation of official statistics as unreliable is purely intuitive. Thus, he cites as a "scientific student" of the problem, of all people, Durkheim, who made extensive use of official suicide statistics. Simpson's rejection of official data is equally dubious. He rests his judgment in part on the failure of persons to agree as to whether suicide increases or decreases with civilization.[13] He also questions official statistics because they indicate that suicide is rare among children, whereas Zilboorg considered suicide among children significant enough for a study of it.[14]

All things considered, present knowledge precludes an adequate evaluation of official statistics. Probably they are not very accurate, but the amount of error is another question. Moreover, reliability probably varies not only by place and time but also according to the

---

[11] Durkheim, *Suicide,* p. 44.

[12] Gregory Zilboorg, "Suicide Among Civilized and Primitive Races," *American Journal of Psychiatry,* Vol. 92 (May, 1936), p. 1350.

[13] George Simpson, "Methodological Problems in Determining the Aetiology of Suicide," *American Sociological Review,* Vol. 15 (October, 1950), p. 660.

[14] *Ibid.,* p. 660. Simpson fails to report that Zilboorg presents no evidence to show that suicide is actually common among children. See Gregory Zilboorg, "Considerations on Suicide, With Particular Reference to That of the Young," *American Journal of Orthopsychiatry,* Vol. 7 (January, 1937), pp. 15-31.

source of official statistics. Gargas reports that during 1900-1925 suicide rates for the Netherlands based on criminal statistics were generally 32 percent higher than those based on the statistics of the registrar's office.[15] This is one of the few studies that have offered concrete evidence of the questionable reliability of suicide rates based on official data. Other research, however, suggests that some rates are more reliable than is generally assumed. This conclusion was reached after applying Durkheim's definition of self-destruction to each coroner's report of a death in New Zealand during the period 1946-1951. Inspection of these records produced an estimate of 955 cases of suicide over the six years,[16] as compared with 1036 cases reported in official statistics.[17] The rates computed on the basis of the two figures differ very little. More noteworthy, perhaps, is that the officially reported number exceeds the count reached by careful inspection of all coroner reports. This contradicts the often expressed belief that official figures always seriously underestimate the amount of suicide, but it does not prove that all suicide rates are reliable, any more than Gargas' findings demonstrate that the reverse is true. We can only conclude that the question of the reliability of suicide statistics remains unsolved. (See Chapter 3, page 141.)

Although the foremost task for sociological studies of suicide is to explain differences in rates, other aspects of suicide also warrant study. Of these, variation in societal reaction to self-destruction is certainly sociological subject matter beyond its being a possible etiological factor.

A final problem remains—explanation of individual cases of suicide. The question can be put simply: what characteristics distinguish persons who kill themselves from those who do not? Note however that the problem of differences between victims and nonvictims is logically distinct from inquiry into the determinants of suicide rates. Simpson and MacIver [18] notwithstanding, such inquiry is not merely a step toward explaining why some persons end their existence and others do not. Moreover, a theory about rates of suicide need not, and pos-

---

[15] S. Gargas, "Suicide in the Netherlands," *American Journal of Sociology*, Vol. 37 (March, 1932), p. 699. The figures provided by Gargas suggest that the discrepancy between the two sets of rates over the years indicated is on the average far less than 32 percent.

[16] This research was made possible by a Fulbright grant and the cooperation of New Zealand's Department of Justice.

[17] *New Zealand Official Year-Book, 1947-49, 1950, 1951-52,* and *1954,* Census and Statistics Dept. (Wellington: Government Printer).

[18] Simpson, "Methodological Problems." R. M. MacIver, *Social Causation* (Boston: Ginn, 1942), pp. 140-44.

sibly cannot, apply to individual cases, nor is its validity contingent on such application.

Despite the logical distinction between rates and individual suicides, there has been and doubtless will continue to be sociological interest in the latter. For one thing, the characteristics that distinguish suicides may be largely social. For another, the characteristics that differentiate suicide victims may vary from one society to the next.

Viewpoints and Interests of the Various Disciplines

The foremost concern in this survey is with differences in suicide rates as a sociological problem. However, the study of suicide is not the exclusive property of any particular field. Accordingly, before undertaking an analysis of differences in suicide rates the viewpoints and interests of several disciplines warrant attention.

Psychological Studies and Observations

Understandably, psychological and psychiatric studies of suicide have focused on explaining the individual case. Several types of inquiries have sought this explanation. One type is based on all cases (or a sample taken as representative) occurring in a population over a specified period.[19] Such studies may consider the social characteristics of victims and the epidemiology of suicide, but, as a rule, they focus on possible motives or reasons for the act and the psychological or psychiatric classification of the victim. At least three serious difficulties confront this type of research. First, the ascription of motives or reasons is likely to be arbitrary. Second, the victims cannot be classified psychologically on the basis of direct observation. And, third, even when particular motives or psychological-psychiatric types are known to have prevailed among the cases, they can seldom be evaluated because the prevalence of these factors in the total population is generally unknown. Accordingly, such studies can at best isolate only the necessary and not the sufficient conditions for suicide.[20]

These psychological-psychiatric studies suggest that completed or attempted suicides often are persons with some mental or emotional disorder; however, the proportion so diagnosed has been in some in-

---

[19] A number of these studies are cited in James M. A. Weiss, "Suicide: An Epidemiologic Analysis," *Psychiatric Quarterly*, Vol. 28 (April, 1954), pp. 250-52.

[20] The first and third problems apply to some extent to studies of attempted suicide. See Margarethe von Andics, *Suicide and the Meaning of Life* (London: Hodge, 1947); and other studies cited in Weiss, "Suicide," pp. 250-52.

stances as small as 15 percent, and it varies considerably from one population to the next. Although depressive psychotics are particularly prone to take their own lives, suicide occurs among almost every type of psychiatric disorder.[21]

A second type of inquiry employs control groups. One such investigation compared four groups of persons with psychiatric histories: persons (1) who had committed suicide, (2) with a history of attempted suicide, (3) with a history of having threatened suicide, and (4) without a history of suicidal behavior. The investigators found that a potentially suicidal person could not be reliably distinguished on the basis of details in his case history.[22] No significant differences were detected among the four groups other than that a disproportionate number of actual suicides had been diagnosed previously as suffering from either reactive depression or paranoid schizophrenia and had one or more relatives with a history of mental hospitalization.

A third type of inquiry, the psychoanalytic approach, relies on random case history data and clinical experience. Typically, it is guided by one of two major ideas. The first is that the "suicidal person is the victim of strong aggressive impulses which he fails to express outwardly and which he, as a result, turns inward, i.e., on himself." [23] Whatever its merits, this conception clearly does not adequately explain the act, because nothing is said concerning the conditions that generate aggression and determine the direction of its expression. The second idea suggests a death instinct as underlying suicide.[24] But this view is subject to the following objection:

> Valid as they are, one must nevertheless remark that the psychological speculations built around the death instinct as a pivotal point explain comparatively little since they are essentially restatements of the observation that, under certain known and mostly unknown circumstances, the impulse to die becomes greater than the impulse to live, at which time man will injure or kill himself. To say that the death instinct gains the upper hand over the life instinct is merely an elaborate way of stating that man does die or kill himself.[25]

---

[21] Sainsbury, *Suicide in London,* pp. 84-86. Weiss, "Suicide," p. 236. Zilboorg, "Considerations on Suicide." Gregory Zilboorg, "Differential Diagnostic Types of Suicide," *Archives of Neurology and Psychiatry,* Vol. 35 (January, 1936), pp. 270-91.

[22] Edwin S. Shneidman and Norman L. Farberow, "Clues to Suicide," *Public Health Reports,* Vol. 71 (February, 1956), pp. 109-14.

[23] Zilboorg, "Differential Diagnostic Types of Suicide," p. 272.

[24] See Menninger, *Man Against Himself.*

[25] Zilboorg, "Considerations on Suicide," p. 17.

Thus, with regard to explaining why some individuals kill themselves and others do not, the results of the three types of psychological-psychiatric inquiries appear generally inconclusive.

Anthropological Observations

Observations on suicide appear occasionally in anthropological literature, usually in a larger report on a particular culture. These observations (and a few special studies) generally deal with three aspects of suicide in a society—alleged typical motives or reasons, incidence, and societal reaction.

Accounts of ritual suicide suggest a peculiarity and a homogeneity of motives or reasons for suicide among some non-European peoples. The fact is, however, that suicide occurs among non-Europeans in a variety of situations and probably has widely diverse motives. Consider the following list of typical reasons or motives given for suicide in various populations: among the natives of Dobu—domestic quarrels; among the Iroquois—for the females, mistreatment in love and marriage and, for the males, the desire to escape apprehension for a violent crime; among the Mohave—longing for the dead; among the Lepchas of Sikkim—disgrace by public reproof; among the Eskimos of St. Lawrence Island—sickness, suffering, and a feeling of uselessness; and among the Chukchee—quarrels, suffering, longing for the dead, or a feeling of *taedium vitae*.[26] These and other reports confirm the earlier findings of Steinmetz and Westermarck,[27] both of whom reached the conclusion that a wide variety of motives or reasons are ascribed to suicides among nonliterates.

One thing is clear. Whatever their relevance to etiological inquiry, it appears that the alleged motives among nonliterates and other non-Europeans are much more akin to those among Europeans than the

---

[26] R. F. Fortune, *Sorcerers of Dobu* (New York: Dutton, 1932), pp. 2-21. William N. Fenton, "Iroquois Suicide: A Study of the Stability of a Cultural Pattern," *Anthropological Papers*, No. 14, U.S. Bureau of American Ethnology, Bulletin No. 128 (Washington, D. C., 1941), p. 90 and pp. 130-34. George Devereux, "Mohave Soul Concepts," *American Anthropologist*, Vol. 39 (New Series, 1937), p. 422. Geoffrey Gorer, *Himalayan Village* (London: Joseph, 1938), p. 269. Alexander Leighton and Charles C. Hughes, "Notes on Eskimo Patterns of Suicide," *Southwestern Journal of Anthropology*, Vol. 11 (Winter, 1955), pp. 327-28. Waldemar Bogoras, "The Chukchee," American Museum of Natural History, *Memoirs* (New York: Stechert, 1904), Vol. 11, Pt. 3, pp. 560-68.

[27] S. R. Steinmetz, "Suicide Among Primitive People," *American Anthropologist*, Vol. 7 (January, 1894), pp. 53-60. Edward Westermarck, *Origin and Development of Moral Ideas* (London: Macmillan, 1908), Vol. 2, pp. 229-64.

presence of ritual suicide in some non-European societies might suggest.[28]

Anthropological observations on the incidence of suicide are difficult to interpret, and the inferences drawn from them are hazardous at best. The reason why this is so should be clear from the observations cited below (Table 3).

These reports are not without value, but some of them treat incidence so impressionistically that they are inadequate for systematic comparisons. Only a rate of suicide is suited for comparisons, and descriptions of the act as "common," "rare," etc., are poor substitutes. These accounts report neither the probable rate of suicide nor the basis for the observer's vague estimate. One danger is that a few exotic cases may give the impression that suicide is rampant in the society. For example, reports on ritual suicide and on the special case of *suttee* (a ceremony in which the wife kills herself on the death of her husband)[29] suggest that suicide was once rampant in India. But was this the case? We do not have the historical statistics needed to provide the answer. But it has been estimated that the rate for the whole of India was only about 4.8 in 1907, with a high of 8.1 in the Central Provinces, as compared, for example, with a rate of 32.6 for Saxony during 1906-1910.[30]

The case of Japan serves as another warning against confusing the occurrence of ritual self-destruction with a high rate of suicide. Ceremonial self-destruction, known as *hara-kiri*, has long prevailed in the country; however, Japan's suicide rate during 1881-1885 may have been less than that of the United States for 1906-1915, and it appears that only since the turn of the century has the suicide rate in Japan substantially exceeded that in the United States.[31]

Until such time as we have something other than impressionistic accounts of suicide in nonliterate and other non-European societies any cross-cultural generalization is suspect. For the time being one

---

[28] The similarity of motives for suicide in different types of societies is stressed in Louis I. Dublin and Bessie Bunzel, *To Be or Not To Be* (New York: Harrison Smith and Robert Haas, 1933), p. 142. Revised version: Louis I. Dublin, *Suicide: A Sociological and Statistical Study* (New York: Ronald Press, 1963).

[29] R. V. Russell and Rai Bahadur Hira Lal, *The Tribes and Castes of the Central Provinces of India* (London: Macmillan, 1916), Vol. 2, pp. 259-67. N. M. Penzer, *The Ocean of Story* (London: Sawyer, 1925), Vol. 4, pp. 255-72.

[30] John Rice Miner, "Suicide and Its Relation to Climatic and Other Factors," *American Journal of Hygiene,* Monographic Series No. 2 (July, 1922), pp. 2-3 and 17.

[31] *Ibid.,* p. 3.

TABLE 3

Incidence of Suicide in Some Non-European Populations

Population	Observations on the Incidence of Suicide
Mohave [1]	"The conflict between longing for the dead and the impossibility of catching up with them should one live too long after they died leads to an appalling number of suicides. . . ."
Kwakiutl [2]	"In practice suicide was comparatively common."
Tanaina [3]	"Suicide is more common now, when old men live to see the last of their sons die."
Havasupai [4]	"Suicides, like the insane, are rare. The practice is referred to in myths and funeral speeches, and is credited to the Walapai, yet there have been no instances for a generation."
Lepchas of Sikkim [5]	"Considering the size of the community suicide is fairly frequent among the Lepchas. There have been six suicides in Lingthem and the neighbouring smaller villages in the last twenty years. . . ."
Indians of the Southwestern U.S. and Northern Mexico [6]	"Suicides occur among most of the tribes visited, but on the whole they are rare, especially among women."
White Mountain Apache [7]	". . . one or more cases of self-destruction occur every year."
Southern Ute [8]	"No instance of death by suicide was learned of. . . ."
Papago [9]	". . . suicide is seldom heard of."
Puma [10]	". . . suicide is rare."

Sources:

[1] Devereux, "Mohave Soul Concepts," *American Anthropologist*, Vol. 39, p. 422.

[2] Benedict, *Patterns of Culture* (Boston: Houghton Mifflin, 1934), p. 219.

[3] Osgood, *American Anthropologist*, Vol. 35, p. 714.

[4] Spier, American Museum of Natural History, *Anthropological Papers*, Vol. 29, Part 3, p. 343.

[5] Gorer, *Himalayan Village*, p. 269.

[6,7,8,9,10] Hrdlicka, U.S. Bureau of American Ethnology, Bulletin No. 34, p. 171.

tentative conclusion is that the suicide rates of nonliterate peoples are probably low on the average, but also that the rates for some of them now exceed or have exceeded those of several European countries.

On the whole, anthropologists have devoted little attention to accounting for cross-cultural variation in the incidence of suicide. This probably reflects the primary interest of individual anthropologists in a particular culture and a strong bias against generalization in the discipline. This may also underlie the preference for clearly *ad hoc* or parochial explanations. As an example, it is said that the suicide rate of the Bison-horn Maria is higher than that of the neighboring Muria because Maria children do not grow up in a village dormitory.[32] The village dormitory is held to be pertinent because it supposedly fosters respect for cultural values and discipline and discourages individualistic attachment to personal property and jealousy. Benedict, as another example, attributes the allegedly high frequency of suicide among the Kwakiutl to a value system which extolled rivalry and envy.[33] These and similar explanations are stated as though their validity is not contingent on how well they apply to other cultures.

We have previously noted marked historical changes in societal reaction to self-destruction. Anthropological reports suggest that pronounced variation also occurs cross-culturally. Among the Pueblos, for example:

> The taking of one's life, however, is entirely outlawed. Suicide is too violent an act, even in its most casual forms, for the Pueblos to contemplate. They have no idea what it could be.[34]

But a quite different reaction prevailed among the Chukchee.

> That voluntary death is considered praiseworthy, may be seen also from the fact that, in descriptions of the other world, those who have died in this way are given one of the best dwelling places. They dwell on the red blaze of the aurora borealis, and pass their time playing ball with a walrus skull.[35]

These and other observations [36] indicate clearly that societal reaction to voluntary death varies, both historically and cross-culturally, from glorification through moral indifference to severe condemnation. However, these variations remain unexplained.

Actuarial Studies

As one might expect, actuaries have focused almost exclusively on the incidence of suicide. They have brought together a vast amount of data on suicide by countries and other political units, age groups,

---

[32] Verrier Elwin, *Maria Murder and Suicide* (London: Oxford University Press, 1950), pp. xxi-xxii.
[33] Ruth Benedict, *Patterns of Culture* (Boston: Houghton Mifflin, 1934), pp. 189-222.
[34] *Ibid.*, p. 117.
[35] Bogoras, "The Chukchee," pp. 562-63.
[36] See Westermarck, *Origin and Development of Moral Ideas*, pp. 236-54.

sex, race, marital status, religion, occupation, and trends in the rates of a variety of populations.[37]

These studies have contributed to our fund of knowledge, but they have not led to a general theory. Explanatory observations by actuaries are limited to two types. In one kind a particularly high or low suicide rate is explained in terms of the composition of the population. Thus, the low suicide rate in the South is attributed in part to the large proportion of Negroes.[38] Since Negroes do have a much lower suicide rate than whites, the "explanation" of course holds for the particular case; but it scarcely can explain why, for example, Austria's suicide rate is now more than ten times that of Ireland.

The second type of actuarial explanation is purely conjectural and *ad hoc*. Consider, for instance, Frenay's observations on the excess of female over male suicides in the age group 15-19 during the period 1911-1920 in the United States: "The greater frequency of the female sex at this particular age may be doubtlessly attributed to the sexual problem." [39] Two questions are in order. First, did the females actually have a greater sexual problem? Second, how do these alleged problems explain why the suicide rate of the age group 75-84 in the United States was in 1960 over five times the rate of persons 15-24? Actuaries do not seek general theories; they assume that each rate has a unique cause.

Sociological Studies

Sociologists have tended to follow Durkheim's lead in considering variation in suicide rates as the major problem. This has produced three types of studies: those concerned primarily with the fact of variation,[40] those that represent an extension of Durkheim's theories and concepts,[41] and those that rest on theories not derived from Durkheim's work.

As suggested earlier, sociologists have all but ignored the reliability of suicide statistics as a problem. This is understandable, considering the obstacles posed by the task of verification and its unrewarding

---

[37] Representative studies: Dublin and Bunzel, *To Be or Not To Be.* Frederick L. Hoffman, *Suicide Problems* (Newark, N. J.: Prudential Press, 1927). Frenay's study also exemplifies the actuarial approach; see Adolph Frenay, *The Suicide Problem in the United States* (Boston: Gorham, 1927).

[38] Dublin and Bunzel, *To Be or Not To Be*, pp. 80-81.

[39] Frenay, *The Suicide Problem*, p. 78.

[40] See, for example, Walter A. Lunden, "Suicides in France, 1910-1943," *American Journal of Sociology*, Vol. 52 (January, 1947), pp. 321-34; Gargas, "Suicide in the Netherlands."

[41] See Maurice Halbwachs, *Les Causes du Suicide* (Paris: Alcan, 1930).

nature, but it is nevertheless, for obvious reasons, most unfortunate. Less understandable is the sociologists' lack of concern with variation in societal reaction to suicide. An adequate explanation of such variation is, of course, a sociological goal in itself, but it is doubly important because of a possible relationship between societal reaction and the incidence of suicide.

The remaining problem—accounting for individual cases of suicide —has received spotty treatment at the hands of sociologists, though it has by no means been ignored. Numerous studies have analyzed the case histories of individual victims,[42] but the results have been uniformly poor. Analyses of alleged motives or reasons have proved to be fruitless, and attempts to find purely sociological characteristics that consistently differentiate victims have been unsuccessful. True, we can speak of certain statuses (such as being divorced or being of a certain age) as representing a greater suicide "risk" than others, but virtually no status provides absolute immunity. Accordingly, the "risk" approach is not adequate.

A far more sophisticated approach looks to conditions that do not influence all individuals in the same way, but that, at the same time, prevail more in some statuses and societies than in others. The isolation of such conditions and the demonstration that they are linked to suicide would be a great achievement, solving two theoretical problems—differentiating persons who commit suicide from those who do not and predicting the magnitude of suicide rates.

Two recent studies which have moved in this direction will be considered. Powell, in line with Durkheim, points to anomie as a crucial factor in the etiology of suicide:

> When the ends of action become contradictory, unaccessible or insignificant, a condition of anomie arises. Characterized by general loss of orientation and accompanied by feelings of "emptiness" and apathy, anomie can be simply conceived as meaninglessness.[43]

Having so described anomie, Powell judged its prevalence in various occupational categories and sought confirmation through inspection of the suicide rates of the categories.[44] Unfortunately, he did not state the operations by which the prevalence of anomie may be gauged; his procedure seemed completely intuitive. Because the conditions which

---

[42] See, for example, Cavan, *Suicide*.

[43] Elwin H. Powell, "Occupation, Status, and Suicide: Toward a Redefinition of Anomie," *American Sociological Review*, Vol. 23 (April, 1958), p. 132.

[44] Here Powell is concerned with suicide rates and not individual cases, but otherwise his observations suggest that the theory applies to both levels.

constitute or give rise to anomie are not described in strictly empirical terms, the theory cannot be subjected to a systematic test on either individual cases or suicide rates.

Far more empirical is Porterfield's analysis of rifts in social relations as factors in suicide.[45] He distinguishes between rifts in *Gesellschaft* relations (e.g., a loss of economic position) and rifts in *Gemeinschaft* relations (e.g., divorce) as being more important in some cases than in others. Porterfield's findings suggest that rifts of both types occur with surprising frequency in cases of voluntary death, but there are some obvious problems that confront an explanation of suicide in such terms. First, the conditions that determine the relative importance of one type of relational rift over the other are not clearly specified. Second, there are numerous instances in which self-destruction is not preceded by a relational rift of either type. Third, it is probably true that the vast majority of disruptions in social relations are not followed by suicide. Despite these problems, Porterfield's approach has merit in that it attempts to achieve a synthesis of the explanation of individual cases and several theories of the incidence of suicide.

Variation in Amount of Suicide

A general theory of the incidence of suicide must account for variation among all types of populations. Accordingly, before considering some general theories, let us examine some further detailed evidence of the kinds of differences in suicide rates. (See Chapter 3, pages 146-60.)

Variation by Political Units

For more than a century it has been known that rates of suicide differ among nations;[46] this continues to the present, as can be seen in Table 4. It is not at all unusual to find a suicide rate in one country that is more than five times the rate in another. General observations do not suggest a close relation between the suicide rate and either climatic factors or any apparent cultural characteristics. True, the majority of high rates are found far north of the equator, but sharp differences between Finland, Sweden, and Norway suggest that this is not a matter of climatic factors. The six countries with the highest rate of suicide are technologically advanced, but the rates for the

---

[45] Austin L. Porterfield, "Suicide and Crime in the Social Structure of an Urban Setting: Fort Worth, 1930-50," *American Sociological Review,* Vol. 17 (June, 1952), pp. 341-49.

[46] See Henry Morselli, *Suicide: An Essay on Comparative Moral Statistics* (New York: Appleton, 1882), pp. 1-35, for a detailed study of European suicide rates in the nineteenth century.

TABLE 4

Suicide Rates for 41 Countries, *circa* 1962

Country	Suicide Rate per 100,000 Population	Year	Country	Suicide Rate per 100,000 Population	Year
Australia	13.7	1962	Japan	17.3	1962
Austria	22.4	1962	Jordan	0.2	1962
Belgium	14.7	1961	Luxembourg	9.3	1962
Bulgaria	8.0	1962	Mexico	1.9	1960
Canada	7.2	1962	Netherlands	6.6	1962
Ceylon	9.9	1960	New Zealand	8.4	1962
Chile	7.7	1961	Nicaragua	0.4	1962
Colombia	4.8	1962	Norway	6.6	1961
Costa Rica	2.4	1962	Panama	6.4	1962
Czechoslovakia	20.6	1961	Peru	1.4	1959
Denmark	16.9	1961	Poland	8.8	1961
Dominican Republic	1.0	1960	Portugal	8.6	1962
Finland	22.1	1962	Spain	5.5	1960
France	15.1	1962	Sweden	16.9	1961
Germany, West	18.7	1961	Switzerland	18.2	1961
Greece	3.4	1962	Union of South Africa	14.2[a]	1960
Guatemala	3.1	1962	United Arab Republic	0.1[b]	1961
Hungary	24.9	1962	United Kingdom	11.6[c]	1962
Iceland	9.4	1962	United States	10.8	1962
Ireland	1.8	1962	Uruguay	11.3	1955
Italy	5.6	1961			

Source: Demographic Yearbook, 1963 (New York: United Nations, 1964), Table 25.
Qualifications: [a] White population only. [b] Population within Health Bureau localities only. [c] Rate based on 1961 population.

United Kingdom, the United States, Australia, New Zealand, and Canada are clearly deviant cases in this regard. Also, the fact that the predominantly Catholic countries generally have very low suicide rates does not, of course, explain the comparative rates of Japan, Ceylon, Jordan, and the United Arab Republic. Moreover, Austria, a predominantly Catholic nation with the second highest suicide rate, is a crucial negative case.

A general theory must also deal with variation within nations. Evidence indicates that suicide rates for political divisions of a nation are never uniform; they vary to a degree approaching that of differences between nations, as can be seen from Table 5. The suicide rate of one state (California) is nearly twice that of the other (Texas), and the cities exhibit a wide range of differences.[47]

---

[47] For a thorough treatment of interstate and intercity variation in U.S. suicide rates, see Austin L. Porterfield, "Indices of Suicide and Homicide by States and Cities," *American Sociological Review*, Vol. 14 (August, 1949), pp. 481-90.

TABLE 5

Suicide Rate of Some Political Divisions of the United States, 1960

Political Divisions	Suicide Rate per 100,000 Population
States	
California	16.0
Texas	8.8
Cities	
Los Angeles, California	20.4
San Jose, California	19.1
Midland, Texas	14.4
Waco, Texas	5.1

Source: Rates computed from suicide data in *Vital Statistics of the United States, 1960*, Vol. II, Pt. B, Table 9-9.

Differences by Sex

As is generally known, women enjoy greater immunity to suicide than men. Less widely known is the great variation in the suicide rates of women, as attested by Table 6. This variation suggests that a biological explanation of differences in the suicide rates of males and females is untenable.

In Iceland, the male suicide rate exceeds the female rate by only 2.1, while the difference in the case of Finland is 23.8. Viewed another way, the extreme cases are Costa Rica and (again) Iceland, with the male rate 13.0 times the female rate in the former country but only 1.3 in the latter. The varying character of female immunity is further reflected by the fact that the female suicide rate in Japan exceeds that of males in 14 of the countries listed in Table 6.

That in all countries listed women are less prone to commit suicide is not as instructive as the variation in the rates, which is so wide that we might expect to find cases where the usual male excess does not obtain. This was found in Bengal, where in 1907 there were 177 female suicides for every 100 male suicides.[48]

Variation by Age

Suicide rates in the United States vary consistently by age. In 1960, for example, the rate (per 100,000 population) was 0.3 for persons 5-14 and increased somewhat regularly from one age group to the next

---

[48] Miner, "Suicide and Its Relation to Climatic and Other Factors," p. 31.

TABLE 6

Male and Female Suicide Rates by Countries, *circa* 1960

Country and Year	Suicide Rate per 100,000 Population		Ratio of Male to Female Rate	Excess of Male Rate
	Male	Female		
Australia, 1960	15.0	6.2	2.4	8.8
Austria, 1959	35.8	15.2	2.4	20.6
Belgium, 1959	18.9	7.6	2.5	11.3
Bulgaria, 1960	10.5	4.7	2.2	5.8
Canada, 1960	12.0	3.0	4.0	9.0
Costa Rica, 1960	3.9	0.3	13.0	3.6
Denmark, 1959	28.7	13.5	2.1	15.2
England and Wales, 1959	14.2	8.9	1.6	5.3
Finland, 1960	32.7	8.9	3.7	23.8
France, 1960	24.0	8.2	2.9	15.8
Germany, West, 1960	25.7	12.6	2.0	13.1
Hungary, 1960	35.6	14.9	2.4	20.7
Iceland, 1960	9.0	6.9	1.3	2.1
Italy, 1959	8.9	3.6	2.5	5.3
Japan, 1959	26.6	18.9	1.4	7.7
Luxembourg, 1959	13.4	5.6	2.4	7.8
Netherlands, 1960	8.2	5.1	1.6	3.1
New Zealand, 1959[a]	13.8	4.3	3.2	9.5
Norway, 1959	11.7	4.0	2.9	7.7
Panama, 1960	7.9	2.4	3.3	5.5
Portugal, 1960	13.6	3.7	3.7	9.9
Sweden, 1959	27.2	9.0	3.0	18.2
Switzerland, 1959	30.1	9.4	3.2	20.7
Union of South Africa, 1958[b]	18.9	6.0	3.2	12.9
United States, 1960	16.6	4.7	3.5	11.9

Source: Demographic Yearbook, 1961 (New York: United Nations, 1962), Table 19.
Qualifications: [a] European population only. [b] White population only.

up to 27.9 for persons 75-84 and then declined slightly to 26.0 for the 85-and-over category. This pattern is often found in European nations but the relationship between suicide rates and age varies tremendously, as is illustrated in Figure 1.

The data illustrate both common and uncommon patterns. American males exhibit the frequently found direct relation between suicide and age, while American females exhibit another common pattern—a decrease in the suicide rate beyond a certain age.[49] The pattern in Japan is most unusual. The rate increases rapidly up to age 24, then plunges to a low between 30 and 50, and then rises again

---

[49] A decrease beyond a certain age is also characteristic of the male suicide rate in some countries.

FIGURE 1

Suicide Rates by Age and Sex in the United States and Japan, 1956-58

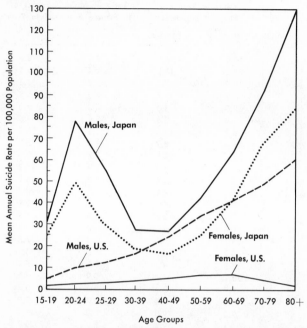

Source: World Health Organization, *Epidemiological and Vital Statistics Report,* Vol. 14, No. 5 (1961), Table 1.4.

with advancing age. These and other patterns indicate that there is nothing biologically inherent in aging which produces self-destruction.

Racial Differences

Our knowledge of suicide by race is clearly inadequate because it is restricted to rates in a small number of countries, and some relevant observations are not comparable. For example, in the United States Negroes have a low suicide rate, but it is reported that suicide is "rather common" among certain Negro tribes in Africa.[50]

The evidence permits only one general conclusion: the immunity of any race to suicide is extremely variable. This conclusion is suggested by data in Table 7. Here we find that Negroes have a suicide rate

---

[50] Frenay, *The Suicide Problem,* pp. 150-52.

TABLE 7

Suicide Rates by Race: A Variety of Cases

Race	Location	Years	Suicide Rate per 100,000 Population
Oriental (Chinese)	United States	1960	22.3
Caucasian[a]	United States	1938-40	15.7[b]
Oriental[c]	United States	1949-51	14.6[b]
Caucasian[a]	United States	1960	11.4
Oriental[c]	United States	1960	11.1
Negro	Seattle, Washington	1948-52	10.2[b]
Caucasian[b]	Mississippi	1949-51	9.7[b]
Negro	United States	1960	3.9

Sources: Vital Statistics, Special Reports, Vol. 43, No. 30, p. 471; Vital Statistics of The United States (1949, 1950, 1951); American Sociological Review, Vol. 20, p. 279; Vital Statistics of The United States, 1960, Vol. II, Pt. A, Tables 5-8.

Qualifications: [a] White. [b] Average annual rate. [c] Identified racially as other than Negro or white.

much lower than that of Caucasians in the United States, but instances of a higher Negro rate can be found. Compare the Negro rate in Seattle, Washington, with the Caucasian rate in Mississippi.

It is perhaps surprising to find that during the period 1949-1951 Orientals in the United States had a suicide rate higher than Caucasians. There are, however, instances where the Caucasian rate exceeds the Oriental rate. The suicide rate for whites in Seattle, 1948-1952, was nearly twice the Japanese rate and nearly three times the Chinese rate.[51] Finally, while the 1960 suicide rates of Caucasians and Orientals in the United States are virtually identical, both are much lower than the 1960 rate for Chinese (a segment of the Oriental population), which clearly suggests that ethnicity is much more important than race.

The Rural-Urban Difference

During the nineteenth century, the urban suicide rate exceeded the rural rate in virtually all countries and provinces.[52] Yet, during recent decades the rural-urban difference in rates has changed sharply in

---

[51] Calvin F. Schmid and Maurice D. Van Arsdol, Jr., "Completed and Attempted Suicides: A Comparative Analysis," American Sociological Review, Vol. 20 (June, 1955), p. 279.

[52] Pitirim Sorokin and Carl C. Zimmerman, Principles of Rural-Urban Sociology (New York: Holt, 1929), Chapter 7.

TABLE 8

Rural and Urban Suicide Rates,
United States, 1960

Territorial Categories	Suicide Rate per 100,000 Population
Metropolitan counties	10.6
Urban	10.7
Rural	10.4
Nonmetropolitan counties	10.7
Urban	10.1
Rural	11.0
Total urban	10.5
Total rural	10.8

Source and qualification: Rates computed from suicide data in *Vital Statistics of The United States, 1960,* Vol. II, Pt. B, Table 9-9. Census figures for the urban and rural populations have been adjusted (in the way of estimates) to make them correspond to the urban-rural distinction employed in gathering and reporting vital statistics. For all practical purposes, the urban population is restricted to persons residing in incorporated places of 2500 or more inhabitants, which is a much more narrow definition of urban than that employed in the 1960 population census.

some countries. For example, during the period 1904-1913, the urban suicide rate in the United States Registration States was 17.7, while the rural rate was only 12.2.[53] Over the decades the rural-urban difference has declined, and, as shown in Table 8, by 1960 the rural rate actually was slightly higher.[54] What is truly remarkable about the data in Table 8 is the minute variation in the suicide rate from one territorial category to the next, and it is all the more remarkable when one considers that such small differences could be due to minor errors in the vital statistics and/or the population estimates employed to compute the rates. However, granted the possibility of errors, it is

---

[53] Hoffman, *Suicide Problems,* p. 182.

[54] Exceptions to the relation between urbanization and suicide are not peculiar to the United States; it was the situation in the Netherlands as early as 1911-1920. See Gargas, "Suicide in the Netherlands," p. 700. Note, however, that the spread of urban population beyond the political limits of cities may produce higher rates for administrative rural areas. This is particularly true for the U.S., where urban suicides are reported only for incorporated places. The rural-urban difference consequently remains subject to question.

perhaps significant that a higher suicide rate for rural males has been reported previously.[55]

Some Occupational Differences

Official statistics on suicide by occupation are reported in only a few countries, and the occupations considered are seldom strictly comparable. Consequently, observations on the subject are sketchy and questionable.

What little is known on the subject suggests extreme variation in the suicide rates of different occupations. An example of this is provided by Powell's study in Tulsa County, in which he found the rate for pharmacists to be 24 times that of carpenters.[56] Such contrasts are peculiar neither to Tulsa, the United States, nor the twentieth century. In Italy, during 1866-1876, the suicide rate was 61.8 for persons engaged in "letters and science," as compared to a rate of only 2.5 for persons engaged in "production of raw materials" and one of only 6.8 for "domestic servants." [57]

Extremely high suicide rates generally prevail in occupations at the extremes—those with either very high income and prestige or very low income and prestige. For example, high rates are often found in both the professional-managerial category and the category of unskilled laborers, with occupations ranking midway between these two in status having lower rates.[58] The high rate that typically prevails among the unemployed and retired appears to fit the low-income–low-prestige pattern.

Again, there are exceptions to the general rule. In some countries, several occupations in both the professional-managerial and the unskilled categories do not have high suicide rates. Also to be noted are data for England and Wales, 1921-1923, which show that the highest and lowest rates among five major occupational groups (designated as social classes) vary from one age group to the next.[59] Moreover,

---

[55] W. Widwick Schroeder and J. Allan Beegle, "Suicide: An Instance of High Rural Rates," *Rural Sociology*, Vol. 18 (March, 1953), pp. 45-52.

[56] Powell, "Occupation, Status, and Suicide," p. 136. For statistics on occupation and suicide for the United States, see National Office of Vital Statistics, *Vital Statistics–Special Reports*, Vol. 53, Nos. 1-5 (June, 1961-September, 1963). Certain questions concerning reliability preclude an analysis of these data.

[57] Morselli, *Suicide*, p. 244.

[58] See Powell, "Occupation, Status, and Suicide," p. 137. *The Registrar General's Decennial Supplement, England and Wales, 1951, Occupational Mortality*, Pt. 1 (London: H.M.S.O., 1954), p. 11.

[59] See Dublin and Bunzel, *To Be or Not To Be*, pp. 95, 96, 108-09, and 399.

the suicide rate of an occupational category may increase or decrease considerably without any apparent corresponding change in income or prestige. For example, the rate for the professional-managerial category in Tulsa County dropped from 63.0 in 1937-1941 to 21.2 in 1947-1951; in the latter period the rate was lower than that for all other occupations combined.[60]

Differences by Religion

A series of studies have shown that Catholics and Jews are much less prone to take their lives than Protestants are. In most cases this is true, but Table 9 shows that the immunity enjoyed by Jews and Catholics is clearly relative to place and time.

Of religious groups in 20 different locations and periods the Jews have both the highest and the lowest suicide rate. The highest Catholic rate is seen to exceed Protestant rates in 7 cases. On occasion, either the Jewish rate or the Catholic rate exceeds the Protestant rate in the same location and period. Finally, as the New Zealand data show, the suicide rates of various Protestant denominations are by no means uniform.

Some of the rates shown in Table 9 doubtless represent unusual cases, but more systematic data lead to the same conclusion.[61] For example, the suicide rate of Jews in Prussia was 4.6 during the period 1849-1855, or about one-third the Protestant rate; but by the period 1901-1907 it had increased to 29.4, at which point it exceeded the Protestant rate by some 17 percent; and by 1925 it had reached 53.0, nearly twice the Protestant rate.

Variation by Marital Status

It is generally, not universally, true that married persons are less prone to suicide than the widowed, single, and the divorced are. For one thing, when age is ignored, the single may have a suicide rate lower than that of the married. This was the case in the United States during 1949-1951: single, 4.7; married, 13.4; widowed, 24.9; and divorced, 45.8.

Only when age is taken into account, as in Figure 2, is the greater immunity of the married made evident. But even here exceptions are present. In the age group 15-19, the lowest suicide rate is found among

---

[60] Powell, "Occupation, Status, and Suicide," p. 135. For some statistics and theoretical observations on the relation between occupational mobility and suicide, see Warren Breed, "Occupational Mobility and Suicide Among White Males," *American Sociological Review*, Vol. 28 (April, 1963), pp. 179-88.

[61] Dublin and Bunzel, *To Be or Not To Be,* pp. 117-18.

TABLE 9

Suicide Rates by Religion: Selected Cases

Religious Group	Location	Mean Annual Suicide Rate per 100,000 Population	Years
Jewish	Netherlands	28.3 [1]	1900-10
Protestant	Prussia	18.7 [2]	1869-72
Protestant	Netherlands	17.1 [1]	1900-10
Congregational	New Zealand	15.1 [3]	1946-51
Methodist	New Zealand	12.9 [3]	1946-51
Catholic	Toronto	11.0 [4]	1928-35
Church of England	New Zealand	9.7 [3]	1946-51
Jewish	Prussia	9.6 [2]	1869-72
Baptist	New Zealand	9.5 [3]	1946-51
Presbyterian	New Zealand	9.5 [3]	1946-51
Protestant	Austria	8.0 [2]	1852-59
Catholic	New Zealand	7.3 [3]	1946-51
Catholic	Netherlands	7.0 [1]	1900-10
Catholic	Prussia	6.9 [2]	1869-72
Church of Christ	New Zealand	6.9 [3]	1946-51
Ringatu and Ratana[a]	New Zealand	6.6 [3]	1946-51
Jewish	Toronto	5.6 [4]	1928-35
Catholic	Austria	5.1 [2]	1852-59
Protestant	Toronto	4.5 [4]	1928-35
Jewish	Austria	2.1 [2]	1852-59

Sources:

[1] S. Gargas, "Suicide in the Netherlands," *American Journal of Sociology*, Vol. 37 (March, 1932), p. 709.

[2] Émile Durkheim, *Suicide: A Study in Sociology*, translated by John A. Spaulding and George Simpson (New York: Free Press, 1951), p. 154.

[3] From records of New Zealand's Registrar-General (Wellington).

[4] Cited by James M. A. Weiss, "Suicide: An Epidemiologic Analysis," *The Psychiatric Quarterly*, Vol. 28, p. 235.

[a] Predominantly Maori faiths.

the single, not the married; and the suicide rate of the married comes to exceed that of the widowed in the ages 70-74.

Instances where the suicide rate of the single or the widowed corresponds closely to, or is less than, that of the married in certain age groups are not peculiar to the United States; they have been noted in other countries,[62] but such exceptions have yet to be explained by a general theory.

Relativity of Suicide Rates

Throughout we have noted that the rate of suicide in a particular status (or social category) varies from place to place and time to

---

[62] See Durkheim, *Suicide*, pp. 175-80.

FIGURE 2

Suicide Rates by Marital Status in the United States, 1949-51

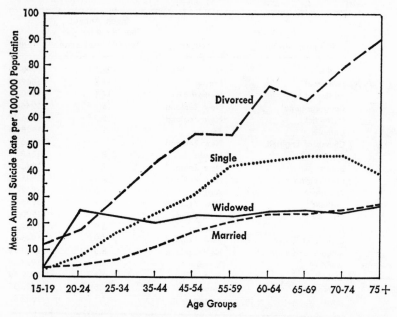

Source: *Vital Statistics—Special Reports, Selected Studies*, Vol. 39, No. 7 (May 8, 1956), pp. 370 and 426.

time. This should always be recognized in attempts to explain differences in suicide rates, if only to avoid the dubious assumption that there is something inherent in each status that generates a certain rate. Thus, more than one investigator has noted increasing suicide with advancing age in a particular country and explained it by postulating something suicidal in the aging process, without recognizing that some elderly populations actually have very low rates.

The universal picture is one of extreme contrast in the suicide rates of different statuses. This suggests that status is in some way linked to the incidence of suicide, but beyond this little can be said. Any doubts as to the relative character of the immunity provided by a particular status should be resolved by the data presented below (Table 10).

Note that under certain conditions females may have a suicide rate that is as much as 186 times that of males under other conditions. The data also indicate that there is no inherent connection between aging and suicide—the young (20-24) may have a rate 150 times that of the old (70 and over). The idea that nonwhites in the United States

TABLE 10

Suicide Rates by Status: Selected Extreme Cases

Status	Lowest Suicide Rate Noted and Conditions	Highest Suicide Rate Noted and Conditions
Male	Nonwhite, single, under 20 years of age, United States, 1949-51 Rate: 0.4	White, divorced, over 75 years of age, United States, 1949-51 Rate: 139.1
Female	Nonwhite, single, under 20 years of age, United States, 1949-51 Rate: 0.3	70 years of age and over, Japan, 1947-49 Rate: 74.3
Young (20-24)	Female, Ireland, 1945-54 Rate: 0.3	Male, Japan, 1952-54 Rate: 60.0
Old (70+)	Female, Chile, 1947-49 Rate: 0.4	White, divorced, male, 70-74 years of age, United States, 1949-51 Rate: 124.4
White	Single, female, under 20 years of age, United States, 1949-51 Rate: 0.3	Divorced, male, over 75 years of age, United States, 1949-51 Rate: 139.1
Nonwhite	Single, female, under 20 years of age, United States, 1949-51 Rate: 0.3	Male, single, 70-74 years of age, United States, 1949-51 Rate: 56.7
Married	Nonwhite, female, under 20 years of age, United States, 1949-51 Rate: 1.0	White, male, over 75 years of age, United States, 1949-51 Rate: 40.8
Divorced	Nonwhite, female, 35-44 years of age, United States, 1949-51 Rate: 0.7	White, male, over 75 years of age, United States, 1949-51 Rate: 139.1

are "naturally" immune to suicide is incompatible with the fact that certain groups of them may have a rate some 189 times that of a particular segment of the white population. Also to be noted is the existence of a suicide rate for certain married persons which is some 58 times that of certain divorced persons.

These cases have, of course, been deliberately selected to show that there is nothing inherent in any one status which generates a particular rate of suicide under all conditions. A possible exception is the status of "child" (i.e., persons under ten years of age), which seems universally associated with extremely low rates of suicide.

Temporal Variation

Cases of a suicide rate remaining stable over an extended period have been noted and stressed by earlier investigators, particularly Durkheim.[63] There are recent instances of such constancy over the short run, as, for example, the suicide rate in Canada: 1956, 7.6; 1957, 7.5; 1958, 7.5; 1959, 7.4; 1960, 7.6.[64] But generally there have been marked changes in suicide rates during recent decades.

The course of the suicide rate in six countries between 1901 and 1960 is shown in Figure 3. Of the six, only Ireland has exhibited a remarkably constant rate over the 60 years. The changes in the rates of the other five are not purely random fluctuations; several long-range trends appear. The United States rate climbed somewhat regularly from 10.4 in 1901 to 16.2 in 1915, and after a decline it again moved up almost continually from 10.2 in 1920 to 17.4 in 1932. Finland provides an even better example of a trend; its rate increased fairly consistently from 10.6 in 1920 to 23.4 in 1931.

Figure 3 also reveals an association between suicide trends and periods of war and depression. In most cases, wars are associated with decreases in suicide rates, while economic depressions are accompanied by increases. These patterns often have been noted.[65] But wars and economic depressions in themselves do not provide an adequate explanation of suicide trends. Obviously, there are numerous instances of definite trends in rates without wars or depressions. Moreover, any explanation of temporal variation should be set forth in the context of a general theory, in which explaining why wars and depressions are associated with change in the suicide rate (and why they are not in some cases) is a special case of a more general problem.

Particular Theories on Variation in Suicide Rates

The data in the previous section point out the general character of variation in suicide rates. In this section we will consider several theories on the subject and, in doing so, rely heavily on the predictive power of each theory as a criterion of its explanatory adequacy. This criterion cannot be applied rigorously, however, as most theories are

---

[63] Durkheim, *Suicide*, pp. 46-53.
[64] *Demographic Yearbook, 1961* (New York: United Nations, 1962), Table 17.
[65] See Frenay, *The Suicide Problem*, Chapters 2 and 8; Durkheim, *Suicide*, pp. 202-08 and 241-46; Halbwachs, *Les Causes du Suicide*, Chapters 11 and 12.

FIGURE **3**

Trends in the Suicide Rates of Finland, Ireland, Japan, Norway, Sweden, and the United States, 1901-60

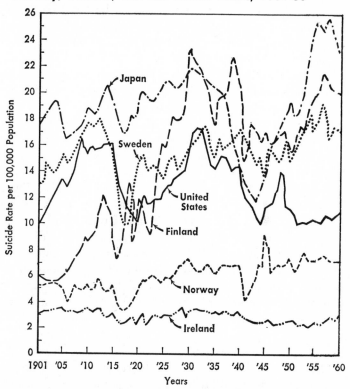

Sources: World Health Organization, *Epidemiological and Vital Statistics Report*, Vol. 9, No. 4 (1956), Table 2, and Vol. 15, No. 10 (1962), Table 2; *Demographic Yearbook, 1957* (New York: United Nations, 1958), Table 14; *Demographic Yearbook, 1961*, Table 17.

far from systematic and the operations necessary for empirical tests often are not specified.

Psychopathology and the Suicide Rate

Running through much speculation on the subject is the suggestion that the suicide rate varies directly with the prevalence or incidence of psychopathology. (See Chapter 2, page 105.) This hypothesized relationship is apparently not the product of a formal theory; it appears, rather, to stem from the common belief that any individual who commits suicide is mentally ill. Whatever the source of the hypothesized relationship, it is not possible to subject it to a definitive test, primarily because of the problem of obtaining reliable statistics on the incidence of mental disorders.[66]

Granting that the negative results may be due to deficiencies in the data, we must nevertheless recognize that some careful investigations have not found evidence to support the assertion of a direct relationship between the incidence of psychopathology and suicide. Some 70 years ago, Durkheim found no close relationship between the number of institutionalized "insane" and the number of suicides by age, sex, religious affiliation, provinces, and countries in Europe. Using a wide variety of data, a more recent investigation [67] found no close direct relationship between any of four measures of the incidence or prevalence of mental disorder and suicide rates by states in the United States.

It may be that a particular type of psychopathology holds the key to variation in suicide rates; this possibility remains to be investigated thoroughly. However, at least in the United States, only rates for total mental disorders exhibit a uniform increase with advancing age that corresponds to a similar increase in the suicide rate, but this type of mental disorder rate bears no close relationship to variation in suicide rates by states. Moreover, there is no evidence to show that mental disorder varies by race and sex in a manner corresponding to the suicide rate.

Societal Reaction to Suicide

Concern with societal reaction to voluntary death has produced a candidate for a general theory of variation in suicide rates.

> Where custom and tradition accept or condone it, many persons will take their own lives; where it is sternly condemned by the rules of the Church and State, suicide will be an unusual occurrence.[68]

This idea can be formally restated: the suicide rate varies inversely with the degree of societal condemnation of suicide.

In terms of general cross-cultural and historical observation, this proposition is not without some support.[69] However, apart from its

---

[66] For a discussion of the problems as they relate to United States data, see U.S. Federal Security Agency, *Patients in Mental Institutions, 1949* (Washington, D. C., 1952), p. 9.

[67] Jack P. Gibbs, "A Sociological Study of Suicide," Ph.D. dissertation, University of Oregon, 1957, pp. 363-75.

[68] Dublin and Bunzel, *To Be or Not To Be*, p. 15.

[69] *Ibid.*, Pt. 4.

seemingly self-evident character, the thesis requires a more exacting measure, or at least classification, of the degree of societal condemnation.

Even before a formal measure is devised, we can anticipate cases in which the predictive power of the proposition might well be negligible. It is unlikely that the range of reaction to suicide among the different statuses in a society (i.e., age, sex, race, marital status, occupation, etc.) is as wide as differences in their suicide rates. For example, there is no reason to suppose that suicide among Negroes and females in the United States is more severely disapproved than it is among whites and males. There is no evidence that all increases or decreases in the suicide rates of countries reflect corresponding changes in the norms pertaining to suicide, and this would seem particularly true for the recent decrease of the rate in the United States.

Social Disorganization

Studies of suicide in the United States and in England have been largely oriented toward the concept of social disorganization. These studies suggest a general theory: the suicide rate varies directly with the extent of social disorganization.

The initial problem in evaluating this theory is to distinguish between social disorganization and its alleged effects. The treatment of the concept at the hands of Mowrer, Elliott and Merrill, Faris, and Cavan [70] does not provide an adequate distinction; on the contrary, it often appears that the concept simply means a lack of conformity to social norms, and, accordingly, the relationship between social disorganization and deviant behavior is essentially tautological.[71] More recent treatments of the concept make a better distinction between social disorganization and its alleged effects,[72] but they do not clearly specify the operations by which the prevalence of social disorganization is to be gauged.

---

[70] Mowrer, *Disorganization*. Mabel A. Elliott and Francis E. Merrill, *Social Disorganization* (New York: Harper, 1941). Robert E. L. Faris, *Social Disorganization* (New York: Ronald Press, 1948). Cavan, *Suicide*.

[71] Mowrer, for example, refers to suicide as "a form" of social disorganization (*Disorganization*, p. 19). Cavan (*Suicide*, p. 330) states that social disorganization is the loss of control of the mores over the members of a group, which suggests that the concept is defined in terms of deviant behavior.

[72] Arnold M. Rose, *Theory and Methods in the Social Sciences* (Minneapolis: University of Minnesota Press, 1954), pp. 3-24. Turner, "Value Conflict." Albert K. Cohen, "The Study of Social Disorganization and Deviant Behavior," in Robert K. Merton *et al.*, eds., *Sociology Today* (New York: Basic Books, 1959), pp. 461-84.

As a consequence of the nebulous character of the concept, the alleged relation between social disorganization and suicide does not rest on direct empirical confirmation; it rests instead on correlations between suicide and other alleged effects of social disorganization. As previously noted, it has been found in some American cities that suicide occurs most frequently in urban subareas that abound with other forms of deviant behavior. But there are contradictory observations. Porterfield has shown that rates of suicide may be *unrelated to or actually vary inversely with* other alleged effects of social disorganization (e.g., crime).[73]

It is of course methodologically indefensible to ignore cases where suicide rates do not correlate directly with other alleged effects of social disorganization. Sainsbury, for example, in testing the hypothesis found suicide rates in the boroughs of London to be fairly closely related to rates of divorce and illegitimacy but not with the rate of juvenile delinquency.[74] He accepted these findings as support for the hypothesis by suggesting that juvenile delinquency is not after all indicative of social disorganization in London.[75] This suggests that the only valid indicators of social disorganization are those which vary directly with the suicide rate, but this makes the relation between the two tautological.

Schmid has attempted to substantiate the social disorganization theory more directly. After designating population mobility as indicative of social disorganization, he demonstrated a fairly high correlation (+.60) among American cities between a measure of mobility and suicide rates.[76] A similar relation has been reported for the boroughs of London.[77]

Measures of population mobility may produce correct predictions of spatial variation in the suicide rate, but this does not extend to statuses and social categories. In the United States, during 1949-1951, the least mobile age groups had the highest suicide rates; that is, the suicide rate varied inversely by age groups with each of six measures of mobility.[78]

---

[73] Porterfield, "Suicide and Crime in the Social Structure of an Urban Setting: Fort Worth, 1930-1950" and "Indices of Suicide and Homocide by States and Cities," p. 489.

[74] Sainsbury, *Suicide in London,* p. 41.

[75] *Ibid.,* pp. 78-79.

[76] Calvin F. Schmid, "Suicides in Seattle, 1914-1925: An Ecological and Behavioristic Study," p. 12, and "Suicide in Minneapolis, Minnesota: 1928-32," *American Journal of Sociology,* Vol. 39 (July, 1933), p. 30.

[77] Sainsbury, *Suicide in London,* p. 41.

[78] Gibbs, "A Sociological Study of Suicide," p. 354.

Secularization and Suicide

Porterfield's observations on the incidence of suicide by types of society suggest a general proposition: the suicide rate varies directly with the degree of secularization. In tests of the proposition on states in the United States, Porterfield found a fairly close relationship between an index of secularization (based on the degree of urbanization, industrialization, membership in churches, and nonnativity) and the suicide rate.[79]

Two points should be noted in evaluating the proposition. First, even if we assume that it applies only to differences among societies, secularization does not seem to account for the moderate suicide rates of the United States, the United Kingdom, New Zealand, Canada, and Australia, all of which are, presumably, highly "secularized." And, second, the proposition does not generate predictions of differences in suicide rates by age, sex, and marital status. The same may be said for any theory which links the incidence of suicide to civilization, modernization, urbanization, and so on. (See Chapter 1, page 60.)

Social Integration and Suicide

The most influential sociological theory of suicide was advanced by Durkheim at the end of the nineteenth century. Having produced an impressive body of evidence to refute explanations of variations in suicide rates in terms of extrasocial variables (psychopathy, race, heredity, climate, and imitation), he turned to the nature of social life for an answer.

Durkheim's inspection of nineteenth-century European data led him to postulate three types of suicide. High suicide rates for Protestants, the unmarried, and married couples without children suggested the *egoistic* type: the suicide which stems from excessive individualism or, put another way, a lack of social integration. On the other hand, insufficient individuation or excessive social integration produces the *altruistic* type of suicide. This type was suggested to Durkheim by reports that suicide (particularly the ritual form) was common in "lower" societies and by high suicide rates for the military, especially among elite troops. And, finally, the connection between the incidence of suicide and economic crisis, divorce, and certain business occupations suggested to Durkheim a third type of suicide—the *anomic*—which is produced by insufficient social regulation of the individual.[80]

---

[79] Austin L. Porterfield, "Suicide and Crime in Folk and Secular Society," *American Journal of Sociology,* Vol. 57 (January, 1952), pp. 331-38.

[80] Durkheim, *Suicide,* pp. 152-216, 217-40, and 241-76.

Most discussions of Durkheim's study center on his conceptions of egoistic, anomic, and altruistic suicide; and only rarely is it recognized that the translation of his observations on the three types into a theory of variation in suicide rates is fraught with difficulties. At first glance it might appear that any test of his theory would necessarily have to be based on separate rates for egoistic, anomic, and altruistic suicide. But, since the three types are defined in terms of their causes, and only vaguely so, it is doubtful if individual cases can be classified as either egoistic, altruistic, or anomic; Durkheim certainly did not apply his typology to all cases of suicide in a population, nor did he compute a rate for each of the three types. Even if separate rates could be established, there would still remain the problem of distinguishing the cause of variation in one of the rates from the causes of variation in the other two. *Altruistic* and *egoistic* suicides are distinguished, on the conceptual level, by designating the former as a product of excessive social integration and the latter as a product of insufficient social integration. But Durkheim's distinction between the causes of *anomic* and *egoistic* suicide is by no means clear, and it is doubtful whether an adequate distinction can be drawn even on the conceptual level, much less in strictly empirical terms.[81] In the face of no clear-cut empirical distinction between the causes of anomic and egoistic suicide, we can only resort to what appears to be the most general and certainly the least ambiguous statement of Durkheim's theory:

> So we reach the general conclusion: suicide varies inversely with the degree of integration of the social groups of which the individual forms a part.[82]

This general statement should perhaps be qualified by noting that Durkheim's observations on altruism suggest that beyond a certain point an increase in social integration results in more suicide.[83]

What can be said in support of Durkheim's general theory that suicide rates vary inversely with the degree of social integration? Relatively little, because Durkheim did not conduct a series of rigorous tests. There is not one instance in which he correlates a measure of

---

[81] Sainsbury (*Suicide in London,* p. 22) has voiced a similar opinion. For a statement of a contrary position (i.e., Durkheim's concepts can be distinguished), see Bruce P. Dohrenwend, "Egoism, Altruism, Anomie, and Fatalism: A Conceptual Analysis of Durkheim's Types," *American Sociological Review,* Vol. 24 (August, 1959), pp. 466-73.

[82] Durkheim, *Suicide,* p. 209.

[83] Little can be said for this side of Durkheim's theory; he uncritically accepted reports of ritual suicide in supposedly highly integrated societies as evidence of a high suicide rate and attempted to account for such cases by invoking altruism.

integration with suicide rates. Moreover, at no time does he provide either a real or nominal definition of social integration, much less an operational one. It is not even made clear whether social integration relates to consensus in values or whether it is found in actual behavior (e.g., the frequency, duration, and regularity of social interaction).

The support for the theory lies not in its demonstrated predictive power but rather in Durkheim's forceful argument. As long as no universal measure of integration was involved, he could argue from knowledge of suicide rates and ascribe degrees of integration to each population accordingly. Perhaps we can sense that Catholics, Jews, and married persons with children are highly integrated (i.e., enveloped in binding social relations), but sensing that something is true and demonstrating it are two different things. Moreover, what is the appropriate conclusion when the usual differences in suicide rates no longer prevail? One can say that the usual degree of integration has also changed, but this is merely arguing backward from knowledge of suicide rates. Interpretation and *ex post facto* explanations are a poor substitute for predictions. Durkheim provided no basis for predictions, and consequently his theory cannot be subjected to any rigorous test. Nonetheless, his achievement was not a small one, for his basic ideas have guided numerous subsequent investigations.

Status and Suicide

Durkheim's influence is particularly marked in a theory advanced by Henry and Short.[84] Their theory rests on three postulates: (1) the suicide rate of a population varies inversely with the strength of the relational systems of the members, (2) the strength of the relational systems of the members of a population varies directly with the external restraints placed on their behavior, and (3) the external restraints placed on the behavior of the members varies inversely with their status (position in the prestige hierarchy).

Since Henry and Short do not specify the operations necessary for gauging either the strength of relational systems or the extent of external restraints,[85] we must be content to consider the proposition that the suicide rate of a population varies directly with its status, a relation which can be derived from the three postulates above.

---

[84] Andrew F. Henry and James F. Short, Jr., *Suicide and Homicide* (New York: Free Press, 1954).

[85] Henry and Short define the strength of a relational system as the degree of involvement in cathectic relations with other persons, and they define the strength of external restraints as the degree to which behavior is required to conform to the demands and expectations of other persons.

Even in the case of status there are no actual measures provided; it is only described conceptually in terms of achievement, possession, authority, and power. Rather than use actual measures in testing hypotheses, Henry and Short assume that in terms of status in the United States the whites exceed Negroes, males exceed females, high-income groups exceed low-income groups, and the young and the middle-aged exceed those past the age of 65, and that army officers exceed enlisted men.

These assumptions appear to be sound, but certain problems come to mind. For one thing, how are predictions to be made in cultures where status cannot be determined on an intuitive basis? Of equal importance, how does the proposition apply to countries and political units?

Apart from these two crucial questions, there appear to be cases where the status of certain segments of the United States population is not in line with the suicide rates. The suicide rate of Orientals in the United States is typically higher than that of whites. Note also that in the United States the rate for persons over 65 exceeds that of persons 15-64, yet the older segment of the population supposedly has less status. This discrepancy is recognized by Henry and Short, but they appear to shift ground in attempting to account for it. They suggest that the strength of the relational system decreases with age; and this contradicts their suggestion that status and the strength of the relational system vary inversely. Another inconsistency is found in the treatment of the lower suicide rate of the married. Their low rate can hardly be attributed to low status, so it is described as the product of external restraints and strong relational systems. Even here, however, there is no real basis for anticipating the close correspondence of the suicide rates of the married and the widowed in the older age groups. Finally, we should note again that high suicide rates have been known to prevail among occupations on the lower end of the status hierarchy.

Status Integration and Suicide

Running throughout Durkheim's observations is the suggestion that the suicide rate varies inversely with the stability and durability of social relations. This suggestion served as a point of departure for a recent theory which links the suicide rate to a particular *pattern* of status occupancy.[86] Through a series of postulates and assumptions it is deduced that in populations where the occupancy of one particu-

---

[86] Jack P. Gibbs and Walter T. Martin, *Status Integration and Suicide: A Sociological Study* (Eugene, Oregon: University of Oregon Books, 1964).

lar status tends to be closely associated with the occupancy of certain other statuses the members are less subject to role conflict, more capable of conforming to the demands and expectations of others, more capable of maintaining stable and durable social relations, and consequently less prone to suicide.[87] The extent of association in the occupancy of statuses is referred to as the degree of *status integration,* which is at a maximum in a society or other population where knowledge of all but one of an individual's statuses enables an observer to predict correctly the remaining undisclosed status of the individual (e.g., all of the persons with a certain occupation, age, sex, race, and religion are married).

The major theorem is: *the suicide rate varies inversely with the degree of status integration in the population.* This theorem applies both to societies and to different segments of any one society. Those societies characterized by a high degree of status integration would be expected to have low suicide rates. *Within* a society those status configurations (i.e., clusters of statuses, such as a particular age, sex, race, marital status, etc.) which are infrequently occupied would be expected to have a high suicide rate. Consider, as an illustration, data on marital status by age in the United States. In 1950, of the males 60-64 years of age, 79.3 percent were married, 9.6 percent widowed, 8.6 percent single, and 2.5 percent divorced. The corresponding average annual suicide rates during 1949-1951 for the four marital statuses in this age group are: for the married, 36.2; for the widowed, 64.7; for the single, 76.4; and for the divorced, 111.1. Consistent with the major theorem, there is a perfect inverse relation between the proportion in a marital status and the suicide rate of the status. The prediction of such a relation (and all other predictions generated by the theory) rests on the assumption that the relative frequency with which a cluster of statuses is actually occupied reflects the extent of role conflict among the statuses, with infrequently occupied clusters assumed to be characterized by role conflict and, consequently, weak social relations.

Because status integration can be measured, the major theorem can be subjected to systematic tests. An initial series of tests has produced positive results,[88] but an adequate evaluation of the theory must await further tests and judgment by impartial critics.[89]

---

[87] *Ibid.,* Chapter 2.
[88] *Ibid.*
[89] The present author hardly qualifies as an impartial critic in this instance.

Needs and Prospects

After more than six decades we still lack an adequate treatment of suicide as a social and sociological problem. It behooves us, then, to look more to the future than to the past.

Future Sociological Investigations

One problem that will confront future studies is the idea of multiple causation, the notion that populations may have high or low suicide rates for different reasons, as, for example, when the difference between the suicide rates of men and women is explained in one way, while the difference between the rates of the old and the young is explained in another way.

However real the case for multiple causation may appear, the very idea defeats the quest for a truly general theory through a search for a common denominator that underlies all instances of high rates. This quest carries on the tradition of Durkheim's approach. But future investigations must not slavishly follow Durkheim, if only because the search must go beyond the generation of indefinite concepts. Little is accomplished by suggesting that the common denominator is "anomie," or some other equally vague term. Future investigations must not only locate a common denominator and describe it conceptually but must also specify the operations necessary for assessment of its prevalence in populations.

As we have seen, the concern of sociologists with individual cases of self-destruction has yielded very little. Future studies must thus choose among a wide variety of possible approaches, one of which is suggested by George Simpson in his plea for a greater integration of sociological and psychoanalytic views on suicide.[90] It is not clear, however, just how the observations of two fields with quite different, if not opposing, perspectives are to be integrated. In the writer's opinion the opportunities for a distinctly sociological contribution lie not in a forced marriage with psychoanalysis but rather in cross-cultural investigations of the characteristics of suicide cases and in the analysis of the sociological past of victims.

In regard to the sociological past of victims, it has become a truism that purely social conditions cannot explain the individual suicide because persons react differently to apparently identical conditions. This is true, but that which is purely social is a part of each person's past as well as the present, and the former may be of greater importance

---

[90] Editor's Introduction to Durkheim, *Suicide,* pp. 20-25.

than the latter in the etiology of suicide. We remain largely ignorant of the influence of the sociological past on behavior, but an investigation of past statuses of suicide victims and the timing of their status changes could serve as a point of departure.

Finally, future studies must come to grips with the problems posed by suicide statistics. There is a real need for more studies that investigate cases of death in particular populations and compute suicide rates independent of official statistics. Such studies would necessarily be limited in scope, but the suicide data gathered by them could be used in strategic tests of any given theory—strategic in that the data are far more reliable than the official statistics are assumed to be. Moreover, the compilation of data on this basis would provide an opportunity to consider types of suicide. In official compilations, suicides are generally lumped into one category, and this one category may be far too heterogeneous to permit valid generalizations.

Suicide as a Social Problem

There is general agreement that current efforts to prevent suicide are not effective. In this case, however, it is senseless to call for an aroused citizenry to demand action, for the brutal truth is that no existing program appears capable of substantially reducing the incidence of suicide.

Practically all attempts to prevent suicide focus on individuals who have shown symptoms of self-destructive tendencies. In the case of attempted suicide the would-be victim may be directed by the court, the police, or relatives to the care of a physician, a psychiatrist, a clinic, a mental institution, or to a special antisuicide organization.[91] Persons who are contemplating suicide or who have in some way exhibited self-destructive symptoms may also be brought to the attention of these agencies.

However humane or helpful the program that focuses on individual cases may be, it has some definite limitations in reducing the incidence of suicide. Such a program could be effective only if those who are about to commit suicide show definite signs of their intentions. The author's study of all cases of suicide in New Zealand, 1946-1951, indicates that suicidal symptoms are by no means always conspicuous. Judging from the testimony of witnesses before the investigating coroner, a previous attempt was reported for only 7 percent of the 955

---

[91] For a discussion of antisuicide organizations see Dublin and Bunzel, *To Be or Not To Be*, pp. 321-25. For references to more recent suicide prevention programs and a relevant theory see Arthur L. Kobler and Ezra Stotland, *The End of Hope* (New York: Free Press, 1964), particularly Chapters I and IX.

cases. This represents the minimum number, of course, since some previous attempts may have gone undetected or unreported. The figure does agree somewhat closely, however, with Sainsbury's findings in London where a previous attempt was reported for 9 percent of the victims.[92] Moreover, it appears that the majority of the New Zealand victims did not suggest, directly or indirectly, that they were contemplating suicide; judging from testimony some 26 percent of them did so. Once again this represents the minimum because of the difficulties of assessing indications and because witnesses are probably reluctant to report that the victim's behavior suggested suicide and that they did not prevent it. Reports of intensive studies of suicide cases indicate that as many as 83 percent of the victims "communicated" their intent,[93] but the problem is that the typical layman may not: (1) recognize at the time the communications of intent that are detected later by trained investigators in the reconstruction of cases, or (2) take effective action even if a suicidal intent is communicated and if he recognizes it as such.

Finally, there is a widespread belief that suicide is preceded by mental disorder and that signs of this disorder can be used to detect and predict attempts at suicide. An analysis of the New Zealand cases indicates that 34 percent of the victims may have suffered from some form of mental disorder (neuroses or psychoses), a number almost identical with an average of 33 percent reported in 16 studies of completed and attempted suicide.[94] We have noted the difficulty of judging psychopathology, particularly on the basis of testimony rather than observation, and therefore know that these figures represent only rough estimates. But it does seem that symptoms of psychopathology are not adequate for identifying potential suicides.

The conclusion is thus inescapable. Even if all persons who show definite suicidal symptoms were brought to the attention of authorities and even if the treatment administered were effective, suicide would still take a heavy toll. What then is the answer? Realistic students of social problems have long recognized that the volume of deviant behavior can be reduced only by removing the conditions that give rise to it, and not through treatment of individual cases. This presupposes,

---

[92] Sainsbury, *Suicide in London*, p. 92. Note, however, that other studies of suicide have reported that between 14 and 33 percent of the victims had made previous attempts. See Kobler and Stotland, *The End of Hope*, p. 5. Nonetheless, there appears to be general agreement that a previous attempt is not a reliable indicator of a potential suicide victim.

[93] For references to and summaries of these studies, see *ibid.*, Chapter I, particularly p. 8.

[94] Sainsbury, *Suicide in London*, p. 85.

of course, that the conditions are known, which leads us again to theory and the uncomfortable recognition that a fully adequate theory has yet to be demonstrated. Furthermore, most theories deal with such basic structural components of society that few would dare contemplate altering society in the direction indicated by the theory. If any of these theories are valid, suicide cannot be eliminated by superficial tampering with the social structure. The major problem set for future students of social problems is thus not the treatment of the would-be suicide but rather how to implement the theories which deal with the incidence of suicide.

7

Sexual Behavior

by Kingsley Davis

EVERY SOCIETY HAS A SYSTEM OF NORMS PURPORTING TO REGULATE sexual behavior, some supported by strong sentiments and painful sanctions. Two of the Christian Ten Commandments deal with sexual conduct. Yet no society, apparently, is able to enforce its sexual norms to a degree commensurate with their number and intensity. The theory of sexual regulation is thus faced at the start with two broad questions: first, why do sexual norms exist, and particularly why do they show such strength and profusion? Second, given the norms, why are they violated so frequently? To these we can readily add a third question: how do norms so strongly held ever change? Do they adapt to social and economic changes?

The present chapter tries to answer these general questions at least briefly, because the answers help to provide an understanding of sexual problems that goes beyond popular conceptions and proposed "liberal" and "conservative" solutions. After this initial discussion of sexual norms, the analysis will turn to sexual problems themselves, trying to explain their types and causes. Finally, by way of illustrating the points made in the general sections, the chapter will conclude with a detailed consideration of two widespread forms of violation—homosexuality and prostitution.[1]

---

[1] Our purpose is objective analysis rather than social reform. Discussions of social problems are often intended to persuade people that certain policies are right and others wrong. The "liberal" approach is normally to condemn certain of the existing norms and advocate their replacement by "more enlightened" ones, which raises the question of why his (the "liberal's") norms happen to be "enlightened." The "conservative" feels that the existing norms *are* the most "enlightened" and that therefore the problem is how to induce or compel people to conform to them. Sociological analysis, on the other hand, simply tries to understand why the norms exist, why deviancy occurs, why certain conditions are viewed as problems, why there is disagreement on norms and policies. Such analysis differs from advocacy and usually deteriorates when combined with it.

Why Sexual Norms?

An *avant-garde* theme since at least the time of Jean-Jacques Rousseau has been to paint certain of the sexual mores as mere matters of prejudice. Sexual expression, it is claimed, is "natural" and therefore should be freely allowed. It is also a private affair, a matter of taste. Hence attempts to regulate it are contrary to nature and represent invasions of privacy. At best they make sex ugly and at worst they give rise to hypocrisy, neurosis, crime, and blackmail.

Although phrased broadly, this argument is usually directed only at *particular* regulations, such as bans on homosexuality or mixed nude bathing; it almost invariably takes other sexual mores for granted. Few people would contend that *no* regulation of sexual behavior whatsoever is called for. To do so would be to treat a conspicuous part of every social system as if it were somehow extraneous, or accidental. It would be as unscientific as the opposite view which treats the sexual norms as absolute and God-given.

The basic explanation of why sexual norms are found in every society is the same as that for other kinds of norms.[2] Human behavior is primarily learned from others by symbolic transmission and example. Social interaction is therefore not organized chiefly through instinct but through patterns received from and enforced by other members of the society. At any stage of social evolution, the norms have presumably gone through a long selective process in which they proved advantageous for collective survival according to the conditions of the time. They are not stated exclusively in negative (proscribed) terms but also in positive (prescribed) and neutral (permitted) forms. They help to regulate activities in such a way as to get things accomplished for the life of the community. Human beings are so dependent on acquired patterns that they would not survive without them.

Yet it would be patently false to claim that behavior automatically conforms to norms. The very existence of regulation implies that there is something to regulate, and we know that certain norms are violated more frequently than they are obeyed. Conformity occurs from habit, ignorance of alternatives, and fear of the consequences of nonconformity. Violation occurs because the individual cannot help himself (as in drug addiction), because the norms themselves are in conflict (obeying

---

[2] For a fuller presentation of the theory of norms, together with citations to much of the literature, see Judith Blake and Kingsley Davis, "Norms, Values, and Sanctions," in Robert E. L. Faris, ed., *Handbook of Modern Sociology* (Chicago: Rand McNally, 1964), Chapter 13.

one requires disobeying another), or because the risk of sanctions is less than the potential advantage. A man who successfully embezzles a million dollars reaps a big reward for nonconformity, just as a wife does who, without detection, murders her rich but unloved husband. In the arena of everyday existence the factors making for nonconformity are so powerful, and so much a part of the society itself, that the battle of social control is never-ending. The norms are perennially being disobeyed, reinterpreted, challenged, misused.

Sexual norms differ from others only by virtue of what they regulate, but this difference has important implications. First, the libidinal drive is powerful. It can be conditioned but not extinguished.[3] Like other strong motives, it can disrupt orderly social interaction when left uncontrolled but, when controlled, can induce individuals to perform in socially advantageous ways. Second, though quite uniform in the sheer physiological mechanism of its gratification, the sexual urge is capable of an extraordinary amount of both situational and emotional conditioning. Third, this potentiality for conditioning is made especially complex and problematic by the fact that sexual gratification normally requires the direct, intimate cooperation of another person. As a consequence, erotic motivation tends to be closely associated with interpersonal relations; it becomes involved with affection, trust, dependence, esteem, and their opposites. In satisfying any individual desire, people compete with others for the means of satisfaction, and social efficiency requires an orderly system for producing and distributing the means; but in the case of sexual desire the objects of satisfaction are themselves persons. Consequently, the task of assigning rights in the means of gratification becomes extremely complicated. Sexual attractiveness becomes a value that can be traded for economic and social advantage, and unattractiveness becomes a handicap that can be overcome by control of nonsexual means—but all within emotional and personal contexts in which competition from third parties is an ever present danger. Competition for the same sexual object inflames passions and

---

[3] Kinsey and his associates found only about one-third of one percent of physiologically normal males to have a "low" sex drive. They found none with no drive at all and concluded that "sublimation" is a myth. Alfred C. Kinsey et al., Sexual Behavior in the Human Male (Philadelphia: Saunders, 1948), pp. 205-13. They found about 2 percent of females to evince no sexual impulse. Sexual Behavior in the Human Female (Philadelphia: Saunders, 1953), pp. 512, 526-27. W. S. Taylor, studying a small sample of males in various walks of life, concluded that there are no males without a sexual outlet. A Critique of Sublimation in Males, Genetic Psychology Monographs, Vol. 13 (1933). See also Hugo G. Beigel, "Abstinence," Encyclopedia of Sexual Behavior (New York: Hawthorn Books, 1961).

engenders conflicts; failure injures one's self-esteem.[4] Fourth, as if this were not enough, sexual intercourse is necessary for procreation and is thus linked in the normative system with the institutional mechanisms that guarantee the bearing and rearing of children. The sexual norms and the reproductive norms become intertwined, so to speak; to the possibility of illicit sexual expression is added the possibility of illegitimate parenthood.

These primary features imply certain additional characteristics of sexual norms, regardless of the particular society. We would expect the sexual mores, at least the main ones, to be seriously regarded and strongly sanctioned in law and religion. We would expect them to reinforce, or at least not interfere with, the formation and maintenance of family relationships. We would expect them to help define the roles assigned to men and women and to vary sharply according to age, sex, and marital status. We would expect the sex norms to be highly ramified, not in the technological sense that characterizes rules of physical property for instance, but in the symbolic and emotional sense. We would expect the evasions of the rules to be numerous and to be subject to subsidiary norms.

Among these characteristics, the most important for an understanding of control systems is the connection with the family. This connection enables us to explain most of the patterns of sexual behavior found everywhere and most of the variations connected with particular kinds of societies. It accounts for the ubiquity and strength of the incest taboo; the widespread preoccupation with norms governing premarital relationships, adultery, and pregnancy; virtually all forms of obligatory sexual relations; and the sharp differentiation in sexual norms as between men and women. Within the limits set by these regularities, the connection of sexual rules with the family helps explain the variation of norms from one society to another. To illustrate this variability, let us consider some alternative schemes of sexual regulation as found in different types of society.

Alternative Schemes of Regulation

Although all societies make sexual intercourse obligatory within marriage, they vary in the degree to which they seek to confine it to the married pair. The polar hypothetical case is the society that attempts to confine all coitus to marriage. This, one might say, is the ideal of contemporary Ireland, or the purest ideal of official Christi-

---

[4] See Kingsley Davis, "Jealousy and Sexual Property," *Social Forces*, Vol. 14 (March, 1936), pp. 395-405. Reprinted with slight revision in *Human Society* (New York: Macmillan, 1948), Chapter 7.

anity. If observed to the letter, the strength it would give to wedlock is clear. But in practice there is a cost to linking marriage too exclusively with sexual expression. If the marital bond is given primacy and is guaranteed to be secure, then confining sex expression to it is a strait jacket which many people seem unable to endure. Under such circumstances they tend to postpone marriage or to forgo it altogether (as in Ireland) or to seek other arrangements. Also, it is unrealistic to ban all sex experience prior to marriage and suddenly to start it with marriage. If, on the other hand, marriage is made dependent solely on sexual love (an ideal sometimes voiced in the United States), it loses greatly in stability, because sexual desire in and of itself is often anarchic and fickle. Actually, in their operating moralities, most societies fall into one or another of two types neither of which goes quite to either of these extremes.

One type has a Rock-of-Gibraltar concept of marriage—fixed, durable, impervious to the waves of change and passion. In return the male is given sexual freedom to indulge himself both before and after marriage. The wife, however, chaperoned before marriage and jealously confined to the home afterwards, has little institutionalized opportunity to escape sexual dependence on her husband. The feminine sphere is sharply demarcated from the masculine in many ways, thus reinforcing a double standard of sexual morality. Obviously, the system requires controlled courtship, and it requires two classes of women— the one respectable and the other readily available. The latter, generally from the lower economic strata, enter prostitution, become concubines, or combine easy virtue with a menial occupation. The separation between good and bad women is carried so far in some countries that sexual intercourse, at least for enjoyment, is felt to be almost inappropriate for a married couple. Puerto Rican husbands, for instance, draw

> a sharp distinction between prostitutes, easy women, and their wives. The former are women to be enjoyed because they are evil. The wife, on the other hand, is like one's mother—holy, pure, and saintly. . . . Husbands seem concerned about the fidelity of their wives and the chastity of the daughters to an almost phobic extent.[5]

This kind of organization of sexual behavior survives well in an agrarian and highly stratified society. It tends to disintegrate under urban-industrial conditions.

---

[5] J. Mayone Stycos and Reuben Hill, "The Prospects of Birth Control in Puerto Rico," *Annals of the American Academy of Political and Social Science,* Vol. 285 (January, 1953), p. 141.

An alternative system is one that involves a romantic, or cooperative, view of marriage. Stressing mutual sexual love between husband and wife, it implies the permissive dissolution of wedlock when love has been replaced by animosity or indifference, but hedges against this eventuality by certain institutional mechanisms. One important hedge is the custom of intimate courtship, which allows self-selection on the basis of compatibility and permits the couple to enter marriage with an already established personal bond. The unchaperoned courtship tends to involve premarital intercourse either officially sanctioned (a sort of trial marriage) as in some Scandinavian countries [6] or unofficially tolerated as in many circles in the United States. The main requirement for such relations is that the two be sincere in their affection and likely to marry each other. Stability in the marriage of the cooperative type is further supported by a merging of male and female interests. Women receive an education comparable to that of men; they often participate in the labor force outside the home; and their rules for sexual behavior differ from those of men in degree rather than kind. Promiscuity and adultery are frowned on for either sex. Both parents tend to be involved in the details of child rearing, which gives them a common bond; yet their use of birth control prevents reproduction from completely dominating their mutual relationship.

The Scale of Sexual Norms

The connection between sexual norms and family structure helps us interpret some of the baffling complexities in sexual control. It has often been alleged, for example, that some societies are much "stricter" than others. The claim has even been made that some (usually those least known to the author) hardly regulate sex at all. "There are cultures," say Kinsey and his associates, "which more freely accept sexual activities as matters of everyday physiology, while maintaining extensive rituals and establishing taboos around feeding activities." [7]

---

[6] Harold T. Christensen, "Cultural Relativism and Premarital Sex Norms," *American Sociological Review*, Vol. 25 (February, 1960), pp. 31-39. Thomas D. Eliot and Arthur Hillman, eds., *Norway's Families* (Philadelphia: University of Pennsylvania Press, 1960).

[7] Kinsey *et al., Sexual Behavior in the Human Male*, p. 4. The sole evidence given is a reference to Bronislaw Malinowski, *The Sexual Life of Savages in Northwestern Melanesia* (New York: Halcyon, 1929), but this work, a description of the Trobriand Islanders, gives plenty of evidence of sexual control. For instance, women of a man's own clan (roughly a fourth of the women in the society) are forbidden to him as sexual objects; adultery by either husband or wife is forbidden; "many things which we regard as natural, proper, and moral are anathema to the Trobriander."

The implied conclusion is that sexual control is merely a matter of prejudice and that "our" society is abnormal and sadistic in having such "rigid" controls. Such comparisons, however, even when made in good faith, are dubious. They often have only one aspect of sexual regulation in mind, the other aspects being ignored. One looks at court-ship in Norway and claims that Norway has more sexual freedom than, say, Mexico—overlooking the greater license of a large class of females and of all males in the latter country. Such comparisons also tend to ignore the gradation of norms, the "highest" norms of one society being compared with the everyday ones of another. "Our own culture," says Murdock, "includes . . . an over-all prohibition of all sexual inter-course outside of the marital relationship." [8] Perhaps so, if one takes official religious statements as descriptive of our norms, but actual surveys and field studies show that these are remote from popular opinion. A national survey in 1963, for instance, found 19.5 percent of adults approving of premarital intercourse for males and 16.9 per-cent approving of it for females. The percentages were much higher among some groups—43.2 percent of Negroes approved for men and 40.3 percent for women; among white New York college students in a companion study, the proportion approving of male premarital inter-course was 78.3, and of female premarital intercourse, 74.3 percent.[9] A majority of Americans favor premarital "petting," a practice that would strike hundreds of millions of Hindus and Muslims as immoral.

Norms exist in "layers," so to speak. At the top are the remote and official ideals; then follow the secondary norms that conflict with the official ideals but nevertheless regulate behavior because conformity to them is rewarded and deviation punished. Beyond these are tertiary norms, and so on down the scale of respectability and rightness. For instance, by a strict interpretation, absolute celibacy is the highest Catholic ideal; but in practice lay celibacy is looked at askance by Catholics, sexual pleasure within marriage is approved of, and physical contact with nonmates (e.g., in dancing) is facilitated. There are even "countermores," which approve of behavior for the very reason that it is morally disapproved. Thus among youth a "real man" may be one adept at seducing girls, and a "real sport" a girl willing to be seduced. It makes a difference *whose* behavior is being judged, since people usually favor more license for themselves than for others. In practice,

---

[8] George P. Murdock, *Social Structure* (New York: Macmillan, 1949), p. 263.
[9] Ira L. Reiss, "The Scaling of Premarital Sexual Permissiveness," *Journal of Marriage and the Family,* Vol. 26 (May, 1964), pp. 188-98. This article also contains references to other research on American attitudes toward sexual behavior.

then, normative rightness is relative rather than absolute. Bad behavior has extenuating circumstances; good behavior has impure motives and dubious consequences. In comparing societies one should therefore compare similar gradations on the scale of normative rightness. One should not compare "Judeo-Christian" morality as contained in the more puritanical sections of the Bible with day-to-day norms in a "savage" society, even if the purpose is to show that the former is abnormal and the latter "natural." An illiterate society has no sacred books in which to encrust an unused set of norms.

The scale of norms has some order to it, despite its bewildering variety and inconsistency. One way to perceive the order is to look at the differential evaluation of roles. For instance, family roles have more prestige than other roles in which sexual relations play a part. The primacy of marriage as a sexual relationship is evidenced by the greater economic and legal security and the higher respectability accorded the status of being a wife as against any other role for a woman. A concubine has a lower position than the wife even in societies where concubinage is customary. In all societies the "single woman"— that is, one who has remained unmarried past the customary age of marriage—has done nothing illegal, yet she is punished by her inability to be a "legitimate" mother and her exclusion from economic and social advantages accruing to wives. She is assumed to be single by necessity rather than by choice.

Another way of seeing order in normative systems is to look for the recurrence of rules from one society to another. Norms that appear over and over again as a part of the working apparatus of each society can be assumed to have basic sociological significance. Thus the incest taboos that form part of the structure of the nuclear family itself are found in every society, and their violation is seldom tolerated or institutionalized. Premarital sexual expression, on the other hand, is variable from one normative system to another. It is freely permitted and abetted in some societies, outlawed in others; but when it is outlawed, there are customary and institutionalized modes of violation, especially for males and some females. The conclusion suggests itself that the specific rule about premarital sexual behavior makes little difference to the efficiency of the economic and social system; the important thing is that there be *some* rules defining the rights and obligations of young people with respect to one another as sexual objects. We thus come back to our earlier point that a viable society is one in which the means of sexual gratification, like the means of satisfying other needs and desires, must be distributed in some regulated fashion. The particular rules may vary randomly or according to the type of society, but rules themselves cannot be dispensed with.

The Problem of Enforcement

Sexual behavior, however, is inherently difficult to control. Not only is the organic urge strong and recurrent, but its release can occur in utter solitude; even normal coitus can be brief and clandestine; the stimuli to prurient arousal are almost limitless in variety; and illicit behavior does not necessarily leave tangible consequences by which to trace the guilty. For these reasons, the regulation of sexual conduct tends to be characterized by certain mechanisms that have evolved to meet the inherent refractoriness. One such mechanism is emotional conditioning, by which the rules become part of the sacred realm, surrounded with mystery, stamped with deep moral significance. Another is the belief in supernatural and magical sanctions; these make punishment inescapable because God sees everything and magic acts automatically. With such controls, the individual contemplates "sin" with deep fear of inevitable sanction, horror of discovery, shame, and guilt. In addition, the rules are reinforced by ignorance and silence. Knowledge of sexual phenomena is withheld; erotic stimuli are banned except under special circumstances. In particular, women and children are protected from information by censorship of communication media; suggestive dress or gestures are tabooed. Finally, certain indirect mechanisms, such as chaperonage and female seclusion, limit the social situations in which assignations could be made.

Controls over sexual conduct are enforced more by interpersonal resentment and retaliation, by gossip and loss of face, than by official action. In Java, for instance, husbands and wives are suspicious of any contact between the spouse and a person of the opposite sex. They tend to interpret minute deviations of behavior as indications of possible infidelity. When asked the meaning of *tjemburu* (jealousy-suspicion), they give examples showing "an almost paranoid watchfulness between spouses." Such surveillance, with anger and reprisal when violation is discovered, undoubtedly helps to control behavior.[10]

The enforcement problem accounts for the significance that religion and public sentiment attach to sexual behavior. In most civilizations, sex is singled out for such attention that when the word "morality" is used alone it is assumed to refer to sexual morality. Evidently such preoccupation is not due to any direct economic or political effect of

---

[10] Hildred Geertz, *The Javenese Family* (New York: Free Press, 1961), pp. 128-33.

erotic misconduct. The British Empire is not crumbling because of increased premarital intercourse in Britain; Ireland is not saved from being the poorest nation in northwestern Europe by its puritanical attitude toward courtship; Denmark has not suffered in comparison to Chile because it has legalized abortion. The preoccupation is due rather to the difficulty of enforcement on the one hand and the familial and interpersonal significance of sexual regulation on the other. The fact that a powerful drive is involved, that its satisfaction can be concealed, and that it generally involves another person explains the enforcement problem. The need for enforcement arises from the potentially disruptive power of sexual passions and from the connection of sex with the family. Although coitus normally signifies private consent between two people, disappointed expectations and triangular struggles often inflame the passions and bring deceit, intrigue, blackmail, and violence. The role of variety in erotic stimulation places a strain on any stable relationship, including marriage. In short, an orderly integration of the sexual drive with social life taxes to the utmost the normative machinery.

Social Change and Sexual Control

In modern times the question of control has been greatly complicated by the urban-industrial transformation. This change, more profound than any other, has not simply made the detection and control of violations harder but has also led people to call into question certain of the sexual mores themselves. It has thus made control problematic in a double sense. If a social problem is some present or future condition that people view as unfortunate and as requiring collective action, then there is the possibility of a secondary problem—that of conflict. Such conflict can occur in two ways: disagreement on whether there *is* a problem, some viewing the condition in question as good and others as bad; or, if there is consensus on the existence of a problem, disagreement on the proper means for solving it. Conflicts of both types have undoubtedly weakened the effort to regulate sexual behavior in modern society. Premarital intercourse is viewed by some as an evil requiring collective action, by others as a justifiable practice. The sale of pornography is widely condemned, but many persons believe its suppression violates the freedom of the press. Nudity is regarded by some as wholesome and by others as obscene. Birth control within marriage by efficient means is seen by some people as the solution of a problem but by others as a problem in itself.

The old mores ingrained in tradition and religion were formed in agricultural societies with high death rates. In these societies, one of the main problems was how to bear and rear enough children to maintain the population. The rules governing sexual behavior accordingly evolved in such a way as to encourage, or at least not interfere with, marriage and reproduction. Moreover, the supernatural sanctions for these rules were taken literally by people steeped in religion and magic. The small size and cultural homogeneity of communities tended to create agreement on the rules and to facilitate face-to-face surveillance of behavior and informal enforcement of the norms. Now, however, our science and technology have enabled us to lower death rates to an unprecedented level, with the result that we have an unintended and unwanted population explosion. (See Chapter 8.) The old rules that sought to tie sex to reproduction—rules such as the ban on contraception and abortion—have accordingly become anachronistic. At the same time, we have massive societies composed of people who represent diverse cultural backgrounds, who utilize scientific technology and thus are skeptical about supernatural punishments, who escape surveillance in the anonymity of the city, and who express their hostilities and psychic insecurities by attacking the validity of whatever rules restrict their freedom. Under such circumstances, criticism of the sexual norms tends to carry with it the impression of "having an open mind" and of "bringing things up to date"; a disposition to enforce the norms is viewed as evidence of "an authoritarian personality" or a "medieval outlook." Inevitably, the fundamental changes in society will force changes in some of the sexual rules; but the skepticism and conflict about some as being "arbitrary," once set in motion, tend to undermine all of them and thus to paralyze regulation in general.

Given this modern attitude, the miracle is that there is as much control of sexual behavior as there is in industrialized societies. The explanation lies in the fact that these societies are, after all, societies. Sex is too important and too ramified in the actual lives of people to be treated as a mere appetite. Individuals still have a stake in how and when their bodies are used by others, and since they are not always wise or strong enough to protect their interests, the community at large helps to secure them against force and fraud in this sphere. Children and youth are particularly vulnerable to sexual aggression and thus in need of parental and community guidance. There is a firm consensus with respect to the desirability of minimizing the tragic consequences of sexual activity outside of marriage. Few people really favor illegal abortions, venereal diseases, illegitimate births, jealous homicides, and "white slavery."

Disagreement arises, however, over the best means of reducing the tragic consequences of "indiscretions." Certainly it is true, as many argue, that a major cause of these would be eliminated by strict observance of existing sexual norms. Others argue, on the other hand, that it is not only sexual intercourse, whether licit or illicit, that creates the subsequent tragedy, but another factor added or omitted. If contraception is efficiently practiced, illicit coitus will *not* lead to an induced abortion or an illegitimate birth. If prophylactic precautions are taken, sexual license will *not* lead to venereal disease. "Why, then," ask the adherents of greater sexual liberty, "try to cure these obvious evils by the very difficult route of limiting sexual pleasure? Why not simply teach people contraception and prophylaxis?" This argument further contends that much of the trouble lies in the oppressive sex rules themselves. Induced abortion, for instance, is dangerous *because* it is illegal, not vice versa. In nations that freely permit abortion and provide facilities for it, as many do today, abortion is not dangerous.[11] Similarly, illegitimacy arises from ignorance about contraception and legislation condemning abortion. Jealousy would not be a cause of mayhem and homicide if it were not for the rules treating others as sexual property. For dealing with recognized sexual problems there is thus an antithesis between the puritanical and the libertarian points of view. The first sees sexual expression itself as the culprit, the second something else. If pushed far enough, both views become extreme—one banning all sexual behavior except for reproduction, the other banning all sexual control; few adherents go so far.

Although people in modern society agree on the undesirability of venereal disease and illegitimacy, can they agree on less tangible problems? Can they agree that incest is wrong, for instance, or statutory rape, masturbation, transvestism, exhibitionism, homosexuality? The answer is that even in modern societies there is considerable consensus on some of these matters. Although one might expect libertarians to favor free sexual expression within the entire family (harmful genetic effects being avoided by contraception), the fact is that the incest ban

---

[11] The Soviet Union, Japan, Scandinavian countries, and satellite countries in eastern Europe (except Albania and East Germany) have all permitted abortion and made facilities available. Studies of the outcomes of abortion in those countries show that it is a safe operation when performed properly. In Denmark and Sweden, for example, there were only six or seven deaths per 10,000 legal abortions during 1953-57. See Christopher Tietze, "The Current Status of Fertility Control," *Law and Contemporary Problems,* Vol. 25 (Summer, 1960), p. 442; "Legal Abortion in Eastern Europe," *Journal of the American Medical Association,* Vol. 175 (April, 1961), pp. 1149-54.

is not even questioned; it is so deeply instilled and powerfully sanctioned that it is seldom violated.[12] There is an almost equal disapproval of rape, child molestation, and the sale of girls into prostitution.

The conflict over sexual norms is then not a simple division between a view that sexual pleasure is always sinful and a notion that it is always desirable. Only certain kinds of sexual expression are in question—principally those outside of marriage (premarital intercourse, prostitution, and homosexuality); the control of pregnancy by contraception, abortion, and sterilization; and the display of erotic stimuli through nudity and lewd motion pictures and magazines. In such cases, the argument against regulation is generally that the behavior in question does no measurable harm—a proposition hard to refute because most of the readily observable consequences have already been assumed away. Prostitution does no harm (at least to the customer) *if* there is protection against disease; adultery does no harm *if* the spouse approves. The antiregulation argument also holds that psychological harm comes from the ban itself rather than from the sexual activity because of the sense of guilt. Since by definition a violation inevitably presents the possibility of guilt feelings, this objection too is hard to refute; but care must be used to avoid confusing the issue. Sexual expression as an organic phenomenon involves a mechanical tension and release of that tension. The normative neutrality of sex per se cannot, however, be used as a justification for eliminating a sexual norm, because the issue is not the occurrence or nonoccurrence of sheer physical release but the kinds of social circumstances and commitments it involves. How sex is handled is of major economic and social significance for several reasons. First, the possible tangible consequences—illegitimacy, population growth, genetic erosion, venereal diseases—are often very costly, both to individuals and to the community at large. Second, erotic relationships have important effects on the emotional and personal lives of individuals. Third, the patterns of sexual conduct are necessarily linked with the rest of the social order, which means that they involve not merely etiquette or convention but also the efficient operation of a social system.

Conflict over sexual norms is especially intense with respect to youth. Not only is the sex drive at a peak in adolescence (for males at least) but also emancipation from authority and lifetime decisions occur at this time. It is upon the younger generation, therefore, that changed social conditions affecting sex behavior mainly impinge.

---

[12] See S. Kirson Weinberg, *Incest Behavior* (New York: Citadel Press, 1963), Chapters 1-3.

Traditional modes of surveillance and control no longer function properly, and in the face of intellectual criticism and debate, the adults mainly responsible for youth—parents, school officials, leaders of youth groups—tend deliberately to avoid the task of preventive regulation in favor of dealing with individual tragedies when they develop. The operating norms are those worked out by the young people themselves. These, while often effective in controlling behavior under peer surveillance, are not necessarily effective in equipping the individual to make decisions on his own or to perform well as an adult. James Coleman, who has shown that the American high school generally does not succeed in instilling a desire to learn, feels that the excitement of boy-girl interaction is partly responsible.

> The dichotomy . . . between "life-adjustment" and "academic emphasis" is a false one, for it forgets that most of the teen-ager's energy is not directed toward either of these goals. Instead the relative dichotomy is cars and the cruel jungle of rating and dating versus school activities . . .[13]

The absence of clear and enforceable rules apart from the peer group leads to many wrong decisions and personal tragedies. To an unusual degree, each young person must fend for himself by a costly process of trial and error.[14] This is doubtless the reason that the Group for Advancement of Psychiatry in their report *Sex and the College Student*[15] recommends that "if a college has certain expectations about sexual conduct on the campus, it has a responsibility to clarify them. There is also need to provide information about the responsibility to self and to others that is implicit in undertaking sexual relations."

Homosexual Relationships

Turning now by way of illustration to a widely condemned but recurrent form of violation—homosexuality—we can begin by recalling that some of the strongest sexual norms are those defining permissible partners. Masturbation involves no partner at all; adultery involves a partner other than one's spouse; homosexuality, a partner of the same

---

[13] James S. Coleman, *The Adolescent Society* (New York: Free Press, 1961), p. 51.

[14] Physical force and misuse of advantage are often unchallenged because no one wants to cause scandal. See Clifford Kirkpatrick and Eugene Kanin, "Male Sex Aggression on a University Campus," *American Sociological Review*, Vol. 22 (1957), pp. 52-58.

[15] Group for the Advancement of Psychiatry, *Sex and the College Student* (New York: Mental Health Materials Center, Inc., 1965), p. 16.

sex. The partner question often takes priority over other issues. Within marriage, since the partners are appropriate, moral control is focused on the techniques and times of intercourse and on the control of reproduction; but when the partners are not the approved ones, some of these questions are irrelevant.

Given the focus on the partners, the normative assessment of a deviant sex connection varies according to the social and emotional quality of the relationship. For this reason, it is not enough simply to define homosexuality as sexual "intercourse" between persons of the same sex. How it is regarded by the community depends in part on the emotionality of the relationship—whether, at one extreme, it is emotionally indifferent (with the same-sex partner taken temporarily as a necessary but unwelcome substitute for one of the opposite sex) or, at the other extreme, the partner is regarded as an exclusive love object. Some authors hold that "homosexuality" designates only some part of this scale, but this rules out an instructive comparison of the various gradations. It seems better to use the term for any sexual connection between members of the same sex, thus leaving room to discriminate, compare, and analyze various gradations without being hampered by some narrow "definition."

How Widely Is Homosexuality Disapproved?

Sometimes the assertion that "our society taboos homosexuality" is made with the implication that this is an aberration, that many other societies favor it, and that consequently the public should be "educated" to accept it. The facts are different. To be sure, the American public disapproves of homosexuality, but this is far from being an absolute "taboo." Not being able to stop the practice, the public tolerates it to a considerable extent and in effect refuses to put discreet homosexuals in the same class as criminals. Public opinion is much softer than the laws on the books seem; yet most of our state laws do not ban homosexuality as such. Since the law has to be specific in order to control, only specific sexual acts usual in homosexual relations, acts of public indecency, and corruption of minors are banned; homosexual behavior among women is usually not legally banned at all.[16] In these regards the United States is similar to just about every other civilized society. In some European countries all homosexual acts (usually those

---

[16] See Morris Ploscowe, *Sex and the Law* (Englewood Cliffs, N. J.: Prentice-Hall, 1951), Chapter 7; Robert V. Sherwin, "Laws on Sex Crimes," *Encyclopedia of Sexual Behavior* (New York: Hawthorn Books, 1961), pp. 626-27.

of males) are legally punishable, while in others only certain acts, specific public manifestations, or dealings with minors are outlawed.[17] The search for societies that approve of homosexuality yields little. In the case of advanced civilizations the idea is ambiguous because opinion is not uniform and because various gradations exist between strictly public and strictly private morality. Such societies have groups who engage in homosexual practices and some writers who apologize for them, but the public at large rejects these views. The assessment is particularly difficult for historical civilizations. Certain literary sources can usually be cited as evidence for approval or toleration, but when we try to assess the attitude of the general public we lack evidence. Furthermore, attitudes change over time. A picture of the ancient Greeks as idealizing homosexuality has been vividly painted by Hans Licht, basing his conclusions on art and literature. There can be no doubt that beginning with the fifth century B.C. the love of boys was idealized among the literati, and that this ideal was sometimes if not often expressed in overt homosexuality. There can be no doubt that there was male prostitution.[18] But Greece as late as the fifth century B.C. was still a stratified society and Athens was a small city. The ordinary people were suspicious of the new intellectuals, the sophists ("professors" of the time). Among these, Anaxagoras was condemned for impiety, Protagoras was driven out and his books burned, and Socrates was condemned to death. Although these men were charged with "corruption of youth," the chances are that the charges were based on their questioning of Greek mores, including religious beliefs. However, we do know that parents put great care into the education of Greek citizen-boys.

> Far from casting out their sons into public schools, with the full knowledge that they will there lose all their simplicity and innocence, Greek parents of the better sort kept their sons constantly under the eye of a slave tutor or pedagogue, . . . who never let them out of their sight.[19]

Actual public opinion concerning homosexual relations in the various periods of ancient Greece will never be known. The hypothesis of general approval seems unproved, and it may be as shaky as the rationalization sometimes given to the effect that Greek wives were

---

[17] *Report of the Committee on Homosexual Offences and Prostitution* (London: Her Majesty's Stationery Office, 1957, Cmnd. 247), pp. 149-51.

[18] Hans Licht, *Sexual Life in Ancient Greece* (London: Routledge and Kegan Paul, 1932).

[19] J. P. Mahaffy, *Social Life in Greece,* 5th ed. (London: Macmillan, 1883), p. 331.

uneducated bores.[20] The Romans, after losing their early rustic morality, evidently tolerated a considerable amount of homosexuality, and the poets of the empire generally adopted a matter-of-fact attitude toward it.[21] However, ascetic and stoic philosophy was also a strong current in Rome, and again it seems difficult to document actual public opinion in this matter. The Hebrew moral code of course strongly condemned homosexuality, as did that of classical Hinduism. The Hindu attitude, however, did not prevent homosexual behavior or homosexual prostitution.[22] In sum, highly complex societies seem to tolerate a certain amount of homosexual behavior (and literary praise of it) without its necessarily ranking high in public opinion. Public opinion appears either to condemn the practice or at best simply to tolerate it.

Primitive societies furnish some, but not many, examples of accepted homosexuality. "Nearly all societies," says Murdock, "seek to confine marriage and sex relations to persons of complementary sex. Some permit homosexuality in specifically delimited contexts, and a very few manifest wide latitude in this respect." [23] Ford and Beach list, in a total of 77 societies, 49 (all primitive) in which "homosexual activities of one sort or another are considered normal and socially acceptable for certain members of the community." [24] Most of these cases represent acceptance of the berdache or transvestite. "The berdache is a male who dresses like a woman, performs women's tasks, and adopts some aspects of the feminine role in sexual behavior with male partners. Less frequently a woman dresses like a man and seeks to adopt the male sex role." [25] Among the Siberian Chukchee the berdache was regarded as a powerful *shaman* (magician). Among the Koniag, an Alaskan tribe, some male children were reared from infancy to play the female role. In such instances, the reversal of roles is rare and not approved for men generally. The Chukchee shaman assuming the female role was "believed to have been involuntarily transformed by supernatural power and some men fear being thus changed . . . ." [26]

---

[20] H. D. Kitto has made a convincing case against the view that Greek citizen-women were an oppressed, uneducated lot. The ordinary male citizen of Athens, even in its late individualistic phase, took a deep interest in his family. *The Greeks* (Baltimore: Penguin Books, 1951), pp. 219-36.

[21] Otto Kiefer, *Sexual Life in Rome* (New York: Dutton, 1935), Chapter 5.

[22] Robert Wood, "Sex Life in Ancient Civilizations," *Encyclopedia of Sexual Behavior,* pp. 130-31; and Jelal M. Shah, "Sex Life in India and Pakistan," *ibid.,* pp. 533-34.

[23] Murdock, *Social Structure,* p. 317.

[24] Clellan S. Ford and Frank A. Beach, *Patterns of Sexual Behavior* (New York: Harper, 1951), p. 130.

[25] *Ibid.*

[26] *Ibid.,* p. 131.

Among the Lango of Uganda, the men who assumed the feminine role were "believed to be impotent and to have been afflicted by some supernatural agency." [27] In other words, the existence of institutionalized homosexuality does not necessarily mean that it has high standing in the scale of desirability or that it is practiced by a large proportion of the population.

Why the Tendency to Disapprove of Homosexual Relations?

If public opinion and official morality tend either to condemn or to place a low value on homosexual intercourse, the next question is why. The answer lies in the theory of sexual norms already sketched. In evolving an orderly system of sexual rights and obligations, societies have linked this system with the rest of the social structure, particularly with the family. They have also tended to economize by having only one such system, which has the advantage of giving each person only one role to worry about in his sex life—namely, a male or female role—which can thus be ascribed and will vary only with age. Homosexuality in itself cannot lead to reproduction and the formation of normal family life; it also involves, for one partner or the other, a reversal of sex role, though sex is one of the most fundamental bases for status ascription. A male who assumes the feminine role, or a woman who assumes the masculine role, is looked down upon—interestingly enough, even by homosexuals themselves.

One reason homosexuality is not more completely and universally disapproved is that the same individual may function in both a homosexual and a heterosexual relationship, either simultaneously or serially. The degree to which this is possible and the amount of strain it places on both the individual and the social order depend on the degree of homosexual commitment. Here we encounter a curious conflict in the evaluation of homosexuality—a conflict that seems comprehensible only in terms of the framework already mentioned. The threat to normal family relationships and to what may be called the main system of sex relations is least when the homosexuality is purely instrumental—that is, when it is simply a means of gaining sexual release in the absence of a normal partner. A person with no emotional fixation on others of the same sex can, when the occasion arises, become attached to a marriageable individual. When boys indulge in sexual play among themselves as a passing sport in the absence of girls, or when prisoners are forced into it by their isolation, it usually carries no implication of a "homosexual way of life," although in certain cases

[27] *Ibid.*

it does lead to emotional commitment. However, such opportunistic behavior—especially if indulged in repeatedly and frequently or for money (as when boys prostitute themselves to older males)—is looked down on for another reason: it affronts the norms not simply in the sense of being homosexual but also in the sense of treating sex as a purely organic release, whereas the intent of the norms is somehow to "civilize" the sex impulse by linking it with acceptable social relations and sentiments. On the other hand, homosexual love is often justified as "elevating" sex to an emotional plane; it may be as romantic, as suffused with "intellectualism" and self-justifying idealism as male-female love.[28] At this level, however, although it meets the "vulgarization" objection, homosexual devotion directly competes with male-female relationships because it is exclusive. While it lasts, it precludes a similar relationship with a normal partner, and if the attitude is generalized to the point where the individual can experience such emotion only with members of the same sex, the antagonism to normal sexuality is complete.

The conflict between homosexuality and the institutionalization of male-female relationships is further intensified by the reversal of sex roles. Such reversal occurs because homosexual relations mimic the heterosexual (in itself a tribute to the power of the male-female image). Homosexual pairs often act as if they are "married"; they set up "housekeeping," demand mutual fidelity, and differentiate themselves according to which one is the dominant (masculine) and which the subordinate (feminine) type. Public contempt is greater for the person who switches his role than for the one who does not, not only because of the obvious inappropriateness of physiology for the role [29] but also because the resumption of a normal role is made more difficult, especially when the relationship is emotional in character. In purely instrumental homosexual intercourse, the male who plays the

---

[28] Homosexual idealism, like the heterosexual kind, can be carried to the point of excluding physical consummation. Plato, for example, built his ideas of beauty and immortality around the idea of male friendship but frowned on the idea of physical contact, the "black horse" of the *Phaedrus*. One can see in such idealism the influence of the sexual norms that, in part, deprecate the purely organic part of sexual expression.

[29] It is interesting that many of the dominant homosexuals in a women's prison prefer to remain fully dressed while they stimulate their subordinate partners—the reason apparently being that they hate to reveal to the partner the inescapable feminine character of their anatomy, which otherwise can be somewhat hidden by masculine clothing, hair-style, and mannerisms. See David A. Ward and Gene G. Kassebaum, *Women's Prison: Sex and Social Structure* (Chicago: Aldine, 1965), p. 179.

dominant role is disdained more for his coarseness than for his homosexuality; he retains his masculine character but has temporarily altered the object of his sexual drive, often to a minimum degree because the object is a youth (beardless and with other juvenile and therefore feminine characteristics) or a deliberately self-feminized man. Similarly, the female who plays the female role in a lesbian relationship can more easily resume normal relations with a man.[30] The role-changer, on the other hand, tends to be either a committed homosexual or to have ulterior goals in view that are themselves despised—such as prostitution by adolescent boys or self-feminized men, or dominance and self-assertion by female "butches."

In sum, one can explain the generally negative attitude toward homosexuality by the fact that every viable society evolves an institutional system fostering durable sexual unions between men and women and a complementary division of functions between the two sexes. To do this, it cannot at the same time equally foster homosexual relations. At most it can permit the latter in special cases—e.g., in prisons, at a particular age, or for persons with a peculiar occupation. Even in these cases the perverted relation tends to mimic, and thus show its inferiority to, the normal one.

So much for societies in general, but conditions have changed. Today the problem is not how to get a birth rate high enough to overcome a high death rate, but how to get one low enough to fit a low death rate. We no longer blatantly subordinate one sex to the other, and we have released heterosexual behavior from the old fetters by contraception, the independence of the young, and more liberal attitudes. Why should homosexuality continue to be disapproved? Insofar as this question refers to the future, it is unanswerable because nobody knows the future. However, in urbanized, mobile industrial societies, familial relationships seem to be particularly valued because they are virtually the only ones that are both personal and enduring; marital and parental ties therefore receive strong sentimental support. Furthermore, the differentiation of role as between the sexes shows a surprising persistence, even if less invidious than formerly. Homosexual relations are notoriously ephemeral by comparison; and, if they involve exclusive emotional commitment, they preclude marital and parental bonds except on a fraudulent basis. If homosexuality were to be generally approved, it would, like heterosexuality, have to be normatively

---

[30] In prison populations it is most often the partner who has kept his regular sex-role (the "femme" in lesbian and the "wolf" in homosexual relations) who returns to heterosexual conduct after release. *Ibid.*, p. 194.

regulated. The young would have to be protected against force, fraud, and economic enticement; the rights, obligations, and role differentiation of homosexual partners would have to be specified; a licensing or identification system would have to be utilized so that normal individuals would not innocently be deceived into marriage with homosexual ones. In short, an institutional system governing such relationships, paralleling the system governing normal sexual relations, would have to be evolved. As yet there is no sign that such an evolution will occur; the complications of the dual system would no doubt exceed even those that characterize the present single system.

Doubtless homosexuality will be increasingly discussed, its merits and morality freely defended. More reports will appear such as the 1957 Wolfenden Report to Parliament in Britain, which recommended "that homosexual behavior between consenting adults in private be no longer a criminal offense," [31] and the 1965 report in the United States by the Group for the Advancement of Psychiatry,[32] which recommends:

> In the social context of the college community, individual incidents of homosexuality may be viewed in different ways: as a psychiatric problem requiring treatment; as antisocial behavior requiring external control; as a transitional phenomenon of late adolescence not properly described as illness or as antisocial behavior; or as a mutant life pattern acceptable so long as it does not disrupt the college community.

Such discussion may portend a softening of laws and attitudes, but not necessarily, because an increased understanding, and especially an increased prevalence, may bring both a greater public rejection of homosexuality and more ingenious methods of controlling it. In any case, a Gallup Poll taken in Britain shortly after the Wolfenden report was issued showed 38 percent favoring legalization of private homosexual acts, 47 percent against, and 15 percent uncertain.[33] Ira L. Reiss, an American analyst of sex standards, says:

> There is little evidence of an exact nature on trends in standards concerning homosexual behavior, but I believe that just as the rates have remained stable so have the attitudes toward such behavior. By and large, there is a strong feeling against homosexual contact, despite its apparent frequency.[34]

[31] *Report of the Committee on Homosexual Offences and Prostitution,* p. 115.

[32] *Sex and the College Student,* p. 59.

[33] J. E. Hall Williams, "Sex Offenses: The British Experience," *Law and Contemporary Problems,* Vol. 25 (Spring, 1960), pp. 354-55.

[34] "Standards of Sexual Behavior," *Encyclopedia of Sexual Behavior,* p. 1001.

Why Homosexual Behavior?

If the public attitude is one of hostility, why does homosexual practice nevertheless occur in all complex societies? Kinsey found that 37 percent of his white male sample had at some time or other had an overt homosexual experience, and 4 percent had been exclusively homosexual.[35] Among his white females the two percentages were 13 and 1 percent.[36]

Objectively considered, the surprising fact is how little homosexuality there is, because we unwittingly facilitate the formation of homosexual habits and attachments. Boys are encouraged to be with boys and girls with girls, in rooming and sleeping together in dormitories, prisons, youth hostelries, and the like. This is intended to reduce heterosexual violations, but it causes the control of homosexual offenses to rest heavily on internalized norms. This is not a dilemma of our society alone, but of every society. To capitalize on the sexual drive and hitch it to an institutional system, societies tend to channel sex in favor of marriage, which entails an entire set of social and legal involvements. The interests of the two sexes being different, sexual attractiveness becomes a valuable good not to be bargained away easily. To some persons, therefore, heterosexual attachments may seem almost unobtainable, or obtainable at too high a price; by contrast, uncomplicated homosexual relations may seem to them to provide an escape from such involvements.

If homosexuality were the consequence of a biological condition—say, a hormone imbalance—then the social pressures favoring it would have no particular effect.[37] But the evidence all indicates that the human sexual drive is capable of wide and complicated conditioning. The object, the situation, the symbols associated with sexual stimulation are subject to habit-formation. For instance, the amount of homosexual behavior varies according to the social situation. The sociologists David A. Ward and Gene G. Kassebaum began a study of a women's prison in California with the aim of determining personality types. They soon found so much lesbianism there, and found it to be such a key feature of inmate social organization, that they entitled their book

---

[35] Kinsey *et al.*, *Sexual Behavior in the Human Male*, pp. 650-51.

[36] *Sexual Behavior in the Human Female*, pp. 474-75.

[37] A biological, or genetic, explanation of homosexuality would seem improbable. Since people committed to this mode of gratification would reproduce very little, they would not diffuse their mutant genetic constitution very far. Thus homosexuality would be constantly bred against.

Women's Prison: Sex and Social Structure. They estimate that at least 50 percent of the inmates participate in homosexual relations while at the institution.[38] Donald Clemmer estimates that 30 percent of 2300 adult male prisoners he studied were partly homosexual and 10 percent were "true homosexuals."[39] Experiments demonstrate that homosexual behavior can be induced even in rats. For example, by supplying ample food and water to caged rats, thus allowing them to breed until very high population densities were reached, Calhoun observed homosexual as well as other pathological forms of behavior. "The general level of activity of these [homosexual] animals was only moderate. They were frequently attacked by their dominant associates, but they very rarely contended for status."[40]

The manner in which human beings are inducted into homosexual practices shows the influence of cultural patterning, persuasion, and example. Ward and Kassebaum, for example, have a chapter describing how new prisoners are skillfully brought into homosexual activities by various techniques of persuasion and compulsion.[41] The variation in style and amount of homosexuality from one society to another shows its dependence on social determinants. In some primitive societies there is no homosexuality at all;[42] in most civilized societies there is a good deal of it. In some societies boys are reared to be homosexual prostitutes, and in still others *everybody* must engage in homosexual behavior as a sort of *rite de passage*.[43] In cases in which an individual has been reared as a member of the wrong sex, he prefers to remain a member of that sex even after discovery of his true sex. "Observations of this nature emphasize the tremendous importance of early experience and social conditioning upon human sexuality."[44]

---

[38] *Women's Prison*, p. 92.

[39] *The Prison Community* (New York: Rinehart, 1958), pp. 257-64, cited by Ward and Kassebaum, *Women's Prison*, p. 94.

[40] John B. Calhoun, "Population Density and Social Pathology," *Scientific American*, Vol. 206 (February, 1962), p. 146.

[41] *Women's Prison*, Chapter 6. See also Ford and Beach, *Patterns of Sexual Behavior*, p. 126.

[42] In the Trobriand Islands, homosexuality "was known to exist in other tribes and regarded as a filthy and ridiculous practice. It cropped up in the Trobriands only with the influence of white man. . . . The boys and girls on a Mission Station, penned in separate and strictly isolated houses, cooped up together, had to help themselves out as best they could . . ." Bronislaw Malinowski, *Sex and Repression in Savage Society* (London: Kegan Paul, Trench, Trubner, 1927), p. 90.

[43] Ford and Beach, *Patterns*, pp. 131-32. Jelal M. Shah, "Sex Life in India and Pakistan," pp. 533-34.

[44] Ford and Beach, *Patterns*, p. 134, citing Havelock Ellis.

Let us now return to our question, why so little homosexuality? Obviously, there is more instrumental than dedicated behavior of this sort. Not all youths who engage in homosexual practices, either among themselves or with older men for money, become emotionally committed to this way of life. What deters most of them is no doubt the strength of the internalized norms and of peer opinion. The few who turn into "true" homosexuals are presumably like the few drinkers who turn into confirmed alcoholics: they do so because they cannot make the normal adjustments in life. Relations between men and women involve obligations in various spheres, including intimate personal adequacy. One way for a man to escape the dominance struggle among men is to give up and assume a feminine role: he retreats into being a woman and yet has few of the obligations that an actual woman has. A dominant male homosexual has no need to assume the obligations that relations with women require. "His problem is not so much that he is attracted to males, but that he is in flight from females." [45]

We can understand why homosexual commitment represents a response to the dynamics of social life. Sex is woven into social relations in a complex way, so that one's self-image, one's motives and emotions, depend not on the sheer organic gratification of sex (which in itself has not much more status than defecation) but on the meaning of sexual activity as a form of companionship and sentimental participation with others. But one participates and shares one's emotions with others of the same as well as those of different sex. The same elements—dominance, devotion, loyalty, dislike, dependence—appear in social relations generally. Therefore, it is a complex process to learn to discriminate between the social emotions and relations that can have an erotic motif and those that cannot. A relatively slight derangement in the mechanics of personal-social development may cause a failure in this discrimination, facilitated by exposure to homosexual practices.

If this view is correct, there is an implication that is seldom drawn. If homosexuality were institutionalized and given the same normative status as heterosexuality, it would then involve the fulfillment of obligations and conformity to norms. It would no longer constitute an avenue of escape, an expression of social hostility, a means of protest. Under these circumstances there would be no neurotic appeal in a homosexual way of life. Would anyone choose that way of life as a commitment?

This, however, is speculation. The reality is that homosexuality is publicly disapproved and yet widely practiced on a hidden and un-

---

[45] Donald Webster Cory, "Homosexuality," *Encyclopedia of Sexual Behavior*, p. 492.

regulated basis. It thus presents certain problems for the community, among which the most important are apparently homosexual prostitution, the spread of venereal disease, and the induction of youth into a homosexual way of life. These are somewhat interrelated. A good share of male prostitutes are lower-class adolescent boys who find this an easy way to make money.

> The delinquent boy often is inducted into this form of hustling by his older peers. He learns how contacts are to be made and where they are easily effected. Above all, he learns the norms and sanctions attached to the relationship. . . . For [some] delinquent gangs, the practice becomes one of "queer-baiting," to roll the "queer" for his money, since he fears legal recourse to charge he has been robbed.[46]

Homosexual prostitution is harder to control than the heterosexual variety because members of the same sex are ordinarily together anyway. Men's lavatories, for example, are such favorite places for homosexual contact that in most large cities they now require special policing. Because of the greater promiscuity of homosexual individuals and the greater lack of prophylaxis, homosexual relationships apparently spread venereal disease proportionately more than do heterosexual relations (wherein prophylaxis serves both an antivenereal and a contraceptive function).

Obviously the homosexual world would be depopulated if it did not constantly get recruits. A part of the recruitment (just how much is not known) is through seduction of the young by older persons. The Wolfenden Report commended "the steps taken by the Ministry of Education and the Scottish Education Department to ensure that men guilty of homosexual offences are not allowed to continue in the teaching profession," [47] but it admitted that detection was difficult. These are, of course, community problems. In addition, there are acute personal and private problems—those of homosexuals themselves and those of normal individuals whose lives have been affected by them.

Prostitution [48]

The attitude toward prostitution, like that toward homosexuality, grows out of the necessity for, and yet special difficulties of, regulat-

---

[46] Albert J. Reiss, "Sex Offenses: The Marginal Status of the Adolescent," *Law and Contemporary Problems,* Vol. 25 (Spring, 1960), p. 323. Reiss' account is graphic and excellent.

[47] *Report of the Committee on Homosexual Offenses and Prostitution,* p. 78.

[48] A revision and expansion of the writer's "The Sociology of Prostitution," *American Sociological Review,* Vol. 2 (October, 1937), pp. 744-55.

ing sexual relationships. It is not a major social problem in the sense that it affects a society's economic development, political stability, or military strength. Except insofar as it forms part of organized, or syndicated crime, it does not have cumulative, long-term consequences such as civil war, economic depression, or breakdown of law and order. Even its oft-cited effect in spreading venereal disease is partly a myth, because carelessness and promiscuity are the main factors in spreading such disease, and not prostitution per se.

The concern over prostitution is due rather to its being regarded as a vice—that is, as a sinful and/or degrading indulgence of a natural appetite for itself alone rather than for any worthwhile purpose. Vice by definition is an activity viewed as reprehensible in itself, regardless of whether it does damage to society at large. Throughout much of the world today prostitution is viewed officially and popularly as a vice, as a moral problem. As a consequence it is not only condemned by spokesmen for religious and civic groups, but is often legally prohibited or restricted as well; and the prostitute and her pimp are treated with a mixture of pity, scorn, fascination, and persecution. Sometimes important social consequences are alleged to flow from prostitution (e.g., drugs, scandal, venereal disease, deterioration of neighborhoods), but these are rationalizations. The disapproval is of prostitution itself, not of its consequences.

The interest of this subject for the student of social problems accordingly lies in the sociological explanation of moral attitudes. Why is prostitution widely condemned today, and under what circumstances, if any, is it tolerated or even approved? Further, granting that in some societies it is condemned in the strongest terms, and is hounded and suppressed, we must ask why it still survives. Regardless of the attitude taken toward it, it is a ubiquitous institution, present wherever civilization has achieved any sort of complexity and often existing even in primitive societies. It therefore raises the question of what there is about the nature of human society that causes it to give rise to, and maintain, an institution that it simultaneously condemns.

In order to reduce the task to manageable size, the present discussion will focus on female prostitution. Occasional references will be made to homosexual prostitution, and to the small amount of masculine prostitution that caters to women, but these forms are distinct. Our mention of them will therefore be mainly for the purpose of comparison, to bring out the features of the familiar form of prostitution in which the male is the buyer and the female the seller.

Let us get beyond the superficial view that prostitution is an evil that can readily be abolished, or the equally superficial idea that the persistence of prostitution is due simply to "human nature" or "the lessons of history." What we seek is a sociological analysis, not an off-hand dismissal of the scientific question. We must seek to understand the ways in which prostitution is bound to other institutions, particularly those involving sexual relations, and how its structure evolves as the organization of these other institutions changes.

Why the Attitudes Toward Prostitution?

Actually, as we shall see, prostitution has not always and everywhere been condemned. Some forms of it have been highly regarded, and even in industrial nations today opinion is by no means unanimous. Although it is generally condemned in official statements by politicians, ministers, priests, and community leaders, it is sometimes defended by liberal writers. Perhaps the modal attitude is reflected (except for the reference to "sociologists") in the following statement of the British Wolfenden Report:

> Prostitution is a social fact deplorable in the eyes of moralists, sociologists and, we believe, the great majority of ordinary people.[49]

Prostitution is condemned in contemporary industrial societies mainly because it involves a high degree of sexual promiscuity that fulfills no publicly recognized societal goal. The promiscuous element was brought out by a student who defined prostitution as "engaging in a primary contact in a secondary relationship." As we have seen, the norms of every society tend to harness and control the sexual appetite, and one of the ways of doing this is to link the sexual act to

---

[49] *Report of the Committee on Homosexual Offences and Prostitution,* p. 79. Defense of prostitution seems to have been most common in the 1930's when reformers aiming to stamp it out, or at least get rid of "red light districts," were most active. See, for example, T. Swann Harding, "The Endless War on 'Vice,'" *Medical Record,* April 20, 1938. Since that time, with prostitution less obvious to the public, the reformist zeal and the liberal's defense both seem to have ebbed. Prostitution in the 1960's seems less a public issue than it was from 1910 to 1940.

Although hounded by the police, the streetwalker is not necessarily felt to be objectionable by the public at large. A survey conducted by *McCalls Magazine* and reported there in February, 1965, found that only 7 percent of the persons questioned said they would bother to clear the streets of prostitutes if they had the chance. Conducted in New York City and Newark, New Jersey, the survey found that 67 percent said they would not clear the streets of prostitution if they could, and another 26 percent gave no opinion, leaving only 7 percent who would definitely take action.

A readable account of the history of organized prostitution and organized reform movements in New York City is to be found in John M. Murtagh and Sara Harris, *Cast the First Stone* (New York: McGraw-Hill, 1957).

some stable, or potentially stable, social relationship. This is hard to do, because sexual intercourse can be accomplished briefly and secretly and because sexual attraction is changeable. But, for this very reason, the moral condemnation of promiscuity is strong. Promiscuity means sexual contacts not only with numerous people but also with strangers. Men consider women to some extent as sexual property to be prohibited to other males. They therefore find promiscuity on the part of women repugnant, and object to it far more than they object to similar behavior on their own part. Furthermore, since one woman can satisfy many men, the prostitute is more promiscuous than her customers. Her extreme promiscuity, which flies in the face of what is considered proper for women, brings down upon her the obloquy of society.[50]

One may protest that what is regarded as objectionable about prostitution is not the prostitute's promiscuity but her willingness to *sell* her favors and her feeling of *emotional indifference,* both of which are usually mentioned in definitions of prostitution.[51] But these two traits are condemned because they imply promiscuity. From a moral point of view, there is nothing wrong with female indifference to sexuality; indeed, a wife who submits dutifully but reluctantly to intercourse is often considered virtuous for that reason, although she is expected to cherish her husband in a spiritual sense. Also, there is nothing morally wrong with a woman trading her sexual favors for a consideration. This is what is done in marriage, for in consenting to get married a woman exchanges her sexual favors for economic support. She usually contributes other things as well, such as housework and child-care, but these are not exclusive; she can render such services to others outside the home without betraying the bargain, whereas having intercourse with men other than the husband is, in complex societies, a violation

---

[50] The line of reasoning used here helps to explain why male prostitution for the benefit of women is relatively rare. Since the sexual division of labor is such that men bear the main economic burden while women bear the child-rearing and domestic burden, women gain economic status through their attachment to men, rather than vice versa. In a traditional society where the sexual division of labor is fully enforced and the kinship system strong, women have neither the economic means nor the freedom to hire men for sexual purposes. In a more complex society, they may have both, but to a limited degree; furthermore, men who serve women in this capacity are condemned, not for their promiscuity, but for taking an unmasculine role. Also, regardless of the type of society, the physiological fact remains that a man cannot have repeated intercourse to the extent that a woman can.

[51] Geoffrey May in the *Encyclopedia of the Social Sources* (New York: Macmillan, 1933) defines prostitution as "characterized by three elements: payment, usually involving the passing of money, although gifts or pleasures may constitute equivalent consideration; promiscuity, with the possible exercise of choice; and emotional indifference, which may be inferred from payment and promiscuity."

of the marriage. In other words, so long as the bargain struck is one that achieves for the woman a stable relationship with a man, especially a relationship like marriage where reproduction is officially sanctioned, the mores offer praise rather than condemnation for the exchange of feminine sexual favors. The prostitute's affront is that she trades promiscuously. She takes money or other valuables for each act of intercourse. She is indifferent not only to sexual pleasure but also to the partner. Her "selling" and her indifference therefore reflect a pure commercialization of the sexual relation.

What has just been said is illustrated by the American law. "In its restricted legal sense prostitution is the practice of a female offering her body to indiscriminate sexual intercourse with men. . . . It is a popular misconception that the element of money remuneration is essential to the crime. It is not an element in it unless specifically made so by statute." [52]

But why is promiscuity itself objected to? The answer has already been given. By linking sexual gratification to a stable social relationship, the society harnesses man's organic drive. It also avoids some of the conflicts and tensions that arise when a strong drive, especially one involving human relations, is left uncontrolled. Unless there is some kind of social order in the distribution of sexual favors, a war of all against all will tend to result. The objection to promiscuity tends to arise and persist because the societies that have this sentiment are, in this respect at least, more capable of surviving than those that do not have it. In the eyes of the members of a society, a woman's sexual favors should ideally be given only in a situation that is an operating part of the social structure. In most of the world's major religions—in the Hindu, Moslem, Christian, and Hebrew faiths, for example—the highest ideal is to confine the woman's sexual activity to marriage, where it is linked to reproduction, the rearing of children, and a domestic division of labor on the basis of sex. This does not mean that in these regions there is no sex freedom outside of marriage. In many Western countries, as noted earlier, premarital sex relations are tolerated if entered into discreetly by couples who are in love and have the prospect of getting married.[53] Such relations, however, and even

---

[52] Isabel Drummond, *The Sex Paradox* (New York: Putnam, 1953), p. 208.

[53] See Christensen, "Cultural Relativism and Premarital Sex Norms," pp. 31-39. Nels Anderson, ed., *Studies of the Family* (Gottingen, Germany: Vanderhoeck & Ruprecht, 1958). Sydney H. Croog, "Aspects of the Cultural Background of Premarital Pregnancy in Denmark," *Social Forces*, Vol. 30 (December, 1951), pp. 215-19. Kaare Svalastoga, "The Family in Scandinavia," *Marriage and Family Living*, Vol. 16 (November, 1954), pp. 374-80. Alva Myrdal, *Nation and Family* (London: Kegan Paul, Trench, Trubner, 1945), Chapter 3. Jerome Himelhoch and

more an extramarital liaison, are viewed with less approval than marriage itself; and everywhere in the areas mentioned, wanton promiscuity on the part of women is deplored. Prostitution is at the bottom end of the scale: not only does it involve promiscuity, but it flaunts this promiscuity by offering sexual favors in the market place to the highest bidder, irrespective of personal inclination. The frequently used expression, "common prostitute," conveys this meaning. Prostitution is therefore at the opposite end of a scale of gradation in esteem that leads from marriage at the top to the "pick-up" and then to the prostitute at the bottom.[54]

There is nothing inherently social about the sexual appetite. Like other organic needs, it can be satisfied in a variety of ways and situations. Its integration in society is therefore a matter of control, not of instinct or happenstance. The social control of sex follows two correlative lines. First, it permits, encourages, or requires various degrees of sexual intimacy within specific customary relations, such as courtship, concubinage, and/or marriage. Second, to bolster this positive control, it follows a negative policy of discouraging or forbidding sexual intimacy in other situations. Generally, for example, sexual intercourse is forbidden or discouraged when the parties cannot get married, especially when the reason is that they are married to someone else. Between certain persons the taboo on intercourse may be absolute, as in the case of incest. These lines of control are present no matter what the specific kind of institutional system. There may be monogamy, polygamy, polyandry, or concubinage; wife exchange, sexual hospitality, or religious prostitution; premarital chastity or unchastity. The important point is not the particular kind of concrete institution, but the fact that without the positive and negative norms there could be no institutional control of sex at all.

The institutional arrangement in which sexual relations are most approved is one in which the two parties are publicly committed to bearing and rearing children. Accordingly, marriage is the most respectable sexual relationship (in which intercourse is not only permitted but is generally required), with others diminishing in respec-

Sylvia Fleis Fava, eds., *Sexual Behavior in American Society* (New York: Norton, 1955), especially Chapters 16, 30, 31.

[54] An opinion survey in Britain in 1949 showed that "Marriage is still regarded as the vitally important center of sex relationship, and only one person in six condones prostitution. But . . . there is a fairly widespread belief that many cases of extramarital and premarital relationship have a good justification, and often people who are living together without being married are cited as providing a better 'example' than the married." L. R. England, "Little Kinsey: An Outline of Sex Attitudes in Britain" in Himelhoch and Fava, *Sexual Behavior,* p. 350.

tability as they stand further away from wedlock. When coitus is practiced purely as a means of personal income, as in straight commercial prostitution, its social effect is left uncontrolled. The buyer clearly has personal pleasure and not reproduction in mind. The seller uses the money for any purpose she wishes. The sexual relation between the buyer and seller is therefore illegitimate, ephemeral, and condemned.

If our analysis is correct, we should expect that both prostitution and the prostitute herself will rise in social esteem insofar as one or more of three conditions are present: (1) the promiscuity is lessened by some basis of discrimination; (2) the earnings of prostitution are used for a goal considered socially desirable; (3) the prostitute combines other roles with that of sexual gratification. This generalization appears to hold true, as shown by instances outside our own society.

In ancient Greece, the lowest rank of prostitutes were those who practiced in brothels. These were open to anybody who had the price, which was not high, and were concentrated mainly in the neighborhood of docks and markets. They resembled in many ways the houses in red light districts in the United States a few decades ago. Ranking almost as low as the brothel inmates were the streetwalkers, but far above both were the *hetairae,* who were distinguished by being educated in the arts, by being available only to the wealthy and powerful, and by providing entertainment and intellectual companionship as well as sexual gratification. The *hetairae* were a focus of Greek cultural and literary interests. Their portrait statues appeared in public buildings alongside those of the great men. They were the heroines of plays and poems.[55] They were even influential in public affairs. Aspasia, daughter of the most celebrated of the Greek *hetairae,* captured the love of Pericles and became his concubine, supplanting his wife. Her house became the center of Athenian literary and philosophical society, frequented by no less a person than Socrates. The *hetairae,* drawn from the alien population, were providers of entertainment and intellectual companionship because respectable wives and daughters (that is, women of Greek citizen families) were not permitted to entertain or to enter the labor market. Instead they were confined to the home, an uninteresting lot. Often cited in this connection is a statement attributed to Demosthenes: "Man has the hetairae for erotic enjoyments, concubines for daily use, and wives of equal rank to bring up

---

[55] Licht, *Sexual Life in Ancient Greece,* pp. 332-63, 395-410.

children and to be faithful housewives." [56] The *hetairae*, then, had an influential and enviable position, but they were still not respectable. There was no forgetting that they were prostitutes; they had a reputation for being faithless, avaricious, vain, and shrewd.[57]

We do not have to rely solely on evidence from the ancient world to provide an example of factors elevating prostitution in the social scale. Japan until recently had three classes of women outside the pale of respectable family life—the *joro* in brothels; the *jogoku*, or unlicensed prostitutes on the streets or in bath houses; and the *geisha*, or dancing girls. The last-named were taken as little girls, often by arrangement with their parents and sometimes through adoption by the proprietors of the *geisha ya*. They were trained in dancing, singing, samisen playing, and other methods of entertaining and serving guests in tea houses. They were an indispensable adjunct at every Japanese affair and entertainment. Not all of them were open to outright prostitution; they were selective, were usually available as concubines, and some of them married.

> . . . trained thoroughly in all the arts and accomplishments that please,—witty, quick at repartee, pretty, and always well dressed,—the geisha has proved a formidable rival for the demure, quiet maiden of good family, who can only give her husband an unsullied name, silent obedience, and faithful service all her life.[58]

The analogy with the Greek *hetairae* is striking, though of course not perfect.

Another way in which prostitution may enjoy social esteem is by association with religion. Throughout much of the ancient world, including Greece apart from Athens,[59] there was the custom of attaching prostitutes to religious temples and using them in religious and festive ceremonies.[60] But again we do not have to rely exclusively

---

[56] Cited by Licht, *Sexual Life in Ancient Greece,* p. 399. See also Alfred Zimmern, *The Greek Commonwealth* (Oxford: Clarendon Press, 1931), pp. 341-44, who has an excellent discussion of the class of alien-born women versus the citizen women.

[57] Licht, *Sexual Life in Ancient Greece,* pp. 354-56; 358-63.

[58] Alice Bacon, *Japanese Girls and Women,* rev. and enlarged ed. (Boston: Houghton Mifflin, 1919), first published in 1891, pp. 286-87, 288-89. Douglas C. McMurtrie, "Prostitution in Japan," *New York Medical Journal* (Feb. 8, 1913). McMurtrie evidently cribbed from Miss Bacon, for entire passages in his article are word-for-word the same as hers and yet no reference is made to her book.

[59] Licht, *Sexual Life in Ancient Greece,* pp. 388-95.

[60] A custom frequently referred to as temple-prostitution, but which was so only in a very special sense, was the requirement that respectable women spend time in a temple until chosen by some stranger for intercourse. The stranger contributed

upon the ancient world for examples. In West Africa the Ewe-speaking peoples were found, late in the last century, to prostitute the wives of the gods.

> In every town there is at least one institution in which the best-looking girls, between ten and twelve years of age, are received. Here they remain for three years, learning the chants and dances peculiar to the worship of the gods, and prostituting themselves to the priests and the inmates of the male seminaries; and at the termination of their novitiate they become public prostitutes.[61]

In India until recently the temples contained dancing girls. The Abbé Dubois, describing southern India as he saw it during the years 1792 to 1823, had this to say:

> The courtesans or dancing-girls attached to each temple . . . are called *deva-dasis* (servants or slaves of the gods), but the public call them by the more vulgar name of prostitutes. . . . Every temple of any importance has in its service a band of eight, twelve, or more. Their official duties consist in dancing and singing within the temple twice a day, morning and evening, and also at public ceremonies. . . .
> These women are also present at marriages and other solemn family meetings. . . . They are brought up in this shameful licentiousness from infancy and are recruited from various castes, some among them belonging to respectable families. It is not unusual for pregnant women, with the object of obtaining a safe delivery, to make a vow, with the consent of their husbands, to devote the child . . . , if it should turn out a girl, to the temple service. . . . No shame whatever is attached to parents whose daughters adopt this career.
> The courtesans are the only women in India who enjoy the privilege of learning to read, to dance, and to sing. A well-bred and respectable woman would for this reason blush to acquire any one of these accomplishments.
> The *deva-dasis* receive a fixed salary for the religious duties which they perform; but as the amount is small they supplement it by selling their favours in as profitable a manner as possible.[62]

Religious prostitution differs from commercial prostitution because the woman is a religious ministrant, the money given her can be used for religious purposes, and the act of intercourse itself can be viewed

---

money or some material gift, but after this episode the woman apparently went back to ordinary life. This custom was reported as occurring in Babylon by both Herodotus and the Bible.

[61] A. B. Ellis, *Ewe-Speaking Peoples of the Slave Coast of West Africa* (London: Chapman and Hall, 1890), p. 140.

[62] Abbé J. A. Dubois, *Hindu Manners, Customs, and Ceremonies,* 3rd ed. (Oxford: Clarendon Press, 1906), pp. 584-86.

as religious ritual.[63] Similar considerations apply to the type of prostitution in which the girl obtains a dowry for her subsequent marriage.[64] This last could hardly cause the woman to lose respect, because it is instrumental to marriage. In religious prostitution such as that found in India or in the entertainment type such as that in Japan or ancient Greece, the prostitute is a female class set apart. Although this class is in some ways superior to the respectable women, its members are somehow felt to be morally suspect. It is worth noting that the *geisha* and *hetairae* were usually of lowly origin, as were many of the *deva-dasis*.

We can now answer our initial question more concisely. All prostitution involves some disapprobation of the prostitute, because she indulges in sex promiscuously and apart from the family. The disapprobation is less when the prostitution is tied to some worthy purpose. Modern Western society strongly dislikes prostitution and classifies the prostitute as being among the dregs of society because, for reasons to be given presently, all that is left now is the purely commercial form of prostitution. In the commercial form, both parties use sex for a purpose not socially acceptable, the one for pleasure, the other for money. To tie intercourse to sheer pleasure is to divorce it both from reproduction and from any sentimental social relationship. To tie it to money, the most impersonal and atomistic type of reward, with no stipulation as to how this reward is to be used, does the same thing. In such a situation, the relationship between the prostitute and her customer is merely a means to a private end, a contractual rather than a personal association. Such purely commercial prostitution will be denigrated in any society, and the women who practice it will have a despised status, regardless of whether the religion be Christian, Buddhist, Communist, Pagan, or Islamic.

The "Causes" of Prostitution

Why is it that something so widely disapproved should still persist, and that an occupation so disrespected should find recruits? In the past, especially under the influence of the great depression and Marxism, the "cause" of prostitution was frequently said to be eco-

---

[63] Edward Westermarck, *Origin and Development of Moral Ideas* (London: Macmillan, 1908), Vol. 1, p. 224: "In Morocco supernatural benefits are to this day expected not only from heterosexual but also from homosexual intercourse with a holy person."

[64] Havelock Ellis, *Studies in the Psychology of Sex* (Philadelphia: Davis, 1913), Vol. 6, p. 233.

nomic.[65] Since prostitution is defined as selling sexual favors, the fact that it has economic causes should hardly occasion surprise. One might as well say, with equal perspicacity, that retail merchandising has economic causes. Prostitution is naturally connected with the economic system, but to jump from this truism to the conclusion that the factors are solely economic, or that prostitution can be abolished by eliminating its economic causes, is erroneous. Economic causes seldom act alone, and hence their removal is seldom a panacea.

Discussions of the "causes" of prostitution usually overlook certain questions. For instance, the assumption is often made that the sole question concerns the factors leading women to enter the business.[66] Actually, there are at least five separable, though of course interrelated, questions: (1) the causes of the *existence of prostitution;* (2) the causes of the *different forms or types* of prostitution; (3) the causes of the *rate or amount* of prostitution; (4) the causes leading *some women to enter,* and other women not to enter, the profession; and (5) the causes leading *some men to patronize,* and others not to patronize, the prostitute.

The Existence of Prostitution

Since prostitution is virtually universal, its sheer existence has to be explained in terms of the organic nature of man, on the one hand, and the sociological nature of his communal life, on the other. On the physical side, it is to be noted that the human female, like other primate females but unlike her lower mammalian sisters, has no *season* of sexual dormancy. In many nonprimate mammalian species the two sexes split apart and form separate social groups during the dormant season. The primate female, at least in many species, has instead a menstrual cycle. A part of this cycle may be anoestrus (involving unresponsiveness to sexual stimuli and sexual unattractiveness to the male). But since this part is usually short, and since the anoestrus period of one female will be unrelated to that of another (a troupe of monkeys, for example, always contains sexually attractive females), sex is a permanent feature of the social group, holding

---

[65] See, for example, the article on "Prostitution" in the old *Encyclopaedia Sexualis* (New York: Dingwall-Rock, 1936). Only slightly less economically deterministic is the article on the same subject in *Encyclopedia of the Social Sciences.*

[66] Both of the encyclopedic treatments just cited make this assumption. Under the heading, "Causes of Prostitution," the article in *Encyclopaedia Sexualis* has this to say (p. 643): "Is the prostitute 'born' or 'made'? That is the core of the question." Later treatments, such as that by Harry Benjamin in *Encyclopedia of Sexual Behavior* (1961), are less narrow.

males and females together.[67] The uninterrupted capacity of the human female for sexual activity and sexual attraction has fundamentally the same effect on human society, but more intensely. It introduces sex as a permanent element in social life and insures constant association of the two sexes.

Moreover, the primates (and particularly man) possess a more complex sensorimotor equipment than lower mammals and have a longer period of infancy. These possessions, plus the fact of continuous sexuality in the group (and, in the case of *Homo sapiens*, in the individual), facilitate an extensive conditioning of the sexual response, with the result that sexual behavior is not simply automatic but is linked with numerous nonsexual stimuli. The sexual response may thus be used, not only or not at all for the individual's own erotic gratification, but as a means to some ulterior purpose.

What leads to this use of sex for ulterior goals? Here we turn from physiological to sociological factors. The reproductive physiology and neural complexity of the human organism *permit* learned behavior linking sex to nonsexual activities, but sociological forces alone *compel* it. The key to these forces is to be found in competition within the group. As has long been observed, mammalian groups are characterized by a system of dominance. Zuckerman early stressed that in the simian group every individual enjoys a precarious position determined by the interrelation of his own dominant characteristics with those of his fellows. The degree of dominance determines what command over the group's resources he will exercise—the amount of food, access to females, and degree of safety he will enjoy.[68] Zuckerman may have exaggerated the role of competition and dominance—not only does dominance vary in degree and character from one species to another, but his own observations were mainly of captive baboons in a London zoo. However, the fact of some competition and dominance in primate groups has often been demonstrated.[69] Also, the analogy with human society is probably better when the primate group is captive or domesticated than when it is in the wild, for man is a highly self-

[67] C. R. Carpenter, "Societies of Monkeys and Apes," in Robert Redfield, ed., *Levels of Integration in Biological and Social Systems* (Lancaster, Pa.: Jaques Cattell Press, 1942), pp. 197-99.

[68] S. Zuckerman, *The Social Life of Monkeys and Apes* (New York: Harcourt, Brace & World, 1932), especially Chapters 3, 4, 6, 8, and 9.

[69] See, for example, Carpenter, "Societies of Monkeys and Apes," and W. C. Allee, "Social Dominance and Subordination among Vertebrates" in Redfield, ed., *Levels of Integration,* pp. 139-62. Various sections in Irven deVore, ed., *Primate Behavior: Field Studies of Monkeys and Apes* (New York: Holt, 1965).

captured and self-domesticated species. In any case, human society exhibits to an extreme degree the role of social competition, of dominance and subordination, in the distribution of the resources of the group. Not only are the organic drives therefore elaborately conditioned by and integrated with the social system, but secondary drives are created which, like the desire for the good opinion of others, seemingly have no strictly organic basis whatever.

We can now see how the basic ingredient of prostitution—the use of sexual response for ulterior purposes—arises. But, as suggested at the start of our discussion, this ingredient characterizes not only prostitution but all the social arrangements whereby sex is traded for an advantage, including marriage, engagement, concubinage, the use of pretty girls in stores, charity drives, advertisements, etc. The next step, then, is to differentiate prostitution from these other forms of relationship in which sex is fitted into the social system. It is differentiated from some of the milder forms of sexual commercialization in that it involves sexual intercourse. But further, it maximizes promiscuity and therefore divorces intercourse from any stable or affectional social relationship. It is these features which explain the predominant attitude of disesteem toward prostitution and its personnel, especially in the case of purely commercial prostitution.

The Customer's Motivation

When it is made illegal, prostitution falls into a peculiar category of crime that is exceedingly hard to deal with—the type in which one of the willful parties is the ordinary law-abiding citizen. This kind of crime, of which bootlegging and bookmaking are other good examples, is supported by the money and behavior of a sizable portion of the citizenry, because in it the citizen receives a service. Although the service is illegitimate, the citizen cannot ordinarily be held guilty, for it is inadvisable to punish a large portion of the populace for a crime, particularly for one that has no political significance. Each such citizen participates in the basic activities of the society, in business, government, the home, the church, etc. To disrupt all of these by throwing him in jail for a mere vice would cause more social disruption and inefficiency than correcting the alleged crime would be worth.

> The professional prostitute being a social outcast may be periodically punished without disturbing the usual course of society; no one misses her while she is serving out her turn—no one, at least, about whom society has any concern. The man, however, is something more than partner in an immoral act: he discharges important social and business relations, is as father or brother responsible for the maintenance of

others, has commercial or industrial duties to meet. He can not be imprisoned without deranging society.[70]

Although the demand for the prostitute's services would seem to be, in economic phraseology, relatively inelastic because it is based on a biological appetite, one must remember that sex is connected with the social order in a complex fashion. Not all males visit prostitutes, nor do those who do so necessarily depend on them for a major share of their sexual outlet. In Kinsey's sample of white American males, for example, about 30 percent never had any contact with these women at all. Of the rest, many "never have more than a single experience or two, and not more than 15 or 20 percent of them ever have such relations more often than a few times a year, over as much as a five-year period in their lives." [71] The question must therefore be asked: what does prostitution provide that other institutional outlets do not provide, and why are its particular appeals greater for some men than for others?

For one thing, prostitution's great advantage is precisely its commercial impartiality and impersonality. Available to anyone who has the price, with gradations in quality and price that will fit almost any pocketbook, it is an ever available resource for those who cannot find sexual satisfaction at the moment in any other relationship. When all other sources of gratification fail, due to defects of person or fortuitous circumstances, prostitution can be relied upon to furnish relief. It also is attractive to the practical male because of its simplicity. The exacting requirements of attracting and persuading a female, or perhaps getting entangled with her in courtship or even marriage, are unnecessary. All that is needed is the cash, and this can be obtained in a thousand ways. Kinsey states that before World War II the average cost of intercourse with a prostitute "was less than the cost of a single supper date with a girl who was not a prostitute." He continues: "Men go to prostitutes because they can pay for the sexual relations and forget other responsibilities, . . ." [72] In other words, it is partly by its very effort to harness the sex drive by making it part of a meaningful and enduring social relationship that society creates certain of the unique advantages of prostitution.

Mention should also be made of the fact that by defining certain techniques or methods of sexual gratification as immoral and hence out of bounds for wives and sweethearts, the moral order gives an

---

[70] Abraham Flexner, *Prostitution in Europe* (New York: Century, 1920), p. 108.
[71] Kinsey *et al., Sexual Behavior in the Human Male,* p. 597.
[72] *Ibid.,* p. 607.

additional advantage to the prostitute; for the latter, motivated by a monetary reward rather than by any aesthetic or moral concern with the act, is more willing to indulge in so-called perversions (usually at an enhanced price). In addition, the man who is in a stable relationship with a woman and who theoretically should have ample opportunity for legitimate or semilegitimate sexual expression, may nevertheless find such expression thwarted by the vicissitudes of interpersonal relations. A stable relationship between a man and a woman is not necessarily harmonious, and, because of its symbolic significance, sexual intercourse may be affected adversely by quarreling and hostility.

The impersonality of prostitution makes it particularly suited to strangers. A man usually cannot take his family with him everywhere he goes, a soldier certainly cannot. The man away from home, away from his wife or the circle of girls that he knows, cannot in a short time count on seducing a respectable woman in the place he happens to be. Yet the sexual appetite is a repetitive one and can become overpowering regardless of where one is. The prostitute's availability to a stranger is thus one of her appeals.

In short, the attempt of society to control sexual expression, to tie it to social requirements, especially the attempt to tie it to the durable relation of marriage and the rearing of children, or to attach men to a celibate order, or to base sexual expression on love, creates the opportunity for prostitution. It is analogous to the black market, which is the illegal but inevitable response to an attempt fully to control the economy. The craving for sexual variety, for perverse gratification, for novel and provocative surroundings, for ready and cheap release, for intercourse free from entangling cares and civilized pretense—all can be demanded from the woman whose interest lies solely in the price. The sole limitation on the man's satisfactions is in this instance not morality or convention, but his ability to pay. "The common and ignorant assumption that prostitution exists to satisfy the gross sensuality of the young unmarried man, and that if he is taught to bridle gross sexual impulse or induced to marry early, the prostitute must be idle, is altogether incorrect." [73]

---

[73] Ellis, *Studies in the Psychology of Sex,* pp. 295-96. Kinsey's sample, *Sexual Behavior in the Human Male,* p. 288, shows that, age for age, a greater proportion of the unmarried male's sexual expression is with prostitutes than is that of the married man. At age 21-25 the ratio is 5.4 to 1; at age 26-30, it is 7.5 to 1; at age 31-35, it is 11.5 to 1. Of course, above age 25 the number of men married is so much greater than the number single that even though the ratio of individual experience is higher, the clientele of prostitutes tends to be mostly composed of married men.

There is no reason to believe that a change in the *economic* system will eliminate or seriously alter the *demand* side of prostitution. In any kind of economic system the effective demand as expressed by price will vary somewhat with current conditions, but the underlying basis for the demand is noneconomic and therefore not subject to change by virtue of economic changes alone.

Recruitment to the Profession

The economic thesis is scarcely more satisfactory on the supply side. Any particular woman's entry into the profession is a result of her own life history, into which many strands are woven, some economic and some not. The crudest expression of the economic thesis is the suggestion, once occasionally heard, that prostitution could be abolished or seriously curtailed if the salaries of working girls were raised. More subtle is the claim, also less often made now than formerly, that it is the capitalistic system itself which engenders prostitution by its pecuniary organization of society.

Such a view tends to rest on the assumption that girls enter the profession because of economic necessity—a view that can most easily be seen to be false if we assume it to be true. Why, for example, should a girl enter prostitution only when she is forced to by financial need? Is the occupation so arduous? On the contrary, we often speak as if harlots "would rather prostitute themselves than work." [74] It is even true that some women physically enjoy the intercourse they sell. From a purely economic point of view, prostitution comes near the situation of getting something for nothing. Since the occupation is lucrative, the interesting question is not why so many women become prostitutes, but why so few of them do.

The answer of course is that the harlot's return is not primarily a reward for labor, skill, capital, or land (rent). It is a reward for loss of social standing. She loses esteem because the moral system—especially one in which the only form of prostitution is purely commercial—condemns the outright promiscuous selling of intercourse. If, then, she refuses to take up the profession until forced by sheer want, the basic cause of her hesitation is not economic but moral. Only when the moral condition is assumed, do wages or economic want take on any importance.

---

[74] W. L. George's novel, *Bed of Roses*, vividly contrasts the hard life of the working girl with the easy life of the prostitute. The novel by Caroline Slade, *Sterile Sun*, does not depict the work as particularly arduous. The economic justification is a rationalization. If a woman enters the profession because she is about to starve, people can hardly blame her for her action. Thus the title of Sheila Cousins' autobiographical account, *To Beg I Am Ashamed.*

In a competitive system, as soon as the economic condition of women improved, the supply of prostitutes would diminish. But the resulting scarcity would increase the effective demand (the demand, remember, is itself inelastic in the sense of remaining relatively uninfluenced by economic conditions). As a result, the price would rise and the flow of recruits into the occupation would increase. The net result would be as much prostitution as before, and in terms of actual money invested and changing hands, there might be more.

As a matter of fact, the wages of prostitution are already far above the wages of ordinary women's work. "No practicable rise in the rate of wages paid to women in ordinary industries can possibly compete with the wages which fairly attractive women of quite ordinary ability can earn by prostitution." [75] The discrepancy between the wages of ordinary work and the wages of this kind of sin results from the fact that the latter is morally tabooed. This increases the wage differential until there is *every economic* incentive for entering. It should be noted, too, that the wages of one class cannot be arbitrarily raised without affecting those of other classes. Women's wages could scarcely be raised significantly without also raising men's. Men would then have more to spend on prostitution. One author concluded that as wealth and prosperity increased, so did prostitution.[76]

In a book called *Red Virtue*,[77] published in 1933 when the Soviet Union was popularly regarded as the almost completed utopia of the world, there was a chapter entitled "Ending Prostitution." At the head of this chapter stood a quotation from a Soviet physician: "Soviet life does not permit of prostitution." Widely accepted and frequently repeated in the 1930's, this belief was taken for granted and used as evidence that the basic cause of prostitution is the capitalistic system.[78] In 1959, the following account appeared by a reporter who had just completed a long stay in Russia:

---

[75] Ellis, *Studies in the Psychology of Sex*, p. 263. "There are call-girls who earn between fifty and a hundred thousand dollars a year." Murtagh and Harris, *Cast the First Stone*, p. 2.

[76] A. Depres, *La Prostitution en France* (Paris: 1883).

[77] By Ella Winter (New York: Harcourt, Brace & World, 1933).

[78] The *Encyclopaedia Sexualis* (1936), pp. 666-67, said: "As to Russia, even those unfriendly to the new regime will admit that prostitution has been obliterated there. . . . [It] has been not so much outlawed as rendered superfluous, through a removal of the economic cause in the form of grinding poverty, and through a radical revision of the marriage and divorce laws." Maurice Hindus, in his *The Great Offensive* (New York: Smith and Haas, 1933), left the same impression. The *Reader's Digest* for February, 1934, condensed his conclusions under the title, "Russia Bans Mrs. Warren's Profession." The article ended with "Prostitutes have practically disappeared from the Russian scene."

During World War II, foreigners were sometimes approached by telephone in their rooms at the Metropole Hotel. But street walking had not been seen in Moscow since the early Nineteen Thirties.

Today a stroller in the central Moscow streets of an early evening is apt to be approached near big hotels. The women are strange sights —heavily rouged, gaunt-faced and costumed as in sketches by Hogarth.

Around the Hotel Astoria in Leningrad prostitutes may also be seen. Typically, the Leningrad women are smartly attired, affect high heels and pony-tail hairdos.[79]

It will take more than communism to eliminate the world's oldest profession. The changes the Russians tried to make are in fact much like the changes the so-called capitalist countries tried to make. For instance, virtually all countries have tried to stop the highly organized aspects of prostitution. They have consistently legislated against third parties—pimps, landlords, bookers—who abet and profit from prostitution. The reason for this is clear. A vice to which large sections of the public are addicted is potentially profitable to those who organize it, especially if the vice is officially banned and thus made inaccessible except with illicit help. In a complex society, accordingly, the pandering to forbidden pleasures can become big business, just as can the pandering to legitimate pleasures. This has been shown by bootlegging in India and the United States under prohibition, by bookmaking under a ban on off-track horse-race betting, and by black-market operations under wartime trading controls. If such illegal big business were allowed to operate with no official harassment, the outlawing of the vice in question would be nullified and the practice of the vice would be encouraged. The organized underworld business of providing opportunities for forbidden indulgence necessarily does what it can to stimulate the desire in question, and it can do this better if not officially harassed. Any government that undertakes to forbid or restrict a vice, then, must be prepared to make war on the organizations that inevitably spring up to cater to the vice.

In the case of prostitution, the so-called vice syndicates did a fabulous business in the United States during the first half of the present century. Their greatest prosperity occurred during the prohibition era, when bootlegging became a principal source of profit, but they could always rely on prostitution as either a main or a subsidiary activity. For example, when William Hale Thompson was returned to office as mayor of Chicago in 1927, it was with the help of a fund, alleged to be $5,000,000, which organized vice and crime had paid

[79] Harrison Salisbury, *The New York Times*, Sept. 10, 1959, p. 10.

his machine through the America First campaign. The following year, 2000 vice establishments were reported to be paying $100 to $750 per week in return for police protection. The police reportedly raided only the resorts that did not pay for protection. Police, politicians, and judges were paid by vice lords such as Al Capone, Dan Jackson, and Jack Zuta. So complete was official protection that the only threat to the vice kings was murder by competitors or prosecution by the federal government for income-tax evasion. Al Capone's delinquent taxes for the years 1924-1929 were originally estimated to be $1,038,654, but in the course of the trial they were scaled down to $266,000.[80] Other cities, and even small places both domestic and foreign, were affected by syndicated vice. In 1936, "Motzie" Di Nicola, overlord of a chain of Connecticut vice resorts, was sentenced to seven years in the Lewisburg federal penitentiary and fined $1,000 for income-tax evasion. His business in prostitution yielded approximately $2,500,000 annually.[81]

Organized crime continues to find prostitution profitable, but the linkage with bootlegging has been replaced by labor-union racketeering, coin-machine control, record pirating, pornographic distribution, and other technologically advanced criminal activity. In 1954, for example, two underworld figures from Seattle worked out a scheme to take over vice operations in Portland, Oregon. By including top officials of the Teamsters Union, they elected a district attorney who then worked with them to set up facilities for pinball, punchboard, cardroom, off-track betting, and prostitution. The Teamsters Union killed all competition by threatening to stop deliveries to restaurants, cafeterias, and bars that refused to use the syndicate's equipment. The United States Senate Select Committee on Improper Activities in the Labor and Management Field revealed the extent to which gangster control spreads like a network over the country:

> Evidence developed by the Committee showed that gangsters today control steel companies, laundry and dry-cleaning establishments, frozen food operations, and many other kinds of businesses. Hoodlums living reputable lives in Los Angeles have major vice and gambling holdings in the Midwest. They seek to corrupt and do corrupt public officials to an alarming extent.[82]

---

[80] Walter C. Reckless, *Vice in Chicago* (Chicago: University of Chicago Press, 1933), Chapter 3.

[81] *The New York Times*, November 11, 1936. See also Murtagh and Harris, *Cast the First Stone*, Chapters 12-13.

[82] Robert F. Kennedy, *The Enemy Within* (New York: Popular Library, 1960), pp. 245-50.

Prostitution has probably declined as an underworld business in America; not only have demand and supply (for reasons to be discussed) slackened, but other activities, such as labor-union control, have proved immensely profitable and easier to organize.

Undoubtedly the attempts to legislate against third parties and organized profiteering in prostitution in various countries have had some effect.[83] Even if completely successful, however, these efforts would not mean an end to the ancient trade. Unorganized prostitution, in which seller, manager, and worker are all the same woman, cannot be eliminated. It should be remembered, also, that payment for sexual favors need not be in terms of money. It may be in terms of privilege, power, food, clothing, almost any form of exchangeable value. Ordinarily, since every complex society must have a medium of exchange, the payment for the harlot's services will be in money; but the possibilities of other forms of payment, particularly in a regime where free market activities are restricted, should not be overlooked.

Prostitution and Social Change

To get reliable data on the prevalence of prostitution, or on changes in prevalence, is impossible. It is possible, however, to learn something about alterations in the types and manifestations of this profession, and to understand how these are connected with the particular kinds of societies in which they are found. This gives us some basis for deducing the circumstances under which prostitution is likely to be most or least prevalent.

We have seen that in classical Greece there were distinct classes of prostitutes, and that the strong position of one of these classes, the *hetairae,* was due to the circumscribed home life and lack of education among the respectable Greek women of the citizen class (except in Sparta). Japan until recently had a somewhat analogous situation. The conclusion emerges that whenever the role of the wife is sharply separated from that of the man, so that her sphere is limited to the household and the children, and respectable women are kept secluded, uneducated, and jealously guarded against outside contacts, a distinct class of women will tend to emerge who furnish sexual diversion, skilled entertainment, and intellectual companionship for men. In other words, a sharp separation between the family and the outer

---

[83] See United Nations, "The Suppression of the Traffic in Persons and of the Exploitation of the Prostitution of Others," Document E/CN.5/338 (New York: United Nations, March 26, 1959).

world, the one being a private and segregated domain, strictly traditional and legitimate, and the other being the bustling stage for business, politics, news, change, and the exercise of talent and wit, will produce two classes of women—the one legitimate and boring, the other illegitimate and interesting. These classes represent two sides of the male character, if you will—the desire to have women for himself, under his dominance and protected from other men; and the desire to have feminine companionship that understands and appreciates, and to some extent participates in, his world of affairs with other men. The second class of women, the free class so to speak, must be economically supported, and since they cannot at the same time be legitimate wives, they must have some less secure position as paid companions, concubines, mistresses, or high-class prostitutes.

As is well known, the Romans did not develop a class of skilled courtesans. To be sure, they had an amazing variety of prostitutes and an amazing variety of places where they practiced, but Roman society in the times of the Republic, when the family was still traditional and respectable women were confined to the home, was still too simple to develop the refinements of Attica in the age of Pericles. By the time of the Empire—that is, in the Rome of Domitian and Trajan, of Tacitus, Juvenal, and Martial—the Roman wife was already a free agent. Furthermore, Rome was a bigger place than Athens, and the Roman Empire a far larger world than that of the Greeks. The numerous Roman social classes, the circulation of slaves and foreigners, plus the freedom and education that wives of all classes had gained, broke down the rigid division of women into groups according to their respectability. Roman men of affairs did not have to rely upon an elite class of paid women to find sexual diversion and intellectual companionship. There were expensive prostitutes, to be sure, but not a socially recognized and established aristocracy of them.

The medieval period in Europe was one of social rudeness again. Prostitutes were numerous, but their position was not high, and they were both taxed and persecuted by state as well as church. "Paul Lacroix has likened the position of mediaeval prostitutes to that of mediaeval Jews: they were persecuted socially, civilly and ecclesiastically, yet all classes were glad to have recourse to them and recognized their indispensability." [84]

With the coming of the Renaissance and the industrial age in western Europe, the emancipation of women from the family, and their education and participation in economic life, were sufficiently great

---

[84] "Prostitution," *Encyclopedia of the Social Sciences*, p. 554.

to keep the *hetaira* type of institution from developing. The prostitute as skilled entertainer, as companion of powerful men and adjunct to festive occasions, came nearer to developing in countries, such as those of Spanish culture, where the traditional family and the seclusion of women were retained. However, these were precisely the countries most influenced by the puritanical and anti-intellectual attitudes of the Roman Catholic clergy. Furthermore, the conquest of primitive peoples in the New World and the consequent intermingling of races made women on a servant basis available to upper-class men in such abundance that there was little incentive to develop a higher class of courtesans, even if the man had wanted feminine intellectual companionship.

The evolution of the family and woman's position in relation to the rest of the social structure have thus deprived prostitution in Western society, particularly during the industrial age, of the extrasexual functions it had in more classical times. Feminine companionship, sexual, intellectual, and recreational, is available to men from the ranks of ordinary women. There is no need to set aside a special class who are directly paid in proportion to their special services. At the same time there are the persistent, age-old demands for the strictly commercial prostitution that gives sheer sexual release. The profession has thus been reduced in modern industrial society to the strictly commercial type. Since this type has always ranked low in social esteem, the result is that prostitution today is viewed with almost unrelieved distaste.

There can be little doubt that during the present century in industrial societies a rise in feminine sex freedom has occurred, especially among the single, widowed, and divorced. Kinsey found that among the women born before 1900 the proportion who experienced premarital intercourse was less than half the proportion for those born after 1900. Among the women still single by age 25, only 14 percent of the old generation had had coitus, as opposed to 36 percent of those born in the next decade.

> This increase in the incidence of premarital coitus, and the similar increase in the incidence of premarital petting, constitute the greatest changes which we have found between the patterns of sexual behavior in the older and younger generations of American females.[85]

With the greater availability of ordinary women for sexual companionship, we should expect the role of the prostitute, in both volume

---

[85] Kinsey *et al., Sexual Behavior in the Human Female,* p. 298. Here will be found a bibliography of other studies and analyses confirming this same trend.

and status, to decline. This is what the available evidence seems to show. Kinsey found that his males of recent generations were down to two-thirds to one-half the frequencies of contact with prostitutes recorded by the older generation.[86] There have been many explanations for this decline. It has been stated that elimination of red light districts, legal drives against organized vice, campaigns against streetwalkers, and educational efforts concerning venereal disease and prostitution have been responsible. The skeptic, however, will point out that such efforts have been tried sporadically throughout modern times with little success. The change in the present century seems more likely to be due to the greater sexual companionship, on a temporary and friendly basis, available to men from ordinary women. Otherwise, we would have to assume that the male himself has reformed, but Kinsey finds that what the male has lost in frequency of intercourse with prostitutes he has gained in frequency with nonprostitutes. As between the older and newer generations of males, "the frequencies of the total amount of premarital coitus were not materially modified for the males, because the frequencies of coitus with females who were not prostitutes had increased to an extent which largely compensated for the decreased frequencies with prostitutes.[87]

If we reverse the proposition that increased sex freedom among women of all classes reduces the role of prostitution, we find ourselves admitting that increased prostitution may reduce the sexual irregularities of respectable women. This, in fact, has been the ancient justification for tolerated prostitution—that it "protected" the family and kept the wives and daughters of the respectable citizenry pure. Lecky states this thesis with Victorian sentimentality:

> There has arisen in society a figure which is certainly the most mournful, and in respects the most awful, upon which the eye of the moralist can dwell. That unhappy being whose very name is a shame to speak; who counterfeits with a cold heart the transports of affection, and submits herself as the passive instrument of lust; who is scorned and insulted as the vilest of her sex, and doomed, for the most part, to disease and abject wretchedness and an early death, appears in every age as the perpetual symbol of the degradation and the sinfulness of man. Herself the supreme type of vice, she is ultimately the most efficient guardian of virtue. But for her, the unchallenged purity of countless happy homes would be polluted, and not a few who, in the pride of their untempted chastity, think of her with an indignant

---

[86] Kinsey *et al., Sexual Behavior in the Human Male,* p. 411. He gives additional references substantiating this change.

[87] Kinsey *et al., Sexual Behavior in the Human Female,* p. 300.

shudder, would have known the agony of remorse and despair. On that one degraded and ignoble form are concentrated the passions that might have filled the world with shame. She remains, while creeds and civilizations rise and fall, the eternal priestess of humanity, blasted for the sins of the people.[88]

Such a view strikes us as paradoxical, because in popular discourse an evil such as prostitution cannot cause a good such as feminine virtue, or vice versa. Yet, as our analysis has implied throughout, there is a close connection between prostitution and the structure of the family. Whether this connection means that where prostitution is weak the family must also be "weak," is another question. The fact that pre-marital intercourse on the part of girls is an accepted practice in Scandinavian countries does not mean that the family is "disappear-ing," or is "bankrupt," in those countries. On the contrary, one gets the impression that the Swedish or Norwegian family is somehow a more viable institution, certainly one more adapted to modern conditions, than the typical Latin American family where the wives and daughters of the upper and middle classes are sedulously "protected" while the daughters of the lower class are used for concubines, prostitutes, and "servants."

In practice, the contemporary attitude toward sex expression on the part of the single, widowed, or divorced woman is one of quiet toler-ance, a tolerance that is not extended to adultery on the part of the wife. The attitude toward prostitution is similarly one of tolerance for the thing itself as a necessary evil, but an intolerance of its open mani-festation and a distaste for the prostitute and the pimp. Moralistic pressure groups exercising a disproportionate influence on official ac-tions, and individual citizens frantically seeking to avoid any identifi-cation with a despised occupation, both support policies designed to banish the open and public manifestations of sexual barter. The very conception of sexual connection as a voluntary and friendly relation-ship between social equals is alien to prostitution, and helps to degrade it in the eyes of the public. Consequently, the history of prostitution in the last 40 years has been a history of the fight to eliminate third parties and open manifestations. In Britain, for example, prostitution itself is not illegal, and the Wolfenden report recommended against making it so.[89] But the laws are being tightened so as to penalize more

---

[88] W. E. H. Lecky, *History of European Morals,* 3rd ed. rev., Vol. 2 (London: Longmans, Green, 1877), pp. 282-83.

[89] *Report of the Committee on Homosexual Offences and Prostitution,* p. 79. It is not illegal in the United States either under common law, but is made so by statute in many states.

heavily street solicitation, the maintenance of a brothel, the willful taking of rent derived from habitual prostitution in the premises, etc. People do not wish to be reminded of prostitution. They do not wish to see streetwalkers on the streets, to see districts where prostitutes are known to be, to live in a building or a block where men in large numbers are seen to be visiting women. As long as they do not see it, they can forget about it.

The General Theory of Prostitution

We can imagine a social system in which the motive for prostitution would be completely absent, but we cannot imagine that the system will ever come to pass. It would be a regime of absolute sexual freedom with intercourse practiced solely for pleasure by both parties. This would entail at least two conditions: first, there would be no institutional control of sexual expression. Marriage, with its concomitants of engagement, exclusiveness, jealousy, legitimacy, and permanence except by divorce, could not exist. Such an institution builds upon and limits the sexual urge, making sexual expression contingent upon nonsexual considerations and thereby paving the way for intercourse against one's inclination. Second, all sexual desire would have to be mutually complementary. One person could not be erotically attracted to a nonresponsive individual because such a situation would inevitably involve frustration and provide a motive for using force, fraud, authority, or money to induce the unwilling person to cooperate.

Neither of these conditions can in the nature of things come to pass. As we have seen, every society attempts to control, and for its own operation must control, the sexual impulse in the interest of social order, procreation, and socialization. Moreover, not all men are born handsome nor all women beautiful. Instead there is a gradation from extremely attractive to extremely unattractive, with an unfavorable balance of the old, ugly, and/or deformed. This being true, the persons at the wrong end of the scale must, and inevitably will, use extraneous means to obtain gratification.

Between the sexes, men have authority and economic means to a greater degree than women. They are directly involved in the competitive struggle for scarce goods, whereas women are more restricted by pregnancy and child-care. Women are therefore more frequently prostitutes than men (and male prostitution is usually homosexual), because men are in a more favorable situation to offer payment or to use authority or force to obtain sexual gratification. Out of the total female population there are relatively few who are young and pretty; they are in great demand by virtually the entire adult male population. Most of these young and attractive women are acquired by the inducement of a definite and presumably permanent social status—marriage—which gives them security against age and loss of beauty. The remainder are still in a favorable position to profit from their attractiveness. They can readily enter the labor force in a clerical, sales, or service position. They can fit particularly into an occupation where sexual attractiveness is important. If, in a more traditional society, participation in the labor force is forbidden them because of the insistence that women must be attached to the home, then the alternative for the woman is an unproductive spinsterhood in the home or an inferior status such as that of the concubine or the prostitute. In that case the women of the dominant class will generally be forced to follow the first alternative, but the second alternative will be followed by the women of inferior or alien classes, the masculine demand for their services being particularly strong because of the "protected" position of women who are the men's equals in social status.

Since the basic causes of prostitution—the institutional control of sex, the unequal scale of attractiveness, and the presence of economic and social inequality between classes and between male and female— are not likely to disappear, prostitution is not likely to disappear either. However, the particular form and scope of the institution may change. One such alteration follows from the appearance of sex freedom among the women of the middle and upper classes. The greater the proportion of free, mutually pleasurable intercourse, the lesser is the demand for paid prostitution. This, it seems, is the true explanation of the diminution of prostitution in contemporary Western industrial countries.

Why modern industrial society should pursue the path of widespread sex freedom instead of the path of companionate prostitution is a complex question that would take us too far afield to try to answer. Basically it is a matter of the social mobility and anonymity inevitably associated with an urban-industrial system. The difference between a distinguished prostitute and a citizen wife in a small town like Athens was known to everyone because the identity of the parties themselves was known. In Paris, New York, or Moscow the case is different. There being no barriers to the transition, the girls capable of being high-class prostitutes will enter marriage by preference, and movement in and out of the profession will make status distinctions difficult and pointless. In other words, in a complex mobile society any sexual status except marriage is a temporary and anonymous one for a woman, not supported by any institutional regularities or securities.

The most persistent form of prostitution is the pure commercial form. Whether in brothels or in the streets, under bridges or in automobiles, this form is practiced everywhere and remains at the bottom of the social scale. Although its scope may be contracted by sex freedom and "amateur competition," the practice itself is not likely to be displaced. Not only will there always be a system of social dominance that gives a motive for selling sexual favors, and a scale of attractiveness that creates the need for buying them, but this form of prostitution is, in the last analysis, economical. Enabling a small number of women to take care of the needs of a large number of men, it is the most convenient sexual outlet for armies and for the legions of strangers, perverts, and physically repulsive in our midst. It performs a role which apparently no other institution fully performs.

Conclusion

Both homosexuality and prostitution illustrate the sociological principle that to understand a type of deviancy one must understand the norm that defines it as deviancy. In both cases the norms are part of the system of sexual control, the key to which seemingly lies in the family. Yet each case also illustrates that there are degrees of legitimacy and illegitimacy in any society, and that violations have their rewards and rules just as conformity does. The persistence of both kinds of deviancy considered here can be seen as due to the counterforces set in motion by the very control of sex itself.

PART TWO
SOCIAL DISORGANIZATION

8

The World's Population Crisis

by Kingsley Davis

THE DEMOGRAPHIC CONDITION MOST OFTEN VIEWED AS A SOCIAL PROB-
lem is the growth in the sheer number of people. When told that the
world's population (3.4 billion in 1965) is growing so fast that a
continuance of the same rate would double the figure every 33 years,
the average person can do the arithmetic that shows where this would
ultimately lead. Within 200 years, for example, the earth's population
would be 230 billion, or 68 times the 1965 total. Particular countries
are faced with even more bizarre increases if the present trend continues. Mexico's population, for instance, is growing at more than
one and a half times the world's rate. Nearly 37 million in 1965, it
will grow, if the current rate keeps up, to some 111 million by the end
of the century and to 860 million in a hundred years.

No one believes that such a frightening human multiplication will
actually occur. But the fact that the current trend would lead to im-
possibly high figures demonstrates that the trend must stop. *How* it
is to be brought to a halt, and the possible consequences *before* it is
halted, pose a social problem of the first magnitude.

The spectacular character of the present rate of increase should not
blind us, however, to the fact that there are other population problems, some of them independent of the question of growth in total
numbers. There are problems arising, for instance, from a high birth
rate regardless of whether the population is growing or not. There are
also problems arising from a very low birth rate. One of the latter
problems, and one that is very much in the public eye, is the aging
population.

In the present chapter we shall deal with the several major population problems, starting with the question of world population growth.
In trying to understand the causes and consequences of this growth,
we shall necessarily discuss changes in death rates, birth rates, and

the age structure. This will enable us to see how the various population problems are interrelated, all part of a fundamental transition that has been, and still is, occurring in human society. An examination of the differences in population growth around the world will quickly show that the situation in the industrial countries is different from that in the peasant-agrarian countries. Consequently, once the world view is sketched, our consideration of the major problems will be divided into two sections, the one dealing with the less developed and the other with the advanced nations.

Accelerating Growth and Its World Distribution

The unprecedented speed and magnitude of the world population increase in recent decades have earned for it the name "population explosion," an apt metaphor that sums up the situation in a single phrase. During countless millennia the human species expanded with infinite slowness, multiplying temporarily in some areas, declining in others, but remaining sparse everywhere. Even such a revolutionary change as the domestication of plants and animals came so gradually that it barely raised the rate of population growth, though in some regions it ultimately gave rise to far greater density of settlement. Compared then to all previous times (embracing more than 99.9 percent of human history), the modern rise in human numbers is utterly revolutionary. The gain in the 65 years from 1900 to 1965 was greater than the total population of the earth in 1900. But, even within the modern period, the rate has been accelerating, as the figures in Table 1 show. From 1750 to 1930, although the rate of increase (Column B) kept rising, the speed with which it rose (Column C) showed little change; but from 1930 to 1965 the speed with which the increase rate rose (Column C again) showed a steep gain. This double acceleration indicates that to extrapolate the past population trend into the future would be a dubious basis of prediction. We cannot safely assume that from 1965 to 1990 the population will grow at the same rate it grew during 1930-1965, because Column C in our table suggests that it may grow faster than that! Although the spurt from 1930 to 1965 seems by far the most explosive part of modern population growth, the gains in the decades immediately following 1965 may prove even more astonishing.

Is this unprecedented population growth a social problem? Although opinion is not unanimous, nearly all demographers and sociologists, most economists, many Roman Catholics, and even some Communists think that the answer is, "Yes." They do not believe that rapid popu-

TABLE 1

Growth of World Population, 1650-1965

	Estimated Population (millions)	Average Yearly Growth (%) in Prior Period	Average Rise (%) in Growth Rate per Decade	Years Required to Double at Growth Rate
	A	B	C	D
1650	545	—	—	—
1750	728	0.29	—	239
1800	906	0.44	8.6	158
1850	1,171	0.51	3.0	135
1900	1,608	0.64	4.6	110
1930	2,015	0.75	5.4	93
1950	2,509	1.10	21.4	63
1960	3,010	1.81	64.5	38
1965	3,361	2.23	51.7	31

Sources: The estimates up to and including 1900 are taken from A. M. Carr-Saunders, *World Population* (Oxford: Clarendon Press, 1936), p. 42. For 1930, 1950, and 1960 they are taken from *Demographic Yearbook, 1963* (New York: United Nations, 1964), p. 142. The 1965 figure is estimated by the author on the basis of United Nations, *Population and Vital Statistics Report* (October 1, 1964), p. 3, and the 1963 *Yearbook.*

lation growth is an inherent evil apart from its consequences, but simply that the consequences are regrettable. If we define as a social problem any condition or threatened condition that is regarded by a substantial portion of the citizenry as bad in itself or in its consequences, then the extremely rapid population growth of today is such a problem. However, before analyzing the precise reasons usually given for viewing it or not viewing it as a problem, let us try to understand the actual situation. There is clearly a large body of reliable information about population which makes possible a scientific analysis, quite apart from the evaluations, sentiments, and taboos that people bring to their reaction to the facts.

Shift of Population Growth to Less Developed Countries

One of the salient facts is that population is growing faster in the poorer countries than in the richer ones. This trend is recent, dating from sometime around 1920. Prior to World War I, the most rapid numerical gains occurred in the more successful nations—in those that were expanding economically and raising their level of living. As a consequence the northwest Europeans, both in Europe and overseas, multiplied more rapidly than the rest of the world's people. In a little more than two and a half centuries the proportion of Europeans in

TABLE **2**

**Population Growth
in Developed vs. Underdeveloped Regions, 1920-80**

	Developed Regions[a]		Underdeveloped Regions[a]	
	Population (millions)	Increase (%) per Decade	Population (millions)	Increase (%) per Decade
1920	574	—	1,247	—
1930	625	8.9	1,390	11.5
1940	673	7.7	1,577	13.5
1950	702	4.3	1,808	14.6
1960	801	14.0	2,209	22.1
1965	857	14.4[b]	2,504	28.3[b]
1980	1,015	7.8[b]	3,253	19.1[b]

Sources: For 1920-60 the populations are from *Demographic Yearbook, 1960* (New York: United Nations, 1961), p. 118, and *1963* (New York: United Nations, 1964), p. 142. The 1965 populations are estimated by the author on the basis of 1962-64 census data and 1960-64 increase rates as found in *Demographic Yearbook, 1963* and United Nations, *Population and Vital Statistics Report* (October 1, 1964). For 1980, the populations are "medium" projections from *Provisional Report on World Population Prospects, as Assessed in 1963* (New York: United Nations, 1964), p. 57.

[a] "Developed" includes Australia-New Zealand, Japan, northwest and central Europe, U.S.A.-Canada, U.S.S.R.; "underdeveloped" includes all the rest. In 1980, all of Europe except southern Europe is assumed to be developed.

[b] Percentages calculated on a decade basis, hence comparable to others.

the world nearly doubled, rising from about 18 percent in 1650 to approximately 35 percent in 1920. After 1920, as Table 2 shows, the underdeveloped countries (overwhelmingly non-European in race and culture) have exhibited the more rapid growth, and their advantage has been accelerating. If we take the gain in the underdeveloped regions as a ratio to the gain in the developed ones, the following results emerge:

Period	*Ratio*
1920-30	1.3
1930-40	1.8
1940-50	3.4
1950-60	1.6
1960-65	2.0
1965-80	2.5 (projected)

From 1920 to 1930, the underdeveloped regions still had high death rates which virtually wiped out their advantage in birth rates. From

1940 to 1950, on the other hand, the industrial nations were caught in a world war which increased their death rates and reduced their immigration, whereas the nonindustrial countries lowered their death rates precipitously and continued their high reproductive rates. In the 1950-1960 decade, the industrial countries maintained their steady gain in mortality, maintained fairly well their postwar high plateau in fertility, and gained in immigration from agrarian countries. By 1965, however, their birth rates had generally dropped, and they were expected to drop further behind the backward countries in population growth.

That the poorer countries are increasing their populations almost twice as fast as the richer ones is one of the most tragic circumstances of the modern demographic situation, for it is these countries which have the least need for, and which can least afford, inflated numbers of human beings. Some of the countries are already overcrowded to an extreme degree. It is at least fortunate that, among the underdeveloped regions, Latin America, on the whole less crowded and less impoverished than Asia or Africa, is exhibiting the fastest population increase.[1] But on whichever underdeveloped continent one looks, one finds exceedingly poor countries struggling to take care of an ever rising tide of humanity. El Salvador, a poor Central American country whose population density is one and a half times that of France, has a human increment of approximately 3.8 percent per year. Egypt, another agrarian country whose poverty is notorious and whose density in settled areas is more than 3 times that of the highly industrial United Kingdom, has an annual increase of 2.6 percent, considerably faster than that of the United States. In Asia there is Ceylon, a country whose economy is in the doldrums and whose politics is chaotic, yet whose population is gaining at the incongruous rate of 2.7 percent per year. Other crowded agrarian countries with annual population increments of between 2.5 and 3.5 percent are Mexico, Taiwan, Lebanon, Albania, Rwanda, Sudan, Trinidad, and South Korea. Among others that could probably be put in this class if we had the data are Nigeria, Ghana, Dominican Republic, and Thailand.

It must be remembered that a population increasing at 3 percent per year will double in 23 years and will multiply 10 times in 77 years; a population increasing at 2 percent per year will double in 35 years and increase 10 times in 116 years.

---

[1] See *Provisional Report on World Population Prospects* (New York: United Nations, 1964), pp. 57, 237-270; Kingsley Davis, ed., "A Crowding Hemisphere: Population Change in the Americas," *Annals of the American Academy of Political and Social Science,* Vol. 316 (March, 1958), pp. 1-10, 84-136.

Why the Rapid Population Growth?

In explaining modern population growth we are faced with two questions: Why has the world's population as a whole increased at an accelerating pace? Why has the fastest growth shifted from the more advanced to the less advanced nations? Although the two questions are interrelated, the answer to the first does not suffice to answer the second.

In strictly demographic terms, the explanation of the great wave of population growth in the last two centuries is the decline in the death rate, not a rise in the birth rate. The long-run trend of the birth rate, taking the world as a whole, has been generally downward, but it has not fallen as fast, or as consistently and widely, as the death rate.

The standard explanation of why the death rate has declined has been economic. At first the decline was limited to those countries experiencing real economic progress. It began gradually but gained momentum as the Industrial Revolution proceeded. The Western gains in agriculture, transportation, and commerce during the eighteenth and nineteenth centuries made better diets possible; the gains in industrial manufacturing made clothing, housing, and other amenities more widely available; the rise in real income facilitated the growth of public sanitation, medical science, and popular education. "It is no disparagement of medical science and practice," said Warren Thompson in 1953, "to recognize that the great decline in the death rate that has taken place during the last two centuries in the West is due, basically, to improvement in production and economic conditions." [2]

This traditional explanation of the death-rate decline seems correct as an interpretation of Western history. But when it is applied to contemporary underdeveloped areas, it is substantially wrong. These areas, since 1920, have benefited from a much faster drop in death rates than the northwest European peoples ever experienced, and they have had this experience without a comparable rate of economic development—in some cases without any visible gain in per capita income at all. Death rates have been brought down with revolutionary speed in the economically backward countries because the latest medical discoveries, made and financed in the industrial nations, can be immediately applied everywhere. Historically in the West, medical advances had to be slowly invented and diffused, with the result that

---

[2] Warren S. Thompson, *Population Problems*, 4th ed. (New York: McGraw-Hill, 1953), p. 77.

death rates were lowered gradually. Today, on the other hand, the nonindustrial nations are suddenly getting the benefit of these accumulated inventions and such new ones as are produced each year, with the result that their death rates are declining almost miraculously. The most important source of death being eliminated is infectious disease. Such diseases are being conquered through the transfer of medical techniques and personnel and funds from the industrial nations, especially under the auspices of international agencies like the World Health Organization, Pan American Health Organization, UNICEF, FAO, etc. It is being demonstrated in country after country that widespread diseases such as malaria, yellow fever, yaws, syphilis, trachoma, cholera, plague, typhoid, smallpox, tuberculosis, and dysentery can be controlled on a mass basis at low cost. Most of the discoveries making this possible are recent: insecticides like DDT, antibiotics like penicillin, vaccines like BCG, drugs like sulfanilamide, better instruments like portable X-ray machines, and rationalized public health campaigns and statistical reporting. To people in industrial countries habituated to paying extremely high fees to private physicians for curative medicine, it is hard to realize that preventive public health measures, instituted and organized by the government and employing only a handful of specialists, can save millions of lives at costs ranging from a few cents to a few dollars per person per year.

An illustrative case is that of Ceylon. A country suffering from chronic malaria, it had a crude death rate averaging 26.9 per 1000 population during 1920-1929 and 24.5 during 1930-1939. In 1946 the rate was still 20.3, but in 1947 it was 14.3, a 43 percent decline in one year! By 1954 it was down to 10.4. The main cause of this unexampled drop was the use of DDT as a residual spray to control malaria. This measure not only greatly reduced malarial infection but it also lowered mortality from other causes. The costs were negligible (less than $2.00 annually per head for all medical services), but even these were partly met from WHO funds; the DDT, first invented in Switzerland, was imported; the experts involved either originated or were trained outside the country. Furthermore, nothing was required of the Ceylonese themselves. Their houses were sprayed *for* them. They were not required to change their habits or institutions, to acquire a knowledge of malaria, or to take any initiative. We can see, then, how the spectacular decline in the death rate of the island came about through no basic economic development or change in the institutional structure.

Similar developments have occurred in other underdeveloped countries. The World Health Organization reported in 1965 that antimalarial efforts since World War II had rid 815 million people of the threat of malaria.[3] Numerous other causes of death have also been, or are being, conquered. Between 1940 and 1964, the recorded death rate fell by 61 percent in Puerto Rico, 71 percent in Taiwan, and 81 percent in Cyprus. For 18 underdeveloped countries, the average decline during the 24-year period was 57 percent.[4]

Since disease control has not involved basic changes in social institutions or education, birth rates have remained high in nonindustrial regions. They were higher to begin with in most of these regions than they ever were in northwestern Europe, and they have in most cases declined little if at all. Furthermore, whereas the presently industrial countries began lowering their birth rates *before* their sharpest declines in mortality, the backward areas of today will do so, if at all, long *after* their mortality has reached a modern low level. It is this dual fact—the unprecedented conquest of mortality by bringing mid-twentieth-century public health to impoverished peoples and the continuance of high birth rates among these peoples—that explains the extraordinarily fast population growth in the three-fourths of the world that still remains underdeveloped. It also explains, along with the postwar rise in birth rates and continued gradual lowering of mortality in the industrial nations, the accelerating trend of the total world population.

Consequences of Population Change: The Agrarian Countries

With this explanation of how the modern upsurge in population has come about, we can more clearly understand the consequences. If, for example, the most rapid multiplication is occurring in the underdeveloped countries, and if this is attributable to causes other than economic development, we can see at once that the human increase may be retarding the rise in level of living or thwarting it altogether. For this to happen, the country does not have to be densely settled already. An area may be sparsely settled, e.g., Brazil, and still have too fast a population growth from an economic point of view. Fur-

---

[3] *The New York Times*, March 26, 1965. Malaria has been almost entirely eliminated in many countries, including such formerly afflicted areas as Corsica, Barbados, Cyprus, and Ukraine.

[4] For fuller analysis and references on the spectacular declines in death rates, see George J. Stolnitz, "A Century of International Mortality Trends," *Population Studies*, Vol. 9 (July, 1955), pp. 24-55; Vol. 10 (July, 1956), pp. 17-42; Kingsley Davis, "The Amazing Decline of Mortality in Underdeveloped Areas," *Journal of the American Economic Association*, Vol. 46 (May, 1956), pp. 305-18; Milbank Memorial Fund, *Trends and Differentials in Mortality* (New York: Milbank Fund, 1956); and the *Proceedings of the World Population Conference* (Belgrade, 1965).

thermore, a country may be prosperous, even heavily industrialized, and still have too fast an increase and other population problems. Since the problems and the reasons for them differ in the two kinds of country, let us consider them separately, beginning with the agrarian nations.

Rising Numbers, Poverty, and Economic Development

Strictly speaking, economic development does not mean simply a gain in total national income. It means a gain in *per capita* income. This requires that capital be added to production faster than labor, which in turn means that the rate of investment must be adequate. With a constant population, a rate of investment of 3 to 5 percent of national income is required to produce a 1 percent increase in per capita income; whereas, with a population growing at 3 percent per year, an investment of between 12 and 20 percent of the national income is required. A poor country finds it extremely difficult to invest even 10 percent of its national income in economic development. Since most underdeveloped countries now have a rate of population growth that is between 2 and 3.5 percent, we can see that they have come dangerously close to making genuine economic development impossible for themselves. Even if they achieve such development, it will be at a slower rate than would be the case with a less climactic population growth.[5]

A graphic appreciation of the difficulties can be obtained by looking at particular cases. We have seen how rapidly Ceylon's death rate declined after 1946. Even before that its population had been growing rapidly. From 2.8 million in 1871 it rose to 4 million in 1901 and 7 million in 1946. In 19 years after 1946, it gained by almost two-thirds, reaching 11 million in 1965. This phenomenal rise was not accompanied by a comparable economic gain, but rather by political instability and economic gyrations. The country has remained predominantly agricultural. "Industry is only slightly developed . . . ; excluding the processing of tea, rubber, and coconut, it contributed only about 5

---

[5] For a brief but lucid analysis of the relation of population growth to economic development, see Arnold C. Harberger, "Variations on a Theme by Malthus," in Roy G. Francis, ed., *The Population Ahead* (Minneapolis: University of Minnesota Press, 1958). See also Norman S. Buchanan and Howard S. Ellis, *Approaches to Economic Development* (New York: Twentieth Century Fund, 1955), Chapter 5; Simon Kuznets, Wilbert E. Moore, and Joseph J. Spengler, eds., *Economic Growth: Brazil, India, Japan* (Durham, N. C.: Duke University Press, 1955), Chapter 4, pp. 7-10; and Ansley J. Coale and Edgar M. Hoover, *Population Growth and Economic Development in Low-Income Countries* (Princeton, N. J.: Princeton University Press, 1958).

percent to the gross national product in 1955." [6] Yet the land under cultivation has increased slowly, and the rising density on the land is a melancholy measure of economic stagnation. In 1921 there were 1.4 rural persons in Ceylon for each cultivated acre; by 1963 the figure had risen to 2.4. A sample study made in 1936-1939 found that 66 percent of village families either owned no land at all or owned less than one acre; a second study in 1950 found 71 percent of village families in this category.[7] On the assumption that each family could support itself on 5 acres of land, it was calculated that the surplus peasant population in Ceylon in 1901 was 660,000; in 1946, 2,766,000.[8] And this is on the assumption that each family could "live" on 5 acres! The nation's 10-year plan for the 1960's envisaged an increase of 64 percent in the irrigated area. As splendid as that sounds, the truth is that the ambitious goal will probably not be realized, and yet the rural population will continue to grow at a rate of about 30 percent per decade. From 1955 to 1963, Ceylon drew heavily on her foreign assets because government expenditures were running about 50 percent above revenues.[9]

Egypt's situation is worse. Its already dense population grew from 14.2 million in 1927 to 28 million in 1963. This huge increase came exclusively from a steep fall in the death rate—from an average of 26.9 deaths per 1000 population per year in 1935-1939 to 15.3 in 1963. The birth rate continued to remain around 40 per 1000; in 1963 it was 42.1, and the population was growing at a rate of 2.7 percent per year. Indeed, as in Ceylon, the population has grown faster than the area under crops, with approximately 1250 persons directly dependent on agriculture per square mile of cultivated land. Efforts to expand irrigation, to grow two or three crops on the same soil, and to improve agricultural technology have greatly increased agricultural production, but at only about a third the rate of population growth. As a consequence, the rising need to import foodstuffs has helped to cripple Egypt's ambitious effort to industrialize. The Aswan dam will add considerably to the country's irrigated area, but it has been calculated that the agricultural population will have grown commensurately by the time the land is available.

[6] *Economic Survey of Asia and the Far East, 1956* (Bangkok: United Nations, 1957), p. 74.

[7] N. K. Sarkar, *The Demography of Ceylon* (Colombo: Ceylon Government Press, 1957), pp. 217-18.

[8] *Ibid.*, pp. 220-21.

[9] *Economic Survey of Asia and the Far East, 1963* (Bangkok: United Nations, 1964), pp. 126, 174-75.

Unlike most underdeveloped countries, Egypt has had its Agricultural Revolution, but the fruits of this process have been largely absorbed in maintaining a greatly expanded population at the same low (and in recent years declining) level of subsistence, instead of providing the surplus necessary to build up other sectors of the economy, notably industry. The standard of living of the Egyptian peasants today is much lower than that of seventeenth-century English peasants, a fact which correspondingly reduces the country's capacity to carry out the large-scale saving required for development.[10]

In many other agrarian countries—India, Pakistan, Lebanon, Haiti, Uganda, to mention only a few—per capita income has risen little if at all, despite a rise in national income. An economist who had worked in Ceylon had this to say:

> The issue is plain: Any check to population growth will make economic progress more likely or speed it up. Continued or accelerated population growth will make progress slow down or stop. In one meeting of government officials I attended, the problem of development was put as that of keeping the standard of living from falling—not of raising it.[11]

Youthful Populations, Unemployment, and Political Instability

When mortality is reduced rapidly with little or no reduction in the high birth rate, the resulting population is abnormally young. The reason for this is that the greatest gains in saving lives are made at the younger ages—in infancy and childhood. As a consequence, the drastic fall in the death rate acts like a sharp rise in births: it greatly increases the proportion of children in the population. Many of the underdeveloped countries of the world accordingly have now the youngest populations the world has ever known. Costa Rica, whose death rate dropped 57 percent in 20 years but whose birth rate has remained high (in fact, during the period of 1959-1963 the average birth rate was 4.9 times the average death rate), has 126 children under 15 years of age for each 100 adults aged 20 to 59. Belgium, on the other hand, being a country that has long had both a low death rate and a low birth rate, has only 44 children per 100 adults in their prime. (See Table 3.) Such young populations mean that the underdeveloped countries are struggling not only with the problem of rapidly rising numbers of people but also with the problem of a burdensome child-dependency ratio. The work the adults do has to be

---

[10] Charles Issawi, *Egypt at Mid-Century* (London: Oxford University Press, 1954), p. 93.

[11] Theodore Morgan, "The Economic Development of Ceylon," *Annals of the American Academy of Political and Social Science*, Vol. 305 (May, 1956), p. 94.

TABLE 3

Indices of the Age Structure in Selected Countries

	Child-Dependency Ratio (Children under 15 per 100 adults 20-59)	Youth-Adult Ratio (Youths 15-19 per 100 adults 20-59)	Old-Age Dependency Ratio (Oldsters 60-plus per 100 adults 20-59)
Underdeveloped Countries			
Costa Rica, 1963	126	25	14
Mauritius, 1962	113	23	13
Taiwan, 1956	106	24	10
Ceylon, 1956	90	19	12
Industrial Countries			
Old World			
Belgium, 1960	44	11	33
Denmark, 1960	49	16	30
France, 1962	50	15	36
New World			
United States, 1960	64	15	27
New Zealand, 1961	70	16	26
Life-Table Populations [a]			
U.S. white female (1963)			
with life expectancy of 73	39	13	45
Hypothetical future U.S.			
with life expectancy of 83	38	13	60

Sources: Census age-data from *Demographic Yearbook, 1962 and 1963* (New York: United Nations, 1963 and 1964), Table 5. U.S. white female life-table population from National Center for Health Statistics, *Vital Statistics of the United States, 1963*, Vol. 2, Section 5, pp. 5-7. Hypothetical U.S. life-table population taken from a projected life table made by the author, unpublished.

[a] A life-table population is the one that would result from the age-specific death rates of a given period, assuming a birth rate equal to the death rate.

used, to an unusual degree, to support large numbers of children rather than to lay the long-run basis for economic improvement. Furthermore, the women are so burdened with constant childbearing and child rearing that they cannot participate in economic production beyond the traditional and usually inefficient tasks of the home and garden. In an unconscious effort to compensate for the heavy child-dependency drag, the agrarian countries tend to start children to work at an early age. Child labor, however, is neither efficient in the short run nor conducive to economic development in the long run. What is required for social and economic development is the acquisition of skills by the population, which means careful and systematic education of children. When children are kept out of school in order to work, the work is normally unskilled and inefficient. Furthermore, especially in an agrarian economy, a failure to educate children in schools deprives them of their main chance of acquiring ideas and attitudes conducive to social change rather than traditionalism. Underdeveloped countries have a hard enough time getting sufficient funds for education, despite heroic proportions of the national budget spent for this purpose. The massive waves of children coming as a result of demographic changes make the problem all the worse. (See Chapter 11, page 572.)

The problem is not solely the swollen ranks of children. It is also the engorged contingents of youth. It can be seen from Table 3 that Costa Rica, for example, has 25 young people aged 15-19 for each hundred adults aged 20-59; whereas in Belgium the ratio is only 11 to each 100. With ever larger waves of youths entering the labor market each year, the underdeveloped country must have a very rapid economic development to absorb them all. If it falters, large numbers of youths become unemployed. They may go to school, but this may merely succeed in making them a class of "educated unemployed." Possessed of youthful energy and idealism, having no stake in the existing situation, being extremely numerous in relation to the adult population, these youths are politically explosive, often ready to follow the leader who promises the quickest and most violent solution. Their role in making and breaking dictators has often been demonstrated in backward countries, whether in Latin America or the Middle East. Their fiery impatience makes it hard for a ruler to follow a policy of basic economic development, for that seems too slow and too prosaic. It is easier for the ruler to satisfy the youthful rabble by threatening war, casting out the foreign devils, seizing property, and insulting the enemy—all in the name of sacred nationalistic sentiment and holy religious emotion.

Functionless Fertility and the Family

The dilemmas of rapid population growth can be seen not only in nations but also, on a minute scale, in families. As the head of the household in an agrarian country often sees it, the problem is how to get enough land. This is why a scheme of land-distribution will generally receive popular support, regardless of how uneconomic it may be. But, as the cases of Ceylon and Egypt show, there may not be any more land to be had, at least without large-scale collective investment. Failing additional land, the peasant finds it hard to maintain his children, much less educate them. His aspirations for his children may be high, because he sees the lack of opportunity in the village and he knows of schools and urban employment, but he cannot meet these aspirations. His wife, on the other hand, is burdened with the same round of childbearing that her ancestors experienced, but with one difference—a far greater proportion of the children remain alive. With a larger family than normal, child-care is a more constant burden, the available land is even more inadequate, the aspirations even more unreachable.

The Geographical Shift of People

Another problem plagues the underdeveloped country growing rapidly in population, especially when the peasantry is already densely settled on the land. This is the necessity of moving something like 60 percent of the people from the country to the cities. It is a problem so formidable that few governments seem willing to face it realistically; yet, if rapid economic development is to be achieved, the territorial shift must take place rapidly.

The necessity of the rural-urban migration arises from the fact that an agrarian population is all located in the wrong places for purposes of an industrial economy. The chief instrument of agriculture is land. When the level of technology is low, as it is in peasant farming, it takes a great deal of labor in ratio to land to produce the crops. For this reason, the population tends to be spread out thickly over the land, and it is generally most numerous where the land is fertile unless the pattern of land-ownership interferes. In industrial societies, on the other hand, the character of agriculture is transformed by the substitution of technology for labor on the farms. The people are emptied off the farm land; they go to the cities where occupations in manufacturing and services are opening up. The growth of urban economic activity contributes to the technological revolution on farms both by furnishing the science, engineering, education, and machinery for better agriculture and by increasing the demand for agricultural products. The superior productivity of urban enterprise pulls labor from the farms by offering higher wages and at the same time increases farm capitalization by increasing demand. As a consequence, the loss of labor to the cities does not lower farm production but raises it, and the few farmers who remain make a much better living than did their more numerous predecessors.

The magnitude of the transformation can be seen from the data for the United States (Table 4). Even during the period 1940 to 1960, the average annual net migration from American farms was 3.7 percent of the farm population at the start of each year. Since the average natural increase was 1.2 percent, the net migration was large enough

TABLE 4

Shift of Population from Farm to City in the United States

Year	Percentage of Population	
	On farms	Not on farms
1820	72 [a]	28
1964	7 [b]	93

Sources:

[a] Commerce Dept., Bureau of the Census, *Historical Statistics of the United States, Colonial Times to 1957* (Washington, D. C., 1960), p. 74. This is the percentage of *gainful workers* engaged in agriculture. We do not have data on the farm population for 1820, but its proportion of the total population should not vary greatly from the proportion of farmers among gainful workers.

[b] Departments of Commerce and Agriculture, *Farm Population,* Current Population Reports, Series Census-ERS, P-27, No. 35 (June 4, 1965).

not only to cancel the natural increase but also to reduce the farm population at an average rate of 1.5 percent each year. After 1910 the farm population, despite the rapid growth of the total United States population, showed no increase. The number of farmers in the country remained at a plateau during the years 1910-1917, after which it declined gradually at first and then rapidly. In 1917 the farm population in the country was approximately 32,236,000; in 1959 it was down to 21,172,000 and in 1964 down to 12,954,000.

The effect of rapid population growth in a still underdeveloped country is to aggravate the problem of rural-urban migration. For this there are two reasons: first, the size of the annual increments to the population is such that the economy, if it is to achieve gains in per capita income, must grow at a rate more rapid than that experienced by industrial countries during their history. From 1820 to 1900, the population of the United States grew at an average rate of 2.8 percent per year. This very fast rate was achieved only because it was helped along by massive immigration from overseas and by expansion of territory. However, as we have seen, many of today's underdeveloped countries, without either immigration or territorial expansion, are eclipsing this rate by their own natural increase. They must therefore find a way to achieve a rate of economic development (i.e., an industrial revolution) more rapid than that experienced by the United States, and this means that the geographic redistribution of their people must be achieved more quickly. Second, rapid population growth in an agrarian country today causes cities to grow rapidly and thereby multiplies urban problems and yet does not succeed in removing the surplus population from the countryside. An analysis of the data for 34 underdeveloped countries between 1940 and 1960 shows that their urban population grew at an average rate of 4.5 percent per year. This figure is half again as high as the rate of urban population growth in 14 industrialized countries *when they were at the peak of their urbanization.*

The main factor explaining the rapid city growth in the underdeveloped countries today is not rural-urban migration but sheer population growth. As a consequence, their rural populations are also growing rapidly and are piling up on the land. In the early history of the now industrial countries, the growth of cities, modest as it was, took the surplus population from the countryside and thus helped in the modernization of agriculture. In those days, the cities had low birth rates and high death rates compared to the rural areas. Today in the underdeveloped nations the cities often have lower death rates than the farm areas and birth rates that are as high or nearly as high. As a result, the city populations are skyrocketing simply by their own natural increase. It is the rapid city growth, engendered mainly by the high rates of natural increase, that is causing the great squatter problem in the cities throughout the underdeveloped parts of the world. In all of these cities there are thousands of people living in self-built shacks in thickly settled shantytowns without sanitary facilities. They settle in parks, schoolgrounds, vacant lots. It is said that in the metropolitan areas of Peru there were nearly a million squatters in 1960; in Manila the number of squatters is expected to reach 800,000 by 1980; in Caracas squatters make up over 35 percent of the city's population; in Ankara, nearly 50 percent. Under such circumstances, rapid city growth is not solving the agricultural problem and is creating urban crises on an unprecedented scale.[12]

The governments of nonindustrial countries often harbor a well-founded suspicion of their growing urban masses. They know that city growth brings problems of frightening dimensions—problems of housing, sanitation, education, public order. They know that swollen city populations tend to become unruly and that they easily resort to riots and strife if the political leaders do not please them. The danger

---

[12] For further analysis, see Kingsley Davis, "The Urbanization of the Human Population," *Scientific American*, Vol. 213 (September, 1965), pp. 40-53. This entire issue is devoted to "Cities"; the data on squatters are taken from the article by Charles Abrams, "The Uses of Land in Cities," p. 152.

TABLE 5

Population Growth in Industrialized Regions, 1950 to 1980

| | Actual Population | | | Projected Population | |
| | Millions | | Percent Gain | Millions | Percent Gain |
	1950	1965	1950-65	1980	1965-80
Australia-New Zealand	10	14	40	18	29
Northern America [a]	167	216	29	262	21
Soviet Union	180	231	28	278	20
Japan	83	98	18	111	14
Europe	392	446	14	479	7
Total	832	1,005	21	1,148	14

Sources: Data for 1950 from Demographic Yearbook, 1963 (New York: United Nations, 1964); for 1965, estimated by the writer on basis of 1960-62 growth rates and latest census data in United Nations, Population and Vital Statistics Report, Series A, Vol. 17, No. 3 (July 1, 1965). Projected 1980 populations are the "medium" ones in Provisional Report on World Population Prospects, 1963 (New York: United Nations, 1964).

[a] Canada, United States, and their possessions north of the Rio Grande.

of urban mobs is all the greater in view of the fact that the city populations are bulging with youth. As noted already, a population with recently and drastically reduced mortality and a continuing high fertility is young, and this feature is made extreme by the added migration of young adults from the rural areas.

It is thus for good reason that governments are suspicious of growing urban masses, but they are generally mistaken as to the chief cause of the growth. They think of rural-urban migration as the chief culprit and sometimes advocate a policy of preventing such movement. Since World War I, however, the main factor in city growth in the underdeveloped areas has increasingly become sheer population growth.

Consequences of Population Change: The Industrialized Countries

One should not assume that rapid population growth is confined to the poorer countries or that it has deleterious effects only in them. The advanced countries of the world, although showing less growth than the poorer ones, are nevertheless characterized by soaring populations. As a whole, they are expected, as shown in Table 5, to increase by 14 percent between 1965 and 1980. It is interesting that, among the advanced areas, the ones showing the most rapid growth are the

TABLE 6

Growth Rate of United States and Canadian Populations

Decade	Percent Increase per Decade U.S.[a]	Canada [b]
1850-60	35.6	32.6
1860-70	26.6	14.2
1870-80	26.0	17.2
1880-90	25.5	11.8
1890-1900	20.7	11.1
1900-10	21.0	34.2
1910-20	14.9	21.9
1920-30	16.1	18.9
1930-40	7.2	11.4
1940-50	14.5	17.4
1950-60	18.7	30.4
1960-65	15.1	19.8

Sources:

[a] Computed from Commerce Dept., Bureau of the Census, *Historical Statistics of the United States, Colonial Times to 1957* (Washington, D. C., 1960), p. 8; and *Demographic Yearbook, 1963* (New York: United Nations, 1964); and *U.S. Population Estimates*, Census Series P-25, No. 309 (June 11, 1965).

[b] Computed from *Demographic Yearbook, 1955*, p. 132, and *1963*, p. 151; and United Nations, *Population and Vital Statistics Report* (July 1, 1965).

newer and less crowded ones. Europe's growth is less than half of the Soviet Union's rate. The newer industrial countries are showing the greater growth because their postwar baby boom was more extreme and has lasted longer, and because some of them—particularly Australia, Canada, and the United States—are receiving huge numbers of immigrants. The United States, for example, has a birth rate higher than that of most industrial countries and regularly receives more immigrants (counting both the legal and illegal ones) than any country in the world. Its population is still growing at a rate that will, if continued, double the number in 50 years, although the postwar growth was reduced after 1960 (see Table 6).

Paradoxically, the prosperous countries find rapid population growth troublesome precisely because of their prosperity. As the goods and services used by each individual mount, and as the number of individuals multiplies, the complications become fantastic. The United States, for example, increased its consumption of energy by more than 16 percent in two years, from 1954 to 1956. In the latter year each man, woman, and child consumed on the average an amount of commercially produced energy equal to 9.5 short tons of coal. This was well over a hundred times the amount of such energy consumed per person in Ceylon. Also, the congestion of people and their material possessions causes an increasing proportion of effort and resources to be used simply to mitigate the effects of congestion. As we have seen, the attainment of a high level of living is accompanied by a crowding of people into cities. In Australia and the United States, for example, about 60 percent of the inhabitants live in metropolitan areas of more than 100,000, and in Canada nearly half do so. Already the New York metropolitan region contains about 16 million people, the Buenos Aires agglomeration about 7 million, and Los Angeles around 8 million.

As these giant urban aggregates grow more populous and the per capita apparatus more complex, the resulting congestion becomes ever more costly. Automobiles, radios, television antennas, boats, houses, freezers, and myriad other possessions multiply much faster than the population, which itself is multiplying. To acquire room to enjoy and store their goods, city families move to the suburbs where a house, yard, and garage can be obtained. The cost of this gain in space is, of course, a longer and more expensive commuting trip for the head of the family. Not only is it burdensome for him but it is also costly to the entire economy, because elaborate throughways and transportation networks have to be built. In addition, utility lines have to be extended, water mains laid, schools built. But the problems of urban crowding cannot be permanently solved by metropolitan deconcentration, because more people each year are trying to find space in each expanding metropolis.

Ultimately the combined human and material multiplication is self-defeating. The effort to escape mounting congestion simply creates more congestion. Every economic activity seeks more space: retailers want one-floor supermarkets and acres for parking, manufacturers want one-floor factories and parklike grounds, commuters and truckers want eight-lane highways and cloverleaf turns. In addition, municipalities want parks and unpolluted watersheds, and families want ranch homes on half-acre plots. As the urban population grows, as each new area fills up, the quest for space takes the suburbs farther out and multiplies the connecting links. The home that was once "in the country" or "in a pleasant little suburb" is presently a dot in a continuous sea of housing developments and shopping centers. The throughway that was so spacious and convenient when it was finished soon becomes an exasperating trap at rush hours. Also, the industries that supply the material wealth, the autos and buses that travel ever greater distances between home and work, the dumps where the mounting refuse is burned—all combine to create a social disease of the twentieth century, smog. This air pollution is extending far beyond the cities themselves; in California, for example, it is beginning to affect the crops in the Central Valley, the richest agricultural region in the world. The movement to the suburbs winds up, not as an escape from the city but as an extension of the city outward in space, with smog, traffic congestion, and crowds appearing all over again. The urban sprawl may cover 20 to 40 miles today; it will cover 40 to 60, or even 100, tomorrow.

The cost of all this becomes staggering. Not only is land increasingly removed from agricultural use, not only do freeways and transit lines cost billions, but the individual himself pays dearly. The man who commutes 45 minutes to reach his job, the family that maintains a summer home some scores or hundreds of miles from its regular home, the woman who abandons her career because she is stuck deep in the suburbs—all are paying a heavy price for what is in the end a fruitless search for escape from the city. As time goes by, as the population doubles or triples and material possessions get more numerous, the additional costs will mount until they cancel the gains in wealth.[13]

Proposed Solutions and Public Controversy

The demographic facts given above in general outline are indisputable. More controversial are the social and economic consequences alluded to, and there is accordingly no universal agreement that a "population problem" exists. Interestingly enough, however, the greatest overt controversy arises over the question of the means suggested for solving the population problem by some of those who believe there is such a problem. Let us begin with the debate over the problem itself and then consider the proposed solutions.

The Debate over the Existence of a Population Problem

The contention that there is at bottom no population problem at all has been maintained more consistently by Soviet spokesmen than by

---

[13] For a lengthier analysis of the ways in which the multiplication of people and possessions is impinging on human adjustment, see R. A. Piddington, *The Limits of Mankind* (Bristol: Wright, 1956). For analyses of urban problems, see William Dobriner, ed., *The Suburban Community* (New York: Putnam, 1958); Wilfred Owen, *Cities in the Motor Age* (New York: Viking, 1959); Robert C. Wood, *Suburbia* (New York: Houghton Mifflin, 1958); Morroe Berger, ed., *The New Metropolis in the Arab World* (New York: Allied, 1963); *Scientific American* (September, 1965), entire issue.

anyone else. As repeatedly expressed in the United Nations, this Marx-Leninist line regards so-called overpopulation as a myth invented by capitalist apologists for the purpose of distracting attention from the real problem, capitalism itself. Such evils as poverty, unemployment, war, or hunger, according to this view, cannot be attributed to the number of people or their rate of increase, but only to the particular social order. In the words of the then Soviet member of the United Nations Population Commission:

> Under the conditions of a capitalistic mode of production a certain part of the population systematically becomes relatively superfluous [because] as a result of the very process of capitalistic production a part of working power (and consequently still greater part of population) is found to be superfluous for the purposes of production. Here lies the root of unemployment, an incurable chronic disease of capitalism. . . .

> In socialist society where the immediate purpose of production is satisfaction of the requirements of society but not the gaining of maximum profits, the problem of excessive population no longer arises.[14]

Logically, what is at issue here is the question of causation. The Soviet spokesmen do not deny that unemployment, poverty, or economic stagnation exists in some places and times; they simply say that the causation of these evils is to be found in the social system, never in the demographic sphere. Obviously, such evils as poverty and hunger cannot be due to a communist mode of organization, because communism, as the greatest good, cannot cause any evil. The cause of the aforesaid evils, therefore, must lie in the even greater evil, capitalism.

A similar view that there is no population problem, that "overpopulation" is therefore a myth, is maintained by some noncommunists, but for different reasons. They hold that science *will* or *can keep ahead* of population growth, no matter how rapid this growth may be. In statements to this effect, one should keep an eye out for the small unobtrusive words. If the view is that science *will* do something, the speaker is presumably resting his case on a notion of automatic or inevitable change; yet others maintain that science depends on human activity and volition, and that its accomplishments are anything but

---

[14] T. V. Ryabushkin, "Social Aspects of Population Structure and Movement," *Papers of the World Population Conference, 1954* (New York: United Nations, 1955), Vol. 5, pp. 1032-33. The Marxist view has tended to be modified, both in the Soviet and the Chinese camps. A greater recognition of the population problem can be seen in the Communist contributions to the World Population Conference in Belgrade, 1965.

automatic. If instead the statement holds that science *can* do something, then the important question is "under what conditions"? Also, a little phrase like "keep ahead" may contain significant ambiguities. Does it mean merely feeding the population, or does it mean giving people a better life? Finally, does the speaker set a time limit on how long he thinks that science will automatically, or can possibly, keep ahead of population growth? Unless some time limit is set, the position becomes absurd, because the world's population, if it continued the growth exhibited from 1950 to 1960, would weigh as much as the entire earth within approximately 1750 years. In other words, in less time than has passed since Julius Caesar, the earth would be entirely absorbed in human beings.

On the other hand, many observers believe that there *is* a population problem in the sense that certain evils are caused by too high a population density and/or too rapid a rate of increase. They do not all agree on which evils, or when or where, but they do agree that overpopulation can have deleterious consequences. The most common view is that overpopulation is responsible for hunger and famine in various parts of the world.[15] In fact, this conception has dominated the thinking about population ever since Malthus' day, perhaps as a result of his inspiration but also partly as a result of an untutored impulse to visualize the population problem in terms of mere physical survival. More subtle is the idea that, under certain conditions, rapid population growth may prevent or reduce economic development.[16] Sometimes this view is challenged on the ground that a gain in per capita income "is not the highest goal." Be that as it may, the fact remains that economic means are necessary for a wide variety of purposes—better education and health, more security and leisure, finer arts and churches, and stronger defense and public order. Any damper on economic development is therefore a danger to these goals.

Of course, there are additional population problems that have nothing to do with poverty. Some people, for example, find sheer crowding objectionable; they go to great lengths to escape being surrounded by

---

[15] Works concerned with population and the food supply are legion. Some examples are Sir John Russell, *World Population and World Food Supplies* (London: Allen & Unwin, 1954). F. Le Gros Clark and N. W. Pirie, eds., *Four Thousand Million Mouths* (London: Oxford, 1951). Michel Cépède *et al.*, *Population and Food* (New York: Sheed & Ward, 1964).

[16] For a history of population theory, see *The Determinants and Consequences of Population Trends* (New York: United Nations, 1953), Chapter 3. This volume also contains chapters on the effects of population growth on economic development. Also, D. E. C. Eversley, *Social Theories of Fertility and the Malthusian Debate* (Oxford: Clarendon Press, 1959).

hordes of other people. There are also objections to other conditions to which population growth contributes, such as air and water pollution, increased exposure to disease, destruction of natural beauty, and elimination of all animal life except man and his domesticated beasts and parasites. Sometimes such arguments are pilloried as being misanthropic. William Vogt, for example, was accused by *Time* magazine of preferring birds to men because he pointed out in his famous book, *Road to Survival*,[17] that many species of birds are becoming extinct as the earth's human population burgeons. But the disappearance of wildlife is a distinct loss to mankind, and it is hardly misanthropic to feel that 3 billion people on earth with the enjoyment of wildlife and with other enjoyments is better than 6 or 10 billion without them. As time goes by, we shall probably hear population increasingly discussed from the standpoint of the sociological, esthetic, and mental health problems involved.

The Debate over the Means

If there is a population problem, it requires a demographic solution. The evils said to flow from too many people or too fast a rate of increase are real enough, but they do not constitute a population problem unless they in fact do flow from such causes. The Soviet theorists quite consistently hold the view that, since the evils are due to capitalism, it makes no sense to try to deal with them by demographic measures. Sometimes others are less consistent. Roman Catholics, for example, sometimes maintain that there is a population problem but refuse to admit any demographic solution.[18] Actually, there are only three possible demographic solutions: a rise in the death rate, a drop in the birth rate, or emigration. If we are thinking of the entire world, emigration is not a solution.[19]

A CHANGE IN THE DEATH RATE. Practically no one wants to see a rise in the death rate, and certainly such a rise is not likely to be adopted as a policy. In the past, death has frequently been used as a population control measure, sometimes by killing the aged or other incapacitated persons but more often by infanticide.[20] In modern eyes, however, keeping people alive is a supreme value; a policy of deliberately de-

---

[17] New York: Sloane, 1948.

[18] See the discussion of economic development below.

[19] Except, of course, for the possibility of travel away from the earth—a possibility we shall show in a moment is remote indeed.

[20] See Herbert Aptekar, *Anjea* (New York: Godwin, 1931), Chapter 7; Knud Rasmussen, *The Netsilik Eskimos* (Copenhagen, 1931), pp. 139-40; Olga Lang, *Chinese Family and Society* (New Haven: Yale University Press, 1946), p. 150; Raymond Firth, *We, the Tikopia*, 2nd ed. (London: Allen & Unwin, 1957).

stroying life is so tabooed that the capital penalty for even the most heinous crimes is outlawed in some countries. Indeed, the genius of modern civilization in keeping people alive has been, as we have seen, the major factor in creating the fantastic population increase of recent times.

Still, even though it will not be adopted as a population policy, a rise in the death rate may prove to be an unintended and unwanted solution. There is no guarantee that the mounting population pressure will not ultimately give rise to catastrophic rises in mortality. Warfare alone could decimate hundreds of millions, especially if fought with thermonuclear weapons. The Russians are estimated to have lost 25,000,000 through deaths caused by World War II.[21] It must be remembered that there is no inherent limit to the death rate. Entire populations can be wiped out, and with modern weapons the attackers could succeed in killing themselves as well as their enemies. In other words, as is usually the case, destruction can be more rapid than construction. Populations can be destroyed much faster than they can be built up by reproduction. The threat of mortality as a terrible solution to the population problem is one of the dangers that drives people to try to find other solutions.

REDUCTION OF THE BIRTH RATE. In industrial countries the rate of population growth has been greatly reduced by a long-run decline in the birth rate. For instance, in four countries of northwest Europe, the average annual births per 1000 population were as shown by the figures in Table 7. In the first half-century, the rate of natural increase was held down by a high death rate, whereas in the last period the birth rate had dropped faster than mortality. This reduction came primarily from the use of contraception and abortion within marriage, rather than by permanent celibacy or by postponement of marriage.

The thought has naturally arisen, then, that birth rates could be further reduced in industrial countries (to the point where, on the average, they match the low death rates and the population does not grow) and that they could be drastically reduced in the underdeveloped countries (to begin to catch up with the spectacular declines in mortality).

This solution, however, encounters opposition from those who cling to the rules and sentiments that prevailed when death rates were high. At that time—say, during the Middle Ages in Europe—the problem was not too many babies but too few, because, the death rate being high,

---

[21] Warren W. Eason, "The Soviet Population Today," *Foreign Affairs,* Vol. 37 (July, 1959), pp. 600-02.

TABLE 7

Historical Changes in Natural Increase of Advanced European Countries

Year	Birth Rate	Death Rate	Natural Increase Rate
1731-49	31.9	28.9	3.0
1750-99	32.6	26.9	5.7
1800-49	31.5	22.5	9.0
1850-99	31.5	18.9	12.6
1900-49	21.0	12.5	8.5

Sources: The average is for three countries—Denmark, Norway, and Sweden—until 1841; after that the average is for four countries, England and Wales being added. Computed from data in H. Gille, "Demographic History of the Northern European Countries in the Eighteenth Century," *Population Studies,* Vol. 3 (June, 1949), p. 63; *Demographic Yearbook, 1953* and *1954* (New York: United Nations, 1954, 1955); *Statistik Aarbog 1922* and *1954* (Denmark); the Registrar General's *Statistical Review of England and Wales, 1941* and *1950.*

a prolific rate of reproduction was required merely to replace the population. The modern fall in the death rate, which has more than doubled the average lifetime, eliminated the need for prolific reproduction but did not immediately alter the old religious and moral rules supporting it. Eventually, in Western countries, individual couples took matters in their own hands, using contraception and abortion to reduce their offspring. Although all religious groups opposed such practices at first, some of them—e.g., Methodists, Lutherans, Presbyterians, Episcopalians, Reformed Jews—changed their views to conform to the changed conditions, holding that the limitation and spacing of births are morally obligatory. The Roman Catholic Church, perhaps because of its celibate clergy, which can be expected to take a negative attitude toward sexual enjoyment, remained more strongly opposed to birth control; but when the notion of the "safe period" was announced in the early 1930's (coincident with the onset of the great economic depression), the Catholic clergy declared this method to be morally acceptable under certain circumstances and thus left itself opposed only to what it called "artificial" methods. Some Protestant sects and Orthodox Judaism have remained opposed to birth control, but not with the vehemence or influence that characterized the Catholic attack on "artificial" methods. In the 1960's, however, with the continued acceleration of world population growth and with growing interest in family planning, public opinion strongly favored birth control. The Gallup Poll reported in June, 1963, that eight out of every ten persons interviewed in the United States favored giving birth control information *to anyone who wants it,* and 53 percent of the Catholics interviewed took this advanced position. A year and a half later, in early 1965, the Gallup Poll found that 78 percent of the Catholics held this view.[22] No wonder the Ecumenical Council in 1965 debated this matter at long length, looking toward a modification of the clergy's traditional stand.

It seems likely, if civilization continues, that birth control will eventually become an established practice everywhere in the world. There is no guarantee, however, that it will come soon enough or be used thoroughly enough to solve the worsening problems of runaway population growth. What is being proposed as a demographic solution, therefore, is not a passive waiting for contraceptive practice to spread, but a deliberate attempt to speed its diffusion. Otherwise, it is feared, the interim population growth will be so enormous as to interfere with economic development and civilized progress. Also, there are reasons for family planning that are independent of the question of population growth. The proper spacing and limitation of births are held to be good for the health and welfare of both parents and children and to be advantageous for the education and employment of youth. The proponents of family planning, therefore, wish to have efficient contraceptive methods and materials made available as soon as possible to all people, in lower as well as in upper classes and in agrarian as well as in industrial countries. They believe that in peasant countries the governments can play a crucial role in speeding this availability, and that international aid should be expended not just to reduce deaths and finance economic projects, but also to reduce births. Only in this way, the proponents of family planning say, can the heavy burdens of functionless fertility among the poorer peoples of the world be reduced.

Of course, if one maintains the view that there is no population problem, then no demographic amelioration of such problems can be admitted. For instance, at the 1947 meeting of the United Nations Population Commission, the Ukrainian representative, Vasil Rjabichko, stated: "We consider as barbarous all propositions formulated in this commission in favor of the limitation of marriages or the limitation

---

[22] The Poll results are cited and discussed in *National Catholic Reporter* (December 2, 1964), p. 10. For history and discussion of Roman Catholic attitudes, see Alvah W. Sulloway, *Birth Control and Catholic Doctrine* (Boston: Beacon Press, 1959); John P. Murphy and John D. Laux, *The Rhythm Way to Family Happiness* (Ithaca, N. Y.: Practical Publishers, 1955); Kingsley Davis and Judith Blake, "Birth Control and Public Policy," *Commentary*, Vol. 29 (February, 1960), pp. 115-21; John T. Noonan, Jr., *Contraception* (Cambridge, Mass.: Harvard University Press, 1965).

of births within marriage." [23] This view was softened by later Soviet writers. In 1965, V. E. Ovsienko, head of statistics at the Moscow Institute of Economics and Statistics, said:

> Of course, population growth raises before Governments additional demands of ensuring food, footwear, housing, schools, health facilities, employment, etc. . . . which brings about additional difficulties. [But] we feel that it is not the size of the population that should be brought in line with the economy but on the contrary, economy, the level of production, should be brought in line with the population size. . . .[24]

Meanwhile, the governments of underdeveloped countries are not waiting for the theoreticians in Moscow or the Vatican to decide whether birth limitation is correct or not. Faced with the problems of poverty, human crowding, and unprecedented population growth, they are forging new and imaginative policies aimed at reducing the birth date. We shall examine these policies in a moment.

INTERNATIONAL MIGRATION AS A SOLUTION. Apparently because migration is not a morally tabooed topic, as is birth control in some circles, it is often set forth as a preferred solution to population problems. Obviously, if one is thinking of the world's population as a whole, migration offers no help. It is at best a local aid, and in some cases—for example, Puerto Rico since World War II, Ireland after the famine of the 1840's, Palestine at the creation of the Israeli state, and Norway, Sweden, and Switzerland in the latter nineteenth century—it can bring substantial relief from population pressure. But such local relief is always temporary unless accompanied by a decline in the birth rate. Thus, China sent out millions of emigrants over the world, as did India, with no lessening of population growth, because the gap left by migration was quickly filled by a continuation of the same high birth rate. In fact, what emigration seems to do in many cases is to postpone the reduction of the birth rate. At the same time, it is exceedingly costly, because the migrants, mainly in the young working ages, have been reared and educated, if educated at all, at the expense of the sending country and are then lost to the labor force. This effect is compensated for to some extent, but usually not sufficiently, by remittances received from emigrants. Sometimes it is the more skilled people who leave, thus depriving the sending country of human resources for which it has paid.

---

[23] Cited by Alfred Sauvy, *De Malthus à Mao Tsé-Toung* (Paris: Denoël, 1958), p. 257.

[24] "Influence of Social and Demographic Factors on Demographic Characteristics," World Population Conference, Belgrade, 1965.

Migration can also have disadvantages from the standpoint of the receiving country. Unless the migrants are very similar in culture to the people whose country they enter, they are not assimilated. Thus, the Irish in the United States have kept their own religion by going to parochial schools where this religion is reinforced, marrying among their own co-religionists, advocating laws for the entire community based on their own religious principles, etc. The Indians in South Africa, Malaya, Fiji, and Burma have remained a separate community, as have the Chinese in Indonesia, Malaya, Borneo, Thailand, and many other places where they have gone. When assimilation does not occur, friction inevitably develops between the immigrant minority or majority and the rest of the population. Some observers therefore maintain that migration often creates far greater problems than it solves. This would seem to be the case with the Arab refugees from territory now constituting Israel, with the Chinese in Indonesia, with the Indians in Burma, with the West Indian and West African Negroes in Britain. In time of war or international tension, unassimilated bodies of immigrants—e.g., the Japanese and Germans in Brazil, the Turkish Moslems in Communist Bulgaria, the French in Algeria, the Tamils in Ceylon—are sometimes more loyal to a country other than the local one, or else are feared to be. Furthermore, various groups in a country are economically injured, or feel injured, by immigration. Employers often want immigrants for precisely the same reason that labor unions do not want them—their cheap labor. Religious groups do not want immigrants who have sinful customs, and political groups do not want those of opposite political persuasion. A democratic country is hardly likely to welcome Communists or fascists as immigrants, and vice versa.[25]

There is little wonder, then, that each nation jealously guards its right to determine whom it will admit and whom it will exclude. Some nations, such as Japan and Russia, have been extremely exclusionist in policy, whereas others such as the United States and Australia have been extremely liberal; but in the last analysis the past record of migration, whereby whole continents were conquered by people from overseas, is not likely to be repeated. The very fact that the fastest

---

[25] For a skeptical but penetrating analysis of migration as a solution of population problems, see William Petersen, *Planned Migration* (Berkeley: University of California Press, 1955). A debunking work published earlier is W. D. Forsyth, *The Myth of Open Spaces* (Melbourne: Melbourne University Press, 1942). For a less critical analysis, see Julius Isaac, *Economics of Migration* (New York: Oxford University Press, 1947); J. A. G. Griffith *et al., Coloured Immigrants in Britain* (London: Oxford University Press, 1960).

growth of population is now occurring in the poorer rather than the wealthier lands indicates the immensity of the migration that would have to take place to make a dent on regional problems. The nonindustrial countries contain about three-fourths of the world's people. Their rate of growth, as projected by the United Nations, is such that they will add approximately one billion to their population by 1980, or an average of 63 million per year. Merely to relieve these areas of their natural increase would therefore require a volume of migration which, *in a single year,* would exceed the total intercontinental migration estimated for the world *during the 83 years* from 1846 to 1932.[26] In other words, the volume of migration would have to be some 80 times what it was during the heyday of international migration in the nineteenth and early twentieth centuries. It seems inconceivable that the countries to which migrants would be attracted will admit such an enormous influx, or that the ships and money for it could be found in any case.

As for interplanetary travel, there are several moot questions: Can human beings be landed alive on another sphere? If so, is there any heavenly body that would be both accessible and livable? And will anybody want to go there? If not, how would the potential interplanetary migrants (victims) be chosen? Assuming that the answers to all these questions were favorable, there would still be the question of costs. At present, merely to remove the earth's natural increase, approximately 250,000 persons would have to be shot into space *each day.* The economic problem would obviously be staggering. It is expensive to move people even from one country to another on *this* globe. If we assume that the cost of sending one person into space could be reduced to one million dollars, the cost *per day* would be, under present conditions, 250 billion dollars. This is many times the daily value of the total world's production. Of course, the cost might eventually be brought down. In 40 years, say, it might be cut in half —down to $500,000 per person; but by that time, while we were waiting for interplanetary travel, the population would have doubled, so that the daily cost of getting rid of the world's natural increase would be the same—250 billion dollars. The striking thing about this solution of the world's population problem is not its impracticality, but why anyone should feel compelled to suggest it at all.

ECONOMIC DEVELOPMENT AS A SOLUTION. The Ukrainian representa-

---

[26] A. M. Carr-Saunders, *World Population* (Oxford: Clarendon Press, 1936), p. 49, estimates the total intercontinental *em*igration during 1846-1932 at 53.45 million, and the total *im*migration during 1821-1932 at 59.19 million.

tive, in a statement already cited, said, "Overpopulation is nothing but the fruit of capitalism; with an adequate social regime, it is possible to face any growth of population. It is the economy that must be adapted to the population, not the reverse." [27] This statement has been echoed time and again. In 1959, for example, the Roman Catholic bishops of the United States issued a statement in which they declared:

> United States Catholics do not wish to ignore or minimize the problem of population pressure, but they do deplore the studious omission of adequate reference to the role of modern agriculture in food production. The "population explosion" alarmists do not place in proper focus the idea of increasing the acreage yield to meet the food demands of an increasing population. . . . It seems never to dawn on them that in a chronic condition where we have more people than food, the logical answer would be, not to decrease the number of people but to increase the food supply which is almost unlimited in potential. [28]

At first, these statements may seem plausible. But let us ask again, what is the problem? Apparently the problem is poverty—a low level of living. Now, if the sole solution proposed is economic development, then we have to ask, once again, what "economic development" is. It is a *rise* in the level of living—that is, a movement away from poverty. By definition, obviously, to the extent that we have economic development we will not have poverty. But this is merely a play on words, not an intelligent proposal for solving a problem. It is like telling a man who has pneumonia that the remedy is simple, what he needs to do is get rid of the pneumonia. The solution for poverty is economic development, that is, getting rid of poverty.

The question still remains, how to get economic development (i.e., release from poverty). What the demographers and many economists are proposing is that, along with specific economic measures such as the use of international funds and domestic savings for the financing of factories, highways, research laboratories, irrigation schemes, public health programs, etc., attention also should be given to bringing down the birth rate and thus relieving the mounting pressure for consumer goods and the mounting costs of schooling and other immediate services for children. In other words, the *demographic* measure is proposed as an aid to, not a substitute for, economic development. It is like saying that the pneumonia patient should have both medicine and rest.

---

[27] Cited in Sauvy, *De Malthus à Mao Tsé-Toung*, p. 257.
[28] From the text of the statement appearing in *The New York Times*, November 25, 1959.

He might be able to recover with no rest, or with no medicine, but his chances are fewer.

The conception of economic development reflected in the statement by the Roman Catholic bishops appears to be limited to agriculture and reflects the old "food-supply" view of the population problem. The truth is that the people of the world are not, and never have been, satisfied with simply enough to eat. They want education, recreation, freedom, security, social position, national recognition, and a hundred other things over and beyond what they eat and wear. In other words, they want genuine economic development in the sense of more goods and services *per person*, not more goods and services simply for more persons at the same old subsistence level. It is easier to achieve a rise in per capita income if the number of persons is not doubling every 20 to 30 years. As mentioned already, the Catholic clergy has been reexamining its position since the bishops' statement.

SCIENCE AS THE SOLUTION. The notion that science can be made to take care of any population growth has already been dealt with. All that need be added is that this idea is usually held by those who think in "food-supply" terms. Because of this, their reasoning is paradoxical. If it be assumed that science is to support an ever larger population, then, to an increasing degree, that population cannot be at the subsistence level. The reason is that science is not maintained and advanced by people living at a subsistence level, but only by people having the means to acquire advanced education and technical skills, to support research laboratories and research personnel, to finance libraries and technical journals, and to reward scientific and academic achievement. A really large world population can therefore be supported only at a very high, not at a subsistence, standard of living. In view of the present poverty in much of the world, the burden of proof is on those who believe that science will soon provide even an adequate food supply, much less an adequate level of living for the nurturing of scientific work. The idea naturally comes to an observer, therefore, that the application of science is out of balance today. It is being applied with remarkable success to the control of deaths. It can also be applied, and with equal success (even at far less cost), to the control of births. If this is done, population pressure will be removed as a major obstacle to scientific development.

National Population Policies

The assumption that skyrocketing population growth will not hinder economic development and other goals is so dubious that many governments have abandoned it. Instead, they are striving to bring fertility control to their people in order to insure and hasten material progress.

The most impressive antinatalist policy in the world has been that of Japan. After World War II, that nation, whose total territory is no bigger than Montana, felt itself to be in a population crisis. The population had risen from 55 million in 1920 to 76 million in 1946. By 1948, the birth rate was 34, the death rate 12, and the resulting population growth enough to double the population every 32 years. In that year the Diet passed a law, supported by the five major political parties, legalizing abortions and sterilizations and setting up birth-control centers throughout the country. Subsequent liberalization of that law was accompanied by a semiofficial nationwide propaganda campaign for family planning, by the formation of a Population Problem Council under the Japanese Cabinet, and by the emergence of private family-planning associations and publications. Emphasis was placed on contraception, with more than 800 government-subsidized health centers and with some 30,000 birth-control guidance officers. There was an amazing drop in the Japanese birth rate. In 1957, the crude birth rate, 17.2, was only half as high as it had been in 1948. Yet the crude rate was held up by an age structure in which there was a high proportion of young adults. After 1958, the age-specific fertility rates were so low that, if they continued indefinitely, and given the current age-specific mortality, the Japanese population would eventually start to decline.[29]

As yet no underdeveloped country has pursued such a vigorous population-control policy, but many have either inaugurated or planned comprehensive measures to achieve this effect. India has long been a leader in this movement. Nehru and his Congress Party held that avoidance of excessive population growth would help promote the social and economic welfare of India's then 350 million people. India's first Five-Year Plan allotted a budget for family planning under the Minister of Health, and each subsequent plan has enlarged the budget. In addition to the central government program, various Indian states have had their own programs, in some cases stressing sterilization as well as contraception. Much government-sponsored and private research has been undertaken on public attitudes, demographic behavior, and on the improvement of contraceptives; many thousands

---

[29] See Yoshio Koya, *Pioneering in Family Planning* (New York: Population Council; Tokyo: Japan Medical Publishers, 1963). Irene B. Taeuber, *The Population of Japan* (Princeton, N. J.: Princeton University Press, 1958), Chapters 13 and 17.

of birth-control clinics have been opened, and sterilization camps have been maintained in some states.[30]

Similarly, the governments of Puerto Rico, Pakistan, Taiwan, Barbados, Korea, and Poland have pursued antinatalist policies, and commissions in Egypt, Mauritius, Turkey, Tunisia, and other countries have recommended such policies. It should not be assumed, however, that government policies designed to restrain population growth are, or will be, automatically successful. In the case of Japan, it can be argued that the birth rate would have dropped even without the government policy, although probably not so fast: age-specific fertility had been declining ever since about 1920; some of the factors in the decline from 1920 to 1957 were not a result of government policy— for instance, a sharp rise in the age at marriage; and the measure most stressed by the government, contraception, was less responsible for the drop in the birth rate than were abortions.

The acid test of family-planning policy lies not in highly urbanized and industrialized countries, like Japan, but in countries that are trying to reduce fertility in advance of industrial and social modernization. In these countries, where the problem is how to alter the circumstances of life for people in such a way as to motivate them to have few children, there has been a tendency to think that the sole important consideration is an efficient and cheap contraceptive—the birth-control pill, the intra-uterine coil, the reversible vasectomy; however, even the best instrument will not be used unless people *want* to use it. Surveys around the world have shown that women do not want big families, and certainly not as many children as "nature" can send them. On the other hand, they want about three or four children on the average—more than just enough to replace the population. With the low death rates now prevailing in even the backward nations, an average of three or four children per couple will yield substantial population growth. Unless the family structure and economic conditions are altered in ways that will motivate people to have fewer children, rapid population growth will not be stopped. In the past, social modernization has tended to introduce new conditions that motivated fertility control, although usually not enough to stop population growth. Now, if fertility control is to precede and facilitate social modernization, government population policy must include comprehensive social and economic measures that alter the old system

---

[30] See the serial publication, *Studies in Family Planning*, issued by the Population Council. This source describes population-control programs, both actual and planned, around the world. See also an issue of *Law and Contemporary Problems*, Vol. 25 (Summer, 1960), devoted to "Population Control."

in specific and relevant ways. This is necessarily difficult, because it would alter what people, including statesmen, consider right and proper. For instance, a rapid decline in fertility would probably follow if women were systematically taken out of the home and put into the labor force; if education for women included instruction in birth control, and preparation for a lifelong career; if small families were given preference in housing and schooling; if the age at marriage were drastically raised; and if abortions were legalized and sterilization rewarded. Yet one or more of these measures would offend the sentiments of all but the most advanced countries. These sentiments were formed, it must be remembered, in times when the problem was how to have enough births to replace the population, and one cannot expect, therefore, that government population policies will have spectacular success. But even if they have a little success, they will be worth the effort, according to the judgment of most experts.[31]

Even if birth rates around the world are reduced, the question still remains as to whether they will be reduced enough to match the low mortality. If so, they will solve one problem (rapid population growth and excessive child-dependency) while creating another, for by greatly altering the age structure in favor of older persons they enormously expand the old-age-dependency problem. Already, in countries where the birth rate has long been rather low, the population has become top-heavy with oldsters. France, for example, has 36 persons aged 60 or over for each hundred aged 20-59, as contrasted to 14 in Costa Rica and 12 in Ceylon (see Table 3). In the future, as life expectancy is continually lengthened, a rate of reproduction low enough just to replace the population will yield an even higher proportion of the elderly. For example, if life expectancy climbs to 83, there will be 60 oldsters for each hundred adults of working age. The result of this aging of the population is to increase medical and welfare costs, to lower the efficiency of the labor force, to reduce technical and economic innovation, and to make life more orderly perhaps but also more somber and boring.

---

[31] For an interpretation of the Japanese case, see Kingsley Davis, "The Theory of Change and Response in Modern Demographic History," *Population Index*, Vol. 29 (October, 1963), pp. 345-66. For an analysis of dilemmas in population policy, see Judith Blake, "Demographic Science and the Redirection of Population Policy," *Journal of Chronic Diseases*, Vol. 18 (1966), pp. 1181-1200; papers in "Population Control," *Law and Contemporary Problems;* Judith Blake, *Family Structure in Jamaica: The Social Context of Reproduction* (New York: Free Press, 1961); Reuben Hill *et al., The Family and Population Control* (Chapel Hill, N. C.: University of North Carolina Press, 1959).

Conclusion

In the demographic realm one is struck by the human tendency to create new social problems by solving old ones. Throughout human history until only yesterday, life has been tragically short. Then, by using science and ingenuity, a remarkable lengthening of the average lifetime was achieved. As this achievement has spread, however, it has created an unanticipated problem of formidable dimensions—the problem of extremely rapid and massive population growth and child-dependency. The humane way out of this difficulty is doubtless to reduce the birth rate. Yet the old moral and religious injunctions that once supported a high fertility tend to persist, so that this solution cannot be adopted without bitter debate and struggle. Furthermore, a lowering of the birth rate so drastic that it would match the extremely low mortality of the present and future would itself create problems, notably the excessive aging of the population.

When presented with dilemmas of this sort, human societies usually do not seize upon any single solution, but muddle through in several directions at once. In the case of population, we must be prepared for the possibility that death rates may rise suddenly and halt the long-run growth trend. We must expect more discussion of birth control and more policies designed to lower birth rates. We must anticipate the possibility that wars will be fought for space and for raw materials, with surplus populations fed recklessly into the deadliest battles ever known. We must look forward to new institutional arrangements adjusted to demographic conditions never before experienced by human society. The prospects ahead do not suggest tranquil progress, but then progress has never been tranquil.

9

Race and Ethnic Relations

by Arnold M. Rose

THE PROBLEMS TO BE CONSIDERED IN THIS CHAPTER ARE THOSE OF THE relationships between "dominant" and "minority" groups in a given society. While such problems are found in many, although not all, societies, this chapter will concentrate on those in the United States.

Nature and Range of the Problem

Definition and History of Minorities

The term "national minorities" had its origin in Europe and was used to describe the particular social position of some people in relation to the rest of the population. In Europe, people with a certain common cultural background frequently shared an ancient attachment to a given piece of land. These people were known as a nationality group, and the land they occupied bore their name. But in the course of many wars, political trades, and migrations, small groups of people belonging to one nationality group frequently found themselves within the political boundaries of a nation where another nationality group was in the majority. As modern political boundaries replaced historical ones, the territories covered by political nations soon ceased to be exactly the same as the territories inhabited by the historical nationality groups.[1] Some nationality groups would occupy only small areas within a national boundary; others would be dispersed by residence and place of occupation throughout the territory of another, larger nationality group. Since the modern conception of a political

---

[1] Failure to understand this point led President Woodrow Wilson to proclaim the ideal of "self-determination for nationalities." Since political self-determination for one nationality was incompatible with political self-determination for other nationalities, as well as being incompatible with economic and military needs, the statement led to endless friction.

nation included a belief that it was to serve the interests of a particular nationality, the smaller groups within the physical boundaries of a nation became known as minorities. Most nations had laws to establish the political conditions of existence of their minorities: sometimes the minorities were enjoined to live within a certain area, sometimes they were restricted to certain occupations, sometimes they sent their own group representatives to the national parliament instead of voting as individuals, and so forth. In nearly all countries, they were regarded as a group apart.[2] For example, a Slovak living in the Austro-Hungarian Empire would never be regarded as an Austrian or a Hungarian, even though he were a subject of the emperor, and a Ruthenian would never be regarded as a Pole, even though he were a citizen of the Polish Republic. Each person was a member of a nationality group determined by his ancestry, not by the country within whose borders he happened to dwell. If his nationality group was dominant in the political control of a nation, he was a member of a majority group. If his nationality group was not dominant, he was a member of a minority group, and he had a different status determined both by law and by custom.

The United States grew up with a different political ideology. There was no conception that a single historical nationality was to be the politically dominant group in this country. It was expected that people of various nationalities and religious faiths would migrate to this country and form a new nationality called American. As a matter of fact, after about 1830 no one nationality group from Europe had either a political or numerical dominance in the population. By numerical count, a large number of people of German or of English background would be found in this country, but even they would not form a majority. Since the United States has a democratic form of government, and since few groups are denied access to the ballot box, no one group has political control. Nor are there special laws to govern the political status of each of the nationality groups. In other words, there are no "national minorities"—in the European sense of the term—in the United States.

Rather, the term "minority groups" [3] has come to be applied to those groups in the United States who face certain handicaps, who are sub-

---

[2] After World War I, a body of international law came into existence in order to protect the national minorities within the boundaries of both the defeated nations and the newly created nations.

[3] According to the best information, the term "minority group"—as distinguished from "national minority"—was introduced into sociology by Donald Young, in his *American Minority Peoples* (New York: Harper, 1932).

ject to discrimination, and who are objects of prejudice from most other people. There is no one "majority group" with a distinctive history and a special claim to the land.[4] Any numerical majority would consist of a heterogeneous mixture of historical nationalities, with few intergroup attitudes in common except an antagonism toward a particular minority group. Many of the people who have a certain nationality background from Europe and who today are not the objects of any discrimination as a group—the Germans or the Swedes, for example—were once minority groups in this country. They were once looked down on, and they once felt themselves to be a group discriminated against. But in the course of time, these groups were no longer regarded as minority groups, and they no longer tended to think of themselves as such. They were no longer Germans or Swedes but were now "Americans." Being a member of a minority group in the United States, then, is a function of the state of mind of the general population and of the person himself rather than a function only of his ancestry. Some groups are allowed and encouraged to merge their group distinctiveness and identity into the general body of "Americans," but certain other groups—the Negroes, for instance—are not. The former are the "majority"; the latter are the minorities. This does not mean that members of assimilating groups in the majority completely lose all their memories of ancestry; they may pass along to succeeding generations selected aspects of traditional culture—often of a ceremonial nature; at the very least, they pass along an awareness of their ancestral identity.

Composition of Minorities

Minority groups today can be objectively distinguished by one or more of four different characteristics. These are race, nationality, religion, and language.[5] A minority group in the United States is thus not of the white race, or not of American nationality, or not of the Protestant Christian religious faith, or does not use primarily the English language. The traits just mentioned characterize the dominant "majority group" when considered on grounds of race, religion, nationality, or language alone. By no means are all groups distinguishable by these characteristics to be considered as minority groups.

---

[4] Closest to such a group—on the basis of historical attachment to the land—would be the American Indians. But the Indians are relatively very few in number, and they are the objects of discrimination from the dominant "majority."

[5] Some writers consider sex to be a fifth characteristic distinguishing a minority group. But the problem of women's status has such different dimensions that it had best be considered in another context.

During most of the eighteenth and nineteenth centuries, Jews were not a religious minority group in this country.[6] At the present time, Americans of Irish descent are no longer a nationality minority, although they once were. A group is a minority group if it is the object of prejudice and discrimination from the dominant groups and if the members think of themselves as a minority. It is not a minority *because* its members have a distinctive racial or nationality background or *because* its members adopt a certain religion or language, although minority status in the United States is attached to at least one of these four characteristics.

Minority Groups in the United States

Race is a biological category; the people of a given race have certain inherited physical features that tend to distinguish them from any other race. There is variation within the race, and there is overlap in regard to some of the specific features among the races, but a certain combination of physical features on the average distinguishes one race from another. These unique, inherited features have resulted from thousands of years of endogamy, so that a racial group has a common and distinguishable ancestry. Among the racial minorities in the United States are the Negroes, the Chinese, the Japanese, the Filipinos, and the American Indians. These groups are not pure biological races, since many people in each of them have some Caucasoid, that is, "white," ancestry. Also, the dominant white race in the United States has a certain proportion of people with some Negroid or Mongoloid ancestry. It is not strictly on biological grounds, therefore, that a person is classified as belonging to a racial minority. For example, a person will be called Negro, even though he has only one grandparent who was Negro, and his other grandparents were white. A Negro is defined in the United States as any person who has any known Negroid ancestry.[7]

The nationality groups in the United States are mostly from Europe, although Americans generally consider some of the peoples from Asia

---

[6] Jewish immigrants might have been temporary minority groups, but then it was on the basis of their nationality background, rather than their religious affiliation. There was a period in which German Jews were a minority group, then Jews from Eastern Europe, but not all identifiable Jews.

[7] Southern state laws define "Negro" with fictitious precision—as having one-fourth or one-eighth Negro ancestry—but in practice the law-enforcement officials treat as Negro anyone with any known Negro ancestry. In other countries—Brazil, for example—mixed bloods are defined as whites, while in South Africa, the mixed population is placed in a third category, distinguished from both "natives" and "Europeans."

Minor as nationality groups also. They are all predominantly of the white race, although there has been a significant admixture of Negro ancestry in some of the people from Spain and Sicily, and there is some Mongoloid ancestry among some of the Russians. While the nationality groups have a distinctive common ancestry, their separation from one another does not extend back into history for the tens of thousands of years necessary to differentiate racial groups. The nationality groups, as we have already suggested, are characterized mainly by a distinctive culture and a sense that they are a distinctive people with a distinctive history. Since the various peoples of Europe and Asia Minor have had a good deal of cultural contact, at least over the past 2000 years, they have many culture traits in common. It is their unique culture traits to which most attention is paid, however. These range from food preferences to the expected pattern of mutual obligations within the family. Usually a distinctive language is also associated with a given nationality, but occasionally we may find two or more nationalities using the same language. (The Germans and Austrians, for example, both use the German language.) Most immigrants gradually learn to speak English, and their children grow up speaking two languages with facility. In other respects, too, immigrants of the second generation are part of both cultures—the minority culture of their ancestors and the dominant culture of the United States. By the third and subsequent generations, the language and cultural patterns tend to be predominantly those of the dominant group. Since there are no permanent physical features associated with their minority status, the third and subsequent generations among the nationality minorities are usually no longer considered members of a minority group.[8]

There are some major exceptions to this pattern. Some members of the various nationality minorities live and work in isolated rural areas. Out of contact with the "dominant Americans," and therefore not faced with the necessity of adopting a second set of cultural practices and values, they maintain the ways of their ancestors for generation after generation. Such is the situation, for example, among many of the German and Scandinavian groups that live in Wisconsin, Minnesota, and the Dakotas. Although they may be third generation Americans and exercise fully the privileges of citizenship, they speak the language of their grandparents or great-grandparents and maintain a cultural

---

[8] An excellent study of present-day identifications of nationality minorities in New York City is Nathan Glazer and Daniel P. Moynihan, *Beyond the Melting Pot* (Cambridge, Mass.: M.I.T. Press, 1963). For a summary of what is known about American assimilation, see Milton M. Gordon, *Assimilation in American Life* (New York: Oxford University Press, 1964).

life not greatly different in some respects from that found in Germany or Sweden some 75 years ago. These groups are minorities, not so much by virtue of discrimination and prejudice (although some seem to feel hostility from other minority nationalities living not far away), but by virtue of their physical isolation and the consequent lack of opportunity to adapt to dominant American culture patterns and of pressure on them to do so. A new type of nationality minority is being created by political persecution in the Communist countries; the best example are the Cubans, concentrated mainly in south Florida and New York City, who plan to return to their home country after an expected future political revolution there.

Similar to the nationality minorities are the language minorities. They can be differentiated from the former mainly by the fact that they are not composed of recent immigrants. They are distinguished by their retaining a language other than English over many generations. They also tend to have other distinctive culture traits. One of the largest of these groups is the so-called Hispano group, concentrated in New Mexico and southern Colorado. These are Spanish-speaking people who did not migrate from Spain to the United States in recent generations. Most of their ancestors were instead incorporated into this country after the United States defeated Mexico in the war of 1846-1848. They are similar to some of the European national minorities in that the political jurisdiction over the land they occupied changed, whereas their nationality did not. Their isolation in the sparsely populated Southwest has allowed them to maintain their traditional uniqueness. Although subjected to a certain amount of discrimination when they come in contact with a large number of "Anglos" (as English-speaking Americans are known to them), their isolation prevents most of them from suffering legal or political disabilities. Most of them are poor, but their poverty stems from the sparse soil on which they choose to live, rather than because of discrimination from the outside. Except for their retention of the Spanish language and some archaic Spanish-Mexican folkways, their cultural uniqueness and their backwardness are reminiscent of the hillbillies of English or Scottish descent who live in the mountain regions of Kentucky and Tennessee.

The religious minorities in the United States include the Jews, the Eastern Orthodox, the Moslems, the members of certain small sects that have broken away from the major Protestant or Orthodox faiths (such as the Amish,[9] the Hutterites, and the Doukhobors), members of

---

[9] John A. Hostetler, *Amish Society* (Baltimore: Johns Hopkins Press, 1963).

the major Asiatic faiths, and—in certain respects—the Roman Catholics. Each of these groups has a heterogeneous composition of race, nationality, or language background. Discrimination and prejudice against them on the part of the dominant groups in the United States are associated with their religious faith and the historical background of that faith. Most of the members of these religious minorities have acquired their faith from their parents, but some have voluntarily adopted it themselves. This fact indicates that one can join a minority; it is not necesary to be born into one.

The Jews constitute a unique minority in that there is no adequate single basis for categorizing them. They have about as diverse racial, national, and linguistic characteristics and backgrounds as possible. Many—perhaps more than half—do not today adhere to the Jewish faith. The most satisfactory way of describing them is to say that, for all of them, their recent forebears are known to have believed in the Jewish religion. As we mentioned before, many ignorant or malicious persons think of Jews as a race; [10] this mistake is also made—though perhaps to a lesser extent—about other religious or nationality minorities.

Size and Distribution of Minority Groups

Table 1 lists the minorities of the United States and indicates their approximate numbers in the population. The figures are not exact: (a) The decennial census does not ask a question on religion; hence the number of Catholics and Jews is an estimate. (b) Some members of the colored minorities pass as whites, either because they deliberately do so, or because they are mistaken for whites by the census takers. (c) There is a small amount of overlap that cannot be eliminated with existing statistics (for example, there are some Chinese Catholics, and, on the other hand, not all Mexicans are Catholics and so should not be deducted completely from the Catholic total). (d) All Protestant European immigrants are excluded from the table. It is felt that they should be because they are rapidly declining in numbers, and discrimination is not being inflicted on their offspring to nearly the same extent. (e) Also excluded are the offspring of the French-Canadian immigrants, even though they maintain a rather separate social existence.

Despite these limitations, the figures are approximately correct; if anything, they underestimate the total minority population. There can

---

[10] One of the better studies of prejudice against Jews in the United States is Bruno Bettelheim and Morris Janowitz, *Social Change and Prejudice* (New York: Free Press, 1964).

TABLE 1

Size of Minority Groups in the United States, 1960-1963

	Year	Number	Percent
Roman Catholics (42,876,665)			
Exclusive of Catholics enumerated below: Mexicans, other Latin Americans, Negro Catholics, Indian Catholics, Puerto Ricans, Spanish-speaking Americans living in the Southwest	1960	38,231,210	21.32
Negroes (including 64,569 foreign-born and 703,443 Catholics)	1960	18,848,619	10.51
Jews	1963	5,365,000	2.99
Southwestern Spanish Americans	1960	3,464,999	1.93
Mexicans			
Foreign-born	1960	572,564	0.32
Native-born whites with one or both parents from Mexico	1960	1,152,274	0.64
Indians (including 129,070 Catholics)	1963	546,228	0.30
Foreign-born from Balkan nations with few Roman Catholics (Greece, Turkey, Bulgaria, Rumania)	1960	324,173	0.18
Puerto Ricans	1960	855,724	0.47
Whites from Central and South America and West Indies			
Foreign-born	1960	801,152	0.45
Native-born white with one or both parents from Latin America	1960	1,312,437	0.73
Japanese (including 109,175 foreign-born)	1960	473,170	0.26
Chinese (including 99,735 foreign-born)	1960	236,084	0.13
Mennonites	1959-61	162,135	0.09
Minor Asiatic races (including: 201,746 Filipino; 1,976 Korean; 27,538 other Asians)	1960	249,040	0.14
Sub Total (all minorities except for Catholics not excluded in first entry)		34,363,599	19.16
Total (all minorities, including Catholics)		72,594,809	40.48
Total Population of the United States	1960	179,325,657	

Sources: Felician A. Foy, ed., *1964 National Catholic Almanac* (Garden City, N. Y.: Doubleday), Negro Catholics, p. 516, Indian Catholics, p. 517; Benson Y. Landis, ed., *Year Book of American Churches for 1963*, National Council of the Churches of Christ in the USA (January, 1963), Roman Catholics, Jews, p. 248, Mennonites, p. 253; U.S. Bureau of the Census, *U.S. Census of Population: 1960, Subject Reports, Persons of Spanish Surname, Final Report* PC (2)—1B, Southwestern Spanish American, Table A, p. ix; U.S. Bureau of the Census, *U.S. Census of Population: 1960, Subject Reports, Nonwhite Population by Race, Final Report* PC (2)—1C, Population Estimates for Negroes, Indians, Japanese, Chinese, and Filipinos, Tables 1-7, pp. 1-7; U.S. Bureau of the Census, *U.S. Census of Population, Detailed Characteristics, U.S. Summary, Final Report* PC (1)—1D, Balkan Nations, Table 163, p. 367, Whites from Central and South America and West Indies, Mexicans, Table 162, p. 366, Population Estimate, Table 155, p. 349.

be no doubt that over a third of America's population consists of minority groups. Over half of the minority population consists of white Catholics. About 10 percent of the total American population is Negro. Less than 4 percent is Jewish. Catholics, Negroes, and Jews, in that order, are the largest minorities. At the other end of the scale, the Orientals are only a tiny proportion of the total American population.

Table 2 shows the geographic distribution of minorities. The Catholics are somewhat concentrated in the East and are relatively absent from the South. About half of the Negroes live in the South and are sparse in the West (although World War II brought significant numbers of them to cities on the Pacific coast). The Jews are fairly well distributed throughout the regions, except for a heavy concentration in New York City. Mexicans are disproportionately represented in the Southwest and in California. The Indians are concentrated in the Southwest and the Mountain states. The foreign-born French Canadians are mainly to be found in New England. Puerto Ricans and other Latin Americans are found mostly on the Eastern seaboard, especially in New York City. About 70 percent of the Filipinos live in California. The Japanese were overwhelmingly concentrated in the three Pacific coast states until World War II, but today more than a fourth of them are dispersed to other sections of the country. The Chinese have some concentration on the Pacific coast, but are much more scattered than the Japanese. Some minority is found in sizable numbers in every section of the country.

Some of the minorities live predominantly in urban settings; others live predominantly in small towns or rural areas. In the first category are included the Catholics, the Jews, the Chinese, the Puerto Ricans. In the second category are included the Negroes, the Indians, the French Canadians. Fairly balanced between urban and rural residence are the Japanese, the Mexicans, the Filipinos.

Race and Ethnic Relations as a Social Problem

Only during the last generation or so have relations between majority and minority groups been thought of as social problems. One reason for this is that social scientists of the majority group formerly believed that minorities were satisfied with their subordinate position. Since there was believed to be no dissatisfaction, there could be no problem. Now it is known that members of minorities do not like to be discriminated against and that, since they are hated, they hate back. It has more recently been discovered that practically all members of the majority group in the United States also believe, at least occasion-

TABLE **2**

Distribution of Selected Minority Groups in the United States by Regions: 1960-64

(Figures are percentages of the total number of each group in the United States)

Region	Indian 1960	Negro 1960	Mexican-born 1960	Japanese 1960	Chinese 1960	Latin-American-born 1960
Northeast	6.4	16.0	1.1	4.0	22.3	30.7
North Central	19.2	18.3	8.8	6.1	7.7	15.1
South	24.3	60.0	39.0	3.6	7.1	14.4
West	50.1	5.7	51.1	86.3	62.9	39.8
Total	100.0	100.0	100.0	100.0	100.0	100.0
Number of Persons (in millions)	.5	18.8	1.7	.5	.2	.8

ally and perhaps then in only a corner of their minds, that intergroup relations are not satisfactory and that they are mistreating the minorities.[11] Another reason why intergroup relations in the United States were formerly not included under the category of social problems is that conflict between groups was thought to be natural and inevitable. Since "strangers" of different races or cultures were thought to be biologically predestined to hate each other, or at least to be suspicious of each other, whenever they came together, it was assumed that nothing could be done to improve intergroup relations, and they were therefore not a problem. Today we know that intergroup hatred and conflict are socially caused, are not inevitable, and can be reduced or eliminated. Thus, intergroup relations in the United States are today considered to be a social problem.

There are many facets of minority problems, and not all of them are identical for each minority even within one country. Nor are the causes of all minority problems the same. Nevertheless certain broad categories apply to all minority problems, and they may be given preliminary definition at this point. Later sections will take them up in detail.

In the first place, there is an attitude of antagonism, sometimes called prejudice, toward all minority groups. Sometimes the specific

---

[11] This seems to have been explicitly recognized first by Myrdal: Gunnar Myrdal, with the assistance of Richard Sterner and Arnold M. Rose, *An American Dilemma* (New York: Harper, 1944), Chapters 1 and 2.

Jewish 1962	Roman Catholic 1962	Total Population 1960
66.3	41.8	24.9
13.6	30.1	28.8
8.8	13.8	30.6
11.3	14.3	15.7
100.0	100.0	100.0
5.4	43.8	179.3

Sources: Figures for Indians, Negroes, Japanese, and Chinese taken from *U.S. Census of Population: 1960, Subject Reports, Nonwhite Population by Race,* PC(2)—1C, Tables 1, 2, 3, 4. Figures for Mexican-born and Latin-American–born (officially called "Other American-Born") from *U.S. Census of Population, 1960, U.S. Summary on Ethnic Origins,* PC(1)—1C, Table 110. Figures for Jews from the *American Jewish Yearbook, 1963* (New York, 1964), Table 2, page 75. Figures for Catholics from the *1964 National Catholic Almanac* (New York, 1964), pp. 472-75.

content of the attitude is predominantly that of fear; at other times it seems to be composed mainly of disgust. Although fear and disgust are both attitudes that tend to be associated with separation and withdrawal, the main type of action that the majority takes with respect to the minority is that of maintaining its own superiority. Withdrawal is only superficial; the main effort is directed at holding the minority group down.

The deliberate holding down of the minority group is commonly called discrimination. The term "discrimination" is also used to refer to the ability to see distinctions and to express individual tastes, but that is not what is meant by discrimination in intergroup relations. Discrimination can simply be defined as the majority group's not allowing members of the minority group to have the same or equivalent opportunities as are afforded members of the majority group. Discrimination is usually considered under four general categories: in economic relations, in law, in politics, and in sociable relations. The discrimination under consideration is that which comes into operation solely because of an individual's race, language, religion, or national origin, and not because of his ability, manners, personality, wealth, or anything else.

Economic discrimination not only affects occupational opportunity and size of income, but indirectly increases the impact of discrimination in law, in politics, and in sociable relations. Included under discrimination in economic relations are not only refusal to hire and payment of lower wages, but also difficulty in securing business loans, failure in securing customers for salable goods or services, difficulty in securing an education under the same terms and of the same type available to members of the majority group, difficulty in getting into trade unions and securing advancement therein. Discrimination in education is included under economic discrimination since education is a means of economic advancement, whether directly through vocational courses or indirectly through academic courses.

Since economic position is basic to the achievement of higher cultural needs and to political power, economic discrimination may be thought of as the most important obstacle created by prejudice. Since the majority frequently gains economic advantage through discrimination in employment [12] and by paying lower wages, some scholars theorize that it is the basic reason for the entire system of discrimination. It is possible to recognize the great importance of economic discrimination in helping to maintain discrimination of other types without accepting the doctrine that economic discrimination is the only reason for the existence of the other types.

Discrimination in law takes several forms. First, the enacted law may contain provisions that single out by name a racial or religious group for inferior treatment. Since 1867, there has been no such law in any city or state in the United States or in the statutes of the federal government.[13] Moreover, it would be unconstitutional to pass such a law, since amendments to the United States Constitution forbid discrimination by law. The only partial exception is that aliens (persons with foreign citizenship) do not have all the privileges under law that citizens do, and there is probably a larger proportion of aliens among minorities than among the majority. The second type of discrimination in law occurs when governments or administrators ignore the Constitution and pass laws or issue decrees that hurt minorities. These are illegal, of course, but a long period of years may elapse before such laws or decrees can be tested in the federal courts and so be nullified. In the meantime, the law effectively discriminates. During times of war, the federal government sometimes deliberately acts in an illegal manner, knowing that the war will be over before the law or decree can be declared unconstitutional. This occurred in World War II when American citizens of Japanese descent were interned without formal

---

[12] Norval D. Glenn, "Occupational Benefits to Whites from the Subordination of Negroes," *American Sociological Review,* Vol. 28 (June, 1963), pp. 443-48.

[13] We are referring solely to American citizens. There have been laws directed at specific groups of aliens.

accusation or presentation of evidence against them.[14] States or cities have passed unconstitutional acts to test the Constitution or to show minority groups that the Constitution can be temporarily ignored, and southern states have passed "laws" to deprive Negroes of their vote. A third type of discrimination in law occurs when there is misapplication of the law by its administrators. Members of the minority may not be able to secure the protection of the law or may not be allowed to take full advantage of government services. This is the most pervasive and most frequent type of discrimination in law in the United States. It creates a condition of insecurity among members of minorities which hurts their activities in many spheres of life. For some it creates a constant threat to life and property. A fourth type of discrimination in law occurs when persons lacking legal authority take the law into their own hands. Of course, although such discrimination is not effected solely against members of minorities, it is especially significant and frequent when used against them because then it is coupled with the tendency of the regular legal authorities to wink at the illegal activities. This type occurs most frequently in the southern states, where it is usually directed against Negroes. Discrimination in law has its greatest effects on the minds of the members of the subordinated minorities, rather than on their bodies or their property. While by itself it usually does not prevent a person from getting a livelihood or enjoying the better things of life, it creates a feeling that these things will not last and that one's very existence is constantly under threat.

Discrimination in politics is frequently basic to discrimination in law, since people who cannot vote can usually be safely ignored by legislators and by administrators of the laws. If they are beaten or their property is destroyed, they frequently cannot call upon the law-enforcement agencies to stop the criminal, punish him, and prevent further depredations. Since employment by federal, state, or local government is a significant type of employment, lack of a vote also means the loss of a certain number of jobs. Since politicians exert power through their offices, and members of minorities who cannot vote also cannot place any of their own group in office, the minorities lack power and prestige. Two major types of minority people are without a vote in the United States. One is the aliens, who have come from other countries and have never become American citizens. In

---

[14] Dorothy S. Thomas and Richard S. Nishimoto, *The Spoilage* (Berkeley: University of California Press, 1946), Chapter 1.

many cases the failure to become citizens is the deliberate choice of the aliens, and—without the strong enforcement of criminal law characteristic of the United States—such aliens take a knowing risk. Aliens are visited with certain special discriminations by the law itself, such as the prohibition against their purchasing land in some states. The second major group without a vote in the United States has been the great majority of the Negro population in the South. Negroes, of course, are citizens, and the Fifteenth Amendment to the Constitution guarantees them the vote. Nevertheless most of them were disfranchised in the South. The lack of a vote for southern Negroes put them in a most precarious legal position, even when there was not a single law in any city or state that specifically discriminated against them. A Supreme Court decision in 1944, and especially federal legislation passed in 1957, 1964, and 1965, greatly diminished this discrimination, although it still exists in large parts of Mississippi, Alabama, South Carolina, and Louisiana.

Discrimination in sociable relations [15] (called, for convenience, social discrimination) would seem not to be discrimination at all by American standards. Any American can avoid associating with anyone he does not choose to associate with, and avoidance of association is not in itself discrimination. However, this is not always simple. In the first place, while Mr. A has the right to avoid associating with Mr. B, he has no right to compel Mr. C also to avoid associating with Mr. B. In a good number of cases of segregation, especially those involving housing segregation, this is what actually occurs. Similarly, an actor or entertainer may wish to perform for Negro customers as well as for white ones; yet he cannot, because the theater does not admit Negroes. A second difficulty is that certain facilities, whether publicly or privately owned, are intended for public use, and Negroes cannot gain the advantages of the facilities if they are prohibited from using them. This applies to parks, playgrounds, museums; to railroad stations, privately sponsored exhibits, concerts; and to hotels, restaurants, theaters. A Negro in such large cities with many facilities as Atlanta or New Orleans might almost as well be in an isolated rural area for all the advantages he can get from the city. The same principle applies to private colleges that refuse to admit Negroes. They are nonprofit-making and so nontaxable; their aim is to give education to those who can afford it and to those who can best use it, unless those persons

---

[15] By sociable relations we mean social contacts of any degree of duration or intimacy; it is used in distinction to economic, political, and legal relations, all of which can be considered "social relations."

happen to be Negro. It can be said that there are private and state-supported colleges for Negroes; but these are often not near the homes of Negro students or do not offer the courses that they want. While there is probably nothing illegal about privately owned segregated institutions, they are discriminatory. Publicly owned or publicly supported institutions that segregate are not only discriminatory, but also usually illegal.

There are still other facets of discrimination that are characteristic of segregation. Before World War II developed a housing shortage for whites, the typical situation in northern cities was that there were plenty of vacant dwelling units for whites, at low rents, but practically no vacant dwelling units for Negroes, and they paid high rents for the mostly inferior accommodations they did occupy. This situation had two causes: one was the heavy migration of Negroes from South to North, which had taken the place of the heavy migration of whites from Europe to America; the other was the system of restrictive covenants by which northern whites put into property deeds a prohibition against selling or renting living quarters to Negroes. The latter created a pattern of residential segregation in northern cities which, in effect, became a major deterrent to Negroes who wanted to move to these cities. The United States Constitution provides that American citizens may move around freely in this country, unless by due process of law they are adjudged to be criminal or insane. Yet residential segregation prevents Negroes from moving nearly as freely as whites can. This, coupled with the higher rents arising from restrictions on renting, constitutes a major form of discrimination. The United States Supreme Court implicitly recognized this fact when, in May, 1948, it held that restrictive covenants could not be enforced in court.

Thus segregation, which purports to rest on the individual's freedom to choose his companions, is inevitably a form of discrimination. It is not only accidentally discrimination in effect, but it is, in most cases, deliberately discrimination in intent. The proposition "separate, but equal" is practically always used as legal defense or argument by those who make little or no effort to create equal opportunities for minority groups. Social discrimination is also sometimes used as an excuse for other kinds of economic discrimination, for political disfranchisement, and for creating legal insecurity.

Minority Problems Abroad: A Résumé

While this short chapter cannot give systematic consideration to minority problems in countries other than the United States, a few very brief descriptions will be given to suggest the range of the problem:

1. THE INDIANS OF LATIN AMERICA. The Spanish and Portuguese conquerors were, with few exceptions, interested only in the wealth they could extract from the New World. They felt assured of their superiority by virtue of their religion, but it was their possession of guns and gunpowder that gave them their real superiority. In many other respects, the Indians of Mexico and Peru had a more developed culture than did their conquerors. This culture was systematically destroyed, even to the burning of the many books written by the preconquest Mexicans. Their wealth was seized, and the Indians themselves were set to work in the fields for the benefit of the whites. The whites did not hold themselves sexually aloof, and during the course of centuries, the dominant group became racially mixed. During the nineteenth century, the Latin Americans threw out their Spanish and Portuguese suzerains, but the domination of the mixed group over the Indians continues with some modifications up to the present day. The domination has mainly involved economic exploitation in an extreme form, but it also has taken the form of political exclusion and personal antagonism.

2. HINDUS AND MOSLEMS. When the British assumed control of India in the eighteenth and nineteenth centuries, they found a fairly high degree of accommodation between Hindus and Moslems, although the latter were dominant in most places. While both religions required some separation between members of the two religious groups, the British accentuated the religious separation. A movement for political separation among the Moslems was encouraged by the British, and this movement grew stronger as it became apparent the British were going to leave India. When the new nations of India and Pakistan were set up after World War II, and the British left the subcontinent, great riots broke out between the two religious groups. There was considerable violence, and millions of minority persons, in both of the new countries, were killed. The violence and discrimination were so extreme that scores of millions of persons had to move from the communities where they had always lived to the country where their own religious group was dominant. After a few years, the remaining persons in each religious minority in both countries were tolerated, although subject to some discrimination.

3. FINNS AND SWEDES. Since the Middle Ages, the country of Finland had a majority of people who spoke Finnish and a minority who spoke Swedish. While there was some concentration of the Swedish-speaking minority on Finland's West Coast, enough of them were

dispersed throughout the southern part of the country to be the basis of a problem in intergroup relations. There was a good deal of mutual discrimination, and feelings between the two groups often ran high. The Swedes tended to be merchants, while the Finns were mostly farmers; when industries began, the Swedes tended to be the entrepreneurs while the Finns were the workers. The Swedes tended to be better educated and have more access to "higher culture." Thus the conflict had a class character, with the numerical minority being in the dominant position. During most of its history, Finland was not an independent nation, but when it became independent during World War I, the Finnish government set about to equalize the position of the two language groups. With democratization of privilege, the status differences between the two groups diminished, and higher cultural opportunities and economic leadership became available to Finnish-speaking persons. The conflict is scarcely apparent today, although memories of the past situation keep it alive in the older generation.

4. APARTHEID. The Dutch who settled in South Africa in the eighteenth and nineteenth centuries quickly assumed dominance over the greater numbers of native Africans because of their greater cohesiveness and organization. A full caste system, based on racism, soon developed, and there was systematic exploitation and discrimination. When the natives developed a small educated class and began to agitate for more equal treatment, the dominant white group instead set up plans for a thoroughgoing system of segregation (*apartheid*). These plans are only in part being put into effect since absolute segregation would diminish economic exploitation, and many of the whites do not really want that. Discrimination and social segregation remain in extreme form in South Africa, and there is frequent violence, although the impact of all this on the natives is diminished by the general prosperity of the country. Tension is very high in South Africa, and unless the caste system is relaxed or complete physical separation is put into effect, there is likely to be a social explosion, especially if the country should experience a depression.

5. GREEKS AND TURKS. Turkey once had a great empire that included many minority groups, most of which formed separate communities. But when the empire broke up, and the modern national state was formed by Kemal Pasha after World War I, there were only a few minorities left within the national boundaries. One of these was the Greeks, who had the same nationality and language as the inhabitants of the nation of Greece. The hostility between Greek and Turk was centuries old, and the dominant Turks had been discriminatory against the Greeks although the latter had worked into favorable

economic positions. Local violence flared up frequently, and there were some exchanges of population between Greece and Turkey. The tension and hostility have been exacerbated in recent years by the Greek effort to take over the island of Cyprus, which has a Greek majority and a Turkish minority but had been politically controlled by Great Britain. When violent riots broke out on Cyprus, it was reflected in violence directed at the Greek minority within Turkey, and many Greeks were forced to leave that country.

Causes of the Problem

The sources of intergroup discrimination and prejudice may be placed in five categories: Power conflict, ideological conflict, racism, social structure, and individual psychology. These categories are virtually exclusive only for theoretical purposes; in any concrete situation, several causes are likely to be operating at once and in such an integrated manner that it is difficult to disentangle their respective influences. Each concrete problem of intergroup relations has its own unique historical-cultural context, and the sociologist's effort to draw some generalizations from the "seamless web" of social facts is based on theoretical conceptualizations and arbitrary distinctions, which are, however, necessary for understanding and scientific prediction. Further, in attempting to explain the nature and causes of intergroup conflict, we must use different levels of explanation that, even though they are different, have a simultaneous validity. For example, we shall explain intergroup antagonism in terms of historical development, contemporary social forces, and mechanisms of individual psychology. These are different levels of explanation, but all are operating simultaneously to "cause" a given concrete problem of intergroup relations.

In considering these causes of intergroup conflict, we shall mention their connections to the more general theories of sociology and psychology and to specific researches that analyze and measure their impact in concrete social situations. Most theories in the social sciences have not been presented in systematic fashion, and most researches fail to meet all the requirements of scientific research; hence we are restricted in our ability to present a theoretical framework and a research buttress for all our statements.

Power Conflict

Power conflict may be defined as a struggle for control of scarce values. The scarce values may be economic, in which case one group seeks domination over another in order to take its wealth or labor at less than its recognized value. The minority group may be enslaved or simply underpaid. Karl Marx is the best-known writer to explain intergroup antagonism in terms of power conflict over economic values. He observed that the English and Irish proletariat was split into hostile camps, hating one another as competitors and so coming to feel a national and religious antipathy toward one another. Believing that such conflicts are spurious in view of a basically common interest among all members of the proletariat, he also held that the antipathies were artificially nurtured by the bourgeois class.[16]

Other scarce values for which groups struggle, and for which one group seeks domination over another, include prestige, symbolic expressions of ascendancy, and sexual access. John Dollard has emphasized conflict over these values in his study of Negro-white relations in the southern United States.[17]

When there is a power conflict, the dominant group practically never seeks to exterminate the minority group: it seeks only its wealth, its labor, its according of prestige and ascendancy, or its women for sexual purposes; in other respects it leaves the minority group alone. Power conflict is rational in the sense that it involves a weighing of costs against the values gained. Slavery in ancient Greece and Rome, and in the Moslem world today, may be taken as examples of power conflict between "groups." The relationship between the ancient Roman conquerors and their conquered peoples involved not only economic exploitation; in many areas, in fact, the only gains to the Romans were those of prestige and ascendancy. This situation also obtains in some parts of some modern empires—for example, in Mussolini's conquest of Ethiopia in the late 1930's. Piracy as it has existed down through the ages in many parts of the world involved only power conflict. Power conflict is the main factor in the explanation of conflicts between the American colonists and the Indians and Negroes down to about the year 1810.

Ideological Conflict

Ideological conflict may be defined as a struggle for the supremacy or maintenance of a given way of life or belief system. In ideological

---

[16] American writers who have attempted to explain intergroup relations in Marxist terms include Carey McWilliams, *A Mask for Privilege* (Boston: Little, Brown, 1948) and Oliver C. Cox, *Caste, Class, and Race: A Study in Social Dynamics* (New York: Doubleday, 1948).

[17] John Dollard, *Caste and Class in a Southern Town* (New Haven: Yale University Press, 1937).

conflict, two groups have opposing sets of values, each of which is believed to contain the only right and good and even necessary values. Historically, most ideological group conflicts have been between organized religions. In recent centuries, the ideological conflicts have been less religious and metaphysical and more political and economic in the specific content of the values contested.

Conflict over political and economic ideologies is to be sharply distinguished from conflict for the possession of scarce political and economic values. Whereas the aim of the power type of conflict is to assume possession of the scarce values, the aim of ideological conflict is to annihilate or convert those who do not accept what the group considers to be true or necessary values; or, if victory is out of the question, the aim is to avoid annihilation or conversion. Whereas power conflict is selfishly motivated, ideological conflict is selfless and even self-sacrificing. In religious conflict, the true values are supposed to emanate from a supernatural source, and the motivation to superimpose these values on nonbelievers is considered to be service for this supernatural power. A group that denies the true God is insulting to this highest good, and therefore must be destroyed or converted.

Groups engaged in ideological conflict that is not religious in nature have substituted such forces as history or the true happiness of mankind for God. If history is believed to decree that the bourgeoisie must disappear, then the bourgeoisie must be annihilated or converted to a proletarian way of life; or if the perfect Utopia does not have a class of employers, then present employers must be convinced that they should not continue to perform their current role. Ideologies that are the source of ideological conflict invariably are absolutistic. The values and forces of God, history, or Utopia are in some way transcendent over all others.

Racism

A third major source of intergroup conflict is racism. It rests on the desire to maintain what is believed to be biological purity and caste separation. While the goal of power conflict is the seizure of scarce values and the goal of ideological conflict is annihilation or conversion of nonbelievers, the goal of racist conflict is complete separation, and the strongest demands are for the avoidance of personal contact. One group, members of which consider themselves to be a biological unit or race, takes positive steps to segregate all other groups in the society from all spheres of life where they may come in contact with the active group. The segregation is on the basis of physical distance where possible, without interference with economic exploitation; otherwise it is on the basis of symbolic separation. It is also possible for nondominant numerical minorities to have racist motives and to initiate conflict. Such minorities generally segregate themselves to keep their biological condition uncontaminated, and conflicts set in when out-groups find the self-segregating activities of the minorities a nuisance obstructing the maintenance of the functions of the society. Groups with racist beliefs regard themselves as biologically superior, and any publicity given to that belief encourages bad relations.

Racist conflict is almost entirely a modern development, since knowledge and interest about the biological composition of a population began at the end of the eighteenth century. However, there are certain weak parallels in the "chosen people" concept of the ancient Hebrews, in the ancient Greeks' concept of their distinctiveness from barbarians, and in the tendency of many societies to regard their members as the only true "people," to be distinguished from other "semianimals." But the main and true examples of racist conflict come from the United States, Germany, and South Africa, in the nineteenth and twentieth centuries.[18] A later section of this chapter will give a more extensive analysis of American racism.

Social Structure

Certain social structural factors have been found to be associated with prejudice and discrimination against minorities. In a comparative study of 40 societies, it was found that absolute monarchies showed the greatest harshness toward minorities, especially in regard to personal violence and economic exploitation.[19] The same study showed personal violence toward minorities to be associated with feudal economies, with low respect for law, and with well-defined class systems. Cultural traditions of prejudice and discrimination, while they should not be considered as causes in their own right, have carried on patterns of harshness toward minorities even when the causes which gave rise to them have disappeared.

Deliberate propaganda may originate antagonism toward minorities, or accentuate an antagonism that already exists. There was very little anti-Japanese feeling in the United States until the Hearst and other newspapers took up an anti-Japanese theme, apparently as a means

---

[18] A history of racist ideology in Europe is given in Erich Voegelin, *Die Rassenidee in der Geistesgeschichte* (Berlin: Junker und Dünnhaupt, 1933). Also see Friedrich O. Hertz, *Race and Civilization* (New York: Macmillan, 1928); Hannah Arendt, *The Origins of Totalitarianism* (New York: Harcourt, Brace & World, 1951), Chapter 2.

[19] Arnold M. Rose, "The Comparative Study of Intergroup Conflict," *Sociological Quarterly*, Vol. 1 (January, 1960), pp. 57-66.

of building circulation.[20] There was little anti-Semitism in the United States until the White Russian emigrés after World War I brought the Czar's propaganda to the United States and persuaded Henry Ford of its authenticity as fact, so that he had it disseminated at his own expense.[21] Shortly after Ford stopped this propaganda, the German Nazi government agents in the United States (in the 1930's) used many new forms of anti-Semitic propaganda, and they were successful in creating a widespread anti-Semitism.[22] The Nazi purpose was to create sympathy for its own anti-Semitic policy and to divide Americans among themselves so that they would be less likely to resist Germany when it declared war on France and England. Some propaganda is not deliberate, but effective nevertheless. A study by L. L. Thurstone and Ruth Peterson [23] indicated that certain American entertainment movies, notably the Fu Manchu films, were perpetuating anti-Chinese sentiment in the United States, and the government discouraged Hollywood from producing such films when it sought to build friendly attitudes toward China during the 1930's.

Psychological Factors of Prejudice

In recent years there have been many studies of psychological factors in prejudice. They fall into diverse theoretical frameworks, which will now be considered in sequence. Two older hypotheses concerning prejudice—stemming respectively from the Instinct school and the original Behaviorist school—have been discarded by contemporary psychologists. Some of the Instinctivists posited a natural "dislike of differences" but this was soon seen as far from universal, and its object was found to be social variation just as often as racial or ethnic differences. Some of the early Behaviorists held that unpleasant experiences with members of minority groups resulted in negative conditioning that could be called prejudice. While this no doubt occurs, it is far from general, and studies have found that prejudice may be just as strong where members of the minority are few or even nonexistent as where they are numerous and hence are available as conditioned stimuli.[24]

---

[20] Carey McWilliams, *Prejudice: Japanese-Americans, Symbol of Racial Intolerance* (Boston: Little, Brown, 1944).

[21] Oscar and Mary Handlin, *Danger in Discord* (New York: Anti-Defamation League of B'nai B'rith, 1959).

[22] Donald S. Strong, *Organized Anti-Semitism in the United States* (Washington, D. C.: American Council on Public Affairs, 1941).

[23] Ruth C. Peterson and L. L. Thurstone, *Motion Pictures and the Social Attitudes of Children* (New York: Macmillan, 1933).

[24] Eugene Hartley, *Problems in Prejudice* (New York: King's Crown Press, 1946).

The contemporary Neo-Behaviorist school is inclined to explain prejudice in terms of the theory of frustration-aggression, which has a similarity to the Freudian theory of displacement. Studies [25] have shown that when people are prevented from doing the things they want to do, they are likely to react by hitting at something or trying to make someone else unhappy. Thus frustration stimulates aggression. Now, if a person cannot hit back at the thing that makes him unhappy, he finds a substitute. When a group of people—perhaps a whole country—feels frustrated, its substitute for the object of needed aggression must be something widely available and yet weak. Minority groups serve that function and become a scapegoat for the feelings of frustration felt by a whole nation. People may feel frustrated by bad economic conditions, unemployment, low wages—conditions that especially many southerners in the United States have been subject to for a long time. Or they may feel frustrated by failure to become a leading nation of the world, as the Germans did when they lost World War I. A people in this condition is ripe for a scapegoat or substitute object of aggression. It is frequently a seeker after political power who may name the object, since such a person can thereby gain leadership and also divert attention from his own deficiencies.

Frustration explains the force behind prejudice, but it does not explain why certain of the weak available objects are chosen to be scapegoats. To explain this choice, psychologists and sociologists have provided us with another theory—the symbolic theory, based on the important fact that one thing can stand for something else in our unconscious minds. We often find ourselves liking something—a certain house or scene, for example—without knowing why we like it. If we could trace our feelings back to their origin, we would find that this newly seen house or scene "reminds" us of something important and desirable. There does not have to be any real connection at all. Our unconscious minds are always making connections for us, so that one thing will substitute for another. The question is: why are certain minority groups disliked by so many people? Obviously, they must be symbolically connected with something very important to, and in this case hated by, many people. Among the things that are important to many people are an interesting life, money, opportunities for advancement, a belief in being kind and just to others, family life and sexual satisfaction, good health, and so forth. Concerning all of these,

---

[25] E.g., John Dollard et al., *Frustration and Aggression* (New Haven: Yale University Press, 1939). Also see Gordon W. Allport, "Catharsis and the Reduction of Prejudice," *Journal of Social Issues*, Vol. 1 (August, 1945), pp. 3-10.

many people have mixed attitudes. They at once like them and also dislike them. They might be a little afraid of some of them. They might wish to rebel against them. But they cannot say so. It is not proper or even desirable from a personal standpoint to dislike these values and goals. So the dislike becomes unconscious and can be expressed only through a substitute. Minority groups become symbolic substitutes for useful and important values in the culture with which they have deep psychological and historical connections. We cannot publicly admit dislike or fear, or admit that we would like to revolt against these things, so we express the attitude against their substitutes—which are frequently minority groups. Analyses by Samuel, McLean, Halsey, Rose, Smith, and others [26] illustrate the symbolic theory, which falls into the general theoretical orientations in social psychology known as psychoanalysis and symbolic interaction.

A more characteristic psychoanalytic explanation of prejudice is the hypothesis of "the authoritarian personality." Some mental disorders can be traced to inadequacies in personality development, and prejudice may be regarded under this theory as the result of a particular kind of development. Most of the studies in support of this theory take the form of comparing groups of prejudiced and unprejudiced persons on a number of questions about personality characteristics and personality development. The items where significant differences appear are then integrated into a clinical picture of the prejudiced personality. Using this approach, Adorno, Frenkel-Brunswik, and their colleagues at the University of California,[27] for example, have discovered the typical anti-Semite to be a compulsive conformist, exhibiting anxiety at the appearance of any social deviation. He appears

[26] Sigmund Freud, *Moses and Monotheism* (New York: Knopf, 1939); Maurice Samuel, *The Great Hatred* (New York: Knopf, 1940); Carl J. Friedrich, in I. Graeber and S. Britt, eds., *Jews in a Gentile World* (New York: Macmillan, 1942), pp. 8, 18; Jacques Maritain, *A Christian Looks at the Jewish Question* (New York: Longmans, 1939), p. 41; Joshua Trachtenberg, *The Devil and the Jews* (New Haven: Yale University Press, 1943); Lewis Browne, *How Odd of God: An Introduction to the Jews* (New York: Macmillan, 1934), especially pp. 225-38; Arnold M. Rose, "Anti-Semitism's Root in City Hatred," *Commentary*, Vol. 6 (October, 1948), pp. 374-78; Margaret Halsey, *Color Blind* (New York: Simon and Schuster, 1946); Helen V. McLean, "Psychodynamic Factors in Racial Relations," *Annals of the American Academy of Political and Social Science*, Vol. 244 (March, 1946), pp. 159-66; Lillian Smith, *Killers of the Dream* (New York: Norton, 1949).

[27] T. W. Adorno *et al.*, *The Authoritarian Personality* (New York: Harper, 1950); Richard Christie and Marie Jahoda, *Studies in the Scope and Method of "The Authoritarian Personality"* (New York: Free Press, 1954). A more careful sociological study is contained in Robin M. Williams, Jr., *Stranger Next Door* (Englewood Cliffs, N. J.: Prentice-Hall, Inc., 1964), Chapter 5.

to be a person with no insight into himself, who projects his own undesired traits onto other people. He has a tendency toward stereotyped thinking and is unimaginative. He has unconscious inferiority feelings centering around a feeling of sexual inadequacy. He expresses strong parental and religious devotion, but unconsciously manifests hatred of parents and social values. He exhibits aversion against emotionalism, but unconsciously has feelings of inferiority because he cannot feel emotion. He is prone to aggressive fantasies. Such a personality development is a product of rigid and repressive childhood training. It expresses itself in many ways, but prominent among them is prejudice against minority groups.

Still another Freudian concept used to explain prejudice is that of "projection," which refers to the tendency of people, under some circumstances, to attribute to others motives they sense in themselves but do not wish to acknowledge openly. Fascists whose aim is world-dominance accuse the Jews of plotting to seize control of all countries. White southerners who hunger for an unbounded sex life accuse Negroes of being naturally immoral and "animal-like." People who are fearful because of the many uncertainties of modern existence are likely to persecute all the people they can, and that includes the minorities because they are weak. In Petegorsky's words, the fearful "persecute so that they may project upon others the fear that is gnawing at their own hearts. By creating in others terrors greater than they themselves experience, men seek to build up for themselves an illusion of security and safety." [28]

Mass Society

Having considered the various psychological theories of prejudice, we may turn to one other social factor that may help in the explanation of prejudice since it seems to activate some of the psychological mechanisms. This is the condition of the "mass society" that is partially characteristic of modern Western culture.[29] It is a state of society in which individuals have diminished communications with each other, and in which most communication is one-way from certain cen-

---

[28] David W. Petegorsky, "The Strategy of Hatred," *Antioch Review*, Vol. 1 (September, 1941), p. 377.

[29] Arnold M. Rose, *Theory and Method in the Social Sciences* (Minneapolis: University of Minnesota Press, 1954), Chapter 2. For some political implications of mass society, see the following: Arendt, *The Origins of Totalitarianism;* Franz L. Neumann, *Behemoth* (New York: Oxford University Press, 1942); and William Kornhauser, *The Politics of Mass Society* (New York: Free Press, 1959).

tral sources through the mass media. It is created by urbanization, relatively rapid mobility, and the development of the mass media which do not allow for two-way communication. Under these conditions, members of a society cannot get together to develop new meanings and values to cope with the changed situation. The consequence of the mass society for the individual is a pervasive feeling that one does not understand, or participate in the control of, the forces that shape the society. Also contributing to this sense of social alienation in the mass society is the weakening of traditional cultural values under conditions of rapid change so that the traditional ways of regarding social forces are inadequate. Consequently, there is a tendency to consider these forces as "mysterious" and to attribute their control to uncomprehended powers such as "Wall Street," "labor bosses," "international bankers," and "Jews." Jews and Catholics receive the brunt of antagonism stimulated in this way, but the general anxiety characteristic of the mass society may find its outlet in violence and prejudice directed to any minority group.

The mass society has a special set of relationships to the psychological mechanisms already considered. Many of the frustrations of modern life are associated with its mass characteristics. The relatively rapid movements of the individual, both in terms of the groups with which he is associated and in terms of his economic employment, may satisfy his wants, but they create problems for him as well. The movements are not always voluntary, but are frequently the function of impersonal economic and political forces (depressions and wars, for example) and of the rapid turnover of social groups when communication and interests are segmentalized. Even when the movements are voluntary, it is only seldom that the desired goals are achieved unattended by some losses and disappointments. Among the losses resulting from almost any movement is a loss of friends and acquaintances and, consequently, a further weakening in the possibilities for communication. Thus rapid movement—whether it be physical movement or simply a change in group affiliation—is bound to create frustration, and rapid movement is a characteristic of a mass society.

There are several ways in which a decrease or segmentalization of communication is frustrating. First, there is the loss of affection and the decrease in a sense of security in interpersonal relationships. In a society in which group affiliations are generally rapidly changing— on the job, in the neighborhood, in voluntary associations, and even in the family through divorce—the possibilities for the expression of intimate affection are reduced. Second, there is less ability to handle new problems, which arise at an increasing rate in a changing society. One of the first impulses a person has when a new problem arises is to talk it over with other people. The person who faces or sees the new problem seeks reassurance as well as ideas for coping with the problem. If the same new problem faces a large number of people, the development of a collective adjustment to it may be necessary or at least considered desirable. Insofar as communication is decreased, segmentalized, or made impersonal, these satisfactions become weakened or nonexistent. Of course, during times of collective catastrophe, the desire for communication is so great that it can be established with astonishing rapidity outside the ordinary rules. Bombs falling on a city will quickly make most people friendly toward each other, and even a minor accident on a public vehicle will establish social contact between the bodies that were only physically packed together a few minutes before. But it may be questioned whether this talking to strangers during times of crisis or stress is as satisfying as talking to friends, whose honesty, intelligence, and personality characteristics have already been gauged.

We have noted some of the frustrating effects of economic and political insecurity and of competitive striving for wealth or prestige and have seen that some studies try to tie these frustrations directly to race prejudice. A correlation can be established between the general economic status of a minority group and the average class position of the members of the majority group most antagonistic to it.[30] For example, there is a relatively greater concentration of anti-Semitism in the upper- and middle-income brackets than there is of anti-Negro prejudice, which finds its relative concentration in the lower-income brackets. Thus, competition seems to be a factor. A study by Hovland and Sears has demonstrated that lynchings in the South regularly increased when the price of cotton fell.[31]

While our major concern is to ascertain the specific character of the frustrations of modern society, we may raise the question as to whether there have been more or fewer frustrations in other societies. Ancient and medieval peoples were undoubtedly afflicted with greater hazards to life and well-being than ourselves, if we neglect the dangers of the atomic era. That famine and disease created great anxiety there

---

[30] Frank K. Westie, "Negro-White Status Differentials and Social Distance," *American Sociological Review*, Vol. 17 (October, 1952), pp. 550-58. Also see E. L. Horowitz, "Race Attitudes" in O. Klineberg, *Characteristics of the American Negro* (New York: Harper, 1944), Part 4.

[31] C. I. Hovland and R. R. Sears, "Minor Studies of Aggression: Correlation of Lynching with Economic Indices," *Journal of Psychology*, Vol. 9 (1940), pp. 301-10. This particular correlation no longer holds, as the changing culture has all but wiped out lynching.

can be no doubt. Certain natural phenomena—such as eclipses, freak storms, and so on—when interpreted in terms of superstitious beliefs, presented threats to their felt security, whereas few people are concerned with such things in our own culture. However, most other cultures had a more integrated and definite set of values, including a cosmology and metaphysics as well as an ethics, which nearly everyone accepted without question. These "explained" catastrophes and also told people how to act in regard to them. In some cultures, where catastrophes were regarded as manifestations of the deity's will, they could even be regarded as having an ultimately benign purpose. These are among the major reasons why contemporary observers of the remains of some preliterate cultures and of Oriental cultures regard them as fatalistic, even in the face of disaster. It seems likely that hazards to life and well-being are less frustrating when people are "fatalistic." In modern mass society, where fewer persons accept any philosophy or value-system unreservedly, there is less fatalism and more anxiety concerning catastrophes and new problems. This situation would seem to be more productive of psychological frustration.

Insofar as displacement is a mechanism involved in race prejudice and intergroup antagonism, it also is affected by the conditions of the modern mass society. An integrated and completely accepted philosophy and value-system would channelize the direction of displacement. The displacement of hostile impulses might be directed toward minority groups or out-groups, but again it might not—depending on the specific cultural definitions. In a mass society, where traditional philosophies and value-systems are much less able to direct displacement, hostile attitudes are likely to be displaced onto weaker groups, which become—by definition—minorities. In preliterate societies, hostility was displaced onto lambs or goats, dolls, imagined devils, or human sacrifices, as well as onto other groups, and this displacement often occurred on ceremonial occasions. In modern society, hostility is more regularly displaced onto minority groups, without benefit of ceremony.

The breakdown of complete communication within the community would seem to contribute to the displacement of hostility toward minority groups. Where people are in regular communication with each other they are less likely to pick each other for displacing hostility in any regular fashion. It should be noted that in medieval society it was the persons estranged from the rest of the community—by virtue of feeblemindedness, psychosis, or belief in their own supernatural powers—who were regarded as witches or other allies of the devil and, therefore, proper objects for the displacement of aggression. In both medieval and preliterate societies there was a good deal of hostility against out-groups—such as people in nearby areas—and these, too, were cut off from communication. In modern mass society there are all sorts of estrangements and barriers to communication within the community, and thus any group can become a minority group chosen for the displacement of hostility.

Most of what has been said about the direction of displacement could also be said about the direction of projection. Further, insofar as the motive force behind projection is divided conscience, it is more likely to occur in a mass society than in any other kind of society. Where there is a single value-system and the pressures of society on the individual are solely in terms of this one system, the individual is not likely to contain within himself differing conceptions of how to think and act. But when he does have such differing conceptions— resulting from contact with a variety of value-systems and incomplete indoctrination in any one of them—he may have an internal conflict over what is right. When this occurs, he needs to eliminate the vanquished desires and thoughts to avoid conscious guilt, and projection is a mechanism for such elimination. This hypothesis, like the others previously presented, needs testing by comparison of cultures.

The mechanism of unconscious symbolism operates largely through projection, and it also comes into use when there is ambivalence of attitude. If an object is both liked and disliked, and is also considered so important that the individual feels the need to take a conscious stand for or against it, the rejected features of the object may be projected onto something else with which it is culturally associated, and the stand opposed to the one consciously taken toward the object is taken toward its substitute. This may result in either love or hate toward the substitute or symbol. Ambivalence, which is the basis of all unconscious symbolism, is to a considerable extent the product of a society containing diverse value-systems and communication inadequate to reduce conflicts of attitudes. Our society offers its members all sorts of mental conflicts and does not provide them adequate means of resolving them. Hence, there is extensive use of the kind of symbolism we are discussing. The direction of repressed attitudes onto minority groups in a mass society has already been discussed. This shows up most clearly in the case of unconscious symbolisms. Of all the things Negroes might stand for, the thing they are most often chosen to stand for by prejudiced persons is uninhibited and passionate sexuality. Of all the things Jews might stand for, they are chosen to stand as symbols of urbanism, rational capitalism, radicalism, and pacifism. While Negroes and Jews do have some cultural connection with these things, the things are important objects of culture toward which there are ambivalent attitudes. Thus, it is to ambivalence that we must trace the use of the symbolism mechanism as a source of race prejudice.

The personality type shown in the several researches by psychologists to be high on prejudice—the type called the "authoritarian personality" by the California group—is hypothesized to be the product of rigid, overdemanding, nonaffectionate childhood experience. The pattern of child rearing is largely a function of a specific culture, as the "culture and personality" school of anthropology has demonstrated.[32] But within any given culture there are variations in child-rearing practices, and the culture itself may show trends away from or toward a more permissive and affectionate attitude toward children. The question before us is whether any of these variations and changes are associated with the characteristics of the mass society. To a considerable extent, parents and other adults who manifest affection and permissiveness toward children are those who are themselves secure and not highly frustrated. We have already seen that insecurity and frustration are partly a function of mass society. Further, the general attitude toward children is partly a result of attitudes toward alternative uses of wealth and time. Especially in an urban civilization, children are expensive to raise, and many a parent weighs the advantages of having had children against the advantages of conspicuous consumption, to the frustration of the child. Any value system in a society places a high premium on children, else the culture would cease to exist. But when values weaken, attitudes toward children may deteriorate. These are among the factors in the mass society which contribute toward the development of children into authoritarian personalities. (See Chapter 10, page 549.)

Racism and Caste in the United States

There was little evidence of racism in what is now the United States before the beginning of the nineteenth century. Although Negroes had been forcibly brought to serve white persons for the two preceding centuries, the relationship of master and servant was quite different before the development of racism than it was thereafter. A brief historical survey will provide the basis for understanding this

---

[32] For example: Abram Kardiner, *The Psychological Frontiers of Society* (New York: Columbia University Press, 1945); Ralph Linton, *The Cultural Background of Personality* (New York: Appleton, 1945); Ruth Benedict, *The Chrysanthemum and the Sword* (Boston: Houghton Mifflin, 1946).

difference and hence what racism is; it will also analyze the causes of racism in one country.[33]

It seems likely that the first Negro in the New World came with Columbus; certainly there were some Negroes among the Spanish explorers and colonists. Spain in the fifteenth and sixteenth centuries was a racial melting pot. The Moors had a significant admixture of Negro ancestry, and Negro slaves had been brought from central Africa to serve in the Christian kingdoms of late medieval Spain. At the time of the Spanish settlement of Florida, Louisiana, and the Southwest, however, Negroes were still not yet completely amalgamated with whites as they are today in Spain.

The English colonists at Jamestown, Virginia, bought their first "negars" from a ship captain in 1619—a year before the first colonists landed at Plymouth Rock. Slavery was then unknown in English law, so the Negroes were treated as indentured servants—that is, they were required to work without pay for a period of time—usually the legal maximum of seven years—to pay for their cost. Their legal and economic status was exactly that of white indentured servants who came from Britain. The latter included: (a) volunteers who wanted to get a new start in the New World but had no funds to pay for the voyage and so "contracted" themselves to a ship captain; (b) children "sold" to a ship captain by their impoverished parents; (c) debtors who were allowed to leave English jails if they would go to America as indentured servants. Negroes, on the other hand, were either (a) slaves in African lands who were bought from their original masters by English and other sea captains; or were (b) captured by raiding parties in west central Africa. In both cases, indentured servitude was a legal-economic arrangement in which the servant was released from bondage after a few years. After his release, an indentured servant, Negro as well as white, could take his place in lower-class colonial society, and sometimes rose to a position of wealth and status.

Thus, the early relationship of Negroes and whites in the colonies (mostly Virginia, where Negroes worked on the tobacco plantations and as house servants) was one in which the Negro's position was about equal to that of a lower-class white servant or ex-servant. Relations between Negro and white ex-servants were close, and there was frequent intermarriage. Still, there were some differences: Negroes had serious cultural handicaps in the English colonies, and their distinctive languages, customs, and provenience gradually distinguished

[33] The best history of this topic is John Hope Franklin, *From Slavery to Freedom* (New York: Knopf, 1956).

them from the whites. In 1661, Virginia passed the first law permitting servitude in perpetuity. This first manifestation of slavery was gradually copied by other colonies during the following three-quarters of a century. At the same time, white indentured servitude was declining, as a movement against it spread in England (it was finally abolished in 1832 for all English colonies, but not before Australia had been partly settled by English indentured servants). Social distinctions—including barriers to intermarriage—gradually grew up in eighteenth-century America, although free Negroes either amalgamated into white society or established themselves as distinct from slaves. Their ranks were constantly replenished by Negroes freed by those masters who were opposed to "servitude in perpetuity."

Such was the situation at the outbreak of the Revolutionary War, when distinguishable Negroes constituted about 20 percent of the population of the 13 original states. Their position was low, on the average, and they were socially distinguished because of this position and the legal status of the slaves. But relationships between Negroes and whites were not marked by noteworthy difficulties or tensions. Negroes were distinguished, not by race, but primarily by legal and economic position (secondarily by "cultural backwardness" of those who came from Africa). In short, there was no racism.

The American Revolution was, in part, a manifestation of a libertarian and equalitarian ideology. Some revolutionists were in favor of the immediate abolition of slavery, and the author of the Declaration of Independence, himself a Virginian, Thomas Jefferson, wrote this into the first draft of the Declaration. But economic interests, particularly from South Carolina and Georgia, insisted on having the decision postponed. The question came again when the Constitution was being written, and this time there was a compromise: (a) the northern states abolished slavery immediately; (b) further importation of slaves would be abolished, although not before 1809; (c) it was expected that the individual manumission of slaves would continue, so that slavery would disappear very gradually. There is no doubt that the majority at the Constitutional Convention were in favor of immediate abolition, but the states of the deep South exacted this compromise as their price of adherence to the Constitution. These states had by this time acquired sufficient economic interests in slavery to wish to retain it, at least for a generation or two.

Almost immediately after the adoption of the Constitution, a sequence of events occurred that changed the whole character of the institution of slavery and hence the nature of Negro-white relations. The main event was the invention of the cotton gin, which made it possible to produce cotton at a price competitive to that of wool and linen, provided someone could be found to grow and pick the cotton bolls in the hot, humid climate necessary for their growth. The new markets created by a rapid increase of the western European population in the early nineteenth century and by the finding of ever new uses for cotton, made cotton a tremendous new source of wealth for planters in the southern states. Accessory also were the improvements in sea transportation and the discovery that the southern states were good places to raise sugar cane and rice. The result was that the deep South, which now expanded toward the west, became a center of wealth and population. Slave labor was an essential ingredient in this wealth, since efforts to introduce free labor into southern agriculture were unsuccessful because of the unpleasant work of growing and harvesting cotton, sugar cane, and rice. The price of slaves rose several hundred percent. Virginia, which had many slaves but did not grow the new crops, found itself with a new industry of slave breeding. The importation of slaves increased rapidly, and when Congress passed legislation in 1809 to outlaw their importation, they were smuggled into the country in ever increasing numbers.[34]

Meanwhile, the United States—along with France, Britain, and other western European countries—was continuing its ideological revolution in favor of liberty, equality, and fraternity. It became apparent that slavery was incompatible with modernity and democracy. There were strong movements to abolish slavery and indentured servitude, which soon became successful in all Western lands except the United States. Yet even the southern planters shared this ideology, and were torn between their desire to be modern and democratic and their desire to retain the wealth and power based on slavery. They found a solution in a series of subsidiary ideologies, which served as rationalizations to permit them to retain both slavery and democracy. At first the most popular among such ideologies was the concept of "Athenian democracy." The best society would be one in which a small number of cultured persons would devote themselves to art, literature, philosophy, and politics, while the bulk of the population would produce the material necessities to allow the leisure class to engage in these high-level activities. Another set of popular ideologies was religious in nature. Slavery was desirable as it permitted the Christianization of the heathen (this worked until the slaves were already

---

[34] It has been estimated that almost as many slaves were imported illegally into the United States between 1810 and 1860 as were imported legally during the two preceding centuries. See: Gunnar Myrdal, *An American Dilemma*, pp. 118-19.

converted to Christianity); slavery was sanctioned and even ordained in the Bible (that is, if one searched for, and "properly" interpreted, the appropriate passages).

As the nineteenth century moved along, a new rationalizing ideology developed. This arose out of some alleged discoveries of the newly developing biological sciences, centering on the assumption of the biological inferiority of the Negro. The ideology is generally called racism, and consisted of the following elements:

1. The various races were offshoots of the evolutionary tree at different stages of development so that the Negro race is lowest, not far above the apes, while the white race is highest. (This theory of "polygenesis" is no longer held by most biological scientists. The present theory, of "monogenesis," is that man—the species Homo sapiens —evolved only once and then divided into races after migration to different parts of the globe. However, no scientific biologists ever held that the races of men were distinct species, that is, as far apart as horse and ponies, for example—which seems to be the popular theory.)

2. Culture is a product solely of biological capacity, so that each race produces the artifacts and institutions of which it is capable, and a lower race is not capable of carrying on the cultural life of a higher race.

3. The offspring of a mixed racial union would at best be midway, in biological capacity, between his two parents and sometimes an anomaly would be created so that he might even be inferior, in certain respects, to his lower parent.

4. Amalgamation of two races would therefore result in the rapid deterioration of the culture of the higher race. Specifically, if the white race of North America should intermarry with any lower race, its great achievements in art and literature could no longer be maintained and appreciated, and its institutions of government (democracy and federalism), economy (free enterprise), religion (Christianity), and family (monogamy) would disappear. "Savage life," such as was believed to be characteristic of central African culture, would replace these. Thus, in order to maintain all the good things of Western culture, the races must be kept biologically separated.

This ideology of racism provided a most effective rationalization for keeping both slavery and democracy: the Negroes were not capable of having democracy and the rest of Western culture but could experience some of its benefits by serving the white race. The analogy was the superiority of the domesticated animal over the wild animal. The Negro was "all right in his place," but if he aspired to equality or intermarriage, he was dangerous and had to be beaten back. ("Dogs are fine animals, but if they should seek to be equal to us or to marry our daughters, they would have to be exterminated.") Democracy and the rest of Western culture could *only* be maintained by slavery.

Racism transformed the relationships between Negroes and whites. Slavery (or its post-Civil War equivalent of systematic discrimination) was no longer regarded as a mere economic arrangement, but rather the basis of a way of life. Any efforts by Negroes to improve themselves outside the status of slaves had to be immediately repressed. Any effort to eliminate slavery had to be fought against with every resource. All the other institutions of society had to be mobilized to maintain slavery (or its later equivalent). For example, the family had to be based on the sexual "purity" of the white woman (since white men had extramarital relations with Negro women); the economy must never allow Negro workers to work at the same occupations as white workers (this inhibited the South from adopting industrialization); the government must never allow Negroes to vote or hold public office; education for the Negro must be limited to agriculture and handicrafts; literature and art had the task of explaining and glorifying these racist requirements. A new social system had to be developed to carry out all the implied requirements of racism; sociologists usually call this "the caste system" because its forms and manifestations (although not its causes) are almost identical with the caste system that developed much earlier in Hindu society. Specifically, the caste system took off from the last element of the racist ideology and has the following provisions:

1. Systematic separation of the races, called segregation or "Jim Crow." If facilities have to be provided for Negroes, they must be separate from those for whites, so that there can be no social equality and no opportunity for Negro men and white women ever to see each other as potential mates.

2. Negro men and white women must never have sex relations, and the frequent relations between white men and Negro women must be illicit and the children classed as Negroes.

3. When whites and Negroes have to come together, usually for economic reasons, a rigid and pervasive series of "customs" must formalize and limit their contacts so that they will never become equalitarian. Sociologists have called this the "etiquette of race relations" [35] since there are hundreds of rules specifying "proper behavior." But it should be understood that this is not etiquette in the usual sense,

---

[35] See Bertram Doyle, *The Etiquette of Race Relations in the South* (Chicago: University of Chicago Press, 1937).

since the rules often require impoliteness rather than politeness. In general, the rules of interpersonal relations require a continuing demonstration that the Negro is inferior to the white man: Negroes and whites must not shake hands when they meet; the white man must start the conversation (although the Negro can hint that he wants to talk); the Negro must address the white person as Mr., Mrs., or Miss, but he must never be addressed by these titles himself (Negroes are addressed by their first name, or called uncle, aunty, darky, nigger, or in some cases—for politeness' sake—may be called by their last name or by such titles as doctor, professor, or preacher). The topics of conversation must be limited to specific job matters or to personal niceties (e.g., inquiries after one's health); it must never stray over to bigger matters of politics or economics or to personal matters such as white husband-wife relationships. Negroes should never look into the eyes of white people when they talk to them but generally should keep their eyes on the ground or shifting, and their physical posture in front of white people when they talk to them should be humble and self-demeaning. The hundreds of such rules differ slightly from one area to the next.

4. Negroes must not have the same occupations as white people. The major exception has been in agriculture, but outside of this Negroes could only be servants, in one capacity or another, and white people were generally not allowed to be servants. Negroes could be entertainers, provided they did not perform alongside whites, because entertainment could be considered a type of service. Of course, Negroes could serve other Negroes in all sorts of occupations (including the liberal professions), but this was strictly to prevent Negroes from coming into contact with whites in these capacities. The main occupational significance of the caste system is that Negroes could not work in manufacturing, commerce, or transportation except in such servant capacities as janitor, elevator operator, or porter.

5. Negroes must not be allowed to vote or to hold political office.

6. Negroes must not be allowed to have legal rights vis-à-vis whites. This means that whites could commit crimes against Negroes without fear of punishment (for over 50 years—1890 to 1945—there was no known case in eight of the southern states in which a white who committed a crime against a Negro was punished by law in any way). It also means that Negroes who commit crimes against whites were punished severely by the southern courts. Negroes who commit crimes against other Negroes are regarded as children and punished lightly, or not at all if some white man asks that they not be punished.

7. Violations of the caste rules must also be punished, usually not

by the courts, since most of the rules were not in law, but by individual or group act. The most severe punishment is meted out for sex relations between white women and Negro men: the men are immediately killed (by a lynching mob or by group-appointed individuals) and the women are exiled (unless they are declared to be innocent and the relationship forced on them). Severe punishment is also usually inflicted on those Negroes who "pass" or attempt to "pass" as whites. Such Negroes are either killed, severely beaten, or their property destroyed. Still, few "passing" Negroes are ever detected because many more Negroes appear to be whites than the whites know about; the passers do so in communities (usually cities) where they are virtually unknown, and the Negro community has seldom been known to betray a passer no matter what the resentment against him as an individual might be.

The most important thing about the caste system, as outlined above, is that it transformed the whole culture of the southern states. It made its mark on every institution, whether of whites or Negroes, and it created suspicion, antagonism, and violence in the relations between the races. It permeated the conversation, the thought, and the literature of the South. This caste system developed only gradually during the nineteenth century; in fact, it did not take complete form until several decades after the end of slavery, around the 1890's.[36] It remained almost intact until about 1940; thereafter, parts of it began to crumble. Today, as we shall see, it is much modified, and it can be forecast, from the rate of change since 1940, that it is doomed to disappear despite the efforts of a vigorous minority of white southerners to keep it alive. Racism, the ideology which underlies caste, is still very strong, and is more closely linked with other aspects of American culture (like the belief in biological determinism) than is caste—which has always seemed to most to be at least a little un-American.

It should be understood that the ideology of racism and the social system of caste are linked only in the United States and a few other places (such as South Africa). In certain other countries, one occurs without the other. In Germany, for example, racism developed in the nineteenth century and reached extreme form in the 1930's and 1940's under the National Socialist government, but there was very little caste accompanying racism in Germany until 1933. Racism apparently first began in Germany in the "Romantic period" following the end of the Napoleonic era. What is now Germany, but was then many

---

[36] C. Vann Woodward, *The Strange Career of Jim Crow* (New York: Oxford University Press, 1957).

different states, was occupied by Napoleon, and while the French control was very mild, there was a sense of humiliation and of discovery of a new national identity. Some intellectuals began to express the idea that the Germans were truly a superior people, whose only defect was that they had never come together to form a single nation. There was much glorification of German history and culture. The deficiencies of other peoples were emphasized. This antagonism was expressed toward all others who did not speak natively a Teutonic language: toward the French and Italians, for example, but especially toward "foreigners" living in Germany—Poles, Jews, and gypsies. When biological ideas about race were popularized, these ideas about German superiority immediately became transformed into racism. Racism was expressed in literature and philosophy and even in art forms (Richard Wagner, for example, was an ardent racist and tried to express this ideology in his operas). Racism was used as a justification in the political unification of Germany (1866-1871) and played a strong role in national politics: the court chaplain to Kaiser Wilhelm I, Adolph Stoecker, was an outspoken racist, and the statesman Otto von Bismarck used racism for political expediency. The racist movement vowed to exterminate the Jews and to dominate the world; in fact, there was very little segregation or discrimination until Hitler gained control of the German government in 1933, after which he attempted—and temporarily succeeded in—putting the racist goals into practice. He first established a caste system; then in a few years he began to exterminate the Jews, Poles, and gypsies (killing over six million). Racism has not completely disappeared from Germany today —nor from certain nearby countries to which German racism spread earlier, such as Poland, Rumania, and Russia—but it is no longer openly supported by the government or by national leaders.

Just as there can be racism without caste, so there can be caste without racism. India provides the classic example of caste.[37] Its origins are lost in prehistory, but for well over 1000 years the caste system has been associated with the Hindu religion. Hindu ideology clearly specifies that the various castes are various stages in an eternal life, and that one moves from caste to caste, not during one's lifetime,

---

[37] For descriptions of the caste system of India, see John H. Hutton, *Caste in India: Its Nature, Function, and Origins* (Cambridge, England: The University Press, 1946); Radhakamal Mukerjee *et al., Inter-Caste Tensions,* a survey under the auspices of UNESCO (India: University of Lucknow, 1951); G. S. Ghurye, *Caste, Class, and Occupation* (Bombay: Popular Book Depot, 1961); Noel P. Gist, "Caste Differentials in South India," *American Sociological Review,* Vol. 19 (April, 1954), pp. 126-37; Harold R. Isaacs, *India's Ex-Untouchables* (New York: John Day, 1965).

but after reincarnation, according to how one behaved in his most recent life. There are hundreds of castes, each associated with a different occupation, but they are classed into five great groups: the Brahmans, originally the priestly caste but now including all the learned professions; the Kshatriyas, originally the warriors but now including all the governmental occupations; the Vaisyas, including all kinds of merchants and now the industrialists; the Sudras, or all workers in both city and country; and the Untouchables, who perform the scavenging tasks. Individuals cannot change their caste, they must marry within their caste, they must adopt the occupation of their caste, they must associate generally only with other members of their caste group, and they must behave toward members of other castes in prescribed ways that demonstrate their position in the caste hierarchy. The caste system is breaking down somewhat in India, especially in the past several decades as a result of modern technology and economics, the teachings of Mahatma Gandhi,[38] and the laws of the new Republic of India. The caste system bred some antagonism among the castes, especially between the deprived Untouchables and all the others. But the antagonism never became racist.

Certain other aspects of racism must be pointed out. It is a complex of deep-seated feelings and attitudes that manifest themselves in behavior, both consciously and unconsciously. The specific behavioral manifestations vary from culture to culture, but since the ideology is based on a conception that men belong to different races, each with its own distinctive biological potentialities, there is always a manifestation of the belief that men can be ranked in terms of biological worth and this cannot be changed by any amount of learning or new environment. One racist society will define people as belonging to different races that another racist society will not: there is little relationship between a scientist's categorization by race—based on biologically inherited physical traits—and the racist's categorization by race—which may just as well be based on religion, language, nationality, or anything else. Racism in the United States, which first developed in connection with Negroes, quickly got transferred not only to Indians and Asians, but also to the Irish, Italians, Poles, Jews, Catholics, Hispanos, Mennonites, and dozens of other groups. Racism, once it exists within a culture, has a tendency to be directed toward ever different groups of people as objects. The history of the United States from 1820 to 1940 exemplifies the spread of racism from one

---

[38] But see B. R. Ambedkar, *Mr. Gandhi and the Emancipation of the Untouchables* (Bombay, Thacker, 1943).

group to another. So does the history of South Africa, now probably the most violently racist nation in the world, which developed racism first in connection with white-native relations, then transferred many of the attitudes toward Indian and south European immigrants.

Racism has also a tendency to spread rapidly from person to person within a society. Thus, while racism began in the southern states, it very rapidly spread to the North, although only a few aspects of the caste system came along with it. Racism does not require an object in the immediate locality to exist: in certain northern states there are areas that have never seen a Negro, but in which there are well-developed racist attitudes toward Negroes. There are few Turks in the United States, and those few probably would not be identified as Turks, but for a long time there were strong racist attitudes toward Turks.

Since racism purports to base itself on unchanging biological differences and includes a belief that people have an instinct to hold themselves aloof from people of differing race, racists believe that their ideology has always existed and is, in a real sense, natural and timeless. They honestly believe that the group relationships they practice have always existed. Racists are surprised and unbelieving when they hear that racism began in the nineteenth century, that most people in the world are not racists, and that racism can be rapidly eliminated if certain institutional changes occur in a society. In a subsequent section, we shall see that changes making it unlikely that racism will remain much longer are now taking place in the United States.

Racism is an ideology, a set of popular beliefs serving to explain or justify a cultural practice. It presumes to state certain facts, but in the case of racism these are false. Mankind is largely divided into races, it is true, although a large proportion of the world's population is mixed and there are no untoward consequences because of this mixture. But there is no scientific basis for the belief that one race is biologically inferior to another. There are minor differences in certain body characteristics—skin color, hair form, nose and lip shape, height, shape of certain bones—and these are what distinguished the races. But there are no proved inherited differences in any psychological traits—despite a century of effort by scientists to find them. This is partly because psychological "traits" are shaped by the environment as well as by heredity, whereas most physical traits are determined by heredity alone. All mankind belongs to the same species, has a common origin, and is capable of fertile and eugenic reproduction in any racial combination. Further, there is no necessary relationship between race and culture. A culture is developed out of historical circumstances operating within geographical limits and is modified by forces operating within itself and by contact with other cultures; there is no known biological influence on culture within the species of man. All normal men, whatever their race, are capable of learning and participating fully in any culture of the world, provided they have been appropriately socialized in that culture since infancy. These facts, which scientists have known for some time, show racism to have a false basis.

Nevertheless, racism itself is a social fact and, in some societies, a very important one. It has probably been the single most significant social fact, influencing profoundly all other aspects of the culture, in societies such as the southern United States, the Union of South Africa, and Nazi Germany; and it has dominated intergroup relations at least in such societies as the northern United States, eastern Europe, and possibly Japan. It plays a role in intergroup relations in some western European countries and in their colonies. In countries where racism is dominant, it is believed deeply and profoundly, and any efforts to change it or to treat it lightly are received with great resistance, anxiety, and reaction. Racism is to be understood as a series of social facts of considerable significance, but not as a series of scientific biological facts.

Social Change and the American Caste System

The American caste system did not come to dominate southern society fully until the 1890's, as we have noted, and its limited spread to the northern states cannot be said to have been completed before the 1920's. But there have always existed forces of opposition, which began to have some effect in the first decade of the twentieth century. The opposition was weak at first, but by the 1940's it impaired noticeably parts of the caste system. These historical forces of social change are:

1. THE INCREASING EDUCATION OF NEGROES. A public school system was established in the South for the first time by the Reconstruction governments that held political control from 1868 to about 1875, and both whites and Negroes had a chance to get an education in public as well as privately supported schools. The further development of the caste system all but wiped out the Negro public schools by the 1890's, but private funds—coming mainly from northern philanthropists and from the Negroes themselves—continued the schooling of perhaps half the southern Negro population, so that there were always some Negroes who had learned to read and write. Meanwhile, the

privately supported Negro colleges were training a "talented tenth" among the Negroes, who could provide some leadership for the Negroes and articulation of their feelings and needs.

2. A SMALL GROUP OF WHITE "SOUTHERN LIBERALS." While only one articulate white southerner—George W. Cable—was speaking out in favor of humane and equal treatment of Negroes by the end of the nineteenth century, there was always a small group of southerners who tried to stem violence against Negroes and to modify the harshness of the caste system. They supported the caste system, but sought to make it benevolent toward Negroes who "kept their place" as inferiors. Their effectiveness was limited to maintenance of order in some localities, except possibly for a larger role in diminishing the number of lynchings.

3. THE RISE OF THE "NEW NEGRO" PRESS. In 1901, Monroe Trotter established the *Boston Guardian,* which was the first of an increasing number of Negro newspapers and magazines that voiced the protest against caste. Since these newspapers had a national circulation and their contents were repeated by word of mouth even to the illiterate masses of Negroes, they had the effect of creating a sense of group consciousness among Negroes throughout the country.

4. THE FORMATION OF A PROTEST MOVEMENT BY EDUCATED NEGROES. In 1905, W. E. B. Du Bois led in the formation of the first Negro protest organization. In 1909, this group joined a group of like-minded northern whites—to be mentioned next—to form the National Association for the Advancement of Colored People (NAACP). The latter organization has used two methods with increasing effectiveness over the years to chop away at the caste system: (a) lawsuits in the federal courts to enforce the Thirteenth, Fourteenth, and Fifteenth Amendments to the Constitution, which render illegal any government support for the caste system; (b) seeking to get new laws designed to gain equal rights for persons to whom such civil rights are not awarded. Since 1915, the NAACP has succeeded in carrying some 65 lawsuits to the United States Supreme Court and has won all but four of them. Since 1915 also, Negroes have formed additional effective protest organizations, which use a variety of means to encourage social action against caste.

5. THE RESURGENCE OF THE NORTHERN CONSCIENCE WITH RESPECT TO THE NEGRO. While the abolitionist spirit was all but dead by the end of the nineteenth century, there have always been some northern liberals willing to do something about violations of civil liberties. Some of these took the leadership in forming the NAACP, and others became active in defense of minority rights in other ways.

6. THE MIGRATION OF MILLIONS OF NEGROES TO THE NORTH AND WEST AFTER 1915. The job opportunities in the North created by World War I, coupled with the cutting off of migration from Europe, encouraged many Negroes to move North. Once the migration began it never stopped, not even during the great unemployment of the 1930's, for migration came to mean a partial escape from the caste system. The North offered the Negro the equal right to vote, and the Negro vote has become highly significant in national and some local politics for it is concentrated in areas where the two political parties are balanced in strength and because it is relatively responsive to political benefits. The President of the United States first showed himself responsive to Negro political influence in 1942 when he set up the Fair Employment Practices Commission to reduce discrimination against Negroes in the war industries (at a time when they were desperately short of manpower). The majority of Congress first showed itself responsive to the Negro vote in 1957, when it passed its first civil rights law since Reconstruction days—to investigate southern disfranchisement of the Negro in violation of the Fifteenth Amendment (Congress has never sought to enforce the voting clause in the Fourteenth Amendment). Congress' increasing responsiveness to the Negro vote is evidenced by subsequent civil rights legislation in 1960, 1964, and 1965.

7. ACHIEVEMENTS OF TALENTED NEGROES, PARTICULARLY IN THE ARTS AND SPORTS. Particularly after World War I, significant numbers of whites slowly came to appreciate the achievements of certain Negro musicians, writers, and athletes, and this encouraged further achievements in these fields. Some of the white applauders gained a broader understanding and sympathy for the Negro's handicaps under caste.

8. THE GRADUAL INDUSTRIALIZATION OF THE SOUTH. The caste system in its full form is possible only in a rural society. Industrialization is bound to bring white and Negro workers into contact with each other; make entrepreneurs more concerned about efficiency than about maintaining a caste system that wastes manpower; move Negroes into cities where it is more difficult to use day-to-day violence against them and where a Negro middle class can develop. The partial urbanization of southern whites has also tended to modernize them, particularly with regard to politics, and during the past two decades a new breed of responsible southern politician has largely replaced the old-time, ignorant rabble-rousers (even though the public is more aware of the exceptions). Of equal importance is the decline of "King Cotton"— which depended on exploitation of Negro labor—as the major basis for the southern economy. As the Negro is no longer vital to the

southern economy, he is more likely to be treated like a white laborer, according to the standards of a free labor market.

9. EXPANSION OF FEDERAL GOVERNMENT ACTIVITIES FOR THE BENEFIT OF ALL UNDERPRIVILEGED PERSONS. The New Deal of the 1930's, partly as a way of softening the impact of the Depression on the individual and partly as an expression of a new political philosophy, expanded federal activities for the security and benefit of all citizens, particularly the poorer ones. Since Negroes were concentrated in the poorer classes, they benefited considerably. Contrary to popular impression, the Roosevelt administration was not partial to Negroes; there was much race discrimination by most New Deal agencies. But the federal government was never as discriminatory as any of the southern state governments, and under the Truman, Eisenhower, Kennedy, and Johnson administrations even this degree of race discrimination was markedly diminished.

10. THE EXPANSION OF THE AMERICAN CONSCIENCE DURING WORLD WAR II. When the chief enemy was arch-racist Nazi Germany, Americans become more aware of their own racism and its implications. The negative reactions of Asians, Africans, and even some Europeans to American racism began to gain American attention. The broadening effect of overseas experience extended to the servicemen, who were a cross section of the American people. A number of scholarly researches, notably *An American Dilemma* by Gunnar Myrdal and associates, and a number of novels sympathetic to Negroes, disseminated information about the Negro problem and helped to make criticism of the caste system respectable.

11. UNPARALLELED ECONOMIC PROSPERITY SINCE 1940. The extreme shortage of labor during World War II helped to encourage industrialists to try using Negro labor in their factories. Almost overnight the myth that Negroes were mentally or physically incapable of working at machines disappeared. While Negroes are discriminated against by many employers and most of them still have not developed traditions of skill and training, they are no longer completely excluded from factories and commercial establishments. Even during the brief periods of high unemployment since 1940, the proportion of Negroes laid off jobs has been only slightly greater than that of whites. Higher and steadier income has allowed Negroes to make progress in getting an education, in achieving a higher standard of living, in making their consumer dollars mean more to tradesmen, and in creating a large middle class.

12. THE LEADING ROLE OF THE FEDERAL COURTS IN THE ENFORCEMENT OF THE FIFTEENTH AMENDMENT AND THE DUE PROCESS CLAUSE OF THE

FOURTEENTH AMENDMENT. The failure to enforce these amendments meant that southern public officials could impose and sanction the caste system by force. Systematic enforcement by the Supreme Court began in 1944; until that time the courts hedged and decided cases on *ad hoc* grounds. In regular succession since 1944, the Supreme Court—by unanimous decisions—has destroyed the legal buttresses of the caste system. What remains of the caste system is largely a private matter; the remaining enforcement by public officials is illegal. The 1954 decision in the *Brown* case rendered illegal segregation in public facilities, and thus struck at the very heart of the caste system. While this decision has been put into operation in only a token way by most of the southern states, it has meant that some Negro and white children are associating on an equal basis; that there have been greater efforts to improve the education provided by the Negro schools; and that in the border states (Missouri, Kentucky, Oklahoma, West Virginia, Maryland, Delaware) desegregation has proceeded to the point where they are more like northern states than southern ones.

13. THE DEVELOPMENT OF A NEW NATIONAL CONSENSUS THAT OVERT DISCRIMINATION AGAINST MINORITY GROUPS IS OUT OF PLACE IN A MODERN DEMOCRATIC SOCIETY. Especially during and after 1963, the great majority of the white people of the United States—as a result of the above-mentioned forces—developed the opinion that legal and other overt forms of discrimination had no place in modern society (although private discriminations continued to be practiced). There were many degrees of this opinion and somewhat different motives behind it, but a strong public awareness did emerge, sometimes catalyzed by an outrageous example of caste violence: the bombings of a Negro church in Birmingham, which killed four children, and, in Selma, Alabama, the fatal beating of a white minister and the shooting of a white northern housewife, who had come to help Negroes demonstrate against voting restrictions. This consensus was manifested in the federal government by the passage of a comprehensive civil rights bill in 1964 and a voting rights bill in 1965 (supported by the majority of both political parties), in speeches favoring civil rights by Presidents Kennedy and Johnson, in a Congressional decision to investigate the Ku Klux Klan for possible subversion, in active participation in civil rights demonstrations by northern white people (especially clergymen and college students), and even in the overwhelming election, in 1964, of Lyndon Johnson over Barry Goldwater as President after the latter had voted against the 1964 civil rights bill. This new public opinion, while developing out of the previously mentioned social forces, became an overwhelming social force in itself.

It is important to note that some of the above-mentioned 13 forces can hardly be reversed, and it seems likely that their long-run effect will be to destroy the caste system. In assessing the present status of Negro-white relations—to which we shall turn next—several counterforces must be listed. However, it can probably be said that the pressures of industrialization, world opinion, and the removal of the legal underpinning to the caste system are more potent than the counterforces.

Patterns of Discrimination Against Minority Groups in the United States

It is not possible, of course, to describe systematically all aspects of minority problems in the United States in the space of this chapter. Rather, we shall present selected aspects of problems, using each to illustrate a problem facing several minorities. It is convenient to classify these into economic, legal, political, and social problems.

Negroes in Southern Agriculture

In 1960, 60 percent of the Negroes in the United States lived in the South. Of these about 12 percent lived on farms, although 42 percent lived in rural areas. These proportions have been much higher in the past, so it can be said that southern agriculture has been one of the major economic problems of Negroes. In 1959, Negro farm operators comprised only one-sixth of all farm operators in the South. Of these, two-fifths were sharecroppers. The average size of farms operated by whites was 382 acres; Negro farms averaged 56 acres. The average value of land and buildings on white farms was $37,816; for Negro farms it was $7,328. Of those Negroes engaged in agriculture, only 48 percent were farm owners or managers as compared to 83 percent among the whites.

Regardless of the position of Negroes, southern agriculture is in a precarious condition.[39] Too many people are trying to earn a living from agriculture; a sizable part of the land has not been properly cared for and so is eroded; a considerable portion of the land is in large plantations, so that most farmers must be tenants or sharecroppers rather than owners; most agriculture is devoted to growing cotton rather than being diversified; the demand for cotton is gradually falling off as new types of cloth become popular and as other

---

[39] James H. Street, *The New Revolution in the Cotton Economy* (Chapel Hill: University of North Carolina Press, 1957).

nations learn to grow their own cotton; a cotton-picking machine is now available that could replace most of the human labor; the boll weevil is a special menace to the cotton crop; the federal government pays farmers not to grow cotton, and there is thus less demand for agricultural laborers.

For all these reasons, the southern agricultural economy has long been a sick economy, from which only a few large plantation owners could make a consistently satisfactory livelihood. The position of the Negro has been especially bad.[40] Never given any land to start out with after the end of the Civil War, Negroes only very gradually acquired ownership of land. But even this reached its peak as far back as 1910, when the factors discouraging Negro farm ownership became so strong that the absolute as well as relative number of Negro farm owners began to decline. Negroes owned the small and poorer farms and so were especially afflicted by the hard conditions of southern agriculture. Because they were Negroes, they could get hardly any bank credit; demands from mortgagors were much more stringent; the possibilities of getting tax reductions were slimmer; the chances of getting cheated by middlemen who bought the crop were greater; and—most important of all—in many areas of the South, Negroes were not allowed to buy land at all. Thus, there have been few opportunities for successful farm ownership for Negroes in the South.

Negro sharecroppers and farm laborers face still other special difficulties in the South. They are systematically cheated by white farm owners who hire them. The sharecropper or laborer is practically never paid in cash, but in credit advances at a general store. On the larger plantations, the store is owned by the plantation owner, but whether owned by him or not, there is a general agreement that the store advancing credit charges high prices (for usually inferior merchandise). Records of purchases are kept by the storekeeper, who turns them over to the farm owner, who uses them to balance the wages or profit share he owes the laborer or cropper. While purchases are kept to a minimum, seldom are wages or profits calculated to be higher than purchases, so that the cropper or laborer usually ends the year with a debt rather than a cash balance.

With all the law-enforcement agencies on their side, white farm owners sometimes use this debt as an excuse to restrain croppers or

---

[40] Charles S. Johnson, *Shadow of the Plantation* (Chicago: University of Chicago Press, 1934). Arthur F. Raper and Ira De A. Reid, *Sharecroppers All* (Chapel Hill: University of North Carolina Press, 1941). Rupert B. Vance, *All These People* (Chapel Hill: University of North Carolina Press, 1945).

laborers from ever leaving the farm. A legalized peonage may result, from which there is no escape. Negro croppers and laborers, unlike white ones, cannot demand to look at, or complain about, the records of purchases or crop sales, nor can they default on their debts. Unless the owner turns honest, or gets disgusted with the Negro, or the Negro steals away under cover of darkness (very difficult if there is a family and no cars or horses), the Negro cropper or laborer is doomed to a marginal existence the rest of his working days. When past the working age, he has no savings or source of income except what his children may be able to provide. Where the owner allows the cropper or laborer to leave at the end of the season—and this is much more common these days—he may still cheat him out of his cash balance. Croppers move from one plantation to another, year after year, looking for more productive land or for more honest owners. This moving discourages repairs on houses, the development of year-round vegetable gardens, or the maintenance of the soil. Both Negro cropper and white owner are caught by the unbalanced cotton economy and the caste system.

During the 1930's, the federal government (through the Agricultural Adjustment Administration) stepped in to aid the southern farmer, but its influence has been generally detrimental to the Negroes. Seeking to operate democratically, the AAA carried on most of its crop reduction activities through elected committees of farmers. In accord with southern practices of keeping all political matters in the hands of whites, these committees were dominated by whites who often made their decisions to match their racial interests. In the first years, large government bounties for crop reduction were kept entirely by farm owners, although the owners were supposed to share with croppers and tenants. Even when this practice was stopped, the tenants and laborers lost thereby were not completely replaced with new ones, and these groups were thus driven out of agriculture. In the long run, this proved beneficial to them, as they moved to cities in both the South and the North, where eventually they obtained better jobs than they ever could have had on the farm. But its immediate effect was harmful. Negroes were more affected than whites, even though they were fewer in number on the southern farms, because they had no recourse to the legal authorities if the owner wished to drive them out. There were 192,000 fewer Negro tenants and 150,000 fewer white tenants in the South in 1940 than in 1930.

The government's other farm program during the 1930's (the Farm Security Administration) was designed to aid small farm owners and thus helped Negroes and whites alike. Still the program did not compensate for the economic devastation caused by the AAA. World War II created temporary economic relief for the cotton economy, as there was an unusual demand for cotton. But the old problems remained and are exerting their full pressure in the postwar years. While general prosperity continues, it is ultimately good for Negroes to be especially hurt by the cotton economy, since they are thereby forced into the cities where they are gradually able to improve themselves economically. Since 1930, the proportion of the Negro population that lives in cities has more than doubled, so that a considerable majority of Negroes are urban today—more proportionately than the whites.

Fair Employment Practice Acts

If we exclude the laws and treaties specifying that the United States has certain obligations toward the Indians (because the latter were deprived of their lands and other natural resources), the first positive effort of the government to prevent private discrimination against minority groups was made during World War II. In the first year of the war, when industry was scraping the bottom of the manpower barrel and war contracts were going unfilled for lack of labor, there were large numbers of minority persons—predominantly Negroes—who could not get jobs because of prejudice. It was said that Negroes were inherently incapable of handling machines and that white workers would quit, even in wartime, if Negro workers were brought into the shop.

The situation was so serious that Negroes organized a "March-on-Washington" movement in 1942 to bring their plight to the world's attention. President Roosevelt pleaded with them not to display disunity in wartime, but they argued back that they could make a greater contribution to the war effort if allowed to work in war plants. Finally, just before the march was scheduled, the President issued an Executive Order specifying that all contracts with firms supplying war materials should contain clauses prohibiting discrimination in employment on grounds of race, religion, or national origin, and that a Commission (called the Fair Employment Practices Commission) should be set up to watch for violations of the contracts.

The FEPC had no way of enforcing the rules except by persuasion and publicity.[41] But it did have a staff to which individuals or organizations representing minorities could appeal, and it did have a certain amount of prestige. The FEPC was able to help many minority

---

[41] On the functioning of the federal FEPC, see Robert C. Weaver, *Negro Labor* (New York: Harcourt, Brace & World, 1946).

members to obtain jobs from which they had formerly been barred. Three things helped the FEPC: (a) highly organized protests from minorities, particularly the Negro groups, against discrimination; (b) an extreme shortage of labor; and (c) a heightened consciousness of democratic ideals during the war. Since the FEPC was a product of an Executive Order under wartime powers, it died when Congress refused to appropriate money for it at the end of the war. Bills to set up a permanent FEPC were introduced into Congress, and one was finally passed in 1964, which will have its main effect on the South.

In 1946, the State of New York passed an FEP law modeled after the President's defunct order, except that it applied to all employers instead of only to those working on a state contract.[42] Even though there was no longer such a drastic manpower shortage, and even though the state FEPC was deliberately so gentle with discriminatory employers that it did not even threaten to bring them to court, the Act had great success. The mere existence of the law, and the presence of a distinguished FEPC to present the facts to employers and unions, served to make many employers hire qualified Negroes, Puerto Ricans, Italians, and Jews (who are the groups mainly discriminated against in New York). Not only did an efficient person in a minority have a better chance of getting a job, but Negroes got the *kinds* of jobs from which they had previously been completely barred —such as department store selling and office clerical work. Employers encountered much less opposition from customers and white workers than they seem to have expected.

After observing the operation of the New York FEPC for a year or more, various other states and cities in the North and West passed similar laws. Some of these laws went considerably further in giving powers of enforcement to the committees, but such powers have been used very little. Everywhere the FEPCs have relied on education, on persuasion, and—at most—on publicity regarding a firm or union violating the law. By 1963, 20 states and 40 cities outside those states had FEP laws. These states and cities include over 90 percent of the nonwhites living in the North and West, and it has been the Negroes who have been most helped by them. On the whole, it would seem that the North and West are not opposed to the principle of "fair employment practice." Major opposition remains in the South. Even there, however, the existence of successful FEP laws in other

---

[42] On the functioning of the New York FEPC, see Felix Rackow, *Combating Discrimination in Employment in New York State* (Ithaca: New York State School of Industrial and Labor Relations, 1949).

states has greatly reduced the belief that Negroes cannot learn to run machines or to appear for work on time and dressed neatly. The South is much more willing to give Negroes jobs of various kinds than it was 15 or so years ago, but it is still not willing to pass laws permitting Negroes to make complaints against discrimination. The opposition of white workers to working side by side with Negroes seems to be more important today than the opposition of employers to hiring them. In 1965, the FEP provisions of the 1964 Federal Civil Rights Act went into operation to bring the legal principle of non-discrimination to the major employers of the South.

Minorities Under American Law and Justice

American law is based on the principle of equal treatment of all citizens, and of regarding each person as an individual rather than as a representative of a group. But these principles do not always operate. Lawmakers and judges may be prejudiced against certain ethnic groups, or they may feel that certain groups need special consideration to make up for the discriminations they suffer. Justice is sometimes taken out of the hands of the law and violated by some despotic official or by a mob. Let us consider certain problems of law and justice facing minorities.

IMMIGRATION LAWS. One of the strong ideals of the United States until the latter part of the nineteenth century was that this country should be open to free immigration and that it would be a haven for the oppressed and a land of opportunity for the ambitious from other lands. Despite this, however, the racism first expressed against Negroes and Indians was gradually transferred to Orientals and to white foreigners. The first legal manifestation of this racism appeared in the immigration laws, since this is one of the few kinds of law which the Constitution permits the federal government to make discriminatory. In 1882, a Chinese Exclusion Act was passed by Congress to keep out all Chinese working people. By 1907, agitation against Japanese immigration in California had become so strong that President Theodore Roosevelt negotiated a "Gentlemen's Agreement" with the Japanese Government, whereby that government would issue no visas to workers, but only to students and businessmen for temporary visits, with the understanding that the United States would pass no formal law to achieve this same aim. In 1917, most other Asians were excluded, and by 1921, the antiforeign feeling had grown so strong that a drastic new law was passed.

The 1921 law prohibited the immigration of Japanese (thereby violating the "Gentlemen's Agreement" of 1907) and contained a "national origins" clause directed primarily against immigrants from southern and eastern Europe. With later modifications, that clause limited the total immigration in any one year to 150,000 and set up a quota from each country that was in proportion to the number of persons in the United States in 1920 "having that national origin." This Act marked the end of free immigration into the United States and acknowledged in law the group antagonisms that had grown up in this country. Although North and South Americans do not come under the quota system, they must meet other qualifications for entry, some of which are quite severe. In 1930 President Hoover by Executive Order further limited immigration, especially that of Mexicans and Canadians. The immigration law bars anyone "liable to become a public charge." By interpreting this clause with severity, officials were able to refuse entrance to practically all members of the working classes. The prospective immigrant must get an American citizen to sign an affidavit that a job is awaiting him and that he will not become a public charge. Persons without resources in savings find this extremely difficult to do, unless they can persuade relatives who are American citizens to take a risk and sign for them. As a result of all these limitations on immigration, there have been a number of years since 1930 when emigration from the United States exceeded immigration. In 1934, as part of the law establishing the independence of the Philippine Islands, a clause was inserted specifying that no Filipinos would be allowed to come to the United States except on temporary business. The immigration laws were modified in the 1950's but the quota principle remained and served to exclude most would-be immigrants outside those from northern and western Europe. It was not until 1965 that Congress, strongly urged by the Johnson administration, abolished the national origins quota, although it retained a maximum limit on the number who could immigrate to the United States from areas outside the Americas.

The motives behind these various laws up to 1965, were partially, at least, based on the racist beliefs that Orientals, Africans, and people of southern and eastern Europe are biologically inferior to other Americans and incapable of assimilation. Naturally, this provoked much international ill will. The militarists in Japan used the United States Immigration Act of 1921 as an example of American treachery and hostility. They were helped thereby to gain control of the Japanese government and eventually to declare war on the United States. Other Asian leaders who collaborated with Japan during the war—notably Laurel of the Philippines and Bose of India—were motivated partly by the hostility shown toward them by Americans. When the United

States was trying to rebuild international good will during World War II, one of the things it did was to pass laws repealing the exclusion of Chinese, Filipinos, and Indians and allowing them to immigrate on a quota basis. That relieved some of the special sting for Orientals, although in practice no more than about one hundred persons a year may enter from each country. Those who do immigrate are for the most part wives or intended wives of those already here. The complete exclusion of the Japanese remained on the statute books until 1951.

The quota system applied to all nations outside the Americas and prevented this country from aiding in the relief of the "displaced persons" who have been victims of the German and Russian dictatorships. In 1948, a Displaced Persons Act was passed by Congress—not to change the quota system but to help displaced persons take full advantage of past unfilled quotas. This Act was so written, however, as to discriminate pointedly against Catholic and Jewish refugees, a fact that increased the insecurity feelings of Americans of those religious faiths. A somewhat less discriminatory law was passed in 1953 to aid the victims of Communist dictatorships, but it applied to relatively few persons.

There is no law against the immigration of Mexicans, but they are kept out by the "public charge" rule and by Presidential order. In view of the heavy demand for agricultural labor, border authorities have winked at the illegal entry of Mexican laborers. But any time that a large employer wants to frighten Mexican workers, or any time white workers believe there is too much competition from Mexicans, they get the immigration officials to raid Mexican communities to arrest and deport these illegals. This practice has proved more than annoying to those Mexicans legally in this country, and even American citizens of Mexican birth or ancestry, who are frequently arrested temporarily during these raids because they do not have immigration papers with them. It has also created some friction with the Mexican government.

A PATTERN OF VIOLENCE. Prejudiced people occasionally take the law into their own hands in relations with minority members, if they believe they can get away with it. In the South, illegal violence is used frequently by whites against Negroes who have committed crimes, against Negroes who have not committed crimes but who have violated one of the hundreds of caste rules, and occasionally against Negroes who simply happen to be around when whites are angry. The frequent use of violence against Negroes in the South occurs largely because there is practically no punishment for whites who engage in such violence. Even where Negroes are murdered, there is seldom a conviction if the murderer is a white man. The fear of organized white revenge is so great that, until recently, few but psychopathic Negroes ever retaliated upon white men who beat them or stole their property. In the late 1950's, however, some Negroes in a few southern communities organized to meet violence with violence.

Illegal violence in the North used to take the form of riots.[43] They occurred infrequently, but when they did occur many people were hurt or killed and much property destroyed. In a riot, both majority and minority groups are aggressive. Usually highly prejudiced members of the majority group start the illegal violence, but there are exceptions (as in the Harlem riot of 1935). Once the riot begins, minority members also engage in violence against the majority. Riots in the United States have, at different times, involved many minority groups. We shall describe one riot involving Mexican-Americans, which occurred in Los Angeles in 1943.[44]

As soon as the Japanese had been forcibly removed from the West Coast in 1942, the newspapers of Los Angeles substituted the Mexicans as the major scapegoat group and played up a number of incidents of Mexican juvenile delinquency. When a young Mexican was killed under mysterious circumstances, the press and the police made a case against a "gang" of Mexican youths who were alleged to be taking the law into their own hands. The trial was almost a ritual of race prejudice, lashed on by the press and by the court officials who took advantage of the publicity. A citizen's committee successfully obtained an appeal, and the higher court established the innocence of the defendants. But the public had been convinced that Mexican youths were dangerous criminals. Egged on by the press and the public, Los Angeles police conducted raids on the Mexican communities, in which hundreds of people were taken into custody on charges of suspicion and on charges of possessing "implements that might have been used in assault cases."

Since it was during the war, the Axis radio was gleefully reporting all evidences of cleavage between the Allies. Representatives of the

---

[43] See, for example, Elliott M. Rudwick, *Race Riot at East St. Louis: July 2, 1917* (Carbondale, Ill.: Southern Illinois University Press, 1964).

[44] This summary description is taken from Carey McWilliams, *North From Mexico* (Philadelphia: Lippincott, 1949), pp. 227-58. For a description of other riots: the one in Detroit in 1942, see Alfred M. Lee and Norman D. Humphrey, *Race Riot* (New York: Dryden, 1943); the riot in Chicago in 1919, see Chicago Commission on Race Relations, *The Negro in Chicago* (Chicago: University of Chicago Press, 1922).

federal government therefore urged newspapers not to feature the word "Mexican" in stories of crime. The press agreed, but soon substituted the words "zoot-suiters" and "Pachucos," which more effectively labeled the Mexican youth as criminals. This went on for over a year, and there was constant friction between whites and Mexicans. On June 3, 1943, 11 white sailors were beaten by a gang of Mexican boys, and some 200 sailors organized to take revenge by following the police raid model. They hired a fleet of 20 taxicabs, swooped down on every Mexican they could find, and beat him. The newspapers pushed the war news from the front page and devoted headlines and front-page articles to the "sailor-zooter clash." The next night the sailors were joined by soldiers and marines who paraded through downtown Los Angeles. Only a few incidents happened that evening, but on the following two evenings there were full-scale operations. At first there was no resistance from the Mexicans, but all the arrests made by the police were of Mexicans. ". . . the press now whipped public opinion into a frenzy by dire warnings that Mexican zoot-suiters planned mass retaliations. To insure a riot, the precise street corners were named at which retaliatory action was expected and the time of the anticipated action was carefully specified. In effect these stories announced a riot and invited public participation." [45]

The mobs of June 7 and 8 numbered several thousand servicemen and civilians. They marched through the streets, beating up every young Mexican they could find. They searched movie houses, bars, and streetcars to pull Mexicans into the street, tear off their clothes, and beat them up. Dozens of youths were left lying, sometimes bare and bloody, on the sidewalks. No white person was arrested for longer than a few hours. The riot stopped when the Navy declared downtown Los Angeles "out of bounds" to sailors, the Mexican ambassador addressed a formal inquiry to the Secretary of State, and the federal government appealed to the Los Angeles press and police. Isolated incidents occurred for some time afterward, and in other sections of the country there began a series of Negro-white riots that continued until responsible committees were formed to stop the practices that caused them. There were few riots in the North after 1944, except in the city of Chicago, which failed to develop effective riot prevention techniques found in other northern cities. In the 1950's, riots occurred in several southern localities as part of the reaction to desegregation.

In the summer of 1964, a new pattern of violence began in several

---

[45] McWilliams, *North from Mexico*, p. 248.

northern cities.[46] An incident of real or fancied discrimination set off thousands of Negroes—mostly young men of the lower-income groups that were unemployed—on an orgy of destruction and looting of white-owned property and of stone throwing at the police. This seems to have had several causes: frustration of the participating youth because of their unemployment, a tradition of friction with the police in lower-income Negro neighborhoods, a desire of the participating youth to join the protest movement without submitting to its discipline, a response to several small nationalist Negro organizations, and a desire for just plain excitement and deviltry (such as were being expressed by groups of white youth of all classes at the same time). In the summer of 1965, the major Negro area of Los Angeles, which had been calm in 1964, saw an even more violent outbreak of the same type. By this time the other northern cities, including those that had experienced Negro violence in 1964, were peaceful (with the partial exception of Chicago where there was a continuous protest against a school board policy of maintaining school segregation), having made, with the aid of the federal government, significant efforts to improve conditions for Negroes.

Minorities in American Political Life

Minority group members have two major interests in politics: (a) to be able to participate in local, state, and federal political processes as first-class citizens; and (b) to be able to use the political process to better their condition. Both interests reflect the abnormal position of minorities in America. Some minority groups are deprived of their vote, and some minority members who are candidates for public office cannot draw votes from outside their group because of prejudice. Members of some minority groups vote as a bloc rather than as individuals because they believe that this is the only way to get their rights recognized by politicians. We shall consider only one of these situations.

Except for the earliest arrivals, Japanese immigrants were not allowed to become citizens until the McCarran-Walter Act was passed in 1951. They were not permitted to go through the naturalization process, as were all white immigrants. Thus there were many elderly Japanese who were brought to this country as children, who never had any loyalty to any other country but the United States, and who

---

[46] For an analysis of the conditions which create the contemporary riots, see Kenneth B. Clark, *Dark Ghetto: Dilemmas of Social Power* (New York: Harper, 1965).

had sufficient knowledge of American history and law to pass the naturalization test; but they never became American citizens. However, under American law, their children were automatically American citizens, since they were born on American soil without the privileges of extraterritoriality accorded to foreign diplomats.

About the time that a significant proportion of second-generation Japanese had reached the voting age, Japan declared war on the United States. All Japanese on the West Coast (who then constituted some 88 percent of all Japanese in the United States) were ordered into "relocation camps" inland. They were not allowed to vote in federal or state elections from these camps, and local matters were controlled by the white camp authorities. In the 1944 election, the only Japanese-Americans theoretically allowed to vote were those who were volunteers in the American Army and the few civilians not interned (and with established residence). Even this privilege was largely theoretical, for the soldiers had to send their ballots to their original home communities on the West Coast, where they were frequently ignored.

After the war, when Japanese-Americans were released from the relocation camps and the Army, they had to reestablish residence (usually taking a full year) and register before they could vote. After 1952, Japanese-born persons could apply for citizenship, and many did so. The long delay in admitting Hawaii as a state in the union was due to the many Orientals in its population. It was not until 1959 that Hawaii became a state, and the deliberate disfranchisement of the Japanese-Americans was ended. Negroes are now the only minority group still partly disfranchised (in some of the Southern states). Not only is this unconstitutional, and so declared in many court decisions, but Congress legislated against this disfranchisement in 1957, in 1960, and again in 1964 and 1965—on the last two occasions much more forcefully.

Minorities in American Social Life

THE SOCIAL STATUS OF JEWS. Jews experience a great deal of segregation and discrimination, despite the fact that they belong to the white race and generally adopt the cultural forms of America after the second generation.[47] It is impossible to identify most American-

---

[47] N. C. Belth, ed., *Barriers: Patterns of Discrimination Against Jews* (New York: Anti-Defamation League of B'nai B'rith, 1958). Elmo Roper, *Factors Affecting the Admission of High School Seniors to College* (Washington, D. C.: American Council on Education, 1949). Alfred M. Lee, *Fraternities Without Brotherhood* (Boston: Beacon Press, 1955).

born Jews on the basis either of physical appearance or manners. But when one *is* identified by other people, he may be subjected to social segregation and discrimination. Although there are no laws against marriage between Jews and non-Jews in the United States, in contrast to laws in 23 states (1960) that prohibit intermarriage between whites and Negroes, Orientals, and Indians, feeling against it tends to be strong.[48] Nevertheless, a significant number of such marriages do occur. While Jews are seldom excluded from commercial hotels, they are frequently excluded from resort and residential hotels. There are no segregation laws against Jews, and hence no legal discrimination in public services, although individual officials occasionally manifest discrimination. Private schools and colleges are sometimes "restricted" to non-Jews completely, or they have "quotas" under which Jews are allowed to enter. Many medical colleges in the United States have a quota system against Jews, and so do some other professional schools.

Certain types of employment also tend to be closed to Jews—notably banking and insurance. Sometimes only one Jewish salesperson is employed to take care of the Jewish clientele. Informal restrictive covenants are in force against Jews in nearly every urban area where they dwell in significant numbers, and there is strong feeling against selling or renting property to Jews in many upper-class Gentile areas. Voluntary associations with sociable or recreational purposes (especially those whose membership is drawn from the upper classes) frequently exclude Jews, although voluntary associations with other purposes tend not to exclude them. Fraternities, country clubs, sports groups, and social clubs are among the most completely segregated associations in the United States, although practices have been changing here, too, in recent years.

It is in interpersonal relations that segregation of Jews is most extensive—not only are they kept out of social clubs, but they are not invited to informal gatherings or parties in many circles. They are talked about behind their backs and kept at a distance in neighborly relations. The rationalization usually advanced to justify this behavior is that Jews are unmannerly or "pushing," but the rationalization is even more frequently applied to Jews who do not have these traits than to those who do. The latter tend to be first- or second-generation Jews who have not yet learned American cultural forms, but who also make little effort to associate with non-Jews. Scorn, disgust, and

---

[48] See, for example, Milton L. Barron, *People Who Intermarry* (Syracuse: Syracuse University Press, 1947).

studied indifference are frequent attitudes manifested by non-Jews in their personal relations with Jews.

THE RESIDENTIAL SEGREGATION OF NEGROES. Housing segregation occurs almost as frequently in northern cities as in southern cities,[49] since in some of the latter a large proportion of Negroes live in what were formerly slave quarters behind the white men's houses. White southerners have effective ways of separating Negroes and whites other than by residential segregation, and they often want Negroes who work as domestic servants to live close to them. In the North, residential segregation plays a relatively greater role.[50] Since there are no laws requiring segregation, people use those institutional and public facilities that are closest to them. If Negroes live in separate areas, their institutions and public facilities thus also tend to be separate. For the same reason, residential segregation prevents Negroes and whites from crossing each other's paths so often on the street. In the South, Negro streets are less likely to be paved or to have adequate street lighting, cleaning, garbage and sewage disposal. In the North, the segregated Negro areas are more likely than not to be slums, with worn-out and obsolete sidewalks and streets, schools, and other public institutions. Discrimination arising from residential segregation is less intentional than the systematic kind used in the South, since whites who live in slum areas experience it too. But it nevertheless affects Negroes with special intensity. Also, Negroes cannot move out of the slums, even if they raise their incomes.

Residential segregation has been maintained by various formal and informal pressures. At first laws were used, but they were unequivocally declared unconstitutional by the Supreme Court in 1917. Then the restrictive covenants came into use, and operated through most of the period of northward Negro migration. The Supreme Court in 1948 declared the covenants to be unenforceable in the courts. Extralegal (including illegal) devices—ranging from persuasion to bombing—have also been used to keep members of minority groups out of certain areas. The refusal of individual owners to sell or rent is, of course, the main way of preventing minorities from coming in, and this is not illegal (except in a few states recently). However, the pressure for housing is so great among Negroes that a few of the wealthier ones pay huge sums to acquire a residence in a white area bordering on the Negro area.

---

[49] On the extent and patterns of residential segregation, see Karl E. and Alma F. Taeuber, *Negroes in Cities: Residential Segregation and Neighborhood Change* (Chicago: Aldine, 1965).

[50] Charles Abrams, *Forbidden Neighbors* (New York: Harper, 1955).

Frequently real-estate speculators organize the initial invasion, since they know they can get higher prices from Negroes. The informal pressures, including the illegal ones, are then used by the white residents of the area. If they prove ineffective, because the Negroes are so desperately in need of housing, the whites become panicky and start to move out of the neighborhood. Other Negroes buy or rent the vacated residences, though often not until the latter have passed through the hands of real-estate speculators. Whites who sell out during the panic get low value on their property, although usually the Negroes buying it still pay high prices to the speculators. After the panic is over, in a year or two, the value of the property rises above the original level, because the Negroes are still overcrowded and still have to pay high prices for housing. The whites who moved out have lost money and have had their hatred of the Negro reinforced. Although residential segregation caused the trouble in the first place, the whites are more determined than ever not to allow a single Negro to gain a foothold in their areas.

Formal segregation in northern cities has tended to keep Negroes bottled up in small areas, while their numbers have grown considerably. By far the most densely populated areas of the United States are the few square miles alloted to Negroes in Chicago and New York City. The overcrowding makes for bad health conditions, lack of privacy, and friction between people, as well as for high rents. The Supreme Court decision caused a rapid outward movement of Negroes into previously all-white areas in those cities where Negroes were not too frightened by threatened violence. A good number could pay high rents and higher prices for houses than could many of the whites with whom they competed for housing.

In Chicago, for example, Negroes found it possible to move both eastward and southward for several miles outside the old "Black Belt." In some of the areas, some of the whites gave way to panic and formed mobs to intimidate the Negro families moving in. In other northern cities, there were also reactions among the whites, but they did not usually lead to violence. Negroes are now to be found in many parts of most large northern cities, although there is also considerable segregation. Most whites still refuse to rent or sell to Negroes. But when a few do rent or sell, neighborhoods become mixed only when the whites do not panic and move out, as is sometimes now the case. One of the important factors for the future is that the rate of migration of Negroes from the South will soon slow down, as so many Negroes have already moved and the older caste patterns are breaking down in the South. Other forces promising further housing desegregation in the future are the passage of state "fair housing laws" in 17 northern states and cities (1964) and President Kennedy's Executive Order (1962) preventing the use of federal guarantees on certain types of loans to construct new housing.

School Segregation

In recent years, the issue of school segregation in the southern states has symbolized the whole struggle over the position of minority groups in the United States. In one sense, of course, school segregation is only one among hundreds of problems of intergroup relations. It affects only part of one minority in one section of the country. On the other hand, it is an appropriate symbol: it is a manifestation of the very essence of racism and the caste system—that certain people are kept separate from others because they are believed to be biologically inferior—and is thus directly or indirectly related to practically all aspects of the problems of intergroup relations in the United States. Furthermore, it is a situation that has been maintained by law and government since racism reached its peak in the South around 1890, and thus involves public action rather than merely private attitudes. The southern proponents of racism and caste are acting as though the abolition of school segregation will mean the end of the caste system entirely (they have reacted in a much milder fashion to elimination of other aspects of discrimination and segregation), and they may be right. It is of considerable interest to students of group psychology and social change that, whereas the effort for change and the Supreme Court order have been directed only at school *desegregation*, white southern racists have identified these as movements toward *integration*. This is not mere labeling for propaganda purposes, but involves a genuine belief that the heart of the caste system ("the southern way of life") is being attacked, and that, if school segregation disappears, so will the rest of the caste system. To northerners and others, this would simply mean that the South would become like the North ("the South would join the Union again," as one northerner semifacetiously put it). To southern racists it would mean eventual amalgamation of the races ("mongrelization") and subsequent decay of civilization.

The school segregation laws of the southern states were passed in the late 1870's and 1880's when the caste system generally was being molded in the South. At first there were some doubts as to their constitutionality, but the *Plessy* v. *Ferguson* decision of the Supreme Court in 1896 laid these doubts to rest. This eight-to-one decision held that public facilities could be separate for the races if they were equal and therefore nondiscriminatory. Actually, the schools of the South were not equal for Negroes, although this information was not presented to the Court, and they became markedly less so during the following two decades. The Court's principle of "separate but equal" was a fiction that was used as a justification for segregation under democracy but that everyone knew did not exist.

When the NAACP began to bring cases before the federal courts in the 1930's on the grounds that public educational facilities for Negroes were in fact not equal, the courts invariably decided for the Negro plaintiffs, but on narrow legal grounds that improved only special conditions—such as teachers' salaries, the size of school libraries, and the availability of professional courses in the Negro colleges. But the legal fiction of "separate but equal" remained the ruling principle. While the southern schools did not in fact provide equal conditions for Negroes very rapidly, the court decisions did—in theory.

By 1950, a crucial legal situation was reached: the wealthy state of Texas, required to provide a law school education for a single Negro applicant, set up an expensive law school complete with a few highly qualified professors and a library—for the one student. This student, with NAACP backing, did not consider it equal and carried his plea to the Supreme Court. The argument was no longer in terms of physical facilities or even measurable quality of training, but in terms of segregated facilities being inevitably unequal. The decision—in this crucial case of *Sweatt* v. *Painter*—was that the state university must admit the Negro to its law school because the school for the Negro was inferior in "those qualities which are incapable of objective measurement but which made for greatness in a law school," such as accessibility to other students who would become the future lawyers and judges of the state. In the same year, the Supreme Court heard the case of *McLaurin* v. *Oklahoma* and also arrived at a unanimous decision read by the Chief Justice. The Negro was admitted to the state university's graduate school, but was required to sit in a special assigned row in classes, use books at an assigned table in the library, and eat at an assigned table in the cafeteria. The Chief Justice found this unequal: "Such restrictions impair and inhibit his ability to study, to engage in discussions, and exchange views with other students, and, in general, to learn his profession." These two decisions were still within the framework of "separate but equal," but the Court now so strictly interpreted "equality" of facilities that any kind of segregation would appear to be a violation of Negroes' constitutional rights.

The straightforward court decision that segregation in and of itself inevitably involved discrimination, and hence was illegal, did not come until the *Brown* case in 1954. This involved elementary school children in five states, and the argument included reports of a number of social science studies which showed that segregation made Negro children aware that whites regarded them as inferior and thus impaired their studies. The Court's unanimous decision in effect nullified the *Plessy* "separate but equal" doctrine, since it said that it was impossible. The segregating states began to abolish segregation in schools, libraries, and recreational facilities after an implementing court decision in 1955, which held that all states must begin to take some steps toward desegregation and proceed toward complete desegregation "with all deliberate speed." Some southern citizens' groups, governments, and politicians began to react against this desegregation—especially in the public schools—and a new stage of intergroup conflict developed.

To understand this present conflict, some points must be clarified. (a) The court did not say anything in the *Brown* decision which really went against southerners' beliefs. The court in effect merely said that "separate but equal" was factually impossible; every southerner knew this and there never had been any southern support for making public facilities equal. The white South wanted segregation, and the Court had set up a legal fiction in 1896 which permitted this. (b) While the Court in 1954 took cognizance of some social science studies, it did not base its decision on these. Its decision was based on *logical* recognition of the fact that "separate but equal" was impossible; segregation was instituted to create and implement inequality. (c) The 1954 *Brown* decision was not an about-face for the Court. The Court had never decided for inequality, and since 1944 it had been giving unanimous decisions for strict implementation of equality. The two decisions of 1950 mentioned above even took cognizance that segregation created intangible inequalities and thus made the *Brown* decision of 1954 a natural consequence. The prosegregationists' delay in reacting until 1954-1955 indicated that the caste system was not nearly so strong as it had been in the earlier decades.

The situation since 1954 has been very complicated, but a number of facts and interpretations can be specified. First, desegregation was quickly begun in many of the states which formerly had compulsory segregation.[51] By 1958, the school systems of the border states—Mis-

---

[51] Some studies of the desegregation process are: Robin M. Williams and Margaret W. Ryan, *Schools in Transition* (Chapel Hill, N. C.: University of North Carolina Press, 1954); Bonita Valien, *The St. Louis Story* (New York: Anti-Defamation League of B'nai B'rith, 1956); Melvin M. Tumin, *Desegregation: Resistance and Readiness* (Princeton: Princeton University Press, 1958); Carl F. Hansen, *Miracle of Social Adjustment: Desegregation in the Washington, D. C., Schools* (New York: Anti-Defamation League of B'nai B'rith, 1957).

souri, Oklahoma, Kentucky, West Virginia, Maryland, and Delaware—were practically completely desegregated, and desegregation had begun in the states of the upper South such as Arkansas, Texas, Tennessee, and North Carolina (only Virginia in this group held out until 1959). In many other social patterns, such as having a two-party political system, the old border states had joined the North, and their affiliation with the South was a matter of history only. Second, the deep South—Mississippi, Alabama, Louisiana, Georgia, South Carolina, and Florida—resisted desegregation with legislative action, public pronouncements, organization of white Citizens' Councils and other groups, and even violence and threats of violence. But even here there were breaks in the caste system: some public facilities other than schools were quietly desegregated (for example, the libraries in Atlanta, Georgia); some southern politicians—especially those in Alabama and Florida—acknowledged that they should follow the law and that all they would or should do was to delay desegregation; some private organizations—even though the court decision did not apply to them—began to desegregate their meetings and even memberships. By 1964, the most resisting of the southern states—Mississippi—adopted some token desegregation in the public schools. In 1965, Congress passed a "federal aid to education" act, which provided that federal funds could be given only to nonsegregated schools. This law immediately hastened the trend toward formal school desegregation, but it may have less effect on *de facto* school segregation based on residential segregation.

Third, violence occurred in only a few localities during the process of transition, and in practically all of these the violence was stimulated by an outside (often northern) agitator, who was motivated by ambition or greed. The major exception occurred in Little Rock, Arkansas, where the opposition was stirred up by the governor of the state, after the local public authorities had commenced a gradual and practically unopposed program of desegregation. The incident, which gained international attention, involved federal troop intervention and resulted in a victory for the forces of moderation (although the governor has since been reelected). The instances of violence against desegregation were seldom protracted, and few resulted in deaths, but they received much more publicity and attention than did the many times more numerous instances of peaceful and unopposed desegregation. While it was mainly the lower-income white population that responded to demagogic appeals for violence against desegregation, the upper- and middle-income population tended to join in a movement called Citizens Councils, Inc. This organization sought to stop desegregation by economic boycott and general harassment of Negroes (and their white friends) who sought to effectuate desegregation. They succeeded in slowing down the pace of desegregation and also in cutting off communication between responsible Negroes and whites in many southern communities. The white "moderates" have not formed organizations, but they are influential in some communities and succeed in minimizing racial "incidents" even in the deep South.

The strongest external forces toward desegregation in the South are the federal government and northern and international public opinion. From the inside, the "moderate" forces tend to include businessmen, intellectuals, and politicians with connections at the national level. The segregationists have joined a nationwide conservative attack on the federal courts, in an effort to restrict their powers. They have also begun to try to swing northern opinion away from sympathy with Negroes and civil rights by appealing—through advertisements and speeches—to the principle of nonintervention in others' affairs. Some northerners, especially among the intellectuals, have been convinced by this propaganda, and if enough of them are convinced, the pressure on the South to eliminate the caste system will be relaxed for a while. Eventually, forces within the South toward modernization and "Americanization" will probably become dominant, but in the meantime they are mainly sustained by the northern conscience and northern pressure. There is now a good chance that the upper South will join the border states in eliminating the caste system, if the public discussion continues. The struggle over desegregation will then be limited to the six states of the deep South. On the other hand, if northern public opinion loses interest in the South and its "problem" and considers that these have no consequences for the well-being of the United States as a whole or its reputation, the caste system will be temporarily strengthened. Eventually, the economic and political forces operating in the South, and the rapid rate of migration out of the South, are likely to render the caste system obsolete.

As noted in an earlier section, race relations in the South have been changing continuously and, in recent years, even rapidly. Yet the justification for the caste system that reached its peak in the decades 1890-1910 has remained unchanged. This is an interesting, but not unusual, social phenomenon—that ideologies remain long after the behavior that they justify disappears. The situation is analogous to that of a man whose health and vigor has been running down for years unnoticed. Then someone—perhaps a physician—tells him that his body is weak and that he is no longer capable of heavy physical exertion.

The man cries out in anguish: he has suddenly realized what has been true for years. His body has been changing gradually, but his conception of himself has changed suddenly. So it is with the South: suddenly, since 1954, it has been forced to begin to change its conception of itself as a region. It is rapidly becoming aware that it can no longer think of itself as a region of romantic old plantations, with lots of old-fashioned courage but no modern tools or weapons, an ancient antagonist of the materialistic and technologically developed North which has always been thought of as exploiting the South. A large number of southerners have suddenly come to realize that their region is becoming quite like the North, industrially and culturally. Those who loved the old romantic myth are now crying out; they are shouting that they will defend to the death something that has largely passed out of existence. They are defending a memory, not a living institution. How long they will go on doing this, how many persons they can recruit to join them, how successful they will be in staving off economic and social change remains to be seen.

New Problems of Intergroup Relations

New kinds of problems arise on the forefront of progress in solving the old problems, and they arise because the old problems of prejudice and discrimination were recently so dominant. Among lower-class Negroes and American Indians, particularly, there is what might be called the "tradition of backwardness." Because they have no particular occupational training and because their families have not encouraged them to prepare for good jobs, many Negroes and Indians are not prepared to take advantage of all the job opportunities that are available. Another problem is that members of racial minorities and of the white majority do not know how to associate with each other; they are excessively formal and sensitive in interpersonal relations.

The ignorance and lack of skill among Negroes are especially serious as the United States has entered a period of automation in industry and clerical work, which forces the unskilled out of employment. While the average income of Negroes climbed from about 33 percent that of the whites in 1930 to about 61 percent that of the whites in 1955, it fell to 58 percent that of the whites by 1962. The recent fall was not due to increased discrimination but to the inability of uneducated Negroes to adjust to the demands of increasing automation. Of course, structural features, such as union seniority rules and high initiation fees, also bar Negroes from desirable employment.

There is little of the simple form of job discrimination left in the North.

A second problem is that the development of housing segregation—since 1910 in the North and more recently in the South—and the segregation of community institutions, especially the schools, have been "de facto" rather than by discriminatory statute or ordinance.[52] Since 1954, northern Negroes and their white sympathizers have held organized protests against de facto school segregation. A number of northern cities—especially New York and Detroit—have taken action to reduce it and also to raise the educational level of "culturally deprived" youth, especially Negroes and other racial minorities. There has been resistance from some white parents, not only because of prejudice, but also because desegregation often interferes with the principle of organizing schools on a neighborhood basis and because the backward Negro children lower the standards of teaching. To raise the level of teaching and to break the pattern of de facto segregation are perhaps the most serious problems in race relations facing the northern states today. While much is being done by many northern cities, the problems will be solved only when the residential concentration of minorities—because of poverty and discrimination—is eliminated.

A third problem is the age-old one of immigrants who do not know how to make an adjustment to big-city life. This probably is most serious for Indians right now, but it is also a problem of Negro migrants from the deep South. For most of the Indians who do not migrate from the reservations there is the problem of living in an underdeveloped economy. The great majority of reservation Indians in the United States practice agriculture without the equipment, knowledge, or organization to derive a decent living from it. The location and quality of most reservation lands make it dubious that their agriculture can ever be made competitive. Their location and local resources also make them fairly unsuitable for industry. Thus most Indians face a marginal economic existence, often without local self-government, unless they choose to leave the reservation. If they leave, however, they have to compete as immigrants who are not very knowledgeable about the ways of the modern white man, and they lose some of the marginal economic benefits that are provided by the federal government for reservation Indians. So many Indians today are torn between two unsatisfactory ways of living, and those who

---

[52] For a review of the whole issue, see Arnold M. Rose, *De Facto School Segregation* (New York: National Conference of Christians and Jews, 1964).

move from one to the other get the disadvantages of both. Discrimination against Indians is not strong in areas not close to the reservations, and Indians can make successful economic and political adjustments in the large metropolitan areas of the United States. But here, as far as Indian culture is concerned, they cease to be Indians and in a generation blend into the dominant American population.

Discrimination against the Chinese, which reached extreme forms at the end of the nineteenth century, and against the Japanese, which had its peak in the early 1940's, has now markedly subsided. Orientals now have access to economic opportunities, to housing, to education, to the ballot, to justice in the courts, to professional and civic associations, and to the other measurable aspects of American life to almost the same extent as white people. The change in the past 15 years has been little short of phenomenal, and has been symbolized by the admission of Hawaii to the Union in 1959 and the seating of its Chinese-American senator and Japanese-American representatives in Congress. There is still considerable social segregation of Orientals, but this does not seem to hamper Oriental-Americans from taking an almost full role in American society.

Immigrants from southern and eastern Europe earlier attained the degree of acceptance into American society which has more recently occurred for the Orientals. Though they are still subject to social discrimination, and their relatives and compatriots are still the object of discrimination in immigration, they have made marked progress toward economic, political, and legal equality. The barriers that separate them from full acceptance into American society have largely shifted from those of caste to those of class and thus out of the context of the problem we are examining in this chapter. Much of what remains by way of caste barriers for the European immigrants are connected with religion rather than national origin, and these might be symbolized by the political prejudice against Catholic candidates for high public office.

Prejudice and discrimination against Jews should be given special consideration in this context, as they arose partly as a product of the general pattern of relationships between old Americans and European immigrants. Particularly in the 1920's and 1930's, however, anti-Semitism in the United States took on a distinctive character, largely as a result of deliberate propaganda from organizations and individuals having political ambitions. The chief discrimination against Jews in the United States today is on the social level; it restricts their admission to housing in certain neighborhoods, to privately owned but publicly available recreational establishments, to service and social clubs, and to free social relationships with non-Jews generally. There are also some restrictions on economic opportunities, particularly in banking and insurance, and "quotas" maintained by medical schools and other segments of higher education. Perhaps most significant of all is a continuing stream of defamation, passed along largely by word of mouth and by the publications of extremist political organizations of the "crackpot fringe."

One of the more serious of contemporary minority problems in the United States is that involving the immigrants from Latin America, particularly from Mexico and Puerto Rico.[53] These are people of mixed Indian-white or Negro-white ancestry, largely of peasant, rural backgrounds, who move to the United States primarily for economic self-betterment. In addition to having all of the problems of rural immigrants, they are faced with serious economic discriminations, both in the types of employment available to them and in the remuneration they receive for their work. They are also excluded from most social relationships with the dominant group and face severe restrictions against dwelling in many residential areas. While the federal government restrains their immigration in only minor respects, especially in the case of Puerto Ricans who are native American citizens, local governments often clandestinely cooperate with private interests to control their immigration. While the rapidity of their cultural assimilation is not dissimilar to that of earlier immigrant groups, the proximity of their homeland offers them a constant temptation to escape from the discrimination and other difficulties of American life.

There are other smaller minorities in the United States who face certain special difficulties. The Hispanos—Spanish-speaking Americans who have lived in New Mexico and Colorado for centuries—are restricted from jury service and certain kinds of employment in those states.[54] The French Canadians who constitute sizable communities in certain New England areas are faced with widespread social exclusion.[55] Periodic efforts are made to prevent Hutterites who dwell in

[53] John H. Burma, *Spanish-Speaking Groups in the United States* (Durham, N. C.: Duke University Press, 1954). C. W. Mills *et al.*, *The Puerto Rican Journey* (New York: Harper, 1950). Oscar Handlin, *The Newcomers* (Cambridge, Mass.: Harvard University Press, 1959). Elena Padilla, *Up From Puerto Rico* (New York: Columbia University Press, 1958).

[54] John H. Burma, "The Present Status of the Spanish-Americans of New Mexico," *Social Forces*, Vol. 28 (December, 1949), pp. 133-48.

[55] B. B. Wessel, *An Ethnic Survey of Woonsocket, Rhode Island* (Chicago: University of Chicago Press, 1931). E. L. Anderson, *We Americans* (Cambridge, Mass.: Harvard University Press, 1937).

the Dakotas and Minnesota from acquiring agricultural land.[56] Filipinos, who are found in small numbers in California, face severe economic and social discrimination.[57] Cajuns, the descendants of French
Canadians who have intermarried with Negroes over the course of
centuries in southern Louisiana, are treated as Negroes by the whites,
although the Cajuns hold themselves aloof from other persons with
Negro ancestry.

Thus, while most minority problems have diminished considerably
since 1900—when Indians were frequently slaughtered and cheated,
when Negroes were all but reduced again to slavery and when violence against them reached an all-time high, and when Chinese were
scarcely allowed outside Chinatowns—these problems have by no
means disappeared. The position of the racial minorities has never
been better, and it is improving in all parts of the country. Anti-
Catholic sentiment has similarly diminished. While anti-Semitism did
not reach its peak until the 1930's, organized anti-Semitism is now
quite rare, although informal anti-Semitism is still quite pervasive.
The nationality and linguistic minorities are on the way to disappearance as distinct groups, largely because of gradual acculturation
and the diminution of prejudice against them. Various prejudices
against minorities are quite common throughout the United States,
but racism as an ideology is no longer adhered to so consciously and
so tenaciously. The caste system, while easily observable in several
areas of the country, has cracked, and is nowhere nearly as complete
as it once was. What is more, most of the social forces likely to effect
intergroup relations in the future are operating to diminish racism
and caste.

---

[56] Joseph W. Eaton and Robert J. Weil, *Culture and Mental Disorders* (New
York: Free Press, 1955). Also see, The Canadian Mental Health Association, *The
Hutterites and Saskatchewan: A Study of Intergroup Relations* (Regina, 1953).

[57] Grayson Kirk, "The Filipinos," *Annals of the American Academy of Political
and Social Science*, Vol. 223 (September, 1942), pp. 45-48. N. T. Catapusan, *The
Filipino's Social Adjustment in the United States* (Los Angeles: University of
Southern California, 1940).

10

Family Disorganization

by William J. Goode

ALL MARRIAGES, LIKE ALL LIVES, MUST END. SOME MARRIAGES ARE dissolved by divorce, some by death, and some gradually come apart, to exist for years as a mere formality. Since family life is suffused with emotion, those who are unhappy in their family relationships usually learn that this kind of misery, like a toothache, cannot easily be set apart, compartmentalized, or controlled by an effort of will. It affects much of their lives. Almost everyone will eventually experience one or another of the various forms of disorganization at some time in their lives; the patterns and processes of family disorganization deserve analysis.

Types of Family Disorganization

If family disorganization may be defined as the breakup of a family unit, the dissolution or fracture of a structure of social roles when one or more members fail to perform adequately their role obligations, then several modes of disorganization may be analyzed separately. Such an examination need not confine itself to the contemporary United States and may properly extend to the consideration of larger social structures in which family processes take place.

In the sections which follow, certain major forms of family disorganization will be sketched first. Data from other societies will be used at times, especially in the analyses of illegitimacy and divorce, to throw light on certain broader aspects of family systems. Considerable space will be given to divorce, because so many other types of family disorganization are likely to issue eventually in divorce, because it is the focus of so much moral concern on the part of the

---

I wish to acknowledge the help of Nicholas Tavuchis in the revision of this chapter.

public, and because changes in the divorce rate are usually an index of changes in other elements in the family patterns of any society.

As a foundation for the later analysis of these forms, a general view of their meaning for social structures will first be outlined.

The major forms of family disorganization may be classified as follows:

1. The uncompleted family unit: *illegitimacy*. Although the family unit may not be said to "dissolve" if it never existed, illegitimacy may nevertheless be viewed as one form of family disorganization for two reasons: (a) the potential "father-husband" conspicuously fails in his role obligations as these are defined by the society, mother, and child; and (b) the role failure of members of the families of both mother and father, especially with regard to social control, is a major indirect cause of illegitimacy.

2. Family dissolution by virtue of the willed departure of one spouse: *annulment, separation, divorce, and desertion.* "Job desertion" may also be included here, when the individual uses the excuse of a job to stay away from home for a long period of time.

3. The "empty shell" family, in which individuals live together, but have minimal communication and contact with one another, failing especially in the role obligation to give emotional support to one another.

4. The family crisis caused by "external" events, such as the temporary or permanent unwilled absence of one of the spouses because of death or incarceration in jail or because of such impersonal catastrophes as flood, war, and depression.

5. Internal catastrophes which cause "unwilled" major role failures through mental, emotional, or physical pathologies: severe mental retardation of the child, psychosis of child or spouse, or chronic and incurable physical conditions.

Such a rough classification emphasizes that the family is, like other institutional patterns, an organization of roles, and that a continuing pattern of role performances is necessary if a particular family is to continue to exist.[1] In addition, the classification anticipates one theme of subsequent discussion: that the larger kinship structure or society is concerned about certain forms of family dissolution more than

---

[1] Obviously, other modes of measurement or classification might also be useful. Among recent suggestions, see those of L. L. Geismar, Michael A. LaSorte, and Beverly Ayres, "Measuring Family Disorganization," *Marriage and Family Living,* Vol. 25 (November, 1963), pp. 479-81; and Alice L. Voiland and Bradley Bull, "A Classification of Disordered Family Types," *Social Work,* Vol. 6 (October, 1961), pp. 3-11.

about others (the family of the deserter, as against that of the prisoner); that the society furnishes social patterns for certain participants, but not others, to follow (death, as against divorce); that it avoids any inquiry into some forms which may nevertheless be emotionally important to the participants (the "empty shell" family, or the family adjusting to the strain of the severe pathology of one of its members); and that even when the society does concern itself with the problem, it may focus on only one of the participants (the deserter or the illegitimate father) but not the entire family.

Family Disorganization and the Larger Society

These various forms of family disorganization may best be understood after a brief consideration of their meaning for the larger social structure. They are found in all societies, but the *rates* of family dissolution from different causes will vary from one society to another. The way individuals adjust to these forms and the interlinkages of each type of form within the social structure will also vary.

Because family relations are emotional and involve much of the individual's life and because each individual is unique, family members are likely to experience any disorganizing experience as highly particular, different from the experiences of other families. Each child feels the death of *his* mother is different from that of any other mother, and the divorcing husband looks back on a series of conflicts which seem to him to be different from those of any other divorcing husband. Each event is, of course, unique, if viewed in all its particularity and detail. However, in this as in other areas of social action, when research inquires systematically into a large aggregate of cases, common patterns are usually uncovered. Often people are unaware that they are adjusting in ways which are similar to those of others who have had similar disorganizing experiences, but the observer may nevertheless chart the similarities. Even if research is scanty, so that knowledge about the area is as yet neither systematic nor certain, sociology can be expected nevertheless to locate some regularities in these forms of family disorganization and to suggest where others might be found eventually. Thus, order and pattern are to be sought, even in social events which are experienced as unique.

A distinction must also be maintained between the disorganization of a family *unit* and that of the family *system* in a particular society, and both of these must be distinguished from *change* in a family system.

All enduring marriages inevitably end with the death of one or both spouses, but the family system which is common throughout that society is not thereby affected. The family customs of the society may continue without change, and indeed they contain provisions for the contingency of death. A society may also have a high divorce rate, but the family *system* may remain unchanged. It is likely, for example, that high divorce rates have been part of Arab family systems for many generations, as they are now. We can ask whether the family system contains provisions for coping with the problems generated by the dissolution of particular family units, but no data exist to show that even if the answer is negative the system as a whole will dissolve.

Wherever the world's population is experiencing industrialization, family systems are also undergoing some changes, though not all these are being recorded. This means that at least some of the elements of the old family patterns, such as arranged marriages in China, are dissolving. Of course, if a family *system* is undergoing change, the rates of occurrence of these forms of disorganization, such as divorce, separation, illegitimacy, or desertion, may change.

However, the new system may have *lower* rates of occurrence of certain forms of disorganization. For example, the divorce rates in Arab Algeria and in Japan have been *declining* for half a century. In several Latin-American countries, the rate of illegitimacy has apparently been decreasing. Prolonging life in industrialized countries has meant that fewer children must face orphanhood. Aside from these facts, the main structure of a family system may be altered only slightly by such changes in rates. Finally, though the old set of patterns is in part dissolved, it is usually replaced by a new set of patterns which is as determinate and controlling as the old one was.

Despite the importance of these forms of family disorganization for the individuals in the family, and thus for the society, the legal and formal structures of the society reflect little concern with these problems. If a couple in the United States decides to separate, no agency of the society acts, or is even empowered to find out that a separation occurred, unless the wife seeks financial support. There are few customs to guide the illegitimate mother or father, and once again the state moves only in narrowly defined circumstances (e.g., if the mother wants to get on the relief rolls). If a wife becomes schizophrenic, or a child is born an idiot, few customs exist to help guide the family members, and the formal agencies of the society do not act unless asked to do so.

This relative autonomy of the family simply expresses the fact that no one outside the family has any "rights" in its deliberations and decisions. Which kin may be included varies from one family system to another, but in general the *state* may interfere only where (a) family members themselves initiate state action; or (b) someone in the family is officially reported to be receiving inadequate physical care. In a modern industrial society, where the network of relatives in close interaction is likely to be small, the breakup of a particular family unit is more likely than in prior centuries, or in other family systems, to leave one or more members without anyone who feels any responsibility for even their physical care. Consequently, state initiative in these matters continues to increase in importance.

The analysis of family disorganization of any kind must also keep in view the extent to which the pressures and structures of the *society itself* help to *create* the problems which family units, or at times some agency of the society, must solve, e.g., illegitimacy, incarceration, war, or divorce.

The Uncompleted Family: Illegitimacy

A generation ago, Bronislaw Malinowski formulated the Rule of Legitimacy, which asserts that every society has a rule that each child should have a legitimate father, to act as its protector, guardian, and representative in the society.[2] Like all other rules, this one is violated, and those who violate the rule will be punished in some way. Where the rule is strongly enforced, the illegitimacy rate is low, and individuals who do not conform, together with their illegitimate children, suffer more severe sanctions. The regulations that form and sustain the family system function to move eligible young men and women toward marriage, to place the child in a definite position in a unit within the kinship and social structure, and to fix responsibility for its maintenance and socialization on that specific family unit. These regulations define "legitimacy" in the society, and thereby "illegitimacy" as well. In a much quoted statement, Crane Brinton has epitomized the close relation between legitimacy and illegitimacy:

> Bastardy and marriage in this world are quite supplementary—you cannot have one without the other. In another world, you may indeed separate the two institutions and eliminate one of them, either by having marriage so perfect—in various senses—that no one will ever commit fornication or adultery, or by having fornication so perfect that no one will ever commit marriage.[3]

---

[2] One such statement is to be found in his "Parenthood, the Basis of Social Structure," in V. F. Calverton and Samuel D. Schmalhausen, eds., *The New Generation* (New York: Macaulay, 1930), pp. 137-38.

[3] Crane Brinton, *French Revolutionary Legislation on Illegitimacy, 1789-1804* (Cambridge, Mass.: Harvard University Press, 1936), pp. 82-83.

Such a view of illegitimacy has important implications. One is that the humanitarian notion is incorrect which suggests that the "problem" of illegitimacy may be "solved" if the law defines all children as legitimate, or the birth certificate omits any information about illegitimacy (as of 1956, 33 states did this). As long as no family unit has been established according to the norms of the society, the child's status is unchanged, and there will be considerable ambiguity as to the father's, mother's, and blood relatives' role obligations toward him or her.

The answer to the questions, "Why illegitimacy?" and "Why legitimacy?" are the same—that the maintenance of the social structure requires that the obligation to create the next generation biologically and socially be assigned to a socially approved family unit.

Let us pursue this question further. In the United States and in Western society generally, illegitimacy is condemned partly because it is evidence of sexual relations outside marriage. However, this connection is not usual, for some degree of premarital sexual license is found in about 70 percent of the societies for which we have information available,[4] but childbirth outside marriage is not approved in those societies. This fact suggests that most societies are more concerned with illegitimacy than with sexual intercourse outside marriage. Public opinion in the United States condemns illegitimacy more strongly than a simple violation of the norms of sexual conduct.[5] Indeed, the disapproval of sex relations outside marriage is less strong when a marriage between the couple is imminent than when it is unlikely or even impossible.

Thus the question posed by Kingsley Davis must be asked: why does society not "solve" the problem by requiring the use of contraception and, when this fails, abortion?[6] His answer is that to break the normative relations between sexuality and the family, so that adults would as a matter of course decide rationally whether they would enjoy sex within or outside of the family, would also reduce the strength of the motive to marry and found a family. The radical changes necessary to eliminate illegitimacy almost completely would very likely come close to eliminating the family system too.

But though societies generally condemn illegitimacy, they vary in

---

[4] George P. Murdock, *Social Structure* (New York: Macmillan, 1949), p. 265.

[5] For the different reactions to different types of illegitimacy, see Kingsley Davis, "The Forms of Illegitimacy," *Social Forces*, Vol. 18 (October, 1939), pp. 77-89.

[6] Kingsley Davis, "Illegitimacy and the Social Structure," *American Journal of Sociology*, Vol. 45 (September, 1939), pp. 221-22, 231-33. Davis also "proposes," not seriously, that some penalties be provided for violation.

TABLE 1

Illegitimacy Rates in Selected Countries

Country	Percent Illegitimate of All Live Births
United States (1963)[a]	6.3
Sweden (1961)	11.7
Italy (1961)	2.3
England and Wales (1962)	6.6
Japan (1962)	1.1
Egypt (1957)[b]	1.0

Source: Personal communication with United Nations Statistical Division (May, 1965).

[a] Estimate.

[b] Data from official *Statistical Yearbook of Egypt*.

the intensity of this disapproval, the strength of the sanctions visited on the child and parents, and the place in the social structure which the child is permitted to occupy. In different class strata of a society, too, illegitimacy arouses different responses. If the sociological view sketched so far is correct, where family norms are upheld vigorously, illegitimacy rates are low. It should then be useful to compare societies having high illegitimacy rates with those having low rates.

Although numerical data are not available for all these societies, it seems likely that the lowest illegitimacy rates are to be found in Arab countries, where the rate is about 1 to 2 percent of live births, and in India. Most African societies prior to industrialization had low rates. In these societies, marriages were arranged, for the most part, when the girl was still in her teens. In India and the Arab countries, social contact between a nubile girl and a man occurred, if at all, only under the close supervision of her relatives, and often his as well. African tribes varied greatly in this respect, but great value was set on children, so that there was little chance that a marriage could not be arranged before childbirth.

In western Europe, numerical data are more exact than in other culture areas (except Japan). For recent rates see Table 1.

A slight downward trend in these rates has occurred over the past half-century. Although the sexual freedom of young adults has increased greatly, social pressures to enter marriage before childbirth have evidently not decreased.

One northwestern European rural pattern, now disappearing, throws light on the effect of social controls on illegitimacy rates. In the Scandinavian countries and in parts of Germany, adolescent children of farmers were permitted considerable sexual freedom so that illegitimacy rates were high in some regions (e.g., 17 percent to 28 percent in certain Swedish departments in the years 1921-1925). However, the courtships were publicly known, and guided by both peer group and adult norms. The father was likely to be known in case of pregnancy, and by that stage in the relationship, both families had at least tentatively approved the match as well. The legal fact that the child might be born out of wedlock was important to both Church and State, but of little concern to the local community, since the marriage was a "settled matter" and would take place at the convenience of the couple's parents.

Evidence from the United States suggests that about 1 out of 5 marriages is preceded by conception.[7] A comparison with Denmark shows that the rate is even higher, more than 1 in 3.[8] However, because the Danes have greater tolerance of sexual intercourse between engaged couples, there are no great pressures to rush into marriage. Thus, the modal time of conception for these cases is 5 months prior to marriage. In the United States sample, it is 2 months. Of course, in both countries almost all these couples do marry, so that the official illegitimacy rate is low: 7 percent in Denmark, 2.9 percent in the Indiana county, and 0.9 percent in the Utah county. In both countries, the likelihood of divorce is greater for couples who conceive premaritally than for couples who do not, but the difference between the former and the latter is smaller in Denmark. Here, the premarital pregnancy is more likely than in Scandinavia to happen to a couple who had, up to that point, no intention of marrying. Thus, the forced marriage which forestalls an illegitimate birth takes place between a young man and woman who have not adjusted to one another, or even to the idea of being married.

The New World south of the Rio Grande offers an instructive contrast to both the United States and Europe generally. Illegitimacy

---

[7] The sociologist traced each birth for a given period in counties in Indiana and Utah to the specific date of the couple's marriage. See Harold T. Christensen, "The Method of Record Linkage Applied to Family Data," *Marriage and Family Living*, Vol. 20 (February, 1958), pp. 38-43; and his "Cultural Relativism and Premarital Sex Norms," *American Sociological Review*, Vol. 25 (February, 1960), pp. 31-39. Cf. Sidney G. Croog, "Aspects of the Cultural Background of Premarital Pregnancy in Denmark," *Social Forces*, Vol. 30 (December, 1951), pp. 215-19.

[8] The United States cases were drawn from records in selected years between 1905 and 1941, the Danish cases from 1948; thus, very likely the rate is higher now.

TABLE 2

Selected New World Illegitimacy Rates

Country	Percent Illegitimate of All Live Births
Brazil (1960) [a]	12.9
Mexico (1962)	25.0
Argentina (1962)	24.3
Peru (1961)	41.7
Paraguay (1955)	48.0
Guatemala (1962)	59.3
Venezuela (1962)	37.3
Jamaica (1958)	71.6
Panama (1962)	61.5

Source: Personal communication with United Nations Statistical Division (May, 1965).
[a] Federal District.

rates are higher than recorded anywhere else, except for urbanized slums in sub-Saharan Africa. Some of these rates are presented here (Table 2).

Here, as so often in analyzing a social pattern, two questions must be considered: (a) are there recurring situations of decision in which the elements important for the decision are similar? and (b) are there larger social structures which permit or cause that type of decision situation to occur frequently?

These high rates are not a product of "Indian" or "transplanted African" cultures, in which "illegitimacy in the white man's sense" has no social value. Descriptions of the older Indian and African family systems show that illegitimacy was not approved. Moreover, the New World nations are Western in culture, and only here and there can one find pockets of "natives" who have maintained any great part of their Indian or African culture (the Bush Negroes in the Guianas, the northwestern highlands of Guatemala, and the Andean highlands of Peru, Ecuador, and Bolivia). Finally, every study of a specific community, even in the countries with the highest rates, proves that illegitimacy is not approved and that the ideal is childbirth within wedlock.[9]

On the other hand, where a high proportion of the people in a given area or social stratum are illegitimate themselves, no one can be

[9] The best study of this point may be found in Judith Blake, *Family Structure in Jamaica* (New York: Free Press, 1961). See also William J. Goode, "Illegitimacy in the Caribbean Social Structure," *American Sociological Review*, Vol. 25 (February, 1960), pp. 21-30.

singled out for much punishment or reward for deviation or conformity to the norm. More central, however, is the immediate situation of decision for the young woman. Courtship is anonymous, or without supervision by either adult kin or adolescent peers. Illegitimacy occurs primarily in lower-class families, which are themselves unstable and have little family honor to lose, so that motivation to control courtship is not high. Consequently, the young girl establishes essentially an individual role bargain with a male and is in a poor bargaining position unless she has outstanding personal qualities. She must be willing to accept the risk of childbirth out of wedlock if she is to have a chance at marriage. These "consensual" unions are less stable than legal ones, but from one of them a stable relationship may emerge. Eventually, most people do marry.

This pattern of individual courtship outside family controls results from cultural and social disorganization in New World countries, comparable to the dissolution of immigrant social and cultural patterns in the United States, and the disintegration of African patterns under United States slavery and, in modern times, under African industrialization. The courtship structure just noted has, in fact, not entirely disappeared among the Negro population of the South, where illegitimacy rates now range from 18 percent to 32 percent. The cultural and social destruction in the New World was on a larger scale than any similar conquest since Rome and was more complete than that of the Chinese under the Manchus, the Indians under the English, or the Indonesians under the Dutch. In the New World, the native religious systems were undermined, and the political systems were effectively destroyed. Populations experienced high mortality, and were also dispersed or moved geographically, so that the social unity of tribes was dissolved. But though the Western norms were gradually accepted as "right," the peasants were not given full social rewards for complete assimilation, as were immigrants to the United States. In most countries, a caste or semicaste system kept the peasants from full participation in the Western patterns. Thus, the new norms were not entirely accepted, and the villages were not unified enough to impose adequate social controls over such matters as courtship. The rulers in turn had no interest in insisting on peasant conformity to the norm of legitimacy. In this respect, too, the South in the United States was similar to the rest of the New World. However, as peasant (and in the United States, the Negro) populations have become more integrated into the national cultural and social patterns, conformity to the rule of legitimacy has increased.

Of course, these general relationships should also be found in many of our Indian populations, who have experienced a similar fate. This is not true of all, of course, since many have been completely assimilated into the United States population. And, following these hypotheses, where the Indian group has managed to maintain its own cultural and social integrity, its illegitimacy rate should not be high. Philip K. Bock adapted these ideas ingeniously to a test *over time*— i.e., when the Indian tribe had a higher level of social or cultural integration, its rate should be lower, and vice-versa. Over the period of a century, these patterns seemed to hold up.[10]

Implicit reference has already been made to the class and caste pattern of illegitimacy, and further patterns should be noted. In the United States, illegitimacy rates are higher among the segments of the population aged 17 to 21 [11] than among those older, and higher among those in lower social strata than in higher strata. The differences are partly a function of higher "exposure frequencies," i.e., frequency of sexual intercourse, and partly the result of a lesser willingness to use contraceptives. On the other hand, older people and those in middle or higher social strata are less likely either to be pressured into marriage by an unwanted pregnancy or to bear the child. They are more able to obtain the services of an abortionist in the United States or nearby countries.

However, public outcry with reference to this problem has been far more strident than the facts suggest. The striking change in the United States over the past generation is that illegitimacy has changed from a personal or family problem to a *social* problem, in the sense that the state and private agencies are far more concerned with the fate of the illegitimate child and mother, believe that they should be helped, and are in fact contributing to their support. This very transformation has, however, created strong sentiments against "helping mothers to have more illegitimate children," or against "paying to increase the illegitimacy rate."

In fact, however, contrary to the apparent trend, Negro illegitimacy has certainly dropped over the past half-century or more and without question will drop in the future. In the post-Civil War period, a large majority of Negroes were not born in a legal marriage. In most southern states, no serious effort was made to collect accurate data on

---

[10] Philip K. Bock, "Patterns of Illegitimacy on a Canadian Indian Reserve: 1860-1960," *Journal of Marriage and the Family*, Vol. 26 (May, 1964), pp. 142-48.

[11] Between 1947-1957, girls less than 18 years of age bore slightly more than 20 percent of all illegitimate children. See *Illegitimacy and Its Impact on the Aid to Dependent Children Program*, Dept. of Health, Education, and Welfare, Bureau of Public Assistance (Washington, D. C., 1960), p. 9.

Negro births, illegitimate or legitimate. Some part of the recent rise (since 1938) arises from a higher level of record keeping, rather than from a change in family patterns. Indeed, our illegitimacy records even now come from only 35 states, and, at earlier periods, they were even scantier. It is not at all clear that there has been a genuine rise in illegitimacy rates, White or Negro, but it is unlikely that the rise has been sharp.[12] Over the period 1940-1960, the illegitimacy rate based on such data has risen from about 4 percent to 4.8 percent.

Since much of the public outcry has also centered on the behavior of teen-agers, it is important to comment that the teen-age illegitimate mother is the *one* age group that has not increased its *rate* of illegitimate births in the recent years. Over the period of almost a generation, since 1938, the trend is even more striking: in 1938, the rate for teen-agers was higher than that for any age group except those 20-24 years old. Now, the rate for this younger group is lower than for any age group under 35.[13]

The Negro revolution of the 1960's demonstrates the extent to which the Negro population is actually entering the mainstream of United States society. Far from an index of disorganization, it is evidence of a major step toward integration, and presages, in fact, a substantial decrease in the illegitimacy rate among the Negro citizens of the United States.

In American society, the unwed mother has a difficult personal adjustment. There is little toleration for the young mother who wishes to keep her child as her own. Some families try to deny the connection of the child with the mother and say that it belongs to a relative. More often, the solution is simply to have the girl bear the child in a nursing home run for this purpose and to leave it there for adoption. The economic problems and the problem of parental control are likely to be too great to handle when there is no father available and no community support (other than economic) is forthcoming. The mother may undergo much emotional suffering, because of the social disapproval to which she is exposed and because she may develop a strong love for her child when it is born. For these reasons, the modern nursing home may enlist the services of social workers whose aim it is to help the young mother to adjust.

---

[12] On these points, see Elizabeth Herzog, "Unmarried Mothers: Some Questions to Be Answered and Some Answers to Be Questioned," *Child Welfare*, Vol. 41 (October, 1962), pp. 341 ff.

[13] For these and other relevant facts of illegitimacy, see "Illegitimate Births: Fact Sheet (Washington, D. C.: National Office of Vital Statistics, April 15, 1960); and Joseph Schachter and Mary McCarthy, *Illegitimate Births: United States, 1938-1957* (Washington, D. C.: National Office of Vital Statistics, 1960).

The problem of the illegitimate Negro child is especially acute, since a shortage of children available for adoption exists only among the white population.[14] The rigorous economic and educational standards now applied in adoption procedures accentuates this oversupply or underdemand, since many Negro couples who might be adequate parents cannot meet such standards. As a consequence, many illegitimate Negro children have no parents during their early childhood, but remain in foundling homes or are shuttled about from one foster home to another on a temporary basis.

It is not surprising, then, that the simple statistical chances of survival, health, or economic success are low for illegitimate children. They are more likely than legitimate children to die at birth or in the first year, to do poorly in school, to become juvenile delinquents, and to land eventually in unskilled jobs. The growth of social work services can perform no more than some individual therapy here and there to lessen somewhat the impact of the disadvantages with which the illegitimate child must cope.

No simple moral or technical solution exists for these problems. The mechanical process of marriage does not automatically create a family relationship, though it may confer the status of legitimacy on the child. Illegitimacy in the United States most often occurs precisely among those who are not deeply involved with one another emotionally and who have shared mainly a sexual experience. Often, the pregnancy occurred partly because of carelessness on both sides and partly because the father has little feeling of responsibility about the relationship, the girl, or the consequences. Marriage would "give a name," but not a father, to the child. Fundamental changes in the social structure would be required to give full social rights to the illegitimate child, and these are not likely to take place in the next few generations.

Willed Departures: Separation, Divorce, Annulment, and Desertion

If one spouse willfully abandons his or her place in the family unit, the family pattern is undermined, even though in the final phase of their interaction the other spouse was equally willing to go. *Separation* may be an informal preliminary step toward divorce, a temporary ex-

---

[14] About "70% of all white illegitimate children are given for adoption, but only between 3 and 5% of the nonwhite illegitimate children." The estimated number of surviving illegitimate children under 18 years of age, Nov. 1, 1958, was 2,512,000 (*Illegitimacy and Its Impact on the Aid to Dependent Children Program,* pp. 35, 37). See also Clark E. Vincent, *Unmarried Mothers* (New York: Free Press, 1961).

TABLE 3

Status of Married United States Population, 1960

(Persons 14 years old and over)

	Males	Females
Total Married	42,630,422 (100%)	42,905,285 (100%)
Spouse Present	94.9	94.0
Spouse Absent	5.1	6.0
Separated	2.1	3.1
Other	3.0	2.9

Sources: Calculated from Bureau of the Census, *U.S. Census of Population: 1960,* Vol. 1, *Characteristics of the Population,* Part 1, United States Summary (Washington, D. C.: U.S. Government Printing Office, 1964), Table 176, p. 424.

pedient to lessen the immediate conflict, or a legally recognized decision to live separately without divorcing. In the 1950 United States Census, 1.6 percent of husbands reported wives absent, and 2 percent of wives reported husbands absent—though no further data exist as to the marital relations of these husbands and wives. In 1960, the married population was divided as shown in Table 3 above.

Annulment is a court decision that the marriage contained some legal flaw (coercion, fraud, unwillingness to consummate the union, nonage, bigamy, etc.). In New York State, where absolute divorce may be granted only for adultery, annulments amounted to about 35 percent of all marital dissolutions since 1960.[15] In the United States, they amount to only about 3 percent; the numerical total in 1960 was 11,181.[16] Children are rarely involved in annulment cases, as compared with half of all divorce cases, but, in general, this pattern appears to be socially defined as a type of divorce. *Desertion* differs from the prior types in that one spouse not only leaves, but tries (at least for a while) to disappear or avoid contact with the family.[17]

These differences may not be ignored, but they should not obscure the similarity of conflict behavior in this large category of marital dissolution. To focus mainly on divorce patterns in the succeeding

[15] *Vital Statistics of the United States, 1960,* Volume III, Sections 3, 4, and 7; *Divorces,* Dept. of Health, Education, and Welfare, Public Health Service, National Vital Statistics Division, pp. 3-17, 3-18.

[16] *Ibid.*

[17] For a presentation of technical aspects of divorce procedure, see William M. Kephart, "Legal and Procedural Aspects of Marriage and Divorce," in Harold T. Christensen, ed., *Handbook of Marriage and the Family* (Chicago: Rand McNally, 1964), pp. 968 ff.

sections will simplify exposition without distorting reality, if available data on the other subtypes are also used where they are relevant.

Divorce as a Part of the Family System

The Western reader tends to view divorce as a misfortune or a tragedy, and high divorce rates as evidence that the family system is not working well. This attitude is part of our religious heritage, which was strong enough to make divorce a rare event until the early part of the present century, although various sects in the Protestant Reformation asserted the right to divorce as early as the sixteenth century, and Milton's famous plea for this right was written in the seventeenth century.[18] Our Western bias in favor of romantic love views marriage as based on love, so that divorce means failure.

All marriage systems require that at least two people, with their individual desires, needs, and values, live together, and all systems create some tensions and unhappiness. In this basic sense, then, marriage "causes" divorce, annulment, separation, or desertion. But though a social pattern must be able to survive even when many individuals in it are unsatisfied, it will also contain various mechanisms for keeping interpersonal hostilities within certain limits. Some family systems prevent the development of severe marital strains, but offer few solutions if they do develop. Two main patterns of prevention are discernible. One is to *lower the expectations* about what the individual may expect from marriage. For example, the Chinese praised family life as the most important institution, but taught their children that they were not to expect romance or happiness from it. At best, they might achieve contentment or peace.

A second pattern, widespread in preindustrial societies and also found among the Chinese, is to value the kinship network more than the relation between husband and wife. Elders direct the affairs of the family, arrange the marriages of the young, and intervene in quarrels between husband and wife. The success of the marriage is rated not so much by the intimate emotional harmony of husband and wife as by the contribution of the couple to the lineage or extended kin. Consequently, tensions between husband and wife would be less likely to build up to an unbearable level.

In addition, there are some social patterns in all groups by which marital tensions may be *avoided*. One pattern is considering certain disagreements trivial. For example, individuals in the United States are told that disagreement on the relative value of bowling and bridge

---

[18] *The Doctrine and Discipline of Divorce* was first published in 1643.

is not important. Another pattern is suppressing some irritations. As individuals become adult, they are increasingly forced to control their anger, unless the problem is serious. Still another is training children and adolescents to expect similar things in marriage, so that what one spouse does is in harmony with the demands of the other.

Societies vary in their definitions of what is a *bearable* level of dissension between husband and wife, as well as in their *solutions* for a difficult marriage. It seems likely that public opinion in the United States during the nineteenth century considered bearable a degree of disharmony which modern couples would not tolerate. People took for granted that spouses who no longer loved one another and who found life together distasteful should at least live together in public amity for the sake of their children and of their standing in the community.

As to what should be done about an unsatisfying marriage, even Western countries vary considerably. Spain, Ireland, Italy, and Brazil permit only legal separations, which are common in the last two of these four countries. In Chile, marriages are mostly dissolved by annulments.[19] In societies with extended kinship networks, but without divorce as an alternative, husband and wife may continue their daily tasks but confine their contacts to a minimum. In a polygynous society, a man may refuse to spend any time with one of his wives if their relationship is an unhappy one. Under the family systems of Manchu China and Tokugawa Japan, a man could take an additional wife or bring a concubine into his house. In China, a dissatisfied husband might be unable to afford a concubine, but might instead stay away from his home for long periods of time with distant relatives or on business trips—thus, a form of separation.

These devices to avoid trouble, to divert dissension, to train individuals to put up with difficulties, or to seek alternative relationships to ease the burden of marriage, show that societies generally do not value divorce highly. In no society, with the possible exception of the Crow, has divorce been treated as an ideal mode of marital behavior. The reasons for this are easily seen. Divorce grows out of dissension but creates additional conflict between both sides of the family lines. Prior marriage agreements are broken, and prior harmonious relationships among in-laws are disrupted. There are problems of custody, child support, and remarriage, as will be analyzed in more detail later on.

In no society, however, are the mechanisms for avoiding or reducing

---

[19] Paul H. Jacobson, *American Marriage and Divorce* (New York: Rinehart, 1959), p. 97.

marital conflict enough to make all couples able to tolerate their marriage. Divorce is, then, one of the safety valves for the inevitable tensions of married life. At present we cannot say why a particular society adopts the pattern of divorce rather than that of separation, or of living together but enlarging the household to take in additional wives, but divorce is clearly a widespread solution for the problems of marital living. Moreover, the alternative solutions that various societies offer are only a variation on the pattern of divorce.

Divorce differs from these variations principally in that it permits remarriage to both partners. In societies without divorce, ordinarily only the man can enter a new union, even if it is not entirely a legal one. Thus, in India, a man might take an additional wife or, in China or Japan, a concubine, but no such possibility was open to the woman who was dissatisfied with her marriage. In a polygynous society, a man might marry additional wives in order to have a tolerable marital life, but the woman whom he disliked was not permitted additional husbands. In Western nations where separation is permitted, but not divorce, the attitudes opposing a wife's entering into an unsanctioned public union are very strong, but the husband is usually permitted to have a mistress outside his household.

It is not correct to speak of divorce as a more extreme solution than some of the other patterns already described. Whether divorce creates more unhappiness, for example, than the introduction of a concubine into the household, is unknown. Whether it is more extreme to divorce or to bear the misery of an unhappy marriage is not measurable, and in any event is partly a matter of personal or social evaluation.

Divorce in Primitive Societies

There are two common stereotypes about family life in primitive societies: (a) everyone lives in a state of simple marital harmony; (b) everyone wears a hibiscus behind the ear and engages in constant amorous pursuit. Neither is true, although both have some small basis in reality. Nonindustrial societies vary greatly in their divorce rates. In general, patrilineal societies (in which the family line is traced through the male side) has lower divorce rates than matrilineal societies. However, about 60 percent of primitive societies for which data are available seem to have higher rates than the contemporary United States.[20] Such high rates do not seem to undermine those so-

---

[20] G. P. Murdock, "Family Stability in Non-European Cultures," *Annals of the American Academy of Political and Social Science,* Vol. 272 (November, 1950), p. 197.

cieties, contrary to the dark predictions in the United States that a high divorce rate foretells the breakdown of the culture.

At first glance this marital instability may seem curious, since in primitive societies most economic and religious activities are guided and structured by a complex family system. People own property through their position in a family and take political or religious responsibilities according to their position in the family lineage. No one lives as a solitary individual, and it is not possible to carry out the normal functions of an adult except through family ties. Yet the social structures of such societies seem to be better able than our own to handle the problem of divorce adjustment. To begin with, marriages are not usually based upon a deep romantic attachment, so that the emotional trauma of marital breakup is not so great. More important, however, is the circumstance that the positions of husband, wife, and children are all clearly defined in advance, so that when the marriage does break up, each knows what he must do. The child, for example, is part of a known lineage, and belongs to that lineage no matter what happens to the individual marriage. If the family system is patrilineal, the child belongs to the father's line, and it will take care of him. In a matrilineal system, the husband goes back to his mother's household, to be received once more as part of the family. As a consequence, no one depends entirely upon his emotional relationship with a particular spouse.

Ackerman has published a crosscultural inquiry into the kinds of *social affiliations* that might create a higher or lower divorce rate: what kinds of relationships are created by marriage, and what kinds are maintained in spite of marriage, but sometimes to its detriment; and how important is the marital union within the network of kin. For example, in a matrilineal system, a woman's children must look to her brother for certain kinds of authority and command, and the woman is linked closely to her blood kin and very little with those of her husband. By asking these and other questions, Ackerman has made a forward step in understanding why some societies have high, and others have low, divorce rates.[21]

This is not to say that there are no problems of divorce adjustment in societies with high divorce rates. It does mean, however, that many of the problems are taken care of by existing family structures. A divorced wife will receive help from her family in establishing a new marriage, and though she is considered a less desirable mate than

---

[21] Charles Ackerman, "Affiliations: Structural Determinants of Differential Divorce Rates," *American Journal of Sociology,* Vol. 69 (July, 1963), pp. 13-20.

before, her chances of remarriage will be relatively high. Finally, of course, where the rate of divorce is high, the amount of social disapproval of divorce is likely to be low.

Countries with High Divorce Rates

The United States has the highest divorce rate among Western nations. Nevertheless, various countries in the past have had higher rates than the United States; e.g., Israel (1935-1944), Egypt (1935-1954), Japan (1887-1919), Algeria (1887-1940). It is perhaps useful to look at some of these briefly in order to understand better the relationship between divorce and the family system. In the following table (Table 4) various divorce rates are presented for comparison.

Westerners are likely to think of Japan as having a stable society. It is therefore instructive to consider that in 1887 there were 320 divorces per 1000 marriages and that this level of marital instability continued until the late 1890's, when certain changes in the marriage law were made. Indeed, not until the 1920's did Japan's divorce rate begin to fall below that of the United States, the present rate being considerably lower. Yet there is no evidence to suggest that the higher degree of marital instability in the past has, in any way, undermined the Japanese social structure.

The high Japanese divorce rate during the early years of the Meiji Restoration is based on calculation from family registers, rather than on the modern system of vital statistics of registration. Consequently, the exact figures may be questioned. Nevertheless, known sources of error could not have inflated the rate substantially; indeed, since a divorce was unlikely to be registered unless the marriage had been registered, and many unstable marriages were never registered at all, the correct figure might be higher still.

Why was the Japanese rate so high? In Japan as in China, marriages were arranged by the elders of the two families through a go-between. The young man and woman themselves took little part in these negotiations, although both were likely to be adults. Child marriage was not an ideal in Japan, and at the turn of the century the average age of recorded first marriage was 27 for men and 23 for women.[22] The couple were, however, likely to be younger if the family had wealth and position, since the couple were not expected to live independently; if the groom was the eldest son, he would not ordinarily set up a separate household.

---

[22] The date is 1910. Irene Taeuber, *The Population of Japan* (Princeton, N. J.: Princeton University Press, 1958), p. 227.

TABLE 4

Divorces per 1000 Marriages in Selected Countries, 1890-1963

Country	Year							
	1890	1900	1910	1920	1930	1940	1950	1963
U.S.	55.6	75.3	87.4	133.3	173.9	165.3	231.7	258 (1960)
Germany		17.6	29.9	40.7	72.4	125.7	145.8	80 (1962)
England & Wales				8.0	11.1	16.5	86.1	81 (1962)
Australia		13.6	12.4	20.4	41.2	41.6	97.3	91
France	24.3	26.1	46.3	49.4	68.6	80.3	106.9	96 (1962)
Sweden		12.9	18.4	30.5	50.6	65.1	147.7	165 (1961)
Iran						194	211	173 (1960)
Egypt					269 (1935)	273	273	238 (1962)
Japan	335	184	131	100	98	76	100	87 (1961)
Algeria	370 (1897)	352	288	396	286	292	a	161 (1955)

Sources:

All figures calculated from governmental sources and from *United Nations Demographic Yearbook*, 15th Issue (New York: United Nations, 1963).

a 1950 Algerian figures are not used, because in that year over 200,000 marriages from previous years were registered civilly, for the first time, thus reducing the true level of divorce rates. How much this under-registration in previous years inflated the divorce rate is not known. Decennial years are used in the table, but in a few cases the true year is one year off.

A better measure of divorce frequency is the number of divorces per 1000 *existing* marriages, but the latter figure is not often available. The above rate compares marriages in a given year, with divorces occurring to marriages from *previous* years. However, changes from one year to another, or differences among countries, may be seen just as clearly by this procedure.

The negotiations took account of such matters as good health, social position, wealth, good temper, but after the marriage the prime matter of importance was whether the young bride would or could adjust well to her elder in-laws. She was under a stern obligation to pay great respect to them, to defer to their wishes, and to obey them even against the opposed wishes of her husband. If she could not obtain or retain the approval of her in-laws, she would be sent back to her parents with little regard to whether she and her husband got along well. The "divorce" in Japan was then a repudiation of the bride by her in-laws.

There is reason to suppose that the divorce rate was lower in the upper social strata than in the lower strata, in part because the Japanese noble could adjust to marital problems by obtaining a concubine. His wife's position was secure enough if she obtained the favor of her in-laws and bore sons for the family. The average man could not afford an additional wife or concubine, and if his family did not accept his wife, she would simply have to be returned. And, since marriage among the nobility was often a family alliance, a divorce would be more likely to cause conflict between the two families.

Changes in the Japanese family system have been extensive over the past 50 years and cannot be analyzed in detail here. For our purposes, however, the important fact has been the steady decline of the divorce rate since the 1920's, as shown in the previous table. One important shift has been toward an increasing proportion of marriages based either on personal choice or on personal preferences which are then approved by parents. As a consequence, the young wife has only to adjust to her husband's needs, not to the needs of a group of elders. Industrialization and urban living have meant that more families are small and are housed in small dwelling units, so that fewer young brides now live with their in-laws. At the same time, although the Japanese are the most industrialized of all Eastern countries, the culture remains family-centered to a considerable degree.

Divorce rates are also high in Arab countries, where divorce and remarriage have been described as the "poor man's polygyny." In all polygynous societies, except those in which a large proportion of men are killed in war, generally men must marry late while women marry early, or an excess of women must be obtained by capture or purchase. Even where females marry early and men late, so that there are more "female years in marriage," most men must be content with only one wife at a time. This general observation also holds in Arab countries, and divorce has always been easy. A man could divorce a woman with only the formality of saying, "I divorce thee." If he said this three times, the divorce was final, and they could not remarry each other until the wife married, cohabited with, and divorced another man. Even said once, however, the phrase betokened a divorce. The financial consequences of divorce were not serious for the man. Remarriage was easy, especially for the man, and both divorcees and children were able to return to their parental circle.

The only Moslem country for which divorce rates of half a century ago can be calculated is Algeria. In 1897, the number of divorces per 1000 marriages was 370; and this rate did not fall substantially until the 1940's, as seen in the previous table. For Egypt and Moslem (but not Arab) Iran, data are available for only the recent period. Thus, divorce rates higher than those of the United States have been observed in several Moslem countries, where, except for Algeria, there seems to be little evidence of any substantial change. In the better educated Arab strata, of course, Western ideas about the rights of women have penetrated, so that divorce is less frequent and the age at marriage is higher.

As yet, there is no adequate analysis of contemporary Arab families, so that a precise statement of the reason for the extremely high rates cannot be made. Of course, the consequence of divorce for the wife and her family would not usually be overwhelming, since (a) the man had to complete his payment of the bride price if there was a divorce; (b) if the woman had brought a dowry or personal wealth to the marriage, these remained in her possession; (c) her family did not have to support the children, since they belonged to the husband's line; and (d) though the second union would not be so advantageous a match, the repudiated wife would usually be able to remarry. There was no great excess of females, and since each man typically had only one wife, the high divorce rate simply means a high rate of marital turnover.

Changes in Divorce Rates as Indices of Other Social Changes

Such changes in the rate of divorce in various countries need not indicate that these societies are becoming disorganized. They do provide an index of change within the family system and an index of change in the larger social structure. Clearly, the industrialization under way in most countries does not imply an increase in divorce rates. In Japan, the divorce rate has been dropping for well over half a century, and the recorded drop in the Arab Algerian rate suggests that other Arab countries may eventually experience a decline as well. By contrast, divorce rates have risen in every western European country where divorce is possible and at a faster *rate* than the increase in the United States. For example, the divorce rate in England a generation ago was about 6 percent and is now 30 percent that of the United States. In the industrializing areas of sub-Saharan Africa and in Communist China, divorce rates are rising. As noted earlier, the Indian Marriage Act of 1955 extends the privilege of divorce to the entire Indian population, so that the divorce rate is also rising there.

Both of these opposite developments are the result of a change in all these family systems toward an emphasis on the independent conjugal family unit. This new type of system has a relatively high divorce rate, but the rate may be lower than in the system which it replaces. Let us look at this conjugal system briefly. (See Chapter 8, page 386.)

Under the fully developed conjugal pattern, as in the United States, people have greater freedom of action and the right to choose their own mates. Under industrialization, people can begin their marriages on the basis of the jobs to be had in the new occupations, in factories or offices; they no longer require land in order to make a living. They depend less upon their older relatives, feel fewer obligations to take care of their elders, and, of course, receive less aid from them. Correlatively, the social controls on both sides are less exacting and effective.

This type of family system, characteristic of the West for several generations, therefore requires that husband and wife obtain most of their emotional solace within the small family unit made up of husband, wife, and children; the extended kin network no longer serves as a buffer against the outside world. The conjugal family unit carries a heavier emotional burden when it exists independently than when it is a small unit within a larger kin fabric. As a consequence, this unit is relatively fragile. When husband or wife fails to find emotional satisfaction within this unit, there are few other sources of satisfaction and few other bases for common living. The specialization of service in an industrialized economy permits the man to purchase many domestic services if he has no wife, and the woman is increasingly able to support herself, even if she has no property and no husband. For these reasons, the independent conjugal family is not highly stable. On the other hand, where the union was fragile because of the elders, as in Japan, or dependent on the whim of the man, as in Arab countries, the new independence of the young couple, their emotional ties with one another, and the increased bargaining power of the woman may mean somewhat greater stability of the family unit.

A large change in the divorce rate betokens a "breakdown" of the older system, but the fundamental functions of the family—the reproduction, social placement, maintenance, and socialization of the child, and social controls over members of the family—may be as well served as they once were. In addition, the freedom and mobility of this newer system seem to fit better the needs of an industrializing economy. If these systems were truly becoming disorganized, illegitimacy rates would rise, if the preceding analysis of illegitimacy was correct. However, in Western countries the data show a slight decline (as also in Japan). Moreover, the percentage of men and women who are willing to take the gamble of marriage has not dropped at all, and there is even a slight rise in some countries. In spite of the many changes ocurring in the family systems and the larger social structures and the changes in the personal fortunes of individuals who do marry, the blanket term, "disorganization," seems not to be applicable.

Fluctuations and Trends in United States Divorce Rates

Divorce rates in the United States have fluctuated a good deal over the past century, but have shown a consistent trend upward. Table 5 presents this trend.

Both divorce and marriage tend to follow the business cycle, increasing during periods of prosperity and decreasing during periods of depression. Of course, people do not lead more contented family lives during depressions. It is rather that the cost of the divorce itself and the still greater cost of establishing new households prevent people from embarking on such a venture. The effect can be seen dramatically in the swift change after the stock market crash in 1929. Up to that point, "the divorce rate had climbed to a new peak of 7.9 per 1000 existing marriages. . . . In the deepening depression that ensued, the rate dropped more than one-fifth to a low of 6.1 per 1000 in 1932 and 1933." [23] The frequency of divorce declined for marriages of long duration as well as those of short duration. The return of better economic conditions soon pushed divorce rates once more to a new high.

The effect of war on divorce rates is somewhat less clear, but after the Civil War and both World Wars the rate rose sharply and then fell off somewhat, only to begin once more its upward trend.[24] During the Civil War and World War I, there was at first a *drop* in the divorce rate. However, in World War II, the rate continued to *rise* during the war, and in the later period of the Civil War the rate rose also. It seems clear that both wartime marriages and unions immediately upon the return of soldiers are less stable than marriages begun at other times. In addition, after World War II many divorces occurred because the returning soldier and his wife could not adjust to one another, so that the record total of 629,000 divorces and annulments took place in 1946.

In part, however, the higher number of divorces after a war is due to the increased number of marriages. There are more marriages exposed to the risk of divorce, and the risks are greater in the first years of marriage. After the first few months of marriage, the risk quickly

---

[23] Jacobson, *American Marriage and Divorce*, p. 95.
[24] *Ibid.*, p. 91.

TABLE 5

Number of United States Divorces per 1000 Existing Marriages, 1860-1956 [a]

Year	Number
1860	1.2
1880	2.2
1900	4.0
1920	7.7
1940	8.7
1956	9.3
1960	258 divorces per 1000 marriage ceremonies [b]

Sources:

[a] Paul H. Jacobson, *American Marriage and Divorce* (New York: Rinehart, 1959), p. 90. The data from 1920 on contain annulments, and all these data are partly estimated, since not all states are included in the divorce registration system. The earlier rates are, of course, even more open to question than the later.

[b] Bureau of the Census, *Statistical Abstract of the United States: 1964*, 85th ed. (Washington, D. C., 1964), p. 64.

rises, to reach a maximum during the third year. For example, in 1955, the rate per 1000 existing marriages was 18 during the first year, 25.1 in the second (i.e., less than two years), 25.4 during the third, and 22.1 during the fourth. Thus, after the third, the rate begins to drop.[25] In general, there has been a trend for divorces to occur earlier in the marriage.[26] At the turn of the century, the peak divorce frequency was found among those married four years (during the fifth year). Consequently, some part of the decrease in the number of divorces during the 1950's can be ascribed to the drop in the number of marriages—which in turn is due to the low fertility of the 1930's, causing a smaller number of young men and women to be available for marriage.

Examination of the long-term trend in United States divorce rates poses the question, "What are the changes in social structure that have taken place in the last 100 years, and that have had an effect on the family system and thus on the divorce rate?"

Perhaps the most striking changes have occurred in the general *values* and *norms* relating to divorce. Certainly there has been no

---

[25] *Ibid.*, pp. 144-47.

[26] In *Summary of Marriage and Divorce Statistics, 1957*, Dept. of Health, Education, and Welfare, National Office of Vital Statistics, National Summaries, Vol. 50, No. 18 (November 25, 1959), p. 48, the claim is made that this trend has been reversed since 1952. I believe this is a statistical variation, and the trend will continue.

acceptance of a philosophy that divorce is good, a thing to be desired, but divorce is no longer viewed as a shameful episode that one must hide from others, or as a sufficient reason for casting a person out of respectable social circles. It is an experience to be regretted, one which commands some sympathy, but it is not viewed as a violation of public decency. Whether the individual sinned or was sinned against, his divorce is generally understood as one possible solution for his family difficulties.

No public opinion surveys of this change of attitudes during the last half of the nineteenth century were made, but newspaper debates, the novelist's increasing use of divorce as a solution for bad marriages, and congressional debates in various states where new divorce legislation was being considered, all throw some light on the growing toleration of divorce.[27] It must not be supposed that public opinion, even 100 years ago, was unequivocally set against divorce. Churches and their leaders fulminated against divorce, and most public figures drew freely on Biblical sources to denounce it, but strong opponents of the indissolubility of marriage did not cease their attacks. The border and frontier states, with their shifting and rootless populations, seemed not to have had rigid views against divorce, and Connecticut on the seaboard had liberal laws.[28] The growing feminist movement sought freedom for women, especially from the disabilities which existing family laws imposed; and though feminist leaders could not muster compelling theological arguments, they were able to best their opponents on humanitarian grounds.[29]

It is not possible to state the "causes" of this basic change in attitude. It is merely one facet of a broader set of changes in Western society, called "secularization": patterns that were once weighed by strong moral norms come to be evaluated by instrumental norms. Instead of asking, "Is this moral?" the individual is more likely to ask, "Is this a more useful or better procedure for my needs?" Sometimes the term "individualism" is applied to this change, for instead of asking whether one's church or one's community approves divorce, the individual rather asks, "Is it the right thing for *me* to do?"

However, a change in values alone does not necessarily lead to a great change in action patterns; other elements are always involved.

---

[27] A good compilation of this material, concentrating on the novel, may be found in James H. Barnett, *Divorce and the American Divorce Novel, 1858-1937* (Philadelphia: University of Pennsylvania, 1939, privately printed), especially Chapters 3-5.

[28] *Ibid.*, p. 36.

[29] *Ibid.*, pp. 40 ff.

Certainly, one important change has been in the types of *social pressures* from kinfolk and friends when there is marital discord. A hundred years ago, these pressures were essentially unidirectional. The individual was told by everyone to adjust, to bear the burden, and to accept his fate. He was told that for the sake of the children it was necessary to remain with his spouse, and he recognized that a divorce would mean losing his standing in his social circle. Although, in contemporary society, friends and kin do give advice to people who are involved in marital difficulties, and though it is safe to say that in the initial stages, at least, the advice is to stay together, especially when there are children, these pressures are not nearly so strong as they once were. They relax even more when those within the social circle recognize that the marriage cannot be mended.

A substantial change has also taken place in the *alternatives* which the husband or wife faces when considering a divorce. Formerly a man found it very difficult to get along from day to day unless he had a wife. This was especially true on the farm, where many activities were defined as female activities, but it was true in urban areas as well. Women had almost no opportunities for employment outside of domestic work. Few women were technically trained, and even when a woman's family had money, a return to her family was always viewed as a shameful alternative to continuing her marriage. These alternatives have radically changed. The man can get along quite well without a wife, for he can purchase most of the services which a wife would perform. Women's alternatives have, of course, expanded even more. Many more women are trained to handle jobs that pay substantial salaries. Finally, and most central in this change, is the fact that since being divorced is no longer a stigma, and since there are many people who have been either widowed or divorced, the person in marital difficulty can hope for another marriage as an alternative.

We should also consider some deeper factors that have influenced the continued rise in the divorce rate. The egalitarian ethos, which has spread throughout much of the Western culture complex during the past 150 years, has argued consistently for equality of rights for women. Men have fought a rear-guard action, winning this battle and losing that one, but in general retreating. This change has a philosophical basis, but it is also rooted in the demands of an industrialized system, which offers each person the opportunity to develop his skills as fully as possible and to utilize them in the economy. An industrial economy apparently requires the services of women as well as men, and only to a limited extent are these services defined by sex roles.

Men typically exaggerate when they assert that women have achieved equal rights. It seems fair to say that women demand a greater range of *rights* than men are willing to concede, just as men are willing to impose a few more *obligations* than women are willing to accept. In a period of great change of sex roles, there is necessarily considerable tension in the day-to-day interaction of husbands and wives. Love is likely to be the crystallizing element in the decision to marry, both in fact and ideal, and the assumption that married life has personal happiness as its aim has come to be widely accepted. Combined with these two factors, the existence of tensions in sex roles means that there are bound to be more conflicts between husbands and wives now than a hundred years ago; and that when such conflicts do arise, individuals feel that the *primary* aim of marriage has not been achieved. Since the only common enterprise is now the family itself, when this fails to yield the expected personal satisfactions, it cannot be surprising that the likelihood of divorce is greater than a century ago.

These pressures and patterns are not at all peculiar to the United States. The general rise in the divorce rate in Europe is not caused by the insidious influence of "bad" American customs, like Coca-Cola and chewing gum. Rather, the United States is in the vanguard of a process which is becoming worldwide. The European countries follow behind simply because they are going through similar phases at a later date. The same processes have been taking place in Communist China, Japan, and parts of Africa.[30]

Where will this process end? Will the ratio of divorces to marriages rise until there are as many divorces each year as marriages? The prediction of a future event is always dubious. We cannot simply extend the curve of the divorce rate indefinitely upward in the future, unless we are absolutely sure that (a) we have located the important factors in its rise, and (b) these factors will continue to increase in the future. It is, however, possible to make a guess, one which is worth some debate. In the post-World War II epoch, the fertility pattern suggests that a change in family attitudes is taking place, especially in the middle and upper-middle strata, which seem to be

---

[30] For these data see William J. Goode, *World Revolution and Family Patterns* (New York: Free Press, 1963). For China, see especially C. K. Yang, *The Chinese Family in the Communist Revolution* (Cambridge, Mass.: Harvard University Press, 1959) and Olga Lang, *Chinese Family and Society* (New Haven: Yale University Press, 1946). See also R. P. Dore, *City Life in Japan* (Berkeley: University of California Press, 1958) and Arthur Phillips, ed., *Survey of African Marriage and Family Life* (London: Oxford University Press, 1953).

at present the vanguard of new styles of life. This change may be summarized by saying that the style of life now held to be ideal is one that is centered around the home to a greater extent than a generation ago, that values children far more than the prior generation, that seeks professional help when there are marital difficulties, and that in general opposes divorce simply because it does not solve the individual problem. This slight exaggeration of an emerging pattern would suggest that the divorce rate will not continue upward indefinitely, but that it may stabilize, or even drop (but only a bit) within the next decade.

Divorce and Desertion in Different Segments of the United States Population

The similarities of people in the United States to one another form the basis of national unity, but individuals in different positions *within* the social structure have different experiences since childhood from those undergone by others in the society, interpret them differently, and are subjected to different social influences. Consequently, it is to be expected that differentials in divorce, annulment, and desertion might be found among people from different socioeconomic strata, religions, race, and rural-urban backgrounds. In the succeeding pages, some of these differentials are presented and analyzed.

Common sense has long suggested that economic factors may be of great significance in the breakup of marriages, while many family analyses have tried to show that differences over money matters often hide underlying bases of conflict, such as definitions of sex roles, personality differences, divergent styles of life. Doubtless, both positions contain some truth. Although most married couples in the United States earn enough to "get by," surveys show that families feel they need 50 percent to 100 percent more to be "comfortable," [31] and believe that they really cannot get along on their income. Spouses tend to have separate ideals of proper economic behavior, different attitudes toward spending money on one thing rather than another, different measures of economic success, and so on. If husband and wife have temperamental incompatibilities and do not meet each other's *emotional* needs, they can express them in conflicts about economic matters, for economic problems pervade much of the family's life. Since economic difficulties are more severe in lower economic strata, divorces might be supposed to be more common there, contrary to

---

[31] Hadley Cantril and Mildred Strunk, *Public Opinion, 1935-1946* (Princeton, N. J.: Princeton University Press, 1951), p. 66.

popular opinion as expressed in editorials and fiction for well over a generation. In fact, divorce rates *are* higher in the lower socioeconomic strata. It is therefore useful to look at the basis for such an opinion, as well as the survey data which show that in fact the upper strata are less prone to divorce.

Census and survey data cannot ascertain the class pattern of divorce of a generation or more ago. Probably it was mainly the rich who could afford divorce. Unquestionably this was so from the early period of United States history until about the Civil War, for in some states divorce required, as in England, a special act of the legislature. But there is no reason to suppose that the marital *stability* of the lower strata was greater. The popular picture of lower-class family life as warm and inviting, with frequent exchange of kinship obligations, tightly knit against the outside world, was a literary stereotype, often written by authors who had never observed a lower-class family. Instability was probably expressed in separation and desertion, as is still true of the lowest strata in our population. In addition, divorces in middle and upper social strata were given much more publicity.

At just what date the lower strata began to exceed the middle and upper in turning to the divorce cannot be known, although the pattern was definite by the 1920's.[32]

A recent summary of various research studies, sample surveys, and census data has clearly demonstrated this inverse relationship between socioeconomic rank and divorce rate.[33] Two tables from this summary, both calculated from national data, show this relationship (Tables 6 and 7).

The relationship between education and proneness to divorce is not simple, in part because social pressures force most people to go through high school, so that they share a similar *formal* educational experience,

---

[32] J. H. S. Bossard uses data from the 1930 Census, and thus the results of family behavior of the 1920's, to show that divorced women were predominantly to be found in the poorer census tracts of Philadelphia. "Spatial Distribution of Divorced Women," *American Journal of Sociology*, Vol. 40 (1935), especially pp. 503, 507. Similarly, Clarence H. Schroeder, in a more elaborate study, used 1930 Census data to corroborate this conclusion. *Divorce in a City of 100,000 Population* (Peoria, Ill.: Bradley Polytechnic Institute Library, 1939), pp. 83, 84.

[33] William J. Goode, *Women in Divorce* (New York: Free Press, 1965), Chapters 4 and 5. See also W. J. Goode, "Marital Satisfaction and Instability: A Cross-cultural Class Analysis of Divorce Rates," *International Social Science Journal*, Vol. 14, No. 3 (1962), pp. 507-26; and Karen G. Hillman, "Marital Instability and Its Relation to Education, Income, and Occupation: An Analysis Based on Census Data," in Robert F. Winch, Robert McGinnis, and Herbert R. Barringer, eds., *Selected Studies in Marriage and the Family*, rev. ed. (New York: Holt, 1962), pp. 603-08.

TABLE **6**

Proneness to Divorce by Urban Occupation, United States, April, 1949

Occupation	Index of Proneness to Divorce
Professional, semiprofessional	67.7
Proprietors, managers, officials	68.6
Clerical, sales	71.8
Craftsmen, foremen	86.6
Operators (semiskilled)	94.5
Service workers	254.7
Laborers (except farm and mine)	180.3

Source: William J. Goode, *After Divorce* (New York: Free Press, 1956), p. 46. Of course a wide range of occupations is included under "service," such as night watchmen and hair-dressers. Properly speaking, this survey used the category, "Other Marital Status" (other than single or married). The survey from which these data were calculated is found in *Current Population Reports, Labor Force,* Series 3-R50, No. 22 (April 19, 1950), Table 5. If different occupational categories are used, a somewhat different ranking may be obtained, but the basic relationship between socioeconomic position and divorce remains the same.

when in fact their social experiences and backgrounds are heterogeneous. Nevertheless, the connection is clear at the extremes of education. Americans with only an elementary school education or less are much more prone to divorce than those who have completed high school or attended college. The lowest rate is found among college graduates.

Interestingly, the relationship between education and proneness to divorce is more marked among Negroes than whites, but reverses the pattern: the higher the level of education, the higher the divorce rate.[34] Detailed analysis of the data suggests that the divorce rate of Negroes who actually *finish* college, however, is almost as low as that of those who have very little education. We cannot interpret these data satisfactorily. It is likely, however, that Negroes with very little education, like similarly placed whites of more than a generation ago, simply do not use the divorce courts as much. Whether the higher rates for the segments with greater education are also an index of the tensions in middle-class Negro living, cannot be ascertained from these data.

What do such correlations mean? Husbands and wives do not ordinarily quarrel about their respective social or economic positions, or their education. It is rather that socioeconomic factors are among the social influences playing on the family, and thus indirectly affect many decisions within the family. For example, in our society most individ-

---

[34] William J. Goode, *After Divorce* (New York: Free Press, 1956), p. 54.

TABLE 7

Proneness to Divorce Index by Income, Age 25 to 44 Years, United States, 1950

Income (1949)	Index
$0	199.0
$1 to $999	188.6
$1000 to $1999	134.8
$2000 to $2999	92.9
$3000 to $3999	89.2
$4000 and over	66.7

Source: Commerce Dept., Bureau of the Census, *U.S. Census of Population, 1950,* Vol. 4, *Special Reports,* Pt. 2 (Washington, D. C.: U.S. Government Printing Office), Chapter D, Table 6, p. 47.

uals come to want a wide range of material things that their limited incomes deny them. Individuals are not reared to accept *normative* limits on their economic goals, although of course many people realistically accept the limits of *fact;* that is to say, although they know they cannot afford a fine car, a house, or fur coat, they do not feel they have no right to these goods. As a consequence, most families feel that their income is insufficient. The responsibility for satisfying these desires rests primarily with the husband, and any failure is his failure. At the same time, almost every study of job satisfaction shows that men in jobs with greater responsibility and prestige enjoy those jobs more than men in lower-ranking jobs enjoy theirs. Thus, both job satisfaction and economic reward point to a similar possibility: that there is more socioeconomic dissatisfaction in the lower strata, and thus possibly more marital tension from this source. Just as personality problems can be displaced onto economic factors within a marriage, so too may economic strains be displaced onto noneconomic relationships, such as sex and marital adjustment.

Other factors varying by socioeconomic position also affect divorce rates. Upper and lower social strata contrast in these relevant ways: (a) More of the income in the upper strata is alloted to long-term investment expenditures, such as houses, insurance, annuities, and so on, while more income in the lower strata is allocated to consumer goods such as cars and television sets. One consequence is that the husband in the upper strata cannot simply "walk out" on his obligations. (b) The difference between the potential earnings of the lower-class wife and her husband is smaller than between those of the wife and husband in the upper strata. Consequently, the wife's potential loss is much greater in the upper strata. (c) The network of both kin and friends is larger and more tightly knit among the upper strata than among the lower strata, so that the consequences of divorce are likely to be greater. It is easier for the lower-class husband simply to abandon his marital duties, either by separation or desertion. He cannot be so easily traced, and often loses little if he obtains an equal job in another city where he is unknown. Men are now more easily traceable than formerly, through social security, FBI, Veterans Administration, and other bureaucratic records, but a differential between upper and lower levels nevertheless remains.

We now see that even if tensions from economic factors were the same at all economic levels, the objective complexities and difficulties ensuing from divorce are greater for upper-strata marriages, so that these are more likely to stay together.

The foregoing analysis also applies to Negro and white divorce and desertion differentials. Divorce and desertion rates are higher among Negroes and the poor than among whites and the well-to-do. Some attention to desertion as a specific separate phenomenon may throw some light on these divorce differentials before we proceed to other divorce patterns.

The amount of social research on desertion does not correspond to its importance as a type of family disorganization. Since the time of World War I, no full-scale analysis of the problem has appeared.[35] Yet of the 2,600,000 children receiving aid-to-dependent-children grants in 1955, 1,400,000 had fathers who were separated from their families.[36] In Pennsylvania, estrangement of the husband accounted for 52 percent of children receiving such aid in 1948, and in Philadelphia, the new cases of nonsupport and desertion in the period 1920-1950 amounted to twice the number of divorces granted.[37] The number of divorces granted in the United States for desertion has increased during most of the decades for which data are available, reaching a peak

---

[35] See E. E. Eubank, *A Study of Family Desertions*, unpublished Ph.D. dissertation, University of Chicago, 1916; J. C. Colcord, *Broken Homes* (New York: Russell Sage Foundation, 1919). Perhaps E. R. Mowrer's study of desertion in Chicago should be added: *Family Disorganization* (Chicago: University of Chicago Press, 1927).

[36] Jessie Bernard, *Social Problems at Midcentury* (New York: Dryden, 1957), p. 383, from a report by the Social Security Commissioner.

[37] William M. Kephart and Thomas P. Monahan, "Desertion and Divorce in Philadelphia," *American Sociological Review*, Vol. 17 (December, 1952), pp. 719-20.

of 112,000 in 1946 and falling (along with divorces from other causes) to about 68,000 in 1950.[38] The National Desertion Bureau estimated in 1950 that desertions cost New York City more than $27 million annually. Desertion has often been called the poor man's divorce, and certainly it has been a common solution for marital difficulties among southern Negroes, Negro migrants to northern cities, and whites in the lowest occupational strata.[39]

One family analyst has asked, "How many days' absence constitutes desertion?" [40] thus suggesting that a "separation" cannot always be sharply distinguished from desertion. A separation presumably includes some agreement about the support of the family left behind, but this agreement may be violated, and even when there is no such agreement a husband may send money to the family and keep in indirect touch with the family. One of the older studies cited above found that 87 percent of deserters were "repeaters," leading to the notion that desertion is often a "holiday" from marital obligations.[41] This form of marital behavior violates central moral values of family life, so that it is most common in strata where social controls are weaker and the difficulties of family life are greater. However, desertion is also more common among Catholics than Protestants, because of their objection to a formal divorce.[42]

Since many separations become desertions *or* divorces, and perhaps most desertions end in a return to the family, no firm estimate can be made of the number of desertions each year. There were 4.3 women whose husbands were absent per 1000 married women aged 15-54 in the 1960 Census, and 3.8 divorced women. For nonwhites the percentages were 20.3 and 5.8 respectively. In 1950, the percentage for women with 4 years of college education was 2.0, but 6.9 for women with 0 to 8 years of education.[43] The *recorded* desertions appear in

---

[38] Jacobson, *American Marriage and Divorce*, p. 124. In 1960, desertion—including abandonment, absence, and combinations of desertion with other grounds—was the alleged ground in about one-quarter of the divorces granted in the Divorce Registration Area (18 states). The total was 24,943.

[39] For a good description of the older rural southern pattern, and the Negro adjustment to the northern slum, see E. Franklin Frazier, *The Negro Family in the United States*, rev. ed. (New York: Dryden, 1948), Chapters 7 and 15.

[40] Thomas D. Eliot, "Handling Family Strains and Shocks," in Howard Becker and Reuben Hill, eds., *Family, Marriage, and Parenthood* (Boston: Heath, 1948), p. 623.

[41] Colcord, *Broken Homes*, pp. 7-8.

[42] Thomas P. Monahan and William M. Kephart, "Divorce and Desertion by Religious and Mixed-Religious Groups," *American Journal of Sociology*, Vol. 59 (March, 1954), pp. 462-65.

[43] Data for 1950 from Paul C. Glick, *American Families* (New York: Wiley & Sons, 1957), p. 154. 1960 data calculated from Bureau of the Census, *U.S. Cen-*

3 situations: the divorce courts, applications for compulsory support from the husband, and applications for aid to dependent children. The apparent increase over the past decades in the number of desertions may actually be due to the present-day existence of machinery for giving help to the deserted family. Increasingly, too, as noted before, it is possible to *find* the husband or wife who abandons the family, so that the family is more likely to report this abandonment.[44]

To continue the analysis of divorce rate differentials, three broad patterns in Negro divorce rates are worthy of comment. One, noted previously, is that in contrast to whites, the higher the educational level of Negroes, the higher the divorce rate, except for the small stratum of those who have *completed* college. A second is the apparently greater effect of depression and prosperity on the Negro divorce rate. The third is that as the Negro population has become more assimilated into the dominant white culture, both their marriage and divorce behavior has become much like that of the whites.

The reason for the second pattern is that depression has, in the past, put Negroes out of work earlier than whites, because Negroes have had proportionately fewer white-collar jobs where employment is steadier. During a depression, Negro women have been better able than men to get jobs (primarily as domestics). One study which illustrated this general divorce pattern found that during 1918-1928, for the most part a prosperous period, the Negro divorce rate in Virginia was higher than the white, but during 1929-1940 the Negro rate dropped below the white rate.[45] An even sharper relative change was recorded in Mississippi during the same period. The total Negro divorce rate in the United States also dropped below the white level during the 1930's, so that in the 1940 Census, for the first time since 1890, there was a lower percentage of Negro divorcees than of white divorcees.[46] These changes may be seen in Table 8.

The data show that in only one censal year, 1940, was the Negro rate lower than the white, the result of a lower divorce rate during the 1930's. However, we must examine the *meaning* of these figures.

---

sus of Population: 1960, Vol. 1, *Characteristics of the Population,* Part 1, United States Summary (Washington, D. C.: U.S. Government Printing Office, 1964), Table 176, p. 424.

[44] In 1955, the National Desertion Bureau changed its name to the Family Location Service, to emphasize its concern with reconciliation and rehabilitation, rather than merely tracking down the missing husband (Bernard, *Social Problems at Midcentury,* p. 383).

[45] Jacobson, *American Marriage and Divorce,* p. 174.

[46] For this reason, Kephart and Monahan, "Desertion and Divorce in Philadelphia," p. 724, could report that the nonwhite divorce rate in Philadelphia was lower than the white: their data were primarily from the 1930's.

TABLE 8

Ratios of Percent Nonwhite Divorced to Percent White Divorced, 1890-1960

	1890	1900	1910	1920	1930	1940	1950	1960 [a]
Ratios:	1.24	1.95	1.67	1.52	1.50	0.95	1.05	1.25

Source: Calculated from William J. Goode, *After Divorce* (New York: Free Press, 1956), p. 49. The original data refer to the population in the marital status of "divorced," and thus exclude those who have divorced but remarried. The above table essentially shows the extent to which the two population segments furnish more or fewer divorcees, relative to the size of their respective populations. The table on p. 51 of that book is in error, because it compares the Negro rate with the rate of the *total* U.S. population.

[a] Calculated from Bureau of the Census, *U.S. Census of Population: 1960*, Vol. 1, *Characteristics of the Population*, Part 1, United States Summary (Washington, D. C.: U.S. Government Printing Office, 1964), Table 48, p. 155.

In 1890, most Negroes were in the rural South; the major migration to northern cities did not take place until World War I. It is doubtful that Negroes were in fact using southern divorce *courts* to a greater extent than whites. A substantial minority of Negroes lived together without marrying legally, and in many southern communities they would have been laughed at had they attempted to obtain a formal divorce. When they gave the answer, "divorced," to the census enumerator, they were merely saying that they were no longer living with their mates, who had probably deserted. On the other hand, the figures do show that Negro marital *instability* was greater, whether or not legally recorded.

The table also suggests that the Negro and white rates are converging, especially if it can be assumed that in the past two decades the census category "divorced" has increasingly come to mean that a legal divorce actually did take place. As a higher proportion of Negroes acquire middle-class patterns, it seems likely that they will resort to the courts more, but their rates will be about the same as those of whites.[47]

To ascertain divorce differentials by religion is especially difficult, since the United States Census has never asked about religion, the occasional Census of Religious Bodies uses only the reports made by churches, and the last published data from even this source were obtained in 1936. The religious beliefs of Catholic, Protestant, and

---

[47] See Frazier, *The Negro Family in the United States,* Chapter 20, and also his *The Negro in the United States,* rev. ed. (New York: Macmillan, 1957), Chapter 13.

Jewish churches generally stand in opposition to divorce but vary in the intensity of their disapproval. The Catholic Church takes the most extreme position, since it does not accept divorce at all (legal separation is permitted), and thus denies the right of a Catholic to remarry. As in other doctrinal matters, Catholics vary among themselves in their conformity to this proscription. The following statements summarize much of what we know about the relationship between marital dissolution and religion, but the student must keep in mind that no technically adequate national study of this problem has been carried out:

In two-thirds of the new desertion cases in Philadelphia, one or both parties were Catholic; some of these cases ended in divorce.[48]

The proportion of Jews was about the same in the total population as in the divorce courts; i.e., they were not "overrepresented." [49] However, two studies (1938 and 1949) suggest that when both spouses are Jewish, the divorce rate is as low as when both are Catholic.[50]

When both spouses are of the same religion, the divorce rate is low, and two studies have found that the Catholic-Catholic marriage is not more stable than the Jewish-Jewish or Protestant-Protestant.[51] However, most evidence suggests that the Catholic-Catholic rate of divorce is from one-half to two-thirds the Protestant-Protestant rate.[52]

In general, the highest divorce rates are found among spouses with no religious affiliation, and the next highest among the mixed-faith marriages (Protestant-Catholic, Jewish-Catholic, Jewish-Protestant). Among the many combinations possible, the Catholic husband married to the Protestant wife is most prone to divorce. Mixed-faith marriages of Catholics are becoming more common, varying between 4% and 50% or more in different regions of the United States.[53]

---

[48] Monahan and Kephart, "Divorce and Desertion by Religious and Mixed-Religious Groups," p. 460.

[49] Ibid., p. 461. For Detroit, Goode, After Divorce, p. 35, found the same result.

[50] Judson T. Landis, "Marriages of Mixed and Nonmixed Religious Faith," American Sociological Review, Vol. 14 (June, 1949), p. 403.

[51] Ibid.

[52] Loren E. Chancellor and Thomas P. Monahan, "Religious Preference and Interracial Mixture in Marriage and Divorce in Loua," American Journal of Sociology, Vol. 61 (November, 1955), pp. 238-39. Monahan and Kephart, "Divorce and Desertion by Religious and Mixed-Religious Groups," pp. 460-61.

[53] Landis, "Marriages of Mixed and Nonmixed Religious Faith," p. 403. Chancellor and Monahan, "Religious Preference and Interracial Mixture in Marriage and Divorce in Loua," pp. 238-39. In general, the larger the percentage of Catholics in a city or region, the lower the proportion of out-marriages. See John L. Thomas, "The Factor of Religion in the Selection of Marriage Mates," American Sociological Review, Vol. 16 (August, 1951), pp. 487-91; Harvey J. Locke, Georges Sabagh, and Mary Margaret Thomas, "Interfaith Marriages," Social Problems, Vol. 4 (April, 1957), pp. 329-33.

This summary requires only little comment. Several general factors interact to produce these results: (a) Groups strongly opposing divorce do have lower divorce rates, but their total voluntary marital dissolution rate may be almost as high as that of other groups. (b) People who claim no church membership are less strongly opposed to divorce, but they may be deviant in other ways, too, so that their divorce rate is higher. (c) Interfaith marriages are less stable, partly because of other differences in social background to be found in such unions, and partly because of religious conflict. However, in general, those who marry outside their church are less committed to its belief. (d) Mothers generally control the religious education of the children.[54] When a Catholic father marries a Protestant, however, he is likely to insist that his children become Catholics. Protestant fathers seem not to insist so strongly that their children become Protestants, when the mother is Catholic. Consequently, the divorce rate is relatively high when the union is Catholic father-Protestant mother. Note, too, that since it is women who ordinarily initiate the divorce suit, the Catholic mother would likely tolerate more conflict than the Protestant mother before bringing suit. The writer speculates that when there are male children, the Jewish father–Christian mother combination is also less stable than the reverse combination because of similar processes at work.

Two final comments should be added here, (a) that most analysts of religious behavior argue that the differences among members of different churches have been declining over the past two decades, and (b) that the differences between nonattenders and those who attend church regularly are often greater than the differences among people affiliated with different churches.

The Meaning of Differences in Social Background

This analysis of voluntary dissolutions of families has moved from a consideration of the broad institutional structures in which marital breakup occurs to a focus on the differences in marital instability that arise at different locations of individuals in the social structure, as these are determined by class, race, and religion. In the present section, an assessment is made of still more specific background traits of couples who marry. These experiences cannot be called "causes" of divorce, except in the sense that they help to generate (or lower) the tensions that may finally erupt in annulment, desertion, or divorce. Later, the

---

[54] Landis, "Marriages of Mixed and Nonmixed Religious Faith," pp. 404-06.

specific complaints and countercharges of the divorcing couples will be analyzed.

To the extent that certain characteristics of social position and background experiences increase or decrease the likelihood of marital dissolution, it may almost be said that divorce "begins" before the first quarrel, or before the couple even meet. It is not possible to review here all of the factors which have been related to eventual marital breakup, but those which seem to be based on good evidence can be presented, together with their sociological meaning. These may be summarized in the following comparisons:

BACKGROUND CHARACTERISTICS ASSOCIATED WITH
A GREATER OR LESSER PRONENESS TO DIVORCE

Greater Proneness to Divorce	*Lesser Proneness*
Urban background	Rural background
Marriage at very young ages (15-19 years)	Marriage at average age (males, 23; females, 20)
Short acquaintanceship before marriage	Acquaintanceship of 2 years or more prior to marriage
Short engagement, or none	Engagement of 6 months or more
Couples whose parents had unhappy marriages	Couples with happily married parents
Nonattendance at church, or mixed faith	Regular church attendance, Catholics, and adherence to the same church
Disapproval by kin and friends of the marriage	Approval of kin and friends
General *dis*similarity in background	Similarity ("homogamy") of background
Different definitions of husband and wife as to their mutual role obligations	Agreement of wife and husband as to the role obligations

These findings are in conformity with common sense, but they also deserve sociological annotation. First, the evidence on which they are based varies considerably, for some are derived from national samples or censuses of individuals, analyzed by marital status, and other characteristics, for example, the finding that the divorce rate of women 15 to 19 years of age is about 50 percent higher than that for women in higher age categories.[55] Other studies have taken small samples of people who are still married and have measured their *marital adjustment*, sometimes comparing a happily married sample with a sample of couples whose marriages ended in divorce.[56] The important sociological factors contributing to these and similar findings may be placed under four main headings:

1. The likelihood that an individual from a particular background has a stronger set of *values* against divorce.
2. Various types of *social pressures* against divorce.
3. The way the processes of mate selection sort out the marriage partners.
4. The ease of marital adjustment between people of similar social backgrounds.

Although a specific factor may play some part in more than one of these sets of processes, the general categories will help to clarify exposition somewhat.

There is greater tolerance of divorce in the United States today than there was a century ago, but many groups still oppose it strongly and view it as a nearly inconceivable alternative to even a bad marriage. Catholics are strongly against divorce, but many Protestant sects also oppose it. Rural populations are more strongly against divorce than urban areas. It seems likely that those with less education are less tolerant of divorce (but more tolerant of other marital deviations) than those with more education. In general, people from a "conventional" background and circle feel more strongly opposed to divorce than those with a less conventional background.

These differences may not lessen the *possibility* of conflict, but they do lessen the likelihood that individuals strongly opposed to divorce will accept that solution for their marital difficulties. However, these differences in opposition to divorce have lessened in the United States. For example, rural-urban social differences are gradually being erased, because the country as a whole is becoming more concentrated in large urban agglomerations and the remaining rural areas have increasingly taken on urban characteristics.

Values in opposition to divorce work in reinforcing ways. The individual who has such values is less likely to think of divorce in the

---

[55] Glick, *American Families*, p. 154.

[56] Harvey J. Locke, *Predicting Adjustment in Marriage* (New York: Holt, 1951). Goode's study, *After Divorce*, often compares divorced couples with the married population.

first place.[57] He is also more likely to be involved in *circles* that are opposed to divorce and press him toward reconciliation or some other adjustment to the conflict. For example, the individual who regularly attends church is also part of a social circle whose general advice and pressure are against divorce. When kinfolk and friends approve a marriage, they are likely to advise the couple to adjust and not to take their conflict seriously. Since a divorce within any social network threatens to some extent the ties which bind it together, the members of the network have a personal stake in attempting to prevent the divorce of any couple.

Some of these background factors, especially the approval of kin or friends, also help an individual to find a congenial companion, and to adjust to that person even before marriage. We should, therefore, think of the approval of kin and friends as having a double aspect. On the one hand it represents a kind of *prediction* that the engaged couple seem fitted for one another. Such circles know one or both of the individuals and judge whether they will fit together. On the other hand, the approval actually helps to bind them together, since their approval makes the interaction between the engaged or the married couple easier and more pleasant. Similarly, the length of acquaintance and the length of engagement may be viewed as an *index* of their adjustment to one another, but it is also a *period* of shared experience, during which adjustment can further take place. If a man and woman know one another for a long period of time, it is likely first of all that they have already, or acquire, common and mutually congenial characteristics. Next, if they stay together during a long period of time, their interaction has likely been productive or pleasant. Finally, a long period of acquaintanceship or engagement gives an opportunity either to become better adjusted or to break the tie. It is not surprising then that both of these background characteristics are associated with stability in marriage.

The length of the engagement is in part, however, a reflection of still other factors. Often, for example, marriages which take place without any engagement at all are really forced marriages, and marriages based upon premarital conception are more likely to end in divorce. Next, short engagements seem to be much more characteristic of lower-strata families, and we have already seen that the divorce

---

[57] Marriage demands a certain amount of repression from the partners, who must in a sense "not see" all of each other's faults, or all the ramifications of a quarrel. Cf. Willard Waller and Reuben Hill, *The Family* (New York: Dryden, 1952), pp. 516-17. An important phase in the dissolution process occurs when one or both spouses first consider divorce seriously as a possibility.

rate is higher in such strata. Thus, a short engagement may be either a cause or an effect. Finally, it seems likely that the length of engagement has a different social meaning in different strata. A very short engagement in a middle- or upper-class stratum is more likely to be a deviant union in some respects than it would be in the lower strata. It at least suggests that there may be background characteristics of the two couples that are incompatible.

Throughout this and earlier discussions, the theme has been developed that the disorganization of a marriage is much more likely to occur if the couple have very different social characteristics. In nearly all the world's marriage systems, whether marriages are arranged by elders or by the young couples themselves, the process of mate selection results in marriages between men and women who are similar to each other in a wide range of social characteristics, but especially with respect to family prestige and wealth.[58] Elders have an interest in establishing a stable marriage, since they invest some of their own time and wealth in it, and common sense has long recognized that a young couple will be more compatible if they are alike in important ways. The elders are also interested in maintaining the prestige and financial standing of their own family, and so will attempt to find a mate who is the *equal* of the young representative of their own family. When marriage choice is formally free, the informal associations and acquaintanceships of young people are nevertheless restricted, so that even if they marry someone whom they fall in love with, they can fall in love with only the people they meet, and these tend to be generally of the same class level and social background.

The more than a hundred studies of homogamy have shown that the likelihood of husband and wife sharing almost any characteristic is greater than chance expectation, whether this characteristic is a physical one, such as height or color of eyes, or an economic factor such as occupational background. Not all of these are of great importance in marital adjustment, but a smaller problem of adjustment exists when the couple can count on finding in each other quite similar attitudes, habits, and tastes. This general range of elements relates also to the factors already mentioned. It is probable, for example, that those who are alike in many respects will share a similar and approving social circle. The selection process itself will often break up the relationship between people of very different backgrounds.

---

[58] For a summary of research on homogamy, see Ernest W. Burgess and Harvey J. Locke, *The Family*, 2nd ed. (New York: American Book, 1953), pp. 369-72; Ruth S. Cavan, *The American Family* (New York: Crowell, 1953), p. 377.

Social Homogamy and Complementarity of Needs

One line of psychological research suggests that, though marital stability is higher among socially homogamous marriages, two individuals may be more contented in marriage if certain of their psychological characteristics are *not* alike.[59] The theory of complementary needs is not an explanation of divorce, but merely says: "in mate selection each individual seeks, within his or her field of eligibles, for that person who gives the greatest promise of providing him or her with maximum need gratification." [60] These needs have been developed from an earlier classification worked out by Henry A. Murray and include such characteristics as: autonomy—to be unattached; independence—to avoid or escape from domination and constraint; deference—to admire and praise a person; nurturance—to give sympathy and aid to a weak, helpless, ill, or dejected person or animal; recognition—to excite the admiration and approval of others; succorance—to be helped by a sympathetic person, to be nursed, loved, protected, indulged.[61] Three general traits are also postulated: anxiety, emotionality, and vicariousness ("the gratification of a need derived from the perception that another person is deriving gratification").

The above list includes only part of the full classification of 13 needs. Although some modification of this list may be necessary in the future, it includes many of the individual's basic personality needs. Once the young people in a given circle of eligibles having similar social characteristics begin to pair off in marriage—"what Jane sees in Tom" is not only his future earning capacity or his handsomeness. What she feels is an attraction based upon the fact that some of her needs are gratified when she is with Tom. For example, if she likes to take care of people and Tom in turn likes to be taken care of, it is much more likely that they will get along well, and feel drawn to one another, than if both share the same need in the same quantity.

However, the theory can be pushed beyond the mere matter of choice of mate. One possible direction of inquiry, for example, should be a study of the extent to which people *mis*perceive others' ability to gratify given needs, especially in our own courtship system, which puts a premium on a "smooth line" and teaches all of us to fit ourselves to the apparent wishes of the other. The dating situation creates a socially *structured* misperception on both sides. Long acquaintance-

---

[59] See Robert F. Winch, *The Modern Family,* 3rd ed. (New York: Holt, 1963), Chapter 18; and his *Mate Selection* (New York: Harper, 1958).

[60] Winch, *The Modern Family,* p. 404.

[61] See H. A. Murray *et al., Explorations in Personality* (New York: Oxford University Press, 1938), Chapter 3; Winch, *The Modern Family,* pp. 408-09.

ship and engagement are conducive to marital stability, in part because the chances of such misconceptions are diminished over time.

The theory of complementary needs also throws light on adjustment and conflict in marriage. Individuals may fit well along one dimension, but not along another. For example, Jane may like to take care of Tom and Tom like to be taken care of by Jane—that is, her need for nurturance complements his need for succorance. However, Jane's deference need may be frustrated by the fact that Tom has no great need to excite the admiration and approval of others. It may happen, then, that the attraction and the later marriage are based upon *some* complementary needs, but there may be *other* needs which are not well met. How the later situation of marriage changes the relative weight of satisfaction of some needs as against some dissatisfactions is a matter for further study.

From this point of view, the stable marriage is likely to be one in which a range of the wife's and husband's needs are mutually gratified. An unhappy marriage leading to divorce may well be one in which some few needs are met, but others are frustrated or ignored, so that the union means a continued unhappiness for either or both persons. How far the adjustment of husband and wife to the reality of their situation is generally sufficient to tolerate this failure of need gratification is a question yet to be answered.

Grounds for Divorce and Complaints and Conflicts

South Carolina reinstituted the absolute divorce in 1949, and now all states permit both absolute divorce and annulment. Because domestic law is decided by the individual states, there are many variations in the grounds which are acceptable for divorce suit. The most popular of these is cruelty; almost three-fifths of all divorces are granted on these grounds. This type of complaint has been used in some jurisdictions for a hundred years, but its meaning has gradually changed in almost all of them. Formerly it meant physical cruelty, an attack upon the spouse's life, or unusual personal indignities. However, in most jurisdictions it has now come to mean little more than "incompatibility," and almost any complaint can be used in support of the charge.

The only other category of complaint that is used in any substantial number of divorces is desertion. In the 1880's, about 40 percent of all divorces were granted for desertion, but the proportion now is less than 18 percent.[62] The other most common complaints are adultery,

---

[62] Jacobson, *American Marriage and Divorce*, p. 124. The total number of divorces on grounds of desertion was 68,000 in 1950.

drunkenness, and neglect to provide, none of which amounts to more than 5 percent of all divorces in the United States. About three-fifths of the total number of marital dissolutions in New York are granted for adultery, the only ground for divorce in that state.

However, it is common knowledge that tabulations of divorces by grounds for complaint do not necessarily reflect the reality of the divorce conflict. They reflect rather the fact that our legal system requires the "innocent" party to prove that the other is "guilty" in his marital behavior. By the time the suit is filed, both husband and wife have usually agreed to obtain a divorce, and they simply utilize the grounds that are legally most effective and socially least accusatory against the other partner. Of course, when such relatively rare charges as drunkenness or adultery are used, the chances are greater that in fact the accused party was guilty, and that the accusing party still feels resentful.

What then are the *real* complaints of husbands and wives against one another? Many studies have attempted to unravel the complex web of their charges and countercharges. Such listings of marital difficulties are worth examining, but they are not necessarily the "true" causes of the marital disorganization. Such lists merely reflect the various areas of marital *interaction*. How much *weight* to give each of them is not known, even when a given wife or husband believes that a particular complaint was the most serious matter involved. A wife may complain that her husband has had an affair, but she does not probe into the meaning of that affair, or inquire what failures in her own family relationships made an outside solace attractive to her husband. A husband may complain that sexual relations with his wife were always unsatisfactory, and never know that his own ineptitude was the major factor in her frigidity. Neither may make a complaint about financial matters, but both may have lived under great tension because of their economic problems.

Two such lists were derived from a comparison of happily married couples with divorcees, and from a study of divorced women.[63] The first study asked each spouse or ex-spouse to check the items in a list of possible marital problems, if the item had in their opinion caused *serious* difficulties in their marriage.[64] The other study, however, asked the divorced woman to use her own words to state what in her opinion was the *main* cause of the divorce. The differences in the questions created differences in the results; a check-list question will usually

---

[63] See Locke, *Predicting Adjustment in Marriage.* See also Goode, *After Divorce.*
[64] Locke, *Predicting Adjustment in Marriage,* pp. 75-76, 377-78.

TABLE 9

Common Complaints of Happily Married and Divorced Couples

Complaints	Locke Study ("Check . . . the following things which . . . have caused serious difficulties . . . .")[a]				Goode Study ("What was the main cause . . . ?")[b]
	Happily Married		Divorced		Divorced
	Men	Women	Men	Women	Women
	(Percent)		(Percent)		(Percent)
Affectional and Sex Relationships					
1. Mate paid attention to another person	3	6	66	74	
2. No longer in love	4	2	60	61	
3. Adultery	1	2	44	55	
4. Unsatisfying sex relations	8	6	46	33	
5. Triangle					16
6. Home life					25
Socially Disapproved Behavior					
1. Drunkenness	3	2	26	56	30
2. Gambling	3	3	6	26	
3. "Drinking, gambling, & helling around"					31
Nonsupport	0	0	7	49	33
Desertion	0	0	20	27	8
Relatives	17	20	53	30	4
Values					21
1. Religion	6	5	8	8	
2. Amusements	29	20	34	29	
Personality					29
Selfishness, Lack of Cooperation	6	12	22	30	
Husband's Attempt to Dominate					32

Sources:

[a] Harvey J. Locke, *Predicting Adjustment in Marriage* (New York: Holt, 1951), pp. 75-76.
[b] William J. Goode, *After Divorce* (New York: Free Press, 1956), p. 123.

elicit more complaints than an open-ended question. Nevertheless, a study of the results (Table 9) helps to understand these complaints.

One set of differences is created by sex roles. Fewer men than women complain about nonsupport, adultery, gambling, drunkenness, or desertion. On the other hand, both happily married and divorced men in Locke's study complained more than women about unsatisfactory sex relations, a difference which grows from the lesser importance of the sexual act itself in the woman's happiness. And men and women complained about equally in regard to purely affectional relations.

The table also shows how few areas there are in which the divorced couples do not remember having had serious difficulties. The happily married, by contrast, reported serious difficulties only with respect to in-laws, amusements, and "other difficulties over money" (men, 14 percent; women, 19 percent); while 39 percent of the men and 27 percent of the women reported "no difficulties at all." By the time of the divorce, most of the interaction between husband and wife has become unpleasant.

All such lists require some interpretation of what each item *meant* to the spouses. Some wives complain that their husbands are simply too "bossy," but others use a more sophisticated vocabulary and refer to the "personality problems" of their husbands. Lower-class wives may accept a degree of domination by their husbands, which middle-class wives would find intolerable. A lower-class wife married to a middle-class husband may feel that their income level is adequate, while (with the same income) a middle-class wife married to a factory worker may feel that they have to scrimp too much. Finally, in all these studies, the specific *answers* of each spouse to the charges of the other are missing.[65]

This analysis has laid relatively little stress upon sexual factors in family disorganization. This is not because divorcees fail to complain that at times their sex relations were unsatisfactory in their former marriage. (Cf. Locke's figures of 46 percent for men, 33 percent for women.) It is rather that this area of dissatisfaction is less likely than others to be crucial. Until about the time of World War II, many marital analysts and counselors were convinced, on the basis of psychodynamic speculations, that sexual dissatisfaction was at the root of much marital conflict. It is quite possible that marital dissatisfaction *was* greater a generation ago, particularly in the period after World War I, when sexual expectations became higher as a result of the general sexual emancipation of that time. By contrast, though the expectations of modern couples have doubtless dropped not at all,

---

[65] For further analyses of the kinds of complaints made by husbands and wives, see Judson T. Landis, "Social Correlates of Divorce or Nondivorce Among the Unhappily Married," *Marriage and Family Living*, Vol. 25 (May, 1963), pp. 178-80; and Howard E. Mitchell, James W. Bullard, and Emily H. Mudd, "Areas of Marital Conflict in Successfully and Unsuccessfully Functioning Families," *Journal of Health and Human Behavior*, Vol. 3 (Summer, 1962), pp. 88-93.

young people today are much better prepared for sex in marriage than their parents or grandparents were, and hence they probably experience less actual sexual dissatisfaction.

A change has also taken place with respect to the supposed *meaning* of sexual dissatisfactions. Family analysts have come increasingly to accept the view that when sexual dissatisfaction is great it is a reflection of dissatisfaction in *other* areas of life. Neither husband nor wife is able to give emotional solace, tenderness, and pleasure in sex when conflicts are severe in other areas. Consequently, even though one focus of complaint may be sexual dissatisfaction, it is usually now viewed as no more than a symptom.[66] This view, however, should be separated sharply from the psychodynamic interpretation of the sexual *bases* of personality. A considerable body of the theory used in psychotherapy now includes the notion that much of the personality conflict within an individual may have originated from sexual problems at some stage in his development. One might then view much of marital disorganization as having ultimately a sexual basis. This is, however, different from the matter of sexual dissatisfaction *within* marriage.

In a deeper analysis of family disorganization, we must know not only exactly what the behavior was, but also the standards or *norms* by which that behavior was judged. Even casual observation of families known to the reader will underline the importance of doing so. Some husbands, for example, are fairly contented with wives who, even by the standards of their own group, seem to be poor housekeepers and relatively unaffectionate. What is needed is a more precise disentangling of the standards by which people judge similar marital behavior and the responses they make to that behavior; their various patterns of behavior; and the words and phrases they use to describe the behavior.

PATTERNS OF CONFLICT. Although divorce conflict is often depicted in dramatic terms in newspaper accounts, novels, and even in sociology textbooks, such accounts really telescope a long series of relatively minor maladjustments, difficulties, and disagreements. A recital of them would be extremely boring. Not many marriages end by the husband or wife simply storming out of the house in rage, or informing the other that he or she has found a new love. More often the period of conflict extends over years (in Goode's study [p. 137], the median time from serious consideration to decree was two years) punctuated

---

[66] Burgess and Locke, *The Family*, pp. 524-25.

by relatively harmonious periods as well as by incidents of anger and disillusionment. Mostly, however, it is merely the slow dragging out of a life together, becoming increasingly unsatisfying. A curve of divorce conflict would not be a simple upward or downward line; it would rather take the form of a spiral, in which the husband and wife come back again and again to points of disagreement, rehashing them interminably. An apparent agreement about some point is accepted for a while, and then later rejected. A disagreement seems to be forgotten, and then reappears. Sometimes even their friends do not know until late in the marriage that it is a failure, because they see them only under happy circumstances. Nevertheless, a full tape recording of their entire life together would make it evident that the marriage has become intolerable for one or both of them.

Two primary patterns are evident in the gradual intensification of conflict. First, husband and wife are wounded in a disagreement over some matter, and one or the other withdraws some of his emotion; the affectional commitment is decreased as a means of protection against further hurt. However, this very withdrawal is coupled with the second pattern, the requirement that they in fact cooperate, work together, live together, day by day. Husband and wife can give sympathy, understanding, and support precisely because they ordinarily do have affection for one another, but living together when that affection is diminished makes any further hurt or wound increasingly hard to bear. However, if the individual cannot obtain comfort from his spouse, there is no other place to go, except eventually to leave the marriage and establish a new one.

At some point in this progressive withdrawal of affection and increasing discomfort in the relationship itself, there comes a time when one spouse decides that he no longer cares a great deal what the other does. The husband no longer hopes for improvement from his wife.[67] The wife looks from a great distance at the foibles and idiosyncrasies of her husband and no longer sees any reason why she should tolerate them at all. In a sense, the conflict process leads to the point where they look at each other as strangers, and, after all, one need not tolerate the bad habits, the domineering qualities, the selfishness, or the nagging of strangers.

It often happens that one spouse either continues to love the partner who has withdrawn his affection, or else is so embedded in a

---

[67] For a fuller discussion of the process of alienation, see Waller and Hill, *The Family,* Chapter 23.

fabric of marital habit that it is painful to face changes in it. One individual may be very dependent on the other, and the conflict process itself will take a longer time. In order to drive his spouse out, the individual who has withdrawn his affection may have to show considerable hostility as well. He or she may commit some dramatic act such as moving out of the house or engaging in an affair with another, in order to crystallize the decision. It must be kept in mind, of course, that the mere withdrawal of affection is not a sufficient "cause" for divorce. Many couples, especially those who have been married a long time, have at best a mild affection for one another; but their habit systems are so meshed, and their expectations are so closely geared to the actual performances of their spouses, that living in the same social space is not at all a burden. It has the comfortable qualities of an old shoe. Marriages that have held together for a long time are not necessarily "better adjusted" as time goes on, but certainly their stability is greater.

It is this *reciprocality* of the conflict process, the contribution that *both* husband and wife make to the eventual divorce, that makes the legal theory of divorce so hollow. Legal procedure requires that the offended party bring suit against the offender and prove that the erring spouse has indeed broken the rules of marriage. The legal theory also assumes that there is no collusion between the spouses with respect to getting a divorce. Both these elements fail to reflect the facts. In every divorce, both parties are offenders, even when one party has offended more than the other, and in practically every divorce both husband and wife agree on the terms of the suit beforehand. Indeed, one might claim that the tragedy of divorce is not so much the breakup of a marriage as it is the apparent destruction of two seemingly honest and decent people, to the point where they behave evilly toward one another. They may come to attack one another savagely for minor wrongs, while showing tolerance and sympathy to their acquaintances and friends for the same faults.

In the United States, nearly three-fourths of all divorces are granted to wives. Presumably, women are not the innocent parties in three-fourths of divorces. Rather, the kinds of charges which can be brought without opprobrium are most easily brought against the husband. Even the charge of adultery damages the man's reputation less than it does the woman's. Cruelty is the most common charge, and the phrasing of legal grounds makes it easier to prove this charge against the husband.

One study has made the claim that the divorces are more frequently granted to wives because it is more often the husband than the wife who first wants to break up the marriage.[68] This general process may be outlined as follows. In spite of the substantial change in the position of women in our society, men remain dominant, in the family as in the occupational sphere. The socialization of the female is still primarily toward the ultimate assumption of the roles of wife, mother, and housekeeper. The male never makes a decision as to whether he will "take a job *or* stay home and take care of the children." Much of his attention, time, and energy are directed to things outside the home. He has a greater scope of activity and his choices are less restricted than those of his wife. Behavior that might be criticized as questionable for the wife is viewed as legitimate and innocent for the husband.

One consequence of these differences is that the husband is less likely than the wife to have his emotional commitments focused on the home and is more likely to find pleasurable or exciting activities away from the home, including some involving the opposite sex. Because the wife's commitment to the home remains dominant, and because in the twentieth century she increasingly applies an equalitarian standard to her husband's activity, she is likely to object to these interests. At least she will object to some of their consequences, such as the apparently lessened interest of the husband in the family, his willingness to spend money and time outside the home, his failure to appear for dinner on time, and so on. From the husband's viewpoint, many of his activities are perfectly innocent, in part because he is permitted by society to wander farther afield, and in part because he does not at first intend to move away from his family.

It is no paradox, then, to assert that wives more often than husbands first suggest the divorce, and eventually get the divorce, yet husbands more often first lose interest in the marriage. Since the wife's commitment to the marriage is likely to be greater, and her potential loss through divorce is greater, the husband is more likely to create a situation in which his wife also wants to break the bond. Perhaps without intending to do so, he must eventually make himself so obnoxious that she desires to break up the marriage as much as he does. Since his position in society depends far less on his family behavior than on his other activities, he may continue to be a congenial and effective co-worker or companion, all the while acting offensively toward his wife. One consequence of her initiative is that it frees him, at least to some extent, from feelings of guilt he might otherwise suffer because he set in motion the train of events leading to the divorce.

---

[68] Goode, *After Divorce*, Chapter 11.

CASES OF CONFLICT. This has been only a very general pattern of conflict, as structured by the status positions of husband and wife in our society. We shall now present two brief vignettes of a divorce conflict, to show these processes in greater detail. Of course, these cases must not be viewed as typical.

John and Anna first met when he was a sophomore and she was a freshman in an excellent undergraduate liberal arts college in the West. John was the son of a brilliant scientist whose marriage broke up while the boy was still young. However, he spent all of his vacations with his father. He early developed a shy, inhibited pattern of meeting the world. He constantly deprecated himself, and expressed his inferiority feelings by refusing to tackle difficult assignments, or by giving up easily. His basic talents were considerable, but his father was rather domineering and seemed able to do almost anything well, whether it was sports, the arts, or his own field of biology. John expanded considerably in college, but did not begin making good grades until late. However, he found Anna a most congenial companion, because she too had had a domineering, successful father, and enjoyed John's expression of rebellion. In her eyes, John was bohemian, daring, and restless. He basked in this admiration.

Very early in their relationship they decided to marry, and when John was a senior, preparing to go to graduate school, they did marry. Their adjustment was not good even at this stage, because Anna had been reared very strictly, and though she admired John's unconventional ways, she was uncomfortable in following them. Their plan was for John to continue in graduate school, and for her to begin teaching elementary school, to let him finish his doctorate. They counted on a little help from either side of the family. Actually, they did receive substantial help from both sides, but Anna's continued effort to approximate a middle-class household, imitating her own home, meant that they constantly had economic problems. John was not especially practical in money matters, and they both blamed one another frequently for a failure to budget properly.

Because John was not well organized personally, and often was in despair because his work did not seem good enough, his work on the doctorate went slowly. However, he continued to broaden and deepen intellectually, and to take on new standards as he entered professional life as a young instructor in a midwestern university. His talent expressed itself increasingly in good research work, and in being accepted by those already established in his field. Anna, meanwhile, tried to combine the roles of full-time teacher and householder, and increasingly found herself falling behind. She could no longer be an adequate companion, and tried to find her security in an increasing rigidity about the way the household should be run. She wanted to buy more things than they could afford, and berated John constantly if he deviated at all from patterns which she thought of as proper middle-class behavior. As his work demanded more and more of his time, and as their household appeared increasingly a stereotype of a middle-class pattern, John spent more of his time in the laboratory and with a younger group of intellectuals around the university. As the conflict between John and Anna deepened and widened, they indulged very little in violent arguments. Both tried to reach out for the other from time to time, but their styles of life, their intellectual levels, their goals and standards, all seemed too different to be bridged by sympathetic human gestures. They remained civil to one another, even when alone together, and their discussions were more often sorrowful self-analysis than accusations.

Finally, John met a brilliant girl graduate student, who seemed to embody all the excitement, creativity, and freedom from restraint that he had missed so far in his marriage. The things that had given him some security and courage early in his career now seemed to be a set of fetters. His affair with the graduate student continued for a long time before he had the courage to inform Anna and ask for a divorce. Whether his new marriage will be stable remains to be seen.

The case of the wife who gradually falls behind while her husband continues to grow is not uncommon. A very different pattern emerges in the following case.

Fred and Mary met at a high school senior prom, when Mary was trying to get over her first unfortunate love affair, and Fred, who had already graduated and was working for a construction company, was visiting Detroit with a cousin of his. To him, she seemed glamorous, with a faintly tragic air about her. Fred seemed to be a strong, silent, masculine type, self-sufficient, and with many depths of character which she could only dimly see. They dated one another for about six months, but Fred's job with the construction company outside Detroit meant that they could only see one another primarily on dates. As a consequence, Mary, her family, and her friends knew very little about him. After their marriage, Fred moved to Detroit, where he again found work with a construction company. They bought a small house, and soon Mary was engaged in setting up her little dream bungalow. She still saw Fred only little, because he attempted to put in as many overtime hours as possible, in order to pay for the many things they wanted to buy. Mary was soon pregnant, and her first pregnancy was quickly followed by another. Although their initial sexual adjustment was adequate, Mary always felt some emotional lack in their relationship. At home Fred was the same strong, silent person she had met at the dance, but she never felt any greater intimacy with him. She soon found that he expressed little affection for their baby son, and though he did not object to any of the decorating she did in the house, neither did he praise it. Rather, he seemed to view his home as something which he slept in, visited, but kept apart from his inner life.

Mary joined the circle of young wives in her neighborhood, and filled her days with taking care of the house, the babies, shopping, and preparing for the few hours that she and Fred would spend together. They had never discussed their futures, and she was thus dismayed to find that Fred had no particular ambition to succeed economically. He made an adequate salary as a semiskilled worker, and his additional wages from overtime work seemed to him sufficient. After about two years of marriage, he suggested that he would like to go to Minnesota where he thought the wages would be somewhat better. Mary realized for the first time that he had invested no emotion in their joint friendship at all. From his side, he had a reasonably comfortable relationship with a pretty woman, and all of the household problems and duties were hers. He did not bother with them, because they were simply not part of his inner life. She gradually came to see also that his apparent "depth" was nothing at all. His silence did not mean that he was thinking important thoughts. Rather he was likely not to be thinking at all. Her frantic efforts to interest him in their first boy, and then their second, remained futile. He treated them as dolls, something which women and young girls play with, but nothing of interest to himself. He was angry if she was not there when he came home, and resented to some extent the time that she spent in the evenings with other wives. However he seemed not to be more resentful on the few occasions when he found her sitting in a local bar, gossiping with another man. He was simply not concerned with her emotional relationships; he was only concerned with whether his needs were being taken care of. If he came home and found that a babysitter was there instead of his wife he simply made himself at home and did not bother to look for her.

She was therefore not surprised, although she was crushed and humiliated by the experience, when she came home from shopping one day and found that he had simply packed all of his clothes and left, without leaving a note. He disappeared, and she never heard from him directly again, although once or twice she heard from friends that he was in Mississippi, and later in New Jersey, still continuing in construction work.

Internal Dissolution: The "Empty Shell" Family

The Bureau of the Census estimates that in 1960 among the population 14 years and older there were about 99 million who had been married at some time in their lives.[69] This category of "ever-married" included those currently married (over four-fifths) as well as those who had been widowed, separated, or divorced. The state may ask many questions of the individual, but so far it has not yet dared to ask whether a supposedly intact family is in truth merely a physical location in which the individuals have no satisfying emotional connections with one another. There is no way by which sociologists and marital counselors can locate a reliable sample of such cases, although a few will turn up in almost any family study. This brief section, then, can present only

---

[69] Bureau of the Census, U.S. *Census of Population: 1960,* Vol. 1, *Characteristics of the Population,* Part 1, United States Summary, p. LV.

a few unsystematic observations on this type of family dissolution, not a series of firm conclusions drawn from research studies.

As noted earlier, most families that divorce pass through a state—granted, sometimes *after* the divorce—in which husband and wife no longer feel bound to each other, cease to cooperate or share with each other, and look on one another as almost strangers. The "empty shell" family is in such a state, for its members no longer feel any strong commitment to many of their mutual role obligations; but for various reasons the husband and wife do not separate or divorce.

Violent, open quarrels are not common in this family. The atmosphere is without laughter or fun, and a sullen gloom pervades the household. Members do not discuss their problems or experiences with each other, and communication is kept to a minimum. Parents and children fulfill their *instrumental* obligations, but not their expressive ones. The husband holds a job and provides for the family. The wife takes care of the house and meals, and nurses those who become ill. The children go to school and at home do their chores. But any spontaneous expression of affection, or even of delight in a personal experience, is rebuffed by the others. Each tells the others whatever is necessary to integrate their instrumental activities—when one will be home for a meal, how much school supplies cost, or what is the next chore to be done.

Usually, one or both of the spouses are strong personalities, at least passively. Their rationalization for avoiding divorce is, on the part of one or both, "sacrifice for the children," "neighborhood respectability," and a religious conviction that divorce is morally wrong. The first two of these are factually erroneous, in that children in such a family unit are usually starved for love, embarrassed when friends visit them, and ashamed to be forced to "explain" their parents' behavior to others. The neighborhood always knows about the internal dissolution of the family, for the couple engage in few activities together, show no pleasure in one another's company, and exhibit innumerable if tiny differences from normal families.

The repression of emotion extends, naturally, to sex as well. This type of family is usually highly conventional with respect to sex roles, and considerably less liberal in its sex attitudes than other families in its neighborhood. The daughters are given less freedom than their age mates, as to type of permissible activity, places where they may go, and when they must be home. Sex relations between husband and wife are rare and unsatisfactory. Most dating activities of the adolescents are kept secret from the parents, or are reported erroneously so as not to arouse punishment.

The hostility in such a home is great, but arguments focus on the small issues, not the large ones. Facing the latter would, of course, lead directly to separation or divorce, but the couple has decided that staying together overrides other values, including each other's happiness and the psychological health of their children. The casual visitor may believe that the members are cold, callous, and insensitive to each other's needs, but closer observation usually discloses that at certain levels they are sensitive: they prove they do know each other's weaknesses and guilts, since they manage frequently to hurt each other.

The members of such a family do not often live a full and satisfactory life outside the family, for they are not really independent of one another, and their relations with outsiders are crippled by their emotional experiences within the family. When the children grow up and begin to think of marriage, often they make their decision without informing their parents until shortly before the marriage, and frequently marry as an escape from their own family.

Until an adequate study of such families is made, these observations cannot be properly assessed. The nearly unrelieved bleakness of this picture may be erroneous, in that the writer may have overlooked some possible rewards that members get from one another in such a unit. It must at least be conceded that these people rarely violate any of the important mores of the society. Finally, the student must remember that this type of family is less likely to occur when large family units live together as in other, non-Western cultures, since each member of such a nuclear family unit may enjoy satisfactory relations with other relatives, and the need for the sharing of direct emotional solace among parents and children is not so great as in the Western family system.

The Externally Induced Crisis: Depression, War, Separations, Natural Catastrophes, Incarceration, and Death

This section focuses primarily on the family's *adjustment* to crisis, since in this type of marital breakup the "development" of the problem lies outside the family itself. Space does not permit a full variety of such problems, and indeed little research has been done in this area. Because adjustment to death has often been related to post-divorce adjustment, the two patterns will be compared, although the divorce crisis does not logically fall in this category of marital problems. Thereafter, brief attention will be given to the adjustment to war separations and to the depression crisis.

Divorce and Bereavement

The main similarities between divorce and bereavement have to do with the basic sociological fact that a set of role relationships has been disrupted, requiring a profound adjustment throughout the family network. Moreover, the old habit patterns tend to continue, making it difficult for an individual to find immediate substitutes or to fill his life with alternate satisfactions. In both events, the removal of the spouse means the cessation of sexual satisfaction which in divorce conflict often occurs before the divorce itself. In both, emotional problems may be so intense that the sex drive is not felt so strongly as before; but there is at most only a temporary abatement, and the sex hunger returns. If the divorced or dead spouse was the husband, his initiative and leadership in the family are missing. Economic problems may become pressing. If the missing spouse was the wife, profound adjustments in household management are necessary. In either case emotional solace, friendship, or love are missing. Children no longer have an adult model to follow, and the spouse remaining with the children is likely to find the problem of controlling and supervising them difficult and wearying. In both situations there are likely to be endless discussions with friends and kinfolk about the spouse and the problems of the adjustment.

The institutionalized character of death contrasts it sharply with divorce.[70] In all societies, the rituals and customs of death are an important part of the social structure. The removal of one person by death from the social network weakens the social structure, and this threat is met by a set of observances that serve to rally the feeling of community, to alleviate sorrow, and to move the bereaved individuals into a new state of adjustment. We all accept intellectually the inevitability of death, but a particular death hurts emotionally. It always calls forth the question, "Why did he have to die?" and the answer cannot be given in biological terms. The death has to be invested with some kind of meaning. It must be placed somewhere in the total cosmos, and this meaning is usually drawn from religious beliefs, which are acted out in religious rituals. Even in a society as secular as our own, these customs remain strong. When the death is marked by nonreligious ceremonials, they still retain a quasi-religious character.

---

[70] In this immediate section we shall draw upon the summary of Thomas D. Eliot, "Bereavement: Inevitable But Not Insurmountable," in Becker and Hill, eds., *Family, Marriage, and Parenthood,* pp. 665-67. We also have utilized Willard Waller, *The Family* (New York: Dryden, 1938), pp. 480-522, and Waller and Hill, *The Family,* Chapter 22.

Unlike the situation of divorce, that of death formally requires kinfolk and friends to attend the bereaved person, to offer services, to give support. They must be at the funeral if possible, and may offer financial help, even if it is insufficient. The bereaved person is not only permitted to express his grief, but is even encouraged to do so. He is told, "Go ahead and cry it out." It is recognized that the crying itself helps the grief psychodynamically. The very fact there is so much social support at this moment makes it possible to give way completely to grief.

The rituals and observances also give the bereaved person some definite tasks to carry out. These are not difficult, and may be no more than moving from one part of the funeral parlor to another, sitting in one place rather than another at the cemetery, greeting and talking with relatives and kin, and so on. The bereaved person is not permitted to grieve alone but is forced almost mechanically to go through various activities that serve to keep him within the social network. The funeral service itself expresses the finality of death; there is nothing in the sequence of steps toward divorce which has this character.

The bereaved person does not usually feel hostility toward the wife or husband who has died; there is a tendency to idealize the past relationship and the person. Both sides of the kin network are encouraged to praise the dead one, unlike the situation of divorce. Wounded pride is less likely to figure in death than in divorce and of course the widower or widow is less likely to feel a sense of failure simply because the relationship has been broken.

Although the customs of mourning do not specify solutions for many of the problems of death, they do offer some solutions; divorce offers none, simply because the social responses to divorce are not deeply institutionalized. There is no set of agreed-upon rights and obligations concerning the divorced person. It is not entirely clear whether either kin line has any obligation to the divorced person, or to his or her children. The relationship of ex-husband and ex-wife after the divorce is not spelled out either. Although the husband may have financial obligations for the care of his children, his obligations for their supervision, socialization, and even emotional health are not stated by custom. Finally, the institutions of our society do not specify whether friends or kin should sympathize with the divorced person, congratulate him, or help him to search for a new mate. Although there is considerable similarity in the adjustment patterns of divorcees, these are not so much the results of specific *customs* about these matters as they are the results of common social *experiences,* the economic needs of a broken family unit, the lonesomeness of the divorced person, and the difficulty in our society of working out an easy adjustment outside of marriage.

Some of the structural differences between the situations of divorce and bereavement also make for differences in the emotional situation of the divorcee as against that of the widower or widow. The divorced person is likely to have gone through a long process, on the average about two years, during which his emotional attachment to the spouse was gradually undermined or destroyed. Consequently, some of the emotional "work of adjustment" is accomplished even before the divorce. Also, under most circumstances, the divorced spouse can give certain types of help, especially if there are children. The divorced person is unlikely to idealize the departed spouse. Divorce is not so irrevocable as death, and of course a much higher proportion of people who lose their spouses by death are older people, for whom the loss may be emotionally crushing.

Psychodynamically, the bereaved person must grieve if he is to adjust to the death. This process may be called the "work of grief," which means simply that the bereaved relives many of his experiences with the dead person, suffering with each memory, but gradually accepting the fact of death and integrating it into his present life. The dead person is "re-created," in the sense that some memories are gradually repressed, and others are kept intact, to form an image of the dead, largely idealized. The numbing experience upon first learning of the death may include episodes in which the bereaved person actually denies the death, and a few individuals never accept the death of a beloved one. Since many persons feel guilt at the death of a beloved person, berating themselves for not having done more for him, this created image of the dead includes usually an idealized version of the relationship between the living and the dead.

The widow and widower, as noted, are guided more than the divorced by social customs. These customs include a period of mourning, in which the individual is supposed to conform especially in his relations with the opposite sex. It is a violation of the dead to engage in a love affair soon after his death. There are always some who praise the widow who so reveres the dead husband that she never remarries, and this was the ideal in both China and India. The widow is less able than the widower to find a new spouse, in part because an older man is not criticized for marrying a considerably younger woman. Twice as many widowers as widows remarry during the first five years after the death of their spouses. On the other hand, widows and widowers are much more likely to remarry than a generation ago.[71]

War and Depression

Although the crisis of war removes a husband from the family, and a depression may not, the existing analyses of these two problems have focused on a common problem, role impairment caused by an external event, and have shared a common perspective, that the major variables in the continuing functioning of the family are (a) its internal integration and (b) its adaptability.[72] Although space does not permit a full discussion of the problems faced or the solutions that families use to solve them, a brief summary of certain research findings may be presented.

A not surprising finding in these inquiries was that a considerable number of families seem to undergo no crisis at all. When the husband went away to war, either the family welcomed his departure as a relief, or each member took on added duties with willingness and a renewed sense of devotion. At the height of the last great depression in 1932-1933, some 14 to 16 million people were unemployed, about one out of four in the labor force, but many families suffering from economic difficulties were able to maintain the integrity and happiness of their family relations by adjusting easily to the new demands of the situation.

Families face a set of similar problems when the father goes away to war: the income is likely to be less, many household tasks defined as "male" must be taken over by others, the mother gets no relief from disciplining or nursing the children and administering the household, and the children both miss their father and lack an important role relationship in their socialization process. The adjustment to both the departure and the later return depends not alone on (a) the *difficulties* of the event itself, however, but equally on (b) the *resources* (both material and social) that the family commands, and on (c) how the family *defines* the situation. The family that defines

---

[71] Waller and Hill, *The Family*, p. 395.

[72] See Robert C. Angell, *The Family Encounters the Depression* (New York: Scribner, 1936), especially Chapter 13; E. Wight Bakke, *Citizens Without Work* (New Haven: Yale University Press, 1940); Mirra Komarovsky, *The Unemployed Man and His Family* (New York: Dryden, 1940); Reuben Hill, *Families Under Stress* (New York: Harper, 1949), especially Chapters 5 and 6; Elise Boulding, "Family Adjustments to War Separation and Reunion," *Annals of the American Academy of Political and Social Science*, Vol. 272 (November, 1950), pp. 59-67. See also S. A. Stouffer and Paul F. Lazarsfeld, *Research Memorandum on the Family in the Depression* (New York: Social Science Research Council, 1937).

the departure or reunion as a catastrophe is more likely than others to respond in uncoordinated and mutually unsatisfactory ways.

The impact of the depression crisis is felt more slowly, and many families literally face no problems until late in the economic cycle. White-collar workers may suffer no loss of pay for a time, while manual laborers or skilled workers in construction begin to lose their jobs early. The lower class generally is economically even more disadvantaged in a depression than in normal times, but it is not certain that their definition of the situation leads to less effective handling of the problems. Middle-class families work far more toward future goals, many of which have meaning for their prestige, so that even when they do not starve or become homeless, the emotional hurt of giving up club memberships, frequent dinners and parties, plans for college, modish clothes, or—apparently among the most hurtful of experiences, accepting relief—may be as great as the lower-class anxiety from the difficulties of simple economic survival.[73] In addition, even in normal times many lower-class families exist close to a minimum standard of living, or lower still, often being without work, and expecting each member of the family to contribute economically when he can. To accept relief is not pleasant, but it is not so degrading as it is for middle-class families that have never even considered that possibility.

The depression crisis has the greater impact on the husband's position, just as the war crisis affects the wife's position more. The role obligations of family head, husband, father, and breadwinner are not ordinarily distinguished from one another by members of the family. Being without a job for months, and the gradual understanding that a new job is unlikely, may therefore reveal weaknesses in the family that were not previously visible. Sometimes, for example, the family is tightly integrated, but is absolutely dependent on the father's leadership and unable to adapt easily when he loses his status as breadwinner.[74] Or the family has instead been held together only because everyone has been dependent on his earnings, while secretly everyone hated him. In all cases, however, some role adjustments of family members are created by his job loss, especially as this continues over time. Many men are psychologically crushed by this loss, and some may desert their families because they are unable to adjust to the wife's taking a job and the children earning much of the family income.

---

[73] Cavan, *The American Family*, p. 538.
[74] See, for example, Angell's type, highly integrated, unadaptable (*The Family Encounters the Depression*, p. 261).

Lip service, at least, is paid to the ideal of the "democratic" family, in which all members have an equal voice in important decisions, and public opinion seems to assert that such families are "more adaptable." The previously cited research on the crisis of wartime separations found that a majority of the families thought of themselves as "equalitarian," but slightly less than 7 percent were so in practice—and that though the *marital* adjustment scores of equalitarian families were higher than other types, their ability to adjust to the crisis of separation and reunion was *not* higher. Effective handling of this type of crisis was found among many different kinds of family, including the "old-fashioned patriarchal" type.[75] Effectiveness was greater when adaptability and integration were high, when affection was strong among family members, the marital adjustment (i.e., between husband and wife) was high, and the family had previously experienced some success in handling similar crises.[76] These findings parallel the findings from the research on the response of families to the depression crisis.

The Internal Social Catastrophe: Major, Unwilled Role Failures Due to Mental, Emotional, or Physical Pathologies

The philosophical question of "blame" seems remote from the kind of crises now to be discussed. In this type of problem, the individual may be physically present, but his pathology prevents him from effectively carrying out his role obligations. Mental and physical illness are discussed elsewhere in this volume; the present context concerns only their impact on the family. As in the external crises which the family must face, the varieties of individual pathology affecting role behavior are so many that it is not possible here to deal with all of them. The onset of blindness or poliomyelitis may destroy a husband's earning capacity, and transform a capable family head into a physical and psychological invalid. Schizophrenia may change an apparently healthy and happy mother into a suspicious and incoherent individual, bent on hurting everyone she once loved. (See Chapter 1, pages 27-29.)

The exposition will be simplified somewhat by calling attention to certain aspects of adult mental illness in the family, and then discussing at greater length the problem of severe mental retardation in children, since in certain respects the effect of this problem is similar to that of mental illness.

---

[75] Hill, *Families Under Stress,* pp. 120-21.
[76] *Ibid.,* pp. 324, 326.

Of course, a high (but unknown) percentage of the mentally and emotionally ill and those with severe physical pathologies never marry because they cannot find a partner.[77] On the other hand, some do, and after marriage some individuals fall victims to these problems. Two stages of family adjustment to adult mental illness may be singled out here for attention: the onset of the disease and the return of the victim to his family for shorter or longer periods after therapy.

The most significant fact about the first behavioral symptoms of mental illness is that the members of the family are typically not competent to judge their meaning, unless the behavior is violent or "hysterical."[78] Role failure is first viewed as some sort of moral problem, deliberate or careless, and the response to it is anger, scolding, withdrawal, or the advice to "get a grip on yourself." A man with a brain tumor may begin to be suspicious, moody, and distracted, and so may a person who is a paranoid schizophrenic, but everyone has at times had a friend or acquaintance who behaved similarly. The husband thinks of laziness, weakness of character, or even organic difficulties, before he begins to guess that his wife may need psychiatric care. Often, the victim behaves normally in many respects, and perhaps (for a while) most of the time. Since the layman considers the acts of others as deliberate, the marriage may actually break up before the husband or wife understands that the problem is one of mental illness.

Once this possibility is faced, most families act to obtain professional help, whether tax-supported services or private psychotherapy. Only a few remain whose attitude is like that of a half-century ago: a family should "take care of its own" as long as there is no threat of violence. Most psychotherapy of a limited type is done by psychiatric social workers. Both clinical psychologists and psychiatrists—within mental institutions and on an outpatient basis—are engaged in deeper therapy. The layman, however loving and sensitive, cannot substitute for these services. Members of the family can contribute best by readjusting the family structure and shouldering the additional burdens.

These additional burdens are in some ways similar to those caused by desertion, divorce, or death, if the patient is hospitalized. However,

---

[77] For a review of this matter, see Aubrey Lewis, "Fertility and Mental Illness," *Eugenics Review*, Vol. 50 (July, 1958), pp. 91-105.

[78] For more detailed data on the family's response to mental illness, see Jerome K. Myers and Bertram H. Roberts, *Family and Class Dynamics in Mental Illness* (New York: Wiley & Sons, 1959), Chapter 8. See also Joan K. Jackson, "The adjustment of the Family to Alcoholism," *Marriage and Family Living*, Vol. 18 (1956), pp. 361-69.

the increasing use of drugs in psychotherapy, permitting the patient to function normally while (or, often, without) undergoing treatment, has meant that he may return to his family for varying periods of time. Preliminary research has thrown some light on this adjustment. It is not entirely certain that a loving permissive reception is most effective for continued rehabilitation. More important, patients who are not very effective in interpersonal relations after leaving a mental hospital are likely to have returned to a parental home where their relatives have strongly negative attitudes toward hospitalization and believe that the illness is inborn and that people who have once been mentally ill are never the same again. As a consequence, the family feels there is nothing they can do except accept the patient's quirks. By contrast, some patients return to families who seem to expect more from them. There is some evidence that these expectations may aid the patient in his rehabilitation.[79] Thus, a diagnosis of the fit between the patient's needs and the structure of family relations may some-times lead to a decision that he should not return to his family at first, but to other groups which will expect him to behave normally.[80]

Interesting work has recently been carried out in the area of the family adjustment to various problems of mental disease. This prob-lem has come to be of special importance because of the greater use of drugs that permit the mental patient to function outside the walls of the asylum. These drugs do not cure, but they shorten the pa-tient's stay in the hospital, and give the patient some promise of quasi-normality. The family, however, has new problems of adjust-ment. Several findings can be noted here.

One significant line of research focuses on what kind of family setting is most helpful for the returning mental patient, and what kinds of roles he can play.[81] For example, one of the more destructive

[79] James A. Davis, Howard E. Freeman, and Ozzie G. Simmons, "Rehospitali-zation and Performance Level among Former Mental Patients," *Social Problems*, Vol. 5 (July, 1957), pp. 37-44.

[80] For a good analysis of the extent to which there may be destructive tolerance in a family, see Lyman C. Wynne, Irving M. Ryckoff, Juliana Day, and Stanley I. Hirsch, "Pseudo-Mutuality in the Family Relations of Schizophrenics," in Nor-man W. Bell and Ezra F. Vogel, eds., *The Family* (New York: Free Press, 1960), especially pp. 579 ff.

[81] For both analyses and descriptive data on these problems, see James C. Baxter, Joseph Becker, and Walter Hooks, "Defensive Style in the Families of Schizophrenics and Controls," *Journal of Abnormal and Social Psychology*, Vol. 66 (May 5, 1963), pp. 512-18; Walter Kempler, Robert Iverson, and Arnold Beisser, "The Adult Schizophrenic and his Siblings," *Family Process*, Vol. 1 (September, 1962), pp. 224-35; Christian F. Midelfort, "Use of Members of the Family in the Treatment of Schizophrenia," *Family Process*, Vol. 1 (March, 1962), pp. 114-18; and Robert D. Towne, Sheldon L. Messinger, and Harold Sampson, "Schizophrenia

family configurations occurs when the *son* returns, and especially if his family is lower class—precisely because of their greater tolerance of his "queerness." That is, they "accept" him "as he is," take care of him as well as they can, but make few demands on him.

A somewhat contrasting situation awaits the male breadwinner, for he is likely to return to an *over*demanding configuration. He is not likely to be able to produce as much as when he was well, but there is no substitute for his services. Correlatively, his performance and prognosis are better if he returns to a large household in which there are *other adult males*. A somewhat less demanding environment is encountered by the wife who returns home from the mental hospital, since other members of the household can take over as many of her functions as she is unable to perform, but thereby they can gauge the challenge to her fitness.

What is evident from these and related findings is that though the onset of mental disease is a catastrophe that threatens the foundations of the family, thousands of families not only meet it adequately, but later develop a family situation in which the returning patient not only can perform reasonably well, but can even sometimes be helped on the slow road back to health.

In most discussions of marital disorganization the impact of marital problems on the emotional and mental health of the child is emphasized. The potentially destructive impact of children upon the marriage is usually ignored. Leaving aside the problem of the unwanted child who enters a marriage in which the mother and father are unprepared to handle the problem of parenthood, a more tragic set of cases is to be found when the child is severely mentally retarded, suffers a brain injury at birth, or becomes psychotic during his childhood. To a lesser extent, the impact is experienced when a child is severely neurotic without being psychotic.

Many families are nearly destroyed by the impact of such children upon them. When the child is born, both parents typically respond with considerable love and pleasure, even though all children are necessarily a burden upon both the family's energy and its pocketbook. Whether the child is viewed as a "doll" or as a young person, his first months are a period in which he gets considerable love and attention. He has no role obligation to perform, so that everything he does causes delight in those about him. In the earliest months, even an expert may

and the Marital Family: Accommodations to Symbiosis," *Family Process*, Vol. 1 (September, 1962), pp. 304-18; and Paul H. Glasser, "Changes in Family Equilibrium During Psychotherapy," *ibid.*, pp. 245-64.

find it difficult to tell that a retarded child will never become normal. In some instances the parents themselves are the last to know. Sometimes the pediatrician first ascertains the fact. The child may be brought to a doctor only for a physical illness; he undergoes no systematic tests to ascertain his normality, so that the question is never raised. Gradually it becomes apparent that the child is not normal in some way. He does not begin to sit up at the proper age. He does not fix his eyes properly, or does not respond to people within the first six months. Neighbors may talk among themselves about the child, but do not bring their suspicions to the attention of the parents.

Gradually, however, the parents begin to suspect that something is wrong, and are shocked when they find that others have long thought so. Then there begins a tragic series of journeys, complicated and more extensive among parents with money, but disheartening and frustrating for all parents. They take the child to medical or psychological clinics for testing periods and receive from each report a gloomy prognosis, but they do not easily give up. Instead, they continue to hope, sometimes for years, that a new drug, some form of therapy, or simple maturation will solve the problem.

Emotional feelings of parents in such situations are complex. Aside from the mourning that they undergo, most of them also suffer from deep guilt feelings.[82] They feel that in some manner it was their fault. This is especially so when the child becomes psychotic, since nearly all parents know that there is likely to be some relationship between the child's social experiences and the development of the psychosis. Even when there is an injury to the brain at birth, parents feel guilty. They wish to assuage their guilt by finding a cure and are willing to bankrupt themselves in order to seek a solution. It is a rare couple who are able to put the child in an institution at an early stage in this process. Rather, they lavish love on the child, and desperately try to compensate for his deficiencies. The child cannot dress himself or take care of himself, and the parents spend their energies in hovering over him. When there are other children, who suffer from the stigma of having such a child in their midst, considerable hostility may develop between the normal children and the parents. The strains of role relationship become intense, and the hostilities and aggressions between husband and wife may grow severe.

A few of the findings from current research on the impact of the

---

[82] "Having a severely mentally retarded child frequently creates a situation of utter chaos." See Bernard Farber, *Family Organization and Crisis*, Society for Research in Child Development (Indiana), Serial No. 75, Vol. 25, No. 1 (1960), p. 5.

severely mentally retarded child on the family may be summarized here:

1. The initial emotional impact on the wife is greater than on the husband.
2. Initially, her reaction is about the same, whether the child is a boy or girl, but the husband's is greater if the child is a boy.
3. Later on, the impact on the wife is greater if the child is a boy, primarily because of the impact on the husband.[83]
4. Families are more willing to place a boy in an institution than a girl; and lower-class families are still more willing to do so than middle-class families.[84]
5. Institutionalization of the child especially relieves the pressures on the retarded child's sister.[85]
6. As the retarded boy grows older, he has a greater disruptive effect on the family; and placing him in an institution helps the family integration.[86]

The case of the psychotic child is, however, somewhat less gloomy than it was a generation ago. Child psychiatry has improved considerably in recent decades, and some radical techniques have been developed in an effort to solve these problems; but all of them still require the separation of the child from the family for any degree of success.

Adjustment to Divorce and Bereavement: The New Courtship

Some quantitative data are available on the emotional impact of divorce upon mothers, but no correlative data exist for men. One interesting finding is that a higher proportion of these women experience more emotional difficulty at the time of *separation* than at any other time in the divorce process, from the time of first consideration to the final decree. Although the filing of the suit is a public act, it is not necessarily known to the important social groups of the wife or husband. The final separation, however, means a public acknowledgment of failure, and the onset of the first genuine impact of all of the prob-

---

[83] *Ibid.*, p. 39.
[84] *Ibid.*, pp. 46-47.
[85] *Ibid.*, p. 58.
[86] Bernard Farber, *Effects of a Severely Mentally Retarded Child on Family Integration,* Society for Research in Child Development (Indiana), Serial No. 71, Vol. 24, No. 2 (1959), pp. 55-58. See also Bernard Farber, W. C. Jenne, Romolo Toigo, *Family Crisis and the Decision to Institutionalize the Retarded Child,* Institute for Research on Exceptional Children (1960).

lems of post-divorce adjustment. By contrast, at the time of the final decree, occurring as it sometimes does many months after the final separation, many of the first problems of adjustment have already been met.

As might be supposed, a longer duration of marriage is associated with a greater impact of the divorce on the divorcee, and, similarly, older wives are more affected by divorce than younger wives. When the divorce was suggested first by the husband, the greatest degree of trauma is experienced, and the least when the divorce was suggested by both husband and wife at about the same time. In general, there is less likelihood of much emotional impact from the divorce if both the husband's and the wife's relatives and friends are relatively indifferent to the divorce, rather than being highly disapproving or approving.

No matter how the family unit was ended, or how intense the emotional impact of death or divorce, those who remain must continue to meet their role obligations. Although poetic literature contains many wails of despair about the loss of a beloved spouse, by death or divorce, old habits are insistent, and acquaintances cannot carry the individual's grief for him. Children demand attention, bills require payment, jobs must be completed, and in general the network of friends, acquaintances, and relatives soon show that whatever sympathies they may still feel, they nevertheless expect continued interaction, some fulfillment of obligation. Many husbands and wives feel that without their spouses they could not carry on, but in fact almost all of them do.

In China, the ideal widow did not remarry, and the ideal was still stronger and more likely to be met in India, where most Brahman widows never remarried. In our own society, by contrast, the social structure gently but firmly encourages the widowed or divorced person to reenter marriage as a mode of adjustment. Indeed, except for the youngest ages, both widowed and divorced men and women have a higher marriage rate than single people of the same ages. Well over 90 percent of the men and women whose divorce or bereavement occur when they are in their twenties will eventually remarry.[87]

As noted earlier, Arab countries have had very high divorce rates, but these did not indicate any breakdown of the family *system:* it continued in this fashion for centuries. However, the divorce adjustment was eased by several factors. First, some part of the bride price was usually not paid by the husband at the marriage, but it was required when he divorced his wife. Thus, when she was sent home, she did

---

[87] Jacobson, *American Marriage and Divorce,* pp. 83-85.

not go empty-handed. Second, her share in her family's property was one-half that of her brothers, and although she seldom took it, she had at least a moral right to share in its fruits. Consequently, her family could not properly begrudge her reentrance into the household. Third, and most important, since divorce rates were high, husbands were likely to be available, and thus the family could actually look forward to another bride price in time. The rules regarding custody of the children were clear: at the early ages, children were taken care of by their mother, but without question they belonged to their father's line, and eventually were returned to his home.

All this is not to imply that there were no heartaches in the Arab divorce system, but the fragility of the family unit in the early years of marriage did not create as many adjustmental difficulties in the woman's network of blood kin relations, and many matters were settled by custom and, therefore, with less argument over principle and right.[88]

It seems safe to say that there is no strong moral norm which asserts that people *should* remarry. It is rather that the institutional patterns of our society leave little room for the individual who wishes to "go it alone." This is of course especially true if there are children, but even if there are no children the pressures are strong. Invitations among adults are typically from one couple to another. Adult conversations focus on families and children. Few adults are unmarried, and those who are unmarried are usually engaged in courtship behavior which leads to marriage. Couples often view the widowed or divorced person, whether male or female, as a potential threat to existing marriage, and often try a bit of matchmaking to see to it that everyone moves back into the married state. When the individual has married, he no longer has to answer questions about his former marital experiences.

For the woman, and especially the mother, the pressures are even stronger. The common judgment is that children need both parents, and parents also need each other to handle children. Sexual problems also press the individual toward remarriage. Although in our era it is possible to engage in sexual relations outside of marriage, social patterns do not make this easy on an extended basis. If a man and woman intend to continue a sexual relationship, they are likely to become involved in many awkward situations if it is not finally legitimated by marriage.

---

[88] For a more elaborate description of divorce in Arabic Islam, see William J. Goode, *World Revolution and Family Patterns* (New York: Free Press, 1963), pp. 115-61.

None of the above pressures is likely to be very strong, but they are recurrent. The consequence is that the pattern of adjustment that is followed by most widowed and divorced persons is eventually to establish a new marriage.

The beginning of courtship and the process of courtship interaction are both an *index* of gradual adjustment to divorce or bereavement, and important causal factors in that adjustment. Successful dating indicates that the hurt pride or the sense of loss of the individual have diminished somewhat. At the same time, the date helps the process of adjustment by discouraging constant references to the former husband or wife. The spouse begins to think of himself gradually as no longer the "ex-spouse of ——," but as a date, friend, or sweetheart, in short, a person with a particular identity.

Children in Marital Disorganization

Refined statistical calculations suggest that childern have only a small effect on the maintenance of a marriage. Of the divorces involving children, the average number of children has been slightly less than two for the past half-century. However, slightly more than half of all divorced couples have no children. Childless couples are more likely to divorce, but only because couples in great marital conflict are less likely to have children. Nevertheless, the number of children involved in various forms of social disorganization is substantial. About 537,000 children were involved in divorce and annulment cases during 1962.[89] As of the year 1960 there were approximately 3,098,000 children 17 years of age and under in the United States who had been orphaned by the loss of one or both parents.[90] In 1960, there were 2,100,000 families with at least one child under 18 years of age, but headed by only one parent because the other parent was dead or divorced, or had simply left.[91]

It is difficult to measure exactly the impact of family disorganization upon children. Without question, children are more likely to grow up to be law-abiding, healthy, and happy adults if they spend their entire childhood in a happy family than they are if the family unit is broken by divorce or death. However, the family can be equally split by vio-

---

[89] *Divorce Statistics Analysis, United States—1962*, Public Health Service Publication No. 1000—Series 21, No. 7 (Washington, D. C., 1965), p. 26.

[90] Bureau of the Census, *Statistical Abstract of the United States: 1965*, 86th ed. (Washington, D. C., 1965), Table 431, p. 312.

[91] Bureau of the Census Population Series, 1960, Final Report PC(2)-4A, *Families*, Table 6.

lent disagreement and by the unhappiness of either spouse within marriage. Keeping the marriage together "in spite of everything" does not necessarily make happier children.

The general association of broken homes with delinquency has been demonstrated by many studies. This association has been traced to two large sets of factors. One of these has to do with the fact that both divorce rates and mortality rates are higher in slum areas, where delinquency rates are also higher. To this extent, the association may be in part a spurious one. The other large set of factors has to do with the role models that parents offer to their children, and the social controls that they impose upon them. If either parent is missing, the boy or girl may not have an adequate role model to emulate and may not learn adequate patterns of behavior. It is also likely that the boy or girl needs a parent of the opposite sex as a *complementary* figure with whom to enact role relations. More fundamentally, both parents are needed to control the children, simply because of the time and energy required to socialize them.

All this is true whether the marriage is broken by death or by divorce, and the relationship between broken homes and delinquency is not spurious. Even when the class position of parents is held constant, the delinquency rate of children is higher for broken than for unbroken homes. Similarly, the rate of delinquency among boys and girls is higher for those whose parents are separated or divorced than it is for those who have lost a parent by death.[92] (See Chapter 2, page 119.)

Unfortunately for those who seek easy solutions of family disorganization, it also seems likely that a family in which there is continued marital conflict, or separation, is more likely to produce children with problems of personal adjustment than a family in which there is divorce or death.[93] In general, separation and continued conflict may have a greater disorganizing effect upon children than divorce, and divorce a greater effect than death because the degree of intimate acceptance, love, support, and control given by the parent or substitute parent is likely to be greater in that same order: separation and conflict, divorce, and death. It is the quality of the childhood experience, not the mere fact of divorce, which is crucial.

Parents in conflict, therefore, must face a critical choice: of course,

---

[92] Myer F. Nimkoff, *Marriage and the Family* (Boston: Houghton Mifflin, 1947), p. 645. See also Sheldon and Eleanor Glueck, *Unraveling Juvenile Delinquency* (New York: Commonwealth Fund, 1951).

[93] Paul H. Landis, "The Broken Home in Teen-age Adjustments," *Rural Sociology Series on the Family*, No. 4 (Pullman, Wash.: Institute of Agricultural Sciences, State College of Washington, 1953), p. 10.

they cannot choose whether the marriage will end in death, but neither do they have a clear alternative in the matter of divorce and conflict. They can choose not to divorce, but they cannot by conscious decision create the happy home that would be the most healthful environment in which to rear their children. Their choice usually has to be between a continuing conflict or a divorce. And the evidence so far suggests that it is the *conflict of divorce*, not the divorce itself, that has an impact on children.[94]

Finally, we must keep in mind that most spouses who lose their husbands or wives will remarry, so that most of these children will eventually enter a new family relationship. The problems of adjustment in this new relationship have been insufficiently explored; we cannot now state just how much it improves the chances of emotional health in children who have gone through the experience of divorce or bereavement. There is at least some evidence that their adjustment is likely to be better with a stepfather than with a stepmother.[95] The reasons are not difficult to ascertain. It is the woman after all who must have the closest contact with the children, who must take their daily burdens on her shoulder, and who must pick up the pieces when there is breakage. It is then easier for the man to adjust to a set of children not his own than it is for the woman.

Marital Counseling

We shall end this chapter on at least a mild note of optimism. Two developments of the last generation may be of some importance in alleviating the problems of marital disorganization. One of these is the spread of courses in marital education in colleges and high schools. These courses are of varying quality. Often they are no more than lectures on morality; but some are relatively sophisticated analyses of the problems of marriage, giving the students a better insight into the problems they will later meet, and suggesting possible solutions for them. Since such courses grow out of the moral concerns felt by our generation, and since they are supported by taxes, they do not offer radical solutions for the marital problems of our time. They are likely

---

[94] For more recent findings on these points, see Judson T. Landis, "A Comparison of Children from Divorced and Nondivorced Unhappy Marriages," *Family Life Coordinator*, Vol. 11 (July, 1962), pp. 61-65; and Harry Pannor and Sylvia Schild, "Impact of Divorce on Children," *Child Welfare*, Vol. 39 (February, 1960), pp. 6-10.

[95] Bernard, *Remarriage*, pp. 220-21.

to be most successful when they offer good practical advice about budgeting, sexual adjustment, contraceptives, and so on. They are likely to be least successful when they venture into moral exhortations about the dangers of petting and premarital intercourse for later marital adjustment. Their impact is also likely to be somewhat less than might be hoped, since they are most common in colleges and thus the people who experience them are less likely to divorce in any event. College people have stabler marriages than noncollege people, and students who are inclined to be serious about their future marital careers are more likely to take such courses. Thus there is a process of preselection in the exposure to such courses. Nevertheless, they may be of some utility, and it is safe to say that in the future an increasing proportion of young people will take such courses.

The other development is that of marital counseling. At the present time a tiny fraction of people in marital difficulties seek counseling. In only a few major cities is there a substantial development of competently staffed professional agencies (usually a Family Service Society) to help people in marital trouble. In most areas there is no one available, or at best a few self-appointed experts with little specific training for this task. Moreover, seeking such advice is not as yet accepted by the American public. New professions emerge only gradually. A generation ago, seeking psychiatric help for a neurosis was viewed as a personal failure. A person with emotional difficulties was told to "buck up and pull himself together." Gradually, however, and most especially in the middle classes, it is taken for granted that if the family can afford it, a person with emotional problems should seek some kind of psychiatric help. The field of marital counseling has not yet gained the acceptance which is now enjoyed by psychotherapy.

Public acceptance of a profession also depends on the development of recognizable skills and knowledge which can be applied to a known problem. Here the public is not yet willing to concede that anyone has the skill necessary to bind the wounds of marital conflict. Since many marital counselors in the past have not had adequate training, the suspicion may be partly justified. However, during the past decade the standards for marital counseling have been gradually raised, so that a steadily increasing number of private practitioners and therapists working in public and private agencies are trained for the task. They are joined, too, by the growing profession of the social worker, especially the psychiatric social worker. The psychotherapist, whether psychiatrist or clinical psychologist, often deals with marital problems as well, because they are one expression of the emotional difficulties felt by the individual who seeks psychotherapy. There is, then, a growing number of professionals whose aim it is to help solve marital problems.

Sometimes the therapy required is nothing less than a full-scale attack on a neurosis in one or both of the spouses. Often, however, the marital counselor can help by merely defining the conflict more clearly to each spouse. It is useful sometimes to learn that the things about which one is fighting are not the real problems. If the husband can move from becoming angry at some minor event such as overcooked eggs to a recognition that he is still annoyed about the aloof way his wife treated him in their courtship, at least one step forward has been made. Sometimes it is possible to help matters by giving the wife or husband an opportunity to pour out his grievances to someone who will not retaliate. In some counseling procedures it may be useful to ask the wife to play the husband's role, and the husband to play the wife's role, so that each may obtain some perspective of the other's problems. Sometimes even so simple a matter as teaching the spouses how to budget properly, or how to improve their sexual technique, may be sufficient to reestablish the marriage on a more harmonious footing.

If our society is creating more marital conflict, it is also trying to develop some techniques for lessening the impact of that conflict. Of course, therapy is individual. Just as the physician cures a disease in the individual without solving the situation from which the disease arose, so the marital counselor attempts to solve the problems of an individual family without being able to change the social structure that created the conflict. In medicine, the professional public health worker engages in the problem of prevention. So far, no such profession has arisen in the field of the family. Even without the emergence of such a profession, however, it is clear that people in our society have not lost faith in marriage as an institution. In spite of the great number of divorces, and the large segment of our population that is hurt by marital disorganization, almost every adult does marry eventually. Almost every person who is widowed or divorced tries marriage once more, and even the children who had unhappy experiences in their own families grow up with enough faith to try marriage themselves when they are grown.

11

Work and Automation:
Problems and Prospects

by Robert S. Weiss and David Riesman

EXCEPT FOR A FEW SCIENCE FICTION WRITERS AND OTHER UTOPIANS, we Americans have never proposed as an eventual aim of national policy the elimination of work. There are people said to work harder than we, such as the Germans and Swiss, but it is doubtful if there are any people on earth to whom work is as important to a man's sense of self.[1] Our problems arise when we must do work that has too little meaning, or when work invades other areas of our lives, or when there is too little work for us, or when the rewards of work are insufficient, or its conditions oppressive. Just because work is so important to us, these difficulties are severely disturbing to us as individuals, and, if widespread enough, to the society in which we live.

We probably never will see a time when there are in our society no problems related to work, if only because of the constancy of change in our technological structure. We have in the past moved from a

---

[1] It is true that in the pre-Civil War South, slavery put a curse on work in the plantation areas, but even so the gentlemanly code of the planter could never completely subdue the effect of Protestantism in making idleness suspect. In a mobile, democratic society, people cannot readily coast on ancestral inheritance, and we have been a society which is inhospitable to playboys while we have a high regard for those who, as the phrase goes, work hard and play hard.

We are indebted to the Center for the Study of Leisure, established at the University of Chicago under a grant from the Ford Foundation, for assistance in studying work in relation to leisure; and to the Survey Research Center and the Institute of Labor and Industrial Relations (Wayne State University-University of Michigan) for assistance in the study of American attitudes toward work. We also want to acknowledge the help given us by Paul Campanis, Pauline Swift, Wyatt Jones, and Alfred Olerio. Work on this chapter has been facilitated by Dr. Gerald Caplan, Director of the Laboratory of Community Psychiatry, Harvard Medical School.

country whose labor force was, in good part, absorbed in agriculture, to a country whose labor force was concentrated in manufacturing and associated activities. We seem now to be moving to a new technological structure, in which more and more men will be employed in professional, technical, and service work, and fewer in the process by which raw materials become product for market. The disruption of lives and dislocations of the match between jobs and job-seekers, careers and those who would follow them, which are inevitable accompaniments of technological change, have long been with us, and will continue, perhaps at an accelerating pace, into the future.[2]

The importance that work has for us is represented by its weight in the seesaw when other values are placed on the other side. Many men in the professional and managerial occupations willingly and even eagerly accept occupations and preoccupations that give them little time with their families and almost no time for reflection; they suffer from ulcers and heart attacks and die leaving widows whose roles as wives and mothers shielded them from the more stringent blasts of careerism. The doctor, the manager, the professor—all relatively affluent—work harder in America than elsewhere, and, of course, set standards of performance that even those capable of greater indolence often seek to live up to. Furthermore, whereas in preindustrial societies those without employment do not feel especially deprived as long as their subsistence needs are met, most Americans temporarily or permanently laid-off feel lost and ill at ease. There are, as we shall see, exceptions, but within most groups in the United States work is an almost irreplaceable element in establishing one's sense of worth, and this gives rise to overwork when there are jobs to be had and to dismay when there is no work or when it uses too little of a man.

This is not to say that the problems of work in America are unchanging. Had this chapter been written a generation or so ago, its contents would have been very different from what we shall present here. Unemployment, the then endemic disease of all industrial societies, would have had the highest priority and would have been discussed as a threat or an actuality for a large part of our population. Here, though unemployment is as damaging as ever to those who experience it, we will give it less space and deal with it primarily in terms of its concentration within certain groups and occupations, and

---

[2] Excellent texts discussing the outlines of the worlds of work, as well as its problems, include: Sigmund Nosow and William H. Form, eds., *Man, Work, and Society* (New York: Basic Books, 1962); Delbert C. Miller and William H. Form, *Industrial Sociology* (New York: Harper, 1964); and Theodore Caplow, *The Sociology of Work* (Minneapolis: University of Minnesota Press, 1954).

its possible relationship to the reshuffling of jobs which automation and technological change bring about. Strikes and lockouts also have a smaller place here than they would have had a generation ago, not because we have solved the problem of industrial conflict, but because we have learned to live with strikes, to reduce the violence and hazard they can bring, to interrupt by government mediation those which seem most dangerous to the economy, and even to manipulate them as part of the process of balancing production and consumption.[3]

So, too, sweatshop wages and exploited workmen, subject to arbitrary domination by management, might once have taken much space, but in this chapter we shall have almost nothing to say about wages per se, only a little about industrial accidents and diseases, and very little about minimum wage laws, social security, and other ways of alleviating industrial depression. Some decades ago, before the Great Depression of the 1930's made the discussion academic, men argued as to whether human beings naturally wanted to work (a doubt implicit in Veblen's polemical concept of the instinct of workmanship) and about the incentives that might be needed to drive men to work if hunger and plain necessity could no longer be relied upon. The complex motivation that brings men to work was, at that time, obscured. Most people obviously had to work to acquire a bare subsistence, and the society, short both of consumer goods and capital goods, obviously needed their production, although the idea that men were inherently lazy was useful to justify a policy of governmental nonintervention in the economic sphere. Today we understand ourselves better and recognize that we will still work, even when bare subsistence is not an issue, so long as we can find in our job a basis for self-esteem. For us, the problem of the incentives compelling men to work looms less large than that of making the work men are willing to do more meaningful and satisfying, and making it possible for men who otherwise could be forced into unwanted separation from the world of work through technological displacement or early retirement to continue to contribute to their society.

The old problems—those to which we shall pay scant attention here—have not disappeared; rather, they have become less visible as we have learned to deal with them with partial success and as other problems have begun to assume increased importance. While the worst forms of sweated exploitation in industry have been abolished by a combination of government regulation, union policing, and the

---

[3] See the clarifying article by Daniel Bell, "The Subversion of Collective Bargaining," *Commentary*, Vol. 29 (March, 1960), pp. 185-97.

civilizing of management, migrant agricultural laborers still often live a kind of life that is not essentially superior to that of the Okies in John Steinbeck's *The Grapes of Wrath*. If violence is not today an expected part of a strike, it is not unknown either. And while it is no longer conceivable that a government that tolerated an unemployment level of 30 percent could stay in power, as was the case in the Great Depression, the relative stability of the economy since 1940 has been assured at least in part by the leverage of the defense spending program; moreover, as these lines are written, unemployment is officially estimated at somewhere around 4 percent of the labor force, a large, if not politically explosive, pool of misery.

Nevertheless, with better management and clearer goals for our economy, it seems now quite possible to ensure that jobs at living wages and under decent working conditions can be made available for all our labor force. But this very promise of abundance raises the questions of "abundance for what." As we have suggested, in many strata of our society much of the richness of life comes from work and from the process of achievement, of creating or cooperating. The assembly line has become a symbol of inanity because it is so largely barren of these potentialities. While assembly lines may not be "makers of morons," as once was feared, since men are not easily turned into automata but can maintain a certain solidarity and enliven with banter even the most grim conditions, we are no longer satisfied with work whose only justification is that it is bearable and pays the rent.[4]

The situation in which jobs, though abundant, fail to meet the needs or hopes of workers is not necessarily an example of social *disorganization*, though we insist that it be considered a serious social *problem*. Disorganization enters in relation to problems which "systems must solve in order to secure their own viability";[5] such would be the case if men suddenly stopped working, as in the dream of a general strike that sustained European radicals 50 years ago. However, viability of a social system, though a necessary condition for life, is not an end in itself. The social system may function in the sense that people are fed, goods distributed, and work performed, while many of those who

---

[4] See David Riesman, "Abundance for What?" in his *Abundance for What?* (Garden City, N. Y.: Doubleday, 1964), pp. 300-08. At the same time there are some individuals who find certain kinds of apparently monotonous work of value just because it leaves their mind free. See Georges Friedmann, *Industrial Society* (New York: Free Press, 1955), pp. 129-56.

[5] We draw here on Albert Cohen's clarifying treatment of the concept of social disorganization, "The Study of Social Disorganization and Deviant Behavior," in Robert K. Merton, Leonard Broom, and Leonard S. Cottrell, Jr., *Sociology Today: Problems and Prospects* (New York: Basic Books, 1959), p. 21.

participate in the system believe their energies largely wasted and gain little satisfaction or sense of worth from what they feel forced to do.[6]

On the whole, American society shows a discrepancy between the almost exuberant viability of the system and the dissatisfaction of many of those who are at once the producers and the consumers of its products. People tend to accept the institutions of their society, even while their satirists may poke fun at them; they learn the motivations these institutions demand; and they manage to find sufficient satisfaction somewhere in the society to make life tolerable. Nevertheless, there *are* difficulties in our economic system, and these are difficulties of overorganization as well as disorganization, for in both we may find that the needs of human beings for challenge, solidarity, and freedom are frustrated.[7] In addition, as we shall point out in this chapter, there are many points of incoherence; some result from technological change, some are the product of conflict between the interests of workers and managers, and some reflect the irrationality of the distribution of rewards among the various occupational groups.

However, even where wide agreement exists that something constitutes a "problem," we must inquire whether the assessment does not depend on a limitation of perspective. For any really exigent problem is apt to be a product of a more general malaise, and, often enough, to represent an uneasy solution. For instance, we later discuss quota restriction, the institution virtually omnipresent in industries where workers set an informal limit on production. From the point of view of management, quota restriction is nothing more than organized insubordination, a way of getting paid without working. With a broader perspective we might recognize that quota restriction is not only a problem, but is itself something of a solution to another problem, created by the inability of managements in the structure of American industry to set production goals cooperatively with the workers.

---

[6] Suggestive in this connection is Ruth Benedict's idea of "synergy," the extent to which a social structure makes individual effort cumulative, noted in Margaret Mead's *An Anthropologist at Work* (Boston: Houghton Mifflin, 1959), p. 351. See also the development of this idea by Abraham Maslow in "Synergy in the Society and in the Individual," *Journal of Individual Psychology,* Vol. 20 (November, 1964), pp. 1953-64.

[7] For a vivid and influential statement of the thesis that American society suffers from overorganization as well as disorganization, see William H. Whyte's *The Organization Man* (New York: Simon and Schuster, 1956). More recently, Paul Goodman has made sharp criticisms of what he believes to be misdirected organization of life. See his *Growing Up Absurd* (New York: Random House, 1956). In our judgment, both Whyte and Goodman at times overstate their case and present as examples quite atypical situations, even while at other times they are brilliantly acute.

(However, in truth, it is far from clear that workers would want formal responsibility for issues such as these.) Quota restriction then becomes a way in which workers can contribute, at least negatively, to the determination of a day's work, without changing the basic organization of industry.

Let us take another example. The work of an ambitious executive requires him to spend long hours away from his family. While once American values would have condoned this, now the family is regarded, even in executive circles, as at least as precious as work. Yet if we look at the executive as an individual, we may find that this very tension, this overallocation of time, is what keeps him going and that he would not really be benefited by time to relax with his family. Describing the zest for work of older executives, William H. Whyte quotes a company president: "Overwork, as I see it, is simply work that you don't like. But I dearly love this work. You live only one time and you might as well do something you like." [8] Such men sometimes pretend to dislike their work lest their wives be jealous. So here too, as in the preceding example, what seems on first sight to be a problem—in this instance, one within the family—appears on further examination to have advantages as well as drawbacks; so much so that the "overworked" executive frequently encounters real psychological trouble only when he is compelled to retire.

How then identify what ought to be changed, when different contexts and different points of view alter the way in which we evaluate any situation? With some hesitancy regarding the effectiveness of this rule, we believe that social forms which tend toward the suppression or frustration of meaning and purpose in life are inferior forms. Thus, work that is too dull, that involves a man too little, that places him under demeaning supervision, or that pays him too little to allow him to maintain a place of some dignity in his community is damaging to him, and on this basis we would consider the form that gives rise to the situation to be inferior, and susceptible to improvement. To the extent that we can make them explicit, these are our assumptions.

What Is Work?

At first glance we might assume that what is work is self-evident, but further scrutiny leads us into a maze of cultural and idiosyncratic definitions. Some people define as work whatever in their daily realm

---

[8] Whyte, *The Organization Man,* p. 147

is irksome; others, only that which is paid or which is obligatory.[9] From the point of view of doing something that makes one feel "worthwhile," which is probably one of the most important psychological functions of work, it is not necessary that one be paid. Consider a rich man who does not "have to work" but who out of a feeling of responsibility serves, without salary, as an executive officer of a foundation; he comes to the office each day at the time the secretarial staff arrives, and leaves when they leave or after. Some of us would insist that he is not working because he is not paid and because there is somehow less constraint in his service. But probably, from his point of view, he is doing a job and may feel that he is neither a member of the unemployed nor a man of leisure. Quite possibly in the future we shall have to widen our societal understanding of what constitutes work to include such occupations. Another important inconsistency in our view of work disparages what the housewife does as not really working, though she herself may complain of the constant demands of her children and endless chores in the house.

The United States Census attempts to achieve a working definition of the idea of "employment" in this way:

> . . . Employed persons comprise those who were either (a) "at work"—those who did any work for pay or profit, or worked without pay for thirteen hours or more on a family farm or business or (b) "with a job but not at work"—those who did not work and were not looking for work but had a job or business from which they were temporarily absent . . .

So, too, we limit ourselves in this chapter to the discussion of work as it is associated with employment, with what a man does for a living. The unpaid activity of the housewife lies outside this area, as do, in fact, many activities in that broad class of constructive behaviors that Freud considered work: activities that are serious and directed toward the shaping of reality, though they are not immediately necessitated by the problems of making a living.

Most Americans, we believe, would agree with us in restricting discussion of work to those activities associated with a job. In many preindustrial societies, this would not be so: there work tends to be an almost undifferentiated part of the routine of life, inseparable

---

[9] A fuller discussion of social and individual definitions of work can be found in the report of a survey in which male respondents were asked what made the difference, for them, between something that was work and something that was not work. See Robert S. Weiss and Robert L. Kahn, "Definition of Work and Occupation," *Social Problems*, Vol. 8, No. 2 (Fall, 1960), pp. 142-51.

from religious ceremonial, the duties owed other members of an extended family, and what we would call play or leisure. The notion of "a job," of work as an activity separated from other activities of life, is largely a characteristic of the modern industrial society. And even here, it is not as valid as many of us would, on first thought, believe; many professionals, for example, use their "leisure" to catch up on the journals, or to plan future work.

Who Holds a Job?

European travelers noted, often with surprise, that America was a country in which all men were expected to have jobs.[10] Actually the expectation that all adult men will work seems to hold only for those men between the ages of 25 and 55. So, at any rate, we would interpret the column "Not in the labor force, for other reasons," in Table 1, which displays the employment status of the civilian, non-institutional male population as of September, 1964. The classifications in Table 1 depend on a definition of who is in the labor force, which may not be beyond debate. An individual is considered in the labor force if (a) he held a job during a specified week; or (b) he reported seeking a job during that same week. In the first case he is considered employed, in the second, unemployed.[11] The category, "not in the labor force, other reasons," includes individuals who are able to work but who did not seek work for some reason: for those over 60, this state may be defined as retirement, whatever the process that brought them there. We would think of those men listed in this category who are under 25 as not yet having "found themselves"— not yet having committed themselves to search out a place in the occupational structure.

Because our statistics do not consider a man unemployed if he is not looking for work, we underestimate the seriousness of the lack of work for men who have just left high school and for men near the close of their careers. If we add together the officially "unemployed" and the "not in the labor force, other reasons" percentages, in the 18-20 year-old category, we find that almost a quarter of the men in that age group lack work. And well over half the men over the

---

[10] Robert W. Smuts, *European Impression of the American Worker* (New York: Columbia University Press, 1953), p. 5.

[11] Abraham J. Jaffe, "Working Force," in Philip M. Hauser and Otis Dudley Duncan, eds., *The Study of Population* (Chicago: University of Chicago Press, 1959), p. 609.

TABLE 1

Employment Status of Civilian Noninstitutional Population

(Month of September, 1964)

	Percentage of Men in Labor Force		Percentage of Men Not in Labor Force				
Age	Employed	Unemployed	In School	Keeping House	Unable to Work	Other	Number in Thousands
14–15	16	1	72	—	—	11	3,511
16–17	34	5	50	—	—	11	3,551
18–19	58	9	19	—	—	14	2,393
20–24	81	6	9	—	—	7	5,574
25–29	95	3	1	—	—	1	5,044
30–34	96	2	—	—	1	1	5,101
35–39	96	2	—	—	1	1	5,657
40–44	95	2	—	—	1	2	5,806
45–49	95	2	—	—	1	2	5,414
50–54	93	2	—	—	2	3	5,014
55–59	88	3	—	—	3	6	4,306
60–64	77	3	—	—	3	17	3,595
65–69	42	2	—	—	4	52	2,799
70+	19	—	—	1	7	73	4,791

Source: U.S. Department of Labor, Bureau of Labor Statistics, *Employment and Earnings,* Vol. II, No. 4 (October, 1964), p. 9.

age of 65 have dropped out of the labor force, undoubtedly not entirely by free choice.

Women are under considerably less social compulsion to work, as is shown by the percentage listed as "keeping house" in Table 2, though it is today far less customary than it once was for the well-bred, unmarried girl to stay home, demure and without function, until she might be taken in marriage. Once such unmarried women could make themselves useful in a large family, where the mother needed help and neither precooked foods nor babysitters existed. Today the girl who is not yet married would feel in the way and useless in the small modern home or apartment. She marries earlier than hitherto; college is much more likely to be available to her; and increasingly she enters the labor force and gets a job. And, often enough, she drops out of the labor force only for the period when her children are small and require almost constant attention, and returns to the labor force as soon as they are old enough to go to school. Thus, while only 35 percent of women in the 30-34 year-old bracket are in the labor force, this percentage rises to 50 percent for the 45-55 year-old groups. Given the fact that the very great majority of women will hold

TABLE 2

Employment Status of Civilian Noninstitutional Population

(Month of September, 1964)

	Percentage of Women in Labor Force		Percentage of Women Not in Labor Force				
Age	Employed	Unemployed	In School	Keeping House	Unable to Work	Other	Number in Thousands
14–15	11	—	75	2	—	12	3,411
16–17	22	4	57	8	—	9	3,517
18–19	42	7	17	22	—	12	2,804
20–24	46	4	4	43	—	3	6,550
25–29	35	3	—	61	—	1	5,613
30–34	35	2	—	62	—	1	5,611
35–39	39	2	—	58	—	1	6,153
40–44	46	2	—	51	—	1	6,317
45–49	51	2	—	46	—	1	5,772
50–54	50	2	—	47	—	1	5,314
55–59	45	1	—	53	—	1	4,617
60–64	32	1	—	64	1	2	3,989
65–69	15	1	—	80	1	3	3,342
70+	6	—	—	83	6	5	6,280

Source: U.S. Department of Labor, Bureau of Labor Statistics, *Employment and Earnings*, Vol. II, No. 4 (October, 1964), p. 9.

a job at some time in their lives, it is regrettable that the jobs they hold are often routine, subordinate, and underpaid.[12]

It is worth noting that women past the age of 65 are listed as "keeping house," rather than within the "not in the labor force, other reasons" category. In contrast to men, women may turn from work to the alternative task of "keeping house" when there no longer is a place for them in the labor force. A man's social situation, on the other hand, is determined almost solely by his relationship to the activity of work.

What Jobs Do People Hold?

An industrial society like ours manifests a staggering array of occupations, thousands of different ones, related to one another by complex chains of interdependence, but each requiring a different set of skills, a different kind of training, which will allow the performance

---

[12] For general discussion, see Eli Ginzberg *et al.*, *Womanpower* (New York: Columbia University Press, 1957); and also, for some hint as to how boys and girls learn different attitudes toward the world of work, David Riesman, "Permissiveness and Sex Roles," *Journal of Marriage and Family*, Vol. 21 (August, 1959), pp. 1-11.

TABLE **3**

Percentage of Labor Force in Various Occupational Groups

(Month of March, 1964)

	Male Percent	Female Percent
Professional, technical, and kindred (e.g., accountants, engineers, teachers, physicians, nurses)	12.1	13.5
Farmers and farm managers	4.7	.5
Managers, officials, and proprietors	14.4	4.8
Clerical and kindred (e.g., bookkeepers, clerks, and typists)	7.3	31.3
Sales	5.9	7.0
Crafts, foremen and kindred (e.g., carpenters, mechanics, electricians)	18.5	1.0
Operatives and kindred workers (e.g., truck drivers, semiskilled factory workers)	20.5	15.2
Private household workers	.1	9.4
Service workers, except private household (e.g., janitors, barbers, police, cooks, beauticians)	7.2	15.4
Farm laborers and foremen	2.5	1.7
Laborers	7.0	.4
Total	100.0	100.0

Source: Bureau of the Census, *Statistical Abstract of the United States: 1964*, 85th ed. (Washington, D. C., 1964), p. 228.

of activities as different as driving a bus and sewing a seam. There is hardly a human aptitude that is not put into play by some job somewhere.[13] A large company like United States Steel will itself have several thousand job categories, many of which will be lumped together by the outsider.

The census, faced with the task of devising some way of grouping occupations that would permit a manageable social accounting, emerged with a scheme utilizing 11 major headings. The categorization of Table 3 suggests not only the tasks that individuals perform, but the educational level they have reached, and, for men, the prestige they are likely to have in the community. (Family status tends to be defined by the occupation of the chief breadwinner of the family: a woman's prestige largely follows that of her husband or father. Thus, a woman in a clerical job, if married to a professional, would not have less social standing than a woman in a managerial or pro-

---

[13] Here, as elsewhere, we are indebted to the work of Everett C. Hughes. See "The Study of Occupations," in Merton, Broom, and Cottrell, eds., *Sociology Today*, Chapter 20.

TABLE 4

Income Distribution of Men within Various Occupational Groups, 1960

	Income of Indicated Percentile Rank [a]			
	20th	50th	80th	95th
Professional, technical, and kindred	$4,225	$6,611	$10,271	$19,191
Farmers and farm managers	606	1,911	4,189	7,791
Managers, officials, and proprietors	3,554	6,436	10,825	22,470
Clerical and kindred	3,192	4,921	6,219	8,419
Sales	2,063	4,917	7,825	12,856
Crafts, foremen, and kindred	3,715	5,507	7,379	9,490
Operatives and kindred	2,640	4,421	6,134	7,865
Service workers	1,605	3,370	5,275	7,265
Farm laborers and foremen	363	1,087	4,330	4,330
Laborers	1,092	2,825	4,813	6,439

Source: Bureau of the Census, *Trends in the Income of Families and Persons in the United States, 1947 to 1960,* Technical Paper No. 8 (Washington, D. C.: U.S. Government Printing Office, 1963), adapted from Table 14, pp. 276-77.

[a] Figures give the annual income of individuals who earn more than the indicated percentage of those in their occupational categories. For example, professionals whose annual income is $4,225 earn more than 20 percent of other professionals.

fessional position.) In addition, the occupational categories suggest the income an individual is likely to receive, as is shown in Table 4.

Table 4 presents information on the distribution of annual incomes within the various occupational categories. Notice the range of incomes as we move from the upper white-collar professional and managerial group to the blue-collar laborer, but notice too that the blue-collar skilled worker is likely to earn more than the white-collar clerical and sales worker. Although verbal and conceptual skills are rewarded more highy than manual skills, there is much overlap. Notice too that the median annual income (the 50th percentile rank) of the unskilled blue-collar worker and the service worker suggests that many in these categories are close to the line of real poverty and deprivation. The even lower median incomes of farmers and farm laborers are shocking, yet difficult to interpret, since the value of fuel, food, or other farm products used for family living is not included in the accounting of income.

The ranges in Table 4 are as important as the medians. A highly skilled tool and die worker, who has had to undergo a long period of apprenticeship, will be near the top of the "crafts, foremen, and kindred" category, and may earn as much as $9,000 a year. The best-paid 5 percent of managers earn over $20,000 a year, and, at the very top, chief executives of large corporations seldom earn less than six-figure

TABLE 5

Specific Occupations of Men and Women Listed as "Professional, Technical, and Kindred"

	Numbers (in thousands)	
	Men	Women
All professions, technical, and kindred [a]	2,970	1,939
Engineers	519	6
Lawyers and Judges	174	6
Clergymen	161	7
Draftsmen	113	8
Physicians and surgeons	180	12
Accountants and auditors	321	56
Nurses	10	389
Teachers	286	835

Source: Bureau of the Census, *Statistical Abstract of the United States, 1957,* 78th ed. (Washington, D. C., 1957).

[a] Only professions in which at least 100,000 men or 100,000 women reported membership are listed in the table.

salaries. Examination of median salaries gives insufficient evidence of the enormous discrepancy in potential income in the different occupations.[14]

The distribution of jobs for women is, as we would expect, quite different from that of jobs for men. While the category of "private household work" is almost solely filled by women, it is men who are the farmers, craftsmen, and laborers. The different distributions of men and women across the gross occupational categories represented in Table 3 suggest part of the story, but only part. Within each of these categories, certain jobs are marked as appropriate for women, and as a result, women tend to work in only a few of the many possible job classifications: in nursing, teaching, bookkeeping, typing or other clerical work, saleswork, dressmaking, as laundry help, semi-skilled hands in factories, beauticians, cooks, institutional attendants, waitresses, private household workers, farm laborers, and as holders of occasional jobs in unskilled labor. Other occupations tend to be seen as "man's work"; these occupations include all but two of the professions, much saleswork, most managerial positions, most factory jobs, including all supervisory jobs, all driving jobs, many jobs in services, and all heavy labor. Table 5 shows the distribution of jobs in the professions. These divide rather clearly into those in which

---

[14] See also Herman P. Miller, *Rich Man, Poor Man* (New York: Crowell, 1964).

there is a preponderance of men (only one percent of engineers are women, and fewer than 10 percent of physicians) and those in which there is a preponderance of women (teaching, where almost 75 percent of those employed are women, and nursing, where over 97 percent are women).

If we were able to make a finer classification than that in Table 5, we should find even greater specialization by sex: women in medicine, for example, are more likely to specialize in pediatrics than in surgery.

The occupational structure which is reflected in Table 3 has been constantly changing since the beginnings of our nation. (See Table 6.) Farmers and farm laborers now represent 9 percent of the male labor force; only two generations ago they represented 42 percent. In recent years, the proportion of the male labor force in this category has continued to decline, although more slowly, as has the proportion in the category of unskilled workers, while the proportion of the male labor force in the categories of professionals, managers, and service workers have increased. This changing distribution of manpower undoubtedly marks the end of one era and the beginning of another. The shift from a society in which most people were farmers to one in which most people are involved, in one way or another, in manufacturing, is almost completed, and a second process is beginning, in which sophisticated self-correcting machinery more and more replaces the blue-collar worker, as well as the white-collar worker whose job is more or less routine, and so makes possible a society in which most people become engaged in what the economist, Colin Clark, calls "tertiary employment"; distribution, services, the "knowledge industry," and related fields.

We can see today, in the developing nations, the same shift away from the farms, the same development of an urban population of producers and consumers of manufactured products, which this country has virtually completed. In the United States, this process occurred over a long historical period, beginning over a hundred years ago.[15] The mechanization of our farms, in considerable degree, freed a great part of our working population for manufacturing and commerce. Here we refer to the complex series of developments that include not only the installation of machinery for plowing, harvesting, and handling of crops, but also the more generic application of rational processes to agricultural production, including scientific soil

---

[15] Seymour Martin Lipset, *The First New Nation: The United States in Historical Perspective* (New York: Basic Books, 1963).

TABLE 6

Distribution of Males and Females in the Labor Force by Major Occupation Group, 1900-1960

Men	Percent						
	1960	1950	1940	1930	1920	1910	1900
Professional and technical	11	7	6	5	4	4	3
Managerial	14	11	9	9	8	8	7
Clerical	7	6	6	6	5	4	3
Sales	6	6	6	6	5	5	5
Skilled	19	19	16	16	16	14	13
Semiskilled	20	20	18	15	14	12	10
Unskilled	7	9	12	14	14	15	15
Service	7	6	6	5	4	4	3
Farming	9	15	22	25	30	35	42
	100	100	100	100	100	100	100

Women	Percent						
Professional and technical	13	12	13	14	12	10	8
Managerial	5	4	3	3	2	2	1
Clerical	30	27	21	21	19	9	4
Sales	7	9	7	7	6	5	4
Skilled	1	2	1	1	1	1	1
Semiskilled	16	20	20	17	20	23	24
Unskilled	—	1	1	2	2	1	3
Service	25	22	29	28	24	32	35
Farming	2	4	4	8	14	16	19
	100	100	100	100	100	100	100

Source: Delbert C. Miller and William H. Form, *Industrial Sociology* (New York: Harper, 1964, pp. 62-63. They credit 1900-1950 data to David L. Kaplan and M. Claire Casey, *Occupational Trends in the United States 1900-1950*, Working Paper #5, Bureau of the Census, U.S. Dept. of Commerce, 1958, pp. 6, 7.

analysis, the use of intensive fertilizers, and scientific breeding, which all together led to the greater rationalization of farming and the ability to produce more crops with fewer workers. In truth, some of this sophistication of farming required that each seemingly independent farmer be supplemented with a host of ancillary services, often supplied by the government, ranging from architectural advice on the building of barns to helicopters for the spraying of crops. The same general process seems to be at work in today's rationalization of manufacturing: more goods are turned out with fewer factory workers, although with increased dependence on ancillary and supervisory workers in related fields. These developments result in gains in industrial *productivity*, the market value of output per man-hour of work, but also in human dislocation, as old jobs disappear, and as other jobs—in different regions and requiring different skills—appear in their place.

Bringing People and Jobs Together

What underlies the fact that in our society almost all men between the ages of 25 and 55 who are capable of working are either employed or looking for work? The common sense of the matter has been that men are brought to work by a combination of "carrot and stick," the "carrot" referring to the rewards obtainable through work and the "stick" referring to the penalties of unemployment. We know that this cannot be the whole story, for although there are some men who prefer to live off their unemployment benefits as long as these last, or on welfare, rather than to work for very low wages at disagreeable jobs, the fact is that few choose this alternative. The importance of work is not to be explained simply by reference to financial rewards.

As we have said before, work, for Americans, is essential to the maintenance of a sense of worth. One's place in the community may be derived from the status implications of one's occupation. In addition, the occupational sphere is the sphere in which most men strive for success and for the reassurance of their basic worth that success brings. The consequence is that the loss of a job is not only a blow to livelihood, but to much else that makes life worthwhile. There are, to be sure, other ways in which men establish their worth, especially through being a good husband and father, but even these roles are dependent to some extent on the man's ability as a breadwinner. There may be less tolerance in American life than there once was for the man so dedicated to his work that he has no time for his family, and there may be more appreciation than there once was of the value of the limited achievement that brings "a good life." But though our lives today can, if we wish, contain more leisure than was possible for most of us to have had a few generations ago, working remains an essential activity for American men.[16]

A measure of the importance of work may be given by a study in which a representative sample of American men was asked, "If by

---

[16] For a discussion of the historical emphasis on performance and achievement in American life, and of how this remains the case today under altered conditions, see Talcott Parsons and Winston White, "The Link Between Character and Society," in Seymour M. Lipset and Leo Lowenthal, eds., *The Sociology of Culture and the Analysis of Social Character* (New York: Free Press, 1961), Chapter 6. For a discussion of changes in the relative primacy of work in American life, see David Riesman *et al.*, *The Lonely Crowd* (New Haven: Yale, 1961).

some chance you inherited enough money to live comfortably without working, do you think you would work anyway or not?" Eighty percent replied that they would work anyway.[17] Their motives for wanting to continue to work were not entirely clear to themselves and were often explained in such terms as: "In order to keep occupied"; or "I'd be nervous otherwise." They recognized that work is functional, without understanding why this should be so. Other studies suggest that work may be important because it is a way of structuring life, a basis for a sense of competence and a source of feelings of worth. All these elements, singly or in combination, support self-esteem and make for participation in community life.[18]

Just as the craving for success may lead away from the world of work as well as toward it, so too the striving for a sense of competence or feelings of worth may not always propel people into useful and legitimate economic activity. Thus, a burglar may take pride in his craftsmanship, and beggars and tramps may feel that they are top-notch at beating the system.[19] As the chapter on juvenile delinquency in this volume argues, each way of life tends to develop its own skills, its own argot, its own way of assigning status. But these are small, marginal worlds, and the great majority of American men look to legitimate work as the area within which to validate themselves.

Although, as we have shown, work is expected of all American men and, also, though perhaps less insistently, of most American women not burdened by child rearing, everyone knows that jobs differ, not only in the nature of the work they require, but in the opportunities for companionship, the chances for self-expression, and the degree of security or insecurity they provide. And, of course, they also differ in prestige, responsibility, and income. Beyond that, they bring people in touch with different worlds; thus a chemist maintains different kinds of relationships, follows a different schedule, and probably has a different social life, than does a banker, and some men would prefer one, and

---

[17] Nancy C. Morse and Robert S. Weiss, "The Function and Meaning of Work and the Job," *American Sociological Review*, Vol. 20, No. 2 (April, 1955), pp. 191-98.

[18] See Eugene A. Friedmann and Robert J. Havighurst, "A Comparison of the Meanings of Work and Retirement Among Different Occupational Groups," in Friedmann and Havighurst, eds., *The Meaning of Work and Retirement* (Chicago: University of Chicago Press, 1954), pp. 170-86.

[19] See Edwin Sutherland, *The Professional Thief* (Chicago: University of Chicago Press, 1937). Harlan W. Gilmore, *The Beggar* (Chapel Hill, N. C.: University of North Carolina Press, 1940). David W. Maurer, *Whiz Mob* (Gainesville, Fla.: American Dialect Society, University of Florida, 1955).

some the other. Similarly, a machinist's life is different from a truck driver's, though the two occupations are similar in prestige. Choice of occupation will therefore help determine not only the status of an individual in the community, but also the nature of his life.

Young people, in thinking ahead to their future occupations, are often vague and even romantic. Yet, if one analyzes the choices they make, one sees that most of them aim to do at least as well as, and often better than, their fathers did. For example, when a survey was made of adolescent boys across the country, over half of those whose fathers were in the manual skilled trades hoped themselves to move into the ranks of the "middle class" and become white-collar workers (clerical or sales workers) or even move into the more prestigious level of managers and professionals. Among those young men whose fathers already were in the category of white-collar worker, almost half hoped themselves to rise to managerial or professional positions. The group that seemed to have renounced the hope of success through mobility included for the most part boys who were unequipped, intellectually or emotionally, to succeed. The goal of "getting somewhere" characterized the youths who appeared most normal in development.[20] This is not to suggest that any renunciation of the drive for outward success, for "getting somewhere," is an indication of abnormality. It may, on the contrary, characterize some exceptional individuals, too unusual to have much effect on survey results, whose personal strength gives them freedom from social pressure. Some of the most gifted college students have turned from the goal of success and have aimed instead at teaching in secondary school, or in some other way have based their occupational choice on what they would like to do rather than on the social status of an occupation.

While the United States has probably gone further than any other large society in providing the conditions necessary for anyone to reach any occupational niche, it nevertheless remains true that where people end up in the occupational world depends in large part on where they began.[21]

---

[20] Elizabeth Douvan and Joseph Adelson, "Social Mobility in Adolescent Boys," *Journal of Abnormal and Social Psychology*, Vol. 56, No. 1 (January, 1958), pp. 31-44.

[21] Lipset and Bendix have found that actual rates of mobility, in terms of progression in one generation from manual to nonmanual status, are very similar in all industrialized countries for which data exist. America may be distinctive in the support and encouragement it gives such mobility rather than the extent to which such mobility is possible. Here the mobile man is considered a "success," rather than a "parvenu." See Seymour M. Lipset and Reinhard Bendix, *Social Mobility in Industrial Society* (Berkeley: University of California Press, 1959).

TABLE 7

Current Occupation by Father's Occupation, Noninstitutional Male Population 25 to 64 Years Old, United States

(Month of March, 1962)

Father's Occupation	Current Occupation		
	Percent Professional or Managerial	Percent Sales or Clerical	Percent Total White Collar
Professional	56	15	70
Managerial	52	15	67
Sales	46	20	66
Clerical	42	16	58
Skilled workers, foremen, etc.	27	12	39
Semiskilled	22	10	32
Service (including private household)	23	14	37
Laborers (excluding mine and farm)	13	11	24
Farmers and farm managers	16	7	23
Farm laborers	9	5	14

Source: Bureau of the Census, Current Population Reports, "Lifetime Occupational Mobility of Adult Males, March, 1962" (Washington, D. C., May 12, 1964). Based on a study conducted by Peter M. Blau and Otis D. Duncan.

As Table 7 shows, over half of those American men aged 25 to 64 whose fathers were professionals or managers are themselves in a professional or managerial job. Over two-thirds of the men whose fathers were professionals or managers are now in white-collar positions. Among those whose fathers were skilled workers, 27 percent are now in a profession or a managerial job, and 39 percent hold a white-collar position. Among those whose fathers were laborers, 13 percent are now in a professional or managerial job, and 24 percent in a white-collar position. Sons of farm laborers are particularly unlikely to make it into a white-collar position: only 14 percent of these men have done so. It is a question of judgment whether to consider these high or low proportions of upward mobility. Certainly the data of Table 7 documents what is only common observation: how well one's father has done has much to do with how well one does oneself. A great many factors contribute to this result. The very ability to conceive of social mobility as a practical goal tends to be found primarily in families that can grasp and communicate the character of the occupational spectrum and that can provide the moral impetus and the educational means for acting on that knowledge. Furthermore, even in our own society where each individual is supposed to be on his own, and not the prisoner of his family, one can still find children, especially girls, who have been saddled with the care of an aged parent or relative and who, as a result, have never been able to make the break to an independent life and career. Nor are all parents eager to see their children move far from them either geographically or socially. And there may be, on occasion, good reason for this hesitancy. Mobility often makes for strain, and many novels as well as research reports tell of the psychological cost to the individual who has moved into a new way of life as a result of occupational mobility.[22]

Occupation and Schooling

The point at which a boy leaves the educational escalator is crucial in determining his future occupational opportunities. If he leaves high school before graduation he is unlikely ever to do anything other than manual work, unless it be to have a fling at running a small business, such as a gas station or a TV repair shop. In contrast, a boy who continues on from high school to college is preparing himself with more and more certainty for a life in one of the middle-class occupations. A number of studies have shown the inducements on the one side and the pressures on the other that tend to impel a lower-class youth, even if he is fairly talented academically, to withdraw from school in fact or in feeling. To such a youth, the immediate rewards of a job—both spending money and the right to spend it—contrast with the immediate irksomeness of school, and weigh the decision in favor of leaving school. Self-esteem too plays a role, as students with low self-esteem have been shown to come disproportionately from groups of lower socioeconomic status and to be less confident of their ability to succeed in a demanding enterprise.[23] Finally, the lower-class youth is less likely than the middle-class youth to see the relevance of education for his later occupational activity. He is more likely to see education as a task set by an arbitrary society, rather than as an opportunity to prepare for a gratifying adulthood.[24] His understanding of the occupational world, and the way in which one

---

[22] For a discerning treatment of such matters, see John P. Marquand, *Point of No Return* (Boston: Little, Brown, 1949).

[23] See Morris Rosenberg, *Society and the Adolescent Self-Image* (Princeton, N. J.: Princeton University Press, 1965.)

[24] See Joseph A. Kahl's perceptive comparison of a group of Boston high school seniors who are going on to college with a group of like ability who are not: "Educational and Occupational Aspirations of 'Common Man' Boys," *Harvard Educational Review*, Vol. 23 (1953), pp. 186-203. He finds that "of the high ability children [of men] in top-level occupations approximately 90 percent planned to attend college, but of the children of similar ability who had fathers who were factory workers, only 55 percent planned to attend college . . . ." There may be

aims for a definite niche in it, is in every way inferior. It has been found (even in kindergartens) that middle-class children are consistently more sophisticated than are the working-class children in their conceptions of the variety of jobs and in their understanding of the instrumental value of education.[25]

Thus it is inevitable that school authorities will encounter many difficulties in communicating with working-class children. Even so, they are often in a quandary as to how to employ such influence as they do have over the educational, and hence the occupational, future of their charges. Lacking sufficient resources, schools are under pressure to concentrate attention upon the students who are clearly middle-class. Otherwise, they would face the possible apathy or even antagonism of lower-class parents who suspected them of holding out impossible goals to their children, as well as the certain resentment of any middle-class parents who believed their children were receiving insufficient attention.[26]

The working-class boy who will eventually drop out of high school experiences a kind of progressive alienation from the high school situation, sometimes initiated by a single difficult relationship with a teacher, sometimes by a complex of factors, including poor grades and close friends who share a view of the school as a hostile environment.[27]

The casualness and the truncation of time perspective that characterize the act of dropping out of school lead to a similar casualness in finding a job. Reynolds and Shister, in a study of manual workers in a New England community, found that over 85 percent discovered

---

some improvement in this situation today, because of our increased awareness of the problem. See also Ralph Turner, *The Social Context of Ambition* (San Francisco: Chandler, 1965).

[25] Donald B. O'Dowd and David C. Beardslee, *College Student Images of Professions and Occupations* (Middletown, Conn.: Wesleyan University Press, 1960).

[26] For a now somewhat outdated but still valuable discussion of these dilemmas of the school, see W. Lloyd Warner, Robert J. Havighurst, and Martin Loeb, *Who Shall Be Educated?* (New York: Harper, 1944); and see, in addition, for discussion of the forms of discrimination against working-class children in a middle-class school, August B. Hollingshead, *Elmtown's Youth* (New York: Wiley & Sons, 1949).

[27] The various reasons boys may have for dropping out of school are vividly described by S. M. Miller and Ira E. Harrison in "Types of Dropouts: 'The Unemployables,'" in Arthur B. Shostak and William Gomberg, eds., *Blue-Collar World* (Englewood Cliffs, N. J.: Prentice-Hall, 1964), pp. 469-84. The boy who gets a "bad reputation" in the school may find he is almost forced by teachers and fellow students into a role antagonistic to the school. See Robert B. Vinter and Rosemary C. Sarri, "Malperformance in the Public School: A Group Work Approach," *Social Work* (January, 1965), pp. 3-13.

the first job through random application or the chance of a personal contact. Almost all took the first job they were offered. They felt, even in relatively good times, that jobs were scarce and that there was a good deal to be said for just having a job. Even more to the point, they felt that since they lacked skill and experience, and didn't know what they wanted in the long run, the first job offered them was as good as any. They did not have the resources to shop around, were impatient to get to work, and were in any case not clear about what they wanted a job to provide. A not atypical example is the following:

> Well, I was out walking with one of my friends, and we happened to be passing by a plant, and he said "Why don't you get a job in there?" So I went in and they gave me a job. (Screw machine operator.) [28]

What follows for many of these youths is a series of shifts among jobs within the blue-collar world, before finally some job turns out to be relatively permanent.[29] In his novel, *On the Line*, Harvey Swados describes the way in which a number of men of very different origins, ambitions, and abilities come to find themselves working next to each other on an automobile assembly line. Many of these men who took a job on the line "temporarily" found themselves stuck there, even though they resented the work, while others left without great hope of finding anything more satisfying.[30]

For working-class children the barriers to mobility are many. Perhaps the first problem is that the occupational system itself is so little understood by them; so little of its range is exposed to their view. In addition, financial and moral resources are so untrustworthy that the children find themselves unable to plan for their futures at all. Indeed, in many sectors of the lower class, the whole culture is opposed to planning, and calculation for the future may be looked down upon as showing a lack of solidarity with one's peers, and per-

---

[28] Lloyd G. Reynolds and Joseph Shister, *Job Horizons* (New York: Harper, 1949), p. 54.

[29] See, for discussion of the careers of blue-collar workers, William H. Form and Delbert C. Miller, "Occupational Career Pattern as a Sociological Instrument," in Nosow and Form, eds., *Man, Work, and Society*, pp. 287-97. Among the conclusions of the authors is, "Once started on an occupational level, a worker tends to remain on that level."

[30] Harvey Swados, *On the Line* (Boston: Little, Brown, 1957). See also Gladys Palmer, "Epilogue: Social Values in Labor Mobility," in the collection of essays, *Labor, Mobility, and Economic Opportunity* (New York: Wiley & Sons, 1954), pp. 47-67. Where accidental factors play a significant role in the choice of first jobs, over time, many workers develop a sense of what kind of "careers" are open to them and, when they shift jobs, do so in the hope of bettering their situation.

haps a certain amount of gullibility in relation to the occupational structure.

Increasingly, attempts to help the working-class youth understand the occupational system, and make realistic plans for his own future within it, have resulted in the development of guidance programs in the schools. A full guidance program would include both individual guidance and group activities in which classrooms, schools, or self-selected groups of students interested in specific occupations would be given information about a specialty.[31] But in consonance with the ancient judgment that to him "that hath shall be given," such guidance programs work best in the well-staffed middle-class schools. The guidance officer in the crowded metropolitan school, when the luxury of such a post can be afforded at all, seldom has time for a conference with every student in which to discover his "needs" and help him set realistic goals; indeed, he would have to know more than he generally does about the milieu, as well as about the individual, in order to grasp the level of attainment that might be possible. Often enough he becomes someone who keeps records and concerns himself primarily with those students who get into trouble.

More effective guidance programs are only part of the answer. The working-class youth, and especially the member of the more disadvantaged segment within the working class, needs some social or institutional support for continuing in the educational system when such support is not forthcoming from parents and peers. New York City, in particular, has attempted to introduce such programs, in part through its Mobilization for Youth program. The difficulties such programs face are enormous. They fight the current of prevailing opinion and existent structures. Much experimentation and patience will be needed before they will succeed.

In contrast with working-class youths, middle-class youths are likely to find the school system congenial, though they may disparage the educational value of the content of their high school and even their college courses. To some extent, school is seen by middle-class youths as a place where one learns to "get along with people" and to acquire the social skills necessary for many white-collar jobs—and many white-collar marriages. In the broadest sense, whatever teachers may think, this is education too.[32] In other words, we see the high school as in-

---

[31] See M. S. Baer and E. C. Rober, *Occupational Information* (Chicago: Science Research Associates, 1951).

[32] See the criticism of antieducational elements in the high schools by James Coleman, *The Adolescent Society* (New York: Free Press, 1960). See also, for different and critical assessments of the types of teachers who have Coleman's

structing young people about their society and their place in it as much through extra-academic activities as through the curriculum. What may seem to be frivolities interfering with preprofessional and professional education are easily afforded by our rich society and may well furnish students with bases for more realistic and more self-expressive occupational choices.

Middle-class children characteristically see their vocational problem as one of deciding what they want to do; they are eager to assess their own talents, interests, and abilities as a means of establishing occupational goals, and their position in the social system gives them opportunity for insight into the occupational world. The fortunate youngster will have a family member or family friend who is a member of the occupational group at which he aims, and from whom he can get a more intimate view of the work of the physician, executive, scientist, or teacher. The less fortunate youngster may have to depend on an occasional article and what can be picked up in school, in the content of courses and in conversation with teachers, for his image of his chosen work.[33] However, the occupational system is surprisingly opaque even for those privileged enough to have an unobstructed view of it. It is difficult to empathize with someone whose concerns are different from one's own; thus, many college students do not have a realistic picture of what their instructor's life is like, let alone a doctor's, or a businessman's.

The problem of the adolescent is intensified by the fact that, while some fields, such as the law and teaching, admit those who have decided fairly late in life to enter, other fields, including some branches of science and many of the skilled trades, require early career decisions of prospective entrance.[34] Thus, for example, those who want

---

approval, Edgar Z. Friedenburg, *Growing Up in America: Adolescence in Mass Society* (New York: Random House, 1965).

[33] Eli Ginzberg *et al.*, *Occupational Choice* (New York: Columbia University Press, 1951). Herman Case has studied the difference between college students whose choice of occupation is in fact a committing choice and those whose choice is only apparently firm. In this he is using the distinctions, suggested by Ginzberg *et al.*, between those whose occupational choice is *crystallized* and those who rather exhibit *pseudocrystallization*. He finds that the *pseudocrystallized* students, who will shift their aims despite apparent commitment, are *less likely* to have been influenced by parents, teachers, or acquaintances in the occupation, are *more likely* to be manifestly motivated by hopes for material success, and are *more likely* to come from a working-class background, though they are headed themselves for the middle-class occupations. See Herman A. Case, "Two Kinds of Crystallized Occupational Choice Behavior: A Problem in Delineation and Relationship," *American Sociological Review*, Vol. 19 (February, 1954), pp. 85-87.

[34] For material on the decision to enter medicine, see Natalie Rogoff, "The Decision to Study Medicine," and Wagner Thielens, Jr., "Some Comparisons of En-

to become physicists must decide in high school to take the right kinds of science and enough mathematics to qualify them for the physics department of an undergraduate college where they may then acquire the training adequate to prepare them for graduate school.[35]

This demand for early choice intensifies the pressure on guidance counselors or, in their absence, puts emphasis on the use of those actuarial guidance counselors, the interest tests. The Strong Interest Test, for example, permits a youngster to compare his profile of likes and dislikes with those of successful members of several occupational groups.[36] Such a test may at least help a youngster determine whether he would like the kinds of things offered by an occupation, including some elements not visible to any except those already participating in it. But neither guidance counselors nor interest tests are capable of overcoming for all, or even for most, the hazards inherent in choosing one's life work without adequate information about one's self.

An evaluation of the extent to which our system for bringing people and jobs together is a good one would have to consider to what extent members of our society truly have equal opportunity to find the jobs that have for them the optimum mixture of intrinsic and extrinsic value, and to what extent our society is able to fill the jobs that need to be done. These two aims are not always complementary. In a less sensitive age than ours, the comforting thought prevailed that people who held the most monotonous or degrading jobs were stupid fellows, often of inferior race, who were lucky to have a job at all. Today, in contrast, we are aware of the conflict between the needs and desires of individual workers and the demands of the society, as presently constituted, that certain tasks be performed for which individuals, given the values of the society, would seldom volunteer. We find it necessary to conscript men for military service, although some of the more glamorous services have been able to rely on volunteers, and volunteers suffice—just barely—for police duty. Street cleaning is looked on as degrading if done by hand, though less so if done by machine; and domestic service, perhaps because of the continual unprofessional supervision, is considered demeaning. Some industrial and agricul-

---

trants to Medical and Law School," in Robert K. Merton, George G. Reader, and Patricia L. Kendall, eds., *The Student-Physician* (Cambridge, Mass.: Harvard University Press, 1957), pp. 109-29, pp. 131-52.

[35] See Everett C. Hughes, *Men and Their Work* (New York: Free Press, 1958).

[36] E. K. Strong, Jr., *Vocational Interests of Men and Women* (Stanford, Calif.: Stanford University Press, 1943). Also see Charles MacArthur and L. B. Stevens, "The Validation of Expressed Interests as Compared with Inventoried Interest, a Fourteen-Year Followup," *Journal of Applied Psychology*, Vol. 39 (1955), pp. 184-89.

tural jobs are still onerous, and despite unionization and minimum wage laws, the rule probably still prevails that the more unpleasant the work (at least in terms of social definition) the less likely that it will be well paid and secure. Yet all these jobs are required, or at least are thought to be required, if our society is to function reasonably well, and so they are left to those who for one reason or another are among the losers in the contest for places in the occupational system.

Because we do not assign our young to jobs, but instead permit individuals to choose their fields, there is always the possibility that potentially gifted people will fail to choose the field in which their contributions might be most needed by the society. This seems now to be the case in nursing and not very long ago seemed to be the case in science. In both fields the demand for trained people far exceeds the supply. Guidance counselors may attempt to direct students into occupations that are at the moment in great demand, but the technological structure is changing rapidly, and it is by no means sure that, for example, engineers or servicemen for household goods or even automobile mechanics will be required in ten years in anywhere near the number required now. Our young people need to have as much knowledge about the future of our occupational structure as can be gathered, and as much opportunity for exercise of intelligent choice as can be made available. Hopefully, we are moving, though perhaps still too slowly, toward the realization of each of these aims.

The Job Itself

In some countries a sagging economy or the absence of an industrial tradition has produced a situation in which merely to have a job and to make a living wage are themselves achievements. In the more affluent sectors of American life, men often can choose, or believe they might once have chosen, among many different ways in which they might earn their living, and they ask of their work that it be more than merely a means toward subsistence. At the same time, in the less affluent sectors, much of the work that is done has little to recommend it beyond the living wage and the absence of alternatives. In a great many industries, a majority of the workers would prefer, if it were only possible, to be doing something else.[37]

---

[37] See Robert Blauner, *Alienation and Freedom* (Chicago: University of Chicago Press, 1964), especially Table 37, p. 202, which presents the proportions of men desiring different occupations by industry. See also Table 8, this chapter.

Managers, recognizing the problems of unsatisfying work, and recognizing also the value to their organizations of good morale, have sometimes attempted to take into account their workers, as well as their production processes, in the design of their factories and offices. The Polaroid Corporation, for example, has attempted to introduce career lines, which permit a worker to move up out of the machine-tending ranks to the laboratory, the office, or even to management. To help men make these moves, part of its plant has been turned into schoolrooms, and men are encouraged to register for classes that teach verbal skills as well as industrial know-how. As a second example, the International Business Machines Corporation has rearranged some of its shops so that machine operators have become responsible not for just one operation on a piece, but for the entire manufacture of the piece, from raw material and blueprint to final inspection.[38]

Any effort to reorganize work with the effect of the job on the worker in mind, rather than over-all efficiency, must overcome the obstacle that reorganization is hardly possible in a fiercely competitive industry, or in one that lacks the financial resources necessary for experimentation. Still, many companies with sufficient resources assume the necessity for the traditional organization and scale of work with its dehumanizing potentialities, never asking themselves whether new methods could not be more creative without, in fact, being too costly in terms of the balance sheet. The objection that industry ought not bear the cost of measures that are not necessary for profit-making is hardly appropriate in the densely organized society of today; it is almost impossible to separate clearly what is the concern of a privately owned industrial organization and what is a public concern. For example, a great many "costs" of particular enterprises are not borne by the enterprise: the workers' time spent in getting to and from work, the cost of their cars, the upkeep of the roads—all are free to the plant, though it is the plant's operation that necessitates their use.

It has often been suggested in the past, and is increasingly suggested as the inroads of automation into the supply of low-level jobs become recognized, that a highly productive society such as ours should attempt to minimize the importance of work and instead devote its energies to developing a more creative use of leisure. The difficulty

---

[38] For a discussion of "job enlargement" at IBM, see Charles R. Walker, "The Problem of the Repetitive Job," *Harvard Business Review*, Vol. 28 (May, 1950), pp. 54-58. The Polaroid program is described in Paul Campanis, "Blue-Collar Careers," unpublished Ph.D. dissertation, Sociology Department, Brandeis University, 1965.

with this course of action is, as we have repeatedly noted, that American men tend to look to their performance on a job, even if it is a repetitive one, as a basis for recognition of their worth. We have already pointed out that few Americans would want to do without work, even if they were not forced by economic necessity to stay at a job. In this respect, most Americans are incapable of viewing their work as do, for instance, many Spanish-Americans, who recognize work as necessary for making a living, but for whom the idea of work as important in itself has no currency at all:

> . . . [Among Spanish-Americans] work is an accepted and inevitable part of everyday life. It is a certain amount of trouble but there it is. . . . Spanish-Americans are good, persistent workers when they see a reason to work, but they do not consider work itself a virtue. It is not common sense . . . to work just to keep the hands occupied, or even to earn money where there is money for the current needs of the family because some other adult male is employed.[39]

For Americans, irrespective of the job they hold, work is itself important, though the reasons for its importance will vary with the particular responsibilities and rewards of particular occupations. This underlying similarity in the valuing of work may be held in mind through the following sections, in which we discuss the different problems associated with work of different kinds. First, we discuss those jobs that emphasize manual rather than verbal skills, carry limited responsibility and limited prestige, and that might generally be referred to as "working-class jobs"; then we turn to jobs, typically within organizations, that emphasize verbal skills, require some responsibility of those who hold them, but are limited, repetitive, and subject to the informal, but nevertheless real, discipline of life on the lower ranks of an organizational hierarchy; and finally we talk about the jobs that carry the greatest variety of task, scope, and prestige in the world of work—the managerial and professional occupations.

The Working-Class Job

At the beginning of the Industrial Revolution, Adam Smith was so impressed with the stultifying nature of factory life that he could only hope that the hours away from work might somehow maintain those qualities of character he regarded as essentially human. Marx went much further in seeing the factory as an ambush of brutishness, of long hours, prison-like conditions, virtual contempt for the well-

---

[39] Margaret Mead, ed., *Cultural Patterns and Technical Change* (New York: New American Library, 1955), p. 164.

being of the worker, and throughout, a job that "exhausts the nervous system to the uttermost, does away with the many-sided play of the muscles, and confiscates every atom of freedom, both in bodily and intellectual activity," which, in sum, makes the worker "a mere living appendage" to the machine.[40]

In the perspective of hindsight, we can see that observers of the evils of factory life may have neglected the elements of passivity and boredom in the life of the peasant and yeoman prior to the coming of industry. And it is likely too that both the nineteenth-century and the contemporary observers who have commented on the factory have failed to see the elements of creativity, disguised in tricks of the trade or sabotage, by which seemingly oppressed workers maintain a certain amount of control over the conditions of work. Furthermore, small talk and "kidding around" can sometimes make bearable the most repetitive task.[41]

However, the sharpest criticism of the industrial job, made by Karl Marx and other nineteenth-century observers of factory life, was not aimed at the immediate discomfort produced by the job, but rather at a condition they characterized as "alienation." They argued that when men engage in activities that have no inner meanings for them as individuals, but are merely a part of the productive process— merely means to an end—then the human beings themselves become alienated from their own deepest passions. Work comes to be something "out there," its processes dwarfing the men who perform them, its products bearing no recognizable relationship to the individual effort of the individual worker. The workers' only awareness of the state of alienation may be the recognition that their work life is unrewarding: the possibility that work might become meaningful is beyond their vision. While many of these specific abuses of early capitalism have been overcome or nearly so in this country, the theme of alienation remains as salient as ever. It turns up not only among blue-collar workers but also in the way white-collar workers and professionals speak of their jobs as the "rat race" and look forward, not to more challenging or more interesting work, but to shorter hours now, and early retirement later.[42]

---

[40] Karl Marx, *Capital* (New York: Modern Library), p. 462.

[41] The work of Donald Roy is particularly useful here. See "Quota Restrictions and Goldbricking in a Machine Shop," *American Journal of Sociology* (March, 1952), pp. 427-42, and also "Banana Time" in Warren G. Bennis, Edgar H. Schein, David E. Berlew, and Fred I. Steele, eds., *Interpersonal Dynamics* (Homewood, Ill.: Dorsey, 1964), pp. 583-99.

[42] See Karl Marx and Friedrich Engels, "On Alienation," in C. Wright Mills, ed., *Images of Man* (New York: Braziller, 1960), pp. 486-507. For a discussion

For the last three generations, workers at all levels have demanded shorter hours, preferring to take part of their increased productivity in the form of time off, rather than in an increase in real income. It is part of the same demand that leads men, not themselves close to retirement and thus not faced with its financial and psychological hazards, to press for an ever earlier age of retirement "so that a man can do all those things in life you can't do while you're working." Warner Bloomberg, Jr., a sociologist who worked in the Gary steel mills and elsewhere, reports that steelworkers from 25 to 55 almost unanimously advocate retirement commencing at 55 or earlier. They blithely dismiss the inevitable economic questions with assertions that they will be able to "make out," based, perhaps, on secret hopes that better stipends for the retired are just around the political corner.[43]

Retirement, when it is in fact reached, turns out to be much less desirable than had been anticipated. For while the job itself may have been oppressive, the absence of work is, in a different way, equally so. Consider these comments by the son of a retired steel worker:

> He (speaking of the retired father) does not see anyone else (besides family). He goes out and watches the card games in the park during the summer. He stands on the sidewalk just standing around. He spends most of his time with the chickens. He has chickens, doves, pigeons in the back yard. If it weren't for those chickens, he wouldn't have anything to do. For the first time after he retired, he spent all his time just walking up and down in the living room. He could not stand it having nothing to do. (Wife, to interviewer: "You wait until you retire, see if you have anything to do!")[44]

In the working class, in fact, jobs are often so unsatisfactory that there is no social pressure to say that one enjoys one's work; it is socially permitted to regard it with dislike or at best detachment. The Morse-Weiss study, referred to earlier, shows that while the great majority of men would continue to work even if work were not economically required of them, only in the middle-class occupations

---

of the Marxist and pre-Marxist use of the concept, see Daniel Bell, *The End of Ideology* (New York: Free Press, 1960), pp. 388-402. A compact review of the meanings the term carries in current sociological thought is given by Melvin Seeman, "On the meaning of Alienation," *American Sociological Review*, Vol. 24 (December, 1959), pp. 783-91. Blauner, *Alienation and Freedom*, is a careful study of the relation between work and alienation in five industries. See also Hannah Arendt, *The Human Condition* (New York: Doubleday, 1959).

[43] Warren Peterson in a study of Kansas City school teachers also found this growing demand for early retirement, expressing boredom and defeatism about work as much as any specific desires for postwork activities. (Unpublished dissertation, Department of Sociology, University of Chicago, 1956.)

[44] Friedmann and Havighurst, eds., *The Meaning of Work and Retirement*, p. 48.

TABLE 8

Percent of Respondents Who Would Continue to Work and Percent Who Would Continue on the Same Job

	Would Continue to Work	Would Continue in Same Type of Work
Middle Class		
Professional	86	68
Manager	82	55
Sales	91	59
Working Class		
Trades	79	40
Operatives	78	32
Unskilled	58	16
Service	71	33

Source: Nancy C. Morse and Robert S. Weiss, "The Function and Meaning of Work and the Job," *American Sociological Review* (April, 1965).

would the majority of men continue in the same type of work (see Table 8). Less than one in six among unskilled workers, and about one in three among the workers in service occupations or in the semiskilled occupations would continue at their present work. It is in these groups that the social and personal function of working at any job together with pure economic compulsion serve to hold the individual to a job he does not really want.

One of the things wrong with the working-class job is simply that it is working class. In a culture where the worth of a man is measured by how far he has gotten, the unskilled laborer or service worker, despite the pieties that may be uttered periodically about the dignity of labor, knows that he has not gotten very far. In most industries many workers would not want their children to wind up as they have. A Negro packing-house worker, for example, responded to an interviewer's question about getting his kids into the plant to work by saying, "I wouldn't want a kid of mine to ever have a job like this." [45]

The sense of being in an inferior position, and the muffled resentment toward those who have been luckier, which characterizes many of the men in factory jobs, is expressed by a machine worker, talking to a sociologist who in the course of his field work had taken a job in a factory:

---

[45] Theodore V. Purcell, S.J., "The Hopes of Negro Workers for Their Children," in Shostak and Gomberg, eds., *Blue-Collar World*, pp. 144-53.

Sure I'm a high school grad, but where does that get me. I didn't know there was such a thing as a college prep course until after I graduated. I went to _____ Tech and over there nobody was going to teach me anything to set me up in competition with the boss' son. All those guys want you to learn is how to read a blueprint and you can learn enough of that to do this work in six months. It's different with you, Slim. You got off to a good start and I wish you well for it, but if you'd come up through the Depression in a trade school the way I did you'd be in the same boat I am. You make the most of it, Slim, and some day you'll be boss. Then you can walk through here and say "Hi there, Jack" and walk along thinking "Old Jack never got very far," and I'll say "Good morning, Mr. _____," and after you're gone I'll say, "I knew that so-and-so when he was a white man." [46]

It is widely recognized that the modern factory offers virtually no opportunity for advancement from the blue-collar ranks. In one study, almost half of all factory workers in a large group of firms felt that there was no opportunity for promotion in their jobs; they believed that no matter how well they did their jobs, they were stuck in them, unless seniority and good luck combined to give them a break. [47] Generally, factory workers cannot move into highly skilled work since it is controlled by the union, and they can obtain entrance only after completing an apprenticeship that a man with a family can seldom afford. Nor would the unions in the skilled trades permit entry to all applicants: the electricians, like the physicians, have no desire to increase greatly the numbers of those licensed to compete for available work.

In this situation of blocked mobility there develops an emphasis on the small differences that make one job slightly better than another: a somewhat better machine, a better shift, a fractionally higher hourly wage, a little more freedom to move around on the job floor. These gradations are controlled by seniority, and seniority also determines what comes to be the most important advantage of all: one's security in the plant in case there is a reduction of the work force. "Getting ahead" does not entirely lose its meaning, but comes to be redefined so that it refers to his life as a consumer, not as a producer. The better-paid workers can find some status in the plant by means of their extracurricular activities—extravagant hunting trips, expensive travels, a new home in a pleasant suburb, or a new car. And, of

---

[46] Orville Collins, Melville Dalton, and Donald Roy, "Restriction of Output and Social Cleavage in Industry," *Applied Anthropology* (Summer, 1946), pp. 1-14.

[47] Blauner, *Alienation and Freedom*, Table 45, p. 206.

course, it is always possible for the worker to dream that he may one day be able to get out of the plant.[48]

Chinoy noted that "a dozen men spontaneously observed that 'almost everybody' talks about getting out of the shop," and reports an assembly-line tender as saying, "It makes the time go quicker and easier if I keep thinking about that turkey farm I'd like to buy." The small business is simply a daydream for most men. Some men try it, but many—if not most—of them fail; they lack capital, contacts, and experience in what is at best a hazardous undertaking.[49]

It must be remembered that even though factory work has come to represent the blue-collar occupations, in fact only a minority of blue-collar workers tend assembly lines. A good many blue-collar jobs, particularly those which allow freedom of movement—such as a milk-route salesman, a telephone lineman, a trucker, a maintenance worker —do provide variety, a considerable amount of challenge and responsibility, and give many who hold them a sense of achievement. Moreover, there are factory jobs such as crane operator, though declining in number, which carry a kind of Paul Bunyan status because of their difficulty and danger. Mining, a declining, dangerous, and depressed industry, nevertheless has a certain allure for those brought up in it. What characterizes all these jobs is the avoidance of that extreme subdivision of work in which the worker repeats operations over and over again through the day.

This extreme subdivision of work is the achievement of decades of engineering effort motivated by a belief that a total work process can be carried out most efficiently if it is broken down into many smaller processes, each of which is allocated to specific workers who specialize in its performance. Instead of having a single man grind, bore, and polish a piece of metal, the engineers would have many pieces ground by one man, then all of them bored by another, and finally polished by a third. (Referring to men in this example may be misleading: thoroughly repetitive work, when it is neither dirty nor heavy nor dangerous, seems likely to be defined as women's jobs.) Only

---

[48] Ely Chinoy, "The Traditions of Opportunity and the Aspirations of Automobile Workers," *American Journal of Sociology,* Vol. 57, No. 5 (March, 1952), pp. 453-59.

[49] Mayer and Goldstein found that of 81 small business firms which began operating in the Providence, Rhode Island, area in the first part of 1958, 78 percent survived their first year in business, and 51 percent survived their second. See Kurt B. Mayer and Sidney Goldstein, *The First Two Years: Problems of Small Firm Growth and Survival* (Washington, D. C.: Small Business Administration, 1961).

rarely, in such a system, would a worker carry through the complete processing of a part and when the system is carried far enough the worker may find his task so routine that his mind and spirit are left free for daydreaming, casual kidding, and boredom.

Though the repetitive job can be justified by the logic of efficiency, its disagreeable qualities have long been recognized. Tocqueville noted:

> When a workman is unceasingly and exclusively engaged in the fabrication of one thing, he ultimately does his work with singular dexterity; but at the same time he loses the general faculty of applying his mind to the direction of the work. He every day becomes more adroit and less industrious; so that it may be said of him that in proportion as the workman improves, the man is degraded.[50]

In fact, as research on the effect of monotonous jobs has shown, the situation is much more complicated than this would suggest. Some workers may willingly perform monotonous jobs that strike them as important, but resist jobs no more monotonous because they seem meaningless. Individuals differ greatly in the extent to which they value a steady rhythm in their work, or require work that is continually presenting new problems. Although a highly repetitive job is likely to be resented by most workers, still some repetitive jobs are better than others, and some workers can tolerate monotony better than can others.[51]

Moreover, as has already been suggested, workers are not helpless cogs in a system, no matter how carefully the system has been worked out, or how closely it is supervised. Workers very often find ways of doing jobs a little more easily, of controlling their own work pace, and of introducing variety into their days. The assembly-line system reduces the freedom of the worker about as much as any factory system can, but even here, if the line is speeded up beyond the point that workers will accept, there may be a sudden, almost spontaneous, refusal to work, or the line may mysteriously break down, or the number of defective parts greatly increase. Human beings make great efforts to control their environment and, in concert, are often able to do so, in a factory setting as well as elsewhere. Even in a nonunion plant, factory workers manage to collaborate, to form work groups and cliques, primarily to humanize the bleakness and impersonality of

---

[50] Alexis de Tocqueville, *Democracy in America,* Vol. 2 (New York: Vintage Books, 1959), p. 168.

[51] See Friedmann, *Industrial Society,* especially the chapters on problems of monotony, rhythm of work, and assembly-line work.

the factory, but also to control through joint action the conditions under which they work.[52]

This informal social group is extremely important to each of its members. The groups give each worker the sense of acceptance as an individual, of value to others, of ability to participate in easy give-and-take, which is so totally absent in other aspects of the factory. The work group forms a supportive environment within which the worker can get through what would otherwise be a painfully tedious day. Yet it should not be thought that the group, despite its very great importance on the job, continues to be so important to the individual off the job. Most factory workers do not carry their friendships at work into their lives off the job. Their commitments to fellow workers, though strong, are largely confined to the work situation.[53]

Managements tend to see the informal social groups which workers form as implacably hostile to the aims of management. And, often enough, informal social groups do act in ways which reduce the efficiency of the factory's operation. They may hoard work secrets for the members of the group, and refuse them to newcomers until the newcomers are accepted into the group; they may define certain jobs as appropriate only for individuals who have much seniority in the plant, and refuse to allow management to assign a new man to these jobs, no matter how competent he may be because of experience outside the plant; and, often, they will set work standards at odds with those set by management. But it is not simply the case that the informal work group is management's antagonist. Studies of factories have often found that the most valued member of such a group is the man who can most easily turn out the "fair day's work" which the group agrees it owes management in return for its "fair day's pay." Correspondingly, when the group restricts output to a level below that which management would consider optimal, it nevertheless tends to keep output up to a level which seems to it fair.[54]

The ability of the work group to restrict the output of its members limits the effectiveness of any piecework or incentive-pay plan that

---

[52] See, in this connection, Charles R. Walker and Robert H. Guest, *The Man on the Assembly Line* (Cambridge, Mass.: Harvard University Press, 1952).

[53] Robert Dubin, "Industrial Workers' Worlds: A Study of the Central Life Interests of Industrial Workers," *Social Problems*, Vol. 3, No. 3 (January, 1956), pp. 131-42.

[54] For a study indicating that a work group may set quite high levels of productivity where management is favorably regarded, see Stanley Seashore, *Group Cohesiveness and the Industrial Work Group* (Ann Arbor, Mich.: University of Michigan, Institute for Social Research, Survey Research Center, Publication No. 14, 1955).

management may institute. Even so, the group may welcome an incentive plan because, while it does not mean extra income, since the amount of product turned out will be limited, it does allow the members of the group to control the pace of their own work. With incentive pay, the workers can calculate how many pieces they will report, and then attempt to turn out that many in, say, five or six hours of an eight-hour day: the remaining time to be spent in washroom conversation, in making equipment they can use in their own homes, in fashioning toys for the children, or in stockpiling pieces for the following day's production record. Collins, Dalton, and Roy quote one worker:

> When you're on piece work you're working against the clock. That makes the time go faster. That old hand moves right around because it's trying to beat you and you're trying to beat it. Then when you've got a pool built up you can spend your time the way you please so long as you keep out of sight of the office crowd.[55]

The Union

The worker may see his union as an institution in which he is treated with more respect than he is in the factory, and in which he has an occasional opportunity to express his solidarity with his fellow workers, as he would in a strike. However, now that unions are well established, the average union member is apathetic and takes little interest in the affairs of his union. This apathy is most pronounced in the large industrial unions; in one study it was found that only one half of one percent of the membership of a steel workers' local attended a biweekly membership meeting.[56] For the early members of the union, many of whom experienced the great organizing strikes of the late thirties, membership in the union meant opposing the clear wishes of their management; now, those who are still working are older and less militant. The younger union members treat the union as an institution that, as far as they can tell, has always been a part of the industrial scene. Though they do not quite take it for granted, they do not have to make as much of a commit-

---

[55] Collins, Dalton, and Roy, "Restrictions of Output and Social Cleavage in Industry," p. 8.

[56] Joel Seidman, "The Labor Union as an Organization," in Arthur Kornhauser, Robert Dubin, and Arthur M. Ross, eds., *Industrial Conflict* (New York: McGraw-Hill, 1954). For further discussion see William Spinrad, "Correlates of Trade Union Participation: Summary of the Literature," *American Sociological Review*, Vol. 25 (April, 1960), pp. 237-44; and also Arnold S. Tannenbaum and Robert L. Kahn, *Participation in Local Unions* (Evanston, Ill.: Row, Peterson, 1958).

ment to it as did the original members. Instead, they see today's union as a reassuring latent power that keeps management from going too far. A steel worker, asked what would happen if the union were to disappear, put it this way:

> You'd lose everything, the company would really throw you around and put the pressure on. They'd be demanding, and high-pressuring everybody. They'd demote people any time they wanted to. There wouldn't be any seniority.[57]

There have been many criticisms of unions, directed both at the extent to which leadership is responsive to the rank and file, and also at the impact that unions have had on their industry and on the economy of the society as a whole. Unions are sometimes criticized as undemocratic and, with a few exceptions, the characterization is probably just. A union leader who has lost an election usually has nowhere to go except back to the factory: this situation sometimes leads union leaders, as an analogous situation sometimes leads college presidents, to put great energy into making their positions secure. Nevertheless, often enough the positions proposed by the leadership of a "good" union, such as the United Auto Workers, in relation to education, opposition to racial discrimination, and the like, seem both in vision and humaneness to be ahead of the thinking of the rank and file. At the same time, democracy, in a town-meeting sense, is as rare among unions as among most other institutions: not only is the leadership anxious to maintain its position, but generally it has built a political machine within the union to accomplish this, and often the rank and file are indifferent as to who is elected to union posts.[58]

Unions are frequently suspected of being autocratic and of exploiting their members. Yet racketeering is not nearly as common in unions as one might assume from news stories. It can seldom persist without being tolerated by management or even without its active cooperation. Hence it tends to occur primarily in such fields as trucking, building, and restaurant trades, where managements are small, decentralized, and beset by competitive pressures. In such situations, it is not unknown for a business agent of the union to make

---

[57] Seidman, "The Labor Union as an Organization," p. 112.

[58] See Miller and Form, "Power and Union Organization," in *Industrial Sociology*, Chapter 8, pp. 288-325. For a discussion of an exceptional union, in which two competing parties provide alternative slates to the membership, see Seymour Lipset, Martin Trow, and James Coleman, *Union Democracy: The Internal Politics of the International Typographical Union* (New York: Free Press, 1956).

a deal with a management representative that is profitable for each, though costly to the members of the union. This should not suggest, however, that all such industrial situations give rise to union racketeering. In the garment industry where firms are also small and highly competitive, the union has brought a certain measure of stability without racketeering. In fact, the International Ladies Garment Workers Union is representative of the majority of unions in that it is led by honest and even dedicated men, no more and often less allergic to democracy than are other Americans, men whose work, like that of the social worker, the physician, or the teacher, necessarily brings them into contact with the lives of others, and often broadens their perspectives.

The union movement grew to a potent force in American economic life between the two World Wars, and has been remarkably successful, for so short a life, in achieving most of its short-run objectives. Wages have been raised; welfare and security measures for workers are now frequently to be found in the union contract; managements are not so often able to act capriciously in layoffs and promotions. Yet economists differ as to whether labor unions have to any appreciable extent actually succeeded in raising the real income of workers as a whole. One view is that they have raised the wage rates for some unionized workers, especially for members of the strong unions in steel, automobiles, rubber, and so forth, at the expense of the nonunionized, who must pay for the goods turned out by the unionized workers. In addition, industries that are in a strong market position—and in general these are the industries where strong incorruptible unions have developed—tend to use a wage concession to labor as an excuse for raising prices to a level that not only covers the wage concession, but increases the profit margin. For this reason Daniel Bell concludes that "the net effect of the union pressure—apart from the gains which have been won for the small group of highly organized workers—has been to help install a mechanism whereby the large corporation is able to strengthen its price position in the market." [59] He would like to see the unions press for the elimination of the distinction between blue-collar workers paid on an hourly basis and white-collar workers who have the dignity and security of a salary; he believes that big industry could now well afford to put all its workers on an annual basis. Beyond that, he would like to see the unions become less insular, concerned not only with the well-being of their own members and of

[59] See Daniel Bell, "The Subversion of Collective Bargaining," *Commentary*, Vol. 29 (March, 1960), pp. 185-97.

the "labor movement," but with lower-income families in general; he would like to see a renewal, not of union militancy, but of union idealism—a prescription that of course applies also to other vested interests in society.

As a way of bringing wages in the unorganized (nonunion) part of the economy closer to the level of those in the organized sector (in part because they wish to reduce the competition of nonunion shops with lower wage scales), unions have rather successfully lobbied for a minimum wage law. However, although on first thought such a law would seem to be to the unquestionable advantage of all members of the work force, in practice this does not prove to be so. A farmer, for example, can sometimes choose to work his farm either with migrant labor or with machines, and he may well base his decision on how much he has to pay to the migrant labor. A minimum wage law is likely to make jobs even more scarce for such marginal workers. Perhaps this is all to the good, but it is a consequence of the minimum wage law that is not apt to be envisioned by its proposers.

Unions have at times been accused of making it difficult for members of some minority groups to work as craftsmen. For example, the building-trades locals maintain monopolistic control over the right to perform electrical work, plumbing, masonry, and the like. These craft unions typically restrict entrance to individuals who are acceptable to the membership, often to relatives of some member, almost always to members of an ethnic group acceptable to the members. It is primarily these trade unions, rather than management, that keep Negroes out of the construction industry. In many of these union groups, work gangs are small in size and have a team spirit, and, as might be the case in a cohesive working-class neighborhood, they are not likely to welcome a member of an ethnic out-group. Add the fact that members of building-trades unions are likely to feel that there are few jobs and that these must be protected for relatives and ethnic co-members to whom they have some commitment, and it becomes clear why plumbers or masons may feel that membership in their union belongs by right to their particular group. As people become more nearly "middle class" in life style and more distant from their immigrant background and the deprivations this once produced, these loyalties may fade. Yet Negroes and members of other out-groups can scarcely be expected to wait for this to happen.

But even as the unions try to meet these more traditional problems, new threats are arising with the advent of automation. One is that the unions will lose their membership base; in fact, the major industrial unions, the Steel Workers, the Auto Workers, and Rubber

Workers, all have registered decreases in membership over the past few years. Union leaders sometimes express hope that it will be possible to organize white-collar workers and in this way prevent the dissolution of the union movement, but their experience thus far has been disappointing. Even before this long-run crisis comes to pass, however, unions must deal with the threat posed by automation to the jobs of current members. Most unions have attempted to regulate the pace of automation while accepting its inevitability. The United Auto Workers has negotiated a provision for voluntary early retirement that may ease some of the internal pressure. Other unions have negotiated programs for retraining workers displaced by automation. Still, the rank and file in many unions are anxious about the safety of their jobs, and union leadership is feeling its way.

The Strike

In the period of the great organizing drives in the 1930's, the strike was often a way in which the union created itself out of the sporadic and isolated discontents of clusters of workers. Today, however, the strike is increasingly institutionalized and less often involves the violence or the emotional excitement of earlier periods. Instead, it is part of a process of bargaining, indeed often a step to which management may not be entirely opposed, since then management may feel itself justified in raising prices after the strike is settled.[60]

There are other strikes, however, that are much less the result of carefully planned maneuvers and much more a sudden eruption of long-smoldering discontent. Most "wildcat" strikes are of this nature. These are strikes unauthorized by the central executive body of the union. Their leaders are not the formally authorized union leaders (or, if they are, they are defying the central authority) and their objectives, if they are formulated at all, may be quite different from the union's objectives. One student of wildcat strikes suggests that the wildcat strike constitutes the workers' expression of aggression against a management that has failed to give them a proper hearing and whose treatment of the workers has been construed by them as a run-around.[61] By the same token, wildcat strikes could serve to tell the national office of the union that the local members would not be controlled by it. While the "causes" of the strike may appear trivial—the reassignment

---

[60] See "Problems of Viewpoints," in Kornhauser, Dubin, and Ross, eds., *Industrial Conflicts*.

[61] Alvin W. Gouldner, *Wildcat Strike* (Yellow Springs, Ohio: Antioch Press, 1954). See also Jerome F. Scott and George C. Homans, "Reflections on the Wildcat Strikes," *American Sociological Review*, Vol. 12 (1947), pp. 278-87.

of a man or the installation of a new machine—the real import of the strike is to give the members a sense of having made themselves felt, of no longer being pushed around.

Over the years, the larger corporations have increasingly accepted unions as part of the industrial landscape, even if a sometimes unwelcome part, and the bitter and bloody conflicts of the past have disappeared (except in the South and Southwest, where there is still virulent resistance to unionization). Increasingly, law and administrative procedure, as represented in the work of the National Labor Relations Board and the comparable state boards, take the place of litigation and fights between pickets and police. Except in crucial industries, such as steel or transport, where strikes can bring the whole national economy grinding to a halt, or in such sensitive areas as education or social work, where the public is apt to be shocked by unexpected militancy, strikes are more and more likely to go unnoticed by those not directly concerned.

It is difficult to determine how costly a strike is to the national economy. On the one hand, a strike may have some positive effects on the economy. Production may have been stepped up in anticipation of the strike or may be increased in one locality because there is a strike in another. The end of a strike may be followed by greatly increased production, as manufacturers work to catch up with the backlog of orders. The strike may simply have replaced an otherwise inevitable layoff in an industry where a full year's production would not be sold, as is reported to have been the case with many strikes in the coal fields. On the other hand, a strike may be extremely costly to the men involved, who may lose most of their savings; it may shut down plants not themselves involved in the strike but which use the materials made by a striking plant; it may force merchants in a strike area to close, or else to extend unlimited credit; and it may strain the budget of public assistance agencies.

Irritation with a particular strike or with a wave of strikes sometimes leads to demands that strikes be eliminated. This could be accomplished if the government were given power, as it is in some Western countries, to arbitrate all differences. Managements generally oppose government arbitration, not only because strikes are a good excuse for price increases, but because they are jealous of any restrictions on their own power to settle affairs. Organized labor almost always opposes compulsory arbitration, believing that the strike or the threat of a strike is its most effective weapon, and often its only effective weapon, in dealing with management. But for the union the strike is very much a two-edged weapon, damaging not only to a firm but also to the workers and to their families (management personnel, however, continue on salary throughout the course of a strike). It seems, therefore, that the most rational strategy from the union standpoint often is to use the threat of a strike while avoiding an actual walkout.

Middle Management and White-Collar Jobs

Some leaders of large industrial unions, as they contemplate the decreasing membership of their unions, and the increasing number of technical, white-collar, and middle-management personnel—the draftsmen, accountants, salesmen, office managers, and junior executives who make up more and more of our urban labor force—wonder if the future of unionization does not lie in the organization of these lower- and middle-level "mind workers." Yet, with only occasional exceptions, such workers have been extremely difficult to unionize. The problem, as many union people have noted, is that men and women in these ranks do not think of themselves as "workers" set off from management by opposing interests and absence of sympathy. Rather they think of themselves as full-fledged members of their organization, identify themselves with top management, and feel, in fact, more kinship with professionals and top executives than with manual workers, though their income would place them with the latter.

To quite an extent individuals in these occupational slots can be characterized, as foremen have been, as "men in the middle." Many observers of the contemporary scene have suggested that, while the top executives and professional men have a good deal of freedom in terms of how and when they do their work, and while the blue-collar workers have another kind of freedom, in that their jobs do not depend on their maintaining an acceptable social reputation, those in most white-collar jobs have neither the elbow room of the top nor that of the bottom. Erich Fromm has written with passionate intensity about the emptiness of the lives of junior executives, salesmen, and other suburbanites in the United States today.[62] C. Wright Mills quotes George Orwell's salesman-hero in *Coming Up For Air*:

> In every one of those little stucco boxes there's some poor bastard who's never free except when he's fast asleep and dreaming he's got the boss down the bottom of a well and is bunging lumps of coal at

---

[62] Erich Fromm, *The Sane Society* (New York: Holt, 1955).

him. Of course the basic trouble with people like that is that we all imagine we've got something to lose.[63]

And Mills himself goes on to describe the constricted and anemic life of many people in middle-class occupations, especially of those who work in large organizations, where great emphasis is put on ability to work with others:

> In many strata of white-collar employment, such traits as courtesy, helpfulness, and kindness, once intimate, are now part of the impersonal means of livelihood. Self-alienation is thus an accompaniment of . . . alienated labor. . . . When white-collar people get jobs, they sell not only their time and energy but their personalities as well.[64]

Mills, in his general indictment, neglects somewhat the concrete differences in the climate of organizations: one department store may demand a submissive conformity and fake amiability from all its employees, while another may welcome or permit a wider spectrum of behavior. Some oil companies, for example, maintain an atmosphere of kindly paternalism toward their administrative staff, even maintaining lunchrooms in which food is sold below cost. Of course even these "permissive" organizations may be subtly constricting in their bland assumption that those who set policy for the organization know best, and in their equating the questioning of policy with disloyalty.[65] Other companies, including some in highly competitive fields, such as automobile manufacturing, demand that an executive "deliver," and woe to him whose work seems less than adequate. Since some companies are run by sales people, others by men whose background is accounting, and still others by production people, the organizational climate will vary from company to company.

Many middle-level, white-collar employees are in positions where they need no special skill (except perhaps an amorphous administrative "know-how") but rather are hired for their personalities. Their tenure depends on getting the job done while still "getting along"

---

[63] C. Wright Mills, *White Collar* (New York: Oxford University Press, 1951), p. xi.

[64] *Ibid.*, p. xvii.

[65] For a description of life as a member of such an organization, see Alan Harrington, *Life in the Crystal Palace* (New York: Knopf, 1959). There are always some individuals who, because of their own personal qualities, can function in any situation with a subjective sense of freedom, and there are other individuals who may be fortunate in finding in their work situation just the combination of constriction and support that suits their personalites; much depends on the specific person and the specific job.

with those above and around them in the organization and with the organization's customers. They are hired less because of a specific gift than because of a general social facility. Those who have specialized skills are perhaps less accountable for their personalities; yet even bookkeepers, cashiers, or nurses are expected not only to perform specific tasks, but to be good members of their organization. The question for them is how much freedom they have to be themselves and to concentrate on their work rather than on subtle interplay with their co-workers.

Outside the sphere of the white-collar worker's specific duties, how does he relate himself to the organization within which his work life is embedded? Does the organization, like Big Brother, demand his allegiance to unexplained and apparently inexplicable directives? Or does he have some say in or at least some understanding of company policies? Also, do the aims of every organization really make sense to its members? Some organizations turn out unquestionably valuable products or services, but others turn out products that, while commercially rewarded, are dispensable, if not actually parasitic. Such questions haunt many who work in advertising; they must either separate themselves from their work or justify advertising as being important to the economy, or else become cynical about their own relationship to society. Analogous questions may haunt the more reflective workers in the defense industries, who are paid to invent, prepare, and maintain devices that may result in a contaminated or even a decimated world.

Compared to these questions concerning ultimate ends, the issue of conformity, now so commonly raised, seems far less important. Depending on one's perspective, one may poke fun at or express fear of large organizations because all their male employees wear white shirts or dark suits or cultivate a certain careful informality when addressing each other. William H. Whyte's *The Organization Man* has helped give rise to this discussion and has led to a certain amount of exaggeration, beyond its own penetrating statement, of the degree of conformity usually required in these matters, such as the now common idea that the wives of management personnel must pass muster before their husbands can be promoted.[66] Issues of this sort can easily shift the focus of attention away from the deeper significance of the meaning of the job to the more superficial level of

---

[66] Whyte, *The Organization Man.* "Society As Hero," pp. 287-88, was perhaps the first and most influential statement of this theme. Other writers, including Louis Kronenberger, in his *Company Manners* (Indianapolis: Bobbs-Merrill, 1954), have developed and elaborated it.

freedom to disobey minor rituals of organizational etiquette. At the same time, this preoccupation with conformity and nonconformity could be an attempt to give shape to a vaguely sensed malaise in the relation of the individual to himself, to others, and to his work, which perhaps is endemic within organizational contexts even while the stability of relationships within organizations can protect the individual and support his work.

Acceptance by co-workers is necessary to effective performance as an organizational member. In the particular form of large-scale organization that has developed in the United States, informal ties based on mutual acceptance carry a great deal of the organizational load.[67] Yet though one needs acceptance to get one's work done, dependence on this "being liked" for a sense of well-being is unnecessary and may make organizational work distasteful and, for some, painful.

The need to feel some independence of those with whom one works, while retaining good cooperative relations, is only one of the difficulties intrinsic to many organizational jobs. Members of organizations must also be able to delegate authority while retaining responsibility; to display initiative without violating the limitations of their prerogatives; and to ask help from others when needed, while maintaining a reputation for competence. They must resolve these and other conflicting pressures day in and day out through the work year.[68]

No one really knows how widespread these difficulties are, nor how keenly they are felt. It has been contended that those who write on social issues, themselves intellectuals sensitive to the world around them, read their own discontents into the lives of others. Certainly, there are great differences among individuals: people of different temperaments and training will interpret the "same" experiences quite differently. Still, it would be a mistake to dismiss as a mere epiphenomenon the unrest that often shows up in the lives of middle-level people, as they comment on the inner bleakness of what is apparently a "good life"; and equally it would be a mistake to blame "the sub-

---

[67] There have been a great many case studies of American organizations. An extensive listing is given by Delbert C. Miller, in his "Industry and the Worker," in Henry Borow, ed., *Man in a World at Work* (Boston: Houghton Mifflin, 1964), pp. 107-09.

[68] For a careful and detailed discussion of the difficulties which may be encountered by the member of an organization, see Robert L. Kahn *et al.*, *Organizational Stress: Studies in Role Conflict and Ambiguity* (New York: Wiley & Sons, 1964), especially Chapter 18, "Conflict and Attempted Solution," pp. 337-74.

urbs" or "conformity" for this unrest. Here as elsewhere we find that the nature of one's work is inextricably a part of a total social context.

The Managerial and Professional Stratum

To the blue-collar worker a managerial or professional job seems so desirable that he may think of it as not being work at all. For one thing, the sense of working under external compulsion, which may be so oppressive within the factory, is less likely to be present; also, there is generally some basis for a sense of personal accomplishment, tasks may be varied and intrinsically interesting, and often the position may bring with it great prestige within the community. We have already noted that most men in managerial and professional occupations would continue in their present work even if they did not have to work to earn a living. This is not an unassailable test of the value of an occupation—for one thing, an occupation may narrow a man's interest to the point that he does not know what else to do with himself—but still it is clear that the professions and the managerial tasks have attractions of their own and are not clung to merely because no better work is available.

The problems that must be coped with by men in these positions differ substantially from those of the industrial worker whose day is spent at a disliked task in a subordinate position. Rather, they have to do with the very great personal commitment to one's work required by these occupations; self-esteem depends on accomplishment and its recognition, while baffled frustration awaits the man who achieves neither. There is strong pressure for an individual to evaluate success not only in terms of a job, but in terms of a career, the sequence of jobs that, ideally, will be ever increasing in responsibility and prestige. Professionals and managers run the risk that because of personal error, incapacity, or plain bad luck their career may come to a halt. In many professional and managerial situations this risk is very great:

> A doctor's career consists of an up grade, a plateau, and a down grade. Doctors don't usually discuss the reasons for the down grade. Partly it is the competition of the younger men coming in. Partly it is a matter of patients retiring the doctor. Many doctors end up with a shriveled practice. . . .[69]

---

[69] Oswald Hall, "The Stages of a Medical Career," in Nosow and Form, eds., Man, Work, and Society, p. 482. See, also, in this collection, the article by Dero A. Saunders, "Executive Discontent," pp. 461-67.

There is some logic in discussing the managerial and professional occupations together, beyond the fact that they carry about the same social ranking and that each is concerned with career lines. The managerial occupation is becoming more and more professionalized: such distinctively professional institutions as the graduate school and the professional journal have found their place in the business world. The modern manager is no longer a man who has built and is running his own business, but instead is a paid employee whose stake in ownership is likely to be minimal (although stock option plans give him a speculative take in profits). While he may receive a handsome salary and perquisites and may feel surrounded by the trappings of rank, he can seldom afford to be autocratic; he must exercise his power with restraint and tact. The most successful managers, like the most successful professionals, are concerned primarily with doing their work well and not simply with making money.[70]

The job of the modern manager is only in part measured by the firm's balance sheet. The manager must maintain in the black his company's reputation among suppliers, consumers, stockholders, employees, government agencies, and the general public. Coping with all these publics is often more than a full-time job, and managers frequently pay for the stimulus their responsibilities give them by working 70-hour weeks with a good deal of their limited "leisure" devoted to their jobs. Some businessmen, asked their hobby, would respond, "work," and insist that not only do they work constantly, but it is only at work that they truly enjoy themselves. Some professions, too, require long hours: Wilensky reports that only a fifth of all lawyers and a quarter of professors work *fewer* than 45 hours per week.[71] When such men are forced to retire, though they may have more than adequate financial resources, they are often bereft of psychological ones. If they have been successful enough in their business or profession to have the power to do so, they may phase their retirement gradually, always maintaining enough touch with affairs so that they may feel in the swim of things. A few retired businessmen have been able to spend their declining years in government or other public service, and a few retired professors have become emeriti at universities that might not have been able to attract their services earlier in their careers.

---

[70] See William Henry, "The Business Executive: A Study of the Psychodynamics of a Social Role," *American Journal of Sociology,* Vol. 54 (1949), pp. 286-91.

[71] Harold L. Wilensky, "The Uneven Distribution of Leisure: The Impact of Economic Growth on 'Free Time,'" in Erwin O. Smigel, ed., *Work and Leisure* (New Haven: College and University Press, 1963), pp. 107-45.

The self-employed professional can often work as long as he cares to, since he does not belong to a bureaucracy that forcibly retires him at a certain age. His job remains as long as patients, clients, or students continue to come to him. But America values youth and vigor as well as age and wisdom, and a lawyer may well find himself losing clients before he begins losing cases. In fact the dependence of the professional man on his customers or clients always has elements of tension in it, no matter how much these may be glossed over by friendliness and tact on both sides; [72] the clients will judge the professional's competence without understanding how to do so, and the professional, though he may reject their conclusion, will prosper or fail according to it.

That the professions are freely chosen is by no means the unalloyed good it might seem at first. Just as in one's choice of husband or wife, one's choice of profession is sometimes misguided and this is the more likely as the profession, unlike the future spouse, allows for no "getting acquainted," but demands full commitment simply on the basis of its public image. These images frequently prove false; medicine, for example, seems to provide unrivaled opportunity for service, but the medical student must in the course of training learn to see his patients as problems as well as persons, and the doctor as someone with a function rather than a mission.[73] Often the problems that will be met in the course of the career are not visible to aspirants, whose models may be furnished by the most prominent "stars" of the career. Thus, Lawrence Kubie, a psychiatrist, has argued that the scientific career and its hazards are little understood by the young people attracted to it. He believes they underestimate the length of time they will be forced to live on inadequate salaries, and even more important, the possibility that they may devote themselves to science without ever realizing the reward of making a significant contribution to their field.[74]

The fact that occupations look different to the occupant than they did to the aspirant is of greater importance in the professions and in the managerial ranks then it is elsewhere in the occupational world,

[72] Everett C. Hughes, "Work and the Self," in John H. Rohrer and Muzafer Sherif, eds., *Social Psychology at the Crossroads* (New York: Harper, 1951).

[73] See Howard S. Becker and Blanche Geer, "The Fate of Idealism in Medical School," *American Sociological Review*, Vol. 23, No. 1 (February, 1958), pp. 50-56. See also, for the extent to which psychiatry seems to promise intimate communication and then erects barriers to its being a two-way process, Allan Wheelis, *The Quest for Identity* (New York: Norton, 1958).

[74] Lawrence S. Kubie, "Psychoneurotic Problems of the American Scientist," *Chicago Review*, Vol. 8, No. 3 (1954), pp. 65-80.

both because in these ranks more time is spent at work, and because the commitment to the specific tasks is more important in the formation of the individual's identity. To be sure, in many professional careers, it is possible to shift one's actual activities without a drastic change of occupational title. A physician, for example, may decide that he doesn't really like to have to deal with patients and may become a research man in a hospital, or become an anesthesiologist dealing with patients only when they are "out," or find a new career as a hospital administrator or as the editor of a medical journal. But these shifts always require one to find new colleagues and to develop new skills, in the process hazarding whatever reputation one has already developed. As one gets older, shifting becomes increasingly difficult. Of course, it is not only in the professions that people are in effect frozen into their jobs by the contingencies of their careers. A machinist might want to try his hand at a business of his own but hesitates to lose his seniority at his present factory job. Many occupations—most of the managerial and professional occupations and many in entertainment and in sales—require maintenance of a large number of "contacts"; the individual who leaves any of these fields for a time risks not being able to return.[75]

Each occupation within the managerial and professional group has its own distinct career line, and some of these are more likely to permit the realization of hopes for success than are others. Some career lines are marked by early rises and high plateaus, as is the case in many areas of government service. Others provide a relatively steady increase in responsibilities and rewards and a degree of advancement for all those who overcome the hurdles of entry; some parts of the academic profession, with steady progression from fairly elevated floor to moderate ceiling may illustrate this pattern. The academic profession may also illustrate the divergencies that exist even within what to an outsider might appear to be a single occupation. In the sciences an unusually able and successful man may become a full professor, running an enormous operation, while in his early 30's; an equally able and equally well-regarded man teaching Greek, on the other hand, may be unable to advance until that time when an already occupied position will be vacated by the death or retirement of the incumbent.

The progress of one's career may be assessed by matching how far one has progressed against one's age or length of time in the field.

---

[75] See, in this connection, Fred E. Katz, "Occupational Contact Networks," in Nosow and Form, eds., *Man, Work, and Society,* pp. 317-21.

Executives, for example, sometimes say that the man who has not entered top management by the age of 40 will never enter it at all. As people age, their aspirations often shrink to meet the "reality" they have come to perceive, and this is as true of professionals and managers as it is of industrial workers. They may then redefine professional success in terms of their personal relations with clients, or their ability to support their family and lead a pleasant life away from work. Since we tend to know more about the frustrations of the literate and articulate, it is sometimes believed that men in professional and managerial occupations lead lives that are particularly harried and full of tension. But comparative studies seem to indicate clearly that the chances, if not for happiness, then for contentment, are on the whole greater in these more elevated strata.[76]

To balance our discussion of the meaning of a career we should add that a career consists of more than the reflected images of glory or of failure associated with having attained a certain outward status. This is certainly one aspect of the story, which shows up in a lack of attention to the work itself and to its potential challenges and exhilarations, and in an often excessive attention to the egocentric self engaged in doing the work—a misplaced focus that leads to boredom and anxiety. But one's career is not only the trace-line of one's journey through life; a running record of places and statuses, tasks and rewards; a skeleton autobiography. It may also furnish a rationale for life, a sense of whether one's work is at every phase related to one's ultimate aims and one's growing abilities. The professional and the managerial occupations are unique in that they permit the individual to hope that his efforts will be cumulative, that his jobs taken altogether may represent a coherent contribution to some end. Thus, the priest hopes not only to become a bishop, but also to save souls; the doctor not only to "make good" in the conventional sense, but also to save lives; and the business executive not only to "get to the top," but also to contribute to the functioning of his society.

Unemployment

In an earlier day, unemployment was discussed in terms of the business cycle, and economists took it for granted that economic booms brought full employment whereas depression brought unemploy-

---

[76] See, for example, the data quoted by Gerald Gurin, Joseph Veroff, and Sheila Feld in *America Looks At Its Mental Health* (New York: Basic Books, 1960), especially in Chapter VI, "The Job."

ment. Today government and business planning have tended to smooth out the business cycle, but, to the dismay of many, without eliminating unemployment. As a result, some observers have come to the conclusion that unemployment now reflects long-term structural changes in the economy. There is much support for this view, including the fact that against a background of a generally expanding economy and high employment levels, there are yet large groups of men in certain regions of the nation and in certain strata of our cities, who cannot find jobs no matter how hard they try. Some experts insist that this is still a business cycle problem and that unemployment could be mitigated, if not entirely eliminated, through increases in the purchasing power of consumers. Producers would then be forced to employ more men to turn out the greater volume of goods needed to meet increased demand. Other observers note, however, that many large corporations are now able to increase their output all the while cutting the size of their labor force. Hence, increased demand might very well be met with only minimal increases in staff.

Unemployment today, because of its concentration in certain regions and in a few demographic categories, appears to differ from the unemployment of an earlier day (e.g., in the Great Depression) when almost every field (with the possible exception of social work) was affected, and when even new college graduates worried about what they might do. Not only was a fourth of the working force without jobs, but whole careers were without jobs: there were no buildings for architects or engineers to plan, few houses to be bought and sold, no boats to be built, and few citizens affluent enough to hire a lawyer, or a music teacher, or to send their children to a dentist. In that epoch, college-trained people took jobs as post office clerks just to be sure of work. For millions there were simply no jobs at all, although reactionaries, opposed to government help for the unemployed, continued to claim that anyone who really wanted to work could find a job.[77]

---

[77] One of the authors (D. R.), while a law student in the 1930's, decided to test the belief of his prosperous New England friends that the unemployed were lazy and "anybody who wants to work can get a job." He naively took off in workmen's clothes for Detroit and Chicago in search of a job. After tramping the streets and lining up at plants, he caught nothing except the flu and the only job he came close to was a very temporary one, helping a street vender sell fruit. In a short spell spent in a federal transient shelter, hastily constructed in Detroit when local relief gave out, he encountered destitute though surprisingly undesperate men who had worked for years as electricians, pattern-makers, miners, or farmers, and who had left their families (whose snapshots they still carried in their pockets) to mingle with hoboes and bums in a wandering and desultory search for nonexistent work.

TABLE 9

Unemployment: Annual Average, 1900-1963

Year	Percent	Year	Percent	Year	Percent	Year	Percent
1900	5	1916	5	1932	24	1948	3
1901	2	1917	5	1933	25	1949	6
1902	3	1918	1	1934	22	1950	5
1903	3	1919	2	1935	20	1951	3
1904	5	1920	4	1936	17	1952	3
1905	3	1921	12	1937	14	1953	2
1906	1	1922	8	1938	19	1954	5
1907	2	1923	3	1939	17	1955	4
1908	8	1924	6	1940	15	1956	4
1909	5	1925	4	1941	10	1957	4
1910	6	1926	2	1942	5	1958	7
1911	6	1927	4	1943	2	1959	6
1912	5	1928	4	1944	1	1960	6
1913	4	1929	3	1945	2	1961	7
1914	8	1930	9	1946	4	1962	6
1915	10	1931	16	1947	4	1963	6

Sources: Years 1900-1957 from Bureau of the Census, *Historical Statistics of the United States, Colonial Times to 1957* (Washington, D. C.), Series D 46-47, p. 73. Years 1958-1963 from Bureau of the Census, *Statistical Abstract of the United States: 1964*, 85th ed. (Washington, D. C., 1964), pp. 229-32.

The pool of unemployed was not finally absorbed in this country until our entry into World War II, first as an arsenal of the allies and then as a belligerent. The war showed that it was possible for the American economy, despite a greatly reduced labor force, to produce both guns and butter in quantities hitherto deemed impossible by all but a few visionaries, and to move, in only a few years, from bust to boom. One result of this economic lesson may be that no government in this country will permit a depression of the scope of earlier downturns to develop: the success of the 1964 reduction in taxes as a spur to economic activity supports this belief. However, as Table 9 shows, not since 1953 has unemployment been down to the 2 or 3 percent that economists call "frictional unemployment"—the unemployment considered unavoidable as workers change jobs, or as temporary layoffs are caused by annual modal changes, bad weather, or the failure of a particular business in an otherwise prosperous industry.[78] (Table 9, it should be noted, does not separate

---

[78] For a general discussion of unemployment, frictional and otherwise, see Neal W. Chamberlain, *Labor* (New York: McGraw-Hill, 1958). Material on the nature of unemployment today is given by Harry Caudill, *Night Comes to the Cumberland* (Boston: Little, Brown, 1963); Michael Harrington, *The Other*

urban unemployment from rural unemployment, though rural unemployment is typically underemployment: two or three family members doing work which, if there were greater opportunity or better use of resources, would be done by one. An unemployment figure of around 5 percent may seem low when compared with the staggering unemployment rate of the 1930's, but it means that three or four million people are without work and unable to find it. Unemployment rates by themselves, however, may be misleading because they assume that unemployment is spread more or less evenly throughout the labor force. A level of 5 percent, for example, suggests that if a man looked hard enough, he could find a job. That this is not the case is made clear by the fact that within some groups, especially nonwhites who have little education, 20 percent or more are without jobs. For members of these groups jobs are as hard to find as they were for many men during the Great Depression.

Unemployment affects not only an individual's income, but again, because of what work means in America, his self-respect as well. To quote from a study that followed the later experiences of men who had lost their jobs when their factories closed down:

> The unemployed man or woman who is responsible for his own livelihood and that of others can come to feel that there is no place in industry for him. He can lose confidence in himself. In his search for a scapegoat he may take his frustration out on his family. As the wife of a former . . . worker put it: "My husband never used to get upset at anything, but since the shutdown he's been hell on me and on the kids." Even more likely is a feeling of bitterness toward the system that permits a man to work in a plant for many years only to be displaced from his job and to find that his age and industrial experience count against him in the job market. . . . For the older worker, particularly, lengthy unemployment is apt to be a traumatic shock. His age, as a result of long company service and the seniority system, had given him an advantage in moving to higher-paying jobs. When permanently laid off, however, age suddenly becomes an economic disadvantage.[79]

The authors go on to point out that unemployment disrupts a man's view of himself and his role in his family, removes one of his

America (New York: Macmillan, 1962); and Ewan Clague, _Profile of Unemployment_ (Washington, D. C.: U.S. Department of Labor, 1963). These three books present very different treatments of unemployment: the first, a moving description of life in one depressed area; the second, equally concrete, eloquent, polemical, and highly influential; the third, factual and detailed.

[79] Richard C. Wilcock and Walter H. Franke, _Unwanted Workers_ (New York: Free Press, 1963), p. 85.

most important ties to the economic and social system, and, to cap it all, stigmatizes the individual as "somebody who isn't working."

Among the unemployed it is the young single man who suffers least when out of work. He generally has friends also without work, and he has not yet formed a sense of himself as essentially a worker and head of a family. The older head of a family suffers most, particularly if his role in the family is dependent on his being the source of income and if he experiences real rejection as a result of unemployment. The head of a family always finds unemployment an attack on his role; how he withstands the attack depends on the resilience of his character and the flexibility of his relations with others. At its worst, unemployment can be among the most tragic of the events that may befall a family.[80]

The process of finding a job is not an easy one no matter what the occupation of the individual. For the blue-collar worker in a community where jobs are scarce, particularly if there is something about him that suggests to the employing staff that he is less than thoroughly desirable, the job-finding process may be harrowing. Applications may be made to dozens of plant employment offices, friends and relatives may be canvassed for a lead, and both public and private employment agencies may be consulted. If all these efforts fail, the man may eventually settle down at home—dispirited, bitter, perhaps maintaining a faint hope that he will yet hear of something. An older worker who has been laid off may find that he has, in fact, been retired from the labor market.[81]

Unemployment is not leisure. The unemployed man does not increase his reading, or take part in neighborhood activities to a greater extent than he did when working, nor does he spend much more time playing with his children. Typically, he withdraws from social contact except for an occasional conversation with other men in the same situation. An unemployed man, quite apart from financial difficulties, is only in an ironic sense a man of leisure.[82]

Observations of men out of work today correspond in every way to observations made during the Depression. In fact, it may be that the unemployed man is in even a more painful situation when his

---

[80] See Robert C. Angell, *The Family Encounters the Depression* (New York: Scribner, 1936).

[81] Wilcock and Franke, *Unwanted Workers*, pp. 94-126.

[82] The inability of the unemployed to treat their now unoccupied time as leisure has been noted repeatedly, perhaps first by Marie Jahoda, *Die Arbeitslosen von Marienthal* (Leipzig, Germany: S. Hirzel, 1933). See also E. Wight Bakke, *Citizens Without Work* (New Haven: Yale University Press, 1940).

community is generally prosperous. There will be few who share his situation and with whom he can talk; also, he cannot easily explain away his unemployment when being interviewed by a prospective employer: if there is no general unemployment, then something must be wrong with the individual. In this situation, there is a tendency for long-term unemployment to feed on itself, and the longer the individual is out of work, the poorer his chances of finding a job, or at any rate of finding a job as good as the one at which he last worked.

These observations cannot, however, be extrapolated to an important group in the "new" unemployment—the young men who have no experience with employment and cannot find a first job. Official Labor Department figures place the rate of unemployment among teen-agers in the labor force across the country at 16 percent and add that teen-agers make up about a quarter of all unemployment. Within the Negro group the report described the situation as "dramatically worse": 23 percent of the Negro teen-age boys and 31 percent of the Negro teen-age girls who were in the labor force were unemployed in 1964.[83] It should be remembered that the government definition of unemployment requires that one be actively looking for work. If the total of unemployed included those youngsters who were so discouraged by their poor prospects that they only sporadically searched for work the figures would be much higher.[84]

A number of programs supported by the national and local government have been developed to help young people enter the occupational system. The nature of the programs has depended on the diagnosis of the difficulty. Almost all observers agree that a key difficulty is insufficient education. In the words of one observer of the

---

[83] *The New York Times,* March 4, 1965.

[84] Negroes, with the possible exception of a fortunate few who become beneficiaries of societal attempts to make amends, and despite the recent civil rights legislation, are severely discriminated against by the job world. In every field, the salaries of Negroes are lower than those of whites, and where figures are available it is clear that the unemployment level of Negroes is much higher than that of whites. Whitney Young, a Negro spokesman, after noting that it is easy to find jobs for the exceptionally able Negro, says this to businessmen: ". . . we run out of Lena Hornes and Ralph Bunches pretty fast. But we know that you have some jobs for ordinary, even dumb, white people, and we want some of those jobs too. We have some ordinary dumb Negroes, and we need jobs all up and down—for the whole group." See his "Jobs and Income," in Eli Ginzberg, ed., *The Negro Challenge to the Business Community* (New York: McGraw-Hill, 1965). For many reasons, including social conscience within American industry and education, this situation is changing rapidly and cannot be summed up in a simple estimate. Increasingly institutions attempt, with varying degrees of inventiveness and commitment, to compensate for inferior early education and continuing social discrimination.

situation in New York City, "If you can't get through college, you are a problem. If you can't get through high school, you are hopeless. There is almost nothing the non-high-school graduate can do." Because so many high school graduates are looking for work, employers tend to require a high school diploma for a stock clerk, an errand boy, in fact any job at all. To an extent, racial discrimination results from this practice since Negro and Puerto Rican youths are more likely than white youths to drop out of school before high school graduation. But employers who require high school diplomas may have some arguments on their side. When high school education is available for the asking to those youths who are able to function in the school system, failure to get a diploma suggests a certain alienation from the larger society. Programs that will keep youths in school, at least to the end of high school, are, therefore, one way of trying to meet the problem. Mobilization for Youth, in New York City, which is supported both federally and by the city, has attempted to develop a program which might remedy some of the reading and learning difficulties that cause some youths to drop out of school, though the success of this program is not yet established. One may argue that youths should not be forced to continue in the uncomfortable role of student only because possession of a diploma is being used by employers to sort out desirable and undesirable applicants. Yet perhaps all education, even the most dispirited, is potentially of value to everyone.

Other current programs for jobless youth begin with the assessment that the difficulty is that these young people's experiences with work have been so discouraging that their current attitudes toward it are thoroughly negative; in consequence, they are either unable to convince a potential employer of their worth, or, if by some chance they should be hired, unable to perform responsibly. At least two of the programs in President Johnson's antipoverty effort are animated in part by this belief—the Neighborhood Youth Corps, which offers to youths no longer in school on-the-job training as machinists, garage workers, and clerical workers; and the Job Corps, which has aims similar to those of the Youth Corps, but will move young people away from home to camps and centers.[85] The question is whether experience with either of these programs will make a youth more attractive to a prospective employer. Still other suggestions have been made, including that of offering two or three years of occupation-directed education at the high school or junior college level to currently unemployed and

---

[85] *The New York Times,* January 17, 1965.

unemployable youths.[86] Although each of these programs—keeping students in school until they get at least a high school diploma, helping them get actual work experience, and giving them vocational skills—has arguments in its favor, one cannot help but wonder whether these programs are responsive to the real problem, which may be that there are not enough jobs which do not require more technical training than could be furnished in the course of two or three years vocational schooling. It may be that some youths are going to be out of work, no matter what. If this is the case, then the Job Corps takes on another meaning and becomes a way of using constructively the energies of youth rather than a way of preparing them for the private labor market. And increased education becomes a way of using constructively the time of still other young people for whom there is no call from the labor market.

Perhaps we must face the possibility that we will be unable to develop jobs for these young people, or for others among our unemployed, and that we must nevertheless ensure them some means of support. John K. Galbraith has argued that people out of work through no fault of their own should receive an income very close to that which they would normally make. He points out that such an income would support the economy as a whole, while preventing hardships to individuals. He notes also that most men want to work and that few would exploit opportunities for paid nonwork.[87] To an extent we have begun such a program, with Unemployment Insurance which pays up to 50 percent of a once-employed man's former wages, for a limited time. We may, in fact, be moving, unevenly, in this direction.

Technological Change: Automation

At several points in this chapter we have remarked in passing on the effect of technological change, especially that due to automation. Let us now turn our full attention to automation, to discuss what it is, and what its implications are for us.

The promise of automation is that it will rid us of work which is

---

[86] Grant Venn, *Man, Education, and Work: Postsecondary Vocational and Technical Education* (Washington, D. C.: American Council on Education, 1964).

[87] John K. Galbraith, *The Affluent Society* (Boston: Houghton Mifflin, 1958). However, the argument that most men want to work and so would not exploit support during a period when they could not find work may be inaccurate in relation to the young people who have not yet worked. They may well have established other ways of gaining recognition or, perhaps, have become accustomed to the inability to find support for a sense of worth in the larger society.

exploitive, destructive of human powers, or demeaning; that without an increase in the work force, more and better products will become possible; and that with its aid, processes, such as almost instant information retrieval, which would otherwise be visionary, will become everyday realities. The threat of automation is the ending of jobs and the misery this can bring. There is much controversy today about the extent to which automation does in fact imply a great reduction in the jobs in the society. On the one hand there are observers who assert that automation has already helped bring about a serious reduction in the number of jobs.[88] In contrast other observers believe that the threat of automation has been greatly exaggerated, that it is being introduced slowly, and even where it is introduced, does not appreciably decrease management's need for people, though it may change the jobs management has for them to do.[89]

Secretary of Labor Wirtz has asserted that we have not as yet enough experience or evidence to allow us to judge the meaning of automation: "The conclusions so far reached about the manpower implications of automation are actually compounded very little of re-

[88] Leon Keyserling, in testimony to Congress, took the position that jobs are *created* by somehow giving purchasing power to those who would consume the products of our economy, including the aged and the poor, while jobs are *erased* by automation. He suggests further that our present economic policies are such that "the private demand for goods and services, and the public demand for goods and services, are not keeping up with the investment in plant and equipment." See his testimony in *Hearings Before the Joint Economic Committee, Congress of the United States,* Part I (Washington, D. C.: U.S. Government Printing Office, 1965), p. 137. A very strong statement of the extent to which automation threatens the job structure was offered by "The Ad Hoc Committee on the Triple Revolution," and appears in the U.S. Congress, House Committee on Education and Labor, *Report of the National Commission on Technology, Automation, and Economic Progress* (Washington, D. C.: U.S. Government Printing Office, 1964), pp. 125-35. Donald M. Michael has also pointed to the dangers of automation in a number of influential articles. See his "Automation: The Silent Conquest," in Morris Philipson, ed., *Automation: Implications for the Future* (New York: Vintage Books, 1962). Informed opinion now would seem to be that increased effort toward the attainment of national goals will absorb the potentially displaced.

[89] See, for a sharp rebuttal to the Michael article, Charles E. Silberman, "The Real News About Automation," *Fortune* (January, 1965). See also the review of the automation literature by Daniel Bell, which appeared in the *New York Review of Books,* Vol. 5, No. 2 (August 26, 1965), pp. 23-25, and the debate between Bell and Michael in the "Letters" column of a later issue of the *New York Review of Books,* Vol. 5, No. 8, pp. 36-38. Bell's position rests on two points: first, that while automation has had dramatic effects in some industries, it has not produced drastic increase in productivity for the society as a whole; and second, that the problem is not one of finding work to be done, but rather one of stimulating demand, which is a problem easily solved by appropriate fiscal policies. His position is thus not entirely unlike Keyserling's, described below, except in his assumption that the government will act to ameliorate the damage of automation, an assumption that now seems correct.

liable analysis and very largely of intuition." [90] One attempt to develop reliable estimates comes from Secretary Wirtz's own department: a study of technological trends in 36 major American industries concludes that employment prospects are mixed. Increased demand may result in employment gains in air transportation, construction, insurance, and trade. In electric power, government, steel, and motor vehicles, increased demand is likely to be offset by technological improvement. And in a variety of industries, ranging from bakery products to railroads and the space industries, technological improvement, including automation, is likely to result in employment losses.[91]

It seems abundantly clear that for a complex of reasons, prominently including automation, as well as the fact that in a competitive economy the more efficient survive, many, if not most, of the industries of our nation are able to increase production while holding relatively constant, or even decreasing, the size of their labor force. Ewan Clague, Commissioner of Labor Statistics, has said:

> If we use 1953 as a base (with an index number of 100) we find that the gross national product in the first quarter of 1964 had risen about 40% while at the same time the index of employment had risen only 12%.
>
> The stumbling block is that over the same period, the nation's labor force (those employed and those seeking employment) increased 15%.[92]

The "gross national product" is a measure of the goods and services produced in our country obtained by adding together the sales of business enterprises, the increase of business inventories, and the value of services rendered to individuals and the government.[93] Thus what Commissioner Clague is asserting is that we as a nation are increasing our production of goods and services at a remarkable rate, while we yet have not yet developed enough new jobs to take care of the new people we are adding to the labor force.

What is automation? We can do no better than quote the discussion of a congressional committee:

> Automation is the third phase in the development of technology that began with the Industrial Revolution of the eighteenth century. First

---

[90] Quoted by Irving Litner, "The Automation Era: A Mysterious Revolution Defies Generalization," *The New York Times,* January 11, 1965.

[91] U.S. Bureau of Labor Statistics, *Technological Trends in Thirty-Six Major American Industries* (Washington, D. C.: U.S. Government Printing Office, 1964).

[92] Quoted by Litner, *The New York Times.*

[93] Theodore Morgan, *Income and Employment* (Englewood Cliffs, N. J.: Prentice-Hall), pp. 56-59.

came mechanization which created the factory system and separated labor and management in production. In the early twentieth century, mass production brought the assembly line and other machinery so expensive that the ownership of industry had to be divorced from management and atomized into millions of separate share holdings. Finally, since World War II automation has added the elements of automatic control and decision making, turning the factory from a haphazard collection of machines into a single, integrated unit and requiring production on an enormous scale. Mechanization was a technology based on forms and applications of power. Mass production was a technology based on principles of production organization. Automation is a technology based on communication and control.

. . . But automation is more than a technology. It is a concept of manufacturing. It requires that the entire productive process, from raw material to final product, be analyzed so that every operation contributes most efficiently to the achievement of the goals of the enterprise. For the purpose of analysis, automation can best be defined as any continuous and integrated operation of a production system that uses electronic or other equipment to regulate and coordinate the quantity and quality of production.[94]

As is indicated in the above discussion, automation suggests something more than the continued development of labor-saving machines: it suggests also the development of *systems* integrating these machines into new and more efficient methods of production. The systems introduced by automation have never, to this date, been capable of operation entirely without human supervision; the day of the "automatic factory," the factory that turns out products without involving any men, has not yet arrived. Yet in some cases the changes in the production process associated with the introduction of automatic equipment have been so drastic that the firms have chosen to build an entirely new plant, often in a new section of the country, rather than redesign their old plant.

The different kinds of automation that have been developed might be classified in this way:

Office Automation: The handling of information involved in record-keeping, billing, etc., by means of computers and punched-card machines.

"Detroit" Automation: An assembly line, in which machines doing many separate operations are linked together by automatic devices for transferring materials.

---

[94] U.S. Congress, House Committee on Education and Labor, *Impact of Automation on Employment Report* (Washington, D. C.: U.S. Government Printing Office, 1961).

Continuous-Processing Systems: The processing of chemicals, oil, and similar substances, in treatment systems that are controlled and integrated by men reading dials and operating valves. It is said that in such systems workers may go for days without ever seeing the material being handled.

Numerical-Control Machines: Machines which can be made to perform a series of complicated operations by means of instructions punched into tape or other control devices.

The continuous-processing system was the first development of automation. In fact, as one observer notes, the oil and chemical industries were "automated" years before the term "automation" was invented.[95] Because the continuous-process plant has contributed to our sense of what an automatic factory might look like, we quote a description of such a plant:

> A continuous-process plant is quite different from a typical factory. There are no recognizable machines and very few workers visible except for a few maintenance workers in colored helmets welding or painting pipes, you see very few people doing anything and nobody making anything. Instead, one sees a large number of individual buildings with vast areas of open space between them, huge networks of pipes, and large towers and other equipment which one later learns are various types of distillation units or chemical reactors. The chemicals which are made and the oils which are refined flow through these pipes from one stage of their processing to another usually without being handled at all by the workers.[96]

In continuous processing we are willing to accept that only through equipment so imposing and awe-inspiring could the work be done at all. In "Detroit" automation we are more likely to feel that machines have taken over men's jobs:

> Among the first examples of the "Detroit" type of automation are two Brooks Park engine plants of the Ford Motor Company near Cleveland, which since 1951 have been turning out 6-cylinder engine blocks from rough castings. The castings, which are first produced in an automated foundry, are fed into a broaching machine, which then "just goes 'Whoosh' and it is done," as one startled observer described the process. . . . A rough casting goes through the line and emerges as a finished engine block in just 14.6 minutes as against 9 hours in a conventional plant.[97]

---

[95] Blauner, *Alienation and Freedom,* p. 124.
[96] *Ibid.,* pp. 124-25.
[97] John Diebold, "Congressional Testimony," in Philipson, ed., *Automation: Implications for the Future.*

Office automation and numerical-control machines are less dramatic in the extent to which machines seem in charge of the productive process, although to be sure the computers and computer-controlled production machines that these systems use are impressive enough. In office automation, the conventional rows and rows of young women sitting at desks or working on files are replaced by a computer, auxiliary machines, and a small team of specially trained technicians. In numerical-control automation the displacement of men is less marked, but the kinds of skills that are required of the men are changed, since a technician operating a programmed machine can turn out more work more quickly and with greater accuracy than a highly trained machinist.

Thus far, the impact of automation has not been catastrophic. Many organizations have minimized layoffs by relying on ordinary turnover to reduce their labor force and absorbing any displaced personnel in nonautomated positions. For example, an organization that has installed automatic equipment in its clerical department may decide not to fire anyone (though quite a few may be underemployed for a time) but simply to wait until the single women who make up the bulk of the clerical staff leave the organization to marry. Here the impact of automation is invisible, since it affects only those who might have been hired for the now nonexistent jobs. In other cases the impact of automation is felt not by the firm installing the new equipment, but by another firm, which had been a supplier of parts now produced, in the first firm, by its automatic machinery. In addition, because firms and industries are automating unevenly, at different times, and with different degrees of completeness, individuals displaced from one setting may yet find jobs in another. Nor is it always clear that automation is the factor responsible for a change in the relationship between an industry's productivity and the number of jobs it affords. Yet many industries, including the manufacture of electrical appliances, instrument production, meat production, the production of leather goods, and canning and preserving [98] show increased production with a shrinking labor force.

There can be little doubt that automation will continue to alter our technological structure. In many lines of work, not only those within factories, the introduction of automatic equipment has required people to learn new skills, or to risk technological obsolescence; occupations as diverse as cargo handling and sociological research require of those

---

[98] These examples are cited in the U.S. Congress, House Committee on Education and Labor, *Impact of Automation on Employment Report.*

who follow them that they come to terms with one form or another of the new automatic equipment. But although every occupation is likely to be affected in some way, it is the semiskilled workers, whose tasks can be performed more accurately and, in the long run, more economically by automatic equipment, and the clerical workers, who cannot begin to rival automatic equipment in either quantity or quality of work, who are most vulnerable to the inroads of automation. In contrast, personal service work, where personal contact is important (barbering, fancy restaurants), work of a craft nature (though not in every case, as the situation of the printers should remind us), and of course managers and professionals, though their jobs may change, are unlikely to be dispensed with by the economy.

Even before automation entered our social scene, science-fiction writers proposed the fantasy of a society in which work was a privilege reserved for a very few highly skilled professionals and managers, and the task of the remainder of the society was to consume the enormous product that was turned out (in sorcerer's apprentice fashion) by the automatic industrial plant. In truth, there is at present an ever increasing demand for professional and managerial personnel. Executives of all kinds are needed to manage our growing, and increasingly complex economy, despite the threat, as yet nothing more than speculation, that their functions may some day be performed by properly programmed thinking machines. The flourishing state of the professions also reflects the widespread affluence of our society; in many professions, not only medicine, but also the apparently more leisurely academic professions, the ubiquity of overwork reflects not a condition of too little pay, but rather a condition of too much demand and the difficulty professionals have in turning customers away. There is at present much more demand for professional services of almost every kind than there are people trained to provide them. Education is itself a growing industry, perhaps the most flourishing of all, with constant demand for instructors. In fact, we may find in time that the education industry has become one of the major supports for our economy, that formal education occupies the energies of more and more young people, continuing for many of them into their twenties, and that the production and distribution of knowledge become an increasing part of the everyday life of other adults.[99]

---

[99] Fritz Machlup points out that "Over the . . . nine years from 1950 to 1959, the increase in the labor force was 17%, the increase in all knowledge-producing occupations 30%, and the group of professional and technical workers grew at the fastest rate, 43%." *The Production and Distribution of Knowledge in the United States* (Princeton, N. J.: Princeton University Press, 1962), p. 388.

Examining the number and nature of jobs allocated to men today, Gerard Piel argues that we would even now be in the midst of a level of unemployment close to that of depression days were it not for our defense economy.

> The rolls of the unemployed include today the 2,500,000 in the armed forces; they are certainly not employed in the production and distribution of goods. To their numbers should be added the 1,000,000 civilian employees of the Department of Defense, whose principal employment is that of housekeeping and procurement for those in uniform. Finally, we must add the 2,500,000 workers in industry engaged in filling the procurement orders of the military. The total of those unemployed or employed outside the civilian economy thus comes to 12,000,000, close to 20% of the labor force, only 5% below the unemployment peak of 1933—and this at the time when the gross national product has reached an all time high.[100]

This suggests that our technological development has already made it possible for us to supply the products at present used by our population, while employing 80 percent of our labor force. As our technological skills develop even further, we will have to choose between greatly reducing our labor force or greatly increasing our national demand.

Automation presents us with two problems—one short-run, the other long-range. The short-run problem is how to reduce the hardships of those individuals now being displaced by automatic equipment. One proposed "solution" is to make early retirement available—much as is done by the armed services, where the rate of obsolescence of men and materiel is notoriously high. Severance pay is still another possible solution, especially if it is coupled with provisions for retraining in the new skills demanded by automatic equipment or required by other jobs if there are such, for which labor is in short supply. "Displacement Insurance" has also been recommended. Unemployment Insurance Benefits meet this need to some extent, though they are not fully satisfactory, because they supply only a part of an individual's normal income and last only a short time.[101]

It is more difficult to visualize possible solutions to the long-run problem of a society with fewer jobs than men in the labor market. One approach is to adjust men to the presumptive fact that we don't really need them. Or we may attempt to spread work by shortening

---

[100] Gerard Piel, *Consumers of Abundance,* Center for the Study of Democratic Institutions, Fund for the Republic, Inc. (Santa Barbara, Calif., 1961).

[101] Wilcock and Franke, *Unwanted Workers.* See also Warner Bloomberg, Jr., *The Age of Automation* (New York: League for Industrial Democracy, 1955).

the work week to 25 or 20 hours, and, of course, hope that the resulting inefficiencies will create still more work. Yet again, we may try to develop "labor intensive" industries—industries that by their very nature absorb many man-hours of work—such as landscape architecture or hand-crafted building façades and sidewalks. Finally, we may encourage young people to stay in school and in this way to become more highly trained and more valuable members of society while withholding their participation from the work force.[102]

Another approach, however, questions whether all the tasks of our society have been accomplished, or will be accomplished as soon as we install the proper automatic equipment. Instead, we may take the position that our problem is one of directing our energies to tasks that are as yet badly performed or unperformed. Mr. Keyserling has testified:

> We are developing two Americas. Eighty-five percent of the children in the schools in Washington, D. C. . . . are Negroes. . . . What is it a reflection of? It is a city of the poor, and so is New York, and so is Chicago. So we have two Americas, the poor people living in the cities, the well-to-do people living on the outside. The affluent people don't care, because their schools are good. Meanwhile, cities can't raise the money to finance education and to finance their other needs. . . . If we budgeted a long-range 10-year program to rebuild America and to rebuild our cities this would take care, in view of the new technology and automation, of one-half of the whole 22 to 27 million job problems over the next 10 years.[103]

Our society still finds it easier to alleviate distress than to prevent it by careful foresight and planning. Without planning, the burden of change falls unevenly on those least able to endure it. The development of the techniques of automation is a testimonial to the ingenuity of scientists, engineers, and industrial architects. The in-

---

[102] Still another way of dealing with the problems which would be posed by a society that can produce the goods and services it needs with a skeleton labor force is suggested by Professor Thomas Green of the University of Syracuse in an as yet unpublished manuscript, "Work, Leisure, and the Structure of Hope." He argues that the way people get income, whether through jobs or through government support, should be divorced from the way they contribute to the society; then, even though their job might be trivial or nonexistent, their "work" could involve them in civic activities or educational enterprises that would permit expression of important commitments and provide a basis for a sense of accomplishment.

[103] Testimony in U.S. Congress, Joint Economic Committee, *Economic Report of the President, 1965* (Washington, D. C.: U.S. Government Printing Office, 1965), pp. 140-41. We believe Mr. Keyserling's prepared statement and testimony are each worth the most careful attention. See pp. 94-159 of the *Economic Report.*

stallation of such equipment is a testimonial to the ability of many corporate managements to plan ahead, not too much hampered by the annual balance sheet that, in so many cases, forces into a short-run prison the planning of both government and business. The planning which extends beyond the corporation and looks at the labor force as a whole not only transcends our present political framework, but also our intellectual one. We hardly know how to think about such matters. The Industrial Revolution caught the Western world unawares, and we are still recovering from the shock; automation has been called the Second Industrial Revolution and, while we are still engaged in liquidating the legacy of problems from the first, we are being plunged into the second.[104]

---

[104] As this book goes to press, we have been in touch with the work of the National Commission on America's Goals and Resources of the National Planning Association, in Washington, which has sought to "cost out" the money and the labor required if we are to move toward such ambitious national goals as the eradication of poverty, the reconstruction of our cities, and the like. Their findings are that even goals which could in no sense be termed utopian would require the services of more individuals than are likely to be in our labor force in the near future, and their assessment is that despite the increase in productivity due to automation, we shall soon experience labor shortage, and not labor glut. This assessment is, of course, based on the assumption that we as a nation are embarking on an attempt to meet these national goals—an assumption we hope is correct.

12

Poverty and Disrepute

by David Matza

A SOCIOLOGICAL CONSIDERATION OF POVERTY REQUIRES AT THE OUTSET a working distinction among various kinds of poverty, and a working assessment of which varieties are *social* and *cultural* problems rather than merely economic problems. The thesis of this chapter is that disreputable poverty, and not poverty in general, presents a serious social problem to society, and a profound challenge to its capacities and ingenuity. This is not to suggest that the elimination of other forms of poverty is a simple task, or that we are making rapid progress in that endeavor. It is to suggest, however, that many forms of poverty are basically *economic* problems to be ameliorated through economic growth and appropriate governmental policy. With the exception of disreputable poverty—the kind of poverty where demoralization appears as a key feature—Robert Lampman's observation is still appropriate: "A more aggressive government policy could hasten the elimination of poverty and bring about its virtual elimination in one generation. Poverty in the economic sense is not an insuperable problem in America. Our deficiencies are of will, not capacity." [1] When demoralization has set in, when the poor become disreputable, our deficiencies are of capacity and knowledge as well as of will. The disreputable poor may be considered—indeed, they may be defined—as that limited section of the poor whose moral and social condition is relatively impervious to economic growth and progress. [2]

---

[1] Robert Lampman, "The Low-Income Population and Economic Growth," Study Paper #12 (Washington, D. C.: United States Congress Joint Economic Committee, 1959), p. 4.

[2] For a good discussion and statistical analysis of the close relationship between the decline from 1957 onward in the poverty-elimination rate, the high levels of unemployment since 1957, and the lagging rate of economic growth, see Lowell Gallaway, "The Foundations of the War on Poverty," *American Economic Review* (March, 1965), pp. 122-30.

A discussion of the varieties of poverty is facilitated—though necessarily oversimplified—by conceiving of concentric circles: the widest
circle is composed of all the poor; an intermediary circle, considerably
smaller, consists of those who are poor and on welfare assistance; and
the smallest circle, the disreputable poor, represents those who are
poor, sporadically or permanently on welfare, and, additionally, suffer
the special defects and stigma of demoralization.

Description and analysis of the disreputable poor is seriously hin-
dered by several difficulties. They are not only hard to reach, but also
hard to identify or designate in any rigorous statistical fashion. Part
of the problem is institutionally created, especially by the character
of the Aid to Families with Dependent Children program—the largest
single welfare program in America. Until very recently, this program
was limited to families in which the father, from an official standpoint,
was no longer in the home. One defect of this provision—there were
many others—was that very little information regarding the males
was officially collected. However, the more important difficulty is theoretical, and rooted in public sentiments of America and other Western nations. The aim of clearly distinguishing the disreputable poor
from others who superficially resemble them is systematically frustrated because a certain element of disrepute attaches even to the
poor who are deemed deserving and morally above reproach. Poverty
itself is slightly disreputable, and being on welfare somewhat more
disreputable. The inner circle—the so-called hard core—is not alone in
living in disrepute. That feature is shared to some extent with all who
are poor or on welfare. But the "hard core" is further along on a range
of disrepute. To the minor shortcoming of being poor is added the
more substantial vice of requiring assistance, and, finally, the major
moral defects of demoralization and immorality. These last features
are the special defects of the disreputable poor and distinguish them
from portions of the population whose moral shortcomings are more
limited and more tolerable.

The distinction between poverty, welfare, and disrepute is further
complicated by a public tendency, echoed by certain sociologists, to
gratuitously extend the features of the inner circle—the hard core—
to the wider but next-removed circle of the welfare poor, and then
to the furthest removed circle of the poor altogether.[3] This tendency
must be guarded against, partly for reasons of sociological precision,

---

[3] See, for instance, Walter Miller, "Lower-Class Culture as a Generating Milieu
of Gang Delinquency," *Journal of Social Issues,* Vol. 14, No. 3 (1958), pp. 5-19.

but more generally for the public purpose of avoiding defamation.

Despite these problems, the concept of the three concentric circles seems useful, subject to the qualification that actual persons and families move from one circle to the other and even to social circles beyond the realm of poverty.[4] This conception will be a rough guide in considering the extent and composition of the various populations under discussion.

The Poor

In estimating the extent of poverty in America, and subsequently in describing its composition, one may choose between an absolute or relative conception. An absolute conception defines poverty in terms of a reasonable dividing line usually expressed in yearly dollar income which remains fixed over time. In recent years, $2,500 and $3,000 have been the dividing lines most frequently used with appropriate modifications made for size of the earning unit. In Robert Lampman's definition, for instance, a "low-income person" is "one with an income equivalent to that of a four-person family with total income of not more than $2,500 in 1957 dollars. Thus, an unattached individual would be classified as a low-income person if he had income under $1,157; a member of a six-person family, if his family had income under $3,236." [5]

Herman Miller in a somewhat more recent study used $3,000 as the dividing line. Needless to say, the proportion found poor will vary according to the exact figure chosen. But the defining feature of the absolute conception is that whatever the exact line chosen it is applied over time without provision for rising customary standards or "needs." Once the dollar value is fixed by standardization, as is typically done, it is applied to a population and yields a historical estimate of poverty for a particular nation. As Herman Miller puts it: "If poverty and affluence are defined as absolutes, no allowance is made for the increase in customary 'needs' or standards." [6]

Paradoxically, an absolute definition of poverty is highly useful in

---

[4] For related distinctions, see S. M. Miller, "The American Lower Classes: A Typological Approach," *Sociology and Social Research*, Vol. 48 (April, 1964). Reprinted in Arthur Shostak and William Gomberg, eds., *Blue-Collar World* (Englewood Cliffs, N. J.: Prentice-Hall, 1964), pp. 12-13.

[5] Lampman, "The Low-Income Population and Economic Growth," p. 4.

[6] Herman Miller, *Trends in the Income of Families and Persons in the United States, 1947-1960*, U.S. Dept. of Commerce, Bureau of the Census, Technical Paper No. 8, pp. 1-2.

stressing the relative deprivation [7] experienced by segments of society. Subjectively, making less than $2,000 means one thing in a setting where most others make no more and quite another when only a small minority earn so little. The point is that the possibilities of relative deprivation are most fully appreciated when we use an *absolute* or fixed conception of poverty. If the poverty line were allowed to float according to rising customary standards or needs, one aspect of relative deprivation would be obscured. There would be a tendency for the proportion of persons experiencing poverty to remain relatively constant and thus there would be little insight into the psychic significance of how many others are in the same boat. However, a fixed or absolute conception has shortcomings. The main difficulty is that it reckons without shifting customary definitions of an acceptable minimal standard of life. Rising aspirations, which are hardly limited to underdeveloped economies, not only allude to the highest possibilities; they also affect the minimal standards of life acceptable in a society.

Each conception of poverty has advantages and disadvantages. Herman Miller goes on to summarize these:

> If poverty and affluence are defined as absolutes, no allowance is made for the increase in customary "needs" or standards. For example, if the analysis had been extended back to 1929, it would have been found that about one-third of the families and individuals would have had incomes under $2,000 as compared with only about one-eighth at present. At the turn of the century, the great majority of families had incomes well below this amount. The use of constant dollar income limits, therefore, *provides a rough measure of the proportion of families that could afford a given level of living at various points in time* [my stress], but it makes no allowance for the fact that "needs" are relative and are quite likely to be much different in a society where half the families have incomes under $2,000 than they are in a society where a much smaller proportion . . . are at this low level. Relative measures of income focus on income position rather than on absolute income and thereby take into rough account the increases in "needs" that accompany rising levels of living. The lowest 20 percent of the families in the United States today may have higher standards of living than the highest 20 percent had 50 years ago. They may also have better food, clothing, and shelter and greater life expectancy than the top income groups in many other parts of the world. This

---

[7] Relative deprivation refers to the idea that subjective feelings of deprivation depend on how one's own experiences compare to those close at hand, to what one has become accustomed in the past, or to what one anticipates. Thus, profound degradation in an absolute sense may be tolerable or even pass unnoticed if others close at hand fare no better or if one never had reason to expect any better. A general discussion of relative deprivation may be found in Robert Merton, *Social Theory and Social Structure* (New York: Free Press, 1957), pp. 225-36.

fact, however, provides little consolation when they see how little they have in comparison with their neighbors.[8]

Thus the relative conception reflects the plausible contention that those in, say, the bottom fifth or tenth of an income distribution will feel deprived irrespective of their level of income. But it does so by obscuring the proportion of the population with whom their lot must be shared. In the relative conception, the proportion of the populations are fixed while in an absolute conception the dollar income levels are fixed. Both are important measures.

Miller found that in 1960 the number of families in the United States with incomes under $3,000 (in constant 1959 dollars) was 10,063,000. This was somewhat lower than in previous years. In 1947, there were 12,628,000 families under $3,000; in 1954, 12,012,000.[9] Lampman's earlier study, using $2,500 income for a four-person family as the poverty line, found 32.2 million persons living below that level. This comprised about 19 percent of the population.[10] Thus, in Lampman's study there tends to be a rough coincidence between the figures that would be arrived at through using a reasonable absolute conception of poverty ($2,500) and a reasonable relative conception (the lowest fifth). The same rough coincidence maintains in Miller's slightly later study. Table 1 below combines the absolute and relative conceptions by showing the income intervals by each fifth of the American population. Note that in 1960, the time of the study, the upper limit for the lowest fifth ($2,798) is very close to the $3,000 used by Miller as the poverty line. This table also graphically demonstrates the considerable amelioration of absolute poverty that occurred between 1947 and 1960.

Thus, whatever the theoretical disputes, it is fair to say that *empirically* the lowest fifth of the American income distribution roughly coincides with the population deemed poor in recent years through use of a dollar income poverty line. A very rough approximation of the number of poor persons in America—nothing more than a rough approximation is warranted—is about 35 million persons.

Composition of the Poor

The emergent tendency with regard to the composition of the poor in America seems clear enough. The tendency is summarized by Simon Kuznets. He says: "If the lower-income groups are defined as

---

[8] Miller, *Trends in the Income of Families and Persons in the United States, 1947-1960,* pp. 1-2.
[9] *Ibid.,* p. 7.
[10] Lampman, "The Low-Income Population and Economic Growth," p. 4.

TABLE 1

Income Intervals by Income Fifths: 1947 and 1960

	1947	1960
Lowest fifth	under $1,580	under $2,798
Second fifth	$1,581-2,561	$2,799-4,812
Middle fifth	$2,562-3,469	$4,813-6,472
Fourth fifth	$3,470-4,926	$6,473-8,992
Highest fifth	$4,927 and over	$8,993 and over
Top five percent	$8,968 and over	$14,385 and over

Source: These figures are adapted from a more detailed table in Herman Miller, *Trends in the Income of Families and Persons in the United States, 1947-1960*, U.S. Dept. of Commerce, Bureau of the Census, Technical Paper No. 8, p. 17.

families with incomes under $3,000 in constant dollars we find in the post-World War II years, this group was increasingly characterized by a small consuming unit, with either an aged or female head, with a smaller than average number of children—in short, either a semi- or fully retired, or a broken family unit." [11]

The details of this tendency, and the close relation between broken family units and nonwhite sectors of the population, are apparent in Lampman's summary of the composition of the poor in 1957. Of the 32.2 million persons deemed poor in Lampman's estimate, 8 million were 65 years of age or more; 8 million were in consumer units without a father, and thus headed by women; and 6.4 million were nonwhite persons. About half of all the poor had one or more of these three main characteristics. The other main characteristic of the low-income population was, of course, being a member of a consuming unit headed by a person with little education. Twenty-one million of the 32.2 million poor persons were "in units headed by a person with less than 8 grades of school." [12]

Miller attempts to summarize the composition of 9,650,000 poor families in 1959 by assigning each of the units to one of five categories, despite the fact that a single unit might possess more than one of the poverty-risk characteristics. Of the 9,650,000 families, 1,570,000 were farmers; 2,581,000 were aged; families consisting of mothers and children numbered 1,561,000; nonwhite families totaled 950,000; and all

---

[11] Simon Kuznets, "Income Distribution and Changes in Consumption," *The Changing American Population* (New York: Institute of Life Insurance, 1962), p. 36.

[12] Lampman, "The Low-Income Population and Economic Growth," p. 4.

TABLE **2**

**Median Income by Family Status
for Whites and Nonwhites, 1961**

Family status	Median income	Average number of children per family
White		
Husband and wife	$6,510	2.4
Mother only	2,675	2.1
Nonwhite		
Husband and wife	3,895	3.0
Mother only	1,665	2.8

Source: Mollie Orshansky, "Children of the Poor," *Social Security Bulletin,* Vol. 26, No. 7 (July, 1963), p. 7.

of the others numbered 2,988,000. Though a useful and legitimate device, Miller's method underestimates the significance of race; for example, about a quarter million of the farm families and a half million of the broken families were nonwhite.[13]

Irrespective of race, however, the absence of a husband in family units is an obvious but crucial correlate of being poor. The role played by the husband's presence may be detected by comparing the average income of intact families with those that are broken within racial categories. Table 2 above summarizes the differences for whites and nonwhites.

We must keep in mind, however, that the proportion of broken families varies by race. While the absence of a father has a profoundly adverse effect on income for both whites and nonwhites, nonwhites more frequently experience this income-debilitating condition. In 1961, there were 1,933,000 intact nonwhite families with one or more children; there were 571,000 with a female head. For whites, there were 21,815,000 intact families with children and about 1,654,000 with female heads.[14] Thus, about 23 percent of nonwhite families were headed by females as compared to 7 percent for white families. And, finally, the special predicament of nonwhites will be evident when one notes in Table 2 the large differences in income between white and nonwhite intact families as well as those between white and nonwhite broken families.

---

[13] Herman Miller, *Rich Man, Poor Man* (New York: Crowell, 1964), pp. 80-93.
[14] Mollie Orshansky, "Children of the Poor," *Social Security Bulletin,* Vol. 26, No. 7 (July, 1963), p. 7.

The Welfare Poor

The welfare poor correspond to the intermediary circle, considerably narrower than that comprising the poor, and considerably wider than the disreputable poor.

The majority of those whose poverty is relieved—the welfare poor—bear no disrepute beyond that implicit in their failure to be self-supporting. But as suggested earlier, dependency itself emits a hint of disrepute in a nation whose official values stress independence, initiative, and capacity. Thus, a public stereotype tends to emerge—but only *tends*—in which the minimal disrepute inherent in the sheer fact of dependency is coupled with the maximal disrepute implicit in demoralization. (Demoralization should be understood in the double sense of the withering of conscientious effort and the decline of moral standards.) The unhampered tendency to couple dependency with demoralization would yield a public stereotype equating the welfare poor with the disreputable poor. But the tendency is partly offset by another tendency, also traditional. Certain forms of dependency are understood, tolerated, and subsequently exempted from the special stigma of demoralization. In this tendency, already apparent in early English Poor Laws, the disabled, the aged, the blind are regarded as occupying a special moral place in society—a place where the normally assumed relation between dependency and demoralization is either inoperative or irrelevant. The two tendencies operate simultaneously. A main mechanism by which the public equates families "on welfare" with the disreputable poor is through a systematic forgetting—a collective repressing—of the composition of the publicly aided population.

The welfare poor are defined by the fact that they depend wholly or partly on some manner of public assistance for sustenance. Morgan and his associates in their survey of consumption units found that "less than one-fourth of the poor families received public assistance during 1959." [15]

This estimate corresponds closely with one derived from totaling the numbers assisted by the variety of aid programs in existence. There are five major aid programs in the United States. This does not —and should not—include Unemployment Insurance and Old-Age, Survivors, and Disability Insurance. Assistance programs are not insurance programs. They are a relief to the needy to which the recipient does not contribute. The major programs that relieve poverty are Old-Age Assistance, Aid to Families with Dependent Children,

---

[15] James Morgan, Martin David, Wilbur Cohen, and Harvey Brazer, *Income and Welfare in the United States* (New York: McGraw-Hill, 1962), p. 216.

Aid to the Permanently and Total Disabled, Aid to the Blind, and General Assistance. All but the last are federally subsidized. General Assistance is locally financed and administered and is typically reserved for persons who are not covered by any of the other programs but are nonetheless deemed needy and thus eligible.

In June of 1963, slightly more than 7.5 million Americans were receiving some manner of public welfare assistance. Of the total, about 2.2 million were 65 or over and receiving Old-Age Assistance; about 462,000 persons were receiving Aid to the Permanently and Total Disabled; and about 98,000 were receiving Aid to the Blind. That means that about 2.8 million of the 7.5 million welfare poor can by crude but reasonable standards be immediately eliminated from the population that harbors and includes the disreputable poor. About 4.7 million adults and children are relieved by Aid to Families with Dependent Children or local General Assistance programs. Of that total, 3,935,000 were on Aid to Families with Dependent Children—2,952,000 children and 983,000 adults—and assorted local General Assistance programs relieved 775,000 persons.[16]

The composition of persons receiving Aid to Families with Dependent Children shows two main features. It is disproportionately nonwhite and is concentrated in the central city areas of the large metropolis. Robert Mugge summarizes the racial composition of AFDC recipients:

> Almost half the cases receiving Aid to Families with Dependent Children were reported to be white, two-fifths were reported as Negro, 2 percent American Indian, and 9 percent "other nonwhite and unknown." [The last category is so large because Puerto Rico and the Virgin Islands reported all cases as "race unknown," and New York state erroneously classified all cases of Puerto Rican origin as "other nonwhite."] It appears . . . reasonable . . . that at least half of the 9 percent . . . were actually white. Therefore, according to a rough estimate, about 54 percent of all cases were white, 44 percent Negro, and 2 percent Indian and other nonwhite.[17]

The concentration of AFDC recipients in central cities is evident in Table 3 below in which recipient rates are shown for different types of area. (A recipient rate is the number of child recipients per 1000 children under age 18.)

---

[16] The figures in this section are all from *Health, Education, and Welfare Indicators* (December, 1963), p. 40.

[17] Robert Mugge, "Aid to Families With Dependent Children," *Social Security Bulletin*, Vol. 26, No. 3 (March, 1963), p. 3.

TABLE **3**

AFDC Recipient Rates by Place of Residence

Place of Residence	Recipient Rate
Standard metropolitan statistical areas	39
Central cities	63
Outside central cities	17
Outside standard metropolitan statistical areas	38
Urban places	39
Rural-nonfarm	41
Rural-farm	27
Total (excluding Puerto Rico and Virgin Islands)	38

Source: Robert Mugge, "Aid to Families with Dependent Children," *Social Security Bulletin,* Vol. 26, No. 3 (March, 1963), p. 4.

The Disreputable Poor

In the phrase, "the disreputable poor," "disreputable" is intended to distinguish a segment of the poor rather than to describe all those who are poor. Though there is considerable variation, at any given time only a portion of those who can reasonably be considered poor are disreputable. The term disreputable introduces no personal judgment but takes account of the judgments made by other members of society; to ignore the stigma that adheres to this special kind of poverty is to miss one of its key aspects.

The disreputable poor are the people who remain unemployed, or casually and irregularly employed, even during periods approaching full employment and prosperity; for that reason, and others, they live in disrepute. They do not include the majority of those who are unemployed or irregularly employed during a period of mass unemployment. To locate the section of the able-bodied poor that remains unemployed or casually employed during periods of full employment is a difficult task, particularly in the American setting where the number unemployed is subject to frequent and relatively drastic fluctuations. The economist Stanley Lebergott finds that, "no decade [in the twentieth century] has passed without severe unemployment (over 7 percent of the labor force) occurring at least once. And none, except for that of the 1930's has passed without seeing at least one year of what we may call minimal unemployment (3 percent or less)." [18] Con-

---

[18] Stanley Lebergott, "Economic Crises in the United States," in Special Committee on Unemployment Problems, *Readings in Unemployment* (Washington, D. C.: U.S. Government Printing Office, 1960), pp. 86-87.

sequently, the line between those who are unemployed only during periods of depression or recession and those who are more permanently unoccupied is especially difficult to draw in America.

The search for the disreputable poor will, of necessity, yield extremely crude estimates subject to wide margins of error. This is due to four major obstacles. First, it is extremely difficult to obtain data on persons receiving General Assistance. States vary widely in the conditions of eligibility for that program and persons are often on the programs for short periods of time awaiting placement in one of the federally subsidized programs. Accordingly, the discussion will be focused on persons relieved by the Aid to Families with Dependent Children Program. Secondly, the character of AFDC makes partly invisible males who are socially associated and culturally similar to the women and children relieved by the program. These men are not typically relieved by AFDC, but frequently they live in the same neighborhoods as those who are, share and perhaps dominate the style of communal life in these neighborhoods, father many of the children, allegedly expend some of the monthly welfare payments, and in many other ways are part of the same social milieu. Thirdly, the indicators used here to estimate the proportion of AFDC recipients who can reasonably be deemed disreputable by general community standards are, of necessity, extremely crude. Fourth, there are undoubtedly persons living in disreputable poverty who are for a variety of reasons temporarily—or perhaps even permanently—off the welfare rolls. For all of these reasons, the reader is cautioned regarding the accuracy of the estimate. The main reason for proposing an estimate is the somewhat shaky belief that some thoughtful estimate—however crude —is better than the half-conscious estimates, based on public stereotype, that all of us carry in mind.

One indication of disrepute revolves around the question of a man's relationship with the children he has fathered and the women with whom he has cohabited. Bastardy, or illegitimacy, has been a persistent sign of disrepute despite the somewhat variable reaction to it by social class, race, and nation.[19] Even if illegitimacy is somewhat tolerated in neighborhoods where it is relatively prevalent, a person's status may be derogated by allusions to the questionable moral character of his mother and the dubious existence of his father.[20]

---

[19] For a more detailed discussion of this point, see William J. Goode, "Family Disorganization," in this volume; also see Judith Blake and Kingsley Davis, "Norms, Values, and Sanctions," in Robert Faris, ed., *Handbook of Modern Sociology* (Chicago: Rand McNally, 1964), Chapter 13.

[20] See, in this connection, the interesting discussion of ranking, the "dozens," and other forms of cutting, albeit playful, talk in Roger D. Abrahams, *Deep Down*

TABLE 4

Status of Father in AFDC Families

Father's Status	Percentage of 910,000 AFDC Families
Dead	7.7
Incapacitated	17.8
Absent from Home	67.2
Divorced or legally separated	14.3
Separated without court decree	8.3
Deserting	18.3
Not married to mother	21.2
Imprisoned	4.2
Other reason	.6
Unemployed	5.1
Other Status	2.2

Source: These figures are reported in Robert Mugge, "Aid to Families with Dependent Children," *Social Security Bulletin*, Vol. 26, No. 3 (March, 1963), p. 8.

The reader will note in Table 4 that in 21.2 percent of the 910,000 families on AFDC at the time of collection of data the man was not married to the mother.[21] A key, but unfortunately unanswerable, question in arriving at an estimate of the population living in disreputable poverty is: how many men have fathered the children in any given family?

Being imprisoned may be taken as another indicator of disrepute. Despite variable levels of tolerance toward criminality, there is typically some acknowledgment of official morality, and this minimal acknowledgment is reflected in the potentially stigmatic character of being or having been imprisoned.

One may add to these two indicators of disrepute—illegitimacy and imprisonment—desertion and separation without court decree. But there we are on somewhat shakier grounds, especially with regard to acknowledged separation, even if without court decree. One may arrive at low and high estimates of the magnitude of disreputable poverty; illegitimacy and imprisonment should be used to derive low estimates and desertion should be added to arrive at a high estimate.

---

in the Jungle: Negro Narrative Folklore from the Streets of Philadelphia (Hatboro, Pa.: Folklore Associates, 1964).

[21] For data bearing on a similar point, see also Gordon Blackwell and Raymond Gould, *Future Citizens All* (Chicago: Public Welfare Association, 1952), pp. 8-9; and M. Elaine Burgess and Daniel Price, *An American Dependency Challenge* (Chicago: Public Welfare Association, 1963), p. 40.

TABLE 5

Usual Occupational Class of Fathers in Assistance Families and that of Employed Men

Occupational Class	Percent AFDC Fathers	Percent Employed Men In General Population
Professional and semiprofessional	.6	10.3
Farmowners, renters, and managers	1.5	5.5
Proprietors, managers, and officials	.5	10.7
Clerical, sales, and kindred workers	2.3	13.8
Craftsmen, foremen, and kindred workers	6.6	19.9
Operatives and kindred semiskilled and skilled workers	13.9	19.9
Farm laborers, including sharecroppers	10.2	2.8
Service workers	5.6	6.1
Unskilled laborers	33.7	6.9
Never had full-time employment	3.1	—
Unknown	22.0	4.6

Source: Robert Mugge, "Aid to Families with Dependent Children," *Social Security Bulletin*, Vol. 26, No. 3 (March, 1963), p. 10.

Accordingly, a low estimate would be that about 25 percent of AFDC families may be regarded as disreputable by general community standards, and a high estimate would be about 45 percent.

The same general impression may be derived from additional data bearing on the usual occupation of the father officially associated with the AFDC family. Table 5 above shows the usual occupation reported for such fathers and compares that distribution to that of employed men.

A crude indicator of the proportion of men living in disrepute can be inferred from Table 5. Any sort of usual occupation confers a minimal legitimacy. Disrepute is most apt to follow from the absence of any occupation or the lack of public knowledge regarding an occupational pursuit. Thus, a crude estimate of the proportion living in disrepute may be derived from adding the last two categories—*occupation unknown* and *never had full-time employment*. This could be considered a low estimate since some proportion of those doing unskilled work are apt to be relatively casual or irregular laborers.[22]

---

[22] The fact that the occupation of the father associated with an AFDC family is unknown can hardly be attributed to mere administrative oversight since the question of eligibility for AFDC turns on the earning capacity of the father. Welfare officials look into the matter carefully. That his occupation is unknown will usually mean that the alliance culminating in a child was so casual that the mother hardly knew the man's name or location—itself an indication of disrepute—or that the man has no known usual legitimate occupation.

TABLE 6

Length of Time on Assistance for AFDC Families

Length of Time	Percent of AFDC Families
Less than 6 months	17
Six months but less than 1 year	15
One year but less than 2	17
Two years but less than 3	12
Three years but less than 5	16
Five years or more	24

Source: Robert Mugge, "Aid to Families with Dependent Children," *Social Security Bulletin*, Vol. 26, No. 3 (March, 1963), p. 4.

A final indication of the proportion living in disrepute may be suggested. A common social assumption is that relief should be a *temporary* matter. Persons who maintain dependent status over a seemingly permanent period are suspect, unless they are aged or otherwise infirm. Thus, long-term dependency may be taken as another crude indicator of the proportion of AFDC families living in disrepute. Table 6 shows the distribution of AFDC families by length of time on assistance. By this indication, too, somewhere between 25 and 45 percent of AFDC families bear the onus of disrepute.

Thus, we may hazard the guess that from one-quarter to about two-fifths of the families on AFDC, and the men who live in the same social circles, can be regarded as disreputable by general community standards.

Welfare Chiseling

It is hardly possible to write on the subject of welfare and disrepute without considering the phenomenon, "welfare chiseling." This trait is often imputed to the welfare poor, and especially to the disreputable among them. This understandable—one might even say reasonable—response to being on the dole received considerable attention as a result of the "Newburgh affair" [23] and subsequently achieved some prominence in the ill-fated Goldwater campaign of 1964.

Welfare chiseling may be defined as the receipt of assistance despite ineligibility or the receipt of more assistance than is legitimately warranted, given prevailing rules and rates. Needless to say, such illi-

---

[23] For a good review of the Newburgh affair, see Edgar May, *The Wasted Americans* (New York: Harper, 1964), Chapter 2.

cit receipt should be *intentional* if it is to be regarded as chiseling. The beneficiaries of modest windfalls in an inefficient welfare system should hardly be regarded as chiselers unless they knowingly contrived toward that end.

There is little adequate knowledge of the number or proportion of chiselers among those who are assisted—no more, say, than exists for wealthy tax-chiselers. What little research exists has been limited to recipients of AFDC, and the research that has been done is handicapped by the obvious fact that if welfare investigators can be defrauded, so can researchers.[24]

That some amount of welfare chiseling occurs is hardly disputable. Almost by definition, the disreputable poor would be more inclined to fraud and other abuses than the deserving, who are more closely bound by moral scruples. The disreputable poor, as has been stressed thus far, are a minority among the poor and even among the welfare poor. This contention receives indirect support from a national study of the proportion of AFDC recipients who were ineligible but nonetheless received support. The main finding of the report is that a relatively small proportion of recipients were engaged in apparent or detectable chiseling. Despite the inconclusiveness of research in this area, some of the main findings of this national study are worth summarizing.

The proportion of ineligible families found to be receiving assistance under AFDC in 1963 varied considerably according to state of residence. Generally, southern states had relatively high proportions; northern and western states low proportions. In West Virginia, 19 percent of the families receiving AFDC assistance were found by special investigators to be wholly or partly ineligible; in Georgia, 17.9 percent, and in South Carolina, 16.8 percent. At the other extreme were Massachusetts, California, Montana, North Dakota, Idaho, Iowa, New Jersey, and Nebraska where less than 2.5 percent of families receiving AFDC assistance were found wholly or partly ineligible.[25] The full range of the proportion of families found wholly or partly ineligible according to state of residence is shown in Table 7 below.

The reason that ineligible families receive assistance, however, may

---

[24] Studies dealing with this and related questions have included Greenleigh Associates, *Facts, Fallacies, and Future,* A Study of the Aid to Dependent Children Program of Cook County, Illinois (New York: 1960); and a National Study requested by the United States Senate Appropriations Committee, *Eligibility of Families Receiving Aid to Families with Dependent Children,* Department of Health, Education, and Welfare (Washington, D. C., July, 1963).

[25] *Eligibility of Families Receiving Aid to Families with Dependent Children,* p. 11.

TABLE 7

Eligibility of Families Receiving Assistance According to State Requirements Governing Eligibility, by State

State	Families Receiving AFDC in March 1963	Percent of Eligible Families			
		Total	All persons in Family Eligible	Family Eligible, But Not All Members Eligible	Percent of Ineligible Families
Alabama	22,550	91.6	89.5	2.1	8.4
Alaska	1,245	92.0	89.1	2.9	8.0
Arizona	9,535	93.2	88.2	5.0	6.8
Arkansas	7,045	93.4	92.3	1.1	6.6
California	91,422	98.9	97.8	1.1	1.2
Colorado	9,656	98.1	97.1	1.0	1.9
Connecticut	12,712	89.0	87.1	1.9	11.0
Delaware	2,465	89.8	88.3	1.5	10.2
Florida	27,801	91.0	89.5	1.5	9.0
Georgia	17,146	83.7	82.2	1.5	16.4
Hawaii	3,239	93.8	92.8	1.0	6.2
Idaho	2,563	98.8	97.6	1.2	1.1
Illinois	59,212	95.1	92.6	2.5	4.9
Indiana	12,181	97.4	96.4	1.0	2.6
Iowa	10,652	98.5	97.4	1.1	1.5
Kansas	6,940	99.1	97.9	1.2	.8
Kentucky	21,600	87.2	78.5	8.7	12.8
Louisiana	22,629	96.8	93.6	3.2	3.2
Maine	6,175	97.6	96.1	1.5	2.4
Maryland	14,183	97.4	96.5	.9	2.6
Massachusetts	20,366	99.1	98.6	.5	.8
Michigan	33,376	94.2	94.0	.2	5.8
Minnesota	11,725	97.9	96.5	1.4	2.1
Mississippi	20,463	88.5	84.0	4.5	11.6
Missouri	26,334	95.5	94.8	.7	4.5
Montana	1,811	100.0	97.9	2.1	—
Nebraska	3,337	99.1	99.1	—	.9
Nevada	1,310	87.6	84.8	2.8	12.4
New Hampshire	1,024	93.8	93.5	.3	6.2
New Jersey	22,914	98.1	97.8	.3	2.0
New Mexico	7,435	90.3	88.9	1.4	9.8
New York	100,473	96.5	94.4	2.1	3.7
North Carolina	28,660	96.6	94.6	2.0	3.5
North Dakota	1,726	100.0	100.0	—	—
Ohio	37,344	95.0	93.0	2.0	5.0
Oklahoma	18,275	98.3	97.1	1.2	1.7
Oregon	8,603	94.7	92.7	2.0	5.4
Pennsylvania	80,522	97.1	95.9	1.2	2.9
Rhode Island	5,464	96.8	95.1	1.7	3.3
South Carolina	8,540	86.7	83.3	3.4	13.4
South Dakota	2,818	96.9	94.4	2.5	3.1
Tennessee	21,485	85.7	83.8	1.9	14.3
Texas	18,317	90.5	89.4	1.1	9.6
Utah	4,597	99.1	97.2	1.9	.9
Vermont	1,358	96.9	96.9	—	3.1
Virginia	10,736	95.5	91.0	4.5	4.5
Washington	12,072	95.4	91.7	3.7	4.6
West Virginia	31,018	82.7	81.0	1.7	17.3
Wisconsin	11,131	97.1	96.0	1.1	2.9
Wyoming	851	94.7	91.0	3.7	5.3

Source: Eligibility of Families Receiving Aid to Families with Dependent Children, Department of Health, Education and Welfare (Washington, D. C., July, 1963).

be rooted in agency oversights or administrative errors as well as in the recipient's deceitful or naive failure to report relevant information or a change in conditions. Though actual situations were highly complicated, the national study under discussion attempted to assign the main responsibility to either agency or recipient. In West Virginia, for instance, where 19 percent of AFDC families were found to be wholly or partly ineligible, 13 percent, in the assessment of the researchers, were due to agency errors or oversights, and 6 percent to changes not reported by the recipient.[26]

In almost all the states, there is apparently the same pattern in which agency error or oversight predominates over recipient culpability. Among the very few exceptions is Nevada where, perhaps for reasons of local custom, a kind of gaming relationship between the citizenry and the state seems to maintain. At least, that is one inference that can be drawn from the investigators findings. In Nevada, where 15.2 percent of AFDC families were found wholly or partly ineligible, the researchers judged that 6.3 percent were due to agency error and oversight and 8.9 percent due to changes not reported by the recipient. The full range of the assessed responsibility for receipt of assistance despite ineligibility is shown by state in Table 8 below.

With this brief consideration of poverty, welfare, and disrepute, and the possible statistical bases for differentiation among them, we may proceed to focus on the concepts and nature of disreputable poverty itself.

Conceptions of Disreputable Poverty

The historical continuity of disreputable poverty has been obscured by the obsessive shifting of terms. One predictable consequence has

---

[26] *Ibid.*, p. 16. Furthermore, the researchers in each state tried to assess whether the recipient's failure to report a relevant change was willful or not. Such an attempt seems idle. The variations in these assessments by state indicate the arbitrary character of such imputations. The results in this regard from our two newest states will serve to illustrate my point. In Alaska, *nobody* among the 3.1 percent who failed to report a change "appears to have intentionally concealed or misrepresented the facts." In Hawaii, *everybody* among the 2 percent who failed to report a change "appears to have intentionally concealed or misrepresented the facts." Accordingly, it would seem best to treat these imputations with extreme skepticism, despite the fact that they are reproduced in Table 8. Else, we should be driven to rescind statehood for one or the other according to our moral preferences.

TABLE 8

Percent of AFDC Families in Which All or Some Members Were Found Ineligible, Listed by State and by Principal Reason that Ineligibility Was Not Previously Known or Acted Upon by the Local Agency

| State | Total | Percent of Errors in Agency Practice | | | Percent of Change Not Reported by Recipient | | Other Reasons [a] |
		Inadequate Determination of Initial or Continuing Eligibility	Agency Failure to Follow Up on Indicated or Known Changes in Family Circumstances	Staff Misinterpretations of Eligibility Policy and Administrative Errors	No Evidence of Intent to Conceal or Misrepresent Facts	Appears to Have Intentionally Concealed or Misrepresented Facts	
Alabama	10.5	4.4	0.5	0.3	2.5	2.2	0.6
Alaska	10.9	1.4	2.9	1.8	3.1	—	1.6
Arizona	11.8	4.3	2.3	1.4	1.8	1.9	—
Arkansas	7.7	5.1	.4	—	.4	1.6	—
California	2.3	.2	.6	.2	.3	.7	.1
Colorado	2.9	1.6	.3	.9	.1	—	—
Connecticut	12.9	3.4	1.1	1.2	2.0	4.5	.8
Delaware	11.7	1.6	1.4	—	1.4	7.4	—
Florida	10.5	3.5	1.3	.2	2.0	3.3	.2
Georgia	17.9	9.3	.3	1.1	3.8	2.1	1.3
Hawaii	7.2	3.3	—	.9	—	2.0	1.0
Idaho	2.3	1.1	—	—	—	1.2	—
Illinois	7.4	2.2	1.6	.4	1.0	1.6	.5
Indiana	3.6	1.0	.9	.4	.6	.6	.3
Iowa	2.6	1.8	.4	.1	—	.2	—
Kansas	2.0	.5	.1	1.0	.4	—	—
Kentucky	21.5	7.4	2.7	1.4	3.3	2.8	4.0
Louisiana	6.4	.7	.8	.7	2.3	1.8	—
Maine	3.9	2.8	.1	—	.5	.5	—
Maryland	3.5	.8	—	.5	.5	1.8	—
Massachusetts	1.3	.7	.2	.3	.2	—	—
Michigan	6.0	.4	—	.1	.5	3.6	1.4
Minnesota	3.5	.8	.4	.5	1.6	.3	—
Mississippi	16.1	7.7	3.0	.2	2.8	1.1	1.2
Missouri	5.2	.4	—	.2	1.5	2.6	.6
Montana	2.1	—	2.2	—	—	—	—
Nebraska	.9	—	.9	—	—	—	—
Nevada	15.2	4.8	—	1.5	1.5	7.4	—
New Hampshire	6.5	—	—	—	—	6.5	—
New Jersey	2.3	.5	—	—	.3	1.2	.3
New Mexico	11.2	2.6	2.9	1.7	2.0	2.1	—
New York	5.8	2.2	1.0	.4	.8	1.3	.1
North Carolina	5.5	2.4	.5	—	1.0	1.6	—
North Dakota	0.0	—	—	—	—	—	—
Ohio	7.0	2.2	2.4	.2	1.1	.9	.5
Oklahoma	2.9	.5	—	—	1.2	.6	.5
Oregon	7.4	.8	2.2	.8	.2	3.5	—
Pennsylvania	4.1	.8	—	.4	.5	1.8	.5
Rhode Island	5.0	3.6	.4	.2	—	.8	—

TABLE **8** (cont.)

State	Total	Percent of Errors in Agency Practice			Percent of Change Not Reported by Recipient		
		Inadequate Determination of Initial or Continuing Eligibility	Agency Failure to Follow Up on Indicated or Known Changes in Family Circumstances	Staff Misinterpretations of Eligibility Policy and Administrative Errors	No Evidence of Intent to Conceal or Misrepresent Facts	Appears to Have Intentionally Concealed or Misrepresented Facts	Other Reasons [a]
South Carolina	16.8	8.6	2.4	1.2	2.4	1.8	.4
South Dakota	5.6	1.5	1.2	—	2.8	—	—
Tennessee	16.2	4.4	1.0	4.3	2.0	3.8	.6
Texas	10.7	4.4	.5	.3	3.7	1.8	—
Utah	2.8	.2	.7	—	—	1.8	—
Vermont	3.1	.1	—	—	1.6	1.6	—
Virginia	9.0	2.4	1.3	3.2	.8	.8	.4
Washington	8.3	2.9	1.1	1.0	.9	2.6	—
West Virginia	19.0	7.6	4.8	.5	4.5	1.5	—
Wisconsin	4.0	1.6	—	.3	.5	1.7	—
Wyoming	9.0	4.9	1.6	—	—	2.6	—

Source: *Eligibility of Families Receiving Aid to Families with Dependent Children,* Department of Health, Education and Welfare (Washington, D. C., July, 1963).

[a] The most frequently reported reasons in this column were: (1) recent changes in agency policy which were to be first applied in each case as it came up for periodic reinvestigation in 1963 (Connecticut and Kentucky); and (2) cases closed before any improper payments of assistance were made (Illinois, Missouri, Ohio).

been the continual rediscovery of the poor—an example of what Pitirim Sorokin called the Columbus complex. The poor, it seems, are perennially hidden, and the enterprising publicists of each decade reiterate their previous invisibility and regularly proclaim the distinctive and special qualities of the "new poor." Dr. John Griscom, commenting on the wretchedness of slum life in the 1840's said, "one half of the world does not know how the other half lives." [27] Griscom's language and viewpoint were echoed almost a half-century later by Jacob Riis,[28] and now, more than another half-century later, Michael

---

[27] Robert H. Bremner, *From the Depths* (New York: New York University Press, 1956), pp. 5-6.
[28] Jacob A. Riis, *How the Other Half Lives* (New York: Sagamore Press, 1957). (Originally published in 1890.)

Harrington [29] again rediscovers a heretofore invisible class of submerged poor and again stresses the novelty of their predicament. Actually, the idea that this segment is "invisible" can be highly misleading. From time to time, it may be invisible to intellectuals, publicists, radicals, and the middle-class students who read their tracts, but it is highly and persistently visible from two social perspectives that are more relevant for those who are themselves disreputably poor. As will be elaborated below, the disreputable poor are highly visible to officials and to the respectable working classes. For officials, they come close to living in a fishbowl. For the respectable working classes, they are part of what is seen and commented on when looking out through the lace curtain.

Disreputable poverty has gone under many names in the past two centuries. The major thrust and purpose of word substitution has been to reduce and remove the stigma, and perhaps the reason for its obsessiveness is that the effort is fruitless. The stigma inheres mostly in the referent and not in the concept. In five years or so, if not already, the term "hard to reach" will be considered stigmatizing and will be relegated to the dead file of offensive labels. The culmination of this process is not hard to predict since it has already occurred in a discipline even more addicted to word substitution and mystification than ours—the field of education. It may turn out that we shall eventually refer to the poor as "exceptional families."

Each conception of disreputable poverty harbors some measure of wisdom and thus illuminates the referent; each makes us one-eyed and thus obscures it. Thus, a sample of conceptions of disreputable poverty may serve to introduce a consideration of its persistent features.

The current conception, "hard to reach," considers and defines the disreputable poor from the vantage point of the administrator of public welfare activities. Implicit in the concept is a view of the disreputable poor as human material that can be worked on, helped, and hopefully transformed.[30] Reasonably enough, this conception implies that one crucial difficulty is that the material cannot even be got hold of. It is hard to reach; to do so requires great expenditures of time and effort. Only a short step is required to transform the concept from one rooted in administrative perspective to one suggesting an important insight. Surely, they are not hard to reach only because the

---

[29] Michael Harrington, *The Other America* (New York: Macmillan, 1962).

[30] For a brief discussion of the administrative welfare perspective, see Thomas Gladwin, "The Anthropologist's View of Poverty," *The Social Welfare Forum* (New York: Columbia University Press, 1961), pp. 73-74.

welfare establishment is deficient. Rather, the elusiveness resides at least partially in the stratum itself. The disreputable poor are disaffiliated; they exist in the crevices or at the margins of modern society. The disreputable poor are probably the only authentic outsiders, for modern democratic industrial life, contrary to romantic opinion, has had a remarkable capacity for integrating increasingly larger proportions of society. For this reason, perhaps, they have been consistently romanticized, glamorized, and misunderstood by intellectuals, especially radicals and Bohemians who frequently aspire to be outsiders but never quite make it.

Beyond this, the concept "hard to reach" tells us little. We should not be discouraged, however, since one insight per concept is doing well. Many concepts are completely nondescript, being the bland and neutral labels best exemplified in the usage of British and American sociologists when they refer as they do to Class 5 or Class E. There is nothing wrong with this. Indeed, from the viewpoint of science it is meritorious. Strictly speaking, concepts should not contain implicit theories since this permits one to smuggle in hypotheses better left to empirical investigation. But concepts that imply specific theories are a boon, providing the theory is empirically sound rather than romantically foolish. The theory implicit, for instance, in a concept of the "happy poor" is mostly romantic foolishness.

Almost nondescript, but not quite, is the phrase initiated by Warner and still fashionable among sociologists—the lower-lower class. Since Warner's categories were ostensibly supplied by members of the community, it implies that, from their perspective, the distinction between two sections of the lower class is meaningful. The difference between lower-lowers and upper-lowers above all pertains to reputation—the one disreputable, the other reputable.

More suggestive is the British term, "problem family." Implicit in this concept are two points. First, to refer to problem families is to observe with typical English understatement that the disreputable poor are a bit of a pain in the neck. They are bothersome and disproportionately costly in terms of the amount of care, welfare, and policing they elicit. Second, and more important, the term suggests that these families collect problems. They contribute far more than their share to the relief recipients, to crime and delinquency rates, to rates of alcoholism, to the list of unmarried mothers and thus illegitimate children, to divorces, desertions, and to the mentally ill. The idea of plural problems, reinforcing and nurturing each other in the manner of a vicious circle, was well stated and developed in the English notion. Thus, the American adaptation, "multiproblem" family, unnecessarily reiterates. Moreover, the American term loses the *double-entendre* implicit in the British formulation.

The remaining concepts, unlike those already discussed, were not attempts to reduce stigma, but, on the contrary, are decidedly offensive terms developed outside the circle of sociologists, social workers, and psychiatrists. The first term, *Lumpenproletariat,* which despite its wide usage among Marxists was never really clarified or developed systematically, refers to the dirt or scum that inhabits the lower orders, nearby, but not of, the working class. The *Lumpenproletariat,* according to Bukharin, was one of the "categories of persons outside the outlines of social labor" and barred from being a revolutionary class "chiefly by the circumstance that it performs no productive work." [31] For the Marxist, this stratum was fundamentally reactionary and, in the revolutionary situation, would either remain apathetic or its members would become mercenaries in the service of the bourgeoisie. Bukharin maintains that in the *Lumpenproletariat* we find, "shiftlessness, lack of discipline, hatred of the old, but impotence to construct or organize anything new, an individualistic declassed 'personality,' whose actions are based only on foolish caprices." [32]

Frequently, *Lumpenproletariat* was used as a derogatory term in the struggles for power among various revolutionaries. If an opponent could be associated with the *Lumpenproletariat,* his stature might be lessened. Despite frequent abuse, the term maintained some distinctive meaning. It continued to refer to the disreputable poor, and implicit in the Marxian conception are a number of suggestive insights regarding their character, background, and destiny. The description given by Victor Chernov, a Russian social revolutionary, is typical since it is garbed in highly evaluative language and since he uses the designation to attack an opponent, Lenin.

> Besides the proletarian *"demos"* there exists in all capitalist countries a proletarian *"ochlos,"* the enormous mass of *déclassés,* chronic paupers, *Lumpenproletariat,* what may be termed the "capitalistically superfluous industrial reserve army." Like the proletariat, it is a product of capitalist civilization, but it reflects the destructive, not the constructive aspects of capitalism. Exploited and down-trodden, it is full of bitterness and despair, but has none of the traditions and none of the potentialities of organization, of a new consciousness, a new law, and a new culture, which distinguish the genuine "hereditary" proletariat. In Russia the growth of capitalism has been strong-

---

[31] Nikolai Bukharin, *Historical Materialism* (New York: International, 1925), pp. 284 and 290.

[32] *Ibid.,* p. 290.

est in its destructive, predatory aspects, while its constructive achievements have lagged. It was accompanied by a catastrophic growth of the *"ochlos,"* a tremendous mass of uprooted, drifting humanity. Wrongly idealized at times, as in Gorky's early works, this mob supplied the contingents for those sporadic mass outbursts, pogroms, anti-Jewish and others, for which old Russia was famous. During the war, "the personnel of industry had . . . been completely transformed. . . . The ranks of factory workers, severely depleted by indiscriminate mobilizations, were filled with whatever human material came to hand: peasants, small shopkeepers, clerks, janitors, porters, people of indeterminate trade. . . . The genuine proletariat was submerged in a motley crowd of *Lumpenproletarians* and *Lumpenbourgeois*.[33]

What may we infer from this description? First, the *Lumpenproletariat* differs in economic function from the proletariat. It is not an industrial working class; instead, it consists of a heterogeneous mass of casual and irregular laborers, farmworkers, artisans, tradesmen, service workers, and petty thieves. They work in traditional and increasingly obsolete jobs rather than, in the Marxian phrase, in the technologically advanced sectors of the economy. They are not of stable working-class stock, but include declassed persons of every stratum. Because of its background and character, the *Lumpenproletariat* is not easily amenable to organization for political and economic protest. It is apathetic. It has been "hard to reach" for agitators as well as for social workers, or at least so thought the Marxists. In point of fact, it has frequently been amenable to political organization, but as soon as it was organized, it was no longer *Lumpenproletariat,* at least not by Marxian standards.

Another concept worth exploring is one suggested by Thorstein Veblen: the concept of a spurious leisure class. It too was never fully developed. Veblen intimated that at the very bottom of the class system, as at the very top, there developed a stratum that lived in leisure and was given to predatory sentiments and behavior.[34] The resemblance between the genuine and spurious leisure class was also noted by George Dowling in 1893. He wrote in *Scribner's,* "The opulent who are not rich by the results of their own industry . . . suffer atrophy of virile and moral powers, and like paupers live on the world's surplus without adding to it or giving any fair equivalent for their maintenance."[35] The spurious leisure class, like Veblen's pe-

[33] Victor Chernov, *The Great Russian Revolution* (New Haven: Yale University Press, 1936), pp. 414-15.

[34] Thorstein Veblen, *The Theory of the Leisure Class* (New York: Huebsch, 1919), Chapter 10.

[35] Bremner, *From the Depths,* p. 22.

cuniary masters of society, lived in industrial society but temperamentally and functionally were not part of it. Because they were not dedicated to the spirit of industrial workmanship, they never evinced the matter-of-fact, mechanistic, and sober frame of mind so admired by Veblen. Instead, this class, like the genuine leisure class, was parasitic and useless, barbaric and military-minded, and given to wasteful display and frequent excess. The major difference was that its leisure was spurious, bolstered by neither aristocratic right nor financial wherewithal.[36] A spurious leisure class, then, must be peculiarly embittered and resentful. It is dedicated to luxury without the necessary finances, and thus its members are given to pose, pretense, and bluster. Veblen's caricature is as harsh as anything he had to say about the pecuniary captains of society. Though there is a ring of truth in Veblen's caricature, there is just as surely distortion.

A final conception pertaining to disreputable poverty was that of pauper. The distinction between paupers and the poor, maintained during the nineteenth and early twentieth centuries, is a useful one, and its demise was one of the major casualties of obsessive word substitution. Harriet Martineau commenting on England in the early nineteenth century, observed that "Except for the distinction between sovereign and subject, there is no social difference . . . so wide as that between independent laborer and the pauper." [37] Paupers, as distinguished from the poor, were often characterized as apathetic regarding their condition. While they were not romantically deemed happy, they were considered less miserable or unhappy than the poor. They had adapted to their poverty, and that was their distinctive feature. Robert Hunter said:

> Paupers are not, as a rule, unhappy. They are not ashamed; they are not keen to become independent; they are not bitter or discontented. They have passed over the line which separates poverty from pauperism. . . . This distinction between the poor and paupers may be seen everywhere. They are in all large cities in America and abroad, streets and courts and alleys where a class of people live who have lost all self-respect and ambition, who rarely, if ever, work, who are aimless and drifting, who like drink, who have no thought for their children, and who live more or less contentedly on rubbish and alms.

---

[36] In like manner, Boulding has referred to "poor aristocrats" who pass easily into the criminal and purely exploitative subcultures which survive on "transfer of commodities and . . . produce very little." See Kenneth Boulding, "Reflections on Poverty," *The Social Welfare Forum* (New York: Columbia University Press, 1961), p. 52.

[37] Cited in Karl Polanyi, *The Great Transformation* (New York: Rinehart, 1944), p. 100.

Such districts are. . . . in all cities everywhere. The lowest level of humanity is reached in these districts. . . . This is pauperism. There is no mental agony here; they do not work sore; there is no dread; they live miserably, but they do not care.[38]

Of all the conceptions reviewed, pauperism comes closest to what is conveyed by the term, "disreputable poverty." Though there are differences,[39] many of the features of disreputable poverty are implicit in the conception of pauperism. The concept of pauperism harbored the ideas of disaffiliation and immobilization that, taken together, indicate the outcasting from modern society suggested by Thomas and Znaniecki. Pauperism, like vice, "declasses a man definitely, puts him outside both the old and new hierarchy. Beggars, tramps, criminals, prostitutes, have no place in the class hierarchy." [40]

Among laymen, the common conception of disreputable poverty has persisted in relatively stable fashion, despite the shifting conceptions held by intellectuals, social scientists, and public welfare practitioners. This persistence is implicit in a lay conception of pauperism that throughout has insisted on a distinction, radical or measured, between the deserving and undeserving poor. Ordinary members of society still maintain the views expressed in 1851 by Robert Harley, the founder of the New York Association for Improving the Condition of the Poor. The debased poor, he said, "love to clan together in some out-of-the-way place, are content to live in filth and disorder with a bare subsistence, provided they can drink, and smoke, and gossip, and enjoy their balls, and wakes, and frolics, without molestation." [41] One need not concur with Harley's sentiment, still pervasive today, that the debased poor do not deserve sympathy, to concur with the wisdom in the common understanding of the differences between pauper and independent laborer. A distinction between the two, measured instead of radical, refined rather than obtuse, is a preface to understanding the working classes and especially the unemployed among them. A similar point is made by S. M. Miller and Frank Riessman in their discussion of the implications of failing to distinguish between the working and lower class. They observe:

---

[38] Robert Hunter, *Poverty* (New York: Macmillan, 1912), pp. 3-4.
[39] For instance, a pauper, strictly speaking, depends on public or private charity for sustenance while in my conception, the disreputable poor are sometime recipients of welfare. They also work casually or irregularly and occasionally engage in petty crime and other forms of hustling.
[40] William I. Thomas and Florian Znaniecki, *The Polish Peasant in America* (New York: Dover, reissued 1958), p. 136.
[41] Bremner, *From the Depths*, p. 5.

This reluctance to make the distinction between "working class" and "lower class," despite useful discussions by Kahl and others . . . leads to errors. For example, the findings of Hollingshead and Redlich . . . have been interpreted as: The lower the class, the higher the rate of mental illness. Close examination of their data reveals, however, that the working class (Class IV) is closer to the upper and middle class (Classes I, II, and III) than to the lower class (Class V). Classes I through IV are similar, whereas Class V is quite dissimilar from all other classes, including the working class.[42]

The Situation of the Disreputable Poor

To understand disreputable poverty, and to appreciate its complexity, one must distinguish among the various components that constitute its milieu. Disreputable poverty and the tradition it sustains are a compote, blending together the distinctive contribution of each ingredient.

Dregs

The core of disreputable poverty consists of dregs—persons spawned in poverty and belonging to families who have been left behind by otherwise mobile ethnic populations. In these families there is at least the beginning of some tradition of disreputable poverty.[43] In America, the primary examples include immobile descendants of Italian and Polish immigrants and of the remnants of even earlier arrivals—Germans, Irish, and Yankees and Negroes who have already become habituated to the regions in which disreputable poverty flourishes. The situation of dregs is well described in a Russell Sage Foundation report on Hell's Kitchen in New York shortly before World War I.

> The district is like a spider's web. Of those who come to it very few, either by their own efforts or through outside agency, ever leave it. Usually those who come to live here find at first . . . that they cannot get out, and presently that they do not want to. . . . It is not [just] that conditions throughout the district are economically extreme, although greater misery and worse poverty cannot be found in other parts of New York. But there is something of the dullness of these West Side streets and the traditional apathy of their tenants

[42] S. M. Miller and Frank Riessman, "The Working-Class Subculture: A New View," *Social Problems,* Vol. IX (Summer, 1961), p. 26.

[43] Boulding suggests that there is perhaps some cause for alarm when "the dependent children who have been aided ask for aid for *their* dependent children," i.e., when a sort of tradition is formed. See Boulding, "Reflections on Poverty." Burgess and Price estimate that "more than 40 percent of the mothers and/or fathers [who were on AFDC] were raised in homes where some form of assistance had been received at some time." See Burgess and Price, *An American Dependency Challenge,* p. 21.

that crushes the wish for anything better and kills the hope of change. It is as though decades of lawlessness and neglect have formed an atmospheric monster, beyond the power and understanding of its creators, overwhelming German and Irish alike.[44]

This description refers to the dregs of the mid-nineteenth-century Irish and German migrations, to those who did not advance along with their ethnic brethren. Only a small proportion of the Irish and Germans living in New York at the time were trapped in the "spider's web" of Hell's Kitchen. Putting Hell's Kitchen in its proper context, Handlin says:

> From 1870 onward the Irish and Germans were dynamically moving groups. . . . [However] some remained unskilled laborers. They stayed either downtown or in the middle West Side, beyond Eighth Avenue and between 23rd and 59th streets, where the other shanty towns were transformed into Hell's Kitchen, a teeming neighborhood that housed laborers from the docks and from the nearby . . . factories, and also a good portion of the city's vice and crime.[45]

Rural immigrants to urban areas in the United States and other nations usually entered the system at the very bottom, but in the course of a few generations—depending on the availability of new ethnic or regional replacements and numerous other factors—their descendants achieved conventional, reputable positions in society. But some proportion of each cohort, the majority of which advances to the reputable working class or the lower rungs of the middle class, remains behind. Each experience of ethnic mobility leaves a sediment that appears to be trapped in slum life, whether as a result of insistence on maintaining traditional peasant values, or as a result of family disorganization, relatively lower intelligence, more emotional problems, or just plain misfortune. These are the dregs who settle into the milieu of disreputable poverty and perpetuate its distinctive characteristics.

An excellent description of this sort of area in England is provided by Josephine Klein in her summary account of "Branch Street":

> Branch Street is a "residual area." All those who can get away from it have left. That includes not only those capable of achieving respectability under their own steam, but also those who, in the opinion of the

---

[44] *West Side Studies*, Vol. 1 (New York: Russell Sage Foundation, 1914), pp. 8-9; also see Richard O'Connor, *Hell's Kitchen* (Philadelphia: Lippincott, 1958), p. 176.

[45] Oscar Handlin, *The Newcomers* (Cambridge, Mass.: Harvard University Press, 1959), p. 31.

housing authorities, are capable of doing better in more favorable circumstances. . . . Branch street is also a "transitional area." Immigrants into the city come here, but they do not stay if they have any chance of going somewhere better. A large proportion of the inhabitants [during 1944-1949] are Irish.[46]

Neighborhoods in which this style of life flourishes possess diversified populations that, like the layers of a geological specimen, reflect their dim history. Handlin describes a single tenement in such an area.

> The poor and the unsuccessful [of each ethnic group] were generally lost in the characterless enclaves scattered throughout the city, in part of the West Side, in Greenwich Village, in Brooklyn, and later in Queens where they were surrounded by communities of the foreignborn. The very poorest were left behind, immobilized by their failure, and swamped by successive waves of immigrants. In the notorious "Big Flat" tenement on Mott Street, for instance, lived 478 residents, of whom 368 were Jews and 31 Italians, who were just entering the neighborhood. But there were also 31 Irish, 30 Germans, and 4 natives, a kind of sediment left behind when their groups departed.[47]

Dregs are the key components of the milieu of disreputable poverty also because they link new cohorts entering the lowest level of society and the old cohorts leaving it. In the conflict between new and old ethnic arrivals, the unseemly traditions of disreputable poverty are transmitted. These traditions are manifested in a style of life distinctive to disreputable poverty and apparently similar in different parts of the world. What are the main features of this style? [48]

Income in this stratum is obviously low, but "more important even than the size of income is its regularity." [49] Unemployment and under-

---

[46] Josephine Klein, *Samples from English Cultures* (London: Routledge & Kegan Paul, 1965), pp. 3-4.

[47] Handlin, *The Newcomers*, p. 29.

[48] It should be reiterated that these characteristics pertain most to the disreputable poor and considerably less so to categories like the welfare poor or the lower class. The latter two are broader categories that include the disreputable poor as a small segment. If one appreciates these distinctions, the skeptical and critical discussion of the thesis positing a close relationship between poverty and pathology by Barbara Wooten will not be seen as inconsistent with the view taken here. See the excellent summary of studies bearing on the presumed general relationship between poverty and pathology in Barbara Wooten, *Social Science and Social Pathology* (New York: Macmillan, 1959), Chapter 2, "Social Pathology and Social Hierarchy." For a more recent and more limited consideration, guided by the same skeptical spirit, see Henry Miller, "Characteristics of AFDC Families," *Social Service Review* (December, 1965), pp. 399-409.

[49] Tom Stephens, ed., *Problem Families* (London: Victor Gollancz, 1946), p. 3. The coincidence between the nature of work and style of life was succinctly and classically summarized by Charles Booth in 1896. He said: "The character of

employment are common. When work can be found it is typically unskilled or at best semiskilled. Job duration is relatively short; hiring
is frequently on a day-to-day basis. Child labor lingers on,[50] and in
many of these families, the wage earner, if there is one, suffers from
frequent ill health resulting in intermittent employment. Savings, even
over a very short time, are virtually unknown, and, as a result, small
quantities of food may be bought many times a day, as the need
arises. Also evident is "the pawning of personal possessions, borrow-
ing from local money lenders at usurious rates, and the use of second-
hand clothing and furniture." [51] The Brock Committee in England in-
dignantly observed that "an important feature of this group is misspending." "Misspending," the committee asserted, "is the visible
expression of thriftlessness and improvidence." The Brock Committee
was impressed with the frequency with which "money is squandered
on gambling, drinking, cigarettes, and unnecessary household luxuries
when bare necessities are lacking." [52] Available resources are frequently
mismanaged. "Rent is typically in arrears . . . and similar irresponsibility is shown towards bills and debts." [53]

To British investigators, the most obvious common feature of these
families is the disorder of family life.[54] People frequently resort to
violence in training children and in settling quarrels; wifebeating,
early initiation into sex, and free unions or consensual marriage are
common, and the incidence of abandoned mothers and children is
high.[55] "The children play outside until late in the evening . . . and are
sent to bed, all ages at the same time, when the parents are tired. . . ."
In many of these homes there is no clock, and "one may visit at
ten in the morning to find the entire household asleep." [56] Relations
between parents are often characterized by constant dissension and an
absence of affection and mutual trust.[57] As a result, family dissolution
is frequent, and there is a distinct pressure toward a mother-centered
family—a rather disorganized version of what anthropologists call

---

the men matched well with the character of the work and that of its remuneration. All alike were low and irregular."
   [50] Oscar Lewis, *The Children of Sanchez* (New York: Random House, 1961),
p. xxvi.
   [51] *Ibid.*
   [52] Cited in C. P. Blacker, ed., *Problem Families: Five Inquiries* (London: Eugenics Society, 1952), p. 3.
   [53] Stephens, *Problem Families*, p. 3.
   [54] *Ibid.*, p. 4.
   [55] Lewis, *The Children of Sanchez*, p. xxvi.
   [56] Stephens, *Problem Families*, p. 4.
   [57] *Ibid.*, p. 5.

serial monogamy with a female-based household.[58] Although family solidarity is emphasized as an ideal, it is rarely even approximated.[59] The disposition to paternal authoritarianism is strong, but since paternal authority is frequently challenged, its implementing frequently requires a show of power or force. The discipline of children has been described "as a mixture of spoiling affection and impatient chastisement or mental and physical cruelty." [60] Moreover, the household is extremely complex. It may contain "in addition to the joint offspring children of diverse parentage." There may be children from previous marriages, illegitimate children, and children of near-relatives and friends who have deserted, died, or been imprisoned.[61] Thus, the normal manifestations of sibling rivalry are perhaps heightened.

The disreputable poor are "the least educated group in the population and the least interested in education." [62] Returning to the Brock Committee, we learn that this group suffers from "an intractable ineducability which expresses itself in a refusal, or else an incapacity, to make effective use of the technical advice available." [63] But the assumption that these families seem content with squalor obviously arises from a failure to distinguish between satisfaction and apathy.

The disreputable poor "react to their economic situation and to their degradation in the eyes of respectable people by becoming fatalistic; they feel that they are down and out, and that there is no point in trying to improve. . . ." [64] Their life is provincial and locally oriented. "Its members are only partly integrated into national institutions and are a marginal people even when they live in the heart of a great city." [65] Typically, they neither belong to trade unions nor support

---

[58] Some are so taken by the durability of this style that, straight-faced, they hold the adjective "disorganized" to be an unwarranted ethnocentric imputation. See *Delinquent Behavior: Culture and the Individual* (Washington, D. C.: National Education Association, 1959), pp. 94-97.

[59] Lewis, *The Children of Sanchez*, p. xxvi.

[60] Stephens, *Problem Families*, p. 5.

[61] Blacker, *Problem Families: Five Inquiries*, p. 32, and for a perceptive documentation, Lewis, *The Children of Sanchez*, in its entirety.

[62] Joseph A. Kahl, *The American Class Structure* (New York: Rinehart, 1953), p. 211. In recent years, a theory stressing "stimulus deprivation" during the formative years has become fashionable in accounting for the relatively dull performance of poor children in school. See Martin P. Deutsch, "The Disadvantaged Child and the Learning Process," in Frank Riessman, Jerome Cohen, and Arthur Pearl, eds., *Mental Health and the Poor* (New York: Free Press, 1964), pp. 172-87.

[63] Blacker, *Problem Families: Five Inquiries*, p. 16.

[64] Kahl, *The American Class Structure*, p. 211.

[65] Lewis, *The Children of Sanchez*, p. xxvi.

any political party.[66] They are immobilized in that they do not participate in the two responses to discontent characteristic of Western working classes—collective mobilization culminating in trade unions, ethnic federations, or political action, and familial mobilization culminating in individual mobility. Despite characteristic apathy, however, members of this group are attracted episodically to revolutionary incidents [67] or at the individual level to criminal behavior in the form of a quick score or hustle.[68] Both are best viewed as forms of only quasi-protest, however, since they contemplate quick and easy remedy without recognizing the onerous necessities of sustained and conscientious effort.

Thus, the style of disreputable poverty apparently transcends national boundaries, though it is perhaps most noticeable in nations with strong puritan traditions. Transmission of this style from one cohort to the next is a major contribution of dregs, but it is not the only mark they make on the texture of disreputable poverty. Just as important, perhaps, is the unmistakable tone of embittered resentment emanating from their immobility. Dregs are immobile within a context of considerable mobility in their ethnic reference groups. Consequently, they are apt to see the good fortunes of ethnic brethren as desertion and obsequious ambition. Their view of those who have been successfully mobile is likely to be jaundiced and defensive. How else explain their own failure? What the reputable applaud as sobriety and effort must seem to those left behind an implicit, if not explicit, rejection of their way of life, and thus a rejection of themselves as persons.

From this perspective, coupled with a peculiarly seamy view of law-enforcement agencies, slum denizens develop a cynical sense of superiority based on the partially accurate belief that they are privy to guilty knowledge shared only with influential insiders. In a word, they are "hip," free of the delusions regarding ethics and propriety that guide the "square" citizenry. Thus, for instance, "hip" slum dwellers in New York knew or claimed to know of the incidents underlying the famous basketball scandals years before the public was shocked by exposés just as "hip" slum dwellers in Chicago knew or claimed to

---

[66] Genevieve Knupfer, "Portrait of the Underdog," *Public Opinion Quarterly* (Spring, 1947), pp. 103-14.

[67] E. J. Hobsbaum, *Social Bandits and Primitive Rebels* (New York: Free Press, 1960).

[68] Miller, "Lower-Class Culture as a Generating Milieu of Gang Delinquency," pp. 5-19.

know of the incidents underlying the police scandals there a few years ago.

Newcomers

Recent arrivals are the second component of disreputable poverty. Not all newcomers gravitate to these regions—mostly, those without marketable skills or financial resources. Irish newcomers escaping to America, even before the great famine, settled in neighborhoods already infamous and in disrepute. Ernst describes one of the most notorious of these neighborhoods in New York:

> To live in the lower wards required some money. The penniless stranger, wholly without means, could not afford the relative luxury of a boardinghouse. His search for shelter led him to the sparsely populated sections north of the settled part of town. In the twenties and thirties Irish immigrants clustered around the "Five Points," a depressed and unhealthy area on the site of the filled-in Collect swamp in the old Sixth ward. Here, at little or no cost, the poorest of the Irish occupied dilapidated old dwellings and built flimsy shanties. . . . In the heart of the Five Points was the Old Brewery, erected in 1792. . . . Transformed into a dwelling in 1837, the Old Brewery came to house several hundred men, women, and children, almost equally divided between Irish and Negroes, including an assortment of "thieves, murderers, pickpockets, beggars, harlots, and degenerates of every type." . . . As early as 1830 the Sixth ward, and the Five Points in particular, had become notorious as a center of crime. . . . The criminality of the area was usually overemphasized, but poverty was widespread, and thousands of law-abiding inhabitants led wretched lives in cellars and garrets.[69]

Numerically, newcomers are probably the largest component of the disreputable poor, but it is important to recall that except for a small proportion their collective destiny is eventually to enter reputable society. Thus, the new ethnics do not fully exhibit the features of disreputable poverty described above nor do they manifest the embittered sense of defeat and resignation characteristic of dregs.[70] They are more apt to express a sort of naive optimism, especially since their new urban standard of life is, if anything, higher than standards previously experienced.

---

[69] Robert Ernst, *Immigrant Life in New York City, 1825-1863* (New York: King's Crown Press, 1949), p. 39.

[70] For a suggestive discussion of the ambition and optimism of new European migrants in contrast with the resignation and apathy of old Americans of Scotch-Irish descent, see Herman Lantz, "Resignation, Industrialization and the Problem of Social Change," in Shostak and Gomberg, eds., *Blue-Collar World*, pp. 258-70. Also see Herman Lantz, *People of Coal Town* (New York: Columbia University Press, 1958).

Newcomers contribute an exotic element, whether they are European, Latin American, or indigenously American as in the case of southern Negroes and whites. Typically backward peoples, they season the streets of the metropolis with peasant traditions. It is this element that has excited the imagination of Bohemians and other intellectuals and led to the persistent romanticizing of life among the disreputable poor. Unfortunately, however, this exotic quality is double-edged, and one of the edges is considerably sharper than the other. Admiration from intellectuals was of little consequence for newly arrived ethnics compared with their persistent humiliation and degradation by resident ethnics.

A negative, degrading conception of newcomers seems a general feature of their reception by older, established members of the community. The description of recent Appalachian migrants to the big city illustrates the stereotypical mold into which the agrarian newcomer has been placed. William Powles reports the stereotype and comments on its validity.

> The outside world claims that the people of Appalachia "look odd," "talk funny," "act stupid." They are lampooned as "Newfies," "Arkies," "brierhoppers," "hillbillies," "poor white trash," fit only for the hills or the slums. No doubt a minority may have gone under, stupefied, demoralized, debauched, debased, inbred, reverted over generations to the status of near-savages, without (so it is broadly hinted by their detractors) even the incest-taboo of . . . respectable savages. But the majority, despite their lack of emphasis on formal learning and their shyness of the great, busy, city world, are warm, friendly, intelligent people, loving their land, creating a folk music both cheerful and sad, and, when transplanted to the city, coping with characteristic vigor with that forbidding world. Their misfortune is that the stable and successful evoke little notice. Only the minority come to the attention of social agencies, the law, and the press. In the city, this minority probably amounts to no more than 10 percent.[71]

The style of disreputable poverty was transmitted in the context of humiliation and victimization. In the folklore of slum traditions and, to a considerable degree, in reality, the newcomers are untutored in the ways of slum sophistication. "Greenhorns," "banana boaters," whatever they are called, they learn the style of disreputable poverty primarily through being victims of it. They learn not by doing but, initially, by "being had." This traditional pattern is neatly summarized in an older description of the environment of newcomers in American

---

[71] William E. Powles, "The Southern Appalachian Migrant: Country Boy Turned Blue-Collarite," in Shostak and Gomberg, eds., *Blue-Collar World*, p. 272.

slums, a description refreshingly free of the contrived relativism that currently misleads some anthropologists and sociologists.

> The moral surroundings are . . . bad for them. In tenement districts the unsophisticated Italian peasant or the quiet, inoffensive Hebrew is thrown into contact with the degenerate remnants of former immigrant populations, who bring influence to bear to rob, persecute, and corrupt the newcomers.[72]

Why have the newly arrived ethnics been so persistently humiliated and degraded by the old ethnic remnants? At one level, the answer seems simple. Despite all their failings, those who were left behind could lord it over the new arrivals for they at least were Americanized, though not sufficiently Americanized to be confident. Embittered and resentful on the one hand, and anxious and uncertain about their Americanism on the other, the ethnic dregs suffered from the classic conditions under which groups seek out scapegoats.

Transmission of the style of disreputable poverty in the context of humiliation and victimization helped to dampen the optimism with which newcomers frequently arrived, and thus facilitated its adoption by a segment of them. Optimism and other cultural resistances were never completely obliterated, however, and only a small proportion succumbed to the temptations of disreputable poverty. Ethnic groups entering America and other nations have varied considerably in their vulnerability,[73] but in each one at least a few families became dregs.

Skidders

Skidders are a third component in the milieu of disreputable poverty. These are men and women who have fallen from higher social standing. They include alcoholics, addicts, perverts, and otherwise disturbed individuals who come, after a long history of skidding, to live in the run-down sections of the metropolis.[74] To a slight extent, low-cost public housing has concealed skidders from immediate view, but it still serves only a small proportion of the poor and at any rate tends to be reserved for the deserving poor. Among the disreputable poor, the visibility of skidders remains high.

---

[72] *United States Industrial Commission on Immigration,* Volume XV of the Commission's Report (Washington, D. C.: U.S. Government Printing Office, 1901), p. xlvii.

[73] The reasons for this variability are complicated; some of them will be suggested in the final section on "The Process of Pauperization."

[74] For a recent empirical study of skidders in Chicago, see Donald Bogue, *Skid Row in American Cities* (Chicago: Community and Family Study Center, 1963).

Occasionally, along with the skidders, one finds some especially hardy Bohemians who take their ideology seriously enough to live among their folk. But it is the skidders rather than Bohemians who contribute importantly to the culture of disreputable poverty. Even when they live in sections of this sort, Bohemians tend to be insulated partially by their clannishness but primarily because they are ungratefully rejected by the authentic outsiders they romanticize.

Skidders contribute a tone of neuroticism and flagrant degradation. They are pathetic and dramatic symbols of the ultimate in disreputable poverty. Perhaps more important, they are visible evidence of the flimsy foundations of success and standing in society and, as such, furnish yet another argument against sustained and conscientious effort. These are the fallen; they have achieved at least modest success and found it somehow lacking in worth. Skidders are important not because they are very numerous among the disreputable poor, but rather because they dramatically exemplify the worthlessness of effort. While their degradation may sometimes goad others, particularly the new ethnic, to conscientious efforts to escape a similar fate, the old ethnic dregs take the skidder's fall as additional evidence of the meanness of social life and the whimsy of destiny. With such a view of life, grave doubts are cast on the efficacy of mobilizing effort or maintaining morality.

The Infirm

The infirm are the fourth element in the milieu of disreputable poverty. Before age, injury, or illness made them infirm, these people belonged to other strata—especially in the reputable sections of the working class. Their downward shift may take the form of physically moving from a reputable to a disreputable neighborhood, but more frequently, perhaps, the infirm stay put, and the neighborhood moves out from under them. Frequently, they belong to old ethnic groups, but not to the dregs, since they have achieved or maintained reputable status. They slip because of some misfortune, aging being the most common.[75] Their contribution is, in part, similar to the skidders, but without the blatant elements of neuroticism and degradation. Like the skidders, they testify to the flimsy foundations of respectability, the worthlessness of sustained effort, and the whimsical nature of fate

---

[75] For good reviews of the economic situation of the aged, see Charles Linninger, "Some Aspects of the Economic Situation of the Aged," and Lenore Epstein, "The Income Position of the Aged," both in Harold Orbach and Clark Tibbits, eds., *Aging and the Economy* (Ann Arbor: University of Michigan Press, 1963), pp. 71-90 and 91-102.

or destiny. Like the skidders—even more so because they have done less to provoke their fate—they symbolize the "beat" conception of life among the disreputable poor.

But the infirm have a distinctive contribution of their own to make. In a completely ineffective way, the infirm oppose the tradition of disreputable poverty. Their cantankerous complaints and what is perceived as their nosy interference frequently precipitate a flagrant and vengeful show of license and sin. The infirm become a captive and powerless audience before whom the flaunting and mischievous youth who inhabit this world can perform. Intruders in this world because they are of different stock, because they claim reputability, or both, they are simultaneously powerless and rejected. Those who claim reputability in a disreputable milieu inevitably give the appearance of taking on airs and are thus vulnerable to ridicule and sarcasm—the typical sanctions for that minor vice. Furthermore, their opposition is weakened because before long the law-enforcement agencies begin viewing them as pests, for the police cannot, after all, bother with their complaints if they are to attend to the serious violations that abound in these areas. The infirm are the one indigenous source of opposition, but their marginal status makes them powerless to effect change. Thus, their distinctive contribution is to demonstrate the pettiness of character and the incredible impotence of those who oppose disreputable poverty.

Functionaries

Functionaries occupy a special and persistent place in the lives of the disreputable poor. The regions they inhabit are inundated by a variety of agents and officials whose conventional purposes include regulation, control, and moral restoration.[76] "Branch Street," which may be regarded as typical of such regions, is marked by many characteristics. One pertinent feature is that "social workers of all kinds are in and out of such houses continually." [77] Not only are the disreputable poor dependent—a feature they share with others—they have deviated from conventional standards. For both reasons, their habits are seen as a suitable topic for inquiry, their paths seen as warranting redirection, and their lives as requiring intervention. The direct responsibility for these tasks falls to welfare functionaries.

Part of the authority of welfare functionaries is to oversee the

---

[76] For a general discussion of the relations between the poor and officials, see Warren C. Haggstrom, "The Power of the Poor," in Riessman, Cohen, and Pearl, eds., *Mental Health and the Poor*, pp. 212-13.

[77] Klein, *Samples from English Cultures*, pp. 4-5.

conduct of those who require assistance. Consequently, they are appropriately placed to pass judgment on the moral character of the welfare poor. The distinction between deserving and undeserving poor and the moral classification of persons as one or the other originate in the functionary perspective and continue to be a matter of special moment among those who share that perspective. Though welfare functionaries possess no monopoly in making the distinction between reputable and disreputable poverty, and none in morally classifying persons within these categories, they claim and are accorded special competence in these endeavors. For welfare functionaries, these are not matters of idle gossip or spirited indignation. For them, these matters are the substance of career and profession. They are the duly authorized overseers of the assisted. Though it may be felt, it is hard for recipients to utter the phrase, "It's none of your business," to welfare functionaries—a phrase regarded as legitimate when directed to those for whom moral judgment is a mere avocation. For welfare functionaries, moral classification is a vocation. In the strictest possible sense, it *is* their business.[78]

Moral classification is implicit in the work of functionaries because it is, first, necessary in determining eligibility for assistance, and, subsequently, part of what is taken into account in reviewing the advisability of continued assistance. Such classification must be based on systematic scrutiny. As a condition of assistance, the modern state (and private charities before it) requires that its agents become privy to matters that are otherwise regarded as private. Welfare functionaries possess a license to scrutinize. Many writers have suggested the stigmatizing consequences of such scrutiny. It is because the recipients of aid are subjected to extraordinary scrutiny and regulation that Lewis Coser goes so far as to suggest that public assistance is forthcoming "only at the price of . . . degradation."[79]

Though Coser's comments apply to the welfare poor, generally, it will be evident that they have special meaning for the disreputable

---

[78] The observation that psychiatric or casework "diagnosis" frequently harbors moral judgments has been made many times. For a discussion of the transition from the explicit moral classification of the Charity Organization Societies to the implicit moral judgments of "casework diagnosis," see Roy Lubove, *The Professional Altruist* (Cambridge, Mass.: Harvard University Press, 1965). For more general discussions of the persistence of moral classification in "scientific" disciplines, see Kingsley Davis, "Mental Hygiene and the Class Structure," *Psychiatry*, Vol. 1 (February, 1938); C. W. Mills, "The Professional Ideology of Social Pathologists," *American Journal of Sociology* (September, 1943); and Erving Goffman, *Asylums* (New York: Doubleday [Anchor], 1961).

[79] Lewis Coser, "The Sociology of Poverty," *Social Problems* (forthcoming).

poor among them. Coser attributes the degradation of being assisted to the fact that recipients are obliged, as a condition of assistance, to partly forfeit their privacy and partly surrender key symbols of maturity. With regard to the partial forfeiture of privacy, Coser says:

> Members of nearly all status groups in society can make use of a variety of legitimate mechanisms to shield their behavior from observability by others; society recognizes a right to privacy, that is the right to conceal parts of his role behavior from public observation. But this right is denied to the poor. At least in principle, facets of his behavior which ordinarily are not public are . . . under public control and are open to scrutiny by social workers and other investigators.[80]

And in connection with the partial surrender of key symbols of maturity, he observes:

> When money is allocated to members of any other status group in society, they have the freedom to dispose of it in almost any way they see fit. Here again, the treatment of the poor differs sharply. When monies are allocated to them, they do not have free disposition over their use. They must account to the donors for their expenses and the donors decide whether the money is spent "wisely" or "foolishly." . . . The poor are treated in this respect much like children who have to account to their parents for the wise use of their pocket money; the poor are infantilized through such procedures.[81]

Thus, Coser argues that degradation is implicit in the situation of assistance since the ordinarily conceived rights of privacy and maturity are partly abrogated. This applies generally to the welfare poor. For the disreputable poor, however, an additional degradation is implicit in the official scrutiny to which they are subjected. They are reminded of their undeserving character; their disrepute is noted, commented on, and filed away. Irrespective of whether sanctions are taken—the main sanction being the "holding of checks"—the negative moral judgments of officials and the wider society they represent are subtly cued or loudly proclaimed.[82]

---

[80] *Ibid.*

[81] *Ibid.* Also on the point of "infantilizing," see Charles Silberman, *Crisis in Black and White* (New York: Random House, 1964), pp. 313-15. For a detailed and documented discussion of the special legal status and special penalties of the assisted that bears directly on the partial forfeitures of privacy and maturity, see Jacobus TenBroek, "California's Dual System of Family Law: Its Origin, Development, and Present Status," *Stanford Law Review*, Vol. 16 (March, 1964), pp. 257-317; (July, 1964), pp. 900-81; and Vol. 17 (April, 1965), pp. 614-82.

[82] For a journalistic description of checkholding, and other matters relating to the treatment of disreputable clients by welfare caseworkers, see Joseph P. Mullen, *Room 103* (Philadelphia: Dorrance, 1963).

In either case, the common conception of the disreputable poor as something less than human is apt to be confirmed and reinforced. It is in this light, perhaps, that the piercing cry of a nameless Negro welfare recipient is best understood. "I'm human! I'm human! I'm human! You dirty son of a bitch, can't you see I'm human!" [83] And it is in their encounters with functionaries that the disreputable poor are most apt to be reminded of their dismal moral condition and of their basic differences with the rest of humanity. Perhaps that is why Julius Horwitz observed that "the cry of being human was the most commonplace cry in the service. I heard it daily." [84]

In the situation of disreputable poverty, the various elements that coincidentally inhabit its regions conspire to perpetuate immobilization. Thus, part of the explanation for its anachronistic persistence lies in the relations among its components. But at best this is a partial explanation; at worst it begs the more basic questions. To understand how disreputable poverty is produced and maintained, we must turn to the process of pauperization.

The Process of Pauperization

Although disreputable poverty has always existed, we do not yet know how the ranks of the disreputable poor are periodically replenished on something approximating a mass basis, or how fractions of newcomers are selected to join them. These two related questions make up the topic of pauperization. The following answers are intended only to illustrate certain facets of the process, not to present a general theory of pauperization.

Pauperization is the process that results in disreputable poverty. That aspect of it by which the population is periodically replenished may be termed *massive generation;* that by which newcomers pass into the ranks of disreputable poverty may be termed *fractional selection.*

Massive Generation

Let us begin cautiously by guarding against two antithetical beliefs—both common—one connected with that hardy variety of humanitarian conservatism we now call "liberalism," the other associated with that harsh variety of economic liberalism we now call "conservatism." The first view all but denies the possibility of pauperization, claiming that

---

[83] Julius Horwitz, *The Inhabitants* (Cleveland: World, 1960), p. 104.
[84] *Ibid.*

the very category of disreputable poverty is a prejudice with no substantive foundation, and that pauperization is merely an unwarranted imputation. The second view assumes that pauperization occurs whenever the compulsion to work is relieved. This view was nicely summarized by Josephine Shaw Lowell. In 1884, she wrote, "human nature is so constituted that no man can receive as a gift what he should earn by his own labor without a moral deterioration." [85]

According to this view, the poor are readily susceptible to the immobilization and demoralization implicit in disreputable poverty and will succumb whenever they are given the slightest opportunity. The view developed here is intermediate: pauperization, in the form of massive generation, is always a possibility, and occasionally occurs, but it requires extreme and special conditions. Pauperizing a significant part of a population is possible, but relatively difficult to accomplish. It must be worked at conscientiously, even if unwittingly.

The circumstances attending the early phases of industrialization in England offer a classic illustration of massive pauperization. As far as can be told, mass pauperization is not, and never has been, a necessary or even a normal feature or by-product of industrialization or, more specifically, of what Marx called primitive accumulation. Instead, it was probably an unanticipated consequence of purposive social action regarding the poor during the early phases of English industrialization.

Mass pauperization was implicit in the sequence of Poor Laws by which the harsh reform of 1834 was built on the indulgent and slovenly base provided by the Speenhamland System ("the decision of the Berkshire Justices at Speenhamland in 1795 to supplement wages from the [poor] rates on a sliding scale in accordance with the price of bread and the size of families concerned"). [86] Neither the reform of 1834 nor Speenhamland alone was sufficient to accomplish a massive generation of disreputable poverty. But together they achieved a major replenishing.

The principal consequence of Speenhamland was *potentially* to enlarge the ranks of the disreputable poor. This was accomplished through the moral confusion associated with a policy that in essence violated normal expectations regarding the relation between conscien-

---

[85] Josephine Shaw Lowell, *Public Relief and Private Charity* (New York: Putnam, 1884), p. 66.

[86] Maurice Bruce, *The Coming of the Welfare State* (London: Batsford, 1961), pp. 41-42.

tious effort and economic reward.[87] Thus, one major aspect of Speen-hamland was a peculiar system of outdoor relief in which "aid-in-wages" was regularly endorsed in such a way as to make indistinguish-able independent laborers and paupers. The wage of the former was depressed,[88] while the lot of the latter was obviously improved.

> The poor-rate had become public spoil. . . . To obtain their share the brutal bullied the administrators, the profligate exhibited their bastards which must be fed, the idle folded their arms and waited till they got it; ignorant boys and girls married upon it; poachers, thieves, and prostitutes extorted it by intimidation; country justices lavished it for popularity and Guardians for convenience. This was the way the fund went.[89]

Consequently, Speenhamland potentially enlarged the ranks of dis-reputable poverty by obscuring and confounding the time-honored distinction between the independent laborer and the pauper. Karl Polanyi has suggested the effect of this confounding on the produc-tivity of a labor force so indiscriminately subsidized:

> Under Speenhamland . . . a man was relieved even if he was in employment, as long as his wages amounted to less than the family income granted him by the scale. Hence, no laborer had any material interest in satisfying his employer, his income being the same whatever wages he earned. . . . The employer could obtain labor at almost any wages; however little he paid, the subsidy from the rates brought the worker's income up to scale. Within a few years the productivity of labor began to sink to that of pauper labor, thus providing an added reason for employers not to raise wages above the scale. For once the intensity of labor, the care and efficiency with which it was performed, dropped below a definite level, it became indistinguish-able from "boondoggling," or the semblance of work maintained for the sake of appearance.[90]

Though boondoggling and other forms of demotivation were im-plicit in Speenhamland's peculiarly indiscriminate system of outdoor relief, that in itself was probably not sufficient for the massive genera-tion of paupers. Pauperization implies more than demotivation of effort; it also implies a more general demoralization, the emergence of a view in which work is taken as punishment or penalty. These

---

[87] This interpretation is based on, but departs somewhat from, that suggested in Polanyi, *The Great Transformation*, p. 100. See also Bruce, *The Coming of the Welfare State*, pp. 41-42.

[88] Polanyi, *The Great Transformation*, p. 280.

[89] *Ibid.*, p. 99.

[90] *Ibid.*, p. 79; also see Marcus Lee Hansen, *The Atlantic Migration, 1607-1860* (Cambridge, Mass.: Harvard University Press, 1940), p. 128.

features of pauperization both appeared in substantial, though obviously limited, sections of the amorphous mass in which laborers and paupers were confounded, and both may perhaps be traced to an institution that was already apparent under Speenhamland and before but came to full fruition in the subsequent policies enacted in the Poor Law reforms of 1834. Pauperization awaited an institution in which persistent poverty was *penalized* and in which the form taken by penalization was *coerced labor* administered on an *indoor* basis.

Under Speenhamland, the penalizing of poverty in the workhouse was a minor appendage to its major feature, indiscriminate outdoor relief. Under the reform of 1834, poverty was penalized on an indoor basis as the major governmental policy in regulating the poor. Since this policy of penalization was pursued first side by side with, and, subsequently, in the wake of, a policy that confounded laborers with paupers, it was well suited to realize the enormous potential for massive pauperization implicit in that confounding. Penalizing poverty through the workhouse reinforced and established, inadvertently but effectively, whatever mere propensities resulted from the indiscriminate use of outdoor relief under Speenhamland. The indolence and boondoggling occasioned by Speenhamland created the propensity for mass pauperization, but to be transformed into true paupers, those exhibiting indolence had to be stigmatized or defamed, work had to be reconstituted as penal sanction, and demoralization centralized under the roof of a facilitating institution. All of this was accomplished by the workhouse system.

In the poorhouse, the ancient culture of paupers could now be disseminated to those who had been thrown together with them, and the potential for massive generation of disreputable poverty could be realized. Moreover, the confusion regarding the moral value of work could be compounded and finally resolved by the unmistakable lesson of the workhouse—work is a penalty and thus to be avoided and viewed with resentment.[91]

Collecting the indolent in an indoor setting was important for another reason. Persons receiving poor relief during Speenhamland were not yet overwhelmingly concentrated in the urban slums we have come to associate with a tradition of disreputable poverty. Most were still distributed over chiefly agricultural areas.[92] Thus, the concentra-

---

[91] The moral confusion regarding the status of work occasioned by this dual aspect of Speenhamland is discussed by Reinhard Bendix, *Work and Authority in Industry* (New York: Harper, 1963), pp. 40-42.

[92] Neil J. Smelser, *Social Change in the Industrial Revolution* (Chicago: University of Chicago Press, 1959), p. 350.

tion that facilitates the formation of a subculture was aided by the poorhouse system. The poorhouses and workhouses served the same function for the disreputable poor that Marx assigned the factories in the development of an industrial proletariat and the same function assigned by criminologists to prisons in disseminating the standards and techniques of criminality. Each is a center for the collection of traits that can then be conveniently disseminated.

The defamation of character implicit in commitment to a workhouse is clearest after the Poor Law reform of 1834. This reform was a direct reaction to Speenhamland.[93] It was calculated to avoid the indulgence of indolence apparent in the previous system, but instead of undoing the effects of Speenhamland, it compounded them. Penalizing poverty completed the historic process of pauperization begun by the moral confusion occasioned by Speenhamland. The abolition of Speenhamland, in some respects, was as Polanyi suggests, "the true birthday of the modern working classes" because it forced them to mobilize on their own behalf. But just as surely, the same abolition and the same enactment of the 1834 reform was the "true birthday of the modern disreputable poor," for it signaled the last phase of the pauperization process. If "Speenhamland was an automaton for demolishing the standards on which any kind of society could be based," then the reform was an instrument for institutionalizing the standards that replaced those "on which any kind of society could be based."

The reform of 1834 was designed in the hope that the poor would be severely discouraged from going on the rates by the stigma now attached to the workhouse and the conditions characterizing it.

> The new law provided that in the future no outdoor relief should be given. . . . Aid-in-wages was . . . discontinued. . . . It was now left to the applicant to decide whether he was so utterly destitute of all means that he would voluntarily repair to a shelter which was deliberately made a place of horror. The workhouse was invested with a stigma; and staying in it was made a psychological and moral torture. . . . the very burial of a pauper was made an act by which his fellow men renounced solidarity with him even in death.[94]

Surely, this was to reinstitute the distinction between independent laborer and pauper, but only after 40 years of confounding precisely that issue. Together the two policies (Speenhamland and the Reform

---

[93] Sidney and Beatrice Webb, *English Poor Law History,* Vol. 8 of *English Local Government* (London: Longmans, Green, 1929), pp. 14-15.

[94] Polanyi, *The Great Transformation,* pp. 101-02.

Act) comprise the classic way to generate a mass population of paupers.

Doubtless, pauperization is easier to accomplish when the population in question is a subjugated national or ethnic group rather than an indigenous group of subjects or citizens. Subjugated people are regarded as moral inferiors to begin with, capable of a variety of vices that typically include indolence and immorality. Pauperizing an indigenous population is more difficult in the measure that national affinities limit, though without necessarily precluding the possibilities of imputing subhuman stature. The English case is classic precisely because pauperizing some part of an indigenous population is difficult. But in that case too, the extent of indigenous pauperization is easily exaggerated, for many who were caught in the curious combination of Speenhamland indulgence and reform penalization were in fact not English but Irish. Some of the Irish in England were pauperized by the same circumstances that affected indigenous Englishmen, but many more were pauperized by a separate process, one that illustrates the pattern of extreme subjugation by which the poor among captive or conquered peoples are commonly pauperized. This second pattern of massive pauperization is of paramount importance in the United States because it perhaps produced the two major ethnic contributors to the tradition of disreputable poverty—the Irish and the Negro.[95]

The great Irish famine was only the culmination of a long period of subjugated poverty which drove the Irish eastward across the channel to England and westward to America. Both before and during the famine it is likely that England rather than America received the most profoundly pauperized sections of the Irish poor,[96] if only because migration to nearby England was economically more feasible. Ireland was an impoverished colony, before, during, and after its great famine, and perhaps, as travelers during the period suggested, impoverished to an extent unrivaled in the rest of Europe.[97] Impoverishment, however, is not the same as pauperization. In the Irish experience, extreme economic impoverishment was combined with profound political subjugation. Just as penalization pauperizes an indigenous population, political subjugation of a captive or colonized

<hr>

[95] For a general sense in which Irish and Negroes were at least somewhat different from other immigrant groups in America, see Nathan Glazer and Daniel P. Moynihan, *Beyond the Melting Pot* (Cambridge, Mass.: The M.I.T. Press and Harvard University Press, 1963).

[96] John A. Jackson, *The Irish in Britain* (London: Routledge & Kegan Paul, 1963), p. 9; also see Cecil Woodham-Smith, *The Great Hunger* (London: Hamish Hamilton, 1962), p. 270.

[97] Woodham-Smith, *The Great Hunger*, pp. 19-20.

people may transform the merely poor into paupers through the agency of oppression and degradation. The political subjugation experienced by the Irish was tantamount to the penalization of the entire island.

Beginning in 1695, the Irish were subjected to the infamous Penal Laws which Edmund Burke aptly described as "a machine of wise and elaborate contrivance, and as well fitted for the oppression, impoverishment, and degradation of a people and the debasement in them of human nature itself, as ever proceeded from the perverted ingenuity of man." The effects of the Penal Laws are suggested by Woodham-Smith. She says:

> The material damage suffered through the penal laws was great; ruin was widespread, old families disappeared and old estates were broken up; but the most disastrous effects were moral. The Penal Laws brought lawlessness, dissimulation, and revenge in their train, and the Irish character, above all the character of the peasantry, did become in Burke's words degraded and debased. The upper classes were able to leave the country and many middle-class merchants contrived, with guile, to survive, but the poor Catholic peasant bore the full hardship. His religion made him an outlaw; in the Irish House of Commons he was described as "the common enemy," and whatever was inflicted on him, he must bear, for where could he look for redress? To his landlord? Almost invariably an alien conqueror. To the law? Not when every person connected with the law, from the jailer to the judge, was a Protestant who regarded him as "the common enemy." [98]

The lingering effects of the Penal Laws were instrumental in creating the two traditions for which the Irish later became noted, terrorist rebellion and disreputable poverty.

The pauperization of the Irish peasantry was also facilitated by the Irish system of land tenure, headed by absentee landlords and managed largely by local agents. Under the policy of surrender and regrant of land, most Irish farmers had become rent-paying tenants.[99] Moreover, the land system, and especially the institution of "cant," seemed almost calculated to punish conscientious effort and reward slovenliness.

> The most calloused abuse by the landlord of his ownership was the practice of putting up farms for "cant" [or public auction] when leases expired. No matter how faithfully a tenant paid his rent, how dutifully he had observed regulations, or how well he had improved the property by his own labors, he was in constant danger of being

---

[98] *Ibid.*, pp. 27-28.
[99] Ernst, *Immigrant Life in New York City, 1825-1863*, p. 5.

outbid for his farm by the "grabber" upon the expiration of the lease.
. . . Moreover, in the Catholic parts of Ireland . . . the tenant was
not entitled to compensation for improvements brought by himself. . . .
Hard experience had taught the tenant the penalties of improving the
property he leased or hired and the self-interest of slovenliness. If he
improved the property, his rent was raised! . . . progress and improvement, instead of being encouraged by the landlord for his own
interests, were penalized. This upside-down system withered the
character, destroyed the initiative, and squelched the ambition of the
Irish tenant.[100]

A key factor in pauperization, as in the English Poor Law policy,
was the negative association of work with sanction. In one instance,
conscientious effort was punished, whereas in the other it was used
as a punishment. Either form of association of work with a negative
sanction facilitates pauperization. Mere indolence is converted to
an active antagonism to work. By the time the Irish began to emigrate
to America, the policy of political subjugation along with the economic impoverishment of the island had had its effect. A substantial
proportion of the population had been pauperized though, almost
certainly, it was nothing approaching a majority. So difficult is the
process of pauperization that no more than a substantial minority are
likely to succumb to it. Counteracting the forces for degradation and
demoralization are always the stabilizing and moralizing forces of
family, religion, and primary group solidarity; these are weakened
but never obliterated.

In the years just before the famine and great emigration, the Irish
poor were subjected to the workhouse system, which was instituted in
the English Parliament as part of the Irish Poor Law Act of 1838.
Thus, in Ireland the penalizing of poverty in a workhouse system
came in the wake of the political subjugation epitomized by the Penal
Laws, whereas in the English case, the penalizing of poverty followed
the indulgence of Speenhamland. The major effect of the Act was to
spur "Assisted Emigration" from Ireland, mostly to America via
Quebec.[101]

The penalization of poverty was the last phase in a long history of
the English pauperization of the Irish poor. It occurred shortly before
the great emigration to America. Thus, a substantial proportion of
emigrants to America had experienced *both* the punishing of conscientious effort, as a result of the cant system, and the use of con-

---

[100] George Potter, *To the Golden Door* (Boston: Little, Brown, 1960), p. 44.
[101] Bruce, *The Coming of the Welfare State*, pp. 76-77; and Ernst, *Immigrant Life in New York City, 1825-1863*, p. 5.

scientious effort as punishment in the workhouse, along with political subjugation under the English. The disreputable poverty of the Irish immigrant in America is best understood in the context of this dubious legacy, and the subsequent tradition of disreputable poverty in urban America is best understood by stressing that our first massive immigration of the very poor was that of already pauperized Irish fleeing in "assisted" fashion from the great famine.[102]

In America, the Irish were almost immediately considered worthless paupers. This stigma was applied not only to those who were already truly pauperized but also to those who had somehow remained simply poor. Since worthy poor too were frequently out of work, they were lumped together with their more disreputable brethren. Potter summarizes their predicament:

> The "indolent Irish" had been a characterization, fixed on the race by the English in Ireland, that America inherited. Superficial observation gave it currency in America for two major reasons. One was the frequent spells of unemployment the Irishman suffered from the nature of his manual work—inclement weather, cyclical depressions, and job competition. On this score the description was unjust because of the elements beyond the individual Irishman's control. The other [reason] was the shiftlessness of a ragtag and bobtail minority, noisy, dissolute, troublesome, gravitating to public relief, which unfairly settled a distorted reputation on the race in the minds of people often initially prejudiced.[103]

Given the disreputability of the Irish, they probably encountered greater discrimination than other minorities in America. "Potential employers disliked and even feared their religion, shuddered at 'Irish impulsiveness' and turbulence, and were disgusted and morally shocked at the Irish propensity for strong drink." In all likelihood, "no other immigrant nationality was proscribed as the Catholic Irish were." [104]

Fractional Selection

Fractional selection is the process whereby some fraction of newcomers pass into the ranks of disreputable poverty. It is the more

---

[102] Of course, there is another more familiar stream that feeds into this tradition in America and massively replenishes the population of disreputable poverty. It derives from the pauperization of substantial sections of the Negro population implicit in their enslavement and continued subjugation after formal emancipation. Suggestive in this respect is Stanley Elkins, *Slavery* (Chicago: University of Chicago Press, 1959).

[103] Potter, *To the Golden Door*, pp. 84-85.

[104] Ernst, *Immigrant Life in New York City, 1825-1863*, pp. 66-67.

normal, less dramatic process of pauperization, depending on existing traditions of disreputable poverty, which are only occasionally replenished on a massive scale by newly generated cohorts. Given the relative infrequency of massive generation, the process of fractional selection is the major hindrance to the gradual attrition of disreputable poverty. The conversion of newcomers to dregs provides for the partial replacement of the pauperized individuals who somehow transcend their circumstance and pass into the reputable sections of society. Consequently, the survival of disreputable poverty has partly depended on barring newcomers from the normal routes of social mobility. Thus, the general conditions underlying fractional selection into the ranks of disreputable poverty are for the most part simply the reverse of those favoring social mobility. These general conditions need no special restatement; instead, we need to emphasize the temporal context of the circumstances favoring mobility.

Strong family organization, a cultural heritage stressing achievement, an expanding economy, an upgraded labor force, a facilitating demographic context, and other conditions generally favoring mobility, have their effect within a temporal context. Once a given period is over, these general circumstances favoring advancement are hampered by demoralization, first in the form of severe discouragement or immobilization, and subsequently in the form of relaxed moral standards. Demoralization signals the culmination of the process by which some proportion of newcomers are selected for disreputable poverty.

The period during which newcomers enjoy relatively high morale is the temporal context within which the general factors favoring social mobility flourish. Its length varies, but the limits can be identified. Demoralization may be avoided until newcomers are reduced to dregs, and the reduction of newcomers to dregs occurs when the steady desertion of mobile ethnic brethren is dramatically climaxed by an ecological invasion of new bands of ethnic or regional newcomers. When newcomers to the milieu of disreputable poverty predominate as neighbors and workmates, the remnants of earlier cohorts resentfully begin to notice what they have finally come to. They must now live and work with "them," and suddenly the previously obscured relation between their lot and that of their more fortunate or successful brethren from the original cohort is clear. They have become dregs, reduced to actually living and working with "Niggers," or some other newcomers in the milieu of disreputable poverty. Pauperization through fractional selection occurs, then, when newcomers take over the neighborhood and workplace. This kind of pauperization becomes more pronounced when the newcomers who have overtaken the dregs are themselves replaced by yet another cohort of newcomers. Thus, the milieu of disreputable poverty is temporally stratified: the older the vintage, the more thorough the pauperization.

The spiteful and condescending clucking of the now reputable segments of the original ethnic cohort is a main agency in demoralizing those who still live in a disreputable milieu. The attitudes of the reputable are illustrated by the comments of upper-lower-class Irish, reported by Warner and Srole:

> "Maybe we haven't made a million dollars, but our house is paid for and out of honest wages, too," said Tim.

> "Still, Tim, we haven't done so bad. The Flanagans came here when we did and what's happened to them? None of them is any good. Not one of them has moved out of the clam flats."

> "You're right, Annie, we are a lot better than some. Old Pat Flanagan, what is he? He is worse than the clam diggers themselves. He has got ten or twelve kids—some of them born in wedlock, and with the blessings of the church, but some of them are from those women in the clam flats. He has no shame."

> "His children," said Annie, "are growing into heathens. Two of them are in the reform school, and that oldest girl of his has had two or three babies without nobody admitting he was the father." [105]

However, the rejection by significant members of one's ethnic community may be relatively unimportant in meaning, especially when compared to rejection by kinsmen. Rejection by kinsmen may be especially damaging and productive of apathy and demoralization. That it occurs even in close-knit families and extended kinship units is apparent. Powles describes the strong bonds that tie contemporary Appalachian migrants to their kinsmen, but also points to a pertinent special situation in which certain members may be cut off or excluded.

> The family of people into which the Appalachian workingman was born retains a particularly intense meaning for him throughout his life, emotionally sustaining him but also in a special way being a piece of social machinery of great personal assistance. . . . The wider or "extended" family is not a vital part of most city-dwellers' experience. But for the Appalachian migrant, its strengths, resources and ramifications play a crucial role. . . . He works his way into city-life [through] kinfolk who already have a toehold, however precarious, in the community. He negates his family ties only in one

---

[105] W. Lloyd Warner and Leo Srole, *The Social Systems of American Ethnic Groups* (New Haven: Yale University Press, 1945), pp. 12-13.

special case. This occurs when he begins to feel contempt for, and to cut himself off from, kinfolk whom he has bypassed on the urbanization ladder, who have gone to the devil, failed to make it, remained trash in the slums.[106]

We may conjecture that the closer the bonds of kinship, the greater the disparagement felt when cut off from them. Those who are thus excluded or left behind come eventually to live among yet another cohort of newcomers.

When they are forced to live and work with newcomers, the remnants need no longer overhear the disparaging comments of the reputable members of their ethnic cohort or extended kinship units. They disparage themselves. They know what they have come to, for they share the wider social view that the newcomers are profoundly inferior and detestable. The irony here is that the demoralization of old ethnics and their subsequent transformation to dregs result partly from the provincialism that simultaneously maintains ethnic identity long after it has been partially obscured in other parts of society and manifests itself in pervasive prejudices perhaps unmatched elsewhere.[107] The measure in which the old cohorts are reduced to dregs depends partly on the extent to which they themselves denigrate newcomers. For now they become in the eyes of significant others, and in that measure in their own eyes, "just like them." [108]

We have noted that the general conditions facilitating social mobility and, thus, the departure of newcomers from the milieu of disreputable poverty are rendered ineffective by the demoralizing encounter with a new contingent of ethnic or regional poor. Thereafter, though the conditions normally favoring social mobility persist, they are dampened by the pauperization of the remnant ethnic stock.

Conclusion

The disreputable poor are an immobilized segment of society located at a point in the social structure where poverty intersects with illicit

---

[106] Powles, "The Southern Appalachian Migrant: Country Boy Turned Blue-Collarite," pp. 275-76.

[107] See Seymour M. Lipset, "Working-Class Authoritarianism," in *Political Man* (New York: Doubleday, 1960), Chapter 4.

[108] The viciousness and bigotry with which the previous ethnic cohort treats newcomers is not just a consequence of their higher levels of provincialism and prejudice; what we regard as residential and occupational desegregation is to ethnic remnants a visible social indication of pauperization. Their intolerant response may be taken as an indication of the extent to which they wish to avoid the visible stigmata of pauperization.

pursuits. They are, in the evocative words of Charles Brace, "the dangerous classes" who live in "regions of squalid want and wicked woe." [109] This stratum is replenished only rarely through massive generation, and there is little evidence that anything in the current American political economy fosters this sort of pauperization. Still, the tradition of disreputable poverty persists, partly because the legacy of the pauperized Irish immigrants has been continued in some measure by the fractional selection of subsequent immigrants, and partly because the internal situation of disreputable poverty persists. Moreover, it persists for a reason hardly touched on in this chapter: because the other main carrier of the tradition of disreputable poverty in America has only now begun to mobilize and, thus, to undo the effects of its enduring pauperization. When the Negro mobilization has run its course, and if no other massive pauperization occurs, the tradition of disreputable poverty will have used up its main capital and be reduced to squandering the interest drawn from fractional selection and its own internal situation—a fitting fate for so improvident a tradition.

---

[109] Bremner, *From the Depths,* p. 6.

13

Community Disorganization

by James S. Coleman

TO STUDY FRUITFULLY WHAT MAKES MEN ILL AND WHAT MAKES THEM die, we must know something about what makes them live. It is similar with social communities of men. To know what makes these communities languish and die, we must know what makes them live. We must know the processes that transform an aggregate of men into a community and keep them one.

Introduction

Thus the first part of this study of community disorganization will be a study of the "vital processes" of the community—the processes that keep it alive as a community, and prevent its disorganization. While examining each process, we shall study its malfunctioning as well, to see how community disorganization comes about. The second part of the study will consist of *conditions* that interrupt or inhibit the vital processes. There are many such conditions, and the ones of interest to us here are those which exist today, in American society and to some degree in all Western society, and those which will exist tomorrow, as our society continues to change. Thus the focus in the second section is on contemporary conditions that impede the vital

I thank Robert K. Merton and Arthur Stinchcombe for detailed critiques of an earlier draft, and Jan Hajda for aid in reorganizing the chapter. Earlier discussions and joint teaching with Messrs. Hajda and Stinchcombe at Johns Hopkins and Peter Rossi at the University of Chicago have played an important part in my thinking. My initial concern with community organization and disorganization stems from research in community conflict, begun in collaboration with Louis Kriesberg at the Bureau of Applied Social Research at Columbia University, and research on measurement of group properties which was initiated by Paul Lazarsfeld at Columbia University. It is hardly necessary to acknowledge the debt that all students of community disorganization owe to the pioneering work of Robert Ezra Park.

processes of social communities. If this were a book on medical pathology, the first part might be titled, "Vital processes of the body, and their malfunctioning," while the second part would be titled "Factors that commonly bring on disease." As it is, they are titled, not so differently: "Social processes that create a community, and their malfunctioning," and "Contemporary conditions leading to disorganization."

What Is a Community?

At the very outset, it is necessary to restrict the area of vision. To the sociologist and the layman alike, the term "community" concerns things held in common. Some of these "things" may be tangible objects, such as the common property of a family or the common pasture lands held by a tribal community. Others are less tangible: common ideas, beliefs, and values, common customs and norms held by all, and finally, common or joint actions of the community as a whole. Furthermore, when we speak of *a* community, we ordinarily mean a set of people who have not just *one* element in common, but *many*.

There are numerous kinds of communities in the larger society: the adolescent community, the Negro community, the academic community, to name three. Yet this chapter will concern itself with none of these, for it is not their disorganization that is of interest. Our focus will be on geographic communities, on neighborhoods, villages, towns, cities, suburbs, farming communities, any geographic clustering of families. Some of these clusters, in fact, show hardly enough organization, hardly enough "commonness" among their members to be called communities. But this is precisely part of our inquiry. The geographic clustering that constitutes a village or town or city ordinarily sets in motion certain processes that tend to make these localities into communities. But sometimes these natural processes fail, or are blocked, and a community fails to develop or falls apart.

This failure to develop is well exemplified by a would-be community that never became one. In the 1930's, the United States government established a cooperative farming "community" in the West. Community organization did not take place, for several reasons. The administrators of the project acted precisely *as* administrators, attempting to solve community problems through executive order. Under such authority, no organization developed to bind the community together when problems arose. Along with the organizational vacuum was a vacuum of previous experience on the part of the residents: in their previous communities, few had played any part in community organizations, and all were ill-equipped for such activity. These two elements together left an absence of organization in the community, which resulted in a final split and disintegration.[1]

The focus of our inquiry, then, will be upon geographic localities and the processes that make of them communities, or by their breakdown lead to community disorganization. But a further clarification is necessary. Consider a metropolitan area, such as Chicago. What is the unit (or units) under consideration: the whole metropolitan area? the city as defined by its political boundaries? the suburb of Oak Park as a separate unit? the neighborhood of Hyde Park (within the city limits) as a separate unit? The answer is quite simple: all of these will be within our focus.[2] To study the community disorganization of the city of Chicago does not preclude a study of the community disorganization of its parts, considered as communities within the city. In general, however, our major concern will not be with the larger geographic entities so much as with the smaller ones. The reason for this is more than convenience: the larger entities tend to have far more extensive governmental machinery for carrying out their social action. Smaller localities are more often dependent upon the natural processes which develop a sense of community and provide informal norms and informal structures for collective action. It is, as a consequence, these communities that are most vulnerable when the natural processes fail to operate.

What Is Community Disorganization?

Social organization is important for one reason alone: to enable the social unit to take action as a unit. If bridges are to be built, wars won, food grown, criminals caught, then there must be organization. Thus our examination of community disorganization will concern the community's inability to *act* as a community.[3] If a community can act

---

[1] See Edward Banfield, *Government Project* (New York: Free Press, 1951).

[2] Some urban sociologists who have studied Chicago have, in fact, suggested that it is the very strength of Chicago's separate neighborhoods as communities that inhibited collective action at the level of the larger community when it became necessary. Sociologists have explicitly studied the city of Chicago as a set of 75 "community areas." See Philip M. Hauser and Evelyn Kitagawa, *Local Community Fact Book for Chicago, 1950* (Chicago: Chicago Community Inventory, 1953). This publication is the third fact book on Chicago's community areas, an enterprise begun by Louis Wirth, a sociologist who had a deep interest in the study of Chicago as a community and a set of subcommunities.

[3] As a number of authors have pointed out, from William Thomas and Florian Znaniecki (*The Polish Peasant in Europe and America* [New York: Dover, reissued 1958]) to Albert Cohen ("The Study of Social Disorganization and Deviant Behavior," in R. K. Merton, L. Broom, L. S. Cottrell, Jr., eds., *Sociology Today* [New York: Basic Books, 1959]), social disorganization is distinct from personal disorganization, just as psychological conflict within an individual is dis-

collectively toward the problems that face it, then it is well organized. If it cannot, then it is disorganized relative to these problems, though there may be a great amount of apparent organization.

Such inability to act can come about in two ways: through an absence of any collective effort, or through the existence of conflicting collective efforts that cancel each other out. That is, in some systems, there is no collective energy available for unitary action; in others, there is collective energy, but in mutual opposition, thereby setting up tension without action. The first can be likened to the wasting away of tissue in a body, the second to paralysis.

These have been the two elements of community disorganization pointed to by many authors. The first is often termed a decline in common consensus, or a weakening of social norms and constraints. This will be called *disintegration* in the succeeding pages. The second concerns culture conflict, social conflict, or normative conflict. It will be called *conflict* in the succeeding pages.

Social Processes That Create a Community, and Their Malfunctioning

Nothing in the definition of "community" implies a geographic locality. Yet we often speak of such a locality (a village, town, or city) as a "community." How does this happen? Certainly not through purposive, rational organization, as occurs in the establishment of business organizations, schools, and other formal organizations. Ferdinand Tönnies, who illuminated the special character of the community, wrote about this in 1887, in a general discussion of *Gemeinschaft* or community:

> Neighborhood describes the general character of living together in the rural village. The proximity of dwellings, the communal fields, and even the mere contiguity of holdings necessitate many contacts of human beings and cause inurement to and intimate knowledge of one another. They also necessitate co-operation in labor, order, and management, and lead to common supplication for grace and mercy to the gods and spirits of land and water who bring blessing or menace with disaster.[4]

Tönnies suggests some of the elements that are responsible for these community-generating processes. The key lies in the *activities*

---

tinct from social conflict. Similarly, societal disorganization is distinct from community disorganization, though in the past there has been empirical connection.

[4] Ferdinand Tönnies, *Community and Society*, translated and edited by C. P. Loomis (East Lansing: Michigan State University Press, 1957), pp. 42, 43.

that men carry out in pursing their own ends. Some of the more important ones should be listed:

> work
> education of children
> religiously related activities
> organized leisure activities
> unorganized social play of children
> unorganized social play of adults
> voluntary activities for charitable or other purposes
> treatment of sickness, birth, death
> buying and selling of property
> buying consumable goods (food, etc.)
> saving and borrowing money
> maintenance of physical facilities (roads, sewers, water, light)
> protection from fire
> protection from criminal acts

Some of these activities can be carried out by individuals. But for most of them, conjunction with other persons is either necessary or desirable. Education of children in modern society could hardly be carried out by most parents; yet this is an activity that must be carried out locally, at least in its early stages. Other activities, such as work, can more easily be carried on outside the local community, and it is such activities that, in modern society, have become less and less local, have moved increasingly out of the local community.

How do these activities form a community out of a set of people? They do so through several processes which will be outlined in some detail below.

Similar Activities, and the Development of Similar Values, Attitudes, Beliefs

One of the elements of commonness composing a community is similarity of activities. In any community where people are engaged in similar activities and subject to the same or similar events, the very similarity generates topics for conversation, leads people to enjoy one another's company, and creates bonds of mutual understanding. This is evident in such disparate situations as those indicated below:

1. In a small southern community:

> The drug stores serve as social centers and are rarely empty. People come, not merely to buy a toothbrush or a cake of soap, but to linger over their Coca-Colas, which they take in small, leisurely sips interspersed with long drafts of gossip. The proprietor is always at hand and always ready with conversation. The habitués are mainly young women, clerks and stenographers from the courthouse, and "men

about town," which may mean a lawyer, a county official, a planter from the country. Upon inquiring for the owner of a plantation ten or twelve miles away, one is told that he can be found any day at his favorite drug store.[5]

2. In a London slum:

> "My Mum comes around at about 3:15—she comes round regularly at that time to spend the afternoon"; "Mum's always popping in here— 12 times a day I should say"; "Then my Mum and I collect Stephen from the school and go back to her place for tea"; "We usually have dinner round at her place"; "She's always popping in here"; "We've got four keys—one for each of us, one for Mum, and one for Mary. That's so they can come in any time they like." "Popping in" for a chat and a cup of tea is the routine of normal life.[6]

3. In a prison:

> As a result of contacts between cell mates, types of relationships develop that are interesting to observe. Including the nine hours supposedly given over to sleep, cell mates spend between eleven and fifteen hours a day in each other's presence. The time in the cell is spent in reading, card playing, idleness, studying, listening to the radio, or in other similar activities.[7]

The similar activities and experiences of these people in their respective communities are an important element in the development of a sense of community. It shapes similar attitudes and behavior, and it creates among people the sympathy, or mutual identification, which pulls them together.[8] Though these in themselves give no cause for social organization, they do provide a basis from which organization may spring, and their absence takes this basis away, as the next section will indicate.

Common Dependence of Activities on the Same Events

There is more, of course, to the development of a community from a locality than mere similarity of activities and problems. Consider, for example, crime prevention. Almost everyone in society has the same

---

[5] Hortense Powdermaker, *After Freedom* (New York: Viking, 1939), p. 10.

[6] Michael Young and Peter Wilmott, *Family and Kinship in East London* (New York: Free Press, 1957), p. 31.

[7] Donald Clemmer, *Prison Community* (New York: Rinehart, 1958), p. 102.

[8] One of the earliest social scientists to discuss such mutual identification in a detailed way was the eighteenth-century author of *Wealth of Nations*, Adam Smith. In his *Theory of Moral Sentiments*, Smith shows how society is held together by "sympathy" or, as we would term it today more commonly, identification or empathy.

interest in protecting himself from robbery, murder, and other criminal actions. But a resident of Los Angeles and a resident of Portland, Maine, have few *common* interests in crime prevention. Different criminals operate in the two places. Most actions that the residents of Portland might take to prevent crime would have no effect on criminal activity in Los Angeles.[9]

The matter is different, however, within a city and, even more strikingly, within a neighborhood. Men's *similar* interests in self-protection become *common* interests, since their safety is dependent upon the same events. A crime wave may set off neighborhood meetings, vigilante groups, decisions of the town council to hire more policemen, grouping of neighbors when venturing out in the evening, and other such activities. A crime wave constitutes a common problem for those living close together, and by the very problem it creates, it spawns social organization.

Crime is but one of many matters in which similar interests become common interests for people who are in the same geographic locality. Fire is much the same. All persons have similar interests in protecting themselves and their possessions from fire; but within a neighborhood, this becomes a common interest. The individual can hardly protect himself from fire as well as he and his neighbors can jointly protect themselves by means of a fire department. Thus fire, like crime, is a problem that generates community organization. The example below suggests just how:

> The City Council was approached several times in 1870 and early 1871 by groups of citizens requesting the building of cisterns in various parts of the town to aid in the extinguishment of fire. There was also some discussion of what was referred to in the minutes of the council proceedings as an "Artesian" well, but no action of any sort was taken. However, when the council met on October 9, 1871, the embers of the great Chicago fire were still smoldering. After some discussion as to what should be done in the way of aid to the people of Chicago the heretofore sadly neglected fire brigade received top priority.[10]

Before the "Artesian well" venture ended in this community, it had caused widespread discussion, controversy, legislation, action, and counteraction in the community. These families' similar problems of

---

[9] Certain types of crime, of course, have nationwide networks, so that certain kinds of crime prevention (e.g., of drug traffic) in one city have important repercussions for other cities.

[10] Kenneth B. Butler *et al.*, *Magnificent Whistle Stop* (Mendota, Ill.: Wayside Press, 1953), p. 47.

fire protection constituted a common problem, and thus stimulated joint activity to solve the problem, with the end result that the locality was more a community after the problem than before.

The comparison of this situation with modern suburban developments is instructive. Most suburbs are served by city water facilities; consequently no fire and drinking-water problems that might be solved by community activity are faced by householders. The problems are already solved, thus obviating the necessity for common action. It is not only in suburban America, however, that such an attenuation of common problems occurs. A study of a neighborhood in Tokyo discusses the decline in neighbor relations, and suggests they are in part due to the reduction of common problems:

> In districts like Shitayama-cho the formal maintenance of neighbor relations still serves some important economic ends such as dealing with emergencies like death and illness, as well as being a means to the less calculable satisfactions of meeting smiling faces instead of blank stares as soon as one steps outside one's door. But these economic considerations are far less important than they are for the farmer whose livelihood depends on various forms of cooperation with his neighbors. Fire insurance, life insurance, and post-office savings schemes are widely employed; in the last resort there is always public assistance.[11]

Thus, one of the fundamental processes in the development of a community is the existence of common problems that can best be solved by joint action. If the problems cannot be solved (as in an extended drought) or if there are formal structures established to solve them outside the community (such as fire insurance, or city water extended to the suburbs, or federal financing for neighborhood rehabilitation), then no community action on these problems can take place, and no perceptible strengthening of the community can occur as a consequence.

Interdependence of Dissimilar Activities

The preceding section indicated how common dependence of similar activities upon the same events creates a common interest and a common goal. But any community is made up of a host of different activities, activities that may even have conflicting goals. Many of the activities of a community are complementary, involving an exchange of goods or services. The merchants in a farm town live off the farm-

---

[11] Ronald P. Dore, *City Life in Japan* (Berkeley: University of California Press, 1958), p. 258.

ers: the merchants in a suburb live off the commuters. A public school teacher is engaged in activities very different from those of a real estate dealer; but the schoolteacher must have a place to live, and the real estate dealer's children must be educated. That is, any community in modern society contains specialists, engaged in activities that are not similar, but do depend on one another.

A modern community, then, includes a great many relations of rational self-interest, in which the different parties to the relation have differing interests. This does not mean that community organization and community action cannot develop from such interdependent activities. But community organization does develop in somewhat different ways in this case than in the case of similar activities and common interests.

The question can be posed as before: how do these interdependent activities help create a community, and under what circumstances do they instead lead to conflict?

The matter is somewhat more complex here than in the case of similar activities with common dependence. *Similar* activities and problems, carried out in physical contiguity, often generate common dependence on the same events, and thus common interests. But interrelated and *different* activities generate interests that are sometimes conflicting, sometimes common. A real estate dealer and a schoolteacher are differently affected by a proposal to increase property taxes so that teachers' salaries can be increased. The real estate dealer's business may decrease, while the teacher's salary will increase. But a proposal for a bond issue to build a new school building generates a common interest, for both the real estate man and the teacher may profit.

Such an alternation between the common and the conflicting is typical of these interdependent activities. In contrast to the similar activities that share a joint dependence, they cannot build up a strong bond of mutual identification. The common interests are soon supplanted by conflicting ones, and the initial impulses to identify with the other person are stifled. Hostility may develop when the activities generate conflicting interests over a period of time; but the impulses toward hostility too may be stifled by a new event that again generates common interests.

Within a geographic locality, these interdependent interests may often lead to community action. For example, industrial firms are mobile these days; communities do much to attract new industries and to hold those they have. Such action requires a high amount of community organization, for it often involves bond issues for new plant construction, creation of new water, electricity, or sewage facilities, promotional activity, and in some cases, even individual donations for a new plant building. The following example shows a community whose organization was not sufficient to hold an industry. As a consequence, many persons were hurt. There were fewer jobs in town for workers, less inflow of money for merchants, less tax money for schools and community services.

> We lost Sampsel, who invented and makes the time controls which stop and start your furnace, because Mendota did not do that which was essential to keep him and his company. Mr. Sampsel apparently did not want to move. This was his home. Most of his employees lived here, being approximately 100 in number. But his growing business demanded more ample quarters. The neighboring community of Spring Valley got its business men and civic leaders together and made a proposal which Mendota did not meet. We now view with regret his large and repeatedly expanded plant in our neighboring city, where he employs upward of 550 people. This payroll might have been ours.[12]

In this case, people engaged in various activities, whose interests were often conflicting, suffered a common setback, a loss shared by all. Yet this was but one event. During much of the time, these interdependent activities, of worker and manager, customer and shopkeeper, merchant and farmer, banker and borrower, had conflicting interests. These conflicting interests do not lead to "common action," but to inaction or to community conflicts. Thus, the same interdependence of activities that, upon occasion, creates common goals and thus community action also upon occasion creates conflicting goals and thus community conflict or a failure to act.

The independent small town of rural America has contained a great diversity of economic activities. As a microcosm of the larger economy, it has contained within its small area most of the economic segments and strata of American society. As a consequence, it has contained much potential for conflict as well as for community action.

Community Action Through Identification with Others or Self-interest

In the processes examined above, community action occurs (if it occurs at all) through common interests or joint interests of the community members in a given course of action. The picture this gives of the community is that of independent persons, each set on personal goals that happen sometimes to coincide with others—either through

---

[12] Butler *et al.*, *Magnificent Whistle Stop*, p. 271.

common dependence of similar activities on an event, or through interdependence of different activities. The coincidence of goals results in common action. In turn, interdependent activities may have opposing goals, and community conflict rather than unitary action results. The view this gives of a community is, however, an incomplete one. Community action takes place through two fundamentally different mechanisms, as the example below will illustrate.

Suppose there are some bricks loose in the cornice of a hotel, and I see them from my hotel room. These bricks could fall, injuring or killing a passer-by on the sidewalk below. If action is to take place, I, out of concern for the passer-by or the hotel, must report this to the desk clerk, the desk clerk must report it to the manager, and the manager must call a bricklayer to have the loose bricks repaired. All this is no simple matter, for it requires a chain of organization: from me to the desk clerk to the manager to the repairman. Each person in this chain must be sufficiently motivated to carry out his particular action, or there is effectively no organization. The bricklayer's motivation is simple: he is paid for the job he does. The manager's is somewhat more complex: if the hotel (and he as manager) will not be held liable for an accident to a passer-by, and if he has no sympathy with the passer-by, he may not be motivated to action. The desk clerk's motivation is even more problematic: he is not held liable for such accidents, and unless he has identification with the hotel or with the passer-by, he may not carry out his action. Finally, my motivation as a hotel guest is most problematic, for I have little attachment to either the hotel or the unknown passer-by, and nothing to lose personally by failing to act.

The essence of the problem of organization for action in this instance is that the consequence of each person's action or inaction must somehow be felt by him. It takes effort to carry out the action, and to compensate for this effort there must be some reward or punishment to him, contingent upon his carrying out the action or failing to do so.

There are two very different mechanisms that can insure such motivation, the mechanisms outlined by Tönnies in his concepts of *Gemeinschaft* and *Gesellschaft*, and by Émile Durkheim in his distinction between repressive and restitutive law.[13] The mechanism of

---

[13] Durkheim's major concern was with the difference between the kind of solidarity that develops through mutual identification and that which develops through self-interests. His discussion of repressive law (resulting from community solidarity) and restitutive law (resulting from a network of self-interests) shows an important consequence of these different forms of organization. See his *Division of Labor* (New York: Free Press, 1947), Chapters 1-4.

Gemeinschaft operates through a strong identification of each with all others. If each person in the chain of action is strongly identified with both the passer-by and the hotel, if he feels their fates as *his*, then he will carry out action to insure their well-being. Such a situation most nearly obtains in small, close communities, where all the members have known each other for a long time, and close bonds of identification with one another and with the institutions of the community have grown up. Even in large cities, such identification is present in some degree: the desk clerk usually feels some sense of identification with the hotel, and is thus motivated to see it fare well; and even though the hotel may be in a large city, all participants in the action-sequence may feel some slight identification with the passer-by who might be injured. But in modern, large, mobile society, such identification is slight indeed, and can hardly be counted on as sufficient motive-power for action.

The second mechanism that may furnish the force for action is that of *Gesellschaft*—the interdependence of self-interests. If my acting or failing to act can be made to have consequences for *me*, then I will act, and the same holds for the other participants in this chain of action. Such mechanisms are in force for a workman, who is not paid if he does a poor job, or a manager, who may lose his job if accidents occur. But in this example there are no such mechanisms in force for a desk clerk or a room occupant. The genius of social organization in *Gesellschaft* (where mutual identification is attenuated and is no longer sufficient motive for community action) is the existence of such mechanisms. In factories, one example of such a mechanism is the suggestion box, with rewards for accepted suggestions. The large factory is not, generally, a *gemeinschaft,* in which there is mutual identification and sympathy between worker and manager; thus the worker has little or no motivation to make suggestions that will aid the manager.[14] But if he is paid for accepted suggestions, there is potential benefit to him, not through the *Gemeinschaft* mechanism of identification with company goals, but through the self-interest mechanism of *Gesellschaft*. (The desire of some managers to operate their business like a "big happy family" shows their awareness that the self-interest mechanism of *Gesellschaft* is often not as efficient in insuring that the organization's interest is met as is the kind of identification involved in *Gemeinschaft*.)

---

[14] Often, the interpersonal punishment he would receive from the foreman for making a suggestion in person would be sufficient to overcome whatever motivation he might have. The impersonal suggestion box reduces the possibility of such punishment.

Most complex actions in society depend upon both these mechanisms. Some institutions, however, depend more on one than on the other. The formally organized rational bureaucracy depends most fully upon relations involving self-interest, such as the rewarded-suggestion scheme mentioned above. Communities have traditionally included a higher component of sympathetic identification. But even a community often depends greatly upon actions that derive from pure self-interest.

The combination of identification-with-the-other and pure self-interest in a community is particularly well exemplified by the formalized neighbor-obligations that exist in Japan. This relation is called *giri,* and actions are said to be done from *giri* when they have the following characteristics:

1. They spring from a sense of obligation rather than from spontaneous inclination.
2. The obligation is spoken of as an obligation *toward* a specific person or group of persons.
3. The immediate sanction that would attend nonfulfillment of the obligation is the displeasure or the distress of this specific person or group of persons.[15]

As point 3 above indicates, the sanction upon which this action depends is the displeasure of the other person, the neighbor with whom many common actions have traditionally been carried out. With such a neighbor, bonds of identification have grown up, and the obligation of *giri* formalizes the actions that would spring from such identification. However, in examining the reduced observance of *giri*-obligation in present-day Tokyo, Dore notes that the action depends also upon self-interest:

> In the foregoing definition of a giri-relation it was said that the *immediate* sanction for the performance of a giri-act is the displeasure or distress of the person towards whom the obligation is felt. It is generally also the case that there is additionally the *ultimate* sanction of possible material disadvantage. . . . A clear appreciation of the economic implications of giri-relations was apparent in some of the replies to interview questions about giri-relations—"support and be supported," "live together, prosper together" were traditional phrases quoted as justifications for maintaining such relationships.[16]

The earlier discussion indicated how common interests and joint interests come about through the intersection of activities, so that the

---

[15] Dore, *City Life in Japan,* p. 254.
[16] *Ibid.,* p. 257.

self-interest mechanism can operate to bring about community action. But the second mechanism for action, identification-with-the-other, does not derive so directly. It is necessary to ask how such identification comes about.

Identification and Hostility as a Residuum of Intersecting Interests

There is a crucial difference between similar activities and interdependent but dissimilar activities. Activities that are alike, and from which persons mutually derive benefit or loss, create similar and shared experiences in each participant. These experiences make it possible for each to identify with the other, to feel the other's problems as if they were his own. Examples of this are abundant in times of difficulty and stress. The following example shows how such mutual identification occurred in one case:

> The following spring promised to be a good year, and, optimists and gamblers that all farmers must be, they got seed on credit, and everyone worked hard and planted his crops. Things seemed to be working out again for all of us. People became a little more dependent on each other, using one plough because each couldn't afford repairs. People became closer because they had common experiences. Again the summer months became intensely hot and people were fearing what might happen. Then about noon one day everything became black. At first we couldn't imagine what was happening. Dust was sifting through the open doors and windows. Our priceless seeds were gradually being blown from the soil. I shall never forget that night as we sat silently eating our supper. It was happening to us again.[17]

These farmers were experiencing the same problems, problems that allowed them to feel sympathy for, and identification with, one another, problems that led to mutual aid. As the drought continued, they could take no community action to solve the problem fully. Yet they were drawn closer by the experience, and a sense of common identity emerged.

Through this mutual identification, each family in a sense "invested" a part of itself in the others, creating a solidary unit. The common interests had left a residuum, binding together the community, so that later events affecting one would be sympathetically felt and reacted to by all. In such a community, bricks that might fall on a passer-by would immediately be reported and fixed, because every member of

---

[17] S. M. Lipset, *Agrarian Socialism* (Berkeley: University of California Press, 1950), p. 99.

the community had invested a part of himself in every other, and the pain felt by the other would be sympathetically felt by him.

It is important to emphasize that such solidarity, which perhaps expresses the concept of community in its purest form, does not develop automatically. It develops through *time,* as a consequence of the *amount of shared activities* and *experiences* of the members of the community. Tönnies lists the following pairs of people as involved more or less in identification with others in communal relationships:

More Identification	Less Identification
peasant	urbanite
those with families	those without families
natives	strangers
religious persons	free thinkers
inland dwellers	those dwelling by the sea
isolated persons	those living by the rivers
mountain people	valley people
religious leaders	worldly rulers
landed nobility	capitalistic leaders [18]

In most of the cases, the persons on the left differ from those on the right in having more prolonged and intensive relations with fewer people. Those on the right are involved—less intensively and less continuously—with a greater number. Thus bonds of mutual identification with any particular person have a smaller chance to build up.

Perhaps the best present-day example of communities where such identification grows is military service, particularly in wartime. Soldiers share a multitude of experiences over a long, continuous stretch of time. They "go through hell together," as they are fond of saying; the bonds of mutual identity that grow among them are recorded in innumerable wartime tales.

However, when activities are interdependent but dissimilar, mutual identification is not the only sentiment that develops. Hostility can develop as well. It is paradoxical that close, continued contact, which can create strong solidarity, can also create strong hostility. Murder, the most violent of crimes, is the one crime most characteristic of small, stable communities. In the United States, murder rates are as high in rural areas as in urban areas, while most other crimes are far higher in urban areas (for example, the rate of robberies is about 3.5 times as high in urban areas as in rural). (See Chapter 3, pages 155-57.)

How can the close association of small communities generate such intense hostility? When activities and experiences are dissimilar but

---

[18] Tönnies, *Community and Society,* p. 276.

highly interdependent in a community, this interdependence often leads to an opposition of interests. Though husband and wife may have common interests in raising the family, their interests are often opposed in specific action-situations: how to distribute work in the family, how to allocate finances, what interest the husband should have in other women, or with friends at the tavern, etc. If, when opposition of interests occurs, the relations are easy to break, they will be broken; on the other hand, there are usually other forces to hold them in place, so that the individuals tend to swallow their anger and keep it inside as a residue of mutual hostility.

A parenthetical note should be added here. The term "mutual" is used for convenience, but it should not be overlooked that there are certain social situations that lead to an asymmetric hostility; that is, in but one member of the relationship. Probably the most important case is that of power differential: if I can affect your destiny, but you cannot affect mine, and if my actions frustrate your goals, then hostility will build up in you, though not in me. For example, the wheat farmers of Saskatchewan developed strong hostility to the owners of the grain elevators, who controlled their fortunes. However, until the farmers organized enough power to thwart the goals of the elevator owners, the owners did not have the same hostility toward the farmers. It is as if the hostility were stored-up energy that cannot be immediately released in action against the other. In a society, the lower classes may build up hostility toward the upper classes who have power; meanwhile, the latter may be either totally unaware of the lower classes and their problems, or have mild sympathy for them so long as the lower classes do not themselves gain power. In a high school (which is one of the closest communities in American society), the members of the powerless out-cliques can often set down, in grim detail, the social structure of the school, while the members of the in-clique, which has power, are often unaware of the existence of other cliques, since they constitute no problem.

Many community conflicts take on this asymmetric character (as will be examined in more detail later), for they represent the outburst of an out-group against the administrative structure of the community, toward which the out-group has built up hostility.

For the moment, considerations of such asymmetry may be put aside; our concern is with the general processes that build hostility within a community. As suggested earlier, interdependent activities often cause low levels of hostility—not enough to provoke disruption of the relation, but hostility nevertheless. Communities take action as communities; and whether that action is taken as the result of a town meeting, the city council, the city manager, or a popular vote, it will seldom be an action favored by all. A farmer's orchard may be condemned in order to provide a site for a new school building; such action opposes the interests of this farmer, and to a lesser extent his fellow farmers who are identified with him. He cannot prevent it, he cannot resign from the community, which benefits him in other ways, but he can build up internal hostility. Or merchants along one street may find themselves faced with an action to forbid parking on that street. They feel it will hurt their trade, as indeed it may. They cannot prevent the action, nor can they easily leave the community; but they can build up hostility toward those who are in favor of the action, or toward the community as a whole.

Such frustrations, stored up as unexpressed hostility, can create community disorganization in two ways: by building up to the point where the hostility becomes a basis for conflict in the community, and by preventing common action when the need for it arises. Consider the latter first. Organized action is necessary to attract a plant to a community or to keep one from leaving after there are initial plans to leave. If there are barriers of hostility between the segments of the community that must cooperate, no action will be taken. Roads will not be built, school bonds will not pass, parks will not be cared for, simply because the hostility arising from frustrated goals erects a barrier to community action. The drift of responsibility for social action from towns and cities to the state and federal governments may be in part a result of such community paralysis-through-hostility,[19] itself a product of the social and economic polarities in the community.

The other consequence of this stored-up hostility is found in overt conflict. Particularly revealing is the community dominated by one group, with a separate, subjugated minority. In such a case, the subjugated minority, with no chance to win a dispute, may erupt in unorganized outbursts of violence. For example, Zimmerman finds such behavior in the lower class in two rigidly dominated communities, one in Mississippi and one in Siam; and Hughes finds this behavior among the English minority in French Canadian towns.[20]

In cases where the sides are more evenly split, hostility may lead to a real conflict and perhaps a realignment of community power. Many conflicts over the city-manager plan have been of this sort. Often, the

---

[19] In part, of course, it is due to a different cause: community indifference resulting from the lack of common or interdependent activities at the local level.
[20] Carle C. Zimmerman, *The Changing Community* (New York: Harper, 1938) and Everett C. Hughes, *French Canada in Transition* (London: Kegan Paul, Trench, Trubner, 1946).

city manager is not responsive to the electorate and sees his job as one purely of physical management of the community (in one study, 96 out of 112 city managers who had completed college had engineering degrees). As a consequence, the manager often aligns himself with business interests and alienates working-class members of the community. In one case (Mason City, Iowa) a letter to the editor appeared in the town newspaper from a carpenter complaining that the creek overflowed into his home. The existing antagonism to the city manager was so great that a controversy developed, resulting finally in abandonment of the city-manager plan.[21]

Thus interdependent activities, with their consequent conflicting goals alternating with the common ones, may produce not only identification of community members with one another—and thus the basis for community action—but also hostility and the basis for barriers to action.

Identification With or Hostility
Toward the Community as a Whole

A special case of the processes discussed above occurs when the community as a unit takes some action. For example, when a community high school football team wins a game against another community, this is an action by the community *as* a community.[22] When a nation's armies make war, this is an action of the nation *as* a nation. Such actions tend to generate strong identification with the community or nation, not only among those who actually take part, but among those who participate only vicariously. A girl who attends every football game and cheers her team on to victory will, as a result, become identified with team and school by her vicarious participation. A winning team will produce a sense of community identity, or increase that which exists. Thus, it has been said that Los Angeles became a city for the first time, rather than merely a collection of suburbs, when its Dodgers won the National League baseball pennant.

The same sort of thing can occur in reverse. When the police apprehend a man accused of a crime, a jury convicts him, and a judge sentences him, this may result in the man's hostility toward the community as a whole. Similar actions by other community officials may generate antagonism on the part of those adversely affected. For ex-

---

[21] Edwin K. Stene and George K. Floro, *Abandonment of the City-Manager Plan* (Lawrence, Kan.: University of Kansas, 1953).
[22] This is less true in modern suburban communities or in cities without distinct neighborhoods, for the school does not represent the community.

ample, some persons have an antagonism toward Chicago because of corruption within the police force which they have felt at one time or another (most often in the case of traffic violations and subsequent maneuvering by individual police for bribes). More important, in some large cities, members of the Negro community develop hostility toward the police force, a hostility that sometimes generalizes to the city as a whole.

As a consequence of such processes, members of the community come to have feelings toward the community as a whole that are important in the development and maintenance of community organization. Such feelings are important elements in the preservation of the community itself, when threatened by an outside force or by disruptive conflict. In Table 1, on page 695, these feelings of identification or hostility will be considered together with those feelings among community members themselves for the sake of simplicity, but it should be remembered that they constitute an important "extra" element in the organization or disorganization of the community.

Community Organization as a Residuum of Past Action

Action toward community problems requires organization. Sometimes appropriate organization is not forthcoming, as in the earlier example of Mendota, Illinois, which lost an industry when it failed to match the attractive offer of a neighboring community. Sometimes no organization of effort can solve the problem. This was the case, for example, in the dust storms of the 1930's, for which farmers had no immediate solution, individual or collective. But when collective action does take place and the problem is solved, two types of residue are left. One is a residue of sentiments, either identification or hostility (or in many cases, both), as discussed above. The second is an organizational residue. The organization of effort that resulted in solution of the problem continues. Organizations, once in existence, tend to perpetuate themselves, as many sociologists have pointed out.[23] Even when these are informal organizations, as in the case of many community groups, the bonds between the members keep them in place.

One example illustrates this well. A new community was constructed during World War II for shipyard workers. Because of the contractor's

---

[23] An interesting present example at the societal level is the National Foundation for Infantile Paralysis, which sponsors the March of Dimes. When polio vaccine was proved successful (in part through this organization's efforts), the foundation did not go out of existence, but searched about for a new goal. A part of that search included a survey of its facilities, reported by David L. Sills, *The Volunteers* (New York: Free Press, 1958).

malfeasance and wartime problems, the community was beset by problem after problem: sidewalks caved in, electricity did not work, and so on. Because these problems involved similar interests, because they could only be solved by joint action, and because they were important and repetitive problems, they generated an extremely strong nucleus of community organization. After the problems were solved, the organizations became engaged in various social, civic, and other activities on which voluntary community groups subsist. But like a volunteer fire department, they also constituted standby organizations which could mobilize to meet problems as they arose. Merton and associates, in studying this community at a later time, found that its rich community organization contrasted strikingly with the unorganized state of another development that had not been faced with such problems. The second development had been well constructed, was well managed, and offered no difficulties to be overcome. Its management, in fact, provided few opportunities for organizational activity to develop. Government was administered from above, not generated from below.[24]

Other community histories show such effects of past problems. The study of Saskatchewan farmers mentioned earlier shows in detail how organization developed among these farmers. The difficulties they suffered at the hands of the Grain Exchange and the elevator owners generated strong cooperative organization. At the same time, they constituted almost a one-class community, with few townspeople and merchants to serve in the various organizations that were necessary. Lipset reports:

> The most important single factor differentiating the Saskatchewan social scene from other regions is the high degree of individual participation in community organizations in rural districts. There are from 40,000 to 60,000 different elective rural posts that must be filled by the 125,000 farmers. There is, then, approximately one position available for every two or three farmers. . . .
>
> This situation is a result of an almost unique combination of factors that have created the formal structural conditions for widespread individual participation in community affairs. The farmers have been faced, in the forty years since the province was created, with a series of major social and economic challenges requiring the establishment of a large number of community institutions to meet them. Pioneering on the unsettled prairie in the two decades before the First World War, farmers had to establish local rural governments, hospitals, schools,

---

[24] Robert K. Merton, Patricia S. West, and Marie Jahoda, *Patterns of Social Life: Explorations in the Sociology of Housing,* 1948 (hectographed).

and a telephone system. They were faced with the hazards of a one-crop wheat economy that was subject to extreme fluctuations in income because of variability in grain prices and climatic conditions. Their position as isolated individual producers and consumers at the end of the distribution system left them exposed to monopolistic exploitation by the railroads, the grain companies, and the retailers. Through the formation of cooperatives and political pressure groups, Saskatchewan farmers sought to improve their competitive position in the fluctuating price economy and to reduce the cost of the articles they bought. All these community and economic associations had to be organized by a handful of people.[25]

The community organization thus generated was extremely powerful, not only in informal associations, but in formal organizations. It spawned a powerful political party, the socialist Cooperative Commonwealth Federation, which gained control of the Saskatchewan provincial government and became a power in national politics. In short, the problems of these wheat farmers, like those of the shipyard workers in their community, generated organizations that could mobilize efforts when later problems arose.

A third example is even more striking than these two, because it concerns a community in the heart of a large city. This community's struggles in rebuilding itself are examined in graphic detail by Peter Rossi and Robert Dentler.[26] Hyde Park, in Chicago, found itself faced with sharp change: rapid decay of many of its buildings and a sudden influx of Negroes. The prospect was one of quick transformation of a university community into a lower-class Negro semislum area, similar to much of the rest of Chicago's south side. But there existed in this community a high level of organization. This was true in part because men worked and lived in the same community (more than 90 percent of the faculty of the University of Chicago lived in the Hyde Park area or in areas immediately surrounding) and thus had many of their interests localized within the community. The community also subsisted on the talents and experience of many of its members in organized community activity. For these and other reasons, the grass-roots organization, which took the form of block groups and a larger "Community Conference," as well as churches, neighborhood recreation centers, and other associations, played an important part in rebuilding the community, stabilizing the population, and preventing further decay. The community appears to have achieved that extremely rare condition in modern America: a stable racially integrated neigh-

---

[25] Lipset, *Agrarian Socialism*, pp. 200-01.
[26] Peter Rossi and Robert Dentler, *Rebuilding the City* (New York: Free Press, 1960).

borhood. A most important factor in this achievement has been, as Rossi and Dentler show, the extremely high degree of community organization.

Not all cases have such optimistic endings. The government farmers' project mentioned at the beginning of the chapter failed, after the administrators had provided no possibility for organization. Many housing projects fail as neighborhoods, because there are no community problems and no organizational life.

It may seem paradoxical that problems create community organization, but such is nevertheless the case. A community without common problems, as many modern bedroom suburbs tend to be today, has little cause for community organization; neither does a community that has been largely subject to the administration of persons outside the community. When community problems subsequently arise, there is then no latent structure of organization, no "fire brigade" that can become activated to meet the problem.

A new town, a budding community, is much like a child: if it faces no problems, if it is not challenged, it cannot grow. Each problem successfully met leaves its residue of sentiments and organization; without these sentiments and organization, future problems could not be solved.

Inability to Act and Rigid Organization

Despite the importance of organization-for-action, it can sometimes impede action and prevent a community from carrying out any positive plan. For instance, a legislature subject to highly organized pressure groups may find itself immobilized by them. The following example, relevant to the present plight of many cities, provides a good indication of the problem.

One of the most powerful reasons families have for moving from city to suburb is schools. A middle-class family finds itself able to choose between a school in a suburb with new buildings, small classes, highly paid teachers and the school its children presently attend, with old buildings, poorly paid teachers, large classes, and other obvious shortcomings reported daily by the children.[27]

The middle-class family, interested in education, can have almost no effect upon the city school. If it succeeds in arousing the local

---

[27] This is not to say that the facilities of the suburban schools, *on the average,* are better than those of the city, for they may not be. But there is ordinarily more *variation* among them. In most places, the suburban schools are financed by the community itself, which can invest as much money in the schools as its members desire.

neighborhood about the lack of classroom space or the size of classes or the poor teachers, this has no effect. The local neighborhood is unable to act because the schools are centrally financed. Classroom size and teacher quality must remain roughly the same in each school. If pay, physical plant, and classroom size are to be significantly changed in one neighborhood, city-wide action is required, changing them in all neighborhoods. As a consequence, the expenditure for schools tends to be drawn down to a fairly low level. Those interested in education cannot raise their schools much above this level, except in informal ways.

Because schools are such an important determinant of residence for middle-class families, they constitute not only a reason for movement to the suburbs, but also a potential force for movement into the city. If a city had, in one or two of its neighborhoods, obviously better schools than those in any suburb, this fact alone would provide an important force to pull people into these neighborhoods. This would be a positive, powerful reason for families to move back into the city —a positive device for reconstituting city neighborhoods on the verge of decay. In other words, such an action would provide one means by which cities could combat the residential decay that most of them are undergoing with the flight of the middle class to the suburbs.

A related problem faced by many cities is neighborhood instability that comes about when Negroes begin to move into a white neighborhood, making racially integrated neighborhoods almost impossible to maintain, except as a transitional stage. Again, if the city could make schools in such fringe areas strikingly better than others in the city and outside, this would serve as a powerful counterforce helping to hold enough whites in the city to maintain an integrated neighborhood.

Yet such action is nearly impossible to take. A city cannot "unequalize" its schools, because of its very organization. In a city council, most of the members would be required to vote heavier taxes for their own districts, for the benefit of a district not their own. These members would face grave problems at the polls when their constituents could review such action. Nor would interest cleavage lie along racial lines. The interests of middle-class Negroes in fringe areas would favor improving the schools in their neighborhoods; the interests of lower-class Negroes, whose children are farthest behind, would favor improving those in the Negro core of the city.

Thus it is safe to say that such a policy of consciously unequalizing its schools to pull suburbanites back into the city or to stabilize changing neighborhoods will not be carried out by any city.[28] This failure to act will not, of course, make American schools more nearly equal; the disparity will grow greater and greater, and the process of city decay will continue unabated, reinforcing, and being reinforced by, the disparity between city and suburban schools. If this growing disparity is to be halted at all, it can only be by action at the state or national level.

This inability to act is not due to lack of social organization, but to organization inappropriate to solve the problem. Whether in this instance there could be organization appropriate to the problem, yet not grossly inappropriate for other problems, is questionable. Yet the important fact is that *organization* impedes action in this case. Paradoxically, in this instance organization itself helps bring about disorganization and disintegration of the city.

This example is not a special case, for the phenomenon is general. Organization must exist if an acting unit is to cope with its problems; yet it must not be so strong, so rigid, that it cannot meet a change in the problems created by its environment. The path of biological evolution is strewn with organisms whose activities became so rigidly organized that they could not survive in a modified environment. Business organizations face the same challenge. Automobile companies in early days faced problems of production and were accordingly organized to meet these problems. When the problems shifted from those of producing cars to those of selling cars, the Ford Motor Company's organization was not appropriate to cope with the new problems. The manufacturing department had too much power, the sales department had too little. It required a major reorganization of the company to regain its market and survive.[29]

Similarly, many primitive tribes were so rigidly organized that they could not survive the coming of Westerners and their civilization. Other tribes were not so rigidly organized; they were able to withstand the onslaughts of civilization, and to continue their society by incorporating some aspects of civilization. For example, Tahitian society broke down quickly under white colonialism, and the popula-

---

[28] The policy of making schools unequal to compensate for cultural handicaps, however, has been and will increasingly be carried out in cities and towns. In this case, the political pressures toward equality are more than counterbalanced by the intensity of political action of Negro civil rights groups.

[29] I am indebted to Arthur Stinchcombe for bringing this example to my attention. See Philip Selznick, *Leadership in Administration* (Evanston, Ill.: Row, Peterson, 1957), pp. 109-10.

tion threatened to die out. In nearby Samoa, however, the society was able to survive, with the necessary changes of structure.

Social Processes and Their Consequences for Community Disorganization

The processes described above provide the basis for concerted community action, or for inaction and conflict—the basis for organization or disorganization. They all stem from the activities in which people engage, and the events which may befall them. Table 1 summarizes the processes as discussed in earlier sections, showing how they lead to certain types of actions, which in turn leave psychological and social residues to influence the subsequent path of the community.

The motives or springs for individuals to act in concert, in conflict, or separately lie in *interests* and *sentiments;* the residual *organization* (or lack of it) provides a further structuring of sentiments and interests to influence the community's future. The importance of these bases of action is evident in the preceding examples. In the case of the loose hotel bricks, strong bonds of identification would have resulted in action, though no immediate interests of the actors were involved; alternatively, a structure involving self-interest at every stage could result in action. Similarly, inaction, opposition, and conflict can arise either from presently opposed interests or from long-suppressed hostility.

Either community action or inaction may result from the distribution of these processes over time and through the structure of the community. It is easy to see that these simple forces, operating with differing frequencies and in different social structures, can produce the most diverse forms of activity: mob action, violent conflict, dictatorial rule, apathy, states of tense inaction, and so on. Community disorganization in its various forms results from the recurrent operation of certain of the above processes to the exclusion of others. Thus the crucial question for present-day communities becomes, what conditions inhibit or encourage these varied processes?

Contemporary Conditions Leading to Disorganization

Contemporary changes in society have a great impact upon community organization. Changes in patterns of leisure, in styles of living, in organization of the larger society, all have special implications for the local community.

Community disintegration and conflict may result from diverse conditions. Certain present social changes are producing disintegration of

TABLE 1

The Processes Leading to Organization and Disorganization: Summary of Preceding Sections

Intersection of Activities	Effects of Activities	Present Interests	Resulting Action	Residues: Sentiments and Organization
Similar activities dependent on same events	→ Action which benefits A benefits B	→ Common interests	→ Collective action	→ Identification and community organization
Dissimilar interdependent activities	→ Action which benefits A benefits B	→ Common interests	→ Collective action / Conflict	→ Identification and community organization
	→ Action which benefits A hurts B	→ Opposed interests	→ Unilateral action / Inaction	→ Hostility and organized cleavage
Independent activities	→ Action which benefits A does not affect B	→ Independent interests	→ Individual action	→ Indifference and mass

community norms, but not necessarily producing conflicts. Other changes (such as the proposal for a fluoridated water supply) are producing conflicts, but without weakening the normative constraints of the community.

These factors will be examined separately in the following pages, with attention first to those conditions whose principal effect makes for the disintegration of the common consensus in a community. Some of these conditions may also bring about conflict, although, as we shall see below, other conditions particularly foster conflict.

The Historical Trend Toward Locality Specialization

Many changes in present-day society tend toward community disintegration. Of all these changes, the one which appears to be the most pervasive, and the basis of other changes, is the trend toward specialization of locality. This trend is not new. As the German sociologist, Georg Simmel, noted more than 50 years ago:

> At first the individual sees himself in an environment which is relatively indifferent to his individuality, but which has implicated him in a web of circumstances. These circumstances impose on him a

close coexistence with those whom the accident of birth has placed next to him. . . . However, as the development of society progresses, each individual establishes for himself contacts with persons who stand outside this original group-affiliation, but who are "related" to him by virtue of an actual similarity of talents, inclinations, activities, and so on.[30]

This tendency of society to be less organized around communities in which one was born and more toward specialized groups has produced a qualitative change in the structure of society, as Simmel goes on to note.[31] In the Middle Ages an individual was surrounded by a series of concentric groups, all based on the particular position into which he had been born. The development of specialized voluntary associations, each containing only a "part" of an individual, came about only slowly, and with difficulty. Earlier, the whole man was specialized (a soldier could not even marry, but was totally a soldier). The fragmentation of men into many roles, some dependent on purposive desires, was not common in the Middle Ages.

Such fragmentation, the result of affiliation with multiple groups transcending locality, has important implications for the organization of a community. Obviously, if all of a man's activities were contained within one community, the processes discussed earlier could operate without inhibition. Common, joint, and opposed interests would arise in abundance; mutual identification and hostility could grow unabated. Only when man broke out of this set of concentric circles did he become an individual through his particular combination of group-affiliations. As he became an individual, his common activities and common interests were spread over a more and more diverse range of groups: those persons with whom he shared one activity were not the same ones with whom he shared another. Thus, the processes that tend to make a *community* out of a *geographic locality* are interrupted and diverted.

The most recent development in this fragmentation into multiple group-affiliations is physical mobility in and out of one's living-place. Modern transportation has made possible part-time residence in several localities. Not only is the community no longer a rigid circle confining men's activities totally within it; it is increasingly a less important and less permanent one of several circles of which the man is a part. At the same time, as geographic mobility becomes more frequent, communities more and more take on the character of purposive associations. Many men are now able to choose with a consid-

---

[30] Georg Simmel, *Conflict* (New York: Free Press, 1955), pp. 127-28.
[31] *Ibid.*, p. 148.

erable amount of freedom where they want to live and how much of themselves they invest in their living-place.

Locality Specialization and Kinds of Communities in Modern Society

As a consequence of mobility and fragmentation, there have come to be very specialized types of communities, specialized according to the kinds of activities they contain for their members.[32]

INDEPENDENT TOWNS AND CITIES. The most complete community is a type that is slowly vanishing in industrial society, except in its larger forms: the community that contains most of its members' activities—work, leisure, education, trade, and services. It was once true, when transportation was less developed, that all cities and towns were by necessity independent, with permanent members spending full time in the community. But now only large metropolitan areas and geographically isolated towns are even in part like this.

The very independence and isolation of such towns and cities create common problems. They must have police and fire protection, they must have water and sewage systems, they must educate their children, provide jobs for their members, regulate their drunkards, mend their roads, tend their sick, and bury their dead. If these communities were not physically set apart, isolated from other towns or cities, many such problems would not be community problems, but would be problems of the larger aggregate. But in independent towns, each of these ordinary everyday activities of living creates problems that can ordinarily be best solved jointly, within this community. Recent controversies in many communities, large and small, over fluoridation of the water system suggest one such problem. Independent towns (unlike city suburbs) have their own water systems, so fluoridation is a

---

[32] There are, of course, many ways of classifying communities. The classification here is based upon the problem at hand: community disorganization. Because community organization depends intrinsically upon the activities of which the community consists, as indicated in earlier sections, the classification must be in terms of these activities. For other classifications, see Albert J. Reiss, Jr., "Functional Specialization of Cities," in A. J. Reiss and Paul K. Hatt, *Cities in Society,* 2nd ed. (New York: Free Press, 1957), pp. 555-75. Also, Otis Dudley Duncan and Albert J. Reiss, Jr., *Social Characteristics of Urban and Rural Communities* (New York: Wiley & Sons, 1956), p. 217. Chauncy D. Harris, "A Functional Classification of Cities in the United States," *Geographical Review,* Vol. 33 (January, 1943), pp. 86-96. Duncan and Reiss provide one important element used in the classification below: the economic exports of goods and services from the community. Many people in the community make their living off their neighbors, but there must be some segment which provides the income of the community. This segment differs radically in different communities, as the classification below will indicate.

matter that must be decided by the community. It thus poses a problem in these independent towns, and in some cases there is organization sufficient to solve it. In some cases, however, there is not, and an examination of such cases in a later section will suggest some of the causes.

Another problem of such independent towns and cities, in contrast to new forms of communities, is providing for the economic sustenance of their members. In one study of a community, the struggle toward this end occupied much of the attention of the community members during the period of the study. The community was faced with a prospective loss of its steel mills, a prospect it resisted at every turn. The mills finally did leave, but the high degree of organized effort resulted in new industries moving into town and old ones expanding. The community was thus able to survive in spite of an apparent death sentence.[33]

The major point, then, about independent towns is that their physical isolation and the consequent fact that they contain a large part of their members' activities create many community problems of importance to the members. These problems often generate a high degree of formal and informal community organization, through the processes discussed earlier. These communities need more organization than many others, and they tend to have more. If the town is small, the organization largely takes the form of informal norms, customs, and mores, and of loosely organized volunteer groups; if it is a large city, organization takes the form of laws, offices, and other aspects of bureaucracy.

All the remaining types of localities to be examined incorporate only some part of the life which is contained in an independent town or city. Although these localities are themselves sometimes parts of a larger metropolitan community, they may nevertheless face local community problems. It is thus important to examine them as communities in themselves, and not merely as parts of a metropolitan area community.

RESIDENTIAL COMMUNITIES THAT DAILY EXPORT WORKERS. City residential neighborhoods and suburbs outside a city have a very different character from independent towns and cities. They are living-places, where men live who work elsewhere. In the economy of these communities, the major export is *people*—a daily export of people into factories or businesses outside the community. Such communities still contain a number of activities for their members, but many of

---

[33] Charles Walker, *Steeltown* (New York: Harper, 1950).

these are tied to the central city, or to another community.[34] Police and fire protection are partly local, partly centralized in city or county departments. Water, sewage disposal, and other utilities are ordinarily provided by the central city. Roads are repaired by county, state, or city. Such communities have thus lost many of the activities that formerly made them close communities. The processes making for mutual identification and hostility have vanished with the common and interdependent activities on which they were based. Different segments of the community experience this process in varying degrees, and sometimes this variation itself creates further community disorganization.

In many such suburban towns, there are two very different groups of people: the commuters, who are daily exported to their places of work, and the local tradesmen, who provide the goods and services of living. The relative numbers of these two groups vary greatly, because these suburbs take on quite different forms. Some have industries of their own with consequent internal economic life.

In general, older suburbs tend to have a larger component of local tradespeople, and even some manufacturing or other concerns. Many of these suburbs began as independent towns, before transportation made feasible, and city growth made necessary, the daily mass movements into and out of the city. In such suburbs, with their own partial economic life, the bases for strife and conflict exist in abundance. For the commuters, many activities and interests are no longer interdependent with those of fellow community members, but are located in the larger metropolitan area. But the people whose economic and social life is bound up in the town have community problems which must be solved. When the commuters *do* become involved in some such problem, there are few bases of mutual identification and often no mechanism for expression of their desires, in order that divergent positions might be brought together.

For example, Yonkers, New York, was in the past largely made up of lower-middle-class Catholics, many of them employed in local industries. Recently, new developments in East Yonkers have brought in white-collar commuters, mostly Jewish. The resulting problems in community organization (largely centering about the schools) are great. The line that divides the "old nesters" on the West and the

---

[34] Chauncy Harris suggests that there are two major types of modern suburbs: living-places and working-places. Thus some of the men who live in one suburb are commuters not to the central city, but to a neighboring suburb containing outlying industries. See Duncan and Reiss, *Social Characteristics*, p. 7, and Chauncy D. Harris, "Suburbs," *American Journal of Sociology*, Vol. 49 (July, 1943), pp. 1-13.

new "carpetbaggers" on the East is as difficult to cross as the super-highway that separates the two halves of the town.[35]

In the early 1950's, many conflicts in these communities arose as previously inactive, uninterested persons suddenly became aroused over issues of Communist subversion. In Scarsdale, New York, a commuter became actively involved in searching out Communist subversion in the school system as a result of personal experiences in New York City, which had persuaded him of such possibilities. His attacks upon the school library burst upon an unsuspecting superintendent and school board. He had previously been little involved in local community life; therefore little had operated to bring his views into some correspondence with those of the rest of the community. Nor was he sufficiently identified with the community that norms or constraints could soften the intensity of his outburst.[36]

This kind of situation seems to have occurred frequently in suburban communities during the subversion scares of the 1950's. It was in the suburban fringes surrounding mushrooming cities (for example, Houston, Denver, Los Angeles, New York) that such cases were most frequently reported.[37]

Some new suburbs (for example, in the Chicago area, Park Forest, Flossmoor, Oak Lawn, and other southwestern suburbs) have little or no internal economic life, and are almost purely residential. Even local goods and services are provided by a few large shopping centers, whose owners and employees live elsewhere, thus keeping the suburb solely a living-place for commuters. This pure case represents a new type of wholly residential community, homogeneous in age, income level, and style of life. Disorganization in such communities takes the form of community disintegration, in the absence of common problems and common activities.

Such purely residential communities are not confined to suburban developments. New housing projects that have replaced slums in the center of many cities have often become solely places to live for their residents. One observer of such housing projects in New York City reports:

---

[35] Harrison Salisbury's series of articles in *The New York Times* on Yonkers' problems shows well the organizational difficulties of some of these communities. See Harrison E. Salisbury, Four Articles on Yonkers, N. Y., *The New York Times,* April 18-21, 1955.

[36] See James S. Coleman, *Community Conflict* (New York: Free Press, 1957), for a discussion of this case.

[37] See the several cases reported in "The Public School Crisis," *Saturday Review of Literature* (September 8, 1951), pp. 6-20.

Before East Harlem began to resound to the deadly plong of the wreckers' ball and the tattoo of new steel work it was a slum. But it had many institutions that gave stability. There were the Neapolitan blocks, the street fiestas, the interwoven relationship of stores and neighbors. Out it all went. In came the gangs.

The new project may permit a church to survive on a small island like St. Edward's. But an absence of churches and an absence of religious influence is notable among project youngsters. The Negro children seldom go to church. The same is true of the Puerto Ricans. The Irish and Italian gang youngsters are usually described by their priests as "bad Catholics," irregular in church observance.

The projects are political deserts. The precinct bosses have been wiped out with the slum. They do not seem to come back. No one cares whether the new residents vote or not. There is no basket at Thanksgiving. No boss to fix it up when Jerry gets into trouble with the police. The residents have no organization of their own and are discouraged from having any.

"We don't want none of them organizers in here," one manager of a project told me. "All they do is stir up trouble. Used to be some organizers around here. But we cleaned them out good. Lotsa Communists. That's what they were." [38]

In these ways, at least, the urban housing project and the suburban development are alike. They have become segmented, specialized parts of the adults' lives, devoid of many of the institutions that could make them complete communities. Though these dormitories may be in part the consequence of ill-conceived planning by developers, they represent also an advanced stage in the organizational structure of society—a movement away from total institutions in which a person is embedded, toward voluntary, specialized, segmental associations.

INDUSTRIAL AND TRADE CENTERS THAT DAILY IMPORT WORKERS. Central cities today are becoming more and more specialized, as places of work. Central cities are becoming less and less places to *live*, less and less places for retail trade, more and more places where people work, in manufacturing, wholesale trade, service, and governmental activities.[39] Though low-income families continue to live close to the center of the city (many of them in their new purely residential housing projects), middle- and high-income families live farther and far-

---

[38] Harrison E. Salisbury, *The Shook-Up Generation* (New York: Great Books, 1959), p. 67.

[39] See Duncan and Reiss, *Social Characteristics*, p. 229, for a tabulation of amount of wholesale and retail trade by size of place. Though there is no variation in mean per capita *retail* trade, *wholesale* trade in 1950 varied from a low of $667 per capita in the smallest urban places (10,000-25,000) to $3,450 in the largest (500,000 or more).

ther from the center, in suburbs. The difficulties in organization that this creates for the residential suburb were mentioned above; the difficulties it creates for the city are somewhat different. As the residences of upper-income families have moved outside the city, so have their interests and money. Their interests in and support of education and the physical improvement of the community are localized where they live. New York's or Chicago's northern suburbs, for example, have a concentration of business leaders and professional men whose absence from the city's educational and political affairs leaves a real vacuum. Similarly, school boards in suburbs of major cities include impressive arrays of legal and administrative talent, devoting their efforts to the small problems of a simple school system, while the far more complex problems of the city schools await solution.

Though the city has the formal organization for solving its problems, much of its informal support has been lost to the suburbs. It becomes more and more a purely economic center. It imports workers, and by so doing engages some of their interest on which organization can subsist; yet some of that interest remains in the residential communities that daily export these men to their jobs.

COMMUNITIES THAT IMPORT PEOPLE FOR LEISURE OR EDUCATION. Resort communities and college towns differ from all the communities described above. They differ because they contain two sets of people: those who *live* there and carry out most of their activities within the community; and those who *come* there for a special purpose: education, relaxation, or entertainment. As leisure becomes more important in our society, more and more communities are coming to have tourism or entertainment as their major export.[40] Whole states, for example, New Hampshire and Vermont, are undergoing a transition from an economy of subsistence farms and small manufacturing to one of resort and vacation communities.

The communities to which people come for leisure, education, or other activities have certain characteristic problems of organization. They contain both people whose activities are bound up within the community and those for whom the community is a temporary abode, fulfilling for them only one kind of function. This bifurcation of interests tends to split the community into two parts and has given rise to many conflicts: "town *vs.* gown" fights in college towns, and "native *vs.* resorter" disputes in resort towns. There are usually few

---

[40] The term "export" used to describe tourism does not, of course, mean that these activities are physically exported. It means instead that this is the commodity that the community sells to the outside: it is the commodity that provides the income for the community.

bases for community between these two groups, and many bases of cleavage. It is significant that after the Peekskill riots (between the natives and the resorters) several years ago, a measure of community integration was restored by one of the few interests both groups had in common: the volunteer fire department, which had previously included only natives, now added resorters to its ranks.[41]

AGE-SPECIALIZED COMMUNITIES. Some communities are tending toward a different functional character from those discussed above: they are becoming age-specific. In one type of community the matter works somewhat as follows: a couple with young children has no money for a substantial down payment on a house but can buy an inexpensive house with little or no down payment, and monthly payments lower than rent. Some new suburbs come to be filled with such people. But after a few years their income is higher and they have an equity in their house with which they can buy a more expensive one. They leave, and their place is taken by another couple with young children. Such communities have a continual influx and outflow of residents, tending to maintain their special character as communities of young families.

This age specialization of communities is not confined to the example cited above: dormitory suburbs in general are not places for young unmarried persons or for retired persons. At the same time, other communities are becoming primarily retired persons' communities: Florida and California have a large number of such communities. These, in contrast to the dormitory suburb, contain a *large* part of their members' lives, but over a *short* period of time. They have their special problems of community organization, though little is known systematically about these problems. Such communities are a relatively new occurrence in society and represent another element in the vast reorganization that society is presently undergoing.

If we look at the family's life cycle, there seems to be developing a three- or four-stage pattern, with important implications for the age specialization of localities. The cycle is this: (1) early married life in a rented apartment in the central city; (2) the young-children stage in a suburb of inexpensive houses; (3) an optional third move, depending on the accumulation of capital, to a more expensive suburb; and (4) after children leave home, the return of the couple to the central city or the move to a community of retired people.[42]

---

[41] James Rorty and Winifred Raushenbusch, "The Lessons of the Peekskill Riots," *Commentary,* Vol. 10 (October, 1950), pp. 309-23.

[42] For further discussion, see Philip M. Hauser, *Population Perspective* (New Brunswick, N. J.: Rutgers University Press, 1961), Chapter 4.

Disorganizing Consequences of Locality Specialization

The consequence of locality specialization that is of major interest to us is the increasing attenuation of bonds to a particular community, with all the difficulties this creates for community organization. The problem is not due to any "evil" that can be exorcised; it is a historical process that must be recognized. Localities may ultimately cease to be political entities and may no longer have any form of organization involving the residents. As mobility becomes even greater and competition between communities increases, it is possible that the essential functions of a community will become incorporated as a business, whose "product" must be sold on the open market, and whose owner profits from their sale. Perhaps, in contrast, there will be an ever increasing transfer of functions from the local level to a central authority, so that community organization will become almost totally unnecessary.

Both these tendencies are evident today. The first occurs in large-scale suburban developments, in which the developer sells a "package" that includes not only a house, but also roads, sewage disposal, water, a community swimming pool, a country club, a shopping center, and sometimes even a school. The difficulty, of course, is that subsequent actions must be taken by the community. The developer is gone, and the community members are left holding the bag of problems, so to speak, without any structure for solving them. An interesting variation upon this is the planned development by a single developer of small satellite cities, from 50,000 to 100,000 population, containing industry as well as the institutions found in suburbs.

The tendency toward central authority is evident in the increasing number of city and state functions taken on by the federal government. It is also evident in city housing projects. Many city housing projects constitute, in numbers, large communities (Fort Greene project, in New York City, has about 17,000 residents), but have no community organization other than the project administrator. This is little more organization than the even larger suburban developments whose developers have sold their package and left.

Through both tendencies, entrepreneurial activity and administration, community organization withers away. Local activity is still far from dead, but there is no sign that the historical trend is diminishing.

CHILDREN AND PARENTS. One special set of problems created by this historical trend toward community specialization has to do with children. Though suburban residential communities are only living-places for parents, they are total communities for their children. Thus there is a proliferation of community among the children,[43] as community among parents disintegrates.

One result of the highly developed adolescent community and minimal adult community is a relative powerlessness of adults to control their children. Because there is little communication among adults, there are no strong norms about hours for being in at night, frequency of dates, and use of cars. The adolescents have a powerful weapon when they say, "All the other kids do it; why can't I?" The parent simply does not know whether all the other kids do it or not. The "pluralistic ignorance" resulting from absence of an adult community often results in the children having their own way. Many authors have seen the greater freedom enjoyed by children as a consequence of greater permissiveness of the modern generation of parents.[44] While this may be so, it is also true that this greater permissiveness probably results from a lack of strong community organization. Such organization would give norms to the parent to reinforce his otherwise solitary and bewildered struggle in socializing his children.[45]

The formation of gangs in cities, and most recently in suburbs, is facilitated by the same lack of community among parents. The parents do not know what their children are doing, for two reasons: first, much of the parents' lives occurs outside the local community, while the children's lives take place almost totally within it. Second, in a fully developed community, the network of relations gives every parent, in a sense, a community of sentries who can keep him informed of his child's activities. In modern living-places (city or suburban), where such a network is attenuated, he no longer has such sentries. He is a lone agent facing a highly organized community of adolescents.

---

[43] For example, in a recent study of ten high schools (two were suburban schools and the remainder were in independent towns and cities), in the upper-middle-class suburban school the students showed higher sensitivity to the adolescent social system and their position within it than in any of the other nine schools. In answer to a question about whether they would like to be in the "leading crowd" of adolescents (asked of all those who said they were not in the leading crowd), a higher proportion said "yes" in this school than in any of the other nine. Reported in James S. Coleman, "The Competition for Adolescent Energies," *Phi Delta Kappan*, Vol. 42, No. 6 (March, 1961), pp. 231-36.

[44] See, for example, David Riesman, *The Lonely Crowd* (New Haven: Yale University Press, 1952). Many of Riesman's observations about the current scene in modern society are undoubtedly consequences of the historical trends in social organization discussed here, rather than the consequence of personality changes.

[45] A few suburban communities (e.g., Palo Alto, California) have recently attempted to replace the now-vanished norms of the community by a rational procedure: a formal code to govern teen-agers' behavior drawn up after a public opinion poll of parents and teen-agers.

GEOGRAPHIC MOBILITY, DEMOCRACY, AND SOCIAL ISOLATION. The consequences of this historical trend toward free choice of community and toward locality-specialization exhibit peculiar twists. It is not easy to be "for" or "against" such changes when one examines their consequences. For example, a tightly knit community, which captures all a man's activities over his whole life, severely restricts his freedom. He is born into a particular position in the community and finds it difficult to change this position throughout his life. This was most pronounced in the closed communities of the Middle Ages, where a man's life was wholly determined by his birth; it also exists to a lesser degree in independent towns in American society. Some analysts of social stratification in American communities have pointed out that a working-class boy or girl's chances for status mobility lie almost wholly in leaving the community.[46]

Modern dormitory communities, on the other hand, do not entrap their residents by their social structure, for the structure is almost absent. And the freedom of choice of one's living-place means that any ensnarement that develops while one is young, in the highly organized adolescent community, can be easily shed.

Thus the historical trend brings freedom and a greater measure of democracy than could otherwise exist. The other side of this coin, however, is not so bright. Freedom and mobility cut away the bonds of mutual identification and solidarity before they can fully develop. The psychological sustenance provided by such bonds is withdrawn. The result is social isolation and anomie, with their attendant discomforts and debilitating effects.

THE LESSENING IMPORTANCE OF LOCAL INSTITUTIONS. One consequence of locality specialization and the mobility it implies is a decrease in the importance of local institutions. Churches in particular have always been at the core of community organization. They have played such an important part that many conflicts in communities have essentially been conflicts between two church groups in the community.

---

[46] This is well illustrated by A. B. Hollingshead's study of social classes and education in a midwestern town. See his *Elmtown's Youth* (New York: Wiley & Sons, 1949). A possibility of breaking out of one's position in the structure sometimes comes about through the local high school. For boys, athletics provides an avenue for mobility in the adolescent status system, and in the larger community as well. Such possibilities are not so great for girls, and probably as a consequence, girls are more anxious to leave the community than boys, and in fact do leave more frequently. For a documentation of the intent, see James S. Coleman, *The Adolescent Society* (New York: Free Press, 1961), p. 124. For a documentation of the different sex distribution of youth in cities and towns, see Duncan and Reiss, *Social Characteristics*, Chapter 3.

But the church is coming to mean less and less in modern society, and can serve less and less as a core of community organization. In a survey of community conflicts carried out in 1929, 9 out of 40 conflicts reported involved churches. In another survey of more than 40 community conflicts carried out in 1957, none of the conflicts involved churches.[47] Though these surveys are not representative samples of community conflicts at these two times, they suggest what the observer feels: the steady decline in importance of the church as a community institution.

Along with this general decline is the fact that the *local* church need no longer be the one a person attends. For example, with the mass migration of city-dwellers to the suburbs, many city churches are losing their neighborhood base. Some suburbanites continue to attend the city church, making it a collecting-point for persons who were once neighbors but are no longer. When the city church "moves out," as many have done, it again often becomes a collecting-point, rather than a neighborhood or community church. The church often moves to some location that will serve several suburban communities, for its former congregation is dispersed throughout them.

This tendency is not, of course, always followed; but the strain in this direction is evident, because of the dispersion of the congregation and its freedom to travel. Such free movement means that churches with dispersed congregations need not be temporary arrangements. Such a situation can persist, and as it does so, the church becomes less and less an institution of the local community.

LOCALS, COSMOPOLITANS, AND A PECULIAR INVERSION. A study of a community in New Jersey found two sets of influential individuals: those concerned with local community activities, to whom others turned for local problems, and those concerned with external affairs, who served as leaders of opinion in things cosmopolitan.[48] In subsequent studies, similar differences have been found between opinion leaders whose attention is focused inward and those whose attention is focused outward. The preceding examination of kinds of communities suggests that such a bifurcation of interests is becoming more pronounced. Many kinds of communities consist of persons whose activities are wholly local and those whose activities are largely outside

[47] The Inquiry, *Community Conflict* (New York, 1929); and Coleman, *Community Conflict.*

[48] Robert K. Merton, "Patterns of Influence: A Study of Interpersonal Influence and of Communications Behavior in a Local Community," in P. F. Lazarsfeld and Frank Stanton, eds., *Communications Research, 1948-49* (New York: Harper, 1949), pp. 180-219.

the community. The former will ordinarily become the "locals" and the latter the "cosmopolitans."

In many such communities, those persons with segmentalized activities partly in and partly outside the community are more educated, of a higher socioeconomic level, and are by training more fitted for organizational leadership than those who are wholly contained within the community. They represent a later point in the historical trend of role specialization, just as suburban communities represent a later point in community specialization than do independent towns.

But paradoxically, these men who are best fitted by education and organizational experience for positions of local community leadership have the smallest amount of their interest and activities located there. Those who are *interested* in the community, because their own lives are bound up in it, are lower in status, have less education, and are ordinarily the men who would look to others for leadership. In such communities, then, there is a peculiar inversion that would seem to inhibit community organization. Often this inversion creates an inversion of power as well. In Montgomery County, Maryland, contiguous to Washington, the average per capita income is one of the highest in the nation, and the schools are among the highest in production of National Merit and other talent search winners. Both these facts are due to the very high proportion of cosmopolitans, professionals who run the federal government. But in 1963, the locals, though greatly outnumbered, were able to take over control of the school board and cut school budgets. Many of the cosmopolitans were not even registered to vote in that county; others were involved in affairs of national interest and failed to vote.

Thus again, as in the historical trend of community specialization, the prospect is not bright for community organization; the trend seems rather away from organization. This is of course neither bad nor good in itself; its consequences are mixed and only serve to emphasize that it is hardly possible to conceive a world which is the best of all possible worlds. A given change may have both good and bad consequences; and what may be a bad consequence for one community (e.g., a suburb) may be good for another (e.g., the nation).

Locality Specialization and the Difference Between Social and Community Disorganization

The historical trend toward locality specialization has undermined community organization in all the ways suggested above. Yet in doing so it has not necessarily undermined social organization of the larger society. If social disorganization is seen as a deterioration of consensus and a weakening of the norms of society (as many have seen it), this is not a necessary consequence of locality specialization. To be sure, the consequences noted above involve a reduction of consensus and undermining of norms in the *local* community—but consensus and norms may be simultaneously strengthened, through this very locality specialization, in other associations within society.

There was at one time a confusion among students of society between personality disorganization and social disorganization. As long as society was composed of concentric circles surrounding its members, as in the Middle Ages, personalities were little more than reflections of these concentric circles. Thus, personality disorganization and social disorganization were not distinct, even in principle. Their separation came about only with the development of multiple-group affiliations in place of the concentric ones. Because such a highly articulated structure necessarily had points of inconsistency and strain, there could be personality disorganization in the face of strong social organization, or conversely, there could be a highly disorganized society filled with persons not especially afflicted with personality disorganization.

In the same way today, locality specialization is beginning to separate community disorganization from social disorganization. Communities are becoming less and less the "building blocks" of which society is composed. So long as they were so, a deterioration of those building blocks meant a deterioration in the structure of society. But the present changes are of a different sort, changes to different kinds of building blocks for society. The new society emerging in the twentieth century may well have social organization without local community organization.

Invasion of the Community: Mass Communication

The historical trend examined above exhibits a greater and greater freeing of the individual from community bonds. He can choose his residence, and his residence, once chosen, contains only one segment of his life. But there is yet another special development in modern society that results in an invasion of the community by the larger society. This development is mass communication, which has culminated in television. With movies, radio, and television, communication has come to be used as mass entertainment and mass leisure. Into the community's life comes daily entertainment from without—entertainment unrelated to the life of the community and by its very existence supplanting that life. The ultimate effects of television and other mass media on individuals and on communities have yet to be assessed, but it is indisputable that the time spent consuming this entertainment is time subtracted from the potential life of the community.

This is evident in local bars and taverns, which have traditionally been the meeting place of friends and one of the wellsprings of solidarity among neighbors.[49] They have been invaded by television, and though the life of the tavern continues, it is attenuated by the omnipresent visitor from without who demands the attention of those present. Just as a child continually demands its parents' attention and reduces the time they have to themselves, the television set's demands reduce the time members of a family or a tavern or a community have to themselves. The result is a weakening of those relations of identification and hostility of which a community is composed.

Mass communication has a second effect as well, an effect upon the content of norms in the community. Norms in a community have always derived from the structure of activities in the community and have been of such a character to maintain these activities. For example, women have ordinarily been the upholders of norms governing sexual relationships and family responsibility in the community. Why? Georg Simmel explains it this way: women, as the physically weaker sex, have always been subject to the exploitations and aggressions of men. Unable to protect themselves individually and unable to separate themselves into a distinct society, they have depended upon the customs and norms of the community for their protection. They have upheld these norms because it is in their interest to do so. They have most to lose by a disintegration of norms.[50]

Similarly, the laws governing protection of property in a community derive directly from the community's activities. They are made into laws through the efforts of those who have property and are most staunchly upheld by these same property owners. Most laws or norms in a community can be understood in the same way: as serving the interests either of all community members or of some faction having enough power to put them into effect. Norms about childbearing have been handed down by mothers of mothers—both by virtue of their authority in the family and by virtue of their experience. The norms they transmit are designed to uphold the existing structure of the community—they are essentially conservative.

---

[49] See David Gottlieb, "The Neighborhood Tavern and the Cocktail Lounge: A Study of Class Differences," *American Journal of Sociology*, Vol. 62 (May, 1957), pp. 559-62, for a discussion of the role that neighborhood taverns play in the lives of their patrons.

[50] Simmel, *Conflict*, pp. 95, 96. As Simmel points out, the emancipation of women in modern society may tend to invalidate this relationship.

But this is coming to be no longer true in an age of mass communication. Norms can now derive from the movies or the television set, rather than from the local community. Authority no longer rests with age, because of the rapidity of change. Mothers, fathers, and children receive, through mass communication, images of moral acceptability that may be very different from the existing norms of their community. Sometimes these norms are commensurate with those in the larger society, but sometimes they derive from the special needs of ·the medium of communication. The movies that feature sex and violence do so not because these attributes reflect norms of the larger society but because they sell movies. The television quiz shows that were "fixed" were so not because this reflected the existing norms of society, but because this made the shows more interesting, and thus more lucrative for the producers and sponsors. The frequency with which social drinking and requests for "bourbon and water" occur in a movie may reflect less the normative structure of society than it does the success of the bourbon manufacturers' trade association in persuading the movie producer to help them sell bourbon. The prevalence in films of such ceremonial religions as Catholicism and Episcopalianism does not reflect their position in society; they simply make better subjects for visual presentation than do nonceremonial religions, in which a minister dresses like everyone else.

Although these things do not reflect the present structure of society, they do have an effect upon the future structure. They tend to set into operation norms, attitudes, and behavior in an irresponsible way. The community and the larger society have so little control over them that normative patterns can establish themselves in full opposition to the community's previous standards. The public clamor over the television quiz show fixes can be seen in these terms. People recognized that television was *setting* the norms of society, in this case undermining the norm of honesty in one's dealing with others. The public clamor may be seen as an outcry against such irresponsible toying with the traditional values of honesty.

There have, of course, always been changes in the basic activities in society that have produced changes in the norms of the society (often after rigid resistance). But there is a fundamental difference between those changes and the ones cited above. Previously, norms have developed (as they still do to a great extent) through interactions of people with one another. They thus bore a close relation to the basic activities of which society was composed, and supported that structure of activities. But with mass communication, norms may be created in a very different and highly irrelevant way, depending, for example, on which advertising agent is closest to a particular television producer.

Rapidity of Change and the Irrelevance of Existing Constraints

In a stable society, the authority of the elders in a community is well grounded. They have had more experience in life, and that experience can be a valuable aid to those younger than they. Part of that experience has been codified into customs, norms, mores, and laws. These guides and constraints are of utmost relevance to the problems that daily face members of a community.

But in a rapidly changing society, the change itself makes many of these guides and constraints irrelevant. They were relevant to the society in which they developed, and they helped preserve that society. But as that society undergoes change of any sort, they become irrelevant. New guides for action are needed, and these residua of past experience are of little help.

Such a reduction in the authority of elders is likely to occur whenever society is undergoing change, whatever the change may be. The old norms are no longer good guides for action, but before new ones can grow up, the old ones must be cut away. Before new community organization can develop appropriate to the changes (e.g., changes in technology or in population size), the old organization must give way. Thus it seems inevitable that change in the community must be accompanied by a certain amount of community disorganization, until new norms and new organization-for-action can become established.

Considerations like these are particularly relevant to the present. Society seems to be undergoing more than sporadic changes followed by stability; since the industrial revolution, new changes have followed quickly upon previous ones. Such continual change tends to keep community organization at a low level—for the existing norms, customs, and authority structure are undergoing continual erosion, as they become irrelevant for the new conditions.

Community Disorganization as a By-product of Higher-level Policy

All the preceding conditions leading to community disorganization have been a consequence of broad historical changes in society. Yet there are numerous other factors affecting disorganization that have little or nothing to do with historical trends. One of these is governmental policy of a state or nation.

The existence of governmental units above the level of the community, at the level of the state or nation, can have important implications for community disorganization.[51] Community government itself tends to be conservative with respect to its own structure, that is, to preserve the organization that presently exists. But supracommunity government is concerned with preserving the structure of the larger society. Its decisions and laws are made from this perspective.[52] Often this is consistent with maintenance of community organization, but sometimes it is not. In some cases, the by-product of these supra-community decisions is a disorganizing tendency at the community level. Two examples of this will illustrate how it can come about.

FHA MORTGAGE POLICY. It was once true that buying a house required a rather large sum of money for a down payment, a considerable fraction of the total cost of the house. Lending institutions usually made loans only up to two-thirds or three-fourths of the appraised value of the property. Since World War II ended, however, a great stimulus to home ownership and to building has come about through federal insurance of home financing. Through the Federal Housing Administration, the government will insure loans up to 87 percent of the assessed value of the property; through the Veterans Administration, it will insure home loans to veterans of military service up to 100 percent of the assessed value, at a lower rate of interest than conventional financing. Such loans are easily obtained on new houses, often because the developer himself will arrange financing with a lending agency. Also, appraisals tend to be very close to the selling price of the house, in part because builders know how to reduce construction costs (and thus quality) without affecting the appraised value (which is based on certain standard specifications). Thus a prospective buyer can obtain a new house for little or no money down. An older house is much more difficult to obtain FHA or GI financing for, and there is no builder to make prior arrangements with lending agencies.

The government policy, in short, has made very easy the purchase of a *new* house without similarly increasing the ease of purchasing an older house. Even more difficult has been the task of securing government-insured loans for extensive renewal of such older properties as apartment buildings.

---

[51] As in preceding sections, the "community" whose disorganization is in question may be a whole metropolitan area or, alternatively, one of its parts such as a suburb or central city.

[52] It is true that sectional and community interests often play a part in national legislative decisions. But the decision is a balance among these interests, along with others (business interests, union interests, etc.), and by this token seldom satisfies any particular community's interest.

This state of affairs has been a remarkable stimulus to new home construction; but it has meant at the same time a speeding-up of the deterioration of older neighborhoods. A house that would have been sold or rented as a single family dwelling, were it not for the discrepancy between its ease of purchase and that of a suburban house, can no longer be thus sold or rented. It can, however, be a good real estate investment if converted for multiple-family use, that is, converted into a tenement.

Because most new home construction lies outside city limits, this old-new disparity has accelerated the exodus from the city to the suburbs. The city has thus deteriorated, while the construction industry and the suburbs have been favored by the government policy. To be sure, prospective home owners have benefited as well, but no more (certainly less, in fact) than if the policy had made it as easy to purchase or renovate older housing as to purchase a new house.

This is not to say that the policy has been "bad," for community disorganization is not in itself necessarily "bad," as the preceding sections have pointed out. The policy has had differential consequences for different social entities, and cities are one entity for which the consequences have been bad.

DESEGREGATION AND DISORGANIZATION OF SOUTHERN COMMUNITIES. This example will illustrate even more clearly the effect of a decision at the national level on community disorganization. It will illustrate as well that community disorganization is not inherently "bad."

Throughout the history of communities in the American South, the community organization included norms and patterns of behavior insuring racial inequality between Negroes and whites. This inequality was enforced through various means, including laws (such as those requiring separate schools for Negroes and whites), norms about interpersonal relations (such as deference of Negroes to whites), and in rare occurrences, violence beyond the law (such as lynching of a Negro accused of some grossly improper behavior toward a white). This system as established formed a stable community organization, as have other systems based on inequality throughout history.

But one fundamental element in the organization of these communities was inconsistent with a value premise of the nation as a whole, expressed in the Constitution: equality among all, regardless of race. In 1954, the United States Supreme Court decreed that this inconsistency in access to education be resolved in favor of the Constitution. (See Chapter 9, pages 470-71.)

But resolution of the inconsistency between local law and national Constitution did not *do away* with the inconsistency. It merely *shifted* the inconsistency to a different level, to within the community organization itself. In border-state communities, in communities with few Negroes, or in large cities where Negroes and whites interact little and only impersonally, the inconsistency is not great, for few elements of community organization are founded upon the premise of inequality. But in the deep South the inconsistency introduced by integrated schools occurs in almost all walks of life. In every case, a building block in the organization of the community has been pulled out, and the organization that remains is less firm. It may reorganize on a different basis after a period of time, but for the present it will certainly be weakened, because that structure of control has been based in considerable part upon the premise of Negro-white inequality.

Again it is evident that community disorganization is not necessarily a "bad" thing. It is disruptive or disintegrative of the local community, but this disruption may serve some other aim—in this case, maintenance of a value premise of equality, upon which the organization of the nation as a whole is based.

Special Conditions Leading to Conflict

The preceding conditions leading to disorganization are those that lead primarily to disintegration of norms and common consensus, and only secondarily to conflict. Beyond these conditions there are others that lead especially to conflict within a community. Some of these are discussed below.[53]

Internally Generated and Externally Generated Conflict

The interdependent activities of which a community is composed sometimes generate joint action and develop community norms, but they often do just the opposite, as discussed in earlier sections. Probably the best example of interdependent activities that often lead to opposed action are economic activities. Workers and managers have some common interests (for example, high import tariffs for substitutable goods), but many that are opposed (for example, wages per unit of goods produced). Since these interests are crucial ones to both parties, they sometimes lead to open conflict such as a strike. At other times, they generate mutual hostility, which may remain temporarily

---

[53] For a more extended examination of community conflict and its dynamics, see Coleman, *Community Conflict.* For a number of theoretical points in the sociology of conflict, see Simmel, *Conflict,* and Lewis Coser, *The Functions of Social Conflict* (New York: Free Press, 1956). The present examination will be limited to certain conditions that lead to conflict.

unexpressed, but which later provides the dynamics for industrial conflict.

In another quite different way, the system of interdependent activities may lead to conflict. When one person or group has control over an activity in which another is interested as well, antagonism is likely to build up in the other. He cannot express his interests in modifying the activity to his taste, so antagonism develops. This has been a partial source of some public school fights in recent years. In one (Pasadena, California), the school superintendent was unresponsive to community pressures from groups that had been heeded by the previous superintendent. Hostility built up in these groups and was fanned by nationalistic persons who had developed special hostility toward innovations in education. The final result was the removal of the superintendent and a return to the old system of easy accessibility to the administration by interested groups.[54]

Perhaps the best example of a power differential generating hostility and finally community conflict is that between Negroes and whites in the South. The absence of a Negro's control over his destiny in the South has generated the latent hostility that can lead to conflict once the opportunity arises to gain partial control.

In general, community members' lack of control over activities that are of central interest to them creates hostility, which sometimes obtains its outlet through subsequent conflict. In any highly differentiated community, there are control differentials of this sort. Lower classes and newcomers to the community tend to be without control, in contrast to old, established families. Thus, the potential for conflict exists in the very structure of activities, giving some persons control over parts of others' lives and creating situations of opposing interests. Conflicts from such sources need no external event to set them in motion, for they are generated by the activities of the community itself.

Racial conflicts are largely produced by hostilities generated through the interdependent activities of the community itself. The example below illustrates how these hostilities may be responsible for conflict.

> A young mathematician from England was at the University of Chicago for a short period in the late 1950's. When he was walking across the Midway, he was accosted by several Negro boys who demanded his wallet. He objected, one of them produced a knife, and they led

---

[54] See David Hurlburd, *This Happened in Pasadena* (New York: Macmillan, 1950).

him over toward bushes beside the walk. The ensuing conversation went something like this, according to his later account: One boy said, "Come on, now, give us your wallet, or we'll have to get tough with you." He replied, "Look here, I don't want to give up my wallet to you. Besides, I've just arrived here from England, and I don't think this is the way to treat someone who's a visitor here." The boys looked at one another, and then one said, "Oh. We thought you were one of those white guys," and they quickly went away.

To these Negro boys, "white guys" had nothing to do with skin color per se, for the English mathematician was white. "White guys" were their fellow community members, the whites from whom they felt alienated because there had been no processes to create common identity between them, only those creating hostility. The Englishman was not a "white guy" against whom a reserve force of hostility had been built up.

This incident illustrates more than a peculiar, localized abnormality. There was no less integration of Negroes into the local community in the Hyde Park area of Chicago, where this incident occurred, than in other large cities. The absence of integration, the absence of any processes that produce a common bond of identity, is very likely an important source, not only of conflict, such as the Trumbull Park riots in Chicago, but also of the Negro crime that occurs in such areas. The flow of Negroes and Puerto Ricans into large cities is great, and these migrants initially have no stake in the city, no reason for not committing crime other than the fear of getting caught. The existence of such a flow of migrants makes especially important those processes that generate mutual identification between whites and Negroes and processes that generate identification of the new migrants with the community.

Such processes need not be left to chance. If a city has a winning professional football or baseball team, of which the residents are very proud, then an alert city administration will consult with the team officials, to try to find an outstanding Negro player who might become a star of the team. In the common enterprise of winning athletic games, the barriers between whites and Negroes tend to be broken down: the whites begin to identify with the Negro star who brings glory to their city; they begin to see him as a person like themselves, but one with exceptional abilities. The Negroes begin to identify with the team and the city, as they urge their hero and his team on to victory. (See Chapter 9, page 451.)

Such devices are all too few in modern cities, but they are not totally absent. What is more important, they need not be left to fate, but can consciously be instituted to combat the disorganizing tendencies of migration and other "natural processes" in society.

Controversies involving racial or ethnic cleavages ordinarily build up through internal processes of the sort implied above. But they also usually include components that are not developed within the community itself: different backgrounds, cultural values, and norms; and differences due to time of movement into the community (classical examples of migrations inducing conflict are Irish Catholics moving into East Coast cities and New England towns in the nineteenth century; "Okies" moving into Southern California during the 1930's; ex-city dwellers moving into established suburbs in the 1950's, often with a different age and income distribution from that of the existing population; and rural southerners, mostly Negro, moving into the center of cities in the 1950's and 1960's).

Some community conflicts, however, are precipitated by purely external events. A new highway coming through a town may cause social cleavage where no trace had existed before. The opposition of interests between those whose homes would be demolished and those who would profit by increased business may lead to conflict. Another external source of such cleavages exists in some modern suburbs: continuing value differences due to the residential character of the community. This may be illustrated by an example in the suburbs of New York City: in Port Washington, Long Island, there were continuing school controversies in the 1950's maintained by two groups with political values at polar opposites. The persons concerned were employed in New York in activities supporting, respectively, their left-wing and right-wing views. Without this external support, grounded in national organizations for which these men worked, such extremes could not have maintained themselves in the same community. But grounded in New York City as they were, these differences continued to provoke violent school conflicts for a long period of time.[55]

As this example indicates, modern dormitory suburbs allow a great diversity of values to be maintained, held in place by diverse jobs and associations in the city. This value diversity can then become, as it has in numerous instances of school controversies, the basis for an explosive conflict.

To summarize, conflict can arise from the activities of the community itself, from purely external sources, or from some conjunction of the two. The internally induced conflict depends on the structure of

---

[55] See Louis Engel, "Port Washington, N. Y.," *Saturday Review* ("The Public School Crisis"), Vol. 34 (September 8, 1951), pp. 6-20.

interdepodent activities in the community, which can operate over time to generate cleavage between two groups or to generate alienation of one group that has little control over these interdependent activities.

Locality Specialization, the Mass Community, and Conflict

As we have seen, locality specialization has taken out of the hands of the local community many of the activities it once had, resulting, for example, in modern bedroom suburbs. In doing so, it has removed many of the interests of its residents into associations that cut across community bounds. Their interests and activities have become extensive, over a wide range of associations. Most of these associations have a special organizational structure: a large mass of members, who are only tangentially interested in the activities of the organization; and a small corps of officers, whose major interests and activities are bound up in the association, men for whom the organization may even be a livelihood. Voluntary associations of all sorts are like this. Unions are probably the best example; professional associations, such as the American Medical Association; political groups, such as the Americans for Democratic Action or the League of Women Voters; P.T.A.'s, consumer cooperatives, conservation leagues, and other similar groups, are other examples.[56]

The local community, fast becoming a specialized living-place, has begun to take on a form similar to that of these voluntary associations. It holds only a small part of the interests of most of its members, whose other interests have become fractionated into many parts, most of them outside the community. Only those few merchants and others whose livelihood is within the community, or who are part of its government, are centrally involved.

The community thus tends toward a "mass society," with a small organized elite and a large unorganized, undifferentiated mass. This is not, of course, to say that its members are a "mass" from the viewpoint of the larger society. They are members of many groups—occupational, recreational, political, professional, and other interest groups. But many of these are not local. Some have their locus in the central city, some spread over the nation, but so long as they are not within the local community, they contribute nothing to its organization. Their

---

[56] For a general discussion of the "mass society" structure of such organizations, see Bernard Barber, "Participation and Mass Apathy in Associations," in Alvin W. Gouldner, ed., *Studies in Leadership* (New York: Harper, 1950). For an examination of the organizational structure of a mass society, see William Kornhauser, *The Politics of Mass Society* (New York: Free Press, 1959).

members are therefore *in effect* a mass, not organized into interest groups and associations that play a role in community decisions. There are special consequences of such a structure, consequences which have much to do with conflict.

It is interesting to note that such a mass society structure can come about through two exactly opposite societal forms: the members' having no important associations outside the family and close friends, so that no interest groups mediate between individual and government; and the members' having all their associational ties in large associations that go beyond the bounds of the governmental unit (in this case, the community), and thus play no role in its decision-making. Though these associations can and do play a mediating role at the metropolitan, state, or national level, protecting and furthering their members' interests, they cannot do so at the community level.

The first of these two forms of mass society is exemplified by traditional societies like those of Central America, where the large mass of the populace is tied only to family and friends. The second is exemplified by modern suburban communities. Despite the apparent polar extremes that these two social entities exemplify, their mass society form gives rise to similar types of conflicts, as will be evident below. (See Chapter 9, page 434.)

Consequences of the Mass Community for Conflict

Trade unions and Latin-American countries having the elite mass structure described above show a characteristic political cycle: alternations between long periods of apathy and violent revolts. The administrative elite goes on for a long time making decisions that are unchallenged by the mass, but then at some point the mass does rise up and attempt to "throw the rascals out." Such a cyclical pattern of authority seems to be a quality of many voluntary associations that engage only a small part of their members' interest and attention. Until some special issue or a special leader comes along to capture a major part of their attention, they are inactive and let the "authorities" administer the affairs of the association. But then there are no regular political channels through which their intentions may be expressed, and the "normal" processes of government give way to conflict in which the outsiders use any means to gain their ends.

As communities come more and more to take on the form of mass communities, with a small interested elite and an uninterested (though often educated) mass, one might expect that their political processes would take on this apathy-revolt pattern. There are no systematic data to document this, but two kinds of recent controversies exhibit precisely the form of a "revolt of the masses." These are school controversies centering around the question of supposed subversive activities of a teacher, librarian, or principal; and fluoridation controversies over the question of whether the water system should or should not be fluoridated.

Some fluoridation controversies show the pattern perfectly: [57] a town or city council will have considered the question of fluoridation of the water system, and passed favorably upon it, often voting the small sum necessary to install it. Before this action is taken, only a few voices have been raised in opposition through letters to the editor of the local newspaper; until after the action, no real opposition to the plan is evident. All organizations in town favor it: business, labor, the professional associations of doctors and dentists, and others; and all members of the interested elite favor it.

But after the action, sentiment begins to build up against the plan, based partly on the charge that fluoridation is dangerous, but partly on the belief that this was not something for the council to decide without a vote, but a decision of the community as a whole. Fluoridation is then put to a vote, and the revolt is accomplished, resulting (in a majority of cases which have so far come to a popular vote) in defeat of the plan.

The normal procedure of decision-making in these communities is one in which the uninterested mass plays no part at all, since the community is only a segmental part of their lives. Thus the council makes this decision as it does others. But the mass membership, aroused by a few dedicated opponents of fluoridation, does not consider this assumption of authority legitimate in this case, and arises to revolt against the decision-makers. There are no organizational channels through which these beliefs could be transmitted as political pressures *before* the decision; the normal process of decision-making does not include the mass of community membership. Only by using new channels, that is, popular revolt, spread by word of mouth and letters to the editor, do the community members take part. And by this time, their antagonism is directed against the "high-handed behavior" of the city council, so that the vote against fluoridation is in part a vote against the council itself.

Conflicts involving charges of Communist subversion of the school system have taken a similar form. (These conflicts were most prevalent during that curious period of American history in the late 1940's and

---

[57] See Coleman, *Community Conflict,* for a more detailed discussion of the pattern of fluoridation controversies.

early 1950's when the nation was beset by fears of Communist subversion—the period commonly known as the McCarthy era.) The usual form has been something like this: the school system will be functioning well when some member of the community who has previously taken no part in school or community affairs will make a charge of Communist subversion against some part of the school system. The majority of the community, whose attention has been engaged in affairs outside the community and inside the home, will suddenly have its attention focused upon the community and its school. Conflict results, because conflict is the only means by which this newly captured attention can gain an outlet.

In short, the mass society form of local community that is arising through locality specialization generates a special kind of community conflict, a "revolt of the masses" against the administrative elite who have been making decisions. These revolts sometimes explode into real conflicts, because the intermediary associations, through which opinions are both expressed and compromised, are largely missing. This particular form of community conflict is especially prevalent today and is particularly interesting, since it seems to be a consequence of social changes (which promise to become even more widespread) toward locality specialization.

In this, as in other processes of community disorganization, it is only possible to point to over-all tendencies. The details of these processes, some given in references above, most of them yet to be found, provide the means by which community disorganization, and social organization as a whole, can be understood, and in some cases altered.

14

War and Disarmament

by Amitai Etzioni

HARNESSED NUCLEAR FISSION CAN PROVIDE MANKIND WITH BOUNTIFUL, inexpensive energy to serve a large number and variety of goals, from the desalinization of oceans and watering of deserts to the melting of polar ice and traveling in outer space. Unleashed, it is the most devastating explosive, one that could destroy civilization. In this sense, the problem of war today is an ultimate expression of a much more general social problem: the disintegrating effect that new means, that is, new technological inventions and related institutional innovations, can produce in a society. Time and again the introduction of more effective means to serve men's goals has undermined these very goals, their relations with other men, and their commitment to whatever god they worship. Unwilling to return to the stone age—in fact, unable to return since the knowledge to produce new means would remain even if those newly introduced were eliminated—man must find better ways of controlling his technology and his fate. Otherwise, he will be the servant, if not the victim, of the means he created to improve his lot.

The danger of the "irrationality of rationality," as Max Weber referred to this dilemma, was first encountered in depth when the introduction of modern means of production (or industrialization) threatened to subject the relations between man and man to the blind forces of the market and deprive the worker of control over the fruits of his work. The same danger was encountered in the study of bureaucracies, where rules and regulations, intended to increase the efficacy and justice of government ministrations to the citizen-clientele, became a new source of estrangement, of Kafka-like labyrinths in which the needs of citizens were distorted and disregarded rather than served.

This chapter is an outgrowth of research at the Institute of War and Peace Studies of Columbia University.

The advent of nuclear technology has brought the "threat of means," the loss of control, to its apex: rather than endangering man's privacy, freedom, or happiness, nuclear arms endanger the basis on which all such values are predicated—his very survival. The means of warfare, from bow to bomber, have been vehicles of power to serve goals ranging from religious to sacrilegious, from glory to banditry.[1] Whatever their ends, whether legitimate or illegitimate, moral or immoral, these means of violence potentially served those who wielded them; as a means to an end, weapons "worked." But a continual increase in the effectiveness of weapons has undermined this means-ends relationship. The mass possession of nuclear bombs and missiles has created a situation where the possible gains of war hardly justify the losses the use of modern weapons would entail.

The number of Americans who died in World War I was 126,000; in World War II it was 397,000. In a statement before the House Armed Services Committee in 1965, Secretary of Defense McNamara stated that *if* the United States spent an additional 25 billion dollars in the next five years for fallout shelters and antimissile defenses, and *if* the attacker waited an hour after launching his initial nuclear attack on our military targets before striking our cities (in McNamara's words, "an unlikely contingency"), "only" 41 million Americans would be killed. If the attack on cities came at the same time as the attack on military targets, 78 million, or every third American, would die; without the additional expenditure of 25 billion dollars, 71 out of every 100 Americans would die.[2] There are already weapons in stock, a single one of which has a greater yield than the total amount of explosives dropped on Germany and Japan in World War II. The specter of a doomsday machine that would leave no survivors at all has been raised. This would be the ultimate subversion of human goals by human means, the complete loss of man's control over his destiny.

Nuclear War: A Real Threat?

Is nuclear war a real threat? Does not the very existence of nuclear weapons deter such a war? Will not the very enormity of nuclear devastation keep the leaders of the United States and the Soviet Union from triggering such a war? Is it not a "certainty that the deterrence

---

[1] On the varying goals of warfare, see Alfred A. Vagts, *A History of Militarism* (New York: Norton, 1937).

[2] *The New York Times,* February 19, 1965, p. 10.

policy would continue to work so that it never would be really necessary to carry out the threat of nuclear retaliation?"[3]

Social scientists have contributed significantly to answering these questions. Drawing on their knowledge of man and society, they have pointed out that even if no man would deliberately unleash a *Götterdämmerung*, there are many ways in which control over nuclear weapons might be lost and a war might be initiated unintentionally. Man has yet to design a foolproof control system, whether of production, administration, or war. It is generally recognized that there are four ways in which a war might be started unintentionally: mechanical failure, unauthorized use, miscalculation, and brinkmanship.

Mechanical Failure

According to a study of the accident problem made by an independent, nonmilitary group, nuclear weapons have been involved in about a dozen major incidents or accidents, mostly plane crashes, both in the United States and overseas. In one of these incidents, a B-52 bomber had to jettison a 24-megaton bomb over North Carolina. The bomb fell in a field without exploding. The Defense Department has adopted complex devices and strict rules to prevent the accidental arming or firing of nuclear weapons. In this case, the 24-megaton warhead was equipped with six interlocking safety mechanisms, all of which had to be triggered in sequence to explode the bomb. When Air Force experts rushed to the North Carolina farm to examine the weapon after the accident they found that five of the six interlocks had been set off by the fall! Only a single switch prevented the 24-megaton bomb from detonating and spreading fire and destruction over a wide area.[4]

If a nuclear bomb should suddenly turn an area of the United States into a radioactive desert, this might well be viewed as an enemy attack and lead to "retaliation." This, in turn, would lead to retaliation by the other side, which might result in full-scale war.

Unauthorized Use

The danger of unauthorized use of weapons will be with us as long as the social sciences have not developed selection instruments that allow screening of persons who, under pressure, might use the arms they have access to, in violation of their orders. During one year

---

[3] Jay Orear and Lincoln Wolfenstein, "European Scientists Speak," *Bulletin of the Atomic Scientists* (April, 1965), p. 45. See also Maxwell D. Taylor, *The Uncertain Trumpet* (New York: Harper, 1960), p. 184.

[4] Ralph E. Lapp, *Kill and Overkill* (New York: Basic Books, 1962), p. 127.

alone, 1959, the United States Air Force, for example, discharged 4213 men on grounds of disability; one-fourth of this number were released because of psychotic disorders, psychoneurotic disorders, or anxiety reactions.[5] Since it is not possible to detect all the potential psychotics or psychoneurotics in the armed services, it is conceivable that eventually one such person might break through and reach a releasing mechanism, either by commanding the opening of the safety devices or by feeding the system false information that would bring about its triggering by authorized personnel.

Unauthorized action might be undertaken also by people who are not "disturbed." According to an Associated Press message from Saigon, dated September 7, 1965, a Marine unit used tear gas in a clash with the Viet Cong at the Batangan Peninsula.

> The spokesman said the commander of the Marine battalion involved was said to have called for the use of tear gas on his own authority. The spokesman said the commander may not have been aware of a policy [then in effect] against the use of tear gas or any other gas in Viet Nam.

Miscalculation

The danger of war by *miscalculation* by an authorized person is probably even greater than that of war by accident or unauthorized action. One major mistake by any one of the sides, President Kennedy warned, and there will be "150 million fatalities in the first eighteen hours." [6] The student of history can hardly expect each government in command of nuclear arms to avoid, over a long period of time, making one major mistake. Such a mistake might well be the acting on the basis of insufficient or wrong information, as, it is argued, was the case the first time an atomic bomb was dropped on human beings.

The issue is a complicated one. At least a score of books have been written on the decision to drop the bomb. There are also several accounts by various persons who participated in the decision, including President Truman. By and large, the participants tend to justify the decision.

Independent experts, while not all critical of the decision, tend to suggest that the decision was based on a mistaken assumption that more use of military might would be necessary to compel Japan's surrender. Actually, at least according to several authoritative accounts, it seems that the main barrier to Japan's surrender *before* the

---

[5] Seymour Melman, *Peace Race* (New York: Braziller, 1961), p. 15.

[6] Theodore C. Sorensen, *Kennedy* (New York: Harper, 1965), p. 512. On Kennedy's concern that his miscalculation might occur, see p. 513.

bomb was dropped was symbolic and sociological. The Japanese wanted to maintain the status of the emperor, following surrender. The United States insisted on unconditional surrender. As the Emperor was the key symbol of the society, one of an importance that members of a modern Western democratic society find hard to conceive, Japan was willing to continue to fight, rather than give up this symbol. In retrospect it seems, according to some authoritative accounts by American experts, that the 1945 bombing of Hiroshima and Nagasaki "made no essential contribution to Japan's surrender without a last battle." [7]

More recently, the United States government decided to bomb North Vietnam. Not all the considerations that went into this decision are a matter of public record at this point. But an authentic glimpse can be gained from the published statement of General Thomas S. Power, the Commander in Chief of the Strategic Air Command from 1957 till 1964, i.e., till just a few months before the bombing actually began:

> Let us assume that, in the fall of 1964, we would have warned the Communists that unless they cease supporting the guerrillas in South Vietnam, we would destroy a major military supply depot in North Vietnam. Through radio and leaflets, we would have advised the civilian population living near the depot of our ultimatum and of the exact time of our attack so that civilians could be evacuated. If the Communists failed to heed our warning and continued to support the rebels, we would have gone through with the threatened attack and destroyed the depot. And if this act of "persuasive deterrence" had not sufficed, we would have threatened the destruction of another critical target and, if necessary, would have destroyed it also. We would have continued this strategy until the Communists had found their support of the rebels in South Vietnam too expensive and agreed to stop it. *Thus, within a few days and with minimum force, the conflict in South Vietnam would have been ended in our favor.* Beyond this, we would have gained immeasurably in prestige and in the credibility of our determination to prevent further Communist aggression against our allies. [8]

---

[7] Paul Kecskemeti, *Strategic Surrender* (Stanford, Calif.: Stanford University Press, 1958), p. 209. This study was conducted under the auspices of the RAND Corporation. See also, Herbert Feis, *Japan Subdued: The Atomic Bomb and the End of the War in the Pacific* (Princeton, N. J.: Princeton University Press, 1961); William D. Leahy, *I Was There* (New York: McGraw-Hill, 1950); Robert J. C. Butow, *Japan's Decision to Surrender* (Stanford, Calif.: Stanford University Press, 1965); Len Giovannitti and Fred Freed, *The Decision to Drop the Bomb* (New York: Coward-McCann, 1965).

[8] General Thomas S. Power, *Design for Survival* (New York: Coward-McCann, 1965), pp. 224-25. (Italics provided.)

This was obviously a miscalculation of what air power could do. A much larger strike could also be similarly misdirected. This we would know, as in the case of Hiroshima and North Vietnam, only in retrospect—that is, if we remain able to engage in retrospection.

Miscalculation seemed less likely when the nuclear powers consisted of only the United States, the Soviet Union, and Britain. The recent addition of members and aspirants to the nuclear club make a nuclear war seem more likely. The stakes of a nuclear gamble are different for countries that have intense emotional commitments to disputed territories, such as West Germany, United Arab Republic, India, or Pakistan, and for countries that are overpopulated and impoverished, than for the established, wealthy, and reasonably contented nuclear superpowers. The larger the number of countries with access to nuclear arms, the less likely that the cooler heads will prevail. This leads us to the fourth danger of unintentional war, brinkmanship.

Brinkmanship

The essence of brinkmanship strategy is an attempt to gain concessions from the other side by threatening nuclear war without actually expecting to have to engage in it. The strategy has often been compared to the "chicken" game played by hot-rodders, in which two cars race down the center of a road toward each other; the first driver to turn his car away from the collision course loses the contest and is labeled a "chicken." Obviously, the more committed a driver is to victory, the more reckless he will be; the more often the contest of wills is engaged in, the more likely that both drivers, their cars, and all their occupants end in ruins. A typical example of superpowers engaged in brinkmanship is the 1962 Cuban crisis. The Soviet Union positioned missiles in Cuba, probably miscalculating the American response. The United States imposed a naval blockade on Cuba, deploying American ships to intercept Soviet ships that were sailing toward Cuba. The fact that both sides prevented, at the last moment, a confrontation on the high seas and that the United States gained the removal of the missiles should not obscure the fact that the Soviet's initial act and the American response involved leaning far over the nuclear brink.[9]

The recurrent point introduced by this examination of the four ways in which the nuclear balance of power might be unbalanced is that military machinery is a set of means designed and staffed by

---

[9] Sorensen, *Kennedy*, pp. 700 ff.

humans; it is, hence, basically susceptible to the follies and weaknesses of man.[10] But, before we can assess the danger of nuclear war, we must confront the question: *How likely is the war system to trigger itself or be triggered unwittingly?*

Some have claimed that nuclear war is a certainty. The British scientist and author C. P. Snow stated on December 27, 1960, that "within, at the most, ten years, some of these bombs are going off. I am saying this as responsibly as I can. That is the certainty . . . a certainty of disaster."[11] On the other hand, there are some who believe that "current preparations are safe." The nuclear strategist Herman Kahn seems to see as acceptable "a force which is invulnerable but which achieves this invulnerability by having (every year) one chance in a hundred of starting a war accidentally."[12] If, however, the cold war is to last for decades, this probability of one in a hundred per year cannot be particularly comforting to the approximately 100 million Americans under 35 who would like to live at least to retirement age. For the over 40 million American children under ten, this prospect would look even dimmer.

An intermediary position holds that nuclear war is not likely, much less a certainty. Still, there is no reason why, if the cold war continues, a hot war cannot erupt; however low the estimated probability of nuclear war, one must note that such estimates are unreliable, as are all probabilities of events that never occurred, and that events of low probability *do* take place; and when the lives of hundreds of millions, if not all mankind, are at stake, the potential disaster is so ominous that one must concern oneself even with events that are unlikely.

Arms: Cause or Symptom?

Some observers see the main source of danger in the existence of arms themselves, especially the new thermonuclear weapons. In this view, man can regain control of his fate by reasserting his control over the development of weapons. Arms races follow their own "logic." "The increase of armaments that is intended in each nation to produce consciousness of strength and a sense of security, does not produce these effects. On the contrary, it produces a consciousness of the strength of other nations and a sense of fear," wrote the British

---

[10] For a more detailed treatment, see the author's *Winning Without War* (New York: Doubleday-Anchor Books, 1965), pp. 159-69.

[11] *The New York Times,* December 28, 1960, p. 28.

[12] Herman Kahn, *On Thermonuclear War* (Princeton, N. J.: Princeton University Press, 1960), pp. 208-09.

Foreign Secretary, Sir Edward Gray, at the outbreak of World War I.[13] But every nation that arms for its own security is simultaneously an "other nation." Arming for security often leads to arming for defense by the "other nation." The defensive intent of arms built up by the other nation is rarely so regarded by the first nation. It rather sees in the other's new arms evidence of its hostile intent; the first nation often sees no alternative but a new rush of armaments—for security. Hence, one major approach to the prevention of war is to reduce armaments. If the nuclear genie could somehow be returned to the bottle, the main new danger of war would be eliminated. If military arms could be entirely eliminated, it is argued, there would be no war.

An opposing view suggests that arms are chiefly the symptoms of deep-seated conflicts. If there were no hostile motivations, people would not produce arms; even if there were triggers, they would not pull them. The people of Canada do not fear American nuclear bombardment. "War starts in the minds of men," says the charter of UNESCO. Curbing arms, it is said, is like treating only the symptoms of disease, without identifying and treating the illness. The treatment is unlikely to be successful, and if successful, other symptoms will soon break out elsewhere. Disarmament, if ever achieved, will be followed not by peace, but by rearmament. What is needed is a treatment of the underlying conflicts of ideology and interest, the clash of powers.[14]

A third position seems more tenable. This one conceives of arms as both a symptom and a contributory cause that must be treated. The malaise that results in the arms race and wars is a deep one; basically, it expresses man's willingness to treat his fellow man as an object rather than as an objective, to the point of turning him into a perishable utensil. The complete cure of this malaise requires providing the social foundations for a world community, since only members of a community treat each other also as goals and not merely as means. If such a global community can be built at all, it will surely be a long process; meanwhile, mankind might destroy itself. The world society in the nuclear age is like a patient who is running a high fever; until we determine and treat the sources of this fever, some measures must be taken to reduce the fever itself if the patient is to

---

[13] Lewis F. Richardson, *Arms and Insecurity* (Pittsburgh: Boxwood Press, 1960), p. 15.

[14] For both sides of this debate see: John Burton, *Peace Theory* (New York: Knopf, 1962); Herbert C. Kelman, ed., *International Behavior* (New York: Holt, 1965); Evan Luard, *Peace and Opinion* (London: Oxford University Press, 1962); and Walter Millis, *An End to Arms* (New York: Atheneum, 1965).

survive. But, obviously, this treatment of the symptoms must be accompanied and followed by treatment of the disease itself.[15]

Furthermore, while the main causes of war seem to lie outside the propelling force and spell of armaments, the pressures of the military establishments are more than a symptom; they are a contributory cause. The military services, as a rule, demand larger defense budgets, not their curtailment;[16] the military's power, prestige, and—to a degree—income are affected by the size of these budgets. Most industries set up or extended to serve the military can turn elsewhere for their business, but the shift involves, at the least, the costs and pains of transition. Congressmen are known to lobby against the closing of military bases in their districts, and since each district has a congressman—and many at least one military installation—it is hard to sustain a broad reduction of arms without evoking some political resistance. This holds not simply for missile sites or naval yards. The production of nuclear warheads in the United States was continued beyond the point of need, as estimated by most military experts, in part because congressmen whose states had employment problems feared deeper unemployment.[17] On top of these extrinsic interests in production of arms come the intrinsic pressures to continually expand the military system, for the building of one component generates call for others. Bombers are of little use without runways. Runways are of little value if they are not protected from bombardment. The commanders of the bomber fleets have to be sheltered. Thus, armed systems tend to produce some extrinsic and intrinsic pressure for their expansion. Hence, when a point is reached where the original reason for the building up of armaments might have declined or disappeared, special efforts are still required if arms are to be reduced. Simply treating the original causes will not suffice.

Finally, armaments contribute to the potentiality of war through psychological consequences. Arms buildups express and magnify hostilities; arms reductions tend to indicate efforts to move toward an accommodation. For instance, the abrupt resumption of the testing of thermonuclear bombs by Russia in 1961, after a three-year mora-

---

[15] For a good review article of various approaches to the "symptoms and disease" question, see Philip Green, "Alternatives to Overkill: Dream and Reality," *Bulletin of the Atomic Scientists* (November, 1963), pp. 23-27.

[16] This holds for the Soviet Union as well. See, for instance, Col. S. Kozlov, *Armed Forces Communist* (January, 1961), in *Survival* (July-August, 1961), p. 160.

[17] James Reston, *The New York Times*, December 18, 1963, p. 40.

torium on such testing, was taken by the United States as a hostile and aggressive act. The 1963 Soviet-American agreement on partial cessation of thermonuclear tests, though of limited disarmament value, was hailed as heralding a new period in East-West relations. In other words, arms reductions can be used to create the atmosphere in which the "treatment" of the deeper causes of war can be better achieved, in much the way that reducing the fever of the patient enables him to survive long enough for antibiotics to take effect.[18]

Prevention of War: Three Approaches

There are many proposals for preventing war, but behind all of them lie three basic approaches, each containing a treatment plan for armament and a conception of the kind of political world necessary to provide the conditions under which the peace can be preserved. The approaches differ in their estimates of the dangers confronting the world today and the need as well as the ability to shift to a different world order. *Arms control* is, comparatively, the most optimistic approach in evaluating the present world and most pessimistic in estimating the changes that can be realistically expected in the international system. (It is the approach reviewed first below, as its conception of the future is most like the conceptions guiding the policy-makers of today.) *General and complete disarmament* (GCD) is most pessimistic about our ability to survive in an armed world and most optimistic about our ability to drastically change international political institutions to fit our needs and desires.[19] *Arms reduction* is an intermediary position that seeks, through reversing the upward spiral of armament, a gradual transition from the world of arms races (with or without arms control) to a world without arms. In short, arms control seeks to make arms safe; GCD seeks safety from arms; arms reduction—a safe transition from one to the other.

Advocates of arms control, we shall see, expect international relations to continue to be guided by some conception of balance-of-power; GCD requires a world authority and a world community; the

---

[18] Amitai Etzioni, *The Hard Way to Peace* (New York: Collier Books, 1962), Chapter 4.

[19] Much confusion is caused in discussion of this vital subject by not keeping carefully separate the *end state* of a process and the process itself or its various stages; both are often referred to as "disarmament." This allows opponents of any reduction of arms to oppose this by pointing to some danger involved in a state of complete disarmament. To avoid this problem, we shall refer to the end state as "general and complete disarmament" (GCD), as official United States documents do, and to the process leading to GCD as "disarmament."

process of arms reduction provides the time in which a world authority and community might gradually be developed.

1. Balance-of-Power and Arms Control

Although the phrase "balance-of-power" seldom appears in a foreign office dispatch or memorandum, it has for centuries guided policymakers and strategists in the world's capitals. As a historical concept, balance-of-power refers to an international system wherein states sought to maintain their independence through the establishment of a rough equilibrium of power. Maintaining peace was thought to require no central regulatory authority; rather, the balancing of power among states occurred as a result of shifting alliances in time of peace and coalitions against the aggressor in time of war. A would-be aggressor was either deterred from initiating hostilities by perceiving that the odds against success were unfavorable, or, seeking to expand its power to a point at which it could unbalance the system and gain predominancy, found that other states unwilling to tolerate such a course would then wage war to maintain or restore the balance. War is thus seen as a temporary and limited phenomenon, something necessary to insure conditions where no one state or group of states could attempt to dominate the others with impunity.

A balance-of-power system in international relations is thus comparable to a system of full competition and laissez faire in economics. The assumption that no universal political authority is necessary is the equivalent of the assumption that economic units, each seeking to maximize its profits, can be relied upon to generate a desirable state of affairs, without extrinsic mechanisms of control.

Throughout history, from the time of the Greek city-states to Renaissance Italy, numerous interstate systems have been studied as approximating a balance-of-power system.[20] An examination of how a balance-of-power system functions is valuable both for an understanding of its limitations in the contemporary context and for the exploration of sociological factors in international relations.

The conditions for the maintenance of a balance-of-power were particularly favorable during the nineteenth century, as attested to by the absence of a general war from 1815 to 1914. Military power was diffused among several states. Diplomacy was conducted by skilled professionals, and there were few ideological impediments to inter-

---

[20] On the logic of these systems, see Morton Kaplan, *System and Process in International Politics* (New York: Wiley & Sons, 1957), pp. 100 ff.; and Richard N. Rosecrance, *Action and Reaction in World Politics* (Boston: Little, Brown, 1963).

fere with the freedom of statesmen to take their country from one coalition into another on the basis of shifting power relations. The relative strengths of competing states could be calculated with reasonable accuracy. War was seen as a method of implementing policy, but there was a consensus that its objectives should be limited and should not include the destruction of an enemy state, as yesterday's enemy might be tomorrow's ally. Important makeweights in the balance must not be destroyed if conditions of equilibrium were to be preserved, and for this a peace of reconciliation—not alienation—was essential. Great Britain as an island power played the role of balancer, adding its weight to the weaker side when the threat of preponderance arose. Most important, perhaps, the European states that dominated world politics shared a common interest in preserving the system itself, since they saw this as the best method of preserving the independence of each of its members and their domestic regimes.[21]

A classical example of a balance-of-power system at work is provided by the Congress of Vienna, where the statesmen of Europe met in 1815 to achieve a settlement to the chaos brought by the Napoleonic wars. The French domination of the Continent had finally been ended through the military success of a great coalition led by England and including Austria, Russia, and Prussia. This coalition was formed to reestablish the state system and restore the European balance. The work of the statesmen meeting in Vienna was facilitated not only by such objective political factors as the relative equality in power terms of their respective states and the ease with which reciprocal compensation in territorial rewards could be arranged, but also by their relative sociological homogeneity. They shared a comparable ideological outlook based upon the acceptance of monarchy and dynastic legitimacy, an aversion to popular democracy, and a generally conservative political orientation. They were of the same social class, spoke a common language (French), and had long experience in dealing with their diplomatic counterparts. They had more in common with each other than with the masses of the people in their respective states. These social and cultural conditions, together with the shared interest in the restoration of the state system, contributed to the relatively moderate peace terms imposed upon the defeated power, France. An indemnity was extracted and there was a period of military occupation, but with a Bourbon king restored to the French throne (and with

---

[21] Inis L. Claude, Jr., *Power and International Relations* (New York: Random House, 1962), pp. 90-91.

the benefits of Talleyrand's skillful diplomacy) France was almost immediately readmitted to the councils of the Great Powers.

Since World War I, however, the sociological conditions required by a balance-of-power system have undergone erosion, and in an accelerating degree. Power relations among states are no longer characterized by even a rough equality. Diplomacy has often passed into the hands of amateurs chosen for their political reliability. An age of radically opposed ideologies has supplanted the earlier periods of consensus. Statesmen, under pressures of public opinion, are no longer free to make policy apart from the demands of their peoples. War is no longer seen as an alternative policy means but as an unprecedented disaster to be avoided. The statesmen no longer share a common outlook, less often speak a common language, and do not agree on either the nature of the status quo to be established or how long or in what ways it should be preserved. In contrast to the period of 1815-1914, the period since 1914 is characterized by great political and sociological heterogeneity and has been marred by two world wars.

The year 1946 ushered in a period of bipolarity: the European Great Powers of the past were wholly overshadowed by two continent-sized superpowers, the United States and the Soviet Union. A true balance-of-power system was precluded by the bipolar division of power. There were no third, fourth, and fifth powers who could be counted upon to prevent either superpower from gaining absolute dominance. Despite this new development, the old idea of balance-of-power continued to guide statesmen and strategists who molded the relationships between the two superpowers and their camps: the two superpowers were to "balance" each other.

By the early 1950's there was added to the already bipolar pattern the element of *nuclear* bipolarity. Armed with massive nuclear weapons that were increasingly rendered invulnerable to attack by shielding and concealing devices, neither side could rationally launch a war against the heartland of the other since massive nuclear retaliation was likely to follow. The initiation of nuclear war, it was argued, meant national suicide. In this sense, the two nuclear giants "balanced" each other. But, since the balance was achieved not by the actual use of strategic weapons but through threats of their use, the system has come to be described as one of *deterrence*, or, more colloquially, as a balance-of-terror.

While the Communist camp might still have desired to extend its hold, and the Western alliance to "roll" it back, neither side dared to engage in anything but marginal skirmishes—and even these were undertaken with great caution—since an unexpected development could trigger an all-out nuclear war. Many American strategists in the 1950's and early 1960's believed that the balance-of-terror system could be prolonged indefinitely, although they favored eliminating especially hazardous conditions through limited arms-control measures (as we shall see), increasing conventional forces that would allow a military alternative to using nuclear weapons, and foregoing policies of nuclear brinkmanship.[22]

It should be emphasized that even before the advent of nuclear weapons and even when the political and sociological requisites existed, the balance-of-power system could not be relied upon to preserve peace. What this system did was not to prevent war but make major wars less devastating and minor wars less frequent. When hostilities occurred, procedures existed for restoring the balance and, thus, a state of peace. The object of war, as we have seen, was not the destruction of the opponent but a form of sanction that was intended to keep the system—and all its major members—operating. Under balance-of-terror conditions, however, where the total destruction of an opponent is technically possible, fear of retaliation is relied upon to deter a nuclear attack. But whereas a rational statesman would not initiate a nuclear war, it is questionable whether even nuclear weapons would deter a Hitler of tomorrow any more than the fear of a conventional response deterred the Hitler of yesterday. In addition, because of the unprecedented and continuing peacetime preparations for war and the instantaneous impact of modern arms, there is no longer any time cushion between a major mistake and a major war. The enormous destructive capacity of thermonuclear weapons means that even a single breakdown of the balance-of-terror system would be one too many. Moreover, in a time of conflicting ideologies, when competing socioeconomic regimes seek not limited triumphs but each other's elimination, an international system with no margin for error and relying on the rational behavior of *all* of its participants is at best a hazardous one.

Increased recognition of these factors, coupled with the apparent inability of states to agree upon disarmament, has generated interest in proposals for arms control—that is, efforts to reduce the probability of war and to limit its scope should it occur. It is a much less encompassing and fundamental approach to the problem of war than general and complete disarmament, but also a much less demanding

---

[22] Morton H. Halperin, *Limited War in the Nuclear Age* (New York: Wiley & Sons, 1963).

one. The arms-control policy neither aims nor expects to eliminate war and, in principle, it precludes the abolition of large national military establishments. It is largely a trimming operation—one that seeks to temper rather than to change the existing international system, to make the balance-of-terror system less dangerous instead of attempting to institute another system.

There are many arms-control proposals.[23] Some are measures each nation can introduce unilaterally. For instance, the United States installed electronic locks on its strategic missiles, which do not allow the doors of the Minuteman missile silos to be opened unless a command position emits a coded signal intercepted by the lock. This measure reduces the possibility of local unauthorized action or the usurping of nuclear arms by local civilian groups. The United States government hopes that the Soviet Union has taken similar precautions with its missiles but has seen little sense in postponing the introduction of this and other unilateral arms-control measures until the Soviet Union first agreed to reciprocate.

Other arms-control measures are bilateral. One such measure was introduced in 1963, when a teleprinter line, popularly known as the "hot line," was installed to provide a direct communication link between Moscow and Washington. Should, for instance, an American pilot take his bomber on an unauthorized attack toward the Soviet Union, the United States is expected to alert that country and help shoot down the plane.

A well-known multilateral arms-control measure is the 1963 treaty banning the testing of nuclear weapons in the atmosphere, in space, and under the seas. The treaty has less value than often claimed: several military experts believe that the United States and the Soviet Union had tested as many devices as were necessary to test before the test ban was signed; the Big Two have continued to conduct— they have probably even increased—their underground testing; and parties are free under the treaty to withdraw upon three months' notice if new testing in now forbidden areas is in their "supreme interest." [24] China was not prevented from testing atomic weapons in the atmosphere by the treaty.

There have been more encompassing arms-control proposals, in-

---

[23] Arthur T. Hadley, *The Nation's Safety and Arms Control* (New York: Viking, 1961); Louis Henkin, ed., *Arms Control* (Englewood Cliffs, N. J.: Prentice-Hall, 1961).

[24] Hearings before the Committee on Foreign Relations, U.S. Senate, 88th Congress, First Session. *Nuclear Test Ban Treaty*, page 3, letter to the Senate from the State Department.

cluding one that suggests a "freeze" of strategic weapons, that is, an agreement between the major powers not to produce additional long-range missiles, strategic bombers, and nuclear warheads. Another arms-control plan calls for some reduction of armament. For a time some experts favored the bomber bonfire plan, according to which a number of bombers of both sides would be brought together in a neutral spot and burned under joint supervision.

These various arms-control plans, however, are not meant to, and cannot, lead to the elimination of the instruments of warfare, even if these proposals were implemented, which most are not. Actually, the underlying assumption of these measures is that national governments will continue to rely on large national military establishments to protect their security. One might ask, "Why *large* military forces?" Could security not be maintained if all states would cut their arms in half, or even by nine-tenths, as long as the cuts are proportional, since the key is the comparative, not the actual, amount of armament? But the strategists of arms control emphasize that it cannot lead to large arms reductions because of the "principle of high numbers."

> The discussion about nuclear disarmament has revealed the paradoxi-cal fact that there is a certain safety in numbers. And this is true even if both sides scrupulously observe an agreement to limit nuclear weapons or the means of delivery. Instability is greater if each side possesses 10 missiles than if the equilibrium is stabilized at, say, 500. For an attack which is 90 percent successful when the defender has 10 missiles leaves him one—or a number hardly likely to inflict unac-ceptable damage. An attack of similar effectiveness when the de-fender possesses 500 missiles leaves 50—perhaps sufficient to pose an unacceptable risk in retaliation. And of course it is technically more complicated to destroy such a large number. Reduction of numbers is thus not an infallible remedy. A very small and vulnerable retalia-tory force may increase the danger of war by encouraging the op-ponent to risk surprise attack.
>
> It follows that stability is greatest when numbers are sufficiently large to complicate the calculations of the aggressor and to provide a mini-mum incentive for evasion but not so substantial that they defeat control.[25]

Thus, the policy of arms control may be capable of limiting the arms race, but abolishing armaments is not its purpose. It seeks to ensure the balance-of-terror, not to shift to a different system of se-curity. Arms control, at best, reduces the probability of nuclear war

---

[25] Henry A. Kissinger, *The Necessity for Choice* (New York: Harper, 1960, 1961), p. 217.

and, under certain circumstances, might limit devastation in the event of a war. It does not, however, remove any one of the major short-comings of the balance-of-terror system. All the ways the system might be unbalanced are still open. The lesser dangers of unauthorized action and mechanical accident might be somewhat reduced if a wide system of arms control were effected, but the danger of miscalculation, escalation, or a technological breakthrough (discussed below) are with us at least as much as in an uncontrolled arms race.

To demonstrate this point, let us examine the difference between an arms-control system that strives to "stabilize" only nuclear armaments (by improving the balance) and one that attempts to control nuclear *and* conventional armaments. A nuclear arms-control system (which is the one most frequently discussed) intends to make the deliberate initiation of nuclear war even less reasonable than it is under uncontrolled arms race conditions, since it would diminish whatever numerical "superiority" one side might have. In the early 1960's, the United States had at least four times as many long-range missiles as the Soviet Union, but this ratio was not considered to be a significant military advantage. They were produced largely because the United States expected the Russians to produce more, and when this turned out not to be the case, resistance to unilateral arms cuts prevented their curtailment. Psychologically, however, reducing "advantages" in number of arms—let us say, in the number of long-range missiles—has a stabilizing value: it makes the temptation to try to get away with a surprise attack less likely.

But the gain is accompanied by a danger. The more the two sides come to recognize that they have stalemated each other's nuclear might, the larger the premium on conventional means of warfare. The more effectively nuclear war is ruled out, the more feasible conventional wars might seem. And, once initiated, there would be little in the arms-control system to prevent strong pressures toward the escalation of such a war to the use of tactical, then strategic, nuclear arms. There is no assurance that after a major battle with conventional arms the losing side would refrain from resorting to some nuclear weapons, which would unleash, in all likelihood, a response in kind. It is true that East-West clashes have thus far stopped on the conventional level, in Korea and in Vietnam, and have not escalated to nuclear blows. But in each case the sides have come close to escalating to the nuclear level. This does not imply that each drive to the brink will tend to fall over the edge, but only that sooner or later one might, and the brink is 100 megatons high. By its very nature, the security derived from nuclear arms control might well turn out to be illusory without conventional arms control, just as illusory as the false security of auto seat belts to the driver speeding along narrow roads.

Arms-control systems that encompass both nuclear and conventional arms (including subconventional armaments such as those used in guerrilla and counterguerrilla warfare) are extremely difficult to effect for technical reasons that need not be discussed here.[26] But even if such controls were ever successfully introduced, the opposing sides would find themselves in military straitjackets *without* having treated the ideological and political sources of the conflict. For the West, it would mean having to tolerate revolutions in a large number of countries, even if they are Communist-inspired, financed, and engineered, as long as no outside armed intervention occurred. For Communist countries, it would spell the end of armed support for what at least some still consider "just" wars—"wars of national liberation." As hostility is not reduced, both sides would probably channel large parts of their military budgets to secret research efforts, to try to achieve a technological breakthrough or to find a weapon that would give them a strategic advantage. Among the weapons already under consideration and toward which the superpowers are investing heavily are anti-missile missiles, to halt a retaliatory strike following an attack (thus breaking out of the mutual deterrence system); a nerve gas to suddenly incapacitate mentally the other side; and various forms of viruses and bacteria to spread epidemics in an enemy's country.

Since an encompassing arms-control system would not allow piecemeal advances, only a weapon that would provide a swift and all-out advantage would be "useful." (Most experts doubt that a strategic advantage could be gained in this way, but both sides are trying for one anyway.) Tying the hands of the opposed sides without treating the sources of their conflict, without providing supervision to keep them from preparing a blow behind each other's back, and without disarming them, would put a premium on all-out war. In short, most arms-control systems only skirt the problem of war and do not even attempt to come to grips with it. Those that do confront the question of prevention of war do it in a way that, if successful, would completely stalemate the sides without providing an international force to safeguard freedom and justice, and if they fail—they might produce the most devastating war, an all-out strike. In short, arms control seems hardly enough to maintain security, whatever its other virtues may be.

---

[26] Bernard T. Feld, "Inspection Techniques of Arms Control," in Donald G. Brennan, ed., *Arms Control, Disarmament, and National Security* (New York: Braziller, 1961), pp. 317-32.

2. General and Complete Disarmament

GCD is a declared goal of both Soviet and United States foreign policy. As generally envisioned, GCD involves the elimination of both nuclear and conventional armaments, both among major and minor powers. Only armaments needed for police forces (or internal security) are to be allowed. By 1964, both the Soviet Union and the United States agreed that verification would have to be allowed if GCD were to be carried out, but little agreement was in sight on the kinds of verification measures and whether they ought to precede or follow disarmament. The United States position is that verification must precede disarmament, as its disarmament proposals call for both verification of arms eliminated *and* of those retained at various stages of the process. The Soviet Union favors reduction first, verification later.[27]

The disagreement over verification is deeper than it might seem. No sudden "break" in the negotiations in Geneva, or a generous give and take in the mood of a *détente,* is likely to remove it, as it serves as a convenient front to conceal the fear in which disarmament is held by most big and small powers. Governments have shown again and again a gnawing fear of being left "naked," exposed to an attack by another nation, following clandestine violations of a disarmament treaty or international use of arms retained for police purposes. Moreover, it must be noted, in a disarmed world a small country like Cambodia would have to fear an attack by a large country like China, even if the attackers were armed only with pitchforks and empty rice bowls.

The governments entrusted with the defense of their people might consider giving up the means of national defense if there were an alternative force to guard their citizens against violence from without. For better or worse, the fact is that nations are unwilling to trust each other to the degree that they will disarm without such alternative protection. "Educating them to trust each other" will surely take longer than the danger of nuclear war allows us to wait for. Hence, the quest for disarmament inevitably raises the question of where an alternative to *national* security will come from. The most common answer is that it would be provided by a world force. But the proposals for the creation of a world force invariably raise the difficult question of who will guard the guards, i.e., who will control the

---

[27] Richard J. Barnet, *Who Wants Disarmament?* (Boston: Beacon Press, 1960); John W. Spanier and Joseph L. Nogee, *The Politics of Disarmament* (New York: Praeger, 1962).

global force? A police force needs laws to enforce. Laws need to be instituted, interpreted, and altered, and violators must be judged and heard by a court of appeal. The force needs a commander loyal to the law and one who will activate the force against violators of any country.[28]

The prevailing Western answer to the question of who would control a world force, a view held by the United World Federalists as well as embodied in the official United States disarmament proposal, is that a revised United Nations or a similar world authority would control it. Such a global authority would legislate and enforce the laws, establish courts and a machinery for the execution of their judgments, and be, in effect, a world government. To it the basic sociological principle of all governmental institutions would apply: world authority or government will function effectively only after the majority of the world's people, at least of those who are politically active, consider it legitimate, that is, in line with their basic values. A government can force some of the people some of the time, but not most of the people most of the time. Acceptance by a politically conscious citizenry is a basic requirement of stable government.

This acceptance, in turn, is based on consensus—the sharing of ideas on the nature and functions of the government. If a substantial part of the people insists that it desires a Western form of government but another part insists equally as strongly that it wants a Communist form, then there can be no government at all. If part of the citizens were to direct the world government to protect private property and political freedoms, but otherwise to stay out of their lives as much as possible, and the other part were to direct this government to nationalize property and to actively guide the citizens' lives, there could be no shared government to do either. Differences of conception of what a government ought to do run deep. They are supported by basic values and reinforced and augmented by self-interest. For instance, those who favor government regulation of the economy and social welfare tend to have less income than those who favor a free enterprise system. Such differences of interest are as much a bar to political consensus as lack of shared values. So far, basic differences of values and of interests have prevented the evolution of a world community and, hence, of a world government, a world force, and—along with these—the realization of disarmament.

---

[28] Hans J. Morgenthau, "Political Conditions for a Force," in Lincoln P. Bloomfield, ed., *International Military Forces* (Boston: Little, Brown, 1964). See also Grenville Clark and Louis Sohn, *World Peace through World Law* (Cambridge, Mass.: Harvard University Press, 1958).

The fact that the West has, as a rule, marshaled a majority of important votes in the General Assembly of the United Nations does not provide a solution. Within a nation, the majority has—within limits of civil and human rights—the right and the force needed to compel a minority to follow its decisions. But does a "majority" of countries have either the moral right or the force to compel a "minority" of countries to comply with its decisions? The international "minority," the Communist countries, have never agreed to join with the Western "majority" in forming a world state, and all attempts to act as if world government already exists have failed. All plans to eliminate international violence by creating a world government here and now, e.g., through revision of the United Nations Charter, will continue to fail so long as a consensus on the purpose and nature of such a government has not been reached. The United States is aware of this and seems to view its official disarmament proposal, which requires a world authority, more as a sign of good will or counterpropaganda than as a policy it expects to follow. Both Russian and American plans for total disarmament are, as J. W. Fulbright, Chairman of the Senate Foreign Relations Committee, effectively put it, "an exercise in cold war fantasy, a manifestation of the deception and pretense of the new diplomacy. . . . There is nothing but mischief in negotiations which no statesmen seriously expect to succeed. They become a forum for the generation of false hopes and profound disappointment. . . ." [29]

The Soviet Union has proposed total disarmament since 1932, and with increasing intensity since the advent of the nuclear age. The Soviet interest in disarmament, in the narrow sense of the term, might well be keen, because the Soviet Union believes it could reap several strategic gains if disarmament were carried out. In the 1950's and early 1960's the proportion of the Russian economy tied up by military efforts was approximately twice as high as that of the United States (about 16 percent as compared to 8 percent), although the actual sum was about the same (according to one estimate, the United States' defense budget in 1959 was 38 billion dollars and that of the Soviet Union 37 billion).[30] Because the Soviet economy was only about half the size of the American one, the cold war required greater sacrifices in Moscow than in Washington. Also, as Russia has a full employment economy and has accumulated a great consumer demand after two generations of scarcity, release of resources following disarma-

[29] Clayton Lectures, given at Tufts University, April 29, 1963.
[30] Kahn, *On Thermonuclear War*, p. 508. It is difficult to get reliable figures on the Soviet GNP. Figures for neither the United States nor the Soviet defense expenditures are reliable.

ment would benefit the Soviet Union; in the United States, on the other hand, total disarmament might lead to a depression. More important, Russia believes, rightly or wrongly, that if the Western military forces were removed from the underdeveloped countries, indigenous leftist or Communist revolutions would soon take place in many African, Asian, and Latin-American states, *without* outside armed Communist help.

Why then does Russia object to verified disarmament under a world government such as the United States proposes? Could the Soviet Union not expect similar gains under these conditions? Russia seems to fear that a world government might be dominated by Western ideas and votes as was the General Assembly of the United Nations in the 1950's. Such a world government might send its forces to conserve national governments against indigenous Communist uprisings. Thus, in Russia's eyes, a world government would either be deadlocked, as agreement could not be reached since consensus on basic values is lacking, or would serve as a Western front organization. Hence, as a rule, the Soviet Union has favored disarmament without the creation of a world force or government. (A more "sinister" interpretation suggests that the Soviets favor disarmament only if not effectively verified, to allow it to benefit from its ability to secretly support local Communist movements in third countries.)

A suggestion to put to test Communist intentions by providing a "fair," neutral world authority, a kind of international civil service, staffed by nations trusted by both sides or by chosen individuals, neglects a major sociological insight we owe to Max Weber. An ideal civil service is an instrument that, under certain sociological conditions (missing on the world level), acts neutrally, serving all governing authorities without discrimination. But every bureaucracy, Weber pointed out, requires a nonbureaucratic political head.[31] Someone has to set the goals and establish the rules. One might add, in a more psychological vein, someone has to serve as a focus for identification that only a nonbureaucratic leader or group can provide. Identification is needed to build up and maintain the personal normative commitment upon which any government ultimately rests.[32] The Presidency, Congressional leaders, and the Supreme Court (next to the flag and the Constitution) are the foci of identification for the average American citizen. It is through identification with them that the work

---

[31] Max Weber, *The Theory of Social and Economic Organization* (New York: Oxford University Press, 1947), pp. 329-30.

[32] This is developed in Amitai Etzioni, *A Comparative Analysis of Complex Organizations* (New York: Free Press, 1961), pp. 201 ff.

of the government becomes concertized and symbolized, meaningful and accepted. Such identification can be built up only with bodies that deal with values and make decisions, not with the civil servants that staff the offices of the bureaucracy. Thus, for both sociological and psychological reasons, a world force and administration will need a political head, and whoever provides or controls it will, in effect, rule the world. The question of control cannot be circumvented.

The foundation of a world government and the disarmament plans based on it, it follows, will have to await the evolution of a world community of sufficiently shared values and sentiments, strong enough to support the institution of a world state.[33] No constitutional convention could provide such a consensus. A world charter might express and, to a degree, extend whatever consensus exists, but it could not remedy its almost total absence. It is often suggested that the fear of nuclear disaster provides such a consensus, but the record shows that people regularly prefer death to violation of the basic values that give meaning to their lives, and a world law compatible with mutually contradictory sets of values cannot, the record shows, be formulated. Consensus will have to be wider than merely the shared fear of a holocaust. World authority needs the support of positive values and must be—or at least must be perceived to be—active in the advancement of worldwide welfare, justice, and human rights. It cannot serve negative causes alone, even the all-important one of prevention of war. To put it differently, worldwide law and order will be maintained only if the world authority is a just one. This makes the world authority very difficult to attain, an extremely demanding institutional structure.

3. Arms Reduction: A Transition Strategy

The arms-reduction approach calls for a *gradual* transition from a world of armaments and balance-of-terror dangers to a world without war and regulation of force by a world authority. It starts as arms control but ends as general and complete disarmament. The main difference between arms reduction and arms control is that the first seeks to eliminate national military forces while the latter does not. The main difference between arms reduction and most proposals for GCD is the gradual nature of the former; it furnishes the time for sociopolitical processes to mature to the level needed to provide for a viable community foundation for a world authority.

---

[33] Talcott Parsons, "Communism and the West," in Eva and Amitai Etzioni, eds., *Social Change* (New York: Basic Books, 1964), pp. 390-99.

Arms reduction is an arms race in reverse. Arms are to be reduced step by step, each step triggering the next.[34] Initially, reductions might begin by one side, with the other then reciprocating (as in the arms buildup), but significant cuts in advance rounds must be simultaneous to gradually eliminate the deterrence system and to build an alternative system of security without upsetting the strategic balance. Thus, deterrence is maintained, even used, to move toward a world where it would be unnecessary.

Reductions must be effectively *verified*, and through techniques that are more acceptable to the closed Communist societies than inspection (which would involve the presence of a large number of foreigners in their countries) but that would also meet Western demands for effective verification. One such technique might be the destruction of weapons in neutral spots. The turning over of fissionable material to the International Atomic Energy Agency for peaceful uses is another. Satellite verification of the closing of bases in third countries is still another.[35] American experts have pointed out that one could verify reduction of 1962-level armaments by two-thirds or more without inspection, and without undertaking any undue risks. Reductions at more advanced stages of disarmament, however, would require inspection. Even then inspection might be introduced gradually in one zone after another, to diminish the adjustment difficulties. (As "insurance," both sides might maintain a force of nuclear-armed submarines, which are believed to be an invulnerable retaliation force, until the very end of the process.)

The details of such plans need not be discussed here, but several general characteristics and problems should be commented upon. They apply to most other social control systems, not just to supervision of arms reduction.

Risks

To delay the initiation of arms reduction (or any other system) until a *completely safe* verification system is found is to delay forever, for such a system cannot be designed. The question of the risks of arms reduction came up in many congressional hearings when meas-

---

[34] This strategy is spelled out by Charles E. Osgood, *An Alternative to War or Surrender* (Urbana, Ill.: University of Illinois Press, 1962), and Etzioni, *The Hard Way to Peace.*

[35] Seymour Melman, *Inspection for Disarmament* (New York: Columbia University Press, 1958). See also, United States Arms Control and Disarmament Agency, "Verification and Response," in *Disarmament Agreements* (Washington, D.C.: Institute for Defense Analyses, 1962).

ures such as the 1963 test-ban treaty were introduced. In part, to emphasize the residual risks of any arms limitation system (whether control, reduction, or disarmament) serves the political purpose of those who object to these programs on extrinsic grounds. In part, this emphasis on residual risks reflects the strong legal training and approach of many members of Congress and their almost complete lack of scientific training. Like lawyers, they look for loopholes and view a measure in which they can find some as unsatisfactory. From a scientist's point of view, the risks could be treated like laws of modern physics: the probability of a mistake is to be assumed, and measures that have a low probability of failure are to be preferred, as none can exist without any risks. Moreover, the *relative* risks of one measure compared to the risks of others have to be taken into account. The present balance-of-terror system that arms reduction seeks to replace is surely not without risk. Arms reduction seems a superior alternative if the risks of failure of verification are smaller than the risks to our mere survival from the continuation of the arms race, and if the risks to freedom are less than those of a more rapid, less verified disarmament.

Side-Effects

Verification—like other social control mechanisms—can be used for a variety of purposes. Some of these purposes, especially their accumulation, can ultimately destroy the effectiveness of verification and defeat its primary goal. One indirect purpose of verification could be to provide additional tasks for an international authority, thus strengthening it and expanding the administrative foundations of the international political community. Verification can also be used to effect social change inside some of the participating nations.

The social change effect, which verification through inspection is expected to have, is of special interest to the social scientists. Those who favor inspection as a lever of change believe that the presence of thousands of Western observers in free contact with the population of Communist countries will have a liberalizing effect on those countries. However, the sociological validity of this belief has yet to be demonstrated. It might be clarifying to study existing inspection systems, such as those involved in checking the quality of milk, the operations of customs inspectors, or even the effects of "northern" FBI agents in the deep South, to determine whether these systems have discernible effect within intercultural contexts. The general tendency to overvalue communication and interaction to the neglect of other sociological factors has probably exaggerated both Western hopes for and Eastern fears of the influence of Western visitors on citizens of the Eastern countries.

In any event, the designer of any control mechanism must take into account that the more goals he tries to serve and the less these goals are shared by those subject to control, the greater the resistance will be to the mechanism itself. Communist societies seem slowly to be recognizing the need to verify arms reductions, but it can hardly be expected that they will favor the use of inspection for attempts at de-Communization. Since arms reduction is urgent, de-Communization will therefore probably have to draw on means other than inspection.

Response

Verification has little value if the sides have no response (or sanctions) to turn to should a violation be discovered. Here there is a significant difference between intranational and international control systems. Intranational systems can rely largely on punishment of violators after a crime has been committed, since intranational violations are ordinarily less threatening to the survival of a society than most international ones, and since courts, police forces, and juries are readily available. International systems are at once more seriously threatened by violations and have fewer means of response, especially early in the development of their control systems. They must rely more on deterring a violation than on punishing the violator afterwards. The main deterrence against serious violations of arms-reduction systems is the anticipation that the other side, too, will rearm. Such a response will not punish the violator (other than in the sense that the prospect for further arms reduction would be dim, indeed, after such a violation). But after such a round of violation and response, the violator and his "victim" would be in a military position similar to the one they were in before the violation. All parties to a workable arms-reduction agreement would maintain an effective deterrent until the very end of the process, thus denying even a successful violator any significant strategic advantage. It is a general characteristic of international control systems that they are less concerned with justice and more concerned with stability than intranational systems.

Pace

The pace of arms reduction cannot be fully planned ahead of time. If each side were to carry out its initial commitment in good faith, additional reductions might be introduced at ever growing speed, just as tariff reductions by the members of the European Economic Community were advanced much ahead of the original schedule. Initial haggling over details is likely to be exceedingly cumbersome, and first steps are apt to be small, cautious, and reluctant. But once begun, arms reduction might well pick up momentum, especially if the "working toward" effect (explained below), which arms control lacks, produces and accelerates the development of mutual trust and global institutions.

The need to maintain an effective deterrent while the deterrent *system* as a whole, with its redundant and excessive forces, is reduced, whatever the price of the reduction, raises an obvious objection: since nuclear arms are the major threat, if some are retained until the end of the arms-reduction process, what does arms reduction contribute to security? The advocates of arms reduction would counter that, first, they do not object to the immediate removal of all nuclear arms if this could be carried out. They have turned to arms reduction largely because the fear of general and complete disarmament prevented national governments from moving toward it, tightening their grip on their armaments.

Second, there is a significant difference between nuclear weapons under arms-race and arms-control conditions, on the one hand, and the same weapons under arms reduction, on the other. Under arms reduction, the weapons are held as a *temporary* safeguard, with the clear intention of abolishing them. This crucial difference of perspective—the difference between a disarmed and an armed world—is important not only for the long run, but also for the immediate and near future, since it changes significantly the domestic and international psychological climate. This is called the "working toward" effect.

Working Toward Effect

Our attitude toward the bombs depends to a large degree on our orientation to the future. In a rampant arms race, we feel that bombs might be dropped on us at any time, and we see in our bombs protection from attack. Under arms control, bombs are a permanent feature of our life, a necessary condition for maintaining a balance of power. Under arms reduction, we see our opponent slowly destroying his arms as we dismantle ours; our fear that the bombs will be used against us is reduced. We realize that bombs are not here to stay and will be removed in the foreseeable future and that, gradually, we will have to conduct our international relations without them. Finally, as a global community matures, we shall come to perceive nuclear arms as very dangerous devices without a function—relics of an earlier era, capable of wrecking the peace we have gradually and painfully constructed over long years.

Our view of the future, by affecting our present anxieties, thoughts, and actions, affects the future itself, since it is determined in part by what we believe it is going to be. This phenomenon has been referred to by Robert K. Merton as the self-fulfilling prophecy.[36] This is a prophecy that, although false at the time it is pronounced, influences behavior to such an extent that the prophecy is realized. In short, the prophecy fulfills itself by virtue of the aftereffects of its pronouncement. If we believe that we are proceeding toward an armed showdown, we will multiply our arms, strengthen our fortresses, and keep our finger on the trigger—actions that tend to elicit a similar response on the other side, which in turn further intensifies our preparations and, moreover, seems to justify our earlier fear. One major false move in such a situation and we might produce the future we "anticipated." If, on the other hand, we feel that we are working toward a world of peace, we might be able to see ways of limiting our disputes with other powers to nonlethal means.

The feeling of progress toward a set goal, the feeling of advancing step-by-step according to a detailed plan—a feeling that the implementation of arms reduction would generate—is especially supportive to the process. If nations should ever give up one kind of arms after another, according to schedule, turning tanks into tractors, soldiers into workers, military appropriations into expenditures for health, economic growth, and education, our belief in the eventual realization of what now seems to many persons a highly Utopian state would grow fast. Moreover, as military researchers are transferred to peaceful work, as weapons factories begin to produce consumer goods, and as armament appropriations are used to build schools, a large variety of new interests vested in the pursuit of peace would be created, and the vested interests in the arms race would be reduced.

Ultimately, the pace of arms reduction will probably depend more on the development of a world community and authority than on the psychological atmosphere successful reductions would generate. There

---

[36] Robert K. Merton, "The Self-fulfilling Prophecy," in Merton, *Social Theory and Social Structure*, revised edition (New York: Free Press, 1957), pp. 421-36. For other applications of the conception of the self-fulfilling prophecy to problems of disarmament and social control of war, see: Herman Kahn, *Thinking about the Unthinkable* (New York: Horizon Press, 1962), pp. 42, 52, 57n., 236; Charles E. Osgood, "Reciprocal Initiative," in James Roosevelt, ed., *The Liberal Papers* (New York: Doubleday, 1962), pp. 177-78, 185, 197; and Jerome D. Frank, "Breaking the Thought Barrier: Psychological Challenges of the Nuclear Age," *Psychiatry* (August, 1960), pp. 23, 245-66.

are two central reasons for this dependency of arms reduction on the development of world institutions. First, while arms can be reduced considerably as states verify each other's reductions,[37] the removal of the final elements of the deterrence system is hard to imagine without the development of world institutions. Second, so long as world community institutions do not evolve, so long as the international system is lacking in adequate mechanisms for peaceful resolution of conflicts and the force needed to enforce peaceful accommodations reached, the pressure to use arms and, hence, to rearm, is bound to be great. Arms can be reduced very rapidly—at the end of World War II the United States cut back seven-eighths of its military establishment in less than a year—but world community institutions grow very slowly; the need for advancing and accelerating their growth is in a sense more urgent now, even though they are needed at later stages of the arms-reduction process. But, can a world community evolve? What is actually required? What processes might bring it about, satisfying the sociopolitical prerequisites of permanent disarmament?

Prerequisites of a World Community

1. Encapsulation, Not Conflict Resolution

The world community has to grow to provide a "capsule" to contain international conflicts and to prevent them from turning into war. Encapsulation refers to the process by which conflicts are modified in such a way that they become limited by rules (the "capsule"). The rules exclude some earlier modes of conflict, while they legitimatize other modes. Conflicts that are "encapsulated" are not solved in the sense that the parties become necessarily pacified. But the use of arms, or at least some usages of some arms, are effectively ruled out. Many observers deny that the normative views of East and West could become reconciled, suggesting that therefore the basis for disarmament is lacking. They see only two alternatives: powers are basically either hostile or friendly. Encapsulation, however, points to a third kind of relationship. Here, some differences of belief or interests, even a mutually aggressive orientation, might well continue. But states agree to rule out some means and some modes of conflict, i.e., armed ones, and set up the machinery necessary to enforce such an agreement. In this sense encapsulation is less demanding than pacification, since it

---

[37] Lawrence S. Finkelstein, "The Uses of Reciprocal Inspection," in Seymour Melman, ed., *Disarmament: Its Politics and Economics* (Boston: American Academy of Arts and Sciences, 1962), pp. 82-98.

does not require that the conflict be resolved or extinguished, but only that the range of its expression be curbed. Hostile parties are more readily "encapsulated" than pacified.

At the same time, encapsulation tends to provide a more lasting solution than does pacification. When pacified, the parties remain independent units that, after a period of time, might again find their differences of viewpoint or interest provoked, leading to new conflicts or renewal of the old ones. Once encapsulated, the parties lose some of their absolute license by being tied into a community. The community provides the sociopolitical foundations that the formation of consensus requires; this consensus in turn is the basis of the conflict-limiting rule of the "capsule."

If a transition to a world community is to occur, it must be self-propelling. Once a superior authority or once a world government or powerful United Nations police force is viewed as a prerequisite, an authority is assumed that can impose rules on the contending parties and thus keep their conflicts limited to those channels allowed by the community. But such universal authority is not available. The search for pathways to a world community must therefore look to those conflicts in which, through the very process of conflict, the participants initiate a self-imposed limitation on the means and modes of strife.

2. Propelling Forces: The Limits of Communication

How may a conflict curb itself? One theoretical answer was advanced by Robert Ezra Park. He pointed out that conflict generates interaction between its parties, e.g., races; the parties come to know each other and to communicate with each other, which in turn leads to the evolution of shared perspectives and bonds, until the conflict turns into competition. (Competition is used by Park and many other sociologists to refer to a conflict that is limited by a set of rules.) [38] George C. Homans supports this line of analysis by suggesting that communication breeds affinity.[39] A study by Daniel Lerner lends further support to this proposition. Lerner reports that French businessmen who travel, read foreign magazines, and have contact with foreign visitors are more likely to favor the formation of a European community than are those who are less exposed to foreigners. Among the businessmen with no exposure, sentiment in favor of such a community is about two to one, while those who have had much contact with foreigners favor the community by a ratio of six to one. The dif-

---

[38] Robert E. Park, *Human Communities* (New York: Free Press, 1952).
[39] George C. Homans, *The Human Group* (New York: Harcourt, Brace & World, Inc., 1950), pp. 110-17.

ference between these two groups might have been related to factors other than exposure, but Lerner shows that such variables as age, birthplace, socioeconomic status, size of firm, and location of firm do not explain the difference.[40] Thus, the proposition that exposure to foreigners can be credited with the generation of favorable attitudes is strengthened.

The theorem that increased communication between parties is the mechanism through which conflicts are encapsulated, and one that grows out of the conflict itself, seems to hold more for parties that have a similar set of values and sentiments to begin with. Communication can make the parties aware of a latent consensus and draw on it to build up agreed-upon procedures for the further limitation of conflicts and for the legitimization of accommodation. Under these circumstances, communication might also serve to work out limited differences of interest or viewpoint, building on shared foundations.

But when the basic values, sentiments, and interests of the parties are not compatible, increased communication may only stir incompatibility between the parties into conflict, dispel hopes of settlement or accommodation, make the parties more conscious of the deep cleavages that separate them, and increase hostilities. The larger the differences between the parties to a conflict, the smaller the degree of encapsulation that can be attained through increased communication. Or to put it more sharply, the greater the need for communication, the less good it does.

3. The Effect of Various Power Constellations

For encapsulation of international conflicts that are between hostile parties who lack shared values, the distribution of power among the parties seems to be more important than communication. Encapsulation seems to advance when it allows the more powerful participants to protect their positions against the pressure for reallocation of power to rising ones.

The number of actors participating in a system has often been related to the stability of a system. The balance-of-power system seems to require at least four or five participants.[41] Systems with three participants tend to lead to coalitions, in which two gang up against the third.[42] Bipolar systems, i.e., with two participants, have been shown to be particularly difficult to pacify. These highly abstract propositions

---

[40] Daniel Lerner, "French Business Leaders Look at EDC: A Preliminary Report," *Public Opinion Quarterly*, Vol. XX (1956), pp. 212-21.
[41] See Kaplan, *System and Process in International Politics*, pp. 27, 34 ff.
[42] Georg Simmel, *Conflict* (New York: Free Press, 1955).

assume that the participants have the same or similar power. An outstanding characteristic of international reality, however, is that the participants differ drastically in their power, ranging from nuclear superpowers to under-armed, poverty-stricken tribal states. The issue is further complicated by the fact that the relative power of any two nations is significantly different according to the sector of international relations under discussion and the particular matter involved. Thus, militarily, the Soviet Union is one of the two superpowers in the world; economically, it might be ranked only as being clearly second to the United States; and in the politics of the General Assembly of the United Nations, it has just three votes and controls only a few others.

A realistic model must therefore take into account the relative power of the participants relevant to the issue at hand, rather than focus only on the number of participants. Encapsulation or community-building seems to be enhanced by the transition from a relatively duopolistic system to a more pluralistic one, a process that can be briefly described as depolarization.

International relations approximated a state of duopoly between 1946 and 1956. It was in this period, the height of the Cold War, that two fairly monolithic camps, one directed from Moscow, the other from Washington, both increasingly equipped with nuclear armament, faced each other across the globe. While a number of countries were not aligned with either camp, their military and political weight was small. Such a duopolistic situation was highly unfavorable to encapsulation. The sides focused their attention on keeping their respective blocs integrated and on enjoining nonaligned countries from swelling the ranks of the opposite camp. Each bloc eyed the other, hoping for an opportunity to expand its respective area of influence, while waiting for the other's collapse.

Depolarization generated a situation more conducive to encapsulation. Between 1956 and 1964, in each of the two major camps, a secondary power rebelled. There were immense cultural, economic, military, and historical differences between De Gaulle's France and Mao's China and in their relations to their respective nuclear superiors. Nevertheless, both France and China had been weak powers, forced to follow a foreign policy formulated in foreign capitals. Both, however, under reawakening nationalism and augmenting national power, increasingly followed an independent foreign policy. Whatever turns foreign affairs may take, it is unlikely that the duopoly of 1946-1956 will be restored.

In any event, between 1956 and 1964 the net effect of the rebellion of the secondary powers in both camps was to draw the two super-powers closer. Seeking to maintain their superior status and fearing the consequences of conflicts generated by their rebelling client-states, the superpowers set out to formulate some rules binding on all parties. The treaty of partial cessation of nuclear tests, which the United States and the Soviet Union tried to make binding on France and China as well, was a case in point. American-Russian efforts to stem proliferation of nuclear weapons was another. Russia, in this period, stopped whatever technical aid it gave to Chinese nuclear research and development,[43] and the United States refused to help France develop its nuclear force. American-Soviet negotiations to agree on inspection of atomic plants, mainly aimed at insuring the use of atomic research for nonmilitary purposes in third countries, pointed in the same direction. The 1963-1964 *détente*, which isolated Communist China and France, and the Geneva disarmament negotiations in the same years, in which these two countries did not participate, were further reflections of this trend.

These measures have in common the important characteristic that they serve the more "narrow" needs of the superpowers while they also advance the "general welfare" of the world and can, hence, be presented in terms of universal values and implemented through world institutions (i.e., extend the "capsule"). For instance, the prime super-power motivation for the 1963 test treaty might well have been the desire of the United States and Russia to remain the only two great nuclear powers, but it also indirectly reduced the danger of nuclear war. It was presented as if the prime motive were advancement of peace and disarmament and the reduction of fallout to protect human health. It is a familiar strategy of political interest groups to work out solutions among themselves and then clothe them in the values of the community at large. (However, one must not lose sight of the fact that the protection of future generations from the danger of further test fallout was actually accomplished.) Indirectly, these values affect the selection of the course of action an interest group follows from among alternative ones available and provide a common basis on which similar or compatible interests of divergent powers can be harmonized and the shared community broadened.

4. International "Floating Vote"

Another process that has enhanced community-building is the emergence of a "floating vote," i.e., votes not permanently committed

---

[43] G. F. Hudson, Richard Lowenthal, and Roderick MacFarquhar, *The Sino-Soviet Dispute* (New York: Praeger, 1961).

to any one side. The great value of the existence of a sizable floating vote for the *maintenance* of a political system has often been pointed out. It tends to moderate conflict among parties by making violent conflict less "attractive" and reducing the temper of conflict in general. As long as a significant part of the voters is uncommitted, gaining their support tends to be preferred to a violent (and risky) showdown, since moderation tends to appeal to the uncommitted voters who are, as a rule, "between" the parties of a conflict in terms of their interests. It is less often recognized that the *emergence* of a significant floating vote supports the *development* of a community by encouraging encapsulation. In the same period in which depolarization advanced, and the solidarity of the Eastern and Western blocs declined, the bipolar system was further weakened by the large increase in the number of nonaligned countries. And the status of nonalignment rose as both the East and West increasingly recognized it as legitimate.

The growth in number and status of the nonaligned, a kind of international floating vote, made several contributions to encapsulation and community-building. Around it began to evolve the growing *shared norm*, recognition of nonalignment, which limited the conflict between East and West in that it defined, increasingly, one major sector of the international system as outside the conflict *so far as armed means were concerned*. While the norm was occasionally violated (e.g., in Vietnam and Laos), it was widely observed and, over the years, violations became less frequent. At the same time, reliance on nonviolent means, such as trade, aid, and propaganda, commanded an increasing proportion of the investments the United States and the Soviet Union put into their efforts in third countries.[44]

The norm supporting nonalignment is of special interest for the study of community-building, as it does not bar conflicts but only rules out intervention by force in third countries. Peaceful appeals—for instance, those aimed at supporting or blocking internal changes in a country, such as progress toward freedom and social justice, or accelerated economic development—are "allowed." This quality of the norm had a double effect: first, it forbade (quite successfully) the joining of countries to a bloc, a joining that would have weakened the movement toward regulation of the conflict, and if continued, would have reduced and potentially exhausted the floating vote. Second, the norm left room for the expression of the ambitions of both

---

[44] Etzioni, *Winning Without War*, Chapter 2. These statements refer to the 1956-64 period. Both the United States and Russia have re-increased their military budgets with the escalation of the war in Vietnam in 1965.

sides without violating the rules curbing the conflict, a major virtue of encapsulation as distinguished from the conflict-resolution, or pacification. (It is not that conflict-resolution is not desirable, but it seems more difficult to attain and especially to stabilize.)

Above all, the increase in the floating vote, like the decrease in bloc solidarity, significantly *increased the range of political activities and sharply reduced the pressure to resort to military means.* The more rigidly the sources of power (e.g., "votes") and prospective rewards (e.g., economic assets) are divided between two parties, and the more integrated internally each of these parties is, the less the weaker of the two can expect to gain a majority (in a parliament or the United Nations) and improve its share in the allocation of assets by non-violent means. The more the avenues of political efforts such as campaigning (to appeal to the floating vote) and bargaining (to split away a segment of the opposing party or bloc) are or seem to be futile, the greater the pressure toward an armed showdown. As has often been suggested, the more constitutional or otherwise legitimate avenues of effective action are closed, the higher the pressures toward change by force.

These general rules apply with special strength on the international level. Here the use of armed means is not considered as illegitimate as it is inside a national society ("war is the continuation of diplomacy by other means"). The normative bonds among the actors are weaker and hostility among the parties more encompassing. There are fewer constitutional avenues for expression and no central force to curb drives toward violent "solutions" by the participants. Hence, a decrease in solidarity of the blocs and an increase in the "floating vote" are of special importance to reduce the pressure toward armed advances and to increase the premium on other political options, including community-building.

As the floating vote provides a reward that shifts to the side that is favored, *the values according to which the floating vote shifts are among the values the sides seek to promote,* or at least to give the appearance of promoting. In the period under study, the floating vote often rewarded moderation, which is quite common, as it tends to be politically "between" the sides to a conflict. On balance, the non-aligned countries stand to lose from an American-Soviet war but to gain from peaceful competition between them for their support. Hence, it is not surprising that, between 1956 and 1964, the nonaligned countries tended to use their influence to encourage encapsulation. By and large, nonaligned countries favored reduction of armaments and of cold war tensions, increase in the capacities, power, and status of the United Nations, cessation of hostilities in Korea and in Vietnam, and exclusion of armed interventions by superpowers in other countries' conduct.[45]

5. Consensus Formation and Regional Bodies

Sociopolitical processes that reduce the differences of interest and viewpoint of parties and that build ties among them are, in effect, community-building processes. Communities, especially if they have a government, require consensus, which in turn needs to be developed. The evolution of *intermediary bodies* is of special value for consensus formation. To form an effective consensus-formation structure it is essential to divide the process into several levels of representation. Rather than attempting to reach consensus among all parties in one general assembly, the parties are best divided into subgroups that are *more* homogeneous than the community as a whole. These subgroups work out a compromise and are represented as if they were a single unit on the next level of the structure in which consensus is formed. Effectiveness might require that such divisions be repeated several times. (In the American political system, the primaries and the national conventions and, to a degree, postelection negotiations over participation in the cabinet provide, as a rule, such a multilayer consensus-formation structure. Thus, for instance, the struggle over who is to be the presidential and who the vice-presidential candidate is also a struggle over what policy the party is to face the electorate with. Once chosen, most segments of the party—e.g., liberal and conservative—tend, as a rule, to support the candidates and the policy. In the negotiations on participation in the cabinet, the party that lost an election is often given some indirect representation to enhance *national* support for what is a one-party administration.)

Regional organizations, communities, and blocs might serve as "intermediary bodies" for the international community. It would, however, be a mistake to view each and every regional organization as a step on the road toward a world community. Regional organizations that have only sociologically marginal roles, such as the European research organization on peaceful usages of nuclear energy (CERN), tend to have much less impact than those that pool the sovereignties of several nations, as the European Economic Community (EEC) began to do.

---

[45] Francis O. Wilcox, "The Nonaligned States in the U.N.," in Laurence W. Martin, ed., *Neutralism and Nonalignment* (New York: Praeger, 1962).

Regional bodies intended to countervail other regional bodies, especially military alliances such as NATO and the Warsaw Treaty Organization, often retard rather than advance encapsulation of conflict; they tend to reflect, on a large scale, the features of nationalism. Economic associations also may serve as "antiblocs," rather than as a basis for a community. For example, the British-led European Free Trade Areas was formed to "counter" the French-led EEC. Regional bodies aimed at internal improvement, such as "welfare" communities (a foundation of the EEC) or development associations (e.g., in Central America) that stress rapid economic growth or mutual assistance, are more likely to serve as intermediary layers in the process of building a world community.

Above all, only regional bodies that allow the process of *upward transfer* of loyalties to take place are helpful to the building of a world community. Studies of social structures as different as the American federal government and the Southern Baptist Association have shown that *once a center of authority is established, it tends,* under circumstances and because of factors that need not be discussed here, *to grow in power, rights, and command of loyalties* earlier commanded by the units, now increasingly controlled by the central authority of the rising system (as when states' rights decline and those of the federal government grow).[46] But a social unit can, by the use of ideological and political mechanisms, advance or retard this process. Only those units that encourage or, at least, allow the process to occur provide a sociopolitical foundation on which a world community might be erected.

The last phase of this *upward-transfer* process is particularly difficult to chart at this stage of our knowledge. Some crude contours of regional communities have begun to appear, and there are limited clues to their inner workings. But, failures of such communities still outnumber successes by a large margin. The nature of such upward transfer is also obscure at this stage, since the development of intermediary bodies often uses the flame of regional and bloc chauvinism to melt away some national sovereignty in favor of the regional organizations or states. Without the cold war, present efforts to form an Atlantic and an east European community are difficult to imagine. A major driving force behind attempts to form common markets in South America, in various parts of Africa, in the Far East, and elsewhere is the desire to counter actual or anticipated consequences of

---

[46] P. M. Harrison, *Authority and Power in the Free Church Tradition* (Princeton, N. J.: Princeton University Press, 1959).

the European Economic Community.[47] Progress, in short, might not be unilinear but dialectic, with units moving apart to provide the foundation for moving closer.

6. Rules and Enforcement

Another major process of community-building is the *evolution of rules and of agencies for their enforcement.* Here there is much room for the application and development of the sociology of law. There are some obvious applications, such as the insight that one need not wait until all the units involved are ready for progress before it can be initiated. However, other experiences warn against excessive reliance on legislation when there is only a narrow sociopolitical basis. A premature and ineffectual world law might be worse than no law at all. Laws that are not backed by effective enforcement and adequate consensus, as illustrated by the abortive attempt to institute prohibition in the United States, breed contempt for the laws and their makers and nurture a whole breed of previously unknown criminal interests. A premature world law on disarmament might well generate clandestine production of weapons and large profits to arms smugglers, and thereby lead to repeal of the law, rather than to lasting disarmament.

The concern in the study of encapsulation, as distinct from most studies of intrasocietal law and controls, is not mainly with protecting the existing mechanism from erosion, as much as accelerating its extension and growth. Hence, the importance of formalization of implicit and "understood" rules into explicit and enforced international laws. This is neither obvious nor widely agreed upon. There are many who stress the value of implicit, unnegotiated understandings.[48] Such "understandings" are valued by some because they can be reached without interference from dissenting allies and domestic opponents. For instance, in 1963 the United States released a leading Soviet spy who was in an American prison; the Soviet Union, only 22 hours later, released a similarly prominent American spy who was in a Soviet prison. The State Department admitted to no Soviet-American "deal." Probably a few weeks earlier a Western diplomat had subtly hinted that the United States intended to release the spy it held and inquired about the health and well-being of the American. The Soviet diplomat promised to make some inquiries. A few days later, he hinted

---

[47] Jan Tinbergen, *Shaping the World Economy* (New York: Twentieth Century Fund, 1962), pp. 195 ff.

[48] For a discussion of this approach see Robert A. Levine, *The Arms Debate* (Cambridge, Mass.: Harvard University Press, 1963), pp. 56 ff.

that Russia would release the American.[49] Thus the sides communicated and reached an agreement without making a "deal" that public opinion might have found distasteful. In a similar way, shortly after the Soviet Union removed its missiles from Cuba late in 1962, the United States removed its Thor and Jupiter missiles from Turkey and Italy in 1963.

There are several disadvantages in reaching agreement in this particular way, especially for community-building efforts. The danger of misunderstanding is larger, especially when matters are complex. When misunderstandings occur, they generate bitter feelings of betrayal and mistrust, which, in turn, stand in the way of future exchanges. And, to the degree that the public is unaware of the agreements, it remains uneducated and will not support more far-reaching agreements if and when those become possible and desirable. To the degree the public becomes aware that a deal was actually made, it becomes more alienated from the government and distrustful of it. And the world institutions do not gain in experience and responsibility unless implicit understandings are codified and enforced by them. This is not to suggest that the path of implicit understanding should not be traveled; only that unless an enlarging flow of such traffic is directed through world institutions, they will remain the dirt roads rather than the highways of international relations.

When rules are formalized, effective verification and response machinery are necessary. The 1954 agreements to neutralize Laos and limit arms supplies for Vietnam were supervised by an understaffed, underfinanced, ill-equipped, and—above all—a politically deadlocked commission. (Its members were India, Poland, and Canada.) In 1959, East and West accused each other of violating these agreements; the enforcement machinery provided neither a clear picture of who was the first to violate the agreements nor an appropriate response. This is a good example of how not to set up an enforcement mechanism. On the other hand, United Nations troops positioned on the Egyptian-Israeli border at the Gaza Strip in 1957 were successful in pacifying this border, which, before that date, was highly explosive. Open, nonmilitary zones (e.g., Antarctica), neutral zones (e.g., Austria), nonnuclear "clubs," regional security systems, and outer space are all areas in which rules can be made more explicit, more encompassing, better enforced, and serve as components for a gradual transition toward a world community.

---

[49] A similar incident is reported in detail by James B. Donovan in his *Strangers on a Bridge* (New York: Atheneum, 1964).

Consequences and Causes of Failures to Prevent War

We have outlined the dangers of a world armed with nuclear weapons, charged with incompatible ideologies, split between "have" and "have not" countries. We have also charted several solutions that have been offered. Some of these, even if implemented, will not assure the base survival of the human race; others are so difficult to implement that, whatever their virtues, they are unlikely to be tried. Finally, we have briefly examined some of the sociopolitical processes that will have to mature before a stable world authority is to become feasible. Without that authority, peace will be a precarious state resting on a delicate balance of terror or a moment of pause between disarmament and rearmament. A condition of permanent peace has been established successfully on the national level in many states via community-building; it needs now to be provided for on regional and global levels. The processes are slow and difficult, but there is reason to believe that they can be accelerated. Let us review, briefly, some of the problems raised by continued absence of a solution: how quickly shall we recover if we fail? To what degree do military institutions prevent the necessary solutions? And, what role do scientists in general, and social scientists in particular, play in advancing a solution?

1. "Will the Survivors Envy the Dead?" (Postnuclear Recovery)

Whether the survivors of a nuclear exchange would envy the dead depends on many factors. Depending on the size of the exchange, the kind of targets selected, and the degree of prewar preparation, estimates of the chance of recovery after nuclear war range from none at all to the relatively short time period of ten years or so. A leading analyst of the possible consequences of a nuclear war has concluded that "with sufficient study we will be able to make a very convincing case for recuperation, if we survive the war, and, more important, that with sufficient preparation we actually will be able to survive and recuperate if deterrence fails." [50]

The speed and scope of recovery, if there is any, obviously depend on the extent of the initial damage. Theoretically, a "strike" could range from the use of one small atomic weapon (e.g., to show determination) to complete devastation of mankind. It would appear that once a nuclear exchange is initiated, it will be difficult to limit it. War plans to limit the war to military targets but to spare enemy cities

---

[50] Kahn, *On Thermonuclear War*, p. 95.

(technically referred to as "counterforce strategy") tend to ignore the fact that many military targets are close to cities, and, hence, a nation under attack will have a hard time determining which kind of attack it is being subjected to. (Attacking only military targets far from cities would leave the opponent with a major striking force.) Moreover, the more dispersed, varied, and protected the nuclear forces become, the larger an initial attack—if it occurs—is likely to be. Finally, although the national course for a country about to "lose" might be to surrender in order to spare its cities, countries in such situations would rarely react rationally. (For example, the Nazi bombing of London in World War II did not bring Britain to its knees.) All of these reasons suggest that a large nuclear war is much more likely than a small one.

The damages of a large nuclear war are often underestimated rather than overestimated. In part, this might be the case because damage assessments are often financed directly or indirectly by a military service or the Office of Civil Defense Mobilization.[51] (Assessments by scholars or members of peace groups are much higher.[52] There seem to be no comprehensive studies by persons without normative commitments on the subject, perhaps because it is so difficult, almost inhuman, to be completely neutral about it.) Also, some seek to legitimize plans for the use of nuclear arms in the case of war. By the end of 1964, the United States had still refused to pledge itself not to be the first to use nuclear arms. Certain plans for the defense of West Berlin called for the use of nuclear weapons.[53] Some generals favored nuclear bombardment in the case of extension of the war in Vietnam, a showdown with China, or any large-scale conventional war for which the United States was believed to be ill-prepared. Other interests seek larger appropriations for civil defense plans, from shelters to antimissiles, and, hence, need to "demonstrate" the value of such

---

[51] The most often cited materials are those presented by the Office of Civil and Defense Mobilization to the 1959 Holifield hearings. See "Biological and Environmental Effects of Nuclear War" (Washington, D. C.: U.S. Government Printing Office, 1959). See also "The Nature of Radioactive Fallout and Its Effect on Man" (Washington, D. C.: U.S. Government Printing Office, 1957). Other studies were conducted by RAND (see Kahn, *On Thermonuclear War*). More recent studies, for instance, a "Five Cities Study" and "Models and Theories for Initial Postattack," in process at the Hudson Institute, are financed by the Office of Civil Defense.

[52] Arthur I. Waskow and Stanley L. Newman, *America in Hiding* (New York: Ballantine Books, 1962). Saul Azonow, Frank R. Ezvin and Victor W. Sidel, eds., *The Fallen Sky* (New York: Hill and Wang, 1963).

[53] *The New York Times*, March 1, 1961, and June 7, 1961. For Soviet reaction see *Pravda*, October 5, 1961.

defenses for postnuclear recovery. Still others have built their reputations on the feasibility of nuclear war, which they sustain with new projections, statistics, and war games.[54]

Another source of gross error are the projections made from "disaster" studies that have proliferated over the last years, often financed by interested parties. Such studies show that even a highly devastated town has been able to recover, leading to possible inference that therefore a devastated nation could. The flaw in the community example is that other parts of the same state are not damaged and national organizations move in, using their undamaged sources and undiminished federal support. As Allen H. Barton indicated in his review of studies of disaster areas, community resources are invariably limited. Leadership, manpower, and specialized knowledge are often recruited from outside the local disaster area, through agencies like the Red Cross, local branches of national corporations, and local arms of the state government, such as the National Guard.[55] Obviously, after a nuclear attack on the whole country there would be no such resources to draw on since the whole fabric of the American society and, in all likelihood, that of its neighbors and allies, will be damaged.

Next to these sociological sources of underestimation of the damages of nuclear war lie other mistakes, the product of misconceived analysis. One common mistake is to assess the damage to be caused on the basis of the number of bodies to be left in the radioactive deserts on the day after the attack, as compared to those that are believed to be wandering around. Thus, sixty million dead, facile statistics show, still leave about two-thirds of America alive. Morality aside, recovering a third of the population seems not too difficult. However, if we assume for a moment that this will be an attack on cities (as is usually assumed),[56] then also destroyed will be most first- and second-class medical facilities, seats of culture, and centers of commercial and industrial activities and of national communication networks. For instance, an attack on 70 urban areas of the United States might kill "only," as the official statistics have it, 46 percent of the population, but among the dead would be 62 percent of all the physicians, 73 percent of all the architects, 79 percent of all salaried managers of key

---

[54] Irving Louis Horowitz, *The War Game* (New York: Ballantine Books, 1963).

[55] Allen H. Barton, *Social Organization Under Stress: A Sociological Review of Disaster Studies,* Publication #1032 of the National Research Council (Washington, D. C.: National Academy of Science, 1963), pp. 168-74.

[56] See, for instance, the list submitted to the 1959 Holifield hearings by the Office of Civil and Defense Mobilization; and Tom Stonier, *Nuclear Disaster* (New York: Meridian Books, 1964).

industries, etc.[57] There would be 1.3 million hospital beds available (if emergency units are included), for 15 million live casualties.[58] Not all the casualties will need hospitalization, but at least three out of every four who do will not be able to receive such treatment. Hence, no recovery of America, as we know it, is likely at all, although—if lucky—the United States might continue to function as a continent-sized Appalachia.

Finally, studies of nonliterate and other societies have shown that under certain conditions the will of a society can be broken, and complete apathy or anarchy prevail. The following statement, from an interview with a survivor of Hiroshima, illustrates this mood:

> The people seemed stunned by the catastrophe and rushed about as jungle animals suddenly released from a cage. Some few apparently attempted to help others from the wreckage, particularly members of their family or friends. Others assisted those who were unable to walk alone. However, many injured were left trapped beneath collapsed buildings as people fled by them in the streets. Pandemonium reigned as the uninjured and slightly injured fled the city in fearful panic.[59]

Luckily, for Japan, such a blow was aimed at only two cities, and not the nation at large.

All this leads to the conclusion that the balance of data and sociological inferences points to damage assessments larger than those usually provided by researchers whose specializations are not in the social sciences, but in statistics or mathematics, and who therefore tend to count individuals and tons of steel and coal rather than analyze social systems.

2. The Military-Industrial Complex: Economics of the Arms Race and Disarmament

The arms race has been explained by persons as different as C. Wright Mills and Dwight D. Eisenhower as deriving, at least to an important extent, neither from the nature of the international power relations nor from the psychology of those exposed to it, but rather from the nature of the society.[60] The essence of this analysis is that

---

[57] Robert A. Dentler and Phillips Cutright, *Hostage America* (Boston: Beacon Press, 1963), p. 15. The transportation equipment industry is cited.

[58] *Ibid.*, p. 65.

[59] I. L. Janis, *Air War and Emotional Stress* (New York: McGraw-Hill, 1951), p. 29.

[60] C. Wright Mills, *The Causes of World War III* (New York: Simon and Schuster, 1958); Dwight D. Eisenhower, "Farewell Address," January 16, 1961.

the arms race is promoted by business circles who reap profits directly or indirectly from weapons production. These circles include not only the arms manufacturers and those who supply them with parts and raw materials, but also America's millions of stockholders, for whenever preparations for war decline, it is said the entire American economy (and with it the economies of many industrial Western countries) suffers a recession. The Great Depression was not really overcome, it is said, until the arms buildup for World War II started. The postwar recession ended only when rearmament for the Korean War spurred the American economy. Subsequent smaller ups and downs of the economy have been related to ups and downs in the tensions of the cold war. For instance, the American stock market experienced hearty rallies after the breakdown of the 1960 summit conference in Paris, the 1961 Berlin crisis, and with the 1965 escalation of the war in Vietnam. The rallies were led by "defense" stocks, but other stocks benefited as well.

Workers also benefit from the arms race. The close association between employment and international tension, unemployment and relaxation of this tension, is reflected in the following figures: in 1939, 17.2 percent of the American labor force was unemployed. The war reduced unemployment to 1.2 percent in 1944. Unemployment rose after the war in 1946 to 3.9 percent, was reduced by the Korean War to 2.5 percent, rose after this war ended to 5.0 percent by 1954 and continued to rise to 7.0 percent in 1961. In the same year, between 6,500,000 and 7,500,000 American jobs depended on defense spending. Were these jobs abolished and no others created, the United States would have the same percentage of unemployed as in 1939—about 17 percent.

No less important in explaining many international actions by the United States and its over-all strategy, it is suggested, are business investments abroad. United States foreign investments amounted to 44.8 billion dollars in 1959. Earnings from these investments are comparatively 60 percent higher than from investments in the United States (13.8 percent versus 8.5 percent); and much of this investment is held by the powerful 100 top American corporations. It is common among followers of this line of analysis to explain specific United States foreign policy acts by reference to big business interests abroad. For example, intervention in the Middle East (e.g., in 1958 in Lebanon) is explained by the interests of various oil companies; intervention in Latin America (e.g., in Guatemala), by the interests of the United Fruit Company, whose property was nationalized by the Arbenz government; and intervention in Cuba in 1961, by the interests of the sugar industry, whose property was confiscated by Castro.[61]

Two groups other than owners and workers also are listed as having vested interests in the arms race. One is composed of generals and admirals and other senior officers. It is said that such men would, for obvious reasons, object to disarmament, which would leave them unemployed, and so to speak, disinvested. The second interest group is composed of thousands of scientists and technicians directly employed by the military services or the recipients of large military research grants. With the diminution of defense expenditure, many of them would lose income and prestige. These professionals are sometimes accused of supplying the antidisarmament business and military groups with ideologies to cover up their naked self-interest. The RAND Corporation, subsidized by the Air Force, is one of many examples. Thus Harrison Brown and James Real have written:

> Ten thousand scientists and technicians have devoted all of their lives to the invention and construction of weapons. A majority of those who went to work *after* World War II are convinced that weaponry is a way of life for themselves and expect the United States–Soviet Union contest to continue forever. Many of them are articulate and highly valued consultants in every walk of American life, from the Congressional committee to the PTA.[62]

C. Wright Mills, whose *The Causes of World War III* stresses the role of the "military metaphysics" in what seems to many of the left as a "drift toward nuclear disaster," states:

> Technologists and scientists readily develop new weapons; preachers and rabbis and priests bless the great endeavor; newsmen disseminate the official definitions of world reality, labeling for their publics the shifting line-up of friends and enemies; publicists elaborate the "reasons" for the coming war and the "necessity" for the causes of it. They do not set forth alternative policies; they do not politically oppose and politically debate the thrust toward war. . . . They have generally become the Swiss Guard of the power elite . . . .[63]

What can be done to counter these pressures toward war? Most radical analysts doubt that anything constructive can be done within the framework of capitalist society, in particular that of the United

---

[61] Samuel Shapiro, *Invisible Latin America* (Boston: Beacon Press, 1963), pp. 84 ff.
[62] Harrison Brown and James Real, *Community of Fear* (Santa Barbara, Calif.: Center for the Study of Democratic Institutions, 1960).
[63] Mills, *The Causes of World War III*, p. 85.

States; they believe that changing international relations must begin with a revolutionary change at home. Only when public ownership of the means of production abolishes the profit motive will the true incentive for armaments production and the arms race disappear. Only when employment is controlled by the government and not by the business cycle, will the socioeconomic prerequisites of disarmament be met. To work for peace, radicals say, therefore requires working for a socialist revolution.[64]

Liberal economists have worked out several schemes for alleviating pressures toward armament within the framework of a capitalistic society. For instance, various peaceful functions are suggested for ex-armament industries; programs are recommended to keep the economy running at full speed by spending the funds saved by cuts in the military budget. Increased investment in schools, medicine, and underdeveloped countries are the favorite recommendations. In addition, as economist Kenneth E. Boulding points out, disarmament may require as much investment as the arms race, if not more, because of the cost of inspection, monitors, international armies, and international organizations.[65] It is estimated that about 40,000 militarily trained personnel will be required to staff disarmament inspection programs alone. Programs have been suggested to retrain army officers for peaceful vocations while maintaining their salary, status, and security. For instance, military staff members might, in some circumstances, make good college teachers; and medical researchers developing nerve gas and bacteriological weapons could be used to fight cancer and mental illness. In short, disarmament, the liberal economists suggest, can be brought into line with the economic self-interests of members of the society.

An accurate assessment of the economic forces that serve to perpetuate the arms race is extremely difficult. It would require a book at least the size of this one to disentangle truth from half-truth and to analyze the various complications involved. It may be true, for instance, that officers have a vested interest in a military career. On the other hand, many officers are truly devoted to their country and might willingly expose themselves to the hardships of retraining for civil careers, to serve the country's best interests, if they were convinced that disarmament is possible. Moreover, the American government did reduce sharply its military budget after World War II and the Korean

---

[64] This is, roughly, the position taken by publications such as *The Monthly Review* and *The National Guardian,* both on the extreme left.

[65] Kenneth E. Boulding and Emile Benoit, *Disarmament and the Economy* (New York: Harper, 1963).

War, though economists warned that such reductions were likely to bring about recession or depression.

The details of various programs advocated to break down the anticipated resistance to disarmament by businessmen, officers, and scientists are sometimes naive, but they indicate that the situation is not beyond remedy. It is somewhat unlikely that SAC pilots would be welcome in the civilian airlines, already overstaffed as a consequence of the introduction of jets. It is also questionable whether army colonels would relish teaching college freshmen, even if the salary were satisfactory. Yet, it is true that locating alternative employment and subsidizing retraining where necessary will ease the transition. If it is true that enforcing disarmament will, at least initially, require considerable personnel and considerable equipment for which ex-military assembly lines can be used (for example, observation towers, satellites, and monitors), then the economic crisis caused by disarmament would be less severe. It seems safe to conclude that if we investigate the problems involved and plan ahead for them, the transition to a peacetime economy can be eased, the anxiety of vested-interest groups can be alleviated, and with it, resistance to disarmament can be reduced, though not eliminated.

Limitations of space do not allow discussion here of the role occupied by military institutions in other societies. The role of the military in the Soviet society and its relative weight compared to the Communist party is of paramount interest. The military in developing nations, often viewed as a major obstacle to development, is in fact sometimes the only effective force for development. Nor can we study here the effects of outside armed intervention on internal processes or social change. The number of countries in which such intervention has taken place, either on the side of the status quo or on that of social change, or both, is so large that it is almost impossible to study societal change anywhere—in Tanzania, Tibet, Brazil, Vietnam, Cuba, or the Gabonese Republic—without studying the role of outside forces. This is another subject unto itself.

3. The Scientist as a Disarmer

The role of scientists in public policy in general, especially foreign policy, has gained much attention since the advent of the nuclear war. At least 50 books have been written on the subject over the past few years.[66] The issue is complex and some of the main questions involved can only be indicated briefly here.

---

[66] For a good selection of essays see Robert Gilpin and Christopher Wright, eds., *Scientists and National Policy-Making* (New York: Columbia University Press,

One view is that the scientist should not take a position on public issues as a scientist. If he takes a position in his role as a citizen, he should carefully warn his listeners or readers that he does so in his nonscientific capacity, in order to preclude the impression that his position has a sounder foundation than that of others. Policy questions, it is pointed out, involve matters much broader than the expertise of any one scientist. And, even in his narrow specialty, there is no professional consensus on many matters. A policy statement, it is emphasized, involves evaluation, not just information—i.e., value judgments, and the scientist's values are not superior to those of the next man.

According to the same position, the scientist has no special responsibility. He generates new knowledge and makes it available to the public. He neither claims nor commands a control of its usages. The student of the structure of the atom is devoted neither to the use of his findings for nuclear warfare nor to desalting the oceans. The student of bacteria is neither oriented to the improvement of vaccines nor to bacteriological warfare. The use of his findings is not determined by him. This attitude was recently illustrated when Carl Buchalla, an Associated Press reporter, interviewed in Cairo a leader of a group of German scientists who are reported to be helping to build rockets with which Nasser said he could hit Israel. Professor Wolfgang Pilz said: "We are not anti-Semites or old Nazis. We are just scientists doing a job." [67] The view that scientific pursuit is quite separate from the political goals for which the findings are used is held by many scientists.

The opposite position is that the scientist does have a special knowledge. He is an expert in his field, and there is often consensus on the basic tenets in that field. When this consensus is ignored, as when fluoridation is condemned as a poison, fallout as insignificant, and DDT as harmless, he ought to speak up and do so as a scientist. Moreover, since his vocation requires some detachment and a command of logical thinking, he might be able to reason relatively more objectively and better than most citizens. The fact that not all scientists reach the same conclusion is not important as long as all schools

---

1964). The *Bulletin of the Atomic Scientists* and *Science* regularly publish articles devoted to this subject. See also Bernard Barber, "Sociology of Science: A Trend Report," *Current Sociology*, Vol. 5 (1956), pp. 91-153; Norman Kaplan, "Sociology of Science," in Robert E. L. Faris, ed., *Handbook of Modern Sociology* (Chicago: Rand McNally, 1964), pp. 852-81.

[67] *The New York Times*, January 1, 1965, p. 1.

of thought have access to the public and to the decision-makers; their job is to broaden the debate, not to deliver a decision.

Special responsibility is derived from the fact that science has released forces that threaten the very survival of the human race. Scientists ought to (as some did) warn society of the dangers of these forces. And, it is pointed out, scientists are involved (for good or bad) in public policy as advisers, applied researchers, members of boards, etc. For some scientists to refrain from public activity would only result in leaving the field open to others. If Hans Bethe, Nobel Prize winner in physics, an advocate of arms reduction, "minded his own business" at Cornell, this would not keep physicist Edward Teller, "the father of the H-bomb" and a "hard-liner," at home on the Berkeley, California, campus.

Among social scientists in the United States who have expressed themselves on the subject, the majority seem to favor general and complete disarmament or arms reduction; some favor arms control, and only a small minority favor continued reliance on the balance-of-terror system.[68] Many prominent social scientists appealed to the public at various points against armed intervention in Cuba, for the test-ban treaty, for neutralization of Vietnam, etc., and a number of them have taken a "peace movement" position; to mention only a few: C. Wright Mills (*The Causes of World War III*); Erich Fromm (*May Man Prevail?*); Kenneth Boulding (*Conflict and Defense*); Margaret Mead (*Keep Your Powder Dry*); Charles E. Osgood (*An Alternative to War or Surrender*); and David Riesman (numerous articles).[69] They are members of national boards of organizations such as Turn Toward Peace, Committee for Sane Nuclear Policy, and United World Federalists.

Aside from their contribution to the public domain, social scientists have made several contributions to peace and disarmament in their professional capacities. They have shown that certain sociological *facts* have a bearing on foreign policy, especially in connection with questions of peace and disarmament. For instance, an analysis of the rapid change of public attitudes toward a test-ban treaty favored only by about 52 percent of the American people in July, 1963, and 81 per-

---

[68] See Raymond Bowers, "The Uses of Sociology in the Military Establishment," in Paul F. Lazarsfeld, William H. Sewell, and Harold L. Wilensky, eds., *The Uses of Sociology* (New York: Basic Books, forthcoming).

[69] See, especially, his introduction to Arthur I. Waskow, *The Limits of Defense* (New York: Doubleday, 1962), and articles in *The Correspondent*.

cent when it was ratified in September, 1963, suggests that when leadership is exercised, public support for arms limitation can be won.[70] Social scientists applied certain sociological *theorems* about the internal behavior of societies to the study of international relations. For instance, they have shown that just as individuals who are more similar are more likely to form a friendship group, nations that are more similar in the level of education, income, and culture are more likely to initiate successful regional communities. Social scientists have served as consultants to make social science *methods*, especially surveys, available for international study. For instance, the United States continually uses survey methods to probe world public opinion. Summaries of these surveys are circulated among the top decision-makers in Washington. (The Director of the United States Information Agency attends the meetings of the National Security Council.)

While the response to these surveys has occasionally been exaggerated, as was the case when the United States lost a few "prestige" points following the orbiting of Sputnik by the Soviet Union,[71] by and large the effect of these surveys is to make the United States decision-makers more sensitive to public opinion abroad and to have a more accurate picture of it than in earlier periods, when foreign public opinion was judged only on the basis of impressions gained by American diplomats from friends and servants, reading the newspapers, and the like.

Finally, probably the most important contribution social science has made so far to the study of war and peace is its special *perspective* on international relations. When social scientists participated in meetings with policy-makers, the main virtue of their sociological recommendations was the repeated expression of a concern and a viewpoint that might otherwise have been neglected. Psychologists, anthropologists, and sociologists have stressed the need for a margin of safety in international systems to safeguard against the dangers of unintentional and irrational behavior. Social scientists have shown that the patterns a man uses to express his distorted mind are borrowed from the society he lives in and involve the use of instruments it provides. Thus, taking the law into one's hands and the use of firearms as the ultimate arbiter of social conflict are established elements of certain traditions of the

---

[70] *Washington Post*, September 16, 1963.

[71] Gabriel A. Almond, "Public Opinion and the Development of Space Technology," in Joseph M. Goldsen, ed., *International Political Implications of Activities in Outer Space* (RAND Corporation, 1960); cf. Amitai Etzioni, "The Moon as a Status-Symbol," in *The Moon-Doggle* (New York: Doubleday, 1964), pp. 149-62.

nation. They are often celebrated on its television screens and in its history textbooks. The easy access to lethal weapons is another feature that sets the American apart from most other civilized societies. In the same way, if the pilot of a SAC bomber or the commander of a Polaris-armed submarine should one day deviate from his orders, thinking, for instance, that he is called upon to deliver America from a President who has grown "soft" on communism, the American culture will provide him with a pattern for his action and the instruments to carry it out. The same holds for the Soviet Union and other nations.

Similarly, sociologists have pointed out the irrationalities hidden in communication systems: the tendency to distort the content of communications to suit the preferences of the recipients and the misinterpretations due to cultural differences that foreigners unwittingly impose on our communications and we on theirs.[72] Further, sociologists have highlighted the value of having a third, uncommitted party to ease and correct communication, even if he cannot oversee the give-and-take itself.

Most of the points are hardly new, but anyone who has closely examined the national decision-making process knows how often they are overlooked, in Washington and in any other capital, as position papers are hurriedly composed by people whose training has not made awareness of these considerations an integral part of their knowledge and perspectives. The social scientist, to the degree that he has access to decision-makers, contributes greatly to keeping the world in one piece until fundamental solutions can be worked out, by helping the parties to maintain their self-control and move cautiously in an age of big bombs on what has proven to be a small planet.

---

[72] For example, Edwin H. Fedder points out: ". . . the Russian word *mir* means peace; however it does not carry over the full English connotation. Peace in English means both the absence of war and the existence of a condition of 'tranquility.' The condition of tranquility is not included in the concept of *mir*. The word 'compromise' has no equivalent in Russian, to cite another example . . . ." in "Communication and American-Soviet Negotiating Behavior," *Background*, Vol. 8 (1964), p. 109.

EPILOGUE

Social Problems and Sociological Theory

by Robert K. Merton

I N THE MODERN WORLD, THE VISIBLY PRACTICAL ACCOMPLISHMENTS OF a science affect the social value placed upon it. For example, now that the utility of mathematics has become evident even to those in places of political power, mathematicians are being accorded vastly enlarged social support and probably heightened public esteem. To record the fact is not necessarily to applaud it. Indeed, within the subculture of science, things often stand quite the other way, with greatest value attached to new knowledge that has no directly apparent practical outcome. Expressing this sentiment is that often quoted, though possibly apocryphal, toast at a dinner for scientists in Cambridge: To pure mathematics, and may it never be of any use to anybody!

It is plain to see why many scientists assess scientific work apart from its use for purposes other than the enlargement of knowledge itself. For only on this ground can the institution of science become fairly autonomous and scientists remain free to investigate what they, instead of only what others, consider significant. Correlatively, if practical utility becomes the sole measure of significance, then science becomes only a handmaiden—of industry or theology or polity. Its autonomy becomes undermined. That is why, also, many scientists today regard with misgivings the doctrine propounded three centuries ago by Francis Bacon that helped establish the new science as socially valuable because it had valued practical applications. But we should remember that Bacon, undeniably the great apostle of the utility of science, distinguished between what he called experiments of fruit, which could be put to use to help achieve the various purposes of men, and experiments of light, which brought into being new knowledge much to be sought, even though it had, then and there, no evident further uses than an enlarged understanding. Bacon was not addicted to the nothing-but fallacy that science must be *nothing but* a guide to action or that it must be *nothing but* self-contained knowledge, entirely insulated from the world of action and social values.

There is, then, this basic duality in science: it can provide greater understanding of how things happen to be as in fact they are, just as it can provide understanding that enables men to change things from what and where they are. As with most dualities in society and culture, this one has given rise to ambivalent attitudes. And since men find it hard to tolerate ambivalence, they periodically deal with their indecision by swinging violently to one extreme position or the other, emphatically denying the worth of the alternative that is being forcibly suppressed.[1] They become extreme advocates of the position that knowledge not put to practical use is not true knowledge at all or of the position that applied knowledge is at best an inferior sort of knowledge. Some become votaries of pure science, others of applied science; disciples of Plato, badly understood, or disciples of Bacon, badly understood. And so we find Macaulay writing that he greatly prefers the error of Bacon to that of Plato for "we have no patience with a philosophy which, like those Roman matrons who swallowed abortives in order to preserve their shapes, takes pains to be barren for fear of being homely."

To quote Macaulay on this matter is not to consider him a sound exponent of the technical philosophy of science. His unforgettable essay on Bacon,[2] from which this passage is drawn, is every bit as defective in its philosophical part as it is perceptive in its biographical part. But though Macaulay often errs when he attempts to write of philosophical notions, this is not one of those times. Through the use of an adroit and deliberately damaging simile, he has exposed the excessive purism of those thinkers who pride themselves on the absence of practical outcomes of their thought, thus confusing practical uselessness with theoretical worth. Yet it is at least possible that a pragmatically useless idea is not, on that account, a theoretically valuable

---

[1] As we shall see in the later section of this chapter devoted to Social Values and Sociological Analysis, this sort of ambivalence has been conspicuous among sociologists of both the past and the present. For a general formulation of the concept of sociological (as distinct from psychological) ambivalence and of the various forms that this ambivalence takes, see Robert K. Merton and Elinor Barber, "Sociological Ambivalence," in Edward A. Tiryakian, ed., *Sociological Theory, Values, and Sociocultural Change: Essays in Honor of Pitirim A. Sorokin* (New York: Free Press, 1963), pp. 91-120.

[2] To be found in almost all of the many editions of Macaulay's essays; for example, Thomas Babington Macaulay, *Critical and Historical Essays* (London: Longmans, 1864), Vol. 1, pp. 346-414. Quotation is on p. 396.

one. The two aspects of claims to knowledge—the pragmatic and the theoretical—are partly independent of each other, authentically coinciding on occasion, turning up severally, and sometimes being altogether groundless. It is this latter case against which Macaulay has directed his fire. Among those who set great store upon speculative theory for its own sake, it is a short step to the fallacy of assuming that all which is not useful is therefore scientifically important and sound. Yet, as Macaulay (after Bacon) wants us to see, the sterile idea may be pretty because it is not laden down with the burdens that come with the pragmatic test.

This long-standing ambivalence toward pure and applied science is no less current among social scientists than among other scientists. It is particularly expressed in the orientation toward the sociology of social problems or toward applied social science in general. Applied sociology is regarded by some as having distinctly less value than theoretical sociology, if indeed it is not put entirely beyond the pale. In contrast, others hold that theoretical explorations in social science which do not bear directly upon the major social problems of our time are explorations of the trivial and that the pure theorists are, in effect, exploiting their position in society merely to satisfy their own idle curiosity rather than returning to the society that supports them the kind of knowledge that can be used to help solve social problems and to achieve social purposes.[3]

If we entertain the hypothesis that these alternative positions are not imposed upon us, that they are, rather, the results of an ambivalence toward the dual theoretical and applied aspects of all science, we can be a little more relaxed about the matter. We can then consider that in sociology, as in the other sciences, physical, biological, and social, there is an intellectual division of labor rather than an all-or-none commitment to an orientation toward one or the other of these dual aspects. Some men, both by temperament and capacity, are no doubt better suited to the exclusive pursuit of one or the other of these paths of inquiry; some may move back and forth between both paths; and a few may manage to tread a path bordered on one side by the theoretical and on the other by the practical or applied. This path is, in the main, the one that has been followed in the chapters of this book. By personal commitment rather than by express con-

---

[3] Claude C. Bowman has instructively examined these tendencies toward proposing mutually exclusive orientations as alone justifiable, in "Polarities and the Impairment of Science," *American Sociological Review*, Vol. 15 (August, 1950), pp. 580-89.

sent, the authors of this book exhibit in their chapters agreement with
the position set forth by Whitehead:

> Science is a river with two sources, the practical source and the
> theoretical source. The practical source is the desire to direct our
> actions to achieve predetermined ends. . . . The theoretical source
> is the desire to understand. I most emphatically state that I do not
> consider one source as in any sense nobler than the other, or intrinsi-
> cally more interesting. I cannot see why it is nobler to strive to under-
> stand than to busy oneself with the right ordering of one's actions.
> Both have their bad sides; there are evil ends directing actions, and
> there are ignoble curiosities of the understanding.[4]

All the chapters in this book have drawn upon both theoretical
and practical sources of sociological knowledge. This does not mean
that they have uniformly made use of a single comprehensive theory
of social problems—of social disorganization and deviant behavior—
for there is, in truth, no such overarching theory to draw upon. No
qualified sociologist holds that the discipline has evolved a single,
strictly formulated theory that fully encompasses the wide range of
social problems, such as those treated in this book, and so enables us
to account for every significant aspect of all these problems. That sort
of claim must be reserved to those pseudosociologists who turn up in
quantity whenever trouble is brewing in society and announce their
quickly designed cures for everything that ails us socially. Yet in
matters so complex and obscure as much of social organization and
human behavior, we are wise to be on our guard against "explanations" that profess to account for every facet of that organization and
behavior. For, as the ancients knew, he who tries to prove too much
proves next to nothing. In no sphere of systematic knowledge—
whether it be mechanics, biology, linguistics or sociology—do specialists go on the fool's errand of explaining every aspect of concrete
phenomena. Instead, particular aspects, structures, and processes of
the phenomena are singled out, under the guidance of some general
ideas, and methodically investigated, while other aspects are conscientiously neglected as no part of the problem in hand. This responsible,
well-attested, and effective frame of mind has become so definitely
established in the older scientific disciplines that it is soon taken over
by novices as a firm implication of their training; it is seldom taught in
explicit and didactic fashion. But the need for dealing with selected
aspects of concrete events is not so widely or immediately sensed in
the newer social sciences, particularly, perhaps, in psychology and

---

[4] Alfred North Whitehead, *The Aims of Education* (New York: New American
Library, 1951), p. 107.

sociology (since every man considers himself a psychologist by virtue of his being human and a sociologist by virtue of living his life in society). The great didactic emphases in these fields upon methodology and the role of theory can be understood in part as a collective effort to keep their practitioners from falling into the trap of explaining little by trying to explain too much. The tidy and seemingly complete explanation of every aspect of human behavior and organization includes a mess of unrelated and specially concocted assumptions that are to be fitted to each distinct aspect of the complex whole under study.

But if there is nothing remotely resembling a single, rigorous, all-encompassing theory of social problems, there is a general theoretical orientation toward social problems widely current among sociologists and largely reflected in the pages of this book. Similar sociological ideas and similar procedures of sociological analysis are put to work in chapter after chapter that deal with the most varied kinds of social problems. If there is no one theory unifying all the significant questions that can be raised about social problems, there is a sociological perspective from which similar kinds of questions have been raised and, in some cases and in some degree, tentatively answered. The rest of this chapter will consider a few—far from most—of the theoretical questions to be kept in mind in the investigation of social problems.

The Sociological Diagnosis of Social Problems

Just about everyone has at least a gross conception of "social problems." Unsought but undeniable troubles in society, social conflicts and confusions usually described as the "social crisis of our time," the victimizing of people by social institutions that put them at a disadvantage in life, crime, presently curable but uncured disease, the socially unauthorized use of violence—all these and more are caught up in what most of us ordinarily mean by the term "social problems." Nor is this general understanding far removed from the technical sense in which the sociologist employs the term. But since the popular and the technical senses of social problem are not identical, although they overlap, it will be useful to consider what enters into the sociologist's diagnosis of a social problem. In considering this, we must recognize that there is not a strict identity in the conception of a social problem held by all sociologists; but, as can be seen throughout the pages of this book, there is enough agreement to provide a working basis.

In examining the sociological notion of a social problem, we must treat at least six connected questions: (1) the central criterion of a social problem: a significant discrepancy between social standards and social actuality; (2) the sense in which social problems have social origins; (3) the judges of social problems, those people who in fact principally define the great problems in a society; (4) manifest and latent social problems; (5) the social perception of social problems; and finally (6) the ways in which belief in the corrigibility of unwanted social situations enters into the definition of social problems.

Social Standards and Social Actuality

The first and basic ingredient of a social problem consists of a substantial discrepancy between widely shared social standards and actual conditions of social life. Such discrepancies vary in extent and in degree of importance assigned them so that social problems are regarded as differing in magnitude as well as kind. In referring to social standards, we do not mean to imply that they are uniformly shared throughout the sectors of a society. Quite the contrary. As we shall see in some detail when we turn to "the judges of social problems," these standards and their implementation differ, to a degree, among the several social strata and social segments. Nevertheless, we can begin by considering certain aspects of the gap between social standards and social actuality, for this provides a useful way of thinking about widely diversified kinds of social problems.

It takes no great knowledge or effort of mind to realize that the extent of the disparity between what is and what people think ought to be varies from time to time in the same society and from place to place among societies. But it is more difficult to devise acceptable measures of the varying extent of this disjunction between social standards and social reality. I do not refer here to the notorious inadequacies in the statistics officially registering the frequency of various types of deviant behavior and symptoms of social disorganization, for many of our chapters have paused to consider in detail these defects in official statistics. All sociological authorities agree that the statistics of mental illness and suicide, of crime and juvenile delinquency, or prostitution and divorce are subject to all manner of bias owing to difficulties in obtaining a thorough count of comparable units. (It is ironic, perhaps, that the most nearly faultless and most informative social statistics available in American society deal with performance in professional baseball and football, indeed, in sports generally; among statistics dealing with social problems, those of traffic accidents and casualties are perhaps the most adequate.) Beyond these technical shortcomings of the statistics of social troubles lie further difficulties in devising apt measures of the extent of the discrepancy between social standards and social actuality.

In dealing with extremely simplified cases of social casualties—as Bredemeier and Toby describe the people who signally fail to meet social standards [5]—we can adopt simple measures that serve, up to a point. One such measure would be provided, for example, by a full record of the number of homicides in a society, thus indicating the extent of the gap between the norm forbidding homicide and the way things actually are in this respect. But even in this seemingly simplest of instances, instructive ambiguities remain. Some, indeed many, moralities hold every human life to be sacred. For people subscribing to this value, the sheer number of homicides would be the appropriate indicator of the extent of this particular social problem. Since each unlawful killing—unlawful because only a fraction who hold to the general value of the sanctity of human life apply this value to the legally authorized killing of human beings, individually or en masse, in war—violates the value placed on human life, the absolute number of homicides becomes central, entirely apart from the differing probabilities of homicide in populations of widely differing size. For other observers, intent on making standardized comparisons of the scale of the problem among different societies, the absolute number of homicides no longer holds as a measure. Instead, they would use standardized rates of homicide—say, homicides per 100,000 of the population or per 100,000 of the adult population. (For the specimen case of homicide, any other form of deviant behavior can be substituted without change in the logic of the argument: for people holding fast to a value, it is the absolute numbers of violations of that value which register the scale of the problem; for the sociological investigator, intent on ferreting out the sources and consequences of social problems, it will ordinarily be the relative numbers—the rates or proportions—that are used to estimate the magnitude of the problem.)

Furthermore, the frequency of deviant acts—whether counted in absolute or relative numbers—is of course not enough to measure the social significance of the discrepancy between standards and behavior. Social values and their associated standards differ greatly in the importance people assign to them. They are not all of a kind. Everyone knows that petty theft—the very term includes an evaluation of significance—differs in its moral and social significance from homicide,

---

[5] Harry C. Bredemeier and Jackson Toby, *Social Problems in America* (New York: Wiley & Sons, 1960).

this difference being partly registered in the currently [6] different punishments meted out to the two classes of offenders. But how are these two classes of deviant behavior to be compared as to the degree to which they constitute social problems? Is one homicide to be equated with 10 petty thefts? 100? 1000? We may sense that these are incommensurables and so *feel* that the question of comparing their magnitude is a nonsense question. Yet this feeling is only a prelude to recognition of the more general fact that we have no strict common denominator for social problems and so have no workable procedures for comparing the scale of different problems, even when the task is simplified by dealing with two kinds of criminal acts.

When we try to compare the magnitude of very different kinds of social problems, the issue of course becomes all the more difficult to resolve. Shall we conclude that the approximately 8500 murders in 1963 represent about one-fifth as great a social problem in the United States as the approximately 43,500 deaths from vehicular accidents in that year? And, in turn, how are these to be compared in order of magnitude with the 4.2 million unemployed Americans in that same year, the nearly 600,000 patients in mental hospitals and the estimated 341,000 outpatients, the approximately 50,000 drug addicts, or the unnumbered millions who are seriously alienated from their jobs, finding little joy and small purpose in them and at best being resigned to using only part of their capacities in work that is for them little more than a necessary evil?

In short, there are no agreed-upon bases for rigorously appraising the comparative magnitude of different social problems. In the end, it is the values held by people occupying different positions in society that provide the rough bases for the relative importance assigned to social problems and, as we shall see later in this chapter, this sometimes leads to badly distorted impressions of the social significance of various problems, even when these are judged in the light of reigning values.

Social Origins of Social Problems

It is sometimes said that social problems must have social origins. It is not always clear whether such a statement is offered as a partial

---

[6] "Currently" because it was not, of course, always so. What is now defined as petty larceny and subject to mild sanctions was in other times and places defined as a capital offense. In sixteenth- and seventeenth-century England, for example, thieves were savagely punished, with many of them included among the 72,000 estimated to have been executed during the reign of Henry VIII alone. See Jerome Hall, *Theft, Law, and Society* (Boston: Little, Brown, 1935), pp. 84-85.

definition or an empirically testable proposition, as a criterion or a hypothesis. In one sense, the requirement of social origins is redundant. For, as we have just seen, a social problem formally involves a discrepancy, judged intolerable, between social standards and social actuality. Another version of this is found in the observation that

> *social groups create deviance by making the rules whose infraction constitutes deviance,* and by applying those rules to particular people and labeling them as outsiders. From this point of view, deviance is *not* a quality of the act the person commits, but rather a consequence of the application by others of rules and sanctions to an "offender." The deviant is one to whom that label has successfully been applied; deviant behavior is behavior that people so label.[7]

In this Pickwickian sense, all social problems have "social origins" inasmuch as they are not taken to be a problem until actual conditions are judged not to measure up sufficiently to social (i.e., shared) standards.

But more than this is ordinarily meant by the proposal that only the problems that originate in social conditions or processes can usefully be regarded as social problems. It is being proposed that the substantive *causes* of social problems must themselves be social, not merely their formal attributes. According to this version of the idea, crime and suicide and family disorganization constitute social problems inasmuch as they result principally from identifiable social circumstances. On this view, socially disruptive events that are not man-made but nature-made would be excluded from consideration. Earthquakes, tornadoes, cyclones, hurricanes, eruptions of volcanoes, floods, perhaps famines and epidemics—these and all other nature-caused events that greatly affect the lives of men in society would be ruled out.

Like other investigators, sociologists are of course free to delimit the range of their inquiry. They are free to state the criteria of the phenomena that will be regarded as pertinent to systematic investigation. But in proposing particular criteria, sociologists, like other investigators, are required to show that these criteria are theoretically useful, if the proposal is to be taken seriously by others. Freedom to define does not mean license to exclude. And until now, no satisfactory case has been made for confining the scope of social problems to only those problems that are in their origin social in the sense that the events precipitating them are initiated by men in society. Rather, it is proposed that, whatever the precipitating events, they enter into purview

---

[7] Howard S. Becker, *Outsiders: Studies in the Sociology of Deviance* (New York: Free Press, 1963), p. 9 (italics by Becker).

as part of a social problem whenever they give rise to significant discrepancies between social standards and social actuality. For whether the forces disrupting patterns of social life are nature-made or man-made, they will, in the end, confront members of the society with the task of responding to them, and the nature of that response is, in sociological principle, greatly affected by the structure of the society, by its institutions, and its values.[8]

Perhaps later inquiry will find distinct patterns of social problems according to whether they are social both in precipitating origin and consequences or are precipitated by nonsocial events that have socially disruptive consequences. But this would only mean the working out of further discriminations. It would not mean scrapping the conception that social problems are defined by their consequences, whatever their origins.[9]

The Judges of Social Problems

We have noted the difficulties entailed in assessing the comparative scale of diverse social problems and the sense in which the unwanted discrepancy between social standards and social actuality makes for a social problem, irrespective of the character of the precipitating events that help create the discrepancy. A third ingredient entering into the diagnosis of social problems requires us to consider the people who judge that the discrepancy exists and that it matters. Sociologists often say that "many people" or a "functionally significant number of people" or even that "a majority of people" in a society must regard a social circumstance as departing from their standards in order for this circumstance to qualify as a social problem. As a beginning and avowedly rough approximation, this formulation can serve for many cases. When social norms are a matter of overwhelming consensus, as with the norms proscribing murder or rape or kidnapping, a more exacting formulation is not required. But for many other kinds of social behavior and social conditions, this merely numerical cri-

---

[8] This conception is developed and documented in the first edition of this book in Charles Fritz's chapter dealing with disasters and catastrophes, pp. 682-94.

[9] Although they occasionally waver in their judgments of "physical problems"— i.e., the usual array of nature-made catastrophes—as constituting social problems, Fuller and Myers conclude their excellent contribution to a sociological theory of social problems by setting forth much the same position adopted here. For example: "While the earthquake itself may involve no value-judgments, its consequences inevitably will call for moral judgments and decisions of policy. People will not agree on how much should be spent in reconstruction, how it should be spent, or how the funds should be raised." Richard C. Fuller and Richard R. Myers, "Some Aspects of a Theory of Social Problems," *American Sociological Review*, Vol. 6 (February, 1941), p. 27.

terion is no longer adequate. It becomes necessary to distinguish among "the many" who define certain recurrent events or a social condition as a problem.

Social definitions of social problems have this in common with other processes in society: those occupying strategic positions of authority and power of course carry more weight than others in deciding social policy and therefore, among other things, in identifying for the rest what are to be taken as significant departures from social standards. There is not a merely numerical democracy of judgment in which every man's appraisal is assigned the same voting power in defining a condition as a social problem. It is a mistaken, atomistic notion that each member of society sets about to define social problems for himself and that it is the aggregate of these independent judgments that decides the array of problems in the society and the comparative importance of each problem in the array. Even otherwise differing "schools of sociological thought" are agreed on the theoretical conception that all societies are differentiated into a variety of structurally connected social statuses. This is universally the case although societies vary, of course, in the degree of structural differentiation. Furthermore, people occupying different positions in the social structure tend to have distinctive interests and values (as well as sharing some interests and values with others). As a result, not all social standards are evenly distributed among diverse social positions. It follows logically and is found empirically that to the extent that these standards differ among social positions and groups within a society, the same circumstances will be variously evaluated as being at odds with the standards held by some and as consistent with standards held by others. Thus, one group's problem will be another group's asset.

Societies that are highly differentiated into a great variety of social statuses, with their characteristic interests and values, will tend to have correspondingly different, and often strongly conflicting, judgments of what in particular constitutes social problems. Scott Greer points out, for example, that traffic congestion may be defined as a problem by the drivers of automobiles but may be regarded as a distinct asset by the proprietors of stores along the routes of congestion. On the other hand, cheap and speedy transportation to the downtown area of the city is scarcely defined as an asset by the suburban merchant.[10] Or, to turn from structurally induced differences

---

[10] See the discussion by Scott Greer in Chapter 13 of the first edition of this book.

of judgments based on calculations of material self-interest, consider that in American society today, abortion is defined as a social problem by many whose religiously based or otherwise legitimized values are violated by it. Others define abortion as a means of preventing a personal problem—having an unwanted child, whether legitimate or illegitimate—which, aggregated for many cases, could become a serious social problem.[11] Or again, to take a stale and therefore at once evident example, free and easy access to alcoholic drink was defined by many Americans, two generations ago, as the source of an important social problem; therefore, for a time, such access was prohibited by legislation. For a good many others—who also defined alcoholism as a problem—the would-be social cure was worse than the ailment: prohibition was held to violate standards by entering the private lives of Americans to regulate what they regarded as altogether personal decisions.

In short, full or substantial consensus in a complex, differentiated society exists for only a limited number of values, interests, and derived standards for conduct. We must therefore be prepared to find that the same social conditions and behaviors will be defined by some as a social problem and by others as an agreeable and fitting state of affairs. For the latter, indeed, the situation may begin to become a problem only when the presumed remedy is introduced by the former. What is loosely described as "socialized medicine," for example, is defined as a social remedy by Walter Reuther and many others in his constituency of the AFL-CIO just as it is defined as a social problem by the successive presidents of the AMA and many others in their constituency. In the eyes of some, unemployment benefits help solve a problem by providing aid to people for their work in the past and for willingness to work in the present; for others, whose secure positions in society help them sustain the belief, these benefits are at best a dole, morally suspect and socially undesirable. For some, the widespread acceptance of things as they are registers the social problem of public apathy; for others, the problem begins with the appearance of organized social protest. Thus, Kenneth B. Clark observes that

> Continuing evidence of the pervasive moral apathy and political cynicism in the American mass culture is a significant negative in weighing the possibilities for social democracy. If constructive change

---

[11] Edwin M. Schur, *Crimes without Victims: Deviant Behavior and Public Policy: Abortion, Homosexuality, and Drug Addiction* (Englewood Cliffs, N. J.: Prentice-Hall, 1965).

were to depend on the chance of profound moral conversion, there might be cause for pessimism. Negroes must convince the majority, who are white, that continued oppression of the Negro minority hurts the white majority too. Nor is it sophistry to argue that this is indeed the case. If it were not the case, the Negro cause would be hopeless. Certainly the Negro cannot hope to argue his case primarily in terms of ethical concerns, for these historically have had only sentimental and verbal significance in themselves. They have never been the chief source of power for that social change which involves significant alteration of status between privileged versus unprivileged groups. Child labor legislation was not the direct result of a moral indignation against the exploitation of children in factories, mines, mills, but rather reflected a growing manpower shortage and the new rise of the labor unions. The value of ethical appeals is to be found only when they can be harnessed to more concrete appeals such as economic, political, or other power advantages to be derived from those with the power to facilitate or inhibit change. Ethical and moral appeal can be used to give theoretical support for a program of action, or in some cases to obscure and make the pragmatic aspects of that program more palatable to conscience. If moral force opposes economic or political ends, the goal of moral force may be postponed. The reverse may also be true. But where moral force and practical advantage are united, their momentum is hard to deny.[12]

What has been stated here concerning the situation of American Negroes as a social problem, and not merely as a problem of Negroes alone, holds for all manner of other discrepancies between widespread (though not unanimously held) social values and actual social situations. The gap between values and actuality is defined by those who perceive the gap as a problem confronting society. It must be closed by bringing social situations closer to social values, not by accommodating values to currently existing situations. But the judges of the problem who wield power and authority will succeed in inaugurating the change only to the degree that other forces in society work in the same direction as the moral mandate. When we speak of the times "being ripe for a designated social change" we are referring metaphorically to the convergence of moral and social system imperatives.

The fact that the conflicting values and interests of differentiated groups in a complex society result in disparate conceptions of the principal problems of society would at first seem to dissolve the concept of social problems in the acid of extreme relativism. But this is only apparently so; it is not an inevitable intellectual commitment.

---

[12] Kenneth B. Clark, *Dark Ghetto: Dilemmas of Social Power* (New York: Harper, 1965), p. 204.

Sociologists need not and do not limit the scope of social problems to those expressly defined by the people they are studying and trying to understand. Fortunately, they have an alternative to the doctrine that nothing is either a social problem or a social asset but thinking makes it so. They need not become separated from good sense by imprisoning themselves in the set of logically impregnable premises that only those situations constitute social problems which are so defined by the people involved in them. For social problems are not only subjective states of mind; they are also, and equally, objective states of affairs.

Manifest and Latent Social Problems

The sociologist investigating social problems assumes that they, along with other facets of human society, have both their subjective aspect, this appearing in the perceptions and evaluations of people in society who affirm or deny that something is a social problem, and their objective aspect, this appearing in the actual conditions that are being appraised.[13] For the sociologist to confine himself only to the conditions in society that a majority of people regard as undesirable would be to exclude study of all manner of other conditions that are in fact at odds with the declared values and purposes of those who accept or endorse these conditions. Such a limitation would require the sociologist to subscribe to an extreme subjectivism, under the self-deceiving guise of retaining the objectivity of the scientific observer. But it is possible to escape this heedless subjectivism that in effect abandons definition of the scope of sociological inquiry to the decisions of the men and groups under study. For not all conditions and processes of society inimical to the values of men are recognized as such by them. It is the function of the sociologist to discover and to report the human consequences of holding to certain values and practices just as it is his function to discover and to report the human consequences of departing from these values and practices.

Apart from manifest social problems—those objective social conditions identified by problem-definers as at odds with the values of the society—are latent social problems, conditions that are also at odds with values of the society but are not generally recognized as being so. The sociologist does not impose his values upon others when he

---

[13] This double aspect of social problems has been recognized for some time, as in the seminal paper by Fuller and Myers, "Some Aspects of a Theory of Social Problems." But often, recognition of the objective aspect of social problems has been blurred by a subjectivist conclusion as when Fuller and Myers say that "social problems are what people think they are."

undertakes to supply knowledge about latent social problems. When the demographer Kingsley Davis, for example, identifies the social, economic, and cultural consequences of rapidly growing populations in diverse kinds of society, he in effect calls the advocates of alternative population policies to account for the results of one or another policy. They can no longer evade responsibility for the social consequences of policy by claiming these to be fundamentally unforeseeable. Or again, the sociologists who demonstrate the "wastage of talent" that results from marked inequalities of opportunity for the training and exercise of socially prized talent bring to a focus what was experienced by the diffuse many as only a personal problem rather than a problem of society. Or yet again, as our knowledge, still notoriously sparse, of the social, economic, and psychological consequences of racial segregation is enlarged—consequences for the dominant majority as well as for the subordinate minority—advocates of alternative policies will be brought increasingly to account for their distinctive positions. In this sense and in this way, sociological knowledge eventually presses policy-makers to justify their social policies to their constituencies and the larger community.

SOCIAL VALUES AND SOCIOLOGICAL ANALYSIS. We should pause to take note of what is *not* involved in this analytical process of making latent social problems manifest. Else, it will be easily mistaken for another version of an extreme and untenable sociological rationalism. It is not being said that the discovery and diffusion of knowledge about the consequences of adhering to current social beliefs and practices will automatically lead people to abandon the beliefs and practices that are shown to prevent them from realizing some of their own basic values. Man-in-society is not as strictly rational a creature as all that. The sociological truth does not instantly make men free. It does not induce a sudden rupture with demonstrably dysfunctional arrangements in society. But by discovering more and more consequences of accepted practices and by making these known, the sociologist engaged in the study of social problems provides a basis for substantial reappraisals of these practices in the long run, if not necessarily at once. It might be asked, of course, why we should be interested in the long run since, as Maynard Keynes emphatically reminded us, in the long run we are all dead. The reply is as thoroughly evident as the question: because presumably, and contrary to our animal and egoistic faith, the world does not die with us.

In other words, there is a degree of rationalism in the sociological outlook, as there is in every other scientific outlook. But it is not rationalism run riot. New objective knowledge of the probable consequences of action need not lead men to act at once in the light of this knowledge. Sociology need not make men wise or even prudent. But, through its successive uncovering of latent social problems and through its clarification of manifest social problems, sociological inquiry does make men increasingly accountable for the outcome of their collective and institutionalized actions.

There is a further use of this distinction between manifest and latent social problems, between the social conditions currently judged by designated categories of men in society to be undesirable and the social conditions that would be so judged, were their multifarious consequences known. Among other things, the distinction helps sociologists themselves recognize how they can move beyond prevalent social beliefs, practices, and judgments without entering upon the misplaced career of trying to impose their own values upon others.[14] Through his work, the sociologist does not remain aloof from social controversy, but in his capacity as sociologist—rather than as citizen— he takes a distinctive and limited part in it. He introduces pertinent sociological truths so that the substantive morality and the social policy governing the issues at stake can take account of these truths. It does not follow, however, that these truths will shape morality and policy in their every aspect. In his capacity as sociologist, emphatically not in his capacity as citizen, the student of social problems neither exhorts nor denounces, neither advocates nor rejects. It is enough that he uncover to others the great price they sometimes pay for their settled but insufficiently examined convictions and their established but inflexible practices.

Above all, this view of the sociologist's role avoids the opposite and equal errors of assuming that in any society, "whatever is, is right" or that "whatever is, is wrong." It discards the perspectives of both the

---

[14] Students of the enduring debate over the social role of the sociologist and the place of values in his inquiry will note at once that this position differs substantially from that set forth by Gunnar Myrdal in various places. See his celebrated Appendix 2, "A Methodological Note on Facts and Valuations in Social Science," in Gunnar Myrdal, with the assistance of Richard Sterner and Arnold Rose, *An American Dilemma* (New York: Harper, 1944), Vol. 2, pp. 1035-64. Also, G. Myrdal, *Value in Social Theory* (London: Routledge & Kegan Paul, 1958). Robert Bierstedt and, to a degree, Ralph Ross have recently formulated the role of the sociologist in relation to social policy in terms intellectually congenial to those set forth here. In the same symposium, Llewellyn Gross states the case for a partly contrasting position. See: Robert Bierstedt, "Social Science and Public Service," pp. 412-20; Ralph Ross, "Moral Obligations of the Scientist," pp. 429-38; and Llewellyn Gross, "Values and Theory of Social Problems," pp. 383-97; all three papers appearing in Alvin W. Gouldner and S. M. Miller, eds., *Applied Sociology: Opportunities and Problems* (New York: Free Press, 1965).

complacent old men and the angry young men. It repudiates the extravagant optimism that sees everything in society as bound to turn out all right in the end just as it repudiates the extravagant pessimism that sees nothing but catastrophe ahead. Nor does it assume that the middle way is everywhere and always the right way: the disparaging connotations of the word *mediocrity*, the condition of being intermediate between extremes, should be enough to ward us off that bland and simple-minded assumption. Rather, this sociological outlook has us examine each set of social conditions in terms of its diverse and progressively discovered consequences for the condition of men, including all those consequences that bear upon the values held by men in the particular society. In following this path, we avoid both forms of that insolent ignorance that would have us pretend to know that society is bound to move in the one direction of cumulative improvement or in the other of continuing decline. Not least, this sociological perspective has the scientifically extraneous but humanly solid merit of leaving a substantial place for men-making-their-future-history while avoiding the utopianism-that-beguiles by recognizing that the degrees of freedom men have in that task are variously and sometimes severely limited by the objective conditions set by nature, society, and culture.[15]

To some degree, then, the distinction between manifest and latent social problems crystallizes ideas governing the range of matters selected for sociological inquiry and the role of values in such inquiry. The distinction maintains that to confine the study of social problems to only those circumstances that are expressly defined as problems in the society is arbitrarily to discard a complement of conditions that are also dysfunctional to values held by people in that society. To adopt

---

[15] This conception of deliberate social change being forced to operate within the limits set not only by nature (modified through technology) but also by the existing structure of society and culture is found in a variety of sociological theories of notably differing ideological origins. We have encountered it in Kenneth B. Clark's discussion of the Negro-white problem in the United States. It is central to functional analysis in sociology, principally in the form of the concept of structural context (or structural constraint). See, for example, Robert K. Merton, *Social Theory and Social Structure*, rev. ed. (New York: Free Press, 1957), pp. 52-53, 73-74, *passim*. It was also central to Marx's theories of social change (although not necessarily to the work of all those who profess to find the source of their ideas in Marx); see the summary in *ibid.*, pp. 40-41. It is also basic to the theory of sociologists who see themselves as altogether at odds with Marxist theory; to take only one example, the penetrating paper by Willard Waller, "Social Problems and the Mores," *American Sociological Review*, Vol. 1 (December, 1936), pp. 922-33. In short, the conception of structural constraints on social change is one that transcends many, though not all, theoretical and ideological differences in sociology.

this course is to hamstring sociological analysis by setting unnecessary limits on the selection of problems for investigation. Under the philosophy intrinsic to the distinction between manifest and latent social problems, the sociologist neither abdicates his intellectual and professional responsibilities nor usurps the position of sitting in moral judgment on his fellow men.

The Social Perception of Social Problems

Linked with the distinction between manifest and latent social problems is the variability in the degree of public attention accorded diverse manifest problems. We cannot take for granted a reasonably correct public imagery of social problems: of their scale, distribution, causation, consequences, and persistence or change. These public images are often egregiously mistaken, for reasons we are beginning to understand. Some, such as mental illness, are walled off and substantially denied for a time; others, such as "crime waves" and drug addiction, become a focus of popular attention to be regarded as of far greater magnitude and as far more consequential than investigation finds them to be.[16]

A familiar and comparatively simple kind of episode brings out the social-psychological processes that make for a disparity between the objective magnitude of events (even when this is gauged by the express values of those perceiving them) and the social perceptions of them. Many more people are killed each year in the United States by automobile accidents than by airplane accidents. The number of deaths occasioned by the two are of entirely different orders of magnitude: in 1963, for example, about 43,500 Americans were put to death by automobiles and 1294 by planes. Yet the intensity of public attention accorded a dramatic airplane accident in newspapers, radio, and television far outruns that accorded the cumulatively greater number of deaths in automobile accidents. The dramatic collision of two planes in midair late in 1960, for instance, aroused nationwide

---

[16] For cases in point of public misperceptions of various social problems, see the foregoing chapters. See also Gerald Gurin, Joseph Voroff, and Sheila Feld, *Americans View Their Mental Health* (New York: Basic Books, 1960); and Daniel Bell, "The Myth of Crime Waves," in his *The End of Ideology* (New York: Free Press, 1960), Chapter 8. An ingenious study of the reporting of crime news in four Colorado newspapers bears directly on this matter of the social perception of social problems. The amount of crime news varied independently of the amount of crime in the state. What is more, a public opinion survey found that the public perception of violent crimes and theft reflected trends in the amount of crime *news* rather than actual crime *rates*. F. James Davis, "Crime News in Colorado Newspapers," *American Journal of Sociology*, Vol. LVII (1952), pp. 325-30.

interest—assuredly in the nation's press, radio, and television, with even the conservative *New York Times* devoting some ten pages to the event, and probably also in uncounted millions of conversations. Yet during the days that this worst disaster in aviation history, with its toll of 137 killed, remained in the forefront of public attention, several hundred more had been killed by automobiles.

The particular instance of marked disparity between the objective magnitude of human tragedies and the popular perceptions of them only highlights the general point (the very familiarity of the case testifying to the generality of the pattern). Popular perceptions are no safe guide to the actual magnitude of a social problem. Ill-understood but partly known processes of social perception [17] involve the patterned omitting, supplementing, and organizing of what is selectively perceived in the social reality. In the case just under review, perception seems affected by what we are better able to describe than to explain: the dramatic quality of unitary events that evoke popular interest. The airplane disaster is perceived as a *single* event, although it is of course compounded of many occurrences that eventuated in the victims going to their death. In contrast, the hundreds of automobile accidents occurring on the same day, with their, say, 200 dead, comprise a compound event that can be detected only through the aggregation of cold and impersonal numbers.[18] The import of this kind of thing is clear. Pervasive social problems that seldom have dramatic and conspicuous manifestations are apt to arouse smaller public attention than problems, less serious even when judged by the beholder's own values, which erupt in the spotlight of public drama. This is another reason that the sociologist need not order the importance of social problems in the same way as the man in the street. For, as we have noted before, even when we take, as we do, the values of the people we are observing as one basis for assessing social problems—in the present case, the sanctity of life and the tragedy of premature death—the public's perception of these problems is often found to be badly distorted.

The perception of social problems is affected by the structure of

---

[17] Theodore M. Newcomb, *Social Psychology* (New York: Holt, 1950), pp. 88-96. Solomon E. Asch, *Social Psychology* (Englewood Cliffs, N. J.: Prentice-Hall, 1952).

[18] For a psychological theory of what makes things seem to belong together and so to comprise an event or unit, see Fritz Heider, "Social Perception and Phenomenal Causality," *Psychological Review*, Vol. 51 (1954), pp. 358-74; also F. Heider, *The Psychology of Interpersonal Relations* (New York: Wiley & Sons, 1958), pp. 60-64.

social relations between people. A generation ago, Pitirim Sorokin found experimentally that the greater the social distance between victims of catastrophe and the people made aware of it, the less are these people motivated to perceive it as a problem calling for effective action and sympathy.[19] Millions of victims of famine in India or China elicit less effective sympathy from Americans than do scores of victims of castastrophes within their own national borders. Further inquiry is needed to find out whether all kinds of social problems are apt to be perceived as less significant the greater the social distance between the observer and the people most directly and visibly affected by the problem.

Related to this fact is the apparently great disparity in people's concern with public and private troubles. This disparity has been depicted in a prototypical instance by the scientist, civil servant, and novelist C. P. Snow. In his novel, *The New Men*,[20] he has his protagonist, Lewis Eliot, muse on the morning after the bomb had been dropped on Hiroshima:

> I went straight off to sleep, woke before four, and did not get to sleep again. It was not a bad test of how public and private worries compare in depth, I thought, when I remembered the nights I had lain awake because of private trouble. Public trouble—how many such nights of insomnia had *that* given me? The answer was, just one. On the night after Munich, I had lain sleepless—and perhaps, as I went through the early hours of August 7th [1945], I could fairly count another half.

What the novelist Snow observed of his emblematic and thinly fictionalized civil servant Eliot, the sociologist Stouffer found to be true for Americans generally. Stouffer's study [21] was conducted during the summer of 1954, better described as the time when the Army-McCarthy hearings were in full swing and were being avidly watched over television by millions of Americans. During this time of public troubles, less than one percent in each of two matched national samples of Americans reported that "they were worried either about the threat of Communists in the United States or about civil liberties." No more than 8 percent mentioned the danger of war or other forms

---

[19] Pitirim A. Sorokin *et al.*, "An Experimental Study of Efficiency of Work under Various Conditions," *American Journal of Sociology*, Vol. 35 (May, 1930), pp. 765-82.

[20] London: Macmillan, 1954, p. 188.

[21] Samuel A. Stouffer, *Communism, Conformity, and Civil Liberties* (New York: Doubleday, 1955), pp. 59-74, reports the findings summarized here.

of international conflict as a source of anxiety. Even when interviewers directed attention to public concerns by asking whether there are "other problems you worry about or are concerned about, especially political or world problems," as many as 52 percent had nothing to add to their previous account. The number referring to problems of civil liberties doubled, rising from the unimpressive total of one percent to the no more impressive total of 2 percent. When asked to report the kinds of problems they had discussed with friends during the preceding week or so, half of these representative Americans said they had talked about personal or family problems only. Evidently, there was something less than a burning preoccupation with some of the most demanding public troubles of the time. These seemed remote, crowded out by the personal problems in family and place of work that turn up in the day-by-day round of social life. This research, then, provides another indication that the judgments of individual members of the society afford anything but a secure guide to the objective saliency of social problems, even for themselves. The connections between public and private troubles are difficult to detect, and it cannot be assumed that they are perceived by most people as they live out their lives.

Chronic victims of collective suffering have on occasion sensed that their problems are invisible to many in the society and have taken dramatic steps to call public attention to their situation. Boycotts, picketing, sit-ins, teach-ins and all manner of public demonstrations are designed to increase the visibility of problems that are otherwise largely ignored because, being chronic and widespread, they tend to be taken for granted. These expedients are rough functional equivalents for providing the high visibility that automatically comes, in this day of nearly instantaneous communication, from sudden mass disasters.[22] Whatever their other purposes and consequences, such demonstrations aim and sometimes succeed in shaking people loose from the tacit conviction that whatever is, is inevitable, and so might as well be ignored.

---

[22] For an instructive analysis of the differences in social response to large-scale chronic suffering and to sudden and acute episodes of collective stress, see Allen Barton, *Social Organization under Stress: A Sociological Review of Disaster Studies* (Washington, D. C.: National Academy of Sciences—National Research Council, 1963), pp. 60-62, 132-33. For a general formulation of how visibility and observability enter into social processes, see Merton, *Social Theory and Social Structure,* pp. 319-57. For the social consequences of mass demonstrations, see Lewis Coser, "The Functions of Violence," paper presented to the Graduate Sociology Society, Columbia University, October 11, 1965 (to be published).

Value Systems and Corrigibility of Social Problems

Functionally considered, unwanted discrepancies between social standards and social reality qualify as manifest social problems only when people believe that they can do something about them. The discrepancies must be perceived as corrigible. It must be thought possible to cope with the problem, to reduce its scale if not to eliminate it altogether. The social problems most completely manifest encompass those frustrations of human purpose on the large scale that are being subjected to active efforts at prevention or control.

From this it is evident that the value orientations in a society toward the preventability or controllability of unwanted social conditions will affect the perceptions of social problems. At one extreme are the societies—China of the fifth century B.C., for example, and early Islam—appreciably committed to fatalism, a system of beliefs that holds everything to have its appointed outcome, not to be avoided or modified by foreknowledge or by effort. Among those holding to such fatalistic beliefs, there will of course be little indigenous sense of social problems: rampant morbidities, high death rates, widespread poverty, and all the rest in the calendar of troubles are simply taken as inevitable. In such a society, the social problems are chiefly or altogether latent. Only the informed observer, exempt from this philosophy of resignation and quietism, sees the possibility of reducing or eliminating these frustrating conditions.

At the other extreme are societies largely committed to an activist philosophy of life that takes just about everything in society as being in principle subject to human control. Such a society, and this is only saying in so many words what has already been implied, that is in fact coping with many of its problems—actively reducing death rates, but still regarding them as "too high," curbing previously unchecked diseases, and doing away with acute poverty—such a society may have many manifest social problems though fewer problems altogether. The active, dissatisfied society will have the more manifest problems, for people in it not only focus on the discrepancies between what they want and what they have, but try to do something about these discrepancies. The fatalistic society, on the other hand, may have a greater complement of social problems altogether—both manifest and latent—because they are moved to do little about the disparity between what exists and what they would like to exist inasmuch as they come to identify what is with what is inevitable.

This relation between fatalism and social problems is not merely a matter of definition but, empirically, is one of mutual reinforcement.

As many have noted, fatalism tends to develop among those living under conditions of extreme stress or rigorous arbitrary rule. Philosophy and conditions of life interact and reinforce one another: men are apt to think fatalistically under depressed conditions and they are apt to remain under these conditions because they think fatalistically. As this has been put by A. Eustace Haydon:

> For the social process the importance of fatalism lies in the ease with which it may serve as a way of escape from responsibility for social maladjustments. Conditions of unresolved wretchedness are 'fertile soil for the fatalistic attitude. In many cases the anaesthesia of fatalism combines with the rigidity of long established patterns of social behavior and the interests of privileged classes to produce the quietistic resignation which results in toleration of social wrongs and incapacity for experimental change.[23]

The contrast between fatalist and activist value systems and the societies in which they occur has been deliberately exaggerated in order to point up the theoretical idea. In concrete reality, few societies have maintained a wholly passive and fatalistic outlook on all their conditions of life, just as few societies have succeeded in maintaining a wholly active and voluntaristic outlook on all their unapproved conditions of life. Strands of active rebellion against fate are found in dominantly fatalistic societies just as strands of resignation and retreatism are found in dominantly activist societies. Yet if these extremes are seldom encountered in all their detailed contrast, they have nevertheless been approximated. As Max Weber and Karl Mannheim,[24] among others, have pointed out, the ethic of fatalism has often been replaced by the ethic of responsibility, in which knowledge of the sources of social problems and efforts to control them become defined as a moral obligation.

To the extent that the ethic of responsibility spreads in a society, social problems tend to become manifest rather than remaining latent. But even within such a society, largely oriented toward directed social change, countervailing processes make for the continued latency for a time of certain social problems. One of these processes has been described by the German jurist, Jellinek, as "the normative force of the

---

[23] A. Eustace Haydon, "Fatalism," *Encyclopedia of the Social Sciences* (New York: Macmillan, 1931), Vol. 6, p. 147.

[24] Max Weber, *Essays in Sociology*, trans. and ed. by H. H. Gerth and C. W. Mills (New York: Oxford University Press, 1946), pp. 120-25. Karl Mannheim, *Ideology and Utopia*, trans. by Louis Wirth and E. A. Shils (New York: Harcourt, Brace & World, 1936), pp. 170-71.

actual." [25] By this phrase he refers to the tendency, of unknown scope and prevalence, for social practices, whatever their origins, to become converted into normatively prescribed practices. Such legitimatizing of much that exists in society tends to militate against the perception of conditions that are in fact opposed to major values held by many in the society but are themselves regarded as normatively right.

Associated with this tendency to legitimatize the existent is another that makes for tacit acceptance of the existent, if not for its moral legitimacy. According to this attitude, unwanted conditions that are not deliberately intended but are by-products of other sought-for developments rank low in the scale of social problems. These unanticipated and undesired consequences of purposive action may become a focus of attention, but they are less apt to mobilize pressure for preventive or remedial measures than those problems that violate a prevailing morality.[26] Since the problem is unintended by those whose actions in the aggregate lead to it, moral sentiments are not activated by the unfortunate circumstance. Widespread states of anxiety in a population, the wastage of talent resulting from economic inequities of access to opportunity for the development of talent, the choking of transportation in tangled traffic—these are for a long time widely considered to be among the costs of a complex society even by many who pay these costs, partly because, undesirable as they are, they are not the result of deliberate intent. In contrast, the purposed behavior that is directly at odds with socially shared norms is at once defined as a problem of society. Crime is generally regarded as a social problem; widespread alienation from the job is not. In other words, people are less apt to experience social disorganization as a social problem than they are deviant behavior.

This observation on the contrasting public saliency of social disorganization and deviant behavior is of course only a first, loose approxi-

---

[25] Georg Jellinek, *Das Recht des modernen Staates* (Berlin, 1900). William G. Sumner made substantially the same observation, in his classic work, *Folkways* (Boston: Ginn, 1906), when he noted that "the notion of right is in the folkways." In much the same vein, Robert S. Lynd observes that "man's inveterate need to feel pride and rightness in his achievements has prompted him to honor the accidents of his past after the fact by describing them as 'ordained by God' or as arising from the 'inner genius' of his race, culture or nation." *Knowledge For What?* (Princeton, N. J.: Princeton University Press, 1939), p. 64. And finally, N. S. Timasheff has incorporated the notion of the normative force of the actual in his *Introduction to the Sociology of Law* (Cambridge, Mass.: Harvard University Committee on Research in the Social Sciences, 1939).

[26] For the context of this statement, see Robert K. Merton, "The Unanticipated Consequences of Purposive Social Action," *American Sociological Review*, Vol. 1 (December, 1936), pp. 894-904.

mation. It is scarcely true that popular concern with evidences of social disorganization is absent. After all, much organized effort is devoted to the replacing of slum housing by public housing; increasing effort is mounted to rescue talent; the city-planning movement aims to bring under control the unplanned sprawl and self-defeating traffic found in the great urban centers. But this enlarged concern with problems of social disorganization as distinct from problems of deviant behavior is itself a major social change. It is, in large part, the result of an accumulating social technology, just as other social changes are in large part the result of an accumulating physical technology. Whereas deviant behavior at once attracts the indignant notice of people whose norms and values have been violated by it, social disorganization tends not to (except as it eventuates in deviant behavior). Technical specialists, unattached intellectuals, and social critics play a central role in trying to alert greater numbers of people to what they take to be the greater immorality—living complacently under conditions of social disorganization that in principle can be brought under at least partial control. Under the progressive division of social labor it becomes the office of these specialists to try to cope with social disorganization. That the social change in this direction is far from complete can be inferred from the uniform complaints by these specialists about the public apathy toward the problems with which they deal.

Social Disorganization and Deviant Behavior

Social problems have been identified here as the substantial, unwanted discrepancies between what is in a society and what a functionally significant collectivity within that society seriously (rather than in fantasy) desires to be in it. The scale of these discrepancies is affected in either or both of two ways: by a raising of standards and by a deterioration of social conditions. There is no paradox, then, in finding that some complex, industrial societies, having a comparatively high plane of material life and rapid advancement of cultural values, may nevertheless be regarded by people in them as more problem-ridden than other societies with substantially less material wealth and cultural achievement. Like everything else in social life, the discrepancies between socially shared standards and actual conditions have both subjective and objective aspects.

We are now ready to take systematic note of the idea, central to the plan of this book and only touched upon previously in this chapter, that social problems can be usefully divided into two broad classes, the one described as "social disorganization," the other, as "deviant behavior." Even before we examine the theoretical basis for distinguishing these two classes of social problems, we can be reasonably sure that these two concepts are analytical, not depictive; abstract, not concrete. That is to say, they do not describe classes of events in all their actual complexity but refer only to selected aspects of them. That is why we find in each of the concrete social problems examined in this book—for instance, family disorganization, criminal behavior, and community conflict—evidence of both social disorganization and deviant behavior, though in differing compound. Nevertheless, it is possible, and useful, to distinguish in each social problem the components and aspects that are matters of disorganization and those that are matters of deviant behavior, recognizing that the two interact and, under certain conditions, tend to reinforce each other.

Social Disorganization

No single conception of social disorganization is employed by sociologists today, any more than yesterday.[27] But within the diversity of usage, there is an appreciable agreement. And since nothing resembling an official nomenclature exists in sociology, just as there was none in chemistry before Lavoisier set to work, the conception of social disorganization as it is reviewed here cannot claim uniform acceptance by sociologists. Nevertheless, it does approximate a good deal of current usage, being much like some and not much unlike any.

Social disorganization refers to inadequacies or failures in a social system of interrelated statuses and roles such that the collective purposes and individual objectives of its members are less fully realized than they could be in an alternative workable system. Social disorganization is relative and a matter of degree. It is not tied to an ab-

---

[27] The range of variation in usage is roughly bounded by the formulation by Thomas and Znaniecki in 1927 and the formulation by A. K. Cohen in 1959 (although there were numerous accounts before the first of these and even a few since the second). See William I. Thomas and Florian Znaniecki, *The Polish Peasant in Europe and America* (New York: Knopf, 1927), Vol. 2, pp. 1127-33. A. K. Cohen, "The Study of Social Disorganization and Deviant Behavior," in R. K. Merton, L. Broom, and L. S. Cottrell, Jr., eds., *Sociology Today* (New York: Basic Books, 1959), pp. 461-84. Many textbooks have subjected the concept to critical reexamination; for examples, Jessie Bernard, *Social Problems at Midcentury* (New York: Holt, 1957); Marshall B. Clinard, *Sociology of Deviant Behavior*, rev. ed. (New York: Holt, 1963); John F. Cuber, William F. Kenkel, and Robert A. Harper, *Problems of American Society*, 4th ed. (New York: Holt, 1964); S. N. Eisenstadt, ed., *Comparative Social Problems* (New York: Free Press, 1964); Mabel A. Elliott and Francis E. Merrill, *Social Disorganization*, 4th ed. (New York: Harper, 1961); Earl Raab and Gertrude Jaeger Selznick, *Major Social Problems*, 2nd ed. (New York: Harper, 1964); Bernard Rosenberg, Israel Gerver, and F. William Howton, *Mass Society in Crisis* (New York: Macmillan, 1964).

solute standard located in some Platonic empyrean but to a standard of what, so far as we know, could be accomplished under attainable conditions. When we say that a particular group or organization or community or society is disorganized in some degree, we mean that the structure of statuses and roles is not as effectively organized as it, then and there, might be. This statement, then, amounts to *a technical judgment about the workings of a social system.* And each case requires the sociological judge to supply competent evidence that the actual organization of social life can, under attainable conditions, be technically improved to make for the more substantial realization of collective and individual purposes. To find such evidence is no easy task. That is why, perhaps, would-be diagnoses of social disorganization are often little more than moral judgments rather than confirmable technical judgments about the workings of a social system.

The composite of faults in the normative and relational structure of a social system described as social disorganization can be thought of as representing inadequacies in meeting one or more of the functional requirements of the system. Social patterns of behavior fail to be maintained (possibly as a result of inadequate socialization of members of the group, though not alone because of this). Or, personal tensions generated by life within the system are insufficiently controlled, canalized, or siphoned off by social processes so that, for example, anxieties accumulate and get out of hand. Or, the social system is inadequately related to its environment, neither controlling it nor adapted to it. Or, the structure of the system does not allow sufficiently for its members to attain the goals that are its *raison d'être.* Or, finally in this list of functional imperatives of a social system, the relations between its members do not maintain the indispensable minimum of social cohesion needed to carry on both instrumental and intrinsically valued activities. Social disorganization exists in the degree to which patterned activities fail to meet one or more of these functional requirements of the system, whether this be an organization or an institution, a comparatively large and complex group or a small and slightly differentiated one.[28]

---

[28] This account draws upon the list of functional imperatives set forth by Parsons and Bales. See Talcott Parsons, R. F. Bales, and E. A. Shils, *Working Papers in the Theory of Action* (New York: Free Press, 1953), pp. 180-90. For a concise and clear summary of this list, see H. M. Johnson, *Sociology: A Systematic Introduction* (New York: Harcourt, Brace & World, 1960), pp. 51-63; and for a detailed analysis of it, see Chandler Morse, "The Functional Imperatives," in Max Black, ed., *The Social Theories of Talcott Parsons* (Englewood Cliffs, N. J.: Prentice-Hall, 1961), pp. 100-52. Whether this list of functional requirements or another is employed need not be at issue. What is theoretically decisive is the

Rigorous and demonstrably valid measures of the degree of social disorganization have yet to be developed. Even good rough estimates are difficult to come by. It would be no small task, for example, to arrive at a sound comparison of the extent of social disorganization in the United States and in the Soviet Union. Somewhat better results can be achieved in comparing formal organizations in the same sphere of activity in the same society. But even in advance of reasonably precise, reliable, and valid measures of social disorganization, we can identify some of the conditions making for disorganization and some of the forms in which it finds visible expression.

Contributing to social disorganization are inadequacies or partial breakdowns in channels of effective communication between people in a social system—whether a national society, local community, or purposive association—who are reciprocally dependent for doing what they are socially supposed to do and what they individually want to do. By turning to them first, we do not imply, of course, that inadequate avenues of functionally relevant communication comprise the single most consequential source of social disorganization. But as many experimental and observational inquiries have found, faulty communication has led to disorganization even in the absence of opposed interests and values among those in a group.

Superimposed on clogged lines of communication and often contributing to lapses of communication is the structural circumstance, which we have previously noted, of status groups and social strata having not only different but incompatible values and interests. This circumstance enlarges the potential for social disorganization, as can be seen in Chapter 13 concerning community disorganization. People may thus work at cross-purposes, even though, or precisely because, they are living up to the requirements and values of their respective positions in society. When the social organization of an economy, for

---

notion that social disorganization results from the inadequate meeting of one or more such requirements, and that this implication is followed in practice even by theorists of social disorganization who explicitly disavow a functional orientation in sociology.

Even the early formulations by Thomas and Znaniecki that practically equate disorganization and deviant behavior are based on a comparable, though implicit, assumption. They elect to focus on disorganization as a failure in maintaining social patterns of behavior, when they define it as "a decrease of the influence of existing social rules of behavior upon individual members of the group." By the same logic, disorganization stems also from failure to meet other functional requirements of the social system—such as a culturally validated degree of goal attainment (Thomas and Znaniecki, *The Polish Peasant in Europe and America,* Vol. 2, Chapter 1).

example, does not provide for ways of settling the clash between the often opposed interests of, say, workers, management, and owners (stockholders), a degree of disorganization results, with interest groups having only the alternative of acting in terms of their own interests. Conflicts of interests dispose toward disorganization, without entailing it.

Defects in the processes of socialization—the acquisition of attitudes and values, of skills and knowledge needed to fulfill social roles—are another prominent source of disorganization. Not infrequently, for example, rapid social mobility occurs without adequate socialization of the mobile individuals. As a result, these mobile people may not know how to behave in their newly acquired statuses. Not knowing the informal limits on the exercise of his formally designated authority, the new boss may "swing his weight around," making demands which, though they are well within the scope of his formal authority, are far beyond the limits of the normative expectations held by the workers of what the boss may legitimately exact of them. The effectiveness of organized effort declines and problems of disorganization emerge.[29]

Disorganization stems also from faulty arrangements of competing social demands upon people who inevitably occupy a variety of statuses in society. This often gives rise to the familiar clash of the multiple statuses that call for contradictory behavior. The statuses pull in different directions. When the social system fails to provide for a widely shared priority among these potentially conflicting obligations, the individuals subject to them experience strains, with their behavior often becoming unpredictable and socially disruptive. The obligations of work and home, of local mores and national law, of religious commitment and scientific outlook, of the particular expecta-

---

[29] The theoretical basis for the substance of this paragraph was early formulated by Chester I. Barnard, *The Functions of the Executive* (Cambridge, Mass.: Harvard University Press, 1938), especially in his important Chapter XII, "The Theory of Authority." Further theoretical implications have been drawn by Talcott Parsons, *The Social System* (New York: Free Press, 1951), Chapter VI. An imaginative experiment with groups of children found that effective "leadership" was constrained by being required to operate within group norms: F. Merei, "Group Leadership and Institutionalization," *Human Relations*, Vol. 2 (1949), pp. 23-39. For summaries of many researches that have since come to the same results, see H. W. Riecken and G. C. Homans, "Psychological Aspects of Social Structure," in Gardner Lindzey, ed., *Handbook of Social Psychology* (Reading, Mass.: Addison-Wesley, 1954), Vol. II, pp. 786-832, and more recently, David Krech, R. S. Crutchfield, and E. L. Ballachey, *Individual in Society* (New York: McGraw-Hill, 1962).

tions of friends and the universalistic requirements of bureaucracy—these and many other sorts of patterned occasions for conflicting obligations can make for disorganization in the degree that the regulatory system fails to establish shared priorities of obligation. The fault—in the objective, not the moral, sense—lies in the inept organization of potentially conflicting obligations, not in the ineptitude of the people confronted with these conflicts.

Put in general terms, then, *the type of social problem involved in disorganization arises not from people failing to live up to the requirements of their social statuses, as is the case with deviant behavior, but from the faulty organization of these statuses into a reasonably coherent social system.* Rather than role conformity leading to people's realizing their several and collective purposes, it leads to their getting in one another's way.

Seen from a proper time perspective, some recurrent social situations might better be described as involving a lack of organization than as being instances of disorganization. They are cases of un-organization, in which a system of social relations has not yet taken shape, rather than cases of disorganization, in which an acute disruption has occurred in a once more or less effective system of social relations. The difference is a little like the difference between an apartment about to be occupied by new tenants, with furniture still scattered almost at random, lacking structural arrangement and functional order—this situation being un-organization—and an apartment, long lived in, but now a shambles after a knock-down and drag-out fight among its occupants, this, needless to say, being the analogue to disorganization. The latter is a case of disarray; the former, a case of not yet having an array. In society, instances of the first kind are approximated under conditions where the rules themselves and the organization of statuses are vague or still unformulated, as when people find themselves in a sudden and previously unexperienced kind of catastrophe; instances of the second kind are approximated by a complex of statuses that are ill-assorted, incompatible, or so linked as to provide little effective integration among them.

In a word, the kind of social problem that is dominated by social disorganization results from instrumental or technical flaws in the social system. The system comes to operate less effectively than it realistically might, owing to defects in meeting one or more of its functional requirements. The sources of social disorganization are many and diverse, and we still have much to learn about them. But whatever the source, disorganization means that even when people conform to their roles within the system they behave at cross-purposes so that the outcome is substantially different from what they severally or collectively expected and wished for.

Deviant Behavior

Deviant behavior on a sizable scale represents another kind of social problem. Whereas social disorganization refers to faults in the arrangement and working of social statuses and roles, deviant behavior refers to conduct that departs significantly from the norms set for people in their social statuses. The same behavior may be construed as deviant or conforming, depending upon the social statuses of the people exhibiting the behavior. This fact is simply a corollary of the sociological notion that each social status involves its own set of normative obligations (although many statuses may share some of the same obligations). When a man acts "like a woman" or a layman acts "like a physician," he engages in deviant behavior. But as these allusive phrases imply, the same behavior by women and by physicians would of course be conforming. That is why deviant behavior cannot be described in the abstract but must be related to the norms that are socially defined as appropriate and morally binding for people occupying various statuses.

As used by the sociologist, the term deviant behavior is a technical rather than a moral one. It does not signify moral disapproval by the sociologist. Nevertheless, as the term has entered into increasing usage, its morally neutral denotation has become overladen with the connotation of moral censure. The reasons for this are understandable and telling. After all, sustained deviant behavior of almost any kind is apt to be disruptive for those in social interaction with the deviant. His failure to live up to the socially defined expectations of those with whom he is in direct relationship makes life miserable or difficult for them. They cannot count on him, although in fact they must. Whether so intended or not, deviant behavior interferes with the measure of predictability required by social relations and so provides a punitive experience for the associates of the deviant. They, in turn, respond by penalizing him, a familiar and important kind of social control. By intent or by unchecked expression of their feelings, role partners of the deviant person act to bring him back into line with their normative expectations if only so that they can go about their usual business.

Much the same response to observed deviant behavior occurs among orthodox members of a social system, even when they individually are not *directly* engaged in social relations with the deviant. Their hostile reactions can be described as disinterested. They have little or nothing to lose by the deviant's departure from norms that "should" hold for him; their own situation is not, in fact, appreciably damaged by his misbehavior. Nevertheless, once they know of it, they too are apt to respond with hostility. Because they have internalized the moral norms now being violated, they, in a sense, experience the deviant behavior as repudiating these norms or as threatening the social validity of what they hold to be right and important. Reprisals of this kind can be described as stemming from moral indignation, a disinterested attack on people who depart from norms of the group, even when the deviation does not interfere with the performance of one's own roles, since one is not socially connected with the person engaging in the deviant act.

DEVIANT BEHAVIOR AND SOCIAL RESPONSE. When we say that deviant behavior departs from norms set for given statuses we imply that these norms are set by those who have both power and legitimacy. It follows, as has been repeatedly indicated,[30] that deviant behavior must be so defined by members of the social system and particularly by those occupying positions of authority. We have seen throughout the pages of this book, and especially in the chapters on crime and juvenile delinquency, that social sanctions are not uniformly applied to all those engaged in actual infractions of social rules, the class, ethnicity, race, and age of violators being only among the more conspicuous bases of differentials in the application of sanctions. In short, concrete deviant behavior involves both what the purported deviant *does* and what authoritative members of the social system *perceive* that he does.

These observations on the character of deviant behavior have been usefully systematized by Howard Becker in the following typology: [31]

---

[30] A. K. Cohen has indicated the need for classifying types of social response to social deviation and has suggested that the paradigm of "Social Structure and Anomie" (by Robert K. Merton in *American Sociological Review*, Vol. 3 [October, 1938]) can be adapted to this purpose (Cohen, "The Study of Social Disorganization and Deviant Behavior," p. 465). This suggestion is taken up in part by Robert Dubin, "Deviant Behavior and Social Structure: Continuities in Social Theory," *American Sociological Review*, Vol. 24 (April, 1959), pp. 147-64. See also: Robert K. Merton, "Social Conformity, Deviation, and Opportunity-Structures," *ibid.*, pp. 177-89, especially pp. 185-86. Specifically focused on this problem is the paper by John I. Kitsuse, first read at the meetings of the American Sociological Association in 1960 and later published as "Societal Reaction to Deviant Behavior: Problems of Theory and Method," in Howard S. Becker, ed., *The Other Side: Perspectives on Deviance* (New York: Free Press, 1964), pp. 87-102. Reprinted in the same volume is the illuminating paper on the same subject by Kai T. Erikson, "Notes on the Sociology of Deviance," pp. 9-21 (initially published in *Social Problems*, Vol. 9 [Spring, 1962], pp. 307-14). These observations have been further developed by Becker, *Outsiders*, Chapters 1 and 2.

[31] Becker, *Outsiders*, p. 20.

Types of Deviant Behavior

	Obedient Behavior	*Rule-breaking Behavior*
Perceived as deviant:	Falsely accused	Pure deviant
Not perceived as deviant:	Conforming	Secret deviant

Once arranged in this logical syntax, the concrete types of situations corresponding to each of the four more abstract types can be readily identified. Conformity is behavior of a kind that is within allowable margins and is so perceived by the authorities and others in the social system. At the other extreme is the *bona fide* deviant action that both breaks the rules and is recognized to have done so. These are familiar enough and have sometimes been assumed to exhaust the range of deviant behavior situations. But the tabulation reminds us of a third type, the falsely accused, who in the lingo of the criminal subculture is described as "taking a bum rap" or in more conventional circles as "an innocent victim of the law." And finally, we take note of the secret deviant who repeatedly violates certain norms without being perceived as doing so by much of the rest of the social system (as may be the case in such activities as illegal gambling, sex fetishism, homosexuality, and a dedicated absorption in pornography.

Rather than accept this as a self-validating classification, we should ask ourselves why it is important to include the social response as well as the instigating behavior in the concept of deviant behavior. It all hinges on the evident and important fact that social sanctions are not set in motion unless the action breaking the rule has some degree of observability.[32] For, to put it somewhat parochially, the social system does not typically respond to deviant actions as the sociologist does. The sociologist is trained to distinguish between cases of actual deviant behavior and the inference that the individuals engaging in such actions are themselves "deviants" (i.e., chronically devoted to such behavior).[33] In contrast, social systems tend to identify the person apprehended in deviant conduct as a social type: a criminal, a delinquent, a former prisoner, a pervert, a renegade, or a traitor.

---

[32] On the role of observability in processes of social control, see Merton, *Social Theory and Social Structure*, pp. 247, 319-22, 336-57, and 374-77, and Rose L. Coser, "Insulation from Observability and Types of Social Conformity," *American Sociological Review*, Vol. 26 (February, 1961), pp. 28-39.

[33] For example, Merton, "Social Structure and Anomie," pp. 672-82, especially p. 676, where it is noted that the typology refers "to role adjustments in specific situations, not to personality *in toto.*"

Once this process is set in train, the individual so designated becomes the victim of a self-fulfilling prophecy in which

> the community's reluctance to accept the deviant back helps reduce whatever chance he might otherwise have had for a successful readjustment. . . . The common assumption that deviants are not often cured or reformed [which, under current conditions, has a substantial statistical basis] may be based on a faulty premise, but this assumption is stated so frequently and with such conviction that it often creates the facts which later "prove" it to be correct.[34]

And this is the essential process of the self-fulfilling prophecy: widespread beliefs help bring about a social environment that so constrains the individual's range of alternatives that his behavior can only seem to confirm those beliefs.[35]

NONCONFORMING AND ABERRANT BEHAVIOR. As a first approximation, all substantial departures of behavior from social norms can be caught up in a single concept and associated term, such as deviant behavior. But first approximations are useful in the degree that they are recognized for what they are: rough discriminations that are to be progressively replaced by more exacting ones. And so it is with the concept of deviant behavior. Since departures from established norms differ greatly in their character and social consequences, it should be useful to map the contours of major types of such deviation.

Two major varieties of deviant behavior can be usefully distinguished on the basis of their structure and their consequences for social systems. The first can be called nonconforming behavior; the second, aberrant behavior. Both types retain the technical conception of deviant behavior in sociological analysis; the distinction does not smuggle in moral judgments through the back door of connotative language. It only helps us identify systematic differences in kinds of deviant behavior that are alike only in that they move away from what is prescribed by identifiable social norms.

These types of nonconforming behavior and aberrant behavior differ in several conjoint respects. First, the nonconformer announces his dissent publicly; unlike the aberrant, he does not try to hide his departures from social norms. The political or religious dissenter insists on making his dissent known to as many as will look or listen; the aberrant criminal seeks to avoid the limelight of public scrutiny.

---

[34] Erikson, "Notes on the Sociology of Deviance," p. 17; see also Becker, *Outsiders*, pp. 34-39.

[35] On the general process of the self-fulfilling prophecy, see Merton, *Social Theory and Social Structure,* Chapter XI.

Contrast the pacifist who burns his draft card in public with the draft-dodger who tries to escape into obscurity. This patterned attitude toward visibility links up with a second basic difference between the two kinds of deviants. The nonconformer challenges the legitimacy of the social norms he rejects or at least challenges their applicability to certain kinds of situations. Organized "sit-in" campaigns designed to attack local norms of racial segregation in restaurants and schools afford a recent example of this aspect of nonconforming behavior. The aberrant, in contrast, acknowledges the legitimacy of the norms he violates: it is only that he finds it expedient or expressive of his state of mind to violate them. He may try to justify his own behavior, but he does not argue that theft is right and murder virtuous.

Third and correlatively, the nonconformer aims to change the norms he is denying in practice. He wants to replace what he believes to be morally suspect norms with ones having a sound moral basis. The aberrant, in contrast, tries primarily to escape the sanctioning force of existing norms, without proposing substitutes for them. When subject to social sanction, the nonconformer typically appeals to a higher morality; except as an instrumental device, the aberrant does not; at most he appeals to extenuating circumstances.

Fourth, and possibly as a resultant of the preceding components of his behavior, the nonconformer is acknowledged, however reluctantly, by conventional members of the social system to depart from prevailing norms for disinterested purposes and not for what he personally can get out of it. Again in contrast, the aberrant is prevalently assumed to be deviating from the norms in order to serve his own interests. Although the law of the land may not make the formal distinction between the nonconformer and the aberrant in this respect, many members of society do. Whatever the generic concept of deviant behavior might seem to pronounce to the contrary, the two types of social deviants are widely acknowledged as having far different social consequences. Those courageous highwaymen of seventeenth-century England, John Nevinson and his much advertised successor, Dick Turpin, were not of a sociological piece with that courageous nonconformist of their time, Oliver Cromwell. And in the event that one's political or religious sympathies, as well as the detachment made easy by historical distance, serve to make this observation self-evident, one should reexamine those judgments that once made of Trotsky or Nehru little more than criminals heading up a sizable gang of followers.

Fifth, and for present purposes finally, the nonconformer, with his appeal to an allegedly higher morality, can in historically propitious circumstances lay claim to legitimacy by drawing upon the ultimate values, rather than the particular norms, of the society. He is trying to make justice a social reality rather than an institutionalized fiction. He is for genuine freedom of speech rather than its everyday pretense. He would rearrange the social structure to provide actual equality of opportunity for all men to develop prized talents and not allow the social simulacra of equality to be mistaken for the real thing. In these ways, his nonconformity can appeal to the moral values that are in some measure being denied in social practice while being reaffirmed in ideological doctrine. The nonconformer can appeal to the tacit recognition by others of discrepancies between the prized values and the social reality.[36] He thus has at least the prospect of obtaining the assent of other, initially less critical and venturesome, members of society whose ambivalence toward the current social structure can be drawn upon for some degree of support. Nonconformity is not a private dereliction but a thrust toward a new morality or a promise of restoring a morality held to have been thrust aside in social practice. In this respect again, the nonconformer is far removed from the other major type of social deviant, the aberrant, who has nothing new to propose and nothing old to restore, but seeks only to satisfy his private interests or to express his private cravings.[37]

Sociologists have lavished far more attention on the form of deviant behavior we have described as aberrant than on that described as nonconforming. That is one reason why this volume deals at length with the principal kinds of aberrant behavior—with crime, drug addiction, alcoholism, juvenile delinquency, and prostitution. For, as Francis Bacon put it, "Books must follow sciences, and not sciences, books." When a body of sociological investigation of various kinds of nonconforming behavior develops, the shape of books on social problems will change accordingly. More attention will be systematically paid to various kinds of nonconformity, without necessarily paying less attention to various kinds of aberrant behavior.

---

[36] Talcott Parsons has noted that patterns of social deviation differ significantly according to whether they lay claim to legitimation. See *The Social System,* pp. 291-97.

[37] The foregoing account of nonconforming behavior develops somewhat the pattern of behavior identified as "rebellion" in the typology set forth in "Social Structure and Anomie." In that same typology, innovation, ritualism, and retreatism would comprise forms of aberrant behavior. And, as has been indicated in the text, nonconforming and aberrant behavior together compose deviant behavior. See Merton, *Social Theory and Social Structure,* p. 140. For further development of this line of inquiry, see Marshall B. Clinard, ed., *Anomie and Deviant Behavior: A Discussion and Critique* (New York: Free Press, 1964).

These future investigations into nonconformity will need to take care that they do not move from an unthinking orthodoxy to an equally unthinking heterodoxy by valuing nonconformity for its own sake. For what is nonconformity to the norms of one group is often conformity to the norms of another group. There is no joy or merit in escaping the error of taking heterodoxy to be inevitably false or ugly or sinister only to be caught up in the opposite error of thinking heterodoxy to be inevitably true or beautiful or altogether excellent. Put in so many words, this is a commonplace wrapped in banality. Yet people alienated from the world about them often do take heterodoxy as a good in itself, whatever its character. And others, perhaps in recoil against being tagged as hopeless Philistines or in reaction to the cases, familiar in every age, of true merit being neglected or punished because it was unorthodox, are quick to see value, all apart from its substance, in heterodoxy or in countercyclicalism, the automatic denial of worth to whatever is widely accepted or to what has been newly proposed. In every time, apparently, shrewd men have known that an appropriate kind of seeming heterodoxy appeals greatly even to the more orthodox members of society. As British lecturers to American audiences have evidently known for a long period, and as American lecturers to women's clubs, literary societies, and businessmen's associations now know: there is no better way to win their hearts than by attacking part of what they stand for while intimating that they are not beyond redemption.[38] These and other forms of specious nonconformity have long been recognized, particularly by some of the most notable nonconformers of their time. It has been said of Marx, for example, that "all his life [he] detested two phenomena with peculiar passion: disorderly life and histrionic display. It seemed to him that Bohemianism and deliberate flouting of conventions was but inverted Philistinism, emphasizing and paying homage to the very same false values by exaggerated protest against them, and exhibiting therefore the same fundamental vulgarity."[39]

ATTRIBUTES OF SOCIAL NORMS AND DEVIANT BEHAVIOR. Such concepts as conformity, nonconformity, and aberrant behavior can easily become misleading if they are not kept under theoretical control. For one thing, they seem to imply a high degree of clarity about what represents behavioral compliance with a norm or departure from it. But such clarity, however great it may be on the conceptual plane, becomes dif-

---

[38] This paragraph is based on Robert K. Merton, "Recognition and Excellence: Instructive Ambiguities," in *Recognition of Excellence: Working Papers* (New York: Free Press, 1960), pp. 297-328, especially pp. 321-22.

[39] Isaiah Berlin, *Karl Marx* (London: Oxford University Press, 1960), p. 79.

ficult to achieve on the plane of empirical research. The experience of law courts, for example, demonstrates that it is often far from easy to find out whether a particular action was deviant by trying to match up the act and the pertinent norms embodied in the law. This difficulty is perhaps all the greater in trying to compare actions with norms that have not been carefully formulated, as is the case with folkways and mores.

For another thing, social norms have many dimensions and so can differ according to the combination of magnitudes of the several dimensions. Norms may prescribe behavior or proscribe it; or, they may merely indicate what forms of behavior are preferred or simply permitted. The extent of agreement on norms within the group or society may vary: they may be almost universally held, as in the West with the norm against kidnapping, or they may be confined to a functionally significant part of the social system, as apparently with the norms violated by many kinds of white-collar crime. Norms may enlist deep-seated or only superficial support among those who subscribe to them. The social sanctions visited on deviants from the norms may be administered by institutional agencies set up for the purpose, or the sanctions may be diffuse, imposed only by the punitive responses of those exposed to the deviation. The norms may call only for overt behavioral conformity, only for inner assent, or for both. And, in this short listing, finally, the norms may have differing degrees of elasticity, sometimes requiring close adherence to a prescribed form of behavior, sometimes allowing considerable leeway in behavior before it is adjudged significantly deviant.[40]

This last attribute of norms, their degree of elasticity, is of particular importance in the study of deviant behavior. For it reminds us that strict, continued, and ready compliance with rigorously defined norms would be possible only in a society that never existed. It is a conceptual construct, at most only approached in social life. In actual prac-

---

[40] For an application of this set of attributes of social norms, see Aaron Rosenblatt, "The Application of Role Concepts to the Intake Process," *Social Casework*, Vol. XLIII (January, 1962), pp. 8-14. On the specific attribute of the elasticity of norms, see Lewis A. Coser, "Some Functions of Deviant Behavior and Normative Flexibility," *American Journal of Sociology*, Vol. LXVIII (September, 1962), pp. 172-81. And on the relation of observability to other attributes of norms, see Rose L. Coser, "Insulation from Observability and Types of Social Conformity," pp. 28-39. Antecedent literature on social norms is represented by Pitirim A. Sorokin, *Society, Culture, and Personality* (New York: Harper, 1947), Chapter 4; Timasheff, *An Introduction to the Sociology of Law*, which has the further value of an extensive annotated bibliography on the subject; Richard T. Morris, "A Typology of Norms," *American Sociological Review*, Vol. 21 (October, 1956), pp. 610-13.

tice, social norms provide for a band of behavior judged admissible even though it departs from the strict letter of the norms. The extent of this band differs among norms and for the same norm under differing social conditions. For example, when it is widely felt that the group or society is in grave danger—as under conditions of war or after a great catastrophe—this band of permissiveness contracts, as exemplified by martial law. Much remains to be discovered about the social processes affecting the extent of patterned leeway in compliance with norms required by a group. Until this general knowledge of regularities grows considerably larger, variations in expected compliance must be empirically investigated in each case.[41]

INSTITUTIONALIZED EVASIONS OF INSTITUTIONAL RULES. Beyond the elasticity of norms that provides for varying degrees of socially acceptable conformity is another pattern that provides for systematic nonconformity to them. This has been described as the pattern of "institutionalized evasions of institutional rules."[42]

Evasions of institutional rules are themselves institutionalized when they are (1) patterned in fairly well-defined types; (2) adopted by substantial numbers of people rather than being scattered subterfuges independently and privately arrived at; (3) organized in the form of a fairly elaborate social machinery made up of tacitly cooperating participants, including those who are socially charged with implementing the rules; and (4) rarely punished and even when they are, penalized in the form of largely symbolic punishments that serve primarily to reaffirm the sanctity of the rules.[43]

---

[41] Hans L. Zetterberg, *Sociology in a New Key* (Totowa, N. J.: Bedminster Press, in press).

[42] The analysis of institutionalized evasions was developed in lectures at Harvard in the late 1930's, with part of it first seeing print in Robert K. Merton, "Discrimination and the American Creed," in R. M. MacIver, ed., *Discrimination and National Welfare* (New York: Harper, 1949), pp. 99-126, and in Merton, *Social Theory and Social Structure*, pp. 317-18, 343-45. For a variety of institutionalized evasions in various institutional spheres, see Wilbert E. Moore, *Industrial Relations and the Social Order*, rev. ed. (New York: Macmillan, 1951), p. 114; Logan Wilson, *The Academic Man* (New York: Oxford University Press, 1941), pp. 218-19; Kingsley Davis, *Human Society* (New York: Macmillan, 1949), pp. 263-64; Robin M. Williams, Jr., *American Society* (New York: Knopf, 1951), Chapter 10; Joseph Bensman and Israel Gerver, "Crime and Punishment in the Factory: The Function of Deviancy in Maintaining the Social System," *American Sociological Review*, Vol. 28 (August, 1963), pp. 588-98; Charles P. and Zona K. Loomis, *Modern Social Theories* (Princeton, N. J.: Van Nostrand, 1961), pp. 156-57, 270-71, 529-30, 553-54, 615-16.

[43] Robert K. Merton in the Foreword to Hubert J. O'Gorman, *Lawyers and Matrimonial Cases: A Study of Informal Pressures in Private Professional Practice* (New York: Free Press, 1963), pp. ix-xi; Williams, *American Society*, p. 356.

These social patterns of evasion develop when practical exigencies confronting a collectivity require goal-oriented or adaptive behavior that is at odds with long-established norms or when newly formulated norms (most clearly in the form of new legislation) are at odds with long-established social practices and sentiments. Such evasions on the large scale are signs of malintegration between norms and widespread, socially induced needs.

When there is a gross discrepancy between newly instituted legal norms and local mores, all manner of procedures for evading the full force of the norms will be adopted: nullification, circumvention, subterfuge, connivance, and legal fictions. Even such crude qualitative knowledge (as distinct from precise quantitative knowledge) of the conditions making for institutionalized evasions can serve to forecast the occurrence of evasions on a substantial scale. Thus, it was possible to anticipate, a half-dozen years before, the broad outlines of response to a decision such as that taken unanimously by the Supreme Court on May 17, 1954, which declared unconstitutional the separate-but-equal doctrine (Plessy v. Ferguson) that had enabled communities to exclude Negro children from public schools maintained for white children. One such forecast read as follows:

> In an unfavorable cultural climate—and this does not necessarily exclude the benign regions of the Far South—the immediate resort will probably have to be that of working through legal and administrative federal controls over extreme discrimination, with full recognition that, in all probability, these regulations will be systematically evaded for some time to come. In such cultural regions, we may expect nullification of the law as the common practice, perhaps as common as was the case in the nation at large with respect to the Eighteenth Amendment, often with the connivance of local officers of the law. The large gap between the new law and local mores will not *at once* produce significant change of prevailing practices: token punishments of violations will probably be more common than effective control. At best, one may assume that significant change will be fitful, and excruciatingly slow. But secular changes in the economy may in due course lend support to the new legal framework of control over discrimination. As the economic shoe pinches because the illiberals do not fully mobilize the resources of industrial manpower nor extend their local markets through equitable wage-payments, they may slowly abandon some discriminatory practices as they come to find that these do not always pay—even the discriminator.[44]

Another instance of the pattern of institutionalized evasions is provided by widespread social response to the law governing divorce in

---

[44] Merton, "Discrimination and the American Creed," p. 120.

the state of New York. Here we see the law lagging behind the changing interests, values, and wants of a substantial part of the population. This lag has given rise to a social machinery built up of tacitly collaborating clients, lawyers, judges, trained connivers, and specialized inventors of make-believe evidence of adultery. A grand jury investigating the matter "confirmed what had long been suspected: fraud, perjury, collusion, and connivance pervade matrimonial actions of every type." They discovered "a wholesale system of fabricating evidence for a divorce, the service of a correspondent and witness being supplied for a fee." [45] The institutionalized though ostensibly proscribed evasions are thoroughly known to officers of the court. As one lawyer summed it up: "Ninety percent of the undefended matrimonials are based on perjury. They are all arranged. The raids are made with the consent of the defendant. We all know this. The judges know it. It's embarrassing to go [to court]." [46]

We see in this particular case the dynamics of institutionalized evasions. A rule is experienced as excessively restrictive by a substantial number of people whose status in the community is otherwise "respectable" and conforming. This goes far toward subverting the legitimacy of the legal norm. A system of evasive practices develops to close the gap between the law and the socially legitimatized though illegal wants of many people. The law is maintained on the books, not as a result of "inertia" but in response to certain interested groups in the community that are sufficiently powerful to have their way. But they are not powerful enough to prevent the circumvention of the law by other "respectable" segments of the community who find it unduly cramping and who deny its legitimacy. During the interim of this social conflict, the social system evolves a pattern of institutionalized evasions in which the rules remain nominally intact while devices for neutralizing them evolve. Such institutionalized evasions give rise to institutional change—in this case, the change of the law governing divorce—when the balance of power between contending sectors of the "respectable" community shifts to those who have made the evasions in the first place.

Historical instances of institutionalized evasions that have run their full course bring out the connections between the pattern of regularized evasion and subsequent institutional change. A meticulously analyzed case is that of eighteenth-century criminal law in England. The punishments for certain crimes then prescribed by law were so

---

[45] O'Gorman, *Lawyers and Matrimonial Cases*, p. 23.
[46] *Ibid.*, p. 33.

severe as to be at great variance with sentiments and values widely held in the society. As a result, the law was ridden with "absurd technicalities" that were designed to give "a criminal undue chances of escape from conviction by the practical revolt of jurymen against the immorality of penalties out of all proportion to moral guilt, and by the constant commutation of capital for some lighter punishment." [47] In due course, simple theft was no longer treated as a capital crime after generations in which "juries, judges, prosecutors, and complainants collaborated" to evade the full force of the extremely punitive law.[48] Once again we see that the social functionaries charged with administering the widely rejected norms are the best situated to evade their literal force and that they do precisely that. To some extent, all this was recognized by observers of human society long ago. From the time of the ancient Roman adage—*Quid leges sine moribus?* to what avail are laws without support of the mores?—down to the present, men have recognized that legal norms will be evaded on the large scale when they are substantially opposed to other norms or values or to what can be practically carried into effect.

The pattern of institutionalized evasions is not at all peculiar to complex literate societies. It has been amply identified in nonliterate societies by such anthropologists as Malinowski, Radcliffe-Brown, Firth, and others, the gist of their observations being admirably set forth by Macbeath, as when he notes that "even the most rigid rules, those which have a supernatural sanction, can be evaded or circumvented not only with the connivance but with the backing of public

---

[47] A. V. Dicey, *Lectures on the Relation Between Law and Public Opinion in England During the Nineteenth Century* (London: Macmillan, 1905), pp. 79-80. This classic is chock-full of historical materials bearing on the emergence of institutionalized evasions of institutional rules. Another classic, published just about a century ago, Henry Sumner Maine's *Ancient Law*, 5th ed. (New York: Holt, 1887) also sets forth apposite materials in the second chapter.

[48] Hall, *Theft, Law, and Society*, p. 87. Jerome Hall has given us one of the most analytical accounts of the process through which the evasion of institutional rules has led to a new body of rules, especially in his Chapter 3, significantly entitled "The Function of Technicality and Discretion in Criminal Law Administration," pp. 68-121.

Oliver Wendell Holmes, like Roscoe Pound and Benjamin Cardozo after him, has argued that law is inevitably subject to social and cultural lag. He writes: "It cannot be helped, it is as it should be, that the law is behind the times. . . . As law embodies beliefs that have triumphed in the battle of ideas and then have translated themselves into action, while there still is doubt, while opposite convictions still keep a battle front against each other, the time for law has not yet come; the notion destined to prevail is not yet entitled to the field." What we note here is that institutionalized evasions emerge to take up the slack during this interim of changing social interests and lagging legal norms. Holmes, *Collected Legal Papers* (Boston: Little, Brown, 1920), pp. 290, 294.

opinion and legalized usage, when the exceptions are in conformity with the people's sense of what is right." [49]

Since the persistence of institutionalized evasions tends to make for changes in the structure of social norms, what was at one time a distinct kind of deviant behavior later becomes conformity. This, then, reminds us of what we already know: not only is deviant behavior relative to the norms of a designated group, so that it can simultaneously be described as deviation from one set of norms and conformance with another, but it is also relative to changing norms, so that what is regarded in one generation as deviation is in the next a self-evident kind of conformity.

Social Problems and Social Dysfunctions

As has been noted in many of the foregoing chapters, the investigation of social problems has a distinct intellectual interest altogether apart from its possible use in ultimately helping men to cope with the social troubles that confront them. One such point of theoretical interest is that the study of social problems requires sociologists to attend to the dysfunctions of patterns of behavior, belief, and organization rather than focusing primarily or exclusively on their functions. It thus curbs any inadvertent or deliberate tendency in functional sociology to re-institute the philosophy that everything in society works for "harmony" and "the good." [50]

---

[49] A. Macbeath, *Experiments in Living* (London: Macmillan, 1952), pp. 144-47. For some of the factual bases of this summary statement, see B. Malinowski, *Crime and Custom in Savage Society* (New York: Harcourt, Brace & World, 1931), pp. 80-81; A. R. Radcliffe-Brown, "The Social Organization of Australian Tribes," *Oceania*, Vol. 1, Nos. 1-4 (1930-31), pp. 34-63; 206-46; 322-41; 426-56; Raymond Firth, *We, the Tikopia* (London: Allen & Unwin, 1936), p. 129; Edward Norbeck, "African Rituals of Conflict," *American Anthropologist*, Vol. 65 (December, 1963), pp. 1254-79.

[50] Without considering the question of the extent to which current functional sociology has exhibited this tendency—a question that would take us far afield—we might note the claim that such a tendency has been expressed in physiology, especially in that part of physiology heavily influenced by Walter B. Cannon's notion of *homeostasis* (the maintenance of steady states in the organism). For Cannon's ideas were also influential in the recent resurgence of a functional outlook in sociology. The criticism is set forth, in sufficiently nontechnical fashion that even those without a thorough grounding in physiology may learn as they read, by the physician and physiologist, Dickinson W. Richards (who was later to become a Nobel laureate for his work on catheterization of the heart). See his account of "The Stupidity of the Body," designed as a complement to rather than a substitute for Cannon's "The Wisdom of the Body," in his paper, "Homeostasis *versus* Hyperexis," *The Scientific Monthly*, Vol. 77 (December, 1953), pp. 289-94.

The theoretical relation of social dysfunctions to social disorganization can be briefly stated. Social disorganization, it will be remembered, refers to that composite of faults in the operation of a social system that interferes with the fulfillment of functional requirements of the system. Social dysfunction refers to the particular inadequacies of a particular part of the system for a designated requirement.[51] Social disorganization can be thought of as the resultant of multiple social dysfunctions.

1. The first essential point in using the concept of social dysfunction for the analysis of social problems can stand repetitive emphasis if only because the point has so often been blunted in the course of usage. A social dysfunction refers to a *designated* set of consequences of a *designated* pattern of behavior, belief, or organization that interfere with a *designated* functional requirement of a *designated* social system. Otherwise, the term social dysfunction becomes little more than an epithet of disparagement or a largely vacuous expression of attitude. To say, for example, that a high rate of social mobility is "functional" or "dysfunctional," without indicating the particular consequences it has for particular attributes of a designated social system, is to say comparatively little. But it is quite another thing to say, as has been said,[52] that a high rate of social mobility from the working class into the middle class is dysfunctional for effective attainment of its goals by a solidary working class, since mobility involves the ex-

---

[51] A more exact formal statement is provided by Ernest Nagel, "A Formalization of Functionalism," in his *Logic Without Metaphysics* (New York: Free Press, 1956), especially p. 269.

[52] This hypothesis was adopted not long ago by a branch of the Labour Party in Birmingham; that is, by people who were, of course, ideologically and in the abstract, staunch supporters of enlarging opportunity for social mobility. Nevertheless, they officially stated that "from Labour's point of view, the objection to the grammar school system was that it had the effect of taking the brightest children of the working class and in effect de-classing them by separation from children in the modern [essentially vocational] schools. Eventually, they get white-collar jobs and upon marriage go to live in the outer suburbs and vote Tory." Substantially, the same hypothesis about the dysfunctions of rapid and large-scale mobility for maintaining the solidarity and effective goal attainment of a working class was set forth by such ideologically opposed theorists as Karl Marx and Vilfredo Pareto. See Marx, *Capital* (Chicago: Kerr, 1906), pp. 648-49; Pareto, *The Mind and Society* (New York: Harcourt, Brace & World, 1935), Vol. 3, pp. 1419-32; Vol. 4, pp. 1836-46. For an analysis of this pattern of "cognitive agreement and value disagreement," see Robert K. Merton, "Social Conflict Over Styles of Sociological Work," *Transactions* (Fourth World Congress of Sociology, 1959), Vol. III, pp. 21-46, especially pp. 39-40. Most recently, the same ambivalence toward social mobility among a disadvantaged population is found among "the masses of lower-class Negroes [who] regard this movement up the ladder with mixed feelings, both proud and resentful of the success of 'one of their own.'" (Clark, *Dark Ghetto*, pp. 57-58.)

portation of talent from that class and a consequent depletion of its potential leadership. This type of statement is at the least and in principle a testable hypothesis about a dysfunction of social mobility, whatever the practical difficulties in putting it to decisive test. Easy imputations of social function or dysfunction in the abstract are no more defensible than easy imputations of social causation in the abstract. Like social causes, social dysfunctions must be discovered through inquiry. And it is no more to be expected that inquiry will promptly discover previously unknown dysfunctions of social patterns than it is that inquiry will promptly discover previously unknown causes of these same patterns.

2. It must be noted, secondly, that the same social pattern can be dysfunctional for some parts of a social system and functional for other parts. This arises from a characteristic of social structure that has been repeatedly called to our attention in the pages of this book: social patterns have multiple consequences, and, in a differentiated society, these consequences will often differ for individuals, groups, and social strata variously situated in the structure of the society.

The continued persistence of a social pattern makes it improbable, not impossible, that it is uniformly dysfunctional for all groups. Thus, it has been noted in Chapter 9 on race and ethnic relations that relatively free access to higher education, irrespective of racial and other origin, is dysfunctional for maintaining a relatively fixed system of caste. Extended popular education militates against the fixing of caste position or resigned acceptance to it. But of course in the very degree that higher education of the socially subordinate is dysfunctional for maintaining the system of stratification, it is functional for the enlarged attainment of culturally induced goals by those formerly excluded from higher education.

All this is something more than a paraphrase of Lucretius' adage that one man's meat is another man's poison. The general idea that serves as a beginning for the analysis of functions and dysfunctions of the same social pattern is, as we have noted, that various groups and strata in the structure of a society have distinctive interests and values as well as in some degree sharing other interests and values. To the extent that this diversity, and sometimes this conflict, of values and interests is so distributed among statuses in the society, we should naturally be prepared to find social patterns serving the requirements of some and interfering with the requirements of other groups differently located in the society. This structural condition is one of the principal reasons why the periodically popular notion of a society in which everything works together for good is literally utopian, and describes an engaging utopia at that. But to forgo this image of a society entirely free of imperfections does not require us to assume that nothing can be done, through deliberate plan, to reduce the extent to which obsolescent institutions and disorganization work against the realization of values that men respect. Indeed, that is the direction aimed at and sometimes attained by developing public policy.

3. Not only is the same pattern sometimes functional for some groups and dysfunctional for others but it also may serve some and defeat other functional requirements of the *same* group.[53] And the reason for this is of the same general sort as the reason for cases in which the pattern is variously consequential for *different* groups. For a group has diverse functional requirements: to take only one thoroughly investigated example, the requirement of enough social cohesion to keep its members oriented to the group as having value for them and the requirement of working toward the group goals, of getting a job done. It is not unusual, therefore, that the same activities that are functional for one of these requirements prove to be dysfunctional for the other. When this is true to a substantial degree, the group confronts an organizational problem.

This example of composite function-and-dysfunction for distinct properties of the same group can be profitably considered in a little more detail in order to bring out the general idea it exemplifies. In the main, sociologists have found that social cohesion facilitates the productivity of a group. This is what one might expect from everyday experience: in cohesive groups, people feel at one with each other and so are the better prepared to work together for joint ends. But this mutually reinforcing relation between social cohesion and productivity holds only part of the time. A functional imbalance can and typically does develop between the activity that serves chiefly to maintain cohesion and the activity that results chiefly in getting work done. An "excess" of social cohesion can restrict intragroup competition in performance; [54] members of a highly cohesive group may become reciprocally indulgent to the degree that they do not hold one another to exacting standards of performance; or a large fraction of the social

---

[53] Indeed, this conception that activities directed toward instrumental and system-maintenance functions are antithetical is basic to the functional analysis of social problems. This is one of the several respects in which, contrary to much superficial opinion, the assumption of structural and functional *conflict* is inherent in functional sociology.

[54] Considerable observational and experimental work bears on this example of composite function-and-dysfunction; for a summary of this one finding, see James G. March and Herbert A. Simon, *Organizations* (New York: Wiley & Sons, 1958), pp. 60-61.

interaction in the group may be devoted to expressing and reinforcing group cohesiveness at the expense of time and energy for getting the job done.[55] When such functional imbalances obtain, the problem confronting the group is one of establishing or of reestablishing a balance in the distribution of activities such that an optimal combination of the two properties of cohesion and goal attainment is approximated.[56]

It cannot be assumed, of course, that an optimal balance is one that maximizes both social cohesion and productivity. Such simultaneous maxima may turn out to be incompatible; we do not yet know enough to say with any confidence. The optimal balance depends upon the comparative value set upon social cohesion and productivity by members of the group, with their being prepared to reduce the one in order to enlarge the other. This is a prototype of the value decisions that must be made in social systems of all kinds. Morale and productivity, compassion and efficiency, personal ties and impersonal tasks—these are familiar enough pairs of values not simultaneously realizable to the fullest extent.[57] All this comprises a sociological near-equivalent

[55] For a few of the many studies to this effect, see A. B. Horsfall and C. M. Arensberg, "Teamwork and Productivity in a Shoe Factory," *Human Organization,* Vol. 8 (1949), pp. 13-25; J. G. Darley, Neal Gross, and W. E. Martin, "Studies of Group Behavior: Factors Associated with the Productivity of Groups," *Journal of Applied Psychology,* Vol. 36 (1952), pp. 396-403; H. A. Grace, "Conformance and Performance," *Journal of Social Psychology,* Vol. 40 (1954), pp. 333-35.

[56] On the conception of the net balance of an aggregate of social consequences, see Merton, *Social Theory and Social Structure,* pp. 51-52; Ralph M. Stogdill, *Individual Behavior and Group Achievement* (New York: Oxford University Press, 1959), pp. 222 ff. Melvin Tumin has indicated that the difficult problem of measuring this net balance has not yet been solved. That is the case. But it should also be noted that this problem, which has at least been identified in functional sociology as a focus of inquiry and analysis, is of course implicit in other sociological analyses of social disorganization and deviant behavior. In short, the same analytical difficulty is there, whether recognized or implicit. See Melvin Tumin, "The Functionalist Approach to Social Problems," *Social Problems,* Vol. 12 (Spring, 1965), pp. 379-88.

[57] *Cf.* Merton and Barber, "Sociological Ambivalence." A rough analogy with the dysfunctional associates of functional genes does not of course supply evidence for the sociological parallel but does provide a sense that this combination is not confined to the plane of human society. Note, for example, the observation by the biochemist and geneticist, Caryl P. Haskins: ". . . the genes . . . do not assort completely independently in inheritance, but are associated into linkage groups. . . . These linked genes are inherited together, though each group as a whole assorts independently of other groups. This means that genetic characteristics which are disadvantageous or are of neutral value to the organism may be firmly linked to other characteristics which are of predominant survival value. Thus, shielded by them in evolution, as it were, they may persist for very long periods merely by virtue of the fact that, under normal circumstances, they are inseparable

to the economist's conception of opportunity costs, which means, in effect, as Scott Greer has indicated, that under certain conditions one commitment reduces the opportunities to make other commitments. The composite of function-and-dysfunction provides another guard against that form of utopian thinking that, by neglecting the social constraints upon the pursuit of certain objectives that result from the commitment to other objectives differing in kind, assumes that all manner of values in society can be maximized. But as the preceding chapters variously indicate, cost-free social action is only a sociological chimera.

4. Above all, it must be emphasized that the concept of social dysfunction does not harbor an implied moral judgment. Social dysfunction is not a latter-day terminological substitute for immorality, unethical practice, or the socially undesirable. It is an objective concept, not a morally evaluating one. Whether one judges a particular social dysfunction as good or bad, as desirable or regrettable, depends, not on the sociological analysis of the consequences for a particular social system, but upon the further and entirely independent judgment of the moral worth of that system. When we noted, for example, that enlarged opportunities for higher education are dysfunctional for the persistence of a caste system, we did not imply, let alone say, that the dysfunction was being judged as evil or undesirable. Or when it is observed that the extremely authoritarian character of the Nazi bureaucracy proved to be dysfunctional for the work of the bureaucracy by excessively restricting lines of communication among its several echelons, it is not to deplore that circumstance. Sociological analyses of function and dysfunction are in a different universe of discourse from that of moral judgments; they are not merely different expressions for the same thing.[58]

All this would not need emphasis were it not for the frequently made assumption that nonconforming and other kinds of deviant behavior are necessarily dysfunctional to a social system and that social dysfunction, in turn, necessarily violates an ethical code. In the history of every society, one supposes, some of its culture heroes eventually come to be regarded as heroic in part because they are held to have had the courage and the vision to challenge the beliefs and routines of their society. The rebel, revolutionary, nonconformist, heretic, or rene-

---

from the benefactor genes and the damage which they cause the organism is much less serious than the evolutionary advantages conferred by their partners." *Of Societies and Men* (New York: Norton, 1951), pp. 113-14.

[58] Dorothy Emmet, *Function, Purpose, and Powers* (London: Macmillan, 1958), pp. 78-82.

gade of an earlier day is often the culture hero of today. Moreover, the accumulation of dysfunctions in a social system is often the prelude to concerted social change that may bring the system closer to the values that enjoy the respect of members of the society.[59] For reasons of this kind, we end this section as we began it: the concept of social dysfunction is not based on ethical premises for it refers to how things work in society and not to their ethical worth.

The sociological art of drawing practical conclusions from theoretical premises and empirical investigation is of course still in the making. But then, so are all the other arts and sciences, no matter how advanced. At least, for the sake of their practitioners, one must hope so. It would be a sad thing if any branches of knowledge and their application had finished growing, with nothing left to be done in them. The pages of this book give some indication of how things now stand with the unfinished sociology of social problems.

---

[59] Merton, *Social Theory and Social Structure*, p. 53. Alvin Boskoff, "Social Indecision: A Dysfunctional Focus of Transitional Society," *Social Forces*, Vol. 37 (1959), pp. 305-11.

. . . .
. . . .
. . . .

Name Index

Bismarck, Otto von, 446
Bixby, F. Lovell, 131
Black, Max, 801
Blacker, C. P., 647, 648
Blackwell, Gordon, 630
Blake, Judith, 323, 399, 407, 487, 629
Blau, Peter M., 571
Blauner, Robert, 578, 582, 584, 613
Bloch, Herbert A., 87, 99, 119
Bloomberg, Warner, Jr., 582, 616
Bock, Philip K., 489
Bogoras, Waldemar, 290, 293
Bogue, Donald, 650
Booth, Charles, 646
Borinski, E., 252
Borkenstein, R. F., 257
Borow, Henry, 597
Boskoff, Alvin, 823
Bossard, J. H. S., 508
Boulding, Elise, 538
Boulding, Kenneth, 642, 644, 768, 771
Bowers, Raymond, 771
Bowman, Claude C., 777
Brace, Charles, 669
Bradley, Harold, 158
Brancale, Ralph A., 128
Brandt, Paul, 352
Brazer, Harvey, 626
Bredemeier, Harry C., 781
Bremner, Robert H., 637, 641, 643, 669
Brennan, Donald G., 740
Briar, Scott, 121
Brill, Norman Q., 38
Brinton, Crane, 483
Britt, S., 432
Bronner, Augusta F., 102
Broom, Leonard, 98, 179, 556, 563, 672, 800
Brown, Harrison, 767
Browne, Lewis, 432
Bruce, Maurice, 658, 659, 664
Buchalla, Carl, 770
Buchanan, Norman S., 382
Bukharin, Nikolai, 640
Bull, Bradley, 480
Bullard, James W., 525
Bunzel, Bessie, 291, 294, 303, 304, 310, 319
Burgess, Ernest W., 520, 526
Burgess, M. Elaine, 630, 644
Burke, Edmund, 663
Burma, John H., 477
Burton, John, 730
Butler, Kenneth B., 676, 679
Butler, Samuel, 15
Butow, Robert J. C., 727

Cable, George W., 450
Caldwell, M. G., 156, 157
Calhoun, John B., 344
Calverton, V. F., 438
Campanis, Paul, 553, 579
Cannon, Walter B., 817

Cantril, Hadley, 507
Caplan, Gerald, 81, 553
Caplan, N. S., 134
Caplow, Theodore, 554
Capone, Al, 364
Cardozo, Benjamin, 816
Carpenter, C. R., 357
Carpenter, John A., 243, 258
Carr-Saunders, A. M., 376, 402
Cartwright, Desmond S., 117, 189
Case, Herman, 576
Casey, James, 95
Casey, M. Claire, 567
Casriel, Daniel, 232
Catapusan, N. T., 478
Caudill, Harry, 604
Caudill, William, 43
Cavan, Ruth S., 119, 283, 295, 311, 520, 539
Cayton, Horace R., 118
Cépède, Michel, 395
Chamberlain, Neal W., 604
Chancellor, Loren E., 515
Chein, Isadore, 196, 207, 209, 210, 214, 215, 221
Chernov, Victor, 640, 641
Chilton, Roland J., 94
Chinoy, Ely, 585
Christensen, Harold T., 327, 350, 486, 492
Christie, Richard, 432
Clague, Ewan, 605, 611
Clark, F. Le Gros, 395
Clark, Grenville, 742
Clark, Kenneth B., 464, 786-87, 791, 818
Claude, Inis L., Jr., 734
Clausen, John A., 26-83, 193-235
Clemmer, Donald, 344, 675
Clinard, Marshall B., 98, 182, 800, 810
Cloward, Richard A., 115, 118, 181
Coale, Ansley J., 382
Coe, T., 256
Cohen, Albert K., 84-135, 171, 311, 556, 672, 800, 806
Cohen, Jerome, 648, 654
Cohen, Wilbur, 626
Cohn, Norman, 4
Colcord, J. C., 511, 512
Cole, Jonathan O., 79
Coleman, James S., 255, 335, 575-76, 589, 670-722
Collins, Orville, 584, 588
Connor, R., 261
Cooley, Charles H., 18
Cory, Donald Webster, 345
Coser, Lewis, 655-56, 715, 795, 812
Coser, Rose L., 807, 812
Cottrell, Leonard S., Jr., 98, 556, 563, 672, 800
Cousins, Sheila, 361
Cox, Oliver C., 427
Crawford, Paul L., 133

Cressey, Donald R., 110, 136-92, 232
Cromwell, Oliver, 809
Croog, Sidney G., 486
Crutchfield, R. S., 803
Cuber, John F., 800
Cumming, Elaine, 52
Cumming, John, 52, 66
Cutright, Phillips, 765
Cutter, Henry S. G., 95

Dahlberg, Gunnar, 150
Dahlgren, Karl Gustav, 284
Dai, Bingham, 207-08, 209, 210
Dalton, Melville, 584, 588
Darley, J. G., 821
David, Martin, 626
Davis, F. James, 792
Davis, James A., 542
Davis, Kingsley, 55, 322-72, 374-408, 484, 655, 789, 813
Day, Juliana, 542
DeMarche, David, 57
Demosthenes, 352-53
Dentler, Robert, 690, 765
Depres, A., 362
De Quincey, Thomas, 201
Descartes, 7
De Sévigné, Madame, 8-9
Deutsch, Albert, 53-54
Deutsch, Martin P., 648
Devereux, George, 290, 292
DeVore, Irven, 357
Dewey, John, 18
Dicey, A. V., 816
Dickens, Charles, 15
Diebold, John, 613
Dietrich, David C., 113
Di Nicola, "Motzie," 364
Diskind, Meyer H., 230
Disraeli, Benjamin, 7
Dix, Dorothea Lynde, 53
Dobriner, William, 393
Dohrenwend, Bruce P., 314
Dollard, John, 427, 431
Donovan, James B., 761
Dore, Ronald P., 506, 677, 682
Douglass, E. M., 244, 246
Douvan, Elizabeth, 570
Dowling, George, 641
Doyle, Bertram, 443
Drahms, August, 167-68
Drake, St. Clair, 118
Dreiser, Theodore, 15
Drummond, Isabel, 350
Dubin, Robert, 587, 588, 592, 806
Dublin, Louis I., 291, 294, 303, 304, 310, 319
Dubois, Abbé J. A., 354
Du Bois, W. E. B., 450
Dubos, René, 58
Dugdale, Richard, 162
Dumpson, James R., 133

Duncan, Otis Dudley, 560, 571, 697, 699, 701, 706
Dunham, H. Warren, 43, 62
Durkheim, Émile, 5, 13, 17, 18, 22, 185, 186, 283, 284-85, 286, 287, 294, 305, 308, 310, 313, 314, 316-17, 318, 680
Duvall, Henrietta J., 230

Eason, Warren W., 397
Eaton, Joseph W., 61, 478
Efron, V., 248
Eisenhower, Dwight D., 765
Eisenstadt, S. N., 800
Eldridge, William B., 226
Elias, Albert, 131
Eliot, Thomas D., 327, 512, 535
Elkins, Stanley, 665
Ellington, John R., 125
Elliott, Mabel A., 311, 800
Ellis, A. B., 354
Ellis, Havelock, 344, 355, 360, 362
Ellis, Howard S., 382
Ellison, Ralph, 15
Elwin, Verrier, 293
Emmet, Dorothy, 822
Empey, La Mar T., 135
Engel, Louis, 718
Engels, Friedrich, 581
England, L. R., 351
Epstein, Lenore, 653
Erikson, Kai T., 806, 808
Ernst, Robert, 650, 664, 665
Etzioni, Amitai, 723-73
Etzioni, Eva, 745
Eubank, E. E., 511
Eversley, D. E. C., 395
Ezvin, Frank R., 763

Farber, Bernard, 544, 545
Farber, S. M., 194
Farberow, Norman L., 289
Faris, Robert E. L., 62, 311, 323, 629, 770
Farrell, James, 15
Fava, Sylvia Fleis, 351
Fedder, Edwin H., 773
Fein, Rashi, 57
Feis, Herbert, 727
Feld, Bernard T., 740
Feld, Sheila, 57, 602, 792
Felix, R. H., 38
Fenton, William N., 290
Ferri, E., 167
Finestone, Harold, 212, 218-19
Finkelstein, Lawrence S., 751
Firth, Raymond, 396, 817
Flexner, Abraham, 359
Floro, George K., 687
Flynn, Frank T., 87, 99, 119
Ford, Clellan S., 338, 344
Ford, Henry, 430
Ford, John C., S.J., 277

Form, William H., 554, 567, 574, 589, 598, 601
Forsyth, W. D., 401
Fortune, R. F., 290
Fox, B. H., 257, 259
Fox, J. H., 257, 259
Fox, Vernon, 148, 152
Foy, Felician A., 416
Frank, Jerome D., 750
Franke, Walter H., 605, 606, 616
Franklin, John Hope, 439
Frazier, E. Franklin, 512, 514
Freed, Fred, 727
Freeman, Howard E., 80, 542
Frenay, Adolph, 294, 300, 308
Frenkel-Brunswik, Else, 432
Freud, Sigmund, 71, 72, 432, 559
Friedenburg, Edgar Z., 576
Friedmann, Eugene A., 569, 582
Friedmann, Georges, 556, 586
Friedrich, Carl J., 432
Fritz, Charles, 784
Fromm, Erich, 71, 72, 283, 594, 771
Fuller, Richard C., 138, 784, 788

Galbraith, John K., 609
Gallaway, Lowell, 619
Galsworthy, John, 15
Gandhi, Mahatma, 447
Gardner, Elmer A., 78
Gargas, S., 287, 294, 302, 305
Garrity, Donald L., 181
Gaskell, Mrs., 15
Geer, Blanche, 600
Geertz, Hildred S., 95, 330
Geismar, L. L., 480
George, W. L., 361
Gerard, Ralph W., 79
Gerth, H. H., 797
Gerver, Israel, 800, 813
Ghurye, G. S., 446
Gibbons, Don C., 94, 181
Gibbs, Jack P., 281-321
Gille, H., 398
Gillin, John L., 168
Gilmore, Harlan W., 569
Gilpin, Robert, 769
Ginzberg, Eli, 562, 576, 607
Giovannitti, Len, 727
Gladwin, Thomas, 39, 638
Glasser, Paul H., 543
Glazer, Nathan, 413, 662
Glenn, Norval D., 420
Glick, Paul C., 512, 518
Glueck, Bernard, 163
Glueck, Eleanor T., 100-01, 162, 549
Glueck, Sheldon, 100-01, 128, 129, 171, 549
Goddard, Henry H., 165
Goffman, Erving, 43, 655
Gold, Martin, 117
Goldberg, Leonard, 237
Goldhamer, Herbert, 60

Goldsen, Joseph M., 772
Goldstein, Sidney, 585
Goldwater, Barry, 453
Gomberg, William, 573, 583, 621, 650, 651
Goode, William J., 479-552, 629
Goodman, Paul, 255, 557
Gordon, C. W., 269
Gordon, Milton M., 413
Gordon, Robert A., 117
Gorer, Geoffrey, 290, 292
Goring, Charles, 161
Gottlieb, David, 710
Gould, Raymond, 630
Gouldner, Alvin W., 592, 719, 790
Grace, H. A., 821
Graeber, I., 432
Gray, Sir Edward, 730
Greeley, Andrew, 95
Green, Philip, 731
Green, Thomas, 617
Greenberg, Leon, 237, 238, 239
Greer, Scott, 785, 822
Griffith, J. A. G., 401
Griscom, John, 637
Griswold, Manzer J., 94
Gross, Llewellyn, 790
Gross, Neal, 821
Grosser, George, 107
Guest, Robert H., 587
Gurin, Gerald, 57, 602, 792

Haberman, P., 274
Hacker, E., 149
Hadley, Arthur T., 737
Haenszel, William, 199
Hagg, Harvey B., 241
Haggard, H. W., 244
Haggstrom, Warren C., 654
Hajda, Jan, 670
Hakeem, Michael, 102, 164
Halbwachs, Maurice, 294, 308
Haldane, Charlotte, 162
Hall, Jerome, 782, 816
Hall, Oswald, 598
Halperin, Morton H., 736
Halsey, Margaret, 432
Handlin, Mary, 430
Handlin, Oscar, 430, 477, 645, 646
Hansen, Carl F., 471
Hansen, Marcus Lee, 659
Harberger, Arnold C., 382
Harding, T. Swann, 348
Harley, Robert, 643-44
Harper, Robert A., 800
Harrington, Alan, 595
Harrington, Michael, 604-05, 638
Harris, Chauncy D., 697, 699
Harris, Sara, 348, 364
Harrison, Ira E., 573
Harrison, P. M., 759
Hartley, Eugene, 430
Hartung, Frank E., 169

Haskins, Caryl P., 821
Hathaway, S. R., 167
Hatt, Paul K., 697
Hauser, Philip M., 560, 672, 703
Havighurst, Robert J., 569, 573, 582
Haydon, A. Eustace, 797
Hayner, Norman S., 154, 158
Healy, William, 102, 163, 169
Heider, Fritz, 793
Henderson, Charles R., 167
Henkin, Louis, 737
Henry, Andrew F., 315-16
Henry, William, 599
Hertz, Friedrich O., 429
Herzog, Elizabeth, 490
Hewitt, Lester E., 89
Hill, Reuben, 326, 407, 512, 519, 527, 535, 538, 540
Hillman, Arthur, 327
Hillman, Karen G., 508
Himelhoch, Jerome, 95, 350-51
Himmelfarb, Gertrude, 7
Hindus, Maurice, 362
Hira Lal, Rai Bahadur, 291
Hirsch, Stanley I., 542
Hitler, Adolf, 446
Hobsbaum, E. J., 649
Hodges, Harold M., Jr., 118
Hoffman, Frederick L., 294, 302
Hoffman, Lois W., 66
Hoffman, Martin, 66
Hogarth, William, 5
Hollingshead, A. B., 62-68, 266, 573, 706
Holmes, Oliver Wendell, 816
Homans, George C., 592, 752, 803
Hooks, Walter, 542
Hooton, Earnest A., 99, 162
Hoover, Edgar M., 382
Hoover, Herbert, 460
Horney, Karen, 71, 72
Horowitz, E. L., 435
Horowitz, Irving Louis, 764
Horsfall, A. B., 821
Horwitz, Julius, 657
Hostetler, John A., 414
Hovland, C. I., 435
Howard, Kenneth I., 95
Howton, F. William, 800
Hudson, G. F., 755
Hughes, Charles, 290
Hughes, Everett C., 563, 577, 600, 686
Humphrey, Norman D., 462
Hunter, Robert, 642-43
Hurlbud, David, 716
Hutton, John H., 446

Ibsen, Henrik, 15
Inkeles, Alex, 98
Isaac, Julius, 401
Isaacs, Harold R., 446
Isbell, Harris, 197

Issawi, Charles, 384
Iverson, Robert, 542

Jacks, Irving, 61
Jackson, Charles, 15
Jackson, Dan, 364
Jackson, Don, 67
Jackson, Joan K., 261, 274, 541
Jackson, John A., 662
Jacobson, Paul H., 494, 502, 503, 512, 513, 522, 546
Jaffe, Abraham J., 560
Jahoda, Marie, 57, 432, 606, 689
James, William, 17
Janis, I. L., 765
Janowitz, Morris, 415
Jefferson, Thomas, 440
Jellinek, E. M., 243, 244, 248, 259, 267
Jellinek, Georg, 797-98
Jenkins, Richard L., 89
Jenne, W. C., 545
Johnson, Charles S., 455
Johnson, Guy B., 151
Johnson, Harry M., 801
Johnson, Lyndon, 453
Johnston, Norman, 97
Joly, Henri, 155
Jones, Maxwell, 80
Jones, Wyatt, 553

Kahl, Joseph A., 572-73, 648
Kahn, Herman, 729, 743, 750, 762, 763
Kahn, Robert L., 459, 588, 597
Kalant, Harold, 262-63
Kallmann, Franz, 67
Kanin, Eugene, 335
Kaplan, David L., 567
Kaplan, Morton, 733, 753
Kaplan, Norman, 770
Kaplan, Oscar J., 69
Kardiner, Abram, 438
Kassebaum, Gene G., 340, 343-44
Katz, Fred E., 601
Kecskemeti, Paul, 727
Keller, Francis A., 167, 168
Keller, Mark, 238, 248, 259, 260
Kelly, J. I., 167
Kelman, Herbert C., 730
Kempler, Walter, 542
Kendall, Patricia L., 577
Kenkel, William F., 800
Kennedy, John F., 204, 227, 453, 469, 726
Kennedy, Robert F., 364
Kephart, William M., 152, 492, 511, 512, 513, 515
Keynes, Maynard, 789
Keyserling, Leon, 610, 617
Kiefer, Otto, 338
King, Rufus, 200, 203
Kingsley, Charles, 15

Mannheim, Karl, 797
March, James G., 820
Marden, C. F., 250, 251
Maritain, Jacques, 432
Marquand, John P., 572
Marshall, Andrew, 60
Marshall, Harvey, 117
Martin, C. E., 158
Martin, W. E., 821
Martin, Walter T., 316-17
Martineau, Harriet, 642
Marx, Karl, 427, 581, 791, 811, 818
Masland, Richard, 39
Maslow, Abraham, 557
Mattick, H. W., 134
Matza, David, 87, 91, 113, 619-69
Maurer, David W., 569
Maxwell, Milton A., 270
May, Edgar, 632
May, Geoffrey, 349
Mayer, Kurt B., 585
Mead, Margaret, 557, 580, 771
Melman, Seymour, 726, 746, 751
Menninger, Karl A., 283, 289
Merei, F., 803
Merrill, Francis E., 311, 800
Merton, Robert K., 4, 16-17, 98, 99,
    112-13, 127, 173, 179-80, 556, 563,
    577, 622, 670, 672, 689, 707, 750,
    775-823
Messinger, Sheldon L., 542
Michael, Donald M., 610
Michael, J., 167
Michael, Stanley T., 65
Midelfort, Christian F., 542
Miles, Harold C., 78
Miller, Delbert C., 554, 567, 574, 589,
    597
Miller, Henry, 646
Miller, Herman P., 565, 621, 622, 623,
    624-25
Miller, S. M., 118, 573, 621, 643, 790
Miller, Walter B., 95, 116, 126, 620,
    649
Millis, Walter, 730
Mills, C. Wright, 477, 581, 594-95, 655,
    765, 767, 771, 797
Mills, Enid, 51
Milton, John, 493
Miner, John Rice, 291, 298
Mitchell, Howard E., 525
Mitler, Herman P., 199
Moberg, David O., 148
Monachesi, Elio D., 167
Monahan, Thomas P., 97, 511, 512,
    513, 515
Moore, Wilbert E., 382, 813
Morgan, James, 626
Morgan, Theodore, 384, 611
Morgenthau, Hans J., 742
Morris, Richard T., 812
Morse, Chandler, 801
Morse, Nancy C., 569, 582-83

Morselli, Henry, 296, 303
Moses, Earl R., 153
Mowrer, Ernest R., 162, 283, 311, 511
Moynihan, Daniel P., 413, 662
Mudd, Emily H., 525
Mugge, Robert, 627, 630, 631, 632
Mukerjee, Radhakamal, 446
Mulford, Harold A., 250, 251, 252, 276
Mullen, Joseph P., 656
Munsey, Frank, 14
Murchison, Carl, 166
Murdock, George P., 328, 338, 484,
    495
Murphy, John P., 399
Murray, Henry A., 521
Murtagh, John M., 348, 364
Myerhoff, Barbara G., 134
Myers, Jerome K., 45, 541
Myers, Richard R., 784, 788
Myers, Robert, 50
Myrdal, Alva, 350
Myrdal, Gunnar, 418, 441, 452, 790

Nagel, Ernest, 818
Nehru, J., 405, 809
Neumann, Franz L., 433
Nevinson, John, 809
Newcomb, Theodore M., 793
Newman, H. H., 162
Newman, Stanley L., 763
Nimkoff, Myer F., 549
Nisbet, Robert A., 1-24
Nishimoto, Richard S., 421
Nogee, Joseph L., 741
Noonan, John T., Jr., 399
Norbeck, Edward, 817
Nosow, Sigmund, 554, 574, 598, 601
Nunnally, Jum C., 50
Nye, F. Ivan, 89, 95, 119

O'Connor, Richard, 645
O'Dowd, Donald B., 573
O'Gorman, Hubert J., 813, 815
Ohlin, Lloyd E., 115, 118, 181
Olerio, Alfred, 553
Olson, V. J., 95
Orbach, Harold, 653
Orear, Jay, 725
Orshansky, Mollie, 625
Orwell, George, 594-95
Osgood, Charles E., 292, 746, 750, 771
Ovsienko, V. E., 400
Owen, Wilfred, 393

Padilla, Elena, 477
Palmer, Gladys, 574
Pannor, Harry, 550
Pareto, Vilfredo, 818
Park, Robert Ezra, 670, 752
Parmalee, Maurice F., 168
Parsons, Phillip A., 168
Parsons, Talcott, 568, 745, 801, 803,
    810

Pasha, Kemal, 425
Pearl, Arthur, 648, 654
Pellens, Mildred, 200, 201
Peluso, Emil, 118
Penzer, N. M., 291
Pericles, 352, 366
Pescor, Michael J., 206, 207, 216, 219
Petegorsky, David W., 433
Petersen, William, 401
Peterson, Ruth C., 430
Peterson, Warren, 582
Pfautz, Harold W., 98
Philipson, Morris, 610, 613
Phillips, Arthur, 506
Phillips, David Graham, 15
Piddington, R. A., 393
Piel, Gerard, 616
Piliavin, Irving, 121
Pilz, Wolfgang, 770
Pinel, Philippe, 53, 79
Pirie, N. W., 395
Pittman, David J., 244, 256, 269, 270, 272, 277
Plant, James S., 68
Plato, 340, 776
Ploscowe, Morris, 336
Polanyi, Karl, 642, 659, 661
Pollak, Otto, 149
Pomeroy, W. B., 158
Porterfield, Austin L., 296, 297, 312, 313
Potter, George, 664, 665
Pound, Roscoe, 816
Powdermaker, Hortense, 675
Powell, Elwin H., 295, 303, 304
Power, Thomas S., 727
Powers, Edwin, 129
Powles, William E., 651, 667-68
Pray, Kenneth L. M., 128
Price, Daniel, 630, 644
Puntil, Joseph, 118
Purcell, Theodore V., S.J., 583

Raab, Earl, 800
Rabow, Jerome, 135
Rackow, Felix, 458
Radcliffe-Brown, A. R., 817
Radinowicz, L., 149
Ranulf, Svend, 184
Raper, Arthur F., 455
Rapoport, Robert N., 80
Rasmussen, Knud, 396
Raushenbusch, Winifred, 703
Ray, Marsh, 231
Reader, George G., 577
Real, James, 767
Reckless, Walter C., 93, 157, 170, 364
Redfield, Robert, 357
Redl, Fritz, 131
Redlich, F. C., 62-63, 266
Reid, Donald D., 58, 65-66
Reid, Ira De A., 455
Reinemann, John O., 129

Reiss, Albert J., Jr., 346, 697, 699, 701, 706
Reiss, Ira L., 328, 342
Renborg, Bertil, 224
Reston, James, 731
Reuther, Walter, 786
Reynolds, Lloyd G., 573-74
Rice, Roger E., 134
Richards, Dickinson W., 817
Richardson, Lewis F., 730
Riecken, H. W., 803
Riesman, David, 23, 553-618, 705, 771
Riessman, Frank, 643-44, 648, 654
Riewald, Paul, 184
Riis, Jacob A., 637
Riley, J. W., Jr., 250, 251
Ritchie, O. W., 270
Rivera, Ramon, 117
Rjabichko, Vasil, 399
Rober, E. C., 575
Roberts, Bertram H., 541
Robinson, Reginald, 57
Robinson, William S., 172
Roe, Anne, 275
Roemer, Ruth, 42
Rogoff, Natalie, 576
Rohrer, John H., 600
Roosevelt, Franklin D., 457
Roosevelt, James, 750
Roosevelt, Theodore, 201-02, 459
Roper, Elmo, 465
Rorty, James, 703
Rosberg, Judy, 151
Rose, Arnold M., 311, 409-78
Rosecrance, Richard N., 733
Rosenberg, Bernard, 800
Rosenberg, Morris, 572
Rosenblatt, Aaron, 812
Rosenthal, David, 67
Ross, Alan, 97
Ross, Arthur, 588, 592
Ross, Ralph, 790
Rossi, Peter, 670, 690
Rothchild, David, 69
Roucek, Joseph S., 99, 102
Roueché, Berton, 241
Roy, Donald, 581, 584, 588
Rubington, E., 261
Rudwick, Elliott M., 462
Rusch, George, 184
Russell, Sir John, 395
Russell, R. V., 291
Ryabushkin, T. V., 394
Ryan, Margaret W., 471
Ryckoff, Irving M., 542

Sabagh, Georges, 515
Sainsbury, Peter, 283, 289, 312, 314, 320
Salisbury, Harrison E., 363, 700, 701
Sampson, Harold, 542
Samuel, Maurice, 432
Sarason, Seymour, 39

Sarkar, N. K., 383
Sarri, Rosemary C., 573
Saunders, Dero A., 598
Sauvy, Alfred, 400, 403
Savitz, Leonard, 97
Schachter, Joseph, 490
Schaffer, Leslie, 45
Scheff, Thomas, 73
Schein, Edgar H., 581
Schild, Sylvia, 550
Schmalhausen, Samuel D., 483
Schmid, Calvin F., 283, 301, 312
Schroeder, Clarence W., 508
Schroeder, W. Widwick, 303
Schuessler, Karl, 100, 110, 166-67
Schur, Edwin M., 223, 234, 786
Schwartz, Charlotte, 46, 79
Schwartz, Morris S., 43, 46, 79, 188
Scott, Jerome, 592
Scott, John Findley, 89
Scripps, E. H., 14
Sears, R. R., 435
Seashore, Stanley, 587
Seeley, John R., 259, 260, 277
Seeman, Melvin, 582
Seidman, Joel, 588, 589
Sellin, Thorsten, 90, 111, 143, 148, 151, 173, 175-77
Selznick, Gertrude Jaeger, 800
Selznick, Philip, 179, 693
Sewell, William H., 771
Shah, Jelal M., 338
Shapiro, Samuel, 767
Shaw, Clifford, 96, 106, 111, 131
Shaw, George Bernard, 15
Sheldon, William H., 100, 162
Shepherd, E. A., 250
Sherif, Muzafer, 600
Sherivin, Robert V., 336
Shils, E. A., 797, 801
Shimkin, Michael B., 199
Shister, Joseph, 573-74
Shneidman, Edwin S., 289
Short, James F., Jr., 84-135, 315-16
Shostak, Arthur B., 573, 583, 621, 650, 651
Shulman, Harry M., 100
Sidel, Victor W., 763
Silberman, Charles E., 610, 656
Sills, David L., 688
Simmel, Georg, 22, 695-96, 710, 715, 753
Simmons, Ozzie C., 80, 542
Simon, Herbert A., 820
Simpson, Alice, 97
Simpson, George, 185, 283, 286, 287, 305, 318
Sinclair, Upton, 14, 15
Skolnick, Jerome, 124
Slade, Caroline, 361
Sletto, R. F., 151
Smelser, Neil J., 660

Smigel, Erwin O., 599
Smith, Adam, 580, 675
Smith, Lillian, 432
Smuts, Jan C., 236
Smuts, Robert W., 560
Snow, C. P., 729, 794
Snyder, Charles R., 244, 265, 266, 270, 272, 276, 277
Socrates, 352
Sohn, Louis, 742
Sonnedecker, Glenn, 200
Sorensen, Theodore C., 726, 728
Sorokin, Pitirim A., 185, 301, 637, 794, 812
Sorrentino, Anthony, 132
Spanier, John W., 741
Spaulding, John A., 283, 305
Spengler, Joseph J., 382
Spiegel, John P., 67
Spier, 292
Spinley, B. M., 220
Spinrad, William, 588
Srole, Leo, 63, 667
Stanton, Alfred H., 43, 188
Stanton, Frank, 707
Star, Shirley A., 49
Staub, H., 184
Steele, Fred I., 581
Steffens, Lincoln, 14
Steinbeck, John, 15, 556
Steinmetz, S. R., 290
Stene, Edwin K., 687
Stephens, Tom, 646, 647, 648
Sterne, M. W., 256
Sterner, Richard, 418
Stevens, L. B., 577
Stinchcombe, Arthur, 670, 693
Stoecker, Adolph, 446
Stogdill, Ralph M., 821
Stolnitz, George J., 381
Stonier, Tom, 764
Stotland, Ezra, 319, 320
Stott, D. H., 102
Stouffer, Samuel A., 538, 794
Straus, Robert, 236-80
Street, David, 126
Street, James H., 454
Strodtbeck, Fred L., 95, 98, 117, 118
Strong, Donald S., 430
Strong, E. K., Jr., 577
Strunk, Mildred, 507
Stycos, J. Mayone, 326
Sullivan, Harry Stack, 56, 71
Sulloway, Alvah W., 399
Sumner, William G., 798
Sutherland, Edwin H., 140, 145, 156, 166, 168, 173-75, 182, 183, 569
Svalastoga, Kaare, 350
Swados, Harvey, 574
Swift, Pauline, 553
Sykes, Gresham M., 113
Szasz, Thomas, 30

Taeuber, Alma F., 467
Taeuber, Irene B., 405, 497
Taeuber, Karl E., 467
Taft, Donald R., 155, 173, 177-79
Talalay, Paul, 194
Tannenbaum, Arnold S., 588
Tannenbaum, Frank, 88, 106, 122
Tappan, Paul W., 87, 125, 128
Tarbell, Ida, 14
Tarde, Gabriel, 161
Tavuchis, Nicholas, 479
Taylor, Maxwell D., 725
Taylor, W. S., 324
Teeters, Negley K., 91, 129
Teller, Edward, 771
TenBroek, Jacobus, 656
Tennyson, Ray A., 95, 117
Terry, Charles E., 200, 201
Thielens, Wagner, Jr., 576-77
Thomas, Dorothy S., 421
Thomas, John L., 515
Thomas, Mary Margaret, 515
Thomas, William I., 17, 18, 643, 672, 800, 802
Thompson, Warren S., 379
Thompson, William Hale, 363
Thurstone, L. L., 430
Tibbits, Clark, 653
Tietze, Christopher, 333
Timasheff, N. S., 168, 798, 812
Tinbergen, Jan, 760
Tiryakian, Edward A., 776
Toby, Jackson, 151, 781
Tocqueville, Alexis de, 8-10, 586
Tolman, Frank L., 161
Tönnies, Ferdinand, 22, 673, 680, 684
Towne, Robert D., 542
Toynbee, A. J., 4
Trachtenberg, Joshua, 432
Trice, Harrison M., 272
Trotsky, Leon, 809
Trotter, Monroe, 450
Trow, Martin, 589
Trubitt, H. J., 257
Truman, Harry S, 726
Trussell, Ray E., 230
Tufts, Edith, 135
Tulchin, Samuel H., 166
Tumin, Melvin M., 471, 821
Turner, James D., 151
Turner, Ralph H., 282, 573
Turpin, Dick, 809

Vagts, Alfred A., 724
Valien, Bonita, 471
Van Arsdol, Maurice D., Jr., 301
Vance, Rupert B., 455
Van Vechten, C. C., 155
Veblen, Thorstein, 555, 641-42
Venn, Grant, 609
Veroff, Joseph, 57, 602
Vincent, Clark E., 491
Vinter, Robert B., 573

Voegelin, Erich, 429
Vogel, Ezra F., 542
Vogt, William, 396
Voiland, Alice L., 480
Volakakis, Joan, 152
Volkman, Arthur P., 167
Volkman, Rita, 189, 232
Von Andics, Margarethe, 288
Voroff, Joseph, 792

Wade, Andrew L., 182
Wagle, Mildred, 57
Wagner, Richard, 446
Walker, Charles R., 579, 587, 698
Waller, Willard, 519, 527, 535, 538, 791
Wallerstein, J. S., 143
Ward, David A., 340, 343-44
Warner, W. Lloyd, 158, 573, 667
Waskow, Arthur I., 763, 771
Wattenberg, William W., 159
Weaver, Robert C., 457
Webb, Beatrice, 661
Webb, Sidney, 661
Weber, Max, 18, 723, 744, 797
Weeks, Ashley, 131
Weil, Robert J., 61, 478
Weinberg, S. Kirson, 43, 334
Weiss, James M. A., 288, 289, 305
Weiss, Robert S., 553-618
Wells, H. G., 15
Wessel, B. B., 477
West, Patricia S., 689
Westermarck, Edward, 290, 293, 355
Westie, Frank K., 435
Wheelis, Allan, 600
White, Winston, 568
Whitehead, Alfred North, 1, 778
Whyte, William H., 557, 558, 596
Wiers, Paul, 156
Wikler, Abraham, 222
Wilcock, Richard C., 605, 606, 616
Wilcox, Francis O., 758
Wilensky, Harold L., 599, 771
Wilkins, Leslie T., 148
Williams, J. E. Hall, 342
Williams, Jack D., 158
Williams, P. H., 242
Williams, Robin M., Jr., 432, 471, 813
Wilmott, Peter, 675
Wilson, Logan, 813
Wilson, R. H. L., 194
Wilson, Robert N., 71
Wilson, Woodrow, 409
Winch, Robert F., 508, 521
Wineman, David, 131
Wines, Frederick H., 171
Winter, Ella, 362
Wirth, Louis, 672, 797
Wirth, P. H. A., 198
Wirtz, Willard, 610-11
Witmer, Helen L., 129, 135
Wolfenstein, Lincoln, 725

Wolfgang, Marvin, 90, 97
Wood, Arthur Lewis, 154
Wood, Robert C., 338, 393
Woodham-Smith, Cecil, 662, 663
Woodward, C. Vann, 445
Wooten, Barbara, 646
Wright, Carrol D., 168
Wright, Christopher, 769
Wyle, C. J., 143
Wynne, Lyman C., 542

Yablonsky, Lewis, 98, 232
Yang, C. K., 506
Yarrow, Leon, 66
Yarrow, Marian R., 51
Yoke, Helen L., 156
Young, Donald, 410

Young, Kimball, 166
Young, Michael, 675
Young, Pauline V., 155
Young, Whitney, 607

Zald, Mayer, 124
Zeleny, L. D., 165-66
Zetterberg, Hans L., 813
Zilboorg, Gregory, 286, 289
Zimmerman, Carle C., 301, 686
Zimmern, Alfred, 353
Znaniecki, Florian, 17, 185, 643, 672,
    800, 802
Zola, Émile, 15
Zubin, Joseph, 31
Zuckerman, S., 357
Zuta, Jack, 364

Subject Index

Aberrant behavior, 808-11
Abortion, 331, 333
Action for Mental Health, 57
Adolescents
and communities, 704-05; and drinking, 250, 252-56, 275-76; and drug use, 210, 214, 215, 220, 221, 225
AFDC recipients
composition of, 627; as disreputable poor, 629; eligibility of, 633-37; length of assistance for, 632; occupations of fathers among, 631; by residence, 627-28, 633-35, 636-37; status of fathers among, 630; and welfare chiseling, 633
Affluent society, 11
Africa
divorce rate in, 500; illegitimacy in, 485, 487; prostitution in, 354
Age
crime rates by, 146-48; delinquency rates by, 93; and population growth, 384-86; suicide rates by, 298-300; *see also* Old age
Agrarian countries
population growth in, 381-90
Agricultural Adjustment Administration, 456-57
Aid programs, 626-27
Aid to Families with Dependent Children; *see* AFDC recipients
Alaska
homosexuality in, 338
Albania
population growth in, 378
Alcohol
action of on man, 236-44; addiction to, *see* Alcoholism; customs of consumption of, 241-42, 244-52; and the economy, 271-72; and education, 274-76; impact of on family, 273-74; level of in blood, 257-58; physiological effects of, 237-41; psycho-

logical effects of, 242-44; social function of, 2, 241-42; *see also* Drinking
Alcoholics Anonymous, 269-70, 278
Alcoholism, 259-62, 278-80
drinking customs and, 263-64; etiological theories of, 262-67; extent of, 267-68; and the family, 273-74; medical approach to, 277-78; personality factors in, 263; and religion, 264-66; social responses to, 268-71; *see also* Alcohol; Drinking
Algeria
divorce rates in, 482, 497, 498, 499-500
Alienation, 581, 595; *see also* Isolation
Aliens, 421-22
Alternative to War or Surrender, An, 771
Altruistic suicide, 313-14
American Bar Association
narcotics control and, 203, 225
American Dilemma, An, 452
"American" school of criminology, 168
Annulment, 492
Anomic suicide, 313-14
Anomie, 19, 23-24, 706
and crime, 179-81; and delinquency, 112-13; and suicide, 295-96, 313-14
Anti-Semitism, 430, 432-33, 465-67
in Germany, 446
Apache
suicide among, 292
Apartheid, 425
Appalachia
migrants of, 651, 667-68
Area projects
for delinquents, 132-33; for drug users, 205-16
Argentina
illegitimacy in, 487
Arms-control systems, 736-40
Arms race, 729-32, 765-69
Arms reduction, 745-51

Art
as approach to social problems, 15
Australia
crime in, 154; divorce rate in, 498; population growth in, 391-92; suicide in, 297, 299
Austria
suicide in, 282, 297, 299
Authoritarian personality, 432-33, 438
Automation, 609-18
and Negroes, 474

Balance-of-power system, 733-36
Belgium
age structure in, 385; suicide in, 297, 299
Berdaches, 338-39
Biology
and crime, 161-63; and racism, 442
Birth control, 6, 332
Birth rate
and population problem, 397-400
Boston Guardian, 450
Brazil
illegitimacy in, 487; marriage termination in, 494
Brinkmanship strategy, 728-29
Brock Committee, 647, 648
Brown v. *Board of Education*, 470-71
Bulgaria
suicide in, 297, 299
Bureau of Narcotics, 205, 224-25
Bureaucracy, 682

California
drug addiction in, 205, 230; drug control in, 228; suicide in, 298
Canada
and disarmament, 730; mental illness in, 64-65; population growth in, 391-92; suicide in, 297, 299
Caste system
in India, 446-47; opposition to, 449-54; in the United States, 443-45
Catholics
attitudes toward sex among, 328-29; desertion among, 512; and divorce, 514-16; drinking among, 251, 276-77; as minority group, 416, 417, 419; and population problem, 403-04
Causes of World War III, The, 767, 771
Celibacy, 328
CERN, 758
Ceylon
age structure in, 385; death rate in, 380; population growth in, 378, 382-83, 384; suicide in, 297
Chicago
area studies in, 132; community organization in, 690; crime in, 218, 363-64; delinquency in, 91; drug addiction in, 205, 206-08, 209, 218;

gang delinquency in, 117; mental illness in, 62; racial conflict in, 717; riots in, 463-64
Chicago Area Project, 207, 208
Child guidance clinics, 55
Child labor, 385-86
Chile
annulments in, 494; suicide in, 297
Children, 126
of divorce, 546-50; mentally retarded, 543-45; suicide among, 286; *see also* Adolescents
China
divorce rate in, 500, 506; family life in, 493; marriage in, 482, 494, 495; nuclear testing by, 737; widows in, 537, 546
Chinese
discrimination against, 430; as minority group, 416, 417, 418
Chukchee
suicide among, 293
Citizens Councils, Inc., 472-73
Civil rights legislation, 451, 453
Civil rights movement, 10
Class; *see* Social class
Cleveland
delinquency in, 91
Clinic services
for alcoholics, 269; for the mentally ill, 44-46
Colombia
suicide in, 297
Coming Up For Air, 594-95
Committee for Sane Nuclear Policy, 771
Communist subversion, 721-22
Communities
and adolescents, 704-05; age-specialized, 703; alcoholism clinics in, 269; common problems in, 675-77; conflict in, 685, 715-22, 800; conflicting goals in, 677-79; creation of, 673-94; crime rates by, 155-57; definition of, 671-72; disintegration of, 695-715; drug addiction in, 210-12, 230, 231-32; and government policies, 712-15; homosexuality in, 346; identification with others in, 680-81, 683-85; identity with, 687-88; industrial, 701-02; leisure, 702-03; and locality specialization, 695-709, 719; mental patients returned to, 79, 80; norms of, 106, 710-11; organization of, 688-93, 695; residential, 698-701; self-interest in, 681; social processes of, 672-94, 722; *see also* Subcommunities; World community
Compassion, 8
social limit of, 9
Confessions of an English Opium-Eater, 201

Conflict
community, 685, 715-22, 800; of
conduct norms, 176-77; ideological,
426-28; of institutions, 19-20; in
marriage, 526-29, 532-34; Marxist
views on, 427; of multiple statuses,
803; personal, 437
Conflict and Defense, 771
Conformity, 596-97
Connecticut
drinking and driving in, 257, 273;
mental illness in, 62-63; organized
crime in, 364
Correctional agents
nonofficial, 122-23; recruitment of,
123
Correctional institutions
for delinquents, 124-25; *see also*
Prisons
Correctional system, 119-26
Costa Rica
age structure in, 385; suicide in, 297,
299
Courtship
in Ireland, 331; in Norway, 328;
patterns of, 488; for second marriage, 545-48; sex and, 326
Crime
biological approach to, 161-63; and
community organization, 676; definition of, 139-41; drug addiction and,
202-03, 217-19; functional necessity
of, 5; multiple-factor approach to,
169-72; psychiatric approach to, 163-
65; psychometric approach to, 165-
67; social prevention of, 14; sociological approach to, 167-69; statistics of, 141-45; white-collar, 145
Crime rates
by age, 146-48; measurement of,
141-45; by nativity, 153-55; by race,
151-53; by sex, 148-51; by size of
community, 155-57; by social class,
157-59
Criminal law, 137
Criminality, 188-89
and drug addiction, 202-03, 217-19;
sociological theories of, 172-82
Criminology, 160-72
Culture
alcoholism rate and, 264-67; as base
for social problems, 2-4; conflict theory of, 176-81; drug use and, 198-
99, 210-12
Cyprus
Greek minority on, 426
Czechoslovakia
suicide in, 297

Dangerous Drugs Act, 233
Death
adjustment of family to, 534-38

Death rate
decline of, 379
Delinquency
control techniques for, 126-34; data
of, 89-97; definition of, 88; ecological differences in, 96-97; motivation
of, 106-10; as a social role, 87-88;
sociology of, 110-19; and subcultures, 111-19; trends in, 91-93
Delinquency rates
by age, 93; by race, 94-95; and
rural-urban differences, 96; by sex,
93-94; by social class, 95
Delinquency theories, 97-105
psychoanalytic, 101-02; psychobio-
logical, 99-101; psychodynamic, 102-
05
Denmark
age structure in, 385; illegitimacy in,
486; legalized abortion in, 331, 333;
mental disorders in, 66; suicide in,
297, 299
Depersonalization, 22
Depression, the, 555
divorce during, 513; end of, 766; and
family disorganization, 539-40; societal maladjustment in, 55-56; unemployment during, 605
Desegregation, 469-74, 714-15
Desertion
from family, 480, 482, 511-13
Detroit
automation in, 613; crime in, 158-59
Deva-dasis, 354
Deviant behavior, 805-17
character of, 806-07; measurement
of, 781-82; and social norms, 812-
13; types of, 808-11
Differential association, 173-75
Disarmament, 741-45
economics of, 765-69; need for, 729-
32; Russia's attitude toward, 743-44;
by scientists, 769-72; transition strategy of, 745-51
Discrimination, 419-23, 425, 443-45
causes of, 426-38
Diseases, mental; *see* Mental disorders
Disorganization, social, 18-19, 82-83,
282-83, 311-12, 800-04; *see also*
Family disorganization
Displaced Persons Act, 461
Disreputable poverty; *see* Poor, disreputable
Divorce, 479-80, 491-93
adjustment to, 545-48; and bereavement, 535-38; case descriptions of,
530-32; causes of, 511-13, 524; children affected by, 548-50; conflict
patterns leading to, 526-29; economic factors in, 507-08, 510-11;
education and, 508-09; and family
system, 493-95; grounds for, 522-32;
income and, 510; occupation and,

Italy
crime in, 154; illegitimacy in, 485; marriage termination in, 494; suicide in, 297, 299

Jamaica
illegitimacy in, 487

Japan
abortion in, 333; bombing of, 724, 727, 765; divorce rates in, 482, 497, 498, 499, 500; illegitimacy in, 485; marriage in, 494, 495; neighbor-obligations in, 682; population control in, 405; prostitution in, 353, 365; suicide in, 281, 291, 297, 299, 300, 309

Japanese
discrimination against, 429, 459-61, 464-65; as minority group, 416, 417, 418

Java
sexual attitudes in, 330

Jews
discrimination against, see Anti-Semitism; and divorce, 514-16; drinking among, 251, 264, 265, 266, 267, 276; as minority group, 414-15, 416, 417, 419; suicide among, 304, 305

Job enlargement, 579

Jobs; see Occupations

Jogoku, 353

Joint Commission on Mental Health and Illness, 57

Jordan
suicide in, 297

Joro, 353

Journalism
as approach to social problems, 14-15

Jukes, The, 162

Justice
in the United States, 9-10

Juvenile court, 84-87, 90

Juvenile delinquency; see Delinquency

Kansas
use of alcohol in, 250

Keep Your Powder Dry, 771

Kentucky
use of alcohol in, 254

Knowledge
applied and theoretical, 775-79

Ku Klux Klan, 453

Kwakiutl
suicide among, 292, 293

Labor unions, 588-94

Latin Americans
as minority group, 416, 417, 418, 424

Law
as approach to social problems, 13-14; criminal, 137; drug use and, 201-04, 224-28; enforcement, 143-44; and minority groups, 420-21, 459-64; and prostitution, 350, 358, 369-70; and suicide, 283

League of Nations
and narcotics control, 224

Learned behavior, 110, 188-89

Lebanon
population growth in, 378

Leisure
creative use of, 579-80

Leisure class
and poverty, 641-42

Lesbianism, 340, 341, 343-44

Lexington Public Health Service Hospital, 206-08, 216, 219, 229, 230

Locality specialization, 695-709, 719

Lombrosian theory, 99, 161-63, 167

London
bombing of, 763; suicide in, 312, 320

Los Angeles
crime in, 155; riots in, 462-64

Louisiana
drinking in, 254

Lumpenproletariat, 640-41

Luxembourg
suicide in, 297, 299

Marihuana Tax Act, 213

Marital counseling, 550-52

Marriage
characteristics of success in, 516-22; complaints in, 524; disorganization of, see Family disorganization; sex before, 328, 329; sex in, 325-27, 329; "sexual bargain" in, 349-52; status of in United States, 492; terminated by death, 535-38; terminated by divorce, see Divorce; see also Family; Remarriage

Marxist views
on prostitution, 355; on population, 393-94; on group conflicts, 427

Mass communication, 709-11

Mass community, 719-22

Mass society, 433-38

Massachusetts
mental illness in, 60-61

Mauritius
age structure in, 385

May Man Prevail?, 771

Mennonites
as minority group, 416

Mental deficiency, 39-40

Mental disorders
causation of, 57-58; classification of, 30-32; effect of on family, 27-29, 51-52, 540-45; etiology of, 31-32, 57-58; hospitalization for, see Mental hospitals; isolation and, 52, 53,

67; of old age, 36-37, 69-70; prevention of, 81-82; reforms in treatment of, 53-57; social class and, 60-66; social role of, 72-73; society's views of, 49-53; stigma of, 52-53; in war, 54-55, 56, 65-66; see also Neuroses; Psychoses; Psychosomatic disorders; Schizophrenia
Mental Disorders in Urban Areas, 62
Mental health programs
national, 56-57; state, 40
Mental Health Study Act, 57
Mental hospitals, 30
admissions, 32, 33, 74-81; commitment to, 42, 51-52; development of, 73; discharges, 74-81; outpatient services offered by, 44-46, 79; resident population of, 33, 34; in United States, 41-44
Mental hygiene movement, 54-57
Mental illness; see Mental disorders
Mexicans
discrimination against, 460-61; as minority group, 416, 417, 418; and violence, 462-63
Mexico
illegitimacy in, 487; minority problem in, 424; population growth in, 378; sexual freedom in, 328; suicide in, 297
Michigan
drug control in, 226-27; use of alcohol in, 250
Middle class
values of, 113-14; see also Social class
Midtown Manhattan study, 63-64
Migration
of Negroes, 451; and population problem, 400-02
Mind That Found Itself, A, 53
Minority groups
characteristics of, 411-15; distribution of, 417, 418; history of, 409-11; and politics, 464-65; size of, 415-17
Mississippi
Negro divorce rate in, 513; prohibition in, 247
Mobility, social, 20-22, 570, 571
Mobilization for Youth, 135
Mohave
suicide among, 292
Monogenesis, 442
Montana
mental illness in, 61
Moral consciousness, 5-6
Mores, 137
Morocco
sexual attitudes in, 355
Moslems
divorce among, 482, 497, 498, 499-500; illegitimacy among, 485; and relations with Hindus, 424

Motivation, 106-10
Multiple-factor approach
and crime, 169-72

NAACP, 450
Narcotic Drug Control Act, 225
Narcotics; see Drug addiction; Drugs
National Committee for Mental Hygiene, 54
National Desertion Bureau, 512
National Institute of Mental Health, 56
National Labor Relations Board, 593
National Mental Health Act, 56
National Safety Council, 257-58
NATO, 759
Negroes
and automation, 474; and caste system, 443-45; changing position of in United States, 10; courtship structure of in South, 488; crime rate of, 151-53; discrimination against, 421-23, 457-59, 465, 467-74, 591; divorce among, 509-11, 512-14; drug addiction of, 206, 207, 208, 209, 211; illegitimacy among, 489-91; as minority group, 412, 416, 417, 418; and public apathy, 786-87; and school segregation, 469-74; sexual attitudes among, 328; slavery of, 438-43; and social change, 449-54; in southern agriculture, 454-57; suicide among, 300-01; trade-union restriction of, 591; unemployment among, 607; use of alcohol among, 252; and violence, 461-62, 463-64; see also Race
Neo-Freudians; see Fromm, Erich; Horney, Karen; Sullivan, Harry Stack
Netherlands
suicide in, 287, 297, 299
Neuroses, 32, 37-38
etiology of, 71-72
Neurotic Personality of Our Time, The, 72
New Deal, the, 452
New Haven study, 62-63
New Jersey
attitudes toward prostitution in, 348; traffic accidents and drinking in, 256; treatment of mental illness in, 50
New Men, The, 794
New York City
attitudes toward prostitution in, 348; drug addiction in, 205, 206, 209, 210, 214, 230; mental illness in, 63-64; poverty in, 646, 650; sexual attitudes among students in, 328; unemployment in, 607-08
New York State
divorce in, 523; drug addiction in,

New York State (cont.)
205; drug control in, 228; hospitalization for mental illness in, 78; use of alcohol in, 250, 254, 256
New Zealand
age structure in, 385; suicide in, 287, 297, 299, 319-20
Newcomers, 650-52
poverty of, 665-68
Nicaragua
suicide in, 297
Nonconforming behavior, 808-11
Nonliterate societies, 11, 435, 436, 495-96
Normative reference groups, 108-09
Norms, 106, 136, 710-11
sexual, see Sexual norms
North Dakota
mental illness in, 61
Norway
courtship in, 328; suicide in, 297, 299, 309

Occupation
and automation, 609-18; categories of, 562-68; choice of, 568-72; and divorce, 509; and education, 572-78; and father's occupation, 571; managerial, 598-602; and poverty, 631; professional, 598-602; and social class, 572-76, 580-88; suicide rates by, 303-04; value of, 578-80; white-collar, 594-98; of women, 562, 563, 565, 567
Ohio
mental illness hospitalization in, 78
Old age
mental disorders of, 36-37, 69-70; social problems of, 70
Oregon
organized crime in, 364
Organization Man, The, 596

Pakistan
minority problem in, 424
Panama
illegitimacy in, 487; suicide in, 297, 299
Papago
suicide among, 292
Paraguay
illegitimacy in, 487
Parole, 191
Pauperization, 657-68
Paupers, 642-43
Penal Laws, 663
Pennsylvania
divorce in, 511, 515; mental hospital admissions in, 74-75, 76-77
Penology, 9-10
Persia
drug use in, 198
Personal disorganization, 83

Personality
of the alcoholic, 263; authoritarian, 432-33, 438; of the drug addict, 219-24; as factor in divorce, 521-22; and mental disorders, 82-83; of middle-management personnel, 595-96; neurotic, 72
Peru
illegitimacy in, 487; minority problem in, 424; suicide in, 297
Philadelphia
delinquency in, 97
Plessy v. *Ferguson,* 469, 814
Pluralism
institutional, 19-20
Poland
suicide in, 297
Polish Peasant, The, 17
Politics
and crime, 363-65; discrimination in, 421-22, 428
Polygenesis, 442
Poor, disreputable
components of, 644-57; conceptions of, 635-44; definition of, 619-20; and pauperization process, 657-68; see also Poverty
Poor Law reforms of 1834, 658, 660, 661
Population growth, 3
acceleration of, 475-81; and age structure, 384-86; in agrarian countries, 381-90; controversies over, 393-96; demographic solutions for, 396-404; and families, 386-87; in industrialized countries, 390-93; Marxist views on, 393-94; and national policies, 404-07; and rural-urban shift, 387-90; in underdeveloped countries, 376-78
Portugal
suicide in, 297, 299
Poverty
and composition of poor, 623-25; disreputable, see Poor, disreputable; extent of, 621-23; and imprisonment, 630; measures of, 621; moral regard for, 6; and population problem, 402-04; and race, 625; and welfare, 626-27
Prejudice; see Anti-Semitism; Discrimination
President's Advisory Commission on Narcotic and Drug Abuse, 204, 205, 227-28
Prisons
homosexuality in, 339, 340, 341, 343-44; see also Correctional institutions; Rehabilitation, of criminals
Probation, 191
Prohibition legislation, 247
Promiscuity, 350-52

Prostitution, 346-48
attitudes toward, 348-55; causes of, 355-65; elements of, 349; male, 337, 340, 346, 349; Marxist views on, 355; motivation of customer for, 358-61; and organized crime, 363-65; recruitment to, 361-65; in religion, 353-55; and social change, 365-70; theory of, 370-72; universality of, 356-58

Protestants
and divorce, 514-16; drinking among, 251, 276

Psychiatric clinics, 44-45

Psychiatry, 40-41, 46-48
and crime, 163-65; and delinquency, 101-06; and marriage, 550-52; and suicide, 288-90

Psychometry
and crime, 165-67

Psychoneuroses; see Neuroses

Psychopathology
and suicide rate, 309-11

Psychoses, 32
functional, 34-36

Psychosomatic disorders, 32, 38-39

Psychotherapy, 45, 79, 190

Puerto Ricans
attitudes toward women among, 326; drug addiction of, 206, 209; as minority group, 416, 417

Puma
suicide among, 292

Punishment, 183-85

Pursuit of the Millennium, The, 4

Quarterly Journal of Studies on Alcohol, 268

Race
crime rates by, 151-53; delinquency rates by, 94-95; and divorce, 512-14; and poverty, 625; suicide rates by, 300-01; *see also* Ethnic groups

Race relations, 419-23, 426-38
in South Africa, 425; in United States, 443-45

Racial discrimination; *see* Discrimination

Racism, 428-29, 438-49
ideology of, 442

RAND Corporation, 767

Red Virtue, 362-63

Rehabilitation
of criminals, 182-92; of drug addicts, 228-34; of mental patients, 44; and punishment, 183-85; techniques of, 185-92; theories of, 187-92

Religion
as approach to social problems, 13; and divorce, 514-16; and drinking, 251, 264-66, 276-77; and prostitu-

tion, 353-55; suicide rates by, 304 305

Remarriage
after death of spouse, 546, 548; after divorce, 545-48

Road to Survival, 396

Roles
and delinquency, 106-08; failure of, 540-45

Rome (Ancient)
homosexuality in, 338; prostitution in, 366

Rule of legitimacy, 483, 488

Rural-urban contrasts
in delinquency, 96; in suicide rates, 301-03

Rural-urban shift, 387-90

Russia
disarmament proposals of, 743-44; drug use in, 198; legalized abortion in, 333; nuclear testing by, 737; prostitution in, 362-63

Rwanda
population growth in, 378

Saxony
suicide in, 291

Scarsdale
community conflict in, 700

Schizophrenia
case description of, 27-29; effect of on family, 540; social relations and, 66-69; subtypes of, 35-36; symptoms of, 34-35

School segregation, 469-74

Science
and disarmament, 769-72; duality in, 775-78; and population problem, 404

Seattle
crime in, 158

Secular rationalism, 7-8

Segregation, 425, 443
in housing, 467-69; in schools, 469-74

Separation, 491-92

Sex
crime rates by, 148-51; delinquency rates by, 93-94; employment by, 562, 563, 565, 567; suicide rates by, 298, 300

Sex and the College Student, 335

Sexual conduct, 322
norms for, 323-31; social change and, 331-35; sublimation in, 324; *see also* Homosexuality; Prostitution

Sexual norms, 323-25
conflict over, 331-35; enforcement of, 330-31; in marriage, 325-27, 329; scale of, 327-30

Shanghai Commission, 202, 224

Siberian Chukchee
sexual practices among, 338

Sikkim
suicide among Lepchas of, 292
Skidders, 652-53
Slavery, 438-45
Smoking, 198-99, 200
Social actuality, 780-82
Social class
crime rates by, 157-59; delinquency
rates by, 95; and mental health, 55,
61-65, 68; and occupation, 572-76,
580-88; and recognition of suffering,
9-10; and schizophrenia, 68; and
social mobility, 21
Social discrimination, 422-23
Social disorganization, 18-19, 82-83
conception of, 800-04; suicide and,
282-83, 311-12
Social dysfunction, 817-23
Social mobility; *see* Mobility, social
Social novel, 15
Social problems
approaches to, 12-16; comparative
study of, 11-12; corrigibility of, 796-
99; criterion of, 780-82; cultural base
of, 2-4; historical background of, 18-
24; historical variability of, 4-6;
judges of, 784-88; latent, 788-92;
manifest, 788-92; modern view of,
6-10; and social dysfunctions, 817-
23; sociological conception of, 16-18,
779-99
Social standards, 780-82, 796-99
Sociology
of correctional systems, 119-26; of
crime, 172-82; of delinquency, 106-
19; of social problems, 16-18; of suicide, 284-88, 294-96
South Africa
race relations in, 425; suicide in, 299
South Dakota
mental illness in, 61
South Korea
population growth in, 378
Soviet Union; *see* Russia
Spain
marriage termination in, 494; suicide
in, 297
Speenhamland System, 658-62
Status
integration, 316-17; reference groups,
109-10; and suicide, 307, 315-17
Stirling County study, 64-65
Stress
and mental illness, 65-66; role of in
alcoholism, 266-67
Strikes, 592-94
Subcommunities
in Chicago, 208, 209; in New York,
209
Subcultures
of delinquents, 111-19; of drug users,
211-12, 214-15, 216
Suburbs, 698-701

Sudan
population growth in, 378
Suffering
recognition of, 8-10
Suicide, 280-321
actuarial studies of, 293-94; anthropological studies of, 290-93; definition of, 286; Durkheim's theory of,
284-87, 313-15; prevention of, 284;
psychological studies of, 288-90;
rank of as cause of death, 281-82;
rates, *see* Suicide rates; ritual, 290-
91; and secularization, 313; and social disorganization, 282-83, 311-12;
and social integration, 313-15; societal reactions to, 310-11; sociological studies of, 284-88, 294-96; and
status, 307, 315-17
Suicide, 17
Suicide rates
by age, 298-300; by marital status,
304-05, 306; by occupation, 303-04;
by political units, 296-98; and psychopathology, 309-11; by race, 300-
01; relativity of, 305-08; reliability
of statistics of, 286-87; by religion,
304, 305; rural-urban difference in,
301-03; by sex, 298, 300; by status,
307; temporal variation of, 308
Superego, 101-05
Supreme Court
and narcotics, 201-04; and segregation, 451, 453
Suttee, 291
Sweatt v. *Painter*, 470
Sweden
divorce rate in, 498; illegitimacy in,
485, 486; legalized abortion in, 333;
suicide in, 297, 299, 309
Switzerland
suicide in, 297, 299
Synanon, 232-33
Synergy, 557

Taboos, 138, 139
Taiwan
age structure in, 385; population
growth in, 378
Tanaina
suicide among, 292
Technological change, 609-18
Television; *see* Mass communication
Temperance movement, 246-47, 248-
49, 267, 277
Temple-prostitution, 353-54
Texas
commitment to mental hospitals in,
42; suicide in, 298
Therapy
for alcoholics, 269-71; for drug addicts, 230, 231; for juvenile delinquents, 128-29; *see also* Psychotherapy

HN
18
M 414

|8763

CAMROSE LUTHERAN COLLEGE
LIBRARY

B 6
C 7
D 8
E 9
F 0
G 1
H 2
I 3
J 4
  5

1966